World War II in Europe

VOLUME I

MILITARY HISTORY OF THE UNITED STATES (VOL. 6)
GARLAND REFERENCE LIBRARY OF THE HUMANITIES (VOL. 1254)

World War II in Europe

An Encyclopedia

Editor
David T. Zabecki

Assistant Editors
Carl O. Schuster
Paul J. Rose
William H. Van Husen

GARLAND PUBLISHING, INC.
A member of the Taylor & Francis Group
New York & London
1999

Library of Congress Cataloging-in-Publication Data

World War II in Europe : an encyclopedia / editor, David T. Zabecki ; assistant editors,
  Carl O. Schuster, Paul J. Rose, William H. Van Husen.
        p.   cm. — (Garland reference library of the humanities ; 1254.
  Military history of the United States ; v. 6)
      Includes bibliographical references and index.
      Contents: v. 1. Social and political issues and events. Leaders and individuals.
  Units and organizations — v. 2. Weapons and equipment. Strategy, tactics, and
  operational techniques. Battles, campaigns, and operations.
      ISBN 0-8240-7029-1 (alk. paper)
      1. World War, 1939-1945—Europe—Encyclopedias.   I. Zabecki, David T.
  II. Series: Garland reference library of the humanities ; vol. 1254. III. Series: Garland
  reference library of the humanities. Military history of the United States ; v. 6.
  D740.W67   1999
  940.53—dc21   98-27981
                                                                        CIP

Cover design by Lawrence Wolfson Design, New York

Printed on acid-free, 250-year-life paper
Manufactured in the United States of America

In memory of
Professor Richard Blanco,
the founding editor of this series

Contents

Foreword

by Martin Blumenson

Having participated in the Second World War in Europe and having spent my adult life studying it, lecturing and writing about it, and teaching it at the collegiate and graduate levels, I am pleased to endorse Garland's *World War II in Europe: An Encyclopedia,* edited by David T. Zabecki. It is a work of reference beyond my expectations. Its features are unique and rewarding.

What is an encyclopedia supposed to be? It is a volume or series of volumes containing and dispensing useful information arranged systematically. Its purpose is to provide data readily, nay immediately, to those who are curious about an event, figure, group, method, circumstance, condition, or other subject. It deals with all aspects of the matter under consideration and all sides of the subject under review. It is factual and accurate, reliable and authoritative, as well as objective.

Encyclopedias of a general nature present a compendium of universal learning comprehensive in scope, that is to say, encompassing all fields of study. Those of a special nature proffer an exhaustive treatment of a single branch of knowledge, a particular academic discipline, or a large and complex happening.

Whether of a general or special type, an encyclopedia serves a wide variety of users. They range from the expert who requires instant confirmation or correction of a date or of a half-remembered sequence of occurrences, to the lay person who hopes to expand his or her understanding. Some persons consult an encyclopedia the way they do a dictionary; others use it as a research tool. Readers must be able to easily find exactly what they are looking for.

This encyclopedia more than meets the criteria of a special work of reference. It rigorously conforms to the highest standards of completeness and authenticity. Eminently readable, it opens its contents without putting obstacles in the way of meaning.

World War II was the greatest single event of the twentieth century. *World War II in Europe: An Encyclopedia* is concerned with an important segment of it. The unfolding conflict, as well as its deep-ranging roots and far-reaching consequences, has stimulated a huge literature, a veritable library. The most significant books dealing with the struggle are listed here in an admirable *Selected Bibliography* in order to guide those who wish to pursue their interests beyond the encyclopedia's covers. Furthermore, each entry carries its own list of sources for those who seek additional information.

A corps of historians and military experts, the staff of contributors, has distilled and summarized the story of the war in Europe in under a million words—a remarkable achievement. The articles describing what happened, why, and to what ensuing ends are concise, even terse, for they need to utilize available and limited space economically. Yet their prose is smooth, surprisingly leisurely in pace, and quickly assimilated.

Garland's encyclopedia has several features well worth noting, for they are special assets normally absent from works on World War II. Firstly, there is implicit recognition of the Soviet Union's importance. A great deal of attention, much more than usual in Western reference works, is therefore devoted to the area of Soviet activity and the eastern front. Secondly, the encyclopedia narrates the significant role of women in the contest. Many women performed outstanding deeds as individuals and as members of groups. Their accomplishments are here recorded.

Thirdly, the encyclopedia is concerned not only with the war itself and how it was prosecuted, but also with its prewar causes and postwar results. It is, therefore, in its totality a history lesson. It describes how and why the war came about, the confrontation of the adversaries, and what the outcome brought. There are no lacunae in the text. Fourthly, splendid photographs, maps, tables, glossaries, chronologies, appendixes, and a list of code names amplify the facts presented. A comparison of military ranks among the various nations at war is most helpful.

Lastly, the encyclopedia has a unique structure. Most compendia are simply organized alphabetically. The editor of this encyclopedia has separated its information into six different sections. Within each section the articles are arranged alphabetically. Dividing the materials on the war into particular compartments has, somehow, clarified major relationships, that is to say, showed the interaction among the various kinds of data.

For example, the first section, Social and Political Issues and Events, discusses these two aspects of the conflict. The entries concern prewar, wartime, and postwar developments. The intent is to offer an understanding of the nonmilitary factors bringing about and shaping the war and its aftermath. War, Carl von Clausewitz has said, is a political act; therefore an appreciation of the social forces at work in the world and how the politicians and diplomats acted is necessary. Among these entries are "Allied Conferences," the "Beer Hall Putsch," the "Curzon Line," "French Resistance," the "League of Nations," "*Lebensraum,*" the "Morgenthau Plan," and the "Treaty of Rapallo."

The next section is entitled Leaders and Individuals, referring to those who directed vital parts of the war or achieved prominence in some way. Among the individuals discussed are Konrad Adenauer, Władysław Anders, Lavrenty Beria, Anne Frank, and Earle Wheeler.

Logically in turn comes Units and Organizations, the groups that fought the war, how they came into being, what functions they assumed, how they affected the outcome. Some are the "Gestapo," the "Ghurkas," the "Maquis," and "Partisans, Soviet."

Weapons and Equipment follows and makes clear the special technology of the war, the means employed to prosecute the conflict. "Enigma," "Helicopters," and "Jet Aircraft" are some of the entries. Notable in this section are the extensive tables giving precise data on the vast array of weapons systems used during the war.

Strategy, Tactics, and Operational Techniques is concerned with the methods of how the war was fought. The articles deal with arcane knowledge, but are lucid and clear. Among them are "Douhet Doctrine," "Naval Gunnery," "Principles of War," and "Rainbow Plans."

Finally, Battles, Campaigns, and Operations, that is to say, the military side of the war, comprises the largest section. Included are "Byelorussia 1943–1944," "Colmar Pocket," "Gazala Line," and "Rapido River."

The entries I have mentioned indicate not only the makeup of each of the six sections, but also the extraordinary scope of the entire treatment. A model of clarity, Garland's encyclopedia gives easy access to relevant information. Whether you come for a brief visit or an extended journey, you will find an educational experience, an exciting adventure in learning. Resolving questions and issues pertaining to World War II in Europe by using this encyclopedia, I promise, will be pleasant and profitable occasions.

Preface

British military historian John Keegan has called World War II "the single biggest event in human history." No one reference could ever comprehensively cover a topic as vast and as complex. The best that a concise encyclopedia such as this can hope to do is give readers an overview of the war by providing key facts concerning the important people, events, organizations, and ideas that shaped the era. That is not a simple task. This encyclopedia contains 1,400 separate entries. Most would easily rate their own book, and many already have.

The encyclopedia is not limited strictly to the events between 1939 and 1945. While the German invasion of Poland on 1 September 1939 is generally considered the formal start of World War II in Europe, it is impossible to understand the war without considering the events that led up to it and the underlying causes. Ethiopia, for example, set the stage for Italian military operations in North Africa that eventually pulled in Germany, thus fragmenting that country's ability to project military power. Spain was Germany's tactical and technological proving ground. The Russo-Polish War set the stage for the Molotov-Ribbentrop Pact, the Katyń Forest Massacre, and the abortive Warsaw Rising—all of which were major factors in the rocky Polish-Soviet relationship of the Cold War years.

This encyclopedia also covers some of the consequences and results of the war. The world order that existed until the start of the 1990s was a direct product of World War II. In a technically legal sense, World War II in Europe ended only on 3 October 1990 when East and West Germany were reunited and Berlin ended its forty-five-year status as a city occupied by the military forces of the former Allies. Until that date, U.S. forces stationed in Berlin were still awarded the World War II Army of Occupation Medal.

Some readers might wonder why a particular topic was included, or why another was left out. To write history is to make choices. In choosing the topics for this volume the editors selected those they believed to be the most significant and interesting. In writing about the topics, the contributors selected the most relevant facts. This, of course, is a subjective process, which makes the writing of history something of an art.

The interpretation of historical events is not an exact science either. Many World War II topics are still controversial, and interpretation is largely a matter of perspective. Since this encyclopedia was compiled by an international team of contributors, some of the interpretations presented may not necessarily be those most familiar to American or British readers.

World War II is far from a closed book. More than fifty years after the end of the war, new information continues to emerge.

Acknowledgments

Compiling this encyclopedia has truly been a team effort. A total of 155 contributors from at least eight different countries participated in the project. Some contributors wrote one or two articles, others wrote many. The most prolific contributors included John Beatty, Charles Bogart, Boyd Childress, Bernard Cook, James Cooke, Sam Doss, Kevin Dougherty, John Dunn, Francesco Fatutta, Alan Harfield, Robert Hudson, Reiner Martin, Peter Mispelkamp, Elizabeth Schafer, Chris Westhorp, and Richard Wires.

Ulrich Trumpener handled a wide array of German-related topics. Andrzej Suchcitz wrote biographical entries for a number of important military and political leaders from the eastern countries little known to western leaders. Ekkehart Guth wrote about some of the most important western front battles from the German perspective.

One contributor who rates a special mention is Jon Moulton, under whom I studied at both the undergraduate and graduate levels at Xavier University. In essence, I credit to him just about everything I know about the study of history. I must admit, however, that I felt rather odd when it came to editing his articles.

The eight contributing editors all did yeoman work on this project. Jonathan Bailey, Tom Cagley, Sidney Dean, Phillip Green, Steve Rogers, Spencer Tucker, Mike Unsworth, and Bob Waite all wrote more than their share of the articles, plus helped cross-check facts, dig up details, and review articles.

Donald Frazier, in addition to writing articles, produced all the original maps, as well as the map key. Marlies Schweigler translated into English the articles originally written in German. And Morgan Benson spent literally hundreds of hours putting the tables on disk in a clean and concise tabular format.

Many of the individual contributors received assistance from various institutions and organizations in the preparation of their articles. The organizations from which I personally received assistance include the *Bundesarchiv-Militärarchiv* in Freiburg, Germany; the *Militärgeschichtliches Forschungsamt,* formerly in Freiburg, now in Potsdam; the U.S. Army Center for Military History in Washington, D.C.; the U.S. Army Military History Institute at Carlisle Barracks; and the Imperial War Museum (IWM) in London. I am especially grateful to Paul Kemp, Jane Carmichel, Ian Carter, and John Delaney of the IWM Department of Photographs for their wonderful support.

The Military History of the United States series was the result of the vision of the late Professor Dick Blanco, and I am forever grateful for his confidence in trusting me with the editorship of this volume. The editorial and production staffs at Garland Publishing have been patient, flexible, and wonderfully supportive, especially considering that this book took four years longer to produce than originally planned. I am indebted to several former Garland staffers—Phyllis Korper, especially, and Marianne

Lown and Earl Roy. On the current staff, editors Carol Buell and Helga McCue, and Sylvia Ploss and Eric Brearton have been immensely helpful.

A special note of thanks goes to Martin Blumenson, who graciously agreed to write the foreword. In addition to being one of the world's foremost World War II historians, he is a true gentleman of the old school. A special thanks, too, goes to Roger Cirillo. Although his name does not appear in connection with any article, he freely gave us his advice and help on a wide range of problems.

Lastly, and by a wide margin most significantly, I have to pay special thanks to the three assistant editors. Without the extensive efforts of Paul Rose, Carl Schuster, and Bill Van Husen, this project never would have seen completion.

David T. Zabecki
Freiburg, Germany

Introduction

World War II in Europe: An Encyclopedia is part of the Garland series Military History of the United States. The series originated under the general editorship of the late Professor Richard L. Blanco, who also edited the first volume in the series, *The American Revolution 1775–1783: An Encyclopedia.*

Rather than a straight alphabetical arrangement, this encyclopedia is organized into six major sections, with entries arranged alphabetically within each section. The reason for this organization is to make it easier for the reader who wants to focus on a particular aspect of the war. The major sections are arranged in such an order that each section provides background information for understanding the subsequent sections.

SOCIAL AND POLITICAL ISSUES AND EVENTS   This is the basic section for understanding World War II. Topics include the background and underlying conditions of the war, such as the Treaty of Versailles, the League of Nations, isolationism, appeasement, and the rise of National Socialism in Germany. Social and political topics during the war include the wartime governments of the major participants, the Holocaust, the major resistance movements, and the role of women in the principal militaries. Finally, some of the most important postwar results of the conflict are included, such as the Berlin Blockade and Airlift, the Marshall Plan, and the United Nations.

LEADERS AND INDIVIDUALS   This section includes biographical sketches of the major political and military leaders, many of whom—Hitler, Stalin, Eisenhower, Montgomery, Patton—are well known. We have made an attempt to include many of the important but lesser-known figures as well. These mid-level movers and shakers, like Hermann Balck, Tadeusz Bor-Komoroswki, Elwood Quesada, and Mikhail Guryevich, played key roles in some of the war's most important events. Also included are many of the military and political leaders of the smaller and eastern European countries—individuals largely unknown to western readers.

This section also includes many of the prewar military theorists, who may not have participated directly in World War II themselves, but who nonetheless had a profound impact on its conduct. This group includes J.F.C. Fuller, Basil H. Liddell Hart, Billy Mitchell, Adna R. Chaffee, Hans von Seeckt, and Mikhail Tukhachevsky. We have included a small selection of individuals who, although not necessarily prominent in the war, became major figures on the world stage in later years. People like Willy Brandt, Franz Josef Strauss, Earle Wheeler, William Westmoreland, and Nikita Khrushchev were deeply influenced and shaped by their experiences in World War II.

We also have included a small number of individuals who may have had little actual impact on the course of the war, yet who, through their actions, deserve mention. These include Charles Upham, the only double recipient of the Victoria Cross since 1917; Alex Drabik, the first American soldier across the Rhine; Michael Wittmann, perhaps the best individual tank commander in history; and Lilly Litvak, history's first female ace. Finally, we have included a number of individuals who never really existed in the physical sense. Nonetheless, Sad Sack, Willie & Joe, Colonel Blimp, and William Martin were very real to many people in the years 1939 to 1945.

UNITS AND ORGANIZATIONS   This section focuses primarily on the military organizations that fought the war, but paramilitary and political organizations are also included. The core of this section includes organizational profiles (not operational histories) of most of the armies, navies, and air forces participating in the western half of the war. For organizations that operated in the Pacific war as well, the emphasis is on their involvement in Europe. Also included are profiles of some of the most significantly unique and special organizations such as Britain's commandos and SAS, America's rangers and 1st Special Service Force, Germany's *Brandenburgers* and *Afrika Korps,* the Soviets' *Spetznaz* and *Smersh,* Italy's 10th Light Flotilla, the French Foreign Legion, and the Gurkhas.

Many of the articles in this section have order of battle tables. In military operations, order of battle (OB) is the process of determining the identification, disposition, strength, command structure, subordinate units, and equipment of any opposing military force. During military operations, OB is an integral part of the tactical intelligence process, one of the many tools used by military intelligence analysts to determine enemy capabilities and probable courses of action.

All armies go to great lengths to prevent their enemies from obtaining this information. Likewise, all armies engage in deception operations to feed false and misleading information to the opposing forces. For these reasons, OB, like so much else in the realm of military intelligence, is as much an art as it is a science. Intelligence analysts face the daunting task of building a coherent picture of the enemy from partial, often conflicting, and sometimes intentionally misleading information gathered from a wide variety of sources of varying accuracy and reliability.

The OB picture of the enemy force is never complete and never stable. It is a constantly moving picture that changes shape as military units lose or build strength, change location, change commanders, reconstitute, exchange subordinate units and elements, and even change designations. The OB picture can be considered true and accurate only after a war is over—and very often not even then.

The historian uses OB information in much the same manner as the intelligence analyst. While the intelligence analyst tries to predict the future, the historian tries to reconstruct the past. Both use similar research and analytical tools and face similar challenges as to the accuracy and completeness of information. Many years after the event the surviving or available records still might not provide enough information to construct the true picture. The objective of both the intelligence analyst and the military historian, then, is to construct the best picture possible using the best available data.

More than fifty years after the end of history's greatest war, the OB information of World War II remains far from crystal clear. This is especially true for the Soviet and eastern European militaries, and for the German army in the war's final chaotic months. In compiling the order of battle tables for this section, the contributors and editors have made every effort to provide the most accurate and representative data available. Some of this information, however, will continue to remain open to refinement and further analysis.

WEAPONS AND EQUIPMENT   World War II was a full-scale technological war. The weapons and equipment used had a great impact on the tactics and conduct of the fighting. The articles in this section focus on the capabilities and limitations of this equipment, how the equipment was used, how it affected the outcome of the battles, and how the experience of World War II influenced the further development of various weapons systems. Many of the articles in this section have technical data tables that allow the reader to compare operational characteristics—how fast? how far? how high? how heavy?

As with the order of battle tables in the UNITS AND ORGANIZATIONS section, the contributors and editors have tried to present the most accurate data possible in the weapons and equipment tables. This has not been an easy task. From start to finish, World War II was a technological arms race. No sooner did a particular piece of equipment leave the drawing boards and enter production than improved versions were already in the works. Many weapons systems had more than one model, and even within a given model many variants existed. Soldiers, sailors, and airmen on all sides in the war continually tinkered with their weapons and equipment in the field in order to extract the maximum levels of performance—that often meant the difference between life and death in combat. For all these reasons, many published sources provide slightly conflicting numbers on the technical data of World War II weapons. In compiling the tables in this section, our objective has been to provide the most representative data.

STRATEGY, TACTICS, AND OPERATIONAL TECHNIQUES   This short group of topics explains how the war was fought. What were the overall strategies of the major participants? How were military operations conducted? Why were they conducted that way? Why did some fail and others succeed? What was different about airborne operations? amphibious operations? desert operations? What influence did World War II have on the development of subsequent military theory?

BATTLES, CAMPAIGNS, AND OPERATIONS   The articles in this section describe the actual fighting that determined the outcome of World War II. The information in the previous five sections is focused toward enhancing the reader's understanding of the descriptions of the battles. For example, the articles on the Sicily and Normandy landings do not contain any detailed discussion of the technical problems of amphibious warfare. That information is covered in the article on amphibious operations in the Strategy, Tactics, and Operational Techniques section.

The Battles, Campaigns, and Operations section contains 226 articles organized in alphabetical order. The section is preceded by a geographical and chronological index that shows the various battles, campaigns, and operations in relation to each other. The index's five major groupings are I. The Preliminaries, II. Intelligence and Deception, III. Air Actions, IV. Naval Actions, and V. Land and Combined Actions. This last section is further subdivided by geographic region: North Europe, Africa and the Middle East, South Europe, East Europe, and West Europe.

Following the volume's six principal sections are a number of appendixes containing specialized information. Appendix A is a chronology of World War II in Europe. Although the chronology, like the encyclopedia itself, focuses on the events between 1939 and 1945, it also covers the causes and consequences of the war. Thus, the chronology starts with the defeat of Germany in 1918 and runs through the fall of the Berlin Wall in 1989. Appendix B contains a series of tables comparing World War II military ranks of parties to the war in Europe. The purpose of these tables is to help the reader make sense of the often bewildering array of rank titles used by the various militaries. Appendix C is a glossary of acronyms, abbreviations, and foreign military terms, and Appendix D is a list of the more commonly known code names used by the various sides in the war. These four appendices can be very helpful references when reading other books about World War II. Finally, Appendix E is a selected bibliography of books published about World War II in Europe. The bibliography itself is organized into eight subsections, one for general references, one for official histories, and one each for the six major sections of this encyclopedia.

The final resources in this encyclopedia are a special index of all cited army, naval, and air force units—including individual warships, and a comprehensive and detailed general index.

World War II, even just the western half of the war—the war against Germany—was a huge and vastly complex event. For six years it focused and monopolized the attentions and efforts of most of the giant figures of twentieth-century history, as well as literally hundreds of millions of ordinary people. In compiling this encyclopedia, the contributors and editors have attempted to make this important historical event more accessible and more understandable to people who will live in the twenty-first century.

Editorial Team

Contributors

José E. Alvarez
University of Houston

Jonathan B.A. Bailey
British Army

L. Lee Baker
University of Illinois

Tony D. Barnes
University of Maryland

Dennis A. Bartels
Carleton University
Ottawa, Ontario, Canada

John D. Beatty
West Allis, Wisconsin

Philip C. Bechtel
Texas Christian University

Benjamin R. Beede
Rutgers University

John D.C. Bennett
Edith Cavell Hospital
Peterborough, England

M.B. Biskupski
St. John Fisher College

George P. Blum
University of the Pacific

Charles H. Bogart
Frankfurt, Kentucky

William D. Bowman
Texas Christian University

Blaine T. Browne
Broward Community College

Steven D. Cage
Department of the Army

Thomas R. Cagley
U.S. Army Reserve

William Camp
Cradle of Aviation Museum
Garden City, New York

Thomas A. Cardwell, III
U.S. Air Force (Ret.)

Boyd Childress
Auburn University

Mark Conrad
U.S. Air Force

Mark Conversino
U.S. Air Force Academy

Bernard A. Cook
Loyola University

James J. Cooke
The University of Mississippi

Sherwood S. Cordier
Western Michigan University

Stephen M. Cullen
Wolfson College, Oxford University
Oxford, England

John R. Dabrowski
Seventh U.S. Air Force

Terry D. Davenport
University of Maryland

Sidney Dean
Kaiserslautern, Germany

Paul D. Dickson
University of Guelph
Ontario, Canada

Steven Dietrich
U.S. Army Center of Military History

Charles K. Dodd
University of Washington

Stephen Donahue
U.S. Army Counterintelligence Center

Samuel J. Doss
Russia and East European Partnerships, Inc.

Kevin Dougherty
U.S. Army

Donald P. Doumitt
University of Maryland

Richard Dumolt
University of Maryland

John Dunn
Valdosta State University

Serge M. Durflinger
McGill University
Montreal, Quebec, Canada

Marian K. Dziewanowski
University of Wisconsin

William K. Emerson
U.S. Army (Ret.)

Peter R. Faber
U.S. Air Force

Francesco Fatutta
Italian Defense Review

William E. Fischer, Jr.
U.S. Air Force Academy

Robert C. Fisher
Manuscript Division
National Archives of Canada

David A. Foy
Columbia, Maryland

Donald S. Frazier
McMurry University

Stephen L. Frost
Huddersfield, England

Cederic Fry
Department of the Army

Susan Teepe Gaskins
Orange Coast College

Norbert H. Gaworek
University of Wisconsin

Robert Gerlich
Loyola University

Norman J.W. Goda
University of Maine

Sylvia Goodson
Russia and East European Partnerships, Inc.

Philip J. Green
British Army (Ret.)

Howard D. Grier
University of North Carolina

A. Gregory Gutgsell, Jr.
Betendorf, Iowa

Ekkehart Guth
Führungsakademie der Bundeswehr
Hamburg, Germany

Peter L. Hahn
Ohio State University

Thomas Hale
Idaho State University

Jussi Hanhimaki
Boston University

Alan G. Harfield
The Bulletin of the Military Historical Society
Hampshire, England

Russell A. Hart
Ohio State University

Robert Hudson
University of Derby
Derby, England

Radu Ioanid
U.S. Holocaust Memorial Museum

Mark R. Jacobson
Ohio State University

Richard E. James
U.S. Air Force Academy

Paul W. Johnson
Washington, D.C.

Budd A.R. Jones
U.S. Air Force Academy

Roger Kaplan
U.S. Army Center of Military History

Marjorie D. Kemp
University of Maryland

Robert Kirchubel
U.S. Army Reserve

Daniel Kuehl
U.S. Air Force (Ret.)

Glenn Lamar
University of Southern Louisiana

Roger D. Launius
National Aeronautics and Space Administration

Clayton D. Laurie
U.S. Army Center of Military History

Donald L. Layton
Indiana State University

Roland V. Layton
Hiram College

Richard Leiby
Rosemont College

Raymond J. Leisner
U.S. Army

Van Michael Leslie
University of Alabama

Donnie O. Lord
Howard Payne University

James Lussier
University of Maryland

Randy MacDonald
University of Maryland

Jack E. McCallum
Texas Christian University

Joseph M. McCarthy
Suffolk University

Charles McDowell
Springfield, Virginia

Stephen McFarland
Auburn University

Michael G. Mahon
Texas Christian University

Reiner Martin
Europa-Kolleg Hamburg
Hamburg, Germany

Geoffrey P. Megargee
Ohio State University

Phillip S. Meilinger
U.S. Air Force

Peter K.H. Mispelkamp
Pointe Claire, Quebec, Canada

Dennis J. Mitchell
Jackson State University

Alexander Molnar, Jr.
U.S. Navy Oceanographic Office

John Ellis Van Courtland Moon
Fitchburg State College

Jon Moulton
Xavier University

Max Mulholland
U.S. Navy

John F. Murphy, Jr.
Drexel Hill, Pennsylvania

Justin D. Murphy
Howard Payne University

Robert Nadeau
Allentown, New Hampshire

Jozef Ostyn
Ohio State University

Robert F. Pace
Longwood College

Mary Anne Pagliasotti
Texas Christian University

Randy Papadopoulos
George Washington University

Susan Pentlin
Central Missouri State University

Paul G. Pierpaoli
University of Arizona

Judith Podlipnik
Florida State University

Michael Polley
Columbia College

William Rawling
Directorate of History
National Defence Headquarters
Ottawa, Ontario, Canada

Kenneth Reynolds
McGill University
Montreal, Quebec, Canada

Antje Richter
Frankfurt, Germany

Steven B. Rogers
U.S. Department of Justice

Patricia K. Rose
University of Paris

Paul J. Rose
University of Maryland

John P. Rossi
La Salle University

James C. Ruehrmund, Jr.
U.S. Air Force Reserve

Mark Rummage
Grenada, Mississippi

Eric C. Rust
Baylor University

Elizabeth D. Schafer
Auburn University

Carl O. Schuster
Hawaii Pacific University

Franz W. Seidler
Universität der Bundeswehr München
Neubiberg, Germany

V.I. Semenenko
Kharkov State University
Ukraine

Glenn Sharfman
Hiram College

Edward J. Sheehy
La Salle University

Richard J. Smith
Litchfield, Maine

Vivian Stacey
University of Maryland

Edward Steel
Stuttgart, Germany

Truman R. Strobridge
U.S. European Command

Robert C. Stroud
U.S. Air Force Chaplain Service Institute

Andrzej Suchcitz
Polish Institute and Sikorski Museum
London

Brian J. Sullivan
University of Maryland

Kenneth J. Swanson
Idaho State Historical Museum

Wolfgang Terhörst
Albert-Ludwigs University
Freiburg, Germany

Gerhardt B. Thamm
Alexandria, Virginia

Ulrich Trumpener
University of Alberta
Edmonton, Alberta, Canada

Spencer C. Tucker
Virginia Military Institute

Roger Tuller
Texas Christian University

Richard P. Ugino
U.S. Army Reserve

Michael E. Unsworth
Michigan State University Libraries

Karl Van Husen
Rochester Institute of Technology

William H. Van Husen
University of Maryland

Georgi Verbeeck
Katholieke Universiteit Leuven
Leuven, Belgium

Richard A. Voeltz
Cameron University

J. David Waite
Northwestern University

Robert G. Waite
U.S. Department of Justice

David Walker
University of California, Davis

B.K. Warner
British Army (Ret.)

Bernerd C. Weber
The University of Alabama

Chris Westhorp
Arms and Armour Press

Michael J. Whitby
Directorate of History
National Defence Headquarters
Ottawa, Ontario, Canada

Timothy Wilson
Department of the Army

Wes Wilson
Department of the Army

Richard Wires
Sarasota, Florida

Michael Wolfert
U.S. Air Force

Laura Matysek Wood
Tarrant County Junior College

Keith Wooster
U.S. Army

David K. Yelton
Gardner-Webb College

David T. Zabecki
American Military University

Marian Zgórniak
Jagellonian University
Kraków, Poland

Strategic Maps of World War II Military Operations

Strategic Maps Locator

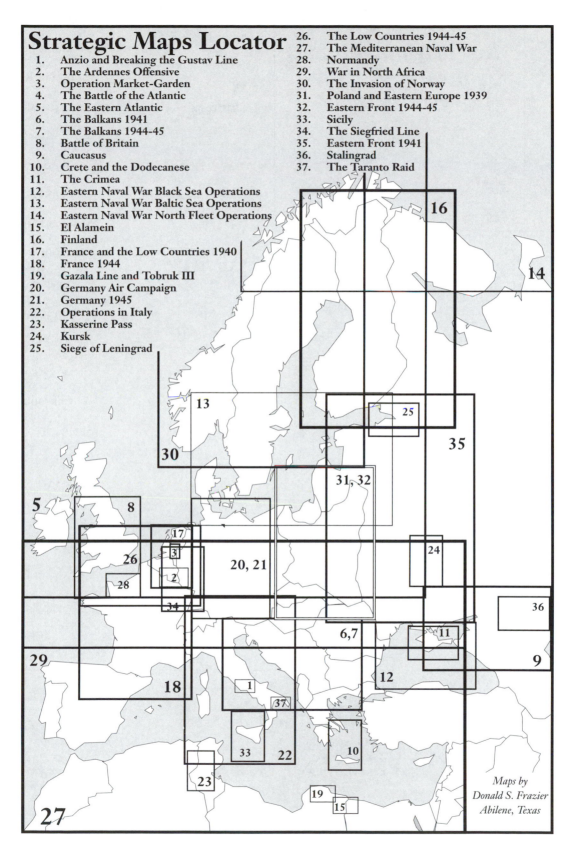

1. Anzio and Breaking the Gustav Line
2. The Ardennes Offensive
3. Operation Market-Garden
4. The Battle of the Atlantic
5. The Eastern Atlantic
6. The Balkans 1941
7. The Balkans 1944-45
8. Battle of Britain
9. Caucasus
10. Crete and the Dodecanese
11. The Crimea
12. Eastern Naval War Black Sea Operations
13. Eastern Naval War Baltic Sea Operations
14. Eastern Naval War North Fleet Operations
15. El Alamein
16. Finland
17. France and the Low Countries 1940
18. France 1944
19. Gazala Line and Tobruk III
20. Germany Air Campaign
21. Germany 1945
22. Operations in Italy
23. Kasserine Pass
24. Kursk
25. Siege of Leningrad
26. The Low Countries 1944-45
27. The Mediterranean Naval War
28. Normandy
29. War in North Africa
30. The Invasion of Norway
31. Poland and Eastern Europe 1939
32. Eastern Front 1944-45
33. Sicily
34. The Siegfried Line
35. Eastern Front 1941
36. Stalingrad
37. The Taranto Raid

Maps by
Donald S. Frazier
Abilene, Texas

Key to Map Symbols and Abbreviations:

				Airbases and Airfields
				Bombing Raids
⊠	Allied Infantry			Axis Minefield
⊠ (filled)	Axis Infantry			Allied Minefield
⊠ (motorized)	Axis Motorized Infantry			Ship Losses
⬭	Allied Armor			Sub Operations
⬭ (filled)	Axis Armor			Paratroop Drops
SF	Special Service Unit			Codenames
U.S. Ninth Army	Allied Army		**Operation** **MARITA**	
FIFTH PANZER ARMY	Axis Army			Engagements
Army Group E (Löhr)	Army Group			Aircraft Industry
				Other Industry
Pol	Polish Units			Strategic Railway
It	Italian Units			Oil Industry
US	United States Units			Submarine Pens
Can	Canadian Units			Missile Base
Br	British Units			Barrage Balloons
Abn	Airborne Units			Capital Ship
SS	Schutzstaffeln Units			Escort Ship
Armd	Allied Armored Units			Oil Field
Bde	Brigade			Fortifications
Grds	Soviet Guards Units			Bridges
Pz	German Panzer Units			Mountains
				Rivers
				Roads
Ⓜ	Allied "Mulberries"			Trees

Maps by
Donald S. Frazier, PhD.
McMurry University
Abilene, Texas

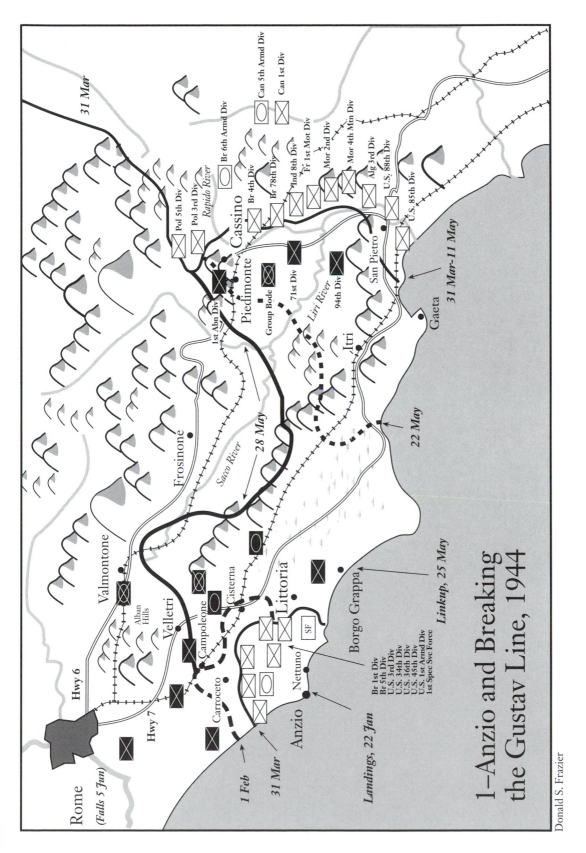

1–Anzio and Breaking the Gustav Line, 1944

Br 6th Armd Div

Can 5th Armd Div
Can 1st Div

Br 4th Div
Br 78th Div
2nd 8th Div
Fr 1st Mot Div
Mor 2nd Div
Mor 4th Mtn Div
Alg 3rd Div
U.S. 88th Div
U.S. 85th Div

Pol 5th Div
Pol 3rd Div
Rapido River

Cassino

31 Mar

Piedimonte
Group Bode
1st Abn Div
71st Div
94th Div
Liri River
San Pietro

Itri

Gaeta
31 Mar–11 May

28 May

22 May

Saco River

Frosinone

Valmontone

Alban Hills
Velletri
Campoleone
Cisterna
Carroceto

Littoria
SF
Borgo Grappa
Nettuno
Anzio

Linkup, 25 May

Landings, 22 Jan   Br 1st Div
Br 5th Div
U.S. 3rd Div
U.S. 34th Div
U.S. 36th Div
U.S. 45th Div
U.S. 1st Armd Div
1st Spec Svc Force

31 Mar

1 Feb

Hwy 7

Hwy 6

Rome
(Falls 5 Jun)

Donald S. Frazier

ANZIO AND BREAKING THE GUSTAV LINE, 1944   xxxi

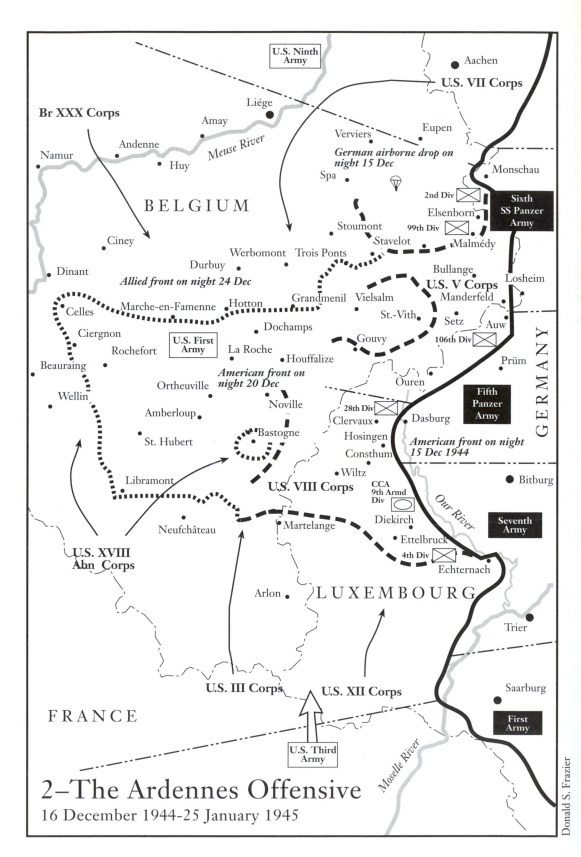

2–The Ardennes Offensive
16 December 1944–25 January 1945

Donald S. Frazier

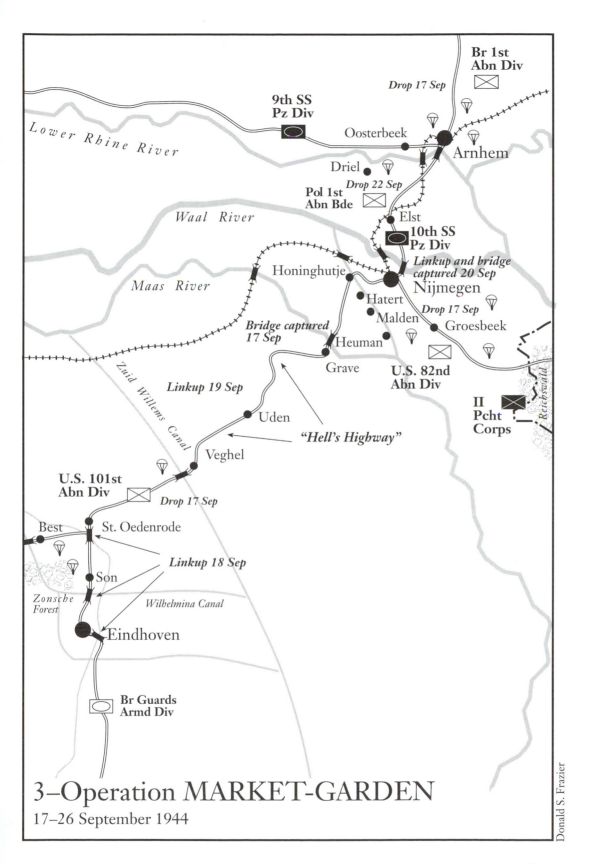

3–Operation MARKET-GARDEN
17–26 September 1944

Br 1st
Abn Div

Drop 17 Sep

9th SS
Pz Div

Lower Rhine River

Oosterbeek

Arnhem

Driel

Drop 22 Sep

Pol 1st
Abn Bde

Waal River

Elst

10th SS
Pz Div

*Linkup and bridge
captured 20 Sep*

Maas River

Honinghutje

Nijmegen

Hatert

Malden

Drop 17 Sep

Groesbeek

*Bridge captured
17 Sep*

Heuman

Grave

U.S. 82nd
Abn Div

Reichswald

II
Pcht
Corps

Linkup 19 Sep

Uden

"Hell's Highway"

Zuid Willems Canal

Veghel

U.S. 101st
Abn Div

Drop 17 Sep

Best

St. Oedenrode

Linkup 18 Sep

Son

*Zonsche
Forest*

Wilhelmina Canal

Eindhoven

Br Guards
Armd Div

Donald S. Frazier

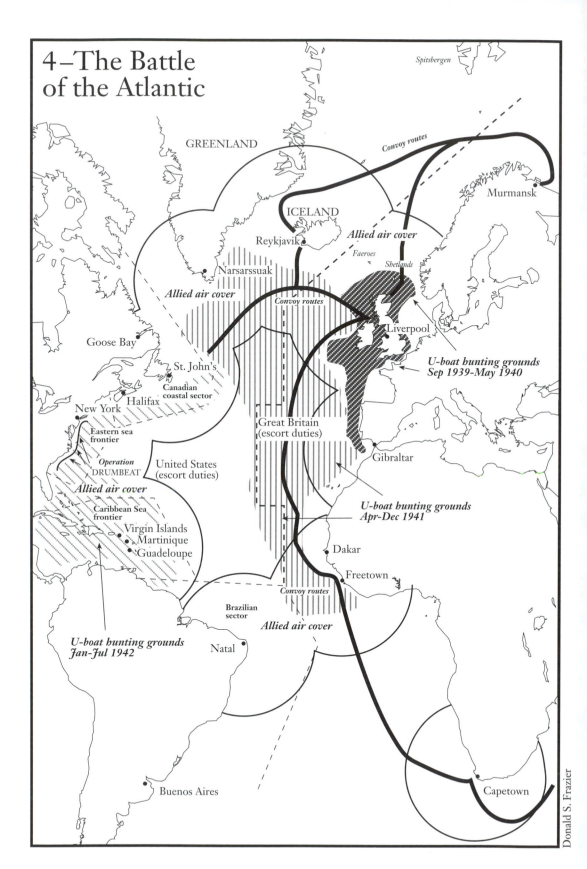

4–The Battle of the Atlantic

Spitsbergen

GREENLAND

Convoy routes

Murmansk

ICELAND

Allied air cover

Reykjavik

Faeroes

Shetlands

Narsarssuak

Allied air cover

Convoy routes

Liverpool

Goose Bay

U-boat hunting grounds Sep 1939–May 1940

St. John's

Canadian coastal sector

New York

Halifax

Great Britain (escort duties)

Gibraltar

Eastern sea frontier

Operation **DRUMBEAT**

United States (escort duties)

Allied air cover

U-boat hunting grounds Apr–Dec 1941

Caribbean Sea frontier

Virgin Islands

Martinique

Guadeloupe

Dakar

Freetown

Convoy routes

Brazilian sector

U-boat hunting grounds Jan–Jul 1942

Natal

Allied air cover

Buenos Aires

Capetown

Donald S. Frazier

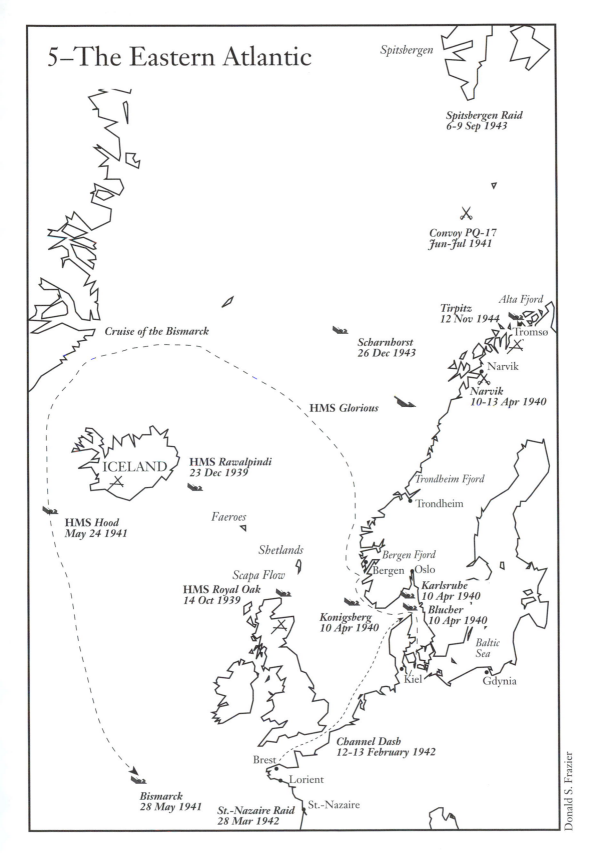

5–The Eastern Atlantic

Spitsbergen

Spitsbergen Raid
6-9 Sep 1943

Convoy PQ-17
Jun-Jul 1941

Alta Fjord

Tirpitz
12 Nov 1944

Tromsø

Cruise of the Bismarck

Scharnhorst
26 Dec 1943

Narvik

Narvik
10-13 Apr 1940

HMS *Glorious*

Trondheim Fjord

Trondheim

ICELAND

HMS *Rawalpindi*
23 Dec 1939

Faeroes

HMS *Hood*
May 24 1941

Shetlands

Bergen Fjord

Bergen   Oslo

Karlsruhe
10 Apr 1940

Scapa Flow

HMS Royal Oak
14 Oct 1939

Blucher
10 Apr 1940

Konigsberg
10 Apr 1940

Baltic
Sea

Kiel

Gdynia

Channel Dash
12-13 February 1942

Brest

Lorient

Bismarck
28 May 1941

St.-Nazaire Raid
28 Mar 1942

St.-Nazaire

Donald S. Frazier

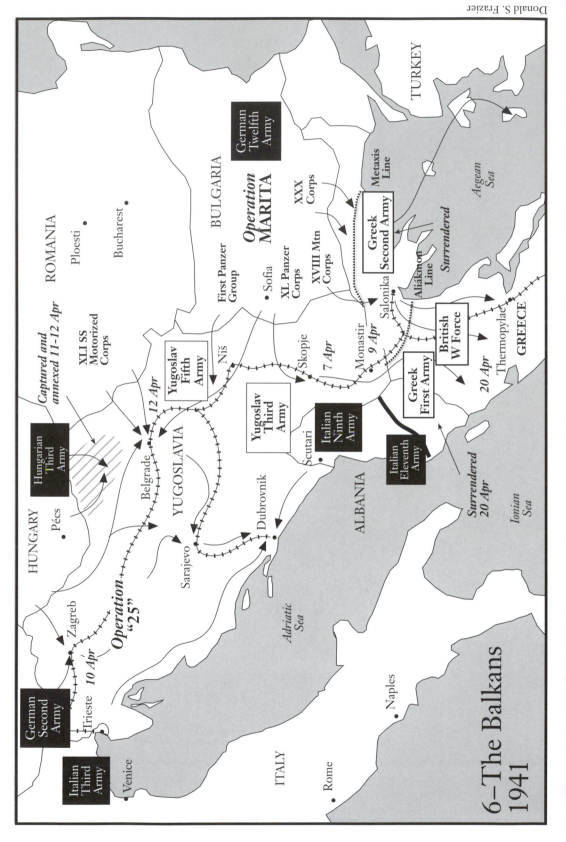

German Twelfth Army

Operation **MARITA**

Metaxis Line

Aegean Sea

TURKEY

BULGARIA

XXX Corps

Surrendered

Greek Second Army

XL Panzer Corps

Aliákmon Line

ROMANIA

First Panzer Group

XVIII Mtn Corps

Ploesti

• Sofia

Salonika

British W Force

Bucharest

Captured and annexed 11-12 Apr

XLI SS Motorized Corps

Yugoslav Fifth Army

Niš

Skopje

7 Apr

Monastir 9 Apr

20 Apr

Thermopylae

GREECE

12 Apr

Yugoslav Third Army

Greek First Army

Hungarian Third Army

Scutari

Italian Ninth Army

Belgrade

YUGOSLAVIA

Dubrovnik

Italian Eleventh Army

Surrendered 20 Apr

Ionian Sea

Péc

ALBANIA

HUNGARY

Sarajevo

Operation "25"

Zagreb

10 Apr

Adriatic Sea

Trieste

German Second Army

ITALY

Naples •

Italian Third Army

Venice

• Rome

6–The Balkans 1941

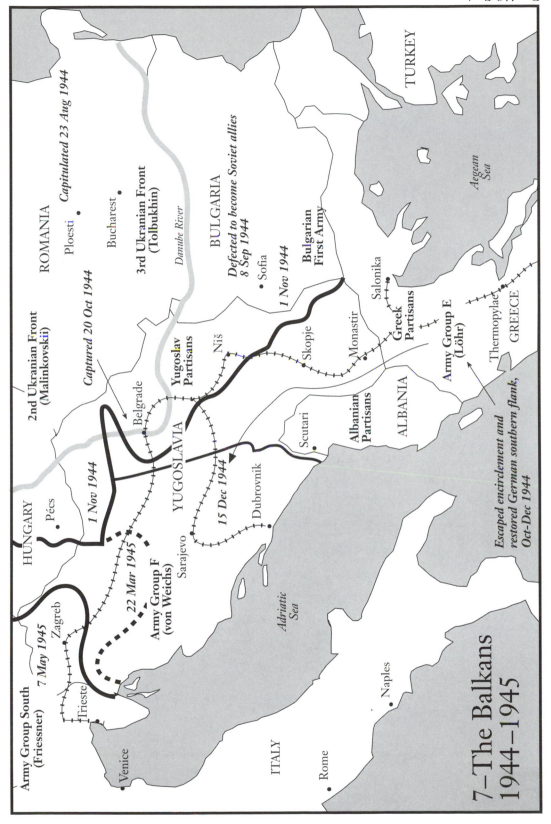

7–The Balkans 1944–1945

Army Group South
(Friessner)

7 May 1945

Zagreb

Trieste

Venice

ITALY

Rome

Naples

Adriatic
Sea

Dubrovnik

15 Dec 1944

Sarajevo

22 Mar 1945

Army Group F
(von Weichs)

YUGOSLAVIA

1 Nov 1944

Pécs

HUNGARY

Belgrade

2nd Ukranian Front
(Malinkovskii)

Captured 20 Oct 1944

1 Nov 1944

Yugoslav
Partisans

Niš

ROMANIA

Ploesti

Capitulated 23 Aug 1944

Bucharest

3rd Ukranian Front
(Tolbukhin)

Danube River

BULGARIA

Defected to become Soviet allies
8 Sep 1944

Sofia

1 Nov 1944

Bulgarian
First Army

Skopje

Monastir

Scutari

Albanian
Partisans

ALBANIA

Greek
Partisans

Salonika

Army Group E
(Löhr)

Thermopylae

GREECE

Escaped encirclement and
restored German southern flank,
Oct–Dec 1944

Aegean
Sea

TURKEY

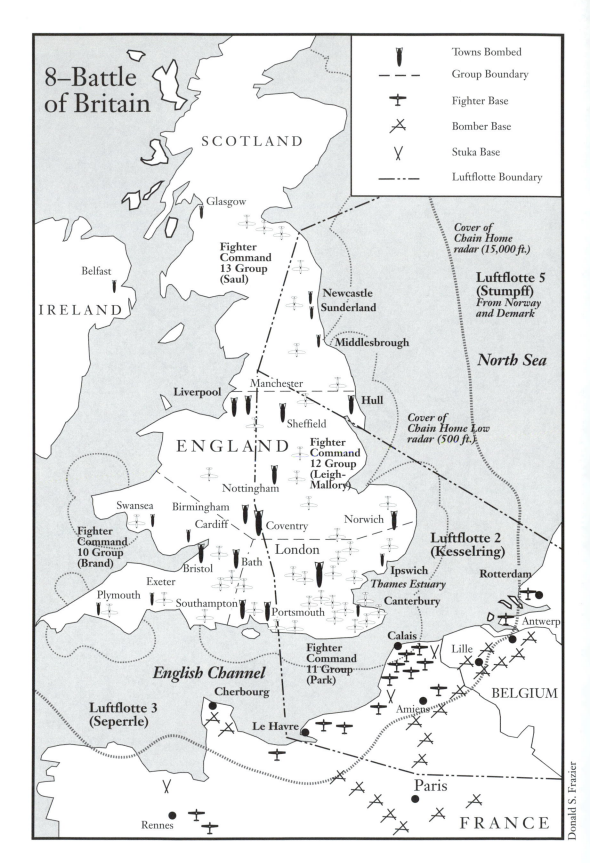

8–Battle of Britain

Legend:
- Towns Bombed
- Group Boundary
- Fighter Base
- Bomber Base
- Stuka Base
- Luftflotte Boundary

SCOTLAND

Glasgow

Belfast

IRELAND

Fighter Command 13 Group (Saul)

Newcastle
Sunderland

Middlesbrough

Cover of Chain Home radar (15,000 ft.)

Luftflotte 5 (Stumpff)
From Norway and Demark

North Sea

Manchester

Liverpool

Hull

Sheffield

ENGLAND

Fighter Command 12 Group (Leigh-Mallory)

Cover of Chain Home Low radar (500 ft.)

Nottingham

Swansea

Birmingham

Cardiff

Coventry

Norwich

Fighter Command 10 Group (Brand)

London

Luftflotte 2 (Kesselring)

Rotterdam

Bristol

Bath

Exeter

Plymouth

Southampton

Portsmouth

Ipswich

Thames Estuary

Canterbury

Antwerp

Calais

Lille

BELGIUM

Fighter Command 11 Group (Park)

English Channel

Cherbourg

Luftflotte 3 (Seperrle)

Le Havre

Amiens

Paris

FRANCE

Rennes

Donald S. Frazier

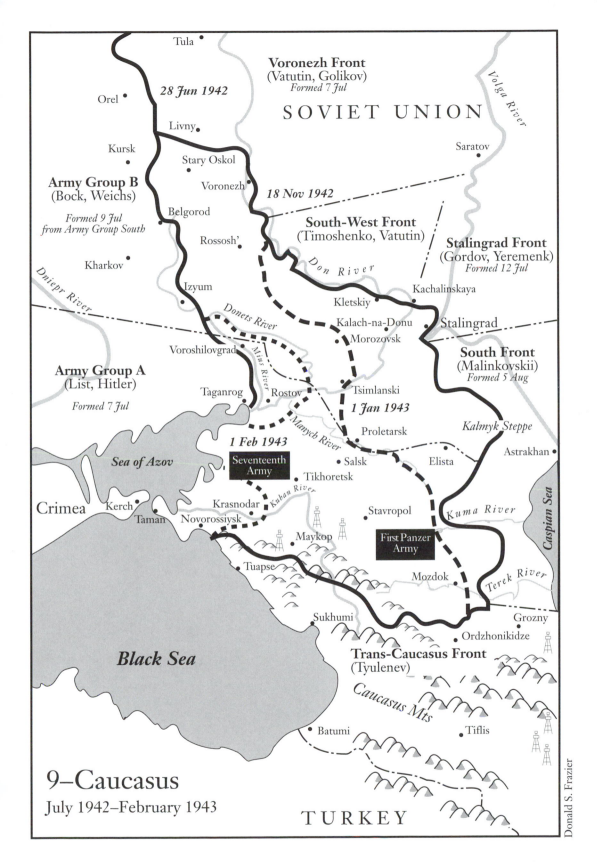

Tula

Orel

Kursk

Army Group B
(Bock, Weichs)

*Formed 9 Jul
from Army Group South*

Kharkov

Dniepr River

Army Group A
(List, Hitler)

Formed 7 Jul

Crimea

Kerch

Taman

Black Sea

28 Jun 1942

Livny

Stary Oskol

Voronezh

Belgorod

Rossosh'

Izyum

Donets River

Voroshilovgrad

Mius River

Taganrog

Rostov

Voronezh Front
(Vatutin, Golikov)
Formed 7 Jul

SOVIET UNION

Saratov

18 Nov 1942

Don River

South-West Front
(Timoshenko, Vatutin)

Volga River

Stalingrad Front
(Gordov, Yeremenk)
Formed 12 Jul

Kachalinskaya

Kletskiy

Kalach-na-Donu

Morozovsk

Stalingrad

South Front
(Malinkovskii)
Formed 5 Aug

Tsimlanski

1 Jan 1943

Manych River

Proletarsk

Kalmyk Steppe

Astrakhan

1 Feb 1943

Sea of Azov

Seventeenth
Army

Tikhoretsk

Kuban River

Salsk

Elista

Caspian Sea

Krasnodar

Novorossiysk

Stavropol

First Panzer
Army

Kuma River

Maykop

Tuapse

Mozdok

Terek River

Sukhumi

Ordzhonikidze

Grozny

Trans-Caucasus Front
(Tyulenev)

Caucasus Mts

Batumi

Tiflis

9–Caucasus

July 1942–February 1943

TURKEY

Donald S. Frazier

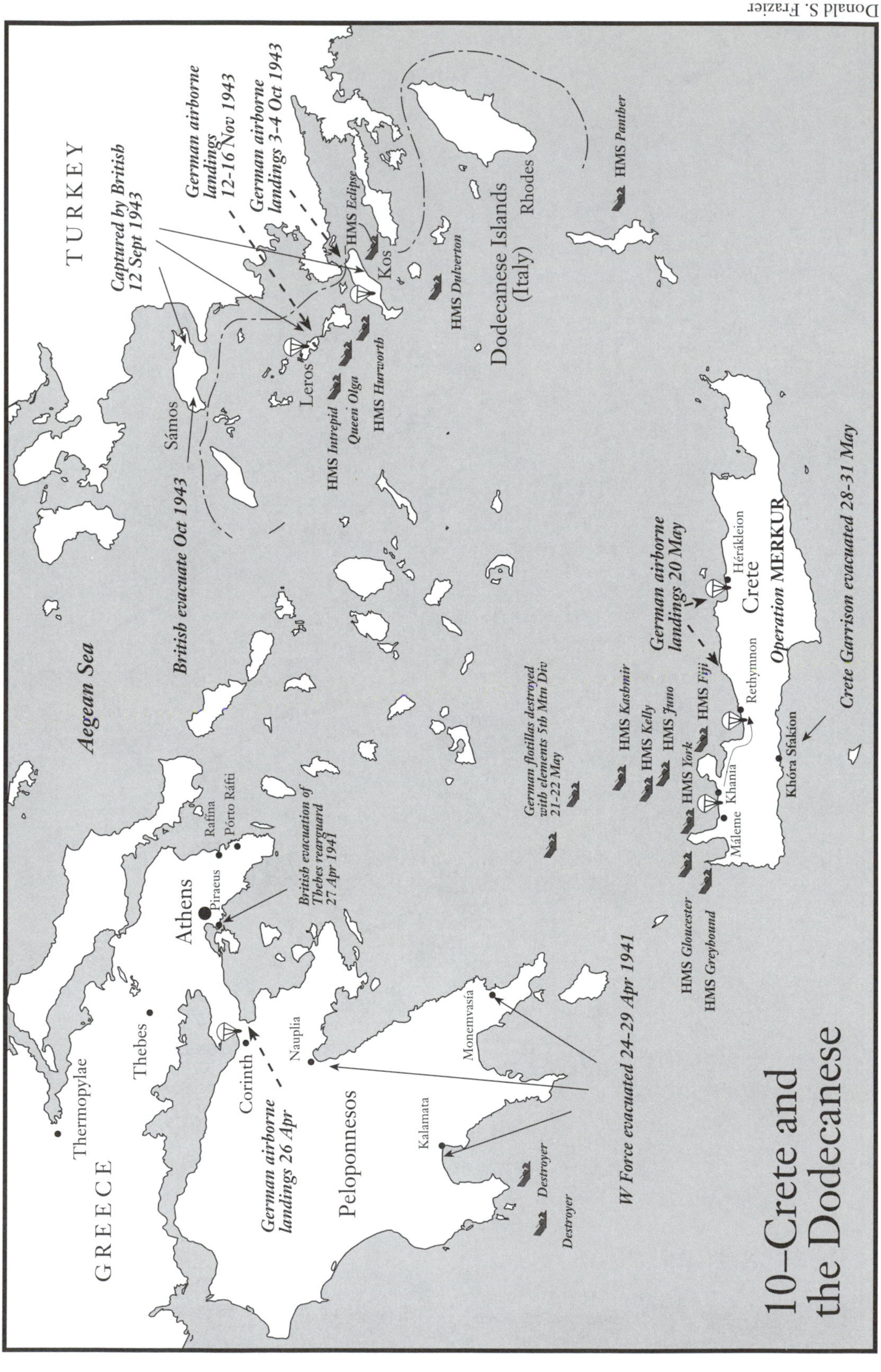

10—Crete and the Dodecanese

GREECE

Thermopylae
Thebes
Athens
Piraeus
Rafina
Pórto Ráfti
Corinth
Nauplia
Peloponnesos
Monemvasia
Kalamata

TURKEY

Sámos
Leros
Kos
Rhodes

Dodecanese Islands (Italy)

Aegean Sea

Crete

Hérakleion
Rethymnon
Khaniá
Máleme
Khóra Sfakíon

Operation MERKUR

Captured by British 12 Sept 1943

German airborne landings 12-16 Nov 1943

German airborne landings 3-4 Oct 1943

British evacuate Oct 1943

German airborne landings 26 Apr

British evacuation of Thebes rearguard 27 Apr 1941

German flotillas destroyed with elements 5th Mtn Div 21-22 May

German airborne landings 20 May

Crete Garrison evacuated 28-31 May

W Force evacuated 24-29 Apr 1941

HMS Eclipse
HMS Dulverton
HMS Panther
HMS Intrepid
Queen Olga
HMS Harworth
HMS Kashmir
HMS Kelly
HMS Juno
HMS York
HMS Fiji
HMS Gloucester
HMS Greyhound
Destroyer
Destroyer

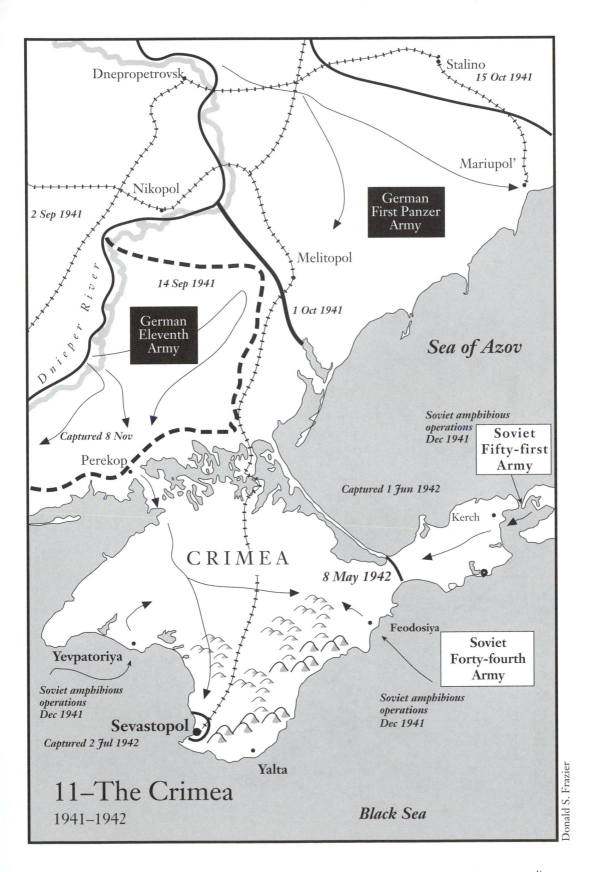

Dnepropetrovsk

Stalino
15 Oct 1941

Mariupol'

Nikopol

2 Sep 1941

**German
First Panzer
Army**

D n i e p e r   R i v e r

Melitopol

14 Sep 1941

1 Oct 1941

**German
Eleventh
Army**

Sea of Azov

Captured 8 Nov

Perekop

*Soviet amphibious
operations
Dec 1941*

**Soviet
Fifty-first
Army**

Captured 1 Jun 1942

Kerch

C R I M E A

8 May 1942

Yevpatoriya

Feodosiya

**Soviet
Forty-fourth
Army**

*Soviet amphibious
operations
Dec 1941*

*Soviet amphibious
operations
Dec 1941*

Sevastopol

Captured 2 Jul 1942

Yalta

11–The Crimea
1941–1942

Black Sea

Donald S. Frazier

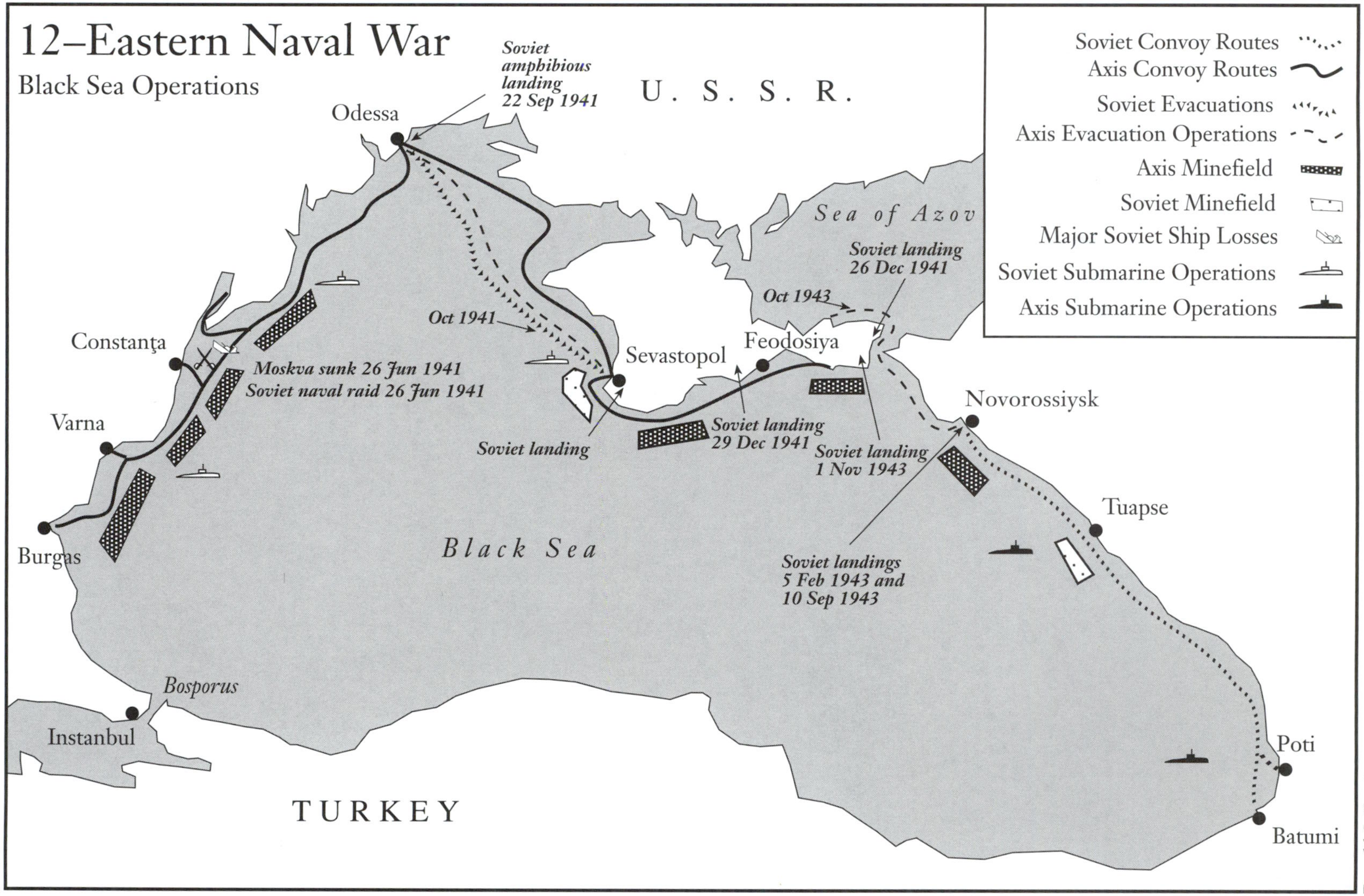

12–Eastern Naval War
Black Sea Operations

Donald S. Frazier

Legend:
- Soviet Convoy Routes
- Axis Convoy Routes
- Soviet Evacuations
- Axis Evacuation Operations
- Axis Minefield
- Soviet Minefield
- Major Soviet Ship Losses
- Soviet Submarine Operations
- Axis Submarine Operations

U. S. S. R.

Sea of Azov

Black Sea

TURKEY

Odessa

Soviet amphibious landing 22 Sep 1941

Oct 1941

Moskva sunk 26 Jun 1941
Soviet naval raid 26 Jun 1941

Constanța

Varna

Burgas

Instanbul

Bosporus

Sevastopol

Soviet landing

Feodosiya

Soviet landing 29 Dec 1941

Soviet landing 26 Dec 1941

Oct 1943

Soviet landing 1 Nov 1943

Novorossiysk

Soviet landings 5 Feb 1943 and 10 Sep 1943

Tuapse

Poti

Batumi

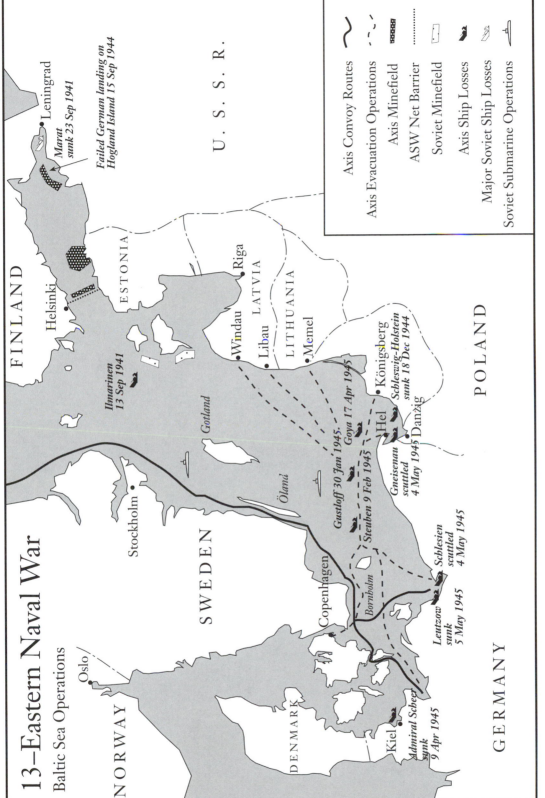

13–Eastern Naval War

Baltic Sea Operations

Donald S. Frazier

Legend:
- Axis Convoy Routes
- Axis Evacuation Operations
- Axis Minefield
- ASW Net Barrier
- Soviet Minefield
- Axis Ship Losses
- Major Soviet Ship Losses
- Soviet Submarine Operations

NORWAY — Oslo

SWEDEN — Stockholm

FINLAND — Helsinki

Leningrad — *Marat sunk 23 Sep 1941*

U. S. S. R.

Failed German landing on Hogland Island 15 Sep 1944

ESTONIA — Riga

LATVIA — Windau, Libau

LITHUANIA — Memel

Ilmarinen 13 Sep 1941

Gotland

Öland

Königsberg — *Schleswig–Holstein sunk 18 Dec 1944*

Danzig

Hel — *Goya 17 Apr 1945*

Gustloff 30 Jan 1945

Steuben 9 Feb 1945

Gneisenau scuttled 4 May 1945

Schlesien scuttled 4 May 1945

Bornholm

Copenhagen

DENMARK

Lützow sunk 5 May 1945

Kiel

Admiral Scheer sunk 9 Apr 1945

POLAND

GERMANY

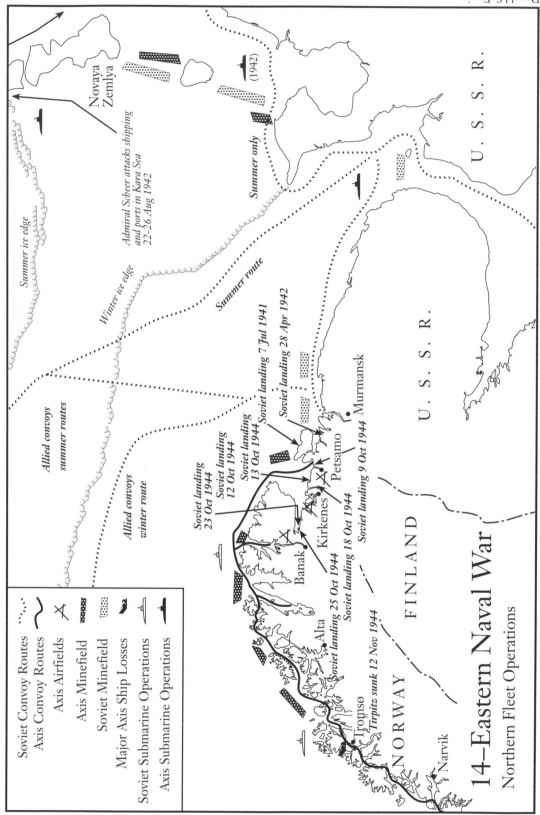

14—Eastern Naval War

Northern Fleet Operations

Narvik

NORWAY

FINLAND

U. S. S. R.

Tromsø
Tirpitz sunk 12 Nov 1944

Alta
Soviet landing 25 Oct 1944
Soviet landing 18 Oct 1944
Soviet landing 9 Oct 1944 Murmansk

Banak

Soviet landing 23 Oct 1944

Soviet landing 12 Oct 1944

Soviet landing 13 Oct 1944

Kirkenes
Petsamo

Soviet landing 7 Jul 1941

Soviet landing 28 Apr 1942

Allied convoys winter route

Allied convoys summer routes

Summer route

Winter ice edge

Summer ice edge

Novaya Zemlya

Admiral Scheer attacks shipping and ports in Kara Sea 22–26 Aug 1942

Summer only

(1942)

U. S. S. R.

U. S. S. R.

Soviet Convoy Routes
Axis Convoy Routes
Axis Airfields
Axis Minefield
Soviet Minefield
Major Axis Ship Losses
Soviet Submarine Operations
Axis Submarine Operations

Donald S. Frazier

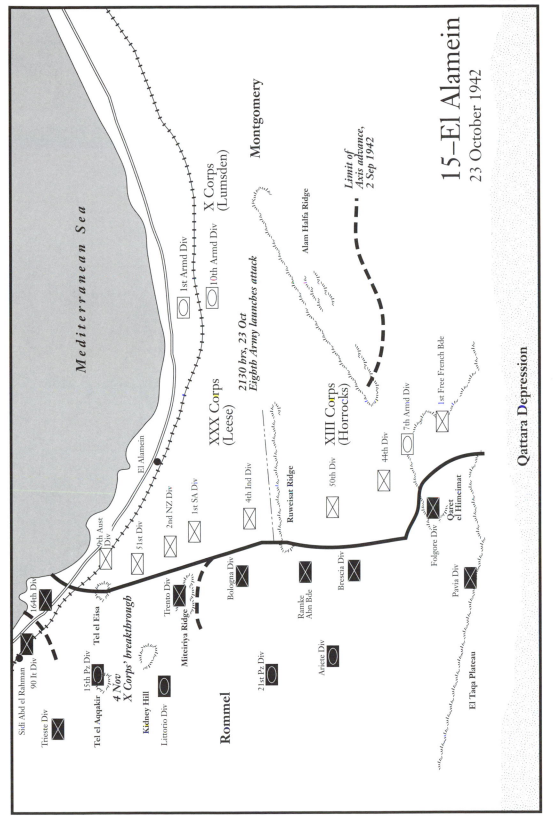

15—El Alamein
23 October 1942

Mediterranean Sea

Montgomery

X Corps
(Lumsden)

1st Armd Div

10th Armd Div

XXX Corps
(Leese)

*2130 hrs, 23 Oct
Eighth Army launches attack*

*Limit of
Axis advance,
2 Sep 1942*

Alam Halfa Ridge

XIII Corps
(Horrocks)

El Alamein

9th Aust Div

51st Div

2nd NZ Div

1st SA Div

4th Ind Div

Ruweisat Ridge

50th Div

44th Div

7th Armd Div

1st Free French Bde

Qattara Depression

164th Div

Tel el Eisa

15th Pz Div

Sidi Abd el Rahman

90 It Div

Tel el Aqqakir

*4 Nov
X Corps' breakthrough*

Kidney Hill

Littorio Div

Trento Div

Miteiriya Ridge

Bologna Div

Ramke
Abn Bde

Brescia Div

Folgore Div

**Qaret
el Himeimat**

Pavia Div

Trieste Div

21st Pz Div

Ariete Div

Rommel

El Taqa Plateau

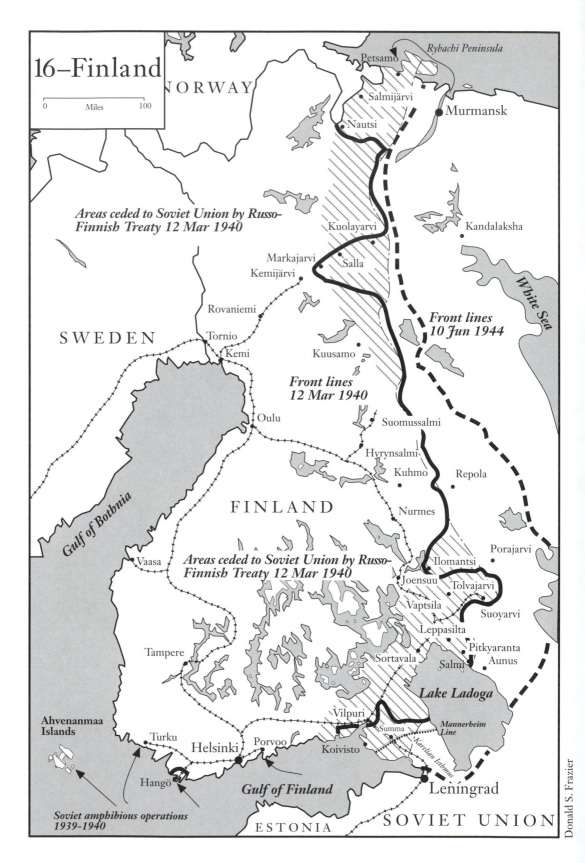

16–Finland

0 — Miles — 100

NORWAY

Rybachi Peninsula

Petsamo

Salmijärvi

Murmansk

Nautsi

Areas ceded to Soviet Union by Russo-Finnish Treaty 12 Mar 1940

Kuolayarvi

Kandalaksha

Markajarvi

Salla

Kemijärvi

Front lines 10 Jun 1944

Rovaniemi

SWEDEN

Tornio

Kemi

Kuusamo

White Sea

Front lines 12 Mar 1940

Oulu

Suomussalmi

Hyrynsalmi

Kuhmo

Repola

Gulf of Bothnia

FINLAND

Nurmes

Porajarvi

Vaasa

Areas ceded to Soviet Union by Russo-Finnish Treaty 12 Mar 1940

Ilomantsi

Joensuu

Tolvajarvi

Vaptsila

Suoyarvi

Leppasilta

Tampere

Sortavala

Pitkyaranta

Aunus

Salmi

Lake Ladoga

Vilpuri

Mannerheim Line

Ahvenanmaa Islands

Turku

Summa

Helsinki

Porvoo

Koivisto

Karelian Isthmus

Hangö

Gulf of Finland

Leningrad

Soviet amphibious operations 1939-1940

ESTONIA

SOVIET UNION

Donald S. Frazier

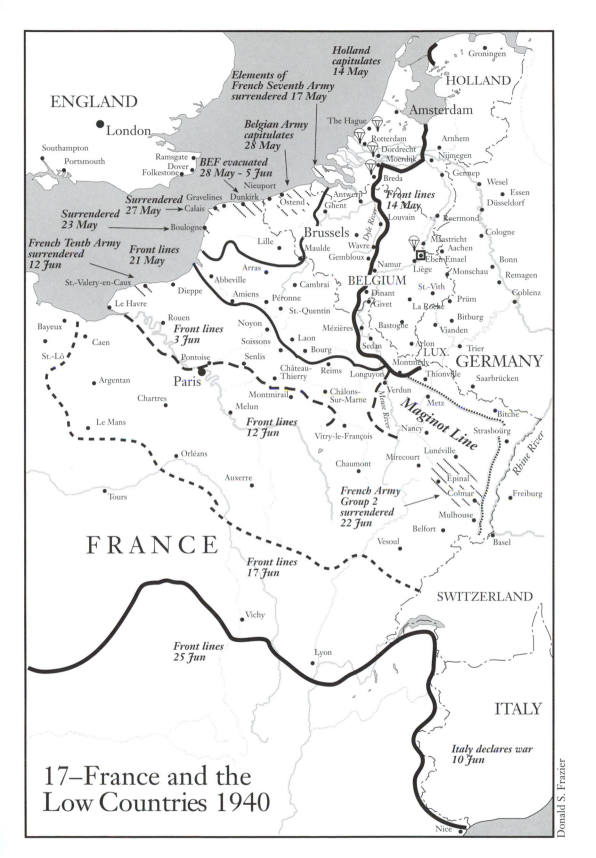

17–France and the Low Countries 1940

ENGLAND

London
Southampton
Portsmouth
Ramsgate
Dover
Folkestone

Holland capitulates 14 May

HOLLAND

Groningen
Amsterdam
The Hague
Arnhem
Rotterdam
Dordrecht
Moerdijk
Nijmegen
Gennep
Breda
Wesel
Essen
Düsseldorf

Elements of French Seventh Army surrendered 17 May

Belgian Army capitulates 28 May

BEF evacuated 28 May - 5 Jun

Nieuport
Dunkirk
Gravelines
Ostend
Antwerp
Ghent
Louvain
Roermond

Surrendered 27 May → Calais

Front lines 14 May

Maastricht
Aachen
Cologne
Bonn

Surrendered 23 May → Boulogne

Lille
Maulde
Wavre
Gembloux
Brussels
Eben Emael
Liège
Monschau
Remagen
Coblenz

French Tenth Army surrendered 12 Jun

Front lines 21 May

St.-Valery-en-Caux

BELGIUM
Namur
Dinant
Givet
St.-Vith
Prüm

Le Havre
Dieppe
Abbeville
Arras
Amiens
Cambrai
Péronne
La Roche
Bitburg

Bayeux
Caen
St.-Lô
Rouen
Front lines 3 Jun
Noyon
Soissons
Laon
Bourg
St.-Quentin
Mézières
Sedan
Bastogne
Vianden
Arlon
Trier

Argentan
Chartres
Pontoise
Senlis
Château-Thierry
Reims
Longuyon
Montmédy
LUX.
Thionville
Saarbrücken

Paris
Melun
Montmirail
Châlons-Sur-Marne
Verdun
GERMANY

Le Mans
Front lines 12 Jun
Vitry-le-François
Nancy
Metz
Maginot Line
Strasbourg
Bitche

Orléans
Auxerre
Chaumont
Mirecourt
Lunéville
Épinal
Colmar
Freiburg

FRANCE

French Army Group 2 surrendered 22 Jun

Mulhouse
Belfort

Tours
Vesoul
Basel

Front lines 17 Jun

SWITZERLAND

Vichy

Front lines 25 Jun

Lyon

ITALY

Italy declares war 10 Jun

Nice

Dyle River
Meuse River
Rhine River

Donald S. Frazier

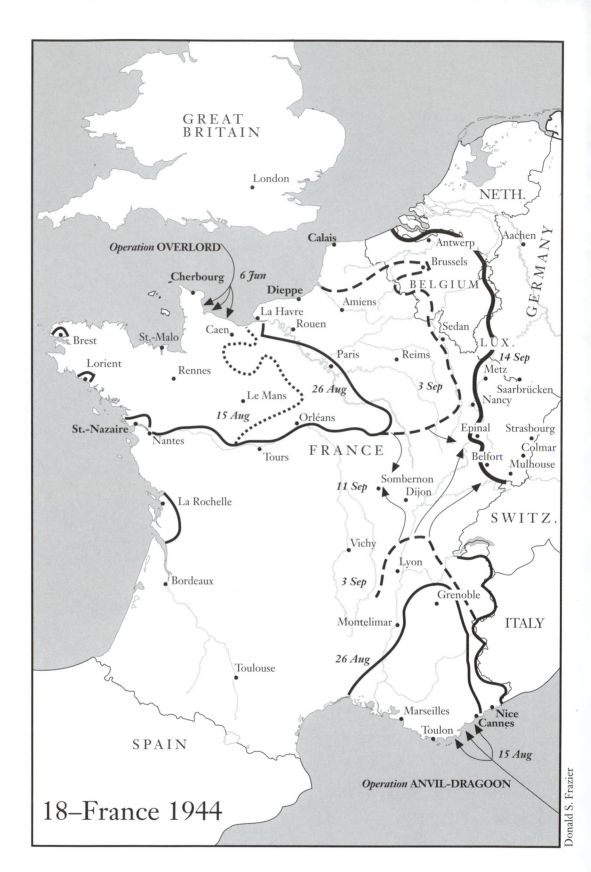

GREAT
BRITAIN

London

NETH.

Aachen

Calais

Operation **OVERLORD**

Cherbourg   *6 Jun*

Dieppe

Antwerp

Brussels

BELGIUM

Amiens

Sedan

LUX.

14 Sep

La Havre

Rouen

Metz

Brest

St.-Malo

Caen

Paris

Reims

Saarbrücken

Lorient

Rennes

Le Mans

26 Aug

3 Sep

Nancy

Epinal

Strasbourg

15 Aug

Orléans

Colmar

St.-Nazaire

Nantes

F R A N C E

Belfort

Mulhouse

Tours

La Rochelle

11 Sep

Sombernon
Dijon

SWITZ.

Vichy

Lyon

Bordeaux

3 Sep

Grenoble

ITALY

Montelimar

Toulouse

26 Aug

SPAIN

Marseilles

Nice
Cannes

Toulon

15 Aug

Operation **ANVIL-DRAGOON**

18–France 1944

Donald S. Frazier

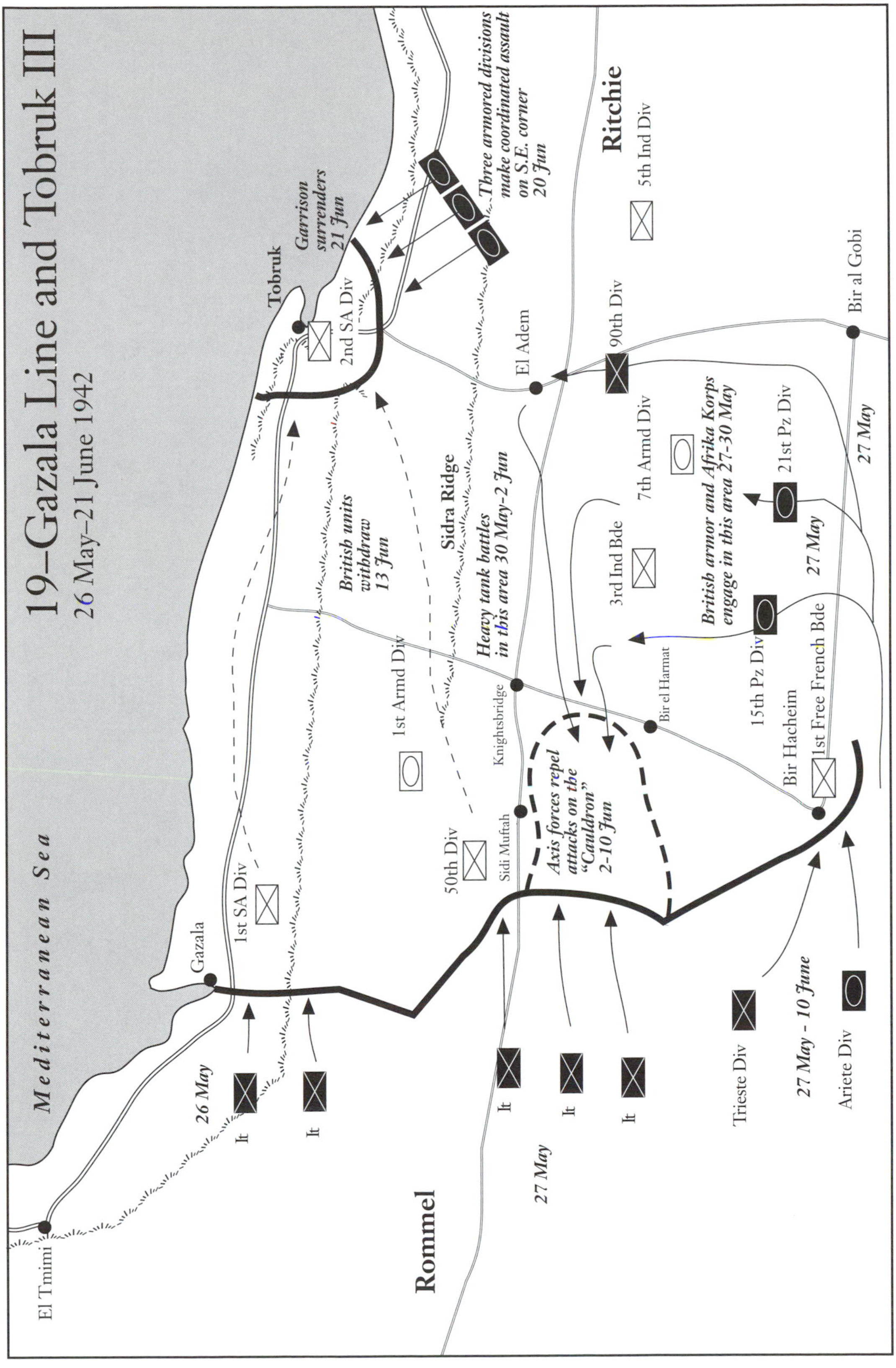

19–Gazala Line and Tobruk III
26 May–21 June 1942

Mediterranean Sea

El Tmimi

Gazala

Tobruk

Garrison surrenders 21 Jun

2nd SA Div

Three armored divisions make coordinated assault on S.E. corner 20 Jun

Ritchie

5th Ind Div

El Adem

90th Div

Rommel

26 May
It
It

27 May
It
It
It

Trieste Div

27 May – 10 June

Ariete Div

British units withdraw 13 Jun

Sidra Ridge

Heavy tank battles in this area 30 May–2 Jun

1st Armd Div

Knightsbridge

1st SA Div

50th Div
Sidi Muftah

Axis forces repel attacks on the "Cauldron" 2–10 Jun

7th Armd Div

3rd Ind Bde

Bir el Harmat

British armor and Afrika Korps engage in this area 27-30 May

21st Pz Div

27 May

15th Pz Div

27 May

Bir Hacheim

1st Free French Bde

Bir al Gobi

27 May

DENMARK

North Sea

Baltic Sea

Flensburg

Kiel

Heide

Warnemünde
Rerik
Wustrow
Rostock

Peenemünde

Anklam
Politz

Lübeck

Stettin

Schwerin

Bremerhaven

Hamburg

Emden

**Fighter escort range
Jul 1943–Feb 1944**

Bremen

NETHERLANDS

**Fighter escort range
Dec 1942–Jul 1943**

Hanover

Brunswick

Magdeburg

Potsdam

Berlin

Scholven Buer

Oschersleben

Dessau

Emmerich
Sterkrade

Essen

Dortmund

Duisburg

Düsseldorf

Kassel

Nordstern

Wanne-Eickel

Cologne

Bonn

Halle

Merseburg

Ruhland

Leipzig
Böhlen

Gotha

Erfurt

Lutzkendorf

Dresden

Zeitz

Chemnitz

Giessen

Suhl

Brüx

Frankfurt

Schweinfurt

Wiesbaden

Mainz

LUX.

Prague

CZECHOSLOVAKIA

Mannheim

Fürth

Nürnberg

Saarbrücken

Ludwigshafen

**Fighter escort range
Feb 1944–Jun 1944**

Stuttgart

Regensburg

FRANCE

Ulm

Augsburg

Munich

Freiburg

	Aircraft Industry
	War Industry
	Marshalling Yards
	Oil Industry
	Sub Pens/Base
	Ballistic Missile Base

20–Germany
Air Campaign

Donald S. Frazier

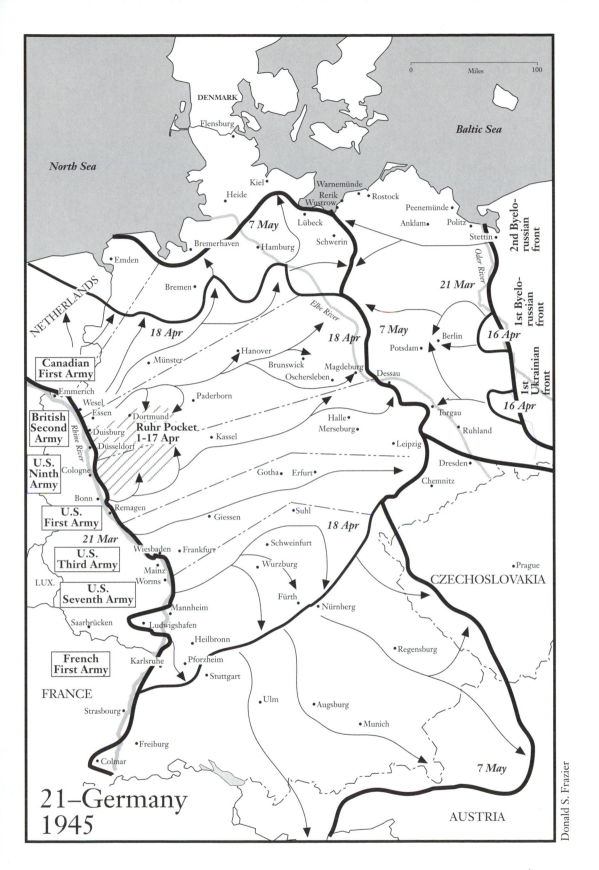

DENMARK

Flensburg

North Sea

Baltic Sea

Kiel

Heide

Warnemünde
Rerik
Wustrow

Rostock

Peenemünde

Anklam

Politz

2nd Byelo-
russian
front

7 May

Lübeck

Schwerin

Stettin

Bremerhaven

Hamburg

Oder River

21 Mar

1st Byelo-
russian
front

Emden

Bremen

Elbe River

18 Apr

16 Apr

NETHERLANDS

18 Apr

Münster

Hanover

Brunswick

Magdeburg

Oschersleben

Dessau

7 May

Potsdam

Berlin

Canadian
First Army

Emmerich

Wesel

Paderborn

Torgau

16 Apr

1st
Ukrainian
front

Essen

British
Second
Army

Dortmund

Ruhr Pocket
1-17 Apr

Halle

Merseburg

Ruhland

Rhine River

Duisburg

Kassel

Leipzig

U.S.
Ninth
Army

Düsseldorf

Cologne

Dresden

Chemnitz

Bonn

Gotha

Erfurt

Remagen

U.S.
First Army

Giessen

Suhl

18 Apr

21 Mar

Wiesbaden

Frankfurt

Schweinfurt

Prague

U.S.
Third Army

Mainz

Wurzburg

CZECHOSLOVAKIA

U.S.
Seventh
Army

Worms

Fürth

LUX.

Mannheim

Nürnberg

Saarbrücken

Ludwigshafen

Heilbronn

Regensburg

French
First Army

Karlsruhe

Pforzheim

FRANCE

Strasbourg

Stuttgart

Ulm

Augsburg

Munich

Freiburg

7 May

Colmar

21–Germany
1945

AUSTRIA

Donald S. Frazier

SWITZ-ERLAND

Line reached by Allied forces in Western Europe 7 May 1945

AUSTRIA

Line reached by Soviet forces 7 May 1945

HUNGARY

Bolzano

7 May

Sondrio · Trento · Belluno · Udine
Aosta · Varese · Como · Vicenza · Pordenone · Gorizia
Novara · Milan · Brescia · Verona · Treviso · Trieste
Vercelli · Pavia · Cremona · Padova · Venice
Turin · Piacenza · Mantova · Rovigo
Asti · Parma · Ferrara
Cuneo · Genoa · *30 Apr* · *23 Apr* · Modena · Bologna · *15 Jan – 8 Apr 1945*

Line reached by Yugoslav partisans 7 May 1945

YUGOSLAVIA

Savona
La Spezia · Ravenna · Rimini
Imperia · Massa · *4 Aug* · **Gothic Line**
Lucca · Pesaro
Ligurian Sea · Pisa · Florence · Ancona
Leghorn · Arezzo
Siena · *17 Jun*
Grosseto · Ascoli Piceno
9 Jun · Teramo
CORSICA (FRANCE) · Pescara · **Gustav Line**
Evacuated by German forces 18 Sep–Oct 1943 · Viterbo · *15 Jan – 11 May 1944*
5 Jun · *Adriatic Sea*
Rome · *28 Sept*
Cassino · Isernia · *25 Sep*
Allies enter Rome 4 Jun 1944 · *8 Oct* · Foggia · *14 Sep*
Anzio · Capua · Benevento · Bari
Sassari · Gaeta · Brindisi
Nuoro · **SHINGLE** · Potenza · Matera · Taranto
22 Jan 1944 · **Naples** · Lecce
Oristano · Salerno
SARDINIA · *Tyrrhenian Sea* · **AVALANCHE** · **SLAPSTICK**
Cagliari · *9 Sep 1943* · *9 Sep 1943*

Evacuated by German forces 18 Sep 1943

Italy surrenders 3 Sep 1943

· Cosenza
Catanzaro
9 Sep

Messina
Palermo · **Reggio di Calabria**
Trapani · **BAYTOWN** · *3 Sep 1943*
Caltanissetta · Enna · Catania
Agrigento · **SICILY** · Siracusa
Strait of Sicily · Ragusa

HUSKY · *10 Jul 1943* · **MALTA**

Mediterranean Sea

0 — Miles — 100

22–Operations in Italy
1943–1945

Donald S. Frazier

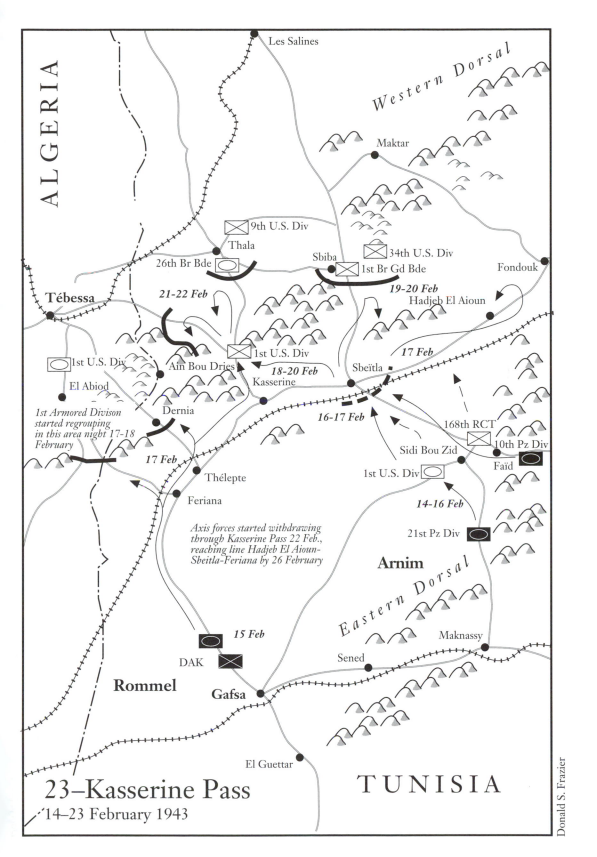

ALGERIA

Les Salines

Western Dorsal

Maktar

9th U.S. Div

Thala

26th Br Bde

Sbiba

34th U.S. Div

1st Br Gd Bde

Fondouk

19-20 Feb

Hadjeb El Aioun

Tébessa

21-22 Feb

17 Feb

1st U.S. Div

1st U.S. Div

Ain Bou Dries

18-20 Feb

Kasserine

Sbeïtla

El Abiod

*1st Armored Divison
started regrouping
in this area night 17-18
February*

Dernia

16-17 Feb

168th RCT

10th Pz Div

Sidi Bou Zid

Faïd

17 Feb

1st U.S. Div

Thélepte

14-16 Feb

Feriana

21st Pz Div

*Axis forces started withdrawing
through Kasserine Pass 22 Feb.,
reaching line Hadjeb El Aioun-
Sbeitla-Feriana by 26 February*

Arnim

Eastern Dorsal

Maknassy

15 Feb

Sened

DAK

Rommel

Gafsa

El Guettar

TUNISIA

23–Kasserine Pass
14–23 February 1943

Donald S. Frazier

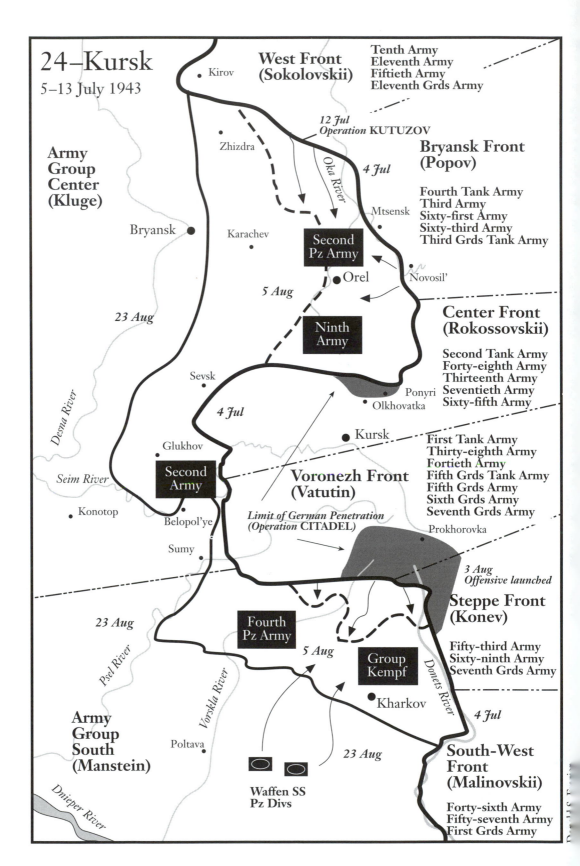

24–Kursk
5–13 July 1943

**West Front
(Sokolovskii)**

Tenth Army
Eleventh Army
Fiftieth Army
Eleventh Grds Army

**Army
Group
Center
(Kluge)**

Kirov

Zhizdra

*12 Jul
Operation* KUTUZOV

Oka River

4 Jul

**Bryansk Front
(Popov)**

Fourth Tank Army
Third Army
Sixty-first Army
Sixty-third Army
Third Grds Tank Army

Bryansk

Karachev

**Second
Pz Army**

Mtsensk

Orel

Novosil'

5 Aug

23 Aug

**Ninth
Army**

**Center Front
(Rokossovskii)**

Second Tank Army
Forty-eighth Army
Thirteenth Army
Seventieth Army
Sixty-fifth Army

Sevsk

Desna River

4 Jul

Ponyri
Olkhovatka

Kursk

Glukhov

**Second
Army**

**Voronezh Front
(Vatutin)**

First Tank Army
Thirty-eighth Army
Fortieth Army
Fifth Grds Tank Army
Fifth Grds Army
Sixth Grds Army
Seventh Grds Army

Seim River

Konotop

Belopol'ye

Sumy

*Limit of German Penetration
(Operation* CITADEL)

Prokhorovka

*3 Aug
Offensive launched*

**Steppe Front
(Konev)**

23 Aug

**Fourth
Pz Army**

5 Aug

**Group
Kempf**

Fifty-third Army
Sixty-ninth Army
Seventh Grds Army

Psel River

Vorskla River

Donets River

Kharkov

4 Jul

**Army
Group
South
(Manstein)**

Poltava

23 Aug

**South-West
Front
(Malinovskii)**

Dnieper River

Forty-sixth Army
Fifty-seventh Army
First Grds Army

Waffen SS
Pz Divs

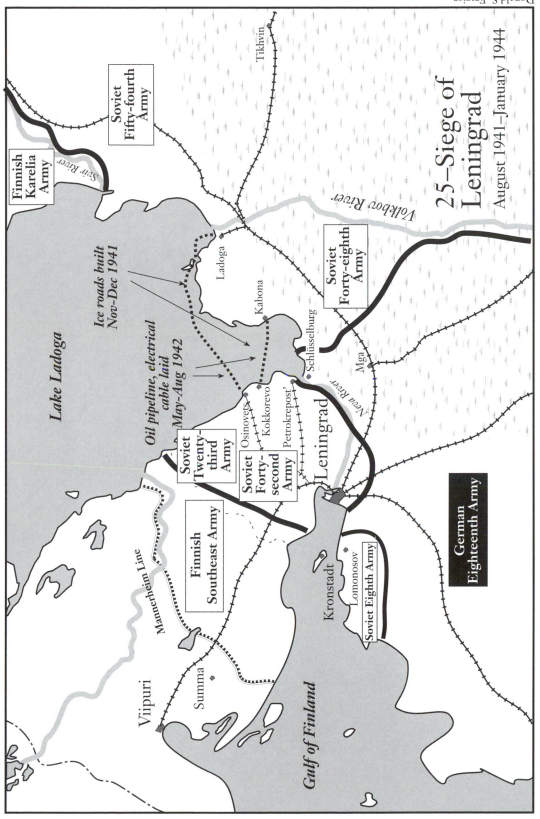

25–Siege of Leningrad
August 1941–January 1944

Tikhvin

Finnish Karelia Army

Svir River

Soviet Fifty-fourth Army

Volkhov River

Ice roads built Nov–Dec 1941

Ladoga

Soviet Forty-eighth Army

Oil pipeline, electrical cable laid May–Aug 1942

Lake Ladoga

Kabona

Schlüsselburg

Mga

Osinovets

Kokkorevo

Petrokrepost'

Soviet Twenty-third Army

Soviet Forty-second Army

Neva River

Leningrad

German Eighteenth Army

Finnish Southeast Army

Mannerheim Line

Kronstadt

Lomonosov

Soviet Eighth Army

Viipuri

Summa

Gulf of Finland

Groningen

18 Apr

HOLLAND

*Operations, against
South Beveland
and Walcheren Island*

Zuider Zee

Amsterdam

The Hague

4 Apr

Rotterdam

Arnhem

Dordrecht

Moerdijk

Nijmegen

Shelde Estuary

Eindhoven

Gennep

Wesel

Nieuport

15 Dec

28 Mar

Essen

Roermond

Düsseldorf

Dunkirk

Ostend

Ghent

Antwerp

Montgomery

Louvain

*Ruhr
Pocket*

Brussels

15 Sep

Maastricht

Aachen

Cologne

Lille

Wavre

Monschau

Bonn

Maulde

Gembloux

Namur

Liège

Remagen

Arras

Coblenz

Cambrai

BELGIUM

Prüm

Péronne

*German Ardennes
Offensive 15-25 Dec*

La Roche

Bitburg

St.-Quentin

Noyon

Mézières

Bastogne

Vianden

Laon

Arlon

Trier

Bourg

Sedan

Bradley

Montmédy

GERMANY

F R A N C E

Thionville

Saarbrücken

Metz

Bitche

26–The Low Countries
1944–1945

Donald S. Frazier

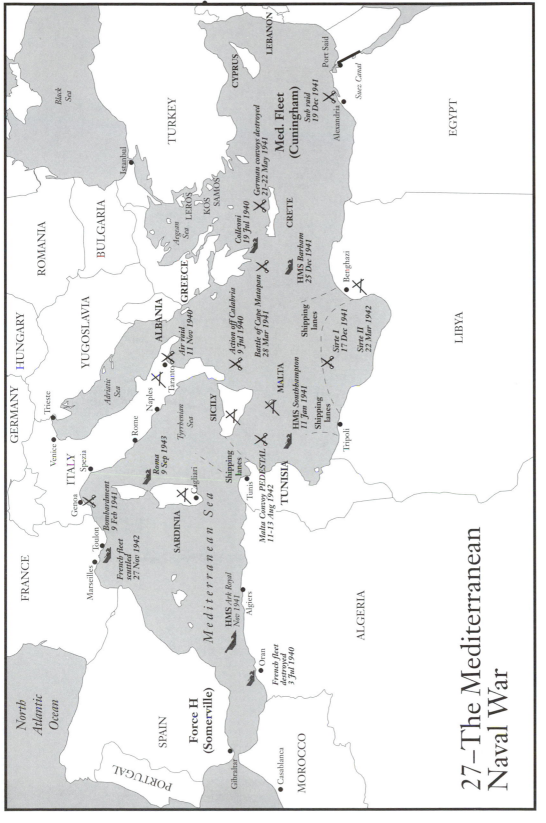

27–The Mediterranean Naval War

North Atlantic Ocean

PORTUGAL

SPAIN

Force H (Somerville)

Gibraltar

Casablanca

MOROCCO

Oran

French fleet destroyed 3 Jul 1940

Algiers

ALGERIA

HMS Ark Royal Nov 1941

Mediterranean Sea

SARDINIA

Cagliari

Shipping lanes

Tunis

TUNISIA

Tripoli

Malta Convoy PEDESTAL 11–13 Aug 1942

FRANCE

Marseilles

Toulon

French fleet scuttled 27 Nov 1942

Bombardment 9 Feb 1941

Genoa

ITALY

Spezia

Venice

GERMANY

Trieste

Adriatic Sea

Tyrrhenian Sea

Rome

Naples

Roma 9 Sep 1943

SICILY

MALTA

HMS Southampton 11 Jan 1941

Shipping lanes

Shipping lanes

Taranto

Air raid 11 Nov 1940

ALBANIA

GREECE

Action off Calabria 9 Jul 1940

Battle of Cape Matapan 28 Mar 1941

Colleoni 19 Jul 1940

LEROS

KOS

SAMOS

Aegean Sea

Sirte I 17 Dec 1941

Sirte II 22 Mar 1942

HMS Barham 25 Dec 1941

Benghazi

LIBYA

EGYPT

YUGOSLAVIA

HUNGARY

ROMANIA

BULGARIA

Black Sea

Istanbul

TURKEY

CRETE

German convoys destroyed 21–22 May 1941

Med. Fleet (Cunningham)

Sub raid 19 Dec 1941

Alexandria

Port Said

Suez Canal

CYPRUS

LEBANON

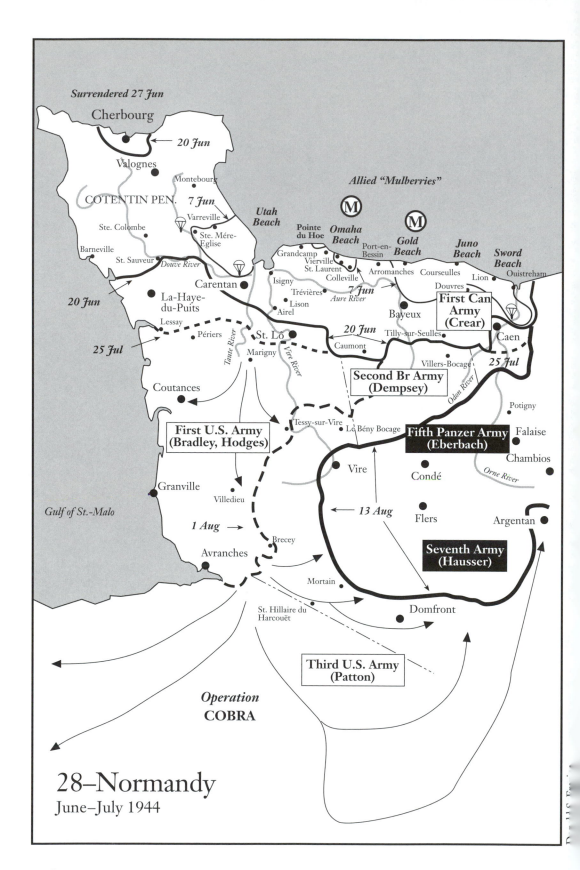

Surrendered 27 Jun

Cherbourg

20 Jun

Valognes

Montebourg

COTENTIN PEN.   7 Jun

Utah Beach

Allied "Mulberries"

Ⓜ   Ⓜ

Ste. Colombe

Varreville

Pointe du Hoe   *Omaha Beach*   *Gold Beach*   *Juno Beach*   *Sword Beach*

Ste. Mére-Eglise

Barneville

St. Sauveur   *Douve River*

Grandcamp   Port-en-Bessin

Vierville   Arromanches   Courseulles   Lion   Ouistreham

St. Laurent

Colleville   Douvres

Carentan

Isigny   7 Jun

First Can Army (Crear)

20 Jun

La-Haye-du-Puits

Trévières   *Aure River*

Lison   Bayeux

Airel

Lessay

St. Lô   20 Jun   Tilly-sur-Seulles

Caen

Périers   Marigny   Caumont

25 Jul

Taute River   *Vire River*   Villers-Bocage   25 Jul

Second Br Army (Dempsey)   *Odon River*

Coutances

Tessy-sur-Vire   Le Bény Bocage

Fifth Panzer Army (Eberbach)   Falaise

First U.S. Army (Bradley, Hodges)   Chambios

Vire   Condé   *Orne River*

Granville   13 Aug   Flers   Argentan

Villedieu

Seventh Army (Hausser)

1 Aug   Brecey

Avranches   Mortain   Domfront

St. Hillaire du Harcouët

Gulf of St.-Malo

Third U.S. Army (Patton)

Operation **COBRA**

28–Normandy
June–July 1944

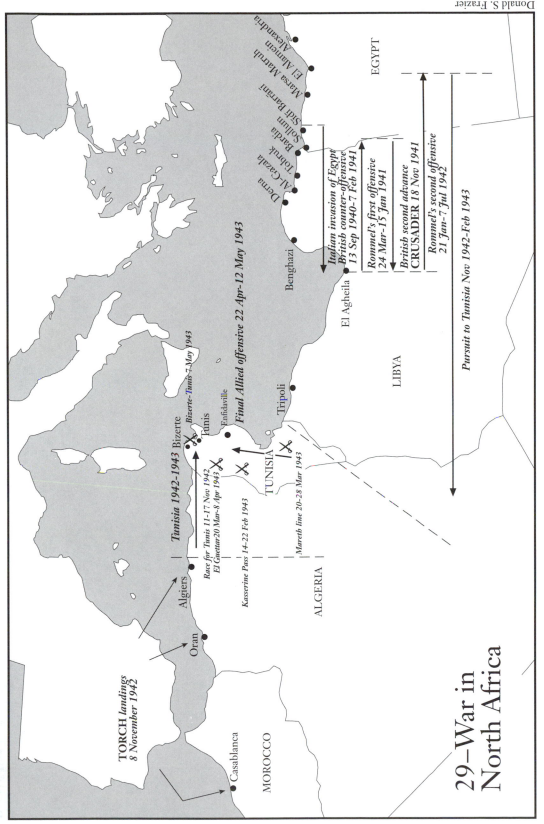

TORCH landings
8 November 1942

MOROCCO

Casablanca

Oran

Algiers

ALGERIA

Race for Tunis 11-17 Nov 1942
El Guettar 20 Mar-8 Apr 1943

Kasserine Pass 14-22 Feb 1943

Tunisia 1942-1943 Bizerte

Bizerte-Tunis 7 May 1943

Tunis

Enfidaville

TUNISIA

Mareth line 20-28 Mar 1943

Final Allied offensive 22 Apr-12 May 1943

Tripoli

El Agheila

Benghazi

Derna
Al-Gazala
Tobruk
Bardia
Sollum
Sidi Barrani
Marsa Matruh
El Alamein
Alexandria

Italian invasion of Egypt
British counter-offensive
13 Sep 1940-7 Feb 1941

Rommel's first offensive
24 Mar-15 Jan 1941

British second advance
CRUSADER 18 Nov 1941

Rommel's second offensive
21 Jan-7 Jul 1942

Pursuit to Tunisia Nov 1942-Feb 1943

LIBYA

EGYPT

29–War in
North Africa

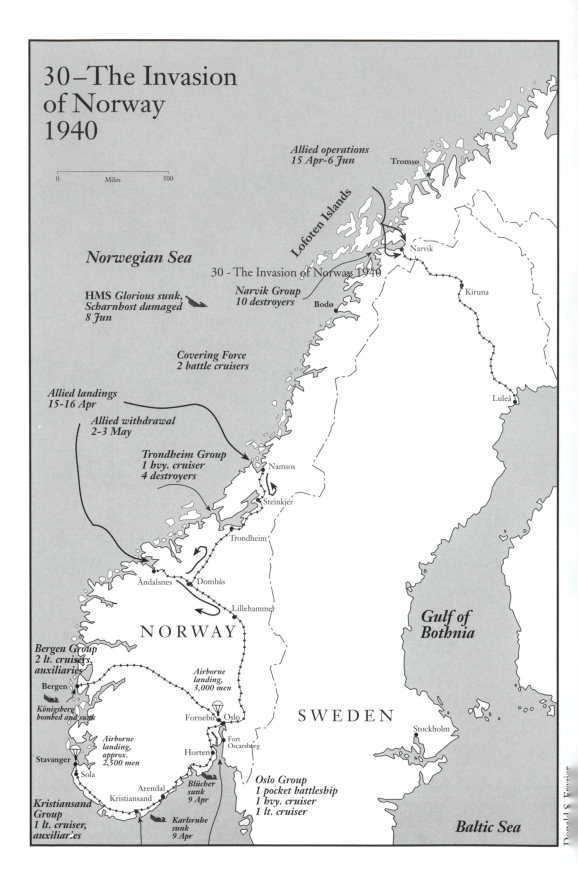

30–The Invasion
of Norway
1940

Miles
0   500

Norwegian Sea

**Allied operations
15 Apr–6 Jun**   Tromsø

Lofoten Islands

30 - The Invasion of Norway 1940

HMS *Glorious sunk,*   **Narvik Group**   Narvik
Scharnhost damaged   **10 destroyers**
8 Jun   Kiruna

Bodø

**Covering Force
2 battle cruisers**

**Allied landings
15–16 Apr**   Luleå

**Allied withdrawal
2–3 May**

**Trondheim Group
1 hvy. cruiser
4 destroyers**   Namsos

Steinkjer

Trondheim

NORWAY

Åndalsnes   Dombås

Lillehammer   *Gulf of
Bothnia*

**Bergen Group
2 lt. cruisers,
auxiliaries**

Bergen   *Airborne
landing,
3,000 men*   **SWEDEN**

*Königsberg
bombed and sunk*   Fornebu Oslo   Stockholm

*Airborne
landing,
approx.
2,500 men*   Horten   Fort
Oscarsborg

Stavanger

Sola   Arendal   *Blücher
sunk
9 Apr*   **Oslo Group
1 pocket battleship
1 hvy. cruiser
1 lt. cruiser**

Kristiansand   Kristiansand
**Group
1 lt. cruiser,   *Karlsruhe*
auxiliaries**   *sunk
9 Apr*   *Baltic Sea*

Donald S. Frazier

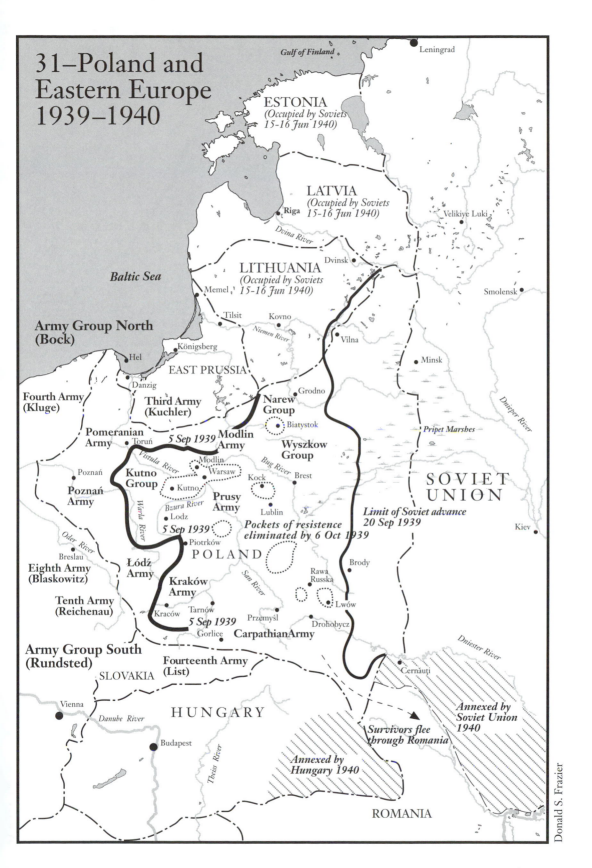

31–Poland and Eastern Europe 1939–1940

Gulf of Finland

Leningrad

ESTONIA
*(Occupied by Soviets
15-16 Jun 1940)*

Baltic Sea

LATVIA
*(Occupied by Soviets
15-16 Jun 1940)*

Riga

Velikiye Luki

Dvina River

Dvinsk

LITHUANIA
*(Occupied by Soviets
15-16 Jun 1940)*

Memel

Smolensk

Tilsit

Kovno

Niemen River

Vilna

**Army Group North
(Bock)**

Hel

Königsberg

Minsk

EAST PRUSSIA

Danzig

Grodno

Pripet Marshes

**Fourth Army
(Kluge)**

**Third Army
(Kuchler)**

**Narew
Group**

Biatystok

Toruń

5 Sep 1939

**Modlin
Army**

**Wyszkow
Group**

**Pomeranian
Army**

Vistula River

Modlin

Warsaw

Bug River

Brest

**S O V I E T
U N I O N**

Poznań

**Kutno
Group**

Kutno

Kock

**Poznań
Army**

Warta River

Bzura River

**Prusy
Army**

Lublin

Dnieper River

**Limit of Soviet advance
20 Sep 1939**

Kiev

Oder River

Lodz

5 Sep 1939

*Pockets of resistance
eliminated by 6 Oct 1939*

Breslau

Piotrków

P O L A N D

**Eighth Army
(Blaskowitz)**

**Łódź
Army**

Brody

**Kraków
Army**

San River

Rawa
Russka

**Tenth Army
(Reichenau)**

Kraców

Tarnów

Przemyśl

Lwów

**Army Group South
(Rundsted)**

Gorlice

CarpathianArmy

Drohobycz

Dniester River

SLOVAKIA

**Fourteenth Army
(List)**

Cernăuţi

**Annexed by
Soviet Union
1940**

Vienna

Danube River

H U N G A R Y

Theiss River

Budapest

*Survivors flee
through Romania*

**Annexed by
Hungary 1940**

R O M A N I A

Donald S. Frazier

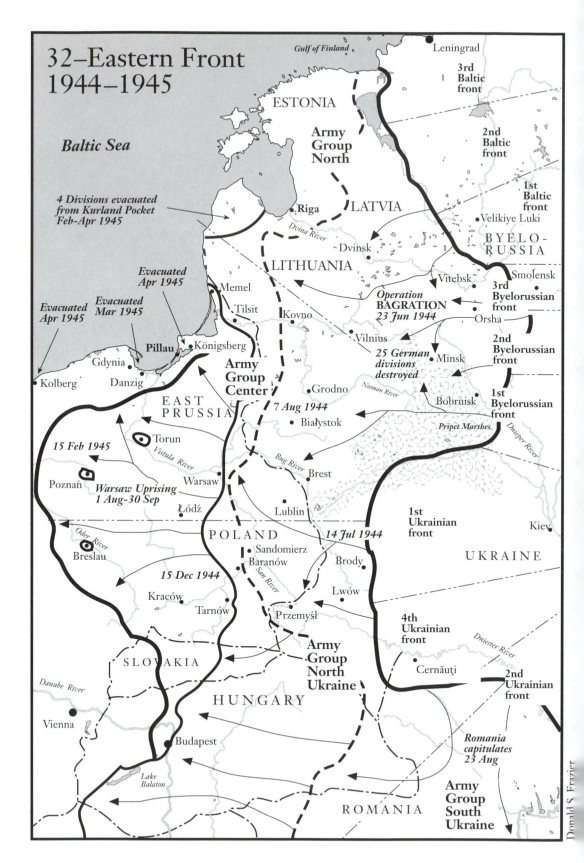

32–Eastern Front 1944–1945

Baltic Sea

Gulf of Finland

Leningrad

3rd Baltic front

2nd Baltic front

1st Baltic front

ESTONIA

Army Group North

LATVIA

Velikiye Luki

BYELO-RUSSIA

4 Divisions evacuated from Kurland Pocket Feb-Apr 1945

Riga

Dvina River

Dvinsk

Smolensk

Vitebsk

3rd Byelorussian front

Operation **BAGRATION** *23 Jun 1944*

Orsha

2nd Byelorussian front

LITHUANIA

Evacuated Apr 1945

Memel

Tilsit

Kovno

Vilnius

25 German divisions destroyed

Minsk

1st Byelorussian front

Evacuated Apr 1945

Evacuated Mar 1945

Pillau

Königsberg

Army Group Center

Grodno

Nieman River

Bobruisk

Kolberg

Gdynia

Danzig

EAST PRUSSIA

7 Aug 1944

Białystok

Pripet Marshes

Dnieper River

15 Feb 1945

Torun

Vistula River

Bug River

Brest

Poznań

Warsaw Uprising 1 Aug-30 Sep

Warsaw

Łódź

Lublin

1st Ukrainian front

Kiev

Oder River

POLAND

14 Jul 1944

UKRAINE

Breslau

15 Dec 1944

Sandomierz

Baranów

San River

Brody

Lwów

Kraców

Tarnów

Przemyśl

4th Ukrainian front

Dniester River

SLOVAKIA

Army Group North Ukraine

Cernăuţi

2nd Ukrainian front

Danube River

HUNGARY

Vienna

Romania capitulates 23 Aug

Budapest

Army Group South Ukraine

Lake Balaton

ROMANIA

Donald S. Frazier

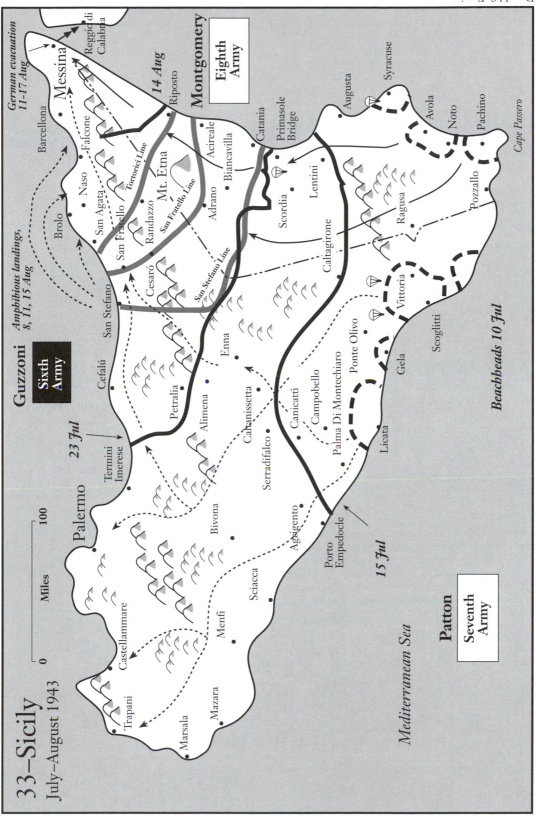

33–Sicily
July–August 1943

Guzzoni
Sixth Army

Montgomery
Eighth Army

Patton
Seventh Army

German evacuation 11–17 Aug

Amphibious landings, 8, 11, 15 Aug

23 Jul

14 Aug

15 Jul

Beachheads 10 Jul

Mediterranean Sea

Miles

0   100

Messina
Reggio di Calabria
Barcellona
Falcone
Naso
Brolo
San Agata
San Fratello
Randazzo
Cesarò
San Stefano
Cefalù
Petralia
Alimena
Enna
Caltanissetta
Serradifalco
Termini Imerese
Palermo
Castellammare
Trapani
Marsala
Mazara
Menfi
Sciacca
Bivona
Agrigento
Porto Empedocle
Licata
Campobello
Palma Di Montechiaro
Canicatti
Ponte Olivo
Gela
Scoglitti
Vittoria
Ragusa
Pozzallo
Scordia
Lentini
Caltagirone
Catania
Primasole Bridge
Augusta
Syracuse
Avola
Noto
Pachino
Cape Passero
Riposto
Acireale
Biancavilla
Adrano
Mt. Etna
Tortorici Line
San Fratello Line
San Stefano Line

Donald S. Frazier

Rotterdam

Dordrecht

Moerdijk

Front lines
15 Dec 1944

Operation MARKET-GARDEN
17 Sep 1944

Arnhem

Nijmegen

Reichswald

Operation VARSITY
24 Mar 1945

Wesel

Front lines
10 Mar 1945

Essen

Ruhr River

Eindhoven

Venlo

Roermond

Düsseldorf

THE RUHR

Antwerp

Ghent

Louvain

Neerpelt

Cologne

GERMANY

Brussels

Front lines
15 Sep 1944

Wavre

Maastricht

Roer River

Aachen

Schmidt

Hurtgen Forest

Bonn

Front lines
21 Mar 1945

Gembloux

Namur

Meuse River

Liège

Remagen

BELGIUM

St.-Vith

Front lines
15 Dec 1944

Coblenz

Givet

German Ardennes
offensive 16–26 Dec

La Roche

Bastogne

Prüm

Bitburg

Moselle River

Mézières

Bourg

Sedan

LUX.

Trier

Front lines
10 Mar 1945

THE RHEINLAND

Mainz

Rhine River

Reims

Montmédy

Saarbrücken

Châlons-sur-Marne

Verdun

Thionville

Metz

Front lines
15 Dec 1944

Bitche

Karlsruhe

Vitry-le-François

Nancy

Strasbourg

The Siegfried Line

Chaumont

Mirecourt

Lunéville

Épinal

Front lines
15 Sep

Colmar

Front lines
21 Mar 1945

Mulhouse

34–The Siegfried Line

and the Advance to the Rhine

September 1944–March 1945

Belfort

SWITZERLAND

Lake Onega

5 Dec

Northwest Front (Voroshilov)

Viipuri

Helsinki

Hango

Gulf of Finland

Lake Ladoga

Leningrad

SOVIET UNION.

Baltic Sea

Narva

Volkov River

Luga

Novgorod

Lake Il'men'

Demyansk

Volga River

West Front (Timoshenko, Zhukov)

Tallinn

Lake Peipus

Dago

Oesel

ESTONIA

Tartu

Staraya Russa

Kholm

Kalinin

Rzhev

Klin

Moscow

Gulf of Riga

Pskov

Riga

Velikiye Luki

Beloj

Mozhaisk

LATVIA

Nevel'

Vyaz'ma

Kaluga

Tula

Army Group North (Leeb)

Dvinsk

Dvina River

Vitebsk

Smolensk

5 Dec

Oka River

LITHUANIA

Orsha

Roslavl

Memel

Kaunas

Minsk

Berezina River

Mogilev

1 Sep

Bryansk

Don River

Tilsit

Vilna

Orel

Livny

Voronezh

Niemen River

Königsberg

Suwałki

Grodno

16 Jul

Gomel

15 Oct

Kursk

EAST PRUSSIA

Desna River

Glukhov

Southwest Front (Budenny, Timoshenko)

Białystok

Army Group Center (Bock)

Pripet River

Konotop

Sumy

Kharkov

Warsaw

Bug River

Brest

Korosten

1 Oct

Lubny

Vistula River

Kowel

UKRAINE

Kiev

Poltava

POLAND

Lublin

Równe

Zhitomir

Dnieper River

Kremenchug

Voroshilovgrad

GERMANY

Lwów

Tarnopol

Cherkassy

Dnepropetrovsk

Stalino

Przemyśl

Uman

Kirovograd

Mariupol'

Dniester River

Southern Bug River

Nikopol

Melitopol

Cernăuti

Nikolayev

Perekop

Sea of Azov

HUNGARY

Army Group South (Rundstedt)

Prut River

Odessa

CRIMEA

Kerch

ROMANIA

Yevpatoriya

Feodosiya

Sevastopol

5 Dec

35–Eastern Front 1941

Yalta

Black Sea

Danube River

Donald S. Frazier

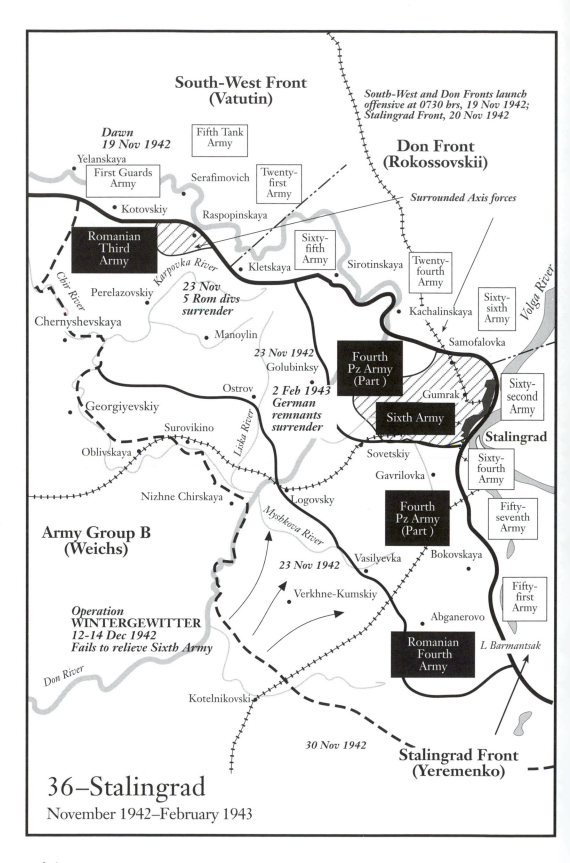

South-West Front (Vatutin)

South-West and Don Fronts launch offensive at 0730 hrs, 19 Nov 1942; Stalingrad Front, 20 Nov 1942

Don Front (Rokossovskii)

Dawn 19 Nov 1942

Fifth Tank Army

Yelanskaya

First Guards Army

Serafimovich

Twenty-first Army

Kotovskiy

Raspopinskaya

Surrounded Axis forces

Romanian Third Army

Karpovka River

Perelazovskiy

Kletskaya

Sixty-fifth Army

Sirotinskaya

Twenty-fourth Army

Chir River

23 Nov 5 Rom divs surrender

Kachalinskaya

Sixty-sixth Army

Volga River

Chernyshevskaya

Manoylin

Samofalovka

23 Nov 1942 Golubinksy

Fourth Pz Army (Part)

Georgiyevskiy

Ostrov

2 Feb 1943 German remnants surrender

Gumrak

Sixty-second Army

Liska River

Sixth Army

Stalingrad

Surovikino

Sovetskiy

Sixty-fourth Army

Oblivskaya

Logovsky

Gavrilovka

Fourth Pz Army (Part)

Fifty-seventh Army

Nizhne Chirskaya

Myshkova River

Army Group B (Weichs)

23 Nov 1942

Vasilyevka

Bokovskaya

Fifty-first Army

Verkhne-Kumskiy

Operation **WINTERGEWITTER** *12-14 Dec 1942 Fails to relieve Sixth Army*

Abganerovo

Romanian Fourth Army

L Barmantsak

Don River

Kotelnikovski

30 Nov 1942

Stalingrad Front (Yeremenko)

36–Stalingrad
November 1942–February 1943

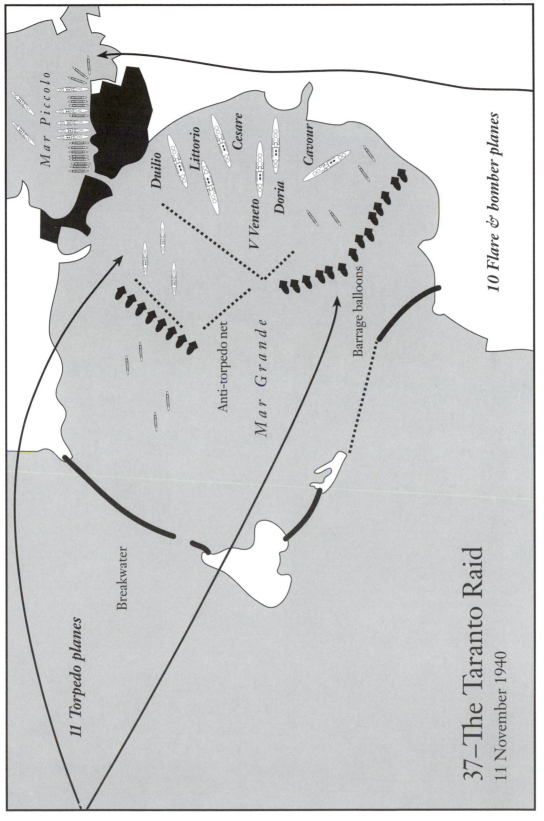

Mar Piccolo

Duilio

Littorio

Cesare

Cavour

V Veneto

Doria

Anti-torpedo net

Mar Grande

Barrage balloons

10 Flare & bomber planes

Breakwater

11 Torpedo planes

37–The Taranto Raid
11 November 1940

Social and Political Issues and Events

A

Allied Military Government (AMG)

International law stipulates that the commander of a military force occupying a territory belonging to another state, or otherwise lacking sovereign rule, assumes certain rights and responsibilities for administering that territory. But even if not required to do so, the commander's own interest would dictate that he control the civilian population and manage the occupied area's resources.

Military government is naturally authoritarian, but it should not be despotic or lawless. Its purpose is to reestablish law and order as a basis for future civilian governing. The Western Allies sought to accomplish this objective in all liberated countries of Western Europe at the end of World War II.

Military governments were tentatively planned well ahead of tactical operations. As part of their early war planning, United States forces established civil affairs sections (designated G-5) as part of their general staffs. A plan to train civil affairs and liaison officers was approved by the U.S. War Department in December 1941, and in May 1942, the School of Military Government began instruction in Charlottesville, Virginia. Students were usually men of experience in public service, local and state government, judicial work, or law enforcement. In retrospect, more emphasis should have been placed on political education.

The aim of military governments was to carry out the military policies and peace objectives of the United Nations, as the Allies came to call themselves during the war. All military governments established during the war were combined Anglo-American operations requiring close consultation and cooperation. At several "Big Three" (the United States, Great Britain, and the Soviet Union) conferences, anticipated problems for the future occupation of Germany were discussed to determine how Allied military governments should be administered. After victory, these problems were approached on a quadripartite basis—with the inclusion of France—for Germany and Austria. In Italy, Belgium, Denmark, Luxembourg, the Netherlands, and Norway, Anglo-American policies generally prevailed. France was a special case because of General Charles de Gaulle (q.v.) and the Free French government already in existence.

The first Anglo-American experience with civil administration came in French North Africa in 1942 with the controversial recognition of Admiral Jean François Darlan (q.v.). Because of French sensitivities, lack of available resources, and experience in such matters, many problems were encountered, but any French regime seemed preferable to an imposed military government.

On 3 June 1943, President Franklin D. Roosevelt (q.v.) directed the establishment of the Office for Economic Coordination (OFEC) under the direction of the State Department, in cooperation with the Treasury, War, and Navy Departments. Its purpose was to consolidate operations of the Board of Economic Warfare, the Lend-Lease Administration, and the Office of Foreign Relief and Rehabilitation Operations for the purpose of "developing overall and area programs for American foreign economic policies." This proved an unhappy marriage, although the War Department welcomed the arrangement because it freed the military from responsibilities for foreign civilian administration.

As Allied forces advanced across Western Europe, an organization known as Allied Military Government of Occupation Territories (AMGOT) was set up to organize, administer, and control liberated areas. AMGOT later was divided into separate Allied military governments to achieve decentralization. The objective was to maintain order, feed the starving population, and provide health, transportation, communications, legal, and financial services.

American and British authorities were responsible, with later French participation, for military governments in all of occupied Europe except for Soviet-controlled areas. The Anglo-Americans generally held the same ideas on the nature of military governments. There were some differences of emphasis on the need for immediate elimination of the influence of Fascism or Nazism, but nothing that could not be overcome. The Americans at first wanted direct military rule; that is, the prefects and mayors of important communities would be removed and replaced by military officers of the occupying force. That idea was first discussed in Italy but not adopted. Instead, it was agreed that Italian officials considered too tainted by Fascism would be removed, but the Italian administrative machinery would be maintained, and Allied rule would be indirect.

General Dwight D. Eisenhower (q.v.), insisted on laying down in advance a single Allied plan to ensure a joint policy concerning civilian and military authority in a given territory. He demanded "joint Anglo-American responsibility and joint conduct of military government" under a "single effective system" that functioned under the Allied area commander. This was a new experience for providing rule, not in individual zones of occupation but rather a complete fusion of personnel divided equally between the two countries.

Allied military government had its first test in Sicily and then in Italy proper. The problems in Italy were incredibly complex. Officials had to cope with a starving population and deplorable hygienic conditions. During the first year, two million tons of drugs, soap, and food were needed. Often, limited transportation facilities had to serve both civilian and military requirements.

The Allied plan for Italy, with modifications based on experience, became the model for military administration in other European countries as they were liberated. Under this plan, a senior civil affairs officer (SCAO) was put in charge of each province or region to supervise the prefect or mayor. Under this officer was a civil affairs officer responsible for general management of various municipalities, assisted by specialist officers for six divisions: civilian supply, legal, financial, public health, public safety, and enemy property.

Following the Italian experience, the next phase was the "revival of administration" in the liberated countries of Belgium, Denmark, France, Holland, Luxembourg, and Norway, where military governments were not established. The term "civil affairs" rather than "military government" was used in these countries to describe the process of "reviving, controlling, and handing over responsibilities" to local authorities after liberation. These matters involved delicate negotiations with General de Gaulle in France and the relief of starvation and chaotic conditions everywhere.

Finally, military governments were imposed on Germany and Austria. The Allied political authorities rejected the Morgenthau Plan (q.v.) for the "pastoralization" of Germany. Both Germany and Austria were divided into four zones of occupation controlled by the U.S., Britain, France, and the Soviet Union.

Efforts were made to overcome zonal division in the economic field in Germany. Disagreements arose when the Soviets insisted on the removal of industrial equipment and other resources that went beyond previous agreements on payment for actual war losses. Soviet paranoia, expansionist tendencies, and dialectic discussion methods made cooperation with them extremely difficult, and excessive French fears of a revived Germany did not contribute to Allied harmony.

United Nations planners anticipated an Allied Control Council with real authority in the direction of German affairs. It was intended that "during the period of occupation, Germany shall be treated as a single economic unit." The control council was charged with developing common policies on a broad range of economic matters. But French and Soviet suspicions of Allied cooperation on German unification ultimately sabotaged the council's effectiveness.

When an understanding among the "Big Four" could not be achieved, the Soviets established their own system of administration in their sphere of influence, including eastern Germany. The Western Allies organized and managed their zones on a tripartite basis, with France as a somewhat reluctant participant.

The three Western Allies generally agreed on the type of military government, its authority, responsibility, and Allied objectives for governing Germany. A similar pattern was followed in Austria. They decided that military government "shall be firm" and at the same time "humane" with respect to the civilian population, consistent with military requirements. It was emphasized to the civilian population that the purpose of military occupation was to "aid military operations, destroy Nazism and the Nazi hierarchy, maintain and preserve law and order, and restore normal conditions among the civilian population as soon as possible."

"Adolf Hitler, his chief Nazi associates, and all

persons suspected of committing war crimes" were to be arrested and held for investigation and subsequent disposition. The Nazi Party was to be dissolved as soon as possible. To accomplish this, military authorities were to take possession of all party records, suspend all party activities, arrest and imprison high party officials, and take control of all party property. A special effort was made to seize and preserve all records and plans of German military organizations, the Nazi Party, and the security, criminal, and ordinary police. All Nazi laws "which discriminate on the basis of race, color, creed or political opinions" were suspended, and all persons imprisoned on such grounds were released. The operation of criminal and civil courts of the Third *Reich* was suspended.

All *Gestapo* and SS (qq.v.) policemen were disarmed, disbanded, and arrested. The Allied supreme commander was authorized to decide whether to work through local government officials on the principle of indirect rule or through direct rule by the appointment of military officers to civilian posts. The principal link for indirect rule was the *Bezirk* (district) or *Kreis* (county) level. Control at the higher levels was discretionary. Appointments of Germans to "important posts" required approval of the Combined Chiefs of Staff.

The entire Nazi leadership had to be removed from any post of authority and no member of the German General Staff or of the Nazi hierarchy could occupy an important governmental post. Generally, freedom of speech and press was allowed and all religious institutions respected, but censorship and control of the press, printing, publications, and dissemination of news or information could be instituted as necessary in the interest of military security. Nazi propaganda in all forms was prohibited. All political activity was prohibited unless authorized by the supreme commander.

All property belonging to the Third *Reich* or to any country at war with the United Nations was seized for future disposition. All property belonging to the United Kingdom, the United States, or other members of the United Nations was protected.

A major humanitarian service required of Anglo-American military governments was caring for and returning to their homelands, or finding homes elsewhere for, millions of POWs, displaced persons, liberated military, and civilian personnel. Approximately a half-million Germans and Italians were returned from the United States, and more than three million Germans were disarmed following their surrender.

Finally, it was strongly emphasized to the civilian population that "Germany's ruthless warfare and the fanatical Nazi resistance destroyed the German economy and made chaos and suffering inevitable" and that the German people could not escape responsibility for what they brought upon themselves.

The Allies considered it their overriding purpose to prevent Germany from ever again becoming a threat to the peace of the world. But they often differed among themselves about how that should be accomplished. Fraternization between Allied forces and German nationals was forbidden. This policy was (and still is) resented by many Germans who felt that the general population was being punished and stigmatized for the behavior of Nazi Party officials.

Generally, the Allied task was twofold: deciding how they would treat the defeated Germans and what would be their relations with each other. The latter proved more difficult than the former. The victors, except for the Soviets, came to the country with few specific ideas of what they wanted to do with Germany. Their policies evolved after the occupation began.

Generally, the British and Americans sought to develop a federal state *(Bundesstaat)* rather than the confederation *(Staatenbund)* sought by France. The form of government mattered little to the Soviets, who sought and obtained a Communist mass-organization with democratic trappings to allow them to control and dominate their area.

Each nation appointed military governors for its area of occupation. The United States had four military governors between 1945 and 1949. They were General Eisenhower until November 1945, General Joseph T. MacNarney from November 1945 to March 1947, General Lucius D. Clay (q.v.) from March 1947 to May 1949, and John J. McCloy from May 1949 until the end of the military government phase in September 1949.

By 1955, the three Western Allies merged their occupation zones into the Federal Republic of Germany, and the Soviet zone became the German Democratic Republic. In 1991, following the collapse of the Soviet Union, the two Germanies merged into a united country.

Paul J. Rose

Additional Reading

Coles, Harry L., and Albert K. Winberg, *Civil Affairs, Soldiers Become Governors* (1964).

Donnison, F.S.V., *Civil Affairs and Military Government in North-West Europe 1944–1946* (1961).

Gimbel, John, *American Occupation of Germany: Politics and the Military* (1968).

Harris, C.R.S., *Allied Military Administration of Italy 1943–1945* (1957).

Alsace and Lorraine

Alsace and Lorraine are two historic provinces whose location on the borders of France, Germany, and Switzerland made them contested areas between France and Germany starting with Louis XIV in the seventeenth century. The people of Alsace are largely of German origin, as are a smaller percentage of the people of Lorraine.

Though originally separate entities, they became linked when, at the end of the Franco-Prussian War in 1871, the German Empire annexed the Alsatian department of Haut-Rhin, Bas-Rhin (except Belfort), and eastern Lorraine into the department of Moselle. Despite a heavy representation of German-speaking people in the annexed regions, the establishment of the *Reichsland* (imperial land), Alsace-Lorraine, provoked a strong protest from the local populace. Additionally, this annexation created bitter enmity in France, which troubled Franco-German relations until World War I.

Efforts of the German imperial government to turn the inhabitants of Alsace-Lorraine into loyal German citizens had only limited success. The presence of the Catholic Church gave the native populace a social base for asserting their autonomy. Prospects for a closer tie to Germany improved after the turn of the century when the people of Alsace-Lorraine were granted greater political autonomy. In 1911, they received a constitution, and French revanchist sentiment also moderated. During World War I, almost 250,000 men from the region were mobilized into the German army, but 70,000 volunteers and numerous deserters joined the French army.

The entry of French troops into Alsace-Lorraine at the end of World War I was greeted with enthusiasm, and the return of the region to France was approved by popular vote. The reintegration of Alsace-Lorraine into France, however, encountered resistance from the native populace when the centralizing efforts of the French government aroused local patriotism and intensified the drive toward regional autonomy. The Catholic population, and the clergy especially, resented the secular policies of the French government. This sentiment could be assuaged only by French concessions in education and religious policies. Even today, the French policy of separation of church and state is not fully applied in Alsace-Lorraine.

At the outbreak of World War II, one-third of the Alsatian population was evacuated. In mid-June 1940, Alsace was occupied by German troops. As a result of the armistice with France, Alsace and Lorraine became occupied territories, remaining legally French. Hitler, however, rather quickly instituted a civilian administration. Against the protests of the Vichy government, Alsace was combined with Baden in the *Oberrheingau* administrative district, and Lorraine with the *Gau* of *Saarpfalz,* later *Westmark.*

The Nazi regime adopted a systematic policy of Germanization, prohibiting the use of the French language, removing French signs and monuments, changing first and last names into German, and imposing strict censorship.

Young people of Alsace and Lorraine were taken into the Hitler Youth (q.v.); older ones had to join the Nazi labor service, and starting in 1942, were drafted into the German army; 20,000 of these soldiers did not return from the war. Additional repressive measures, including arrests, deportation, removal of Jews, and total disregard of native autonomy, led to a decisive rejection of the Nazi regime by much of the populace. Unlike many areas of France, however, Alsace and Lorraine never produced an active resistance movement.

The end of World War II brought the full restoration of Alsace and Lorraine to France. With modified policies of the French government, greater tolerance of bilingualism, and the advancing economic and political integration of Europe, the particularist aspirations of the people have waned and the Alsace-Lorraine question has greatly abated.

George P. Blum

Additional Reading
Silverman, Dan P., *Reluctant Union: Alsace-Lorraine and Imperial Germany 1871–1918* (1972).

American Military Tribunals

Following the trial of the major war criminals before the International Military Tribunal (q.v.) at Nuremberg, the United States conducted a series of war crimes trials in the American Zone of Occupation. The legal basis for the trials was Allied Control Council Law Number Ten of 20 December 1945, which authorized the four occupying powers to conduct prosecutions in their own zones. Although the Soviets made no use of this provision, the British conducted military courts in Hamburg, Wuppertal, and other locations in the north of Germany. The American trials were conducted at Nuremberg.

Starting in November 1946 and lasting to April 1949, American authorities conducted twelve separate trials, proceeding in the order listed in the table. Many of the trials centered on key individuals, such as Erhard Milch, Oswald Pohl, and Alfried Krupp von Bohlen und Halbach (qq.v.). The Judges' Trial, which concluded on 4 December 1947, was the basis for the acclaimed 1961 film, *Judgement at Nuremberg*, staring Spencer Tracy.

Of the 185 individuals indicted, 177 actually came to trial. Four committed suicide before their trials, and another four were declared unfit to stand trial. Twenty-four of those tried were condemned to death. Twelve were actually executed; one was extradited to Belgium, where he later died; and eleven later had their sentences commuted to life. Twenty of the defendants were sentenced to life in prison, and ninety-eight received prison sentences ranging from eighteen months to twenty-five years. Many of those sentenced had their sentences reduced or commuted on 31 January 1951. Thirty-five defendants were acquitted. Some of those acquitted and many of those who were sentenced and released later faced German denazification courts.

David T. Zabecki

Additional Reading

Benton, Wilbourn E. (ed.), *Nuremberg: German Views of the War Trials* (1955).

Rosenbaum, Alan S., *Prosecuting Nazi War Criminals* (1993).

Smith, Bradley F., *Reaching Judgement at Nuremberg* (1977).

Tutorow, N., ed., *War Crimes, War Criminals, and War Crimes Trials: An Annotated Bibliography and Source Book* (1986).

American Military Tribunals at Nuremberg
November 1946–April 1949

Case	Date of Judgment	Focus
Doctors' Trial	19 Aug 47	Doctors who conducted medical experiments at concentration camps.
Milch Trial	17 Jul 47	Forced labor and high altitude and freezing medical experiments at the Dachau concentration camp.
Judges' Trial	4 Dec 47	Judges and the legal system within the Third *Reich*.
Pohl Trial	3 Nov 47	SS officers who ran the concentration camps and slave labor program.
Flick Trial	22 Dec 47	Industrialists who used slave labor and who profited from the confiscation of Jewish property.
I.G. Farben Trial	29 Jul 48	Same as the Flick Trial, but focusing on the giant chemical concern that manufactured *Zyklon-B* gas.
Hostages Trial	19 Oct 48	The treatment of civilians in southeast Europe. In Germany this trial is known as the Southeast Generals' Trial.
RuSHA Trial	10 Mar 48	The involvement of the SS Race and Resettlement Office in genocide.
Einsatzgruppen Trial	10 Apr 48	The SS special action units that conducted mass murders on the eastern front.
Krupp Trial	31 Jul 48	Another trial involving industrialists and their role in property exploitation and slave labor.
Ministries' Trial	11 Apr 49	Officials of the Foreign Office and other ministries who helped the Nazis consolidate power within the Third *Reich*. In Germany this trial is known as the Wilhelm Strasse Trial.
OKW Trial	28 Oct 48	Members of the military high command and their role in the treatment of POWs and civilians in occupied areas.

Anglo-German Naval Agreement of 1935

While Adolf Hitler was rearming Germany, Britain hoped to negotiate a reasonable arms limitation agreement, especially in naval development. Hitler was intent on building a German navy, but he also wanted to keep Britain's goodwill. In November 1934, he communicated his willingness to the British government to negotiate a naval agreement that limited German naval tonnage to about 35 percent of British naval strength. When a similar offer was repeated in March 1935, the British Admiralty expressed interest, hoping to avoid a naval race that might result in the construction of a German fleet that exceeded the 35 percent limitation.

Hitler's formal announcement in the same month of the existence of the German Air Force and the introduction of compulsory military service, all contrary to the Treaty of Versailles (q.v.), temporarily drew Britain, France, and Italy together in the Stresa Front, named after the city in Italy that hosted the conference in April 1935 among Ramsay Mac-Donald of Great Britain, Pierre Etienne Flandin of France, and Benito Mussolini of Italy. The conference was in response to Hitler's repudiation of the Versailles Treaty in March 1935. The front of solidarity among the victorious allies of World War I was short-lived as a result of Mussolini's invasion of Ethiopia. British eagerness to see Germany's naval strength set at a fixed relationship to the Royal Navy prompted British representatives to enter into separate negotiations in early June 1935 with Joachim von Ribbentrop (q.v.), Hitler's special ambassador. The Anglo-German Naval Agreement was signed on 18 June 1935, the 120th anniversary of the Battle of Waterloo.

Apart from limiting German naval tonnage to 35 percent aggregate tonnage of the British Commonwealth fleets, the agreement allowed Germany to build a submarine force comparable to that of Britain and eliminated earlier warship limitations by category or displacement and gun caliber. For Hitler, the Anglo-German Naval Agreement was a major triumph. It exploded the Stresa Front and abrogated the disarmament stipulations of the Versailles Treaty.

France was particularly angered by this British unilateral action, which betrayed the postwar international settlement. France was much less convinced than Britain that Hitler would keep his commitments. Skeptics who distrusted Hitler's intentions were proven right by events that followed. In response to the Anglo-French guarantee to Poland, Hitler formally renounced the Anglo-German Naval Treaty on 28 April 1939.

George P. Blum

Additional Reading

Hildebrand, Klaus, *The Foreign Policy of the Third Reich* (1973).

Weinberg, Gerhard L., *The Foreign Policy of Hitler's Germany: Diplomatic Revolution in Europe, 1933–1936* (1970).

Anschluss (Annexation of Austria)

Anschluss was the name given to Adolf Hitler's forced integration of Austria into Germany on 13 March 1938. The Pan-German idea was an old one, not original with Hitler. The idea, according to Karl Dietrich Bracher, had been "common property" of both the non-monarchist right and the Social Democratic left since 1848, and was reemphasized after the collapse of the Habsburg Empire in 1918. Since the ban on German-Austrian union by the 1919 Treaty of Versailles (q.v.), *Anschluss* became a goal of most political camps in both countries. It was a major foreign policy objective of the Weimar Republic (q.v.).

The National Socialist idea of an all-German union was not the same federalist concept envisioned earlier. To Hitler, a native Austrian, nothing seemed more natural than a National Socialist revolution in Austria resulting in a merger with Germany. The wounded national pride of Germany brought on by military defeat and the loss of territory was easily fed by the idea of a "Greater Germany" united by culture and language. The Nazis found little opposition to this, one of their central ideas.

Nonetheless, Hitler laid his plans very carefully before taking any overt action. After consolidating his hold on the German armed forces, he accused Austrian Chancellor Kurt von Schuschnigg (q.v.) of violating the Austrian-German Pact of 1936 requiring Germany to respect Austria's independence. At a hastily arranged conference in Berchtesgaden in February 1938, von Schuschnigg was browbeaten into appointing Austrian Nazi Party leader Arthur Seyss-Inquart (q.v.) as minister of interior, as the first step toward *Anschluss*.

In an effort to thwart Hitler, von Schuschnigg called for a referendum on Austrian independence. Before it could be conducted, however, he resigned in response to Nazi-provoked riots and unrest, and Seyss-Inquart became chancellor. Even before the new chancellor had time to request aid in restoring public order, German troops moved into Austria to great public acclamation. Hitler immediately annexed Austria and named it *Ostmark*.

The failure of the Western Allies to thwart Hitler's aggression toward Austria convinced Hitler

German troops cross the Austro-German border at Kufstein-Kieferfelden, 13 March 1938. (IWM NYP 68062)

that they would do nothing to block his planned move against Czechoslovakia later that year. The *Anschluss* was a major step on the road to World War II.

Paul J. Rose

Additional Reading

Bracher, Karl Dietrich, *The German Dictatorship* (1971).
David, Claude, *Hitler's Germany* (1963).
Fest, Joachim, *The Face of the Third Reich* (1970).
Pinson, Koppel S., *Modern Germany: Its History and Civilization* (1966).

Anticolonialism

Anticolonialism played a minor role in the European theater of World War II, but the Atlantic Charter (q.v.) electrified colonial peoples because they assumed its promises applied to them. They especially cherished the provisions stating that all peoples should choose their own form of government and that sovereign rights and self-government would be restored to all who had been forcibly deprived of them.

In Great Britain, the West African Student Union (WASU) immediately asked Clement Attlee (q.v.), the deputy prime minister, if the charter ap-plied to British colonies. Attlee answered: "You will not find in the declarations . . . any suggestion that the freedom and social security for which we fight should be denied to any of the races of mankind. We fight this war not just for ourselves alone, but for all peoples." On his return from the Atlantic Conference, Winston S. Churchill (q.v.) attempted to limit the charter to Europe, but neither the United States nor the colonial world would agree.

During the war, anticolonialism was strongest in Great Britain because Britain held the largest empire and allowed the greatest freedom of expression. India demanded its independence, but that political battle had shifted to India. West Indian and African "exiles" were the most active in Britain during the war. A host of organizations such as the WASU and the League of Coloured Peoples questioned government spokesmen, published tracts, and lobbied on behalf of black peoples. The Fabians created a colonial bureau that investigated, held hearings, and published advice to guide the development of postwar policy toward greater independence for colonies. The fall of Singapore to the Japanese and the published accounts of Asian indifference to the change of rulers led the *Times* newspaper to express a general public hostility toward the maintenance of the empire.

The French suppressed anticolonialism more

effectively. Comparable voices were not heard from Paris, Vichy, or Charles de Gaulle's (q.v.) camp. Colonial revolt did worry Vichy enough to keep German inspectors in Africa in civilian clothes and largely out of sight of subject peoples. De Gaulle offered confused concessions for a French "community" in the Brazzaville Conference chaired by a black administrator from Guiana, but both French governments retained a strong belief in the French "civilizing" mission and assimilation that worked to keep colonial opposition inarticulate.

Anticolonialism reached the point of armed conflict only in Eastern Europe when the Germans invaded the Soviet Union in order to turn it into a colony. Because of their commitment to "racial purity," the Germans at first refused to appeal to the Soviet minorities as colonial peoples. When the war turned against them, the *Waffen-SS* (q.v.) recruited and armed legions from many ethnic groups. Only the units from rabidly anti-Russian Estonia and Latvia fought well for Germany. More minorities fought the German imperialists as resistance fighters, but they were offered only a choice of masters, so most fought unenthusiastically on either side.

Europeans ignored the strength of anticolonialism during the war and paid the price in later years.

Dennis J. Mitchell

Additional Reading
Albertini, Rudolf von, *Decolonization: The Administration and Future of the Colonies, 1919–1960* (1971).
Paxton, Robert, *Vichy France: Old Guard and New Order, 1940–1944* (1972).

Anti-Comintern Pact

The Anti-Comintern Pact, signed 25 November 1936 between Germany and Japan, was more noteworthy for show than for substance. The five-year treaty merely called for cooperation between Berlin and Tokyo in combatting the Third (Communist) International. Since Communist elements in Germany and Japan had already ceased to function, the world correctly assumed the pact contained secret supplements. Yet even these private accords had slight meaning, requiring nothing more than consultation between the signatories preceding political agreements with Moscow and benevolent neutrality from each signatory should the Soviet Union without provocation attack the other. Italy joined the pact in November 1937 and in 1939, Hungary, Manchukuo, and Spain joined

under pressure. Still, the pact remained without practical significance.

The pact's true meaning was propagandistic. Joachim von Ribbentrop (q.v.), the architect of the Anti-Comintern system and Hitler's foreign minister after February 1938, prized the pact for its facade of unity among the world's dynamic states as contrasted with the decaying League of Nations (q.v.). Since the practical weaknesses of the pact were generally unknown, it could assist in the intimidation of Germany's potential enemies. There existed the additional possibility of converting the Anti-Comintern system into a full military organization, though the Tripartite Alliance between Berlin, Rome, and Tokyo would not ensue until September 1940. The Anti-Comintern system continued during the war despite the Molotov-Ribbentrop Pact (q.v.) of August 1939, and reached its apex with its renewal on 25 November 1941 when Bulgaria, Croatia, Denmark, Finland, Rumania, and Slovakia joined.

Norman J. W. Goda

Additional Reading
Bracher, Karl Dietrich, *The German Dictatorship* (1970).
Shirer, William L., *The Rise and Fall of the Third Reich* (1960).

Anti-Semitism

Jesus of Nazareth, his life and his crucifixion, are central to understanding anti-Semitism. Biblical tradition holds that his death at the hands of the Romans was demanded by Jewish religious officials because he considered himself king of the Jews—an untrue messiah in Jewish eyes. This false myth, which persists to this day, became a destructive and murderous legend that has been used over the centuries to whip up passions and aggressions against Jews everywhere.

Only in the 1960s did the Catholic Church declare that the Jews of Jesus' time should not be held responsible for the crucifixion. And more importantly, modern Jews should not be held accountable for the alleged sins of their fathers. Yet the false but widely held belief of many Christians to this day that Jews are "Christ killers" lies at the very heart of anti-Semitic beliefs.

In addition, Jews were widely viewed as being somehow different. This difference was in part derived from the Jewish feeling of being a "Chosen People." In history, this proclaimed sense of being chosen was a burden forced on succeeding generations of Jews. There is biblical justification

A banner reading "Jews are not wanted here" hangs over the entrance of the Bavarian village of Rosenheim. (IWM MH 13348)

of this view, for it is written: "for thou art an holy people unto the Lord thy God; the Lord thy God hath chosen thee to be a special people unto himself, above all people that are upon the face of the earth" (Deuteronomy 7:6; fifth book of the Old Testament).

Some of the great figures of Christianity of the early and late Middle Ages held and taught extreme views hateful to Jewish people. Ignatius of Antioch, regarding the supersession of the third century of the Christian Era, taught: "Now the peoplehood of the Jews has been cancelled: the Gentiles rather than the Jews will inherit the Kingdom."

During this period, the church adopted a double and contradictory attitude toward the Jews. Jews were human with souls and could be saved, but only if they gave up their religion and converted to Christianity. Conversion as the only means of salvation is a recurring theme throughout history.

A destructive and morally evil legend that spread throughout early Christianity was the "blood-libel." This belief held that Jews murdered Christian children for religious purposes. Once paganism invaded Christianity, the blood-libel caused untold suffering to the Jewish people. This pernicious belief ignored the very real Jewish concern for the sanctity of human life everywhere and that they were the first to condemn vivisection and the use of even animal blood. Jews became the scapegoats for all evils and sufferings of humanity.

Closer to our time, Martin Luther, who led a split in Christendom in the sixteenth century, held strong anti-Semitic views. In his book, *On Jews and Their Lives,* he wrote that Jewish synagogues should be burned, that Jews be segregated like Gypsies, and that their rabbis be forbidden under the threat of death to teach their prayerbooks and Talmuds. If this did not work, their property should be confiscated and they should be driven from the country.

Even the French Revolution, while proclaiming "Liberty, Equality, and Fraternity," promised to accept the Jews as individuals only if they converted to Christianity.

The term "anti-Semitism" was apparently coined by Wilhelm Marr in *The Victory of Judaism over Germanism,* published in 1879. It implied racial hatred of German Jews. The meaning has since changed to include a whole range of anti-Jewish expressions, including anti-Zionism and a general antipathy to all Jews.

While anti-Semitism is a worldwide phenomenon, it found its most virulent expression in Germany and Eastern Europe. Many writers viewed Jews as culturally, morally, and physically inferior. In addition, they were seen as corruptive and unassimilable. The rise of German nationalism following the German victory in the Franco-Prussian War of 1871 strengthened these views. Further, the presence of prominent Jews in revolutionary causes gave the impression that all Jews were socialists or Communists.

Many Christians viewed Jews as a curse upon mankind. Jews became once again a scapegoat for evils both real and imagined in most European countries. The Dreyfuss Affair in France in 1904–1906 and the publication of the so-called *Protocols of the Elders of Zion* in Russia in 1905 were accepted as "proof" that anti-Semitism had been justified all along. The fact that Dreyfuss was eventually proven innocent and the *Protocols* were false did little to minimize their deadly impact.

The founding of the Nazi Party and the rise of Adolf Hitler in Germany in 1933 gave a powerful impetus to anti-Semitism. Hitler made the Jews scapegoats for the loss of World War I and the terrible economic conditions in Germany. Anti-Semitism became an integral part of Nazi governmental policy. The Nazis blamed the Jews for both capitalism and Communism. Worst of all, Hitler considered the Jews as biologically inferior and a threat to the "purity" of the Aryan population. Jews were barred from the civil service, from the legal and medical professions, and from admission to university. The Nuremberg Laws (q.v.), proclaimed in September 1935, stripped Jews of their citizenship and all civil rights.

In 1938, all "Jewish matters" were turned over to the SS (q.v.) to administer. The outbreak of war in 1939 saw Nazi anti-Semitic policies enter a new and more deadly phase and brought on greatly increased power of the SS. Legal discrimination gave way to the increasing use of violence, and many Jews were forced to leave the country. A terrible fate awaited those who remained. Censorship and secrecy of war provided cover for "resettlement" of Jews as a prelude to the death camps. Much esoteric language was used, but in 1942, the "Final Solution" (q.v.) of the "Jewish problem" was understood to be genocide.

By the end of World War II, almost six million Jews had perished, and only remnants of European Jewry remain today. Sadly, anti-Semitic beliefs are still widespread as we approach the twenty-first century. The Holocaust (q.v.) was a terrible reality, contrary to what the naysayers and revisionists may insist.

Paul J. Rose

Additional Reading

Almong, Shmuel (ed.), *Anti-Semitism Through the Ages* (1988).
Dawidowicz, Lucy S., *The War Against the Jews, 1933–1945* (1976).
Levy, Nora, *The Holocaust* (1973).

Appeasement

The dictionary definition of "appeasement" is "to bring peace to; placate; soothe. To satisfy or relieve. To pacify." Some writers trace appeasement as an instrument of foreign policy back to the Bible. In St. Matthew 5:25, it is written: "Agree with thine adversary quickly, whilst thou art in the way with him."

Before World War II, appeasement was an honorable word, carrying no derogatory connotations. It simply meant to negotiate rather than fight, to peacefully decide disputes not vital to the national interest. Because of events leading up to World War II, and the way in which the Western democracies acquiesced to Adolf Hitler's aggressive demands, the word is now associated with policies granting concessions to dictators based on fear and weakness in order to maintain the semblance of peace.

From 1937 to 1939, British Prime Minister Neville Chamberlain (q.v.) followed a policy of appeasement with Hitler (q.v.), partially because of Britain's military weakness, but also because of a rift within his cabinet and country over what policy to follow in opposition to Hitler's aggression. The appeasement dispute reached its climax during the Munich Crisis (q.v.) and conference over Czechoslovakia in 1938.

World War I had slaughtered humans on a scale not seen since the Thirty-Years' War. People's sensitivities were dulled. As the war progressed, the desire for revenge increased in both Britain and France. In his war memoirs, Britain's World War I prime minister, David Lloyd George, reasoned that the war and the bitterness it engendered had poisoned people's minds with "suspicions, resentments, misunderstandings, and fears." All of these emotions were reflected in the Treaty of Versailles (q.v.), which was seen in certain British circles as being too harsh and unfair to the Germans.

Appeasement did not begin with Chamberlain at Munich; nor did it end there. It had its roots in British shame about the unfair treatment of Germany under the Versailles treaty. But the political stigma of Chamberlain's appeasement policies is still with us today and makes peaceful settlement of even marginal disputes difficult.

Economist John Maynard Keynes blamed the statesmen at Versailles for the harsh treaty provisions, which he said impoverished and humiliated the German people. He saw only folly in the treaty, particularly in how it was imposed. Many Britons agreed with him and attempted to place the blame on France for insisting on such bitter terms—and on the British statesmen who agreed with France.

Britain's postwar efforts at friendship with the Germans failed because they too were embittered. German reluctance to accept cordial relations with the British only increased the latter's sense of guilt. The unsettled years of the Weimar Republic (q.v.) were not propitious times for improving Anglo-German relations.

Hitler's coming to power in 1933 aroused fears of renewed violence, although many people admired his efforts to restore the German nation. Others, however, could not forget that Germany was the traditional enemy, the evil spirit they remembered across "No-man's Land," the killers of a generation of British youth. Attitudes in Britain hardened. Some people favored harsher treatment of Germany, while others favored a rapprochement.

Hugh Dalton wrote that some Englishmen became rabidly anti-French; others unreasonably anti-Soviet, while others became "sentimentally pro-German, based on some myth of special kinship or national resemblance." Anti-German sentiments were also evident in the love-hate affair the British had developed with Germany. Here is where one finds the roots of the appeasement policy that reached its apogee at Munich in 1938.

British proponents of better relations with the Germans, led by Keynes and Lord Lothian, proudly called themselves appeasers and saw no infamy in the term. They sought to crush the anti-German movement led by Sir Robert Vansittart (described as a "professional anti-German"), and Eyre Crowe, whose anti-Germanism knew no bounds. To the German haters, Nazism tended to confirm their darkest fears. They hated the Germans for being German as much as for being Nazi.

The appeasers were optimists from the political school of idealism, willing always to look on the bright side of things and ignore what they did not like about the Nazis. Germany was seen as a "new, strong, outspoken" nation that would oppose the spread of Communism in Europe. Hitler was a dedicated, if not overly exuberant, nationalist. Friendship with Germany was a necessary counterweight to the dangers of international Communism. To many in Britain, the French could not be relied upon as dependable allies. In any coming conflict, France could be expected to side with the Soviets. Had not the alliance between France and Russia dragged Europe into war in 1914?

The policy of appeasement was nothing less than a call to arms to maintain peace in Europe through an Anglo-German alliance. Nazi efforts to intimidate the German population, to round up socialists, Communists and labor leaders and to press their anti-Semitic practices did not sway the appeasers. British historian J. Wheeler-Bennett, while admitting he had not even read *Mein Kampf* (q.v.), stated: "Hitler, I am convinced, does not want war. He is susceptible to reason in matters of foreign policy." He is the "most moderate member of his party."

It was against this background that Hitler began his assault on the Treaty of Versailles through German rearmament, occupation of the Rhineland (q.v.), the *Anschluss* (q.v.) of Austria, and finally the annexation of Czechoslovakia. When Western democratic leaders ignored or made excuses for his every aggression, Hitler took this as a green light to do as he wished. The results should have been predictable. It was during the Munich Conference over the Czech Crisis that appeasement reached its denouement.

Chamberlain's partner at Munich, French Premier Édouard Daladier (q.v.), was of little help, since he had an equally serious appeasement crisis at home where Communists and Fascists battled in the streets daily. One had only to read the graffiti *"pour qui et pour quoi?"* (For whom and why?) on buildings and walls throughout France to realize that no one would lift a hand to oppose Hitler's demands.

Both Chamberlain and Daladier were weak leaders who presided over populations still traumatized by the senseless killing in the trenches during World War I. Both countries had large peace movements, large Fascist movements, and parliamentary divisions over foreign policy objectives. Both countries, the British in particular, were militarily weak. Even the supposedly strong French army, as events would soon prove, was not a reliable instrument to support a strong position at Munich.

It was against this background that Chamberlain and Daladier met with Hitler and Benito Mussolini (q.v.) at Munich on 29–30 September 1938. Chamberlain, a man of seventy, was ill, and in fact, he died within two years of the meeting. He presented a sad spectacle as he pleaded with Hitler for peace. He had few trump cards. His own military chiefs warned him that military resistance was out of the question. He felt that even if his mission failed, ". . . it was right to try it. For the alternative was war."

At the conference to decide their fate, the Czechs were not allowed to participate. British and French leaders, without serious dissent, gave in to Hitler's demands to annex the Sudetenland (q.v.) of Czechoslovakia. All the conference participants then cynically agreed to guarantee the sovereignty of what remained of Czechoslovakia.

A

In triumph, Chamberlain returned to London sporting his black umbrella, waving his agreement with Hitler, while proclaiming "Peace for our Time." Hitler's signature was worthless. Six months later, in a mocking gesture of his insincerity, he occupied what remained of Czechoslovakia. Speaking to the House of Commons on that occasion, Chamberlain refused to discuss any "charges of breaches of faith" by Hitler. He declared that he would not be deterred by what had happened. "We will continue to pursue our policy of appeasement," he vowed. This was no doubt what Hitler wanted to hear.

Historian Telford Taylor (q.v.) wrote that this action "shattered the pre-existing power structure of Europe" and was the "manifest overture" to World War II. Otherwise, what is the legacy of this time and these policies? The stigma of appeasement is so strong today that world leaders often are afraid to negotiate in good faith or to compromise on even marginal issues. It even can be argued that the effects of Chamberlain's policy contributed to the Vietnam War, since a series of American leaders were afraid to compromise negotiable differences for fear of being accused of appeasement and labeled another "Chamberlain."

In 1955, Vice President Richard M. Nixon led a White House delegation to the airport to greet President Dwight D. Eisenhower returning from a summit conference with Soviet leaders in Geneva. Despite a violent rainstorm, Nixon would not allow anyone to carry an umbrella for fear of association with the appeasement policies of Chamberlain. What would Chamberlain think today of his silly, but enduring, notoriety?

Paul J. Rose

Additional Reading
Gilbert, Martin, and Richard Gott, *The Appeasers* (1963).
Rowse, A.L., *Appeasement: A Study in Political Decline, 1933–1939* (1961).
Taylor, Telford, *Munich: The Price of Peace* (1979).

Arab League

The Arab League was formed in 1944, with the formal signing of the pact taking place on 22 March 1945. The founding members include Egypt, Saudi Arabia, Iraq, Syria, Lebanon, Yemen, and Transjordan (later Jordon). Since Egypt sponsored and hosted the talks, and was the most advanced Arab state at that time, Abdul Rahman Azzam Pasha became the first secretary-general of the Arab League. Ironically, Egypt was ousted from the league in 1979 as a result of the Begin-Sadat Peace Treaty, and league headquarters moved from Cairo to Tunis. (Egypt since has been readmitted to the league.) There were two motivating factors for the union. One was greater pan-Arab unity and strength; the other was British encroachment.

As to the second factor, British hegemony in the Arab region resurfaced with the start of the war. On 29 May 1941, British Foreign Minister Anthony Eden (q.v.) called for cultural and economic ties with the Arab peoples. Further, Eden endorsed Arab calls for unity to end the problem of artificial boundaries established at the end of World War I.

Arab rejoicing at Eden's words was short-lived, for barely a week later, British and Free French forces invaded Syria. That occupation restricted Axis encroachment in the Middle East and freed Syria and Lebanon from Vichy French control. It was also hoped that by moving the French out, the "Fertile Crescent" states of Iraq, Syria, Lebanon, Palestine, and Transjordan would unite, preferably under the Hashemites—Arabian rulers aligned with Britain during World War I. Rivalries among clans in Syria and between Hashemite dynasties, however, prevented any political union.

The Arab League confederation fifty years later is loose at best. One protocol calls for collective security among member states. When the new Jewish state gained independence in 1948, the Arab League declared war, but soon fell into disarray because of the lack of coordination of the Arab armies and lack of policy toward the Palestinians. Another protocol rejects full union among its members, but in 1958, Egypt's Gamal Abdul Nasser formed his pan-Arab union with Syria and Jordon. These breaches nearly destroyed the Arab League.

William H. Van Husen

Additional Reading
Hourani, Albert, *A History of the Arab Peoples* (1991).
Lenczowski, George, *The Middle East In World Affairs,* 4th ed. (1980).
Mansfield, Peter, *The Arab World* (1976).

Ardeatine Caves Massacre

On 23 March 1944, a group of partisans ambushed a German SS column on Rome's Via Rasella. The partisans were part of the *Gruppi di Azione Patriotica,* young people organized by the Communist Garibaldi Brigades and the Action

Party to carry out attacks against German and Fascist targets. Of the 150 SS security troops, thirty-three were killed and seventy wounded.

The German response was draconian. Field Marshall Albert Kesselring (q.v.) informed Adolf Hitler that ten Italians would pay with their lives for every dead German. Right after the attack, the Germans took hostages around Via Rasella, and a number of them were Jewish. To these hostages were added prisoners already condemned to death, and individuals selected by Pietro Caruso, the police chief of Rome. On 24 March, 335 victims were taken by truck to caves on the Via Ardeatine just outside of Rome. The victims were shot in the back and the caves were then sealed by explosions.

After the liberation of Rome, the caves were opened and most of the remains identified. Some of those responsible for the crime were subsequently tried. In September 1944, Caruso was tried for this and other offenses and condemned to death. In 1948, Lieutenant Colonel Herbert Kappler, the SS security officer who supervised the rounding up of victims and the murders, was sentenced to life imprisonment by a military tribunal. In 1977, he escaped from prison in Italy and in 1978, died at his home in Germany. In November 1995, former SS captain Erich Priebke was extradited from Argentina to Rome to stand trial for his part in the massacre.

Bernard A. Cook

Additional Reading
Katz, Robert, *Death in Rome* (1967).

Argentia Bay Conference
See CONFERENCES, ALLIED

Arsenal of Democracy
In a radio address on 28 December 1940, President Franklin D. Roosevelt (q.v.) explained and defended his recently announced Lend-Lease (q.v.) policy. Long-term Nazi goals, he warned, included domination of the American hemisphere; the United States could avert this danger only by aiding those nations actively resisting Nazi aggression.

Americans, Roosevelt announced, could help advance the Allied cause by directing all available energy toward the production of the munitions that would keep Great Britain in the fight. "We must," he declared, "be the great arsenal of democracy." Cognizant of public apprehension about American intervention in the conflict, he assured his listeners that the ultimate purpose of the Lend-Lease policy was "to keep war away from our country and our people."

Subsequent public response was overwhelmingly favorable. With his remarkably persuasive skills, Roosevelt portrayed a policy of more direct involvement in the war as a means of staying out of it.

Blaine T. Browne

Additional Reading
Burnes, James MacGregor, *Roosevelt: The Soldier of Freedom, 1940–45* (1970).
Divine, Robert A., *The Reluctant Belligerent: American Entry into World War II* (1965).
Sherwood, Robert E., *Roosevelt and Hopkins* (1948).

Atlantic Charter
In late July 1941, Harry Hopkins (q.v.) told British prime minister Winston S. Churchill (q.v.) that President Franklin D. Roosevelt (q.v.) would like a face-to-face meeting. Although the two leaders had corresponded for two years, they had never met, and Roosevelt was anxious to show U.S. support for a beleaguered Britain. Churchill jumped at the opportunity, hoping to draw the U.S. closer to Britain. The issues discussed included Lend-Lease (q.v.) (which included aid to Britain as well as the Soviet Union), defense policies (especially regarding Atlantic shipping lanes), and a joint policy toward Japan and the Far East.

The meeting was held at Placentia Bay, Newfoundland, 9–12 August 1940. Churchill arrived on the battleship HMS *Prince of Wales* and Roosevelt aboard the cruiser USS *Augusta*. The meeting was an exchange of ship visits between the two men and their respective delegations.

During their first meeting on 9 August, Roosevelt suggested a joint declaration of principles. Churchill, who was under some pressure at home to produce a statement on war aims, agreed and asked Permanent Foreign Undersecretary Sir Alexander Cadogan to prepare a draft. He then made his own revisions and handed it to Roosevelt. Undersecretary of State Sumner Welles made the revisions on the U.S. side. Among the items the Americans struck out was a British reference to "an effective international organization" at the end of the war, thought to be a negative symbol in the United States.

The resultant Atlantic Charter, a joint declaration agreed to on 12 August and issued in the form of a press release, pledged the two states to eight guiding principles:

1. no territorial aggrandizement by either the United States or Great Britain;
2. no territorial changes contrary to the freely expressed wishes of the people concerned;
3. the right of all people to choose their own form of government;
4. equal access of all nations, victors as well as vanquished, to trade and raw materials;
5. international collaboration to bring about improved labor standards, economic advancement, and social security;
6. after the destruction of "Nazi tyranny," the resulting peace should secure "freedom from fear and want";
7. freedom of the seas; and
8. abandonment of force and the disarmament of aggressor nations, pending establishment of a "permanent system of general security."

Although the immediate public reaction in the U.S. to the Atlantic Charter was one disappointment (it seemed largely a mix of President Woodrow Wilson's Fourteen Points and Roosevelt's Four Freedoms [q.v.]), its effects were far-reaching. Unlike the 1918 Fourteen Points, this was no unilateral declaration. It was, in fact, the first formulation of peace aims in the war and an effort to give them an Anglo-Saxon imprint. Churchill was pleased because the charter moved the United States firmly toward intervention in the conflict. As he later noted, the fact that the United States, although technically neutral, had joined in such a declaration was "astonishing." It represented formal acceptance by the U.S. government of responsibility for the defeat of Adolf Hitler (q.v.) and establishment of a just peace, a fact not lost on isolationists in the United States, who were quick to denounce it.

Spencer Tucker

Additional Reading

Burns, James M., *Roosevelt: The Soldier of Freedom (1940–1945)* (1965).

Churchill, Winston S., *The Grand Alliance* (1950).

Lash, Joseph P., *Roosevelt and Churchill, 1939–1941: The Partnership That Saved the West* (1976).

Sherwood, Robert E., *Roosevelt and Hopkins* (1948).

Auschwitz

See CONCENTRATION CAMPS

Axis Pact

The Rome-Berlin Axis was a curious affair. In 1934, Italy was still the predominant military and political power in south-central Europe, and Benito Mussolini (q.v.) was aroused over the attempted Nazi *Putsch* that year in Austria. Rushing troops over the Brenner Pass, he helped stave off the incorporation of that country into the Third *Reich*.

Italy's invasion of Ethiopia (q.v.) in 1934 alienated its Western allies. Although the foreign ministers of France and Britain were prepared to allow an Italian takeover (the Hoare-Laval Proposals of December 1935), public opinion strongly opposed it. The refusal of Britain and France to support Italy in Ethiopia drove a wedge between them. Germany refrained from criticism, and their joint intervention in Spain, in the summer of 1936, facilitated rapprochement.

The Axis Pact was proclaimed on 25 October 1936. It provided for collaboration of the two states in all matters affecting their "parallel interests"; opposition to Communism, economic cooperation, and the maintenance of the territorial and colonial integrity of Spain. This was followed by a trade agreement in December that extended to the Italian colonies the same economic privileges Germany enjoyed in Italy proper. It also divided river and rail traffic in the Danube states.

The first real fruit of the Rome-Berlin Axis for Germany came regarding Austria. In 1937, Mussolini announced that Italy would not fight to prevent the *Anschluss* (q.v.). In September 1940, he staged a highly publicized trip to Germany. With German rearmament, the incorporation of Austria, in March 1938, was virtually a foregone conclusion.

Italian-German relations in World War II were strained. Italy did not join Germany in declaring war in September 1939, pleading shortages of vital materials; the real reason was doubt over the probability of German victory. Italy declared war only when it was obvious that France was defeated. Mussolini hitched his wagon to the German star, although his alliance was never popular with the Italian people.

Mussolini demanded Italian participation in the Battle of Britain (q.v.), deploying air units there that were needed in North Africa. Angry that he was not informed of the invasion of the West beforehand, he did not inform Adolf Hitler (q.v.) of his plans to attack Greece. Nevertheless, in one of the war's most momentous decisions, Hitler came to the relief of the hard-pressed Italians, upsetting his own timetable for the invasion of the Soviet Union. German forces also were dispatched to assist the Italians in North Africa and Sicily. In spite of the North African situation, Mussolini insisted on Italian participation in the invasion of the Soviet Union.

The term "Axis" was coined by Mussolini in a speech given in Milan in 1936. It refers to an "axis" that other countries could work around. In addition to Italy and Germany, other countries in the Axis included Austria, Bulgaria, Hungary, Romania, Finland, and, finally, Japan. When Mussolini was overthrown in September 1943, Hitler ordered him rescued and installed as a puppet ruler in German-controlled northern Italy.

One of the greatest ironies of the Rome-Berlin Axis is that there was virtually no coordination in military efforts between the two powers. Indeed, the failure of all three Axis powers—Germany, Italy, and Japan—in this regard is in marked contrast to the very close and effective coordination of Great Britain and the United States.

Spencer Tucker

Additional Reading

Deakin, F.W., *The Brutal Friendship, Mussolini, Hitler, and the Fall of Italian Fascism* (1962).

Lemkin, R., *Axis Rule over Occupied Europe* (1944).

Smith, Denis Mack, *Mussolini's Roman Empire* (1976).

A

B

Babi Yar

Several days after the Germans entered the Ukrainian city of Kiev in September 1941, a tremendous explosion destroyed the German headquarters at the Continental Hotel. Other buildings mysteriously exploded and a great fire burned in the city center. Although it was Soviet troops that set the explosives and placed land mines around the city, Kiev's Jews paid the price.

SS Colonel Paul Blobel, leading *Sonderkommando* 4a of *Einsatzgruppe* C, ordered the Jews to be rounded up. On 27 and 28 September, placards appeared in the city announcing that all Jews were required to assemble for "resettlement." More than 30,000 gathered in the bitter cold on 29 September at the appointed time and place, believing they were to be relocated.

The Jews were marched to a ravine northwest of Kiev known as Babi Yar, forced to undress, and in two columns marched toward the head of the ravine. They stood, a hundred at a time, at the edge of a twenty- to twenty-five-meter drop, with German machine guns directly opposite them. The machine guns opened fire and the bodies fell into the ravine, the wounded lying among the dead.

The Nazis caused one wall of the ravine to collapse onto the dead and wounded, burying them under tons of earth, which continued to shift from the movement of the people still alive underneath; most suffocated under the crush of bodies and dirt. In a two-day period, 33,771 Jews died at the hands of *Sonderkommado* 4a.

The killings did not end there. During the next week, the slayings of Soviets, Ukrainians, and Jews continued. At regular intervals during the war, Babi Yar was used for the purpose of mass murder. The Babi Yar massacre and others like it showed the Nazis that they could bring about the "Final Solution" (q.v.) to the "Jewish problem."

Beginning in August 1943, the Germans created special *Kommando* 1005, a detail of 400 Jews and Red Army POWs, and sent them back to Babi Yar to conceal the evidence of the killings. The mass grave was unearthed, the decaying bodies, stacked along with railroad ties and iron rails, were doused with gasoline and set afire in huge pyres. It took nearly two days for the flames to burn all the corpses in the pit; a heavy, acrid smoke hung over Kiev during those days.

The workers, knowing they too were slated for execution, covered the bones and ashes. They became determined that at least a few of them should escape and survive to bear witness to what they saw at Babi Yar. In late September 1943, the "corpses," as the SS referred to them, broke out of their barracks and tried to reach some kind of hiding place. Fourteen managed to find shelter; 311 died trying. Ten of the escapees survived the war, while the other four died fighting with the Red Army against the Germans.

Babi Yar serves as a symbol for Jews all over the world. Today, a monument stands near the site of the massacre of 100,000 people. It fails, however, to mention specifically that Jewish citizens died there, and that Babi Yar was one of the first sites of mass killings of Jews during World War II.

Susanne Tepee Gaskins

Additional Reading

Bauer, Yehuda, *A History of the Holocaust* (1982).
Gilbert, Martin, *The Holocaust: A History of the Jews of Europe During the Second World War* (1985).

Baltic States

Conquered by both the Red Army and the Germans during the war, the Baltic states of Latvia and

Estonia first gained their independence after World War I. Prior to that, the Latvians and Estonians lived under a succession of German, Danish, Swedish, Polish-Lithuanian, and Russian dynasties. Lithuania, on the other hand, had existed as a nation since the Middle Ages.

The region continued to be heavily influenced by events in nearby Russia. During the Russian Revolution, the provisional government granted Estonia autonomy in 1917, and complete independence was declared just prior to the arrival of German troops into Tallinn. The collapse of Germany in November 1918 enabled Estonia to reassert its independence and at the same time defend itself against a Soviet invasion. All foreign armies were expelled from the country by March 1919.

Latvia's strong industrial sector made it important to Russia. During the revolution, Latvians split their loyalties between the provisional government and the Bolsheviks. As in Estonia, the German collapse in 1918 led to a Soviet invasion, a situation further complicated by German attempts to create a puppet regime. Both the Soviet and the German attempts to subjugate Latvia ultimately failed, and by 1920, the country was free of foreign armies.

Lithuania was still under German occupation when it declared independence in 1918. It was, however, unable to exercise national sovereignty until the final collapse of the German Empire. The Red Army also invaded Lithuania, but it was driven out, as were the *Freikorps* (q.v.) German troops still operating there after the armistice. Lithuania's postwar nationalist movement was complicated by the creation of a new Polish state that raised territorial claims against parts of Lithuania, including Vilnius, the historic Lithuanian capital.

Russian domination of the Baltic states came to an end in 1920 with the signing of separate peace treaties. All three countries established parliamentary democracies, although none had experience with democratic institutions. The eventual failure of these experiments in democracy led to the creation of centralized authoritarian regimes under the leadership of strong executives in all three states.

During the interwar years, the Baltic states attempted to pursue neutral foreign policies, although the growing power of the Soviet Union and Germany once again threatened their national identities. Estonia and Latvia entered into a defensive alliance in 1923, and each signed a nonaggression pact with the Soviet Union in 1939. Lithuania signed a nonaggression pact with the Soviet Union as early as 1926, but did not join the Estonian-Latvian alliance until 1934. Although neutral, all three countries relied heavily on Great Britain, whose navy guaranteed their independence.

By 1939, Germany and the Soviet Union realized that Britain was no longer able to protect the Baltic states. Following a 1938 Polish ultimatum to Lithuania to relinquish Vilnius, Nazi Germany in March 1939 annexed the coastal strip of Lithuania, including the port city of Klaipeda (Memel). This area had belonged to Germany prior to 1918. Lithuania, nevertheless, refused to enter into a military alliance with Germany against Poland despite Nazi promises to return Vilnius to Lithuanian control.

In August 1939, Adolf Hitler and Josef Stalin (qq.v.) signed the Molotov-Ribbentrop Pact (q.v.), which had a secret protocol assigning Estonia and Latvia to a Soviet sphere of influence while Germany gained control over Lithuania. Following the German and Soviet invasions of Poland in September 1939, and the isolation of the Baltic States, Lithuania came into the Soviet sphere as well.

In late September 1939, the Soviets initiated a policy that eventually would lead to the annexation of all three Baltic states. Through a process of armed intimidation beginning with Estonia, Stalin coerced each country into signing a mutual assistance pact that would provide for the stationing of Soviet troops in its territory. In turn, Lithuania was awarded Vilnius, which the Soviets took from Poland. All three countries tried to maintain good relations with the Soviet Union. It was clear that Britain and the West could no longer protect Baltic interests and neutrality.

Beginning in May 1940, the Soviet government accused the Baltic states of provocative acts in violation of their respective mutual assistance pacts. Threats and acts of intimidation followed. The Soviet Union first targeted Lithuania and delivered an ultimatum that it either form a new government capable of honoring the agreement or additional Soviet troops would be sent into the country. When Lithuania failed to satisfy the first condition, Soviet troops crossed the border on 15 June 1940, and occupied the country. Latvia and Estonia received similar ultimatums the following day, and on 17 June 1940, the Soviets occupied those countries as well.

Following the occupation of the Baltic states, emissaries from the Soviet government went to the Baltic capitals with the task of establishing "peoples' governments," the interim phase preceding official incorporation into the Soviet Union.

During this time, many Baltic leaders were deported to Siberia and were replaced with individuals more amenable to Soviet interests. While these governments initially claimed they had no intention of seeking incorporation, the Soviet emissaries to each country dictated policy to the new governments and oversaw the gradual dismantling, or "Sovietization," of the Baltic states. By mid-July of 1940 each country held elections for the new people's assemblies, with pro-Soviet candidates elected by overwhelming margins. On 21 July, each of the new assemblies convened and proclaimed Soviet-style republics and applied for membership in the Soviet Union. The three Baltic states were formally incorporated on 6 August 1940.

The process of Sovietization of Baltic institutions continued over the next year. During this time, a number of Baltic resistance groups were established to oppose Soviet rule. The largest and most active of these groups was the Lithuanian Activist Front (LAF), which received covert German support through Kazys Skirpa (q.v.), the Lithuanian envoy in Berlin. This group's goal was to reestablish an independent Lithuanian state under a LAF provisional government. There also were small partisan groups in Latvia and Estonia, but none of these was as large or as well organized as the LAF.

The first major act of Soviet repression against the Baltic populations came in the summer of 1941. On 13–14 June, Soviet security forces began massive deportations of anti-Soviet and other undesirable elements, including foreigners. Although many ethnic Germans in the Baltic states had departed for Germany beginning in 1939, those Balts who had ties with Germany were spared from these deportations as the result of a January 1941 repatriation agreement between the Nazis and the Soviet Union.

Just one week after these massive Soviet deportations, Germany invaded the Soviet Union and the Baltic states. On the morning of 22 June 1941, units of German Army Group North, which included the Sixteenth and Eighteenth armies and the Fourth *Panzer* Group, crossed the border into Lithuania. The Lithuanians, followed by the Latvians and the Estonians, viewed the German invasion as a guarantee of Baltic independence after a year of subjugation under Stalin.

On the first day of the invasion, Lithuanian insurgents, led by the LAF, took over key institutions in Kaunas, established a provisional government, and proclaimed an independent Lithuanian state. Whereas Baltic independence did not fit into the Nazi plans for its newly conquered territory,

the German military commander, who arrived in Kaunas on 25 June, did not take any immediate actions against the government as long as its activities did not interfere with German war aims. What the provisional government perceived as tacit Nazi approval permitted it to initiate a number of measures to shed the yoke of Soviet domination while establishing an independent state allied with Germany. In the meantime, the Germans began to disband the Lithuanian government, which had no real means of exercising sovereignty. This process was completed in August 1941.

The Germans pushed the Red Army out of Lithuania within the first three days of the campaign. Advanced units reached Daugavpils, a city in eastern Latvia, on 26 June 1941, and captured Riga, the Latvian capital, by 1 July. The German forces advanced into Russia, and by 9 July, they effectively isolated the Soviet troops still in the Baltic region. By early July, Army Group North held a broad front running from the Baltic Sea in the west, through south-central Estonia, to Pskov in the east. The first week of the campaign marked one of the most dramatic German offenses of the entire war.

Anti-Soviet insurgencies also were active in Latvia and Estonia prior to the consolidation of German control. A short-lived provisional government was established in Riga on 28 June 1941, but the Germans had no official contact with it and it soon collapsed. In Estonia, there was no formal attempt to establish an independent government. Anti-Soviet activities were concentrated in several clandestine partisan groups, some of whom managed to establish effective local administrative units in the southern part of the country weeks before the German arrival in July. Tallinn, the Estonian capital, came under German control in late August, and once the Germans consolidated their control, the Estonian partisans were either disarmed and disbanded or incorporated into German military and police units.

Despite varying degrees of cooperation with the local movements, German leaders never entertained the notion of restoring independence to the Baltic states. The Nazis perceived this area to be a logical extension of German *Lebensraum* (q.v.). This policy could only be realized once the Germans defeated the Red Army on the battlefield, pacified the area, and then relocated parts of the local Baltic populations.

Consolidation of German authority over the Baltic states began in earnest in July 1941 with the establishment of a German civilian administration for each country. Alfred Rosenberg (q.v.), the Nazi

Party ideologue, was named *Reich* minister of the eastern occupied territories on 17 July 1941. Subordinate to him was Heinrich Lohse, the *Reich* commissar for *Ostland,* appointed on 28 July, and responsible for the administration of the three Baltic states and Byelorussia. A general commissar was appointed for each of the jurisdictions.

German authorities did establish locally controlled administrations in each of the Baltic states, but each had little, if any, direct say in the formulation of policy. By routing laws and regulations through these bodies, the Germans attempted to show the Balts that they retained some authority. In fact, they were able to carry out routine administrative functions as long as they did not interfere with duties and responsibilities reserved for the German civil administration.

The Balts soon realized, however, that German liberation did not mean restoration of their countries' independence. Property nationalized by the Soviets was now confiscated by the Germans. The Baltic states were, for all intents and purposes, occupied by the Germans and governed and managed pursuant to the realities and necessities of the German war effort. Ironically, the war prevented the Germans from realizing their proposed Germanization of the Baltic states.

The subjugation of the Baltic states became more apparent in late 1941 when the Germans introduced compulsory labor service, and a force of several thousand was sent to Germany. An additional several thousand men were drafted into German-controlled military and police units. These security battalions were initially placed under the jurisdiction of the German security police and order police and were deployed to pursue Red Army stragglers and other individuals and groups identified as having collaborated with the Soviets. Some of these units were also involved in German-inspired anti-Jewish actions throughout the Baltic states.

Although there were several instances of spontaneous anti-Jewish pogroms in the early days of the German occupation, most of the Baltic Jews were killed during a systematic sweep carried out by German *Einsatzgruppen* (q.v.) and their local collaborators in the summer and autumn of 1941. The Jews who survived were later confined to newly established ghettos. Concentration camps were established near Riga and Tallinn in late 1941 and early 1942, and they became the destination for thousands of deported German and Czech Jews. By the end of 1943, many of the ghettos were liquidated and the residents murdered or transferred to concentration camps. By the end of the German occupation in 1944, nearly a quarter of a million Jews had been murdered or were deported to concentration camps in the Baltic states.

In the final years of the war, Baltic police and military units were deployed outside of the region to combat the advancing Red Army and Soviet partisans (q.v.). The Germans also created "volunteer" *Waffen*-SS (q.v.) divisions in Latvia and Estonia in 1942–1943. Late in the war, remnants of these divisions were evacuated to Germany and eventually surrendered to the Allies. The Germans failed to mobilize the Lithuanians into SS units, and it was not until February 1944 that local Lithuanian military units were created and placed under the command of General Povilas Plechavicius. In May 1944, there was an unsuccessful attempt to incorporate these units into the SS. These units were disbanded and Plechavicius was arrested.

By the summer of 1944, the German offensive against the Soviet Union was collapsing and Germany was no longer able to maintain its occupation of the Baltic states. As a result, the Red Army reoccupied most of this territory by late fall, with only the Kurzeme (Courland) region of western Latvia remaining under German control until May 1945. Despite the chaos of this period, the Soviets managed to rapidly reestablish control over the Baltic states and new Soviet governments were organized in November 1944. New deportations occurred in 1945 and 1946 and a number of territorial concessions were forced upon Estonia and Latvia. Lithuania regained Klaipeda and their coastal strip from the Germans.

The three Baltic states remained under Soviet control until 1990 and 1991, when they regained their independence—a harbinger of the coming disintegration of the Soviet Union.

Steven B. Rogers

Additional Reading

Higgins, Trumbull, *Hitler and Russia* (1966).

Meiksins, Gregory, *Baltic Riddle: Finland, Estonia, Latvia, Lithuania—Key Points of European Peace* (1943).

Misiunas, Romuald J., *The Baltic States: Years of Dependence 1940–1990* (1993).

Oras, Arts, *Baltic Eclipse* (1948).

Suabe, Arveds, *Genocide in the Baltic States* (1952).

Beer Hall *Putsch*

The "Beer Hall *Putsch,*" sometimes called the Munich *Putsch* or *Hitlerputsch,* was Adolf Hitler's (q.v.) abortive attempt on 8 and 9 November 1923 to carry out an insurrection against the Bavarian government and lead a march on Berlin to overthrow the Weimar Republic (q.v.). The Beer Hall *Putsch* got its name from the *Bürgerbräukeller* Beer Hall, (which ironically became a U.S. Army Service Club in 1945) where it began.

Hitler, stunned and dismayed by German defeat in World War I, sought to expose and punish the guilty parties. He blamed the government in Berlin for all of Germany's ills, including the rampant hyperinflation that ravaged the country. In Bavaria, he attracted a weird assortment of supporters, including practitioners of astrology such as Frau Elsbeth Ebertin, who persuaded him that it was his destiny to "sacrifice himself for the German nation."

Whether Hitler personally believed in astrology or not is debatable, but he certainly considered himself a man of destiny. Among his entourage, he "tuned out all but affirmative voices," wrote historian John Toland. One of those voices, Frau Winifrid Wagner, Richard Wagner's daughter-in-law, remarked, "He is destined to be the savior of Germany."

During the same period, Houston Stewart Chamberlain (q.v.), an English racist philosopher and admirer of Wagner, wrote to Hitler: "With one blow you have transformed the state of my soul. That Germany, in the hour of greatest need, brings forth a Hitler—that is the proof of her vitality." All of this was music to Hitler's soul and confirmed his long-held view of himself as a man of destiny. He saw himself as a man with a fateful and urgent mission.

Germany's galloping inflation was a fortunate aspect of his fate. By October 1923, it took more than 30 million marks to equal one 1913 mark. Formerly affluent Germans groped in desperation as the country became a nation of scavengers. A postage stamp cost one million marks. Legless war veterans begged on street corners, while former enemies stripped Germany of its territory. These were supreme irritants to the proud Germans, and Hitler saw the deeper political meanings waiting to be exploited.

Munich was fertile soil for political intrigue. Given these conditions, Hitler's small Nazi Party drew more than 30,000 new members during October 1923. This convinced him that the people were ready for revolution. Hitler's speeches on Germany's woes were electrifying and effective. He knew how to arouse an audience, not solely with what he said, but by the passion with which he said it.

The Bavarian people, conservative and na-

tionalistic, rallied to his cause. Some might have objected to his violent language and crude tactics, but they shared his vision of a strong and united Germany that would throw off the humiliations of the hated Treaty of Versailles (q.v.) and take its rightful place in the world as in the prewar days.

The Bavarian government and General Otto von Lassow, the regional *Reichswehr* Commander, resisted pressure from Berlin to restrain Hitler and ban his newspaper, the *Völkischer Beobachter.* Even the *Münchener Zeitung* newspaper called for an overthrow of Chancellor Gustav Stresemann (q.v.). *Reichswehr* soldiers stationed in Bavaria were taking oaths of allegiance to the Bavarian rather than to the national government.

To resolve the crisis, von Lassow suggested three possible options: continuing the status quo; Bavaria seceding from the *Reich;* or conducting a march on Berlin and taking over the national government. Hitler supported the last option. Alfred Rosenberg (q.v.) and others among Hitler's followers suggested they begin by kidnapping Bavarian Crown Prince Rupprecht and Gustav *Ritter* von Kahr, the right-wing state commissioner of Bavaria. Argued out of this plan by his associates, Hitler sought to split the ruling triumvirate of von Kahr, von Lassow, and Hans von Seisser, chief of the Bavarian state police, by meeting privately with the latter. He tried to convince Seisser that Kahr was unfit to govern and that he and Lassow should align with himself and General Erich Ludendorff (q.v.), head of the World War I German Army. While privately considering the Nazis "trash," Seisser and Lassow did agree to act.

The most important job was to set up a new national regime. All agreed the Weimar Republic must be done away with. On the evening of 6 November, Hitler met with some of his supporters to draw up a plan of action. They agreed to launch a full-fledged *Putsch* on 11 November.

Early the next morning, they met again with other supporters, including Ludendorff, to plan their next move. They would seize telegraph offices, radio stations, public utilities, and railroad stations. Leading Socialists and Communists were to be arrested. Numerically, Hitler's supporters had an advantage of about 1,400 over the police and troops expected to oppose them. That same day, Ernst Pöhner, the Munich police commissioner, and Wilhelm Frick (q.v.), a police official still protecting Hitler, agreed to join the *Putsch.*

A golden opportunity was presented when von Kahr announced a mass meeting that included local government leaders at the *Bürgerbräukeller* the next evening. Hitler decided to move early by going there and confronting them with sufficient force to convince them they should go along with the coup d'état. At this point, he had no specific plan. He sought only to excite the Bavarian public by a dramatic display of power that would defy Berlin. His co-conspirators were doubtful about such action and a long argument ensued. Later, orders went out to the leaders of the Nazi SA (q.v.) to prepare their men for action.

On the evening of 8 November, Hitler's group arrived at the overcrowded beer hall, which was closed to all but important personages. Expecting trouble, the city had mobilized 125 municipal policemen to keep order. Hitler argued his way in with his followers, including the foreign press. He convinced the police to leave and make way for his troops. When he entered the great hall, von Kahr was denouncing Marxism and calling for a new regime in Germany. One of Hitler's aides ordered a beer for him so he would better fit in with the crowd—it cost one billion marks.

Little attention was paid to Hitler until he jumped onto a chair and told the crowd to be quiet. When they failed to respond, he pulled his pistol and fired a shot into the ceiling. He then shouted to the surprised audience: "The national revolution has broken out. The hall is surrounded!"

Faced with such a show of force, von Kahr, Lassow, and Seisser followed Hitler into an adjoining room. Lassow was overheard whispering to his colleagues, "Put on an act." Hitler apologized for proceeding in such a manner, but claimed he had no alternative. When accused of breaking his promise not to make a *Putsch,* he again apologized but stated he had to do it for Germany. He announced that Pöhner would be the new Bavarian prime minister. Ludendorff would command the newly created army, which would include the right-wing *Kampfbund* (Battle League) and the SA, and lead the march on Berlin. Whistles and catcalls followed from the hall floor until Hermann Göring (q.v.), taking his cue from Hitler, fired his pistol into the ceiling.

When the uproar died down, Hitler promised Lassow could join the government as army minister and Seisser as police minister in return for their support. Huge crowds outside the beer hall yelled, "*Ja, Ja,*" when asked by Hitler if he had their support. In a free Germany there will be room for an autonomous Bavaria, he yelled.

Not having been informed of Hitler's premature move, and having arrived at the hall after Hitler, Ludendorff was instrumental in winning over the reluctant triumvirate. A handshake sealed the deal. All promised to cooporate. Hitler was overcome with emotion. His face pale and dripping with perspiration, he told the enthusiastic crowd:

> I am going to fulfill the vow I made to myself five years ago when I was a blind cripple in the military hospital: to know neither rest nor peace until the November Criminals had been overthrown, until on the ruins of the Germany of today there should have risen once more a Germany of power and greatness, of freedom and splendor.

Others among Hitler's close followers present that evening were Hermann Esser, Max Amann, Harvard-educated Helene Hanfstangl, and Rudolph Hess (q.v.). The next day, Gregor Strasser and Julius Streicher (q.v.) joined the group. Frick persuaded his police colleagues not to launch a counterattack against Hitler's followers. Hitler, in a state of euphoria, departed to settle other urgent matters and left Ludendorff in charge. That turned out to be a critical error.

After Hitler's departure, Lassow asked to leave the beer hall to take care of some business and Ludendorff agreed. Von Kahr and Seisser went with him. Later, Hitler was upset with Ludendorff for this action, but the old general replied that a German officer never breaks his oath. Hitler tried to reach Lassow by telephone but to no avail. Now, Lassow could and did sabotage the revolution. He mobilized forces for a counterattack. Ludendorff later stated he would never again trust the word of a German officer, but it was too late.

It was 5:00 o'clock the next morning when Lassow informed Hitler that he and his two associates could not respect their promises, since they were given under duress. Lassow now was going to put down the *Putsch* by force. The coup was coming unraveled and Hitler was stunned. He nevertheless vowed to fight to the death and began a march into the city to win over the people and rescue Ernst Röhm (q.v.), who was being detained.

The march ended in disaster when police fired on the crowd, killing eighteen, including fourteen of Hitler's supporters and four policemen. Hitler was injured when his personal bodyguard was shot and jerked him down so sharply that his arm was pulled from its socket.

Hitler later was arrested and tried for treason by a court that largely sympathized with him. He used the trial to attack the government and gain worldwide fame. Ludendorff was freed and Hitler was given a modest sentence of five years in

B

Landsberg prison; he served barely eight months. While there he wrote his infamous personal manifesto, *Mein Kampf (My Struggle).*

The debacle convinced him to henceforth pursue power by parliamentary means. Ironically, it also left Hitler and his movement in a stronger position. Prior to the *Putsch,* Hitler was little more than a regional agitator. Afterward, he was on center stage of national politics, having supplanted Ludendorff as the head of the *Völkisch* movement in Germany.

Paul J. Rose

Additional Reading
Bullock, Alan, *Hitler: A Study in Tyranny* (1962).
Fest, Joachim C., *Hitler* (1973).
Toland, John, *Adolf Hitler* (1976).

Belzec
See CONCENTRATION CAMPS

Bergen-Belsen
See CONCENTRATION CAMPS

Berlin Blockade
The Berlin Blockade began in 24 June 1948, and continued until 23 May 1949. It happened as a consequence of tensions generated from the inability of the Western Allies and the Soviet Union to resolve their differences over the kind of government postwar Germany should have.

The West viewed the blockade as a step in the Soviet strategy to westward expansion. Berlin became a challenge for the containment of Soviet power. Soviet Premier Josef Stalin (q.v.), on the other hand, was determined to drive out the Western Allies by blocking all land and water routes to the Allied sectors of the city.

Soviet behavior toward Berlin may better be understood by recalling that when Soviet representatives walked out of the Allied Control Council in April 1948, and suddenly halted American, British, and French trains enroute to the city, they acted on deeply held beliefs that Berlin was ". . . the lair of the Fascist beast." The Soviet Union, having defeated the most powerful German military machine in history, at the cost of seven million men, thought it a catastrophe not to be allowed to hold all of Berlin—the major prize, and one of the greatest Soviet achievements of the war.

In May 1945, the Soviets were determined to be in Berlin before the Western armies arrived. But, according to an Allied agreement in London in 1944, Germany and Berlin were to be divided into zones of occupation. As historian Alexander Werth wrote, "The Soviet Union felt cheated when she was obliged to share sectors of Berlin with the Western armies."

In September 1945, the United States, Britain, and France had relinquished to Soviet authorities all operational control and supervision of land and water routes leading to Berlin. With these advantages of control, the Soviets were able to halt the flow of Western traffic on railroads, auto routes, and canals to the city, as well as Western traffic through three air corridors patrolled by the Soviet Air Force.

The blockade of Berlin reportedly was further motivated by Soviet resentment toward a foreign ministers' conference in 1947, when the Western nations vetoed any Soviet access to the iron deposits of the Ruhr Valley.

The Soviets had never questioned the agreement made with the Western powers in June 1945 permitting unrestricted use of the railroad between Magdeburg and Berlin. But in 1948, when the Soviets began boarding and inspecting military trains, they were violating the previously agreed-upon freedom of movement provision. Now, the Soviets were declaring the international agreements of 2 September 1944 and 1 May 1945, concerning zones of occupation in Germany and the city of Berlin, no longer valid. They referred to ". . . the unlawful occupation of West Berlin," and ". . . the severe abuse of occupation rights," as deliberate provocations against the Soviet Union. The Soviets then called for ". . . a demilitarized West Berlin as a free city," yet showed no intention of cooperating with the Western powers in rebuilding Germany economically or socially.

The more immediate cause of the Berlin Blockade came when the Western Allies decided to unite their occupation zones in Germany itself into a single economic unit, and approved a currency that was applicable to West Germany and West Berlin. Assuming this was an American-led attempt to establish itself permanently in the heart of Germany, and an affront to their own assumed preeminence, the Soviets ordered a blockade of all land routes to and from Berlin.

As the Soviet objective was the absorption of all of Berlin into their occupation zone, Soviet propaganda was aimed at convincing the Western occupation forces that they were holding an untenable position, surrounded and heavily outnumbered in manpower. In January 1948, there were

9,000 Americans in Berlin, including about 4,000 combat troops with a combined Allied combat force of 6,500. In contrast, there were more than 70,000 Soviet troops in their sector of Berlin or stationed around the city. An additional 300,000 Soviet troops were stationed in Soviet-occupied eastern Germany—a force that could be easily expanded if needed.

Even with their numerical superiority, the Soviets did not take direct military action. That would have meant a major military confrontation with the West, as well as having to feed and supply Berlin's two million people for an indefinite period of time. Viewing Soviet actions as a war of nerves and a slow squeeze to get control of the city, Berliners felt harassed during the critical winter months when coal and fuel supplies ran short. For Americans, the blockade made Berlin an island deep inside the Soviet zone.

Soviet propaganda was aimed at convincing the German people and Berlin's population that their real enemies were the Western powers. The East German chief of propaganda, Gerhart Eisler, encouraged East Germans to paint "Go Home" signs on American buildings, and orchestrated mass demonstrations appealing to German nationalism. Such efforts had little effect, however, on West Berliners, who worried about Western resolve and rumors that U.S. forces might evacuate the city.

In response to Soviet pressures, American and British officials closed off the Soviet Control Center, preventing its use by the Soviet military, but later withdrew the order. The Soviets then viewed the American move as proof that the U.S. was actually weak when it tried to look strong.

General Lucius D. Clay (q.v.), the U.S. military commander, reaffirmed the U.S. and Allied position in Berlin by declaring he had no intention of moving his office to Frankfurt, as some Americans were doing. Clay reminded the Soviets that the 1945 Potsdam Agreement guaranteed the Western powers a right to joint occupation of Berlin, and thus Western evacuation was unthinkable.

To sustain Berlin's beleaguered population, the Western Allies used the three air corridors running from West Germany to the city. Nearly a quarter of a million flights supplied food, coal, and medical supplies for nearly a year. The Berlin Airlift (q.v.) was the most massive use of airpower for peaceful, political, and humanitarian purposes in history to that time. Its success was especially spectacular because West Berlin remained free. The near paralysis of East-West commerce created by the blockade, however, harmed business confidence. It curtailed orders with Berlin factories, slowed deliveries to a trickle, and increased the risk factor of business investments.

The price tag for not succumbing to the Berlin Blockade came to $6 million a month. Western analysts saw the financial cost as an acceptable burden to pay for preventing the Soviet absorption of West Berlin. Failure there so early in the Cold War would have seriously damaged the West's credibility, as well as confidence in American willingness to stand up to Soviet threats. The loss of Berlin would have shifted the political momentum to the Soviets. The blockade also served to transform the West Germans from a wartime enemy into a cooperative partner in the containment of Soviet advances.

In May 1949, Stalin communicated his willingness to end the blockade. The U.S. initially rebuffed the gesture to show its disdain for Soviet activities in Czechoslovakia and Finland, but later accepted the Soviet bid. Possible reasons why the Soviets extended peace feelers were its loss of political ground in Italy and France, and the success of the Marshall Plan (q.v.), which was pouring billions of dollars into Europe's economy and putting the Soviet Union on the defensive politically and psychologically.

Though the Western Allies could not be dislodged without a war, the Soviets were in a position to dominate Berlin without a major military confrontation. Their decision to launch the blockade was influenced by their belief that the West's capacity to supply Berlin was limited. In retrospect, the Soviets were correct, as an airlift could not have been maintained indefinitely. Yet, Berliners endured beyond Soviet expectations, costing them political ground elsewhere.

On 23 May 1949, the Berlin Blockade was formally ended and a four-power agreement was signed. The Soviet municipal government of Berlin broke up and a separate regime under Soviet military protection was established. The Western sectors of Berlin responded by organizing their own city governments. Thus, the blockade left a divided Berlin and a divided Germany.

Donald Doumit

Additional Reading

Davison, W. Phillips, *The Berlin Blockade* (1957).

Pinson, Koppel S., *Modern Germany* (1966).

Richardson, James L., *Germany and the Atlantic Alliance* (1966).

B

Berlin, Occupation of

Planning for the occupation of Berlin, Germany's capital, began well before the end of the war. In the summer of 1943, the British cabinet issued a report recommending that Berlin be occupied by the three major Allied powers, each with control over a separate zone of occupation. Further discussions came at the Moscow Conference in October 1943, and a formal agreement was signed in Quebec on 12 September 1944.

According to this agreement, Berlin was to be administered as a distinct area within Germany, split into three zones, "jointly occupied by armed forces of the USA, UK and USSR," and administered by an inter-Allied governing authority, an Allied Control Council made up of military commanders from each of the occupation powers. A fourth zone was subsequently arranged for the French at the Yalta Conference in February 1945. The Allied authorities also decided to locate their postwar headquarters in Berlin.

Discussions concerning the occupation and the future of Berlin continued after the conquest of the city by Soviet armed forces and the capitulation of Germany. The Allied commanders in chief met in Berlin on 5 June 1945, and there they defined the occupation zones and sectors. Tensions among the Allies, however, quickly mounted, especially between the Soviets and the other three occupation powers.

When the American and British representatives, General Lucius Clay (q.v.) and General Sir Ronald Weeks, met with Marshal Georgy Zhukov (q.v.), their Soviet counterpart, to finalize arrangements for the entrance of Western forces into the city. Zhukov objected to these arrangements and directed that access be limited to a single main highway, one rail line, and two air corridors.

By the time the Western powers moved their forces into Berlin in July 1945, the Soviet Union had already consolidated its control and had done much to shape the future political and economic life of Berlin. In addition, the Soviets dismantled nearly 500 complete factories and shipped most of the machinery back to the Soviet Union as war reparation. Berlin's economic recovery was further crippled by the restrictions on inter-zonal trade.

A provisional constitution for Berlin was ap-

British and Soviet soldiers on the balcony of Hitler's ruined Chancellery in Berlin. (IWM BU 8635)

proved on 13 August 1946, and it called for free municipal elections to be held on 20 October. More than 92 percent of the electorate went to the polls for the first free election held in Berlin since 1933. While the Soviets clearly expected a victory of the SED (Socialist Unity Party), it received only 20 percent of the vote. The clear winner was the SPD (Social Democratic Party), which secured almost 49 percent of the vote. The conservative CDU (Christian Democratic Union) obtained 22 percent, and the FPD (Free Democratic Party) 10 percent. The October election was, in fact, a critical event for occupied Berlin, marking the rebirth of political freedom and making the city an arena in the Cold War. Recognizing the unpopularity of the Communists and the ineffectiveness of their propaganda, the Soviet Union adopted new techniques to ensure its dominant position in the city.

Following the elections and the resounding commitment to democracy, the resolve of the Western powers was strengthened, as the Soviets continued to resist or refuse to compromise on a variety of issues. Tensions between the Western occupation powers and the Soviet Union rose, and meetings of the control council degenerated into little more than shouting matches. Increasingly, each of the Allied commanders acted unilaterally in his own sector, although the Western leaders cooperated more as a single entity. This cooperation led to the economic unification of the British and American zones on 1 January 1947. The French quickly joined.

Tensions in Berlin continued to mount during early 1948 as the Soviets imposed additional arbitrary restrictions on rail and highway access to the city. The Soviets continued to attack Western policies, and on 20 March, Marshal Vasili Sokolowsky (q.v.) walked out of the control council, thereby effectively ending the formal four-power control of Berlin and of Germany as a whole. With no resolution of the major issue of currency reform, the Western powers introduced a new currency into their three zones on 21 June 1948. The Soviets responded in kind, adopting its own currency reform for the eastern zone and accusing the West of irreparably splitting Germany and transforming their zones into "an instrument for the rebuilding of Germany's war potential."

Next, the Soviet military administration in Germany imposed further restrictions on Berlin, hoping to gain control of the entire city and drive out the Western powers. By 24 June 1948, these restrictions led to the total blockade of Berlin (q.v.). The Soviets fully expected the food short-

ages in the Western zone to lead to unrest, which in turn would force the Western allies out of the city. The blockade caught the Western military leaders unprepared, but they immediately instituted a massive airlift to supply the city by the only means of access still available.

The Berlin Airlift (q.v.), which lasted until 12 May 1949, involved more than 277,800 flights carrying more than 2.3 million tons of food. The Soviets eventually lifted the blockade because they recognized that it would not achieve the objectives of delaying the formation of a West German government or hastening the incorporation of all of Berlin into the Soviet Occupation Zone.

Other political changes followed. With the establishment of the German Democratic Republic in the former Soviet zone on 7 October 1949, the government of the Soviet sector in Berlin promulgated a new constitution and declared itself to be the capital of the new Communist East German state. A month later, the Soviet commander transferred administrative functions to the local German government, thereby deepening the division of the city.

In summer 1950, the municipal assembly in the Western sectors drafted its own constitution, giving the three Western zones the legal status of a *Land* (State) in the new Federal Republic of Germany. This constitution was adopted on 1 September 1950. Later in 1950, it was decided to liberalize Allied controls in Berlin, and by March 1951, the Western military governors sharply reduced their powers and granted more autonomy to the German municipal government of West Berlin.

The Soviets continued to isolate East Berlin from West Berlin, in part to aid economic development in its own area of control. These efforts culminated in the building of the infamous Berlin Wall on 13 August 1961. It stood as a monument to the continued occupation and division of Berlin until 9 November 1989. The fall of the Berlin Wall marked the end of the city's occupation, and its subsequent adoption as the capital of the reunified Federal Republic of Germany.

Robert G. Waite

Additional Reading

Gimbel, John, *The American Occupation of Germany: Politics and the Military 1945–1949* (1968).

Heidelmeyer, Wolfgang, and Guenther Hindrichs (eds.), *Documents on Berlin, 1943–1963* (1963).

McInnis, Edgar, Richard Hiscocks, and Robert Spencer, *The Shaping of Postwar Germany* (1960).

Snowden, J.K., *The German Question 1945–1949: Continuity and Change* (1975).

Bern Incident

In January 1945, with Allied forces advancing rapidly through Italy, a German intelligence agent in Milan initiated discussions with Allen W. Dulles, the Office of Strategic Services (qq.v.) agent in Bern, Switzerland, concerning a possible armistice in northern Italy. First approached by a Swiss intermediary on 25 February, Dulles remained noncommittal. While a growing number of emissaries and messages passed through his office, Dulles negotiated with SS Colonel General Karl Wolff (q.v.) to halt all fighting in northern Italy. The two met on 19 March. Dulles advised Allied leaders of his discussions with the Germans. On 21 April, the Allied Joint Chiefs of Staff ordered him not to proceed.

U.S. president Franklin D. Roosevelt and British prime minister Winston S. Churchill told Soviet premier Josef Stalin (qq.v.) about the negotiations, and Stalin accused them of seeking a separate peace with Adolf Hitler. Dulles, nevertheless, pursued the negotiations with Wolff, and by 29 April 1945, the German military leadership in Italy signed a surrender agreement with the Western Allies. The terms were made public on 2 May. Dulles's efforts to bring an end to the war in Italy and Stalin's angry response became known as the Bern Incident.

Robert G. Waite

Additional Reading
Dulles, Allen W., *The Craft of Intelligence* (1963).
———, *The Secret Surrender* (1966).
Höhne, Heinz, *Der Krieg im Dunkeln: Macht und Einfluss der deutschen und russischen Geheimdienste* (1985).

Birkenau
See CONCENTRATION CAMPS

Blomberg-Fritsch Crisis

By late autumn of 1937, Adolf Hitler was actively planning for the coming war. He wanted the *Wehrmacht* to be ready to fight as soon as possible. The evidence for this is the famous meeting he convened in his Berlin chancellery on 5 November 1937, which has gone down in history as the Hossbach Conference (*see* Hossbach Protocol), named after the military adjutant who took notes

of the meeting. In addition to Hitler and Colonel Friedrich Hossbach, the conference was attended by five men: Field Marshal Werner von Blomberg, the minister of war; General Werner von Fritsch, commander in chief of the Army; Hermann Göring, commander in chief of the *Luftwaffe;* Admiral Erich Raeder, head of the navy; and Konstantin von Neurath, the foreign minister (qq.v.).

Hitler spoke for four hours. He claimed that Germany was faced with a problem of overcrowding that could only be solved by the creation of *Lebensraum* (q.v.), or living space, for the German people. Then he addressed the question of where this space was to come from. His answer: Not from overseas colonies, but from territory in the "immediate proximity of the *Reich* in Europe"; and not from France or elsewhere in the west, but from the east, more precisely, from Russia. Hitler next addressed the "how" question: The only way to obtain this *Lebensraum* was to take it by force.

It was his "irrevocable decision" to solve Germany's space problem by 1943–1945, at the latest, and earlier than that if at all possible, depending on political and other circumstances. He might begin next year, 1938! Time was of the essence. He was getting older, Hitler said, and only he could achieve *Lebensraum* for the German *Volk.* Armament production would have to be stepped up. Hitler also outlined the initial steps he intended to take: the annexation of Austria and the conquest of Czechoslovakia.

The reaction of Blomberg, Fritsch, and von Neurath to these ideas was less than enthusiastic. They felt Hitler's plans entailed too much risk and that the German Army was not ready to fight a war, especially a large-scale war as was implied in Hitler's program. The *Führer* also was unhappy with his *Wehrmacht* leaders for another reason in 1937. On the surface, relations between him and the military looked good. Blomberg, a pro-Nazi general, was appointed minister of war just after Hitler's appointment as chancellor, and with his approval.

On von Hindenberg's (q.v.) death in August 1934, Hitler assumed the title of supreme commander of the armed forces and every member swore personal allegiance to him the same day. But relations with the *Wehrmacht's* leaders had not developed as Hitler had hoped.

Hitler wanted a competent but docile officer corps. Instead, he was met with skepticism from the generals on several occasions, for example, the reoccupation of the Rhineland (q.v.) in 1936. Hitler also felt the officers had shown too little enthusiasm for rearmament. They advised against the introduction of universal military conscription in 1935. Blomberg's and Fritsch's 1937 doubts regarding Hitler's plans for conquest in the east, then, were only the latest in a series of hesitations, the most recent examples of moderation on the army's part that Hitler despised.

In January and February 1938, Hitler took advantage of two chance opportunities in order to eliminate all three of the recalcitrant conservatives who had balked at his plans the previous November. The first to go was the fifty-nine-year-old General Blomberg. His first wife had died in 1932. Later, he fell in love with his secretary, the twenty-four-year-old Eva Gruhn. He married her, with the blessing and attendance of Göring and Hitler. But he made a small error; his new wife had an unsavory past. Several writers claimed she was a prostitute; what is certain is that she had posed for pornographic photographs at one time. Moreover, Blomberg knew about these rumors before he married her. Not knowing whether to marry her, he asked Göring for advice. Göring encouraged Blomberg to fulfill his heart's desire.

Shortly after the ceremony, the lewd photos came into the hands of the police, who passed them on to General Wilhelm Keitel (q.v.), who gave them to Göring. Göring went to Hitler, arguing that it simply would not do for the minister of war of Nazi Germany to be married to such a woman. Hitler agreed. Blomberg's resignation would be required to remove the stain on the *Wehrmacht's* honor. SS chief Heinrich Himmler (q.v.), frustrated by the roadblocks placed by the army in the way of the *Waffen-SS* (q.v.), also was intriguing against Blomberg.

Göring wanted to replace Blomberg as the minister of war, but Hitler placated him with the title of field marshall. He eliminated Blomberg's title altogether, made himself commander in chief of the armed forces in practice as well as in name, and gave the job of chief of the high command of the armed forces (OKW), a new agency that became Hitler's military staff, to the pliable technocrat, Keitel. Blomberg went into exile and obscurity with his new wife.

The next episode in this melodrama concerned General Werner von Fritsch, commander in chief of the army. A bachelor, Fritsch was suddenly confronted with charges that he had committed a homosexual act. His accuser was a professional blackmailer, one Otto Schmidt, who was picked up by the police and testified during interrogation that he had witnessed von Fritsch in the act five years earlier, in 1933.

The news got to Göring, and again, he went to Hitler. Hitler summoned Fritsch to his chancellery and confronted him with the accusation and with Schmidt. Fritsch denied the charge, but ineffectively, probably because he could not believe that this was happening to the highly respected head of the German Army.

Despite the fact that Fritsch gave Hitler his word of honor that he was innocent of the charge, Hitler suspended him pending the outcome of an investigation by the army and the *Gestapo*. The investigation disclosed that the homosexual act witnessed by Schmidt was in fact committed not by von Fritsch, but by a retired cavalry officer named Frisch. Göring and Himmler were aware of the identity mix-up but suppressed the information in order to eliminate Fritsch. Helmuth Krausnick rightly calls this an "infamous maneuver" on their part.

Schmidt later confessed it was Frisch, not von Fritsch, that he had seen, and the informant subsequently was liquidated by the *Gestapo* on Hitler's orders. He had failed as a blackmailer.

By the time von Fritsch's innocence was established, it was too late to reinstate him as army commander in chief. A new one was named, General Walther von Brauchitsch (q.v.), another technocrat. After his exoneration, von Fritsch was appointed commander of his old artillery regiment with the rank of colonel! He never recovered from the dishonor visited upon him by Hitler, however, and he was killed in action during the Polish campaign on 22 September 1939. Fellow officers suspected that he sought his own death.

In February 1938, Hitler also dismissed Foreign Minister von Neurath and replaced him with the obsequious Joachim von Ribbentrop (q.v.). As a consequence of these changes in personnel, Hitler had, in a few weeks' time, eliminated the "defeatist" leaders in the *Wehrmacht* and Foreign Ministry and replaced them with "yes" men. For most authors this was the equivalent of coordinating or Nazifying these two critical institutions. Now Hitler was ready to pursue his foreign policy goals unhindered. His ascendency over the military was close to complete.

Jon Moulton

Additional Reading

Deutsch, Harold C., *Hitler and His Generals* (1974).

O'Neil, Robert J., *The German Army and the Nazi Party, 1933–1939* (1966).

Taylor, Telford, *Sword and Swastika: Generals and Nazis in the Third Reich* (1952).

Wheeler-Bennett, John W., *The Nemesis of Power* (1961).

Bohemia and Moravia

In the geographical center of the European continent, Bohemia and Moravia mark the border between the German and Slavic peoples. With a highly developed agriculture and an abundance of raw materials, Bohemia is one of the principal manufacturing centers of Europe. During the reigns of the Holy Roman and Hapsburg empires, the German minority squelched Bohemian and Moravian independence.

After World War I, in which many Czechs had fought against the Central Powers, the new state of Czechoslovakia incorporated the Czech lands of Bohemia and Moravia together with Slovakia and Ruthenia. The provinces of Bohemia and Moravia consisted of more than 70 percent Czechs, and the whole nation contained only about three million ethnic Germans, living mostly in the western borderland.

By the late 1930s, German expansion under Adolf Hitler (q.v.) threatened Czech independence and old animosities resurfaced. The German minority opposed the new republic and looked to a resurgent Germany. Though Czech leaders sought to stand firm against Hitler, their Western allies fatally compromised Czech independence at the Munich Conference (q.v.) in September 1938. The Czech government was forced to cede to Germany all districts of Bohemia and Moravia that had 50 percent or more Germans. Under heavy German pressure, the Slovaks on 13 March 1939 declared their independence from Czechoslovakia. On 15 March, Hitler and Hermann Göring (q.v.) pressured Czech president Emile Hácha to sign over sovereignty of his rump country to Germany, and German troops occupied Bohemia and Moravia the same day.

Hitler established the "protectorate" of Bohemia and Moravia on 16 March, supposedly to establish Czech autonomy within a "Greater German Empire"; actually, he annexed them. Germany assumed control over foreign affairs and defense; all military equipment was confiscated. A native administration ran internal affairs under the auspices of the "protector," who safeguarded German interests in the country and who had approval over ministers and policies. Konstantin von Neurath (q.v.) was the first protector, beginning on 18 March 1939.

A fifty-member Committee of National Solidarity replaced the National Assembly, and all political parties were abolished. Czech companies were forced to sell stock at prices dictated by German buyers, or to increase capital to an amount to guarantee a German majority among the stockholders.

A Supreme Office of Prices was established in May 1939. *Reich* ministries handled justice and finance; the *Gestapo* (q.v.) controlled the police. Prominent democratic writers, journalists, teachers, and priests were arrested and placed in concentration camps. Universities were closed.

Conditions worsened in September 1941 when the new "protector," Reinhard Heyrich (q.v.), initiated a reign of terror through martial law and appointed a new government fully subordinate to German superiors. His assassination on 27 May 1942 led to a direct German takeover and brutal retribution. On 10 June, the Germans destroyed the town of Lidiče (q.v.) and killed most of its occupants. Resistance in the protectorate lagged, but an intelligence network, which included a spy within German intelligence, provided much information. In the six years of occupation, 360,000 Czechs were sent to concentration camps; 235,000 of them died. In addition, 140,000 Jews perished. With the defeat of Germany in 1945 and liberation by the Red Army, Bohemia and Moravia again became a part of Czechoslovakia.

Laura Matysek Wood

Additional Reading
Duff, Sheila Grant, *A German Protectorate: The Czechs Under Nazi Rule* (1942).
Mastny, Vojtech, *The Czechs Under Nazi Rule: The Failure of National Resistance, 1939–1942* (1971).

Book Burning

During their reign of power in Germany, the Nazis were adamant about controlling public thought by controlling the media. When the Nazis began the practice of book burning, they discovered there were two benefits to this method of censorship. Not only could they purge Germany of undesirable literature, but also they could use these great bonfires to incite and rally the crowds in favor of Adolf Hitler (q.v.).

While there are numerous instances of book burning by the Nazis, the most famous instance occurred on 10 May 1933 in Berlin. Although the Nazis wanted the world to believe the event was the spontaneous initiative of university students, there is evidence that the event was organized by Propaganda Minister Joseph Goebbels and the SA (qq.v.). There is little doubt that both played a role in this symbolic demonstration of intolerance toward all that failed to conform to the Nazi agenda.

The entire day of 10 May saw raiding parties going into public and private libraries and confis-

Nazi book burning in Berlin, 10 May 1933. (IWM NYP 68048)

cating books perceived to be unfit for the Third *Reich*. A variety of literary works were targeted, including authors such as Karl Marx, Sigmund Freud, Voltaire, Thomas Mann, Hermann Hesse, Romain Rolland, and H.G. Wells. Even the writings of the American heroine Helen Keller were targeted. Of those authors who lived in Germany, many went into exile in order to avoid the persecution they expected would follow.

As the day wore on, mobs arrived with more books to pile onto the heap. When the demonstration reached a frenzied pitch, Goebbels arrived and gave a rousing speech that fueled the crowd to even greater heights. As night fell, students from the University of Berlin began to dance around the bonfires shouting Nazi phrases and slogans.

This extreme display of censorship led to continued witch-hunts for literary works viewed as suspect. Most book burning demonstrations occurred in cities that were specifically university towns. During a six-day period in September 1936, thirty-eight searches were conducted in the district of Düsseldorf. The search produced 37,040 forbidden volumes. After sorting, these books were destroyed by the police.

Even though the book burnings were an effective motivational technique to rally the populace, it took the Nazis several years after coming to power to create an effective censorship mechanism. During the period, books that were banned in one state could be found in other states. The instructions given to the police were vague, which resulted in subjective judgments as to whether any certain work was "calculated to endanger public order." Once the censorship machine was organized, absolute censorship authority rested with Goebbels's *Reich* Chamber of Literature.

Tony D. Barnes

Additional Reading

Noakes, J., and G. Pridham (eds.), *Nazism: A History in Documents and Eyewitness Accounts, 1919–1945* (1984).

Wiskemann, Elizabeth, *Europe of the Dictators, 1919–45* (1966).

Buchenwald

See CONCENTRATION CAMPS

C

Cairo Conference

See CONFERENCES, ALLIED

Casablanca Conference

See CONFERENCES, ALLIED

Casualty Figures

Any effort to compile casualty statistics on World War II needs to be accompanied by the disclaimer that there are few entirely reliable statistics available. Figures given here were compiled by U.S. defense agencies and several other sources. These statistics are approximate figures only and frequently given in round numbers. Widely differing figures are available from a variety of other equally reputable sources. Statistics from developed countries tend to be more accurate than those from less developed ones, and battle casualties more accurate than civilian casualties.

World War II caused more material destruction and exacted a greater death toll than any other war in history. Available statistics show that about 70 million people served in all branches of the militaries of all countries involved. Of these, slightly more than 17 million died of combat injuries. The Soviet Union suffered approximately 7.5 million battle deaths, the greatest number of any country. Germany had 3.5 million and Japan 1.25 million service members killed. Statistics on German and Soviet losses, as each country records them, vary significantly.

Total deaths, both military and civilian, from all causes have been estimated at from 35 to 70 million. Battle casualties are the best documented. In many cases, only rough estimates of civilian deaths are available, since they were not nearly as accurately recorded as battle deaths and frequently not recorded at all. This can be explained in part by population shifts and loss of records and family ties as civilians fled before invading armies. Millions of civilians were driven from their homes, died of starvation, or were deported as slave labor and never accounted for.

Civilian deaths in the Soviet Union have been fixed at approximately 2.5 million, and untold millions of other Soviet citizens, both military and civilian, died in German work camps, prison camps, and death camps. The total Soviet loss of population, including both battle and non-battle casualties, is frequently estimated at more than 20 million.

The most accurate statistics available are those on American and British Commonwealth forces. Also, Britain and the United States, perhaps due to superior logistical services, more humane practices, and a great deal of luck, suffered fewer battle casualties than any other major participants. With the United States lying outside the main battle areas, and Britain only on the fringe, both countries could enter the fight at the time, place, and under conditions of their choosing.

World War II was a total war in ways other wars never were. Destruction wreaked by aerial bombing was unprecedented. A German, Japanese, or British soldier was just as likely to hear from home that mother and father were killed in an air raid as the parents were to hear that their son had died in battle. The number of civilians killed in air raids reached approximately 300,000 Germans, 500,000 Japanese, and 150,000 Britains.

The number of homeless or "displaced persons" at the end of the war amounted to 12 million in Europe. This displaced population included prisoners of war afraid to return home, orphans, Nazi death camp survivors, and many people who fled invading armies and war devastated areas.

TABLE 1

Principal Allied and Axis Casualty Figures

Nation	Peak Strength[1]	Battle Deaths	Wounded	Civilian Deaths
The Allied Powers				
Belgium	650,000	7,760	14,000	70,000
Canada	780,000	37,476	53,000	—
Denmark	25,000	4,339[2]	—	2,000+
France	5,000,000	210,000	400,000	300,000+
Greece	414,000	73,700	47,000	350,000+
Netherlands	410,000	6,238	2,800	200,000
Norway	45,000	4,780	—	8,000
Poland	1,000,000	320,000[3]	530,000	3,000,000+
Soviet Union	12,500,000	7,500,000[4]	5,000,000	2,500,000[4]
United Kingdom	5,300,000	244,723	348,403	60,000+
United States	12,300,000	292,131	671,000	6,000
Yugoslavia	500,000	410,000[5]	425,000	1,200,000
Totals	38,924,000	9,111,147	7,491,203	7,696,000
The Axis Powers				
Bulgaria	450,000	10,000	21,878	10,000
Finland	250,000	82,000	50,000	11,000
Germany (includes Austria)	10,200,000	4,000,000	7,600,000	800,000[6]
Hungary	350,000	77,494	89,000	285,000
Italy	4,000,000	262,420	77,494	146,000
Romania	600,000	300,000	—	200,000
Totals	15,850,000	4,731,914	7,838,372	1,452,000

Notes:

1. Peak strength refers to the greatest strength reached at any one time during the war, as distinguished from total strength. For example, the U.S. had a peak strength of 12,300,000, but a total strength of 16,353,000.
2. Included are the deaths of more than 1,200 merchant sailors in the service of the Allied navies.
3. This figure includes more than 400,000 prisoners or missing persons.
4. In addition, more than 5,000,000 Soviet citizens died in prison camps or were permanently missing. An estimated 7.7 million civilians perished.
5. Most of these deaths were suffered in guerrilla campaigns against the German occupiers during the war and involved many men from non-regular military formations.
6. This figure does not include an estimated one million Germans who died fleeing from the east in early 1945.

TABLE 2

Estimated Number of Jews, by Country, Killed Under Nazi Rule

Country	Original Jewish Population	Number Killed	Percentage Killed
Baltic States	253,000	228,000	90
Belgium	65,000	40,000	62
Bulgaria	64,000	14,000	22
Czech Protectorate	90,000	80,000	89
France	350,000	90,000	26
Germany (includes Austria)	240,000	210,000	88

(continued next page)

TABLE 2 *(continued)*

Country	Original Jewish Population	Number Killed	Percentage Killed
Greece	70,000	54,000	77
Hungary	650,000	450,000	69
Italy	40,000	8,000	20
Luxembourg	5,000	1,000	20
Netherlands	140,000	105,000	75
Norway	1,800	900	50
Poland	3,300,000	3,000,000	91
Rumania	600,000	300,000	50
Slovakia	90,000	75,000	83
Soviet Union	2,850,000	1,252,000	44
Yugoslavia	43,000	26,000	60
Totals	8,851,800	5,933,900	67

Note: Jewish populations not included for Denmark and Finland since statistics indicate no Jews perished there.

Changes in national borders made many people homeless. Millions of people, particularly ethnic Germans, fled, or were expelled from, postwar Communist rule in eastern Germany, Poland, Czechoslovakia, and other Eastern European countries. The largest sea disaster of all time occurred on 30 January 1945 in the Baltic when a Soviet submarine torpedoed the *Wilhelm Gustloff*, a refugee ship, entombing 7,700 fleeing Germans. By 1946, an estimated 14 million Germans living east of the Elbe River had been displaced.

The United Nations Relief and Rehabilitation Administration (UNRRA) resettled 11 million stateless people in other countries, particularly in the United States, Canada, Australia, and South America. By 1947, one million stateless persons still remained in camps in Western Europe.

Paul J. Rose

Additional Reading
Dawidowicz, Lucy S., *The War Against the Jews, 1933–1945* (1975).
Dupuy, R. Ernest, *World War II: A Compact History* (1966).
Keegan, John, *The Second World War* (1989).
O'Brien, Terence H., *History of the Second World War: Civil Defense* (1973).

Censorship
Censorship was an activity common to most nations, belligerent and neutral, during World War II. With the increasing importance of technological and economic resources in warfare, coupled with traditional concerns for military security and maintenance of general morale, control of information assumed a critical importance. Yet the growing sophistication of communications presented both opportunities and challenges in providing meaningful control.

Radio broadcasting in particular posed a number of difficulties. Enemy aircraft could "home-in" on the signals of a commercial broadcast operation. Moreover, the immediacy of broadcast news meant that censors had to almost be at a microphone to clear copy. This same immediacy also gave a government the means to rapidly disseminate officially sanctioned material. Motion pictures had to be censored not only for military information but also for propaganda content. Telegraph communications, which routinely used codes and abbreviations, had to be carefully examined.

Newly developed microfilming techniques meant that classified information could be secreted on an innocuous publication with the use of a microdot. Microfilming could also be used to strengthen officials' powers by centralizing procedures that lent themselves to official oversight. For example, the British microfilmed letters from service personnel overseas to their families ("airgrams"), which simplified censorship review.

Many censorship organizations made distinctions between domestic and foreign publications. Totalitarian countries often had publishers and journalists as *de facto* or *de jure* public employees, theoretically practicing self-censorship. Despite such status, the Soviet Union and Nazi Germany reviewed most, if not all, domestic publications. Some countries, such as Britain and France, set up propaganda ministries that handled censorship.

These bureaucracies had initial teething troubles due to a number of factors: the newness of the agencies, the reluctance of the military to release any kind of bad news, and the defeats that these countries suffered in the early war years. By the time of the London Blitz, Britain had liberalized its restrictions, finding that truthful reporting improved civilian morale. Most other warring powers also discovered that selective release of accounts of the war's horrors could actually increase their populations' commitment to the war effort.

In the United States, censorship activities were separate from propaganda, with the U.S. Office of Censorship (OC) and the Office of War Information handling the respective areas. OC relied on voluntary censorship from the press and broadcasters rather than any formal regulation. On occasion, the Roosevelt administration brandished the 1940 Espionage Act that threatened punishment or withdrawal of postal permits to those who provided an "enemy with useful information relating to the nation's defense." All countries, of course, could use wartime paper shortages and their management of broadcast frequencies to control transgressors. Effective censorship was often compromised by two factors. One was when high government officials revealed classified materials. The other was the reporting of censored developments in the media of neutral countries.

Nations could and did treat foreign war correspondents differently from their home media. On one hand, these people could be courted by governments, receiving access to information and places that domestic media did not routinely receive. More likely, they were regarded as annoyances at best and thinly veiled spies at worst. One of the most successful spies of the war, Richard Sorge (q.v.), used his journalist cover in Tokyo to provide the Soviets with detailed information on German plans. Correspondents from neutral countries had to practice self-censorship, which often was more damaging than direct censorship. Reporters had to worry about expulsion and inadvertent compromising of sources.

War correspondents had to negotiate with the military censorship apparatus on matters ranging from delays in clearing copy to arranging transportation and rations. Non-Soviet Allied correspondents, many of whom had scant experience in dealing with military bureaucracies, often chafed at the restrictions they were put under. Most correspondents, however, were patriotic individuals and often practiced self-censorship, saving their public criticisms for the postwar period. Journalists felt particularly abused when censorship was used to block release of news that was not strictly military, such as accounts of corruption in rear areas or of photos of black GIs dancing with British women. Official reasoning for censoring was usually that such publicity would upset fragile social cohesion or that it would be used in enemy propaganda.

A little-known but vital area of press censorship dealt with the dissemination of scientific and technical (sci-tech) publications. By the late 1930s, the scientific community had become internationally interdependent. Scientists avidly scanned professional journals, regardless of their place of publication, to keep abreast of developments in their fields. Germany, for instance, used scarce foreign currency reserves for the purchase of overseas sci-tech journals. It also set up a technical information center to translate, abstract, index, and disseminate the contents of foreign publications.

With the outbreak of war, this worldwide network of scholarly communication between the belligerents collapsed. Neutral nations became locations for purchase of journals (Sweden and Portugal for the Allies; Mexico and Portugal for the Germans) where intelligence agents took out numerous subscriptions. Moreover, the journals themselves were censored to delete sensitive information. The difficulty of determining what was militarily or scientifically significant sometimes caused censorship systems to fail.

German scientists in 1940 learned of important Allied atomic discoveries that were published in the March and April issues of *Physics Review*. The Germans reciprocated by allowing the printing of Otto Hahn's articles on atomic experiments after they decided that atomic weapons were impractical. Thus, despite censorship and other barriers, scientists of the warring powers sometimes received important information from their counterparts in hostile nations.

Perhaps the type of censorship that affected people most directly was that of letters and telegraphs. Written communication gave authorities a major challenge due to sheer mass, yet also provided a number of opportunities. Monitoring a society's letters provided a gauge of morale. It also could become an intelligence asset, informing officials of important domestic and foreign situations. Many countries routinely read all communications, while others did a more selective job.

The U.S. Office of Censorship identified certain types of letters as being more important than others and concentrated on those. The OC did perform random censorship of the "safer" categories. Censors quickly became adept at breaking rudimentary codes that people devised to bypass censorship.

Most military services censored the letters of their own members, generally with officers and senior NCOs doing this task as a collateral duty. Depending on the type of transgression, offending writers received punishments ranging from admonishments to terms in prison camps, as artillery officer and *Gulag Archipelago* author Alexander Solzhenitsyn discovered after he denounced Josef Stalin (q.v.) in a letter. Civilian correspondence was read by designated agencies that could be the well-established ones in totalitarian powers or "for-the-duration" operations such as the U.S. Office of Censorship.

The total effects of censorship operations are hard to gauge. It is likely that strict military censorship did cloak vital operations. On the other hand, morale was often adversely affected by a combination of censorship of true calamities and of unconvincing propaganda. Moreover, overly tight censorship sometimes hid rectifiable situations from view until the postwar period. Perhaps the greatest legacy of World War II censorship was that it made information control a permanent part of governmental operations.

Michael Unsworth

Additional Reading
Gilbert, G.M., *The Psychology of Dictatorship* (1950).
Hale, Oran J., *The Captive Press in the Third Reich* (1964).
Hull, David, *Film in the Third Reich* (1969).

Channel Islands

The fall of France brought Germany's victorious army to the shores of the English Channel. The invasion of England was the next step, and the British Channel Islands, Jersey and Guernsey, were to serve as a springboard for the assault. By capturing these islands, Hitler was able to satisfy one of his strongest obsessions, that of occupying British soil.

When Operation SEA LION (q.v.) was postponed indefinitely, the value of these islands was reduced drastically. Their significance as a propaganda instrument was also diminished after the invasion was called off. On the other hand, the Channel Islands did prove useful to the German war effort as an early warning station for Allied bombers heading for Germany, and as a protective screen for German ships plying the coastal waters between German ports and ports on the French coast.

When the German war machine turned toward the east, the backdoor in the west had to be secured. The Atlantic Wall fortifications began in earnest. From 1941 to 1943, tons of building materials and equipment, along with troops and heavy weapons, poured into the defense of Western Europe. Workers, some contracted, others forced into slave labor, were sent to build the massive structures. Because the Channel Islands were British territory, they received a significant share of building materials and heavy coastal artillery.

In the end, the German garrison of the Channel Islands (30,000 soldiers and sailors) half-starved and diseased, surrendered peacefully to British forces on 9 May 1945.

José Alvarez

Additional Reading
Cruickshank, Charles, *The German Occupation of the Channel Islands* (1975).
Durrand, Ralph, *Guernsey Under German Rule* (1946).
Sinel, L.P., *The German Occupation of Jersey* (1946).

Chelmno

See CONCENTRATION CAMPS

Chemical Warfare Deterrence

On 22 April 1915, the Germans unleashed a chlorine attack against unprepared French divisions near Ypres, Belgium, thereby initiating toxic chemical warfare (CW) in World War I. The public reaction was revulsion and fear: revulsion against a weapon that broke the taboo against the use of poison in warfare; fear of being caught unprepared in any future attack.

In the interwar period, many military experts predicted that any future war would begin with an apocalyptic CW attack, directed against civilian population centers rather than against military positions, an attack causing widespread terror, panic, and casualties. Defensive and offensive preparedness for CW became far more crucial given the generalized nature of the future threat. But the chemical warfare apocalypse never happened. Why?

A number of negatively reinforcing factors conditioned the Allies and the Axis against the initiation of chemical warfare in Europe. Doubts persisted among military men about the tactical effectiveness of chemical weapons. Most professional soldiers shared the popular moral revulsion against the use of such weapons, a revulsion clearly embodied in the 1925 Geneva Protocol essentially prohibiting the first use of chemical and biological weapons in warfare. Chemical weapons, therefore, remained not integrated within the arsenals of the major Atlantic powers. In 1939, none of the belligerents were either prepared or willing to initiate gas warfare.

Allied declaratory policy, therefore, was confined to retaliation and deterrence. In 1942 and 1943, U.S. president Franklin D. Roosevelt and British prime minister Winston S. Churchill (qq.v.) extended the umbrella of CW deterrence to their Allies. A strongly reinforcing factor in the maintenance of this policy was the fear of escalation: use of CW in one theater of war would lead to global gas warfare.

Although the U.S. Army's Chemical Warfare Service pressed repeatedly for a revision of policy, claiming that gas would help to eliminate Japanese island strongholds, its claims were rebuffed by planning officers conscious of the vulnerability of civilian populations and worried about the possible use of gas against Allied troops in the planned invasion of the European continent. Deterrence held in the European theater throughout the war. But the issue of initiation occasionally surfaced within the Allied and Axis commands. Confronted with the German invasion threat in 1940, British leaders considered the use of mustard gas to contain a German landing on the coast of England.

In July 1944, enraged by the indiscriminate V-l and V-2 bombings of London, Churchill directed the British chiefs of staff to study the employment of gas against Germany. Despite energetic prodding, the British chiefs rejected the prime minister's arguments on political and military grounds.

Toward the close of the European war, some of Adolf Hitler's associates recommended the use of gas in retaliation against Allied city bombings. Although Hitler may have considered such an option, the opposition of the German military and key civilian officials, like Albert Speer (q.v.), squelched the proposal. Not surprisingly, however, the end of the war in Europe resurrected the pressure for the initiation of CW in the Pacific theater, especially as a tactical and strategic weapon to eliminate fanatical resistance to the planned Allied invasion of Japan.

World War II ended without the use of chemical weapons by the major belligerents (except for limited use by the Japanese against the Chinese). The threat of retaliation, reinforced by moral considerations, the complications posed by preparedness for global CW, and skepticism regarding the usefulness of gas as a weapon countered momentary pressures for initiation. Dominating all these considerations was the realization of the belligerents that their cities were hostages to one another.

Fortuitous factors reinforced deterrence. The tactical situation in the European theater never lent itself to initiation. During the period of the German *Blitzkrieg* (q.v.) in the west and the east (1939–1942), the use of chemical weapons would have hindered the mobile operations upon which German success hinged, threatening to turn advance into stalemate. Once the initiative passed to the Allies (1943–1945), their air supremacy, combined with their ability to deliver a chemical warfare strike whenever and wherever they chose, negated any defensive advantage that the use of CW might have conferred on German soldiers seeking to repel the 1944 Allied invasion of northwestern France. German restraint was strengthened by ignorance. Fortunately, the Germans, who alone developed powerful nerve gases (tabun and sarin), assumed the Allies also possessed these agents. If they had known otherwise, the temptation to use these unique weapons might have prevailed.

John Ellis Van Courtland Moon

Additional Reading

Adams, Valerie, *Chemical Warfare, Chemical Disarmament* (1990).

Brown, Frederic J., *Chemical Warfare: A Study in Restraints* (1968).

Spiers, Edward M., *Chemical Weaponry: A Continuing Challenge* (1989).

Collaboration

At the Liberation in 1945, Norwegian authorities arrested some 90,000 of their compatriots on suspicion of collaboration. Of these, some 46,000 were eventually convicted of such offenses; this in a country with a population of less than three million.

In the east, some 1.5 million Soviet citizens allied themselves with the Germans against the Red Army. The first such anti-Communists joined the Germans only two months after the opening of Operation BARBAROSSA.

At the bitter end, it was foreign troops—Frenchmen, Norwegians, Danes, and Spaniards—who were the final defense around Adolf Hitler's bunker. Without foreign workers—drivers, militia, police, journalists, and soldiers—the German war effort would undoubtedly have been of a shorter duration. As one former Norwegian resistance fighter put it in a statement that could perhaps be used to cover most occupied countries: "If all the Allied countries had done as much to fight Germany as had Norway, Hitler and his associates would still be ruling Europe today."

Whatever the ultimate truth of that statement, it is clear that collaboration was at least as important to the Germans as the resistance was to the Allies. That it has hitherto received comparatively little attention is evidence of the depth of the scars left by Europe's last fratricidal bloodletting.

One of the problems with writing the history of collaboration is defining exactly what collaboration was. Was the woman who slept with a German as guilty as the businessman whose factory made parts for German radios, the idealist who fought on the eastern front, or the criminal used by the *Gestapo* (q.v.) to assist in the arrest and torture of resisters?

One can identify four broad types of collaboration: economic, literary, political, and uniformed. The enthusiasm with which people and groups collaborated also varied widely, from the *attentiste* attitudes of the early days of occupation, to the bloody last-ditch struggles of collaborationist groups that had no options left in the final months prior to liberation.

Perhaps the most difficult area of collaboration to quantify, because, in part, it was less noticeable than military or journalistic collaboration, was economic collaboration. The Nazis' failure to fully mobilize their civilian population, in particular the slowness with which they replaced male workers with women, presented two problems: a shortage of military personnel and a shortage of war workers.

Neither problem was solved fully, even after 1942 and the arrival of Albert Speer (q.v.). In the end, German attempts to obtain foreign workers led to the strengthening of resistance to their occupation. At first, the Germans tried to entice foreign workers into the *Reich*'s industries. That approach failed to provide the necessary numbers, so in 1942 compulsory direction of labor was introduced. In Holland, the result was to increase the numbers of Dutch moving to work in Germany by less than 80,000—from 277,000 to the final total of 350,000. Thousands more went into hiding.

In France, the move to compulsory labor service in Germany simply led to the expansion of the *Maquis* (q.v.), especially in the more remote rural areas of the country. How far those who went, or were sent, to Germany to work can be regarded as collaborators is a difficult question. Some, like Georges Marchais (later head of the French Com-

munist Party), were unwilling workers—in his case in the German aircraft industry. Others, like the 1,150 Walloons recruited for the German armed forces while working in the *Reich,* were clearly active allies of Germany.

The extent of business collaboration is even harder to estimate, in part because liberation governments were more concerned with rapid economic recovery than meeting the demands of liberation justice. In liberated France, a National Inter-professional Purge Commission was established to investigate the issue, but its investigations were limited. By January 1945, there were some 13,000 cases of collaboration waiting to be investigated. Some cases involved major firms, such as Renault, whose Paris factory was targeted by the Royal Air Force in 1942. Air France was nationalized in 1945 because of its collaboration. Many cases involved the little profiteers that all wars produce.

If many business collaborators went unnoticed and eventually unpunished, this was not the case with the literary and journalistic allies of the Germans. The polarization of European literature in the interwar period continued under the occupation.

Norway's leading writer, Nobel Prize winner Knut Hamsun, had been a long-time admirer of the Germans and a supporter of Vidkun Quisling's (q.v.) *Nasjonal Samling*. By 1940, Hamsun was an old man in his eighties, but he still wrote sympathetically about the German cause. His wife was even more active, going on reading tours of the eastern front, where Hamsun's book *Growth of the Soil* was one of the most popular among the troops there.

It was in Paris where the most active literary collaboration could be found. Pierre Drieu la Rochelle, Robert Brasillach, Louis-Ferdinand Céline, Henry de Montherlant, and a host of other writers contributed to the Fascist and collaborationist press. The collaborationist press in all occupied countries helped boost collaborationist morale, promoted recruitment for service with the Germans, attacked the "terrorists" of the resistance, and singled out unfortunate individuals for their anti-German views. For this activity, some of these collaborators, like Robert Brasillach, paid with their lives with the arrival of liberation courts. Others, like radio propagandist Philippe Henriot, were killed earlier by the resistance—in Henriot's case in June 1944. Interestingly, 400,000 people in four days filed past Henriot's coffin, perhaps a measure of the importance of literary collaboration.

Many factors went to make up the nature of political collaboration in the various occupied countries: the speed of the German conquest, the initial reaction of the democratic authorities, the strength of native Fascist movements, and the development of resistance and German reaction to it.

In Denmark, the German invasion of April 1940 led to the deaths of only thirteen Danish soldiers, and the political system remained intact. In the general election of March 1943, the Germans gave little support to the Danish National Socialist Workers' Party, supporting it only later in the war when resistance became more troublesome.

In other countries, the German invasions were not rapid enough to prevent the escape of governments and heads of state, thus leaving a political vacuum that had to be filled. France's surrender was preceded by the legal appointment of Marshal Henri Pétain (q.v.) as head of the French government. At first, Pétain's policy of *attentisme* was undoubtedly popular. But, as the Vichy (q.v.) government proved increasingly incapable of extracting much in the way of concessions from Hitler, support for Vichy declined, and the Pétainists drifted into an ever-closer collaboration with the Germans.

Other groups and personalities were active collaborators from the start, seeing in the Germans the chance to implement their own varieties of Fascist government, an aim that often ran contrary to the desires of the German authorities (much to the surprise of the collaborators). Foremost in this field was Quisling, and his *Nasjonal Samling*. His quick work in establishing himself as leader of Norway, as the Norwegian government fled, was undone nearly as quickly by the Germans, who only allowed his return to power in early 1942, when German fortunes were on the ebb.

In general, native Fascist groups and movements were the most active political collaborators. But their loyalty to the German "New Order" received scant reward, as the occupiers exploited them as sources of manpower in the fight against the resistance and for troops for the eastern front. Fascists, like Belgian Leon Degrelle (q.v.), the most highly decorated non-German of the war, may have dreamed of a new Europe of Fascist and National Socialist brotherhood, but the dominant German desire was the old one of national aggrandizement.

The occupied countries provided the Germans with a useful source of security and military manpower. The figures here are often quite surprisingly large. Uniformed, or armed, collaboration can be broken down into three areas: police and security; factory, rural, and home defense; and military personnel serving outside their homelands.

The lowest uniformed collaboration could be found in organizations like the Rural Guard, which was raised in both linguistic areas of Belgium. By May 1942, this organization had 28,000 men in Flanders and 38,000 in Wallonia. Their role was to protect crops and food stores against sabotage, which for many, represented their livelihoods.

A more active collaborationist force was the Dutch *Landwacht Nederland* (later the *Landsturm Nederland* when it was under the jurisdiction of the SS), which recruited from the ranks of Dutch National Socialists. Some 11,000 soldiers served with this unit, which saw action against the resistance, and against the British at Arnhem (q.v.).

Collaborationists often proved the most determined anti-resistance fighters, the most notorious being the *Milice Française* of Vichy France, under the control of 1914–1918 and 1940 French hero Joseph Darnand (q.v.). The *Milice Française* (q.v.) had about 13,000 full- and part-time members who actively hunted down, tortured, and killed members of the resistance. The remnants of this organization were later incorporated into the French *Waffen-SS* "Charlemagne" unit.

The non-German units of the *Waffen-SS* are, perhaps, the most famous of the military collaborators. By 1944, more than half of the *Waffen-SS*'s nearly one million troops were non-Germans, mostly volunteers. In the final months of Hitler's German Empire, it was these men who provided the most determined fighters of the *Reich*. Exact figures for total uniformed collaboration are difficult to provide, but they include about 2,000 Norwegian military collaborators, 50,000 Dutch, and, including the Rural Guard, about 95,000 Belgians.

Why did people collaborate with their occupiers? For some there was material gain; for others, it was a chance to give vent to their own brutal personalities, as employees of the *Gestapo*. There was idealism too, the belief that the Nazi "New Order" really did mean something, other than the final propaganda offensive. Also, there was a sort of desperate nihilism, found among some of those who volunteered for almost certain death on the eastern front. Betrayed by the occupiers, attacked by resistance, killed in action, executed at the liberation, or deprived of civil rights, the ultimate reward of many collaborators was as unenviable as that of many in the resistance that they so bitterly opposed.

Stephen M. Cullen

Additional Reading
Griffith, Richard, *Marshal Pétain* (1970).
Littlejohn, David, *The Patriotic Traitors* (1972).

Maziere, Christian de la, *Ashes of Honor: A Frenchman in the Waffen SS, Traitor or Misguided Patriot?* (1976).

Werth, Alexander, *France, 1940–1955* (1956).

Comintern (1919–1943)

The Bolshevik revolution in November 1917 not only failed to unify the former Russian Empire by means of Marxist ideology, but also failed to ignite the worldwide Communist insurgency Vladimir Ilich Lenin had anticipated. By 1917, Lenin hoped that the Bolshevik revolution might revive the traditional internationalist spirit among the working class and provoke worldwide revolution. Not until 1919, however, was the Soviet government able to rejuvenate this internationalism, which had lain dormant since the outbreak of the war.

In January 1919, the Russian Bolshevik Party and Lenin called upon Leon Trotsky to draft a manifesto creating a new International organization. The "Third Communist International" or Comintern was established in March 1919, as Soviet Russia was struggling for its very survival against counterrevolutionaries and foreign invaders. The new organization was to provide a forum for the discussion of Communist ideology, as well as a disciplined and centralized leadership for what Lenin hoped would be the cataclysmic destruction of world capitalism.

The Comintern traced it origins back to the First International established in 1864. Founded in Great Britain by Karl Marx and known as the "International Workingman's Association," it advanced the cause of socialism by demanding public ownership of land and utilities as well as other radical reforms. It was dissolved in 1872 because of Marx's support for the 1871 Paris Commune and the deep internal crisis created with Mikhail Bakunin and the Italian anarchists.

The Second International dates from 1889. Like its predecessor, it was not affiliated with any organized Communist movement although its member parties enjoyed mass support. It served as common ground for European social democracy and organized trade unions. In 1914, its professed internationalism was undermined by the outbreak of war and rising nationalism in its ranks. Socialist parties chose to support their nation's war effort. The Second International ceased to function as a centralized organization, although it was reactivated briefly in 1923 as the Socialist and Labor International, and finally in 1951 as the Socialist International.

The Third Communist International, created in 1919, was the first to be controlled by an organized Communist Party. It evolved out of the left-wing of the Second International, Social Democratic parties, and other socialist factions that rejected reformism and condemned the support of individual socialist parties for the war effort, as well as any attempts to unify these parties in opposition to the war. Its inception, however, was not promising; only nineteen delegations responded to Lenin's call for world revolution and attended the First Congress.

Comintern (*Com*munist *Intern*ational) membership increased to more than forty individual delegations at the Second Congress, during the summer of 1920, when membership qualifications were debated. Lenin presented his "Twenty-One Conditions" of membership, criteria that called on member parties to expel pacifists and moderate socialists, to centralize their internal organization, to henceforth refer to themselves as "Communist" parties, and to reject all alliances with *bourgeois* parties and organizations. All Communist parties willing to accept these conditions outlined by the Soviet Russian Communist Party were invited to send delegates to the Comintern headquarters in Moscow.

Even if these parties operated legally, foreign Communists and revolutionaries pledged to infiltrate nationalist, independence, and workers' movements throughout the world and win them over to the cause of worldwide Communist revolution. Even though Lenin and Trotsky proposed that Soviet Russia would have equal status with other member parties, it soon became evident to all involved that Soviet Russia was the bastion of Communism and that membership in the Comintern's decision-making bodies would remain overwhelmingly Russian.

Organizational and operational policies and procedures passed by the Comintern at its congresses were binding on all national delegations. The executive committee and its ruling presidium, through the policy of democratic centralization, held absolute authority, which ensured policies and procedures were put into practice and national delegations strictly adhered to them.

At the Third Congress in 1921, the Comintern membership realized the anticipated worldwide revolution was not imminent. The Soviet government in Russia experienced military defeat in Poland in 1920 and its Communist Party was still in the process of consolidating power at home. Abroad, other Communist parties, especially the German one, which attempted revolution in March 1921, faced increased repression.

The more moderate delegations called for the creation of "united fronts," the formation of broad coalitions with non-Communist parties, namely those Social Democratic parties from which they had separated the previous year. The Comintern attempted to follow this more moderate path beyond the Fourth Congress in 1922. The socialists, however, fearing that the Communists only wished to subvert them, refused to enter coalitions. In 1923, the left wing of the Comintern under Grigory I. Zinoviev once again assumed control and called for revolution.

The power of the Comintern, particularly its right wing, was fatally weakened with Lenin's death in January 1924. Lenin favored Trotsky as his successor, but Josef Stalin outmaneuvered him as he strengthened his grip on the Soviet Communist Party. The Fifth Congress was held six months after Lenin's death. Supported by Zinoviev and Leo Kaminev, Stalin directed the ruthless purging of the Soviet Communist Party and the international Communist movement. Comintern member parties now had to accept the dictates of the Soviet Communist Party, and become instruments of Soviet foreign policy.

The Comintern did not convene another congress until 1928, an interlude of four years. By 1926, Stalin was attacking the left wing of the Soviet Communist Party and the Comintern. He expelled Zinoviev and Trotsky from the ruling politburo of the party and further consolidated his personal power while making a rapprochement to more moderate factions within the party and the Comintern.

At the Sixth Congress in August 1928, Stalin once again attacked the right wing of the Comintern, purging many of the older leaders and moving it to the left. European social democracy, viewed as an ally to capitalism and the originator of what Stalin now called "social Fascism," became the central target of the Comintern. Totally subservient to Moscow, the new organization would serve as the clarion of a new period of worldwide revolutionary activity. In reality, the influence of the Comintern was further truncated during Stalin's brutal consolidation of power. He demonstrated little faith in the need for the Comintern, believing that foreign Communists would naturally follow the lead of the Soviet Communist Party.

During the summer of 1935, the final Seventh Congress was held in Moscow. With the Nazi takeover in Germany in 1933, the Soviet Union perceived the defeat of Fascism to be foremost in its national interest and a key Soviet foreign policy

issue. The Comintern mirrored this concern and again called for the establishment of "popular fronts," coalitions with socialists and other parties in opposition to Nazi Germany. Soviet support of the international brigades fighting for Republican Spain was the only real manifestation of this policy; other attempts throughout Europe, particularly in France, failed miserably.

This policy of popular fronts served as the Comintern's focal point until 1939, when the Soviet Union and Nazi Germany stunned the world by signing nonaggression and friendship pacts.

The Comintern now existed in name only. Communist parties throughout the world were totally dependent on the Soviets for financial support. Therefore, there was no need for an organizational framework to guarantee their support for Soviet foreign policy. After the Germans invaded the Soviet Union in June 1941, the Soviets joined the Western Allies. The Comintern, whose professed goal was the overthrow of Western *bourgeois* governments, now became an enigma in this renewed international struggle against Fascism. Stalin's eventual dissolution of the Comintern in May 1943 was an empty gesture to his new allies that he would no longer sanction an organization whose primary purpose was the destruction of their governments and national identities.

In a continuing effort to control the international Communist movement after World War II, the Comintern was reconstituted in 1947 under the name Communist Information Bureau (Cominform). To counter criticism that the Comintern had been dominated by the Soviet Union and was not, as alleged, a voluntary association of Communist parties, the Cominform was moved from Moscow to Belgrade, and later to Prague. Its purpose, as with the Comintern, was to control and dominate Communist parties in other countries. Loyalty to the Soviet Union was a precondition to joining either the Comintern or the Cominform. After the death of Stalin and resulting changes in the international political conditions, the Cominform was formally dissolved in 1956.

Steven B. Rogers

Additional Reading

Bottomore, Tom (ed.), *A Dictionary of Marxist Thought* (1983).

Braunthal, Julius, *The History of the International* (1967).

Brown, Anthony Cave, and Charles B. MacDonald, *On a Field of Red: The Communist International and the Coming of World War II* (1981).

Hulse, J.W., *The Forming of the Communist International* (1964).

Commando Order

The Commando Order was issued on Adolf Hitler's (q.v.) instructions on 18 October 1942, two months after the British commando raid on Dieppe (q.v.). All captured Allied commandos were to be turned over to the SD (q.v.) for summary execution. Any German commander who failed to comply with the order would be held accountable before a court-martial. In part, the order read:

> I therefore order that from now on all enemies on so-called commando missions in Europe or Africa, challenged by German troops, even if they are to all appearances soldiers in uniform or demolition troops, whether armed or unarmed, in battle or in flight, are to be slaughtered to the last man. It does not make any difference whether they landed from ships or airplanes for their attacks or whether they were dropped by parachutes. Even if these individuals when found should apparently seem to give themselves up, no pardon is to be granted them on principle.

During the Nuremberg Trials (*see* International Military Tribunal), many senior German officers, Admirals Karl Dönitz and Erich Raeder (qq.v.) among them, were charged with complicity in the Commando Order. In their defense, they argued that the Commando Order was a legitimate reprisal, designed to deter the Allies (particularly the British) from employing their commando forces in ways that violated the Geneva Convention and the laws of war.

There is a certain measure of legitimacy to the argument. British commandos (q.v.) in particular were trained in especially brutal tactics, and evidence exists that on more than one occasion they operated outside the laws of war. Commandos on the Dieppe raid were issued shackling devices called "death slings" that slowly strangled prisoners. Other commandos were outfitted with special firearms concealed in the armpits, designed to fire when a commando raised his arms seemingly to surrender. A training order for British sabotage troops read in part:

> . . . the days when we could practice the rules of sportsmanship are over. For the time be-

ing every soldier must be a potential gangster and must be prepared to adopt their methods whenever necessary.

Compliance to the Commando Order was uneven at best. The difficulty lay in determining just who was a commando and who was not. Some German commanders used the order as a blank check to execute any prisoner they wanted to. Other German commanders virtually ignored the Commando Order. General Erwin Rommel (q.v.), for example, burned his copy as soon as he got it.

David T. Zabecki

Additional Reading

Allied Control Authority for Germany, *Trial of the Major War Criminals Before the International Military Tribunal, Nuremberg, 14 November 1945–10 October 1946*, vol XXII (1949).

Davidson, Eugene, *The Trial of the Germans* (1966).

Commissar Order

The destruction of the Soviet Union, the extirpation of Bolshevism, and the elimination of the Jewish community in Europe had been long-standing goals of Adolf Hitler (q.v.) and the Nazi movement. World War II, especially after the attack on the Soviet Union, provided the opportunity to achieve these aims.

On 30 March 1941, addressing the senior military commanders in Berlin prior to the implementation of Operation BARBAROSSA, Hitler again elaborated his ideas. He wanted political commissars and members of the Soviet security forces killed on the spot: the "Communist-Jewish" intelligentsia was to be destroyed. Eastern Europe was to become a German colony. Hitler ordered his thoughts to be put into directives to all fighting forces.

Hitler sought to impress his generals with the belief that Communism was a mortal danger to Germany and that notions of comradeship between soldiers, chivalrous combat, and observance of international conventions would not apply to the Russian front. According to a diary entry of General Franz Halder (q.v.), army chief of staff, "This fighting will be different from the fighting in the West. In the East, harshness today means leniency in the future. Commanders must make the sacrifice of overcoming their personal scruples." On 6 June 1941, the *Kommissarbefehl* was signed by Field Marshall Wilhelm Keitel (q.v.), chief of the high command of the armed forces and distributed to all major commanders.

Despite some technical caveats—there was concern that the decree would limit the judicial authority of the army in occupied areas, or that full implementation of the decree would affect troop morale—the order was implemented without major objections. A more broadly constructed special decree, *"Nacht und Nebel"* (q.v.) (Night and Fog) of 7 December 1941, was directed against Communists and non-Communists alike who were caught acting against the security and interests of Germany.

It is difficult to assess the damage Germany's war effort suffered because of the implementation of the regime's racial-ideological prejudices in Eastern Europe, especially in regard to people who welcomed German troops as liberators. The shortsighted treatment of Russian nationalists, such as Andrei Vlasov (q.v.), is a case in point. Both decrees became issues at the Nuremberg war crimes trials (*see* International Military Tribunal).

N.H. Gaworek

Additional Reading

Fugate, Bryan I., *Operation Barbarossa: Strategy and Tactics on the Eastern Front, 1941* (1984).

Schulte, Theo, *The German Army and Nazi Policies in Occupied Russia* (1988).

Concentration Camps

Nazi concentration camps can be classified into two types: the regular or labor camps that were used to confine prisoners between 1933 and 1945, and the killing centers erected after 1941. In the regular camps, one might live for a number of years, and some people survived these camps.

In the extermination camps, on the other hand, death often occurred within hours, and few survived. In spring 1945, some of the regular camps were transformed into extermination centers by adding gas chambers. Most of the regular camps already had crematoria. Moreover, some of the labor camps had gas chambers from an early date. The camp at Linz, Hartheim Castle, began operation in August 1941. Other western camps that had gas chambers were Mauthausen, Neuengamme, Ravensbrück, and Dachau. Although there are some similarities between the regular camps and the killing centers, their goals were different. It is preferable, therefore, to discuss them separately.

Regular Concentration Camps

In the Third *Reich's* early months, there were two kinds of regular camps: "wild" and official. Some were set up by Hermann Göring when he was in charge of the *Gestapo,* some by the SS, and some by the SA (qq.v.). The wild camps were largely SA in origin. Examples are Papenburg and the Vulkanwerft in Stettin, both notorious for the brutality of their guards. After the purge of Ernst Röhm (q.v.) and his followers in June 1934, the SS took over all the SA camps.

Most of the wild camps, including Oranienburg, Fehlbüttel, Esterwagen and Columbia-House, were closed down between 1934 and 1939. At the same time, the SS opened a smaller number of official camps. A consolidation took place.

The most important of the official camps were Bergen-Belsen, Buchenwald, Dachau, Flossenbürg, Gross-Rosen, Mauthausen, Natzweiler-Struthof, Ravensbrück, and Sachsenhausen. All were located in Germany, and remained in operation until 1945. Including their satellites, the total number of the regular concentration camps was well over 100. Ravensbrück, the concentration camp for women, alone had at least fifty-five subcamps—factories and other enterprises where the women were farmed out as slave laborers.

Of the official concentration camps, Dachau, just outside Munich, was the first. Established by Heinrich Himmler (q.v.) in March 1933, it became the model for all the camps that followed. The first two commandants of Dachau were Hilmar Wäckerle and Theodor Eicke (q.v.). The earliest concentration camp rules (Wäckerle's regulations) and the most important of these rules (Eicke's disciplinary regulations) were drafted while these men were commandants.

On 4 July 1934, Himmler promoted Eicke to "inspector (chief) of concentration camps" with the task of organizing and administering all Nazi camps. In 1935, Eicke began using concentration camp prisoners as forced laborers in various industrial and other economic enterprises connected with the camps. In 1938, Himmler removed these economic activities from Eicke's control and turned them over to Oswald Pohl, chief of the SS *Wirtschafts-und Verwaltungshauptamt* (WVHA), the Economic amd Administrative Main Office.

Reinhard Heydrich (q.v.) was also involved with the concentration camps. His police determined who would be arrested and sent to the camps, who would be released, and when. In addition, each concentration camp, including the killing centers, had a political section composed of *Gestapo* who reported not to Eicke or Pohl but to Heydrich.

The legal device used by the *Gestapo* and SA to incarcerate persons in the concentration camps was "protective custody" *(Schutzhaft)*. Based largely on the *Reichstag* Fire Decree of 28 February 1933, protective custody arrests were distinct from normal criminal arrests. Protective custody was seen by Göring, Himmler, Heydrich, and other high Nazi leaders as a "preventive instrument" for use against enemies of the state such as Communists and "active" Social Democrats. The purpose was "educational," to deter political crimes.

Protective custody enabled the *Gestapo* to arrest persons who had violated no existing law and place them in a concentration camp for an indefinite period. In the early years of the Third *Reich,* the term of incarceration was usually less than one year, and in many cases a matter of weeks. After 1939, however, the term was often "for the duration"—prison labor was needed for the war effort.

Every inmate in regular concentration camps worked. If a prisoner was incapable of working, he or she was usually "selected" for destruction. Prisoners labored in one of the interior or exterior work details. The degree of danger to the inmate varied greatly from detail to detail. In general, details inside the camp, for example, in the infirmary or a laboratory, were the least dangerous. But some of the interior details could be as lethal as the outside ones.

In Buchenwald, gardening was dangerous, for it consisted in moving large quantities of stone or dirt by wheelbarrow "on the double." Prisoners who failed to keep pace were beaten and sometimes shot. Exterior detail in the stone quarries of Mauthausen and other camps was often fatal. As a rule, the most capable and adaptable inmates secured the best details for themselves and thus had the best chances of survival.

The SS guards and camp officers were notorious for their brutality, which was inculcated in the guards from the start. Eicke devised an "unwritten code of conduct for SS guards" that required them to treat each prisoner "with fanatical hatred as an enemy of the State." In theory, there were limits; Eicke's written regulations called for the guards to be harsh but impersonal toward the prisoners. They were supposed to refrain from "independent brutality." Not surprisingly, the guards were often incapable of distinguishing between acceptable and unacceptable cruelty.

In *The Theory and Practice of Hell,* a memoir of his six years in Buchenwald, Eugen Kogon enumerated some of the consequences of Eicke's training: Fatigue drill was imposed as punishment for the slightest infraction of the rules; the SS held

endless roll calls, summer and winter, and everyone, dead or alive, had to be present and accounted for; arbitrary punishments, especially whippings, were common; inmates were trussed up by their arms with their hands tied behind their backs until they perished. One prisoner who tried to escape was forced into a wooden box in the crouch position; nails were driven through the boards. After two days and three nights of "dreadful screams," the prisoner was put out of his misery.

In a perversion of the Hippocratic Oath, SS camp doctors performed all manner of dreadful experiments on their human guinea pigs. Most of the SS doctors at Ravensbrück, for example, were sadists and murderers. Sterilizations were performed. Karl Gebhardt, a high-ranking SS doctor, conducted crippling vivisection experiments on young Polish women.

Despite Himmler's edicts threatening draconian punishment for any camp guard found guilty by an SS court, corruption was widespread in the camps. Guards accepted bribes, stole the property of condemned prisoners, and had inmates perform various illicit services for them, such as drawing family trees and making furniture.

Illegally acquired gold was so plentiful in Auschwitz II that the guards, including the *Kapos* (prisoner/supervisors) and prisoner/guards, used 140-gram gold cylinders as units of exchange for obtaining all manner of goods and services including food, liquor, tobacco, and even monthly subscriptions to the *Völkischer Beobachter.*

In 1938, Hitler's foreign policy moves against Austria and Czechoslovakia led Himmler to propose that some of the SS concentration camp guard units be enlarged and provided with the requisite arms for future "police" work in conquered nations. Hitler was most receptive. This was the origin of the *Einsatzgruppen* (q.v.) (Task Groups) and marked a turning point in the history of the concentration camps.

Killing Centers
In 1941, Hitler issued a verbal order to murder the Jews. Following the June attack on the Soviet Union, the SS created six death camps. All were located in Poland: Lublin (Majdanek), Chelmno (Kulmhof), Sobibor, Belzec, Treblinka, and Auschwitz. The largest was Auschwitz, which consisted of three parts: the original camp, Birkenau, and Monowitz. They are often referred to as Auschwitz I, II, and III, respectively. Although Auschwitz I had a gas chamber and crematory, most of the assembly-line killing occurred at Auschwitz II (Birkenau), which had four "combination" gas chambers and

Under Allied guard, SS troops are forced to load victims' bodies onto trucks for transport to burial grounds. Bergen-Belsen, 18 April 1945. (IWM BU 4024)

crematoria. Monowitz (Auschwitz III) was a forced labor camp. Auschwitz was a mixture of regular camp and killing center.

Of the Polish camps, four were "pure" extermination centers: Belzec, Chelmno, Sobibor, and Treblinka. These camps had a dual chain of command, one originating in the *Führer*'s office, and another running from Himmler to the RSHA (q.v.), or to a local higher SS and police commander in Poland. Unlike Auschwitz, there were no factories or other forced labor installations in or near these four camps. Because these prisoners were not used for slave labor, Pohl's WVHA was not involved.

The death camps were run by the SS. However, the smooth functioning of these camps depended upon the cooperation of many German governmental and party bodies in Germany, Poland, and the other occupied countries of Europe. Perhaps the best example is the German state-run railroad, which had to work overtime to accommodate the demands of Adolf Eichmann (q.v.) and his colleagues.

Most of the victims brought to these death camps were Jews. Most of the Jews were Polish, but thousands were shipped in from Holland and other Western European states. The Jews from Western Europe were transported to the extermination camps in regular passenger trains. The Polish Jews, on the other hand, were shipped to the camps in freight trains, packed in like sardines with no water and no sanitary facilities beyond a one-gallon bucket. In summer, the heat was often unbearable; many weaker passengers died en route.

All of the inmates in the extermination camps were slated for death. Some were spared for a period of time if the killing centers were temporarily congested, if prisoner labor was needed in the camps, or if their labor was needed in one of the industrial enterprises associated with the camps. The Third *Reich* was schizophrenic in the way it treated the death camp prisoners. On the one hand, prisoners were viewed as enemies of the state; on the other hand, they became increasingly important for the production of weapons and other war-related goods as the fighting progressed.

On arrival, SS officers culled a number of the stronger Jewish prisoners to perform camp duties. The duties ranged from playing in the camp orchestra, to sorting the victims' abandoned clothing and other articles, to removing corpses from the gas chambers and then cleaning the chambers of blood, urine, and excrement. These were the *Arbeitsjuden* (worker-Jews). The "real work" in the mechanism of extermination was done by these "worker-Jews." At least one of them actually had to process his own recently gassed wife, son, and daughter. After they were worn out, they joined the previous victims. In 1943, they revolted at Treblinka and at Sobibor. Not surprisingly, both these rebellions were easily crushed.

Jewish *Kapos* directed the worker-Jews. For this they obtained special privileges, above all, the hope that they might physically survive. A few did. Neither the worker-Jews nor the *Kapos* appear in a favorable light in the literature, for many were as brutal toward their fellow prisoners as the Ukranians and Germans.

The condemned men, women, and children would arrive and unload. They were then directed to a large square inside the camp and given a brief, reassuring lecture by one of the German officers. Next, the men and women were usually separated and directed to a building where they undressed and checked their valuables. Then they walked or were driven, naked, into the chambers and gassed; worker-Jews removed the bodies from the gas chambers, extracted gold fillings from teeth, inspected all body cavities for hidden valuables, and lugged the corpses to a grave for burial or to a crematory for stacking and burning. Most of the victims in these four camps were killed not by the gas *Zyklon B* (q.v.), but by carbon monoxide produced by gasoline or diesel motors.

Some victims, especially babies, the sick, and the elderly, were unloaded from the trains, thrown onto carts, and taken to a special part of the camp (usually identified as the "hospital") and then shot in the nape of the neck. They were too young or weak to walk the short distance to the gas chambers. Much of this shooting was carried out by the Ukrainian "volunteers." The number of German guards and their Ukrainian or Polish assistants in the killing centers was small. Nevertheless, most of the prisoners went to their deaths without resisting. Most of the victims evidently had no idea they were about to be gassed. "The Jews first became suspicious when they were already in the gas chambers." The camp guards made every effort to deceive the inmates as to their true fate. The SS welcoming speeches left the impression that the prisoners were in transit to work camps in Poland or the Ukraine; their present camp was merely a way station. Everyone would now shower and have his/her clothes disinfected. Paths to the gas chambers contained signs reading "To the Baths" or "Ascension Street" *(Himmelfahrtsstrasse)*.

Treblinka's gas chamber had a large, heavy curtain at its entrance with the following inscription in Hebrew: "This is the gate through which the righteous enter." It would be hard to imagine a more cynical message. Hannah Arendt has written that the Jewish councils in some countries, including Poland, cooperated with the Nazis in the selection of Jews for transportation to the concentration camps. Perhaps this accounts in part for the victims' naiveté.

Originally, the victims of the gassing were buried. After a certain point in time, which varied from camp to camp, the corpses were cremated. In addition, the worker-Jews were forced to exhume the previously buried bodies and burn them on grates made of train rails. Trees were cut for fuel. The fires raged day and night and the stench was overwhelming. Bones left over from this cremation were broken or ground up and buried. The ashes were then covered with a thin layer of soil and the area planted with trees and shrubs.

Everything belonging to the victims capable of being used by the Nazis, including the hair of the women, was confiscated. All valuables were supposed to be turned over to the camp administration and forwarded to the WVHA for the eventual benefit of the *Reich.* As in the regular camps, corruption intruded. For example, Sobibor had its own Jewish goldsmith who survived for a time by fashioning jewelry and similar items of gold and silver for the German guards and officers. Other Jewish artisans created shoes and belts for the German personnel. In the Chelmno extermination camp, some of the Poles working for the SS solicited condemned Jewish women for sex. Some consented, but after a night or two they were sent on their way.

Many of the Germans in the four camps participated in Hitler's "euthanasia" program before the war. The skills acquired there were later used in the killing centers. Many of the German camp guards were ordered to work in the camps; they were not volunteers. Most obeyed their SS officers without question. Some guards evidently believed they would end up in a concentration camp themselves if they refused to obey these orders. Many of the lower-ranking guards were of working or lower-middle-class background and of limited intelligence. In order to alleviate the psychological stress brought on by their duties, German guards received extra rations of alcohol. All the Chelmno guards received the War Service Cross.

Treatment of the death camp prisoners by the German guards varied enormously, from rare compassion to far more common sadism and brutality. One guard, identified only as "Kurt B.," even trained his dog "Barry," a large mixed Bernadine, to attack prisoners on the command, "Human, grab the dog!" *(Mensch, hol den Hund!)*. Barry was so large that he often seized the males' genitals, biting them off. The guards made no attempt to prevent this. All the guards carried a leather whip or a wood stock for beating the prisoners, and made frequent use of it. They were authorized to shoot prisoners for almost any reason. The mandatory report was filed, but few questions were asked. The depravity extended to the camp commandants, the worst of whom were Dr. Christian Wirth and Kurt Franz. Wirth was the architect of the gas chamber killing centers.

At least some of the Nazis knew perfectly well that their activity was immoral and illegal. All camp personnel were sworn to secrecy. Violations of this rule were dealt with severely. The camps and their activities were classified as *"geheime Reichssache,"* the highest level of secrecy in the German government. When they dissolved the camps in 1944–1945, the SS ordered all documents destroyed. Euphemisms abounded. The best known is the "Final Solution" (q.v.) of the Jewish problem. People weren't killed, they were "evacuated" or "resettled." The "Operation REINHARD" camps (Treblinka, Belzec, and Sobibor) operated under the name "Charitable Foundation for Institutional Care." There are many more examples.

After World War II, the Allies arrested some of the SS camp guards and tried them at Nuremberg (*see* International Military Tribunal). Others were extradited to Poland or Czechoslovakia; many of these were executed for their crimes. After 1960, the West German government began tracking down camp personnel passed over in 1945–1946 and tried them. Some of these were convicted and sentenced under the German Military Criminal Code *(Militärstrafgesetzbuch),* section 47, paragraph 2.

All of the post-1960 defendants resorted to the plea of superior orders. Many sentences were mild. Those found guilty could not be executed because Article 102 of the West German constitution (the Basic Law) prohibited the death penalty. The most they could get was life in prison, and most were let off with much lighter sentences.

We have only rough estimates of the total number of Jews and others who were murdered. The camp officers either kept loose records or destroyed what records they had. In any case, the numbers were large. At Treblinka alone more than 700,000 died.

Jon Moulton

Additional Reading

Broszat, Martin, "The Concentration Camps 1933–45," in Helmut Krausnich, et al., *Anatomy of the SS State* (1968).
Delarue, Jacques, *The History of the Gestapo* (1964).
Dickinson, John K., *Germany and Jew* (1967).
Hilberg, Raul, *The Destruction of the European Jews,* 3 vols. (1985).
Kogon, Eugen, *The Theory and Practice of Hell* (1960).

Conferences, Allied

Although well over half the independent states of the world eventually joined the fight against the Axis, the Allied effort was dominated by the USA, the USSR, and Britain and its empire. Meetings and discussions between their leaders—the "Big Three," Franklin D. Roosevelt, Josef Stalin, and Winston S. Churchill (qq.v.)—decided major strategic issues, and increasingly as the war approached its end, set the pattern of the postwar settlement. There were twelve meetings involving the Allied leaders, starting at Placentia Bay before America entered the war, and lasting till Potsdam, after V-E Day. Remarkably, it was only twice, at Teheran and Yalta, that all three were present. In contrast, the two Western leaders met on eight occasions, while Stalin and Churchill met twice. To emphasize the extent to which the war was a "Big Three" enterprise, only two other world figures were ever invited: General Charles de Gaulle (q.v.) and Chiang Kai-shek were each given a walk-on part at one conference.

C

The first conference took place between Churchill and Roosevelt aboard the British battleship HMS *Prince of Wales* (sunk by the Japanese off Malaya four months later) anchored in Placentia Bay, Newfoundland, from 9 to 12 August 1941. Also known as the Atlantic Conference, it was an attempt to set out the basic war aims of their two countries. During the meeting, the two leaders discussed U.S. intervention in the Atlantic, aid to the Soviet Union (recently invaded by Germany), U.S. supplies to Britain, and the Japanese menace in the Far East. At the conclusion of the conference, Roosevelt and Churchill issued the Atlantic Charter, "common principles in the national policies of their respective countries on which they base their hopes for a better future of the world."

The Atlantic Charter contained two points of particular interest. That Roosevelt accepted the words "after the final destruction of Nazi tyranny" indicates that despite America's neutrality, he was committed to eventually going to war with Germany. Of even more significance, the whole tone of the Atlantic Charter shows that America had no intention of retreating back into isolation once the war was over.

Four months later and immediately after the Pearl Harbor attack, the two leaders met again in Washington (code named ARCADIA) from 22 December 1941 to 7 January 1942. With the two countries now formal allies, complete Anglo-American understanding on the conduct of the war was essential. Although it was agreed that the immediate priority was to regain naval control of the Pacific, the crucial decision to give precedence to the defeat of Germany was made even at this early stage. It was further decided that the liberation of the European mainland would have to be delayed and that North Africa would be invaded as a preliminary step. At ARCADIA, the Chiefs of Staff Committee also was set up, a body that was to play a key role in implementing Anglo-American cooperation on a routine working level.

During the ARCADIA Conference, the United Nations Pact was drawn up and signed by twenty-six states. The original title was "Associated Powers"; Roosevelt suggested the term "United Nations." The signatories accepted the principles set out in the Atlantic Charter and pledged to continue the fight against the Axis to the end, without separate armistices. Significantly, the Soviet ambassador, Maxim Litvinov, was frightened by the concept of religious freedom and felt it safer to refer the matter to Moscow for agreement.

On 26 December 1941, Churchill was invited to address the U.S. Congress, a rare honor for a foreigner. He was, he later wrote, bolstered by the knowledge that on his mother's side, he was descended from an officer of George Washington's army.

Churchill returned to Washington for another meeting with Roosevelt from 19 to 25 June 1942. The main topic this time was TUBE ALLOYS—the atom bomb. Both countries were making good progress, but there was reason to fear that Germany would beat them to it. The two allies agreed to pool their information and to set up facilities in the United States, away from enemy bombers. It was at this conference that Churchill met General Dwight D. Eisenhower (q.v.), then virtually unknown, for the first time.

The next conference was in Moscow from 13 to 17 September 1942. Roosevelt did not attend, but was represented by Averill Harriman (q.v.). One of the war's key issues was hotly debated: when would America and Britain open a second front? With the Soviet Union bearing the brunt of German power, Stalin reluctantly accepted that there could be no invasion of northwest Europe in 1942, but he pressed hard for a 1943 date. Stalin found it difficult to understand the problems of amphibious operations. "Russia is a land animal," said Churchill to him; "the British are sea animals." Stalin was, however, pleased with plans for the air offensive against Germany, and appreciated the strategic value of the impending North Africa landings.

A few months later, with most of North Africa safely in Allied hands, Roosevelt and Churchill met in Casablanca (code name SYMBOL) from 14 to 23 January 1943. The two countries could not agree on the next step. The Americans favored standing firm in North Africa and making all other resources available for the invasion of Europe across the English Channel. The British favored invading Italy as a preliminary step. The latter view prevailed, and Sicily was chosen as the next objective. The conference reaffirmed that victory over Germany was the first priority. It also emphasized both the need to defeat the U-boat menace in the Atlantic to ensure the buildup of U.S. forces for D-Day could take place safely, and the desirability of sending as many supplies as possible to the Soviet Union. On the diplomatic side it was agreed that efforts to enlist Turkey to the Allied cause should be made.

After initially refusing to attend, de Gaulle arrived on 22 January and discussed with Vichy representatives the cooperation of Vichy and the Free French against the common enemy. He had little success. Casablanca also saw the first use of

Soviet Premier Josef Stalin arrives at Churchill's residence during the Potsdam Conference, 23 July 1945. (IWM BU 9192)

the term "unconditional surrender." Roosevelt used the words at the final press conference. There is some doubt as to whether the British were consulted, though perforce they went along with it. Some historians since have suggested that by giving the Germans and Japanese nothing to gain by surrender, the concept actually lengthened the war and increased the destruction of Europe.

By the spring of 1943, the whole of North Africa was taken. Churchill sailed to Washington for another conference (code name TRIDENT) with Roosevelt from 11 to 17 May. He actually spent only one day with the president; he then flew to Algiers with Generals George C. Marshall and Hastings Ismay (qq.v.) to discuss with Eisenhower and General Harold Alexander (q.v.) what was to follow the capture of Sicily. Sardinia and Corsica were considered, but an invasion of southern Italy was decided upon. The decision to continue offensive operations in the Mediterranean, given the worldwide shortage of landing craft, inevitably meant that D-Day would have to wait until 1944.

The two Western leaders next met in Quebec (code name QUADRANT) from 17 to 24 August 1943 to review Allied strategy worldwide following the success in Sicily. In particular, the time had come for some firm decisions about Operation OVERLORD, as the invasion of northwest Europe was now known. An American officer was to be in command, priority was given to Operation OVERLORD over the Mediterranean (especially in landing craft), and the bombing offensive against Germany was to be stepped up. The decision to invade Italy proper was also confirmed. In the Far East, Lord Louis Mountbatten (q.v.) was appointed supreme Allied commander Southeast Asia, and priority was to be given to offensive operations in Burma to enable an overland route from India to China to be opened.

The Grand Alliance of the three major powers had been in existence two years before the Big Three finally all met at the Teheran Conference (code name EUREKA), from 28 November to 1 December 1943. Even then, Churchill and Roosevelt felt it necessary to meet beforehand in Cairo (code name SEXTANT) on 22 to 26 November to ensure that as far as possible they spoke with one voice. Chiang Kai-shek was present briefly at this mini-conference. They also met again briefly in Cairo immediately after Teheran

Although postwar affairs were discussed in general terms at both the Atlantic and first Washington conferences back in 1941, subsequent meetings between the leaders had concentrated on winning the war. At Teheran, considerable time was now devoted to the shape of central Europe after the war. Stalin was afraid that Germany would recover from defeat, as it had done once already, and pose a further threat to the Soviet Union. A possible permanent partition of Germany was tentatively discussed. New frontiers for Poland, which had the effect of moving the country bodily farther west, were delineated. Finland was to remain an independent state. A strong difference of opinion between Roosevelt and Churchill over postwar Europe became apparent during this conference, with Roosevelt seeming far more sympathetic to Stalin and ready to agree to his territorial and political demands in Eastern Europe.

On the strategic side, it appeared that Stalin suspected the British were lukewarm on Operation OVERLORD, and preferred a push through the Balkans, which could have limited the westward advance of the Red Army. However, he obtained a firm promise from Churchill and Roosevelt that the invasion would take place in May 1944. Additionally, if sufficient landing craft could be gathered, they would also invade southern France (Operation ANVIL). In return, Stalin promised a major offensive to coincide with Operation OVERLORD. He also promised a major offensive against Japan once Germany surrendered.

The Big Three also agreed that further efforts should be made to recruit Turkey to the Allied cause. The main advantage to that would be the opening of another and easier supply route to the Soviet Union as an alternative to the arduous and dangerous Arctic convoys.

During their second meeting in Cairo, Roosevelt and Churchill, together with a representative from Stalin, met with a high-level Turkish delegation on 4 December 1943. They received no clear answer from the Turks, but the Western Allies did make a number of decisions at this post-Teheran mini-conference. Owing to the shortage of landing craft, tentative plans to attack Rhodes and the Andaman Islands were cancelled, and priority was given to Operations OVERLORD and ANVIL. Earlier at Quebec, it was decided an American would command OVERLORD, and at Cairo, Eisenhower was nominated. To replace Eisenhower, British General Sir Henry Wilson (q.v.) was nominated as the Mediterranean commander in chief.

As victory came ever closer, the question of the pattern of the postwar world became increasingly urgent. On 10 September 1944, Roosevelt and Churchill met briefly in Quebec (code name OCTAGON) and drew up an outline plan for the division of a defeated Germany into occupational zones. From August to October 1944, representatives of Britain, China, America, and the Soviet Union met at Dumbarton Oaks (q.v.), in Washington, and set out the basic plan for a permanent United Nations (q.v.) organization, whose main role would be to preserve the peace, then so painfully being won.

This set the scene for the second Stalin-Churchill conference in Moscow, from 9 to 17 October 1944. Nothing pertaining to the war was discussed, and the whole conference was given over to the postwar shape of Eastern Europe and the Balkans. Between themselves, the two leaders settled the degree of influence the Soviet Union and the West were to exercise in each country in that region. In Yugoslavia and Hungary, it was to be shared equally; in Rumania and Bulgaria, the Soviets were to predominate (90 percent and 75 percent influence, respectively); in Greece, the West was to have 90 percent influence. Somewhat understandably, neither Churchill nor Stalin wanted this crude carve-up made public, though Churchill did inform Roosevelt. It is ironic to note that in reporting to his colleagues in the cabinet, Churchill wrote that the proposed settlement "is intended to prevent, for instance, armed strife between Croats and Slovenes on one side, and powerful and numerous elements in Serbia on the other."

At one stage of this second Moscow conference, when Poland's new frontiers were under discussion, two Polish delegations were invited to join the discussion. One was from the strongly Communist "home" government, the other from General Władysław Sikorski's (q.v.) London-based government-in-exile. The former was set up by Stalin immediately after the Teheran Conference and was completely under his thumb, while the latter disagreed with the amount of territory Poland was expected to give up to the Soviet Union, a portent of bitter quarrels to come.

The second and last occasion on which all the Big Three met together was at Yalta (code name ARGONAUT), in the Crimea, from 4 to 11 February 1945. As had been the case with the Teheran Conference, Roosevelt and Churchill held a short prior meeting, this time on Malta, at which Churchill emphasized the importance of not letting the Red Army and Soviet influence come any farther west than was absolutely necessary.

By now it was clear that victory was but a few months away, and thus at Yalta the sole topic was the postwar world, particularly Eastern Europe. Stalin was afraid that at some future date a resurgent Germany would be in a position to launch another attack on the Soviet Union. That Germany should be divided for an unspecified period into occupational zones was readily agreed by the three leaders. But Stalin was determined to enhance the security of the Soviet Union by dominating Poland militarily and politically. Poland's new borders, which had already been discussed at Teheran, were once again a key issue at Yalta. The conference determined to move both its eastern and western borders farther west: in the east to the Curzon Line (q.v.), thus handing over a significant slice of territory to the Soviet Union; in the west, to an unspecified distance to be determined exactly at some later peace conference—at Germany's expense.

There were still two Polish governments, the exiled one in London, which raised an army of 150,000 soldiers who fought with great gallantry under British command, and the Communist-installed government in Lublin. There was no love lost between the two, and the situation was made worse by events in Warsaw the previous August. Pro-Western Polish patriots rose up against the Germans in the last days of the occupation to prevent Warsaw falling under the control of Stalin's puppets. A few miles away the powerful Red Army watched cynically while the Germans crushed the rebellion. The start of the Cold War can be seen in this sinister event.

Two questions arising from the Polish situation bedeviled Yalta. First, which government should be recognized by the Allies? Stalin clearly backed the Lublin government, though he was prepared to concede that it should be enlarged by one or two men from London. Churchill was strongly opposed to this, but with the Red Army firmly in control of Poland there was really very little he and Roosevelt could do. Second, how should a Polish postwar government be elected? With the Red Army firmly in control, how could non-Communists, especially those associated with the London government-in-exile, be assured of fair treatment? The best that the Western leaders could achieve was a vague promise that the elections would be free and that British and American observers could be sent.

Churchill and Roosevelt often have been accused of betraying the Poles at Yalta by their acquiescence to these proposals. Certainly, the subsequent actions of the Soviet Union led to Poland enduring forty-five years of Communist rule. But it is difficult to see what else the two could have done. There was still a war to be won, the Germans still had a substantial military force in the field, and the alliance had to hold together until the end.

Above all, Stalin held the whip hand; it was his army that held Poland.

At Yalta, the new United Nations organization, and the results of the Dumbarton Oaks Conference were deliberated. Stalin feared that a combination of minor states could combine to outvote and thus paralyze the great powers. To counter this, an American idea whereby any one of the five permanent members of the Security Council could veto such a vote was proposed and accepted. In the years to come, the Soviets would take advantage of that with unfailing regularity.

Yalta was the last conference before V-E Day. The Potsdam Conference (code name TERMINAL) was held symbolically in a suburb of the capital of defeated Germany from 17 July to 2 August 1945. It is a watershed in the history of the twentieth century. It marks the break-up of the Big Three. Roosevelt was by then dead and was replaced by Truman, while Churchill was defeated in a general election, and handed the reins over to Clement Attlee (q.v.) in mid-conference.

Potsdam also marks the break-up of the wartime alliance. It was clear by then that any understanding the West thought it had reached with Stalin at Yalta was hollow. Now at Potsdam, there was open disagreement over what reparations the Soviet Union could squeeze out of Germany, and how far into Germany the new Communist government of Poland could push its new western border. The adjustment of these frontiers, decided by statesmen around a table as a matter of *realpolitik,* had an appalling human result, with some eight million Poles and Germans being forced to move in conditions of great hardship.

Although half a world away from Hiroshima, Potsdam marks the political start of the nuclear age as well. The first atomic device was detonated in New Mexico earlier in July, and it was at Potsdam that Truman informed Stalin of its existence. From that moment, this new weapon of war would be a dominant factor in world diplomacy.

This series of conferences makes a fascinating study. No such top-level inter-Allied meetings had ever been held in previous conflicts. That they could take place in World War II, with the leaders and their large entourages of military and diplomatic advisers traveling around the globe in safety, is an indication of the command of the sea and air held by the Allies outside the areas under immediate Axis control. The conferences not only offer an insight into the development of Allied strategy and the conduct of war at the highest level, they also provide evidence of other key themes of twentieth-century history: the

C

emergence of the United States from isolation; the decline of British and European power; the origins of the Cold War; the birth of the United Nations; and the dawn of the nuclear age. What is more, many of the topics discussed by the Big Three are relevant today. Anyone wishing to understand central and Eastern Europe now that the Iron Curtain has come down and Soviet power has shriveled would do well to study these events.

Philip Green

Additional Reading

Charmley, John, *Churchill: The End of Glory* (1993).
Churchill, Winston S., *The Second World War,* 6 vols. (1953).
Edmonds, Robin, *The Big Three: Churchill, Roosevelt, and Stalin in Peace and War* (1991).
McCullough, David, *Truman* (1992).
Sherwood, Robert E., *Roosevelt and Hopkins* (1948).

Conferences, Axis

The word "conference" is hardly the term to describe the fractious, ad hoc diplomatic and military contacts among the Axis powers of World War II. A Mafia "settling of accounts" might be a better term. Most inter-Axis diplomatic initiatives were bilateral contacts either among Adolf Hitler, Benito Mussolini, and Generalissimo Francisco Franco (qq.v.) on the one hand, or their foreign ministers, ambassadors, and military leaders on the other. Most of the meager contact between Germany and Japan was at the ambassadorial level with rare foreign minister involvement. Between September 1939 and January 1945, either Hitler or German Foreign Minister Joachim von Ribbentrop (q.v.) held more than 270 different meetings with representatives of Axis and other friendly governments. Very few produced any real decisions, and most involved the communications flowing in one direction only.

There was no Axis equivalent of the Allies' Atlantic Charter (q.v.) or anything like it. There was nothing comparable to the Winston S. Churchill–Franklin D. Roosevelt (qq.v.) conferences or the "Big Three" conferences when Josef Stalin (q.v.) participated (*see* Conferences, Allied). Nothing the Axis did can be compared to the far-reaching, twenty-six-nation White House conference held on 1 January 1942 that resulted in the Declaration of the United Nations, established the Grand Alliance,

and pledged to destroy the Axis powers, while promising no separate peace initiatives.

At the highest levels, the Axis powers never even attempted anything like the close coordination and collaboration of military efforts that the Americans and British achieved with the Combined Chiefs of Staff (q.v.). For the Axis powers, "cooperation" usually meant the presence of a German military delegation at Axis capitals to ensure that Germany's interests prevailed. The concept of a global strategy against the Allied nations was never seriously considered. Other than the generic term "Axis," the alliance had no name, no plan, no grand strategy, and few common objectives.

From the Axis perspective, the European and Asian-Pacific operations were two distinct wars, fought by entirely different member countries with little or no coordination or cooperation between them. It was only the American participation against the Axis in all theaters of operation that justified the term "world war."

These differences go to the very nature of a totalitarian versus a free democratic alliance. The Tripartite Pact between Germany, Italy, and Japan was not a coalition of equals, while lesser Axis "partners" such as Hungary and Rumania were usually dictated to or intimidated rather than consulted. The Nazis tended to use the same crude, bullying tactics in foreign affairs that had proved effective internally against Hitler's opponents. These tactics worked best where German military power could be brought directly to bear against the "adversary."

Hitler made his decisions unilaterally and presented them to his Axis partners as *faits accomplis*. He did not trust his Axis partners and shared with them very little information, and only that which could not be used secretly to his own advantage. Italy, and more importantly Japan, followed essentially the same techniques as Hitler. Axis decisions usually bore the mark of pure egotism on the part of their initiators. The more desperate the Axis powers became, as defeat loomed on the horizon, the more deception and intimidation played a role in Axis diplomacy. Hitler used deception, threats, and overly optimistic assessments on the progress of the war to keep morale up and prevent the defection of his allies. As a result, the Axis partners never openly admitted military setbacks and seldom sought new, improved techniques of cooperation and collaboration.

Hitler's greatest diplomatic failures came in his relations with Spain and Japan, where bullying and intimidation could not easily be applied. Because of their proximity to Germany and Nazi power, Hitler was usually able to obtain his policy objectives one way or another with Italy and his Eastern European allies. With Spain and Japan, his influence was limited to traditional persuasive and diplomatic methods, techniques Hitler never mastered and even disdained.

In vain, Hitler tried to persuade the wily Franco to become a full-fledged Axis partner and participate in the war. In a meeting at Hendaye, Spain, on 23 October 1940, Franco refused to join the Axis cause. The two dictators talked for nine hours, with Franco refusing either to enter the war or to allow German troops to cross Spanish territory for an attack on Gibraltar. "Rather than go through that again," Hitler stated later, "I would prefer to have three or four teeth yanked out."

A Hitler meeting with Spanish Foreign Minister Serrano Suner at the Berghof on 18 November 1940 also failed to change the Spanish position on the war. As long as Britain remained undefeated and could threaten his Atlantic coast, Franco refused to jeopardize his hard-won position as dictator of Spain. Under intense German pressure, Franco finally accepted a protocol stating his intention to engage in war "against Russian Communism." A division of Spanish volunteers, the famous Blue Division, was activated under the command of General Munoz Grandes and sent to the eastern front to fight under German command. (It was withdrawn in March 1944.) From Hitler's point of view, the lack of Spanish cooperation was inadequate justification for the cancellation of Operation FELIX (q.v.), a planned German attack on Gibraltar.

Hitler's diplomatic failure with Spain had far-reaching implications for the conduct of the war. Diplomatic and political success with Spain could have given the Axis Spanish manpower, resources, additional Atlantic ports, plus the all-important access to Gibraltar and Malta, which in turn could have led to Axis dominance in the Mediterranean. Later, on 2 June 1941, Hitler bluntly rejected a suggestion by Mussolini to cooperate in the Mediterranean. Success in the Mediterranean could have isolated Britain from its Middle Eastern and Asian colonies while assuring Germany access to Arabian oil. The failure of Hitler's diplomacy with Spain and his cavalier attitude toward his most important ally, Mussolini, cost him dearly.

Since he could not bully or intimidate Franco, Hitler lost many important, potential gains. Franco constantly resisted Hitler's demands to declare war, waiting instead to see how the winds of war were blowing. Finally, on 7 May 1945, Spain broke diplomatic relations with Germany without ever declaring war. Nonetheless, Spain's close ties with Germany resulted in it not being among the founding members of the United Nations (q.v.).

The failure of Hitler's political and military policy objectives with Japan may have proved even more disastrous for the worldwide Axis war effort. His primary objective was for Japan to attack the Soviet Union rather than the United States. Japan, for its part, wanted Germany to forgo an attack on the Soviet Union and attack the United States, Japan's principal enemy.

During a meeting in Berlin on 4 April 1941, Japanese Foreign Minister Yosuke Matsuoke obtained a promise from Hitler that if Japan went to war with the United States, Germany would "act accordingly." Matsuoke learned only that conditions were getting worse with respect to the Soviet Union, but gained no knowledge of the impending German attack. When Hitler and Mussolini met at the Brenner Pass on 2 June 1941, the latter too was kept in the dark about Operation BARBAROSSA, to be launched in less than three weeks.

Hitler proposed to the Japanese ambassador, Hiroshi Oshima, on 14 July 1941, that Japan take part in the "occupation of the Soviet Union" by "marching" from Vladivostok to Omsk to link up with German forces. Japan saw no interest in cooperating against the Soviet Union, a move that very probably would have saved Hitler from his worst military predicament of the war by ensuring the defeat of the Soviet Union in 1941. Since Hitler could not bully or threaten the Japanese, his efforts came to naught.

Instead of cooperating against the Soviet Union, Japan further broadened the war on 7 December 1941 by attacking the world's largest industrial power, the United States. The attack came as a complete surprise to the Germans. Hitler and his generals had so little interest in or knowledge of that part of the world that they had difficulty locating Pearl Harbor on a map when they learned of the attack. Nonetheless, Hitler's concept of Axis solidarity led him to declare war on the United States on 11 December, a decision that made certain Germany's ultimate defeat. Italy followed the German lead that same day.

Hitler was much more successful in bending Mussolini to his will. On 18 March 1940, in a meeting with Hitler at the Brenner Pass, Mussolini gave in under pressure, and against his better judgment, offered his support to the German invasion of Western Europe. Mussolini's docile acquiescence assured Hitler peace on his southern flank while he settled accounts with his bitter enemy,

France. It also made Italy a full partner in Hitler's aggressive war. For a while, Mussolini attempted to go his own way, with his invasions of Albania and Greece (qq.v.). The Italians, however, quickly ran into trouble in the Balkans, and the Germans had to bail them out.

As the war progressed, Hitler met frequently with his allies either at the Berghof, in Berlin, or at Rastenberg. He did his best to foster the Axis alliance by stressing the need to maintain it against all odds and by minimizing the dire military situation of the moment.

Hitler ignored any suggestions on ending the war that came up during meetings with Romanian leader Ion Antonescu (q.v.) on 10 January and 12–13 April 1943 and with Hungary's Admiral Miklos von Horthy (q.v.) on 16–17 April. These discussions indicated that leaders in Romania and Hungary were already having serious doubts about an Axis victory and were looking for a way out. On 1 July, Antonescu visited Mussolini in Italy and suggested that Italy, Romania, and Hungary all leave the war together. By this point, however, Mussolini was too intimidated by Hitler to take any action. During a 19 July meeting with Hitler at Feltre in northern Italy, Mussolini hardly spoke. About six weeks later, on 3 September, Italy surrendered to the Allies.

Although under considerable pressure at home to desert the alliance, Antonescu again came to Germany on 26–28 February 1944 to assure Hitler of his continued support of the Axis cause in the face of the impending defeat in the east. Hitler accepted such obedience as his due and was determined to sacrifice his allies to stave off his own certain defeat as long as possible.

Horthy too felt the lash of Hitler's whip when he was so severely browbeaten at the Berghof on 18 March 1944 that he agreed to a German occupation of Hungary and the forced resignation of the Kallay government, which had dared suggest ending the war.

The potential impact of most Axis and Tripartite "conferences" was restricted by their dilatory nature and by Hitler's tendency to burst into impassioned and unintelligible tirades as he refused to face the reality of Axis defeat. As the Axis *Götterdämmerung* came nearer, the Axis options were reduced to two—an unlikely military standoff or a certain fiery immolation. Against this background, Hitler's Eastern European allies scrambled to abandon the Axis cause and make the best political and military arrangements possible with the victorious Soviet Union.

Paul J. Rose

Additional Reading
Deakin, Frederick W., *The Brutal Friendship: Mussolini, Hitler and the Fall of Italian Fascism* (1962).
Feis, Herbert, *The Spanish Story: Franco and the Nations at War* (1948).
Ikle, Frank W., *German-Japanese Relations, 1936–1946* (1956).
Merrill, Johanna M.M., *Hitler and Japan: The Hollow Alliance* (1966).
Presseisen, Ernst L., *Germany and Japan: A Study in Totalitarian Diplomacy* (1958).
Wiskemann, Elizabeth, *The Rome-Berlin Axis: A Study of Relations Between Hitler and Mussolini* (1949).

Conferences, Naval

One of the more interesting aspects of the interwar period was the international effort to monitor and control naval armaments. In those pre-nuclear days, navies were considered the world's strategic arms and a nation's power and prestige was measured by the size and reach of its fleet. Thus, ships and naval armaments, the most expensive and powerful weapons of their day, were the benchmark upon which international tensions and stability were measured. The initial impetus for these developments was financial. The United States, Great Britain, and Japan found themselves in a naval construction race and contending foreign policy interests following the end of World War I, a race and competition none of them could afford.

American Secretary of State Charles Evans Hughes issued invitations to the first naval limitations conference on 8 July 1921. The United States, Japan, Great Britain, France, Italy, Belgium, China, Portugal, and the Netherlands were invited. The conference was intended to resolve tensions in the Far East as well as establish a venue for naval disarmament.

It was at this conference that Secretary Hughes announced and obtained a "ten-year holiday" in capital ship construction and limits on capital ship tonnage in service. It was a daring and provocative proposal that called for the participating nations to scrap nearly two million tons in capital ships, more than that already in service in any one of those countries. Distrustful of Western intentions, Japan was the most reluctant to agree, but did so in the end.

By 15 December 1921, the Washington Naval Conference ended in the world's first disarmament treaty. Signed on 6 February 1922, the so-called Five-Power Naval Treaty of Washington established ratios of 5:5:3:1.7:1.7 in capital ship tonnage between the United States, Great Britain, Japan, France, and Italy, as well as a prohibition against the fortification of naval bases and possessions in Asian waters. Considered a major success in its time, the Washington Naval Treaty did not include provisions for minor fleet units such as submarines and destroyers. Like the later SALT Treaties of the modern era, however, it did place technological limits on the strategic weapons of its day—capital ships.

Under this treaty, a capital ship was described as a warship, not an aircraft carrier, exceeding 10,000 tons displacement or carrying guns 8-inches (208mm) or larger in diameter. No capital ship could surpass 35,000 tons in displacement nor carry a gun larger than 16-inches (435mm) in diameter. Aircraft carriers, a new weapon system at the time, were limited to 27,000 tons displacement and prohibited from carrying guns exceeding 8-inches. These limitations served to reduce international tensions, but they also led to the naval arms race shifting into ship categories not covered by the treaty—light cruisers, destroyers, and submarines. Alarmed by this development, President Coolidge called a second conference to be held in Geneva in the summer of 1927. After six weeks of contentious discussions, it ended in failure in August. Great Britain sponsored the next conference in January 1930. Although not a universal success, the London Conference closed the loopholes of the Washington Treaty by establishing limits on all categories of warships. Moreover, additional capital ships in commission were to be scrapped and their replacements postponed for five years. Japan was given a 10:10:7 ratio in destroyer and a 10:10:6 ratio in cruiser tonnage in relation to the United States and Great Britain. The London Treaty also contained a provision for another conference in 1935; but ultimately that conference was doomed by escalating tensions in the world, Italy's refusal to participate, and Japan's denouncement of the Washington Treaty on 29 December 1934. The second London Conference ended in March 1936 with only a few minor limitations on specialized naval craft. More importantly, the nations adhering to these treaties found themselves at a technical disadvantage in the war's early combats against those nations (Germany and Japan) that did not (*see* Anglo-German Naval Treaty).

Although these treaties did not fully achieve their ultimate intended purpose, total naval disarmament, they did restrict naval construction at great savings to the taxpayers of the countries concerned. Nonetheless, the experience of the inter-war naval treaties shows both the promise and dangers of such agreements: they are only effective as long as no one cheats and the nonsignatories lack the ability to acquire or build something better than the signatories.

Carl O. Schuster

Additional Reading
Bailey, Thomas A., *A Diplomatic History of the American People* (1969).
Carr, E.H., *The Twenty Years' Crisis* (1939).
Hough, Richard, *The Longest Battle* (1986).
Tate, Merze, *The United States and Armaments* (1948).

Conscription

By the end of 1938, Germany had reoccupied the Rhineland and had carried out the *Anschluss* with Austria (qq.v.), Italy had attacked Ethiopia (q.v.), and Japan had invaded Manchuria. Few Americans, nonetheless, were fearful of a threat or felt the need for a military draft. By 1940, with Germany in control of western Europe and Japan encroaching into China, the mood in the United States had changed.

In July 1940, President Franklin D. Roosevelt (q.v.) publicly endorsed the need for a military draft "for the defense of the Western Hemisphere." In September 1940, the U.S. Senate and the House of Representatives passed the Burke-Wadsworth Act, named for its sponsors Senator Edward R. Burke and Representative James W. Wadsworth. On 16 September, Roosevelt signed the act into law and the Selective Service System was born.

Initially the Selective Service Act had a limit of one year. Later the House of Representatives voted to extend it to eighteen months by the razor-thin margin of 203 to 202. Unlike the Civil War's Enrollment Act of 3 March 1863 and World War I's Selective Draft Act of 18 May 1917—both of which terminated when hostilities ended—Selective Service was repeatedly extended, remaining in effect for thirty-three years until 1973.

Selective Service required every male (including resident aliens) between the ages of 21 and 36 to register. If called, the inductee would serve one year of active duty and ten years of reserve service. Conscientious objectors whose stance was based on religious beliefs were offered alternative civilian service in lieu of military duty. The Selective Service Agency was created to manage Selective Service and was placed under civilian control, not under the Navy or War departments. The director of Selective Service could, however, be a military officer. The first director was former University of Wisconsin president Clarence Dykstra. Shortly after, General Lewis B. Hershey (q.v.) became the director of Selective Service, and held that position until 1973.

In the first 30 days of Selective Service, 16 million American men registered at local election boards across the nation. In late October, a lottery system for selection was initiated, with the first lottery taking place on 29 October.

Unlike the two previous draft acts, Selective Service provided reemployment rights for inductees. They were "considered as having been on furlough or leave of absence during their period of military service" and were to be "restored without loss of seniority." No provisions were made, however, for those individuals in highly paid professions to augment the meager military salaries they would receive. A sports figure or corporate executive making upwards of $50,000 a year could suddenly find himself as an army private making $21 a month.

The Selective Service Agency established a classification system for potential inductees. Registrants in Class 1 were immediately eligible for military service. Those in Class 2 were given some level of deferment based on educational or occupational requirements. Those in Class 3 were deferred for dependency or hardship. After 1942, with a large number of eligible men rushing to the altar, this classification was modified so that married men without children and in nonwar-related skills were eligible for military service. Those in Class 4 were permanently disqualified for military service because of age, health, handicap, or other factors. Farmers were given an automatic deferment to meet the food needs of the nation.

The minimum required literacy rate for military service was a fourth-grade reading level. By war's end, over 40 percent of American enlisted men had no more than a primary education—completion of the eighth grade. This may seem low by today's standards, but in 1945, 60 percent of all American civilians had no higher than a primary school education.

In 1942, the U.S. Navy began using the draft as a means of meeting its manpower needs. As a result, the draft itself was expanded to all males between the ages of eighteen and forty-five. This created a manpower pool of roughly 49 million. The length of active duty service also was extended "for the duration" of the war. In the four years following the Pearl Harbor attack, 12 million Americans entered military service. Of that total, 10 million men entered through the draft.

Although there were some incidents of corruption and bribery at local draft boards—particularly in securing deferments—the system was fair overall. Classification proved an effective tool in assigning deferments to those in need of them. Of some 49 million eligible American males, Selective Service chose 19 million and inducted 10 million.

Most other nations in World War II also relied on conscription to meet their military manpower needs. In March 1935, Germany reintroduced the draft. Hugely popular, conscription fit the German tradition that a young man's development was not complete without the discipline of military service. Conscription was necessary to support Chancellor Adolf Hitler's (q.v.) immediate goals of the remilitarization of the Rhineland, the *Anschluss* with Austria, and the annexation of Czechoslovakia. Initially German conscription age started at eighteen years. By January 1945, in a last ditch effort to save the Third *Reich,* Hitler called for the induction of boys of sixteen years and younger.

Germany also relied on conscription to meet industrial and labor shortages. In June 1938, under the industrial service law, 400,000 workers were drafted into the para-military *Reichsarbeitsdienst* (German labor service) to work on the West Wall fortifications. In January 1943, labor conscription called up some three million women between the ages of seventeen and forty-five to meet shortages, primarily in the armaments industries. Of the three million women, less than one million were actually put to work—the rest received deferments for children, health, or other reasons.

Britain introduced conscription on 27 April 1939, following Germany's annexation of Slovakia and Italy's invasion of Albania (qq.v.). The initial law called for all males over the age of twenty to register, but the actual steps to select, train, and equip this surge in military manpower were not immediately addressed. The supporters of the bill had little difficulty mustering the necessary votes in Parliament (380-143) to enact the legislation. In December, the conscription range was extended to those men between the ages of nineteen and forty-one.

Conscientious objectors were given the same consideration in Great Britain as in the United States. In lieu of military service, inductees were offered positions in Civil Defense, particularly in the Auxiliary Fire Service, which suffered manpower shortages because of military conscription.

In February 1940, Britain embarked on a massive military training program. All unemployed men between the ages of seventeen and forty-one, and not selected for military service for whatever reason, were given six months of training in war-related areas to meet the shortages of skilled labor as a result of conscription. In December 1941, this program was expanded to unmarried women between the ages of twenty and thirty. Many of those women served in the police or fire services or in the armed forces as well as in industry.

For political and social reasons, the British draft did not apply in Northern Ireland. Enforcing any form of a draft or draft registration, British political leaders believed, would have resulted in many fleeing south to the Republic of Ireland to avoid service. Nonetheless, Britain did launch an intensive recruiting drive in the North for volunteers. Many northern Irish, both Catholic and Protestant, enlisted in the British forces. Even some 80,000 citizens of the Republic of Ireland served in the British military during the war.

In Canada, a call-up of reservists between the ages of twenty-one and twenty-four was announced in September 1940. Conscription itself was not introduced until February 1942. In response to French-Canadian anti-draft riots throughout Quebec, Prime Minister Mackenzie King (q.v.) initially vowed not to press French-speaking Canadians into military service. His fear was that a pro-Vichy Quebec would break away from Canada. Under pressure from the United States and English-speaking Canadians, however, the Canadian government enacted full conscription in July 1942. Many in Quebec protested, but the draft stood.

On 20 October 1939, Australian Prime Minister Robert Menzies enacted compulsory military training. In the spring of 1942, with the threat of a Japanese invasion looming, Australia imposed conscription along similar lines as Great Britain.

Draft registration was already in effect in the Soviet Union when the war broke out. Although Soviet conscription required all men between the ages of seventeen and fifty to register, the minimum induction age was eighteen. Women who had occupational specialties required by the military, such as those in medical fields, were also eligible for military service. In September 1941, Premier Josef Stalin (q.v.) called for the immediate induction into the armed forces of all men eighteen years and older.

It is noteworthy that after the end of the war in 1945, all but a very few countries throughout Europe continued the draft. This, of course, was a result of the subsequent Cold War between eastern Europe and the West.

William H. Van Husen

Additional Reading
Chambers, John Whiteclay II, *To Raise an Army* (1987).
Churchill, Winston S., *The Second World War: The Gathering Storm* (1948).
Flynn, George Q., *The Draft, 1940–1973* (1993).
Grunberger, Richard, *The 12-Year Reich: A Social History of Nazi Germany, 1933–1945* (1971).

C

Croatia

The "Independent State of Croatia" with its capital at Agram (Zagreb) was proclaimed under Italian-German patronage after the military defeat of Yugoslavia on 10 April 1941. It included parts of the Yugoslav provinces of Croatia, Bosnia, and Herzegovina. It covered an area of about 100,000 square kilometers with a population of 6.5 million; 3.3 million were Roman Catholic Croats, 2.2 million were Greek Orthodox Serbs, 800,000 were Moslem, and 100,000 were ethnic Germans. Croatia also had a population of about 18,000 Jews.

The Croatian economy was preindustrial, with 79 percent of the people working in agriculture and only 9 percent in industry. Mineral resources were the dominant export. The Germans were especially interested in the rich deposits of bauxite and iron ore, which were mined together with brown coal. The German-Croatian economic agreement of 1941 granted broad concessions to Germany, and led to tensions with Italy, which considered Croatia in its sphere of interest. Because of its weaker political position, Italy was powerless to reduce the German influence over the area.

Politically, dominant power in Croatia was the *Ustaša* (q.v.), under Ante Pavelić (q.v.), who called himself *Poglavnik* (leader), using Adolf Hitler and Benito Mussolini (qq.v.) as models. The program of this extremely nationalistic party had many parallels with Italian Fascism and German National Socialism: liberty for Croatia, priority for the Croatian people, exclusion of all non-Croats from the government, peasantry as the base of the state, and priority of the people's community over individual interests. All this amounted to the limitation of private property and the dictatorship of the party.

The press in Croatia was censored. The *Ustaša* took over the police functions, permanent martial law ruled, drumhead courts-martial were established, and concentration camps were set up. The main victims of these policies were the Jews and the Serbs. The anti-Semitic measures of the regime included the prohibition of marriages between Jews and Croatians, expropriation of property, and murdering Jews in the spirit of Germany's "Final Solution" (q.v.).

The persecution of the Serbs started out with prohibition of the Cyrillic alphabet and proceeded to forced conversions to Catholicism, which were fully supported by the local Catholic clergy. In the end, the *Ustaša* tried to expel or mass-murder all the Serbian people. This violence and terror against half of Croatia's population did not lead to the results intended by the government. It only increased support for Tito's (q.v.) partisan movement. Since the Croatian Army, which had about 150,000 men in regular units in 1942, operated without success against the partisans, the territory of the *Ustaša* state began to shrink, especially after Italy's capitulation and the withdrawal of Germany. The Croatian Army surrendered to the British on 14 May 1945 at Bleiburg. Many were handed over to the partisans, who summarily executed about 40,000.

Even though the *Ustaša* linked itself to Croatian nationalism, the government had no popular support. Nationalists in the country rejected the border treaty with Italy, which ceded large areas with Croatian majorities. Violence and terror against minority groups produced counterviolence and strengthened the partisans. The military impotence turned the regime into a pawn in maneuvers between the Italians and the Germans.

Franz Seidler

Additional Reading

Black, C.E., and E.C. Helmreich, *Twentieth Century Europe* (1972).
Deroc, Milan, *British Special Operations Explored: Yugoslavia in Turmoil 1941–1943 and the British Response* (1988).
Strugar, V., *Jugoslavia 1941–1945* (1970).

Curzon Line

Perhaps the most mischievous and misunderstood boundary line ever proposed, the so-called "Curzon Line," had its origins in the Paris Peace Conference of 1919. At the request of the Supreme Council, the Committee on Polish Affairs prepared a proposal for the eastern border of reborn Poland. The results in April 1919 were "a delimitation line of indisputably Polish territories" with the clear proviso that territories further east were ethnographically problematical and would require further study. Significantly, the chief source available to the committee was the 1897 Russian census, which was notoriously and prejudicially inaccurate regarding the Poles. This line stopped at the prewar Austrian border and hence did not include the area of Galicia.

On 8 December 1919, the line was incorporated in a "Declaration of the Supreme Council" that stated: "The rights Poland may be able to establish over the territories situated to the east of the said line are expressly reserved." Hence, the line was minimal and provisional.

However, the declaration contained a map which, for reasons never explained, extended the line south to the Carpathians, thus dividing Galicia. It was this extended line that British Foreign Secretary Lord Curzon telegraphed to the Soviets on 11 July 1920 from the Spa Conference as a proposed armistice line (not a frontier) to halt the Russo-Polish War (q.v.); hence the name "Curzon Line." The Soviets rejected the proposal. Soon after, the Poles won the war and the Polish-Soviet frontier was fixed far to the east at the 1921 Riga Conference.

Early in World War II, Stalin insisted upon Curzon's abortive 1920 armistice line (that corresponded roughly to the 1939 Molotov-Ribbentrop Pact (q.v.) as the future Polish-Soviet frontier. The Western powers acquiesced at the 1943 Teheran Conference. The Poles objected bitterly, but in vain, and lost thousands of square miles of territory.

M.B. Biskupski

Additional Reading

Karski, Jan, *The Great Powers and Poland, 1919–1945: From Versailles to Yalta* (1985).
Lukas, Richard C., *The Strange Allies: The United States and Poland* (1978).

D

Danzig

Danzig, today the Polish city of Gdańsk, was established as a free state after World War I under the terms of the Treaty of Versailles (q.v.). It was placed directly under the supervision of the League of Nations (q.v.). The city had 408,000 inhabitants, 12,000 of whom were Poles. The foreign affairs and the defense policy of the free state lay in the hands of the government of newly reestablished Poland. Danzig sat at the end of what became known as the "Polish Corridor," a strip of formerly German land given to Poland for access to the sea. The Polish Corridor cut East Prussia off from West Prussia and the rest of Germany. The Polish government also controlled the harbor of Danzig and had custom rights and access to the mouth of the Weichsel River.

Danzig was a problem for German-Polish relations right from the start. In 1939, it was played up as a cause of war by Adolf Hitler (q.v.), when he demanded an extraterritorial railroad and a road going through the Polish Corridor (q.v.) to Danzig. Supported by the British and the French, Warsaw rejected the demands without negotiations, and the Poles let the German ultimatum expire.

World War II started in Danzig when on 1 September 1939, the German warship *Schleswig-Holstein* opened fire on a Polish fortification on the Westerplatte (q.v.), located outside Danzig harbor. The same day, the local Nazi Party leader and president of the Danzig senate, Albert Förster, annulled the Danzig constitution and made the city part of the *Reich*. After the German victory over Poland, Danzig became, until 1945, the capital of the *Reichsgau Danzig-Westpreussen*. Förster became the government *Reichsstatthalter* and the *Gauleiter*.

Despite its position in the east of Germany, Danzig was attacked several times during World War II by the air forces of the Western Allies. The bombing was targeted at the shipyards and train stations. During the attacks of 11 July 1942 and 9 October 1943, the old town was completely destroyed. Units of the Soviet Second Shock Army under Colonel General I.I. Fedjuninsky took Danzig on 30 March 1945 against the defense of the German Second Army. Ninty-five percent of the old town, with almost all the churches, was destroyed.

As the result of the Potsdam Conference, Danzig was placed under Polish administration. Förster was sentenced to death by a Polish court in May 1948, his sentence later commuted to life imprisonment. He died in 1954.

Franz W. Seidler

Additional Reading

Benetson, John R., *Nazi War Aims: The Plans for a Thousand-Year Reich* (1962).
Shirer, William L., *The Rise and Fall of the Third Reich* (1960).

Destroyers for Bases Deal

In the summer of 1940, Britain was in desperate straits. The bulk of the British Expeditionary Force was extracted from Dunkirk (q.v.), but virtually all heavy equipment was abandoned in France, leaving only one properly equipped division in the British Isles. Particularly hard hit was the Royal Navy. With the French Channel ports and Norway in German hands, Britain faced a possible invasion with only sixty-eight destroyers fit for service, compared to 433 in 1918. Britain's shipping lanes were even more vulnerable than in 1918: Italy was now in the war and France was lost.

In mid-June 1940, Prime Minister Winston S. Churchill pleaded with U.S. President Franklin

D. Roosevelt (qq.v.) for World War I–era American destroyers: "We must ask therefore as a matter of life or death, to be reinforced with these destroyers." The United States had already repealed the ban on arms sales in November 1939. American interventionists felt that was insufficient. If Germany defeated Britain, the United States might have to face Adolf Hitler (q.v.) alone.

The result was the Destroyers-Bases Deal of 3 September 1940, announced in an executive agreement. In a message to Congress, Roosevelt described it as "the most important action in the reinforcement of our national defense that has been taken since the Louisiana Purchase." He noted that Thomas Jefferson had done this without treaty or vote in the Senate. He defended the executive agreement as a means to save time.

The United States turned over fifty old destroyers to Britain for outright gifts of sites for bases on Newfoundland and Bermuda for ninety-nine years. The British also granted similar rent-free leases on six additional sites from the Bahamas to British Guiana. Separately, at almost the same time, Churchill promised never to surrender the British fleet. This guaranteed that the destroyers would not fall into Hitler's hands and be used against the United States.

The Destroyers-Bases Deal was clearly to the advantage of the United States, particularly as the destroyers were old four-stackers that barely made it across the Atlantic and had to be substantially rebuilt in Britain. Nonetheless, it was a significant boost to British morale, and Churchill believed he had gotten the United States to take a significant step toward more active participation in the war.

The deal touched off a great debate in the United States. Noninterventionists were particularly upset by what was a clear violation of both American neutrality and domestic laws governing the disposal of public property. On the whole, reaction in the country was favorable; even Republican isolationists in the Congress found it difficult to criticize. Wendell Wilkie, Roosevelt's Republican opponent in the election of 1940, approved the plan in substance, although he decried the lack of coordination with Congress. Later he said he regretted even that criticism. Congress indirectly approved the deal by voting money to develop the bases.

The Destroyers-Bases Deal marked a major turning point in American policy toward the war. While still determined to stay out of the war, the United States had shown that it was anxious to do everything else possible to save Britain from defeat.

Spencer Tucker

Additional Reading
Bemis, Samuel Flagg, *A Diplomatic History of the United States* (1965).
Churchill, Winston S., *The Second World War (Volume 2): Their Finest Hour* (1949).

Drang nach Osten (Drive to the East)

The subject of contentious debates, this complex and controversial catchphrase generally denotes the movement of and expansion by Germans into central, eastern, and southeastern Europe since the ninth century. The term was conceptualized in the nineteenth century by German historians, publicists, and politicians, and it was quickly appropriated by their Polish, Czech, and Russian counterparts. The controversy continues today.

Drang nach Osten was intermittent and took many forms. It was facilitated by many factors, including geographic and demographic aspects. One form was the relatively peaceful penetration and colonization, often by invitation of neighboring authorities, by missionaries, traders, craftsmen, and peasants into areas inhabited mostly by Slavs.

The Hanseatic League's economic activities from London to Novgorod, the founding of towns, and Catherine the Great's settlement of German peasants in the middle Volga region of Russia are examples. Additionally, there was Charlemagne's christianizing expedition to the Elbe River, the crusades of orders of knights in the Baltic, the territorial expansion of Austria and Prussia, and Germany's war aims in World War I. And finally there was the virulent and megalomaniac Nazi program to conquer, exploit, and enslave Eastern Europe (as well as remove or exterminate part of its inhabitants) to gain *Lebensraum* (q.v.) for a "people without space."

Although not continuous, and characterized by reversals, German eastward expansion was more persistent than earlier "drives" southward or westward, or colonial expansion after unification in 1871. Russia's *Drang nach Westen* set limits; Napoleon's reordering of Europe temporarily diminished Prussia's reach; and the political-territorial consequences of World war I further reduced German influence.

Adolf Hitler's (q.v.) rise to power in 1933 and the implementation of his annexationist policy, typified by Austria's *Anschluss* (q.v.) and Czechoslovakia's dismemberment, ushered in the new form of *Drang nach Osten*. The Molotov-Ribbentrop Pact (q.v.) of August 1939 and the ensuing world war provided the opportunity to gain vast territories in Eastern Europe and the

Soviet Union and to reach for the domination of all of Europe.

Defeat in World War II moved Germany's divided and occupied boundary to the Oder-Neisse line (q.v.). Flight and expulsion of more than ten million Germans drastically reduced the number of German ethnic minorities eastward of that line. Since the inception of West German Chancellor Willy Brandt's (q.v.) *Ostpolitik,* a steady, albeit intermittent, flow of ethnic Germans from as far as the Soviet Union further reduced the once substantial German presence in eastern and southeastern Europe.

The end of Soviet-controlled Eastern Europe in 1989, which facilitated a reunited and sovereign Germany in 1990 and the establishment of a new German-Soviet relationship, caused new concerns in many quarters, especially in Poland. New questions were posed. What will Germany's place and role be in this new Europe? How will events in the still unstable successor states and a fragmented Soviet Empire affect future German policy, especially if there is an intensification of ethnic and national tensions, conflicts, and, perhaps, rival territorial claims?

Juxtaposed to such speculations, what is the validity of views that maintain that traditional quests for territorial gains have been replaced by the dynamics of transnational politics and economic/financial/technological power? Will Germany conform to this pattern, or will major global or regional upheavals lead to regressive behavior by instability and flux?

Norbert H. Gaworek

Additional Reading

Benetson, John R., *Nazi War Aims: The Plans for a Thousand-Year Reich* (1962).

Higgins, Trumbull, *Hitler and Russia: The Third Reich in a Two-Front War* (1966).

Meyer, Henry Cord, *Mitteleuropa in German Thought and Action, 1815–1945* (1955).

Dumbarton Oaks Conference

Dumbarton Oaks is an estate located in the Georgetown district of Washington, D.C., owned by Robert Woods Bliss, a former U.S. State Department diplomat. Between 21 August and 7 October 1944, it was the site for a conference to frame a new international organization as a successor to the League of Nations (q.v.). The conference consisted of thirty-nine delegates from the United States, Great Britain, and the Soviet Union. China was brought into the discussion on 29 September

1944, to round out the "Big Four." The delegations were headed by U.S. undersecretary of state Edward R. Stettinius, Jr. (q.v.), and ambassadors Sir Alexander Cadogan of Great Britain and Andrei Gromyko of the Soviet Union.

Cadogan and Gromyko selected Stettinius as the permanent chairman of the conference. Within the conference was the Joint Steering Committee composed of delegation heads and key advisors. The committee created four subcommittees to design the principles of the various international organizations. In addition to these subcommittees were two formulation groups to write the proposals from the subcommittees. After each session, short statements would be released to the press.

President Franklin D. Roosevelt (q.v.) endorsed calling this new organization United Nations (q.v.) and was adamant in selecting a headquarters location other than Geneva. The idea was to sever all ties with the defunct League of Nations. In this new organization, the delegates agreed to the formation of a General Assembly consisting of representatives of all member nations. Each nation would have one vote regardless of political or military influence. The General Assembly would discuss questions dealing with the maintenance of peace and make recommendations regarding the promotion of social and economic matters. Gromyko proposed each of the Soviet Union's sixteen republics be added to the General Assembly to increase voting leverage vis-à-vis the smaller states. This "X-matter" was vehemently opposed by both Cadogan and Stettinius. The Soviets felt equally strongly on this matter, and as a result the issue would remain unresolved.

The primary purpose of actually keeping the peace would fall under the responsibility of an executive council, later referred to as the Security Council. All delegations agreed on unanimity among the Big Four. Later in the conference, France was added as a permanent member of the Security Council. Stettinius suggested adding Brazil to the permanent membership to represent Latin America; however, both Cadogan and Gromyko objected strongly and the proposal was dropped. The British and American delegates proposed a ban on voting by nations involved in disputes. The Soviets strongly opposed the idea, and because of the impasse, this, like the X-matter issue, was deferred to a later conference.

The Security Council was tasked to resolve international disputes peacefully by any measures, including diplomatic and economic sanctions, and if necessary, military force. Should military force become necessary, member nations would provide armed forces under the direction of the Military Staff Committee composed of officers from the permanent members.

The delegates agreed on the procedure for the expulsion of "recalcitrant" members—nations whose behavior was deemed unacceptable by other members. Also agreed on at Dumbarton Oaks were the creation of an Economic and Social Council, an International Court of Justice (also known as the World Court), and a permanent Secretariat to administer the General Assembly.

The last session of the conference was 7 October, and the proposals were published 9 October 1944. It must be noted there was a great deal of agreement among the delegations. Roughly 90 percent of the proposals were agreed upon. It was stressed that with little or no agreement, there would be no lasting peace. Apparently, that was the motivation needed to create such a high level of agreement.

William H. Van Husen

Additional Reading

Campbell, Thomas M., and George C. Herring, *The Diaries of Edward R. Stettinius, Jr., 1943–1946* (1975).

Halderman, John W., *The United Nations and the Rule of Law* (1966).

E

Elbe River Meeting

"At 1640 hours on April 25, 1945 . . . American troops of the 12th Army Group joined forces with Soviet elements of Marshal Koniev's First Ukrainian Army Group." This quote was part of a message sent to all unit commanders, from General Omar N. Bradley's (q.v.) headquarters, announcing the meeting of East and West on the field of battle in the struggle against Nazi Germany.

The actual first meeting occurred three hours earlier at 1330 hours. A twenty-six-man U.S. patrol, led by Lieutenant Albert Kotzebue, crossed the Elbe River to investigate scores of dead civilians. Although there were no explanations for these deaths, Kotzebue suspected the Red Army. The patrol met a group of Soviet soldiers; each side saluted without exchanging a word. The official meeting, the one quoted in the message, was at Torgau on the Elbe, seventy-five miles south of Berlin. Leading the American forces was Major General Emil Reinhardt, commander of the U.S. 69th Infantry Division. The Soviet delegation was led by Major General Rusakov of the 58th Guards Rifle Division.

Major General Emil F. Reinhardt (left), commander of the U.S. 69th Infantry Division, shakes hands with the commander of the Ukrainian First Army, Torgau on the Elbe, 3 May 1945. (IWM CP 15906)

The Elbe River meeting was significant for several reasons. First, it bisected what remained of the Third *Reich*. A vise had closed on Germany. As a result, Germany no longer had a unified command. Admiral Karl Dönitz (q.v.) assumed operational command in the north, while Field Marshal Albert Kesselring (q.v.) commanded Axis forces in the south. Second, the Elbe River meeting surrounded Berlin, cutting the city off and slowly strangling Germany's capital. Third, the joining of Allied forces created a significant morale boost for U.S. and Soviet forces. The long war was nearing an end. For the Soviet forces, their struggle had lasted nearly four years.

William H. Van Husen

Additional Reading
Ambrose, Stephen, *Eisenhower and Berlin, 1945: The Decision to Halt at the Elbe* (1967).
Hastings, Max, and George Stevens, *Victory in Europe* (1985).
Lucas, James, *Last Days of the Third Reich* (1986).

Enabling Act
Passed by the German *Reichstag,* on 24 March 1933, the Law for the Alleviation of the Crisis of the *Volk* and the State, provided Adolf Hitler (q.v.) with the authority needed to consolidate his power and establish dictatorial rule. By granting Hitler the power to issue laws for a period of four years, without a parliamentary or presidential check, the Enabling Act released the Hitler regime from effective constitutional control.

Officials in the Ministry of the Interior began developing proposals for an enabling act in early February 1933, but these efforts gained importance only after the victory of the Nazi-led coalition in the general elections of 5 March. With the draft prepared, the Nazi faction in the *Reichstag,* led by Hermann Göring (q.v.), entered intense negotiations to gain the essential support of other political parties. The law passed by 444 to 94 votes, even though the tactics of the Nazis and the wording of the law clearly violated the principles of the Weimar constitution.

The Enabling Act's importance for the consolidation of Nazi rule was immediately summed up by Joseph Goebbels (q.v.), who wrote in his diary, "Now we are also constitutionally the masters of the state." The law had a far-reaching impact—the *Reichstag* lost its legislative role, the *Reich* president had his authority undercut, and Hitler gained control of the bureaucracy and judiciary. Essential safeguards of the Weimar constitution were thereby eliminated.

Although the law was to expire on 1 April 1937, Hitler simply renewed it in January 1937, in 1939, and in 1943 in the name of the *Reichstag,* thereby maintaining the charade of legality for his ongoing dictatorial rule.

Robert G. Waite

Additional Reading
Bracher, Karl Dietrich, et al., *Die nationalsozialistische Machtergreifung,* 2nd ed. (1962).
Morsey, Rudolf (ed.), *Das "Ermächtigungsgesetz" vom 24. März 1933* (1968).
Schneider, Hans, "*Das Ermächtigungsgestez vom 24. März 1933,*" in Gotthard Jasper (ed.), *Von Weimar zu Hitler: 1930–1933* (1968), pp. 405–442.

Estonia
See BALTIC STATES

Evacuation and Resettlement
Evacuation and resettlement are terms describing the forced migration of European populations from 1939 to 1944. One goal of National Socialist policy was to transform Germany into a culturally and ethnically pure homeland for all German-speaking peoples. To this end, Adolf Hitler established the *Reich* Commission for the Strengthening of Germandom (RKFDV), headed by *Reichsführer*-SS Heinrich Himmler (q.v.). This agency coordinated the evacuation and resettlement of newly annexed provinces of Lorraine, Alsace, and Poland.

Jews, Slavs, and other unwanted ethnic groups were expelled to make room for ethnic Germans *(Volksdeutsche)* from Eastern Europe, France, the Low Countries, and Italy. Eventually, the RKFDV resettled populations almost at will, placing them wherever the twisted logic of Nazi population policy dictated.

Possibly four to six million Europeans were dislocated by Nazi resettlement policies. Combined with those populations deported for annihilation during the Holocaust (q.v.), that number may approach 12 million, making the Nazi effort one of the largest forced population migrations in all of history.

Richard Leiby

Additional Reading
Koehl, Robert L., *RKFDV: German Resettlement and Population Policy 1939–1945* (1957).
Schechtman, Joseph B., *European Population Transfers* (1946).

F

Fascism

Fascism was the authoritarian political movement that developed in Italy and other European countries following World War I. It was a reaction against political and social changes, in particular socialism and Communism, resulting from World War I. This original totalitarian movement was founded in Milan, Italy, on 23 March 1919, by Benito Mussolini (*Il Duce,* "The Leader"), a former socialist. Along with Nazism and Communism, Fascism became one of the three ideological scourges of the twentieth century.

Certain characteristics of Fascism are historically related to reactions against eighteenth-century Enlightenment, the French Revolution, and economic, scientific, and political developments of the nineteenth century. The more immediate ideological roots of Italian Fascism can be traced to a group of political thinkers who had adopted, with some weird innovations, the philosophy of Friedrich Hegel (1770–1831).

Consistent with the Hegelian political hypothesis that the state was the manifestation of God on earth, these thinkers demanded that the Italian people submerge their identities and social interests in a united effort to revive the greatness of the Romans. They asserted that Italy had a glorious mission to illuminate the contemporary world as it had during the Roman Empire and the Renaissance. They denounced democracy, pacifism, liberalism, and tourism ("that erotic obsession"), and all other attitudes and values traditionally popular in Italy. They glorified war as a cathartic hygiene that would purge the contemporary world of its many impurities.

First among those early ideologists was Giovanni Gentile (1873–1944), who was a faithful disciple of Hegel, but who took his master's idealism almost to the point of mysticism.

Gentile's political purpose was to merge and unify the "infinite variety of man and nature in an absolute one in which the human is the divine human." Particularly, he was critical of the scientific trend of modern times, and even managed to find fault with the philosophy of Plato as lacking sufficient spirituality. He proudly described his own political views as anti-intellectual.

While saying little about the specific problems of government, Gentile strove to prepare the minds of millions of Italians for "attitudes of unquestioning submission and contempt for reason." Following Hobbesian logic, he wrote that there was never any justification for antagonism between the individual and the state. For him, the ultimate in liberty coincided with the "maximum use of force by the state."

Guiseppi Prezzolini also contributed to Fascist political thought. Like Gentile, he was a disciple of Hegel. He exalted the state above the individual, despised parliamentary democracy, and condemned Italian liberal traditions as a threat to the nation's strength. He proclaimed Fascism as Italy's "true religion" and the embodiment of the "most exalted conception of the patriotic spirit." To him, socialism, Communism, and even trade unionism were alien to, and deeply resented by, the people of Italy, because they set one class against another, incited lawlessness, and caused severe economic losses from labor unrest. Others contributing to Fascist theory were Arthur Schopenhauer, Friedrich Nietzsche, Henri Bergson, and a wide range of social Darwinists.

Although by no means a political philosopher, Mussolini contributed to Fascist ideology. His early political views were a mixture of contradictory forms of extremist doctrines. While professing to be a "Marxian socialist," he mingled his "socialism" with ideas borrowed from the French syndicalist Georges Sorel (1847–1922). In his early career, he condemned the imperialism he later practiced so enthusiastically. Before World War I, he vilified the Italian king, defamed the church, and called the Italian flag a "rag to be planted on a dung hill."

As Mussolini came closer to leadership of a successful movement, he modified his views and became more conservative. In 1919, the Italian Fascist Party endorsed universal suffrage, a capital levy, a large tax on inheritance, and the abolition of the senate. Once he was in power, all reference to reform was omitted. Like their younger brothers, the German Nazis, Italian Fascists used the lure of socialism to gain worker support, but abandoned it once they came to power.

Mussolini staged his "march on Rome" on 28 October 1922 and King Victor Emmanuel III (q.v.) asked him to form a government the next day. This grant of parliamentary approval by the king led to the all too willing surrender of democracy by the Italian people.

Mussolini soon convinced the Italians that the Fascists would restore order and establish a functioning state. Supporters of *Il Duce* liked to boast that "the trains ran on time" in Fascist Italy. The Fascist state was dictatorship governed by a "Grand Council of Fascism," with Mussolini the undisputed leader. Under him, all political parties and any vestiges of democracy were abandoned.

The aggressive face of Fascism was shown to the world during the conquest of Ethiopia in 1935–1936 and the Spanish civil war in 1936–1939, when Italy joined Nazi Germany in supporting General Francisco Franco's (q.v.) Falangist movement, which was inspired by Mussolini's doctrine.

Mussolini once stated that Fascism was not something that could be exported, but his success led to the growth of Fascism across Europe. National Socialism (q.v.), the German equivalent, can be viewed as a subspecies and a further development of Fascism. Once Adolf Hitler (q.v.) was in power, the Nazi movement ran parallel to, but developed faster than, the Italian version.

In addition to its two chief proponents, long-enduring Fascist regimes of Franco and of Antonio Salazar of Portugal followed the same model. Fascist regimes in Europe, particularly Romania and Hungary, were more temporary, perhaps because of their defeat and occupation by the Soviet Union after World War II. Fascist movements also developed in France and Britain during the 1930s.

Generally, national Fascist movements that developed in the 1930s did not survive the death of their founders. Although today Fascism is still a threat to democracy and has many adherents around the world, it has failed to gain hold in a major power. German Nazism died with Hitler in the *Führer* Bunker in Berlin in 1945, with only small, isolated, lunatic fringes remaining in Germany today to remind us of its existence. The same appears to be true in Italy, although a right-wing movement that claims loyalty to Mussolini gained power in Italy by free elections in 1994. At the time of this writing, its future remains in doubt. In both Spain and Portugal, Fascism seems to have been supplanted by successful democratic governments.

Paul J. Rose

Additional Reading

Arendt, Hannah, *The Origins of Totalitarianism* (1966).

Blinkhorn, Martin (ed.), *Fascists and Conservatives* (1990).

Gregor, James, *Young Mussolini and the Intellectual Origins of Fascism* (1979).

Smith, Denis Mack, *Mussolini* (1982).

Final Solution (Endlösung)

Hitler assigned Hermann Göring (q.v.) the task of determining a "final solution of the Jewish problem" in March 1938, and this developed in the hands of Heinrich Himmler and Reinhard Heydrich (qq.v.) into the systematic and deliberate murder of some five to six million European Jews. At first, the planning included various options, such as a Jewish "reservation" in Poland and the deportation of Jews to Madagascar. The latter was abandoned, however, after war spread to the west and cut off transport routes.

The decision to launch a campaign to completely annihilate the Jews of Europe, to achieve a "Final Solution," came from Adolf Hitler in the summer of 1941, as German forces advanced rapidly into the Soviet Union. Hitler gave the order verbally to Himmler, and historians continue to debate the precise date, with some placing it earlier in the year. It was, however, in June and July 1941 that victories of the German forces against the Red Army brought new territories in Eastern Europe with the highest concentration of Jews under German control.

During the early phase of the Final Solution in the summer of 1941, units of the *Einsatzgruppen* (q.v.), mobile forces under the command of the *Reich* Main Security Office (RSHA) (q.v.), carried out an unprecedented wave of mass murder in the Soviet Union. The commanders of these units received verbal orders from Heydrich placing priority on the execution of all Jews encountered. The 3,000 men of the *Einsatzgruppen,* active throughout the Baltic states, White Russia, the Ukraine, and the Black Sea area, were responsible for the killing of more than 568,000 Jewish men, women, and children between the summer of 1941 and spring, 1942. The *Einsatzgruppen* were aided by local forces and auxiliary police units throughout Eastern Europe. Documents prepared from the reports of these units, the *Ereignismeldungen* (Report of Events), record in detail their deadly activities.

The successes of the German Army and the *Einsatzgruppen* led Heydrich, as chief of the security police and the SD (q.v.), to call a conference to plan the next phase of the Final Solution. Held at a villa on the Wannsee in Berlin on 20 January 1942, the meeting brought together fifteen participants from the SS, police, and various other agencies and ministries. They learned more about the Final Solution from Heydrich as he outlined the deportation of the Jews of Europe to killing sites in the east. Heydrich opened the ninety-minute meeting with a review of Jewish emigration since 1933, and went on to estimate the number of Jews remaining in each country of Europe, a total of 11 million.

Heydrich's statements at the Wannsee Conference made it clear that the Jews of Europe were to be herded into transit ghettos and then sent to concentration camps for hard labor or immediate extermination. Those chosen for work were also to be murdered. The Wannsee Conference gave an official stamp of approval to the killing program already started and secured the cooperation of other agencies needed to coordinate the expanding program of genocide.

The massive killings of the Final Solution had already started well before the Wannsee Conference. Along with the operations of the *Einszatgruppen,* the concentration camps (q.v.) at Chelmno and Auschwitz began the mass execution of Jews with poison gas. Starting in early December 1941 at Chelmo, Jewish victims from the nearby area and the ghetto in Lodz were taken in sealed trucks and asphyxiated with carbon monoxide from the vehicle's engine.

Auschwitz began its operations in May 1940, and the gassing of Jewish prisoners commenced immediately. As the war progressed, Auschwitz grew in size and served as both a concentration camp and an extermination center. The killing operations gained in efficiency, with Prussic acid,

or *Zyklon-B* (q.v.), first used in September 1941, becoming the preferred method of annihilation. Large numbers of Jews began to arrive at Auschwitz in January-February 1942, prompting the construction of additional gas chambers at nearby Birkenau. The complex was expanded again in August and achieved its murderous climax in August 1944, when 24,000 Hungarian Jews were killed in one day. The last Jews arrived in November 1944, and Himmler gave the order to destroy the crematoria.

Following the Wannsee Conference, the killings intensified, and more death camps were established under the operation called *Aktion REINHARD,* the systematic annihilation of the Jews in the General Government of Poland (q.v.). Launched in the late spring of 1942, *Aktion REINHARD* was led by SS and police leader of the Lublin District Odilo Globocnik. His staff consisted of some 450 Germans, 92 of whom had gained murderous experience in the euthanasia program, and about 300 Ukrainian volunteers, former POWs from the SS training camp at Trawniki. To carry out the mandate of *Aktion REINHARD,* three death camps were established, each in a remote area, close to a rail line. The first of these killing centers, Belzec, was set up in late 1941, and killings began on 17 March 1942. Sobibor dates from March-April 1942, with operations commencing in early May. Treblinka was constructed in the summer of 1942 and the killings started there on 23 July 1942, when the mass deportations from the Warsaw Ghetto (q.v.) began. The gas chambers at another concentration and forced labor camp, Majdanek, began operation by October 1942, playing a role in *Aktion REINHARD.*

Jews from all parts of Europe were "relocated" to the ghettos of the General Government. They were usually sent to the nearest death camp for annihilation. Other European Jews perished in the concentration camps in Western Europe, the victims of a deliberate policy of mistreatment and abuse. The ghettos were systematically eradicated and the inhabitants sent to their deaths in one of the extermination centers. By the end of December 1942, approximately 300,000 of the two million Jews in the General Government remained alive. The last of the ghettos and remaining survivors were liquidated by June 1943. *Aktion REINHARD* concluded in early November 1943 when the Jews in the Majdanek, Poniatowa, and Trawniki concentration camps were killed in Operation *ERNTEFEST* (Harvest Festival).

By the end of the war, the Final Solution,

F

Nazi Germany's all-out effort to annihilate the Jews of Europe, came close to realizing its objective. Adolf Eichmann (q.v.) maintained that six million Jews had perished, and scholars recently concluded that the figure is somewhere between 5.3 and just over six million. The precise number can, however, never be determined. Even though detailed records of many of the shootings and concentration camps were maintained, the mass deportations to the death camps of Poland led an unknown number of men, women, and children directly to the gas chambers without their ever having been recorded. Most of the victims of the Final Solution were killed in the death camps, others perished in the concentration camps, and a large number died at the hands of the *Einsatzgruppen,* all victims of the Nazi policy of genocide.

Robert G. Waite

Additional Reading

Benz, Wolfgang (ed.), *Dimension des Völkermords: Die Zahl der jüdischen Opfer des Nationalsozialismus* (1991).

Breitman, Richard, *The Architect of Genocide: Himmler and the Final Solution* (1991).

Furet, François, *Unanswered Questions: Nazi Germany and the Genocide of the Jews* (1989).

Hilberg, Raul, *The Destruction of the European Jews,* 3 vols. (1985).

Fortress Europe

The term *Festung Europa* was introduced to the press by the propaganda experts of the German Foreign Office. It described the north, west, and middle European states as a bastion against Communism. After the beginning of the Russian campaign on 20 June 1941, the German *Reich* expected solidarity against Stalinism from all other non-Communist states.

The term also was supposed to describe the invincibility of the combined allied and occupied countries under the control of the *Reich.* The idea was to convey the impregnability of fortresses like Verdun in World War I or the West Wall (q.v.). Since, however, it was becoming obvious that even the most modern fortress construction could not hold up against heavy artillery, air attacks, or air landing troops, Propaganda Minister Joseph Goebbels (q.v.) prohibited further use of the phrase "Fortress Europe" on 7 December 1942. It was a defensive term and only had negative elements. One could besiege a fortress and it would be only a question of time when it would fall.

In 1943, the term Fortress Europe was adopted by the Allied press. At the end of November 1943, Ward Price wrote that, with the attack against Fortress Europe, the biggest siege in world history was about to start. With the Allied landings in France in June 1944, only a few fortresses of the "invincible" Atlantic Wall (q.v.) held for any amount of time. The gates to Fortress Europe were open.

Because of Adolf Hitler's (q.v.) predilection for calling cities fortresses or fortified places, the term "fortress" was widely used anyway. Only a few such places held longer than a couple of days. Because of increasing Allied air attacks and the ineffectiveness of the German air defenses after 1944, it was said in Germany that "Fortress Europe had no roof."

The term "Fortress Europe" was used again in 1990 when the European Free Trade Association considered joining the European Community (EC) and had to face the economic attitudes of the EC members.

Franz W. Seidler

Additional Reading

Hastings, Max, *Bomber Command* (1989).

Shirer, William L., *The Rise and Fall of the Third Reich* (1960).

Four Freedoms

In the course of his annual message to Congress in early 1941, President Franklin D. Roosevelt (q.v.) warned that the United States should not be seduced into a "dictator's peace," but should strive instead to bring about a world founded upon "four essential human freedoms":

The first is freedom of speech and expression—everywhere in the world.

The second is freedom of every person to worship God in his own way—everywhere in the world.

The third is freedom from want—which, translated into world terms, means economic understandings that will secure to every nation a healthy peacetime life for its inhabitants—everywhere in the world.

The fourth is freedom from fear—which, translated into world terms, means a worldwide reduction of armaments to such a point and in such a thorough fashion that no nation will be in a position to commit an act of physical aggression against any neighbor—anywhere in the world.

Though the speech was well received, the Four Freedoms never quite attained the status of a popular fighting creed. They were, however, imprinted on the reverse side of the United States World War II Campaign medal.

Blaine T. Browne

Additional Reading
Perret, Geoffrey, *Days of Sadness, Years of Triumph: The American People, 1939–1945* (1973).

Führerprinzip (Leadership Principle)

Der Führer (The Leader) was the title officially assumed by Adolf Hitler (q.v.) upon the death of President Paul von Hindenburg (q.v.) on 1 August 1934. In that one title, Hitler combined the powers formerly held by von Hindenburg as head of state, and the powers Hitler held as head of government. Henceforth, *Führer* was the mandatory form for addressing Hitler for all Germans.

The purpose of the nation was to give the world the best people, Hitler wrote in *Mein Kampf*. The state must be organized on the principle of rule by natural leaders, not on any concept of majority rule. "The spirit has never had more violence done to it than when mere numbers make themselves its master," wrote Hitler.

The *Führerprinzip* stressed intuitive decision making and mystical means of communicating ideas and concepts. Knowledge was entirely subjective. Science, observation, measurements, and reason provided partial, fragmented, and relative knowledge. Intuitive decisions made by natural leaders were much sounder practices.

Hitler's policy deliberations often consisted of rambling conversations with party comrades during evenings on the Obersalzberg. Observant and ambitious followers, such as Martin Bormann (q.v.), took voluminous notes of Hitler's intuitive and spontaneous ramblings and later wrote them up as policy papers and direct orders.

Strong, unrelenting will was the essential element in success and triumph. In a discussion with historian Basil H. Liddell Hart, General Franz Halder (qq.v.) stated: "Hitler taught and believed that reason and knowledge are nothing and that the unbending will to victory and the relentless pursuit of goals are everything. Mystical speculation replaced consideration of time and space and the careful calculation of the strength of one's own forces in relation to the enemy's."

The *Völkisch* state had no representative bodies deciding questions by majority vote. Instead there were advisory councils standing at the side of the leader or subleader, but authority always came from above. "For humanity blessing has never lain in the masses, but in its creative heads," Hitler wrote.

The same high degree of social Darwinism found in most extreme conservative ideologies was present in the *Führerprinzip*. Elites came to power through struggle and were replaced through struggle if they lost the qualities that brought them to power. Such leaders derived their power from intuitive knowledge, intelligence, and manipulative skills; or if necessary, by brute force. The whole concept had a Machiavellian ring to it.

Philosopher Friedrich Nietzsche, who influenced Nazi ideology, identified leadership with "heroic man," unrestrained by law, who possessed the power and will to dominate lesser souls. Hitler often expressed pleasure at coming to power through the ballot box. Yet, it was clear to him that the German people wanted to be ruled by a strong, willful Leader. And once they had expressed themselves at the polls, no further purpose was served by holding subsequent elections.

Paul J. Rose

Additional Reading
Bullock, Alan, *Hitler: A Study in Tyranny* (1969).
Hitler, Adolf, *Mein Kampf* (1939).
Lang, Jochen von, *Martin Bormann: The Man Who Manipulated Hitler* (1979).
Liddel Hart, Basil H., *The German Generals Talk* (1948).
Manning, Paul, *Martin Bormann: Nazi in Exile* (1981).

G

General Government of Poland

Following the invasion and partition of Poland by Germany and the Soviet Union in September 1939, Adolf Hitler incorporated the western and northern regions of the conquered country into the *Reich* and transformed the remainder, about 95,000 square kilometers with a population of approximately 10.5 million, into the so-called General Government of Poland. Headed by a veteran Nazi, Dr. Hans Frank (q.v.), the General Government was administratively divided into four major districts (Krakow, Lublin, Radom, and Warsaw), each headed by a German district chief, later called governor. In August 1941, after the invasion of the Soviet Union, a fifth district, Galicia, was added to the General Government.

Charged with administering and exploiting the area for the benefit of the Third *Reich,* Frank was assisted by a relatively small group of German civil servants headed by State Secretary Dr. Josef Bühler. In the lower levels of the administration, Polish nationals continued to be employed.

Until May 1940, the *Wehrmacht's* activities in the General Government were supervised by Colonel General Johannes Blaskowitz (q.v.), an old-fashioned soldier who occasionally spoke out against Nazi brutalities. He was succeeded by two reactivated elderly generals, Curt Frieherr von Gienanth (until September 1942) and Siegfried Haenicke.

Practically all "security" matters in the General Government, including the persecution of the Jewish community and the repression of various other target groups, were coordinated by a higher SS and police leader (HSSPF) who, like Frank, had his headquarters at Krakow. Until November 1943, *SS-Obergruppenführer* Friedrich Wilhelm Krüger filled that key post; he was then succeeded by Wilhelm Koppe, who had previously represented Heinrich Himmler's (q.v.) interests in the annexed Poznanian region (*Gau* Wartheland). As in most other German-controlled areas of Europe, investigation and repression of political opponents and "undesirable" population groups were handled primarily by various units of the security police (SIPO) and the SD (q.v.), the security service of the SS.

Probably the most infamous of the SS and police functionaries operating in the General Government was *SS-Brigadeführer* Odilo Globocnik, who presided over various extermination programs in the Lublin District until August 1943. An equally repulsive figure was *SS-Standartenführer* Josef Meisinger, the SIPO/SD chief in Warsaw from 1939 to 1941. He subsequently was posted to Tokyo as police attache, where he displayed singular ineptness in connection with the Richard Sorge (q.v.) spy case.

From 1939 until the arrival of the Red Army in 1944–1945, the population of the General Government experienced a great deal of physical hardship and violence. While the extermination centers within the General Government (Auschwitz, Belzec, Majdanek, Sobibor, Treblinka, etc.) were used primarily to kill Jews, the death rate among Polish Christians as a result of Nazi terror and deprivation was likewise extremely high. Although there were some people in the General Government who collaborated with the Germans (and even joined the *Waffen-SS*), most historians agree that the level of acceptance of Hitler's "New Order" was much lower in Poland than in most other occupied countries of Europe.

Ulrich Trumpener

Additional Reading

Birenbaum, Haliva, *Hope Is the Last to Die: A Personal Documentation of Nazi Terror* (1972).

Gross, Jan T., *Polish Society Under German Occupation: The General-Gouvernement, 1939–1944* (1979).

Lipschutz, Norman, *Victory Through Darkness and Despair* (1960).

Lukas, Richard C., *The Forgotten Holocaust: The Poles Under German Occupation, 1939–1944* (1986).

Germany, Occupation of

By 12 September 1944, representatives of the Allied nations decided that Germany would be occupied and divided into zones of occupation. The postwar Potsdam Conference further determined that Germany must be occupied, Naziism rooted out, democracy established, and reparations paid to the countries conquered and devastated. According to the agreements, the eastern zone would be administered by the Soviet Union; the northwestern zone by Britain, and the southwestern zone by the United States, which carved out an additional zone for France.

After the war, on 5 June 1945, the commanders of the Allied forces—British, American, French, and Soviet—issued a declaration from Berlin that they, as the Allied Control Council, had assumed supreme authority within Germany, and military government was established. German political and legal authority had ceased to exist.

In the pursuit of their objectives, the occupation powers faced formidable problems, including a devastated nation, millions of refugees and displaced persons, war criminals, the need to establish democratic institutions, and a lack of consensus on policies. The economic emergency had to be faced immediately, as Germany's infrastructure was destroyed.

Economic output in 1946 remained a third of the prewar 1939 figure, and food shortages reached crisis proportions, especially in the French and in the highly urbanized British zones. Food was more plentiful in the American zone, thanks to the soldiers' generosity and some 16 million CARE packages that arrived between 1946 and 1949. Even the Soviet zone, which according to the Potsdam agreements was to send foodstuffs from its agriculture regions, was hindered both by the loss of the eastern provinces to Poland and by Soviet policy. It was becoming increasingly apparent to Western authorities that in order to prevent starvation, foodstuffs would have to be sent into Germany, and that the Soviet Union implemented only those parts of the Potsdam agreement it chose to.

Recovery was further hurt by the lack of fuel,

and during the hard winter of 1946–1947, the Ruhr produced only a quarter of its prewar quantity of coal. In an effort to stay warm, people cut down trees, burned furniture, and took refuge in railway stations. An acute shortage of accommodations worsened as six million refugees came into the zones of occupation, joining the five million made homeless through the bombing. The black market flourished, particularly for luxury goods such as coffee, cigarettes, chocolate, and even food.

The military governments quickly initiated a program of reparations payments for occupied Germany—although the Allies could not agree on any firm figure. While the Western powers recognized the connection between industrial disarmament and the German standard of living, they did not desire an impoverished nation unable to support itself. That would place an additional burden on the military governments. The Soviets, however, were determined to seize as much as possible. By July 1945, for example, Soviet forces had dismantled 380 factories in Berlin alone. The policy was to transfer industrial production capability from its zone of occupation to the Soviet Union. In addition to this materiel, the Soviets also received 25 percent of the reparations from the Western zones, but they were to provide the West with food, which they did not.

The military governments initiated a program to democratize Germany immediately following the end of the war. In the American and British zones, as part of the massive de-Nazification program, questionnaires were issued to almost every adult, as the authorities strived to learn about their political past. The vast numbers of those investigated led the American and British military authorities to turn the process over to German courts. Fully 950,000 individuals were punished. In the Soviet zone, more than half a million former Nazis received punishment, usually loss of their jobs. The trial of the major Nazi leaders took place at Nuremberg from November 1945 to August 1946. Twenty-four defendants faced charges of conspiracy against peace, crimes against peace, violation of the laws and customs of war, and/or crimes against humanity (*see* International Military tribunal).

Within the zones of occupation, the military governments pursued the de-Nazification and at the same time worked toward reestablishing a political system. In the American zone, administered by the Office of Military Government for Germany and based in Frankfurt am Main, a resurgence of political life began early. American authorities worked with German nationals and particularly leaders from the individual states. In line with the ideal of building "democracy from the bottom up," local elections were first held in January 1946, and on 20 September 1947, political parties were formally permitted.

The British zone was administered by Control Commission for Germany/British Element (Bad Oeynhausen), and authorities there established a German advisory council on 15 February 1946. Political parties were organized shortly after the war as the British encouraged local democracy.

France's Control Council for Germany (Baden Baden) was led by that nation's enduring concerns over security. Various states were reestablished between autumn 1946 and 1947, but the building of political parties proceeded slowly. Furthermore, France attempted to absorb the Saarland (q.v.), which in May 1945 was separated from the general occupation zone.

In the Soviet zone, governed firmly by the Soviet military administration in Berlin, authority remained highly centralized. In 1945, far-reaching changes were introduced, with land reform and much of the economy placed in the hands of state authorities. Political parties were reestablished as part of the "Anti-Fascist Block," and the communist Socialist Unity Party (SED) predominated.

Increasingly, a split between the Eastern and Western zones emerged and broadened. As more refugees from the east came into the Western zones, it became apparent that German and even European recovery depended upon discontinuing the Potsdam deindustrializing program. While de-Nazification and demilitarization continued, the development of peaceful industries was permitted.

To spur this, American secretary of state James F. Byrnes (q.v.) announced in a September 1946 speech that the Western zones ought to function as a single economic unit. He also stated that U.S. forces would remain in Europe indefinitely, and that a greater measure of local self-government was to be permitted. On 1 January 1947, the American and British zones merged to form the Bi-Zone; and a year later, the French zone also joined.

The German economy did begin a slow but steady recovery after the hard winters of 1946–1947. After the announcement of the Marshall Plan (q.v.) in June 1947, the economic organization of the Bi-Zone was strengthened, with Ludwig Erhard appointed as the director of economic administration, and a central bank was established. On 20 June 1948, currency reform was introduced in the Tri-Zone, and the effect on economic life was immediate and strong. Industrial production rose by 50 percent in the latter half of 1948 and a full 75 percent in 1949. The steady economic buildup of the West aroused both the suspicions and the animosity of the Soviets.

The failure of a four-power conference in London in December 1947 led the Western leaders to conclude that they needed to act on their own, without the Soviets, if a coherent policy was to be applied to Germany. By late 1947, American and British leaders were openly discussing a "union" of the three Western zones. At a March 1948 meeting in London, it was announced that a democratic Germany was to fully participate in the recovery of Europe. Further steps to reestablish an independent Germany, comprising the Western zones, came at the 20 April London Conference. The Soviet Union responded with a meeting of its bloc in Warsaw on 24 June, shortly after the Western zones' currency reform. The split between East and West had become irreparable. Now the movement toward establishing an independent Germany hastened. The military governors of the Western zones met on 1 July 1948 and issued a statement calling for a constitutional convention to assemble by 1 September to draft a new constitution. The German Basic Law took effect on 23 May 1949.

While the Occupation Statute reserved for the Allies important issues such as disarmament, reparations, de-Nazification, foreign policy, and Allied and Soviet military forces stationed in the two German states, the occupation had, in effect, ended with their independence. This was further confirmed by the September 1951 Allied conference in Washington that expressed the Allied objective of "the inclusion of a democratic Germany in a European community on the basis of equal status."

Robert G. Waite

Additional Reading

Backer, John H., *The Decision to Divide Germany* (1978).

Gimbel, John, *The American Occupation of Germany: Politics and the Military 1945–1949* (1968).

Snowden, J.K., *The German Question 1945–1949: Continuity and Change* (1975).

Vogelsang, Thilo, *Das geteilte Deutschland* (1969).

Ziemke, Earl F., *The U.S. Army in the Occupation of Germany* (1975).

GI Bill of Rights

The Servicemen's Readjustment Act of 1944,

popularly known as the GI Bill of Rights, was passed with broad support of the White House, Congress, and the public. After President Franklin D. Roosevelt (q.v.) proposed legislation providing educational benefits to veterans in late 1943, the American Legion veterans organization drafted more sweeping legislation that Senator Champ Clark introduced in January 1944. With eighty-one cosponsors, the bill unanimously passed the Senate on 24 March. The House unanimously approved it with minor amendments on 18 May; conferees reported a compromise on 13 June; and Roosevelt signed it into law on 22 June. The bill provided veterans preference in hiring in certain jobs; unemployment relief for up to one year; low-interest loans for purchases of businesses, farms, and homes; and educational benefits, including full tuition and supplementary allowances.

Several concerns motivated passage of the GI Bill. Roosevelt supported it to restore social programs that Congress had recently dismantled. Other liberals acted to prevent fiscal depression widely predicted once wartime spending subsided. Conservatives desired safeguards against postwar malaise that might push veterans toward political and economic radicalism. The public felt indebted to servicemen, and politicians wished to tap that sentiment in impending election campaigns. The 16 million servicemen and their families constituted one-fourth of the electorate.

Ultimately, 7.8 million veterans received training or education under the bill, approximately 2.2 million at the college level. Some eight million collected unemployment relief, and nearly four million secured home and business loans. GI Bill expenditures eventually surpassed $50 billion. The law helped veterans as a group become educated, satisfied, and productive members of the middle class, and thus pillars of stability in postwar society.

Studies show that the money spent was a good social investment. Veterans educated earned more money and repaid the GI Bill costs by paying more taxes on higher earnings.

Peter L. Hahn

Additional Reading
Olson, Keith, *The G.I. Bill, the Veterans, and the Colleges* (1974).
Severo, Richard, and Lewis Milford, *The Wages of War: When America's Soldiers Came Home—from Valley Forge to Vietnam* (1989).

Gleichschaltung (Coordination)

Gleichschalten (to coordinate) is also a technical electronic term meaning to bring on line. *Gleichschaltung* was the domestic policy through which the Nazi Party (q.v.) leveled the German state and society, bringing every facet of German daily life in line with National Socialist ideology and practice.

Once the Nazis came to power, they quickly consolidated their grip over the country through a series of sham legislations, including the Enabling Act (q.v.) of 23 March 1933 and the National Socialist Civil Service Act of April 1933. All organizations within Germany were forcibly merged under Nazi umbrella organizations. All trade unions, for example, were consolidated into the German labor front *(Deutsche Arbeitsfront)*, and all youth organizations, including the Boy Scouts, lost their individual identity in the Hitler Youth (q.v.).

The ultimate goal of *Gleichschaltung* was a nation based on the principle of "One People, One Empire, One Leader" *(Ein Volk, Ein Reich, Ein Führer)*.

David T. Zabecki

Additional Reading
Bracher, Karl Dietrich, *The German Dictatorship* (1970).
Grunberger, Richard, *The 12-Year Reich: A Social History of Nazi Germany, 1933-1945* (1971).

Governments-in-Exile

The Allies recognized eight exile governments during World War II: Norway, Poland, Czechoslovakia, the Netherlands, Belgium, Luxembourg, Yugoslavia, and Greece. The Free French fought for recognition until the liberation of France in 1944.

The first permanent exile government established in London for the course of the war was the Norwegian government, which fled the German invasion in 1940. Unlike many of the other governments, King Haakon (q.v.) and his ministers took substantial assets with them. They shipped Norway's gold to Ottawa and New York.

From London, the Norwegian government controlled the world's fourth-largest merchant marine, and by 1941, 40 percent of the foreign tonnage entering Great Britain. Its army was negligible, consisting of 1,500 men in Scotland training to return home. Norwegian sailors manned fifty-five vessels in the British Navy by the end of 1941, and "Little Norway" in Ontario, Canada, formed an air force.

Harsh German reprisals kept the resistance at home small and usually ineffective, but late in the war, the Swedish government allowed almost 9,000 Norwegian refugees to assemble in "health camps" where they were trained as a police force to occupy Norway when the war ended. King Haakon served as a nationalistic rallying point for the exiles and for resistors at home. The king returned to Norway 7 June 1945, but only two members of the London exiles obtained places in the restored postwar government.

Queen Wilhelmina's (q.v.) flight to London with her cabinet left the Dutch public feeling deserted at first and the exiles wavered in their commitment to fight Germany. The Dutch made some preparations, moving their gold out of the country and allowing large companies to transfer their headquarters abroad, and saved much of the economy from German control.

Warships, a sizable merchant navy, and a number of large passenger ships escaped and joined the exiles, who also controlled an extensive colonial empire in the East Indies and the Caribbean. These assets made the Dutch feel independent of the British and led them to pursue an independent policy to protect the East Indies from the Japanese. Some ministers suggested relocating to Batavia in order to assert their independence from the British, but the queen forbade it. The Dutch did not declare war on Italy immediately and considered making a separate peace with Germany during the first year of the war.

Gradually their policy changed as the Japanese encroached on the East Indies. The exiles turned to the British and Americans for help but found none because the British had no forces to keep the Japanese out of the East Indies, and the Americans were hostile toward the Dutch for their economic concessions to the Japanese. The East Indies fell in 1942, forcing the exiles to abandon pretensions of being at least a middle-ranking power. The British and Americans treated the Dutch exiles almost as a British dominion.

In the occupied Netherlands, popular attitudes toward the exiles evolved from hostility to support, with Radio Orange playing a major role. The queen inaugurated a quarter-hour series on the BBC (q.v.) with an address in July 1940. Listening constituted an act of resistance and the whole country began to listen and identify with the exiles.

In September 1940, the exiles deposed the prime minister who advocated a negotiated peace and replaced him with P.S. Gerbrandy. Gerbrandy endorsed a "Commentary" written by a leader of the professional bureaucrats at home that advocated passive resistance. The Germans effectively penetrated and disrupted most active resistance efforts; however, there was an underground press that attempted to educate the public.

In July 1944, the London cabinet appointed an underground editor to the post of minister of justice in an effort to incorporate resistance leaders into the exile camp. Gerbrandy appointed seven representatives of the government to act as agents of the London government during the transfer of power from the Germans. These efforts produced a relatively smooth return for the exiled government.

The Belgians fared worst in leaving their homeland and securing resources. King Leopold (q.v.) refused to leave his army or to endorse the exile ministers who fled from Dunkirk to Britain and then flew back to France. The prime minister, Hubert Pierlot, spoke on French radio announcing his break with the king, but when the French retreated to Bordeaux, they exhibited their disdain for the Belgians by assigning them a modest house in Rue Blanc-de-Trouille (white with fear), which made them the butt of jokes.

At Vichy, they reached their nadir when, meeting in cafes and cut off from any reliable information, patriots joined them with the news that most Belgians sided with the king. Only two of the ministers were determined to go to Britain to continue the government-in-exile; the others resigned to maintain legality for the government.

The foreign minister, Paul-Henri Spaak (q.v.), and Pierlot barely escaped from France. Arrested in Spain, they smuggled themselves into Portugal and arrived in England to join two ministers sent earlier to safeguard control of the Congo. So, four men with one African colony as their only real asset constituted the Belgian exile government. They established the policy, which was fiction, that no conflict existed between them and the king. In their BBC broadcasts, they made the captive king the symbol of passive resistance. The ministers interested themselves in the creation of international economic and political organizations. Spaak along with his colleagues created the Benelux as the war raged.

By contrast, Luxembourg's Grand Duchess Charlotte (q.v.) withdrew, according to prepared plans, to France, and then to Britain with her family and ministers. They established a London government with a Montreal branch. At home, the resistance created a general strike in 1942, leading to massive deportations. The British trained a small Luxembourg force that participated in the 1944 liberation. The exiles brought about long-term changes in the duchy. They abandoned Luxembourg's historic commitment to neutrality after the war by joining NATO and cofounding the Benelux.

When Adolf Hitler occupied his country, the former Czechoslovak President Eduard Beneš (q.v.) rushed to France from the University of Chicago, where he was a professor. The French allowed Beneš to organize a Czechoslovak committee and to create a Czech Army of one division and a sizable air force unit.

With the fall of France, Beneš accepted British help, and from the BBC, called for his military units to join him. The air force and half of the infantry made it and took part in the Battle of Britain (q.v.). Beneš's most valuable asset was an extensive intelligence network in Eastern Europe. When Germany invaded the Soviet Union, as he had predicted, all of the Allies recognized Beneš as the head of the Czechoslovak government.

The Soviets recognized Beneš first because he cultivated them. Since before Munich, the Soviets supported Czechoslovakia, and Beneš refused to participate in anti-Soviet activities or plots. He met regularly with the Soviet ambassador in London and kept the Soviets well informed, which cost him some trust from the British and his fellow exiles. Despite that handicap, Beneš worked successfully for several diplomatic goals to reestablish his nation after the war. He got the British and the Free French to repudiate the Munich Agreement (q.v.). After the assassination of the German occupational governor and the fearful revenge the Germans took, he won support for the postwar expulsion of the Sudeten Germans from Czechoslovakia.

Beneš signed an agreement with the Soviets not to interfere in one another's internal affairs. He ignored warnings that he was being naive about Soviet intentions and reached a compromise for a coalition with the Czechoslovak Communists, who had spent the war in Moscow. He established his government after the war, but resigned in 1948 to protest the Soviet takeover of his restored country.

The Polish government, eluding the Germans and the Soviet invaders in 1939, traveled to neutral Romania where German pressure on the Romanians prevented them from leaving. The Poles decided to have the president appoint a successor already in France, but the French rejected the first candidate. The second appointee, in turn, named an opponent of the defeated government, General Władysław Sikorski (q.v.), to be leader of the Polish state in exile. Sikorski possessed ideal qualifi-

cations, including frontline service in the 1919–1920 Russo-Polish War (q.v.), and two short terms as prime minister in coalition cabinets not associated with the dictatorship of the 1930s.

Poland made a substantial contribution to the war effort. In France, an army of 85,000 men, along with substantial airpower, was assembled. A smaller force made its way to French territory in Syria. In 1940, the Germans captured two-thirds of the Polish Army in France, but the other third, the Levant Army, and the air force, escaped to Britain. Polish fighter pilots made up almost 20 percent of the RAF during the Battle of Britain, and the small Polish Navy fought in the North Atlantic.

In 1941, the Soviets allowed Polish survivors in Russia to form an army that journeyed through Persia and joined with existing forces in Palestine to fight under British command in North Africa, and later in southern Europe. By 1945, the Polish exile army was rebuilt to 228,000 men. Polish scientists also played a major role in breaking the German Enigma cipher and creating ULTRA (qq.v.).

Diplomatically, the Polish government attempted to weld the small exile powers into a bloc, and briefly, Poland looked to be moving toward a confederation with Czechoslovakia. However, they succeeded only in creating a regular lunch meeting of the exiled foreign ministers. Most of their diplomatic efforts foundered on their hostility toward the Soviets. That hostility grew after the German discovery of the bodies of 4,000 Polish officers in the Katyń Forest (q.v.) in April 1943.

The London Poles built an excellent relationship with their resistance groups and commanded the largest force, the Home Army, or AK (q.v.). Despite bad relations with the Soviets, the London-based government ordered the AK to cooperate with the advancing Red Army in 1944. In the largest action, the AK revolted in Warsaw during the Soviet approach to the city, only to have the Soviets sit and wait while the Germans destroyed the resistance fighters. The Soviets then imposed their own Lublin government, consisting of their agents, in the country.

The British and Americans withdrew their recognition of the London-based government in return for Josef Stalin's (q.v.) continued support. The British provided the Polish armed forces the option of returning to Poland or resettling in the Commonwealth. The majority chose permanent exile and the London-based government refused to return to Soviet-dominated Poland. The London Polish government-in-exile finally recognized the

Warsaw government in 1991, with the fall of Communism in Eastern Europe.

Perhaps the least effective of the exile governments was the Yugoslav, which had seized power in a coup when the Yugoslav regency signed an alliance with Hitler. Responding to British urging, a group of young officers deposed the regent and proclaimed seventeen-year-old King Peter (q.v.) as having reached his majority. When the Yugoslav Army collapsed in the face of the German and Italian invasion, the king and his ministers fled with 1,500 soldiers, three small naval vessels, and sixty aircraft. The Germans later destroyed the majority of the planes on the ground in Greece and captured most of the soldiers. Peter and his ministers moved from Cairo to London where the coup-created government, according to a British agent who worked with it, was ". . . weak, divided, ignorant, obstinate, proud, and unaccommodating."

When resistance fighting first erupted in Yugoslavia, the London government condemned it as premature. Lack of support for the resistance led to the appointment of a seventy-three-year-old historian as prime minister in January 1942. His role was to support General Draža Mihailović (q.v.), the leader of Serbian resistance fighters, called Četniks (q.v.). The exiles promoted Mihailović to defense minister and a host of other titles, but instead of fighting the Axis, he dealt with them for arms to fight the Yugoslav partisans (q.v.), who were fighting the Axis. The London government split into a host of warring groups along ethnic lines, between those who made the coup and the older military officers, and between the king's court and the ministers.

When the British learned the truth about the situation inside Yugoslavia and tired of the infighting among the exiles, they shifted support to Tito's (q.v.) partisans and urged the appointment of an exile government acceptable to Tito. King Peter, who neglected his education to pursue Princess Alexandra of Greece, listened willingly to the British because his ministers were denying him permission to marry. At the British behest, Peter conducted a coup, installed a leader, and moved the Yugoslavs to Cairo. In March 1945, that government merged with Tito and went out of existence.

When the Italians invaded Greece in 1940, General Ioannis Metaxas (q.v.), who ruled as a military dictator, threw the Italians back. Metaxas died in the midst of the fighting and King George II (q.v.) appointed a mild-mannered banker as prime minister. The banker committed suicide when the Germans and Bulgarians struck, and the king ap-pointed another banker from Crete, where the government quickly took refuge only to be dislodged by German paratroops. The king escaped and received ready recognition, but held no power.

In Egypt, the large Greek colony and some exiles recruited forces to form a small army, navy, and air force under British command. It soon became apparent that the exile force constituted only a small portion of Greece. One part was effectively occupied and the larger portion, consisting of the mountain provinces, created a powerful resistance force independent of outside control. In the mountains, the Communists were strong and anti-monarchist sentiment was high. Despite these realities, the king's exile government did not purge Metaxas's people and promised restoration of constitutional liberties until 1943.

Early in 1944, a mutiny broke out in the exile army in support of the Communist-dominated organization controlling the Greek mountains. Changing prime ministers to deal with the mutiny brought Georgios Papandreou (q.v.), who recently arrived from Greece, to power. He authorized the British to put down the mutiny and convened an all-party conference in Lebanon. His conference formed a government of national unity that even the Communists joined, and he returned to take control of Greece in October 1944. George II came back after a plebiscite in 1946.

After the French government surrendered in 1940, no leading official emerged to carry on the war. Only Charles de Gaulle (q.v.), a brigadier general recently appointed assistant minister of defense, offered to settle in London and continue the war on Germany. He had failed to convince the government to transfer itself to North Africa, and he accepted on his own the British offer of use of the BBC to rally opposition in the empire and at home. Few followed him at first. Not one of the French Embassy staff in London joined him. His early recruits came from ordinary people, soldiers in the ranks, and fishermen who sailed across the Channel. Despite scarce resources, he established the Free French committee with British support. After the British attack on the French fleet at Mers el-Kébir (q.v.), many Frenchmen saw de Gaulle as collaborating with another enemy.

The first turn of the tide in de Gaulle's favor came with the announcement by the governor of Chad that he recognized de Gaulle's authority. Most of the sub-Saharan colonies followed, then the Indian and the Pacific Islands. De Gaulle almost met disaster in 1940 when he attempted and failed to capture Dakar (q.v.) from Vichy forces. He ignored the defeat and in Brazzaville, free of

British control, he issued a manifesto creating a "Defense Council of the Empire" and an "organic declaration" stating that the Vichy government was illegal. These declarations effectively established his committee as a government-in-exile in de Gaulle's mind, but no one recognized it as such.

From the French Empire, de Gaulle attracted soldiers and began to build a fighting force, which probably saved him from destruction by his British hosts. When the British occupied French Syria and refused to turn over control, he assumed that they intended to add Syria to the British Empire; in retaliation, he made himself as disagreeable as possible. He angered the U.S. by seizing Saint-Pierre and Miquelon, two small French islands off the Canadian coast. As a result, the British kept him a virtual prisoner for eleven months, during which he first threatened to move permanently to Equatorial Africa, and then asked the Soviets if they would give his government asylum.

Strained relations eased when the Free French Army won a major victory in North Africa at Bir Hachiem (q.v.). The British Army, in retreat from General Erwin Rommel (q.v.), asked a French general with 5,000 men to cover their retreat, which the French did magnificently. The publicity generated by French bravery led to a reconciliation between the British and de Gaulle, who changed the name of his committee to "The Fighting French."

Despite French contributions, the U.S. and the British did not inform de Gaulle before the North African invasion, and they refused to recognize de Gaulle's authority in the captured territory. Instead, the Americans made a deal with the Vichy officials and turned over administration to Admiral Jean François Darlan (q.v.), who was killed by a mysterious assassin.

President Roosevelt called de Gaulle to the Casablanca Conference and forced him to deal with the Vichy commander, General Henri Giraud (q.v.). De Gaulle and Giraud became co-presidents of a new Committee of National Liberation. They mounted a military operation capturing Corsica, and de Gaulle established a consultative assembly in Algeria as the last step in building a provisional government. Giraud failed to match de Gaulle as a politician, and de Gaulle eliminated him as co-president.

By playing the "Soviet card," de Gaulle united all of the French resistance forces including the communists behind his leadership. From Vichy, leaders swarmed to Algiers to join de Gaulle, but still Roosevelt refused to recognize him. As D-Day approached, plans went ahead for an American military administration in liberated France.

Officially unrecognized, de Gaulle traveled to France, dispatched his agents to claim power, and fought a secret civil war to gain control of France. He defied the Allies by issuing his own money in competition with an Allied invasion currency, and he personally visited many towns where he met rapturous receptions. Despite their dependent position, the other exile governments broke ranks with the Americans and the British and recognized de Gaulle as the legal ruler of France. The "Big Three" did not follow until months later. De Gaulle's only response was "The French Government is satisfied to be called by its name."

De Gaulle summarized the feelings of the exiles in his memoirs. ". . . underneath the externals of the etiquette we could discern the dramas caused in their souls by defeat and exile . . . each one in a shadow lived through his own heart-rending tragedy." Some exiles made material contributions to the war effort; others served mainly symbolic purposes; some returned to rule their homelands; and others suffered permanent exile; but all displayed a degree of bravery to break with their occupied nations and to continue the battle against the Axis, who seemed to be invincible in 1940, when the exiles made their decisions.

Dennis J. Mitchell

Additional Reading

Davies, Norman, *The Heart of Europe: A Short History of Modern Poland* (1984).

De Gaulle, Charles, *Memoirs of Charles de Gaulle,* 3 vols. (1955–1960).

Spaak, Paul Henri, *Continuing the Battle: Memoirs of a European* (1971).

Greenland

Although not a scene of major battles, Greenland was a major strategic concern for both Allied and Axis war leaders. Located just 500 miles northeast of Maine, this barren and isolated Danish territory sat astride the great circle route for aircraft flying to Great Britain. More significantly, Greenland was the largest landmass over which Arctic weather fronts formed before moving across the Atlantic to the European continent. Observing the weather over Greenland therefore enabled military meteorologists to predict the weather over the critical war fronts. This is what made Greenland critical to the Allied war effort and a key battle ground in the "Weather War" (q.v.), fought in the harsh Arctic from 1941–1945.

Greenland first came to Allied attention with Denmark's surrender in April 1940. Although the island's climate and terrain were too harsh to support large-scale military operations, its strategic location suggested to both British and American leaders that German control of Greenland would be disastrous.

On 1 May 1940, President Franklin D. Roosevelt (q.v.) dispatched a special consul, James Pinfold, to Ivigtut, Greenland, to negotiate American protection of the island. The Danish governor for Greenland, Eske Brun, not only accepted American protection, but established the Greenland Army (q.v.), which he designated the Sledge Patrol. The United States agreed to sell arms to Greenland, provide for its defense, patrol its waters, and establish air bases on its territory. Greenland's cryolite mine in Ivigtut was the one facility that would be protected by American forces (cryolite is a key material used in aluminum production). The initial agreement was formalized on 9 April 1941 under the 1940 Act of Havana, which called for the American defense of the Western Hemisphere. Under this agreement, the United States built three airfields and established several seaplane operating bases in Greenland.

Greenland's importance is best demonstrated by the fact that the United States undertook the defense of the island before it made a similar agreement for Iceland. Greenland's coastal defense was the responsibility of the U.S. Coast Guard (q.v.), whose offshore patrols continued well into the postwar period. U.S. Army Air Force survey teams selected air base locations and the island became a familiar area of operations for both American, Danish, and German weather teams throughout the war. More significantly, Greenland retained its importance to the United States well into the Cold War period, providing forward defense radar sites and strategic bomber staging bases well into the late 1980s.

Carl O. Schuster

Additional Reading
Balchen, Bernt, et al., *War Below Zero* (1944).
Howarth, David, *The Sledge Patrol* (1957).
Willoughby, Malcolm F., *The U.S. Coast Guard in World War II* (1989).

Greer Incident

In September 1941, the United States moved a step closer to open hostilities with Germany when the American destroyer USS *Greer* narrowly avoided being torpedoed by a German submarine. The *Greer* was on mail duty in the North Atlantic southwest of Iceland on the morning of 4 September when a British patrol bomber warned of the presence of a submerged U-boat some ten miles ahead. In the subsequent nine-hour action, the *Greer,* acting on orders forbidding attack, doggedly tracked the U-boat and reported its position to the British aircraft, which ineffectually dropped a spread of depth charges. Uncertain of the nationality of his pursuer, the *U-652's* commander turned on the destroyer and fired two torpedoes, both of which missed. The *Greer* unsuccessfully depth-charged the U-boat before breaking off action.

In his account of the incident to a national radio audience, President Franklin D. Roosevelt (q.v.) selectively omitted some key facts to create the impression that the *Greer* was the innocent victim of Nazi "piracy." Hoping to capitalize on the incident in order to turn public opinion toward more direct aid for beleaguered Britain, Roosevelt denounced the U-boats as "rattlesnakes of the seas," and announced that the U.S. Navy now had orders to "shoot on sight." Roosevelt's account of the incident was a blatant pretense, though one that he felt necessary to implement policies that would assure Britain's survival and the ultimate security of the United States. Almost immediately, the *Greer* incident brought about an offer of naval protection for any ship desirous of sheltering in American convoys headed to Iceland. Ultimately, it moved the United States closer to outright conflict with Germany.

Blaine T. Browne

Additional Reading
Langer, William, and S.E. Gleason, *The Undeclared War* (1952).
Wiltz, John, *From Isolation to War, 1931–1941* (1969).

H

Holocaust

The Holocaust, as a historical event, refers to the systematic extermination of approximately six million European Jews and at least 250,000 Sinti and Roma Gypsies by the National Socialist state during World War II and to the annihilation of Eastern European Jewish life. Derived from the Greek word *holokauston,* which refers to a sacrifice by fire, this connotation came into use in the late 1950s. Previously, it had meant, in English, any great destruction or a mass slaughter of human beings.

Initially, the Germans referred to the Holocaust as the *Ausrottung der Juden,* the removal of the Jews, and later to the annihilation as the *Endlösung der Judenfrage,* or "Final Solution" (q.v.). The actual methods of extermination of persons, defined racially as Jews and Gypsies, included shooting, beating, starvation, gassing, or other forms of torture and brutality. This was carried out by the Germans, their Axis allies and *Volksdeutsche,* ethnic Germans, or other persons under German command in occupied countries.

Since 1940, *Shoah,* a Hebrew word meaning devastation or great catastrophe, has often been chosen to emphasize the uniqueness of the event for Jews. The Hebrew word *Hurban,* which traditionally refers to the destruction of the Temple, was used during the war and still appears occasionally in reference to the Jewish genocide.

"Holocaust" also refers to an American novel of that name by Gerald Green and to a television miniseries by the same title. NBC broadcast this story of the fate of a German-Jewish family, a nine-and-one-half-hour dramatization, on American television in April 1978. The following year, it also was viewed in West Germany where a record number of viewers tuned in.

The Gypsies and Jews of Europe were the only groups targeted for total annihilation by the National Socialists. Their extermination was based on a policy of racial and biological definition. Although Jews were less than 1 percent of the prewar German population of 65 million and widely assimilated, from the very beginning of the Third *Reich,* they were singled out by the Nazis for persecution.

Jews had been a part of German culture since the early Middle Ages. The language of the *Shtetl,* of small-town Jewish culture in Eastern Europe, was Yiddish, which is based on Rhenish dialects. Emancipation of the Jews began in Prussia in 1781, and the democratic constitution of the Weimar Republic (q.v.) recognized equal status for Germans of Jewish faith before the law.

German Jews considered Germany their *Vaterland,* their *Heimatland* or homeland. They felt they were, as Germans of Jewish faith, not unlike Germans of Christian faith, and they believed that they were accepted members of the democratic state. This faith was reinforced by the record of Jewish battlefield heroism in World War I. But while their coexistence in Germany seemed harmonious, they were, of course, tragically deceived. The so-called "Jewish Question" became the driving factor of the Third *Reich.*

Though there are differences in the way the policies were arrived at and carried out, the 700,000 Gypsies in Europe suffered the same fate as Jews in the Third *Reich.* Gypsies are a people who left northern India, for reasons unknown, about 2,000 years ago, reaching German-speaking areas by the fifteenth century. Nomadic by tradition, they are descendents of an early Indo-Germanic people, whom Nazi theorists called the "Aryan Race." Like German, the Romani language is Indo-European.

Unlike Jews in Germany, Gypsies were generally not assimilated and rarely were citizens of any European country. Those who owned property often escaped deportation. Early persecution generally came on account of supposed "antisocial" behavior, not race. However, like Jews, they were measured and studied by racist scholars who found them an alien, inferior race and a threat to public health. To rationalize the loss of "Aryan status," they argued that Gypsies had descended from low castes and were of mixed blood. Once Nazi theorists concluded they were not truly Aryan, the policy became a racial "Final Solution of the Gypsy Problem."

Some sources also include the 200,000 patients suffering from mental or congenital diseases killed in the euthanasia program in Germany. After 1 September 1941, the euthanasia program was officially halted in response to public protest, although in the occupied areas, the Germans continued to kill mental patients. Several hundred Jehovah's Witnesses were persecuted for their religious beliefs. Thousands of homosexuals and other "asocials" were persecuted in the *Reich*. However, the Germans applied the policies in these cases less systematically than with Jews and Gypsies.

The Holocaust is only one of many genocides perpetrated by one group against another in the twentieth century. In 1933, the term was invented by Raphael Lemkin, a Jewish jurist, to describe the murder of a people for ethnic, racial, or religious reasons, or actions taken to destroy a national language and culture through random killings or other measures of oppression. The German murder and mistreatment of Poles and other Slavs was genocide, but it should not be understood as the Holocaust. The fate of persons identified as Jews and Gypsies was quite different.

While Poles and other Slavs were victims of the Third *Reich,* the German policy was one of brutal subjugation, not of total, systematic annihilation. Nazi theorists recognized Slavs as Aryan, though of a lower class. The intent was to eliminate Polish nationhood and enslave the population. About 2.5 million Poles were sent to the *Reich* as slave laborers. After the Warsaw Rising (q.v.) in 1944, the city was evacuated and thousands of Poles were sent to concentration camps (q.v.). Collective punishment and retaliation were common.

Several hundred Christian Poles died in the gas chambers of Auschwitz and tens of thousands of Poles and other Slavs lost their lives for underground activities or minor infractions of occupation laws. Soviet prisoners of war suffered horrible conditions in German captivity. Of the 3.3 million captured by the Germans, only 57.5 percent sur-

vived. Of 16,000 interned at Auschwitz, only ninety-six survived.

The Holocaust is the most documented event in human history. When the Jewish historian Simon Dubnov was shot in the Riga Ghetto, his last words were: "Write and record!" An amazing number of diaries and records were preserved, including hidden records from the crematoria workers in Auschwitz, the chronicle of the Lodz Ghetto, and the largest archival project known as the *Oneg Shabbat* in the Warsaw Ghetto. There are also hundreds of memoirs, records of testimony, *Yizkor* remembrance books, films, and oral histories from Jewish victims and from Nazi perpetrators. Comparatively little is available about the Gypsy experience.

The Holocaust began on 30 January 1933 when President Paul von Hindenburg appointed Adolf Hitler (qq.v.) chancellor of the German *Reich.* It came to its tragic end twelve years later with the Allied defeat of Germany on 8 May 1945. Anti-Semitism (q.v.) was part of the basic foundation of the rise of National Socialism (q.v.). Although many Germans who voted for Hitler may have made their choice for other reasons, they nevertheless voted, fully aware of the anti-Semitic nature of the National Socialist Party.

In 1919, Hitler expressed the central themes of his racial philosophy against the Jews. He wrote: ". . . the Jews are definitely a race and not a religious community . . . a Jew who happens to live among us and is thereby compelled to use the German language cannot be called a German. . . . Even the Mosaic faith, however important for the maintenance of this race, cannot be considered as absolutely decisive in the question of whether or not someone is a Jew." The party program, adopted in Munich in 1920, provided the basis for the Nazi state to eliminate Jews after the takeover of power.

Immediately after the seizure of power, political repression began against the Communists, socialists, trade unionists, and other opponents of the Nazis. The first concentration camp was opened at Dachau for political prisoners shortly after the *Reichstag* fire (q.v.). Jews suffered increasing humiliation and harassment as efforts grew to drive them from all aspects of daily life. The first public show of discrimination came on 1 April 1933 with a one-day boycott of Jewish businesses.

One week later, non-Aryan civil servants were pensioned, with the exception of war veterans. Signs appeared on park benches and public beaches announcing "No Jews." Then, the government announced a quota for Jewish students at

German universities. "Non-Aryan" Germans gradually found their lives more and more under totalitarian control. They began to hesitate to share their views of the new government, even with family and friends, for fear of the *Gestapo* (q.v.).

After von Hindenburg's death in the summer of 1934, the process of *Gleichschaltung* (q.v.), of bringing every facet of public and private life under the control of the Nazi Party, intensified. Non-Aryans grew more and more isolated. On 15 September 1935, the Nuremberg Laws (q.v.) were announced, depriving Jews and Gypsies of their citizenship. Based on racial ideology, baptized Jews were not exempted. Obviously aware of world disapproval at the persecution of the Jews, Germany eased the outward signs during the 1936 Olympic Games in Berlin.

Indicative of Germany's descent into criminality, Buchenwald was opened in July 1937, within sight of the city of Weimar, long a symbol of German cultural greatness and democracy. In 1938, anti-Gypsy laws appeared. Many of the 215,000 Jews who remained in the *Reich* were desperately trying to find a haven, to flee Germany, but often they could not find any country willing to accept them. Others hesitated to leave for business or personal reasons.

In July, delegates from thirty-two nations met in Geneva for the Evian Conference to discuss the Jewish refugee situation, with little concrete outcome. The U.S. State Department made it clear at the onset that it had little sympathy for increasing immigration quotas. The British would not consider allowing more Jews to enter Palestine. After 5 October, Jewish passports were stamped "J." In the wake of *Kristallnacht* (q.v.), efforts to emigrate grew more desperate, but it was too late for the vast majority.

The annexation of Austria, the occupation of Bohemia and Moravia in 1938, and the invasion of Poland on 1 September 1939, brought more Jews into German hands. It was clear at the onset that the goal was not just *Lebensraum* (q.v.). It was an ideological war against the Jews, and an opportunity to gain economically from their exploitation. During the invasion, in Poland's western regions, Jews were robbed, humiliated, savagely beaten, and randomly executed by *Einsatzgruppen* (q.v.) with support from the German Army.

To facilitate their plans for the Jews, the Germans established the first of their ghettos at Piotrkow on 28 October 1939. Jews throughout Poland were evacuated and concentrated near railways. The Germans chose a *Judenrat* (Jewish Council) and its head, the *Älteste der Juden*, to facilitate and implement their orders. Ghetto police later assisted in *Aktionen* (roundups). Jews were thus forced to participate in their own deportation and annihilation. The Łódź Ghetto was enclosed on 30 April 1940, and the Warsaw Ghetto was walled closed in November.

Ghetto conditions were devastating. Thousands died of starvation, typhus, and other illnesses brought on by the unsanitary conditions and terrible overcrowding. SS troops intimidated and shot Jews for smuggling or for no reason at all. And yet the desire to live remained fierce. Ghettos developed their own city administrations and services. Many opened schools and had an active cultural life. Yitskhok Rudaschevski, barely sixteen when he perished at Ponary, wrote in his diary: "I often reflect, this is supposedly the ghetto, yet I have such a rich life of intellectual work: I study, I read, I visit club circles."

Young Jews were sent to *Arbeitslager* (work camps) or on forced labor outside the ghetto. In some places, Jews were sent to transit camps. Village Jews were concentrated in ghettos in larger cities. On 30 January 1940, the decision came to expel 30,000 Gypsies from Germany into the Government General of Poland (q.v.). On 12 February 1940, the first German Jews were taken into "protective custody" and then deported by train to Poland.

Then, the German Army invaded Denmark, Norway, Holland, Belgium, and France, bringing even more Jews and Gypsies into danger. Though Christians had lived together with their Jewish neighbors for hundreds of years and had become economically interdependent, few reached out a helping hand, with exceptions such as in Bulgaria and Denmark. German opposition and underground movements in Eastern Europe contributed little to saving Jewish lives. Some partisan groups were openly anti-Semitic.

Though Hitler had suggested gassing 12,000 to 15,000 Jews in *Mein Kampf*, it is likely the actual decision for a "Final Solution" was formulated a few months before the invasion of Russia as alternatives to "solve the Jewish problem" became unlikely. On 22 June 1941, the German Army invaded the Soviet Union and the Baltic states, areas with a population of more than five million Jews. The *Einsatzgruppen* killed, usually by shooting, over one and a half million Jews and Gypsies, including those deported from Western Europe, the Polish ghettos, and former Soviet-held regions in killing fields like Babi Yar (q.v.) and Ponary.

Heinrich Himmler (q.v.) grew concerned at the effect this was having on the perpetrators and

H

he sought more orderly, efficient methods. The SS turned to gas vans in September 1941, but this method was also found to be inefficient. Borrowing personnel and techniques from the euthanasia program, they used carbon monoxide gas at Belzec, Sobibor, and Treblinka. *Zyklon B* (q.v.) gas was employed at Auschwitz-Birkenau.

On 23 July 1942, Adam Czerniakow, head of the *Judenrat* in Warsaw, committed suicide when ordered to participate in mass deportation. Jewish resistance grew in the Warsaw Ghetto as witnesses confirmed that the deportations to Treblinka meant death. On 19 April 1943, armed Jewish resistance met SS troops when they entered the ghetto.

Three weeks later, as troops surrounded his command post, Mordecai Anielewicz (q.v.), wrote proudly in his final hours: "Jewish self-defense has become a fact. Jewish resistance and revenge have become actualities." A few survivors escaped to form armed partisan groups. There were also uprisings in Treblinka, Sobibor, and Auschwitz, and in ghettos, including Byailstok and Czestochowa.

In 1943, Shmuel Zygelboim, a Jewish socialist, committed suicide in London. In his final note, after blaming the Germans for the massacres of Jews, he added: "but indirectly this responsibility lies with all mankind—the Allied nations and governments who have not made any effort toward concrete action to halt the crime. . . ." Halting the Final Solution was not a major aim of Allied forces. On 10 June 1943, Josef Goebbels (q.v.) triumphantly declared Berlin *Judenrein* ("clean of Jews").

The Nazis were hurrying to finish the job. There was a constant conflict between the need for workers versus their fervent desire to kill Jews. Jews in the Łódź Ghetto were deported to Auschwitz in August 1943. Though the military was in great need of troops, Sinti Gypsies serving in the German Army were demobilized and sent to death camps. Trains, which were needed for supplies to the front lines, were diverted to deport Jews. They brought more than 400,000 Hungarian Jews to Auschwitz-Birkenau in May 1944. Himmler waited until 2 August 1944 to liquidate the Gypsy camp at Birkenau. The last Jews were deported from Berlin on 5 January 1945 to Auschwitz and on 27 March to Theresienstadt.

As the war began to turn against Germany, the SS and officials in Berlin realized they might be culpable for their crimes. In 1942, they began *Aktion 1005,* digging up mass graves in Poland and cremating the bodies. The Soviets held the first war crimes trial in July 1943, in Krasnodar, against members of *Einsatzgruppe D.* In October, Himm-

ler spoke to SS officers, explaining the "extermination of the Jews" would be "an unwritten and never to be written page of glory in our history." Hastily, the Germans began destroying records and evidence of the Final Solution.

In July 1944, Majdanek was liberated and the SS began destroying and evacuating the remaining camps as the Allies approached. One-third of the inmates died on death marches back into Germany. The SS also killed many prisoners to prevent them living to be witnesses to the crimes, but they did not always have time; 300,000 inmates lived to see the liberation, though many were in very weakened physical condition.

Allied troops were not prepared for the horrors they found. U.S. Army captain Pletcher, whose division liberated a satellite camp of Mauthausen, recalled: "I doubt if any of us who saw it will ever forget it—the smell, the hundreds of bodies that looked like caricatures of human beings, the frenzy of the thousands when they knew Americans had arrived at last . . ." More than one million survivors came out of hiding and from the forests or survived using false identities or in "protected circumstances."

The Holocaust resulted in the deaths of two-thirds of European Jews. One-third of the world population of those of Jewish faith were exterminated. Ninety percent of the Polish Jews perished.

The majority of the survivors sought refuge in the Soviet Union. The *She'erit ha-Peletah* (survivors) often had no home to return to. They waited in displaced persons camps, recovering their health, searching for family, and hoping to leave Europe. Only about 12 percent of German Gypsies survived. As many as one-third of the world's Gypsies perished in the Holocaust.

While many perpetrators and bystanders want to forget, to deny "the truth of Auschwitz," West German President Richard von Weizsäcker stated, in 1978, on the fortieth anniversary of the *Reichskristallnacht:* "The truth is that all this nevertheless came to pass before the very eyes of a large number of German citizens . . . and that another large number of them gained direct knowledge of the events. The truth is that most people, faint of heart, kept their silence." Of course, the same could be said about many in the occupied countries.

The Holocaust brought to an end the rich traditions of Jews in central and Eastern Europe. Yitzhak Katzelnelson, a Yiddish poet who perished at Auschwitz, wrote in his "Song of the Murdered Jewish People": "Woe unto me, nobody is left . . . There was a people and it is no more. There was a people and it is . . . Gone . . ." After anti-Semites killed forty-two Jewish survivors in Kielce in 1946, 100,000 left Poland, mostly for the United States and Palestine. Today, only about 5,000 to 6,000 Jews remain in Poland and about 40,000 persons of the Jewish faith live in Germany.

In the 1970s, Holocaust deniers began to appear under the guise of scholarly debate. In 1985, Mel Mermelstein, a survivor, won a case against William Carto's Institute for Historical Review, publisher of the *Journal of Historical Review*, which claims the Holocaust never happened. Judge Thomas T. Johnson at Los Angeles Superior Court took judicial notice that "Jews were gassed to death at the Auschwitz Concentration Camp in Poland during the Summer of 1944 . . . it is not reasonably subject to dispute . . . it is simply a fact."

However, the 1980s have seen some German historians like Ernst Nolte open debate on the issue of German guilt. They rationalize and justify support for National Socialism, arguing that Communism in the Soviet Union was the real evil. The Germans were only following the models established by Stalin. Nazism came as a result of a crisis in liberal democracy and may have been the only alternative Germany had. Some even claim that Chaim Weizmann's 1939 statement—that Palestinian Jews would stand by the Allies—justifies Hitler's viewing Jews in Germany as enemies.

The uniqueness of the Holocaust and the great loss of civilian life in World War II have challenged the faith in technological and scientific progress and the religious beliefs of all postwar generations. Elie Wiesel, survivor of Auschwitz, wrote in his memoir *Night:* "Never shall I forget those flames which consumed my faith forever. Never shall I forget that nocturnal silence which deprived me, for all eternity, of the desire to live." In 1949, the United Nations recognized genocide as an international crime against humanity.

In 1957, Israel opened Yad Vashem, a Holocaust memorial commemorating the six million Jewish dead and the non-Jewish "Righteous Among Nations" who risked their lives to save others. West Germany paid reparations to Israel from 1953 to 1965 for Jewish property losses and continues to pay restitution to Jewish survivors, but Gypsies have received none. In 1979, the U.S. Congress established "Days of Remembrance for Victims of the Holocaust," as a time each year for the nation "to reflect upon the horror of the Holocaust." The U.S. Holocaust Memorial Museum opened on the Mall in Washington, D.C., in the spring of 1993.

Susan Pentlin

Additional Reading

Dawidowicz, Lucy, *The War Against the Jews, 1933–1945* (1975).

Hilberg, Raul, *The Destruction of the European Jews* (1961).

Gilbert, Martin, *The Holocaust: A History of the Jews of Europe During the Second World War* (1985).

Gutman, Yisrael, and Shmuel Krakowski, *Unequal Victims: Poles and Jews During World War II* (1986).

Yahil, Leni, *The Holocaust: The Fate of European Jewry* (1990).

H

Home Front

Since few people in America opposed the war after Pearl Harbor, World War II for the civilian front was perceived as a clear-cut case of good versus evil. Almost no American questioned the need or righteousness of the war. Most people viewed it as a conflict between lightness and darkness, or as a "crusade to save Christendom and Christianity from the Axis power of paganism."

The press, Hollywood, and the government put out the popular view of the war; Adolf Hitler, along with his aggressive allies Italy and Japan, used treachery and surprise in their brutal conquest, but the ultimate goal was to conquer the United States. In contrast, the United States was fighting the war for "the right of all people to live in freedom, decency, and security." Later came the Four Freedoms (q.v.) of President Franklin D. Roosevelt; freedom of speech, freedom of worship, freedom from fear, and freedom from want. As one newspaper put it, "Never in our history have issues been so clear."

Even though there had been another war twenty-five years earlier, Americans came into World War II with a wide-eyed sense of credulity. They believed what they read in the papers. When after Pearl Harbor some of the more sensational papers were reporting the imminence of a Japanese invasion, youth from the San Francisco area would arm themselves with .22 rifles and BB guns, take a packed lunch and go down to the shore to await the invaders. Men showed a great desire to join up. In Studs Terkel's oral history of the war, one narrator tells of a short friend who went to bed for a week, stretching himself to meet the minimum height requirement for induction.

The relentlessly upbeat and patriotic tone of movies was matched by a wave of patriotic warlike songs such as *Praise the Lord and Pass the Ammunition,* and songs specifically aimed at the Japanese after Pearl Harbor: *Good-bye, Mama, I'm Off to*

The Aldwych underground station in London during the Blitz, 8 October 1940. (IWM HU 44272)

Yokohama; We Are the Sons of the Rising Guns; Oh, You Little Son of an Oriental; To Be Specific, It's Our Pacific; The Sun Will Soon Be Setting on the Land of the Rising Sun; and *Remember Pearl Harbor.* Then came the biggest hit, the largest record and sheet music seller in the nation, the country-western sounding *There's a Star-Spangled Banner Waving Somewhere:*

> There's a Star-Spangled Banner waving
>   somewhere
> In a distant land, so many miles away.
> Only Uncle Sam's great heroes get to go
>   there.
> Where I wish that I could also live someday.
> I'd see Lincoln, Custer, Washington, and
>   Perry
> And Nathan Hale and Colin Kelly too!
> There's a Star Spangled Banner waving
>   somewhere
> O'er the land of Heroes brave and true.

Stirred by such patriotic songs, Americans seemed willing to believe anything. In Los Angeles, fantastic rumors circulated that a whole Japanese infantry unit was secreted in Fish Harbor, near Terminal Island, in the garb of fishermen. In the 1920s and 1930s, a Japanese fishing community had flourished there, but the Japanese-Americans there, as elsewhere in the West, were brutally expelled from their homes and jobs and placed in so-called relocation centers.

Initially, General John L. DeWitt, who headed the West Coast Defense Command, opposed the arrest and detainment of American citizens of Japanese ancestry; just Japanese aliens should be affected. But, the ferocity of anti-Japanese sentiment on the West Coast became so intense that he changed his mind. Racism was not just limited to California, as this typical hate-filled statement by the governor of Idaho showed: ". . . a good solution to the Jap problem would be to send them all back to Japan; then sink the island. They live like rats, breed like rats, and act like rats."

California Attorney General Earl Warren (later Supreme Court chief justice) fully supported placing the Japanese in California in internment camps. He even went so far as to testify before a congressional committee against the Japanese: "The first generation born Italians and Germans in this country are no different from anybody else. When we deal with the Japanese, we are in an entirely different field . . . because of their method of living . . . If the Japs are released no one will be able to tell a saboteur from any other Jap." Such treatment was entirely unwarranted in fact.

The only significant West Coast spy ring existed in the Los Angeles consulate of the Japanese government. Naval intelligence and the FBI had already penetrated it months before, neutralizing any potential damage. So, while the Navy and FBI knew the truth, the removal and internment continued. President Roosevelt ordered it, the army carried it out, and Congress endorsed it. The one institution that should have realized the damage done to the nation's values, the Supreme Court, simply trailed along.

The Japanese were not the only Americans to suffer persecution in the heated patriotism of World War II. In 1940, the Supreme Court ruled, in *Minersville School District* vs. *Gobitis,* that students could be compelled to give the flag salute. That decision, made at a time when it looked like the United States would soon be in the war in Europe, led to mob violence across the country against Jehovah's Witnesses, who refused to recite the pledge for religious reasons. Neighbors beat them, sacked their homes, and burned their assembly halls. In Richwood, West Virginia, deputy sheriffs and members of the American Legion detained seven Jehovah's Witnesses, forced them to drink large amounts of castor oil, and then paraded them through town on a rope.

All told, the Justice Department received reports of more than 800 incidents of violence and harassment from 1940 to 1942, and schools across the nation expelled more than 2,000 Jehovah's Witness children. In 1943, in *West Virginia State Board of Education* vs. *Barnette,* the U.S. Supreme Court overturned the Minersville School District case.

The issue of racial prejudice in America during World War II was not just confined to the Japanese. At the beginning of the war, the U.S. military had little interest in recruiting black Americans (*see* Black Units in the U.S. Military). They could not enlist in the marines or air corps. The navy accepted blacks only for mess and serving work.

The army accepted them, but then segregated them. A War Department policy paper instructed: "The War Department is not to intermingle colored and white enlisted personnel in the same regimental organization." White officers commanded black combat units. Blacks who became officers were assigned only to black service units. Also, no black officer assigned to a black unit could outrank or command a white officer in the same unit. The "rationale" was the insistence of the army that African Americans had "proved" unsuccessful in combat during World War I because of "racial inferiority." Secretary of War Henry L. Stimson (q.v.) wrote in his diary in 1940, "Leadership is not imbedded in the Negro race yet." Another officer stated, "Colored units are inferior to the performance of white troops, except for service duties." In 1941, General George C. Marshall (q.v.) said any attempt to desegregate the army would cripple morale and hinder the war effort. General Dwight D. Eisenhower (q.v.) referred to black soldiers as "my darkies." Ironically, while the armed forces remained strictly segregated, President Roosevelt in 1941 issued an executive order prohibiting discrimination in defense industries.

Most black Americans deeply resented the practices of the army. Probably one of the most resented practices was the army's segregation and labeling of blood plasma according to race. But during World War II, the draft greatly increased the number of black soldiers, 200,000 in the army by 1944. It was evident there was a great waste of manpower under the old practices, so gradually some changes occurred. After James V. Forrestal (q.v.) became secretary of the navy, integration proceeded rapidly, with blacks serving as seamen, radiomen, and gunners on twenty-five integrated ships. For the army, integration was often ordered, but not implemented—certainly not in the South.

The disruption and dislocation of the war created racial incidents large and small from Vallejo, California, to Detroit, Michigan. A Vallejo *News Chronicle* headline of 28 December 1942 that even edged out war news proclaimed: "NEGRO SAILORS CONFINED TO QUARTERS IN RIOT AFTERMATH." One eyewitness, however, said that what he had seen was not a riot incited by blacks, but an unprovoked attack by armed white servicemen. Following closely on earlier conflicts in Mobile, Alabama, and Beaumont, Texas, the Detroit race riot of 1943 claimed thirty-four lives.

The most famous clash involving Mexican Americans, the so-called "zoot-suit riot," took place in June of 1943 in Los Angeles, where many Mexican American youths joined "Pachuco" gangs and adopted the "zoot suit" as their distinctive dress. The ensemble consisted of a broad felt hat, long key chain with pocket knife, trousers that were flared at the knees and tapered at the ankles, and a long "ducktail" haircut. Trouble started when sailors from the Chavez Ravine Naval Base went into the Mexican American sections of Los Angeles, supposedly to revenge servicemen attacked by "zooters." They looked for anybody wearing a zoot suit. They then grabbed them, proceeded to remove the suit, tear it up or burn it, and then trim the ducktail haircut.

Police did little to stop this violence, which caused Los Angeles to be declared off-limits for a time to naval personnel. Much of this violence was

H

attributed to racial unrest stirred up by Axis enemy agents in order to disrupt production. That was nonsense, of course.

World War II changed many social and sexual attitudes on the home front. To begin with, many American communities became concerned about the "girls who hang about the streets, dance halls, and taverns," and the so-called victory girls and cuddle bunnies who suddenly appeared around army and navy bases. Many feared the rising tide of promiscuity from a moral viewpoint, but a greater fear came from venereal diseases infecting the men of the armed forces, posing a threat to the war effort.

Most localities tried to shut down brothels located near military bases. The May Act of 1944 specifically authorized such action. The few advocates of legal prostitution maintained that close medical supervision would be a better method of handling the spread of venereal diseases. But they lost out to moral reformers who advocated "blitzing the brothels," which they did in 1944, closing some 700 red-light areas. After all, who could stand up to the accusation that brothels furthered gonorrhea and syphilis, decimating our troops like "enemy agents within our midst." Ironically, the rate of infection from venereal diseases was higher among servicemen stationed in the United States than among those overseas.

During the war, the public's reaction to venereal disease changed dramatically. Here the U.S. Army did much to break down the old "taboos" about syphilis and gonorrhea that had made them virtually unmentionable. The subject became quite mentionable because the army instructed all soldiers in the use of prophylaxis. Of course it shocked some people who thought soldiers should solve the problem by practicing "continence," i.e., self-restraint.

Boxing great Gene Tunney wrote an article called "The Bright Shield of Continence," arguing that "sexual indulgence" was not necessary, and in fact weakens the soldier, because any boxer knew continence kept a man "at the peak of physical force." Tunney later expressed doubts, saying "Men don't get medals for practicing it."

The army took the realistic view that many would inevitably expose themselves to infection. Since one could not know ahead of time who these soldiers might be, all soldiers received instruction in the use of prophylaxis and condoms. Various people, including the unit's medical officer, and even chaplains, performed this duty. To withhold the information, the army contended, would cause many soldiers to be infected and would be equivalent to depriving them of a smallpox vaccination.

The war years unleashed dramatic economic changes as well, the first blossoming of prosperity after the long winter of the Depression. On the eve of Pearl Harbor, 10 million people still faced unemployment despite the New Deal. Almost overnight, the war converted the United States into a mammoth, twenty-four-hour-a-day defense plant with abundant jobs. About 20 million people left farms and small towns to seek work in places like San Diego, which doubled its population in three years.

The war created a social melting pot with country people coming into contact with people they had never encountered before—blacks, Hispanics, Jews, and Catholics. Millions of women poured into the defense industry. They would later credit the war with liberating them from domestic frustration. For many women in defense work, "Rosie the Riveter" was the beginning of their emancipation. "I found out that I could do something with my hands besides bake a pie," said one woman.

Though paid less than men for the same work, 80 percent of the women surveyed by the U.S. Labor Department in 1944 said they wanted to keep their jobs after the war. Most of them were dismissed and sent home "where they naturally belonged." For many women, the war meant opportunities for financial independence and even sexual opportunity. Yet, for other women it was a protracted nightmare. Marjorie Cartwright remembers her desolation: "I lived alone for four years during the war, and they were the most painful, lonely years I think I will ever spend." The GIs came home to a nation that was immeasurably different, including marital tension created by long separation. Just as the 1941 marriage rate was the highest in history, the 1946 divorce rate, the byproduct of a passionate relationship and hasty marriage born out of loneliness and fear, was equally high.

For the first time in the history of the United States, women were permitted to serve as volunteers in the armed forces. By war's end, some 216,000 served in the women's auxiliaries of the army, navy, and marines. Initially, though, some conservative commentators eyed women in uniform with suspicion: "Take the women into the armed services and who will then do the cooking, the washing, the mending, the hundred homey tasks to which every women has devoted herself? Think of the humiliation! What has become of the manhood of America?"

Once in uniform, rumor and speculation about sexual activity in the female army ran rampant, especially during the spring of 1943. John Costello wrote that "from New York it was rumored that ship loads of pregnant WAACs [Woman's Army Auxiliary Corps] (q.v.) were being sent back from Britain and North Africa under armed guard to prevent them jumping overboard rather than disgracing their families."

At Camp Lee, Virginia, soldiers believed anyone seen dating a WAAC had to report for medical attention. Despite such misunderstandings, the war did in fact set the stage for the changes in attitude toward the roles of men and women in society that appeared in the postwar years.

Rationing was a part of home front life. Most Americans found themselves limited to three gallons of gasoline a week with an imposed 35 mph speed limit. Meats, fats, oils, tires, liquor, canned fruits and vegetables, oil stoves, and fuel oil were all rationed. But compared to the home fronts of Britain and Germany, Americans suffered little deprivation. In fact, the very austere British rationing shocked American sensibilities. The British, under constant U-Boat attack, took extreme measures in conserving foodstuffs. British adults were rationed to four ounces of meat, two ounces of cheese, two ounces of butter, and one fresh egg per week. Sugar, sweets, and preserves were rationed up until the coronation of Queen Elizabeth II in 1953. The Ministry of Food in Britain supplied a recipe for "oatmeal sausages"; only two ounces of meat, four ounces of oatmeal, some cooking fat and bread crumbs. Made into sausages, this recipe was supposed to feed four people.

The impact of American servicemen on the British home front can best be gauged by noting that in November 1990, the U.S. government agreed to release thousands of pages of information on the whereabouts of Americans stationed in Britain during World War II to a group of British subjects. They believe the men may be their long-lost biological fathers—the final legacy of the British lament, "Oversexed, Overpaid, and Over here."

In Germany and the Soviet Union, the home front was a battle front, thus making the insulated United States home front unique among the major combatants of World War II. To keep all Americans at home intensely involved in the war effort, the government established grease, can, and scrap iron drives—contrived efforts to fire patriotism, rather than real contributions to war production. Overall, the attitude and mood of the home front in the United States can best be described as warlike and patriotic, and out of harm's way. But those who tended the home front had, if unknowingly, helped to change it for those who were to return from war in the Pacific and Europe.

Richard A. Voeltz

Additional Reading

Blum, John Morton, *V Was for Victory* (1976).

Calder, Agnus, *The People's War, Britain 1939–45* (1969).

Charman, Terry, *The German Home Front, 1939–45* (1989).

Costello, John, *Virtue Under Fire, How World War II Changed Our Social and Sexual Attitudes* (1985).

Grunberger, Richard, *The 12–Year Reich, A Social History of Nazi Germany, 1933–1945* (1971).

Harris, Mark J., Franklin D. Mitchell, and Steven J. Schecter, *The Home Front: America During World War II* (1984).

Lingeman, Richard R., *Don't You Know There's a War On? The American Home Front, 1941–1945* (1970).

Terkel, Studs, *The Good War, An Oral History of World War Two* (1984).

Woll, Peter, *American Government: Readings and Cases* (1990).

Hossbach Protocol

At the International Military Tribunal (q.v.) in Nuremberg, the Hossbach Protocol was a prime prosecution document in establishing the charge against the German government of conspiracy to commit crimes against peace. The Hossbach Protocol was the minutes of a meeting, which, in the opinion of the court, proved that German war preparations had already started by 5 November 1937.

The conference took place in the *Reich* Chancellery in Berlin. In attendance were Adolf Hitler, Minister of Foreign Affairs Konstantin von Neurath, Minister of War Werner von Blomberg, the commanders in chief of the army, air force, and navy, Werner von Fritsch, Hermann Göring, and Erich Raeder, respectively, and Colonel Friedrich Hossbach (qq.v.), Hitler's military adjutant. Hossbach wrote the minutes that carried his name a few days later from notes he made at the time.

The main reason for this conference with Hitler was that in the beginning of 1937, the armament situation in the *Wehrmacht,* especially concerning raw material, became so critical that the three service chiefs were concerned about the further rapid buildup of their forces. They had differences concerning the allocations of raw materials, thus, von Blomberg arranged the meeting so that Hitler himself could set the priorities.

For Hitler the matter was not of top importance. He started the meeting talking about politics, presenting his ideas and experiences from his last four-and-a-half years in power. In the beginning of his detailed explanations, he expressed his opinion concerning the existing lack of *Lebensraum* (q.v.) for the German people. This, he felt, would prevent the growth of the German people and lead to a stagnation that would cause social conflicts. The possibility of preventing this consisted in gaining land that was agriculturally useful and in direct proximity to the *Reich*. Hitler admitted that this solution meant force and was not without risk.

Hitler saw the problem coming to a head between 1943 and 1945. He hoped, however, that even before 1943, the tensions among the other European nations would make it possible for him to attempt the annexation of Czechoslovakia. He was convinced that Britain and France had written off that country and would not risk a long European war because of it. The basis of his ideas concerning the time phasing was the ongoing rearmament of the *Wehrmacht* giving him the military-technological lead in Europe for the years to come.

The military leaders did not agree. Von Blomberg and von Fritsch warned him not to turn France and Britain into adversaries at the same time, but Hitler rejected their apprehensions. The main points of the meeting were that Hitler had made it clear he wanted to solve the German "space question" at the beginning of the 1940s, that he therefore needed a *Wehrmacht* ready to march, and that, for that reason, he put the generals under pressure with his political agenda.

Looking at that meeting from its intended purpose, it is difficult to say that a conspiracy was born there against world peace. There were no decisions made, no orders given. Hitler only used his psychological influence on the military chiefs. The real effect of the document was that the International Military Court in Nuremberg used it, among others, to support its judgments against von Neurath, Göring, and Raeder and to convict them of crimes against peace.

Ekkhart Guth

Additional Reading

Hossbach, Friedrich, *Zwischen Wehrmacht und Hitler* (1949).

Kluge, D., *Das Hossbach—"Protokoll"* (1980).

I

Intelligence and National Policy

Recent scholarship has highlighted the importance of intelligence and perception in decision making in World War II. Often, certainly in the first few years of the conflict, this was more important in deciding the fortunes of war than nations' industrial capacities and the quality of their fighting forces. Thus there was a critical difference between intelligence and policy making in Nazi Germany, the Soviet Union, Great Britain, and the United States.

Nazi Germany had an immense hunger for intelligence of all kinds. It perceived potential enemies everywhere, not only among foreign powers, but also at home. Hence the possession of intelligence bestowed power and prestige on government departments, which in turn could lead to greater access to resources for the departments concerned.

Fierce competition among the numerous intelligence-gathering organizations occurred in the Third *Reich,* from the RSHA to the *Abwehr* (qq.v.). On the one hand, this competition was good, because it promoted professionalism. But it also resulted in Nazi leaders being swamped with vast amounts of information; information that was often useless because it was not properly organized or analyzed. This was because intelligence in the Third *Reich* became a commodity; it was no longer a means to uncover the truth, but a device for gaining power.

Hitler preferred the competitive structure, however. It meant that no one organization could achieve dominance in intelligence, a potentially serious threat to his own power. Also, because such a large quantity of raw information reached him, he could choose to regard only that which best supported his own dogmatic opinions. Thus intelligence had little input on policy making in the Third *Reich,* though it did usually shape the implementa-

tion of decisions. For example, military intelligence largely decided the timing and direction of the attack on Poland in 1939, but it had no say in the decision to invade, which was Hitler's prerogative.

The German system worked well in the early war years, when Hitler's shrewd guesses about the enemy's power were backed up by competent tactical and operational intelligence. In 1941, however, the German intelligence community's lack of knowledge of the United States and the Soviet Union led to both policy making and its implementation being based on Hitler's opinions, with ultimately catastrophic consequences. This trend grew worse as the war continued and Hitler became increasingly dominant within the German state.

A central paradox in Soviet history is that despite having very large and usually highly effective intelligence organs, such as the NKVD (q.v.), the Soviet Union was caught almost completely by surprise by Nazi Germany's attack on 22 June 1941.

The initial invasion was compared to a moderate nuclear strike in its effects, and the campaign as a whole came close to annihilating the Soviet Union. While the Soviet leadership received ample indicators of the impending attack from numerous sources, it chose to disregard them, and made no additional defensive preparations that might have mitigated the impact of the invasion. There were two main reasons for this.

The first was Josef Stalin's (q.v.) firmly held notion that war must be avoided at all costs, and his confidence in being able to achieve that. He feared provoking Hitler and believed that any new military undertakings on the Soviet western frontiers, even defensive ones, might precipitate a Nazi invasion. Stalin dismissed all intelligence concerning the upcoming attack as disinformation, attempts by his enemies to involve him prematurely in the war. And after the terrifying purges (q.v.) of 1937–1938, no one, especially in the military, was inclined to challenge him.

The second reason was the Soviet military's lack of understanding of German operational and tactical doctrine, and *Blitzkrieg* (q.v.) warfare in a wider sense. They believed only small countries could be affected by *Blitzkrieg,* and they stuck to World War I principles that held that in a war between major powers an interval would occur between frontier incursions by invading forces and the decisive battle of the campaign, as both sides needed time to deploy their main forces. These outdated notions caused frightful Soviet casualties in the opening weeks of Operation BARBAROSSA.

At no time, however, were the Soviet leaders under any illusions that their ultimate enemy would be other than Nazi Germany. They failed to understand the nature of that enemy, despite receiving a glut of information on the subject, until it was almost too late.

Great Britain had a long-established and for the most part well-organized system for the collection and analysis of intelligence. This included the secret and effective work of MI-5 and MI-6 (qq.v.), and the Government Code and Cypher School, which was responsible for breaking encoded messages sent by foreign governments.

In the 1930s, some problems appeared, most notably in the British government's understanding of the power structure in Nazi Germany, which ascribed too much influence to "moderates" who in reality did not exist. By 1939, this and other misapprehensions had largely disappeared, and intelligence reached decision makers more effectively due to the establishment of a unified government intelligence-evaluating body under Foreign Office auspices. By the beginning of 1940, with more Enigma (q.v.) decrypts being made and a solid network of Czech and Polish stay-behind agents in place, British intelligence was in good shape in Europe, and would remain so for the remainder of the war.

In the United States, a strong aversion to the Axis powers, especially Nazi Germany, went hand in hand with a long-standing desire to keep out of international politics. This produced a confused foreign policy in the 1937–1941 period. Intelligence organizations reflected this uncertainty and were in general underfunded and unsophisticated. In addition, senior policy makers tended to focus on American hemispheric defense needs, and the United States ability to meet them, rather than potential enemy intentions and capabilities.

Intelligence regarding Japan was an important exception and highly valued, although the famous MAGIC decrypts of Japanese signals were by no means comprehensive, as Pearl Harbor showed. The real U.S. intelligence failure at Pearl Harbor, the worst in U.S. history, was due mainly to a lack of a centralized evaluation system. After Pearl Harbor, these problems were less important, as the United States became fully committed to the defeat of the Axis.

David Walker

Additional Reading

Hinsley, F.H., et al., *British Intelligence in the Second World War: Its Influence on Strategy and Operations,* Vols. 1–5 (1979–1990).

Kahn, David, *Hitler's Spies: German Intelligence in World War II* (1978).

May, Ernest R. (ed.), *Knowing One's Enemies: Intelligence Assessment Before the Two World Wars* (1986).

International Military Tribunal

The International Military Tribunal was established shortly after the end of World War II in Europe to conduct a trial of major Nazi leaders on charges of territorial aggression and crimes committed against soldiers and civilians during the war and occupation of European countries. Allied leaders like U.S. Secretary of the Treasury Henry Morgenthau, Jr. (q.v.), Lord Chancellor Simon of Britain, and at times even Winston S. Churchill and Josef Stalin (qq.v.) had favored the summary execution of an unnamed number of Nazi military and political leaders. The U.S. government, however, under pressure from the State and War Departments and other government figures, became the foremost advocate of a trial court to avoid the charge that the victors merely exacted revenge from alleged culprits of a defeated enemy.

There was no precedent in history for the creation of the International Military Tribunal. Jurists representing the American, British, Soviet, and provisional French governments met at a conference in London between 26 June and 8 August 1945 and, after considerable dispute, hammered out the London Agreement. It included the Charter of the International Military Tribunal, which provided the legal basis for the tribunal and the trial procedures. Its principles and procedures reflected a compromise of the different governments but established procedures for the trial of the major war criminals that were largely Anglo-American in form rather than continental.

The jurists defined the categories of crimes to be tried by the tribunal, limited in advance the plea of superior orders, and set aside pleas of official position and impunity. Nineteen other countries subscribed to the IMT Charter. The trial itself, however, was conducted solely under judges and prosecutors of the four Allied Powers. Additional trials of lesser Nazi figures were held in Nuremberg, the occupied zones of Germany, and several countries in Europe, using many of the principles of the IMT but not acting directly under its auspices.

The origins of the IMT go back to the declarations and warnings issued by the Allies in the early years of the war. As early as October 1941, President Franklin D. Roosevelt (q.v.) condemned war crimes and Prime Minister Churchill asserted that retribution for war crimes would become one of the goals of the war. In January and again in April 1942, the Soviet Union issued similar pronouncements. In January 1942, nine governments-in-exile signed the Declaration of St. James' Palace relating to the punishment of war criminals, and further warnings were sounded by Roosevelt, Churchill, and Stalin.

More concrete steps toward the creation of the IMT were taken with the establishment of the United Nations Commission for the Investigation of War Crimes and the joint Moscow Declaration of October 1943 by the foreign ministers of the U.S., Britain, and the Soviet Union. The latter announced that German officers, soldiers, and Nazi Party members who were responsible for massacres would be punished for their offenses in the respective countries, or under the combined action of the governments of the Allies. It was not until June 1945, however, that a declaration by the four powers led to the London Conference that laid the foundation of the IMT.

A largely ceremonial first session of the IMT convened in Berlin on 18 October 1945, under the presidency of Major General I.I. Nikitchenko, the principal Soviet member of the bench.

Regular trial sessions of the court commenced in Nuremberg on 20 November 1945, and concluded on 1 October 1946 with the delivery of the elaborate judgment of the court. Lord Justice Geoffrey Lawrence of Britain served as the permanent president of the court and Mr. Justice William Norman Birkett as the British alternate. Francis Biddle (q.v.) and Judge John J. Parker were the U.S. member and alternate, respectively, on the bench. France was represented by Professor Donnedieu de Vabre and *Monsieur le Conseiller* Robert Falco; and the Soviet Union by Major General I.I.

Nikitchenko as regular member and Lieutenant Colonel A.F. Volchkov as alternate. The prosecutors were also drawn from each Allied country and were led by U.S. Supreme Court Justice Robert H. Jackson (q.v.); Sir Hartley Shawcross of Britain; François de Menthon and later Auguste Champetier de Ribes of France; and General R.A. Rudenko of the Soviet Union.

The formidable task of collecting, summarizing, and translating the documentary evidence, drawn from Nazi archives, affidavits, and interrogations, lay largely in the hands of the American Commission.

The indictment against the Nazi leaders comprised four counts:

1. a common plan or conspiracy to commit the crimes indicated in categories two, three, and four below;
2. crimes against peace, i.e., participation in the "planning, preparation, initiation, or waging of a war of aggression" in violation of international treaties and agreements;
3. war crimes, i.e., violations of the traditional laws of war including the mistreatment and murder of prisoners of war, civilians, deportations of slave labor, destruction not justified by military necessity;
4. crimes against humanity, i.e., enslavement, murder, extermination, and genocide based on ideological and racial grounds.

The major defendants at Nuremberg represented a cross-section of German politicians, military leaders, administrators, and propagandists. With Adolf Hitler, Heinrich Himmler, and Joseph Goebbels dead, Hermann Göring (qq.v.) was the most prominent Nazi. He was *Reichmarshal* and commander in chief of the *Luftwaffe*, and until shortly before Hitler's death, his successor-designate. Göring was indicted on all four counts. Rudolf Hess (q.v.), deputy to Hitler until his bizarre flight to Scotland in 1941, was also charged under all four counts, as was Joachim von Ribbentrop (q.v.), one-time champagne salesman and later Hitler's foreign minister.

Somewhat less in stature among the civilians was Alfred Rosenberg (q.v.), Nazi Party philosopher and *Reich* minister for the occupied eastern territories, also indicted on all four counts. Wilhelm Keitel (q.v.), chief of staff of the high command of the German armed forces, was the most conspicuous military figure and had to answer all four charges.

Ernst Kaltenbrunner, chief of the security police and the SD (q.v.) and head of the RSHA (q.v.), which supervised the murder of Jews, was indicted on counts one, three, and four. So also was Hans Frank (q.v.), Hitler's chief lawyer and governor-general of occupied Poland. Wilhelm Frick (q.v.), minister of the interior, was charged under all four counts.

Julius Streicher (q.v.), publisher of the notorious anti-Semitic weekly *Der Stürmer,* was indicted on counts one and four. Walther Funk, as president of the *Reichsbank* was considered responsible for the exploitation of Jews and others, and therefore charged under all four counts.

Hjalmar Schacht (q.v.), who had served Hitler as minister of economics and president of the *Reichsbank,* but in the end was sent to a concentration camp, was nevertheless indicted on counts one and two. Erich Raeder (q.v.), commander in chief of the German Navy before 1943 was charged under counts one, two, and three, as was Karl Dönitz (q.v.), his successor. Baldur von Schirach, leader of the Hitler Youth (qq.v.) and later *Gauleiter* of Vienna, was indicted on counts one and four. Fritz Sauckel, a lugubrious figure as plenipotentiary for labor mobilization, Alfred Jodl, chief of the operations staff of the German armed forces, and Albert Speer (qq.v.), Hitler's favorite architect and minister of armaments and munitions, were all charged on four counts. So were Arthur Seyss-Inquart, *Reich* commissioner for the Netherlands, and Konstantin von Neurath (qq.v.), Hitler's foreign minister until 1938 and later *Reich* protector of Bohemia and Moravia. Franz von Papen (q.v.), a wily politician and diplomat, who served with Hitler as vice chancellor and subsequently in diplomatic posts, found himself charged under counts one and two. On the insistence of the Soviets, Hans Fritzsche (q.v.), a relatively innocuous figure in Goebbels's ministry, was indicted on counts one, three, and four. Martin Bormann (q.v.), head of the Nazi chancellery and secretary to Hitler, could not be found and was tried *in absentia* on counts one, three, and four.

Absent among the defendants was a representative of heavy industry. Gustav Krupp von Bohlen und Halbach (q.v.), mentally incompetent and physically incontinent, was considered too ill to be tried. An American move, supported by the Soviet and French prosecution, to try Gustav's son Alfried (q.v.) instead was rejected by the British.

In addition to the twenty-two defendants, the prosecution named seven Nazi organizations to be declared criminal: the leadership corps of the Nazi Party, the SS, the SD, the *Gestapo,* the SA, the German General Staff (qq.v.), and the *Reich* cabinet.

When the trial opened, probably no one expected it to last but a few weeks or months. In the end, there were more than 400 open sessions before the court adjourned, and the judges spent much of September 1946 deliberating in secret on the judgment and the verdicts. For the trial of the defendants, the staff of the prosecution scrutinized 100,000 documents, from which 4,000 were entered in evidence.

The prosecution also called thirty-three witnesses to testify in court. The number of witnesses presented by the defense was almost double that. A considerably larger number of witnesses were called by the prosecution against the indicted organizations, and 1,800 affidavits were submitted.

The defense presented close to two dozen witnesses and flooded the court with almost 200,000 affidavits. The trial proceedings, in English, comprise twenty-three volumes with another nineteen volumes of documentary evidence. For the first time in history, a trial was conducted in four languages: English, German, French, and Russian, with simultaneous translation.

Before and during the trial, the Allied jurists enjoyed certain advantages making for an uneven match between prosecution and defense. Several members of the tribunal who served as judges and prosecutors participated in the drafting of the London Agreement and the IMT Charter, and thus shaped the ground rules of the trial. Months before the court proceedings began the prosecution teams were collecting documents without significant legal, financial, or diplomatic restrictions, since they could count on the assistance of the military governments, the Allied Control Council, and the armed forces.

A number of Germans were put under arrest for political reasons, and prosecutors could draw on this pool for witnesses during the trial. In contrast, the defense team encountered very significant difficulties in preparing its cases.

The defendants could choose only from a panel of German lawyers selected by the court, or request a court approval for a German defense counsel of their choice. The defense attorneys had a small number of assistants and lacked the resources and authority the prosecution commanded in collecting evidence or calling witnesses. They were also given little time to prepare before the trial and lacked full knowledge of both the charges and the evidence in the hands of the prosecution.

Even more difficult for German lawyers was the adversary Anglo-American court format, which pitted the prosecution against the defense, with the judges playing the role of umpires. They were used to a more cooperative continental ap-

The Trial of the Major War Criminals

Defendant	Conspiracy	Crimes Against Peace	War Crimes	Crimes Against Humanity	Sentence
Martin Bormann*	NG	NI	G	G	Death
Karl Dönitz	NG	G	G	NI	10 Years
Hans Frank	NG	NI	G	G	Death
Wilhelm Frick	NG	G	G	G	Death
Hans Fritzsche	NG	NI	NG	NG	None
Walther Funk	NG	G	G	G	Life
Hermann Göring	G	G	G	G	Death
Rudolf Hess	G	G	G	NG	Life
Alfred Jodl	G	G	G	G	Death
Ernst Kaltenbrunner	NG	NI	G	G	Death
Wilhelm Keitel	G	G	G	G	Death
Konstantin von Neurath	G	G	G	G	15 Years
Franz von Papen	NG	NG	NI	NI	None
Erich Raeder	G	G	G	NI	Life
Joachim von Ribbentrop	G	G	G	G	Death
Alfred Rosenberg	G	G	G	G	Death
Fritz Sauckel	NG	NG	G	G	Death
Hjalmar Schacht	NG	NG	NI	NI	None
Baldur von Schirach	NG	NI	NI	G	Life
Arthur Seyss-Inquart	NG	G	G	G	Death
Albert Speer	NG	NG	G	G	20 Years
Julius Streicher	NG	NI	NI	G	Death

*Bormann was tried and sentenced *in absentia*

G Guilty
NG Not Guilty
NI Not Indicted

proach in court among attorneys of the defense, attorneys of the prosecution, and the judges. Lastly, the prosecution insisted on using only German documents and benefited greatly from a pretrial decision of the British and American jurists that barred access to U.S. State Department and British Foreign Office records.

Under the leadership of Lord Justice Lawrence, the Nuremberg court did manage to observe more than the mere appearance of due process. Even though the prosecution was the dominant element in the trial proceedings, it also had to accept certain definitive rulings on judgments by the tribunal that limited the conspiratorial planning charge, declared defendants liable for crimes against humanity only between 1939 and 1945, restricted the definition of "aggressive war" (albeit not very satisfactorily to specific instances), and put severe limitations on a blanket condemnation of the so-called criminal organizations. Also, the American prosecutor, Robert Jackson, received no assistance from the bench when he floundered in his cross-examinations of Göring and Schacht.

The finest hour of the German defense came when the counsel for Karl Dönitz was able to obtain an affidavit from U.S. Admiral Chester Nimitz to the effect that unrestricted submarine warfare had been practiced from the outset by the Americans, thereby weakening the charge against Dönitz. Less successful was the German defense effort to pursue the background of the Katyń Forest massacre (q.v.), which the Soviets tried to pin on the Germans.

Some of the discussion of controversial issues between the members of the bench was carried on in open trial sessions. However, the most fascinating debates and "horsetrading" between the eight judges occurred behind closed doors when they deliberated on the verdicts and sentences of each of the defendants, as revealed years later by Francis Biddle's court diaries and declassified material from U.S. and British archives.

Although the defendants were indicted on numerous charges, they were not necessarily declared guilty on all of them. In the end, the court handed down twelve death sentences, three life sentences, four term sentences of ten to twenty years, and three acquittals. The verdicts and death sentences for Göring, Ribbentrop, Keitel, and Jodl aroused little or no discussion among the judges. Frick, Seyss-Inquart, and Sauckel also easily drew death sentences, even though each was acquitted on at least one count.

There was prolonged haggling between the judges before Rosenberg and von Neurath were found guilty on all four counts with the first sentenced to hang and the other to a fifteen-year prison term. Kaltenbrunner and Frank had their guilty counts reduced, but were given death sentences nevertheless without significant juridical disagreement.

Hess's case caused a temporary deadlock among the judges before he was given a life sentence. Raeder and Dönitz were the subject of lengthy deliberation by the judges, resulting in a life sentence for Raeder and a ten-year prison term for Dönitz. Raeder wanted the court to change his life imprisonment to death. Speer and Schirach both drew twenty-year sentences, even though their cases were quite different.

In a somewhat haphazard and casual manner Bormann, who was tried *in absentia,* was sentenced to hang; but with the proviso of a possible change in sentence if found alive. Probably no other action of the tribunal gave it the appearance of a reasonably fair court more than the verdict of acquittal for Schacht, Papen, and Fritzsche. Yet during the judges' deliberations, Schacht's case proved cumbersome, even though in the end, the majority voted him and the others not guilty.

Finally, of the seven organizations indicted for criminality, three also were acquitted, and only the leadership corps of the Nazi Party, the SS, SD, and the *Gestapo* declared criminal. At the time the verdicts were announced, there appeared to be unanimity among the American, British, and French judges. Only the Soviet senior judge publicly dissented from the life sentence for Hess, arguing for death, and against the acquittals of Schacht, Papen, Fritzsche, and the Nazi organizations.

The end of the Nuremberg trial, followed by the hanging of ten of the major leaders of the Third *Reich* (Göring committed suicide), also sparked renewed controversy over the legality and fairness of the Nuremberg tribunal. Scholars occasionally still wrestle with the issue of *ex post facto* elements in the London Charter, though the majority of jurists have found ample principles in international law to defend the establishment of the IMT and the formulation of its charges.

In the final analysis, there were political and practical considerations, since no court functions in a societal vacuum. Since the Germans could not be trusted to deal with accused war criminals and there was no overwhelming sentiment among the Allies to resort to simple summary trials with perhaps thousands of executions, the creation of the IMT may well have been the best possible solution.

Its proceedings, however, would have been more creditable had the tribunal included jurists from at least a representative group of other countries that subscribed to the IMT principles. The legacy of the IMT has nevertheless been significant. Its charter and the Nuremberg trial have passed on certain concepts of wars of aggression, crimes against humanity, and the notion that those who commit them can be held responsible and punished.

Some of the conclusions reached by the tribunal are also manifest in the U.N. Genocide Convention, the U.N. Human Rights Declaration, the Convention on the Abolition of the Statute of Limitations on War Crimes and Crimes Against Humanity, as well as in the Geneva Convention on the Laws and Customs of War and its supplementary protocols.

George P. Blum

Additional Reading

Allied Control Authority for Germany, *Trial of the Major War Criminals Before the International Military Tribunal, Nuremberg, 14 November 1945–1 October 1946* (1949).

Davidson, Eugene, *The Trial of the Germans* (1966).

Maser, Werner, *Nuremberg: A Nation on Trial* (1979).

Smith, Bradley F., *The Road to Nuremberg* (1981).

Tusa, Ann, and John Tusa, *The Nuremberg Trial* (1984).

Iran

After World War I, the Reza Khan came to power in Iran (then called Persia) and assumed the title of Reza Shah Pahlavi. During his reign, he attempted to create a powerful, modern state by molding Iran's various ethnic groups into a nation. Part of the immediate problem was to develop the country economically and above all to prevent foreign dominance of Iran's internal affairs and resources, particularly oil. Pahlavi built a 40,000-man, disciplined military force, which he used to curb the activities of such rebellious ethnic groups as the Kurds, Jangali, Lurs, Baluchi, and Quasqai.

He had his political enemies either murdered or imprisoned.

After suppressing tribal power, Pahlavi immediately set out to emancipate women, build roads, and introduce industry. In foreign policy, he attempted to neutralize Britain and the Soviet Union by playing them off against each other. Close cooperation and coordination with Germany brought an increase in German influence in Teheran during the 1930s. By 1941, several hundred German technicians were in Iran. In return for oil and other support and resources, Germany helped modernize Iran. A reminder of German influence can be seen today in the form of an enormous swastika in the dome of the Teheran train station.

The shah succeeded in suppressing internal dissent, controlling the press, and turning the country's legislative body, the Majlis, into a rubber stamp. His efforts at creating a modern Iran were cut short, not by domestic problems but by the intrusion of external events. The German invasion of the Soviet Union (q.v.) in June 1941 brought an end to German influence in Iran and the violation of Iranian neutrality, because the Allies needed the use of overland routes through Iran to supply the hard-pressed Soviet Army. To gain access to supply the routes, British and Soviet troops jointly invaded Iran in August 1941, two months after the start of Operation BARBAROSSA. The positions of Britain and the Soviet Union in Iran were legitimized by a Tripartite Treaty of Alliance on 29 January 1942. Under that treaty, the Soviet Union and Great Britain agreed to respect Iran's territorial integrity and sovereignty and to withdraw their troops six months after the end of the war. On 1 December 1943, a new four-way agreement was signed that included the United States.

The failure of Reza Shah to cooperate with the Allies brought about his forced abdication on 16 September 1941, in favor of his eldest son, Mohammed Reza Pahlavi. Reza Shah died in South Africa in July 1944. His son initially tried to rule more democratically, accepted the Allied occupation of Iran as a fact, and in 1943, declared war on Germany.

Advisors from the United States arrived in 1942 along with troops to provide some economic help, to improve the railways, and to ensure the safe transit of materiel to the Soviet Union. The volume of supplies flowing through Iran played an important role in the survival of the Soviet Union. Iran itself played no part in the supply operation other than reluctantly providing the supply routes.

In accordance with treaty provisions, American and British troops withdrew six months after the end of the war, but Soviet troops remained in Azerbaijan, in northwest Iran, until May 1946. Soviet dictator Josef Stalin (q.v.) gave every indication that he intended to annex this province until an ultimatum from U.S. President Harry S Truman (q.v.) persuaded him to withdraw the Soviet forces.

Paul J. Rose

Additional Reading

Churchill, Winston S. *The Second World War*. Vol. 3, *The Grand Alliance* (1950).

Motter, T.H. Vail, *The Persian Corridor and Aid to Russia* (1952).

Upton, Joseph M., *The History of Modern Iran* (1960).

Isolationism

The expansionist ambitions of Germany and Japan were already apparent in the mid-1930s, and increasingly the world faced the real possibility of a major war. Public opinion in the United States, however, reacted to these events almost unanimously—America was not to get involved in another foreign conflict. In fact, this prevailing view reflected both a widespread abhorrence of war and the belief that an impending war did not involve the strategic interests of the United States. The debate over isolationism was most intense in American between 1935 and 1941.

Isolationists came from both major political parties, from differing parts of the country, and from wide backgrounds. They were, however, united in agreement that American foreign policy should not be tied to decisions made by international agencies, multinational conferences, or foreign governments, and that political commitments tying American policy to the policies of other countries was dangerous and unnecessary. The isolationists sought to retain the independence in foreign policy that had served this country well during the nineteenth century at a time when the world was coming ever more closely together through trade relations, alliances, and threats of aggression. American isolationists did not favor withdrawing totally from the world; they simply wanted to maintain their country's ability to act unilaterally. In fact, the U.S. preached isolation while practicing intervention around the world.

The commitment to unilateralism and the anxiety about war were the common elements of American isolationism. The mounting crises of the mid-1930s in central Europe and Asia presented new challenges to these beliefs. A war in Europe, it was widely recognized, would mean a land conflict requiring the mobilization of huge numbers of soldiers and an alliance with Great Britain and France. The former meant a challenge to American democracy, and the latter meant joint decision making and possible permanent involvement in European affairs. A conflict in Asia presented less of a threat, isolationists believed, because it would not be a land conflict and would be directed against Japan. America would, in all probability, be able to wage the war independently and not have its wartime or postwar policies determined by its Allies.

Other factors contributed to the widespread isolationism of the mid-1930s. There was, in America, the growing realization that the policies of Germany, Italy, and Japan would lead to a major war, and unless significant action was taken, the United States would be drawn into the conflict. In addition, foreign policy was not nearly as important to most Americans as were the consequences of the Great Depression. According to a December 1936 poll, "the most vital issues before the American people today" were unemployment and economy in government. The economic crisis also served to erode confidence in the strength of the United States and its ability to carry out its historic mission. With the country's economic strength seriously undermined, many believed it was futile and counterproductive to intervene in international matters. Only in May 1939 did the American people identify keeping out of war as the major issue.

The Depression also generated widespread distrust of banks and big business, two institutions with major interests in trade and foreign relations. Another element supporting the position of the isolationists was the revisionist interpretation of America's involvement in World War I. Some scholars argued that the entry of the United States in that conflict was the result of other nations' chicanery, and this served as a powerful warning. Isolationism also increasingly appealed to those who not only questioned American participation in world affairs, but also disappointed idealists who favored internationalism only to see it fail.

After 1939, however, most Americans began to question the adequacy of a policy of unilateral action as the best means of defending American interests. German successes showed that there might in fact be a greater threat to the nation's future. Nevertheless, some individuals remained committed to isolationist principles and maintained that the country was again being tricked into involvement in a foreign war. Chief among the die-hard isolationists were Senator Burton K. Wheeler of Montana, Senator Gerald P. Nye of North Dakota, the two LaFollete brothers of Wisconsin, Representative Hamilton Fish of New York, William Randolph Hearst and his newspaper chain, and Colonel Robert R. McCormick of the Chicago *Tribune*. Norman Thomas, the socialist and pacifist leader joined this group. Working with this group was a well-financed organization known as the "America First Committee," and one of its best known leaders of isolation and appeasement was Charles A. Lindberg.

Even within isolationist ranks, there was no unanimity among the organizations, which, in addition to the America First Committee, included the National Council for the Prevention of War, the Women's International League for Peace and Freedom, the American Peace Mobilization, and the Keep America Out of War Congress.

The Japanese attack on Pearl Harbor, on 7 December 1941, ended any isolationist spirit in America.

Thomas F. Hale
Robert G. Waite

Additional Reading

Adler, Selig, *The Isolationist Impulse: Its Twentieth-Century Reaction* (1974).

Jonas, Manfred, *Isolationism in America, 1935–1941* (1990).

Langer, William L., and S.E. Gleason, *The Challenge of Isolation: The World Crisis of 1937–1940 and American Foreign Policy*, Vol. 1 (1970).

J

July Plot
See OPPOSITION TO HITLER

K

Kapp-Lüttwitz *Putsch*

After the collapse of imperial Germany in November 1918, social and political turmoil accompanied the emergence of the Weimar Republic (q.v.). Disaffected groups and movements from both extremes of the political spectrum attacked it verbally and physically until its demise in January 1933.

Although speculations of an impending attack against the German government were circulating quite openly since Germany was forced to accept the Allied peace terms, such an attack came on 13 March 1920. It was a hastily planned, poorly coordinated and botched attempt to overthrow the socialist-led government of President Friedrich Ebert (q.v.) and Chancellor Gustav Bauer. The coup was led by General Walther Freiherr von Lüttwitz, chief of the Berlin command of the provisional *Reichswehr*, and Chancellor-designate Dr. Wolfgang Kapp, an ex-East Prussian official and ardent nationalist.

Lüttwitz was the military leader of the *Putsch*. His instrument was the 2nd Naval Brigade, led by Captain Hermann Ehrhardt, whose unit was stationed near Berlin. That brigade of disaffected officers and soldiers was forced by the Allies to withdraw from the Baltic, where it was dabbling in local politics under the guise of fighting Bolshevism. It was recently taken away from Lüttwitz's command because, despite his opposition, it was to be disbanded. He again protested and made other demands. He was finally sacked and the government issued orders for the arrest of Kapp and other conspirators. Lüttwitz precipitated the coup by telling Ehrhardt's brigade to march on Berlin. The government left the city.

The circle of conspirators, loosely gathered in the National Union *(Nationale Vereinigung)* was composed of extreme right-wing conservative officers, former officials, and other anti-republicans who, contemptuous of democracy, essentially wanted to establish a military dictatorship of non-party experts. Lüttwitz demanded new elections, a presidential plebiscite, the removal of General Georg-Hans Reinhardt (chief of the army command and loyal to the republic), and an end to demobilization. The government did not give in to Lüttwitz's insurrectionist demands.

"Chancellor" Kapp failed to get the support of the Berlin bureaucracy or the security and police forces of Berlin. The *Reichswehr* and German industrial leaders played an ambiguous role in the affair. But the labor unions, seconded by socialist ministers in the government, called an effective general strike. On 17 March, Kapp fled Berlin; Lüttwitz followed shortly. The *Putsch* collapsed ignominiously. The Weimar Republic survived to face further assaults from left and right. The *Reichswehr* survived intact and continued to play a fateful role in German politics.

The Kapp *Putsch* indicated the early polarization of German politics and the growth of irreconcilable anti-republican circles in Germany resulting from World War I and the Treaty of Versailles (q.v.). The new government of Hermann Müller, installed on 27 March 1920, and the election of 6 June 1920, also demonstrated this polarization. The moderate, middle-of-the-road supporters of Weimar lost eight million votes. Left-wing actions continued to be put down more harshly than right-wing actions, including Adolf Hitler's Beer Hall *Putsch* (q.v.) in 1923.

N.H. Gaworek

Additional Reading

Bracher, Karl Dietrich *The German Dictatorship* (1970).
Pinson, Koppel S., *Modern Germany* (1966).

Katyń Forest Massacre

On 13 April 1943, German radio announced the discovery of mass graves in the Katyń Forest, near Smolensk, containing more than 4,000 corpses of Polish soldiers, mostly officers. The Poles had all been shot in the base of the skull. Germany blamed their deaths on the Soviet Union. To investigate the atrocity, the Germans set up three commissions, including one formed by the Polish Red Cross. Journalists from Sweden and Switzerland were also allowed to examine the grave sites and their grisly contents. The bodies were buried in sandy soil, which resulted in a kind of mummification, so that the bodies were fairly well preserved.

The commissions announced that the Soviets were the guilty party. The Polish government-in-exile, in London, thereupon lambasted the Soviet regime for perpetrating the horror. Moscow then broke relations with the London Poles, accusing them of being collaborators of Adolf Hitler.

When the Red Army overran the Katyń Forest area in the fall of 1943, the Soviet government set up its own commission—not to find out who had committed the atrocity, for Moscow never wavered in blaming the Germans, but rather to investigate the "circumstances of the shooting of Polish officer prisoners by the German-Fascist invaders in the Katyń Forest." The commission was staffed by people who had to answer to Stalin. Foreigners, even Polish Communists, did not participate in the investigation. The commission duly issued a report, giving the "details" of the execution.

After the war, the Nuremberg trials (*see* International Military Tribunal) briefly examined the Katyń Forest massacre, but issued no verdict, because the Soviet side blocked any real inquiry. Independent scholars proceeded to investigate the evidence, which included such facts as the following: the bullets were of German manufacture, but of a type widely sold in Eastern Europe in the 1930s; the rope used to tie the soldiers' hands was of Soviet make; the state of the corpses indicated the spring of 1940 (i.e., long before the German invasion in June 1941) as the date of death; on the bodies were found more than 3,000 documents, and not a single one had a date later than the spring of 1940; some of the bodies showed bayonet wounds, and the bayonet used was the characteristic four-sided Soviet bayonet; young spruce trees were planted on the grave site, and the tree rings showed they were transplanted in 1940. Other evidence is given in specialized studies of the massacre.

By the 1950s, most serious students (including a 1951–1952 Select Committee of the U.S. Congress) concluded that although the Germans could have committed the ghastly deed, in that they were experts at such things, in this case it was the Soviets who had to bear the blame before history. The scholars' deductions were borne out by later events. Under the *Glasnost* period of the late 1980s, the Soviet regime began to allow Polish pilgrims to come to the graves to conduct ceremonies and put up anti-Soviet signs.

On 13 April 1990, the Soviet government finally admitted the blame. On 14 October 1992, the Russian government of Boris Yeltsin released a 5 March 1940 Politburo document that implicated the top Soviet leadership directly. Apparently still nursing a grudge against the Polish Army for the Soviet defeat in 1920, Josef Stalin (q.v.) ordered that the Polish officers be subjected to "the supreme punishment—execution by firing squad." Thus the Communist regime under Stalin, turning its back on every principle of decency, shot in cold blood thousands of honorable soldiers, defenseless prisoners of war.

The 4,321 corpses found at Katyń represent only part of the more than 15,000 Polish officers (including at least 295 generals and colonels) unaccounted for after being captured by the Soviets in September 1939. Those buried at Katyń mostly came from the Soviet POW camp at Kozielsk. The remainder were held initially in at least two other camps. Prisoners from the Starobielsk POW camp were murdered at Kharkov and buried near the village of Piatikhatki. Those from the Ostashkov camp were murdered at Kalinin (now Tver) and buried at Myednoye.

The killings were carried out by the NKVD (q.v.), under the overall direction of Vsevold Nikolayevich Merkulov, deputy minister of the interior and a member of the Communist Party Central Committee. For his part in the action, Merkulov was awarded the Order of Lenin on 27 April 1940. After the war, the NKVD established a resort at the Myednoye site, located about ninety miles north of Moscow.

One may well ask what the Soviet regime could hope to gain from such a horrendous deed. The answer lies in the tortured ethics of Communist ideology. The Polish officers included many reservists from the Polish elite (professors, teachers, doctors, lawyers, clergy), the natural leaders of Polish society. They were all "class enemies." With these men out of the way, it would be easier later to impose a Polish leadership corps manufactured in Moscow. That is indeed what happened beginning in 1944 when the Red Army overran Poland. But it was a hollow victory, because the Katyń Forest massacre poisoned relations between the Soviet Union and Poland, making it impossible for the Polish Communists ever to be accepted as legitimate by the Polish people. It was that illegitimacy that, combined with the chronic economic failures of the Polish Communist government, helped lead to the collapse of Polish Communism in the late 1980s.

In a larger sense, the Katyń Forest massacre is just one more Communist horror that, added to the *Gulags,* the purges (q.v.), the contrived famines, and all the repressions of Communist totalitarianism, made a mockery of Marxist-Leninist claims to be able to build a better world.

Roland V. Layton

Additional Reading

Abarinov, Vladimir, *The Murderers of Katyń* (1993).
Allen, Paul, *Katyń: The Untold Story of Stalin's Polish Massacre* (1991).
Bergh, Hendrik van, *Die Wahrheit über Katyń* (Berg am See: 1986).
Zawodny, Janusz K., *Death in the Forest: The Story of the Katyń Forest Massacre* (1962).

Kearny Incident

On 10 October 1941, Slow Convoy 48 passed through the Strait of Belle Isle heading east into the Atlantic. The convoy consisted of forty-nine merchant ships escorted by two British corvettes and one destroyer. The sea was heavy and the convoy could only make about seven knots. All was quiet until 15 October.

At roughly 400 miles south of Iceland, the convoy was attacked by a U-boat wolf pack that sank three ships. The escort commander requested help from the U.S. Naval Command at Reykjavik. The naval operations staff ordered Destroyer Escort Unit 4.1.4 to disperse westbound convoy ON-24, which it was accompanying, and proceeded to assist SC-48.

After making 23 to 25 knots in heavy seas, the destroyer escort unit took up stations on the stricken convoy. The escort unit consisted of the USS *Plunkett* (flagship), the USS *Kearny* (port flank), the USS *Livermore* (starboard bow), and the USS *Decatur* (starboard flank). The USS *Greer* (q.v.) arrived late. The British destroyer HMS *Broadwater* and the Free French ship *Lobelia* also responded.

On the night of 16–17 October, a wolf pack surfaced and waited for the convoy to come within range. Once within range, the U-boats "fan launched" their torpedoes into the line of ships. Six merchant ships were sunk and several others were ablaze. The *Kearny* slowed to permit the British corvettes to pass. Seeing the destroyer stalled and silhouetted by a burning freighter, the *U-568* fired two torpedoes into what U-boat commander Joachim Preuss thought was a British destroyer.

The *Kearny* was damaged but survived. Eleven of her crew were killed and twenty wounded. The ship was not, as the American public was lead to believe, an innocent victim, but instead was engaged in depth-charging suspected locations of German U-boats when attacked. The Germans earlier had suffered such attacks to avoid a direct conflict with the U.S. Earlier that September, the USS *Greer* (q.v.) had been fired upon but escaped damage, while similarly engaged in depth-charging suspected U-boats. Any reasonable understanding of what was meant by neutrality made both ships engaging in this activity "fair game" for attack by German U-boats.

President Franklin D. Roosevelt (q.v.), however, capitalized on these two incidents in an effort to turn public opinion in favor of additional aid to the British. He referred to the attacks as "piracy" and the U-boats as "rattlesnakes of the sea." He then issued his famous "shoot on sight" order. It is important to note that this order continued a trend that was rapidly making the United States an active participant in the "undeclared war" (q.v.). These two incidents, together with the sinking of the USS *Reuben James* on 31 October, which cost the lives of 115 American seamen, moved the United States closer to a shooting war with Germany. A formal declaration of war was now only a few weeks away.

Terry D. Davenport
Paul J. Rose

Additional Reading

Bailey, Thomas A. and Paul B. Ryan, *Hitler vs. Roosevelt, the Undeclared Naval War* (1979).
Langer, William, and S.E. Gleason, *The Undeclared War* (1952).
Morison, Samuel Eliot, *The Battle of the Atlantic, 1939–1943* (1990).

Kellogg-Briand Pact

Aristide Briand, foreign minister of France (1925–

1932), was determined to maintain the French alliance system and keep the largest army in Europe. One alliance Briand sought was a bilateral pact with the United States to replace the unratified Treaty of Anglo-American Guarantee of the Paris Peace Conference.

At the same time a small but influential group in the United States had been urging that war be outlawed. Professor J.T. Shotwell of Columbia University suggested such a proposal to Briand, who announced in April 1927 that France was prepared to enter into such a pact with the United States in renouncing war as an instrument of national policy.

American Secretary of State Frank Kellogg (1925–1929) was opposed to a bilateral agreement, but petitions with two million signatures supporting a treaty poured into Washington. In December, Kellogg suggested that the pact be expanded to include other nations.

As finally worded, the treaty was composed of only two sentences: "The High Contracting Parties solemnly declare in the names of their respective peoples that they condemn recourse to war for the solution of international controversies, and renounce it as an instrument of national policy in their relations with one another. The High Contracting Parties agree that the settlement or solution of all disputes or conflicts of whatever nature or of whatever origin they may be, which may arise among them, shall never be sought except by pacific means."

In August 1928, it was formally signed by the representatives of fifteen nations, but ultimately sixty-three nations signed it. Although there was some criticism of the pact in the United States, it was undeniably popular with the voters and the Senate ratified it by a vote of 85 to 1.

Although all the powers signed it without reservations, many interpreted it differently. All the major powers insisted on the right to wage defensive war, deciding themselves what was offensive and what was defensive war. It also contributed to the failure of many countries to actually declare war in the apparent belief that war was not war if undeclared. Ironically, Kellogg, the reluctant convert, was awarded the Nobel Peace Prize for the pact in 1929.

The Kellogg-Briand Pact was only one of many treaties that gave the illusion of security. After World War II, it was used as a justification for the prosecution of war criminals.

Spencer Tucker

Additional Reading

Black, C.E., and E.C. Helmreich, *Twentieth-Century History* (1972).

Ferrell, Robert H., *Peace in Their Time: The Origins of the Kellogg-Briand Pact* (1952).

Miller, David H., *The Peace Pact of Paris* (1928).

Kristallnacht (Night of the Broken Glass)

Kristallnacht, or "Night of the Broken Glass," occurred 9 and 10 November 1938, and marked a massive violent attack on Jews in Germany and the recently annexed Austria. It was designed to eliminate them from the economy and to force them into emigration.

The pretext for the violence and terror was the shooting of Ernst vom Rath, a secretary in the German Embassy in Paris, by the seventeen-year-old Polish Jewish youth, Herschel Grynszpan (q.v.).

Joseph Goebbels (q.v.) used the incident to launch an inflammatory tirade against Jews, and soon instructions were sent to all parts of Germany calling for "spontaneous" demonstrations of outrage over the murder of vom Rath. There was limited spontaneous action of crowds, but much systematic violence and destruction was instigated by the SA (q.v.) and members of Nazi organizations. SS men in civilian clothes participated, and the police had instructions not to interfere.

More than 7,000 Jewish businesses were vandalized or destroyed and nearly 200 synagogues burned. Some Jewish women were raped and close to 100 Jews murdered. About 30,000 Jewish males, mostly well to do, were arrested and taken to concentration camps at Dachau, Buchenwald, and Sachsenhausen. Many were released if they could demonstrate their intent to emigrate.

Hermann Göring and Heinrich Himmler (qq.v.) were surprised by Goebbels's initiative and critical of the widespread destruction. Nevertheless, in his capacity as plenipotentiary of the four-year plan, Göring implemented decrees after 12 November that confiscated or "Aryanized" Jewish businesses and factories, barred Jews from public cultural and recreational places, and expelled Jewish children from schools. Whatever compensation Jews received from insurance companies had to be handed over to the German government on the grounds that Jews had provoked the violence. The Jewish community in Germany was also fined one billion marks for the murder of vom Rath.

The ruins of the Berlin Synagogue, torched on the night of 9–10 November 1938. (IWM FRA 204717)

Despite protests and outrage by the Western press and several governments, the Nazis neither relented in their persecution of the Jews nor did Western governments significantly liberalize their emigration policies to enable Jews to escape from Germany.

George P. Blum

Additional Reading

Pinson, Koppel S., *Modern Germany* (1966).

Read, Anthony, and David Fisher, *Kristallnacht: The Night of Terror* (1989).

Thalmann, Rita, and Emmanuel Feinermann, *Crystal Night, 9 and 10 November, 1938* (1974).

L

Laconia Order

The *Laconia* Order was issued by Grand Admiral Karl Dönitz (q.v.) after *U-156* sank the *Laconia,* a 19,695–ton British troop ship, on 12 September 1942. On discovering that the *Laconia* had carried 1,800 Italian prisoners of war, the submarine began recovering victims and called for assistance. During the rescue operation Allied aircraft bombed *U-156* without success.

To prevent future risks, on 17 September, Dönitz prohibited U-boats from rescuing survivors of torpedoed ships, stating that it contradicted the necessity for "the destruction of enemy ships and their crews," and reminded them that bomber raids on German cities killed women and children. During the Nuremberg trials (*see* International Military Tribunal) the prosecution argued that Dönitz had ordered U-boats to kill survivors, a charge that, if proven, would have resulted in a death sentence. The court was not convinced, however, and only convicted him of the lesser charges of waging aggressive war and general war crimes.

Robert C. Fischer

Additional Reading

Dönitz, Karl, *Memoirs: Ten Years and Twenty Days* (1959).
Padfield, Peter, *Dönitz: The Last Führer* (1984).

Lateran Treaty and Concordat

The Lateran Agreements were signed on 11 February 1929 by Benito Mussolini (q.v.) and Cardinal Pietro Gaspari, Vatican secretary of state. The treaty recognized the Vatican as a sovereign, independent state with an area of 108 acres. The pope would be regarded as a foreigner and a foreign ruler. In return, the Vatican renounced all claims to the old Papal States with the exception of select churches in Rome and the Vatican's summer residence in Castel Gandolfo.

The concordat stipulated the rights between Italy and the Vatican in areas of education and Catholicism. The Catholic religion would be recognized as the state religion of Italy, and the church could use its influence and ideologies within Italian society. Religious education became mandatory in all schools. Italy would renounce civil law marriages and recognize canonical, church marriages only. Under civil law, however, divorce was recognized by the state.

The treaty and concordat were mutually beneficial. Italy was able to bring the church back in line with Italian Fascism. Pope Pius XI hoped to reconcile differences between Fascist Italy and the Holy See and restore the church's role in Italian society. On 14 February 1929, the pope referred to Mussolini as "the man sent by Providence." Gaspari's nephew, Enrico Gaspari, also a cardinal, referred to Mussolini as "the only man in the present world chaos with a clear view." For this support, Italy became the protector of the pope and the church. Many catholics and non-Catholics wondered if the church had been sold out to the Fascists. Were the gains the Holy See made worth the religious, and perhaps political, independence lost?

William H. Van Husen

Additional Reading

Lewy, Günter, *The Catholic Church and Nazi Germany* (1964).
Rhodes, Anthony, *The Vatican in the Age of the Dictators, 1922–1945* (1973).

Latvia

See Baltic States

League of Nations

The League of Nations was an international peace-keeping organization established after World War I. The purpose was to "promote international cooperation and achieve peace and security." With its headquarters in Geneva, Switzerland, it operated from 1920 until 1946. Ironically, "nations" could not belong to the League of Nations; only "states" could.

The League was founded on the simple but consistent principle that an association of sovereign states could cooperate in their own and in the world's interest by uniting to maintain "peace and security." That it did not work out as expected is the League's enduring legacy.

While the League did not fulfill the hope of its creators, it played a significant role in world politics and made a positive social and economic contribution. It helped to shape a historical epoch familiar with and friendly to the idea of collective security. The League served as a starting point and role model for the more highly developed United Nations (q.v.) following World War II.

The history and origins of international organization can be traced back through history from the United Nations of today to the League of Nations, to the Hague Peace Conferences of 1899 and 1907 and on back to the point in history where people began living together in political communities. The Achaean League, for example, was created by the city-states of ancient Greece in the hope of avoiding conflict by introducing cooperative measures into their intercity relations. Each historical failure only served to inspire man to try again. Since supranational organizations were not attainable, only voluntary agreements were attempted. So it was after World War I when world leaders once again set out to create another voluntary organization, the League of Nations.

World War I, by introducing total war on such a vast and murderous scale, made the need for international cooperation seem even more urgent. If a local quarrel between Austria-Hungary and Serbia could spread so quickly to engulf most of the world, it was clear that the era of national independence was being replace by one of interdependence. Recognizing this important trend, U.S. President Woodrow Wilson declared in 1916 that the day of the neutral was past. And so it was. The world would never again be the same.

Wilson, a historian and scholar before going into politics, introduced his famous Fourteen Points before a session of the U.S. Congress on 8 January 1918. His Fourteenth Point stated that a "general association of nations must be formed under specific covenants for the purpose of affording mutual guarantees of political independence and territorial integrity to great and small powers alike." The idea was not entirely original with Wilson because many private groups in Britain, France, and the United States had been discussing the idea for some time. It was clearly an idea whose time had come. Nevertheless, Wilson can legitimately be called the League's chief architect.

In taking the leading role, Wilson was responding to the passions of his times. The U.S. decision to save Europe from its own "follies" seemed to inspire Americans with a holy mission to "make the world safe for democracy."

The Covenant of the League of Nations was written at the 1919 Paris Peace Conference. The deliberations were dominated by Britain, France, Italy, and the United States. Like the United Nations a generation later, the League was a victor's initiative and was at first limited to the membership of the victor nations.

Wilson chaired the first commission of the Peace Conference that wrote the League's Covenant. Key U.S. Senate leaders, who would control Senate ratification of the peace treaty, wanted assurances that American participation would not compromise the integrity of the Monroe Doctrine, would guarantee an American veto in major League organs, keep domestic politics beyond League jurisdiction, and ensure their right of withdrawal. These assurances were included in the treaty but Wilson was still unable to obtain Senate ratification, and the United States never did become a member. American absence along with absences at various times of such key nations as Germany, Italy, Japan, and the Soviet Union, denied the League universality and probably doomed it to ultimate failure.

The Covenant contained twenty-six articles. The power it gave to the international body was an accurate measure of the degree of sovereignty nations were willing to cede to the new organization. It turned out to be inadequate for the enormous task at hand. The League's experience revealed the need for a more specific expression of authority, functions, and purpose. This lack of specificity and the resulting failure of the League of Nations later resulted in the Charter of the United Nations containing 111 articles and a more specific expression of authority, functions, and purpose.

The Preamble to The Covenant of the League of Nations states its high purpose thusly:

The High Contracting Parties
In order to promote international cooperation and to achieve international peace and security
by the acceptance of obligations not to resort to war
by the prescription of open, just and honorable relations between nations,
by the firm establishment of the understanding of international law as the actual rule of conduct among Governments, and
by the maintenance of justice and a scrupulous respect for all treaty obligations in the dealings of organized peoples with one another,
Agree to this Covenant of the League of Nations.

The Covenant of the League of Nations was equivalent to the Charter of the United Nations. It was adopted on 28 April 1919, and was part of the Treaty of Versailles (q.v.). The Covenant, with forty-two members participating, took effect in January 1920. The League would eventually include sixty-three members but no more than fifty-eight at any one time. Germany joined the League in 1926 and the Soviet Union joined in 1934. During the 1930s, Germany, Japan, and many South American states withdrew, and the Soviet Union was expelled in 1939.

A large part of the Covenant was dedicated to ways and means of peace keeping. Articles 1 through 7 covered membership and organization. Articles 8 through 17 were concerned with the peacekeeping function, which gave precedence to such early-twentieth-century methods as arbitration, international law, and judicial decision making. The most important of these articles were 10 and 14. Article 10 guaranteed the "territorial integrity and existing political independence of all Members of the League" while Article 11 instructed the League to establish the Permanent Court of International Justice.

Articles 18 through 21 concerned Wilson's First Point, which called for "open covenants openly arrived at." Specifically, Article 18 stated:

Every treaty or international engagement entered into hereafter by any member of the League shall be forthwith registered with the Secretariat and shall as soon as possible be published by it. No such treaty or international engagement shall be binding until so registered.

The Wilsonian doctrine was that "open covenants" would help to ensure peaceful relations among nations. American public opinion was offended by the realization that their European allies had secret treaties specifying how they would divide up the spoils of war after victory was achieved. Ironically, after arriving at the Paris Peace Conference waving his Fourteen Points and calling for "open covenants openly arrived at," Wilson did most of his own important negotiations in secret with the governments of the other big powers. Current American practice does not follow the Wilsonian model. It is a well-established principle of international relations that successful negotiations must be done in secret, with the results then made public.

Article 22 concerned "mandated" territories taken from Germany and Turkey, which were to be held in trust and administered by the Allied powers. A mandate commission was established to guard the rights of populations on these territories. Article 23 set forth humanitarian goals and Article 24 instructed the League to establish the International Labor Organization. Article 25 urged nations to establish national Red Cross organizations and Article 26 provided for amendments to the Covenant.

The main executive organs of the League of Nations, like its successor the United Nations, were the Council and the Assembly, assisted by a permanent Secretariat. For other than procedural matters, all decisions in both bodies were required to be by unanimous vote, with a party to a dispute disqualified from voting. All League members were represented in the Assembly and each state had one vote. At least one session was held annually. The assembly elected its own president, established specialized committees as needed, and approved its own rules of procedure.

The initial plans were that the Council would consist of five great powers, the United States, Britain, France, Italy, and Japan holding permanent seats, plus four non-permanent members chosen by the Assembly. The United States never became a member, and later when Germany and the Soviet Union joined the League, they were granted permanent seats on the Council. Later still the number of nonpermanent members was increased to eleven. Normally, the Council met twice annually and in special session as events required.

During the period between the two world wars, the League managed to settle more than forty disputes; including a boundary dispute between Bulgaria and Greece, the Aaland Island dispute between Sweden and Finland, and the dispute over

L

Leticia between Peru and Colombia. Also, the 1935 Plebiscite that returned the Saarland (q.v.) to Germany was conducted by the League.

The League met its first serious setback when Italy invaded the Greek island of Corfu in August 1923. Big power support for the League was lacking and the crisis had to be handled by the Council of Ambassadors meeting in Paris. This incident left a widely shared view that guaranteeing true international security was beyond the League's capabilities.

During the troubled 1930s, the League became involved in crises of greater magnitude. The Japanese invasion of Manchuria in 1931 was a case in point. The Lyton Commission, the first commission sent to investigate the actions of a great

League of Nations Membership

Asterisks indicate countries that were charter members of the League and remained members during its entire life. A = Admitted, E = Expelled, W = Withdrew.

Country	Remarks	Country	Remarks
Afhganistan	A: Sep 1934	Iraq	A: Oct 1932
Albania	A: Dec 1920; annexed by Italy Apr 1939	Ireland	A: Sep 1923
		Italy	W: Dec 1937
Argentina	*		
Australia	*	Japan	W: Mar 1933
Austria	A: Dec 1920; annexed by Germany Mar 1938	Latvia	A: Sep 1921
		Liberia	*
Belgium	*	Lithuania	A: Sep 1921
Bolivia	*		
Brazil	W: June 1926	Mexico	A: Sep 1931
Bulgaria	A: Dec 1920		
		Netherlands	*
Canada	*	New Zealand	*
Chile	W: Jan 1938	Nicaragua	W: Jun 1936
China	*	Norway	*
Colombia	*		
Costa Rica	A: Dec 1920; W: Jan 1925	Panama	*
Cuba	*	Paraguay	W: Feb 1935
Czechoslovakia	*	Persia (Iran)	*
		Peru	W: Apr 1939
Denmark	*	Poland	*
Dominican Republic	A: Sep 1924	Portugal	*
Ecuador	A: Sep 1934	Romania	W: Jul 1940
Egypt	A: May 1937		
El Salvador	W: Aug 1937	Siam (Thailand)	*
Estonia	A: Dec 1921	Spain	W: May 1939
Ethiopia	A: Sep 1923	Sweden	*
		Switzerland	*
France	*		
		Turkey	A: Jul 1932
Germany	A: Sep 1926; W: Oct 1933		
Greece	*	Union of South Africa	*
Guatemala	W: May 1936	Union of Soviet Socialist Republics (USSR)	A: Sep 1934; E: Dec 1939
Haiti	W: Apr 1942		
Honduras	W: Jul 1936	Uruguay	*
Hungary	A: Sep 1922; W: Apr 1939		
		Venezuela	W: Jul 1938
India	*	Yugoslavia	*

power, named Japan as the aggressor; but the best the League could do was recommend that members not recognize the Japanese puppet state of Manchukuo. Limited sanctions were applied to Italy for the invasion of Ethiopia (q.v.) in 1935, but the conquest stood. Japan's bombing of Chinese cities was condemned by the League, which only urged member states to apply individual sanctions.

The League of Nations played almost no role in the events leading up to World War II, except to expel the Soviet Union for the 1939 invasion of Finland (q.v.). These failures were more the failures of the League's member states than of the League itself. The League was not a supernational organization, nor did it possess sovereignty. It had no existence independent of its members. The League was the members, and they did not measure up to the challenge they faced. The League could have been successful only if its members supported strong economic, political, or military action against aggressors. Unfortunately, they did not.

Nevertheless, there were technical failures in the League's peacekeeping machinery. The requirement for unanimity of both the Council and the Assembly on most substantive matters permitted violators to veto some League countermeasures. The machinery for disarmament was unusually weak and members felt no responsibility to reduce their own armaments. An early interpretation of the Covenant permitted each member to decide for itself whether or not it supported sanctions. Other technical weaknesses existed, but it would be wrong to give too much importance to them. Stronger positions taken by member states could have overcome some technical failures by interpretations that could have provided alternative courses of action.

One of the most popular explanations of the League's failure was the defection of the United States. There is no doubt that the American failure to participate in a world peacekeeping organization inspired and sponsored by its own president created a psychological power vacuum that was almost impossible to overcome. But it is a myth that the small garrison-bound U.S. Army of that period could have turned League failures into successes, for any American power was more potential than actual. Further, until Pearl Harbor awakened them from their deep, isolationist sleep, Americans were not psychologically prepared to play a major international role. Thus, while American defection weakened the League of Nations, it was not the major reason for its ultimate collapse.

Other powers also contributed mightily to the failure of the League as a peacekeeping body.

The actions of such great powers as Germany, Japan, and the Soviet Union were often disruptive and negative. Only Britain and France, of the great powers that were members of the League, played a more or less positive role during its lifetime. In any event, the League of Nations went as far and accomplished as much as its members would permit. And alas, that degree of cooperation was not adequate to prevent World War II.

Paul J. Rose

Additional Reading
Larus, Joel (ed.), *From Collective Security to Preventive Diplomacy* (1965).
Northedge, F.S., *The League of Nations: Its Life and Times 1920–1946* (1986).
Scott, George, *The Rise and Fall of the League of Nations* (1974).

Lebensraum (Living Space)

The direct translation of *Lebensraum* is "living space." The term originated in the nineteenth century by Friedrich Ratzel, a professor at the University of Munich and later at the University of Leipzig. The term was embraced by Adolf Hitler and his Nazi movement. *Lebensraum* has been associated with another German ideological belief, *Drang nach Osten* (q.v.)—the Drive to the East. This drive to the east belief goes back to Charlemagne's reign in the ninth century, with the myth of German superiority over the Slavic races. It produced the catalyst for the Nazi invasion of Poland in 1939 and the Soviet Union in 1941.

Nazi Germany used *Lebensraum* to justify its territorial expansions east. Hitler stated that whatever Germany needed, Germany was entitled to take since the Nordic Germans were the *Herrenvolk*—the Master Race. At the beginning of the twentieth century, British geographer Sir Halford J. MacKinder and German professor of geography Karl Haushofer (a close personal friend and advisor to Rudolf Hess) embraced the "Heartland Theory." Succinctly, this theory states that if a nation controls the heartland of Eurasia (Russia, Eastern Europe, the Moslem states of Central Asia, and China), it will eventually control the rimlands (British Isles, Scandinavia, Iberian Peninsula, Arabia, Indonesia, Philippines, Japan, etc.). Once the rimlands are controlled, that nation can control the destinies of the world. Nazi Germany enthusiastically supported this heartland-rimland theory in its drive for territorial expansion or "living space."

Hitler believed that Germany was overpopulated and needed *Lebensraum* to ease this burden. Hitler would balance his new empire with a highly industrialized Germany and predominantly agricultural, or peasant, eastern territories—all at the expense of Poland, Czechoslovakia, and the Soviet Union. After all, as Hitler believed, German workers needed to eat.

Lebensraum was not a new concept to Hitler, and Hitler's belief in it was not new to the world. In 1924, while in Landsberg prison, Hitler talked about *Lebensraum* in his book *Mein Kampf* (q.v.). Hitler was convinced Germany would again become a leading power on the Continent. Short-sighted European leaders like Édouard Daladier of France and Neville Chamberlain (qq.v.) of Great Britain, wishing to avoid another European war, chose to overlook Hitler's clearly stated expansionistic ambitions. These ambitions eventually found their expression in the remilitarization of the Rheinland in 1936, the *Anschluss* (q.v.) with Austria in 1938, and the Munich Conference (q.v.) and subsequent dismantling of Czechoslovakia in 1938–1939. The final blow, however, came on 1 September 1939 with Hitler's invasion of Poland. With appeasement's (q.v.) failure and Hitler's blatant invasion of Poland, France and Great Britain declared war on Germany on 3 September 1939. Hitler's vision of *Lebensraum* came at a cost, and that cost was the ultimate destruction of the Third *Reich*.

William H. Van Husen

Additional Reading

Liddell Hart, Basil H., *History of the Second World War* (1970).

Pinson, Koppel S., *Modern Germany,* 2nd ed. (1966).

Winks, Robin W., Crane Brinton, John B. Christopher, and Robert Lee Wolff, *A History of Civilization,* 7th ed. (1988).

Lend-Lease

During the 1940 presidential election, President Franklin D. Roosevelt (q.v.) promised the American people that their sons would not be sent to fight in a foreign war. Privately, however, Roosevelt conceded that the United States would have to do everything possible to prevent an Axis victory. Roosevelt went on to win a third term as president in 1940 despite his wavering on the critical issue of aid to Britain and eventual entry into the war.

The British, as well as interventionists in the United States, perceived Roosevelt's reelection as a positive sign that the United States would maintain its opposition to German and Japanese aggression, even at the risk of eventual war. However, on account of continued isolationist sentiment in Congress and among the American electorate, Roosevelt was forced to act cautiously in his policies dealing with wartime aid to Great Britain.

Roosevelt's ultimate test of resolve over the issue of British aid occurred in December 1940. Early on the morning of 9 December, Roosevelt received a lengthy personal cable from British prime minister Winston S. Churchill (q.v.). In that letter, Churchill carefully spelled out the grave turn of events in the war in Europe. He informed Roosevelt that German submarine warfare was taking a devastating toll of Allied shipping in the Atlantic and that Britain was in dire need of critical war materiel.

Furthermore, he confessed to the president that "the moment approaches when we shall no longer be able to pay cash for shipping and other supplies." Churchill then expressed his confidence that Roosevelt would somehow find a way to continue the flow of munitions and goods to Great Britain.

Eight days later, the president held a news conference in which he told reporters that he was devoted to maintaining Britain as America's first line of defense. The president argued that since Britain needed a continual flow of supplies to help maintain America's security, it might become necessary to lend to Great Britain those goods considered essential to the war effort. "What I am trying to do," said Roosevelt, "is eliminate the dollar sign." Thus, Roosevelt accomplished two goals: he superficially adhered to the Neutrality Acts (q.v.) while at the same time he circumvented Britain's cash shortage crisis. The concept of Lend-Lease was Roosevelt's answer to Churchill's plea.

The American public responded enthusiastically to the Lend-Lease proposal. On 29 December, Roosevelt elaborated on the proposal in a "fireside chat" to the American people. Once again, he emphasized Britain's role as America's first line of defense and repeated his pledge to keep the nation out of the war. He concluded by declaring that "we must be the great arsenal of democracy." Thus on 10 January 1941, the Lend-Lease bill, cleverly numbered *H.R. 1776,* was formally introduced into Congress.

The Lend-Lease legislation was simple and straightforward. The bill sought to empower the president "to sell, transfer title to, exchange, lease, lend, or otherwise dispose of" any defense materiel or supplies to any nation whose defense "the president deems vital to the defense of the United

States." During congressional debates over the Lend-Lease legislation, isolationists, led by aviator Charles A. Lindbergh, strenuously lobbied Congress to defeat the legislation. Such legislation, argued the isolationists, would only lead the United States to war. Historian and staunch isolationist Charles A. Beard called upon Congress to "preserve one stronghold of order and sanity even against the gates of hell." But by January 1941, the isolationists were in the minority.

A large majority of Americans lined up behind the president in support of Lend-Lease, and when Republican leader Wendell Willkie endorsed it, the legislation became a bipartisan issue, virtually assuring its passage through Congress. After a period of brief debate, the House passed the Lend-Lease bill by a wide margin. And despite a small group of opponents in the Senate, led by Democrat Burton Wheeler and Republican Gerald Nye, the Lend-Lease bill passed through the upper house by a two-to-one margin. On 11 March 1941, the Lend-Lease Act became law with the president's signature. Shortly thereafter, Congress approved an initial appropriation of $7 billion to support Lend-Lease operations.

In the end, the Lend-Lease Act became the last great battle fought by the isolationists. The enactment of the bill also proved to be a critical turning point in American foreign policy. Many Americans continued to hope that the Axis powers could be defeated without direct American intervention; but by offering Britain access to American resources and supplies, the United States took a major step toward war.

Once the Lend-Lease Act was signed, a new problem arose. In the face of intense German submarine warfare, many advisors warned the president that without American convoys, Lend-Lease goods were unlikely to reach England. Roosevelt again wavered in the face of intense pressure from both the interventionists and the isolationists.

Not until 27 May did the president announce in public his solution to the convoy dilemma. Broadcasting nationwide, he declared that U.S. naval patrols were ready to help protect the delivery of supplies to Britain. But he carefully avoided using the term "convoy." He knew that if the U.S. Navy began formal convoy duty, engagements with German submarines would be unavoidable, and he felt that the American public would not stand for such direct action.

The next major challenge for Lend-Lease operations was the extension of aid to the Soviet Union. In response to the German attack on Russia on 22 June 1941, Roosevelt said, "Of course we are going to give all the aid we possibly can to Russia." But he did not mention the option of extending Lend-Lease aid to the Soviets. Although he had the power to do so, Roosevelt at first hesitated to extend Lend-Lease to the Soviets because there was widespread U.S. antipathy toward the Soviet Union. He nonetheless remained privately committed to extending aid to the Soviet Union.

After having carefully tilled the ground of public opinion, the Roosevelt administration introduced a second Lend-Lease bill into Congress in September 1941. The bill, designed to extend aid to the Soviets, passed the House on 10 October 1941 and the Senate on 23 October. A week later, Roosevelt announced his decision to send $1 billion worth of Lend-Lease aid to the Soviet Union.

Congress mandated the termination of all Lend-Lease aid at the end of the war, although Roosevelt's successor, Harry S Truman (q.v.) tried unsuccessfully to curtail Lend-Lease to the Soviets in May 1945. Lend-Lease assistance to the Soviet Union was formally ended in September 1945, even though Lend-Lease oil continued to be delivered to the Soviets and other recipients well into 1947.

Paul G. Pierpaoli, Jr.

Additional Reading

Dallek, Robert, *Franklin D. Roosevelt and American Foreign Policy, 1932–1945* (1979).

Divine, Robert A., *The Reluctant Belligerent: American Entry into World War II,* 2nd ed. (1979).

Heinrichs, Waldo, *Threshold of War: Franklin D. Roosevelt and American Entry into World War II* (1988).

Lidiče

Within hours after the assassination of Reinhard Heydrich (q.v.) in Prague, Czechoslovakia, on 27 May 1942, Adolf Hitler (q.v.) ordered that "all conceivable" measures be taken to find the attackers. Hostages were arrested and martial law imposed. When Heydrich died of his wounds on 4 June, Hitler threatened more drastic actions if the assassins were not caught. Tips and information came from a variety of sources, and a letter, intercepted by a Czech factory owner, led the *Gestapo* (q.v.) to the village of Lidiče. On 9 June, the day of Heydrich's funeral, Hitler gave the order that Lidiče, located west of Prague, be destroyed in retribution.

According to Horst Böhm, the *Gestapo* chief

The Czech village of Lidiče burns after being torched by the Nazis in reprisal for the assassination of Reinhard Heydrich, 9 June 1942. (IWM K 9332)

in Prague, "On June 9th 1942 at 19:45 *Gruppenführer* [Karl Hermann] Frank telephoned after an interview with Hitler and told me to deal with the commune of Lidiče in the following manner: (1) all men to be executed by shooting. (2) All women to be sent into concentration camps. (3) Children are to be concentrated, those capable of being Germanicized are to be sent to SS families in Germany and the rest elsewhere. (4) The commune is to be burnt down and leveled to the ground."

To a large degree, the destruction of Lidiče resulted from the frustrations of the SS in not being able to capture the assassins of Heydrich. Even though scores of Czechs were arrested and many were executed, the authorities could not locate the assassins. In choosing Lidiče for revenge, the *Gestapo* had seized upon flimsy evidence.

SS-*Gruppenführer* Frank, the leader of the action, later maintained that "during the investigations into the assassination of . . . Heydrich, it was discovered that the village of Lidiče near Kladno was a hideout for English paid parachutist-agents." He added that "the obliteration of the village is a political measure of top significance, for it makes it absolutely clear to the Czechs that the *Reich* will never permit the existence of any center of resistance even in the remotest corner of the Protectorate. This measure has impressed the Czech population in a corresponding manner."

The action against Lidiče was well planned and executed. At 10:00 P.M., 9 June 1942, German troops and police, aided by Czech gendarmerie, encircled the village. They registered the population, searched the houses, evacuated the livestock, and seized valuables. All males over the age of fourteen were held together, while women and children were sent to the local school.

At dawn, in a farmyard, a special squad of regular police shot 173 male inhabitants, all those over the age of sixteen. The women of the village, numbering 198, were transported to another town before being sent to the Ravensbrück concentration camp. The eighty-one children deemed racially unsuitable were sent to the Chelmno concentration camp and later killed. The remaining seventeen children were placed for adoption by German families. The village was then obliterated.

The victims were buried on 11 June in a mass grave dug by Jewish prisoners. Army engineers burned the houses and barns. Units from the *Reich* Labor Service were brought in to level the area and eliminate all traces of the village. Nazi vengeance was not yet complete; an additional twenty-six inhabitants were later put to death, as the SS continued its pursuit of villagers.

On 14 June, several days after the destruction of Lidiče, a member of the Czech resistance panicked and identified the two Heydrich assassins to the gendarmerie. The location of their hiding place, the crypt of the Church St. Cyril and Methodius in Prague, was discovered, and SS troops surrounded the church. The two assassins committed suicide before they could be captured. Nevertheless, Nazi retribution against Czechoslovakia continued.

The destruction of Lidiče and the murder of its inhabitants made headlines around the world, and sparked widespread indignation. The village became a symbol of Nazi barbarity, especially because it was destroyed not as the result of military action, but as a deliberate act of retribution. The Czech puppet government cooperated with the Nazis in their pursuit of the assassins, thereby fully discrediting itself and lending prestige to the government-in-exile led by President Eduard Beneš (q.v.). He assumed the moral leadership of all Czechs and gained recognition from the Allied powers.

John David Waite

Additional Reading
Bradley, John, *Lidice: Sacrificial Village* (1972).
Mastny, Vojtech, *The Czechs Under Nazi Rule: The Failure of National Resistance, 1939–1942* (1971).

Lithuania
See BALTIC STATES

Locarno Pact
The agreement signed at Locarno, Switzerland, in 1925 aimed at bringing peace to Western Europe. Germany, France, Belgium, Great Britain, and Italy agreed to respect their respective borders and not to go to war with each other, except in self-defense or in accordance with an action of the League of Nations (q.v.).

As part of the treaty, Germany sought admission to the League, which enabled it to enter the realm of "acceptable countries." Germany did not, however, accept its eastern border with Po-land, but agreed to change it only by peaceful means.

The leaders at Locarno, Aristide Briand of France, Austen Chamberlain of England, and Gustav Stresemann (q.v.) of Germany, believed the agreement would lead to an era of collective security. Briand echoed the sentiment at Locarno by declaring: "Differences between us still exist, but henceforth it will be for the judge to declare the law . . . Away with rifles, machine guns, cannons! Clear the way for conciliation, arbitration, peace!"

For Germany, Locarno was particularly important. Foreign Minister Stresemann ended Germany's diplomatic isolation and "revised" the hated Treaty of Versailles (q.v.). Germany would no longer have to worry that the French Army would invade over reparation problems, as they had in 1923.

The "Spirit of Locarno" nevertheless, was misleading. It placed faith in the League of Nations, which proved unable to enforce treaties. Germany was still not reconciled to its eastern frontier, and several key European powers, such as the Soviet Union, were left out of the agreements. In addition, many Germans were influenced by nationalist propaganda that scorned Locarno because Germany acknowledged the loss of Alsace and Lorraine.

Glenn R. Sharfman

Additional Reading
Black, C.E., and E.C. Helmreich, *Twentieth Century Europe* (1972).
Jacobson, Jon, *Locarno Diplomacy: Germany and the West, 1925–1929* (1972).
Pinson, Koppel, S., *Modern Germany* (1966).

Loyalty Oath to Hitler
See BLOMBERG-FRITSCH CRISIS AND NIGHT OF THE LONG KNIVES

L

M

Majdanek
See CONCENTRATION CAMPS

MANHATTAN Project

Taking its name from the location of its first office, the organization known as the MANHATTAN Project was brought together in 1942 to develop an atomic bomb for the United States. The original impetus behind the project came from a group of émigré scientists who were concerned by indications that German physicists were making important advances in the area of nuclear fission.

Moved by fear of the consequences of atomic weapons in Nazi hands, the scientists convinced Albert Einstein (q.v.) to convey their apprehensions in a letter to President Franklin D. Roosevelt (q.v.) in October 1939. Intrigued by Einstein's reference to "extremely powerful bombs of a new type," Roosevelt authorized a coordinating commission and later diverted military funds into the top-secret research.

By summer 1942, the MANHATTAN Project, with major facilities in Los Alamos, New Mexico, Oak Ridge, Tennessee, and Hanford, Washington, took shape under the direction of Brigadier General Leslie Groves (q.v.). Eventually, the project absorbed two billion dollars and employed 150,000, including renowned scientists Leo Szilard, Enrico Fermi, and J. Robert Oppenheimer (q.v.). Managed with such compartmentalized secrecy that some employees never knew exactly what they were working on, the MANHATTAN Project produced a successful atomic detonation in the New Mexico desert in July 1945. Concurrently, the 509th Composite Group, which was to deliver the bomb, was completing secret training in the remote Utah desert.

Meanwhile, the Allied advance into Germany in spring 1945 produced evidence that the German scientists were nowhere near harnessing nuclear fission. By August, events dictated that the bomb be used to induce a Japanese surrender. Though a number of the MANHATTAN Project's leading scientists were now warning against use of the new weapon, the new president, Harry S Truman (q.v.), had no serious reservation. His authorization unleashed the products of the MANHATTAN Project on Hiroshima and Nagasaki in August 1945.

Blaine T. Browne

Additional Reading

Herken, Gregg, *The Winning Weapon* (1980).
Jones, Vincent C., *Manhattan: The Army and the Atomic Bomb* (1985).
Rhodes, Robert, *The Making of the Atomic Bomb* (1986).

Marshall Plan

The Marshall Plan, together with the Truman Doctrine that preceded it, and the foundation of NATO that was to follow, can be seen as marking the beginning of the Cold War. From these three events until the collapse of the Warsaw Pact in the early 1990s, the states of the Northern Hemisphere were split militarily, economically, and ideologically into two distinct and opposing power blocs.

The Marshall Plan was also a key event in the recovery of Western Europe from the destruction wrought by the two world wars. At the same time, it is a reminder of how the great European empires that dominated the world scene for more than two centuries were by 1950 subordinate to the two superpowers that emerged from World War II. Its proper title was the "European Recovery Program," but it is more commonly known as the Marshall Plan, after its developer, U.S. Secretary of State George C. Marshall (q.v.), who had been chief of staff of the U.S. Army during the war.

In the aftermath of World War II, political leaders were determined not to repeat the follies of the post–World War I settlement. In 1919, the vicious and vengeful mood of the victors, and the imposition of impossibly heavy reparations on the defeated Germany, which could only be repaid through American and British loans, were both a contributory cause to the economic disasters of the 1930s, and a major cause of World War II. This second global conflict, mainly as a result of aerial bombardment, caused even greater damage and destruction to Europe. Twenty percent of its factories were destroyed or seriously damaged, whole cities needed rebuilding, much of the railway network was ruined, and western Germany was full of millions of refugees fleeing the Red Army.

The might of the Red Army loomed menacingly over a Western Europe too weak to defend itself, and there were strong Communist parties waiting to turn economic distress into political profit. The situation, said Winston S. Churchill (q.v.) in his "Iron Curtain" speech at Fulton, Missouri, in March 1946, was "a growing peril and challenge to Christian civilization."

Early in 1947, Britain informed the United States that though it would continue to provide military support to Greece in its fight against Communist rebellion, it could no longer afford economic aid to Greece or Turkey. The U.S. response was $400 million for the two countries, quickly followed by the announcement of the Truman Doctrine: "It must be the policy of the United States to support free peoples who are resisting attempted subjugation by armed minorities or by outside pressures." In May, a U.S. State Department report spoke of a steadily deteriorating situation in Europe, with the possibility of a return to the economic chaos of the 1930s, a breakdown of international trade, and political gains by the Communists.

Thus it was that on 5 June 1947, U.S. Secretary of State Marshall offered substantial financial aid, not just to Western Europe, but to any government willing to cooperate with America in the task of economic recovery. In contrast to the militancy of the Truman Doctrine, the offer was set out in humanitarian tones: "Our policy is directed not against any country or doctrine, but against hunger, poverty, desperation, and chaos. Its purpose shall be the revival of a working economy . . ." America already had provided $15 billion in aid to Europe since V-E Day. Under the Marshall Plan, a further $23 billion was to follow.

The motives behind the American offer were mixed. On the one hand, there was a considerable element of self-interest, as well as the strategic need to keep Communism out of Western Europe. Only if these countries were on a sound financial footing could they provide a market for U.S. goods. But there also was a large degree of compassion for those who suffered so grievously during the war.

Britain and France took the lead in accepting the offer. The two foreign ministers, Ernest Bevin (q.v.) and Georges Bidault, invited their Soviet counterpart to a meeting on the topic, but he turned them down. They next invited all the European states, except Germany and Spain, to a conference in Paris. The Soviet Union ordered its satellites not to attend, though Poland and Czechoslovakia expressed great interest. Neutral Finland, fearful of provoking the Soviets, also stayed away. Eventually, representatives of fourteen countries assembled in Paris to discuss the American proposal and to list Western Europe's requirements for 1948 through 1951.

The only stipulation made by the United States was that the Europeans should decide on the allocation of Marshall Plan aid themselves. The U.S. government did not want to appear to be meddling in European affairs. This led to the setting up of the Organization for European Economic Cooperation (OEEC) in April 1948. After much hesitation, the OEEC decided on a formula whereby aid was distributed on the basis of each member state's balance of payments and trade deficits. Not an entirely satisfactory solution, as countries with the lowest levels of economic activity, and hence of living standards, inevitably received the least. The OEEC was to outlive the Marshall Plan, and went on to greatly expand the range of its activities. In 1960, it was joined by the U.S. and Canada, and changed its title to the Organization for Economic Cooperation and Development (OECD).

The impact of the Marshall Plan was economic, political, and psychological. It was one of the most important cornerstones for Western Europe's remarkable recovery in the second half of the twentieth century. To quote Churchill: "Without the massive dollar aid provided by the American administration . . . Europe might well have foundered into ruin and misery in which the seeds of Communism might have grown at a deadly pace. General Marshall's decision was on the highest level of statesmanship. . . ."

M

The financial help provided by the plan was used to build modern industrial plants, to replace war-damaged factories, and to modernize the Continent's transport infrastructure. In many instances, war damage proved a blessing in disguise, as much of what was destroyed was obsolete or obsolescent. It is ironic that a Europe largely stripped of its political and military influence in the world was later to reach levels of prosperity undreamed of during the era of its imperial power.

By 1950, Western Europe's combined gross national product (GNP) was equal to the 1938 figure; by 1952 it was twice the prewar figure. The growth, moreover, was sustained. In the decade 1949–1959, America's GNP grew by 6.9 percent. In Western Europe, only Britain (5.0 percent) and Belgium (6.2 percent) had lower growth rates. All other countries grew at a faster rate than the United States, with West Germany (15 percent), Austria (11.4 percent), and Italy (10.4 percent) at the top. Western Europe's wealth tripled in a single generation. Such spectacular economic achievements were the result of many factors, but chief among them, and absolutely indispensable, was the financial assistance of the Marshall Plan.

The plan undoubtedly exacerbated the Cold War split. Marshall offered aid to all countries irrespective of ideology. Had the Eastern European countries been able to accept the aid, they almost surely would have been weaned away from Communism and Soviet domination. For that reason, Josef Stalin (q.v.) forbade them to take the assistance offered. The United States must have foreseen this outcome, and from then on, the U.S. was able to pose as the generous benefactor, in contrast to the stubborn intransigence of its Soviet rival.

In response, Stalin tried to portray the plan as an example of American imperialism, and he ordered the Western Communist parties, particularly the large ones in France and Italy, to stir up unrest and political instability. The success of the Marshall Plan and the consequent speedy economic recovery foiled him in both respects. From 1947 until the demise of the Soviet Empire forty years later, the two halves were not only in different military camps, they were also operating two completely different economic systems. It is idle, but fascinating, to wonder what the state of the Eastern European economies would be today had they been permitted to accept American aid.

Another effect of the Marshall Plan was the impetus it gave to European unity. American insistence on Europe deciding for itself how Marshall Plan aid should be distributed led to the establishment of the OEEC, the first time European states

ever collaborated except in temporary and constantly changing political and military alliances. The lessons learned and the experience of working together toward a common aim were to prove useful to the founding fathers of the European Community.

Phillip Green

Additional Reading

Gimbel, J., *The Origins of the Marshall Plan* (1976).
Hogan, M.J., *The Marshall Plan* (1987).
Urwin, Derek W., *Western Europe since 1945* (1990).

Mauthausen

See CONCENTRATION CAMPS

Mein Kampf

Adolf Hitler (q.v.) began work on his political tract while imprisoned at Landsberg for his participation in the 8–9 November 1923 Beer Hall *Putsch* (q.v.). He actually dictated the two volumes, the first published in 1925 and the second a year later, giving the book the quality of a long and rambling discourse. The best expression of his ideas, *Mein Kampf* depends heavily on nationalist, racist, and anti-democratic tracts popular in late-nineteenth-century Austria and Germany. Rather than simply opposing the current political order, he offered his vision for overthrowing and completely replacing it, a vision to which he remained remarkably true.

More than half of the first volume deals with Hitler's early life, at least as he chose to portray it, the development of his worldview, and his formative experiences during World War I and the German revolution of 1918–1919. The remaining 300 pages ramble on, covering his early political activities, the beginnings of the Nazi Party, and some of his thoughts on race and politics. The second volume, slightly shorter than the first and subtitled "The National Socialist Movement," is clearly the more original of the two. The recurrent themes of both volumes are his vicious anti-Semitism, his expansionist philosophy cloaked as *Lebensraum* (q.v.) or living space, and his ambition for the dictatorial rule of Germany.

Although poorly written and the subject of repeated editing, *Mein Kampf* sold almost 300,000 copies by 1933 and close to 10 million by 1943, earning Hitler substantial royalties. Once he came to power, it was widely purchased in Germany and abroad, having been translated into sixteen languages. Despite its apparent popularity, the book was not widely read, at least not in its entirety. *Mein Kampf* is banned in Germany today.

Robert G. Waite

Additional Reading

Hammer, Hermann, "*Die deutschen Ausgaben von Hitlers 'Mein Kampf,' " Vierteljahreshefte für Zeitgeschichte* (April 1956), pp. 161–178.

Hitler, Adolf, *Mein Kampf* (translated by Ralph Mannheim) (1971).

Maser, Werner, *Hitler's* Mein Kampf: *An Analysis* (1970).

Molotov-Ribbentrop Pact

At dawn on 22 June 1941, the greatest single military operation in history unfolded as the German Army invaded the Soviet Union. Three million German troops launched a 1,000-mile-wide attack, the first invasion of Russia since Napoleon's ill-fated try in 1812. Four years later, the Soviets would drive the German Army out at a cost of more than 20 million lives.

Less than two years earlier, Josef Stalin (q.v.) had signed a nonaggression pact with Adolf Hitler (q.v.). With the Soviet Union as an ally, and not an enemy at his back, Hitler had unleashed the *Blitzkrieg* (q.v.) attacks, first on Poland and then on Western Europe. The Soviets had trusted the nonaggression pact so much that the German invasion came as a complete surprise. How did it happen?

In *Mein Kampf* (q.v.) in 1924, Hitler wrote that expansion in Europe must be obtained

> . . . at the expense of Russia, and that this meant that the new *Reich* must again set itself on the march along the roads of the Teutonic Knights of old to obtain by the German sword sod for the German plough and daily bread for the nation.

Truth and honesty had no place in Hitler's relations with other people. He often contradicted himself and told people what he wanted them to hear at a given time and place. But throughout his many vacillations and falsehoods ran a constant theme: his overriding objective to create a pure, master race and provide it with living space in the east where it could grow and prosper. This was a constant in his thinking. He went to war with the West in 1939 because Britain and France were interfering with his plans to conquer Poland as a first step to moving into the Ukraine.

Stalin read *Mein Kampf* in translation and should have been aware of Hitler's designs in the east. He should have understood clearly the message: "We take up where we left off 600 years ago. We stop the endless German movement to the south and west, and turn our gaze towards the east."

Since Stalin was aware of Hitler's designs on the Soviet Union, why did he sign a nonaggression pact and a treaty of friendship with him? The answer is that he had little choice. For, while Germany had the strongest, best equipped, and most feared army in the world, the Red Army had been devastated by Stalin's purges (q.v.) of the 1930s. The disorganized, inexperienced, and demoralized Soviet Army needed to be completely rebuilt, and that required time that he hoped a pact with Hitler would give him.

Stalin also viewed with alarm the growing might of the German Army, as Hitler assaulted the Treaty of Versailles (q.v.) by rearmament, occupation of the Rhineland (q.v.), annexation of Austria, and the conquest of Czechoslovakia. He was acutely aware of his own weakness against the growing might of Japan, and feared a two-front war with Japan and Germany. Here, Stalin followed the old maxim that countries will behave aggressively when they can and defensively when they must. His own weakness dictated that he must now behave defensively.

Their practical need to cooperate overrode any ideological, personal, or historical enmity between the two dictators. It may have been true, as often alleged, that in the nonaggression pact Marx had been sacrificed upon the altar of Machiavelli, but still there were strong precedents for such cooperation. Bismarck had set the example with czarist Russia. In the 1920s, the two countries were forced into each other's arms by the hostility of the world community. As political outcasts, they signed the Rapallo Treaty (q.v.) and cooperated on trade and military affairs. Soviet attempts to reach a rapprochement with Britain and France were rebuffed as well. Stalin saw that his only acceptable alternative was to reach an agreement with his ideological rival, Hitler.

Foreign Ministers Vyacheslav M. Molotov and Joachim von Ribbentrop (qq.v.) signed the pact in Moscow on 23 August 1939. It bound the two countries to refrain from aggression against each other and not to help any third party at war with either of the signatories, to consult on problems of common interest, and to settle disputes in a friendly manner. A secret protocol provided for *de facto* partitioning of Eastern Europe.

It is doubtful whether either party was sincere

M

in its commitment to the other. Hitler most surely was not. He always intended to invade the Soviet Union once he had settled with Poland, Britain, and France. He too, did not want a two-front war. He needed to protect his rear while attacking Western Europe. Stalin's intentions are less clear. He tried mightily to appease Hitler and avoid war. He was subservient in carrying out his treaty obligations so as to please Hitler. Stalin even neglected the western defenses of the Soviet Union so as not to provoke Hitler. He refused to believe Western reports or even reports from his own spies (Leopold Trepper in Europe and Richard Sorge [qq.v.] in Japan), that Hitler was planning to attack, and he took no precautions to blunt the attack. His surprise appeared to be total.

The pact was demoralizing to Communists throughout the world who could not understand this ideological about-face by the motherland of the international Communist movement. Communist spokesmen have been hard-pressed since to explain why. They have defended the pact as a grave necessity that gave the Soviet Union time to strengthen its military forces in preparation for the struggle to come. Communist apologists also have argued that the Soviet invasion of Poland and the Baltic states was done to protect the local populations from the Germans. The need for time to build up Soviet military forces sounds plausible. But given what is known about Soviet deception, duplicity, tactics, and ideological motives, the explanation for the invasion of the Baltic states and Poland lacks credibility.

Paul J. Rose

Additional Reading
Beloff, Max, *The Foreign Policy of Soviet Russia, Vol. 2, 1936–1941* (1949).
Celil, Robert, *Hitler's Decision to Invade Russia, 1941* (1975).
Read, Anthony, and David Fisher, *The Deadly Embrace* (1988).

Morgenthau Plan

The Morgenthau Plan was a list of proposed policies that were to give direction to the administration of postwar occupied Germany. Drafted in August-September 1944 by the U.S. Treasury Department and endorsed by Treasury Secretary Henry Morgenthau, Jr. (q.v.), the document contained fourteen policies intended to "prevent Germany from starting World War III." Although many of the suggestions mirrored those made by other cabinet offices, the Treasury plan insisted that the key to pacifying Germany was the destruction of its industrial capacity.

Specific proposals called for stripping the Ruhr Valley of its plants and closing its mines, the destruction of all German armaments factories, and the prohibition of future industrial activities. In short, Germany was to be transformed from Europe's leading industrial economy into "a country primarily agricultural and pastoral in character."

The plan was tentatively approved by President Franklin D. Roosevelt and Prime Minister Winston S. Churchill (qq.v.) at the Quebec Conference (*see* Conferences, Allied), but quickly drew criticism from within the U.S. government. Among its opponents were Secretary of State Cordell Hull and Secretary of War Henry Stimson (qq.v.), who argued that the Treasury Department's "Carthaginian" proposals would destroy any hope for a lasting peace in Europe.

When the plan was leaked to the press, this internecine bickering proved quite an embarrassment to the Roosevelt administration. The embarrassment was compounded when Nazi propaganda minister Joseph Goebbels (q.v.) made repeated references to the plan's policies as proof of the harsh treatment that would befall Germany should it surrender. After only two weeks, Roosevelt began to distance himself from the document. Before the year was out, the Morgenthau Plan was officially discarded.

Richard Leiby

Additional Reading
Byrnes, James F., *Speaking Frankly* (1947).
Morgenthau, Henry, Jr., *Germany Is Our Problem* (1945).

Munich Crisis and Agreement

On 14–15 March 1939, the German Army marched into Prague, destroyed the Czechoslovakian government, and occupied the country. This was a flagrant violation of the Munich Agreement signed six months earlier by German dictator Adolf Hitler with Benito Mussolini of Italy, French Premier Édouard Daladier, and British Prime Minister Neville Chamberlain (qq.v.). According to historian Telford Taylor, this action "shattered the pre-existing power structure of Europe" and was the "manifest overture" to World War II. How did it happen?

The Munich Crisis was a complicated and multifaceted affair involving German expansionist ambitions and British, French, and Soviet weakness and vacillation. The fate of the peoples of the

Czech regions of Bohemia and Moravia (q.v.), and the ethnic Sudeten Germans living there, was the immediate cause of the contest of arms and wills known in history as the Munich Crisis. But the background of the crisis involved repercussions over the breakup of the Austro-Hungarian Empire after World War I, German bitterness over territory lost under the Treaty of Versailles (q.v.), and big power rivalry in Europe.

In February 1938, Hitler outlined to the *Reichstag* his intention to protect the rights not only of the Sudeten Germans but of Germans in adjoining nations. In retrospect, this statement foretold future events, not only in Czechoslovakia but also in Poland.

Early in September 1938, at a Nazi Party rally in Nuremberg, Hitler called for the right of the Sudeten Germans to self-determination. To that end, Nazi propaganda became increasingly shrill and bellicose. The Germans stepped up pressure on the Czechs by causing border incidents and threatening war unless their demands were immediately satisfied. The Nazi press continued to excite the population by use of the blackest of propaganda as Hitler prepared for military aggression.

The creation of the Republic of Czechoslovakia was one of the most gratifying outcomes of the

Treaty of Versailles that ended World War I. Created in 1919 out of the Austrian provinces of Bohemia and Moravia, plus the Hungarian provinces of Slovakia and Ruthenia, Czechoslovakia became one of the most liberal, democratic, and industrially advanced states in Eastern Europe. Within its borders were located most of the old Austro-Hungarian industries, including the renowned Skoda steel and armament manufacturers.

The German-speaking Sudetens formed a strident minority. They had long regarded themselves as superior to the Czechs and other Slavs. They frequently complained of discrimination against them by the Czechoslovak regime and claimed to be in economic distress. There originally was a measure of truth in this assertion, although they were treated far better than any other ethnic minority. Not wanting to provoke the Nazi regime in Germany, the Czech government made far-reaching concessions to satisfy Sudeten demands. They were guaranteed access to some administrative offices together with full parliamentary representation.

In May 1938, two Germans were killed in a frontier incident. These two dead men were a godsend to Adolf Hitler. In a display of mock fury, he used the incident as an excuse to further excite the

European leaders at the Munich Conference, 29–30 September 1938 (left to right): British Prime Minister Neville Chamberlain, French Premier Edouard Daladier, Hitler, Mussolini, and Italian Foreign Minister Geleazzo Ciano. (IWM NYP 68066)

German population and to mobilize his troops along the Czech border. This brought the crisis to a white heat. The Czechs, with one of the finest small armies in Europe, were not intimidated. From their standing army of 180,000 men plus more than one million reserves, they rushed 400,000 troops to their frontier with Germany. Dug in as they were behind the Carpathian Mountains, the determined Czechs could have been expected to give an excellent account of themselves, even against the powerful German Army.

In response to these provocations, the French government announced that it would honor its treaty obligations to Czechoslovakia, and Britain promised to support France. The Soviet Union also offered unspecified support in the crisis. Under these circumstances, Hitler backed down and withdrew his troops. But the *Führer,* fearing a loss of prestige, was not willing to accept this setback lightly. On 30 May 1938, in a meeting with his generals at Jüteborg, he announced his "unalterable will" to smash the Czechs by military force at an early date. A military plan, Operation GREEN, was issued setting 1 October as that date.

During the summer of 1938, the controlled Nazi press continued to vilify the Czechs. Inside Czechoslovakia, Konrad Heinlein, leader of the Sudeten German Party, urged his followers on in the use of threats, agitation, and terror. Hitler demanded that the Czechs renounce their military alliances and allow the creation of a Nazi state within Czechoslovakia.

The Western democracies, meanwhile, were having second thoughts about going to war over Czechoslovakia. Both Chamberlain and Daladier were weak leaders who presided over populations still traumatized by the brutal and senseless slaughters of World War I. Both countries had large peace movements, weak governments, and populations overwhelmingly opposed to going to war. In 1936, at Oxford and Cambridge universities, British students were signing statements that under no conditions would they ever again fight for king or country.

Both countries, Britain in particular, were militarily weak. The supposedly strong French Army, as events would soon prove, was not ready for war. Under these circumstances, both Western leaders were dealing from positions of weakness, as Hitler well understood. An alternative to war would have to be found. "Peace at any price" became their objective.

With the consent of the French government, Chamberlain sent Lord Runciman to Prague to unofficially arbitrate the issue. At his urging, the Czech government offered far-reaching additional concessions to the Sudeten Germans. They agreed to divide the country into Swiss-like cantons, to share all state offices proportionately, and to make large grants of money to them for economic relief. But no concessions short of an outright invasion of Czechoslovakia would satisfy Hitler. An alternative to peace would have to be found. "War at any price" became his objective.

Hitler's appetite for aggression was insatiable and the situation was now very much to his liking. Historian Louis L. Snyder noted that with the absorbtion of Austria into the *Reich,* Germany's appearance on the map "gave the impression of a giant wolf's-head, its mouth surrounding western Czechoslovakia, its top canine tooth in Silesia, the bottom tooth in northern Austria."

Hitler had every intention of snapping the jaws shut when the situation was more to his liking. In the 1935 Czech election, the Nazi Party won more than 60 percent of the Sudeten vote, and was demanding the right to "full liberty for Germans to proclaim their Germanism and their adhesion to the ideology of Germans"—that is, to become willing and useful tools of Hitler's movement.

In February 1938, Hitler spoke in the *Reichstag* of the "terrible conditions" of the German minority in Czechoslovakia. He again offered German protection against the horrible atrocities allegedly being inflicted by the Czechs. Other prearranged incidents along the frontier prompted Czech president Eduard Beneš (q.v.) to declare martial law. As a warning to Britain and France, Hitler announced the construction of the West Wall (q.v.), "the most impregnable defense ever constructed by man," along Germany's western frontier.

On 15 September 1938, Neville Chamberlain decided to try personal diplomacy. He was seventy years old and looked every day of it. Hitler was surprised and overjoyed when informed that the aging head of the British government would come all the way to Berchtesgaden (flying in the crude aircraft of that time was both dangerous and tiring), essentially to plead with him for peace. Hitler, a much younger man, did not offer to meet the aged Chamberlain in a more convenient location. *"Ich bin vom Himmel gefallen,"* exclaimed the surprised Hitler in a German expression of surprise, meaning roughly "I fell from the sky," when told that the British prime minister would make the long journey to meet with him.

Chamberlain's intention was to determine Hitler's price for peace, seek French agreement, and then impose the conditions on the Czechs.

The meeting with Hitler was not a conference but rather a one-on-one affair. Hitler demanded the cession to Germany of many of the Sudeten areas of Czechoslovakia. Having no apparent objection himself, Chamberlain consulted the French, who readily agreed. Pressure was immediately put on the Czechs to accept. They did so, on 15 September, subject to new frontiers being established by an international commission.

Elated by these conditions, Chamberlain flew to Germany for a second meeting with Hitler, this time at Bad Godesberg. He found Hitler in a fury and making even more extreme demands. To Chamberlain's dismay, Hitler attacked the accords as entirely inadequate and upped the ante: the Sudeten territory must be incorporated into Germany immediately to avoid a general war. Germany was going to get "what rightly belonged to her," or else.

So astonished he could hardly speak, Chamberlain accepted a map and a note from Hitler indicating the desired areas of Czechoslovakia and returned to London to consult again with his divided cabinet and the French government. On 20 September, without consulting Prague, Britain and France notified the Czech government that those districts principally inhabited by Sudeten Germans must be ceded to Germany immediately to avoid war. If the Czechs agreed, their future security would be guaranteed. The Czechs rejected the ultimatum out of hand.

At that point, Benito Mussolini and President Franklin D. Roosevelt (qq.v.) interceded, proposing a four-power conference. In desperation, Chamberlain jumped at the idea. In a Berlin speech on 26 September, Hitler assured the world that if the Sudeten problem were solved, Germany would present no more "territorial claims in Europe." Wearily, Chamberlain returned once again to Germany, this time to Munich. He presented a sad spectacle as he pleaded anew with the German dictator for peace. He stated that even if his mission should fail, ". . . it was right to attempt it. For the only alternative was war." To the conference to decide their fate, the Czechs were not invited. The British and French accepted, without serious dissent, all of Hitler's demands.

Under the terms of the agreement, Germany would occupy the Sudeten areas of Czechoslovakia on 1 October, and an international commission would supervise plebiscites in all areas where the Czech population was not in the majority. The four powers present at the conference would guarantee the independence of what remained of Czechoslovakia. In the annexed regions, the Czechs would leave behind all valuable materials, especially arms and munitions. To add insult to injury, Britain also signed a peace and friendship treaty with Hitler.

Chamberlain, in a triumphant mood, returned to Britain to receive a hero's welcome. He was diverted from the airport directly to Buckingham Palace to receive congratulations from King George VI (q.v.). Then he went to Number 10 Downing Street, where enthusiasm was also high. Waving the agreement that he and Hitler signed, he told the excited crowd: "My good friends, this is the second time in our history that there has come from Germany to Downing Street, peace with honor. I believe it is peace for our time."

Chamberlain, a gentleman of the old school, seemed not to realize that Hitler's signature was worthless. In short order Hitler produced new demands. He wanted the right to construct a highway across what remained of Czechoslovakia. He insisted on the right to dispose of Slovakia and Ruthenia, and he named himself arbiter of the border dispute between Czechoslovakia and its neighbors, Poland and Hungary.

When Emil Hácha, the new president of Czechoslovakia protested, he was summoned to Berlin and treated to a tirade of abuse and insults. Finally worn down, Hacha gave in and signed the treaty, making his country a protectorate of Germany. In a mocking gesture of his insincerity, Hitler then ordered his army to occupy the rest of Czechoslovakia and the country ceased to exist. On 15 March 1939, Hitler proclaimed the protectorates of Bohemia and Moravia. Slovakia, which seceded from Czechoslovakia, became an "independent" puppet state. Britain and France did nothing, claiming the guarantees they gave at Munich were to the whole of Czechoslovakia, and those guarantees were nullified by the secession of Slovakia.

Snyder has written, ". . . at Munich four men in four hours signed away the peace of Europe." The world at the time, however, reacted with joy, believing incorrectly that a war had been averted. Chamberlain was the central figure in this sorry episode. Was he a hero or a goat? Opinions differ. Winston S. Churchill (q.v.) was among the first to realize what the consequences would be. He stated,

> . . . we have sustained a total and unmitigated defeat and France has suffered even more than we have . . . And do not suppose that this is the end. This is only the beginning of the reckoning. This is only the first sip, the first foretaste of a bitter cup which will be

proffered to us year by year unless, by a supreme recovery of moral health and mortal vigor, we arise and take our stand for freedom as in olden times.

In defense of Chamberlain, it should be noted that he had only two options: either concede to Hitler's demands or resort to a war his country was unprepared to fight. British historian P.K. Kemp pointed out that when Chamberlain asked the British chiefs of staff for their opinion on the military implications of an alliance with France and other European states to resist by force any German attempt to attack Czechoslovakia, they stated without qualification that Britain was not ready for war.

Thus Hitler felt assured that Britain and France would not fight under any circumstances. He later stated that he understood the Western leaders well; he had seen them at Munich and they were "little worms." His next objective would be Poland, then the world.

The German destruction of Czechoslovakia was a threat to the entire world, but a greater di-rect threat to Britain and France. They had a most urgent interest in taking immediate counteraction, but the will, if not the means, was lacking.

Arnold Toynbee cites four reasons why they should have done so. First, Britain and France had joined with Germany in coercing concessions from the Czechs. Second, they had a moral obligation, if not a legal one, to resist any German attempt to take over the rest of the country. Third, these two great democracies were the only two European powers that might have had the ability to challenge Hitler's march toward World War II, if only they had acted. And finally, they had an overriding national interest in taking decisive action without delay. Alas, they did nothing of the sort.

Paul J. Rose

Additional Reading

Baker, James Franklin, *The U.S. and the Czecho-slovakia Crisis, 1938–1939* (1982).

Taylor, Telford, *Munich: The Price of Peace* (1979).

Toynbee, Arnold, and Veronica Toynbee (eds.), *The Eve of War, 1939* (1958).

N

Nacht und Nebel (Night and Fog)

Nacht und Nebel (Night and Fog) involved a practice by the Nazis during World War II of arresting people considered enemies of the *Reich*. Adolf Hitler (q.v.) signed a decree on 7 December 1941, that information would not be provided on arrested people and no contact would be allowed between them and friends, relatives, or other persons outside. Thus, in Germany, arrested people just disappeared as far as their family or friends knew. No exceptions were permitted and arrested persons were given no hearing or trial unless "special circumstances" warranted.

To make the practice even more sinister, arrests were often made on dark, foggy nights (very common weather in Europe) by the SS or *Gestapo* (qq.v.), whose overt agents generally wore long, black, leather overcoats and hobnailed boots that made a fearful and easily recognized metallic sound on cobblestone streets. Thus an atmosphere of terror surrounded any official visit or inquiry. The feared knock on the door was intended to intimidate anyone who might criticize or differ with the regime. Fear of arrest day or night was a major objective of the policy.

Paul J. Rose

Additional Reading

Bullock, Alan, *Hitler: A Study in Tyranny* (1962).
Bracher, Karl Dietrich, *The German Dictatorship* (1970).

National Redoubt

The National Redoubt was a German plan for final resistance in the alpine areas of Germany, Austria, and Italy. It included fortifications and underground factories for armaments production. Although tentative steps were taken in 1944–1945, Hitler did not issue an implementation order until 24 April 1945, when Allied advances made the plan impractical.

American generals took the alpine fortress very seriously, despite British skepticism. To disrupt formation of the National Redoubt, General Dwight D. Eisenhower (q.v.) sent strong forces into southern Germany and into Austria in the spring of 1945. Postwar investigations revealed that the National Redoubt was primarily a German propaganda offensive to convince the Western Allies that the war was far from over and that the only alternative to prolonged fighting was a separate peace with the Third *Reich*.

Benjamin R. Beede

Additional Reading

Minott, Rodney G., *The Fortress That Never Was: The Myth of Hitler's Bavarian Stronghold* (1964).

National Socialism

German Nazism, in many important ways, was an outgrowth or subspecies of Italian Fascism (q.v.). For example, the idea of the Nazi salute, and to a large extent, the uniformed political armies, were borrowed from the Italian Fascists. Also, Adolf Hitler greatly admired Benito Mussolini (qq.v.) and sought his support and endorsement during the 1920s.

The Germans also borrowed and adopted for their own use the totalitarian party structure of Lenin, with its well-developed mechanism for membership, control, and violence. Nazism was, nevertheless, a special German phenomenon with deep roots in the country's historical, political, and social substructure; but unlike Italian Fascism and international Communism, it had few direct ideological antecedents.

Mussolini was an avid reader of such writers as Machiavelli, Sorel, Gentile, and Prezzolini, and the Communist leaders were deeply versed in the philosophical roots of their movement. Hitler, on the other hand, appears to have read very little except for the fiction of Karl May, a smattering of military history, and the rantings of anti-Semitics and other racists.

Hegelian idealism, which glorified the state as the indispensable instrument of all human progress, appears to have influenced the political ideas of Mussolini and the Fascist movement. Hegel's influence upon Nazism, however, was negligible. Hitler had a low opinion of the state, which he saw as a mere artificial "instrument" or a means to an end. He, instead, glorified the *Volk* or nation. The philosophy of Frederick Nietzsche, to the extent that he was a social Darwinist who glorified the survival of the fittest, may have made some contribution to the brutal Nazi ideology.

Possibly, Nazi ideology was influenced to some small and uncertain extent by philosophers Immanuel Kant, Johann G. Fichte, and Hegel as developed and interpreted by such racist thinkers as Arthur de Gobineau and Houston Stewart Chamberlain (q.v.). But a close examination of the basic tenets of Nazism leads one to believe that Carl Schmitt and Alfred Rosenberg (q.v.) had a more direct influence on Nazi thought and action. Proof of other philosophical antecedents is scarce.

To Schmitt, the most important distinction in politics was one between "friend and enemy." Nations, in particular, fell into one or the other of these categories. An enemy nation, for Schmitt, was one that was different and strange in some intense or provocative way. Its "strangeness constitutes the negation of one's own kind of existence, and must therefore be repulsed or fought in order to preserve one's own way of life." From this perspective, it easily followed that war was the law of life among nations. This attitude is clearly evident in the Nazi policies toward the *"Untermenschen"* (Subhumans) of Eastern Europe. War was the natural result when the "strangeness" of another nation becomes intolerable. For Schmitt, universality was impossible and a world state would be a contradiction in terms.

Immediately after meeting Hitler in 1919, Rosenberg began to work within the Nazi Party to prove the superiority of the Nordic race. His argument followed that of General Eric Ludendorff (q.v.), who espoused semi-religious worship of the Teutonic tribal gods: Odin, Hertha, Wotan, and Siegfried. The German people, they believed, should worship their racial heritage, their blood, and their soil. To Rosenberg, Judaism and Catholicism were the two greatest enemies of "Germanity," and he wanted their elimination from German soil. He opposed such Christian values as the belief in the virtues of charity, humility, and mercy. The crucifix as a symbol of sacrifice of these values should be replaced by the swastika or sunwheel. Hitler was to be the new Messiah or savior.

Andres Gyorgy and George D. Blackwood, in their classic study of ideologies, writes that the new pagan faith had twenty-eight articles in its creed. Among them were the following:

The Divine is revealed through the eternal laws of race, blood, and soil in all things; men differ according to values and duty; the Germans must fashion the divine powers of the Nordic race that animate the race; the Nordic Soul is immortal and is the power of the Divine in the universe; and finally, a struggle must be waged for the preservation of the Nordic races on earth.

In applying this creed, two points were hammered home. First, all people are not equal, but are unequal according to their race. Second, if one race is superior (as of course the Nordic race is), then this race need not respect the rights of others. Where the needs of other races conflict with the needs of the Nordic race, as for example the need for *Lebensraum* (q.v.), those needs are void and a war of aggression is then justified on behalf of the "rights" of the superior race.

As seen by Rosenberg, each race possesses a soul that is characterized by mental, physical, and spiritual qualities peculiar to that race. No matter where the members of a race live, their political attachments and racial qualities would not be affected by national politics or cultures. A German living in another country, even if he was a citizen of that country, would remain German and owe his loyalty to Germany. During World War II, the Nazis used this concept in an effort to enlist the aid of ethnic Germans living in the United States and South America.

Rosenberg nationalized the attack on Christianity. Unlike the Italian Fascists who needed the support of the Catholic Church to rule peacefully, the Nazis planned to eliminate the influence of both Catholic and Protestant religions in Germany. Their fears and concerns were based on the consideration that the foundation of Christianity was Jewish and the higher authorities of the Catholic Church lived outside of Germany.

While Hitler was by no means a philosopher,

his emotionally charged garrulity did provide a verbal framework for the aims and methods of his followers. To a very large extent, Nazism was what Hitler said, did, and believed. Born in Austria, he felt more loyalty to Germany and Germanity than to his homeland.

Hitler's father was a minor customs official and his mother a member of the lower middle class, the so-called *petite bourgeoisie*. As a typical Austrian mother, dedicated to home and family, she became Hitler's ideal of the purpose of German womanhood. Very few women went to universities to pursue careers in the Third *Reich*. Predictably, the Germans went down in defeat in World War II without mobilizing their women.

One need look no further than *Mein Kampf* (q.v.), to find nearly all of Hitler's theoretical beliefs. His doctrines are too many and too trivial to be included here, but the following, all taken from *Mein Kampf*, merit special consideration:

Nationalism: Hitler was a nationalist in the sense that he opposed internationalism and deified the nation rather than the state. To him, the nation was a *"Volk"* community, ethnically homogeneous, a kind of tribal brotherhood in which all members worked together toward common goals. The state was primarily an instrument for preserving racial purity and for giving the people a consciousness of their destiny. It was a necessary tool in promoting the victory of the superior races over the inferior ones. To Hitler, nationalism was very useful in indoctrinating the German people to accept many of his other programs.

Racism: Hitler copied his racial concepts from Austrian anti-Semites, especially from Schmitt and Rosenberg, and substituted the word "Aryan" for "Nordic." To Hitler, the Germans, Dutch, Scandinavians, and British were Aryans. Americans could have hopes of cultural success because of their large German population, but they would first have to purge their culturally "inferior" people through the purifying effect of war.

Like Rosenberg, Hitler believed that the basis of all cultural progress was the purity of race. "All of the great cultures of the past." he insisted, "perished only because the original creative race died off through blood-poisoning." These racial ideas were central to the Nazi movement. Ultimately, they brought about the defeat of Nazi Germany when the *"Untermenschen"* of Eastern Europe refused to accept the inferior role prescribed for them.

Führerprinzip (Leadership Principle): Since the purpose of the state was to give the world the best people, it must be ruled by the "natural leaders," and not on any democratic concept of majority rule or any dogma of inborn equality. The *"volkish"* state had no need for democratic institutions. The Nazi Party represented the German people because is was in tune with the needs, fears, and aspirations of the nation. The intuition of natural leaders was a better guide to action than laws. Elites arrived at their positions through power struggles. They represented what Nietzsche called the "heroic" man who has the will and the power to dominate. The future would belong to heroes unrestrained by either law or morality. Hitler had no doubt that he and his major associates met all of these requirements to a very high degree.

Anti-Semitism: Anti-Semitism was common to most European countries because of religious prejudice, economic rivalries, and cultural differences. Also, the Jews were considered "Christ killers." They were blamed for both capitalism and Communism. Efforts were made to show that the Jews planned the domination of the world. To the Nazis, the phony book, *The Protocols of the Elders of Zion,* represented nothing less than revealed wisdom. Worst of all, the Jews were biologically "inferior." A solution had to be found to the "Jewish problem" because the very presence of Jews threatened the "purity" of the German population. Given these clearly and forcefully stated views in *Mein Kampf,* the Holocaust (q.v.) should have surprised no one.

Anti-Communism: Anti-Communist feeling came basically from political and international considerations. It was aimed primarily, not at domestic Communists, but at the Soviet Union, the Mecca and fatherland of Communism. The goal was the elimination of international Communism and the Soviet Union. Roy C. Macridis writes that an ideological struggle against international Communism and the Soviet Union served several "secular, strategic, economic, and geopolitical goals of Germany." It was related to the *Drang nach Osten* (q.v.), the Drive toward the East. These blind, anti-Communist attitudes would cost the Nazis dearly during the invasion of the Soviet Union.

Lebensraum (Living Space): Hitler considered the most important element of any nation to be ample living space. Abundant living space was not only to provide sufficient resources, but also to insure urban population was balanced with an adequate proportion of healthy peasants. The best protection against social disturbances, he insisted, was the presence of a sturdy peasant stock of small and medium land holders. Security considerations were not forgotten. Small nations went down to defeat more quickly when they could not provide for defense in depth. Hitler later learned just how important this concept was when his armies became bogged down deep inside the Soviet Union.

Expansionism: Hitler was an expansionist but not an imperialist as the term is generally understood. He did not seek colonial territory in overseas empires. Instead, he wanted territory for expansion almost exclusively in Europe. As he stated it, he would engage in, "the winning of land for settlement that would increase the area of the motherland itself."

Nazism, like most other right-wing movements, was "anti" almost everything. The Nazis opposed reason, equality, parliamentarianism, democracy, individualism, *bourgeois* society, religion, international law, and much more.

There also were "positive" themes to Nazism, if one can use the term "positive" in relation to the brutal Nazis. In this very limited sense, every negative had its opposite. From this perspective, purity of race would replace anti-Semitism; the communitarian ethic would replace individualism; order would replace chaos; and a new international order would replace the hated Treaty of Versailles.

The Nazis accepted a body of thought that was not rational and that emphasized the importance of emotions and intuition in the place of reason and scientific inquiry. In communitarian values and solidarity, they sought the key to stability and political obligations.

It is easier to describe a movement like Nazism than to explain why it was so easily accepted by a highly educated people like the Germans. Macridis writes:

> With an ideology that appealed, at least in part, to some of the basic cultural traits of the German people, with a militant party to mobilize the people behind it, with a magnetic leader trying to resurrect the national demons of the Germanic racial and national superiority while exploiting all the weakness of a deadlocked parliamentary government, the totalitarian state came to Germany with far greater support than anywhere else.

Right-wing, totalitarian movements like that of the Nazis developed in many European countries after World War I. They grew in Spain, Portugal, Poland, Italy, and throughout the Balkans. Even in countries with long democratic traditions like Britain and France, liberty was threatened seriously. But nowhere did the totalitarian state receive the support, enthusiasm, and uncritical acceptance as in Germany.

The Nazi Party was a mass party in ways that the Russian Bolsheviks, the Italian Fascists, or the Spanish Falangists were not. Its tentacles permeated into every aspect of peoples' lives more thoroughly than did the other mass parties. The Nazis were welcomed by most social and economic groups, including the church, the intellectuals, business groups, the military, middle-class workers, and even the industrial proletariat that is usually socialist or Communist. So pervasive was their appeal that they succeeded in corrupting the medical, legal, academic, and scientific professions.

How can one explain the German people's continued loyalty to Hitler and Nazism until their country had been reduced to ruins? The German people never turned against Hitler, were hardly critical of him, and never blamed him for their terrible sufferings. When things went badly, they could be heard to say, "If only Adolf knew, he would not allow it to happen." They blamed others for the sins of their *Führer.* They never gave up on him or rejected him. The Allies had to fight their way into the rubble of Berlin and take him from them. This says more than words about the mystic appeal of Nazism and its strange leader.

Although certain aspects of Nazism were borrowed from abroad, the body and soul of the movement were German. As Macridis writes, "Nazism was a homemade product. It was made in Germany by the Germans."

Paul J. Rose

Additional Reading

Adorno, T.W., et al., *The Authoritarian Personality* (1969).
Arendt, Hanna, *The Origins of Totalitarianism* (1968).
Aycoberry, Pierre, *The New Nazi Question* (1981).
Bracher, Karl Dietrich, *The German Dictatorship* (1970).
Bullock, Allan, *A Study in Tyranny* (1963).
Gasman, Daniel, *The Scientific Origins of National Socialism* (1971).
Gyorgy, Andres, and George D. Blackwood, *Ideologies of World Affairs* (1967).
Hamilton, Alistair, *The Appeal of Fascism* (1971).
Hitler, Adolf, *Mein Kampf* (1962).
Macridis, Roy C., *Contemporary Political Ideologies: Movements and Regimes* (1983).
Neumann, Franz, *Behemoth: The Structure and Practice of National Socialism* (1944).

Neutral Countries

A widespread discussion of neutrality in international relations began during World War I, and it continued into the postwar years, generating much opposition. In 1917, Woodrow Wilson stated that "neutrality is no longer feasible or desirable where the peace of the world is involved and the freedom of its people." Later, in March 1920, the League of Nations (q.v.) Council announced that "the conception of neutrality of the members of the League is incompatible with the principle that all members will be obliged to co-operate in enforcing respect for their engagements." That statement was affirmed by British and American statesmen.

The inability of the League to enforce its policies, especially after the collapse of sanctions against Benito Mussolini's (q.v.) Italy, led to a new drive for neutrality, particularly among the small nations of Europe. On 1 July 1936, a number of these countries, including Belgium, Denmark, Finland, Norway, Sweden, the Netherlands, Spain, and Switzerland reached agreement and they published a joint declaration cancelling their obligations to the League of Nations. Their neutrality was based on new assumptions, which included the premise that a nation could freely decide to participate or to remain neutral in case of a military conflict—if the belligerents permitted. With the outbreak of war in September 1939, twenty European states declared neutrality, but only five—Sweden, Ireland, Spain, Portugal, and Switzerland—were able to retain that position, though not without difficulty.

In 1920, Sweden joined the League of Nations in spite of opposition from right-wing political parties, and it became an active member. The Swedish government was committed to peace, disarmament, and international understanding. During the 1930s, its hopes for continued peace were shattered, and Sweden recognized that maintaining its neutrality would be difficult.

In spite of strong pressures from Germany, whose fleet dominated the Baltic Sea and whose air force was within striking distance of Swedish cities, the Swedish Foreign Office continued to pursue a policy of neutrality. It believed that neutrality could be maintained if several conditions were met: if the major powers had an interest in respecting that position; if the Swedish military were strong enough to command respect; if the country stayed united; and if it restricted foreign interference.

World War II was the ultimate test for Swedish neutrality. Immediately after the outbreak in 1939, Sweden announced its neutrality, a position it found increasingly difficult to maintain. The Winter War (q.v.), between Finland and the Soviet Union, prompted Sweden to shift its status to non-belligerent, as it provided Finland with weapons, food, and volunteer forces. The pragmatic nature of Swedish neutrality was apparent, but it did have limits. When the British and French asked to send troops through southern Sweden in March 1940, in order to aid Finland, the request was rejected.

Sweden's neutrality was threatened in April 1940 when the Germans occupied Denmark and Norway, thereby virtually encircling it. Sweden did assert its neutrality once again, but on several occasions German troops were permitted to pass through its territory. Furthermore, German pressure remained strong, especially because of its need for Swedish iron ore and ball bearings. Swedish neutrality shifted again in 1943 when it aided Denmark and Norway and permitted refugees, especially Jews, to flee to its territory. Danish and Norwegian police troops trained in Sweden, and they played a roll in the liberation of their countries.

In the spring of 1939, Ireland's political leaders opted for neutrality in any future European war, even if Great Britain and the Commonwealth nations were involved. Not much attention was given to Ireland's neutral stand until November 1940 when British Prime Minister Winston S. Churchill (q.v.) expressed his regret about Britain not being able to use Irish ports for its ships to combat the German submarine threat. Almost immediately, Ireland's neutrality was attacked in the press on both sides of the Atlantic. The Irish leader, Eamon de Valera, pledged that Ireland would not be used against Britain, and effective measures to guarantee that pledge were taken. Still, the attacks in the British press continued and charges were made that, for example, the German Legation in Ireland was a vast center of espionage.

At the outbreak of the war, the ties between Francisco Franco's (q.v.) Spain and the Axis powers were many and strong. The active support and intervention of Italian and German troops in the Spanish civil war (q.v.) led to his victory. He remained indebted to Mussolini and Hitler, ties that led to economic agreements and other commitments. There were also strong indications, however, of Franco's determination to remain neutral. During the Czech crisis of September 1938, for example, he assured both Britain and France that, in case of a European conflict, Spain would remain strictly neutral. Spanish national pride and Franco's genuine need to rebuild the country were important factors. While his victory in the civil war had been complete, it came only after an appalling loss of life and great physical damage to the nation. Consolidation of the Franco regime would take time.

When war broke, out some members of Franco's government were decidedly pro-Nazi, while others favored the British. France and Britain moved quickly with a series of conciliatory gestures toward Franco, including the reestablishment of traditional economic, financial, and diplomatic relations.

The rapid success of German forces, and especially the conquest of France, implied a quick end to the war. These developments led Franco to inform the Nazi government that under certain circumstances his country was ready to enter the war on the side of Germany and Italy. He had ambitions on Gibraltar and much of French North Africa. He was, however, still concerned with Britain's ability to inflict damage on Spain, and with the possibility of Spain becoming a vassal to Hitler's Germany.

Franco continued to stall, however, and in his first meeting with Hitler on 23 October 1940, he assured the Nazi leader of his strong support. Franco also emphasized his nation's problems, particularly its food shortage, and asked for direct assistance. German pressure mounted after Mussolini's forces became bogged down in Greece. By December, Hitler decided that action against Gibraltar was imminent and further plans were drawn up. Once again Franco delayed and refused to act. The invasion of the Soviet Union shifted Hitler's attentions to the eastern front and the Spanish project was abandoned. Falangist support for the Nazi aggression was strong and a division of volunteers, the "Blue Division," was organized to fight under German command against the Soviets.

Germany continued to cultivate Spain's friendship as it desired a nonbelligerent friend over a position of strict neutrality, especially in the strategic location at the tip of the Mediterranean. In fact, a nonbelligerent Spain actually served Germany's needs better than if it had become a staunch ally.

At the Paris Peace Conference in 1919, Switzerland was able to secure formal recognition of its neutrality, whose guarantee was an international obligation to peace. Switzerland joined the League of Nations, formally recognizing it's neutrality on 13 February 1920. It was an active member of that international body, participating in various actions, including economic sanctions, but was absolved from any military involvement. Military preparations were also banned on Swiss territory. The increased difficulties of the League in the 1930s prompted Switzerland to withdraw on 14 May 1938.

At the beginning of World War II, the Swiss legislature issued a declaration of neutrality, as it had done in 1914, and notified formally each belligerent of its status. But Switzerland continued to strengthen its army and mobilized almost 400,000 soldiers during the invasion of Poland. A second general mobilization came in May 1940, which involved about 450,000 troops. For economic reasons, however, it could not maintain such a large force for very long. During the war, its standing army ranged between 100,000 to 150,000. Along with nine divisions and six brigades, the Swiss military was well-equipped, and its air force had ninety Bf-109 fighters. The German Army command did take note of the Swiss fighting forces.

The successes of Nazi Germany's military campaigns placed considerable pressure on Switzerland. This included violations of its airspace, economic pressure, and veiled threats. German military plans for an invasion were drawn up under code name *TANNENBAUM*. The Nazi representative in the Swiss capital of Bern spoke out repeatedly against what he termed the "hostile attitude" of the Swiss press. As a result, the Swiss hoped for an Allied victory in the war.

Late in the war, Swiss neutrality was threatened by the Allies who planned to march through Switzerland to invade Germany. The collapse of Nazi Germany prevented this Allied troop movement and also effectively canceled any further discussion of neutrality.

Thomas F. Hale
Robert G. Waite

Additional Reading

Bindschedler, Rudolf L., et al. (eds.), *Schwedische und Schweizerische Neutralität im Zweiten Weltkrieg* (1985).

Hägglöf, M. Gunnar, "A Test of Neutrality: Sweden in the Second World War," *International Affairs*, Vol. 36 (1960), pp. 153–167.

Lee, J.J., *Ireland, 1912–1985* (1989).

Packard, Jerrold M., *Neither Friend nor Foe: The European Neutrals in World War II* (1992).

Payne, Stanley G., *The Franco Regime, 1936–1975* (1987).

Puzzo, Dante A., *Spain and the Great Powers 1936–1941* (1962).

Neutrality Acts

The Neutrality Acts were a series of four laws, passed between 1935 and 1939, designed to prevent U.S. involvement in overseas wars by restricting American commercial intercourse with belligerent countries. They originated in the belief that unscrupulous American bankers and arms merchants were responsible for dragging the United States into World War I.

This belief gained strength during the 1930s as American disillusionment with the legacy of intervention in World War I grew. It gained quasi-official sanction through the activity, between 1934 and 1936, of the Senate Special Committee Investigating the Munitions Industry, chaired by Gerald P. Nye of North Dakota. The conclusions of the Nye Committee and the growing international crisis created a climate of opinion conducive to the passage of neutrality legislation. The Neutrality Acts became a focal point in the confrontation between American isolationists and internationalists until superseded by America's entry into World War II.

The First Neutrality Act, passed in August 1935, mandated that the president, whenever he found that there existed a state of war between two or more countries, issue a proclamation identifying them as belligerents. Thereupon, it would become illegal to export weapons, munitions, or other war materiel from the United States to the belligerents until the president declared that the state of war between them had ended. The section of the Neutrality Act containing this embargo was scheduled to expire on 29 February 1936.

The First Neutrality Act also created the National Munitions Control Board to regulate the arms and munitions industry and traffic. It further prohibited American ships from carrying weapons, munitions, or war materiel destined for belligerents. Finally, the First Neutrality Act gave the president discretionary power to deny American citizens traveling on belligerent ships the protection of the American government, to ban belligerent submarines from American waters, and to take measures to prevent the use of American harbors for acts of war by belligerents.

The First Neutrality Act was a temporary compromise between isolationists in the Senate and the administration. The aim of the isolationists was to cut all commercial links between the United States and overseas belligerents and to prevent the administration from aiding any overseas belligerent in any way. The administration also wanted to preserve American neutrality, but if possible, without sacrificing either overseas commerce, or the president's ability to discriminate between aggressors and their victims. It should be noted that this was an impossible task.

In January 1936, both the administration and leading isolationist senators tried to gain support in Congress for a new neutrality act. The administration sought to increase the president's ability to discriminate against aggressors, while the isolationists wanted to limit the president's discretionary powers and further restrict American commercial contacts with belligerents. The result of this debate was a new compromise.

The Second Neutrality Act, passed in February 1936, essentially extended the provisions of the First Neutrality Act with only minor modifications. The most important amendment was a ban on American loans to belligerent countries. The Second Neutrality Act, like its predecessor, was a temporary measure and would expire on May 1, 1937.

In early 1937, Congress considered several proposals for permanent neutrality legislation before passing the Third Neutrality Act in April. That act retained the main features of its predecessor and added several new ones. The new law applied the provisions of its predecessor to internal as well as international conflicts, a response to the outbreak of the Spanish civil war (q.v.). The new act also banned Americans from traveling on belligerent ships and prohibited the arming of American merchant ships.

The most important innovation in the Third Neutrality Act was the "cash-and-carry" clause, which required belligerents to pay cash for the nonmilitary goods they bought in the United States and to transport those goods in non-American ships. In actuality, the "cash-and-carry" provision was a pro-British move, since they could "carry" their own goods, while the Axis could not. The "cash-and-carry" clause was the only temporary feature of the Third Neutrality Act and expired in May 1939.

As the European crisis deepened, the administration became more concerned with the limits the Neutrality Act placed on its ability to aid Britain and France in a potential conflict with Germany. The existing neutrality legislation put Britain and France at a disadvantage since they, more than Germany, depended on American loans and arms.

During the spring of 1939, the administration tried to get Congress to pass a revised neutrality law that would be more favorable to the Western democracies, but the isolationists prevailed. The outbreak of war in September 1939, however, resulted in a shift in popular opinion toward sympathy for the Allies. The result was the passage, in November 1939, of the Fourth Neutrality Act.

The Fourth Neutrality Act did away with the impartial arms embargo of previous neutrality legislation and instead subjected all trade with belligerents to "cash-and-carry" provisions. This allowed the Allies to exploit their dominance on the sea by importing arms from the United States while denying Germany access to American exports. The fourth act also gave the president the authority to define war zones from which American merchant ships would be banned. Most of the features of the Third Neutrality Act were retained.

The Fourth Neutrality Act was amended in November 1941 to permit armed American merchant ships to sail through the war zone and into British harbors, a further sign that support for strict neutrality was on the wane. The attack on Pearl Harbor, in December 1941, put an end to the American experiment in neutrality legislation.

Jozef Ostyn

Additional Reading

Adler, Selig, *The Isolationist Impulse: Its Twentieth-Century Reaction* (1957).

Cole, Wayne S., *Roosevelt and the Isolationists, 1932–45* (1983).

Divine, Robert A., *The Illusion of Neutrality* (1962).

Night of the Long Knives

Adolf Hitler (q.v.) came to power in 1933 with the tacit or express support of members of Germany's old ruling class. In the early years, he used his alliance with these conservatives to solidify his power. He was careful not to antagonize three groups: the bureaucracy, big business, and especially the army. Hitler was well aware that some officers in the *Reichswehr* distrusted him and his movement. As a result, initially, Hitler was quite conciliatory toward the army.

In 1934, the Nazi movement was divided between the party, on the one hand, and the *Sturmabteilung* (SA) (q.v.) on the other. The party was generally satisfied with what transpired in Germany after the so-called seizure of power on 30 January 1933. Some members, like Hermann Göring and Joseph Goebbels (qq.v.), were given high government offices. Others, like Rudolf Hess (q.v.), filled important positions in the party organization. The SA, however, was dissatisfied.

Before 1933, Hitler had created Nazi Party offices parallel to the regular governmental bureaucracy and the army. The implied promise to his followers was that they would take over the corresponding positions in government and in the *Reichswehr* once Hitler became chancellor. But this happened only in part.

By the spring of 1933, Ernst Röhm (q.v.) and his SA Brownshirts believed Hitler had sold out to the conservatives, thus betraying the Nazi revolution. Röhm therefore pressed for more radical reforms amounting to a second revolution. By the summer of 1933, the SA was seething. Its leaders were eager for blood and spoils at the expense of the conservatives who had retained their positions in the civil service and army.

The SA demanded compensation for the lean years from 1920 to 1933. Röhm's particular ambition was to replace the old, "reactionary" German *Reichswehr* with a nation in arms on the French model of 1789 or Trotsky's Red Army. He wanted to replace the classic, Prussian-based German army with the SA. In Röhm's own words, "The grey rock must be drowned in the brown fluid." This new "People's Militia" *(Volksheer)*, commanded of course by Röhm, was to be free of the traditional legal and moral restraints of the regular army. This goal, combined with Röhm's personal morals, did not endear him to the army's leaders.

The underlying problem in 1934 was the SA's greatly reduced utility to Hitler. Whereas it was vital in the "time of struggle" before 1933 and was helpful in "coordinating" or Nazifying Germany in early 1933, by 1934 the SA no longer served any essential purpose. It was causing a lot of trouble. Röhm made several key mistakes in 1934. He underestimated the number of enemies he had made in the Nazi Party (he had few friends). He greatly underestimated Hitler, and Röhm failed to state with any precision what it was he wanted.

Franz von Epp (q.v.), the Bavarian *Reichsstatthalter* (*Reich* Governor), put his finger on it: "The SA is continuing the revolution. Against whom? What is its goal? Dissatisfaction by itself doesn't give a right to revolution." These errors by Röhm made it possible for his enemies to claim that his protest movement was directed not against the conservatives, but against Hitler himself.

Despite many provocations, Hitler put up with Röhm's dissent for a long time. Time and again in 1933–1934, he tried to warn Röhm to cease agitating for a second revolution. But Röhm continued to demand an SA takeover of the army.

By the summer of 1934, the SA had grown into a serious protest movement. Röhm was openly grumbling. If Hitler "thinks he can squeeze me forever for his own ends and some fine day throw me on the ash heap, he's wrong."

The army put pressure on Hitler to do something about Röhm. In early summer 1934, matters between Hitler and Röhm finally came to a head. On 3 June, the two men met for five hours in a last attempt to resolve their differences peacefully. At Hitler's insistence, Röhm announced a month-long leave of absence for the entire SA beginning on 1 July.

On 17 June 1934, Vice Chancellor Franz von Papen (q.v.) delivered a famous speech at the University of Marburg critical of German developments under Hitler. This increased pressure on Hitler to do something about the SA. Röhm's enemies within the Nazi Party also coalesced in order to exploit the anti-SA mood for their own ends. One of his most dangerous enemies was Heinrich Himmler (q.v.). With Heydrich's (q.v.) help, Himmler began circulating rumors about Röhm's alleged plans for an SA takeover of the army and a possible coup against Hitler. Hermann Göring was also involved in these machinations. Hitler was falsely led to believe that Röhm was planning a coup d'etat.

At the end of June 1934, Hitler finally decided to eliminate the threat from Röhm once and for all. On 30 June, he struck in a manner never to be forgotten. Using units of the SS (q.v.), Hitler led an early morning raid on Röhm and the other SA leaders vacationing at Bad Wiessee in the Bavarian Alps south of Munich. Arriving unannounced at 7:10 A.M., Hitler and his SS troops went directly to the rooms inhabited by Röhm and other high SA leaders. They found Röhm, a homosexual, in bed with one of his young minions. All were arrested. The charge? They were planning a *Putsch* to overthrow Hitler and his government. Following this *Putsch*, it was alleged, Röhm would carry out his second revolution.

After their arrest, Röhm and the other SA leaders were bundled into cars and transported to Stadelheim prison in Munich. Over the next few days, many of them were shot by SS firing squads. As for Röhm, Hitler vacillated; should he be shot or allowed to go into exile? Finally, on 1 July, Hitler decided that Röhm would have to die. Two SS officers shot Röhm through the observation window in his cell door.

The killings were not restricted to Munich. Many took place in Berlin, Silesia, and other parts of Germany. On the morning of 30 June, a call went out from Munich to Berlin. Only one word was spoken, *Kolibri* (Hummingbird). On receiving it, Göring and Himmler immediately sprang into action. The blood purge was a heaven-sent opportunity for Hitler, Göring, Joseph Goebbels (q.v.), and Himmler to settle some old scores. The victims were not only SA leaders by any means. Hit lists of conservatives and other enemies were drawn up and circulated among the highest Nazi leaders.

These lists included retired Generals Kurt von Schleicher (q.v.) and Ferdinand von Bredow, Gregor Strasser, Bernhard Stempfle and Gustav von Kahr (two close associates of von Papen), and many others, all killed.

How many people were liquidated during the three-day spree? Estimates range from a low of seventy-seven, the number Hitler admitted executed, to a high of 1,000. Bracher fixes the number between 150 and 300, and this is probably the correct range. Alan Bullock admits that we don't know for sure how many perished.

On 30 June, Hitler eliminated the "threat" from Röhm and the other high SA leaders, as the conservatives wished. But those same conservatives should have been troubled by several aspects of the purge. Hundreds of people, including two generals, were liquidated by Hitler without anything approaching due process of law.

In addition, the *Reichswehr* played an indirect role in the entire affair. It provided arms and transportation for the SS troops traveling to Bad Wiessee. The army was also prepared to intervene on Hitler's behalf in case the SA put up a fight, which it didn't. For Gordon Craig, the *Reichswehr's* involvement in the Röhm affair "can only be called a moral capitulation on the part of the Army leadership." The real winner, the SS, would prove to be an even greater threat to the army than the SA had been.

After 30 June, the army's prerogatives and independence were progressively restricted by Hitler. On 2 August 1934, President Paul von Hindenburg (q.v.) died. The same day, Hitler abolished the title of president and transferred the president's constitutional powers to himself as chancellor, thus becoming commander in chief of all the armed forces. Hitler also required that every German soldier swear an oath of allegiance to him personally, in which each promised not only to remain faithful but also to lay down his life for the *Führer*.

There was no open opposition following the 30 June killings. Not even the huge SA made any effort to avenge its fallen leaders. After 30 June, fear of Hitler and his SS grew in Germany. Rightly so. After all, they had literally gotten away with murder.

Jon Moulton

Additional Reading

Bracher, Karl Dietrich, *Die Auflösung der Weimarer Republik* (1964).
Bullock, Alan, *Hitler: A Study in Tyranny* (1964).
Gallo, Max, *Night of the Long Knives* (1973).

Höhne, Heinz, *Mordsache Röhm* (1984).
Mau, Hermann, "The Second Revolution, June 30, 1934," in Holborn, Hajo (ed.), *Republic to Reich* (1973).
Pinson, Koppel S., *Modern Germany* (1966).
Toland, John, *Adolf Hitler* (1976).

Nuremberg Laws

The spring of 1935 marked increased boycotts and violence against Jews in Nazi Germany. *Reich* leaders felt that the violence could lead to conflicts between police enforcing the laws and Nazi Party members. On 11 April, Adolf Hitler's deputy Rudolf Hess (q.v.) warned party members not to commit individual acts of terror against Jews. *Reichsbank* President Hjalmar Schacht (q.v.) indicated that the lawlessness would put the economic basis of rearmament in jeopardy. Hess and Schacht felt that any conflict between the police and party members would "play into the hands of the Jews."

The growth of party-sponsored terror against German Jews prompted Hitler and the *Reich* justice minister to consider laws against the Jews. These laws would direct the police against Jews, not party members. Many laws were considered, but by late summer 1935, the violence had almost ceased. This alleviated the need for the laws, and the only law drafted prohibited Jews from raising the Nazi swastika flag.

The Nazis held their annual rally at Nuremberg from 9 to 15 September 1935. On the last day, the *Reichstag* was scheduled to be present to pass the flag law and listen to a foreign policy speech by Hitler; but during the rally, the "racial experts" of the Nazis, led by Doctor Gerhard Wagner, rallied the party with a speech about the "protection of German blood." Seizing the opportunity, Hitler canceled his final speech and instead concentrated on anti-Jewish laws. Hitler's staff worked hard and fast during the last days of the rally to prepare these laws for the *Reichstag*. Two separate laws presented at the rally became known collectively as the Nuremberg Laws.

The *Law for the Protection of German Blood and German Honor* was based on the premise that "the purity of German blood is essential to the further existence of the German people." The law contained seven articles:

I. Marriage was prohibited between Jews and anyone with "German or racially related blood." Any such marriages were declared null and void, even if contracted outside of Germany.

II. All extramarital relations between Jews and "citizens of German or racially related blood" were prohibited.

III. German females under the age of forty-five were not allowed to be employed in "Jewish households."

IV. Jews were forbidden from displaying the *Reich* or national flag, but "their right to display their own colors is, however, permitted . . ."

V. Persons violating Articles I through IV were subject to a fine and up to one year in prison.

VI. The *Reich* minister of the interior, together with the deputy *Führer* and the minister of justice were responsible for the enforcement of the law.

VII. The law took effect immediately, except Article III, which became effective on 1 January 1936.

The Reich Citizenship Law contained three articles:

I. All "subjects of the state" had certain obligations toward the *Reich,* and their status was established by this law.

II. A "citizen of the *Reich*" was defined as a person of "German or kindred blood," and who, through his conduct, demonstrated his fitness to "serve the German people and *Reich* faithfully." German citizenship was acquired by the granting of *Reich* citizenship papers, and only such a citizen enjoyed full political rights.

III. The *Reich* minister of the interior and the deputy *Führer* were responsible for implementing this law.

This second law deprived all Jews in Germany of their citizenship, making them "subjects." Both laws were passed by the *Reichstag* on 15 September 1935. From 1935 to 1943 some 250 decrees followed these laws, which excluded Jews from professions and official positions, and, progressively, from economic life and obliged them to wear the Star of David and to live where ordered. The final decree, anticipating the Final Solution (q.v.), made Jews outlaws in Germany.

Richard Dumolt

Additional Reading
Arendt, Hannah, *The Origins of Totalitarianism* (1979).

Carr, William, *A History Of Germany: 1815–1990,* 4th ed. (1991).

Hoyt, Edwin P., *Hitler's War* (1988).

Nuremberg Rallies

Contrary to widely held belief, not all the Nazi rallies, the uniformed shows of strength, were held in Nuremberg. The first NSDAP rally was held in Munich in 1923. The first rally held in Nuremberg was the "German Day" rally of September 1923, which was held at the instigation of Julius Streicher (q.v.). After the Munich Beer Hall *Putsch* (q.v.) of 1923, Adolf Hitler (q.v.) was banned from Nuremberg; so despite his desire to hold displays within the historic city, he was unable to do so. It was not until 1927 that the NSDAP was able to use Nuremberg as the focal point of its mass parades and speeches.

The rallies were intended as a concentration of strength of the NSDAP, each branch of the party being represented in the marching columns, bands, and organized displays. As the NSDAP grew in size, so did the time span of the rallies and their content, taking over a whole week in September at their greatest. They included choirs, bands, flyovers, gymnastic displays, and mock battles in addition to the staple diet of marching columns and speeches.

The marches of the NSDAP uniformed contingents were held through the streets of the old town of Nuremberg. Often Hitler took the salute from an open car in the *Hauptplatz* (later renamed *Adolf Hitler Platz*). In the early years, meetings were held in the Town Hall, the Opera House, and the *Kulturvereinhaus,* while the larger open-air events were staged outside the town on the *Luitpoldhein* and the *Zeppelinwiese.* Hitler always stayed at the Deutscher Hof Hotel in the center of Nuremberg, taking the salute from the balcony.

After the Nazis came to power in 1933, the Party Day *(Reichparteitag)* Rallies, as they were known, took on a greater magnitude and importance. The old Zeppelin sheds on the edge of the *Zeppelinwiese* were converted from warehousing into the *Luitpoldhalle* (or Congress Hall), and used for the first time at the 1933 rally. The Party Day rallies became the focal point of the Nazi Party calendar. The sounds and speeches of the events were broadcast on radio across Germany to those who could not be there.

In 1934, German filmmaker Leni Riefenstahl (q.v.) came to Nuremberg at Hitler's request and recorded the events of the *Reichsparteitag,* covering all the stages of the week's proceedings. The final product was *The Triumph of the Will,* a documentary film from which most postwar viewers have built their impressions of the Nuremberg rallies.

The massed standards of the SA and SS on parade in Nuremberg, 1934. (IWM NYP 10979D)

The film is considered by many to be, to this day, the greatest documentary ever produced.

Each rally had its theme; the 1936 rally was "Honor and Freedom." Every day was dedicated to displays by different sections of the NSDAP, the Day of the Hitler Youth (q.v.), the Day of German Labor, etc. The first day of every rally was always the same, the Consecration of the Flags, where, in semi-religious ceremonies, new SS, SA (qq.v.), and other NSDAP formations had their new unit banners consecrated by the *Führer* in person (by touching them to the "blood standard" used in the march through Munich during the Beer Hall *Putsch)*. Mysticism, pageantry, and ritual were all essential ingredients of the Nuremberg rallies.

The rallies continued to grow in importance as statements about the strengths and achievements of the National Socialist state. To accommodate that importance, Hitler ordered architect Albert Speer (q.v.) to provide suitable settings for the grand events. Assisted by a team of designers and architects, Speer went from strength to strength in a series of halls and stadiums planned to house the future rallies. Not all Speer's plans, however, were completed.

The last and greatest Nuremberg rally took place in 1938. It incorporated not only the displays by the NSDAP but also involved delegates from overseas Nazi and Fascist organizations, together with diplomats and international press. Important organizations representing German minorities abroad were allowed to take part, which had particular relevance for staking claims to unity with German minorities across Europe.

Although planned for, even down to sending out official invitations and striking the usual commemorative medallions, the Party Day of 1939 never took place. On 1 September, the usual opening day of the rallies, the Germans started World War II.

Stephen L. Frost

Additional Reading

Grunberger, Richard, *A Social History of the Third Reich* (1971).
Wykes, Alan, *The Nuremberg Rallies* (1969).

Nuremberg Trials

See INTERNATIONAL MILITARY TRIBUNAL AND AMERICAN MILITARY TRIBUNALS

Oder-Neisse Line

The Oder-Neisse Line is the western border of present-day Poland. It lies from fifty to seventy-five miles west of Poland's 1939 western border, and it includes within Poland the former German territories of Pomerania and coal-rich Silesia. (Farther to the east and not adjacent to the Oder-Neisse Line, the former German territory of East Prussia was split between Poland and the Soviet Union.) A direct product of World War II, the Oder-Neisse Line was one of the thorny issues in East-West relations during the era of the Cold War.

The Allied leaders planning the shape of the postwar world were faced with two inescapable realities concerning Poland. The first was that the Soviet Union had occupied about one-third of the former Polish territory in the east, and nothing could induce Josef Stalin (q.v.) to withdraw his troops from the area after the war. The second was that Germany had started the war by attacking Poland, and thus there was almost universal agreement that Poland should not emerge from the war poorer in total resources than before. Recognizing these realities, Winston S. Churchill (q.v.) wrote during the Teheran Conference in November 1943: "Personally, I thought Poland might move westwards like soldiers taking two steps close left. If Poland trod on some German toes, that could not be helped; but there must be a strong Poland."

One of the enduring myths of World War II is that the establishment of the Oder-Neisse Line as Poland's western boundary was primarily a Communist contrivance, designed to penalize Germany, and to partially compensate Poland for the large tracts of territory "returned to the Soviets." It was, in fact, Władysław Sikorski (q.v.), prime minister of the London-based Polish government-in-exile, who was the first statesman to propose such a boundary in a 4 December 1942 memorandum to President Franklin D. Roosevelt (q.v.).

Sikorski did anticipate that postwar Poland would loose the eastern areas to the Soviets. But his justification for the western border was based more on Poland's strategic needs and historical claims to Silesia, which only came under German control when seized by Frederick the Great in the 1740s. Sikorski also advocated a postwar Polish-Czechoslovakian confederation, in which the small states of central Europe would play a balance of power role between east and west.

Sikorski's diplomatic initiatives began to fall apart with the April 1943 discovery of the mass graves of Polish officers in the Katyń Forest (q.v.). From that point on, relations with the Soviets were on a crisis footing, eventually resulting in the establishment of a rival Polish government-in-exile in Moscow. The conflict with the Soviets also weakened the position of Sikorski's government with London and Washington—both went to great lengths to maintain smooth relations with Moscow during the war. In the middle of the crisis, Sikorski and his closest aides were killed on 4 July 1943 in an airplane crash off Gibraltar.

After Sikorski's death, the London Polish government went into a decline from which it never recovered. The West eventually yielded to Stalin's demands for most of prewar eastern Poland, and the Soviets and the Moscow Poles took up the call for the Oder-Neisse Line to become Poland's western boundary. As a result, Poland remained tightly bound into the Soviet orbit throughout the Cold War.

The Oder-Neisse problem had an all-too-human dimension as well. After Silesia, Pomerania, and East Prussia came under Polish control, most of the ethnic German population was expelled over a period of years. Most of the place-names in the areas were changed to their Polish versions. The cities of Breslau, Stettin, and Swinemunde, for example, became Wrocław, Szczecin, and Swioujscie.

Poles living in the former eastern territories now under Soviet control also suffered a similar fate. When Eastern Galicia was incorporated into the Ukraine, most of the ethnic Poles were expelled. Many were relocated into Poland's newly acquired former German territories. Many Polish institutions in the city of Lwów—including Poland's national library, the Ossolińeum—were transferred over a period of years to Wrocław.

For many years after the war the question of the Oder-Neisse Line and the former German lands in the east were touchy subjects in German domestic politics. Finally, on 7 December 1970, Poland and West Germany signed a treaty recognizing the Oder-Neisse Line as the border between Poland and Germany.

David T. Zabecki

Additional Reading

Drzewieniecki, W.M., *The German-Polish Frontier* (1959).

Kulski, W.W., *Germany and Poland: From War to Peaceful Relations* (1976).

Pounds, Norman J.G., *Poland Between East and West* (1964).

Terry, Meiklejohn, *Poland's Place in Europe: General Sikorski and the Origins of the Oder-Neisse Line, 1939–1943* (1983).

Opposition to Hitler

In a totalitarian police state, opposition comes to mean any effort to oppose or protest the policies of the state and its supporters. Such effort may be armed or unarmed and be organized or individual responses. It may involve opposition to the entire political system or only to individual elements of the system. Acts of opposition may even come from supporters of other actions taken by the state. The opposition may be purely altruistic or with some intent of gain. It may have reasonable hope for success or be recognized from the onset as an act of martyrdom.

In the National Socialist state any opposition became dangerous and opponents considered traitors to the cause and to Germany. While there was never a cohesive movement, the opposition included groups and individuals from all levels of education, from the right and the left, liberals and conservatives, socialists and Communists, diplomats and the army, church leaders and civil servants. They joined the ranks of the opposition in response to the fundamental injustice and destructiveness they saw in the Nazi system.

Opposition to the Third *Reich* was rare in Germany and difficult to sustain in view of the popularity of Adolf Hitler. Although the Nazis received only 33 percent of the vote in the last free election and 43.9 percent in the first election after assuming power, the atmosphere in Germany, the mass rallies and cheering crowds, suggested overriding public support for the Third *Reich*. Many Germans saw Communism as the ultimate evil and believed Nazism had become the only alternative.

Undoubtedly influenced by the economic uncertainties of the Weimar era, anti-Semitism (q.v.) proved popular in Germany and there was little resistance to early racial policies. The lack of world response to the suppression of democracy in Germany and the apparent international acceptance of Hitler and the new Germany also contributed to German reluctance to oppose Hitler. Most Germans accepted the new Nazi state as a legal government.

Opposition in Germany was different from that in the countries the Nazis invaded. German opponents of the Nazis were not resisting an invader or a foreign occupier. They were not part of a fifth column. They were opposing colleagues, schoolmates, neighbors, and a government that seemed to be making headway on some of Germany's social problems.

In the vacuum created by the perversion of law, no legal protection afforded citizens the right and the safety of independent action and freedom of thought or speech. After the death of President Paul von Hindenburg (q.v.) and Hitler's consolidation of powers in 1934, the *Gestapo* (q.v.) network and the number of internees in concentration camps grew and with this, public suspicion and fear. All aspects of daily life became *gleichgeschaltet,* Nazified, and it took considerable moral strength on the part of individuals to resist the pressure of conformity. At the same time, those Germans who, by race or politics, were left out were removed from the *Volksgemeinschaft,* the community of the people, and became increasingly isolated.

Popular opposition in small ways was the widest spread. Even German patriots continued buying from Jewish stores. Others avoided flying the German flag or contributing to Nazi charities. In Munich, residents shied from the Odeon Square where passers-by had to give the Hitler salute before a memorial to the fallen "heroes" of Hitler's 1923 Beer Hall *Putsch* (q.v.). Some resisted the state on a personal level by helping a Jewish friend or neighbor. Others chose to ignore anti-Hitler remarks or failed to report someone listening to a foreign radio station.

Working-class groups were among the earliest opponents of National Socialism and were thus first to experience the terror of the new regime. But the left was deeply divided by labor unions, Social Democrats, and Communist groups which, at first, spent more energy opposing each other than the National Socialists. The Communists, in particular, underestimated the danger and naively believed that Nazism was only a stage that would eventually lead to the breakdown of capitalism. When they finally agreed to form a popular front with other workers in 1935, it was too late.

In March 1933, the key leaders of the Social Democratic Party (SPD) in Berlin were arrested when they opposed the Enabling Act (q.v.). The trade unions staged several strikes, but the unions were dissolved on 2 May 1933. Opposition continued underground, when an estimated 1,000 leftist organizations were active from 1935 to 1936. Their leadership was soon imprisoned and they accomplished little. The *Gestapo* counted more than 1,500,000 illegal leaflets published in 1936. They too had little impact.

Communist groups were more immune from *Gestapo* infiltration, but their allegiance to the Soviet Union made them suspect to many Germans. One small Marxist group, led by Walter Löwenheim (known as Miles), prepared early for underground activities, but it was also hounded by the *Gestapo* and became inactive in 1938. This group became known as *Neu Beginnen* (New Beginning), the name of a pamphlet they smuggled into Germany.

Beppo Römer also organized several underground anti-Nazi groups. The most important was the Robby Group, located in Berlin's Osram works. Another group was the *Rote Kapelle*, or Red Orchestra (q.v.), with its Berlin cell led by Harro Schulze-Boysen in the Air Ministry. Most of its members were arrested and executed by 1943. Anton Saefkow's group functioned as a central committee until August 1944, when several hundred members were executed along with Ernst Thälmann, the Communist leader imprisoned since 1933. In fact, none of these groups provided any really effective opposition.

Jews in Germany condemned brutality and racism, but hoped, at least in the short term, for continuance of Jewish life in Germany. Their resistance floundered on the hope of remaining German. The Zionist element failed to see the future course of events soon enough. Rather than offer opposition within Germany, their goal was to build Palestine. Nonetheless, about 35,000 German Jews emigrated. For many who remained behind, surviving one more day, choosing suicide, or dying with dignity became forms of personal opposition.

In Germany, there was no tradition of separation of church and state to form a basis for opposition. The Protestant Church was, in effect, the state church of Prussia. Protestant theologians and leaders served as nationalist leaders and supporters of the nation-state during the Weimar Republic (q.v.). Christian anti-Semitism also supplied a theological basis for Nazi racial philosophy. In 1933, a unified German faith movement, whose members considered themselves "The Storm Troops of Christ," approved the appointment of Ludwig Müller as *Reich* bishop of the German Protestant Church.

In 1934, representatives of all Protestant churches in Germany met and prepared the Barmen Declaration, denying the right of the state to dictate matters of faith. The Oppositional Confessing Church movement originated from this beginning. From prison in 1938, the theologian Martin Niemöller (q.v.) wrote in a letter describing the new church: "The paint is chipped, the masts are broken, its whole appearance is not beautiful; but Christ will stand at the helm and the ship floats! Who would have dared hope it when Ludwig Müller thought he had pirated it!"

Since the German Catholic Church was in the minority and answered to a central authority outside Germany, it proved more immune to outright Nazification. On the other hand, the Vatican appeared to support the new state by signing a concordat with Hitler in 1933. This granted certain church rights, while recognizing the authority of the Nazi state. The churches failed to stand against the racial laws and persecution of the Jews, although they did seek to protect Christians of Jewish descent and raised voices of protest over the euthanasia program in Germany.

But all told, they were ineffective in combating the violence of the state, in spite of the heroism of individual priests, nuns, pastors, and lay people such as Franz Jägerstätter, an Austrian Catholic who refused the call to military service out of individual conscience. He explained: "That we Catholics must make ourselves tools of the worst and most dangerous anti-Christian power that has ever existed is something I cannot and will not believe." He was beheaded in August 1943. The majority of the perpetrators of genocide and war crimes were, of course, believing Christians.

O

Countermovements to the Hitler Youth (q.v.) developed as early as 1937. Most of these youth groups came from the working class and had names such as "*Edelweiss* Pirates" and "Pack of Hounds." They rejected the regimentation of the Nazi state, wore distinctive clothing, and clashed with bands of Hitler Youth. In the early war years, "swing groups" (from the name of the musical style of that time) started in Hamburg. More middle-class in character, they played jazz, wore bowler hats, and carried umbrellas. But these youth were more nonconformists than true opponents of the regime.

The White Rose (q.v.), a student group at the University of Munich, was the first to use the term *Widerstand* or "opposition." Led by Hans Scholl and his sister Sophie Scholl (qq.v.), they wrote and distributed anti-Nazi leaflets in the summer of 1942 and the spring of 1943. They tried to establish contacts with other opposition groups and students at other universities. A janitor, however, saw the Scholls throwing leaflets at the university. They were arrested, tried before the People's Court with their friend Willi Graf, and beheaded. Three other members of the group, including Hans Huber, a professor of philosophy at the university, were executed later, and eleven others were tried for their opposition.

Conservative opposition to Hitler came primarily from aristocrats, diplomats, military staff, and members of the *Abwehr* (q.v.), German military intelligence. Patriots, who believed Hitler was leading Germany to defeat and collapse, began discussions that constituted acts of high treason and sabotage. Before the invasion of Poland, the former mayor of Leipzig, Carl Goerdeler (q.v.), drafted a peace program, asking for international cooperation in combating Hitler. But he hesitated at direct action because he saw Christianity as the basis of reconstruction and believed the opposition should spend its efforts in preparing for postwar Germany.

The Kreisau Circle centered around Count Helmut von Moltke (qq.v.), and took its name from his Silesian estate where the group met clandestinely on several occasions from July 1941 to June 1943. They also drew up documents outlining plans for a postwar German government and had a Christian orientation. Along with Goerdeler, the Kreisau Circle and others made numerous attempts to negotiate with the Allies and to warn European neighbors of Germany's invasion plans.

Even as late as the summer of 1944, the Kreisau Circle continued in efforts to contact the Allies through friends abroad, but the effort proved essentially fruitless. The Allies did not know whom to trust. The opposition failed to recognize that they would view all Germans as Nazis. Its leaders did not understand that the Allied governments saw no more reason to trust them than official government sources. After 1942, the Allied demand for unconditional surrender (q.v.) made the patriots hesitate to negotiate their homeland's defeat.

Dietrich Bonhoeffer (q.v.), a Protestant theologian and member of the Kreisau Circle, joined the armed opposition. The Kreisau Circle realized that opposition was the only way to stop the war and save Germany from complete collapse. In 1941, Bonhoeffer told the secretary general of the World Council of Churches: "I pray for the defeat of my country, for I think that is the only possibility of paying for all the suffering that my country has caused in the world." Of course, it was a difficult struggle for Christians to reconcile the taking of another human life, even Hitler's.

The extent of German crimes against the Jews in Eastern Europe also became a driving concern for many in the opposition. Together with Hans von Dohnanyi and Hans Oster from the *Abwehr,* and the Catholic leader Josef Müller, Bonhoeffer organized an escape route for Jews to Switzerland. But these and other efforts were largely unsuccessful; 90 percent of the Jews remaining in Germany and Austria in 1942 were murdered by the Nazis. Only about 5,000 Jews survived in hiding in the *Reich.*

The military provided a safe cover for the opposition, because soldiers were not under as much surveillance from the *Gestapo* or influence from the Nazi Party. They were reluctant to react because of their military oath to Hitler, initial military successes, and the fear that they would be taking the law into their own hands like the Nazis. Few soldiers refused orders to kill Jews and partisans, even though there is scant evidence they were risking their own lives by refusing.

Franz Halder (q.v.), chief of the general staff of the army, carried a loaded pistol when meeting with Hitler in 1938; but he wanted to wait for the order to attack Czechoslovakia before killing his chief. Due to the course of political events, that order never came. All in all, Hitler had a number of narrow escapes from assassination. In 1939, Georg Elser, a cabinetmaker, planted a bomb in the Bürgerbräu cellar in Munich, awaiting Hitler's speech in commemoration of the 1923 *Putsch.* Though the bomb went off, killing eight party members, Hitler had left the hall early.

After the invasion of Russia, Hitler became more inaccessible. Also, the military was in the best position to attempt an assassination. In March 1943, Fabian von Schlabrendorff (q.v.), a staff member of Army Group Center, succeeded in placing a briefcase containing a British-made bomb on board Hitler's plane. He released the firing pin, but the detonator failed to ignite the explosive.

The central figure recognized by the various groups in the plot was General Ludwig Beck (q.v.), a retired general staff officer. Among the general staff there were other officers who sabotaged criminal orders and were willing to kill Hitler, but they came to fear that, if they killed him, Hermann Göring or Heinrich Himmler (qq.v.) would assume power. They decided a change of government would have to come with his death. After the defeat at Stalingrad and meetings with other conspiracy groups, plans to take over the government were drawn up and volunteers located to serve as the assassin.

Several plans failed to materialize. Then in 1943, Claus Schenk Count von Stauffenberg (q.v.), a severely wounded officer posted as chief of staff to General Friedrich Olbricht (q.v.) of the Home Army in Berlin, agreed to join the plotters. In July 1944, he tried at least three times to assassinate Hitler. Then on 20 July, he flew to Hitler's *Wolfschanze* headquarters where he went to the morning briefing with a fused bomb in his briefcase. After hearing an explosion, he returned to Berlin, assuming Hitler had died, and the coup d'état was set in motion.

The bomb did explode, but von Stauffenberg was able to fuse only one of the two bombs. This may explain why the force was not as severe as anticipated. He was also the leader of the coup d'état plan, so he could not direct Operation VALKYRIE until several hours later. When leaders in Berlin learned that Hitler was alive, they decided not to set the operation in motion, and General Friedrich Fromm (q.v.) refused to call up the Home Army. On his arrival in Berlin, von Stauffenberg sent teletype orders to all military districts, but it was too late. By midnight, the coup had failed.

Fromm ordered von Stauffenberg and three other officers shot that evening in Berlin. Beck committed suicide. Goerdeler, Oster, Major General Henning von Tresckow (q.v.), General Erwin von Witzleben (q.v.), and members of the Kreisau Group, including Peter von Yorck, Adam von Trott zu Solz, Adolf Reichwein, Hans Bernd von Haeften, Adolf Delp, Julius Leber, Wilhelm Leuschner, and other chief conspirators were arrested soon afterwards. Along with Bonhoeffer and von Moltke, they were tried by the People's Court and executed before the end of the war.

The events of 20 July 1944 showed the world another Germany, even though the conspirators failed to greatly affect Nazi policy or to shorten the war. However, von Moltke wrote to his wife in October 1941 that "the realization that what I do is senseless does not stop my doing it." Erwin Planck, a member of Goerdeler's group, also explained for the opposition that "the attempt on Hitler's life must be made if only for the moral rehabilitation of Germany."

In the immediate postwar years, the heroism of the German opponents to Hitler went largely unrecognized and, in some instances, they were regarded as traitors. In a 1984 poll, 63 percent of young West Germans could not give one fact about the 20 July 1944 coup attempt. East Germany only recognized the opposition of the Left. However, the sacrifices of the opposition ultimately helped form the united, democratic Federal Republic of Germany respected by its European neighbors today.

Susan Lee Pentlin

Additional Reading
Balfour, Michael, *Withstanding Hitler in Germany 1933–45* (1988).

Conway, J.S., *The Nazi Persecution of the Churches 1933–1945* (1968).

Galante, Pierre, and Eugene Silianoff, *Opposition Valkyrie: The German Generals' Plot Against Hitler* (1981).

Hoffmann, Peter, *The History of the German Resistance 1933–1945* (1977).

Hoffmann, Peter, *German Resistance to Hitler* (1988).

Moltke, Helmuth J. von, *Letters to Freya 1939–1945* (1990).

Oradour-sur-Glane

A French village in the *Massif Central,* rising a mile high in Auvergne in central France, near the city of Limoges, Oradour was destroyed by the *Waffen-SS* Division *Das Reich* on 10 June 1944. While moving toward Normandy to take part in fighting Allied troops that landed four days earlier on D-Day, *Das Reich* was harassed by French resistance units along the way. Oradour was burned down in reprisal for these acts. The men of the village were shot and the women and children were herded into a church and burned alive. The entire

The ruins of the French village of Oradour-sur-Glane, razed by Waffen SS *troops on 10 June 1944. (IWM KY 30561)*

village was burned down leaving only the stone walls and chimneys standing.

The unit *Das Reich* had many members from the French provinces of Alsace and Lorraine, then under German control. Schoenbrun writes: "As a warning to all towns near Resistance forces, and an example to the Resistance of the consequences of their actions, the Germans selected Oradour to be a lesson of horror." Only ten people, eight of whom were away at the time, survived from the 652 villagers. The two survivors of the massacre later told American investigators what had happened. Their testimony is on file in the National Archives in Washington, D.C., under file number 1501401.

After the war Oradour was fenced off and left as it was in 1944 after the massacre. A new Oradour was built alongside the old. Aged survivors of the massacre and their children can be found there today, passionately and dramatically conducting tours of the ruined village and warning visitors that they "must never forget" what happened on that dreadful day in 1944.

Paul J. Rose

Additional Reading

Kraus, Jens, *Oradour-sur-Glane* (1969).
Mackness, Robin, *Massacre at Oradour* (1988).
Schoenbrun, David, *The Soldiers of the Night: The Story of French Resistance* (1980).

P

Paris Air Agreement

The Paris Air Agreement of 1926 relaxed the restrictions on German aviation placed on it after World War I. The Treaty of Versailles (q.v.) banned German military aviation and restricted the manufacture of civilian planes for six months. In 1922 and again in 1924, however, the Allied nations placed further restrictions on the manufacture of civil aircraft, as well as broadening the definitions for military aircraft as spelled out in the treaty.

Worldwide, rapid advances in aeronautical science during the period resulted in a great passion on the part of the general public for flying. The German people, however, found they were not allowed access to the new technology with the same freedom as the rest of the world. Since Germany's civilian aircraft were limited to a flying range of less than 200 miles, it was common to see superior planes from the other European countries racing past the smaller German aircraft. Germany responded by setting up subsidiary companies in neutral countries. German aeronautical factories could be found in the Soviet Union, Sweden, Turkey, Denmark, Italy, and Switzerland.

As the sport of gliding became popular, the German government began to subsidize it heavily. Gliding was permissible under the provisions of the Versailles Treaty. Germany began covertly using sport gliding as a means of training future military pilots in current aviation technology. Germany also was allowed to stay abreast academically with aeronautical developments, and they organized several agencies to track the new technology. Aviation enthusiasts flocked to these agencies, which later became the nucleus of a new German air force.

Germany bought 100 Fokker D-XIII aircraft to try to counter France's occupation of the Ruhr (q.v.) in 1923. The planes arrived too late. As a result, half were sold to Romania and the other half were taken to Lipetsk in the Soviet Union to be used as trainers. The Germans and Soviets made an alliance which, ironically, resulted in the buildup of the Soviet military with German aid. The Soviets offered the use of airfields and labor, which allowed Germany to test aircraft and related equipment. Germany reciprocated by sharing the technology gained through the tests. The Allied nations complained bitterly of the suspected secret agreements between the two.

Article 314 of the Versailles Treaty stipulated that Allied countries could use German airspace enroute to another country, but they were not allowed to land on German soil. By January 1923, the aerial navigation clauses of the treaty were no longer in effect, and Germany once again controlled its own airspace. France ignored the new situation by repeatedly violating German airspace. Mechanical problems were a recurring feature in these early aircraft, and France had thirteen of its aircraft confiscated by Germany after making emergency landings on German soil.

Since Germany would not allow Allied planes to land, several countries were ready to come to an agreement of some sort. Great Britain regularly flew to India and wanted landing rights in Germany for fuel and maintenance. But since the Versailles Treaty still limited Germany to aircraft with a 200-mile range limit, Germany continued to demanded that Allied planes adhere to the same standards. This, of course, would severely hamper the operations and profitability of Allied aviation. Thus the World War I Allies were eventually forced to return to the negotiating table with Germany.

In May 1926, the Paris Air Agreement was signed. It canceled all restrictions on the quality of German commercial aircraft, lifted all of the technological restrictions, and allowed the Germans to construct dirigibles. In return, Germany agreed to stop subsidizing sport flying. The effect of the new treaty was to restore a large measure of Germany's air sovereignty. Although the Paris Air Agreement did not lift the ban on German military aviation, it did allow some in the military to take up sport flying. By chipping away at the restrictions, the stage thus was set for the rapid military buildup that later occurred during the 1930s under Adolf Hitler.

Tony D. Barnes

Additional Reading

Mason, Herbert M., Jr., *The Rise of the Luftwaffe: Forging the Secret German Air Weapon 1918–1940* (1970).

Phony War

"A rejection of every accepted tenet of military strategy" was Field Marshal Wilhelm Keitel's (q.v.) apt description of the "Phony War." It lasted from 1 September 1939 until the German invasion of France in May 1940, and it represented the nadir of Anglo-French military planning. The beginning of this "campaign" marks one of the lost opportunities of World War II. Franco-Polish agreements called for a two-front campaign against Germany, while the latter's *Fall WEISS* (Plan White) required a weak defense in the west to assure a quick victory in the east.

The reasons for the Allied inactivity were varied and many, including memory of the massive casualties of World War I, doctrinal uncertainties over mobile warfare, and lukewarm British and French domestic support over anti-Fascist policies. Despite the obvious advantages of an offensive into the Rhineland, Allied responses to Germany's *Blitzkrieg* (q.v.) against Poland were minimal. This passive attitude continued into 1940 causing U.S. Senator William Borah to dub the conflict a "phony war." In Britain, it was called the "sitzkrieg," an obvious play on the word *Blitzkrieg*. This Allied inaction was a great advantage to Germany. It allowed the *Wehrmacht* to reorganize and to launch a new *Blitzkrieg* into France.

John Dunn

Additional Reading

Boothe, Clare, *Europe in the Spring* (1940).
Kimche, Jon, *The Unfought Battle* (1968).
Shachtman, Tom, *The Phony War, 1939–1940* (1982)

Polish Corridor

In 1634, the Kingdom of Poland was one of the largest countries in Europe, extending to less than 100 miles from Berlin in the west, and to a little more than 100 miles from Moscow in the east. Over the course of the next 150 years, Poland was successively whittled down by its neighbors. Starting in 1772, Poland underwent three major partitions: first by Russia, Prussia, and Austria; then in 1793 by Russia and Prussia; and finally in 1795 by Russia, Prussia, and Austria. With the final partition, Poland disappeared from the map of Europe. For the next 123 years, Poland existed only in the hearts and minds of the Polish people.

With the conclusion of World War I, the reestablishment of an independent Poland was Point Thirteen of U.S. President Woodrow Wilson's Fourteen Points. Poland declared its independence on 11 November 1918. The resurrected country consisted largely of territory that had been under Russian control, with smaller sections from Germany and Austria. On 28 June 1919, the Treaty of Versailles (q.v.) gave Poland access to the Baltic Sea through the port of Gdynia by awarding it a narrow strip of former German land of approximately 6,000 square miles. The territory had a mixed population, with Poles having a slight majority.

Known as the Polish Corridor, the strip of land was vital to Poland's economy between the wars. It quickly became, however, a major sticking point in German-Polish relations. The corridor separated East Prussia from the rest of Germany, and Germans continued to look on the land as German territory. The Poles considered the corridor historic Polish land, first seized by the Prussian Hohenzollerns in 1772.

Adolf Hitler (q.v.) and his propaganda machine did not create German animosity over Poland and the corridor, but they exploited it to the fullest extent. As early as 1922, General Hans von Seeckt (q.v.) stated, "Poland's existence is intolerable, incompatible with the essential conditions of Germany's life. Poland must go and will go."

In October 1938, Germany demanded the right to build a modern highway and a double-tracked rail line across the corridor, with both routes enjoying extraterritorial rights. When Poland refused, Germany countered by adding a demand for the return of Danzig (q.v.) and extraordinary privileges for the German minority in Poland. Poland again rejected the German demands. In March 1939, Britain and Poland signed a mutual assistance treaty, and Hitler reacted by renouncing the 1934 German-Polish nonaggression pact. Germany followed up with the Molotov-

Ribbentrop Pact (q.v.) with the Soviet Union on 23 August 1939. The stage was now set for Germany to invade Poland in little more than a week's time.

David T. Zabecki

Additional Reading
Kulski, W.W., *Germany and Poland: From War to Peaceful Relations* (1976).
Pounds, Norman J.G., *Poland Between East and West* (1964).
Shirer, William L., *The Rise and Fall of the Third Reich* (1960).

Potsdam Conference
See CONFERENCES, ALLIED

Propaganda
"Propaganda" is a difficult word to define. It has different meanings to different people. One authority holds that propaganda is "official government communications to the public that are designed to influence opinion. The information may be true or false, but is always carefully selected for its political effect." But propaganda is not a governmental monopoly; nongovernmental agencies also practice it. However defined, it consists of a systematic effort to manipulate human beliefs, attitudes, and actions by use of such symbols as pictures, banners, gestures, and words.

The deliberate emphasis on deception sets propaganda apart from other exchanges of ideas. The propagandist usually has a goal to achieve. To reach that goal, selected facts, ideas, and arguments are used in the context expected to achieve the desired objective. Pertinent facts may be omitted and others distorted. Selection, distortion, manipulation, and deception distinguish propaganda from normal educational methods.

The concept of propaganda as a technique to influence human behavior goes back to antiquity. One of the earliest known uses can be found in Kautilya's *Arthasastra,* a treatise on strategy of population manipulation written in India about 300 B.C. It argues that the king should use secret agents to infiltrate congregations, influence the people's views, and keep disloyal subjects silent.

A more contemporary use of the term "propaganda" was derived from the work of Catholic theologians, as expressed in the *Congregatio de Propaganda Fide* (Congregation for Propagation of the Faith), established in the early seventeenth century to aid in conducting missionary work. The Catholic Church still maintains a committee of cardinals to supervise its worldwide missions. By the twentieth century, the term had taken on the secular meaning of influencing the thinking and actions of others. Notwithstanding its religious origin, the word has an underhanded, disingenuous connotation that implies deceptive practices. In the ideologically charged atmosphere of the twentieth century, it has also taken on the meaning of agitation. It often involves the use of parables, slogans, and half-truths to exploit people's fears and hopes.

It is helpful to look at propaganda in three broad, conceptual categories. "Black" or covert propaganda involves secret, deceptive, and disguised sources. This often includes unsigned political tracts, fabricated incidents, false names, and false articles planted in the media to appear as legitimate news. Black propaganda was one of the main tasks of the Office of Strategic Services (OSS) (q.v.) during the war, and is still a major function of the Central Intelligence Agency (CIA) and other clandestine services around the world.

"White" or overt propaganda uses open sources and strives to enhance what is essentially the truth. This form of propaganda is widely used and is considered quite normal in any effort to sell a program, policy, person, or product. An individual job resume, for example, is a bit of propaganda since it attempts to enhance the product without actually stating a falsehood. Programs carried on by the U.S. Office of War Information during World War II fit into this category. So did Cold War radio broadcasts by the Voice of America. To some uncertain degree, the broadcasts of Radio Free Europe and Radio Liberty, engage in "white" propaganda. They also have engaged in "black" propaganda.

"Gray" propaganda could involve a mixture of black and white methods. All effective propaganda will contain a measure of truth or truthful-sounding themes.

Along with rapid advances in communication technology and sophisticated methods of influencing human attitudes and behavior, the use of propaganda attained formidable influence in the twentieth century. These advances have brought us totalitarianism by the skillful use of psychological indoctrination. Totalitarian regimes gain power and stay in power through the clever use of propaganda. But propaganda is a double-edged sword. It can also be turned against the totalitarians. As much as anything else, the communications revolution of the 1970s and 1980s effectively countered Soviet propaganda and brought down the Soviet Union and its satellite system.

German Propaganda

Nazi propaganda was unusual in that it managed to merge the practical and political with the mystical and mythical. Adolf Hitler's (q.v.) oft-repeated themes merged into the mythical whole, that is the Hitlerian ethos of the importance of race. More than any other leader, he emphasized the irrational by the use of myths and symbols. Jews were the clearly defined enemy target around which the nation rallied. Pride in a revived nation was emphasized for those who might be put off by strident anti-Semitic rhetoric. These themes won wide acceptance among the entire population.

While all countries engage in propaganda, the Nazi movement took the practice of exploiting and manipulating the masses to new heights. Hitler's rise to power in Germany relied heavily on the propaganda of both fear and hope as was the case in the 1936 occupation of the Rhineland, the 1938 *Anschluss* of Austria (qq.v.), and the blackmailing of Britain and France in the takeover of Czechoslovakia. Hitler's mouthpiece, Dr. Joseph Goebbels (q.v.), wrote that "propaganda has only one object: to conquer the masses." The Nazis practiced psychological and political persuasion to the ultimate degree.

So pervasive was their appeal that the Nazis were able to corrupt not only the masses, but also the academic, legal, and medical professions. Writing about the high level of education and culture of Hans Frank (q.v.), Gerald L. Posner wondered "how someone of Frank's background ended upon the gallows for crimes that have fascinated historians and anguished his family."

Of the four SS *Einsatzgruppen* (q.v.) operating in Russia, three were commanded by men with Ph.D.s in academic disciplines—men who should have been free spirits and critical thinkers. Instead, their submission to political and propagandistic pressures indicates how easily learned and scholarly doctors, lawyers, and professors, with Renaissance educations, were won over to the tortured, distorted, and warped Nazi views on racial superiority.

The Nazis managed to merge the ideas of traditional German patriotism with Nazi ideological beliefs by exploiting the evils, both real and imagined, of the Treaty of Versailles (q.v.). Also, traditional German prejudices were absorbed into, and not easily distinguishable from, Nazi ideology. This merger of patriotism, ideology, and prejudices proved a compelling propaganda weapon against the *bourgeois* mentality of the leaders of the Weimar Republic (q.v.). As irrational as these views may appear today, they were very effective in winning over the German masses.

The same techniques that worked so well at home were tried abroad, but with less effectiveness. Thomas C. Sorenson has noted that the Germans spent vast sums of money on their efforts to establish "front" groups that exalted Hitler and the Third *Reich* and trumpeted the real and invented weaknesses of the democracies. To prepare for the invasion of Norway in 1940, Britain and France were denounced as blackmailers eager to invade their small, helpless neighbor. The rapid German invasion was intended only to head off the Western Allies. Since Britain and France were actually planning naval action against Norway, this line of reasoning was not entirely fictitious. The Nazi answer was to put Norway under the "protection" of Germany.

Prior to the invasion of France in 1940, Nazi propaganda concentrated on Britain's willingness to "fight to the last Frenchman." A large amount of the work of German armies in the invasion of Western Europe was done by propagandists. Much confusion was spread by the eagerness of many French, Dutch, and Belgian citizens to believe in the purely mythical idea of the fifth column. French troops were subjected to propaganda barrages while sitting in the Maginot Line (q.v.), an effort that contributed greatly to the defeat of the French Army.

Britain's refusal to end the war after France's defeat was used by German propagandists as evidence that the British "warmongers" wanted war, not peace. The British people "proved" that they wanted war by defending themselves and supporting their allies. A distinction was made between the worthy but misguided masses and the selfish English ruling classes. After the Battle of Britain (q.v.) turned out to be a German failure, the highly dramatized stories of Britain's early defeat were played down as emphasis shifted to the theme of Britain's "false hopes" for ultimate victory.

American Propaganda

Today, the United States, like most other countries, engages in all shades of propaganda. Prior to 1940, however, little thought was given to establishing a full-time, governmental organization to influence and exploit foreign populations in peacetime. Many Americans considered it an unworthy and improper function for a democratic government. Yet, manipulating and exploiting foreign populations was a major function of the OSS, established in 1940, and of its successor, the CIA. The OSS used "black," "white," and "gray" propaganda appeals with equal zeal.

The slanted and propagandistic *Why We Fight*

series of films, produced by Frank Capra, were highly effective in convincing Americans of the rightness of their cause. Other films produced, particularly by the Army Information Series, presented the enemy in the worst possible light. American comic strips, published on a mass scale, depicted the enemy as grotesque, inhuman, bestial characters without redeeming moral, social, or ethical principles. World War II was presented as a struggle between the forces of good and evil, or between light and darkness. There was little doubt as to who wore the white hat and who wore the black one. The struggle was less a war than a crusade against evil.

Because of their open democratic traditions, the use of "black" propaganda did not come easily to the Western Allies. They had no alternative but to be rather more open, forthcoming, and truthful than did the Axis. Western leaders knew that the truth would eventually emerge. In the final analysis, telling the truth proved to be the best propaganda. In this respect, the Allies held the high ground and needed only to point to the German record of brutality and large-scale murder in the occupied lands, while emphasizing what they perceived to be their own more humane practices.

Populations under Axis control learned to look to Western broadcasts for factual news on the progress of the war. Allied bombing of German cities was effective psychological warfare since it gave the lie to German claims of winning the war and brought the reality of war and defeat home to the population in an early and unmistakable way.

British Propaganda
The British formed the Political Warfare Executive (q.v.) in 1940 to attack German morale by means of psychological warfare. Some of the blackest of broadcasts were aired by a radio station called *Soldatensender Calais*. These broadcasts contained detailed and accurate information, often obtained from ULTRA (q.v.) sources, about the private lives of German leaders and the Nazi Party. But spiced with it were some of the most lurid, vicious, and false stories designed to undermine German fighting morale. Doubts were cast on the loyalty of the soldiers' wives back home with millions of sex-starved foreign workers. There are no authoritative studies of the effectiveness of such stories, but British officials felt justified in having more than fifty different stations broadcasting them. To enhance their effectiveness and minimize their foreign connections, many of these stations claimed to broadcast from inside German territory, which they did not.

British authorities had little need to convince their own populations of the need to resist, since German bombers performed that purpose for them on a daily basis. Nevertheless, the magnificent rhetoric of Winston S. Churchill (q.v.) was highly effective in countering any defeatism among the population and at the same time reaching across the Atlantic and influencing the war views of his American cousins.

Soviet Propaganda
The Soviets had their own considerable successes in propaganda, aided by the harshness of German policies toward the Soviet population. Working with a population without experience in democracy, authorities easily reasserted tight party control. The Germans defeated themselves by refusing decent treatment to the populations in the occupied Soviet territories. Had their policies been political rather than racial, the Germans could have had a very large ethnic Slavic army (particularly the Ukrainians) marching alongside their ranks. Many in the western areas of the Soviet Union were ready to support any invading army that opposed Communism.

Josef Stalin (q.v.) knew how to exploit the situation. German atrocities were publicized, party loyalties played down, and national institutions and national loyalties emphasized. Even the church was reinstated and the tsars were praised. The "Great Patriotic War" became a rallying cry. Nationalism had far greater appeal than Communism: "Mother Russia," rather than "Socialist Solidarity."

Psychological warfare (q.v.) in World War II used the weapons of newsprint, radio broadcasts, leaflets, and graffiti. Millions of leaflets were printed and dropped by both sides. The results are difficult to appraise.

The letter "V" became a symbol for victory for the Allied cause. The British Broadcasting Corporation (BBC) (q.v.) used the "short-short-short-long" rhythm of the Morse code "V" (also the opening four notes of Beethoven's Fifth Symphony) as its interval sign between broadcasts to German occupied Europe. Soon the letter "V" started to appear in print and on walls, houses, trees, and vehicles.

Following World War II, concern was expressed over the effects of unrestricted propaganda on world peace. Discussions took place in various international forums to bring about regulation on the use of propaganda, but to little effect.

Paul J. Rose

Additional Reading

Baird, Jay W., *The Mythical World of Nazi Propaganda, 1939–1945* (1974).

Balfour, Michael, *Propaganda in War 1939–1945* (1979).

Bramsted, Ernest K., *Goebbels and National Socialist Propaganda 1925–1945* (1965).

Seth, Ronald, *The Truth-Benders: Psychological Warfare in the Second World War* (1969).

Sorenson, Thomas C., *The World War: The Story of American Propaganda* (1968).

Purges, Soviet (1937–1938)

When the Soviet Army was thrust into World War II by the German invasion on 22 June 1941, it had not yet fully recovered from the military purges of 1937–1938. These purges decimated the Soviet officer corps, eliminating leaders who fought in World War I, were bloodied in the civil war, trained in the Soviet military academies, and served as advisors in Spain. Many of them developed the Soviet doctrine and were trainers at the leading academies, indoctrinating junior officers who would suddenly find themselves in the higher leadership roles.

When the Leningrad party leader, Sergei M. Kirov, was assassinated in 1934, Josef Stalin (q.v.) found the excuse he needed to purge the government of those he felt disloyal or threatening to his position. The standard charge was covered by Article 58 of the Criminal Code of 1926. This article listed fourteen crimes against the state, including failure to make a denunciation, intentionally careless execution of duties, subversion of industry, suspicion of espionage, and contacts leading to suspicion of espionage. The law further declared that proof was an unnecessary ingredient for trial, mere intent (however that was defined) was sufficient to convict. The most consistent charge against the condemned officers, particularly the more senior ones, was either collaboration with the Germans or spying for the Germans.

Stalin's principal target was Marshal Mikhail Tukhachevsky (q.v.). By 1937, Stalin was convinced that he commanded enough of a following, or "personality cult," to be dangerous. Tukhachevsky, only forty-four, developed a reputation as a profound military thinker. He commanded Soviet forces against Poland and put down the Kronstadt Uprising at the age of twenty-eight, and was chief of the Soviet Army General Staff at the age of thirty-one. He clearly was a man of immense abilities and appeal.

In addition to Tukhachevsky, Stalin singled out the chief of the Frunze Military Academy, and other men who were leaders of army units during the civil war. There were several common threads that linked the victims: they fought in the civil war with Trotsky (q.v.); they distinguished themselves as leaders; and, most damning, they created a personal following, if only within the Soviet military.

Stalin set to his task with a vengeance. By the time he had wearied of the purges, three of five marshals, all eleven deputy commissars of defense, and thirteen of fifteen generals of the army were purged, most by shooting. Nearly a third of the total officers corps of the army was eliminated, including the commanders of all the military districts. In the line units, fifty-seven of eighty-five corps commanders, 110 of 195 division commanders and 220 of 406 brigade commanders were purged. Additionally, half of the regimental commanders were removed.

The Soviet Navy lost all but one fleet commander. The overall statistics are even more appalling: 93 percent of the officers lieutenant general and above, and 58 percent of the officers between colonel and major general were eliminated. Thus when the Germans invaded the Soviet Union in 1941, only 7 percent of the officers had any military education higher than company-level training, and 37 percent of those had not even completed that.

Accurate figures will never be known, but in excess of 65,000 officers were executed by 1938. Further, it has been estimated that five to ten times that many died in penal colonies or camps. Ironically, 4,000 officers survived the torture and the camps and were released in 1940, regaining leadership positions in the Soviet Army. The best-known of these was Konstantin Rokossovsky (q.v.), who was destined to become one of Stalin's best commanders and eventually a Marshal of the Soviet Union.

The immediate results of the purges were seen in the elevation of junior and inexperienced officers to high-ranking positions. Instead of having the luxury of serving in deputy or similar staff positions and learning by observing or assisting, the Soviet military started World War II with the youngest flag officers of any of the Allied forces.

Three older commanders did survive the purges, but they had no major influence on the course of the war. Dimitri Pavlov (q.v.) was executed after the first major battle; Boris Shaposhnikov (q.v.) was shuffled aside because of ill health; and Kliment Voroshilov (q.v.), losing a major battle early in the war, was reassigned to political and diplomatic duties for the remainder of the war. Thus the purges eliminated the highest-quality senior leadership, forcing the Soviets to rely on the rapid development of mid-level officers when the war came.

There was a positive side to the Soviet purges, brutal as they were. Many older officers with outdated views were eventually replaced by younger, dynamic ones more attuned to modern warfare.

Thomas Cagley

Additional Reading

Bialer, Seweryn (ed.), *Stalin and His Generals* (1984).

Moynahan, Brian, *Claws of the Bear: The History of the Red Army from the Revolution to the Present* (1989).

P

R

Rapallo Treaty

The World Economic Conference at Genoa, Italy, was convened by Great Britain's Prime Minister David Lloyd George and France's Aristide Briand in April 1922. The conference was an attempt to restore international trade by dismantling the many restrictions put in place during and since World War I, and to solve the problem of reintegrating the Soviet Union into the world economy after settling the question of Russia's foreign debts and expropriated property. Germany, represented by Walther Rathenau, and the Soviet Union, represented by Georgy Chicherin, attended.

Meanwhile, on 16 April 1922, representatives of these two pariah states, Germany's Baron Ago von Maltzan and the Soviet Union's Adolf A. Ioffe, met at Rapallo and unexpectedly signed a bilateral agreement. Prior negotiations between German and Soviet officials regarding such a treaty had taken place, and a German-Soviet trade agreement had existed since May 1921. To their profound dismay, the Allied leaders learned that Germany and the Soviet Union reestablished full political and diplomatic relations, renounced financial and other claims against each other, and by promising economic cooperation, reestablished close ties that existed prior to the war.

Allied leaders regarded the treaty as a treacherous circumventing of their own plans and an act of German defiance, because Germany previously had proposed a Western consortium to open up Russia's economy. Other Allied leaders saw it as a sinister plot against the entire postwar settlement. Consequently, German relations with Western nations deteriorated until 1924. The Franco-Belgian occupation of the Ruhr (q.v.) over nonpayment of reparations was the nadir.

The Rapallo Treaty showed that despite ideological and systemic differences, Germany and the Soviet Union were willing to reshape the balance of power in Europe by overcoming their respective isolations. Germany, as it threatened to do before, played its "Russian card," while the Soviet Union played its "German card" against the Allies. Both sides thus made sure that neither of them would join the Allies' side. Although German-Soviet political relations were not free of problems, economic relations improved dramatically. Perhaps more importantly, clandestine military collaboration between the two countries continued.

Some analysts have noted several similarities between Rapallo and the agreements reached in mid-July 1990 between West German chancellor Helmut Kohl and the Soviet Union's president Mikhail Gorbachev regarding issues relating to German unification and future German-Soviet relations. In view of the subsequent fall of Communism and the dissolution of the Soviet Union, those observations probably were overdrawn.

N.H. Gaworek

Additional Reading

Fink, Carole, *The Genoa Conference: European Diplomacy, 1921–1922* (1984).

Pinson, Koppel S., *Modern Germany* (1966).

Rosenbaum, Kurt, *Community of Fate: German Soviet Diplomatic Relations, 1922–1928* (1965).

Reichstag Fire

The burning of the *Reichstag* (German parliament building) on 27 February 1933 was an important event on Adolf Hitler's road to dictatorial power. It has long been believed that the fire was set with the complicity of Propaganda Minister Joseph Goebbels and the *Reichstag* president, Hermann

The ruins of the Reichstag, *burned in 1933 and bombed in 1945. (IWM BU 8573)*

Göring (qq.v.). They allegedly used ten Nazi agents, led by Karl Ernst, who entered the *Reichstag* by a tunnel leading from Göring's official residence. Their purpose was to influence public opinion by blaming the fire on the Jews, Communists, and labor unions to create a crisis in order to gain dictatorial powers in Germany.

The alleged arsonist, Marinus van der Lubbe, a deranged pyromaniac and Dutch Communist, was found on the spot. Many believed he was brought there by Nazi agents. Others hold that he operated on his own without Nazi complicity. Van der Lubbe was convicted and executed. Whether by design or accident, the incident gave Hitler the opportunity he wanted to achieve supreme power. How the fire actually started is still a subject of debate and research.

The very next day, over President Paul von Hindenburg's (q.v.) signature, a series of decrees were issued rescinding all constitutional protection of personal, political, and property rights. If the German people had any doubt about the true nature of Nazism, that doubt was removed as un-bridled terror was unleashed throughout the land. Although the election following the fire failed to give the Nazis an outright majority, they persuaded the now thoroughly intimidated parliament to pass the Enabling Act (q.v.) by a vote of 444 to 94, transferring all legislative power to the *Reich* cabinet. By such measures, Hitler's dictatorship gained official sanctions.

The Enabling Act gave the government the power to take whatever measures considered necessary to restore public security. The death penalty was imposed in place of imprisonment for such crimes as treason, arson, and railroad sabotage. The German people were inundated with propaganda about the imminent Communist revolution from which the nation was saved, but that still allegedly represented a serious threat. Other laws covering high treason were so deliberately ill-defined as to cover every possible form of dissent, including the publishing or distribution of any unauthorized form of printed material. Hitler's control over the German people was now secured until 1945.

Paul J. Rose

Additional Reading

Bracher, Karl Dietrich, *The German Dictatorship* (1970).

Pritchard, R. John, *Reichstag Fire: Ashes of Democracy* (1972).

Tobias, Fritz, *The Reichstag Fire* (1964).

Reprisals

Reprisals are legal or illegal acts executed in retaliation against a state or other group to compel it to agree to the settlement of a dispute resulting from an earlier illegal act done by it. Reprisals can take many forms, and can include the forcible seizure of an enemy's subjects or resources in retaliation for injuries sustained; or the practice of using political, economic, or military force without actually resorting to war.

Reprisals usually are taken in retaliation for an injury, with the intent of inflicting as much injury as was received. International law holds that legal reprisals must be in proportion to injuries sustained. Reprisals were widely employed during World War II. Most of them, like the razing of Oradour-sur-Glane and Lidiče, and the Ardeatine Caves massacre (qq.v.) were illegal.

Paul J. Rose

Additional Reading

Von Glahn, *Law Among Nations* (1981).

Resistance, Danish

In May 1939, the Danish government signed a nonaggression pact with Nazi Germany. On 9 April 1940, Adolf Hitler gave the order to begin Operation *WESERÜBUNG*—the invasion of Norway. To secure the flank of the German forces, Germany also occupied Denmark. The German troops marched through Jutland, but except for some skirmishes, they met hardly any opposition. Denmark capitulated the same day. Hitler promised not to subject Denmark to an oppressive occupation in return for King Christian X's (q.v.) cooperation with the occupation force.

Hitler aimed to make Denmark the "model" occupied country, and for several months, Denmark retained its institutions, including the army and navy, under German control; King Christian reigned; the courts, press, and parliament functioned almost normally; Denmark's 8,000 Jews were not persecuted. Denmark was the only German-occupied country allowed to fly its national colors, the *Dannebrog*.

In return for these privileges, Denmark had to be completely obedient to German demands. By August 1943, German demands grew excessive, and on 29 August 1943, the Danish government declared itself dissolved. The king no longer ruled. The *Wehrmacht* took over and the country was placed under martial law. A seven-person "Freedom Council" made up of resistance leaders then formed and was recognized as the legitimate central authority by the Allied powers.

In the beginning of the occupation, Danish resistance was rather passive. German soldiers were ostracized and ridiculed by the Danish, which was rather a sensation for the Germans, who were used to attention and obedience. In May 1941, the first underground newspaper appeared in Hillerod and the outlawed Danish Communist Party published the first successful anti-Nazi paper, *Land og Folk.* Soon editions were printed in twenty-one Danish cities. Borge Outze, a crime reporter, set up *Information,* the only underground press service in any Nazi-held country. *Information* became the main outlet for the Freedom Council.

Danish resistance fighters from all walks of life began undertaking activities from derailing trains, setting up ambushes, and beating up isolated Nazi sentries, to blowing up the Forum on 24 August 1943, the largest exhibition hall in Scandinavia, which was supposed to have been converted into German Army barracks.

After this coup, Dr. Werner Best, Nazi administrator for Denmark, issued an ultimatum on 1 September 1943 by which all acts of sabotage and possession of firearms and explosives were punishable by death. This ultimatum was ignored by the Danish, like all other orders given by the Nazis. A classic example was the "Star of David Decree," which ordered all Jews to wear a yellow six-pointed star. In solidarity with the Jews, the king and many non-Jewish Danes wore the star, and the decree was finally dropped. Nonetheless, the *Gestapo* (q.v.) had planned to round up all Danish Jews for deportation to concentration camps by 1 October 1943. The Freedom Council, with the help of the Danish population, was able to evacuate 7,200 Jews to Sweden. Only about 600 were captured and deported.

Against the orders of Best, the Danes celebrated their traditional "Midsummer's Night Fest" in Copenhagen. The Nazi answer to this disobedience was the imposition of a curfew and the demolition of the fabled Tivoli Gardens, Copenhagen's beloved recreational park. Open violence broke out for the first time on 30 June 1944. The Danes launched a general strike demanding the lifting of the curfew, and the removal from

Copenhagen of the Schalburg Corps (made up of Danish convicts and Nazi collaborators). On 1 July, the Germans declared a state of emergency, but by 4 July, they were forced to meet some of the Danish demands.

In 1944, the control of Denmark was turned over to the *Gestapo*. In an attempt to eliminate the resistance movements, *Gestapo* headquarters at Aarhus University and at Copenhagen's Shell House compiled files on all members of the various resistance groups. Responding to a Danish request, the RAF attacked both buildings. The destruction of the files saved the resistance movements from capture.

Returning the favor, the Danish resistance blew up Aalborg air base, a strategically important site for the *Luftwaffe*. Probably the most remarkable foray against the Nazis was the bombing of the Globus Radio Factory on D-Day. The destruction of this factory, which produced components for V-2 rockets, effectively slowed their rate of production.

With the help of arms, radios, and agents parachuted in by the Special Operations Executive (SOE) (q.v.), the Danes built an effective resistance movement against the Nazis. Even though the flat country was less than ideal for guerrilla operations, the Danes well understood how to undermine German control by creative, fearless, and most importantly, united action.

Sylvia Goodson

Additional Reading

Hawes, Steven, and Ralph White (eds.), *Resistance in Europe 1939–1945* (1975).

Outze, Borge (ed.), *Denmark During the German Occupation* (1946).

Werstein, Irving, *That Denmark Might Live: The Saga of Danish Resistance in World War II* (1967).

Resistance, French

After the Phony War (q.v.) ended and Germany occupied France in June 1940, decentralized resistance slowly began. French resistance efforts included military, political, and ideological components. As German troops advanced during the Battle of France, French Premier Paul Reynaud (q.v.) and his cabinet fled to southern France. He considered continuing the war against Germany from North Africa, but he was opposed by General Maxime Weygand and Marshal Henri Philippe Pétain (qq.v.), who thought the French Army and government should stay in France and ask for a cease-fire.

The president of the Third Republic, Albert Lebrun, with the approval of the parliament, gave power to Pétain as a virtual dictator and requested Germany to offer an armistice. On 22 June 1940, Adolf Hitler (q.v.) divided France and established a military occupational zone governed by the Germans in northern France, and an unoccupied political zone overseen by Pétain south of the Loire River. Until the end of the war, Pétain ruled over what became known as Vichy France (q.v.).

The capitulation humiliated the French, and they met the German occupation with a slow, gradual resistance movement. In the northern zone, the French were infuriated at German economic and political control, which affected all facets of French life. Minor sabotage and various other actions, such as obscuring directional street signs, changing road signs, wearing the Tricolor, harassing German soldiers verbally, and singing the *Marseillaise,* were methods of expressing anger over the occupation. Initially, such resistance was localized and limited, and often resisters were unaware of the activities of others. The motivations for resistance were patriotism and humanism, stressing the glory of the nation and the value of the individuals trapped in occupied France.

In the northern zone, French citizens immediately were oppressed by the occupying German troops. They resented this intrusion and for the most part did not want to collaborate with the Nazis. Most French citizens abhorred the Nazi's anti-Semitism, ideological control, and exportation of Jews and French labor to Germany.

One of the initial forms of resistance was small groups helping Jews, prisoners of war, and downed Allied pilots escaping to the southern zone, where they then could exit France more easily. Also, many airmen and resistance workers were picked up by light planes at remote landing strips throughout France and flown to Britain. Resistance networks became known by code names that often honored an historic French figure. They were staffed by individuals also using aliases to prevent capture, especially if information leaked during interrogations. These groups arranged escapes by providing contacts for shelter, guides to lead escapees to each checkpoint, false identity cards, and food and clothing.

The Germans sought out all groups helping individuals and Allied airmen escape. They set up tribunals to mete out penalties for such resistance work. The *Gestapo* (q.v.) infiltrated groups and brutally interrogated suspects. Other crimes for which the *Gestapo* arrested resisters included the transmission of military information, strikes, demonstrations, listening to contraband radio broadcasts and speeches, and the distribution of leaflets and other printed material.

Resisters occasionally were exposed by double agents, who were trusted members of the network and who divulged the information to the *Gestapo* in exchange for leniency or other favors.

In the southern zone, many of the French were repulsed by Marshal Pétain's collaboration with the Nazis. Collaborators within the Vichy government and Vichy police units, formed to suppress resistance of their fellow French citizens, were objects of contempt, and became targets of resistance activity. In the surviving French Army, officers hid weapons and ammunition and organized intelligence networks, preparing for future battle against Germany. Other military leaders fled to Britain with Brigadier General Charles de Gaulle (q.v.) to form the Free French movement based in London.

De Gaulle, supported by Winston S. Churchill (q.v.), favored basing Free French troops in North Africa to continue the fight against Germany. On 18 June 1940, de Gaulle broadcast an appeal over the British Broadcasting Corporation (BBC) (q.v.) for French troops to join the *Forces Françaises Libres.* He also addressed French military forces in Chad, French Equatorial Africa, Cameroon, and troops stationed at French posts around the Indian Ocean. By declaring their loyalty and allegiance to France, these unified forces could resist the German occupation through direct military action.

Colonel Gilbert Renault Remy and the French chiefs of staff exiled in London established the *Confrérie Notre-Dame* in November 1940, one of the first organized resistance groups. Early on, the Polish Army in exile had established an espionage network inside France, using the code names F1 and F2. British Intelligence created the ALLIANCE and GILBERT networks. Efforts were fragmented during the first year of resistance, as resisters encountered the vast extent of the occupation. Gradually, however, the resistance cells began to connect with each other, and the efforts became more efficient and effective.

French resistance entered a new aggressive phase after Germany declared war against the Soviet Union in 1941. First organized in London in 1941, the *Forces Françaises de l'Intérieur* (French Forces of the Interior—FFI) (q.v.) planned future uprisings within France to be staged before Allied troops arrived to liberate the country. This resistance was to be aimed at both the Germans and the collaborators. The *Comité National Français* (CNF) was established in September 1941, and by

July 1942, nineteen countries in North America, Africa, and Asia supported it, and it was recognized by the Soviet Union. This external support encouraged resisters within France.

In the occupied zone in the north, five major resistance groups emerged: (1) the *Organisation Civile et Militaire* (OCM); (2) the *Libération-Nord* (whose members included militant socialists and syndicalists); (3) the *Ceux de la Libération-Vengeance;* (4) the *Ceux de la Résistance;* and (5) the *Défense de la France.* Espionage was the focus of much of the northern resistance.

Resisters in the south had more freedom to operate because the absence of a German occupation force (until November 1942) meant there was no immediate oppression. Southern resistance groups included *Combat, Libération-Sud,* and *Franc-Tireur.* Their resistance activities consisted mostly of running escape routes. Later these three merged into *Mouvements Unis de Résistance* (MUR).

In both zones, the Communist Party organized the resistance group *Front National.* Members included both Communists and non-Communists, and they pursued paramilitary aims of sabotage and capturing enemy arms. The *Organisation de Résistance de l'Armée* (ORA) emerged from the intelligence staff of the small army allowed to Vichy under the terms of the armistice. The ORA was non-Gaullist and active in both zones. Other resistance groups established reserve military units to support the Allies at such time as they landed in France. Some church-affiliated resistance groups also formed.

Resistance groups within France each had an intelligence network. The *Cohors Asturies, Centurie, Turma-Vengeance,* and *Fana* groups gathered and distributed information about the German Army and war production, as well as assisting in the rescue of Allied aircrews escaping through France.

By 1942, many Frenchmen believed that the combination of de Gaulle's military force and resistance efforts would eject the occupation forces and mitigate the torturous conditions within France. The British Secret Intelligence Service, MI-6 (q.v.), established a network of contacts inside France and also established a special section called MI-9 to help British prisoners escape from the French interior.

British Special Operations Executive (SOE) (q.v.) conducted sabotage operations against German forces in France and supplied the various resistance movements with weapons and explosives. The SOE had special sections to cooperate with the Free French operations inside the country. In return for this assistance, the Free French used both their intelligence and operational branches to channel information to the British about German plans and operations against Great Britain. The two Free French branches combined in 1942 as the *Bureau Central de Renseignements et d'Action* (BCRA) (q.v.). The French also received assistance from the U.S. Office of Strategic Services (OSS) (q.v.) .

Arms and agents were parachuted into France by the Allies to help the resistance. During the war, almost 700 agents from Free France, Britain, Canada, Poland, and the U.S. landed in both occupied and Vichy France. They built secret landing strips for the *Bureau d'Opérations Aériennes* (BOA), which was responsible for airdrops in the north, and the *Centre d'Opération de Parachutage* in the south.

Within France, railway workers helped sabotage railroads, which were crucial to German transport. When the Germans made forced labor compulsory, strikes and other actions to resist forced labor became the means to attack the occupation. Other daily ways to deride and delude the Germans included forging and altering ration cards and identification papers. Often resisters spontaneously improvised resistance techniques according to local conditions and events.

A major component of the French resistance was intellectual. Most resistance encompassed some form of written resistance: the disseminating of information and ideas, the dispelling of propaganda, or devising ruses against the occupiers. In the southern zone, resisters could meet in public without arousing too much suspicion. They gathered in libraries and cafes. Such public activity was too dangerous in the occupied zone, where most resistance was underground and furtive.

Many resisters were average people who found themselves spurred to resist by the suffocating occupation. Both men and women resisted, and foreign émigrés and refugees contributed to the French effort. Scientists, artists, and lawyers, as well as other professionals, found themselves utilizing their professional abilities for unique expressions of resistance. Doctors, for example, hid Jews and Allied soldiers in clinics and transported them to safety and across borders in ambulances. Students and professors staged massive protest rallies at universities.

The media proved a powerful force of resistance. Most resistance groups had a newspaper or bulletin, whose title was that of the group's name, or very similar. The *Front National,* the Communist front organization, published *L'Humanité,* and the Paris-based resistance movements distributed *Résistance.* For the most part, this media was part of an underground movement by the intellectuals. French citizens who escaped to the United States also published articles in American and international periodicals. Expatriate American authors added to the literature, both inside and outside France.

In addition to encouraging resistance, most newspapers rebutted propaganda issued by the Vichy government that enticed citizens to collaborate. Books and pamphlets were issued by clandestine publishers, with the first full-length work being *La Silence de la Mer* by Vercors (pseudonym of Jean Bruller). Pseudonyms were used by authors to prevent persecution. The BBC broadcasted frequently to the French to provide messages of hope for liberation, as well as coded messages for clandestine operations.

The Germans responded to resistance activity with arrests and punishments, making contact or involvement with the resistance movement dangerous. Torture, deportation to concentration camps, and execution were punishments outlined for resisters. The *Gestapo* did its best to confiscate resistance groups' ammunition and weapons. In response to acts of resistance, they inflicted brutal punishments on local people, sometimes burning entire villages and executing residents indiscriminately as a means of repression (*see* Reprisals).

Jean Moulin (q.v.) was the first president of the *Conseil National de la Résistance* (CNR), which was organized to form a liberation committee in each French department, thereby unifying the resistance effort. De Gaulle sent Moulin on missions to coordinate resistance, to plan for liberation, and to prepare for revolution for France's political future. This movement was assisted with money and arms from Britain. The *Front National*'s guerrilla section, *Francs-Tireurs et Partisans Français,* and MUR's equivalent group, *Armée Secrète,* also helped collect supplies for wresting control of France from Germany. Moulin was tortured to death by the *Gestapo* in June 1943, but his supporters continued his work.

By autumn 1943, a more overt form of resistance was being conducted from hidden locations in forests and caves by guerrillas known as the *Maquis* (q.v.). Many resisters, fleeing south, joined these groups to avoid roundups by German forces for labor and concentration camps. Their efforts contributed directly to the liberation of France. In January 1944, a joint Allied organization, the Special Forces Headquarters, started to coordinate supply to the *Maquis,* which peaked in strength that June.

In June 1944, the French resistance groups came out into the open to support Allied troops as they crossed the English Channel. In southern France, resistance workers tried to delay German troops from moving north to counter the Allied invasion. They also harassed retreating Germans with sniper fire. Joining the Allied forces, the resisters, both military and civilian, expunged the enemy from France. After the liberation, many resistance organizations took the law in their own hands and staged trials for thousands of collaborators.

During World War II, the French resistance kept public hope for liberation alive during the harsh years of the occupation, rescued individuals in danger of imprisonment or extermination, inflicted injury to Germany's occupation and military forces, and planned for France's political future. The resistance enabled French spirit to thrive and to outlast enemy attempts to undermine it at home and abroad, even when that nation was not able to fight at full strength on the battlefield.

Elizabeth D. Schafer

Additional Reading

Ehrlich, Blake, *The French Resistance, 1940–1945* (1966).

Kedward, H.R., *Resistance in Vichy France* (1978).

Kedward, H.R., *Occupied France: Collaboration and Resistance, 1940–1944* (1985).

Lottman, Herbert F., *The Purge* (1986).

Schoenbrun, David, *The Soldiers of the Night: The Story of the French Resistance* (1980).

Sweets, John F., *Choices in Vichy France: The French Under Nazi Rule* (1986).

Resistance, Norwegian

Strategically important, Norway was of prime importance both to Germany and the Allies. Invaded in April 1940, its government escaped to London and never surrendered to Germany. Initially ruling via *Reich* Commissar Josef Terboven (q.v.), the occupiers gave a facade of power to an extremist collaborationist government led by Vidkun Quisling (q.v.). He had secretly encouraged the Germans to invade since 1938.

The Norwegian people, who had never before experienced occupation, were proud of their liberal institutions. With very minor exceptions they were solidly behind their government-in-exile. Norway was a sparsely populated country of small villages with a real sense of community and camaraderie, making it ideal territory for resisters—provided they were of the community themselves.

From the very beginning, the Norwegians demonstrated their opposition to the occupation. This was not always the case in the rest of Europe, with the majority of the people waiting to see which way the war went before committing themselves.

Many Norwegians fled to neutral Sweden, and the large Norwegian merchant and fishing fleet headed for British ports. Of the vessels at sea when Germany invaded, some 90 percent heeded the call not to return to Norway. This is an impressive figure considering the corresponding number for the French merchant fleet was a desultory 5 percent. These boats formed a large network used to smuggle arms, supplies, and agents into Norway. It became known as the "Shetland Bus Route" (after the Scottish island from which most of the boats departed).

The veterans of Norway's armed forces organized themselves into the *Militär Organisasjonen,* or Milorg (q.v.), to prepare for the day when another Allied force would come to oust the Germans. At first, however, they did not undertake large-scale guerrilla warfare for fear of reprisals against the civilian population. This caused some friction with the SOE (q.v.) in London, and in 1942, it was agreed that overt military activity would increase.

A great many Norwegians joined the SOE and were infiltrated back to their native country. Future CIA Director William Colby parachuted into Norway to work with the Norwegian resistance. One SOE instructor remembered the Norwegians as the bravest, the most steadfast, and the most ready to run risks of all his agents. Jan Baalsrud's actions epitomized their spirit.

The Norwegians, in the form of an organized SOE group, were responsible for one of the most significant acts of the war when, in 1943, they successfully sabotaged the Norsk Hydro (q.v.) works at Vermork near Telemark. The Germans were shipping out a byproduct of the plant, heavy water, to further their atomic weapons research. It was felt at the time in Allied circles that the raid was a severe setback to the German program in this field. We now know the German program was not as advanced as was then suspected. Nonetheless, the raid was a daring act, carried out by very brave Norwegians led by Einar Skinnarland. One year later, a group under Knut Haukerlid carried out an attack on a ship transporting more heavy water to Germany.

Norway also staged one of the most impressive acts of civil disobedience in protest to Nazi rule. In the schools, the Quisling regime wanted to introduce a new history syllabus, which offered

Nazified views of the past. Virtually every Norwegian teacher who refused to implement it was arrested. As if this were not impressive enough, when Quisling tried to break the teachers by forcing them into a union of his design, some 85 percent resigned and the school system shut down. They largely maintained their solidarity and Quisling gave in after six months. This almost unique act of defiance against the *Gestapo* (q.v.) remains a tribute to the Norwegians.

Other military acts continued during the occupation, notably railway sabotage, as Milorg prepared to fill the vacuum that would occur between the time the Nazis departed and the proper government could be restored. The Communists were a minor element in the resistance. Collaborators too were small in number, although some 6,000 Norwegians did volunteer for service in Hitler's *Waffen-SS* (q.v.).

At the war's end, some 60,000 members of the Norwegian underground disarmed 365,000 Germans in the country, and the prewar government and monarchy returned virtually unchanged. It was a relatively peaceful transition compared to the violent political upheavals occurring elsewhere. This reflected the solidarity of the Norwegian people. The resistance was of limited effectiveness militarily, as was to be expected in a country of Norway's size and population, but its value socially and psychologically cannot be underestimated.

Chris Westhorp

Additional Reading

Hambro, C.J., *I Saw It Happen in Norway* (1940).

Hawes, Stephen, and Ralph White, *Resistance in Europe 1939–1945* (1975).

Howarth, David, *We Die Alone* (1955).

Johnson Armanda, *Norway—Her Invasion and Occupation* (1948).

Riste, Olav, and Berit Nökleby, *Norway 1940–45: The Resistance Movement* (1970).

Resistance, Polish

Poland historically has suffered from the territorial ambitions of its two large neighbors, Germany and Russia. This relationship has made Polish nationalism a particularly potent force and has fueled the resentment felt against both these countries down through the centuries. Therefore, resistance and independence of action has become part of the spirit of the Polish people. The dismemberment of Poland in 1939 was a terrible consequence of the realization of these neighbors' ambitions, and it gave the Poles two enemies, not just one. At Brest-Litovsk, the NKVD and *Gestapo* (qq.v.) symbolically exchanged prisoners. The Poles never forgot that.

Nazi Germany wanted more territory in the east, and the western part of Poland was annexed and ruled by Hans Frank (q.v.) as the General Government of Poland (q.v.). The Nazis regarded Poles as racially inferior Slavs. The Polish Jews, being two-time losers under Nazi ideology, were considered subhuman. This is important because the degree of subjugation experienced by the Poles naturally created levels of bitterness and hatred that were reflected in their readiness to wage armed resistance.

It is no accident that Poland was practically the only occupied country where there was almost no trace of cooperation between indigenous authority and the occupiers. The imposed regime was harsh and brutal. Its disproportionate reprisals fueled this lack of cooperation. It was only when the war turned against Germany that it became feasible for the Poles to actually wage a violent campaign at any meaningful level.

Poland's Jews, who suffered so much, remained isolated. Initially, this reflected their prewar status in Poland; but soon the German policy of ghettoization formalized and harshly enforced these conditions. The Jews formed their own combat groups in Warsaw and their 1943 rising in the Warsaw Ghetto (q.v.) offered many lessons for those advocating urban insurrection.

Few Poles wished to return to the prewar authoritarian government of Marshal Józef Piłsudski (q.v.). Instead, they wanted political change, and a fertile breeding ground existed for radical resistance groups in Warsaw. In early 1942, the *Polska Partia Robotnicza* (Polish Workers' Party) was formed and from this grew the postwar regime. The political background to Polish resistance was fractious and was made more so by the deliberate actions of the Soviet Union determined to undermine all attempts to restore a non-Communist government.

Thousands of Poles managed to escape the occupation and establish a government-in-exile in France, which later moved to London. These people played a prominent role in the Allied war effort. Many Polish pilots performed heroically with the British Royal Air Force; Polish soldiers formed elite formations (notably the Polish II Corps) that were among the most reliable of combat units. The Poles had a marvelous intelligence network throughout Europe. They were able to break Germany's Enigma (q.v.) code, reported on buzz bomb sites, and actually delivered a V-2 missile to London. They accurately mapped bomb damage in Germany and established large radio networks in France. The Poles formed an underground movement in Auschwitz, which organized 400 escapes, thanks to the bravery of Witold Pilecki, a daring young officer.

Within Poland an alternative underground society was established with factories (including limited arms production), a police force, and legal and educational systems. Its overseas voice was the London-based government-in-exile headed by General Władyław Sikorski (q.v.). Its military arm was called the *Związek Walki Zbrojne* (Association for Armed Struggle), led by General Kazimierz Sosnkowski (q.v.). From this seed grew a more formidable group called the *Armie Krajowa* (Home Army, or AK); a 250,000–plus strong military force led by General Stefan Rowecki (qq.v.) and headquartered in Warsaw. This fighting force was formed from 100 disparate groups, but by 1942, it was generally united.

The AK and its government-in-exile were determined to do what they could to resist Soviet efforts to suborn them in Poland's liberation; but they also realized that the USSR was going to play the vital role in their country's future. In order to insure a crucial say for the Poles themselves, the AK had long planned a coordinated nationwide insurrection at some point. This eventually took place in Warsaw (*see* Warsaw Rising) in 1944; but other events contributed to its failure.

Communications were always a problem. In 1943, the leadership was dealt a series of heavy blows from which it never recovered. Rowecki was captured by the *Gestapo* and had to be replaced by Tadeusz Bor-Komorowski (q.v.). More crucial still, Sikorski was killed in an air crash. His successor, Stanisław Mikołajczyk (q.v.), was not as able, and the suspicion lingered that Stalin's agents played a part in Sikorski's death.

As the tide of the war turned, so for many people did their perceptions of the Red Army. After the exposure by the Germans in 1943 of the Katyń Forest massacre (q.v.) there were many Poles who would never trust the Soviets under any circumstances. With the responsibility for the incident then in doubt, many other Poles, supported with arms and money from the Soviet Union, were quite prepared to join or lend support to pro-Communist military forces siding with the Communist political front named *Krajowa Rada Narodowa* (National Council of the Homeland).

Nurtured by Josef Stalin (q.v.), an alternative Polish government was built from this base. It was established in Lublin as the Polish Committee for National Liberation (PCNL) when the Red Army entered in 1944. Many of its members were from the *Związek Patriotow Polski* (Union of Polish Patriots), a pro-Soviet party composed of exiled Poles in Moscow. The Polish Workers' Party supported the PCNL, and with *de facto* power, it reinforced its own military, *Armia Ludowa* (People's Army), led by General Zygmunt Berling (q.v.), as well as the partisan *Gwardia Ludowa* (People's Guard) working closely with it.

Polish resistance now descended into civil war. All the various political hues were represented, including nationalists such as *Narodowe Siły Zbrojne* (National Armed Forces), who were so extreme that the AK under Sikorski's leadership refused to cooperate with them. The bloodiness and bitterness was exacerbated, if not caused, by the Soviet NKVD, who ruthlessly eliminated non-Communist Poles in Soviet-liberated Poland. They did this after using the local knowledge afforded by such Poles to help defeat the Germans. The AK did not have the weapons to arm its total manpower (it could only field a force of about 30,000) and the well-supplied Communist forces eventually triumphed. The fate of the Warsaw Rising dealt a crushing blow to hopes for an independent Poland.

Shamefully abandoned to its fate by the *realpolitik* of the Western powers, Poland was one of the countries to suffer most in the war. It played primary host to the Holocaust (q.v.) as 90 percent of its Jewish population died; and it was terribly damaged in human and material terms. The final blow came with the arrest, trial, and imprisonment of sixteen prominent anti-Communist Poles on spurious charges of "underground activity." This wiped out Poland's alternative leadership, and, despite vociferous protests from the London exiles, both Britain and the United States failed to act decisively and soon recognized Poland's pro-Soviet regime. The Poles' belief, developed over the centuries, that they could only rely on themselves, proved true once more.

Chris Westhorp

Additional Reading

Bor-Komorowski, Tadeusz, *The Secret Army* (1950).
Foot, M.R.D., *Resistance: European Resistance to Nazism 1940–1945* (1976).
Garliński, Jozef, *Poland, SOE, and the Allies* (1969).

Resistance, Ukrainian

By 1943, three separate resistance movements had emerged in the Ukraine: spontaneous mass actions, Soviet-sponsored partisans, and the independence-minded Ukrainian Insurgent Army (UPA). By the end of that year, there were 58,500 fighters in the Soviet partisan detachments, with 42 percent of the units headed by cadre officers. Between March 1943 and November 1944, their activities were directed by the Ukrainian staff of the partisan movement, headed by T.S. Strokach, general of Peoples' Commissariat of Internal Affairs. In the summer of 1943, the troops under his command were mainly located in North Polesjye near the border of Byelorussia. These units were heavily supported by the Red Army. In 1943, more than half of the flights of civil and military transport aircraft were made in support of various partisan groups.

To reinforce Soviet ideological influence in the Ukraine and to neutralize UPA activity, partisan units started conducting raids in the western Ukraine in early 1943. Between January and March, units under A.F. Fyodorov, I.Y. Shushpanov, Y.I. Melnik, S.A. Kovpak, and M.I. Naumov took to the field. On 12 June 1943, 2,000 partisans under S.A. Kovpak started a sweep of the village of Milashevichi in the Gomel region through Polesjye, Rovno, Lvov, Tarnopol, and toward the oil fields in the Stanislav region. In some areas, their guides were actually men from the UPA.

In August 1943, Kovpak's unit was defeated by the Germans near Delyatine, and the remnants of the force withdrew in the direction of Zhitomir. About the same time, more than 2,000 partisans tried to take control of the regions around Kovel and Lyubomil. After violent fighting with UPA detachments, they withdrew with heavy casualties.

In January 1943, the Germans established their own decoy partisan groups in an attempt to gather more intelligence on these activities. Near Konstantinovka in the Donbass region, the Germans planned to establish a camp for partisans' children. In order to attract the support of the Kharkov population, the Germans sponsored the Ukrainian Liberation Committee in the spring of 1943. The *Wehrmacht* also started to form a Ukrainian Liberation Force, but these units were disbanded in August 1943.

Partisan activity continued. During August 1943 alone, partisans derailed 665 trains—twice the number of any previous two-month period. In the second half of 1943, they caused 3,200 railway accidents and destroyed 260 bridges. In total, the partisans caused the Germans some 36,000 casualties in the Ukraine.

By May 1944, the Soviets had established in the western Ukraine eleven partisan formations, forty detachments, and numerous sabotage groups, involving more than 13,000 people. The organs of the Peoples' Commissariat of Internal Affairs also formed combat groups that, operating under the guise of UPA detachments, discredited the nationalist and insurrectionist movements. There were 156 such groups in operation by 20 June 1945. Partisan detachments fought actions against the UPA at Stanislav, Rovno, and Lwów. In Sarny in the Rovno region alone, the partisans burned fourteen villages and plundered seventy-nine. In September 1944, Kovpak's unit, now under P. Vershigora, was designated for the struggle with the UPA.

At the start of 1943, the principal centers of the Ukrainian Insurgent Army were Polesjye and Volyn. By that spring, UPA detachments south of Volyn controlled a large liberated area bounded by Dubno, Ostrog, Shumok, and Kremenets. The UPA established an "autonomous republic" there, and in July 1943, hundreds of people from the local populace frustrated partisan attempts to consolidate a base in the Surazh Woods, near Teremne.

In the summer of 1944, most of the independent detachments of insurrectionists, under pressure from the Ukrainian Nationalist Organization, were consolidated into UPA groups Sever, Zapad, and Yug.

UPA activities against the Germans began to increase when the Germans changed the occupation administration of the Ukraine to include representatives from the Polish, Russian, and *Volksdeutsche* (ethnic German) populations. Polish persecutions of Ukrainians living west of the Bug and San Rivers drew reaction from the UPA. The situation became more tense when Władysław Sikorski's (q.v.) Polish government-in-exile in London declared its intention of reestablishing postwar Poland with its 1939 boundaries, which included eastern Galicia and parts of the western Ukraine (including the city of Lwów). Bloody confrontations between ethnic Poles and Ukrainians took place in Holmshina, Volyn, Posyanye, Lemkovschina, Galicia, and other regions.

In the spring of 1943, the Polish government-in-exile in London developed its plans for Operation *BURZA* (TEMPEST), which in part called for the Polish *Armia Krajowa* (Home Army, or AK) to liberate Lwów, Stanislav, and other areas in eastern Galicia before the arrival of the Red Army. At the end of 1943, in the Belgoraisk woods and

Holmsk region, more than 15,000 AK troops concentrated to seize the corridor from Przemyśl to Lwów, and to clear it of Ukranians.

For its part, the UPA established its own front in the region from Lyubachiv to Rava Russian to Grubeshov. Between March and July 1944, the UPA fought in turn the Polish AK, the Germans, and the Soviet partisans. The situation in the area became critical when the UPA command issued an order on 2 April 1944 expelling the entire Polish population from eastern Galicia. As a result, 200,000 Poles moved across the Bug River. By the end of 1944, paramilitary units of various political orientation had annihilated more than 32,000 Poles. At the same time, the Polish self-defense units of various political affiliations continued their own terror actions against the Ukrainians, particularly the intelligentsia. In the Holmsk region alone they destroyed twenty Ukrainian villages. All attempts by both sides to stop the undeclared Polish-Ukrainian war were in vain.

The various resistance movements progressively took their toll on the German exploitation of the Ukraine for the needs of the *Reich* and the *Wehrmacht*. In the summer of 1943, in the Volyn, Podolia, Vinnitsa, Zhitomir, and Kiev areas, losses amounted to 400,000 tons of grain, 30,000 tons of oil-bearing plants and meats, 70,000 tons of sugar, and 5,000 tons of fats.

In the summer of 1944, representatives of the UPA concluded a pact with Hungarian military authorities. In November and December of 1944, in Budapest, the problems of future relations were negotiated by a UPA delegation under the leadership of I. Grineh and M. Lutsky. In the spring of 1944, Grineh, L. Shankovsky, and N. Duzhiy negotiated with Romanian authorities. These talks produced little results because the Bucharest government insisted the UPA recognize North Bukovina and Bessarabia as an integral part of Romania.

Between 11 and 15 July 1944, not far from the village of Nedilna, near Sambor, representatives of the National Insurgent Army founded the Ukrainian General Liberation Council (Rada). It was supposed to be a temporary parliament of an independent Ukrainian state. When the Germans withdrew from Ukraine, some local agreements between UPA detachments and the *Wehrmacht* provided arms and ammunition to the insurrectionists. By April 1944, military units of the German Army supplied UPA units with 10,000 rifles, 200 machine guns, twenty cannons, ten antiaircraft guns, 500 submachine guns, 500 pistols, 100 mines, and other armaments. On 18 August 1944,

the German propaganda organs issued an order prohibiting the use of the term "bandits" applied to the UPA.

When the Red Army established Soviet power in western Galicia, the persecution of the families of UPA combatants began. In March 1944, Nikita S. Khruschev sent Josef Stalin (qq.v.) a State Defense Committee memo recommending the expulsion of Ukrainian nationalists to the distant regions of the Soviet Union. By the end of 1944, 5,500 people from the western Ukraine had been deported to Siberia.

To eliminate the armed UPA detachments in the Ukraine, the Soviet government committed about 40,000 soldiers from internal security and regular units, plus five armored trains. Later, those forces were increased to 585,000 troops. Between July and December 1944, Soviet punitive operations annihilated 57,405 people and arrested 50,941 in the western Ukraine. On 9 September 1944, the Soviet-sponsored Polish Committee for National Liberation and the Ukrainian government signed an agreement on moving Ukrainians from Poland and Poles from the Ukraine. The process began on 15 October 1944.

V.I. Semenenko

Additional Reading

Armstrong, John A., *Ukrainian Nationalism* (1990).

Armstrong, John (ed.), *Soviet Partisans in World War II* (1964).

Sodol, P.R., *They Fought Hitler and Stalin: A Brief Overview of Military Aspects from the History of the Ukrainian Insurgent Army, 1942–1949* (1987).

Stetsko, J. *Ukraine and the Subjugated Nations: Their Struggle for National Liberation* (1989).

Resources, National Natural

No nation can long sustain a modern war effort without the strategic raw materials required to build and support its economy and military forces. Oil and iron are the best known of these materials but specialized metals such as nickel, wolfram, aluminum, copper, tin, and chromium are every bit as critical. The building of tanks, cannon, ships, aircraft, and submarines requires thousands of tons of these materials. Therefore, gaining access to those resources, ensuring their delivery, or denying the same to the enemy, was a dominant feature in the strategies of all the war's protagonists.

From a natural resource perspective, World War II was a war between the "haves" and the "have nots," with the Allies being very much the haves. Both the United States and Soviet Union had vast quantities of the most critical strategic materials within their territories. On the other hand, while Great Britain enjoyed similar quantities of these materials within its empire, it had little within the country itself and had to import nearly 52 million tons of these materials to sustain itself. Protecting the sea lanes over which those materials transited was the single most vital element of Britain's war strategy (*see* Atlantic Campaign). Conversely, interdicting those sea lanes was a major feature of German naval strategy, but oddly enough, not a key feature of its overall national strategy.

The Axis countries, primarily Germany and Italy, had neither sufficient quantities of raw materials nor ready access to the areas where they were found. Acquiring the materials themselves was therefore a primary consideration in Adolf Hitler's strategy, if not Benito Mussolini's (qq.v.).

Faced with British naval supremacy, Hitler had to look eastward and northward for his raw materials; in Scandinavia, the Balkans, and the Soviet Union. Of these areas, the Soviet Union was the most important. Although Sweden and Finland offered high qualities of iron ore and nickel, respectively, and the Balkans had copper and bauxite, the Soviet Union had all the raw materials Hitler needed.

Hitler initially got what he wanted via diplomacy (*see* Molotov-Ribbentrop Pact). However, he soon decided to seize these material resources through military conquest and ordered the invasion of the Soviet Union. Beginning on 22 June 1941, that campaign consumed more than 70 percent of the German war effort in World War II and ultimately led to its defeat. The failure to obtain the Soviet Union's material resources spelled doom for the Third *Reich*. For without natural resources, particularly oil, Germany could neither build nor support the mechanized armies, naval fleets, and strategic air forces needed for victory. Allied strategy, conversely, was directed at denying Germany access to those materials. Twice during the war, Great Britain planned major air strikes against Soviet oil fields (1940 and 1943) to deny Hitler their production. The Norwegian campaign was fought to deny Germany access to Swedish iron ore, which was transported through Norwegian waters in the winter. Britain's minelaying campaign in the Baltic Sea was also intended to interdict that traffic.

Additionally, the Allies pressured Spain and Turkey, both diplomatically and economically, to

National Natural Resources Versus Requirements in World War II

Resource	USA	UK	USSR	Germany	Italy
Oil	SS	DD	SS	DD	DD
Coal	SS	SS	S	SS	DD
Iron	S	D	S	DD	D
Bauxite	D	DD	S	DD	SS
Copper	SS	DD	D	DD	DD
Tin	DD	D	DD	DD	DD
Chromium	DD	DD	S	DD	DD
Rubber*	DD	DD	DD	DD	DD
Grain	S	DD	S	DD	S
Meat	S	D	S	D	D

SS = Surplus and export capability; S = self-sufficiency; D = required some imports; DD = imported all or bulk of requirements.

*Countries with a surplus of oil had the capability to produce synthetic rubber.

reduce their sales of wolfram, tungsten, and chromium to Germany. Although not entirely successful, that effort did quadruple the price of those ores. Finally, the costly Allied bombing of the Ploeşti (q.v.) oil fields of Romania was directed at destroying Germany's primary petroleum source.

As prewar exporters of strategic materials, the United States and the Soviet Union initially enjoyed the freedom to shape their forces and strategy on military and political factors alone. The United States retained that independence throughout the war, enabling it to concentrate on a power projection strategy with large fleets, air forces, and a fully mechanized army. The Soviet Union, however, lost that liberty with the 1941 German invasion, which robbed the country of its more highly developed resource areas. The loss of the Ukraine's agricultural production was a particularly severe blow. For Stalin, regaining those areas came second only to protecting the country's capital, Moscow.

Although not the only factor affecting the national strategies of the war, the securing of strategic materials and their transport dictated the pace and direction of the major campaigns from the Atlantic Ocean to the Russian steppes. It also led to some interesting smuggling operations. Germany and Japan, for example, conducted a lively trade in key materials (diamonds, opium, rubber, tin, and tungsten), using both surface and submarine blockade runners to evade the Allied blockade (*see* Blockade Running).

Great Britain and Sweden conducted a similar level of trade in critical ball bearings and special steel alloys, using high-speed motorboats. Also, several nations initiated synthetic materials programs to reduce dependence on key raw materials such as petroleum, aluminum, and rubber. Germany's synthetic fuels program and the American development of synthetic rubber and textiles (such as nylon) represent the best examples of such efforts. These programs, however, only reduced dependence on strategic raw materials, they did not supplant them. No nation successfully eliminated its reliance on these materials.

Carl O. Schuster

Additional Reading

Calvocoressi, Peter, Guy Wint, and John Pritchard, *Total War,* Volume I, *The Western Hemisphere* (1989).

Ellis, John, *The World War II Data Book* (1993).

Eisenhower, Dwight, *Crusade in Europe* (1948).

Goralski, Robert, and Russel W. Freeburg, *Oil and War* (1987).

Reuben James Incident

The USS *Reuben James* was an American destroyer torpedoed by a German submarine on 31 October 1941. In March 1941, the U.S. Congress passed Lend-Lease (q.v.) legislation. The next month, Greenland (q.v.) came under American protection. In July, U.S. troops were sent to Iceland. President Franklin D. Roosevelt (q.v.) announced in August that U.S. warships would escort all North American convoys west of Iceland. Adolf Hitler (q.v.) ordered his naval commanders to avoid attacks on American vessels outside the German blockade zone, but it extended west of Iceland.

On 4 September 1941, within this zone was an incident involving the destroyer USS *Greer* (q.v.). A British plane spotted a German U-boat and the *Greer* pursued; the U-boat fired two torpedoes at the American destroyer. Both missed, but Roosevelt issued a "shoot on sight" order for German submarines.

On 16–17 October 1941, the USS *Kearny* (q.v.) was torpedoed during a night attack against her convoy by German U-boats. Eleven crewmen died, but the destroyer made it back to port safely. On 31 October, the *Reuben James* was attacked at daybreak. One of five destroyers escorting a convoy of forty-four merchantmen, she was struck by a torpedo that ignited the forward magazine. There was an explosion and the destroyer sank in five minutes. Only forty-five members of her 160-man crew were saved. The *Reuben James* was the only U.S. warship sunk by the German Navy before America's entry into World War II.

The incidents involving the American destroyers occurred because they were ordered into combat situations; all three attacks were within the German blockade zone. Roosevelt's naval policy probably would have brought the United States into the conflict had not war come from another quarter. The attacks did help secure congressional revision of the Neutrality Acts (q.v.) in November 1941. As Admiral Harold Stark (q.v.) later testified, by that date the U.S. Navy was already "in the war."

Spencer Tucker

Additional Reading

Bailey, Thomas A., and Paul Ryan, *Hitler Versus Roosevelt: The Undeclared Naval War* (1979).

Compton, James V., *The Swastika and the Eagle: Hitler, the United States, and the Origins of World War II* (1967).

Rhineland

Georges Clemenceau, the French premier, wished to detach the Rhineland from Germany following World War I. For centuries, the Rhineland had been a French objective. Woodrow Wilson and David Lloyd George, the British prime minister, resisted such a blatant violation of the principle of self-determination. Instead, the Rhineland, all of German territory to the west of the Rhine River, and territory to a depth of fifty kilometers on the east bank, was to be permanently demilitarized, and the area to the west of the river occupied by Allied troops for fifteen years.

During the early years of the occupation, the French encouraged Rhenish separatism. In 1920 and 1923, in order to put pressure on Germany, they temporarily extended their occupation to areas across the river.

A prime goal of German Foreign Minister Gustav Stresemann's (q.v.) policy of fulfillment was to gain the early removal of the French from the Rhineland. He finally won their agreement to leave, but the departure did not occur until 30 June 1930, nine months after his death. An earlier departure might have bolstered the prestige of the Weimar Republic (q.v.), but as it was, Adolf Hitler was able to take advantage of German resentment over the Allied treatment of the Rhineland.

On 7 March 1936, a year after Hitler announced that he would abide by the Treaty of Versailles (q.v.) restrictions on the German military, he ordered German troops to occupy the Rhineland. Hitler took a gamble. His occupying

German troops re-enter the demilitarized Rhineland, 7 March 1936. (IWM HU 6898)

force numbered only 22,000 soldiers and 14,000 policemen, and had orders to withdraw across the Rhine if the French attacked. They did not.

France at the time was immersed in a bitterly divisive political campaign, and its army was totally dominated by a defensive mentality. As a result, they were unwilling to take unilateral action. The British, swayed by Hitler's arguments of defensive intent, national rights, and his hint of a naval agreement, also would not act.

The impact of the remilitarization of the Rhineland was significant. It prompted Hitler to believe that his "insight" was superior to that of his military commanders, who expressed trepidation over the venture. It bolstered his domestic popularity and Germany's external prestige. It also had a consequence fatal to French defense. The Belgians, shaken by the development, announced that they would withdraw into neutrality.

Bernard A. Cook

Additional Reading

Eubank, Keith, *The Origins of World War II* (1969).

Haraszti, Eva, *The Invaders: Hitler Occupies the Rhineland* (1983).

Weinberg, Gerard L., *The Foreign Policy of Hitler's Germany: Diplomatic Revolution in Europe, 1933–1936* (1970).

Ruhr Occupation (1923–1925)

French Premier Raymond Poincaré, exasperated by German calls for a moratorium on reparation payments and angered by the 1922 Rapallo Treaty (q.v.) between Germany and the Soviet Union, used German delays in the transfer of 140,000 telephone poles and coal, owed as reparations, as an excuse for a military occupation of the Ruhr, the industrial heart of Weimar Germany. Over British protests, the Germans were declared in default, and a Franco-Belgian technical commission was sent into the Ruhr on 11 January 1923. They were accompanied by a military escort commanded by French General Jean Degoutte.

When the commission arrived, they discovered that the German coal syndicate had shifted its headquarters from the Ruhr to Hamburg. The French sent additional troops in to occupy the region, and the German government immediately suspended further reparation payments and called on the citizens of the Ruhr to meet the French occupation with passive resistance. The French fired German officials who refused to follow their orders. Violence occurred on 1 March at the Krupp Works in Essen, where French soldiers opened fire on a group of striking workers and killed thirteen. By September, more than 100 Germans were killed by the occupying forces, several hundred were jailed, and 180,000 striking workers were thrown out of their homes.

The French occupation of the Ruhr, a region that produced 80 percent of Germany's coal, iron, and steel, was a devastating blow to the German economy. The decision to pay the striking workers of the area without increasing taxes transformed Germany's already serious inflation problem into disastrous hyperinflation. In the midst of this catastrophe, Gustav Stresemann (q.v.) became chancellor on 12 August 1923. With the German mark collapsing toward four trillion to the dollar, the French encouraged separatism in the Ruhr and Rhineland (q.v.). With much of Germany threatened with political chaos, the German government on 26 September called for the workers in the Ruhr to return to work immediately. On 28 September, Germany announced it was resuming reparation deliveries to France and Belgium.

Despite the extraction of 1,392,689,175 francs from the Ruhr and the consequent weakening of the German economy, the episode was a costly one for France. The expense of the occupation more than offset its financial gains; the franc was weakened; Britain was alienated; and German ability to meet the reparation assessment established in 1921 was further undermined.

At the Inter-Allied Conference of July and August 1924, Germany agreed to meet a reduced schedule of reparation payments set by the Dawes Plan. The new French premier, Édouard Herriot, agreed to begin the evacuation of the Ruhr, which was completed in July 1925

Bernard A. Cook

Additional Reading

Halperin, S. William, *Germany Tried Democracy: A Political History of the Reich from 1918 to 1933* (1974).

Schmidt, Royal J., *Versailles and the Ruhr: The Seedbed of World War II* (1968).

S

Saarland

The Saar is an area in western Germany abutting Lorraine (France) and Luxembourg. The Treaty of Versailles (q.v.) placed the Saar basin, with its then rich coal deposits, under the administration of a League of Nations (q.v.) commission for fifteen years. France, in compensation for the destruction of its coal fields, was given the region's coal mines. The treaty stipulated that at the end of the period, the inhabitants of the Saar were to choose, through a plebiscite, whether they wished to remain under the control of the League of Nations, become part of France, or rejoin Germany. If the Saarlanders chose to become once again part of Germany, Germany was to pay France for the value of the mines.

The plebiscite was held on 13 January 1935. Adolf Hitler (q.v.) had been in power for two years, and the economic vitality of Germany and nationalist appeals won over the Saarlanders. Forty-six thousand voters, apparently reacting to Hitler's suppression of independent trade unions and the political parties of the Left, voted for continued administration by the League of Nations. Two thousand voted to join France. An overwhelming 445,000 expressed their desire to return to Germany.

Following World War II, the Saar again was separated from the rest of Germany, and France integrated the area into its economy. In 1947, responding to pro-French sentiment in the Saar, the French allowed the area to have limited local self-government. The French desire to annex the Saar, or at least to separate it from Germany, was opposed both by the new West German state and by the inhabitants of the Saar, who were enticed by the economic dynamics of the new Federal Republic of Germany.

In 1952, the West German parliament stated that it regarded the Saar to be German territory unless its inhabitants, through a plebiscite, were to reject association with Germany. The Paris Treaties of 1954 attempted to establish an independent Saar, supervised by the West European Union and tied economically to France, but the Germans insisted that the arrangement depended upon ratification by the Saarlanders. As the Germans expected, the Saarlanders scuttled the plan. In October 1955, they overwhelmingly voted against supervised independence. Bonn and Paris then reopened negotiations. The cordial relations, which developed between the two countries in the 1950s and the movement toward the economic integration of Western Europe, facilitated French concessions. The Saar was incorporated into the Federal Republic of Germany on 1 January 1957, as a new state *(Land)*, but it remained tied economically to France until 1959.

Bernard A. Cook

Additional Reading

Freymond, Jacques, *The Saar Conflict, 1945–1955* (1960).

Russell, Frank Marion, *The Saar: Battleground and Pawn* (1951).

Sachsenhausen

See CONCENTRATION CAMPS

Slovakia

Created in the wake of World War I and the dismemberment of the Austro-Hungarian Empire, the Czechoslovak republic was established with a parliamentary government. Before the war, Czechs, Slovaks, and South Slav minorities agitated for greater autonomy from the Hapsburg monarchy, and with the outbreak of hostilities, these minorities refused to support imperial war aims, knowing that they had much to gain if France and Serbia won. The Czechs and Slovaks were determined to seek independence once the war was over. In the final weeks of the war, Emperor Karl I, who ascended the Austro-Hungarian throne in 1916, supported a new federal state in which the constituent nationalities would enjoy greater autonomy. The Czechs and Slovaks opposed the concept, however, and on 11 October 1918, jointly declared an independent Czechoslovak republic.

In May 1918, Slovaks living in the United States assembled in Pittsburgh and called for a federated Czech-Slovak state in which each nationality would have its own assembly, judicial system, public administration, and language rights. Tomáš Masaryk (q.v.), a leading Czech nationalist, attended this convention and supported its program, thereby setting the stage for the joint declaration of independence five months later. Once independence was achieved, the Czechs favored a more centralized government based in Prague and the autonomy promised the Slovaks was never realized.

Political development in the new republic was focused on national and religious considerations. Although both Czechs and Slovaks were predominantly Roman Catholic, the new state diminished the powers of the church in the Czech provinces of Bohemia and Moravia (q.v.) where Protestant minorities supported a stronger central government. The church remained strong in Slovakia, however, and supported local aspirations for greater Slovak autonomy.

These aspirations gave rise to Father Andrej Hlinka's (q.v.) Slovak People's Party, which advocated greater Slovak autonomy. This policy was met with growing anti-clericalism throughout the Czech provinces and brought about a general weakening of the central government in Prague. The viability of the government was due primarily to the presidency of Masaryk, who was respected by both Czechs and Slovaks.

Masaryk retired in 1935 and was replaced by Eduard Beneš (q.v.), his perennial foreign minister. Conflicting national and ethnic aspirations and Slovak calls for greater concessions from the central government increased. Adolf Hitler's (q.v.) annexation of Austria in 1938 also isolated Czechoslovakia from its European benefactors and encouraged Hitler to demand that it cede the Sudetenland (q.v.) to Germany, a demand sanctioned by Britain, France, and Italy at Munich in 1938.

Beneš resigned and was replaced by Emil Hácha, who finally granted Slovakia greater internal autonomy with its own government ministers. Monsignor Joseph Tiso (q.v.) organized a new Slovak cabinet dominated by Father Hlinka's party, whose separatist wing continued to gain strength throughout the 1930s. In December 1938, the new cabinet banned all other political parties. In early March 1939, it was accused of having overly cordial relations with Germany and was subsequently dismissed by the central government.

Hitler interceded on Slovakia's behalf and pressured Hácha to finally grant Slovakia its independence, which was declared in Bratislava on 14 March 1939. Two days later, Germany absorbed what remained of Czechoslovakia, contrary to promises made at Munich, and established a *Reich* protectorate. The new Slovak state immediately requested German protection and German troops were sent in. Despite its nominal independence, Slovakia signed a treaty with Germany on 23 March 1939, thereby subordinating its military and foreign affairs to German supervision. Slovakia was not to become simply a puppet state of Nazi Germany, however, for the Catholic Church also strongly influenced the policies and actions of Hlinka's Slovak People's Party, a classical clerico-Fascist entity. Tiso, the new president, was not only pro-Nazi, but he was also a Catholic priest.

Both the *Reich* protectorate and Slovakia remained outside the framework of Allied and Axis military strategies throughout most of the war. The Slovakian government did, however, adhere to Nazi racial policies and cooperated in the systematic destruction of the local Jewish population. Most of the anti-Semitic measures were administered by the Central Economic Office, which was established in August 1940. Jewish property was confiscated and Jews were excluded from national life and the economy. They were also employed in forced labor programs and most were eventually deported or concentrated in a network of camps operated by the Slovak interior ministry and guarded by members of the Hlinka Guard. Nearly 70,000 Jews were deported from Slovakia, most of whom died in concentration camps.

There was also a general lack of local resistance in the *Reich* protectorate except for scattered instances in Moravia in 1944. Slovakia, despite its formal alliance with Germany, was the center of large-scale resistance efforts. A secret Slovak army was established and there were a number of Communist partisan groups operating throughout the country.

More than 8,000 Slovak partisans supported

the Red Army when it invaded over the Carpathian mountains in August 1944, and a general partisan uprising ensued causing the overthrow of the Tiso government. It requested assistance from the Germans, whose troops moved into previously unoccupied areas. Two divisions of the Slovak resistance army went over to the Germans, but the remaining units joined with the partisans to defend "Free Slovakia" with Soviet military aid. This aid never materialized and all resistance was met with savage German reprisals and driven into the mountains. The Soviets finally advanced through Slovakia in March 1945 in the face of a general retreat.

Under Soviet occupation, Slovakia was once again integrated with the Czech provinces resulting in a Communist Czechoslovakia that lasted until the fall of Communism in Eastern Europe. On 1 January 1993, Slovakia and the Czech Republic once again split in what is known as the "Velvet Divorce."

Steven B. Rogers

Additional Reading

Jelinek, Yeshayahu, "Slovakia's Internal Policy and the Third *Reich,* August 1940–February 1941," in *Central European History* (9/71), pp. 242–270.

Jelinek, Yeshayahu, "Storm Troopers in Slovakia: the Rodobrann and the Hlinka-Guard," in *Journal of Contemporary History,* no. 3 (1971), pp. 97–120.

Minkus, Joseph A., *Slovakia: A Political History: 1918–1950* (1963).

"Stab-in-the-Back" Myth

Following the German defeat in World War I and as a result of the punitive measures imposed by the Treaty of Versailles (q.v.), the *"Dolchstosslegende,"* became popular in Germany. According to this premise, adopted from a British general who referred to the collapse of support for the German military on the home front as a "stab in the back," Germany had been defeated by the treachery of the Jews and socialists at home, and not by the Allied forces on the battlefield. Paul von Hindenburg, the *Freikorps* (qq.v.), Adolf Hitler's National Socialists (qq.v.), Erich Ludendorff's (q.v.) *Tannenbergbund,* and the Pan German League put great stock in this idea. They used it in an attempt to convince the German people that the Jews and Communists were responsible for the country's ills, and that the annihilation of this conspiracy would lead to a return of Germany's greatness.

This allegation was without foundation in fact. On 29 September 1918, General von Hindenburg wrote to the chancellor urging him to sue for peace because of the collapse of the armed forces. German nationalists, unwilling to publicly acknowledge the failure of the military, looked for a scapegoat for Germany's defeat and postwar economic chaos. The stab-in-the-back legend became a staple for anti-democratic politicians in Germany.

Steven B. Rogers

Additional Reading

Bracher, Karl Dietrich, *The German Dictatorship* (1970).

Pinson, Koppel S., *Modern Germany* (1966).

Sudetenland

Since 1902, when a journalist coined the term "Sudeten Germans," those areas of Czechoslovakia where ethnic Germans resided were known as the Sudetenland. This narrow strip of border districts, located primarily in Bohemia, Moravia, and Silesia, held 3.2 million ethnic Germans, according to the 1930 census. By that date, most had become intensely nationalistic and wanted to be reunited with Austria. In late 1918, the Sudeten Germans' right of self-determination became the center of their leader's policy, and on 30 October 1918, the province of Sudetenland was established. These strivings for autonomy did not lead further.

After World War I, the Sudetenland was incorporated into the newly created Republic of Czechoslovakia, a nation sensitive to the needs of its minorities. Measures were introduced to meet the concerns of the minorities. In June 1919, the administration of all towns and parishes with a German majority was placed in the hands of that group. In other communities, German minorities secured a proportional share in the legislative and administrative bodies.

Czechoslovakia was, in fact, the only country on the European continent in which national minorities gained representation in the government. Nevertheless, national autonomy remained a strong desire among the Sudeten Germans, but it was unacceptable to the new central government, which feared it would lead to the separation of the German areas from the republic—areas vitally important to the nation's economic well-being.

The rise of Nazism in the early 1930s and the Great Depression led to increased nationalism among the Sudeten Germans, who received support from Nazi organizations. A new policy formulated by the Hitler regime and the German Ministry of Foreign Affairs called for additional and more direct assistance to the Sudeten Germans.

Hurt by the economic crisis, angered at Czech government efforts that did not aid their plight, and heartened by the success of the Nazi Party in revitalizing the economy in Germany, the Sudeten Germans intensified their nationalism. This sentiment was increasingly directed by the Sudeten German Party (the *Heimatfront*), founded in 1913, and its leader, Konrad Henlein. In the May 1935 election, it received 1.2 million votes, 60 percent of the ballots cast by the German minority. With this victory, the *Heimatfront's* leaders looked to Nazi Germany for help in splitting Sudetenland away from Czechoslovakia.

The plight of the Sudeten Germans also aroused interest in London, and in 1935 and 1936, Henlein traveled there to seek support. The Czech president and foreign minister moved to assuage the Germans of the Sudetenland, and far-reaching concessions on representation and other matters were made. The demands of Henlein quickly escalated, and he called for "self-determination and co-determination within the settlement area and also in all central state organizations." If granted, such concessions would have undermined the integrity of the Czech state. While appearing outwardly cooperative, Henlein and his party continued to conspire with Berlin in its efforts to undermine the Czech republic. By late 1937, the situation reached a crisis point.

In March 1938, Adolf Hitler (q.v.) summoned Henlein to Berlin and announced that he had decided to solve the Sudeten German issue in the near future. Henlein was to cooperate by demanding more than the Czech government would concede. Unrest and demonstrations throughout the Sudetenland mounted, as the Sudeten Germans believed nothing short of separation from the Czech state would be acceptable. On 24 April 1938, Henlein publicly announced his eight demands, which called for full and complete autonomy, as well as liberty to profess National Socialism. In September 1938, Sudetenland finally was ceded to Germany as the result of the Munich Agreement (q.v.).

The Sudetenland issue was used by Hitler as an excuse to crush Czechoslovakia. It was a major step on the road to World War II.

John David Waite

Additional Reading

Luza, Radomir, *The Transfer of the Sudeten Germans: A Study of Czech-German Relations, 1933–1962* (1964).

Smelser, Ronald M., *The Sudeten Problem, 1933–1938: Volkstumspolitik and the Formulation of Nazi Foreign Policy* (1975).

T

Teheran Conference
See CONFERENCES, ALLIED

Theresienstadt
See HOLOCAUST

Treaty of Versailles

The Treaty of Versailles, signed by the Allied and Associated Powers and Germany on 28 June 1919 in the palace of Versailles, brought to an end the most destructive war in modern times. In 1918, Western Europe lay bleeding and starving after its greatest catastrophe ever. The war was a dreadful tragedy. A record 60 million men were mobilized to fight a war people variously believed would bring justice, honor, national pride, and an end to all future wars while establishing a new international order of peace, progress, and goodwill. It did nothing of the sort.

At the war's end, 8 million soldiers lay dead, 20 million wounded or gassed, and more than 21 million civilians killed or wounded. Four great empires—Germany, Austro-Hungary, Russia, and the Ottoman Empire—collapsed, and many of their cities and towns were in rubble. Germany in particular was reduced to a nation of scavengers. In addition, Communism and Fascism, those two ideological scourges of the twentieth century, gained roots in European politics.

The war settled nothing. Existing European problems were merely aggravated by massive destruction and upheaval. Germany felt encircled, deceived, and humiliated, and France still felt threatened by Germany. The European countries fought the war for their own ulterior purposes as expressed in secret treaties. The victors, led by Britain, France, and the United States, came to Versailles seeking vengeance and determined to make the Germans pay for Allied losses. "Let the Huns pay" became the overriding principle and rallying cry of the Allies.

When the German government requested U.S. president Woodrow Wilson to arrange an armistice in October 1918, they expected, and were given reason to expect, that it would be a just peace based on Wilson's idealistic Fourteen Points. These Wilsonian principles called for "open covenants, openly arrived at," "absolute freedom of navigation," the "removal of economic barriers," the "impartial adjustment of colonial claims," the "restoration of Alsace and Lorraine to France," the "creation of an independent Polish State," and the formation of a "general association of nations." Wilson also supported the proposition that the conclusion of the war would bring "no annexations, no punitive damages, no retributions."

These Wilsonian ideals offered the hope of addressing every grievance and righting every wrong. But as soon became evident, these utopian principles clashed with the secret treaties and other national demands made by England, France, Italy, and many of the lesser powers.

The treaty was drafted at the Paris Peace Conference during the winter and spring of 1919. The conference was dominated by Wilson of the United States, Georges Clemenceau of France, and David Lloyd George of Great Britain, with Vittorio Orlando of Italy playing a minor role. The defeated nations had no say in what went into the treaty.

Writing of the treaty took place in specialized committees with little coordination between them. Some committee members thought they were drafting position papers listing maximum demands to be discussed and negotiated. Other papers included impossibly harsh terms with the expectation that they would be debated and revised before inclusion in the treaty.

Under the pressure of deadlines, these incomplete and spitefully conceived papers were simply stapled together and presented as a complete work. They were neither rationally considered nor debated. Few people, and none of the major participants, bothered to analyze or consider the political, economic, social, or psychological impact of such a one-sided treaty. Almost everyone's maximum demands, wishes, and fantasies found their way into the treaty. While each provision may not have been individually too devastating, the total impact of the treaty was simply unbelievable in its vengeance, hatred, and unfairness.

On 18 April, the Germans were tersely, even rudely, "invited" to Paris "for the purpose of receiving the text of the treaty" and were reminded that the delegation "must confine itself strictly to its role." They were being invited to receive, not to discuss the treaty.

Count Ulrich von Brockdorff-Rantzan, Germany's most experienced diplomat, headed the German delegation. The train carrying Brockdorff-Rantzan and his principal associates left Berlin on 28 April. From the French border, a French engine pulled them on to Paris, but not directly. The French government wanted the German delegation, who knew little about the war, to have every opportunity to view the devastation their armies had inflicted upon northern France.

In a moon-cratered region roughly the size of Holland, where an estimated 1,000 large artillery rounds had exploded per square meter, the railway was partly rebuilt. The train moved slowly, sometimes stopping for a few minutes to give the passengers a better view, through mile after mile of destroyed villages, ruined farms, and marred landscape. The only people seen were German war prisoners, guarded by French soldiers, rebuilding roads and bridges. Members of the delegation offered food and magazines to the prisoners, but drew back in terror when the men were clubbed back to work by their guards. The psychological impact was all the French government could have desired. In letters home, delegate members described this tour of the battlefield as an "overwhelming experience."

The train halted a few miles before Versailles and the delegates continued by automobile to avoid the possibility of attack by mobs. A French colonel took the delegation to the *Hotel des Reservoirs,* the same hotel where the French peace commission waited in 1872 for peace terms from Prince Otto von Bismarck ending the Franco-

Prussian War. More a prison than a hotel, it was surrounded by barbed wire and guarded by French soldiers with fixed bayonets and live rounds in their rifle chambers.

Later, the Germans received the humiliating treaty in the same room where Emperor Wilhelm I was crowned in 1871. They were seated on a bench labeled *Banc des Accusés*—bench of the accused. The atmosphere was more like that of a court-martial than a peace conference. Far from being a coincidence, these carefully choreographed arrangements were staged to introduce the delegates psychologically to the reality of the low, mean-spirited atmosphere awaiting them at the conference.

It is an understatement to say the Germans were shocked at the severity of the terms. A "Guilt Clause" (Article 231) held Germany responsible for "all the loss to which the Allied and Associated Governments and their nationals" suffered; and a "Blank Check Clause" (Article 233) held the Germans accountable for whatever amount of reparations the Allies might later choose to claim. These articles were referred to by the Germans as the *Schmachparagraphen*—shameful paragraphs—and they had already started using the term *Diktat* to refer to the treaty. They criticized the French "revenge," British "brutality," and the utter "hypocrisy" of Wilson.

The treaty reduced the territory of Germany by approximately 10 percent. Alsace and Lorraine (q.v.), as expected, were returned to France. The Saarland (q.v.) was placed under supervision of the League of Nations (q.v.) to be controlled and exploited by France for fifteen years. Three small areas were transferred to Belgium and, following a plebiscite, northern Schleswig returned to Denmark. A Polish state was established and given most of Posen, Upper Silesia, and a corridor to the Baltic Sea separating East Prussia from the rest of Germany. Danzig (q.v.) became a free city. All German colonies were taken over by the League of Nations and mandated to the Allied powers then occupying them. The German fleet surrendered to the British and was locked up in Scapa Flow, Scotland.

The German army was reduced to 100,000 men; the general staff was abolished; the manufacturing, owning, or using of tanks, planes, submarines, and poison gas was forbidden. German territory west of the Rhine and fifty kilometers east of it was to be demilitarized. Merger with Austria was forbidden. The treaty included the Covenant of the League of Nations and established the Permanent Court of International Justice and the International Labor Organization. The treaty contained 440 separate articles and 75,000 words. Hundreds of paragraphs began with the words "Germany renounces . . . Germany renounces . . ."

The Germans bitterly objected to the harshness of the treaty. They argued, correctly, that they were not legally obligated to any conditions not consistent with Wilson's Fourteen Points. They insisted that Germany had not surrendered unconditionally, but had merely exchanged a strict "pre-armistice agreement," legally binding upon victors and vanquished alike. By any standards of international law, they claimed, it was illegal for the Allies to increase these demands.

Their second defense was that various Allied leaders had stated repeatedly that their quarrel was with the monarchy, not with the German people. Wilson had stated, "We have no quarrel with the German people. We have no feeling toward them except one of sympathy and friendship." He insisted that the enemy was "the government of the German Empire." Now that the kaiser and the monarchy were gone, it was unfair to punish the German people. Surely, the impartial, highly respected Wilson would understand that they had laid down their arms, as he had invited them to do, expecting understanding and mercy. Now that they were disarmed and helpless, they felt betrayed. Where were those high ideals under which the Allies had conducted their crusade against the German kaiser and monarchy?

The Allied reply was to sign the treaty at once and without changes or Germany would be invaded. Having surrendered their own armies, the Germans had no defense. With Germany engaged in virtual revolution between traditional right-wing forces and strong leftist elements, even a *Levée en Masse*—popular uprising—was ruled out. Refusing to sign the treaty, no matter how unfair it was, was not a viable option. With grave misgivings, the Germans signed.

No one was completely satisfied with the treaty. Many individual members of the Allied delegations were appalled at its harshness and unfairness. To many members of the British and American delegations, it was too harsh, but to the French, it was too lenient. The French wanted to move their frontier to the Rhine River and incorporate the Saarland and the Rhineland into the French republic. Only strong British and American objections prevented their doing so. In fact, the French would have been pleased had the Germans refused to sign the treaty. They felt they could gain more by invading Germany and imposing individual peace treaties on the various German regional governments. The fear of this possibility

played a significant role in the final German acceptance of the treaty.

Roy S. Baker, the American press chief, termed the treaty a "terrible document, a dispensation of retribution with scarcely a parallel in history." Wilson himself is quoted as saying, "If I were a German, I think I should never sign it." The U.S. secretary of state, Robert Lansing, wrote, "The terms of peace appear immeasurably harsh and humiliating, while many of them seem to me impossible of performance." French Marshal Ferdinand Foch noted that this was not a peace treaty but a twenty-year truce. How true those words were, for twenty years and two months later, World War II broke out. But neither Wilson nor Clemenceau could be persuaded.

Wilson was adamant that the treaty must be accepted at once and without alteration. A great surprise to many participants at the peace conference was the enormous difference between the idealism of Wilson, as expressed in his Fourteen Points, and the man's harshness, indifference, small-mindedness, and even lack of scruples in dealing with the defeated Germans.

Ill and under pressure from his allies, Wilson agreed to add the indirect cost of pensions to the direct cost of wartime civilian damages, greatly inflating the bill. To the suggestions of his advisors that this was illogical, Wilson blurted out: "Logic! Logic! I don't give a damn about logic. I am going to include pensions." This compromise made it clear that Germany was to become a slave state, shackled to the Allies by its war debts.

Wilson left Versailles a beaten, even a hated man, who, according to his critics, compromised his universal and loudly proclaimed principles in a most dishonorable way.

Among other members of the American and British delegations, Herbert Hoover, John Maynard Keynes, Bernard Baruch (q.v.), Vance McCormick, and John Foster Dulles were disgusted by the severity of the treaty's terms. But it was letters written to David Lloyd George and Woodrow Wilson by General Jan Christian Smuts (q.v.), a South African member of the British delegation, that put the treaty in some perspective. He emphasized its shortcomings, which had the effect of softening the earlier harsh British position, but not that of America or France.

Smuts warned that French occupation of the Rhineland (q.v.), a sort of "Alsace-Lorraine in reverse," would be the root cause of future trouble. Even the fifteen-year limitation was a delusion since the treaty provided an end to the occupation only when Germany had satisfied all the many other impossible conditions of the treaty. Reparation demands alone made any redemption impossible.

With Germany reduced in size, stripped of the Saar and Upper Silesian coal fields, its merchant navy and many of its blast furnaces reduced, it was impossible to generate enough commerce to pay the debts imposed by the treaty. Smuts castigated the Allies for the loss of German land to Poland and accurately predicted future troubles there.

In summary, Smuts warned that unless the treaty was thoroughly revised, the Allies would soon have cause to regret forcing its acceptance on the Germans at the point of a gun. Lloyd George accepted this argument and tried in vain to win over Wilson and Clemenceau.

The Reparations Commission initially imposed a total reparations payment of 269 billion gold marks payable over a thirty-five-year period. This was later reduced to 132 billion marks. After the French occupation of the Ruhr (q.v.) in 1923, to compel payments, Germany lurched into hyperinflation caused partly by governmental design and partly by poor economic policies. Under the U.S.-sponsored Dawes Plan of 1924, America lent Germany money to make payments. This money went full circle when it came back to the United States in the form of reparation payments to satisfy Germany's war debt to America. Germany paid approximately 33 billion marks of the total reparations debt. At the Lausanne Conference of 1932, it was proposed that the whole reparations matter be settled by a German payment of three billion marks. Hitler's rise to power the following January prevented even this modest amount from being paid.

To assuage French fears of a rejuvenated, aggressive Germany, Lloyd George and Wilson offered an Anglo-American guarantee against any future "unprovoked" German aggression. But this guarantee came to naught, when the U.S. Senate failed to ratify the peace treaty. Its failure intensified French fears.

Had the Germans won the war, would they have behaved more humanely? Most likely not. Defenders of the treaty argued, correctly, that it was a tradition of European wars that the loser pay an indemnity to the winner. In fact, the winner usually took all that he conveniently could. The Germans themselves were particularly successful in this practice. Had they not extracted from the French in 1872 an indemnity twice the cost of the German wartime expenditures? And throughout the just concluded war, German leaders repeatedly vowed that the defeated enemy would pay, and pay dearly, for all the German sacrifices and sufferings. *Vae Victis*—Woe to the loser—was a constant German theme. There is little doubt that had Germany won, the British, French, and Italians, among others, would have had ruinous indemnities imposed upon them, as the extremely harsh German treatment of the Russians in the Brest-Litovsk Treaty of March 1918 so clearly foretold.

In analyzing the lessons of the Treaty of Versailles, we are reminded there are seldom "winners" in wars and they are easier to start than to end. Also, we should learn that harshness and vengeance in "peace" settlements can rebound against those who impose them. The harsh provisions of the Treaty of Versailles were intended to maximize the economic and military security of the Allies while minimizing those of the Germans. That it did not turn out exactly as planned holds a profound lesson for future diplomats. It is dangerous to humiliate one's enemy, particularly a strong, proud people like the Germans. Better that today's enemy be left some dignity, resources, and self-respect, because an embittered and humiliated enemy can be the source of grave future difficulties.

The diplomats of 1919 failed miserably to preserve the old or to establish a new world order. Their failure brought us Adolf Hitler, World War II, the Cold War, and a confused legacy that haunts us to this day. All that was predicted in General Smuts's letters to Lloyd George and Wilson came to pass. The harshness of the treaty, instead of providing security for some, brought insecurity to all.

Paul J. Rose

Additional Reading

Bailey, Thomas A., *Woodrow Wilson and the Lost Peace* (1944).

Mee, Charles L., Jr., *The End of an Order: Versailles 1919* (1980).

Watt, Richard M., *The Kings Depart: The Tragedy of Germany: Versailles and the German Revolution* (1968).

Treblinka

See CONCENTRATION CAMPS

U

Unconditional Surrender Policy

This policy was an Allied war aim announced by President Franklin D. Roosevelt during a press briefing held after the Casablanca Conference in January 1943, which stated that the Grand Alliance would accept nothing less than a total and unconditional Axis surrender. Roosevelt was the driving force behind the policy and favored its adoption for several reasons. After the first Allied victories, the American public demanded some further enunciation of war aims beyond the statements of the 1941 Atlantic Charter (q.v.). The unconditional surrender policy satisfied this demand and created Allied unity and resolve to persevere toward the common goal of victory. Roosevelt similarly hoped to reassure Soviet Premier Josef Stalin of the West's determination to fight until the final Axis defeat. Stalin did not understand the policy. He said "just let them surrender and then we can make it unconditional."

The guarantee that the Western Allies would not negotiate a separate peace or armistice with the Axis excluding the Soviets, or make any agreement that allowed enemy governments to remain intact after hostilities, was explicit. In addition, Roosevelt wanted Germany to know that its final defeat would be an undeniable fact, unlike in World War I where an armistice was negotiated only to have the Germans later claim they were not militarily defeated but were "stabbed in the back" (q.v.) by defeatists and treasonous politicians. A final reason was Roosevelt's personal moral outrage about Axis atrocities and his refusal to deal with those he considered ruthless war criminals.

The unconditional surrender policy proved controversial. Critics have charged that it provided ammunition to Axis propagandists to spur their population to greater sacrifices to avoid a defeat they were assured meant the division of their countries and the total annihilation of their peoples and cultures.

Some Allied military leaders, none of whom were consulted in advance about the policy, shared the view that it prolonged enemy resistance and cost the lives of additional Allied troops and increased expenditures of material and financial resources. The policy had its greatest impact on Allied propagandists dealing with Germany who offered hope to "good" Germans that anti-Nazi resistance could shorten the war and bring a "soft" peace.

The majority of Allied military and civilian leaders cited factors other than the unconditional surrender policy that prolonged enemy resistance. Such factors included the Allied insistence on a total victory, the lack of any indigenous resistance movements in most Axis nations, or prominent leaders with whom the Allies could negotiate, and the refusal of Axis leaders to consider any form of capitulation.

While British prime minister Winston S. Churchill and Stalin initially doubted the wisdom of the policy, it was accepted as an Allied war aim. The unconditional surrender policy was not implemented with equal rigor, although it was intended to apply to all Axis nations. It was not extended to the Axis allies in Eastern Europe, which surrendered conditionally to the Soviet Union. Nor was it was strictly applied to Italy, which surrendered unconditionally but gained certain privileges from the Anglo-Americans because of its subsequent membership in the anti-Nazi alliance after September 1943. In the case of Japan, some conditions, such as allowing the emperor to remain on the throne and Japan's national identity to remain intact, were conceded in return for an unconditional military surrender. The doctrine was specifically tailored to Nazi Germany, whose military and political power was totally destroyed before surrender was accepted.

Clayton D. Laurie

Additional Reading

Armstrong, Anne, *Unconditional Surrender: The Impact of the Casablanca Policy on World War II* (1961).

Dallek, Robert, *Franklin D. Roosevelt and American Foreign Policy, 1932–1945* (1979).

Undeclared War, America's (1940–1941)

Responding to the outbreak of the European war in early September 1939, President Franklin D. Roosevelt (q.v.) affirmed that the United States would remain a neutral nation. He was quick to add, however, that he could not ask, as Woodrow Wilson had in 1914, that every American remain neutral in thought as well as deed. It was a frank acknowledgment of political reality; the overwhelming majority of Americans favored the Allied cause.

Roosevelt also asserted that "even a neutral cannot be asked to close his mind or conscience." It was a subtle indication of his own unwillingness to be bound by strict definitions of neutrality. Indeed, over the next two years, he stretched the meaning of neutrality to encompass decidedly unneutral actions and policies aimed at bolstering the Allies in their struggle against Nazi Germany. Together, these activities, which grew in scope between the fall of France and eventual entry of the United States into the war, comprised an "undeclared war" against Hitler's Germany.

His attention drawn to foreign affairs by the late 1930s, Roosevelt was struck by the increasingly dangerous incongruity of domestic opinion and events abroad. Since 1935, the Neutrality Act (q.v.), a concession to isolationist sentiments, limited the president's latitude in dealing with foreign crises.

Subsequent years would see a series of aggressions in Asia and Europe, which the United States seemed helpless to deter. Revision of the Neutrality Act in 1937 had at least permitted the U.S. to sell nonmilitary goods to endangered allies on a "cash-and-carry" basis. Deeply rooted isolationism mitigated against more direct aid. As hopes for European peace through appeasement evaporated in 1939, the Roosevelt administration offered only nominal support to Britain and France, now standing firm in their commitment to defend Poland against German aggression. In anticipation of war with Germany in May 1939, the administration authorized joint Anglo-American naval planning. Only in the aftermath of Poland's collapse was more substantial aid pledged.

In the early stages of the "Phony War" (q.v.), Roosevelt's main concern was to insulate the American hemisphere from the war by declaring oceanic "security zones," in which belligerent naval activity was prohibited, and proscribing hostile submarine operations in American waters.

Other policies allowed U.S. naval units considerable latitude in communicating useful information, such as the position of German vessels, to British patrol units. In an episode that typified this "unneutral neutrality," the German passenger liner *Columbus* was "escorted" out of the U.S. security zone by an American cruiser, which probably alerted a nearby British warship to the liner's position. Ordered to heave to by the British vessel, the *Columbus* was scuttled by her crew. In a similar incident, the German freighter *Arauca* was chased into Port Everglades, Florida, by a British destroyer. There the crew was interned and the ship seized for American use.

The Phony War ended in April 1940 with a stunning sequence of Nazi thrusts into northern and Western Europe. The unexpectedly rapid collapse of France had a discernible impact on American opinion, which registered mounting alarm over the consequences of new Nazi conquests. Roosevelt deftly nurtured the growing public willingness to aid a now-isolated Britain by focusing his rhetoric on the eventual danger that a Nazi-dominated Europe would pose to the American hemisphere. That summer, as the Battle of Britain (q.v.) underscored that nation's role as the sole opponent to Adolf Hitler's design, the Roosevelt administration frantically explored every avenue by which Britain might be aided.

A 1917 law permitting the sale of outmoded or surplus military equipment on a cash-and-carry basis was dusted off to facilitate the sale of nearly 200 aircraft and large quantities of small arms and ammunition to the beleaguered island nation. Additional American aid appeared in the form of "obsolete" tanks that found their way to Canada, the use of aviation training facilities in Florida, and of no small consequence, permission for British warships to seek repairs in U.S. ports.

By fall 1940, however, it was evident that such efforts were insufficient to overcome the losses occurring in the intensifying Battle of the Atlantic (q.v.). What Britain needed most was escorts, which British Prime Minister Winston S. Churchill had requested from Roosevelt as early as May 1940. Still restrained by isolationist sentiment, Roosevelt hesitated for three months before agreeing to the "Destroyers for Bases Deal" (q.v.).

In exchange for fifty World War I–vintage destroyers, the U.S. received ninety-nine-year leases to eight base sites spanning the Atlantic rim from Newfoundland to British Guiana. Though isolationists howled, public opinion was with the president. Most Americans perceived this less-than-neutral act as a good means of keeping Britain in the war and the U.S. out. German response to the trade was surprisingly muted, but later the same month, the formation of a Berlin-Rome-Tokyo Axis through the Tripartite Pact came in part as an effort to restrain the U.S. from further action.

As was clear by December, further American aid would be necessary if Britain were to remain in the war. An urgent plea from Churchill to Roosevelt revealed that Britain no longer had the financial means to meet the terms of "cash-and-carry." The president moved quickly to frame the Lend-Lease Act (q.v.), which was enacted into law in early 1941.

This legislation, later praised by Churchill as "the most unsordid act in the history of any nation," circumvented the troublesome provisions of the Neutrality Act by "lending" Britain urgently needed materials and equipment. If the American people wished to remain out of war, Roosevelt declared in a radio broadcast, they must be prepared to become the "great arsenal of democracy" (q.v.) and supply Britain with the requisite Lend-Lease goods. Though the American public generally supported the act as a means of warding off war, it was a virtual declaration of war against Germany.

The impact of Lend-Lease on Britain's war effort was salutary, but ultimately the renewed flow of war supplies only served to present Roosevelt with another dilemma. The German U-boat campaign in the Atlantic was taking a damaging toll on transatlantic commerce. Unwilling to commit the U.S. Navy to convoy duty, Roosevelt did move to extend U.S. naval patrols and order U.S. Marines to occupy Iceland (q.v.). Even so, convoys still had to pass through a U-boat-infested "No Man's Land" in mid-ocean, where escort protection lapsed. In April 1941, the U-boat threat was compounded by the successful breakout into the Atlantic of the German battleship *Bismarck* (q.v.). Urged by Churchill to forward any information on *Bismarck*'s position, Roosevelt contemplated more direct action. Were *Bismarck* to appear in the Caribbean, and were he to authorize U.S. submarines to attack her, would he be impeached? His specu-

lation became moot as the Royal Navy sank the German warship two days later.

While Roosevelt continued to publicly reaffirm the urgency of supplying Britain during the summer, the more important question of convoy escort went unresolved. Hitler's invasion of the Soviet Union in June complicated matters by posing the question of potential competition for Lend-Lease aid. While the program would eventually be extended to the Soviet Union, Roosevelt's advisers suggested redoubled aid for Britain and U.S. naval protection for convoys. Again he hesitated, bound by public sentiment. Instead he authorized a U.S. occupation of Iceland. More direct involvement rested on some movement in public opinion.

Public opposition to convoying and any remaining pretense of U.S. neutrality disappeared in the aftermath of the *Greer* Incident (q.v.) in September 1941. The USS *Greer*, an American destroyer, was attacked by a U-Boat in the North Atlantic in the course of aiding a British patrol bomber in tracking the submarine. Roosevelt's account of the event disregarded *Greer*'s decidedly unneutral actions and depicted the destroyer as the innocent victim of wanton Nazi aggression. Damning the U-boats as "rattlesnakes of the seas," he announced that henceforth the U.S. Navy would "shoot on sight," and more importantly, would now offer convoy escort protection as far east as Iceland.

In the waning months of 1941, the last vestiges of U.S. neutrality rapidly disappeared. As Congress debated revising the Neutrality Act to permit the arming of U.S. merchantmen, events closed in. On 16–17 October 1941, a German U-boat attacked the destroyer USS *Kearny* (q.v.). This was followed two weeks later by the sinking of the USS *Reuben James* (q.v.) on 31 October. These incidents virtually killed the Neutrality Act.

By November, America's "undeclared war" against Germany had proceeded as far as it could. Tenacious isolationist sentiment still disallowed actual belligerent status. Until some circumstance created a public consensus favoring complete commitment, America's war would remain undeclared and its participation limited. On 7 December, the Japanese attack on Pearl Harbor provided that consensus with a bang.

Blaine T. Browne

Additional Reading

Bailey, Thomas A., and Paul B. Ryan, *Hitler vs. Roosevelt: The Undeclared Naval War* (1979).
Burns, James MacGregor, *Roosevelt: The Soldier of Freedom, 1940–45* (1970).

U

Divine, Robert A., *The Reluctant Belligerent: American Entry into World War II* (1965).

Morison, Samuel Elliot, *The Battle of the Atlantic: History of the United States Naval Operations in World War II,* Vol. I (1947).

United Nations

United Nations, the present world peacekeeping body, is the successor organization to the League of Nations (q.v.) founded after World War I. The U.N. was founded in San Francisco in 1945. Its roots can be traced to a series of international and diplomatic conferences of the nineteenth and early twentieth centuries that led first to the creation of the League of Nations and subsequently to the United Nations. The U.N. had its immediate impetus from the desire of the victorious powers of World War II (i.e., the United Nations) to prevent another world war. It is one of the ironies of history that "nations" cannot belong to the United Nations—only "states" can.

The Covenant of the League of Nations, the precursor of the United Nations, was intended to preserve the peace by establishing the Permanent Court of International Justice, by dealing with such issues as disarmament, by maintaining territorial integrity, and by imposing sanctions on aggressor states. The League's collapse resulted from its inability to keep the peace and prevent World War II. Its final demise came in 1946 when its assets and some of its functions were transferred to the newly born United Nations.

The earliest of several specific steps to establish the United Nations came with an inter-Allied declaration, signed in London on 12 June 1941, by the United Kingdom, Canada, and twelve other nations then at war with Germany and Italy. (The United States and Japan had not yet entered the war.) In August 1941, the Atlantic Charter (q.v.), signed by President Franklin D. Roosevelt and British Prime Minister Winson S. Churchill (qq.v.), called for the defeat of Germany and Italy and the subsequent establishment of international cooperation to help resolve the world's many problems that could lead to future wars.

The twenty-six nations fighting against the Axis powers signed the Declaration of the United Nations in Washington, D.C., on 1 January 1942. The declaration proclaimed the principles and purposes of the Atlantic Charter and called for the defeat of the Axis powers (Germany, Italy, and Japan) at the earliest possible date. The "United Nations" originally was the name of the anti-Axis coalition during World War II. Initially, the United Nations, even in its early role as a world body, was an organization of the victorious powers of World War II, consisting of fifty-one nations. The three Axis powers and their allies were not admitted at first. Membership was later enlarged to include all "peace-loving" nations.

At the Moscow Conference of 30 October 1943, the foreign ministers of the United States, the United Kingdom, the Soviet Union, and the ambassador of China recognized the necessity of establishing an international organization for the maintenance of peace and security in the postwar world. A month later at the Teheran Conference, Roosevelt, Churchill, and Stalin declared:

> We recognize fully the supreme responsibility resting upon us and all the United Nations to make a peace which will command the good will of the overwhelming masses of the peoples of the world and banish the scourge and terror of war for many generations.

At the Dumbarton Oaks Conference (q.v.) in September 1944, representatives of the United States, the United Kingdom, the Soviet Union, and China drew up concrete plans for the United Nations. They agreed on the structure, functions, and aims of the emerging world body. They proposed a Security Council to be charged with keeping the peace. Five permanent seats on the council, with veto power, were proposed for China, France, the Soviet Union, the United Kingdom, and the United States.

The United Nations founding conference was held in San Francisco in April 1945. The fifty-one founding members included the forty-six nations that adhered to the United Nations Declaration of 1 January 1942 and, in addition, which had declared war on at least one of the Axis powers. Subsequently, Argentina, Byelorussia, the Ukraine, and Denmark were added to the total. All "peace-loving" countries were eligible for membership if, in the judgment of the United Nations, they were able and willing to carry out the obligations of the charter.

The U.N. Charter established these six main organs: the Economic and Social Council, the General Assembly, the International Court of Justice, the Secretariat, the Security Council, and the Trusteeship Council. Although the work of the Secretariat is conducted in English and French, other official languages are Arabic, Chinese, Russian, and Spanish.

The central idea of the U.N. was broad and forward-looking. Of the six main organs, the Security Council and the General Assembly were to be the principal political organs. The very ambitious task of collective security was assigned to the Security Council based on the belief that the five permanent members could reach unanimous decisions and be the great guardians of peace through the prompt use of military counterforce when necessary. As John Stoessinger in *The Might of Nations* writes, their task was to "kill another Hitler in his shell ere he become too great."

The General Assembly, where every nation has one vote, functions as what Stoessinger calls the "Parliament of Man in Embryo," a meeting place where all nations great and small can confer on the basis of sovereign equality. This is a world forum where nations can employ the time-honored method of talking things through. In addition, the assembly guides policy and manages general financial affairs. The U.N. is allied with several agencies that work independently, such as the World Bank; the United Nations Educational, Scientific, and Cultural Organization (UNESCO); the Economic and Social Council; and the World Health Organization.

The Preamble to the United Nations Charter states its purpose:

WE THE PEOPLE OF THE UNITED NATIONS DETERMINED to save succeeding generations from the scourge of war, which twice in our lifetime has brought untold sorrow to mankind,

and to affirm faith in fundamental human rights, in the dignity and worth of the human person, in the equal rights of men and women and of nations large and small, and

to establish conditions under which justice and respect for the obligations arising from treaties and other sources of international law can be maintained, and to promote social progress and better standards of life in larger freedom.

At San Francisco, the Soviet representative questioned the use of "We the People" in the Preamble, preferring instead that the role and authority of the states be emphasized. The American belief in "individualism" over "statism" prevailed, and this phrase, borrowed from the Preamble to the American Constitution, was used.

The founders understood that in due course the necessity for changes in the charter would arise. Article 108 of the United Nations Charter provides that an amendment to the present charter would come into force on adoption by a vote of two-thirds of the members of the General Assembly. The new amendment must then be ratified in accordance with the respective constitutional processes of two-thirds of the members of the United Nations, including all permanent members of the Security Council. Most amendments adopted to date have increased the membership of the Security Council and the Economic and Social Council.

By unanimous resolution on 14 December 1945, the United States Congress invited the United Nations to establish its permanent home in the United States. On 14 February 1946, the General Assembly, meeting in London, accepted the invitation. There were both economic and psychological reasons for this decision. The United States was the only major industrial nation to emerge from the war in a strong economic condition. In America, housing facilities were more readily available than in war-torn Europe, resources were plentiful, and the dollar had become the international medium of exchange. More importantly, the United States was expected to initially finance at least 50 percent of U.N. administrative costs.

Psychologically, it was considered a wise move to place the U.N. headquarters in the United States, to give the American people a strong sense of attachment to the world body. International leaders remembered only too well that twenty-six years earlier, the United States Senate had rejected the Treaty of Versailles (q.v.), and by so doing, had denied the League of Nations universality, if not outright doomed it to failure. It was hoped this time the U.S. Senate would be less likely to reject the new world body if it was based in the United States. This time there was little danger of U.S. Senate rejection in any event.

After meeting in temporary locations at Hunter College in the Bronx and at the Sperry Gyroscope plant at Lake Success, New York, the General Assembly accepted an offer of $8.5 million by John D. Rockefeller, Jr., for the purchase of eighteen acres of land between 42nd and 48th Streets on Manhattan's East Side. An American architect, Wallace K. Harrison, was selected by the first secretary general, Trygve Lie, to oversee the construction of the now existing U.N. headquarters, in cooperation with a board of consultants from ten other countries.

In 1947, the U.S. secretary of state signed an agreement with the secretary general of the United Nations prescribing the privileges and immunities of the U.N. headquarters. This agreement gave the United Nations authority to make the necessary regulations for governing the headquarters district. Personnel assigned to the United Nations constitute an international civil service and owe their loyalty to the United Nations, its principles, and its purposes. Each person is under oath not to take instructions from any government or outside authority. In the performance of their official duties, they are expected to avoid any external control or direction.

This principle of neutrality on the part of U.N. civil servants has generally been respected, with the exception of former Soviet bloc personnel who were tightly controlled and directed by their own governments. Even in their official functions as employees of the U.N., they were required by the Soviet Union to promote Soviet objectives and serve as apologists for Soviet power. The Soviet Union regularly placed KGB (Soviet Committee for State Security) and GRU (Soviet military intelligence) agents on the U.N. payroll in violation of the U.N. Charter.

In his book, *Breaking with Moscow,* Arkady N. Shevchenko, one of the highest-ranking Soviet officials ever to defect to the West, noted that as chief of the Security Council and Political Affairs Division of the (Soviet) mission; "I had a staff of more than twenty (i.e., Soviet) diplomats. I soon discovered that in fact there were only seven real diplomats; the remainder were KGB or GRU professionals. . . ." Western intelligence sources estimated that the former Soviet Union kept up to 300 intelligence agents (many of them assigned to U.N. duties) permanently in New York to control and spy on Soviet personnel, as well as to recruit among the other nationalities assigned to the U.N.

Personnel assigned to the U.N. headquarters staff do not possess diplomatic immunity. For this reason, they are subject to the provisions of U.S. law for activities unrelated to their U.N. duties. Over the years, many Soviet bloc personnel have been arrested by the FBI and convicted in American courts for spying activities.

The Secretariat services those other U.N. organs and administers the programs and policies authorized by them. It consists of the secretary general, the U.N.'s chief administrative officer, and his staff. On the recommendation of the Security Council, the General Assembly appoints the secretary general for a term of five years. This means that he must receive the support of the five permanent members of the Security Council. In addition to his regular duties, he is expected to perform any "other functions" entrusted to him by the Security

Council. He is authorized to bring before the Security Council "any matter which in his opinion may threaten the maintenance of international peace and security."

The U.N. is a very complex organization that represents as great an increase in functional development over that of the League of Nations, as the latter did over the poorly developed organizational system of earlier periods. During its more than one-half century of existence, the U.N., in what has been a difficult balancing act, has managed to accommodate both continuity and change in a world that encompasses many divergent and even contradictory interests. As new problems develop, organizations and institutions are created to meet the need for a united effort to solve them. A major function of the U.N. has been its peacekeeping role.

It is clear that the League of Nations failed because it was unable to achieve the critical task of preventing World War II. The United Nations has not yet failed in its primary purpose of preventing World War III. It continues, after more than fifty years, to provide a valuable forum for discussing, and in some cases, resolving, many of the world's problems. The U.N., for example, has been involved in the Arab-Israeli Conflict and the Cuban Missile Crisis. The Korean Conflict of 1950 and the Gulf War of 1991 were officially fought by the United Nations. The U.N. has presided over the decline of Western colonial empires and the growth of the number of nation-states to more than 180.

Like the League of Nations, the United Nations was to a large extent an American creation. Yet, the United States has been very ambivalent toward the world body. Conservative American political opinion is suspicious of the collective security principle envisioned in the U.N. Charter. American liberals feel more comfortable with the idea of the U.N. as an embryonic world government. There is constant tension between the two views.

In its early years, the U.N. was dominated by the United States and used almost as an extension of American foreign policy. In those days, American public support of the world body was high. The United States frequently backed Soviet leaders into a corner and forced them to use their Security Council veto to protect their own perceived interests. Much was made of the fact that the Soviet Union, not the United States, vetoed measures wanted by a majority of U.N. members. Most Americans loved it. But in later years, when the United States found its own interests challenged and could no longer obtain majority support in the greatly expanded General Assembly, the veto was casually resorted to as a valuable parliamentary device. This, of course, was precisely how the veto was intended to serve. But most importantly, American public opinion toward the U.N. soured when U.S. dominance declined.

Since the collapse of the Soviet Union, the United States is left as the "lonely superpower." In that role, the United States is again in a position to frustrate, if not completely dominate, the U.N. Under the Reagan (1981–1989) and Bush (1989–1993) administrations, a very hostile attitude was shown toward the U.N. A Reagan spokesman once virtually invited the U.N. to relocate from the United States. During this period, the United States refused to pay much of its assessed U.N. dues as provided in the charter.

The Bush administration showed an increased willingness to participate in multinational operations (e.g., the Gulf War of 1991 and the Somalia Operation of 1992–1993) only if the United States could command and control them. Bush left office on 20 January 1993 with the United States owing several hundred million dollars in back dues. It remains to be seen how future administrations will relate to the United Nations.

Such American domination on the one hand, and the lack of support on the other, serve to undermine the integrity and neutrality of the world body by making it appear to be an instrument of American foreign policy. This ambivalent American attitude greatly detracts from the U.N.'s potential as a world peacekeeping body. Yet, the U.N. cannot cope with world security problems without American support and cooperation. It is clear that in the 1990s, only the United States possesses the resources and political power to mobilize and lead many of the complex and dangerous multinational operations. Other nations are often reluctant to move into crisis areas until the United States leads the way. If the U.N. finds the United States difficult to live with, it also finds it impossible to operate without strong American support.

The Security Council has an uneven record. It has yet to attain its goal of collective security, but its five permanent members have often agreed to give the secretary general increased powers to use in specific peacekeeping functions. When unanimity exists among the "Big Five" (United States, Soviet Union, Great Britain, France, and China), the Security Council has extensive powers to keep the peace. Security Council resolutions have the force and effect of international law.

The existence of the "big power" veto on the Security Council has proven to be both a curse and a blessing. On the positive side, the provision for the veto recognizes the powerful position of its holders on the international scene and their ability to essentially protect their own vital interests. The veto also prevents powerful nations from being backed into a corner where the only acceptable alternative is to fight. On the negative side, the veto is often used to block progressive action needed by the world community. The present economic power of Germany and Japan merits their receiving a permanent seat on the Security Council. So far, there has been little demand for such an action.

The General Assembly has yet to become the world's parliament, but it has improvised to meet unforeseen world problems better than anyone could have anticipated. Thanks to its availability and versatility, the Cold War was waged, in the words of Stoessinger, "in an atmosphere of parliamentarianism rather than on the battlefield."

The effectiveness of any international body can best be evaluated by analyzing the character and behavior of its members. The U.N. cannot succeed in the absence of a consensus by a majority of its members, including unanimity of the five permanent members of the Security Council. The U.N. is not a supranational organization, nor does it possess sovereignty. Stripped of its membership, the U.N. is an inanimate object; a structure of steel and concrete; an organization of charts, graphs, and computers. It cannot be blamed for how it is used or not used. This much-maligned world peacekeeping body is morally and functionally neutral. It can carry out only those functions that its members empower it to perform. United Nations members must accept the blame for any of its shortcomings.

The record shows that the U.N. can achieve almost any goal that a majority of its members, including the "Big Five," approve. In its early years, the U.N. was to a large degree paralyzed by the polarizing effect of the ideologically motivated East-West struggle. The collapse of the Soviet Union has greatly improved the possibility of concerted United Nations action to meet most conceivable threats to world peace. The United Nations remains the current best hope of humankind if the world is to avoid its own destruction.

Paul J. Rose

Additional Reading

Arne, Sigrid, *The United Nations Primer: The Key to the Conferences* (1948).

Bennett, A. LeRoy, *International Organizations* (1980).

Bentwich, Norman de M., *From Geneva to San Francisco: An Account of the International Organizations of the New Order* (1946).

Claude, Inis L., Jr., *Swords into Plowshares* (1984).

Stoessinger, John G., *The Might of Nations* (1986).

V

Versailles Treaty
See TREATY OF VERSAILLES

Vichy France (1940–1944)
When German armed forces invaded France in the summer of 1940, they occupied the strategic northern, Atlantic, and Channel coastal regions of that country. The remaining one-third of French territory in the southern and interior zones was administered for a period of four years by the *Etat Français* (the French State). The *Etat Français* was known popularly as Vichy, named after the provincial spa town that became the seat of the French government while Paris remained under German occupation.

The Vichy state became the rallying point for all those who blamed the fall of France on what they perceived to be the decadent Third Republic (1871–1946), which apparently had been corrupted by the so-called evils of Jewish, Masonic, Communist, and other "foreign" influences. The Vichy regime based its ideology of "National Revolution" upon the conservative values of homeland, family, and work. It adopted the principles of "Order, Authority, and Patriotism" in preference to the old republican values of Liberty, Equality, and Fraternity. Vichy was xenophobic, anti-Semitic, anti-Communist, anti-socialist, and anti-republican. The Vichy regime scorned all libertarian and democratic values. Yet, despite the development of a considerable number of Fascist organizations in France before and during World War II, Vichy was not overtly Fascist, and in its early days, was the only state to retain some semblance of autonomy in Hitler's Europe.

French Fascism apart, Vichy was, above all, the triumph of the *bourgeoisie,* of the hierarchy of the Catholic Church, and of monarchist and traditionalist elements. The establishment of the new

French state can therefore be interpreted as the revenge of the conservative, traditional, and extreme right upon the French republic. As such, the Vichy period serves as a key moment in the *Guerres Franco-françaises* theory; that is, the idea of a nation continuously divided over ideological, cultural, class, and religious issues. The historiographical controversies over Vichy France are vast and complex; yet arguably, until more recently, the most formative works were produced by non-French historians. It was through the publications of American historians Robert Paxton in 1972 and Stanley Hoffman in 1974 that the French have tried to come to terms with their recent past. On 10 July 1940, the French National Assembly met at Vichy in the unoccupied part of France and by a vote of 569 to 80, with 17 abstentions, authorized the assumption of full powers to the recently nominated prime minister and World War I hero, Marshal Henri Philippe Pétain (q.v.). At the age of eighty-four, Pétain declared himself "Head of the French State" which, between 1940 and 1944, replaced the French Third Republic. At the time, many French people transmogrified him into a saviour figure who would defend France in that nation's darkest hour.

Some historians have excused Pétain as a mere figurehead, manipulated by the more pragmatic and self-seeking Pierre Laval (q.v.), who on 23 July 1940, became Pétain's *vice president du Conseil* and his named successor. Yet, Pétain was no mere puppet. He was the ultimate arbiter of policy at Vichy, and he often advocated outright collaboration with the Germans, as demonstrated by his meeting with Adolf Hitler at Montoire in October 1940. It should be emphasized that Vichy's choice of economic, political, military, and police collaboration (in French, "to collaborate" carries the connotation "to cooperate") was wished for by the French government and not instigated by the Germans. This was motivated by Vichy's wish to have a future role in Europe, with the assumption that the Germans would win the war, and also in a desire to limit the damage of occupation costs and reparations payments.

Thus the administration of Vichy was conditioned by its relations with Nazi Germany, which occupied two-thirds of French territory and annexed Alsace-Lorraine (q.v.), as well as held 1,800,000 prisoners of the former French Army. Yet even Hitler had to come to terms with the Vichy government. It controlled a powerful colonial empire and a navy whose loyalty was tempered by the battle of Mers el-Kébir (q.v.).

Admirals played a considerable role in the administration of the Vichy state. This explains why and how in the postwar years the higher echelons of the French Navy were purged, and many admirals went into exile until the amnesty of 1951. Admiral Jean François Darlan (q.v.), Laval's successor, employed admirals in all the key posts of the Vichy administration. Cardinal Lienart, the bishop of Lille, reportedly once asked Darlan where he would find another admiral to replace him as bishop upon his death. For a time, the Vichy state was even nicknamed by its detractors, the "Society for the Prevention of Cruelty to Admirals."

Members of the ecclesiastical hierarchy who supported Vichy included Cardinal Suhard, archbishop of Paris; Monsignor Piguet, bishop of Clermont-Ferrand; and Cardinal Gerlier, bishop of Lyons. They all hoped that Pétain's Vichy state would bring France back to its Christian roots.

The repressive nature of the Vichy government was clearly demonstrated by a series of laws against secret societies and combinations, most notably against the Freemasons (August 1940) and the proscription of trade union activities (November 1940). This was linked with a number of internments and trials of leading politicians of the Third Republic (the *Riom* trials), as well as a general policy against anti-clericals, Protestants, left-wingers, pacifists, and foreigners.

Of particular note were a series of harsh laws passed in October 1940 attacking the civil rights of the Jewish population. It should again be noted that Vichy was under no pressure from Nazi Germany to implement these laws; that Vichy's anti-Semitism was indigenous; and that some policemen seemed to flinch from rounding up Jews for deportation. As a whole, however, the Vichy police can be blamed for complicity in the deportation of 76,000 Jews.

Vichy mounted a number of anti-Semitic exhibitions and diffused anti-Semitic propaganda.

Reich Marshal Hermann Göring (right) arrives in St. Florent-Vergigny, France, for a meeting with Marshal Henri Pétain and Admiral Jean Darlan. (IWM HU 39706)

French Jews were obliged to wear the yellow Star of David on their clothes. They were excluded from a number of professions and were forced into exile or internment in special camps, such as Drancy, Pithiviers, and Beaune-la-Rolande, before deportation to Nazi Germany. In June 1942 alone, 13,000 French Jews were arrested and interned for a week in the winter sports stadium *(Vel d'Hiv)* in Paris before being transported to concentration and death camps in the east. Among those 13,000 Jews deported were 4,000 children. Less than 400 Jews would return to France at the end of the war; none of the children.

The Vichy French state was supported by an "Armistice Army" of 100,000 troops. There also were protection groups led by Colonel Georges A. Groussard, head of the French Legion of Combatants *(Legion française des combatants)* and the SOL *(Service d'ordre legionnaire)*.

The history of Vichy can be seen as falling into four phases. The first period, between July and December 1940, was dominated by Pierre Laval, and witnessed the resigned acceptance of the German victory. This was the period in which Vichy was looking for an opportunity to collaborate with Germany, stimulated by French resentment at what was perceived as British treachery in the aftermath of Mers el-Kébir. Pétain sent envoys to Berlin, and Laval negotiated directly with Otto Abetz, the German ambassador in Paris. It was these negotiations that led to the meeting between Pétain and Hitler at Montoire on 24 October 1940. Laval wanted closer collaboration with the Germans, and tried to negotiate better deals for Vichy. But when Laval was fired by Pétain and arrested on 13 December 1940, Franco-German relations temporarily froze.

The second phase, January 1941 to April 1942, witnessed the primacy of Admiral Darlan, Laval's successor. Darlan viewed Franco-German relations from a geo-strategic point of view, aiming at Franco-German military cooperation. At this stage, Vichy was of use to the Third *Reich* because of Nazi plans to invade the Soviet Union and to expand into the Middle East. As such, Vichy granted the Germans permission to transport war materials through French Tunisia to help Rommel in his North African campaign.

The Paris Protocols of May 1942 led to further Franco-German military collaboration. This was supported in the northern occupied zone by the French Volunteer Legion (LVF), which had been formed the previous summer by the French Fascist Jacques Doriot. The initiative behind the creation of this force was purely Parisian rather than Vichy, since the Vichy government refused to declare war on the Soviet Union. Early in the war, Hitler did not favor the recruitment of foreign legions, because he did not want to give guarantees to pro-Nazi movements in occupied territories. Also, he was wary of the true military value of such organizations, wrongly considering the French volunteers in this case to be inferior soldiers. Despite Hitler's sensibilities, the SS (q.v.) and the *Wehrmacht* encouraged this kind of collaboration, and the LVF subsequently served on the eastern front. Yet at no single time did more than 10,000 Frenchmen serve in the German military.

The third phase, between April 1942 and January 1944, witnessed the return to power of Laval, as a result of German pressure on Pétain. But Laval's ambitions to further Franco-German collaboration were momentarily checked by a major crisis on 11 November 1942 when, after the Allied landings in North Africa, the Germans invaded and occupied the Vichy zone. Although the *Wehrmacht* disarmed the Vichy Armistice Army, they failed to take the French fleet at Toulon, which in turn scuttled itself on 27 November.

In February 1943, Laval established the *Service de Travail Obligatoire* (Obligatory Work Service, or STO), which forced young men to leave France to work in Germany, supposedly in exchange for French POWs. The plan largely backfired, however, since many refused to leave their homeland, choosing instead to go underground and join a variety of burgeoning resistance (q.v.) groups.

Other youngsters were conscripted into Joseph Darnand's (q.v.) political police, the *Milice* (q.v.), created on 30 January 1943 to fight against the resistance. Alongside units of the German Army, the *Milice* worked hand-in-hand with the *Gestapo* (q.v.). Typical examples of this direct collaboration were the work of local *Gestapo* chief and torturer Klaus Barbie; police chief Paul Touvier (qq.v.); supreme SS chief in France Karl Oberg; and René Bousquet, the general secretary of the French Police, who in July 1942, placed the police in the northern zone completely at the disposition of the Germans. Meanwhile, Vichy reinforced its anti-Jewish policy with the creation of the *Commissariat général aux questions juives* (General Committee for the Jewish Question), which operated under German control.

The final phase, January to July 1944, witnessed the domination of Vichy by French Fascists and pro-German fanatics. By that point, Pétain's authority was curtailed considerably. With the liberation of France and the retreat of the *Wehrmacht* from French territory, the Vichy government was forced into exile, establishing itself in Sigmaringen, Germany, in September 1944. Reportedly, Pétain refused all governmental power, ceding his authority to the Germanophile collaborator Fernand de Brinon.

When the Vichy government and pro-Fascist collaborators withdrew to Germany, the majority of French soldiers in German uniform and the *miliciens* were regrouped into the *Waffen-SS* Charlemagne Division. Numbering between 7,000 and 8,000 troops, they accounted for only between 0.01 percent and 0.02 percent of the French population.

Pierre Laval was tried and executed after the war. Marshal Pétain's death penalty was commuted by Charles de Gaulle (q.v.). Subsequent French governments have resisted pressures to allow Pétain to be buried at Verdun with his men.

Since the end of World War II, echoes of the Vichy state can be seen in the extreme right, reactionary, traditionalist, and monarchist movements extant in France. The Vichy experience has deeply divided French society, and the traumatic shock of this experience continues to reverberate in French political and intellectual life. In the 1980s and 1990s, there have been a series of dramatic legal proceedings against Klaus Barbie, Paul Touvier, René Bousquet, and Maurice Papon. The atmosphere further has been poisoned by the publications of revisionist historians of the period. As in most Eastern and Western European societies, elements of anti-Semitism, racism, and neo-Fascism continue to lurk in French society.

Robert C. Hudson

Additional Reading

Aron, Robert, *The Vichy Regime 1940–1944* (1958).
Griffiths, Richard, *Marshal Pétain* (1970).
Paxton, Robert, *Vichy France: Old Guard and New Order* (1972).

W

Wannsee Protocol
See FINAL SOLUTION

Warsaw Ghetto
As a part of the "Final Solution" (q.v.) of the "Jewish Problem," the German occupation authorities herded the Jewish population of the General Government of Poland (q.v.) into several urban ghettos—the largest being in Warsaw. Surrounded by a brick wall ten feet high, some 400,000 Jews were starving on their meager rations, crowded in at an average of twelve to fourteen people per room, and decimated by hunger and diseases, especially typhoid.

By the end of July 1942, the German authorities began to transfer the fast-shrinking Jewish population of the Warsaw Ghetto to the death camp of Treblinka at the rate of some 5,000 people per day. The Jews were deceived by promises of being resettled in the labor camps in more peaceful and comfortable surroundings.

A few Jews who escaped the Treblinka camp managed to inform their compatriots about the horrors of the camp where the Jews were being murdered in gas chambers. The news spurred into action the segment of the Warsaw Ghetto community that had been secretly organized into the Jewish Fighting Organization, known as ŻOB by its Polish initials. The main leaders of the ŻOB were Mordecai Anielewicz and Itzhak Zuckerman (qq.v.), who believed that the Jews, like the Poles, should defend themselves arms-in-hand against Nazi genocidal practices.

These two leaders got in touch with General Stefan Rowecki (q.v.), the commander of the Polish underground forces, known as the Home Army, or AK (q.v.). Rowecki endorsed the ŻOB as a segment of his forces and dispatched to the ghetto whatever he could spare of his forces' meager armament, a few rifles and pistols, as well as a certain amount of ammunition and explosives. Moreover, the ŻOB purchased some more arms on the Warsaw black market.

On 18 January 1943, the Nazis entered the Warsaw Ghetto to gather the daily contingent of Jews to be sent to Treblinka. To their utter shock they were met with armed resistance by the ŻOB. Street fighting went on for four days, leaving about ten Germans and many more Jews dead, but affording ŻOB an opportunity to seize some German arms. The Germans withdrew and stopped the deportation scheme until 19 April, when SS chief Heinrich Himmler (q.v.), ordered a special operation to clear the ghetto by 20 April—Hitler's birthday. On the day of the operation, 2,000 SS men supported by a handful of army troops moved into the area with tanks, light artillery, and ammunition trailers. The Jewish guerrillas opened fire with their motley weaponry, one machine gun, some pistols, a few rifles, and homemade bombs. They destroyed a number of tanks, killed several German troops, and captured some more weapons, including another machine gun. The Germans withdrew that evening. The next day the fighting resumed. The Germans used gas, police dogs, and flamethrowers in an effort to dislodge the Jews from their bunkers.

Meanwhile, the Jewish fighters were supplied from the Polish side with some 100 pistols, 500 grenades, and explosives with fuzes and detonators. Two flags, the white and blue Jewish banner with the Star of David, and the white and red Polish flag were hoisted on one of the high buildings of the ghetto. At the same time, the Polish resistance tried to fulfill its promise to stage a series of diversionary actions and pierce a hole in the wall surrounding the ghetto in order to allow some of the surviving Jewish population to escape to the "Aryan side." Several groups of Polish underground army soldiers attacked the Germans guarding the outer wall three times, but were repelled with heavy losses by the vastly superior and better armed German forces. Only one Polish soldier managed to penetrate into the ghetto to fight, side by side, with the Jews.

Meanwhile, the Jewish freedom fighters continued their resistance. Not until 8 May did the Germans manage to capture the ŻOB headquarters bunker at number 18 Miła Street. Civilians hiding there surrendered, but many of the surviving ŻOB fighters, including Anielewicz, took their own lives to avoid being captured. The desperate battle continued until 16 May, becoming sporadic as Jewish ammunition was exhausted. The SS burned the Warsaw Ghetto and killed the surviving civilians or sent them to the death camps. SS major general Jürgen Stroop (q.v.), the commander of the operation, ordered the dynamiting of the Great Synagogue of Warsaw. Thereupon he wrote his report to Hitler: "The Warsaw Ghetto Is No More."

The losses of the ŻOB and their Polish supporters amounted to some 1,500. German casualties amounted to sixteen men killed and eighty-five wounded, according to the official German communique. Nazi losses probably were higher, but Berlin purposely wanted to minimize the size and importance of the uprising. The Polish government in London repeatedly intervened with the British and U.S. governments, urging them to assist the ŻOB in its heroic stand. Unfortunately, as the National Committee to Save Jews in Occupied Europe stated, "The world remained completely unmoved while the Germans were destroying the ghetto and slaughtering its inhabitants." As the Allied leaders explained, no resources could be diverted from the main purpose, that is, the rapid winning of the war.

Before the end of the uprising, Zuckerman led some seventy-five ŻOB fighters through the sewers and into underground havens on the Polish side of Warsaw. He continued to lead a Jewish team of guerrillas that joined the Polish underground.

M.K. Dzeiwanowski

Additional Reading

Garliński, Józef, *Poland in the Second World War* (1985).

Gutman, Israel, *Resistance: The Warsaw Ghetto Uprising* (1994).

Hilberg, Raul, *The Destruction of the European Jews* (3 vols.) (1985).

Nowak, Jan, *Courier from Warsaw* (1982).

Penkower, Monty Noam, *The Jews Were Expendable: Free World Diplomacy and the Holocaust* (1983).

Zuckerman, Itzhak, *A Surplus of Memory: Chronicle of the Warsaw Ghetto Uprising* (1991).

Wartime Government, British

The British government entered World War II with carefully prepared plans designed to direct the transition from peacetime to wartime administration. The guidelines for this transition originated in the "War Book," assembled by the Committee of Imperial Defense in the 1930s. The "War Book" covered step-by-step all areas of the transition from peace to war that included mobilization, institution of domestic security measures, broadcast censorship, and the establishment of full government control in wartime. The Ministries of Supply, Economic Warfare, Food, Information, Shipping, and others came into existence to meet the demands of war.

With the outbreak of war, British Prime Minister Neville Chamberlain (q.v.) moved to form a War Cabinet similar to that set up in World War I under David Lloyd George. Chamberlain followed no specific plan in constructing his nine-member War Cabinet except that of forming a cabinet that could work together well. While his War Cabinet included many of his prewar colleagues, he invited Winston S. Churchill (q.v.), a critic of the government's appeasement policy during the 1930s, to fill the post of first lord of the Admiralty and to sit in the War Cabinet. From the beginning, Chamberlain's wartime government found itself weakened by the refusal of the Labour and Liberal Parties to participate.

The supervision of the war effort lay in the hands of a number of War Cabinet committees. The Home Security Committee, the Home Affairs Committee, the Ministerial Priority Committee, the Food Committee, and the Economic Policy Committee held responsibility for organizing and managing the domestic side of the war. Direction of military operations and planning centered on the Military Coordination Committee, chaired by Lord Chatfield as minister of coordination of defense. Military plans originated in the Chiefs of Staff Committee, composed of the three heads of the fighting forces, who made recommendations to the Coordination Committee, which in turn took them up with the War Cabinet. This proved a slow and cumbersome process that lacked strong centralized direction.

By April 1940, Churchill presided over the committee as senior service minister with the authority to issue orders to the chiefs of staff. This proved an awkward and unworkable arrangement. He lacked adequate authority over his colleagues. In frustration, he asked Chamberlain to chair the Military Coordination Committee in order to provide central authority and direction to the conduct of the war.

Chamberlain's fragmented system of wartime direction did not last. Months of inactivity on the military front and mounting frustration with what many believed to be an excess of government regulation and inefficiency led to rising criticism of Chamberlain's handling of the war. Critics charged that the government lacked direction or energy. He responded to these charges by reluctantly adopting a more aggressive military policy that resulted in the Norwegian debacle and the collapse of his government.

On 10 May 1940, Churchill succeeded to the premiership. His arrival at 10 Downing Street ushered in substantial changes in Britain's wartime government. Unlike Chamberlain, he proved able to construct a truly national government that had widespread popular support and included both Labour and Liberal Party leaders. At first, he appointed a War Cabinet of five composed of the leading political figures with only the Foreign Secretary, Lord Halifax (q.v.), having specific departmental responsibilities. As the war continued, the membership in the War Cabinet expanded and the complexion of the cabinet changed as most of its members held departmental positions. A number of new ministries including, for example, Aircraft Production and Reconstruction, evolved to meet the changing demands of the war.

The most decisive change in government structure came in the higher direction of war policy. With the king's approval, Churchill combined the offices of prime minister and the minister of defense. As minister of defense, a position with unspecified powers, he took over many of the functions of the service ministers, who were dropped out of the War Cabinet to the status of departmental administrators with no direct involvement in military planning or operations. A Defense Committee divided into two branches, Operations and Supply, presided over by the prime minister, directed the central management of the war.

The most significant change in Britain's wartime government came when Churchill took over the direction of the Chiefs of Staff Committee. "Thus," he wrote, "for the first time the Chiefs of Staff Committee assumed its due and proper place in direct daily contact with the Executive Head of the Government, and in accord with him had full control over the conduct of the war and the armed forces." Meetings of the Defense Committee grew less frequent as war policy concentrated in the hands of Churchill and the chiefs of staff with whom the prime minister had an excellent working relationship. The War Cabinet evolved in the direction of a central directorate chiefly responsible for domestic issues. Thus the faults in Chamberlain's system of wartime direction which diffused responsibility over too wide an area found a corrective.

More than anything else, Churchill provided confidence, direction, and energy at the center of Britain's war effort that energized and inspired the entire machinery of government. Yet his administration of the war effort did not go without criticism. Critics pressed for a smaller War Cabinet composed of members without departmental duties, and for Churchill to give up the minister of defense post. In 1942, his position as war leader came under direct challenge when a vote of confidence took place in the House of Commons, with 25 voting for the motion and 475 voting against.

The improving tide of war strengthened Churchill's hold on the government and the nation. Throughout the remainder of the war few changes occurred in the government as Churchill had by that time established a team on which he could rely, and a centralized system of administration that worked admirably. Ironically, as the war expanded, his influence over the higher direction of military planning declined in deference to the need to coordinate planning and policy with the United States, which emerged as the senior partner in the wartime alliance.

During World War II, Britain's government successfully responded to the demands of modern war. Prewar planning established the foundations for the transition from peacetime to wartime administration. The period of Chamberlain's wartime government demonstrated the shortcomings of running a war without the centralized direction of war policy and a clear-cut chain of command. Nevertheless, important steps occurred that helped prepare the way for Churchill's success as war leader. With his ascent to the premiership, all the elements came together to create an efficient system of war direction that served Britain well throughout the remaining war years.

Van Michael Leslie

Additional Reading

Colvin, Ian, *The Chamberlain Cabinet* (1971).

Daalder, Hans, *Cabinet Reform in Britain 1914–1963* (1963).

Franklyn, Arthur J., *Defense by Committee* (1960).

MacKintosh, John P., *The British Cabinet* (1968).

Wartime Government, German

By the time World War II broke out, the Western democracies, when they compared themselves to the new dictatorships, had pronounced feelings of inferiority. The democracies compiled a sorry record over the preceding twenty years. They won World War I but made an utter mess of the peace settlement. The economic depression of the 1930s found democratic leaders cowering before their multitudes of unemployed citizens.

By contrast, the Nazi dictatorship in Germany projected an image of ruthless efficiency. Millions of Adolf Hitler's (q.v.) minions were marching willingly, even rapturously, to his commands. Having ended the depression in Germany, or so it seemed, Hitler was using his "genius" to remake Europe to fulfill German ambitions. As Hitler piled up his victories, first in foreign policy, and then, once war broke out, on the field of battle, the democracies took up their task with gloom and premonitions of disaster. How could the inefficient and seemingly outmoded democracies stand up to the smoothly functioning totalitarian state?

It all turned out, of course, much different than even the wisest observer of world affairs would have predicted in the late 1930s. The democracies learned how to be efficient, and the German dictatorship, that is to say Hitler, by a multitude of bizarre military decisions and because of the extreme inefficiency of the ramshackle government he created, actually helped the Allies to their great victory.

Hitler's regime rested on two, quite contradictory, pillars; the Weimar constitution, and the *Führerprinzip* (q.v.) or Leader Principle. Hitler, for all his contempt for the Weimar Republic (q.v.), never abolished its constitution, and indeed based the legitimacy of his dictatorship in part on its constitution.

First, Hitler used Article 48, the Emergency Decree Clause of the constitution, as the sanction for the notorious decree "For protection of People and State," promulgated just after the Nazis came to power early in 1933. This innocuous-sounding decree (for who would not be for "protection" of people and state?) canceled traditional civil rights and enabled Hitler to begin his career as a totalitarian dictator. The Nazi regime continued to cite this decree as justification for its actions all the way to its demise in 1945.

Second, the Enabling Act (q.v.) provided a further basis for Hitler's claim to legal dictatorship. This act, passed by the *Reichstag* acting under its powers granted by the constitution, gave him unlimited power for four years to solve Germany's problems. He renewed the Act at regular intervals right up until his death in 1945.

Hitler's political instincts were at work in all this, for he knew he would have more support from the general population if he came to power "legally" than if he seized power in a coup. But his actions were in fact a long way from true legality. The Enabling Act was passed only after Hitler used violence and intimidation to secure the *Reichstag* votes he needed. Additionally, Article 48 was hardly intended by the framers of the Weimar constitution to make possible a permanent cancellation of democratic civil rights.

Also fundamental to the Nazi state was the *Führerprinzip*. Under this principle all authority was vested in a charismatic leader, whom everyone in the nation obeyed. There was no need for discussion, because the "infallible" leader never erred.

The Third *Reich* was meant to be a mystical union of leader and nation, reaching heights of almost religious ecstasy, as shown by the hysterically screaming multitudes at Hitler's public appearances. The people expressed their support, not only by screaming, but also in plebiscites, which helped give legitimacy to his decisions.

The near 100 percent approval votes were obtained by a flow of propaganda that engulfed the people, by terror and threats of terror, and especially, in the case of the foreign policy successes of the 1930s, by the genuine popularity of Hitler's policies. The *Führerprinzip,* requiring a superman as leader, does not work in the real world of real human beings. Hitler turned out to be a mere man, and an unusually fallible one.

The Leader Principle was at work in all the traditional areas of German government. In foreign affairs, Hitler appointed and fired the diplomats, conducted negotiations, made alliances. His decision, seemingly lightly made, to declare war on the United States in 1941, brought the immense American resources, which were beyond the reach of German bombs, into the scales against him.

In the realm of justice, Hitler was the "supreme judge" of the nation, dismissing judges he thought too lenient and openly interfering in court

Chancellor Adolf Hitler is received by President Paul von Hindenburg at a public ceremony in Berlin early in 1934. Directly behind Hitler are General Hermann Göring (left) and Grand Admiral Erich Raeder. (IWM NYP 22518)

procedures, a process that culminated in the trials of the men who attempted to overthrow him in 1944. The image of his judicial deputy, Judge Roland Freisler (q.v.), screaming hysterically at the pitiable defendants, captured on film for posterity to view, is indelible.

In the German civil service, with its high standards of probity and efficiency and one of the proudest creations of the old Germany, Hitler gave full expression to his evil notions. In a series of steps, the civil servants were broken to his will, a process that reached its culmination in the middle of the war when Hitler, on 26 April 1942, proclaimed to the *Reichstag,* to enthusiastic applause, his legal right to dismiss anyone who did not do his duty as he perceived it. In legislation, that central activity of any government, he was in complete control. His orders, and in the end even his speeches, had the full force of law, without any approval from any other institution or person required.

Given the centrality of Hitler in the process of governing wartime Germany, how well suited was he, in the qualities of mind and character, to be the all-knowing and infallible *Führer?* The most cursory examination by the historian shows that, for Germany's sake, he should never have left Vienna. For all of his life, as shown by memoirs of people who knew him at various ages, he was incapable of sustained work. Rather than work, he was inclined to talk and consume sweets. Instead of engaging in careful discussions, embracing many different points of view that lie at the heart of good governance, Hitler preferred to deliver a harangue.

If choosing capable subordinates is a prime characteristic of a good ruler, then Hitler was an abysmal failure. While he prided himself on his ability to judge men, and would peer searchingly into the eyes of someone being introduced to him, in actuality, in the words of one historian, he chose "a remarkably large number of duds." A dilettante in everything himself, he chose a wine salesman as his foreign minister; his chief ideologue, a writer of unreadable books, as his minister for Eastern Europe; and an overage and overweight ex-fighter pilot as his director of the economy. To be fair, sometimes his intuitions paid off, as in the case of Albert Speer (q.v.), an architect who did outstanding work in the last years of the war (when it was already too late) in producing the weapons needed by the soldiers.

Hitler hated change. When someone's incompetence became obvious to all, he nevertheless retained the person on his staff. Also, it is well authenticated that Hitler, in his public image the most decisive of men, in fact was very prone to postponing decisions, or avoiding them altogether. Even Martin Bormann (q.v.), a man besotted with Hitler, complained about his indecisiveness. Very significant is the degree to which Hitler succumbed to wishful thinking, to a complete inability to adjust to, or even to listen to, unpalatable facts. Finally, he lacked the most essential requirement of effective statecraft—to have some kind of harmony between goals and resources, between what one wishes the state to achieve and the wherewithal possessed by that state.

The structure of Germany's wartime government, as created by Hitler, cut short the life of the "Thousand Year *Reich.*" The traditional ministries continued to exist, but the ministers never met as a cabinet during the whole course of the war. Ministers were known to complain that they heard of important events that concerned their ministries by reading the newspaper.

The *Reichstag,* the basic institution of government, was turned into an applauding and screaming audience for Hitler's pronouncements. In the rest of the government, Hitler followed a "divide and rule" formula, creating agencies that collided head-on with the traditional governmental bodies and thus leading to the fiercest imaginable battles over power and jurisdiction. He welcomed these battles because they helped preserve his own power, since the quarreling figures had to turn to Hitler for arbitration. It may have made him the dominant figure, but it stopped the business of government in its tracks. In the end, he created anarchy, the very state of affairs government is supposed to overcome.

A main source of inefficiency was the position of the Nazi Party, the monopoly party, as separate from the state. Hitler portrayed the party as the embodiment of the union between leader and people. But the party chiefs, the Leader Principle at work at lower levels, quarreled endlessly with each other and with state officials.

The *Gauleiters* (Party Regional Leaders), as they were called, were like feudal barons, operating their regions to suit themselves and openly expressing their contempt for Berlin, although not for Hitler himself. Speer's memoirs are replete with examples of these Nazis actually sabotaging the war effort by, for example, withholding some vital raw material from another Nazi leader's enterprise, in order to make that Nazi look bad in the *Führer's* eyes.

Corruption was general, since there was no scrutiny of any sort over the party's vast wealth. Party members used their political position to enrich themselves, and thereby damaged the process of government. The great Nazi slogan was "public benefit before private gain," but the average Nazi turned it around.

The SS, run by Heinrich Himmler (qq.v.), constituted a second state, alongside the traditional state, though both were presided over by Hitler. Himmler gave the political police the task of creating, not just safeguarding, the new order. One sees the Nazi scorn for law in its purest from in the SS. Himmler, in fact, openly stated that "we National Socialists then went to work not without right, which we carried within us, but, however, without laws." He made that statement in a speech to, of all people, the members of the German Law Academy.

Himmler proceeded, using the most extreme

forms of violence, to destroy actual and potential opponents of the regime (an opponent was anyone who violated a "healthy national spirit" as determined by Hitler and Himmler), and to exterminate the "inferior races," so that Europe after the war would be populated only by "Aryans," except for a few "inferiors" left behind to do slave labor. He pursued this hideous vision with a horrifying single-mindedness. The great writer Hannah Arendt long ago pointed out that the Nazis' main war was against the Jews. They were quite willing to weaken their effort against the Allies if they could thereby use those resources in their campaign against the Jews.

Finally, we must look at Hitler as the commander of the German armed forces. In earlier wars, once the fighting broke out, the German army traditionally had taken over many functions of government. In World War I, for example, the Army high command established a kind of dictatorship, running the economy, setting labor policy, and controlling public information. The German people were accustomed to the army's intrusion into civilian affairs. In World War II, it was entirely opposite, the party taking over areas like the economy, propaganda, and security that would have been at least partly under the army's control. The ultimate shock for the army was to lose control of even battlefield operations to the World War I corporal who had become head of state.

This development would not have been too bad for the *Wehrmacht* had Hitler been a capable strategist or tactician. The memoirs of Germany's World War II generals are full of scorn for Hitler's abilities as a military leader. General Walter Warlimont (q.v.), for example, one of the highest-ranking officers at German general headquarters, spoke of the "spirit of the Reich Chancellery," meaning that any discussion of the pros and cons of a question was regarded as pusillanimity. Total submission to fanatic National Socialist will was the way to win wars, Hitler thought. Field Marshal Erich von Manstein (q.v.) commented in his memoirs that Hitler never realized that the enemy also had will.

Hitler had every failing of an incompetent general: he ignored intelligence about the strength of the enemy; he had only vague notions of space and time; he failed to take into account weaknesses of his own forces; he did not understand how to concentrate his forces at a decisive point; he let nonmilitary factors be the controlling elements in military decisions; he did not know how to inspire his staff (because he regarded almost all officers with suspicion)—the list of his shortcomings go

on. The whole process was aided by toadies around him. These "yes" men believed, apparently sincerely, in Hitler's "second sight" and sixth sense. General Alfred Jodl (q.v.) once remarked to General Adolf Heusinger that the officers on his staff must not shake the *Führer's* inner conviction by arguing with him.

The result of such nonsense was the gigantic loss of the whole German Sixth Army at Stalingrad; and a short time later of the German Army in North Africa, when it was trapped in Tunisia. Defying all principles of common sense, Hitler's single principle of strategy became never to retreat. Of course, not to retreat to a defensible line in the face of a stronger army is to have one's own army overrun and lost.

The observer of these events must spare a little sympathy for the majority of the German generals, steeped in the great professional traditions of the Prussian army, the heirs of von Moltke, as they saw their armies ground to bits by the insane decisions of their *Führer*. To sample the profound vulgarity of the head of the German wartime government, a person need only read the long dialogue between Hitler and his chief of staff, General Kurt Zeitzler (q.v.), after the surrender of the Sixth Army at Stalingrad. Apparently oblivious to the fact that Germany had just suffered its greatest military catastrophe in history, the two men talked on at great length about why Field Marshal Friedrich Paulus (q.v.), the commander of the destroyed army, had not taken his own life, rather than fall prisoner to the Soviets.

The democracies regained their lost prestige because of how they conducted World War II. It was obvious to every European that Hitler lost the war all by himself. The "lessons of history" are sometimes not very obvious, but in this case they are clear enough. The Leader Principle simply does not work, for no one is infallible. The rule of law is essential to any decent society.

Roland V. Layton

Additional Reading
Bracher, Karl Dietrich, *The German Dictatorship* (1970).

Peterson, Edward N., *The Limits of Hitler's Power* (1969).

Speer, Albert, *Inside the Third Reich* (1970).

Steineart, Marlis G., *Die 23 Tage der Regierung Dönitz* (1967).

Warlimont, Walter, *Inside Hitler's Headquarters, 1939–1945* (1964).

Wartime Government, Italian

As World War II approached, Italy had tied itself to Germany. Following the 1936 invasion of Ethiopia (q.v.), Benito Mussolini (q.v.) was gratified by Germany's refusal to support sanctions against Italy; and together with the Germans, he intervened on behalf of the Nationalists in the 1936–1939 Spanish civil war (q.v.).

On 26 October 1936, Germany and Italy joined in the Axis Pact (q.v.) and on 6 November 1937, Italy joined Germany and Japan in the Anti-Comintern Pact (q.v.). During a September 1937 trip to Germany, Mussolini was overawed by German technical efficiency and military prowess. He was courted by Hitler and cheered by a gigantic crowd on the Maifeld. He became convinced of German invincibility and, as a sign of friendship, or even acquiescence, he subsequently accepted the *Anschluss* (q.v.) of Austria in March 1938.

Fearful of being bypassed by destiny, Mussolini, in the aftermath of Hitler's absorption of Czechoslovakia, ordered the invasion of Albania on 7 April 1939. He also acceded to the German demand for a formal military alliance by signing the Pact of Steel on 22 May. Mussolini impulsively directed his submissive and superficial foreign minister, Galeazzo Ciano (q.v.), to pledge Italian support for Germany in the event of a war without gaining any specific German commitment to Italian objectives.

The Molotov-Ribbentrop Pact (q.v.) of 23 August was a sobering shock for the Italians. War now seemed imminent. In an attempt to avoid being pulled into the impending conflict, and encouraged by the Italian ambassador to Berlin, Ciano in panic submitted to Germany an extensive list of materials needed by Italy before it could engage in combat. Germany only agreed to provide a minute part, and on 3 September 1939, Italy announced its "nonbelligerency."

To emphasize this decision on behalf of neutrality, Mussolini introduced a sweeping reorganization of the government. More power was shifted to Ciano and the circle that supported neutrality. With the exception of Ciano, Giuseppi Bottai, the minister of education, and Admiral Paolo Thaon di Revel, the minister of finance, all of the important posts were shuffled.

Although the new government was constructed in line with Ciano's neutral stance, it did not possess any real authority. Mussolini was the sole and ultimate arbiter of power. He was not only prime minister, impeded by no limitation of ministerial responsibility, but also head of all three service ministries, acting commander in chief, and the determiner of foreign policy. The holder of this supreme authority was increasingly feeble. He progressively degenerated in both physical and intellectual stamina, and was increasingly prone to pathological reversals of policy.

Apart from the charismatic aviator, Italo Balbo, there were no individuals with the personal strength or technical ability to temper *Il Duce* and avert disaster. The sycophants and opportunists who surrounded him did not tell him what he did not wish to hear.

Another capital deficiency was the absence of any unified command structure. Neither Mussolini nor the chief of the Supreme General Staff had effective organizational staffs, and interbranch rivalry debilitated the Italian armed forces. There was not any coordinated policy for the procurement of arms until the establishment of limited power for the Ministry of War Production in February 1943.

Pretense and bravado substituted for substance. The corrupt and inefficient regime had not effectively modernized or adequately equipped its military. Italy was less prepared for war in 1940 than it had been in 1915. His failure to attempt a remedy of this situation or to stay out of the war is a testament to his incompetence and irresponsibility. He ignored his realistic naval undersecretary, Admiral Domenico Cavagnari, and he allowed himself to be deluded by the army undersecretary, General Alberto Pariani, and the air force undersecretary, General Giuseppi Valle.

Despite his failure to prepare for war, Mussolini was galled by the passivity of neutrality. Since late 1938, he hammered away at the timidity and softness of the Italian *bourgeoisie*. He believed that war was necessary to toughen the Italian people. On 10 March 1940, he met with Hitler and agreed to enter the war. Three weeks later, he sent Ciano and the service commanders a memorandum in which he argued that war was imperative to establish Italian dominance in the Mediterranean. King Victor Emmanuel III (q.v.) was tempted to capitalize on opposition to war to supplant Mussolini. Marshal Pietro Badoglio (q.v.) and the general staff pointed out serious inadequacies in armor and aircraft, but Hitler's lightning advance through France undercut the king's slowly materializing resolve.

Mussolini, in a panic to share in the spoils, assumed temporary control of the high command at the end of May 1940 and gave the military two weeks to prepare for war. Without consulting the Grand Council of the Fascist Party or the Council of Ministers, he declared war on 10 June 1940.

To Badoglio's warning that war would be suicide, he retorted that it was all but won and Italy needed a few thousand dead in order to join the Germans at the peace conference. His policy was reactive rather than active and Italy was completely subordinate to Germany. German gratitude for Italy's tardy entry into the war was less than overwhelming. Unwilling to absolutely alienate France, Germany thwarted Italy's bid for Nice, Corsica, and Tunisia.

Expecting a complete German victory, Mussolini was anxious to assert Italian interests. Instead of concentrating Italy's limited resources on strategically important Egypt, he ordered the occupation of British Somalia, threatened Yugoslavia, and then, without consulting the Germans, ordered the invasion of Greece (q.v.) on 28 October 1940.

The decision to invade, concocted by Ciano, was made against the advice of the chiefs of staff. The date of the attack, which changed from moment to moment according to Mussolini's whim, was irrationally set during the rainy season. The Italian military headquarters finally learned of the precise date when Mussolini's ultimatum was reported over the radio from London. There was no coordination between various military departments, and he deliberately discounted his military intelligence's estimates of Greek strength.

The campaign was understandably a humiliating disaster. Badoglio was forced to accept the responsibility for Italian ineptitude. He was replaced as chief of the Supreme General Staff by Marshal Ugo Cavallero (q.v.) and Mussolini compounded the national malaise by sending leading members of the government, including Ciano, Bottai, and Dino Grandi, to the front. Cavallero, aware of his total dependance upon Mussolini, cravenly supported his predilection for a bloated but ill-equipped army rather than a smaller but more efficient force. Cavallero also acquiesced to the army's dispersal in the Balkans and in Russia rather than concentrating it in North Africa and Sicily, which proved decisive for Italy.

In the spring of 1941, Germany temporarily salvaged the Italian disaster in the Balkans (q.v.) with a rapid campaign, which left Italy in control of Montenegro and parts of Slovenia and Dalmatia. Although the British overran Italian East Africa (q.v.), the Italian defeat in North Africa was also momentarily reversed by the Germans.

This *deus ex machina* did little for Italian morale or unity. The wartime emergency divided the supporters of the Fascists into self-protective and combative segments. The party, bloated with forced members and a satiated elite, lacked the spirit to mobilize the country. Mussolini failed, and Fascism, which was accepted as a means of providing order and distributing power, lost its appeal and vitality.

By 1942, industrialists were pressing for Italy to leave the war and the Roman Catholic Church was warily working for a postwar regime to its liking. Carmine Senise, the career bureaucrat, who served as chief of the state police, was strengthening contacts with conservative monarchists. Badoglio and other disgruntled or disillusioned military men, such as Marshal Enrico Caviglia, became embroiled in a number of plots to take Italy out of the war. Cavallero supported the Axis alliance, but he was replaced because of the defeat in North Africa. His successor, Vittorio Ambrosio (q.v.), was ambivalent toward the anti-Mussolini conspirators within the military. After the Allied landings in North Africa and the German defeat at Stalingrad, Ciano lost any hope of winning the war. Mussolini alone was steadfast, but he was debilitated by illness. He sank into megalomania and the family of his mistress, Clara Petacci, gained increasing power.

In February 1943, Mussolini ousted Ciano, Grandi, Bottai, Marshal Emilio De Bono, and Cesare De Vecchi from the government. In April, Senise was removed from the leadership of the state police, and Aldo Vidussoni, the secretary of the Fascist Party, was replaced by Carlo Scorza in a futile effort to rejuvenate the movement. Grandi, Bottai, and Senise joined the plotters, and, following the successful Communist-organized strike in Turin and Milan in March, Vittorio Cini, representative of the industrial organization *Confindustria,* resigned from the government.

In November 1942, King Victor Emannuel asked Ciano to contact the enemy, but the king was unwilling to further compromise himself. His effort was taken up by Duke Pietro d'Acquarone, financier, senator, and minister of the royal household, who coordinated two separate conspiracies. One consisted of pre-Fascist political figures, military men, and police officials; the other consisted of moderate Fascists who wished to preserve aspects of their system under a military government headed by Caviglia. When the king was informed by d'Acquarone that some key Fascists were anxious to separate themselves from Mussolini, he hinted that he might act in response to a public appeal.

After the fall of the strategic island of Pantelleria in May 1942, an invasion of Sicily was imminent. Mussolini met with Hitler in April at Klessheim and in July at Feltre. Rather than convey the desire of his military and political advisors to withdraw from the war, he again was seduced by Hitler. On 10 July 1942, Sicily was invaded, and on 19 July, Rome was bombed. His failure to find a way out of the war was his undoing. He was even opposed by hard liners, like Scorza and Roberto Farinacci, who wanted Ambrosio to be replaced by Marshal Rodolfo Graziani (q.v.).

Both the hard line and moderate Fascists, hoping to use a meeting of the Fascist Grand Council to accomplish their goals, pressed Mussolini to call the first meeting of the council since 1939. The session began on 24 July 1942 and lasted until the early morning of 25 July. Relying on the support of the king, he weakly defended his policy. Grandi, Bottai, and Ciano seized the initiative. They denounced the alliance with Germany, and Grandi called upon the king to assume power. His motion carried, nineteen votes to seven, with one abstention. The palace immediately assumed control of the military and the police.

When Mussolini met with the king in the afternoon, he was informed that he had been replaced by Badoglio and was put under arrest. On the order of the king, the Fascist Party was dissolved and Badoglio set up a "nonpolitical" monarchical cabinet drawn from the ranks of the military, the royal household, the police, and the bureaucracy.

Badoglio in a tactical move announced that Italy would remain in the war. He perhaps hoped to play the two sides off against one another. In late August 1942, he began inquiries about a surrender, which his envoy, General Giuseppi Castellano, signed on 3 September. On 8 September, General Dwight D. Eisenhower (q.v.) announced the armistice, but Badoglio failed to take any measures to prevent a German takeover. On 9 September, he and the king sought refuge behind the new Allied lines in Calabria. The royal government established its headquarters in Brindisi. Sicily and most of the south were controlled by the Allied military government.

The Badoglio government, under supervision of an Allied control commission, was initially allowed to administer only Sardinia and four southeastern provinces. It was not welcomed as an ally and became a virtually army-less "cobelligerent" as a result of its 13 October declaration of war on Germany.

The delayed surrender allowed the Germans, virtually without opposition, to consolidate their occupation of Italy, and on 12 September 1943, they rescued Mussolini from his imprisonment on the Gran Sasso. He was taken north where he proclaimed, on 15 September, the Italian Social Re-

public or the Republic of Salò, the site of the Ministry of Popular Culture (or Propaganda).

In theory, Mussolini controlled a segment of Italy; in reality, he was no more than a pawn of the Germans. The Southern Tyrol, Gorizia, and Istria were directly incorporated into the administration of the Third *Reich,* and the Germans exercised real control over the remainder of non-liberated Italy. The Germans set up a parallel administration to supervise Mussolini's impotent pseudo-state, and Rudolf von Rahn, the German ambassador, and SS general Karl Wolff (q.v.) were more powerful than any Salò minister.

The new Salò government was composed of second-rate men. Mussolini served as the foreign minister of a regime recognized solely by their German masters. Largely out of spite against the *bourgeoisie,* he reverted, at least verbally, to the anticapitalism of his earlier days. He revenged himself against De Bono and his son-in-law Ciano, whom he had executed for voting against him in the Grand Council. Graziani became the minister of defense and chief of staff, and he directed the effort against the resistance in northern Italy. He had 45,000 reliable troops. Guido Buffarini Guidi, the minister of interior, had perhaps 150,000 men of questionable loyalty and effectiveness in the Republican National Guard. There also was an array of private bands, which "maintained order" and engaged in private lawlessness.

In attempting to control the resistance, as in other endeavors, it was the Germans who were dominant. With the collapse of Germany's ability to resist, what remained of the Social Republic collapsed, and amid the debris, Mussolini, attempting to flee, was captured by Communist partisans at Dongo and executed on 28 April 1945.

In April 1944 the "nonpolitical" government of Badoglio gave way to a coalition of the six major anti-Fascist parties. Badoglio was pressured by the Americans to accept this change, and the revulsion of the anti-Fascist parties was overcome when Palmiro Togliatti returned from Moscow to express the willingness of the Communists to join the monarchical government.

With the liberation of Rome in June 1944, Crown Prince Umberto, now substituting for his father under the title of lieutenant-general of the kingdom, was forced by the Committee of National Liberation and the Americans to replace Badoglio with the moderate-left reformist Ivanoe Bonomi, who held the post until June 1945. The influx of the more radical northerners at that time, ushered in the Action Party's Ferrucio Parri.

However, the fact that Italy was placed in the

Western camp by the American occupation limited the possibilities of radical change. In December, the Christian Democrat Alcide de Gasperi, who was initially forced to share power with the Communists and socialists, became the leader of a center-left coalition. He remained prime minister until August 1953, and it was de Gasperi who presided over the removal of the Communists from the government and the definitive association of Italy with the West.

Bernard A. Cook

Additional Reading

Ciano, Galeazzo, *The Ciano Diaries* (1973).
Clark, Martin, *Modern Italy, 1871–1982* (1984).
De Grand, Alexander, *Italian Fascism: Its Origin and Developments* (1982).
Knox, MacGregor, *Mussolini Unleashed, 1939–1941: Politics and Strategy in Fascist Italy's Last War* (1982).

Wartime Government, Soviet

On the brink of World War II, Josef Stalin (q.v.), exhibiting ideological correctness, blamed German aggression on the forces of imperialism that drove nations, Allied as well as Axis, to seek the expansion of territory and the domination of people. As tensions increased in the late 1930s, Stalin followed a deliberate course that would protect the Soviet Union from war with Germany for as long as possible. Neither Adolf Hitler's *Anschluss* (q.v.) with Austria nor the diplomatic crisis over Czechoslovakia would draw Stalin into war. In fact, the Soviet leader pursued a rather tolerant stance toward Germany's obvious territorial ambitions.

Stalin wanted two things: to maintain and expand his fledgling economic relationship with Germany, and to see the nations of Western Europe go to war with each other. Stalin hoped for a lengthy war between Germany and the Western Allies, waiting until the fighting between them sufficiently weakened each before Soviet expansion into Eastern Europe.

With this thought in mind, he allowed Foreign Minister Vyacheslav Molotov (q.v.) to negotiate the Molotov-Ribbentrop Pact (q.v.) of 23 August 1939 with his worst ideological enemy. In the two years prior to the German invasion of the Soviet Union, the economic ties between the two nations increased considerably. From Germany, the Soviets received machinery and war materials. In return, the Soviets sent their unlikely trading partner grains, produce, gasoline, manganese, chromium ore, and cotton.

Soviet defenses against invasion by "imperialist" nations took the form of the Stalin Line in White Russia. The Soviets built a defensive system modeled on France's Maginot Line (q.v.), and although quite formidable in places, it was not a continuous string of fortifications. Stalin embarked on a plan that emphasized space rather than stationary defenses along some geographical tier.

Beginning with the nonaggression pact in 1939, Stalin started acquiring territory in order to concentrate more land area in the Red Army's hands and to increase the distance between the Soviet population centers and their enemies to the west. With the 1939 German invasion of Poland and the agreed-upon partitioning, the Soviets gained 60,000 square miles of territory, moving the Soviet Union 200 miles further west. Stalin also obtained the regions of Bessarabia and northern Bukovina from Romania. The Soviet Union menaced the three Baltic states (q.v.) to join the Soviet Union in a mutual defensive alliance, and then annexed them outright in the summer of 1940.

Stalin pressured Finland for territorial concessions, but the tough and determined Finns resisted, precipitating a Soviet invasion on 30 November 1939. Although the Soviets ultimately gained some 17,000 square miles from Finland, particularly possession of the strategic Karelian Isthmus, they suffered considerable casualties and a rather substantial blow to their military reputation and confidence.

The Soviets grappled with the Japanese in the Far East over Manchuria and Mongolia during much of 1939. The Soviets decisively defeated the Japanese in August and by April 1941, the two nations had signed a nonaggression pact, an agreement that allowed Stalin to move forty Siberian divisions from the Far East to Moscow in December. In addition to this, the Japanese decision to attack the United States, as reported by GRU agent Richard Sorge (q.v.), convinced Stalin that his divisions would be of better use in the west against the German *Wehrmacht.*

The time and territory Stalin bought with the Nazi-Soviet agreement turned out to be a rather poor bargain. He assumed France's reputation as one of the greatest military powers in Europe would lead it to resist the *Wehrmacht* at all costs. Here he miscalculated badly; the defeat of France in six weeks shocked Stalin. Knowing his nation remained unprepared for war, Stalin wanted to avoid war with Nazi Germany and to provide his country and the Red Army the time they needed to recover from the purges (q.v.) and the Great Terror.

The Red Army suffered greatly during Stalin's purges of the late 1930s, losing nearly half of its senior commanders. He liquidated or imprisoned those he saw as enemies of the state, removing many of the more capable and experienced men from command positions. Few who came later were adequately qualified to handle the responsibilities thrust upon them. In addition, the rapid expansion of the armed forces after 1939 greatly increased the number of troops, but failed to provide the soldiers with qualified leaders.

In September 1939, Stalin began conscripting young citizens for military service, increasing the Red Army's size by 280 percent over a twenty-one-month period. Between the purges and the explosive growth of the Red Army, its lack of good leadership would prove to be a near-fatal handicap.

Although the Soviet Union signed a nonaggression pact with Germany, it seemed highly probable that war eventually would break out between the two nations. But even as the signs and warnings of the coming invasion grew more obvious and insistent, Stalin refused to acknowledge the tremendous danger the Soviet Union faced.

When Germany's Operation BARBAROSSA commenced on 22 June 1941, he failed to respond to General Georgy Zhukov (q.v.), who relayed the news to him over the telephone. For two hours following the German invasion, Stalin remained silent, unwilling or unable to issue the order to resist. For a week afterward, he received no visitors, leaving it to Molotov to announce publicly that a state of war existed between the USSR and Germany. Finally, on 3 July, the Soviet people heard the voice of their country's leader again over the radio, a voice that sounded shaky and uncertain.

Based on the Red Army's performance against the Finns, Hitler clung to the idea that the Soviet Union's military remained weak and poorly organized. The Nazis lacked intelligence information about the Soviet military, which kept them in the dark about the extent of Soviet preparedness. In some respects, the German perceptions of Soviet military weakness hit the mark.

The primary Soviet shortcoming lay in the fact that Stalin alone acted as head of the Communist Party and the Soviet government, appointing himself president of the Council of People's Commissars, and of the highly centralized command system of the armed forces. He maintained direct control over the Stavka (q.v.), the Supreme High Command, as well as the State Defense Committee (Goko). He behaved as the ultimate political and military master who trusted no one and manipulated everyone.

The structure of the Soviet Army was strongly bureaucratic and compartmentalized, clearly discouraging individual initiative in making decisions on the battlefield. Each unit of the Red Army included a representative of the Communist Party known as a political commissar. Commissars, in many cases, possessed the authority to give orders to the military officer in command and to countermand that officer's orders. Soviet commanders lost their effectiveness and confidence when commissars questioned their decisions on the battlefield and undermined their authority. Soviet officers also knew that the political "education officer" had ties to the firing squads, torture chambers, and the *Gulags* wielded by Lavrenti Beria and the NKVD (qq.v.).

Initially, commissars joined the military units during the 1920s, but Stalin discontinued the practice in 1934. The policy switched back and forth several more times, until he reinstated the authority of the commissars on 16 July 1941, after the previous month's disastrous losses. During the late summer of 1941, the Germans drove deep into Soviet territory and Stalin began to realize that his method of tightly controlling the behavior of his field commanders damaged his army's ability to repel the Germans. By 1942, he learned his lesson and altered the chain of command once again, relegating the commissars to nonmilitary duties and giving more decision-making freedom to field commanders.

A vital factor in the Soviet's ability to resist lay in the patriotic fervor and the morale of the general populace. Initially, Stalin appealed to the people to save Communism, but when the citizens failed to respond enthusiastically, the government began appealing to the populace to save "Mother Russia." Patriotism quickly replaced ideology as the focus and motivation in repelling the *Wehrmacht*.

The Soviet government also eased its strict ban on religion, allowing people freely to express their religious feelings and opening churches again to worship. Even the hierarchy of the Orthodox Church received official sanction from Stalin, following nearly twenty years of repression and torment.

For Soviet citizens, World War II soon became known as the "Great Patriotic War" whose popular slogan was "not one step back!" The Soviet system enjoyed other advantages, for example, the mobilization of the civilian population. As the Germans stood before Moscow preparing for the final push, 500,000 Muscovites, many of them women and children, dug sixty miles of antitank ditches and 5,000 miles of trenches, and readied other defenses for the attack.

Following the massive encircling moves by the Germans, the Stalinist government realized the potential significance of civilian inhabitants and military men living under German occupation. The Soviet high command sponsored, organized, and encouraged much of the partisan (q.v.) activity directed against the Germans. Partisan bands harassing the enemy received equipment, supplies, and specially trained personnel from Stavka.

Even before the war, new industrial centers started to grow beyond the Ural Mountains. As the German *Panzers* rolled over the USSR, whole factories, including raw materials, machinery, and scores of workers, were moved and rebuilt out of reach of the *Wehrmacht*. Between August and October 1941, 80 percent of Soviet war production relocated to the east and turned out goods in record time.

Sources of raw materials fell into German hands, but the evacuations of Soviet industry proceeded apace, sometimes while under attack by the *Luftwaffe*. The factories in the Urals manufactured more than 100,000 tanks, 136,000 airplanes, and 440,000 artillery pieces between 1941 and 1945. If a plant could not be moved out of the German path, the Soviets destroyed it. The Soviets fully intended to deny the Germans the use of their precious resources and the fruits of their industrial production. The Soviets also developed additional oil supplies in the Far East, the Urals, and the Volga area.

Along with the USSR's own output, the Soviets received military aid from the British between June and December 1941. Shortly thereafter, Lend-Lease (q.v.) supplies arrived directly from the United States: food, winter boots, aircraft, petroleum, copper, radios, radar sets, railroad locomotives, boxcars and rails, and 2 1/2 ton Dodge trucks. British and American goods and materials arrived at the Arctic ports of Murmansk and Archangel. After August 1941 and the joint British-Soviet occupation of Iran, supplies came through Persia. Lend-Lease supplies, totaling some $11 billion, allowed the Soviets to concentrate on producing what they made best: tanks, machine guns, and other armaments. By mid-1943, the Soviets were manufacturing 2,000 T-34 tank chassis per month.

The rapid Soviet mobilization, coupled with the speed and early success of the Nazi invasion, greatly affected the already short supply of food and other essential consumer goods. Although the war effort increased industrial production in the Soviet Union, agricultural production fell as a result of farmland overrun by the Germans, crops destroyed, and farmers called to active duty in the military. From October 1941 until the summer of 1944, the German Army controlled Soviet territory containing 45 percent of the population, 64 percent of its coal reserves, 47 percent of its grain cultivating region, 60 percent of its aluminum manufacturing, and more than 60 percent of its iron and steel production.

While the Soviet Union and its people bore the brunt of the German juggernaut, Stalin wanted more from his allies than Lend-Lease supplies. He repeatedly insisted on the opening of a second front to relieve the pressure the Germans directed against the Soviet Union. A second front would force Germany to divide its attention between two fronts rather than focus it all against "Mother Russia." Winston S. Churchill and Franklin D. Roosevelt (qq.v) agreed that, eventually, an offensive must be launched in the west to bring about Hitler's defeat, but Stalin's Western Allies claimed their forces lacked the strength and equipment necessary for a successful operation.

Roosevelt optimistically suggested the second front be opened sometime in 1942. Churchill objected, proposing landings first in North Africa, and then in Sicily and Italy, that "soft underbelly." Suspecting the worst, Stalin grew increasingly restive as the Western Allies demurred several more times. His long-awaited second front came on 6 June 1944, with Operation OVERLORD, the cross-channel invasion.

As the Germans attempted to stave off the conquering Red Army from the east and the Americans and British from the west, Stalin pursued his own political agenda. Despite making public pronouncements favoring the Atlantic Charter (q.v.), he intended to create a buffer zone between his nation and the West, and to render Germany powerless.

Unable to extract promises of territorial gains from the defeated nations out of Churchill and Roosevelt, Stalin planned to install "friendly" (read "Communist") governments in the countries that bordered his western frontier. The growing tensions between the United States and the Soviet Union that resulted from Stalin's taking control of Eastern European governments ushered in the Cold War of the postwar period.

Susanne Tepe Gaskins

Additional Reading
Clark, Alan, *Barbarossa: The Russian-German Conflict, 1941–1945* (1985).

Dallin, Alexander, *German Rule in Russia, 1941–44* (1957).

Dawson, Raymond, *The Decision to Aid Russia, 1941* (1959).

Seaton, Albert, *The Russo-German War, 1941–1945* (1971).

Werth, Alexander, *Russia at War, 1941–1945* (1964).

Wartime Government, U.S.

With no debate and virtual unanimity, the U.S. Congress committed the nation to war against Japan in early December 1941; the single "nay" vote was cast by Montana's pacifist representative Jeanette Rankin. War with the European Axis remained problematic only until 11 December, when Germany and Italy officially declared war against the United States. This time the Congressional response was unanimous. The vote was reflective of an enduring wartime consensus—to get the job done as quickly and efficiently as possible. Though this popular mandate for the cause was a tremendous asset for America's wartime government, it did not ensure the complete absence of conflict; it was a consensus over ends rather than means.

As the government began the awesome task of mobilizing its material and human resources for the unfolding struggle, it became clear that the American people, always contentious, would continue to play out their political dramas on a wartime stage. Such disagreements as occurred never subsumed the ultimate objective of victory over the Axis. They did, however, remain characteristic of the American approach to government, even in wartime.

With all the principals agreeing upon the rightness of the cause and the certainty of victory, the next item on the national political agenda was the obligatory profession of nonpartisan conduct for the duration. Ed Flynn, chairman of the Democratic Party, was quick to affirm that "in the face of war, politics are adjourned." His Republican counterpart pronounced similar sentiments. But this renunciation of partisan politics became one of the war's first casualties.

Though neither party proved willing to go to such extremes as to threaten national unity, both were ready to sacrifice political unity to partisan goals. For the party in power, this meant not-so-subtle hints that supporting Democratic candidates and policies was the only patriotic approach in war. Ed Flynn went so far as to suggest that to vote Republican was to vote for the Axis. "The only ben-eficiaries of the Republican policy of criticism," the Democratic boss asserted, "are in Tokyo . . . in Rome, in Berlin, and in other Axis centers." While President Franklin D. Roosevelt (q.v.) was quick to disavow such sentiments, other Democrats did feel justified in equating criticism of Democratic policies with aid and comfort to the enemy.

The great Republican fear was articulated by Senator Robert Taft, who fretted that "the New Dealers are determined to make the country over under the cover of war if they can." To forestall that possibility, Republicans and some conservative Democrats moved to dismantle the myriad agencies that comprised the New Deal. Thus the great reform program of the 1930s quickly fell victim to the exigencies of war. Already relegated to secondary importance by Roosevelt, who dropped the title "Doctor New Deal" for "Doctor Win-the-War," the New Deal could no longer be justified as necessary to economic recovery.

Hence, public works agencies such as the Works Progress Administration, the Civilian Conservation Corps, and the National Youth Administration succumbed to budgetary strangulation or statutory demise. Reform agencies such as the Farm Security Administration, died gradually through neglect. Many liberals actually agreed that wartime priorities required a reallocation of national resources.

As had been the case in World War I, antitrust programs also fell by the wayside, as the administration focused foremost on production and efficiency. There were other indications that liberalism in general was suffering a wartime setback. The character of the federal bureaucracy changed with the advent of war and the liberals, activists, and reformers so prevalent during the 1930s were eclipsed in influence by lawyers, the military, and businessmen.

Especially abhorred by liberals were the "dollar-a-year men," executives recruited by the government for a nominal salary. Though these businessmen were sought for their expertise in expediting production, liberals claimed that they inevitably sought foremost to serve the interests of their respective corporations.

Though faced with these setbacks, liberals still saw cause for hope. There remained a few areas in which reformers could direct the government's resources to social ends, for example, public housing. Perhaps more importantly, the GI Bill of Rights (q.v.) of 1944 was seen by many liberals as a model of the types of benefits that might someday be extended to a larger segment of the population. Moreover, some liberals reasoned, the end of the Depression and the marshaling of massive economic resources hinted that the postwar period could provide the opportunity for the further extension of the liberal welfare state. Such possibilities, of course, were predicated on an American victory.

To achieve that victory, the government had, as first priority, the mobilization of the nation's economic resources. Having served for a year as the "Arsenal of Democracy" (q.v.), the United States had already taken the first tentative steps toward total mobilization. Belligerent status brought about a further multiplication of federal agencies charged with organizing the war effort. Predictably, the profusion of wartime agencies brought public criticism about overlapping authorities and duplication of effort.

A widespread 1942 anecdote told of the frustrations encountered by a Japanese spy ordered to pinpoint agencies that might be sabotaged to cripple the U.S. war effort. The spy purportedly informed his superiors: "Suggested plan hopeless. Americans brilliantly prepared. For each agency we destroy, two more are already fully staffed and doing exactly the same work."

Such tales, apocryphal or otherwise, reflected reality. The government bulged with new agencies. The superagency charged with developing policies governing all aspects of production was the War Production Board (WPB). The director, Donald Nelson, had the unenviable task of arriving at a *modus vivendi* with the armed services. Though wartime production was the one area in which the military significantly challenged civilian control, truly serious clashes were mitigated by an agreement by which the army and navy were allowed to direct military procurement.

The WPB plunged ahead with its main goal of converting industry to military production. Here the focus was on the automobile industry, which proved reluctant to reduce domestic auto production until ordered to cease altogether in early 1942. The WPB was also responsible for conserving scarce and strategic materials, and did so by imposing limitations on nonessential production and restricting the use of such materials as iron and steel in consumer goods. Raw rubber, 90 percent of which came from areas now under Japanese control, was controlled indirectly through gasoline rationing and banning pleasure driving. Despite all the restrictions and shortages, most industries prospered as lucrative incentive programs drove up both production and corporate profits.

To coordinate labor resources, the War Manpower Commission (WMC) was established in 1942. Like the WPB, it stressed voluntary compliance rather than coercion in its efforts to move workers into war-related industries. By early 1943, that approach was clearly inadequate for manpower needs. As the WMC gained control of the Selective Service System, its director moved closer to compulsion when he issued a "work or fight" order to channel labor into essential jobs.

Closely related to the manpower problem were inflation and wage control. As wages rose and spending increased by 1942, inflation rose 15 percent above the 1939 level. The task of slowing wage increases fell to the National War Labor Board, which struggled to moderate union demands. Inflation could be further offset by raising taxes and pushing the sale of war bonds.

Ultimately, however, controlling inflation was contingent upon reining in prices and rationing consumer goods. The Office of Price Administration (OPA) was created to this end in early 1942. The oft-maligned OPA introduced more than a dozen major rationing programs beginning in 1942, but also championed consumer interests throughout the war.

While America's war effort was greatly facilitated by an organized, coherent bureaucracy, ultimate success was largely contingent upon the quality of executive leadership. As president, Roosevelt faced challenges near the equal to those confronted by Abraham Lincoln. Roosevelt had already seen the country through a debilitating depression, and the advent of war was to further challenge his leadership abilities. Reelected to an unprecedented third term in 1940, Roosevelt focused most of his energies on the conduct of the war. While he did not abrogate his domestic responsibilities, he was willing to entrust many domestic affairs to subordinates.

On some occasions, the president issued executive orders of far-reaching consequence in order to expedite the resolution of important but distractive domestic problems. Executive Order 8022, prohibiting racial discrimination in defense plant hiring, was hurriedly issued in summer 1941 to forestall a threatened civil rights march on Washington, D.C.

The now infamous Executive Order 9066 granted the U.S. Army authority over the disposition of Japanese Americans in the Western defense zone, and led to the internment camp system administered by the War Relocation Authority. Pressed by the exigencies of war, Roosevelt opted to ignore the wider issues inherent in each episode.

This apparent inattention to major domestic issues and willingness to accept the expedient was in part the consequence of Roosevelt's immersion in diplomatic and military affairs. Few presidents have been faced with challenges as great as those involved in keeping the Grand Alliance together.

Yet, through arduous personal diplomacy and serial wartime conferences (q.v.), Roosevelt did much to win the cooperation of oft-contentious Allies toward the accomplishment of complex ends. War aims, such as those expressed in the Atlantic Charter (q.v.), included both the realistic and the idealistic. Roosevelt proved strikingly effective in articulating those aims to his countrymen and the Allies alike. That he failed to attain all of his objectives should not diminish his accomplishment. The greater triumph was in achieving as much as he did in such difficult circumstances.

Secretary of State Cordell Hull (q.v.) recounted that Roosevelt once requested that he be addressed as "commander in chief" rather than as "president." His predilection for the title was a reflection of his determination to fulfill the role. He had missed the chance for military service in World War I, serving instead as Woodrow Wilson's assistant secretary of the navy. Roosevelt's abiding interest in naval affairs blossomed during World War II into a sincere interest in all the services and overall military strategy.

Biographers record Roosevelt's close rapport with his military chieftains, which did not always mean automatic deference to their judgments. On some occasions, the commander in chief did overrule his military advisers, but he never did so in outright showdowns, preferring instead the use of persuasion and low-key pressure.

The president was scrupulous about keeping the selection of generals and admirals free of politics. Similarly, most of his disagreements with his chiefs over military planning decisions stemmed from military rather than political reasons. Overall, disagreements were surprisingly few. He was determined to coordinate political and military strategy, but generally supported the decisions made by the military chiefs. While he did offer sporadic suggestions concerning matters as mundane as rotating personnel, he did not interject himself into the military's conduct of the war to the degree that Winston S. Churchill (q.v.) did. The result was relative autonomy for the Joint Chiefs of Staff and a generally congenial relationship with the president.

The experience of war worked enormous changes on America's government. Ultimately, the conflict had the effect of broadening the depth and scope of federal power. Certainly executive authority underwent an expansion. Perhaps more importantly, the successful prosecution of the war did much to rejuvenate the public's faith in the American political system, so sorely tried in the decade of the 1930s. Victory seemed a very real vindication of national institutions and a national creed that was in dire need of reaffirmation.

Blaine T. Browne

Additional Reading
Brinkley, David, *Washington Goes to War* (1988).
Burns, James M., *Roosevelt: The Soldier of Freedom: 1940–45* (1970).
Larrabee, Eric, *The Commander in Chief: Franklin Delano Roosevelt, His Lieutenants and Their War* (1987).
Perrett, Geoffery, *Days of Sadness, Years of Triumph: The American People, 1939–1945* (1973).
Polenberg, Richard, *War and Society: The United States, 1941–45* (1972).

Washington Conference
See CONFERENCES, ALLIED

Weimar Republic

In the summer of 1917, the Imperial *Reichstag* passed a resolution calling for an end to German participation in the war, an action that signaled the end of the German *Reich*. With the Allies on the offensive in early 1918, the monarchy grew demoralized and stood at the brink of collapse as the basis of its support eroded. Chancellor Georg Hertling resigned in late September 1918 and was replaced by Prince Max von Baden, who urged domestic reform and support for a general armistice based on President Woodrow Wilson's Fourteen Points.

Leaders of the old regime waited too long to act. As a result, German sailors mutinied at Kiel in late October 1918, workers and soldiers rebelled in Berlin, and a socialist Soviet republic was established in Bavaria in early November. Thousands of German workers took to the streets, forcing the government and the military leadership to call for the emperor's abdication. When he refused, Chancellor von Baden unilaterally announced the abdication and appointed Friedrich Ebert, the Social Democratic Party (SPD) leader, as chancellor of a provisional government. On 9 November 1918, just two days before the armistice, the SPD established what would come to be known as the "Weimar Republic." The German *Reich*, established in 1871, had collapsed.

General Wilhelm Gröner, the German Army chief of staff, pledged support to the new republic, and Ebert's provisional government scheduled elections for January 1919. The provisional government fell in late December 1918 amid calls for more democracy. The election of deputies to a constitutional convention was held as scheduled, with the SPD winning 163 of 421 seats. The constitutional assembly met on 9 February 1919 in Weimar, and elected Ebert as president. He, in turn, asked Philipp Scheidemann to form a coalition including representatives of the SPD, the Catholic Center Party, and the Democratic Party. By July, a new Weimar constitution was prepared, one providing for a parliamentary form of government within the framework of a republic headed by a strong executive president, and guaranteeing fundamental rights.

While the government struggled with the creation of democratic institutions, the German delegation to the peace conference at Versailles (*see* Treaty of Versailles) was saddled with full responsibility for the war. The inability of the Scheidemann government to extract more favorable conditions for the infant republic brought about the collapse of his cabinet. The negotiations at Versailles fared no better under the new cabinet led by Gustav Bauer, and on 28 June 1919, the German delegation signed the peace accord.

Under its terms, Alsace-Lorraine (q.v.) was returned to France, territorial concessions were made to Poland, the west bank of the Rhine was demilitarized and occupied by the French, and the German Army was severely restricted in order to prevent its ability to wage aggressive warfare. The victorious Allies imposed harsh reparations on the fledgling Weimar Republic, and forced it to acknowledge German responsibility for the war.

The transition from a monarchy to democracy and the lost war proved difficult, and the early years of the Weimar Republic were characterized by political crises and violence. The unsuccessful Kapp *Putsch* (q.v.) in March 1920 called for a return to the monarchy and brought about the fall of the Bauer government. Foreign Minister Hermann Müller, who signed the Versailles Treaty for Germany, was named as the new chancellor, and he held the ruling coalition together until the elections scheduled for June 1920.

With the emergence of numerous special interest parties, many of the older established political parties suffered defeat at the polls, including those that had formed the earlier coalitions. Governments changed quickly as new coalitions were formed. The former ruling SPD, however, played no significant role in any of these governments.

Political instability was compounded by the country's failure to make the reparation payments required under the provisions of the Versailles Treaty. In late December 1922, a reparations commission ruled that Germany was in arrears and had failed to meet its obligations under the treaty. To compel payment, a joint French and Belgian military force occupied the Ruhr Valley, Germany's industrial heartland, on 11 January 1923, and took direct control of the major industries. The Germans reacted with violence and industrial production was curtailed, thereby exacerbating an already growing inflation. German currency rapidly lost its value making it further impossible for Germany to make the necessary reparation payments. Hyperinflation devastated the German middle class.

By August 1923, the republic was on the brink of collapse, and recognizing this, Ebert turned to the conservatives to form a new government. Gustav Stresemann (q.v.) was appointed chancellor and his government was successful in revitalizing industrial production and monetary stability through the issuing of a new *"Rentenmark."* These policies were welcomed by the British and French, who hoped this new stability would permit Germany to meet its foreign obligations. With the crisis ending, the anti-republican right in Bavaria decided it was time to act. Hoping to imitate Benito Mussolini's (q.v.) march on Rome, Adolf Hitler led the abortive Beer Hall *Putsch* (qq.v.) in Munich on 7 November 1923.

Political and economic stability initiated under Stresemann continued for the remainder of the decade. Despite substantial protests from the political right, Germany accepted the Dawes Plan, which called for a reduction of reparation payments and the removal of French troops from the Ruhr. New foreign loans were made available to Germany and the *"Rentenmark"* was replaced by the new *Reichmark*. This atmosphere of renewal experienced a brief setback when Ebert died in February 1925. The voters chose as his replacement war hero Field Marshal Paul von Hindenburg (q.v.), a decisive statement for authority and tradition. He proved to be a capable and loyal leader.

Other indications of a return to normalcy included the October 1925 Locarno Pact (q.v.), which settled the question of postwar boundaries, and Germany's entry into the League of Nations (q.v.) in 1926. The country continued to revitalize its economy and grew prosperous. Internal economic stabilization and a conciliatory foreign policy, the hallmarks of the 1920s, began to erode in 1929. Stresemann, the architect of this foreign policy, died in October and his death led to a fragmentation of the government coalition that had ruled since 1923. The October 1929 stock market crash led to escalating unemployment and it devastated the German economy, which had, in fact, been supported through foreign aid subsidies that disappeared with the advent of the Great Depression.

The ruling coalition collapsed in late March 1930, and von Hindenburg asked Heinrich Brüning (q.v.), leader of the Catholic Center Party, to form a new government, to continue Germany's conciliatory foreign policy, and to develop a deflationary economic program for the country. These policies, however, were condemned by both the Left and the Right. A failure to reach a consensus led von Hindenburg, in July 1930, to dissolve the *Reichstag* and rule by presidential decree until a new election scheduled for September.

Following a violent and divisive campaign, the elections proved a victory for the Nazi Party, which increased its representation in the *Reichstag* from 12 to 107 seats, thereby becoming the second-most-powerful faction. Brüning continued to serve as chancellor and von Hindenburg was called upon to issue a number of emergency decrees to stem the growing violence and political and economic malaise.

The power and influence of the Nazis grew as they campaigned against the established political and economic order. Their gains were so pronounced that the SPD socialists supported von Hindenburg against Hitler in the March 1932 presidential election. After his reelection in a run-off ballot, von Hindenburg attempted to crack down on the growing influence of the SA and the SS (qq.v.).

Von Hindenburg dissolved the Brüning government in May 1932 and named Franz von Papen (q.v.) as chancellor. Von Papen appointed a more reactionary and aristocratic cabinet, and von Hindenburg once again dissolved the *Reichstag* in June 1932, calling for new elections the following month. Just prior to the election, however, von Papen seized the Prussian government from the ruling SPD, and placed it directly under his control. The elections, held at the end of July, were another major victory for the Nazis who increased their *Reichstag* seats from 107 to 230. Von Papen expressed a willingness to take Nazis into his government, but Hitler demanded nothing less than the chancellorship.

The Nazi leadership persisted in its challenge for the von Papen government, forcing new *Reichstag* elections in November 1932, but the Nazi Party, which had alienated many voters, lost 34 seats. It nevertheless remained the strongest faction in the *Reichstag* with 196 seats. Von Papen resigned and was replaced by Kurt von Schleicher (q.v.), who failed to garner any real support. He resigned in January 1933. Von Papen next met with Hitler to discuss a coalition government, and he urged the reluctant von Hindenburg to appoint the Nazi leader as chancellor. Hitler was named German chancellor on 31 January 1933, and led a coalition government with von Papen holding the position of vice chancellor. Von Papen was convinced he could control Hitler. This was not the case, however, and Hitler set forth immediately to dismantle German democracy.

Steven B. Rogers

Additional Reading

Dorpalen, Andreas, *Hindenburg and the Weimar Republic* (1964).
Pinson, Koppel S., *Modern Germany* (1966).
Watt, Richard N., *The Kings Depart: The Tragedy of Germany: Versailles and the German Revolution* (1968).

Women in the Military, Britain

In the summer of 1938, the British War Office revived the World War I–era auxiliary services to prepare for the coming war. These various female military auxiliaries enabled women to participate actively in the war effort in the hopes of quickly defeating the enemy and preserving the home front. Because of the abnormal conditions that war brought on, women were invited to work in technical military positions previously unavailable or considered too dangerous. By filling vacancies, women enabled war work to proceed without interruption and freed men for the front.

Auxiliary applicants had to be between eighteen and forty-five years old. Older women who were veterans of World War I or who had special qualifications also were welcomed to apply their expertise. Volunteers were interviewed for placement and signed up for a four-year enlistment. Most women enlisted as privates, and some later applied for officer's ranks. The women's auxiliary work, such as radar monitoring, often required specialized technical training.

Women trained for their service at various military schools and colleges in England and were taught by military instructors. Many women's immediate relatives were military men, and they expected women to participate in wartime military work. Foreign women, denied similar opportunities because their countries would not organize women's auxiliaries, joined the British auxiliaries. American women, especially, served Britain because the U.S. War Department delayed establishing similar auxiliaries.

Social segregation of women volunteers existed. Some branches, considered more elite than others, recruited women from the upper classes and required references. Three auxiliaries, Women's Auxiliary Air Force (WAAF), Women's Land Army (WLA), and Women's Royal Naval Service (WRNS) (q.v.), tended to be small and selective. These women often joined as a sense of obligation to their social class, having fathers who were high-ranking officers.

The WAAF, affiliated with the Royal Air Force, monitored the coast, issuing air raid warnings and plotting navigational courses. They also patched, repaired, and maintained airplanes, parachutes, and barrage balloons.

In June 1939, the Ministry of Agriculture established the WLA, which had also been active in World War I. In the WLA, women farmed in the countryside, raising crops and livestock to provide rations. They also cooked, repaired roads, and delivered mail and supplies.

The WRNS also served in World War I. In 1939, the Royal Navy reestablished this auxiliary. The WRNS was the only auxiliary service not regulated by military discipline. It also was considered the most selective and glamorous of the military service groups for women, with mostly upper-class women being permitted to enlist. Their most important function was radio work with shore communication units.

The Air Transport Auxiliary (ATA) also tended to be elitist because it required women to be trained pilots with 600 hours of flight time—indicating a certain socioeconomic status. They ferried new planes as well as training craft to various airfields in Scotland and northern England. The women were not treated equally with male pilots, being paid 20 percent less. Nor were room and board provided for them. Conditions were often dangerous, with intense cold from open cockpits, fatigue, lack of radios and precise navigational aids, occasional attack from enemy aircraft, stray fire from artillery training ranges, and looming barrage balloons all hazards of ferry duty. Fifteen ATA pilots died in service.

The Auxiliary Territorial Service (ATS) (q.v.) was modeled after the Territorials, Britain's voluntary male reserve corps. The ATS was composed mostly of Territorials' wives and daughters, as well as female veterans of a similar branch in World War I. In the ATS, women affiliated with the army relayed messages, dispatched supplies using motorcycles and automobiles (which they also repaired and maintained), photographed shellfire, tested gun sights, and supervised antiaircraft weaponry.

The Field Auxiliary Nursing Yeomanry (FANY) continued a similar World War I medical auxiliary, as did the Mechanized Transport Corps and London Auxiliary Ambulance Service, providing stretcher and ambulatory services during bombing raids. Supplementing the military auxiliaries, the Women's Voluntary Service (WVS) began in 1938, with one million women participating. They cooperated with civil defense, doing such jobs as watching for fires and communicating with victims' families.

Most British officers appreciated the women auxiliary services, especially in branches where there were familial ties between officers and women. Despite their conscientious service, however, many women volunteers encountered slanderous rumors about their morality and occasionally were confronted with verbal and sexual harassment by jealous men. They endured other discriminatory actions, such as receiving lower wages and smaller rations than men. Many women complained of the monotony of their military work.

When the war ended, some women were retained to aid in reconstruction. Married volunteers were demobilized first, and single women were dismissed based on their age and time in service. They received four weeks' pay and clothing coupons. Women discovered their militarily acquired skills were not applicable to civilian employment. Yet many recognized that some obstacles had been removed and that they now had some options to pursue nontraditional professions.

Some women enrolled in universities or applied for jobs using their wartime training; but many decided to discontinue this work, especially because male engineers and technicians resented their intrusion. In the workplace, women had not gained equality and were exploited economically. Many women married and focused on family life after being discouraged from working. From the highly challenging technical atmosphere of wartime service working with planes and radios, they reentered a society that considered women's most appropriate place, unless in time of national emergency, to be in the home.

Elizabeth D. Schafer

Additional Reading

Braybon, Gail, and Penny Summerfield, *Out of the Cage: Women's Experiences in Two World Wars* (1987).

Summerfield, Penny, *Women Workers in the Second World War: Production and Patriarchy in Conflict* (1984).

Women in the Military, Germany

The National Socialist state passed laws regulating the employment of women in the war economy and permitting them to serve in the *Wehrmacht* only in 1942–1943. Up until that point, National Socialist ideology dictated the role of mother and housewife to the German woman. A directive issued on 27 January 1943, however, stated that women between the ages of seventeen and forty-five who did not have children had to report for service in the defense of the *Reich*. The reason for this measure was the first noticeable shortage of soldiers that occurred after major military setbacks in Russia during the winter of 1942–1943. The goal in this employment of women was to use them in rear echelon staffs and units in order to release soldiers for the front. A large portion of this potentially freed-up manpower went to the occupying forces in the conquered regions.

Thus, by the end of World War II, 450,000 German women had served as female defense helpers *(weibliches Wehrmachtsgefolge)*. The air force and navy made use of the women, but not as much as the army. The women, however, had no military status and were considered civilian employees of the *Wehrmacht*. But for security reasons they were still subject to military law and disciplinary rules. Those rules were not applied as strictly as they were for the soldiers. If the women served in any position where they were in danger of being captured, they were given uniforms, which gave them combatant status under the rules of international law.

The German army organized its female workers into three groups. The Troop Helpers *(Truppenhelferinnen)* performed jobs like radio operators and drivers; the Staff Helpers *(Stabshelferinnen)* served as stenographers, typists, or even as interpreters; the Economic Helpers *(Wirtschaftshelferinnen)* were cooks and waitresses, or they worked in other supply areas. The *Luftwaffe* organized its auxiliaries like the army according to different activities: Air Reporting Helpers *(Flugmeldehelferinnen)* and Organizational Helpers *(Betriebshelferinnen)*. The navy had only one group designation, Naval Helpers *(Marinehelferinnen)*.

The female auxiliaries came to play a particularly prominent role for the *Luftwaffe*. They were used in the air reporting service, in the telephone and telegraph service, and in the air warning service. They also served in the air defense service, with large numbers of women on twenty-four-hour duty. They lived in special barracks close to their places of work. The barracks were run by women who reported directly to the military staffs.

None of the women had actual military rank but their functions were designated by special insignia on their service clothes. Within the *Reich*, there were no standardized designs for the female service clothing, but they did conform to the colors of the specific forces. An exception was the *Luftwaffe's* air defense auxiliaries, who were allowed to wear actual uniforms on German territory. In general, however, there were never any plans for putting all the *Wehrmacht's* women into uniform.

By the end of the war, the air information service used most of the *Luftwaffe's* 130,000 female auxiliaries. In some functional areas, like telecommunications, they normally were not exposed to combat. The air reporting staff, however, was a huge organization extending from northern Norway to North Africa. That organization consisted of ground observers, radar operators, fighter aircraft ground controllers, and analysis personnel. A fighter division responsible for a certain area would have as many as 6,000 female auxiliaries operating listening equipment, radio direction finders, light markers for positional maps, and similar equipment. Those women came the closest to purely military work and many were directly endangered because of where they were stationed.

Toward the end of the war, the trend clearly was leading to one of "women in arms." By 1944, the *Luftwaffe's* Air Defense Helpers were manning searchlight and barrage balloon batteries. They also worked measuring radio, sound, and control equipment, in direct contact with enemy aircraft. But the scope of the title "Helper" was continually stretched and the women were never designated as combatants. Thus the German female auxiliaries were never used in "direct combat" nor were they ever issued weapons.

The employment of women in the *Wehrmacht* had little influence on the outcome of the war. Perhaps the main reason was that the use of women was started well into the course of the war, and that the much larger potential that still existed was not fully exploited. It should also be noted that the availability of millions of foreign (slave) laborers made the full mobilization of German women less necessary than in the Soviet Union, Great Britain, or the United States.

Ekkhart Guth

Additional Reading

Gersdorff, U. von, *Frauen im Kriegsdienst* (1969).

Seidler, Franz W., *Blitzmädchen—die Geschichte der Helferinnen der Deutschen Wehrmacht im Zweiten Weltkrieg* (1996).

Women in the Military, Soviet

At the time of the German invasion of the Soviet Union in June 1941, relatively few women served in the Soviet military. The initial Soviet attitude, even after the attack, was that men should do the fighting and women replace them in the factories and workshops of the country. By the end of 1942, more than 60 percent of all defense industry workers were women. Women also helped build fortifications and dig trenches.

As Soviet military losses mounted during 1942, the government began to mobilize women. All childless women not directly engaged in war work were eligible to be called up to serve. Soviet women began to enter all the services and assumed combat roles until the end of the war. They served in infantry, antiaircraft defense, armor, artillery, transportation, communications, air force, nursing, and partisan (q.v.) units. A few women served in the navy, primarily in minesweeping operations. By the end of 1943, women composed 8 percent of Soviet military personnel, with more than 800,000 serving at the front (including nearly 27,000 partisans).

About 250,000 Soviet women trained as mortarwomen, machine gunners, riflewomen, and snipers. The Central Sniping Center for Women, established in May 1943, turned out 150 skilled sharpshooters every few months. One estimate suggests that women snipers killed more than 11,000 enemy troops by war's end. The first separate Women's Reserve Rifle Regiment, formed in February 1942, produced 5,200 women soldiers.

Antiaircraft units became almost a female specialty with their own female officers and several hundred thousand women in their service. Unlike their British counterparts, the Russian women actually fired their guns. Women served as tankers in all capacities. They also made up 75 percent of auto transport services personnel. Additionally, 50,000 women served as communication workers.

Women were less numerous, but perhaps more visible, in the air force. Women trained in air clubs and civilian aviation in the 1930s and were thus available for service when war broke out.

Under the direction of Marina Raskova, three women's combat aviation regiments were formed. In addition, a training unit, the 122nd Air Group, was stationed near Saratov on the Volga River, and eventually graduated 600 pilots who served in these regiments.

The 586th Interceptor Regiment, flying YAK fighters, was active on all fronts and accounted for thirty-eight enemy planes destroyed. Soviet female losses are not known. The 587th Short Range Bomber Regiment was a tactical unit that strafed and bombed enemy positions and supply depots. Its activities ranged from Stalingrad to East Prussia. The third unit was the 588th Night Bomber Regiment, perhaps the most famous of the three. It started in the northern Caucasus with sporadic night bombing raids in light canvas biplanes and ultimately flew missions as far away as Poland. The group sometimes flew as many as 300 sorties a night. Individual women pilots served in male units as well.

Women were quite active in military medicine, constituting 43 percent of military surgeons, 41 percent of frontline doctors, 43 percent of the medics, 40 percent of aides and orderlies, and 100 percent of the nurses. Many medical women also bore arms and were combatants, since the line between medicine and combat virtually disappeared near the front.

Figures of women in partisan units operating behind enemy lines are difficult to come by. Shortly after the German invasion in June 1941, Stalin invited women to join partisan units, and one estimate places 26,707 women among the 287,453 partisans operating in January 1944. In Byelorussia, about 16 percent of all partisans were women.

Women thus played a significant role in Soviet military undertakings beginning in 1942 and made important contributions to the Soviet military victory. Russian women took part in the final assault on Berlin, and a Russian woman helped raise the Soviet flag over the *Reichstag* building.

Donald L. Layton

Additional Reading

Howell, Edgar M., *The Soviet Partisan Movement, 1941–1944* (1956).

Isakov, Ivan S., *The Red Fleet in the Second World War* (1947).

Myles, Bruce, *Night Witches: The Untold Story of Soviet Women in Combat* (1981).

Wagner, Ray (ed.), *The Soviet Air Force in World War II: The Official History* (1973).

Women in the Military, U.S.

Uniforms and factories became the symbols of World War II American women. The war enabled American women to acquire jobs previously denied them. Military service became an option previously unavailable to most American women. Female auxiliary members served in positions that required laborious paperwork and other rote tasks, freeing male workers to go to the front. In assuming these jobs, women broke traditional gender roles.

There were five U.S. military auxiliaries in which a total of 350,000 women served. Thousands more performed as nurses at domestic hospitals and in the European and Asian theaters. Women joined the military for a variety of reasons: patriotism, a desire to end the war quickly and victoriously, the opportunity for vocational training, and adventure.

Because many U.S. military leaders were reluctant to establish auxiliaries, many American women joined Allied auxiliaries in order to participate. Women lobbied with the aid of groups such as the General Federation of Women's Clubs and the American Association of University Women for the right to serve in the U.S. military. As the military situation in Europe worsened, military branches considered including women to release more men for the front. The War Department did not want women to have full military status and carefully worded the Women's Auxiliary Army Corps (WAAC) (q.v.) bill to limit them from military inclusion and benefits. After the WAAC bill passed in 1942, other branch auxiliaries were created in a similar mold.

In most auxiliaries, married women could enlist but not women with children under eighteen. Their families received no benefits unless they could prove the woman was their main source of financial support. Most auxiliaries required enlistees to have completed high school, and officer candidates were required to be at least twenty years old with two years of college and work experience. Women in the military often encountered low-skill jobs beneath their abilities, lack of training for their positions, sexism, and racism for black women who remained in segregated units. Some men opposed the use of women in nontraditional roles, fearing they would be displaced from postwar jobs. This resulted in propagandistic smear campaigns falsely labeling and persecuting women in the military as being overly promiscuous or lesbians.

First Lady Eleanor Roosevelt lauded military women in her newspaper column *My Day*. She thought more women needed to be in military auxiliaries to enhance morale and ease burdens, and she urged women to join. Nurses were readily accepted in the medical corps of the army and navy, because nursing was a traditional occupation for women. Women had nursed casualties in prior American wars. Approximately 60,000 women were in the Army Nurse Corps, and 14,000 in the Navy Nurse Corps.

At least 140,000 American women joined the Women's Auxiliary Army Corps. When the organization became the Women's Army Corps (WAC) in 1943, it was accorded full military status to establish discipline and control. Most WACS performed gender-restrictive tasks such as clerical and administrative jobs that were similar to civilian work. Some managed to get assigned overseas, or to more glamorous assignments like aircrews; but most remained in the United States, performing somewhat monotonous work for the duration of the war.

The navy auxiliary's Women Accepted for Volunteer Emergency Service (WAVES) (q.v.), began in 1942 and had a total of 100,000 women serve during the war. By 1944, the WAVES gained full military status. Auxiliary members to the U.S. Coast Guard, known as SPARS (from the motto *Semper Paratus*), began in 1942 and numbered 13,000. The marines established an auxiliary in early 1943 with 23,000 in the Marine Corps Women's Reserve (MCWR).

As early as 1940, suggestions circulated that women could ferry aircraft to relieve men from this time-consuming duty. Women pilots demanded to be involved, and when denied the opportunity in the U.S., they joined the British Air Transport Auxiliary. Beginning in 1942, the Women's Auxiliary Ferrying Service (WAFS) served under the Army Air Forces' Air Transport Command. WAFS members were required to have a minimum of 500 hours of flying time. They were hired as civilians.

In 1942, with the support of General Henry H. "Hap" Arnold, Jacqueline Cochran (qq.v.) began the Women's Flying Training Detachment to train novices for WAFS. In 1943, WAFS merged with this program into Women's Air Service Pilots (WASP) (q.v.), with a total of 1,100 women. They were hired as civilians attached to the Army Air Forces. They trained in ground and flight schools, towed targets, maintained engines, trained antiaircraft batteries, and ferried a variety of planes, including bombers and, late in the war, jets. Thirty-eight WASPs died in service. The female pilots received less pay than male counterparts and were ineligible for benefits. Although attempts to militarize WASP in 1944 were pursued, they failed, and female pilots lost jobs to men at the end of the war.

U.S. Army nurses arrive in Britain. (IWM EA 18096)

Female veterans were not welcomed home with equivalent receptions and parades as men; nor did they receive similar support or consideration for war-related problems at home. They were permitted to join the American Legion, but not the Veterans of Foreign Wars. They received fewer benefits than male veterans, and their reemployment rights were often disregarded, with some women believing their service was a negative factor in postwar employability. With a renewed societal emphasis on family, many woman submitted to abandoning employment and returning to conventional roles. Women veterans received some benefits for college and tentatively entered predominantly male curricula, such as engineering, as well as striving for previously limited leadership positions.

The initial postwar personnel shortage enabled some women to continue military careers. The 1948 Women's Armed Services Integration Act granted women some benefits but not full equality. Married women, unless they were veterans, were refused, and women were limited to certain occupations.

The inclusion of women in military auxiliaries mitigated military staffing and administrative problems during the war. Women acquired a sense of accomplishment and patriotism as well as new viewpoints concerning their role in society and the workplace. Aware that they were capable of performing nontraditional jobs, and with the destruction of some occupational barriers, women lobbied for postwar choice, initiative, and leadership in their employment. This enlightenment led to the women's movement in the 1960s and 1970s, which achieved goals such as Congress approving retroactive benefits and readjusting the status of female veterans.

Elizabeth D. Schafer

Additional Reading

Anderson, Karen, *Wartime Women: Sex Roles, Family Relations, and the Status of Women During World War II* (1981).

Gruhzit-Hoyt, Olga, *They Also Served: American Women in World War II* (1996).

Hartmann, Susan M., *The Home Front and Beyond: American Women in the 1940s* (1982).

Honey, Maureen, *Creating Rosie the Riveter: Class, Gender, and Propaganda During World War II* (1984).

Y

Yalta Conference
See CONFERENCES, ALLIED

Young Plan
Named after American banker Owen Young, the 1929 Young Plan attempted to restructure the German war debt from World War I. It modified the Dawes Plan concluded five years earlier. The Young Plan set up a Bank of International Settlements, which organized a schedule of fifty-nine yearly payments, averaging two billion *Reichmarks,* payable to the United States and the Allies. The leader of the German negotiations, Foreign Minister Gustav Stresemann (q.v.) pushed hard for the reduction of German debt as well as the stipulation that all international controls on German economic life would be lifted. Additionally, the Allies would agree to remove French and Belgian troops from German soil by 1930.

The agreement, which pleased Stresemann, was short-lived. Stresemann died in October 1929, only four months after the agreement was signed. He hoped that the Young Plan would give support to the more democratic parties in German politics, as well as place Germany on a sound financial footing. The problem, however, came when the worldwide depression hit. The plan was used by rightwing parties, especially the Nazis, as campaign propaganda.

To Hitler and some of his industrialist supporters, the acceptance of the plan admitted German culpability for World War I and signified German weakness. The parties that supported the Young Plan's payment schedule were discredited for "enslaving" Germany with reparations until 1988. In fact, the Young Plan lasted only until June 1932, when, under the impact of the Great Depression, a decision at Lausanne was made to set aside the plan's payments.

Glenn R. Sharfman

Additional Reading
James, Harold, *The German Slump: Politics and Economics, 1924–1936* (1986).

Leaders and Individuals

Abrams, Creighton W., Jr. (1914–1974)

American lieutenant colonel, commander 37th Tank Battalion. Creighton Abrams, a native of Springfield, Massachusetts, was the U.S. Army's premier tank battalion commander in World War II. He graduated from West Point in 1936 as a cavalry officer. In March 1942, Major Abrams assumed command of a battalion of the 37th Armored Regiment of the 4th Armored Division.

During the campaign in northwest Europe, Lieutenant Colonel "Abe" Abrams commanded the 37th Tank Battalion in France, Belgium, and Germany. His competence was well known throughout the army and drew praise from General George S. Patton (q.v.). In September 1944, the 37th Tank Battalion played a key role in the battle for Nancy (q.v.), and Abrams won the Distinguished Service Cross. During Germany's Ardennes offensive (q.v.), Abram's battalion spearheaded Patton's counterattack into the German left flank, and was the first unit to break through to the surrounded U.S. forces at Bastogne (q.v.). Abrams received a second DSC for that action.

After the war Creighton Abrams became a full general. He succeeded William C. Westmoreland (q.v.) as U.S. commander in Vietnam, and succeeded him again in 1972 as chief of staff of the U.S. Army. Abrams was instrumental in introducing the "Total Force" concept, where the reserve components have come to be regarded as equal partners with the regular army. In line with that concept, the structure of the U.S. Army was reconfigured to make it impossible to go to war without first mobilizing the reserves. Abrams did this on purpose, reasoning that the reserves would only be mobilized if the American people fully supported commitment to a future war. In this way Abrams hoped to avoid putting the U.S. Army in another Vietnam situation. The experience of the

1991 Persian Gulf War seems to have proved Abrams right. Abrams died in office on 4 September 1974.

Randy Papadopoulos

Additional Reading
Cole, Hugh M., *The Ardennes: Battle of the Bulge* (1965).

Acheson, Dean G. (1893–1972)

American diplomat. Armed with a conservative political philosophy and an autocratic approach to decision making, Dean Acheson began his diplomatic apprenticeship during World War II in the State Department. His memoirs paint a vivid picture of how he chafed at the lack of recognition of his talents, and include sharp observations of the prominent diplomats of the war. By V-J Day, most of his attitudes toward international relations were firmly set.

Always an advocate of stability and order, Acheson was appalled by the tumult and power plays that shook the Department of State from 1941 to 1945. An example was the failure to develop and execute an effective policy on economic warfare. He rated postwar economic planning more favorably; he saw the Bretton Woods Agreements, which helped establish the World Bank and the International Monetary Fund, as one of the few positive achievements during the war.

Acheson worked hard to promote a bipartisan approach to foreign policy in Congress during the war. Although the policy was initiated by Cordell Hull (q.v.), Acheson literally did the legwork, going from office to office sounding out senators and representatives on crucial legislation. To some degree, it was this wartime experience, not always pleasant, that led Acheson to develop a haughty attitude toward Congress that played a role during his later service as secretary of state.

As important as his achievements were, Acheson's memoirs are his most enduring contribution to the history of World War II. His prickly personality and arrogant bearing do not negate the value of his observations on leaders and policy making. Acheson was a major example of the apprenticeship aspiring leaders acquired from 1941 to 1945 for the Cold War that would soon follow.

Michael Polley

Additional Reading
Acheson, Dean, *Present at the Creation* (1970).

Adam, Wilhelm (1877–1949)
German general, army group commander. The son of a Bavarian merchant, Adam joined the army in 1897, starting out in a railroad unit and transferring later to the combat engineers. After attending the Bavarian War Academy in Munich, he served as the senior general staff officer of a Bavarian reserve division in the latter part of World War I.

During the Weimar period, he rose rapidly through the ranks. In 1930, he was appointed head of the *Truppenamt* (the camouflaged general staff of the German Army). Eight months after Adolf Hitler's (q.v.) rise to power, and following growing friction with the new defense minister, General Werner von Blomberg (q.v.), Adam was sent to Munich as commander of the Bavarian Military District.

In October 1935, Adam was promoted to general and simultaneously placed in charge of the newly created *Wehrmachtakademie* (War Academy) in Berlin. In late March 1938, this advanced staff training college was closed down, and he was appointed commander of Army Group 2, with headquarters at Kassel. Responsible for the defense of Germany's western borders, he took a very dim view of Hitler's policies during the Czech crisis and repeatedly spoke out on that subject. As a result, he was replaced in his post by General Erwin von Witzleben (q.v.) in November 1938, and shortly thereafter retired from active service.

From then on, Adam lived in the Bavarian Alps, at Garmisch-Partenkirchen. Though he maintained contact with some anti-Nazis, he was not involved in any of the major plots against Hitler. In 1945, in response to suggestions by an American journalist, Adam wrote his memoirs but decided not to make them public. Small portions, though, were used as background information at the Nuremberg Trials (*see* International Military Tribunal).

Ulrich Trumpener

Additional Reading
O'Neill, Robert J., *The German Army and the Nazi Party, 1933–1939* (1966).
Deutsch, Harold C., *Hitler and His Generals: The Hidden Crisis, January–June 1938* (1974).

Adenauer, Konrad (1876–1967)
German politician and statesman. Born in Cologne to a poor Catholic family, Adenauer studied law at Freiburg, Munich, and Bonn, eventually becoming an attorney and serving as assistant district court judge in Cologne. He entered politics in 1906 and became leader of the Catholic Center Party. In 1917, he became mayor of Cologne, after serving six years as deputy mayor. He was mayor for the next sixteen years.

During this period, Adenauer also served in the Prussian Council of State of the Weimar Republic (q.v.) and in the Rhineland Provincial Legislature. There he attempted to unify Catholics and Protestants in opposition to the growing power of the socialists. The Nazis expelled Adenauer from political life in 1933, and he retired to a village outside of Cologne. The *Gestapo* (q.v.) constantly harassed him, and in 1944 he was sent to a concentration camp.

After the war, Adenauer returned to politics and became the leading political figure in Germany. The U.S. occupation authorities reinstated Adenauer as mayor of Cologne in 1945, but he was subsequently dismissed by the British. Cofounder and leader of the postwar Christian Democratic Union, a supra-denominational party, he served as the party whip. In 1948–1949, he became chairman of the parliamentary council responsible for drafting the new constitution.

In 1949, he was elected the first chancellor of the new Federal Republic of Germany. He was reelected three times before stepping down from office in 1963. As chancellor, he finally established Germany as a democratic nation, guided it through the famed "Economic Miracle," acknowledged the German crimes against the Jews during the war, and paid reparations to Israel, which he visited shortly before his death.

Steven B. Rogers

Additional Reading
Bucerious, Gerd, *Der Adenauer* (1976).

Hiscocks, Richard, *The Adenauer Era* (1975).
Schwarz, Hans-Peter, *Adenauer,* Vol. 1 (1986).

Aitken, Maxwell (Lord Beaverbrook) (1879–1964)

British minister of aircraft production, lord privy seal. A Canadian self-made millionaire owning major British newspapers, Aitken was elected to the British Parliament in 1910 and had a major role in the World War I coalition government, during which time he became a friend of Winston S. Churchill (q.v.). He was elevated to Lord Beaverbrook in 1917. Between the wars, he became a major offstage player in British politics.

In 1940, he became minister of aircraft production. During the period 1940–1941, he greatly increased aircraft production but at the expense of repair parts. The short-term increase in aircraft was impressive. Production went from 719 aircraft in February 1940 to 1,601 in August 1940, but with a decline in quality. The long-term effect of this program on RAF aircraft availability is still controversial.

A major supporter of direct military aid to the Soviet Union and the opening of a "Second Front," Beaverbrook was at times both a political problem and a fellow conspirator to Churchill, who had to weigh many different needs against limited means. Beaverbrook served as minister of supply (1941–1942), administrator of Lend-Lease (1942), and lord privy seal (1943–1945). After the war, he remained a major behind-the-scenes player in British politics.

Charles A. Bogart

Additional Reading
Taylor, A.J.P., *Beaverbrook* (1972).
Villa, Brian L., *Unauthorized Action* (1989).

Alanbrooke, Lord
See BROOKE, ALAN

Lord Beaverbrook (left) and William S. Knudsen confer in Washington, 19 August 1941. (IWM OEM 251)

Alexander, Harold (1891–1969)

British field marshal, commander in chief of the Mediterranean theater. Harold Rupert Leofric George Alexander, later First Earl Alexander of Tunis, was born in London and raised on his family's estate in County Tyrone in northern Ireland. As a young boy he showed an aptitude for sports and art, especially painting. He attended Harrow and the Royal Military College, Sandhurst, and in 1911, he was commissioned a lieutenant in the prestigious Irish Guards.

During World War I, he served as a regimental officer in France, where he distinguished himself for bravery. He was twice wounded and won the Military Cross and the Distinguished Service Order. He ended the war as lieutenant colonel. After the war, he served with Allied commissions in Poland and the Baltic states where he mastered German and Russian.

Attendance at the Staff College and the Imperial Defence College in the 1920s led to Alexander's appointment as a brigade commander on the northwest frontier in India in 1934. He returned to England in 1937 and was promoted to major general, making him the youngest general in the British Army.

At the outbreak of war in 1939, he was sent to command a division in France. During the German invasion in May–June 1940 in the Low Countries and France, Alexander demonstrated the qualities that made him an outstanding commander, imperturbability, common sense, and quiet bravery. At Dunkirk (q.v.) he helped prepare the withdrawal of British troops after Lord Gort (q.v.) was called home. During three days of command, Alexander oversaw the evacuation of more than 110,000 troops. Before leaving for Britain he toured the beaches to make sure no British troops remained.

Back in England, Alexander helped prepare defenses against a possible German invasion. In February 1942, he was briefly appointed British commander in Burma, where the Japanese were in the process of expelling empire forces. He was brought home in August 1942 by Prime Minister Winston S. Churchill (q.v.), who admired his fighting qualities, to take command of the Middle East. Although credit for the victory over the Germans at El Alamein belonged to General Bernard L. Montgomery (qq.v.), Alexander formed an effective working relationship with the flamboyant "Monty."

In January 1943, Alexander attended the Casablanca Conference where he made a favorable impression on President Franklin D. Roosevelt,

General George C. Marshall, and General Dwight D. Eisenhower (qq.v.). He was chosen to serve as Eisenhower's deputy for the remainder of the Tunisian campaign. Alexander's strategic qualities were an advantage as Allied forces inflicted a major defeat on German General Erwin Rommel's vaunted *Afrika Korps* (qq.v.).

Alexander demonstrated considerable diplomatic tact in his dealings with the American forces. Of all the British generals, Alexander was best at getting along with his American counterparts. His diplomatic skills rivaled Eisenhower's in bringing together different personalities. Even the prickly General George S. Patton (q.v.) admired Alexander—no mean compliment given Patton's view of the British.

After Tunisia, Alexander presided over the complicated invasion of Sicily (q.v.). He had overall command of the two armies, one British under Montgomery and one American led by Patton. Again Alexander showed his grasp of diplomatic skills as he organized the rapid conquest of the island in just thirty-eight days.

After Sicily, the Allies started to concentrate on the eventual invasion of France. Alexander was left in charge of a motley force of Americans, Poles, British, and empire troops with which to oust the Germans from Italy. He directed the Italian campaign, from September 1943 until the final German surrender in May 1945, amid great difficulties. He managed to tie down large numbers of Germans while having to make do with reduced manpower and supplies.

Alexander's command in Italy was characterized by intelligent use of resources, and occasional flashes of operational genius, as in the plans for Salerno and Anzio (qq.v.). But that bitter twenty-one–month war remained a strategic sideshow for the Allies. He constantly lost troops to the French front following the invasion of Europe. As a reward for his valor and his success, just before the fall of Rome in June 1944, Alexander was promoted to field marshal. He replaced General Henry Maitland Wilson (q.v.) as commander in chief of the Mediterranean Theater of Operations (MTO).

After the war, H.C. O'Neill, the highly regarded military commentator for the *Spectator,* told Harold Nicolson that Alexander's Italian campaign was the most brilliant waged by British arms during the war. Following the German surrender, Alexander was named governor-general of Canada. He was a popular choice and served with distinction there from 1946 until 1952, when Churchill, again prime minister, called him home to serve as minister of defense. In that assignment, however,

General Sir Harold Alexander, DSO, MC (later Field Marshal Earl Alexander) with Air Marshal Sir Arthur Coningham, DSO, MC, DFC, in Tunis, 20 May 1943. (IWM NA 3027)

Alexander proved a poor choice. He had no interest in politics, and despite Churchill's great admiration for him, Alexander resigned in the fall of 1954.

In the last fifteen years of his life, he served on a number of boards of directors, edited his military dispatches, and continued painting. He died suddenly of a heart attack on 16 July 1969.

John P. Rossi

Additional Reading

Alexander, Harold R.L.G., *The Alexander Memoirs 1940–1945* (1962).

Hillson, Norman, *Alexander of Tunis: A Biographical Portrait* (1952).

Jackson, William G.F., *Alexander of Tunis As Military Commander* (1971).

Alexandris, Constantine (1894–1976)

Greek rear admiral, commander in chief of the Royal Hellenic Navy. Alexandris commanded a warship during the Italo-Greek war of 1940–1941. From 1941 to 1943, he was naval and air attache in London, where he negotiated the loan of Brit-ish warships to the Greek Navy. In 1943–1944, he was commander in chief of the Royal Hellenic Navy, based at Alexandria and Port Said, operating in the Aegean against the Dodecanese Islands (q.v.). He was dismissed after a short-lived mutiny broke out on several Greek warships.

Andrzej Suchcitz

Additional Reading

Smith, Peter C., and Edwin Walker, *War in the Aegean* (1974).

Zotos, Stephanos, *Greece: The Struggle for Freedom* (1967).

Allen, Terry de la Mesa (1888–1969)

American major general, commander of the U.S. 1st and 104th Infantry Divisions. Allen graduated from Catholic University in 1912 and served as a regimental commander in World War I. In March 1942, he commanded the 1st Infantry Division (the Big Red One). A charismatic and highly aggressive commander, he led his division in the North African campaign, including the battle of Kasserine Pass, and in Sicily (qq.v). He was relieved of his command in Sicily by General Omar N. Bradley (q.v.), who disliked his brash style. Following his relief, Allen trained and commanded the 104th Infantry Division (Timberwolves) in 1944, and fought with that division in France and Germany until the end of the war.

Randy Papadopoulos

Additional Reading

Hoegh, Leo A., and Howard J. Doyle, *Timber Tracks: The History of the 104th Infantry Division, 1942–1945* (1946).

Hurkula, John, *The Fighting First Division* (1958).

Almond, Edward M. (1892–1979)

American major general, commander of the 92nd Infantry Division (Colored). "Ned" Almond was born in Luray, Virginia, and graduated from the Virginia Military Institute in 1915. During World War I he commanded a machine gun battalion of the 4th Infantry Division in France. In the interwar years, Almond was groomed for high command. He attended the Army War College, the Air Corps Tactical School, and the Naval War College.

In March 1942, Almond was promoted to brigadier general and assigned as the assistant commander of the 93rd Infantry Division (Colored). In July 1942, U.S. Army Chief of Staff General George C. Marshall (q.v.) personally selected Almond to command the 92nd Infantry Division (Colored). It was to be one of Marshall's most controversial decisions of World War II.

Almond trained the 92nd in Alabama and Arizona and commanded it in Italy in 1944 and 1945. The 92nd was the only all-black division that fought as a complete division in World War II. Despite the dedication and bravery of the division's soldiers, the 92nd experienced serious problems in both training and combat. To a large degree, this was the result of the general low quality of the white officers assigned to the Army's segregated black units. And although Almond himself harbored strong and well-known prejudices against minority soldiers, he ultimately was not held responsible for the shortcomings of his division.

After World War II, Almond served as United Nations chief of staff in Korea under General of the Army Douglas MacArthur. Almond helped plan the Inchon landings, and commanded U.S. X Corps in that operation. Promoted to the rank of lieutenant general, Almond's final assignment was commandant of the Army War College.

David T. Zabecki

Additional Reading

Lee, Ulysses, *The Employment of Negro Troops* (1966). Stanton, Shelby L., *America's Tenth Legion: X Corps in Korea, 1950* (1989).

Ambrosio, Vittorio (1879–1958)

Italian general, chief of the Italian General Staff. Ambrosio was born in Turin 28 July 1879, and died in Alessio 20 November 1958. He was a leading figure in the efforts of the Italian Army to oust Benito Mussolini (q.v.) in 1943. Ambrosio rose steadily through the ranks of the Italian Army and served in the Libyan campaign as a cavalryman. In World War I he was a divisional chief of staff. During the interwar years, he rose to the position of corps commander, and by 1939, he commanded the Second Army on the Yugoslav border.

In April 1941, Ambrosio cautiously moved his army into Yugoslavia, where he remained until being called in 1942 to replace Mario Roatta as chief of staff of the army. On 1 February 1943, Ambrosio replaced Ugo Cavallero (q.v.) as chief of general staff of armed forces. With Mussolini's full approval, Ambrosio tried to bring back the Italian forces in the Ukraine and the Balkans. After the Axis collapse in Tunisia, he saw nothing but disaster should Italy continue in the war. On 9 July 1943, the Allies invaded Sicily (q.v.), and on 14 July, he sent a note to Mussolini in which he said now is the time to ". . . consider whether it would be expedient to spare the country further sorrow and ruin, and to anticipate the end of the struggle . . ."

At the conference in Feltre on 19 July 1943, Ambrosio, along with others, made one last attempt to get Mussolini to stand up to Adolf Hitler (q.v.) and tell him that Italy could not continue. He was disappointed. To Giuseppe Bastianini, Ambrosio exclaimed, "Did you hear what he said to Hitler after my warning of this morning? He asked him again for that war materiel which they will never send. He still deludes himself . . . He is mad, I tell you, mad." This conclusion led Ambrosio and other conspirators to proceed with arrangements to arrest Mussolini with the approval of King Victor Emmanuel (q.v.). For a short time Ambrosio served as a member of Pietro Badoglio's (q.v.) military provisional cabinet. On 9 September 1943, Ambrosio fled Rome along with Badoglio and the king, after the armistice announcement by the Allies.

Richard A. Voeltz

Additional Reading

Deakin, F.W., *The Brutal Friendship* (1962).

Kirkpatrick, Ivone, *Mussolini, A Study in Power* (1964).

Anders, Władysław (1892–1970)

Polish lieutenant general, commander of Polish II Corps. During the 1939 campaign in Poland, Anders commanded the Nowogrodzka Cavalry Brigade, part of Army "Modlin" defending the northern approaches to Warsaw. He withdrew his force first to Ptock and then southeast, defending the Vistula River at Dobrzyn. A further withdrawal led him to the area of Tomaszow Lubelski, where, during the second phase of the battle, he broke through the German lines and retook Krasnobrod. His cavalry group eventually was destroyed near Sambor on 27 September in fighting against both the German and the Soviet armies. Anders was wounded, taken prisoner by the Soviets, and imprisoned in Lubianka Prison in Moscow.

Following the Polish-Soviet Agreement of July 1941, Anders was appointed commanding general of the Polish Army in the Soviet Union, but continual Soviet chicanery convinced him that the only chance to organize and train his army for combat was to withdraw it to the Middle East. Along with the army, he evacuated several thousand Polish civilians, a total of 114,000 people in all. More than one and a half million Poles remained prisoner in the Soviet Union.

From 1942 to 1943, Anders was commander of the Polish Army in the Middle East. He also commanded the Polish II Corps, designated for operations in Europe. The II Corps, consisting of two infantry divisions and an armored brigade, landed in Italy in the winter of 1943–1944 and became a part of the British Eighth Army.

During the advance on Rome, II Corps was given the Monte Cassino sector of the Gustav Line. All previous Allied attempts to capture the high ground and its Benedictine monastery that controlled the road to Rome failed. The final and successful attack on Monte Cassino (q.v.) lasted from 12 to 18 May 1944 and fell into two phases.

Anders's plan was first to attack two neighboring heights and then launch the main assault from there. The first attempt ended in failure with heavy Polish casualties. On 17 May, he attacked again,

Lieutenant General Władysław Anders (with cigarette) conferring with British officers in Italy, April 1944. (IWM NA 13680)

this time securing the adjoining high ground. The next day, the Poles launched the final attack on Monte Cassino, and the German stronghold fell.

In June 1944, II Corps was transferred to the Adriatic coast, where its main task was to capture the port of Ancona and secure it as a supply base. Feigning an attack along the coast, Anders sent his main forces in a flanking movement, resulting in the capture of the port intact on 18 June 1944. That autumn, II Corps operated in the Appenines.

Following the Yalta Conference, British Prime Minister Winston S. Churchill (q.v.), in a heated exchange with Anders, told him that Polish forces were no longer needed and he could take them away. In the dark days of 1940, Churchill's attitude had been somewhat different. On 26 February 1945, Anders was appointed acting supreme commander in chief of the Polish armed forces. He held that position until the end of the war.

Andrzej Suchcitz

Additional Reading
Anders, Władysław, *An Army in Exile* (1949).
Czarnomski, Francis B. (ed.), *They Fight for Poland* (1941).

Andersen, Lale (1905–1972)
German entertainer. Lale Andersen was a Berlin cabaret singer in 1937 when she introduced the song *Lili Marleen,* based on a 1923 poem by Hans Leip. She later recorded the song, which initially enjoyed only a limited success. In the summer of 1941, a German soldiers' radio station in Belgrade played the song, and was immediately flooded by repeat requests from the troops. Within a short period of time it became the signature song of the German soldier.

During the North African campaign (q.v.) *Lili Marleen* was immensely popular with the soldiers of the *Afrika Korps* (q.v.). British troops liked it just as much, and soon an English version came out as *Lilli Marlene.* The French version, *Lily Marlene,* followed shortly. When American troops entered the war they too adopted the song. In 1944, Hollywood came out with the movie, *Lilli Marlene,* starring Marlene Dietrich.

Lili Marleen was perhaps the only song to enjoy equal popularity on both sides of World War II. Its lyrics, which told of a soldier about to be shipped out to the front and the girl he was leaving behind, transcended all notions of nationality. It was a universal soldier's song that spoke to all soldiers everywhere. Although translated into many languages and recorded by many artists, Lale

Andersen's recording in the original German remains the definitive rendition.

David T. Zabecki

Additional Reading
Mayer, S.L. (ed.), *Signal: Hitler's Wartime Picture Magazine* (1976).

Anderson, Kenneth Arthur Noel (1891–1959)
British Lieutenant General, Commander of the British First Army. Sir Kenneth Anderson was born in Scotland. He entered the British Army in 1911 and served in combat during World War I. In 1930 he commanded the 11th Infantry Brigade, and from 1931 to 1932 he was the commander of British troops in Palestine. In the early stages of World War II, Anderson commanded the British 3rd Division in France in 1940.

During Operation TORCH, Anderson commanded the Allied Eastern Task Force. The actual landing operation at Algiers was conducted on 8 November 1942 by the Eastern Assault Force, under the command of Major General Charles W. Ryder. On 9 November, Anderson assumed command of all Allied troops in Algeria for the 400-mile eastward advance to Tunisia (q.v.). His force, designated the British First Army, took the port of Bône on 12 November.

On 17 November Anderson ordered a halt to consolidate prior to pushing toward Tunis. The Axis forces used that time to build up their own strength in Tunisia. By the time the Allied drive resumed on 25 November, the balance had tipped in the Axis favor. That, combined with heavy seasonal rains, forced the Allies to temporarily abandon the attack on 24 December.

On 26 January 1943, Anderson took command of all Allied forces on the Tunisian front, including U.S. II Corps. On 19 February, General Sir Harold Alexander (q.v.) assumed control of overall ground operations in North Africa as commander of the 18th Army Group—which included Anderson's British First Army and the British Eighth Army of General Sir Bernard Montgomery (q.v.). Alexander was immediately critical of Anderson's command ability and considered replacing him with Major General Oliver Leese (q.v.).

The Allies finally took Tunisia on 13 May 1943. Anderson never again held a major command in combat. He commanded the British Second Army in Britain during the initial preparation stages for the Normandy (q.v.) invasion. Prior to the actual operation, however, Montgomery replaced Anderson with Lieutenant General Miles Dempsey (q.v.).

David T. Zabecki

Additional Reading

Howe, George F., *Northwest Africa: Seizing the Initiative in the West* (1957).

Playfair, I.S.O., et al., *The Destruction of the Axis Forces in Africa, 1942–1943* (1968).

Andrews, Frank M. (1884–1943)

As an American lieutenant general and aviation pioneer, Andrews was one of America's leading architects of military airpower during the interwar years. Born in Nashville, Tennessee, he graduated from the United States Military Academy at West Point in 1906 and was commissioned a cavalry officer. He completed flight training in 1918, too late to fly in combat in France. In mid-1920 Andrews did, however, succeed Brigadier General William Mitchell (q.v.) as Air Service Officer of the American Army of Occupation in Germany.

In March 1935, the U.S. Army Air Corps underwent a major reorganization. Andrews was promoted to temporary brigadier general and named to command the newly created General Headquarters (GHQ) Air Force. For the first time, all of the U.S. Army's air strike elements were consolidated under a single commander. Subsequently promoted to temporary major general, Andrews molded GHQ Air Force into the offensive combat arm that became the model for the U.S. Army Air Forces in World War II.

In 1937 Andrews ran afoul of the Army General Staff when he strongly advocated an independent air force during testimony before the House Military Affairs Committee. As a result, in 1939 he was exiled to Fort Sam Houston, Texas, and reverted to his permanent rank of colonel. Within a few months, the new Chief of Staff of the Army, General George C. Marshall (q.v.), brought Andrews back to Washington as Assistant Chief of Staff of the Army for Training and Operations. Andrews was the first aviator to hold that key general staff position.

In 1941, as a lieutenant general, Andrews assumed command of the Caribbean Defense Command—the first air officer to command a theater. In November 1942, he became the commander of all U.S. forces in the Middle East. On 5 February 1943, Andrews was given supreme command of all U.S. forces in the European Theater of Operations. Three months later he died in the crash of a B-24 bomber, while attempting a low visibility landing in Iceland.

At the time of Frank Andrews's death, many contemporary observers considered him the leading candidate for supreme Allied command. He possessed an almost ideal balance of intellect, strength of character, courage, and military skills. Andrews Air Force Base in Maryland was later named for him.

David T. Zabecki

Additional Reading

Huie, William B., *The Fight for Air Power* (1942).

McClendon, R. Earl, *The Question of Autonomy for the U.S. Air Arm* (1950).

Angelus, Oskar (1892–1959?)

Director for internal affairs of the Estonian Country Directorate. A high-ranking official of the Estonian Interior Ministry, Angelus emigrated to Germany in 1939 and became a German citizen in 1940. He returned to German-occupied Estonia in August 1941 as director of internal affairs in the Estonian self-administration. In 1942, he complained the Germans were usurping the self-administration's authority. By 1943, his goal was the reestablishment of an independent Estonia allied with Germany against the Soviet Union.

Steven B. Rogers

Additional Reading

Misiunas, Romuald J., and Rein Taagepera, *The Baltic States: Years of Dependence, 1940–1980* (1983).

Anielewicz, Mordecai (1920–1943)

Polish-Jewish resistance leader. Anielewicz was one of the organizers of the resistance movement inside the Warsaw Ghetto (q.v.). From November 1942, he commanded the *Żydowska Organizacja Bojowa* (Jewish Combat Organization) and was one of the key commanders of the Warsaw Ghetto Uprising in April 1943. He was killed by German troops in his command bunker at 18 Miła Street, along with other leaders of the uprising.

Andrzej Suchcitz

Additional Reading

Nirenstein, Albert (ed.), *A Tower from the Enemy: Contributions to a History of Jewish Resistance in Poland* (1959).

Orska, Irena, *Silent Is the Vistula: The Story of the Warsaw Uprising* (1946).

Zuckerman, Itzhak, *A Surplus of Memory: Chronicle of the Warsaw Ghetto Uprising*, (1991).

Antonescu, Ion (1882–1946)

Romanian general, leader of "Iron Guard" government. Antonescu was a Romanian general during World War I, chief of the general staff, and minister of defense in the years prior to World War II. He fell from King Carol II's (q.v.) favor in 1940 when he criticized the country's lack of preparation for war. This lack of preparation forced Romania to cede large tracts of its territory to neighboring states.

Eventually appointed prime minister, Antonescu persuaded the king to abdicate. He then assumed total control as de facto leader of the country. He established a so-called National Legionary government, allied Romania with Nazi Germany, and later joined Adolf Hitler in the invasion of the Soviet Union in 1941 in a move to regain lost territory. He was arrested on orders of King Michael (q.v.) in August 1944, tried, and executed as a war criminal.

Steven B. Rogers

Additional Reading

Cretzianu, Alexandre, *The Lost Opportunity* (1957).
Pavel, Pavel, *Why Rumania Failed* (1944).
Ziemke, Earl F., *Stalingrad to Berlin: The German Defeat in the East* (1966).

Antonov, Alexei Innokentievich (1896–1962)

Soviet general, chief of the Soviet General Staff. Antonov, the son of a military officer, attended the Pavlov Military School. He served as an ensign in the tsar's forces in World War I and was demobilized in 1918. He reentered the military as chief of staff of a Red Army brigade during the Russian civil war, and moved up to chief of staff of a military district by 1937. At that time, he attended the Frunze Military Academy and then received additional training at the Academy of the General Staff.

Antonov developed his talents as a staff officer and held various chief of staff positions throughout World War II. As deputy chief of the Soviet General Staff, he participated in the planning of Operation BAGRATION, the action that encircled the German salient in Byelorussia and East Poland, and led to the Soviet counteroffensive that ended at the Elbe.

Antonov was a skilled staff officer, particularly adept at collating and coordinating data and developing operation orders. In his initial planning for BAGRATION, he provided Marshall Georgy Zhukov (q.v.) with the operational objectives down to the corps and divisional units.

Antonov enjoyed the respect of front (army group) and other army commanders, who could rely on his precise and terse statements. During the time he served in his most influential assignments, the Soviet armies were in no position to have long drawn out conferences. He had an exceptional grasp of military matters and was able to condense volumes of material into meaningful and pertinent briefings.

Antonov became the chief of the Soviet General Staff in 1945. He was a Soviet delegate to the Yalta and Potsdam Conferences (*see* Conferences, Allied). With his knowledge of Soviet military strategy he was well qualified to place Soviet interests in correct juxtaposition with Allied desires. In 1955, he capped his military career as chief of staff of Warsaw Pact forces.

Thomas Cagley

Additional Reading

Bialer, Seweryn (ed.), *Stalin and His Generals* (1984).
Guillaume, Augustin L., *Soviet Arms and Soviet Power* (1949).
Shukman, Harold (ed.), *Stalin's Generals* (1993).

Aosta, Duke of

See Savoia, Amadeo di

Arciszewski, Tomasz (1877–1955)

Prime minister of the Polish government-in-exile. Arciszewski was a leading Polish socialist, and one of the party's leaders in occupied Poland. He flew to Britain in 1944 and became prime minister that November. He headed Poland's last wartime government, protesting against the Yalta agreements, reached at Poland's expense and without its participation.

Andrzej Suchcitz

Additional Reading

Czarnomski, Francis B. (ed.), *The Fight for Poland* (1941).
Garliński, Józef, *Poland, S.O.E., and the Allies* (1969).
Mazur, Tradeuz, et al. (eds.), *We Have Not Forgotten 1939–1945* (1960).
Raczyński, Edward, *In Allied London* (1963).

Arnim, Hans-Jürgen von (1889–1971)

German colonel general, commander of German Army Group Africa. Von Arnim served on both fronts during World War I, ending the war as a captain commanding an infantry battalion. He progressed through the ranks in the *Reichswehr*, ultimately rising to major general as an infantry regimental commander. In 1940, he became a *Panzer* lieutenant general. He served in Russia and was a corps commander when he departed for Africa in November 1942. He assumed command of the Fifth *Panzer* Army in Tunisia, and later command of the short-lived Army Group Africa, which he surrendered to the Allies in May 1943. Taken prisoner by the British as colonel general, he was, for a while, the ranking German POW, except for Rudolf Hess (q.v.).

Steven D. Cage

Additional Reading
Barnett, Correlli (ed.), *Hitler's Generals* (1989).

Arnold, Henry Harley (1886–1950)

American general of the air force, chief of the U.S. Army Air Forces. "Hap" Arnold was born in Gladwyne, Pennsylvania, on 25 June 1886, the son of a doctor. After completing his secondary education in neighboring Lower Merion, Arnold entered the U.S. Military Academy in 1907. Although his was not a distinguished academic career, he graduated in 1907 with his West Point nickname "Happy" or "Hap" firmly affixed.

Arnold was commissioned a second lieutenant in the infantry and served a brief stint in the Philippines before returning to the United States to attend a flying school in Dayton, Ohio, operated by Orville and Wilbur Wright. From there, he was assigned to the new Signal Corps Aviation School as an instructor. In 1913, he returned to the Philippines, and by 1916, he was stationed at Rockwell Field in San Diego, where he organized an aero squadron for the Panama Canal Zone.

An experienced and highly resourceful pilot, Arnold rose rapidly through the ranks. His only direct combat service in World War I came very late as an air observer. Between the wars, he remained a strong advocate of airpower. He supported General William Mitchell (q.v.) and was a defense witness at Mitchell's court-martial.

After spending several years in Washington, Arnold was assigned to posts in the Midwest, including commands at Wright Field near Dayton. In 1931, he was promoted to lieutenant colonel and posted to March Field in California where he reorganized the base to house bomber units. Here his considerable skills as a flyer led him to experiment with new aircraft and equipment. In 1933, Arnold moved to a command position at Wright Field, but in 1936 he returned to Washington. In the fall of 1938, as major general, he became chief of the Army Air Corps.

The opening phase of World War II found Arnold uncomfortably at a desk job in Washington. His primary role was to increase awareness of the need for airpower, its expansion, and the needed changes in the aircraft industry to produce adequate air combat resources. By the time America entered the war in December 1941, aircraft production had increased sixfold, and pilot training had kept pace. He attended conferences of the Combined Chiefs of Staff, including those at Casablanca, Quebec, London, and Potsdam, but he was absent from Yalta due to health problems. His most demanding task was satisfying the aircraft needs of the army and navy.

During the spring of 1941, Arnold traveled to Britain to help coordinate the Lend-Lease (q.v.) program. He developed cordial relations with Royal Air Force leaders, and his conception of the coming air war proved very accurate. Later that year, the U.S. Army Air Forces (USAAF) were established and he was given the command. His role as head of the AAF kept him stateside, coordinating strategy and policy. In early 1943, he was promoted to general and then to general of the army (five-star general) in December 1944.

In April 1944, Arnold also assumed direct command of the Twentieth Air Force, although he remained in Washington. The Twentieth Air Force was Arnold's creation, a strategic force of B-29 bombers organized on a global basis. In 1945, it was this unit that devastated Hiroshima and Nagasaki.

Shortly after the war Arnold turned command of the AAF over to General Carl Spaatz (q.v.) and retired in March 1946. Arnold remained a staunch supporter of airpower and national defense, and was one of the prime movers for the independent U.S. Air Force established in 1947. At that time, his rank was converted from general of the army to general of the air force, the only person thus far to hold that rank. His considerable writings, including *This Flying Game* (1936), *Winged Warfare* (1941), *Army Flyer* (1942), all with Ira Eaker (q.v.), and his autobiography, *Global Mission* (1949), reflected his strong views on aviation.

A victim of heart disease, Arnold died after his

Generals Henry H. Arnold (left), Dwight D. Eisenhower (center), and George C. Marshall (right) visit Normandy, 12 June 1944. Admiral Ernest J. King stands directly behind Eisenhower. (IWM EA 26286)

fifth heart attack on 15 January 1950. His funeral at Arlington National Cemetery was attended by the highest-ranking officers of all service branches as well as President Harry S Truman.

Boyd Childress

Additional Reading

Arnold, Henry H., *Global Mission* (1949).

Cate, James L., "Arnold, Henry Harley," *Dictionary of American Biography, 1946–1950* (1974).

Coffey, Thomas E., *Hap: The Story of the U.S. Air Force and the Man Who Built It, General Henry "Hap" Arnold* (1982).

Copp, DeWitt S., *A Few Great Captains: The Men and Events That Shaped the Development of U.S. Air Power* (1980).

Attlee, Clement (1883–1967)

British prime minister 1945–1951. Born in Surrey and educated at Oxford, Attlee rose quickly through the ranks of the Labour Party to be its leader by 1935. He served at Gallipoli and on the western front during World War I. In 1919, he became a member of Parliament (MP). In 1930, he served as a junior minister in Ramsey Mac-Donald's government and became the unquestioned leader of the party shortly thereafter.

During the 1930s, Attlee criticized Britain's policy of appeasement (q.v.). Despite his rejection of Soviet Communism, he encouraged the British government to enter into a political and economic treaty with the USSR and France. He believed collective security was the only way to stop Adolf Hitler's (q.v.) expansion. Attlee also supported the League of Nations (q.v.). In 1937, he led a group of Labour MPs to Spain to show solidarity with the Republican forces fighting Francisco Franco (q.v.). Attlee thought Neville Chamberlain's (q.v.) policy of appeasement was foolish, declaring: "I think that this House and this country ought to say that we will not countenance for a moment the yielding to Hitler and force, what was denied to Stresemann and reason."

In 1940, Attlee joined Winston S. Churchill's (q.v.) coalition national government as lord privy seal, and two years later, he became deputy prime minister. Right after the war, he and the Labour Party defeated Churchill's Conservative Party and

Clement Atlee, visiting Polish paratroops training in Scotland, April 1942. (IWM H 18882)

Attlee became prime minister. His tenure in office (1945–1951) put into place many of the programs Labour had long advocated: nationalization of the railways, coal, electric, gas, steel, and the introduction of a national health service.

Glenn R. Sharfman

Additional Reading

Attlee, Clement R., *A Prime Minister Remembers: The War Memoirs of* . . (1961).

Burridge, Trevor, *Clement Attlee: A Political Biography* (1985).

Auchinleck, Claude (1884–1981)

British field marshal, commander in chief Middle East, and last British commander in chief in India. Sir Claude Auchinleck had the misfortune to be occupying a senior position when the outbreak of war found Britain and the other democracies ill-prepared to face Nazi aggression. Like John Gort, Edmund Ironside, and Archibald Wavell (qq.v.), Auchinleck's task was to hold the fort as best he could in a series of difficult jobs, leaving the glory of success to those who followed.

Coming from a military family, Auchinleck was educated at Wellington and Sandhurst before joining the Indian Army in 1904. He saw extensive active service in Egypt and Mesopotamia in World War I. Between the wars, he instructed at the Indian Staff College, commanded a brigade on operations in Waziristan in 1937, and was prominent in advancing Indians to command positions in an army officered mainly by the British. By the start of World War II, he was a major general commanding the Meerut District.

In 1940, Auchinleck served in Britain and Europe for the only time in his career. He was first commander of the Allied expedition to Narvik (q.v.), then commander in chief southern command, with responsibility for organizing the defense of the British south coast against the German invasion that was expected to follow Dunkirk (q.v.).

In December, Auchinleck returned to India as commander in chief, the professional peak of an Indian Army career. Seven months later, however, Prime Minister Winston S. Churchill (q.v.) removed Wavell as commander in chief Middle East and ordered Auchinleck to replace him in this

General (later Field Marshal) Sir Claude Auchinleck. (IWM JAR 557)

again began to retreat toward the Suez Canal. Taking personal command, Auchinleck fought successful delaying actions at Mersa Matruh (q.v.), before halting Rommel at Ruweisat Ridge (q.v.).

In October 1942, General Bernard L. Montgomery (q.v.), used Auchinleck's success as a springboard for a decisive victory over Rommel, leading to the push of the Axis out of North Africa completely. By then, however, Churchill had come to believe that Auchinleck, like his predecessor Wavell, lacked aggression. Churchill removed him and he returned to India for a second spell as commander in chief. There his drive and organizational skills, applied in a country he knew well, supplied men and resources for General William Slim's Fifteenth Army to reconquer Burma by mid-1945.

Auchinleck remained in India throughout the period of independence and partition, performing a last sad duty of supervising the division of his beloved Indian Army into two parts, Indian and Pakistani. Tragically, they fought each other soon after the British left. He was promoted to field marshal in 1946. He retired the next year and settled in Morocco, where he lived until his death at age ninety-seven.

The "Auk," as he was known, was a big man both physically and morally. He was a professional soldier to the core who never complained at the difficulty of his tasks, or of his sometimes unfair treatment by politicians. It was sufficient for him to do his duty and to know that he was highly esteemed by his comrades in arms, both Indian and British.

Philip Green

Additional Reading
Auchinleck, Claude, and John Connel, *Auchinleck: A Biography of Field Marshal Sir Claude Auchinleck* (1959).
Lucas, James, *Command* (1988).

imperial command, which included Australian, Indian, New Zealand, and South African, as well as British troops. Following the British defeats in Greece and Crete (qq.v.), morale was low and equipment was scarce. The arrival of the dynamic German general Erwin Rommel to lead the *Afrika Korps* (qq.v.) made life no easier, and no fewer than twenty of Auchinleck's subordinate generals became casualties.

Auchinleck's main force was the Eighth Army. Twice he intervened to save it from disaster. In late 1941, a failed British attack followed by a swift German counterattack led the British commander, General Alan Cunningham (q.v.), to order a retreat. Auchinleck countermanded this and ordered the Eighth Army to stand fast. Then in January 1942, the Eighth Army, now under Neil Ritchie (q.v.), found itself outflanked by Rommel, and

Axis Sally
See GILLARS, MILDRED ELIZABETH

B

Bader, Douglas (1910–1972)
Royal Air Force group captain. Bader was born at St. John's Wood in London on 21 February 1910. He was educated at Temple Grove School and St. Edwards School, Oxford. He became a cadet at the officer training school at Royal Air Force Cranwell in September 1928. Having qualified as a pilot, he joined Number 23 Squadron in August 1930, where he flew Gamecock fighters.

On 14 December 1931, Bader joined two friends and flew to Woodley Aerodrome, near Reading. As the three were about to leave to return to Hendon, Bader reluctantly accepted a dare to "beat up" the aerodrome. It was during this demonstration that Bader's Bristol Bulldog fighter was hit by a change of wind, causing the wing tip to hit the ground. Bader had no chance to recover, as he was flying too close to the ground. As a result of the crash, Bader lost both legs, one above the knee, and the other below the knee. Fitted with artificial limbs, Bader taught himself to fly again within a few years, but an RAF medical board still declared him medically unfit for further service.

Bader worked for the Shell Petroleum Company until the outbreak of the war in September 1939. He volunteered to return to the RAF. After several attempts and demonstrations that he could in fact fly, he was accepted. Within a few months Bader was in command of Number 242 Squadron. Bader became one of Britain's leading fighter aces during the Battle of Britain (q.v.), eventually scoring twenty-two-and-a-half air-to-air victories. He was known as the "Legless Wonder" for his skill as a pilot, and he was awarded the Distinguished Service Order and Bar, and the Distinguished Flying Cross. During the Battle of Britain, however, he was a strong advocate of the "big wing" formation, which was strongly opposed by RAF Fighter Command.

Bader eventually rose to command a fighter wing at RAF Tangmere. On 9 August 1941, Bader flew his last sortie, leading his wing of Spitfires on a sweep over France. He became separated from his group, and on seeing six German Bf-109s, he attacked the formation single-handedly. He shot down two of the German aircraft, but then his Spitfire was rammed from the rear by another Messerschmitt. With his Spitfire's tail gone, Bader had to bail out over France, losing one of his artificial legs in the process.

Bader first was confined in a hospital at St. Omer. While he was there, the RAF airdropped another artificial leg for him, which the Germans let him have. Bader then was confined at *Oflag IVB*. After an unsuccessful attempt to escape, he was transferred to Colditz (q.v.), where he remained for the rest of the war.

Bader was released on 14 April 1945. He was promoted to group captain and given command of the RAF Flight Leader School at Tangmere, and later command of the North Weald Fighter Sector. On 15 September 1945, he led 300 aircraft in the victory fly-past over London. Bader resigned his RAF commission in February 1946 and returned to Shell Oil.

Alan Harfield

Additional Reading
Brickhill, Paul, *Reach for the Sky* (1954).

Badoglio, Pietro (1871–1956)
Italian marshal, military head of the post-capitulation Italian government. The son of peasant parents, Badoglio became duke of Addis Ababa and Benito Mussolini's (q.v.) successor. He attended military school in Turin, became a sublieutenant in 1890, and a major in 1911. He fought in

every Italian war from 1895 to 1944. At the end of World War I, he was a general and a national hero, his reputation untarnished by the debacle at Caporetto (a surprise attack by German/Austrian forces in the autumn of 1917, resulting in an Italian rout). He served as chief of the general staff from 1919 to 1920 and from 1925 to 1940.

After Mussolini's arrest in 1943, King Victor Emmanuel III (q.v.) chose Badoglio to head the Italian government. He dissolved the Fascist Party and many of its institutions, freed political prisoners, liberalized laws, and disregarded anti-Semitic decrees. On 3 September 1943, he signed an armistice with the Allies. Five days later, a German attack in the north forced the Italian government to flee south to Brindisi. On 5 June 1944, Badoglio resigned and retired to his birthplace, Grazzano Montferrato, later renamed Grazzano Badoglio.

Mary Anne Pagliasotti

Additional Reading

Badoglio, Pietro, *Italy in the Second World War* (1948).
Delzell, Charles F., *Mussolini's Enemies: The Italian Anti-Fascist Resistance* (1961).

Bagramyan, Ivan Khristoforovich (1897–1982)

Soviet general, commander of the Soviet 1st Baltic Front (army group). Bagramyan was born of working-class parents in Armenia. At the age of eighteen, he joined the army, graduating from officers' school in 1917. He participated in the Russian civil war as a member of the Red Army. After the civil war, he completed various military training courses, including the Frunze Military Academy and the Academy of the General Staff. His principal assignments prior to World War II were in staff positions. In 1941, he became chief of operations and deputy chief of staff of the Kiev Military District, and of the Southwestern Front 1941–1942. In 1942, he became commander of the Sixteenth Guards Army and fought at Kiev and Kursk (qq.v.).

In 1943, Bagramyan replaced General Andrei Yeremenko (q.v.) as commander of the 1st Baltic Front and remained there through 1945. Bagramyan was ordered to capture Riga and encircle the German Army Group North in Memel. His efforts on the Soviet northern flank contributed to the later successes of Ivan Konev and Georgy Zhukov (qq.v.) in capturing Berlin and Germany east of the Elbe. Bagramyan, however, was blamed for the initial failure to take Königsberg.

After the war, Bagramyan became the commander of the Baltic Military District. Promoted to marshal in 1955, he finished his career as deputy minister of defense and chief of rear services of the armed forces in 1958.

Thomas Cagley

Additional Reading

Bialer, Seweryn, *Stalin and His Generals* (1984).
Shukman, Harold (ed.), *Stalin's Generals* (1993).

Baker, George (1915–1975)

American staff sergeant, cartoonist. Baker created the World War II cartoon character Sad Sack (q.v.), whom he described as a "bewildered civilian trying to be a soldier." First printed in *Yank* magazine in May 1942, Sad Sack was a satiric comic strip that depicted the ironies of army life.

An artist, Baker before the war had worked on the animation team of classic movies, including Walt Disney's *Fantasia*. He joined the army in June 1941 and devoted his leisure time to sketching cartoons. He entered his caricature of Sad Sack in a contest and was invited by *Yank* magazine to join the staff. After the war, he continued to draw the Sad Sack cartoons commercially. He died in 1975.

Elizabeth D. Schafer

Additional Reading

Hess, Stephan, and Milton Kaplan, *The Ungentlemanly Art: A History of American Political Cartoons* (1968).

Balck, Hermann (1893–1984)

German general of *Panzer* troops, commander, Army Group G. Balck was born in Danziglangfuhr, Prussia, in 1893. His father, Lieutenant General William Balck, was a noted author on tactics and was awarded the *Pour le Mérite* in World War I. During World War I, the younger Balck served as a mountain infantry officer on the western, eastern, Italian, and Balkan fronts, finishing the war as company commander. He was wounded seven times and was awarded the Iron Cross.

In the interwar period, Balck transferred to the cavalry. He twice refused an opportunity to join the German General Staff, preferring to remain a combat officer. In 1938, Lieutenant Colonel Balck transferred to General Heinz Guderian's (q.v.) Inspectorate of Mobile Troops within the army high command, and consequently oversaw the refitting of German *Panzer* divisions during the Polish campaign.

Immediately following the conquest of Poland, Balck assumed command of a motorized infantry regiment in the 1st *Panzer* Division of Guderian's XIX *Panzer Korps*. On 13 May 1940, Balck's regiment crossed the Meuse River, spearheading Guderian's breakthrough at Sedan. After Sedan, at Balck's suggestion, German tanks and infantry were employed in combined arms *Kampfgruppe* formations. This was a significant development in the doctrine of armored warfare. Until then, infantry and armored regiments were employed separately.

In 1941, Colonel Balck served in the Greek campaign as commander of the 3rd *Panzer* Regiment. When his division broke through the Metaxis Line, Balck assumed command of the *Panzer* battle group that outflanked the British Corps rear guard during the battle of Mount Olympus.

In November 1941, Balck became inspector of mobile troops, the position held by Guderian in 1938. In May 1942, Balck assumed command of the 11th *Panzer* Division, where he fully displayed his impressive command abilities. He emphasized leading from the front to remain in constant touch with the action. His principal axiom was "night marches are lifesavers." In December 1942, during the Soviets' LITTLE SATURN offensive along the Chir River (q.v.), his division successfully outflanked and defeated a serious threat to the German forces outside of Stalingrad. With Balck issuing only verbal orders, the 11th *Panzer* Division accomplished the incredible feat of counterattacking in three different directions within a period of four days. At Tatsinskaya, Balck's division encircled and destroyed a Soviet tank corps; and in another action it defeated a Soviet shock army.

In 1943, Balck commanded the XIV *Panzer Korps* at Salerno (q.v.) until he was injured in an airplane crash. After recovering, he returned to the Ukraine and commanded the XLVIII *Panzer Korps* in the savage 1944 battles at Kiev, Radomyshl, and Tarnopol. During those battles his corps destroyed three Soviet armies. In August 1944, Balck assumed command of the Fourth *Panzer* Army. Counterattacking near Baranov, he brought the Soviet offensive in the great bend of the Vistula to a halt.

On 21 September 1944, Balck assumed command of Army Group G in the west, opposite the U.S. Third and Seventh Armies. On Adolf Hitler's (q.v.) direct orders, Balck's mission was to stop U.S. General George S. Patton (q.v.) and prevent him from interfering in the planned Ardennes offensive (q.v.). Balck was relieved in December 1944 when he ran afoul of Hitler. Balck finished the war com-

General of Panzer *Troops Hermann Balck. (IWM MH 6025)*

manding the German Sixth Army in Austria where he surrendered to American forces at war's end. He remained in captivity until 1947.

Although little remembered today, Balck was one of the greatest battlefield commanders of World War II. He was one of only twenty-seven German soldiers to be awarded the Knight's Cross with Swords, Oak Leaves, and Diamonds. His battles on the Chir River are studied at the U.S. Army Command and General Staff College to this day.

Randy Papadopoulos

Additional Reading
Balck, Hermann, *Ordnung im Chaos: Erinnerungen 1983–1948* (1981).
Mellenthin, F.W. von, *German Generals of World War II: As I Saw Them* (1997).
———, *Panzer Battles* (1956).

Balodis, Jánis (1881–1965)
Latvian general, commander in chief of the Latvian Army. During the 1919–1920 War of Latvian Independence, Balodis was the commander in chief of

the Latvian Army. In June 1940, he was still commander in chief of the army and vice president of Latvia as well. He sympathized with those Latvians who wanted to resist the Red Army. Following the Soviet invasion, he was dismissed from his posts and subsequently deported and imprisoned.

Andrzej Suchcitz

Additional Reading

Bilmanis, Alfred, *Baltic States and World Peace* (1945).
Feld, Mischa J. (pseud.), *The Hug of the Big Bear* (1961).

Barbie, Klaus (1913–1991)

Gestapo chief of Lyons. Barbie grew up in a middle-class and deeply Catholic environment under the brutal domination of his alcoholic father. After finishing school, he joined the Hitler Youth (q.v.) and in 1935, the SS (q.v.). As a member of the elite SD (q.v.), Barbie was sent to Lyons, France, in November 1942 to persecute Jews and other "public enemies." He personally tortured and murdered several victims and even enforced the deportation of forty-one Jewish children to Auschwitz.

After the war, Barbie escaped to Bolivia with the assistance of the U.S. Army Counterintelligence Corps (CIC) (*see* Counterintelligence Operations), and assumed the name Altmann. U.S. Intelligence used Barbie against the Soviets. In 1983, he was extradited to France. On 4 July 1987, he was sentenced to life imprisonment in Lyons for crimes against humanity. His trial in France raised many sensitive and long-suppressed questions concerning French collaboration during the German occupation. He died in prison in 1991.

Wolfgang Terhörst

Additional Reading

Bower, Tom, *Klaus Barbie: Butcher of Lyons* (1984).
Dabringhaus, Erhard, *Klaus Barbie: The Shocking Story of How the U.S. Used This Nazi War Criminal As an Intelligence Agent* (1984).

Barkhorn, Gerhard (1919–1983)

Luftwaffe major, air ace. This popular and charismatic Prussian was the second-highest-scoring ace of World War II, with 301 kills, most in a Bf-109F. Although he failed to score a victory against the British in 1940, he rose to prominence after transferring to the eastern front in July 1941 with

Major Gerhard Barkhorn, history's second-highest-scoring ace. (IWM 6026)

Jagdgeschwader 52. There he scored all his victories and was shot down nine times. His best day came in July 1942 when he shot down four planes on a single sortie.

After receiving the Knight's Cross with Oak Leaves and Swords, Barkhorn joined *Jagdgeschwader* 44 in January 1945 and trained in the Me-262 jet fighter. On his second jet mission he crashed and spent the rest of the war in a hospital. After 1,100 combat missions, he ended the war as a major. He joined the West German *Bundesluftwaffe* in 1955, finally retiring as a major general. In 1983, the second-highest-scoring ace in military history was killed in a traffic accident near Cologne.

Laura Matysek Wood

Additional Reading

Musciano, Walter A., *Messerschmitt Aces* (1982).
Williamson, Gordon, *Aces of the Reich* (1989).

Baruch, Bernard (1870–1965)

Financier and presidential advisor. Born in South Carolina, the son of a former Confederate doctor, Baruch aspired to an appointment to West Point.

Denied because of a hearing loss, he obtained a degree in business and established himself as a financier of the first rank. Politically and philosophically a liberal, he became an advisor to President Woodrow Wilson at the beginning of World War I. He retained his role as a presidential advisor through World War II.

Perhaps Baruch's most significant contribution to the Allied success in World War II occurred in 1934, when he urged President Franklin D. Roosevelt (q.v.) to stockpile two critical war materials: tin and rubber. During the war, he was an important advisor to the president on economic mobilization. Following World War II, he served on the U.N. Atomic Energy Commission. In 1946, he presented the Baruch Plan for the international control of atomic energy. It was rejected by the Soviet Union.

Thomas Cagley

Additional Reading
Divine, R.A., *Roosevelt and World War II* (1969).
Schwarz, Jordan A., *The Speculator: Bernard M. Baruch in Washington, 1917–1965* (1981).

Batov, Pavel Ivanovich (1897–1985)
Soviet general, commander of the Soviet Sixty-fifth Army. Batov, like so many of his contemporaries, was born of working-class parents. He served as a junior officer in the tsar's army, and became a member of the Red Army during the revolution. Apparently he did not display any particularly outstanding leadership traits early on. He found himself assigned to administrative duties during the time many of his fellow officers were attending the various staff schools and serving in staff positions. Although he was slow to work into command channels, he eventually did attend the Frunze Military Academy.

The single thread that runs through Batov's career is his command of occupational troops. He also was one of the few Soviet generals who served in the Spanish Civil War (q.v.). After he returned from Spain, he commanded a corps, and his unit occupied eastern Poland in September 1939. He then participated in the Russo-Finnish War (*see* Winter War, Finnish).

When World War II started, Batov commanded the IX Rifle Corps, the Fifty-first Special Army in the Crimea, and the Third Army in Briansk. He commanded the Sixty-fifth Army during battles for Stalingrad and Kursk (qq.v.), in the Dnieper crossing, and the attack into East Pomerania. His units also participated in the crossing of the Oder and the subsequent drive on Berlin.

After the war, Batov was commander of the Soviet Army of Occupation in Germany from 1945 to 1949. He was a central figure in the Berlin Blockade (q.v.), and the solidifying of East Germany behind the Iron Curtain. In 1956, Batov commanded the Soviet forces occupying Hungary.

Thomas Cagley

Additional Reading
Bialer, Seweryn, *Stalin and His Generals* (1984).
Shukmaan, Harold (ed.), *Stalin's Generals* (1993).

Bayerlein, Fritz (1899–1970)
German *Panzer* commander. Born in Würzburg in 1899, Bayerlein served as an officer candidate in the 2nd *Jäger* Battalion on the western front from 1917 to 1918. After demobilization, he joined the infant *Reichswehr* in 1921 as a lieutenant in the 21st Infantry Regiment. He later transferred to the embryonic armored force, was promoted to major, and served as a staff officer with the 3rd *Panzer* Division in 1938. Between 1939 and 1941, he served in Poland, France, and Russia as a staff officer to General Heinz Guderian (q.v.).

In 1940, Lieutenant Colonel Bayerlein became chief of staff of Erwin Rommel's *Afrika Korps* (qq.v.) in September 1941. He received the Knight's Cross in December and became chief of staff of the new *Panzerarmee Afrika* in February 1942. In November, he was promoted to major general and took temporary command of the *Afrika Korps,* leading the abortive Alam el Halfa (q.v.) offensive. Subsequently wounded, he was evacuated before the final German collapse in Tunisia in May 1943.

In 1943 and 1944, Bayerlein led the 3rd *Panzer* Division in the east. In February 1944, he was given command of the new, elite *Panzer Lehr* Division (the *Panzer* forces school troops). Promoted to lieutenant general in May 1944, he led the *Panzer Lehr* during the Normandy (q.v.) campaign. The division was decimated during the American breakout at St. Lô (q.v.) in July. He rebuilt the *Panzer Lehr* and led it during the Allies' Lorraine campaign in November, and in the German Ardennes offensive (qq.v.). In February 1945, he commanded LIII *Korps.* He was captured in the Ruhr pocket (q.v.) in April 1945.

Bayerlein died in Würzburg on 30 January 1970. He had a keen appreciation of the potential of armored warfare and of the value of tactical airpower as an effective counter to armor.

Russell Hart

Additional Reading
Carrell, Paul (pseud.), trans. E. Osers, *Invasion: They're Coming!* (1962).
Kurowski, Franz, *Die Panzer Lehr Division* (1964).
Ruetgen, Helmut, *Die Geschichte der Panzer Lehr Division in Westen 1944–45* (1979).

Beaverbrook, Lord
See AITKIN, MAXWELL

Beck, Józef (1894–1944)
Polish foreign minister in 1939. Beck was the foreign minister of Poland at the outbreak of World War II. He was the architect of the Anglo-Polish Mutual Assistance Treaty of August 1939. He successfully ensured that any conflict with Germany would not be a local affair isolating Poland politically.

Andrzej Suchcitz

Additional Reading
Kennedy, Robert M., *The German Campaign in Poland, 1939* (1956).
Zajackowska, Anna, *Poland: The Untold Story* (1945).

Beck, Ludwig (1880–1944)
German colonel general, leader of the opposition to Adolf Hitler (q.v.). A general staff officer during World War I, Ludwig Beck served in a variety of staff and command positions in the postwar *Reichswehr*. In October 1933, Lieutenant General Beck, then commander of 1st Cavalry Division, was appointed head of the *Truppenamt*. This "Troop Office," formed in 1919 with its deliberately misleading title, carried on the functions of the general staff prohibited under the Treaty of Versailles (q.v.). In March 1935, it was redesignated the general staff of the army.

Beck presided over the expansion of the general staff, and developed contingency war plans based on a defensive strategy. Considered a master strategist by his peers, he realized any future war would become a multi-front war, with German defeat inevitable. In 1935, he still believed an army-Nazi accord could be reached if the officer corps held together and forced Hitler to reason. As

Hitler pressed to invade Czechoslovakia in 1938, Beck recognized his error, and openly opposed the *Führer*. He wrote a series of memoranda describing the disaster inherent in a policy of aggression. He mobilized other generals but failed to gain sufficient support from army commander in chief Walther von Brauchitsch (q.v.).

Realizing he was getting nowhere, Beck, now colonel general, retired in August 1938 and organized a covert resistance group of active and former officers and other conservatives, maintaining contact with other democratic opposition movements. He contacted London, proposing to stage a coup if supported by Britain and France. British Prime Minister Neville Chamberlain (q.v.), however, preferred "peace in our time."

Beck's group warned Belgium shortly before the 1940 invasion, and maintained close contact with field commanders and staff officers as the war unfolded. By 1943, Beck's group was convinced that only Hitler's assassination could save Germany from destruction. He was aware that surrender and occupation of Germany were inevitable, although some of his co-conspirators hoped a separate peace could be made with the Western Allies.

Beck's group organized several assassination attempts, culminating in von Stauffenberg's (q.v.) 20 July 1944 attempt. The conspirators planned to carry out Operation VALKYRIE after Hitler was killed. The Home Army would declare martial law, arresting Nazi leaders and neutralizing SS garrisons under the pretext of stopping an SS coup. Beck, the designated regent pending free elections, categorically refused to consider the systematic execution of Nazi Party and SS leaders to secure success.

Initially believing Hitler dead, the conspirators contacted field commanders to organize their participation in neutralizing the SS and *Gestapo* (qq.v.) and initiating cease-fires on all the fronts. As news of the failed attempt became known, Beck nonetheless insisted on continuing with VALKYRIE. Aware of the diminished likelihood of success, he stated that Germany deserved the attempt. As troops loyal to Hitler stormed the conspirators headquarters, Beck tried to shoot himself. He inflicted a nonlethal head wound and was killed by a sergeant.

In his function as army chief of staff, Beck helped rebuild the German military into an efficient war machine. His early opposition to Hitler's policy of aggression partially preserved the German Army as an institution from the stigma of undivided identification with Nazism. Beck's later active opposition demonstrated that true German patriotism was not synonymous with National Socialism, but instead, was incompatible with it.

Sidney Dean

Additional Reading

Barnett, Correlli (ed.), *Hitler's Generals* (1989).

Görlitz, Walter, *History of the German General Staff* (1953).

Hoffmann, Peter, *German Resistance to Hitler* (1988).

Liddell Hart, B.H., *The German Generals Talk* (1948).

Belfrage, Bruce (1901–1974)

British broadcast journalist. During the first half of the war and the most desperate time for Britain, the BBC (q.v.) Home Service news consisted of Frank Phillips, Alvar Lidell, Joseph McLeod, Alan Howland, and Bruce Belfrage—probably the best known of all the radio broadcasters. During the German Blitz, with bombs literally raining down on Broadcasting House, the unflappable former stage and screen actor delivered the nine o'clock news in a voice that became as reassuring as that of Prime Minister Winston S. Churchill (q.v.).

On 4 November 1942, following General Bernard L. Montgomery's victory over German General Erwin Rommel at El Alamein (qq.v.), Belfrage read on the air his most famous announcement: "This is London, this is Bruce Belfrage speaking, Rommel is in full retreat." Ironically, he submitted his letter of resignation from the BBC that same day, because of a change in broadcasting assignment that diminished his role as news reader. Following the war, he followed a checkered career in politics and acting. In 1951, he published his autobiography, *One Man in His Time*.

Richard A. Voeltz

Additional Reading

Belfrage, Bruce, *One Man in His Time* (1951).

Briggs, Asa, *The BBC, the First Fifty Years* (1985).

Beneš, Eduard (1884–1948)

Czech statesman. Beneš served as president of his country from 1935 to 1938 and again from 1940 to 1948. He was born to a farm family on 28 May 1884, in Kozlany, Bohemia, and later studied in Prague, Paris, Dijon, and Berlin. After the outbreak of war in 1914, he helped organize a Czech resistance movement in Prague, and in 1919, he was the leader of the Czech delegation to the Paris Peace Conference, where Czechoslovakia gained its independence.

In order to preserve the Treaty of Versailles (q.v.) settlement, Beneš helped establish the Little Entente, an alliance of Czechoslovakia, Romania, and Yugoslavia supported by France. He firmly believed this alliance would guarantee the independence of Czechoslovakia.

Succeeding Tomáš Masaryk (q.v.), Beneš became president of Czechoslovakia on 18 December 1935, at a time when the demands of Nazi Germany for the Sudetenland (q.v.) were increasing. Czechoslovakia's allies abandoned it and permitted the dismemberment of the country under the Munich Agreement (q.v.) in September 1938.

A week later, Beneš resigned the presidency and left the country. After war broke out, he organized a government-in-exile and became its president on 21 July 1940. Throughout the war, he kept international attention focused on Czechoslovakia. He returned to Prague after Germany surrendered in May 1945.

In the elections held the following year, the Communists received 38 percent of the vote, the largest of any party. The Czech Communists and their Soviet allies pressured President Beneš, already in poor health, to appoint a government containing only two non-Communists, allowing himself to remain little more than a figurehead. The constitution of 9 May 1948 served to confirm Communist control, and Beneš resigned the presidency on 7 June 1948. He died on 3 September.

John David Waite

Additional Reading

Beneš, Eduard, *Memoirs: From Munich to New War and New Victory* (1954).

———, *My War Memoirs* (1948).

Mackenzie, Compton, *Dr. Beneš* (1946).

Rothschild, Joseph, *East Central Europe Between the Two World Wars* (1974).

Bennett, Donald Clifford Tyndall (1910–1986)

British air vice-marshal. A childhood visit to a Wright brothers exhibition in his native Australia proved inspiration for Bennett to pursue an aviation career. After a brief period flying seaplanes for Imperial Airways, the forerunner of BOAC, he was commissioned in the Royal Air Force (RAF) in 1941. He distinguished himself on a bombing raid on the German battleship *Tirpitz*. On that raid, he and his copilot were shot down over Norway and made their way to Sweden.

A series of quick promotions soon found Bennett the youngest air vice-marshal in RAF history. He conceived the idea behind Bomber Command's Pathfinder Force, high-speed mosquito aircraft that flew ahead of the main bombing wave to drop flares and incendiaries, pinpointing targets for night strikes (see Pathfinder Technique). He was also behind the Light Night Striking Force, a continual thorn in the *Luftwaffe*'s side; and FIDO, a fog dispersal system designed to offset bad weather. His outspoken, often abrasive style won him few friends, but none questioned his contribution to the success of the Allied bombing offensive against Germany. Ironically, Bennett was the only RAF group commander to serve a full term as air officer commanding (AOC), and not be knighted for his service during World War II.

Mark Rummage

Additional Reading
Maynard, John, *Bennett and the Pathfinders* (1996).
Richards, Dennis, and Hilary St. George Saunders, *The Royal Air Force 1939–1945, Vols. 1–3* (1953–54).

Berg, Paal (1873–1968)

Norwegian resistance leader. When Norway was invaded, Berg was the chief justice of the Norwegian Supreme Court. Following the German occupation of Oslo, he led a group of distinguished civilians in proposing the formation of an administrative council to administer the occupied territories, leaving policy formation still in the hands of the king and government.

After Norway finally fell in June 1940, Berg withdrew from talks aimed at establishing a pro-German government. He then organized and led the Norwegian civilian resistance. The direction of the Norwegian resistance (q.v.) was steered by an inner cabinet, "The Circle," which he headed. He was an opponent of violent action, and he often clashed with Milorg (q.v.), the armed branch of the resistance. An agreement between the two factions was finally reached in 1943, with Berg's policy line taking the upper hand.

Andrzej Suchcitz

Additional Reading
Ash, Bernard, *Norway 1940* (1964).
Derry, Thomas K., *The Campaign in Norway* (1952).

Beria, Lavrenty (1899–1953)

Chief of the Soviet NKVD (q.v.). Beria's name is almost as infamous as Josef Stalin's (q.v.). He joined the Communist Party at the start of the revolution, and participated aggressively in activities in his native Georgia. Right from the start, he found intelligence and counterintelligence work to his liking, and he displayed traits that would serve him well in the paranoia of the Stalin years.

Immediately following the revolution, Beria took charge of the security police in Georgia. He worked his way up through the Communist Party structure, eventually attracting the attention of Stalin. In 1938, shortly after the Soviet purges (q.v.), Stalin elevated Beria to the position of commissariat for internal affairs and chief of the secret police, the NKVD. In July 1939, Beria became a member of Stalin's State Defense Committee.

Under Beria, the NKVD almost paralleled the *Gestapo* under Heinrich Himmler (qq.v.). The NKVD kept dossiers on generals and ran the Soviet POW camps. The NKVD carried out the deportations from Poland, the deportations of the Crimean Tartars, and the executions of Polish officers at Katyn (q.v.). He was also responsible for the conduct of partisan (q.v.) operations behind German lines. His main value to Stalin was that he kept the Soviet premier supplied with current intelligence, often more timely than what the official military intelligence organs could produce.

After the war, Beria continued to serve as minister for internal affairs. Stalin, however, limited some of his roles in order to reduce his power. Upon Stalin's death in 1953, Beria served as one of four coequal deputy prime ministers, but soon fell into disfavor with his cohorts. He was stripped of all power, arrested, tried, and executed in December 1953.

Thomas Cagley

Additional Reading
Dziak, John J., *Chekisty: A History of the KGB* (1988).
Khrushchev, Nikita, *Khrushchev Remembers* (1974).
Moynahan, Brian, *Claws of the Bear: The History of the Red Army from the Revolution to the Present* (1989).

Berling, Zygmunt (1896–1980)

Polish lieutenant general, commander of the Communist First Polish Army. A retired regimental commander, Berling was not called back to active duty in 1939. From 1939 to 1941, he was a prisoner in the Soviet Union were he was wooed by the NKVD (q.v.) along with other Polish officers.

In 1942, Berling defected from the Polish Army to remain in the Soviet Union. There he formed the 1st Kościuszko Infantry Division to fight under the operational command of the Soviets. He commanded the division in the battle of Lenino in October 1943. The Poles suffered heavy casualties, mainly because they were left to their own devices by their Soviet allies.

Berling later became the commander of the Polish I Corps, and then the Polish First Army, formations subordinated to the Polish Communists in Moscow. In September 1944, he unsuccessfully attempted to aid the Home Army during the Warsaw Rising (q.v.). The following month he was unexpectedly relieved of his command.

Andrzej Suchcitz

Additional Reading

Garliński, Józef, *Poland in the Second World War* (1985).
Mikołajczyk, Stanisław, *The Rape of Poland: Pattern of Soviet Aggression* (1948).

Bernadotte, Folke (1895–1948)

Vice president of the Swedish Red Cross. Nephew of Swedish King Gustavus V and veteran Swedish diplomat, Count Bernadotte graduated from the Swedish Military Academy at Karlberg and served in the Swedish Army from 1918 until 1930.

As vice president of the Swedish Boy Scouts, he was responsible for integrating the organization into the Swedish defense network during the war. As vice president of the Swedish Red Cross, he was responsible for arranging British-German prisoner exchanges in 1943–1944. His negotiations with Nazi officials increased in 1944 after his government's decision not to enter the war on the side of the Allies, and its commitment to initiate rescue missions for Scandinavian prisoners held in German prisons and concentration camps. These efforts proved successful when Heinrich Himmler (q.v.), contacted by the Swedish Red Cross in December 1944, agreed to transfer these prisoners to the Neuengamme Camp outside Hamburg.

Bernadotte went to Berlin in February 1945 to finalize the agreement. Himmler left the details of these negotiations to Ernst Kaltenbrunner (q.v.), chief of the *Reich* Security Main Office (RSHA) (q.v.), who agreed in principle to these arrangements, but left the final decision to Himmler. Bernadotte next met with Himmler, and suggested that the prisoners be sent directly to Sweden. After much disagreement and delay, the prisoners were transferred to Neuengamme in April 1945, despite Kaltenbrunner's insistence that the camp was not equipped to handle these new prisoners.

As a result of these negotiations, Himmler came to recognize Bernadotte as an individual trusted by both the Germans and the Allies, and he selected him as an intermediary to present surrender terms to the Western Allies. They were reluctant to deal with Himmler, however, believing he did not have the authority to speak for the German government. Himmler persisted, and once Führer Adolf Hitler (q.v.) indicated he would remain in Berlin to the end, he believed he was now in a position to negotiate. In late April 1945, Himmler met with Bernadotte at the Swedish consulate in Lübeck, and he proposed a German surrender in the west in return for a Western Allied promise to assist the Germans in their war against the Soviet Union. Bernadotte presented Himmler's conditional terms, which were subsequently rejected by the Western Allies.

Bernadotte's role in the release of concentration camp inmates was the subject of criticism after the war because of his apparent disinterest in rescuing Jews. This criticism was due, in part, to an invented letter from the count to Himmler in which he stated that Jews would not be welcomed in Sweden.

After the war, Bernadotte became president of the Swedish Red Cross, and in 1948 he was appointed by the U.N. Security Council to mediate the Jewish-Arab conflict in Palestine. He was assassinated in Jerusalem by Jewish extremists in September 1948.

Steven B. Rogers

Additional Reading

Bernadotte, Folke, *The Curtain Falls: The Last Days of the Third Reich* (1945).
Ilan, Amitzur, *Bernadotte in Palestine* (1948).
Trevor-Roper, Hugh R., "Kersten, Himmler, and Bernadotte," in *Atlantic Monthly*, February 1953, pp. 43–45.

Bernhard, Prince Leopold (1911–)

Commander of the Dutch Forces of the Interior. Bernhard, a German, married into the Dutch Royal family in 1937. Prior to his marriage he was a member of the SS (q.v.). His supporters were quick to point out he was a member at a time when it was more of an elite organization in which socially prominent Germans received honorary ranks, rather than the ruthless murder organization of the later Nazi years.

Bernhard was well liked by the Dutch. When the Dutch government fled to Britain after the German invasion in 1940, he went to Zeeland to join the Dutch forces fighting there. During the years of the German occupation, he worked closely with the Allies, at times reporting directly to General Dwight D. Eisenhower (q.v.) in coordinating Dutch resistance.

Thomas Cagley

Additional Reading
Posthumus, H.W. (ed.), *The Netherlands During German Occupation* (1946).
Warmbrunn, Werner, *The Dutch Under German Occupation: 1940–1945* (1963).

Beurling, George F. (1921–1948)

Canadian flight lieutenant, air ace. "Buzz" Beurling was the leading Canadian fighter ace of World War II, with thirty-one-and-one-third victories. He was best known for his spectacular role in the defense of Malta (q.v.) in the summer of 1942, where he shot down twenty-seven Axis aircraft in four months of intensive combat. He was awarded the Distinguished Service Order, the Distinguished Flying Cross, and the Distinguished Flying Medal with Bar.

Serge M. Durflinger

Additional Reading
Nolan, Brian, *Hero: The Buzz Beurling Story* (1981).

Bevan, John Henry (1894–1978)

British colonel, controlling officer, London Controlling Section. A member of one of Britain's leading financial families, Sir John Bevan's range of connections and previous experience as a general staff officer during World War I led to his appointment to head the London Controlling Section (LCS) in May 1942. Established in 1940 along the lines of Dudley Clarke's successful "A Force," the LCS provided the British chiefs of staff with a framework for coordinating strategic deception plans on a global basis, ranging from Europe and North Africa to the Middle East and India.

While involved in every major deception of the war from BARCLAY to MINCEMEAT (q.v.), the undoubted triumph for Bevan and his LCS staff was the development of BODYGUARD, the successful cover plan for the Normandy (q.v.) in-

vasion. He received a knighthood for his wartime services and was later made privy councilor.

Mark Rummage

Additional Reading
Brown, Anthony Cave, *Bodyguard of Lies* (1975).
Howard, Michael, *British Intelligence in the Second World War,* Volume 5: *Strategic Deception* (1990).

Bevin, Ernest (1881–1951)

British minister of labour and national service. Bevin's life was virtually a British version of "log cabin to Congress." An illegitimate child who never knew his father, orphaned at age eight, his formal education ended at the age of eleven; yet in World War II, he was completely responsible for the direction of all Britain's manpower. Immediately after the war, he was an effective foreign secretary during a difficult and dramatic period of world history.

The Baptist Church and trade unionism, particularly the latter, were the great influences on Bevin's adult life. From the age of thirty until he entered Parliament thirty years later, he was a full-time union official, initially in Bristol and later at the national level. He devoted this period of his life to improving the lot of the working class. In this, he was motivated not by ideology (he was to prove an implacable enemy of communism), but by a humanitarian concern for the sort of people with whom he had grown up.

In May 1940, Bevin was elected to Parliament and appointed minister for labour and national service. He remained in this vitally important post throughout the war, responsible for all manpower and with the authority to direct labor to where it was needed most. From the start, he concentrated on cooperation between management and unions, and placed great emphasis on workers' welfare, as well as on sheer industrial efficiency. Under his guidance more than three million men and women were moved out of nonessential jobs, increasing the armed forces by four million and armaments industries by three million. Significantly, this enormous effort made by a democracy could not be matched by any of the totalitarian regimes engaged in the conflict. The part played personally by Bevin cannot be overestimated.

A feature of this period was Bevin's friendship and easy cooperation with Prime Minister Winston S. Churchill (q.v.). Their shared patriotism and determination to get the job done more than com-

Ernest Bevin campaigning during the 1945 General Election. (IWM HU 59484)

pensated for their differing social backgrounds and fundamental political opposition.

Between the wars, extensive travel to the United States and Australia on trade union business gave Bevin an interest in world affairs. In 1945, he became foreign secretary in Clement Attlee's (q.v.) postwar government at a time when British power was declining and the Cold War starting. Bevin was prominent at Potsdam and other conferences (*see* Conferences, Allied) drawing up the postwar settlement, in British decisions to withdraw from Palestine and Greece, the introduction of the Marshall Plan (q.v.), and the setting up of the North Atlantic Treaty Organization (NATO). At a time of great difficulty, his stewardship of foreign affairs must be judged as much a success as his wartime achievements.

Bevin was a great patriot and a true man of the people. His greatest attributes in all three periods of his life were common sense, forthrightness, and a fundamental decency toward his fellow human beings. He died in London on 14 April 1951.

Philip Green

Additional Reading
Bullock, Alan, *The Life and Times of Ernest Bevin,* 2 vols. (1960–67).

Biddle, Francis (1896–1968)

United States attorney general during the Roosevelt administration. Previous to his appointment as attorney general in September 1941, Biddle was the solicitor general, primarily responsible for administering the Alien Registration Act of June 1940. On 1 January 1945, Biddle, along with Secretary of State Edward Stettenius and Secretary of War Henry Stimson (qq.v.) wrote a memorandum to President Franklin D. Roosevelt (q.v.) for use during the Yalta Conference. The memorandum proposed that the key German leaders be put on trial after the war, rather than being put to death without benefit of a trial. The three cabinet secretaries noted: "The names of the chief German leaders are well known and the proof of their guilt will not offer great difficulties." Despite having already reached a verdict in his own mind, Biddle later served as a judge at the Nuremberg trials (*see* American Military Tribunals). He was, however, known for his compassion.

Paul Rose

Additional Reading
Biddle, Francis, *A Casual Past* (1961).
———, *In Brief Authority* (1962).
Cooper, B.W., *The Nuremberg Trials* (1947).

Billotte, Gaston Henri Gustave (1875–1940)

French general, commander of the French 1st Army Group. A graduate of St. Cyr, Billotte served in the French colonies until 1915. During World War I, he held various staff and command positions. While leading an infantry division, he was gassed twice. In 1937, he became inspector general of colonial troops.

At the outbreak of war in 1939, Billotte received command of the 1st Army Group, which included four French armies plus the British Expeditionary Force (BEF). As he moved the bulk of his forces into Belgium to meet the enemy attacks, the Germans overran his southernmost army, the French Ninth, in the area between Sedan and Givet. Realizing the threat to his flank, he began to pull his units back toward France. He died in a car accident at Ypres on 23 May 1940.

Glenn Lamar

Additional Reading
Chapman, Guy, *Why France Fell* (1968).
Goutard, Adolphe, *The Battle of France, 1940* (1958).
Michel, Henri, *The Second World War,* 2 vols. (1968).

Bily, Josef (1872–1941)

Czech general, resistance leader. Bily was a co-organizer and commander in chief of *Obrana Naroda* (Defense of the Nation), the Czech underground army loyal to Eduard Beneš (q.v.). Formed on a non-conscriptorial basis, its effectiveness was limited mainly to sabotage operations. Bily was arrested in the spring of 1940, imprisoned, and shot by the Germans the following year.

Andrzej Suchcitz

Additional Reading
Beneš, Eduard, *Memoirs: From Munich to New War and New Victory* (1960).
Erdely, Eugene V., *Germany's First European Protectorate: The Fate of Czechs and Slovaks* (1942).
Hronek, Jiri, *Volcano Under Hitler: The Underground War in Czechoslovakia* (1941).
Mastny, Vojtect, *The Czechs Under Nazi Rule* (1971).

Blamey, Thomas Albert (1884–1951)

Australian general, commander of the ANZAC. Australia's senior general, Sir Thomas Blamey com-

manded the Australian I Corps in the Middle East in operations in Libya. He then led the Australian and New Zealand Corps (ANZAC) in the Greek campaign, but was recalled to Egypt as deputy commander in chief, Middle East, a post with little power. Blamey fell out with British general Claude Auchinleck (q.v.) over the use of Australian troops.

Recalled home as commander in chief of the Australian Army, Blamey effectively organized the country's defenses and went over to the attack, repulsing Japanese forces on the Kokoda trail in New Guinea, recapturing Papua and Buna, and directly commanded ground troops as commander in chief, Allied land forces southwest Pacific from September 1942 to January 1943.

Andrzej Suchcitz

Additional Reading
Glenn, John G., *From Tobruk to Tarakan* (1960).
Hetherington, J.A., *Blamey: The Biography of Field Marshal Sir Thomas Blamey* (1955).
Long, Gavin M., *To Benghazi* (1963).

Blanchfield, Florence Aby (1882–1971)

American colonel, director of the U.S. Army Nurse Corps. Blanchfield began her military career with the Army Nurse Corps (ANC) in France in 1917. She joined the surgeon general's staff in 1935 and in 1942, as a lieutenant colonel, she was head of the ANC. Under her leadership, army nurses were trained in military regulations, surgical nurses were assigned to hospitals near the front lines, and the ANC expanded from 639 to 40,000. She worked for full military rank for nurses, and in 1947, became the first woman commissioned into the regular army. She received the Distinguished Service Medal in 1945 and retired from the ANC in 1947.

Laura Matysek Wood

Additional Reading
Archard, Theresa, *G.I. Nightingale: The Story of an American Army Nurse* (1945).
Bartlett, Dorothy, *Nurse in War* (1961).
Roberts, Mary M., *The Army Nurse Corps Yesterday and Today* (1957).

Blaskowitz, Johannes (1883–1948)

German general, commander of Army Group G. Born in Peterswalde on 10 July 1883, Blaskowitz was a professional soldier of the old school who tried to maintain high standards of behavior among his own forces. As military governor of occupied Po-

Colonel General Johannes Blaskowitz. (IWM PL 83971)

land, he protested SS (q.v.) brutalities, forwarding detailed reports of their atrocities to Field Marshal Walther von Brauchitsch (q.v.). Ultimately, Blaskowitz's efforts to prosecute SS personnel led to his dismissal. He later commanded Army Group G in France in 1944. He surrendered to British forces in the Netherlands in March 1945. Arrested as a war criminal in 1946, he committed suicide shortly before his trial.

Carl O. Schuster

Additional Reading
Humble, Richard, *Hitler's Generals* (1974).
Wesphal, Siegfried, *German Army in the West* (1952).

Bleicher, Hugo (1899–1982)

Abwehr sergeant and counterintelligence agent. Bleicher was a brilliant *Abwehr* (q.v.) counterspy who used the terror of the name *Gestapo* (q.v.) to gain cooperation and confessions from captured agents. His exploits were many. Using the disguise of a *Luftwaffe* officer who pretended to believe Germany had lost the war and wanted to defect to the Allies, he penetrated the spy network of Peter Churchill (q.v.) in the Savoy Alps and arrested him and agent Odette Sansom (q.v.) who was posing as his wife.

Through confessions obtained from Raoul Kiffer, Bleicher arrested Mathilde Carré (q.v.) a radio operator for the INTERALLIE network. By pretending he already knew all about the network, he obtained confessions from her permitting him to arrest the entire INTERALLIE network.

Paul Rose

Additional Reading
Churchill, Peter, *Duel of Wits* (1953).
Lauerkühn, Paul, *German Military Intelligence* (1954).

Blimp, Horatio

British cartoon figure. Colonel Blimp was created in the 1930s by British cartoonist David Low (q.v.). Red-faced, potbellied, and with a walrus moustache, Blimp was a caricature of the pompous, ultraconservative military type the British public came to associate with the disasters of World War I. Blimp was known to say, "Gad, sir, Lloyd George is wrong! If things had been left to the High Command the war would have been over in half the time for twice as many troops." Blimp, of course, opposed the replacement of the horse by the tank. Given the inevitable trend of technology, Blimp still believed that the new tank crews should continue to respect cavalry traditions by wearing spurs inside their tanks.

Blimp's name became a byword associated with many of the conservative aspects of the British national character. His name spun off words such as "blimpish," "blimpery," and blimpian." The cartoon character also inspired a sophisticated wartime film, *The Life and Death of Colonel Blimp,* which ultimately cast the figure of Blimp in a sympathetic light. Nonetheless, when Prime Minister Winston S. Churchill (q.v.) saw the movie's premier on 11 June 1943, he was so outraged that he tried to have the film banned.

The real-life model for Colonel Blimp was General Sir Herbert Plumer, who was red-faced, potbellied, and had a walrus moustache. The resemblance, however, stopped at the physical characteristics. Plumer, ironically, was one of the best British generals of World War I, and was thoroughly trusted by his troops.

David T. Zabecki

Additional Reading
Chandler, David (ed.), *The Oxford Illustrated History of the British Army* (1994).

B

Blomberg, Werner von (1878–1946)

German field marshal, minister of defense. Werner von Blomberg played a pivotal role in Adolf Hitler's (q.v.) acquisition of supreme power within Germany. As virtual head of the *Truppenamt* (the thinly disguised German General Staff, outlawed by the Treaty of Versailles [q.v.]) from 1927 to 1929, von Blomberg visited the Soviet Union and became impressed with the power the Red Army enjoyed under a totalitarian regime. By 1930, he was enamored of National Socialism and was one of the first generals to support Hitler. President Paul von Hindenburg (q.v.) recalled von Blomberg from Geneva, where he was serving as the chief military delegate to the disarmament conference, and appointed him minister of defense in Hitler's cabinet on 30 January 1933. As *Reichswehr* minister, he tried to place generals sympathetic to Hitler in positions of authority.

Von Blomberg agreed to support Hitler's succession to the presidency if Hitler purged the SA (q.v.). After the 30 June 1934 "Night of the Long Knives" (q.v.), von Blomberg led the German generals in an oath of unconditional obedience to the *Führer.* Hitler rewarded him by promoting him field marshal on 1 April 1936.

During the Hossbach Conference on 5 November 1937, von Blomberg expressed strong reservations about Hitler's plans to annex Austria and Czechoslovakia. Thus, von Blomberg had to go. His marriage to a former prostitute in January 1938 enabled Hitler to force him into retirement. Hitler then assumed the War Ministry himself. Von Blomberg did not participate in World War II, but he later testified at Nuremberg (*see* International Military Tribunal), where he died on 13 March 1946.

Justin D. Murphy

Additional Reading

Görlitz, Walter, *History of the German General Staff, 1657–1945* (1953).

Mitcham, Samuel W. Jr., *Hitler's Field Marshals and Their Battles* (1988).

Wheeler-Bennett, John W., *The Nemesis of Power: The German Army in Politics, 1918–1945* (1961).

Blum, Leon (1872–1950)

Prewar French prime minister. Born into a middle-class Alsatian family, Blum was brought into active politics as a result of the Dreyfus Affair. In the early 1920s, he played a decisive role in the reconstruction of the French Socialist Party. After the victory of a left-wing alliance *(Front Populaire),* he became prime minister in 1936. A far-reaching program of social reforms and his active foreign policy in favor of the Spanish Republic, brought him into deep conflict with the right-wing parties, which led to his resignation in 1937.

After the French collapse in 1940, Blum was indicted by the Vichy government on charges of war crimes. Although the trial was suspended, he spent several years in French prisons and in a German concentration camp. He retired from public life after a brief period as deputy prime minister in 1948.

Blum is considered as one of the founders of the modern French Socialist Party and as an architect of the Socialist International between the two world wars. The concept of a broader anti-Fascist alliance gained substantial influence among many European politicians and intellectuals in the interwar period.

Georgi Verbeeck

Additional Reading

Blum, Leon, *Leon Blum Before His Judges at the Supreme Court of Riom* (1942).

Lacouture, Jean, *Leon Blum* (1977).

Field Marshal Werner von Blomberg. (IWM HU 2411)

Bock, Fedor von (1880–1945)

German field marshal, army group commander. Fedor von Bock commanded Eighth Army during the *Anschluss* (q.v.) of Austria, and led Army Group North against Poland. He commanded Army Group B during the assault on the Benelux and France. He executed a frontal attack on Holland and Belgium, crushing the Dutch in four days, then pushing the Belgian and Allied forces from their defensive positions along the Dyle River, taking Brussels and Antwerp. After the fall of Dunkirk (q.v.), he drove against the new French defensive line to take Paris and the territory southeast to Bordeaux. In July 1940, he received his marshal's baton.

In Operation BARBAROSSA, von Bock commanded Army Group Center (designated the "center of gravity" for the invasion), winning numerous major battles through November 1941. His advance faltered fifty kilometers from Moscow. Forced back by a Soviet counterattack, he faced Adolf Hitler's dissatisfaction. Stricken by stomach illness, von Bock relinquished command to Field Marshal Günther von Kluge (q.v.) on 18 December 1941.

After recovering, von Bock assumed command of Army Group South in February 1942. When Army Group South was split into Army Groups A and B that April, he took over Army Group B. He directed the defense in the first battle of Kharkov (q.v.) in May 1942. On 28 June, Army Group B struck eastward in true *Blitzkrieg* manner until delayed at Voronezh (q.v.). Hitler ordered von Bock to turn south but remained dissatisfied with the pace of advance. He was relieved of command on 13 July 1942. Ill again, he retired. He died with his family on 5 May 1945 during an Allied air raid.

Von Bock contributed greatly to the early success of *Blitzkrieg* (q.v.). Politically, he vacillated. A true Prussian officer, he despised the Nazis. He ignored the Commissar Order (q.v.), and wrote a horrified report to Hitler concerning SS massacres in Russia. Yet he refused to take a "mutinous" stand, stating he would "defend the *Führer* against any who attacked him." This posture is best defined by historian Walter Görlitz as "a combination of a rather narrow conception of soldierly obedience with personal ambition."

Sidney Dean

Additional Reading

Gerbet, Klaus, ed., *Generalfeldmarschall Fedor von Bock: The War Diary, 1939–1945* (1996).
Görlitz, Walter, *History of the German General Staff* (1953).

Liddell Hart, B.H., *The German Generals Talk* (1948).
Mitcham, Samuel W., Jr., *Hitler's Field Marshals and Their Battles* (1988).

Bohr, Neils Henrik David (1885–1962)

Danish physicist and Nobel Laureate. Born in Copenhagen on 18 November 1885, Bohr was the son of a professor of physical sciences. At age twenty-two, Neils won a gold medal from the Danish Scientific Society for his work relating to the surface tension of water. He earned a doctorate from the University of Copenhagen in 1911. His dissertation was on the electron theory of metals.

Bohr went to Britain and worked at the University of Cambridge under the direction of J.J. Thomson, and later at Victory University of Manchester under E. Rutherford's group, which studied the structure of the atom. On returning to Denmark in 1916, Bohr first worked as a professor, and then, in 1920, he became director of the University of Copenhagen's newly created Institute of Theoretical Physics, a position he held until his death.

During German occupation of Denmark, Bohr was active in the anti-Nazi resistance movement. He escaped to Sweden in a fishing boat and went on in 1944 to participate in the American atomic program at Los Alamos, New Mexico. He feared for the awesomely destructive weapon that resulted from his collaboration and felt that a free exchange of people and ideas among nations would be necessary to control it.

Paul J. Rose

Additional Reading

Bohr, Neils H.D., *Atomic Physics and Human Nature* (1958).
French A.P., and P.J. Kennedy (eds.), *Neils Bohr* (1987).
Moore, R.E., *Neils Bohr* (1966).

Bonhoeffer, Dietrich (1906–1945)

German theologian and opposition leader. During his short life, Bonhoeffer became an outstanding theologian and adherent of the ecumenical movement. He also supported German peace movements and became directly engaged with the anti-Nazi opposition. As the son of the well-known neurologist and psychiatrist, Karl Bonhoeffer, Dietrich received a liberal education. From 1923 to 1927, he studied theology at Tübingen, Rome, and Berlin. From 1931 to 1935, he worked as a pastor and instructor in Berlin and London. He sharply opposed the accommodation between the German churches and the Nazi regime. He demanded his colleagues side with the persecuted minorities and stand up for peace.

From 1935 to 1940, Bonhoeffer guided the illegal seminary known as the "Confessing Church." As the repressions against all "non-Aryans" increased, his twin sister Sabine, who had married a Jew, was forced to emigrate. Bonhoeffer decided to offer active opposition. Through his brother-in-law, Hans von Dohnanyi, he joined the circle around Admiral Wilhelm Canaris (q.v.), and became a party to the plans to overthrow Adolf Hitler (q.v.). Bonhoeffer's role in the conspiracy was to contact the bishop of Chichester, George Bell, in order to win Allied support for the German opposition. In 1943, however, Bonhoeffer was arrested. After enduring harsh treatment in prison, he was killed at Flossenburg concentration camp only days before the Allies arrived. He never gave up hope and lived his theology of the "responsible world" right to the end.

Wolfgang Terhörst

Additional Reading

Bonhoeffer, Dietrich, *Letters and Papers from Prison* (1971).

Robertson, Edwin, *The Shame and the Sacrifice: The Life and Teaching of Dietrich Bonhoeffer* (1987).

Borghese, Prince Junio Valerio (1912–1974)

Italian naval commander, special operations officer. "The Black Prince" achieved early wartime fame through the operations of his special naval forces, the 10th Light Flotilla (q.v.), known as XMAS, which specialized in frogman and "human torpedo" attacks. In Mediterranean operations his unit sank 73,000 tons of Allied shipping. On 19 December 1941, three of his miniature submarines entered the port of Alexandria (q.v.) and crippled the battleships HMS *Valiant* and HMS *Queen Elizabeth*. During the Italian Social Republic, he transformed XMAS into a 25,000-man anti-partisan army. He was a committed Fascist, and as late as 1970, he led an attempted coup in Rome.

Stephen M. Cullen

Additional Reading

Borghese, Junio V., *Sea Devils* (1952).

Bragadin, Marc A., *The Italian Navy in World War II* (1957).

Juardo, Carlos Caballero, *Resistance Warfare, 1940–1945* (1985).

Boris III (1894–1943)

Tsar of Bulgaria. Boris III had extensive blood ties to European royalty; the late Tsar Nicholas II of Russia was his godfather, and his wife was the daughter of the Italian king. Boris's reign was dominated by internal strife in the 1920s. The interwar economic depression forced Bulgaria to be dependent on German supplies. Boris, stabilizing control in the 1930s, preferred that Bulgaria remain neutral.

Discussing Boris's diplomatic manner, Adolf Hitler once labeled Boris a "cunning fox." Germany helped Bulgaria recover southern Dobrudja from Romania, and although he was pressured to join the Tripartite Pact, Boris refused. When the Soviet Union offered Bulgaria sovereignty, Hitler and Joachim von Ribbentrop (q.v.) visited him to discuss bordering territory—Thrace and Macedonia—that Boris wished to occupy. He realized allying with Germany might aid that goal. In addition, the Bulgarian people and military were pro-German.

Boris realized that Germany could be a savage enemy. He estimated that if he allied with Germany and was defeated, he would risk losing Bulgaria to the victorious Communist Soviets. Frustrated, he considered abdication.

Internal chaos, resulting from German threats to deport Bulgarian Jews and the infiltration of Soviet-trained Bulgarian Communists, complicated Boris's neutrality stance. On a trip to *Wolfsschanze*, he was astounded by Hitler's demands for use of Bulgarian military troops and Bulgaria's declaration of war on the Soviet Union. Boris refused, enraging Hitler, who threatened to seize Bulgaria.

When he returned home, Boris succumbed to an embolism and died on 28 August 1943. The actual cause of his death was never verified, but his family, doctors, and even Hitler suspected that he had been poisoned. His six-year-old son assumed the throne under a regency. Although Boris carefully cultivated Bulgaria's neutrality and diplomatic ties with the Soviet Union, that nation declared war on Bulgaria in August 1944, and later forced the abolition of the monarchy.

Elizabeth D. Schafer

Additional Reading

Groueff, Stephane, *Crown of Thorns: The Reign of King Boris III of Bulgaria, 1918–1943* (1987).

Bor-Komorowski, Tadeusz (1895–1966)

Polish lieutenant general, commander of the Polish Home Army. During the 1939 Polish campaign, Bor-Komorowski was deputy commander of an improvised cavalry brigade defending the central Vistula crossings. After Poland fell, he was appointed commander of the underground Kracow Home Army District, which he organized. From 1941 to 1943, he was deputy commander in chief of the *Armia Krajowa* (q.v.) (Home Army or AK) and simultaneously commander of the Western Home Army District. In July 1943, he became commander in chief of the AK. He led the AK during its most active period. By the summer of 1944, the AK had an effective force of 250,000, not counting support personnel.

In January 1944, Bor-Komorowski initiated Operation *BURZA* (TEMPEST), in which Home Army units in eastern Poland came out into the open to assist the Soviet Army in its operations on Polish soil. The AK played key roles in supporting the Soviets in the liberation of Wilno and Lwów. Following these operations, the AK units were forcibly disbanded and their officers either shot or deported by the Soviets.

From 1 August to 3 October 1944, Bor-Komorowski led the Warsaw Rising (q.v.). Betrayed by the Soviets and all but abandoned by the Western Allies, the AK fought for sixty-three days. On 30 September 1944, he was appointed supreme commander in chief of the Polish armed forces. With the final suppression of the Warsaw Rising, Bor-Komorowski became a POW in Colditz (q.v.). After his liberation, he resumed his post as Polish supreme commander in the west.

Andrzej Suchcitz

Additional Reading
Bor-Komorowski, Tadeusz, *The Secret Army* (1950).
Hazpern, Ada, *Liberation Russian Style* (1945).
Kennedy, Robert M., *The German Campaign in Poland, 1939* (1956).

Bormann, Martin (1900–1945)

Adolf Hitler's (q.v.) private secretary. Not well known outside of Hitler's inner circle, Bormann deliberately maintained a low profile and amassed great power and influence in his position as secretary to Hitler. He was born on 17 June 1900 to the family of a postal official in Halberstadt, a central German town. In 1920, he joined an anti-Semitic organization, and in 1923, an illegal *Freikorps* (q.v.) unit.

Martin Bormann. (IWM NYP 77063)

Because of his complicity in the murder of a comrade thought to be a spy, Bormann served two years in jail. On his release in February 1925, he gravitated to a nationalistic group in Weimar where he met Ernst Röhm (q.v.). He obtained a job with the Nazi Party in 1926, and his administrative abilities enabled him to rise steadily from regional offices in Thuringia to SA (q.v.) headquarters in Munich. Another strategic move was his 1929 marriage to Gerda, the daughter of an early Nazi Party member, party chairman, and Hitler's comrade Walther Buch.

After the Nazi seizure of power in 1933, Hitler appointed Bormann chief of staff to his deputy, Rudolf Hess (q.v.), and gave him an office in the party chancellory in Berlin. A fanatical devotee of Hitler, Bormann handled the *Führer's* private financial matters and other personal affairs. Deliberate, calculating, ambitious, and unpretentious, he arranged all meetings of party leaders with Hitler, and he attended every one. In April 1943, he was rewarded for his loyalty and effectiveness with the title "secretary to the *Führer*," and increasingly participated in all policy decisions. He strongly supported the harshest measures against Jews, and vigorously advocated the elimination of all Christian influences in Germany.

Bormann was a functionary who gained

power from the office he held. After the abortive 20 July 1944 attempt on Hitler's life, he became even more important to Hitler. He remained convinced that Hitler would somehow resolve the war in Germany's favor, and he remained true to Hitler to the very end.

Following Hitler's suicide, Bormann fled from the *Führer's* Berlin bunker on the night of 1 May 1945. He was never seen alive again. His fate, however, remained unknown. Bormann was indicted as one of the original defendants at the Nuremberg trials (*see* International Military Tribunal), and was sentenced to death in absentia. It was later learned that Bormann died in Berlin, possibly by suicide, on 2 May.

Robert G. Waite

Additional Reading

Fest, Joachim, *The Face of the Third Reich* (1970).

Lang, Jochem von, *The Secretary Martin Bormann: The Man Who Manipulated Hitler* (1979).

McGovern, James, *Martin Bormann* (1968).

Stevenson, William, *The Bormann Brotherhood* (1973).

Trevor-Roper, H.R. (ed.), *The Bormann Letters* (1954).

Bradley, Omar Nelson (1893–1981)

American general, commander 12th Army Group. Known as the "GI's general," Omar Bradley was a native of Clark, Missouri, where his father was a schoolmaster. The young Bradley attended the United States Military Academy at West Point and graduated forty-fourth in the class of 1915—the year that later came to be known as "the class the stars fell upon." During World War I, Bradley served as an infantry captain in the 14th Infantry Regiment, a training unit in the state of Washington. He finished the war as a temporary major, and then reverted to his permanent rank at the conclusion of the hostilities. He did not reach the grade of major again until 1924.

Unusual for a future senior commander, Bradley never led a unit in combat prior to World War II. During the interwar years he had very little service time with combat arms units. Bradley's interwar service began with duty as a Reserve Officer Training Corps (ROTC) instructor at South Dakota State College, and then as a mathematics instructor at West Point. In 1925, he attended the Infantry Officers' Advanced Course at Fort Benning, Georgia, where he came to the attention of George C. Marshall (q.v.). That connection was a significant factor in Bradley's later rise to high command.

In 1927 and 1928, Bradley served as the officer in charge of National Guard and reserve affairs for the Hawaiian Islands. In 1929, he graduated first in a class of eighty-eight officers from the Army Command and General Staff College. After assignments as the chief of weapons instruction at the Infantry School, and completion of the Army War College in 1934, Lieutenant Colonel Bradley taught tactics at West Point and also served as the academy's plans and training officer.

In 1938, Bradley moved to Washington, D.C., as a general staff officer in the personnel (G-1) division. He then served as the assistant secretary to the general staff until February 1941. That same year he was promoted directly from lieutenant colonel to brigadier general, and he assumed command of the infantry school. He was the first graduate of the Class of 1915 to reach general officer rank, making it seven months ahead of his classmate, Dwight D. Eisenhower (q.v.).

In February 1942, Major General Bradley assumed command of the newly reactivated 82nd Infantry Division. He supervised the division's training prior to its conversion to an airborne unit. Between June and December 1942, he commanded the 28th Infantry Division, a unit federalized from the Pennsylvania National Guard. Early training assignments such as these were very important in the careers of American commanders in World War II. They were used by the army's senior commanders to evaluate the effectiveness of their subordinates for future command. In the mobilization and training of these two divisions for combat, Bradley made good use of his skills as both a teacher and an organizer. The fact that these units went on to become two of the premier divisions of the U.S. Army in the European theater is due in no small part to the influence Bradley exerted on their training in their earliest days.

On General Marshall's recommendation, Bradley's next assignment was to the North African theater of operations, where he served as Eisenhower's "eyes and ears" with U.S. II Corps, which was commanded by Lieutenant General George S. Patton (q.v.). This was the first time Bradley and Patton served in combat together, with Bradley initially working as Patton's subordinate. Bradley later received command of II Corps for the final two months of the Tunisia (q.v.) campaign, completing the conquest of the Axis foothold in North Africa. Bradley largely left the conduct of operations to his subordinate division commanders, although he did take part in the debates over broader issues with the British Allies. This was the first occasion in which American officers served opposite British General Bernard L. Montgomery (q.v.), and it was during this time that both Bradley and Patton developed their dislike for the British commander's cautious command style and prickly personality.

During Operation HUSKY, the conquest of Sicily (q.v.), Bradley continued to command II Corps, under Patton's U.S. Seventh Army. Faced with a skillful German delaying action, Bradley's forces nonetheless captured the western two-thirds of the island and took Messina. During the operation, however, he dealt with a variety of internal problems, including the ever-increasing disputes with Montgomery over operations.

The most significant of Bradley's difficulties consisted of finding suitable higher-level commanders for the rapidly expanded U.S. Army. During the fight for Sicily, Bradley relieved Generals Terry de la Mesa Allen and Theodore Roosevelt, Jr. (qq.v.), largely because of their unwillingness to properly discipline the 1st Infantry Division. Bradley also had to contend with Patton's direct intervention in II Corps operations. When Patton got in trouble for slapping two U.S. soldiers suffering from combat fatigue, Bradley remained openly loyal to his boss. He would, however, tolerate Patton's theatrical outbursts to only a limited degree.

Bradley's reward for a more balanced command style was his selection to command U.S. ground forces in northwest Europe, a role that eventually made him Patton's commanding officer. Following the Sicilian campaign, Bradley was transferred to Britain in October 1943 to command the U.S. First Army. In that role Bradley began planning for Operation OVERLORD, the Normandy (q.v.) landings. All the Allied ground forces for that operation came under the overall command of Montgomery. Bradley was impressed with the ambitious plans laid out for the British units, but he was a bit skeptical of the possibility of their execution.

During the OVERLORD landings on 6 June 1944, Bradley had to face the prospect of failure on OMAHA Beach. The spirited action of several senior officers on the scene, however, firmly established American forces ashore and secured the beachhead in the face of stiff German opposition. Bradley later was critical of the performance of British units on the beaches east of OMAHA, describing the British and Canadian forces as having "sat down" and failing to take the initial objective city of Caen (q.v.).

General Omar N. Bradley and Marshal Ivan S. Konev at Torgau, 5 May 1945. (IWM EA 66097)

After Bradley moved his own headquarters ashore, the Allied ground forces were split into the 12th and 21st Army Groups, with Bradley commanding the former and Montgomery the latter. After Montgomery's forces repeatedly failed to take Caen, Bradley planned and executed Operation COBRA, the breakout at St. Lô (q.v.). In the subsequent Allied drive across France and Belgium, Bradley's 12th Army Group controlled four field armies—the First, Third, Ninth, and Fifteenth, with a total of 1,300,000 troops—the largest single field command ever held by an American officer.

As a consequence of the massive scope and importance of the northwest Europe campaign, Bradley had to contend with leadership difficulties, disagreements over operations with the British Allies, and logistical and manpower problems on an immense scale. When faced with overly cautious or inefficient division and corps commanders, Bradley relieved them without compunction. Yet Bradley remained adept at the intricacies of coalition war. During the German Ardennes offensive (q.v.), for example, Bradley readily accepted Eisenhower's decision to place U.S. forces north of the Bulge under Montgomery's command—although Bradley did not especially agree with that decision. Similarly, Bradley successfully mastered the complexities of supplying his army with material and manpower, despite the tremendous pressures of combat operations.

Bradley's service in World War II marks him as one of the most talented commanders in American military history. While he was not an aggressive commander, and was prone to deliberate planning, Bradley had the judgment to select and give

B

free hands to subordinates such as Patton, J. Lawton Collins, and John S. Wood (qq.v.) He relied on them to exploit successful breakthroughs. Bradley's understated manner masked an intelligent commander who understood his own strengths and weaknesses, and who employed the best human and material resources the U.S. Army had to give him.

Following World War II, Bradley headed the Veterans' Administration from 1945 to 1947, and was chief of staff of the U.S. Army from 1948 to 1949. From 1949 to 1953 he served as the first chairman of the Joint Chiefs of Staff. During that period he was responsible for the strategic direction of the Korean War. In 1950, Bradley was promoted to the rank of General of the Army, making him the last American officer to achieve five-star rank. Five-star generals and admirals receive lifetime tenure and never retire. When General Bradley died on 8 April 1981, he had amassed almost sixty-six years of service in the U.S. Army. Appropriately enough, he died while attending a meeting of the Association of the United States Army.

Randy Papadopoulos

Additional Reading

Bradley, Omar N., *A Soldier's Story* (1951).
Bradley, Omar N., and Clay Blair, *A General's Life* (1983).
Weigley, Russell F., *Eisenhower's Lieutenants: The Campaigns of France and Germany, 1944–1945* (1981).

Brandenberger, Erich (1894–1970)

German General. Erich Brandenberger was bespectacled, bald-headed, and full-jowled. He was meticulous in the handling of his forces, and he never panicked even under the most adverse of conditions. Before being brought to the Western Front, Brandenberger commanded the German XXIX *Korps*—part of Army Group South Ukraine—in the Balkans in August of 1944. Two of his divisions were Romanian, and they collapsed in the face of the late-August Soviet offensive. After the disastrous battle of the Falaise-Argentan Pocket (q.v.) in Normandy, the German Seventh Army commander, Heinz Eberbach, was captured at Amiens. In the first days of September Brandenberger was brought to the West to command and rebuild the shattered Seventh Army.

Brandenberger's Seventh Army was in the Ardennes-Eifel region along the German border, with responsibility for defenses opposite Luxembourg in the south (I *SS Panzer Korps*), along the Belgian border in the center (LXXIV *Korps*), and

astride the Aachen Gap in the north (LXXXI *Korps*). His greatest accomplishments were his rebuilding of the Seventh Army and defense of the Aachen-Hürtgen Forest-Roer Dams areas against the U.S. First Army. The fighting in that sector began in the second week of September 1944. By adroit employment of meager resources, Brandenberger consistently defeated American efforts in the Hürtgen Forest (q.v.). Thus the German Army in the West had a secure northern flank in the Eifel, while preparing for its December 1944 Ardennes offensive (q.v.).

Brandenberger is best known for having commanded one of the three German armies in the Ardennes offensive. Under an elaborate deception plan, the Seventh Army moved from the Eifel region to the southern Ardennes, opposite Luxembourg. His two corps (LXXX and LXXXV *Korps*), composed of mechanized and infantry forces, formed the southern wing of the German offensive. Its mission was to drive to the west as far as the Meuse River, establishing a cordon of infantry and artillery facing south and southwest, protecting the German Fifth *Panzer* Army left flank against any probable counterattack from the U.S. Third Army. It was to advance as far south as Luxembourg City if possible. Brandenberger's objectives were well beyond his means, as many of his troops were ill trained and he received a lower priority in equipment than the two German *Panzer* armies. Although in no place nearly reaching his objectives, nonetheless many of his divisions fought well. His 5th Parachute Division battled nobly against U.S. Third Army units attacking from the south to relieve Bastogne (q.v.). In the end, Seventh Army was slowly forced back.

Over the coming weeks Brandenberger's Seventh Army held tenaciously against U.S. First and Third Army attacks in the Ardennes and into Germany proper, exacting a heavy toll in casualties as the Americans drove for the Rhine River. Often faced with overwhelming odds, Brandenberger at times recommended withdrawing to more favorable defensive terrain. Relations between him and the Army Group Commander, Field Marshall Walther Model (q.v.), were strained. At Seventh Army headquarters on 20 February 1945, Model castigated Brandenberger and relieved him. Moments later, after Brandenberger departed, an American bomb hit the headquarters, killing and wounding several of the staff.

Within weeks Brandenberger was in command of the Nineteenth Army of Army Group G. The Nineteenth Army defended 100 miles of front against the French First Army in the area of the Black Forest. The Nineteenth Army had been badly weakened after the fighting in the Colmar Pocket (q.v.). Attacked relentlessly by the French, by the end of April the Nineteenth Army was in tatters. Brandenberger surrendered himself and his army at Innsbruck, Austria, on 5 May 1945.

Sam Doss

Additional Reading
Cole, Hugh M., *The Ardennes: Battle of the Bulge* (1965).
MacDonald, Charles B., *The Final Offensive* (1973).
————. *The Siegfried Line Campaign* (1963).

Brandt, Willy (1913–1992)

Member of the German opposition and future chancellor of West Germany. Brandt was born in Lübeck, the illegitimate son of Martha Frahm. His proletarian background led him into politics at an early age, and at seventeen, he joined the Social Democratic Party (SPD). In 1933, as a consequence of Nazi pressure on all opposition parties, he emigrated to Norway. For security reasons he gave up his real name, Herbert Ernst Karl Frahm, and assumed the name Willy Brandt. Together with friends he tried to organize a popular front against Adolf Hitler (q.v.), and in 1936, he worked illegally in Berlin. After the Nazis stripped him of his German citizenship in 1938, Brandt became a Norwegian citizen. He escaped the German invasion of Norway disguised as a Norwegian soldier.

After the war Brandt worked as a journalist for various Scandinavian newspapers. In 1947, he resumed his German citizenship and entered politics. From 1957 to 1966, he was mayor of West Berlin, and he acquired a great international reputation during the building of the Berlin Wall. In 1964, he became the chairman of the SPD, and he served as chancellor of the Federal Republic of Germany from 1969 to 1974. He was awarded the Nobel Peace Prize in 1971 for his *Ostpolitik*, a policy of reconciliation with the Soviet Union and Eastern Europe.

In 1974, Brandt was forced to resign as chancellor when one of his top aides was unmasked as an East German agent. He remained active in politics and the SPD. At the time of his death from cancer in 1992, he was president of the Socialist International.

Wolfgang Terhörst

Additional Reading
Binder, David, *The Other German: Willy Brandt's Life and Times* (1975).
Prittie, Terence, *Willy Brandt: Portrait of a Statesman* (1974).

Brauchitsch, Walther von (1881–1948)

German field marshal, commander in chief of the German Army. In 1933, von Brauchitsch was promoted from artillery inspector general to commander of the 1st Military District. In 1937, he became commander of the 4th Army Group. The following year, he replaced Werner von Fritsch (q.v.) as commander in chief of the German Army. An SS opponent, von Brauchitsch was not Adolf Hitler's (q.v.) first choice, although he was expected to be more agreeable than von Fritsch. Hitler hoped to appease the officer corps by appointing a respected professional rather than a political crony.

Von Brauchitsch refused to support active opposition to Hitler, stressing the military's neutrality in politics. He did, however, support Ludwig Beck's (q.v.) contention that Germany was not ready for war and should avoid conflict. Despite these misgivings, von Brauchitsch coordi-

Field Marshal Walther von Brauchitsch. (IWM MH 10684)

nated the campaigns in Poland, France, and later the Balkans. Promoted to field marshal in July 1940, he began the planning for Operation BARBAROSSA.

Awed by the initial successes of 1941 in Russia, Hitler refused the army's suggestions to consolidate gains and assume defensive positions for the winter. Thus von Brauchitsch, following his inclination to avoid conflict with the *Führer*, launched the November 1941 offensive. When it faltered in December, Hitler assumed personal command of the army, in addition to his supreme command of the overall *Wehrmacht*.

Von Brauchitsch retired on 19 December 1941 (at his own request), with a military record distinguished, in Liddell Hart's words, "by the most striking series of victories in modern history." His departure also "registered the final defeat of the soldier's claim to decide questions of strategy and military policy."

Sidney Dean

Additional Reading

Barnett, Correlli (ed.), *Hitler's Generals* (1989).
Görlitz, Walter, *History of the German General Staff* (1953).
Liddell Hart, B.H., *The German Generals Talk* (1948).
Mitcham, Samuel W., Jr., *Hitler's Field Marshals and Their Battles* (1988).

Braun, Eva (1910–1945)

Adolf Hitler's (q.v.) mistress. Born in 1910, Braun was the daughter of a Munich technical school teacher. After attending a local convent school, she went to work for photographer Heinrich Hoffmann as an assistant in his shop and studio in Munich. While working for Hoffmann, who became Hitler's official photographer, she first met Hitler in 1930. After the suicide of Hitler's niece, Geli Raubal, in 1931, she became Hitler's regular female companion. On 1 November 1932, she attempted suicide (unconvincingly), out of jealousy over other women seen in Hitler's company. After a second attempt, Hitler bought her a private apartment in the Munich suburbs where he could see her on a more private and regular basis.

In 1935, Braun joined Hitler at his Berghof retreat on the Obersalzburg, where after a clash of personalities she replaced Hitler's half-sister Angela as housekeeper. Normally out of the public eye, Braun visited Italy with Hitler, later returning without him in 1941. Finally, joining Hitler in Berlin in April 1945, she moved into a small suite in the *Reich* Chancellery bunker. She was married to Hitler on 28 April 1945 and committed suicide with him later that day. She took cyanide and her body was cremated with his.

Stephen L. Frost

Additional Reading

Fest, Joachim, *Hitler* (1973).
Gun, Nerin, *Eva Braun* (1969).
Picker, Henry, and Heinrich Hoffmann, *The Hitler Phenomena* (1974).

Braun, Wernher von (1912–1977)

German rocket pioneer. At the early age of seventeen, von Braun joined the staff of rocket pioneer Hermann Oberth, whose book on space flight thrilled the young man. In 1930, von Braun started his own studies at the Technical University of Berlin; and while still only twenty years old, he became a civil collaborator at the German Army arms office. By 1934, the talented physicist graduated to the problem of fluid-driven rockets. After Adolf Hitler (q.v.) took power in Germany, the army and air force started to show even more interest in von Braun's work. In 1937, he became technical director of the new army research institute at Peenemünde on the Baltic Sea. The institute was charged with the development of rocket weapons, a compromise he was willing to make because he saw no other chance to pursue rocket research.

On 3 October 1942, the "A-4" rocket achieved a range of 200 kilometers at a maximum altitude of ninety kilometers. This event signified a revolution in aviation. As the fortunes of war turned against Germany, the rocket project got increasingly higher priority in Hitler's strategy. Von Braun's "A-4" was renamed the "V-2" *(Vergeltungswaffe-2)* (Revenge Weapon). On 8 September 1944, the first "wonder weapons" hit London, but the rockets caused much less damage than Hitler had hoped.

In May 1945, von Braun and a group of his colleagues surrendered to U.S. forces and he was sent to the United States a few months later. In 1955, he became an American citizen. From 1960 on, he directed the Space Flight Center at Huntsville, Alabama. Under his guidance, the Saturn rockets were developed, and in 1969, the Apollo program was crowned by the landing on the moon. Until his death in 1977, von Braun, as deputy director of NASA, continued to communicate his enthusiasm for astronautics to people all over the world.

Wolfgang Terhörst

Additional Reading
Bar-Zohar, Michael, *The Hunt for German Scientists* (1967).
Braun, Wernher von, *I Reach for the Stars* (1958).

Brereton, Lewis H. (1890–1967)

American lieutenant general, commander of the Allied First Airborne Army. Brereton was one of the early pioneers of airpower. During World War I, he served as chief of aviation for the U.S. I Corps and was operations officer and later aide to General William L. "Billy" Mitchell (q.v.). A debonair type, Brereton loved to fly and was a staunch airpower advocate. Subpoenaed by General Douglas MacArthur, Brereton testified at the Mitchell court-martial. During the interwar period, Brereton commanded the 2nd Bomb Group, one of only three fully combat capable U.S. Army Air Corps units. In 1940–1941, he was commander of the Third Air Force. This unit was responsible for organizing, training, and employing air units in the North Carolina and Louisiana maneuvers that reshaped U.S. tactical doctrine on the eve of World War II.

A close friend of General Henry H. "Hap" Arnold (q.v.), Brereton was chosen to be General MacArthur's air chief in the Philippines, where he organized and trained B-17 and P-40 units prior to the war. After the fall of the Philippines, he was transferred to India to command the U.S. Middle East Air Force, and then to North Africa to command the U.S. Ninth Air Force. His B-17 and B-24 units conducted raids on the oil field at Ploeşti (q.v.), Romania, in 1943. In the spring of 1943, he moved the Ninth Air Force to Britain to prepare the air support for the Normandy invasion (q.v.).

Brereton insisted that his units be well prepared. He went to great efforts to assure an aircraft with the pilot's name, sufficient quarters, and other necessities were waiting for each new arrival. Working closely with General Elwood Quesada (q.v.), Brereton created a training school to assure that all pilots could fly all required missions and that they were exposed to the combat experiences gained by U.S. aircrews in Italy. His crossflow program resulted in minimum casualties for Ninth Air Force crews after the BIG WEEK (q.v.) raids and throughout the Normandy invasion.

In August 1944, Brereton became the commander of the Allied First Airborne Army. All British, Canadian, and American airborne forces fell under his command. In that position, he was responsible for Operation MARKET, the airborne assault portion of MARKET-GARDEN.

Following the war, Brereton served in several command and staff positions, including membership on the Atomic Energy Commission's Military Liaison Committee. A firm believer in interservice, inter-Allied cooperation, he employed an open leadership style and proved an able commander of diverse units.

Michael L. Wolfert

Additional Reading
Gavin, James M., *Airborne Warfare* (1947).
MacDonald, Charles B., *Airborne* (1970).

Brooke, Alan F. (Lord Alanbrooke) (1883–1963)

British field marshal, chief of the Imperial General Staff. Sir Alan F. Brooke was to many the greatest British soldier of this century. He was born and educated in France and was naturalized a British citizen before he could join the army. For the rest of his life, he remained fluent in French, his native tongue. Commissioned into the Royal Artillery in 1902, he spent the next eleven years at regimental duty, mainly in India. A lieutenant commanding an artillery ammunition column at the start of World War I, he was a lieutenant colonel and chief artillery staff officer in the British First Army at the end.

Between the wars, Brooke established himself as one of the coming men in the British Army, widening his military knowledge and expertise far beyond artillery matters. He filled, in turn, the appointments of infantry brigade commander, inspector of artillery, director of military training, and commander of Britain's first armored division. He was a lieutenant general in 1938 with command of the I Anti-Aircraft Corps. When the war started in 1939, he went to France commanding II Corps in the British Expeditionary Force (BEF). One of his divisions, the 3rd, was commanded by Major General Bernard L. Montgomery (q.v.).

The period between September 1939 and June 1940 was Brooke's only experience of commanding a large formation in battle, and it is on that short time that his reputation as a fighting general rests. When the *Blitzkrieg* assault came in May 1940, Brooke, with the four divisions of his corps, steadily withdrew, never allowing a German breakthrough on his front, and then covered the exposed flank opened by the Belgian surrender. By brilliant generalship, he held the German advance long enough to get the BEF into its defended pe-

Field Marshal Sir Alan Brooke (later Viscount Alanbrooke) and Air Vice Marshal Sir Keith Park (right), in Malta. (IWM CH 92345)

rimeter around Dunkirk (q.v.). Prime Minister Winston S. Churchill (q.v.) said at the time "General Brooke and his corps fought a magnificent battle."

Evacuated from Dunkirk, Brooke was immediately sent back to France as commander in chief of the 160,000 British troops still with the French armies in Normandy. Churchill's intention was to reconstitute the BEF by reinforcing Brooke with the troops saved at Dunkirk while the French established a redoubt in Brittany, or failing that, North Africa. Quickly assessing the situation, Brooke had the moral courage to tell the prime minister (whom he had never met) that the French were on the point of collapse and all British troops must be evacuated. Churchill reluctantly agreed. On 17 June 1940, without informing Brooke, and while the British evacuation was only half complete, France capitulated. His biographer states: "Brooke's prescience, decision, and moral courage had made possible the evacuation."

During eighteen months as commander in chief of the home armies, Brooke prepared to repel the German invasion of Britain. When none came, he set to training, hardening, and reequiping formations, a period in which he revitalized the Home Forces from top to bottom. In December 1941, Churchill appointed him head of the British Army, and three months later, chief of the Imperial General Staff. Brooke and his U.S. opposite number, General George C. Marshall (q.v.), were responsible, through President Franklin D. Roosevelt (q.v.) and Churchill, for the global strategy ensuring the defeat of the Axis powers.

The period when Brooke came to the supreme direction of the war was the nadir of Allied fortunes. The British, driven out of Europe and just hanging on in the Middle East, lost the East Indies, Malaya, and Burma, and seemed on the point of losing India. In the Atlantic the U-boat reigned. The Pearl Harbor attack decimated U.S. naval power, and Japan occupied American Pacific bases. In those dark days, Brooke evolved a strategy that he was to adhere to throughout the rest of the war; a strategy that, despite misgivings and disagreements by his colleagues, allies, and political masters, he doggedly fought for.

Brooke's perception was that the overriding strategic factor was shipping. Enough shipping was required to transport sufficient troops and equipment to Britain to allow an assault on mainland Europe, while continuing the logistic support of forces engaged worldwide. He believed the Mediterranean was the key. By clearing that sea of the enemy, a million tons of shipping would be saved by avoiding the Cape of Good Hope route. Possession of the African shores would also protect Soviet oil in the Caucasus and Western oil in Iran and Persia, keep Turkey inviolate, and prevent a junction of Axis forces if Japan continued its advance through Asia and Germany struck south from Russia. When the Middle East was secure, then sufficient strength could be built up in Britain to allow a cross-channel assault, probably by 1944.

Despite American suspicions of this strategy (as being too cautious and designed to save the British Empire) and the American desire to fight on mainland Europe in 1943, Brooke's strategy prevailed. In the event, the massive cross-channel assault in June 1944 was successful, but only after prolonged and bitter fighting. Whether it would have succeeded a year earlier, given the resources used to assault Italy, is debatable. Brooke, by force of argument, brought the Combined Chiefs of Staff (q.v.), Roosevelt, and Churchill to his strategy. It could therefore be said that he, more than any other man, had the strategic vision, balanced by realism, to ensure the defeat of Germany.

These were his achievements. What sort of man was this military paragon? Short, sallow, round-shouldered, bespectacled, he spoke with a nasal, rapid-fire delivery as though his tongue could not keep up with his brain. Despite his uninspiring appearance, the army of which he was head went in awe of him, as did his colleagues, to whom he appeared an iron man with strength, clarity of expression, and incisiveness.

Brooke trusted his field commanders and never interfered with them. The greatest of them, Montgomery, wrote to Brooke after the war, "I could never have achieved anything if you had not been there to help me." One of Montgomery's senior staff officers said years later, "the one person he (Montgomery) was really afraid of and held in enormous respect was Brooke."

Brooke was a remote, austere man who very carefully separated his military and private lives. In the latter, he displayed facets of character very different from his public image: a great lover of animal life, a distinguished ornithologist, and a devoted husband and parent.

Bryant's great works based on Brooke's diaries, while extolling Brooke's contribution to the war and putting his relationship with Churchill into correct perspective, portrayed a man who never made a mistake. Brooke had his faults (excessive caution at times, occasional misjudgments of men, and an intolerance of those whose brains did not work at the same lightning speed as his) and these must have led him into error, albeit rarely. Nonetheless, Brooke stood head and shoulders above all other British military officers in World War II, and was the ideal counterweight to the incomparable Churchill, keeping him tethered to what was realistic and practical. Churchill's wartime powers made him virtual dictator of Great Britain and yet, such was the measure of Brooke that never once did Churchill go against the advice of his chiefs of staff, expressed by Brooke as their spokesman. After the war he was raised to the peerage as 1st Viscount Alanbrooke.

B.K. Warner

Additional Reading
Bryant, Arthur, *Triumph in the West* (1959).
Fraser, David, *Alanbrooke* (1982).
Guingand, Francis de, *Generals at War* (1964).

Brown, George S. (1918–1978)

U.S. Air Force colonel, bomber pilot. Brown graduated from West Point in 1941. He was a 93rd Bombardment Group section leader in the Ninth Air Force's 1 August 1943 raid on the Ploeşti (q.v.) oil refineries. By age twenty-six, and after a total of only three years and four months of military service, Brown was a colonel. His meteoric rise in rank reflected his abilities, but it also illustrated the murderous attrition rate initially suffered by American bomber crews in the European theater. His participation in the Ploesti raid is a case in point. He began as deputy lead of the thirty-nine-aircraft contingent from the 93rd Bombardment Group, but he assumed command when air defenses shot down the lead aircraft. His courage and leadership earned him the Distinguished Service

Cross and anticipated the qualities he later showed as chief of staff of the United States Air Force from 1973 to 1974, and chairman of the Joint Chiefs of Staff from 1974 to 1978.

Peter R. Faber

Additional Reading
Puryear, Edgar F., *George S. Brown, General, U.S. Air Force: Destined for Stars* (1983).
Webb, Willard J., and Ronald Cole, *The Chairmen of the Joint Chiefs of Staff* (1989).

Browning, Frederick (1896–1965)

British lieutenant general, commander of the British I Airborne Corps. Sir Frederick Browning can claim to be the founder of Britain's airborne forces, for he commanded in succession the first airborne division to be raised, and then the only British airborne corps from D-Day to V-E Day. He was born in London in 1896, and after Eton and Sandhurst, joined the Grenadier Guards in France in 1915. His experiences in the trenches of World War I were typical of his generation. Because of heavy casualties, he was a company commander before his twenty-first birthday (hence the nickname "Boy," which stuck with him for the rest of his life). By 1918, he was

Lieutenant General Sir Frederick Browning, DSO, and Major General James Gavin. (IWM EA 44529)

awarded a Distinguished Service Order (DSO) and a French *Croix de Guerre.*

His interwar years were uneventful, the highlight being a spell as adjutant of Sandhurst. In 1932, he married the novelist, Daphne du Maurier. By 1940, he was commanding a brigade in Britain, but at the end of the year, he was ordered to form the 1st Airborne Division from scratch. Despite his age (forty-four), he took easily to parachuting. From the start, he insisted on the highest possible standards of fitness, determination, and professional skills for all members of the new force. In all these respects, he personally set the example. But equally, as a guards officer, he insisted that success in battle demanded discipline and smartness when units were out of the line.

Elements of his division fought in Algeria and Sicily (q.v.), but Browning did not go with them. Instead, in January 1944, he was promoted to lieutenant general and given command of the British I Airborne Corps. He led that unit in airborne operations in Normandy, Arnhem (qq.v.), the crossing of the Rhine, and finally in the advance to the Baltic. During the last months of the war, as the *Wehrmacht* was crumbling, his airborne divisions relied more on physical fitness than gasoline-guzzling vehicles, and advanced at a faster rate than any others on the Allied side. Incidentally, his verdict on Operation MARKET-GARDEN—"a bridge too far"—was chosen as the title of Cornelius Ryan's 1974 book and the subsequent film.

V-E day did not end the war for Browning. Despite the lack of formal staff training, he was sent to the Far East to act as Lord Louis Mountbatten's (q.v.) chief of staff. With his unconventional approach and flexible mind, he successfully dealt with the three services of the many different nations under Mountbatten's command in the chaotic conditions that arose in the aftermath of Japan's surrender.

Retiring from the army in 1948, Browning served the Royal Family as comptroller of Princess (later Queen) Elizabeth's household. He died in 1965, but he lived to see the new airborne forces he had raised and led in battle become a permanent part of the British order of battle. Like the commandos (q.v.), the airborne forces added a touch of aggressiveness and initiative to the traditional endurance and dogged courage of the British Army.

Philip Green

Additional Reading
Gregory, Barry, *British Airborne Troops* (1974).

Norton, Geoffrey G., *The Red Devils: The Story of the British Airborne Forces* (1971).
Saunders, Hilary St.G., *The Red Beret* (1949).

Brüning, Heinrich (1885–1970)

German chancellor, 1930–1932. Born to the family of a Münster industrialist, Brüning received his doctorate from the University of Bonn in 1915. He served in the German Army during World War I, and became active in the League of German Trade Unions in 1920. Elected to the *Reichstag* in 1924 as a member of the conservative Catholic Center Party, he eventually became party chairman in 1929.

President Paul von Hindenburg (q.v.) appointed Brüning chancellor on 28 March 1930, and his government instituted a number of widely unpopular austerity measures to address the economic crises facing the Weimar Republic (q.v.). Lack of any broad-based support compelled von Hindenburg to dissolve the *Reichstag* in July 1930 and rule by decree. The Brüning government was also weakened by the rise of Nazi strength in subsequent elections. Despite his government's foreign policy successes, which included lower reparation payments, right-wing and other anti-democratic elements pressured Hindenburg to appoint Franz von Papen (q.v.) chancellor in May 1932.

Brüning resigned from his party and the *Reichstag* and moved to Switzerland in the summer of 1934. He emigrated to the United States and taught political science at Harvard University from 1937 to 1952. He died in Vermont in 1970.

Steven B. Rogers

Additional Reading
Jarman, Thomas L., *The Rise and Fall of Nazi Germany* (1955).
Mau, Hermann, and Helmut Krausnick, *German History 1933–1945* (1959).

Budenny, Seymon Mikhailovich (1883–1973)

Marshal of the Soviet Union, Soviet deputy commissar of defense. Budenny was born in Voronezh province, the son of a peasant sharecropper. Mustered into the Imperial Russian Army at age twenty, he saw service in the Russo-Japanese War. In 1907, he was transferred from his assignment with a dragoon regiment to become a student at the St. Petersburg Riding School of the Imperial Cavalry. He began World War I as a sergeant major with an elite imperial dragoon regiment, fight-

Marshal Seymon Budenny (left), presenting the Stalingrad Sword to the Mayor of Stalingrad at a Kremlin ceremony, February 1944. (IWM HU 53121)

ing the Turks on the Caucasian front. He won four St. George Crosses, the highest imperial decoration for combat valor. He won four other medals for heroism as well.

In late 1917, Budenny embraced the Bolshevik cause in the Don River basin and at Tsaritsyn (later renamed Stalingrad, now called Volgograd) with his tattered, free-booting cavalry force. At Tsaritsyn in summer 1918, Budenny connected with the military clique then forming under the front's new political commissar, Josef Stalin (q.v.). Later known as the "Tsaritsyn Group," Stalin's coterie was fueled by a shared malevolence toward Leon Trotsky (q.v.), the Bolshevik war commissar. They conducted a war that was openly insubordinate to Trotsky's titular authority in Moscow.

From 1918 to 1920, Budenny's horsemen swept through southern Russia and the Ukraine, contributing to the rout of White Russian forces in the civil war. Transferred to the Russo-Polish War (q.v.) in May 1920, Stalin and his military henchmen, including Budenny, disobeyed orders to provide critical flank support for Mikhail Tukhachevsky's (q.v.) assault on Warsaw. As a result, both wings of the Red Army were mauled by furious Polish counterattacks in August 1920. This debacle sealed a mortal enmity between the Tsaritsyn Group and Tukhachevsky.

In 1935, Budenny was one of the first five officers promoted to the rank of marshal. As commander of the Moscow Military District in 1937, he was a member of the military tribunal that had

Tukhachevsky shot on rigged charges of treason. Budenny consequently rose to deputy commissar of defense in 1939. Of the original five marshals, only Budenny survived Stalin's purges (q.v.).

With the Nazi onslaught in June 1941, Budenny joined the *Stavka* (q.v.), and commanded the southwestern theater in the Ukraine. His armies were quickly smashed and overrun. In the wake of the giant encirclement battles at Uman and Kiev (q.v.) which shredded his command during August–September 1941, he was relieved and banished to a training assignment on the reserve front. He resurfaced in early 1942, as commander of the North Caucasus Front in the months prior to the battle of Stalingrad (q.v.). In January 1943, he was made commander of the cavalry of the Soviet Army.

Stephen Donahue

Additional Reading

Bialer, Seweryn (ed.), *Stalin and His Generals* (1984).
Erikson, John, *The Soviet High Command: A Military-Political History 1918–1941* (1962).
Shukman, Harold (ed.), *Stalin's Generals* (1993).

Bull, Harold Roe (1893–1976)

American major general, deputy chief of staff for operations, SHAEF (q.v.). "Pinky" Bull was born on 6 January 1893 in Massachusetts. He graduated from West Point in 1914 and served as an instructor of logistics at the Fort Benning Infantry School in 1926, under George C. Marshall (q.v.). In 1941, Brigadier General Bull became chief of operations (G-3) at the War Department. In 1943, Marshall sent Bull as a special observer to North Africa. Between June and September 1943, Bull commanded U.S. III Corps.

Bull's next assignment was in London as the deputy G-3 to the chief of staff of the supreme Allied commander. There he became one of the principal planners of Operation OVERLORD. During that period, he persuaded the War Department to take all measures to ease the ammunition shortage in the European theater. In February 1944, Bull became General Dwight D. Eisenhower's (q.v.) chief of operations at HQ, SHAEF, and was promoted to major general. Bull found it increasingly necessary to make quick visits to U.S. battlefield commanders. Often his visits concerned trying to pry loose men and equipment for an upcoming operation.

The bespectacled, balding Bull could be equally difficult to work with and for. He was totally committed to an existing plan. He found it very difficult to accommodate deviations to the plan in order to exploit unexpected battlefield opportunities, such as at the Remagen (q.v.) bridgehead. He was a member of the group of Allied officers to whom General Alfred Jodl (q.v.) surrendered in Reims, France, on 7 May 1945. Bull died in Washington, D.C., on 1 November 1976.

Marjorie D. Kemp

Additional Reading
Eisenhower, Dwight D., *Crusade in Europe* (1948).
Pogue, Forrest C., *The Supreme Command* (1954).

Burns, Eedson L.M. (1897–1985)
Canadian lieutenant general, commander of the Canadian I Corps. Following exemplary service in World War I with the Royal Canadian Engineers, Burns became well-known during the interwar period as a prolific writer on matters of military technology, with emphasis on armored warfare. After commanding the Canadian 4th Armored Brigade and later the Canadian 5th Armored Division in Britain, he quickly rose to command all Canadian troops in Italy by March 1944. Some of the most arduous assignments and greatest successes in the campaign fell to the Canadian I Corps, including the breakthrough in the Liri

Valley and the attack on the Gothic Line (q.v.) that autumn. Outspoken and opinionated, Burns's relations with British Eighth Army headquarters became strained and he relinquished corps command in October 1944. Though not always considered a fully effective operational commander, the war record of Burns's Canadian I Corps in Italy was among the Allies' best of that campaign. In 1956, he commanded the Canadian-led United Nations Emergency Force in the Middle East, and he later vigorously campaigned for an end to the nuclear arms race.

Serge M. Durflinger

Additional Reading
Burns, E.L.M., *General Mud: Memoirs of Two World Wars* (1970).
Nicholson, G.W.L., *The Canadians in Italy, 1943–1945* (1956).

Busch, Ernst (1885–1945)
German field marshal, commander of Army Group Center. Born in Essen-Steele on the Ruhr on 6 July 1885, Busch was an outright Nazi who enjoyed sitting in on the Nazi's "People's Court" and never disobeyed or questioned an order from

Field Marshal Ernst Busch. (IWM MH 6031)

the *Führer*. It was this "loyalty" that ensured his advancement, despite his shortcomings as a leader. He is best remembered as the commander of Army Group Center, whose rigid obedience of Adolf Hitler's (q.v.) stand-fast order led to the destruction of his command during the Soviet summer offensive of 1944. He finished the war as commander of German Forces in Denmark and Schleswig-Holstein. He died in captivity on 17 July 1945.

Carl O. Schuster

Additional Reading
Humble, Richard, *Hitler's Generals* (1974).
Mitcham, Samuel W., Jr, *Hitler's Field Marshals and Their Battles* (1988).

Bush, Vannevar (1890–1974)

Director of the U.S. Office of Scientific Research and Development. Although better known as a pioneer in computational and calculating devices, Bush was the overseer of virtually all scientific research in the United States during World War II. The scope of his responsibility included the MANHATTAN Project (q.v.), the single largest scientific research and industrial development project undertaken to that time. He also advised the government on scientific research and development, and helped convince Albert Einstein (q.v.) to sign a letter to President Franklin D. Roosevelt (q.v.) on the potential status of German nuclear physics activities.

John D. Beatty

Additional Reading
Baxter, James P., *Scientists Against Time* (1946).

Byrnes, James F. (1879–1972)

U.S. secretary of state. Few secretaries of state have assumed that office facing the sort of difficulties Byrnes faced on 2 July 1945. First, he had to deal with the high expectations generated by the recently concluded San Francisco conference of the fledgling United Nations (q.v.) organization. Second, he had to confront rising Soviet-American tensions. Last, he was secretary to Harry S Truman (q.v.), a man Byrnes believed did not deserve to be president.

Given these challenges, Byrnes's career proved moderately successful. He helped formulate a moderate foreign policy that steered a course between the new isolationism of congressional Republicans and the naive internationalism of liberal Democrats like Joseph Davies. On the negative side, his lingering presidential aspirations caused him to crave the public limelight at the expense of his diplomatic obligations.

Byrnes's most important wartime achievement was his attendance at the Potsdam Conference in 1945 (*see* Conferences, Allied). Like most American diplomats, he was vexed by Soviet stubbornness and paranoia. Nevertheless, he returned to America convinced that his moderate approach could soon yield dividends for U.S.-Soviet relations.

Byrnes only served as secretary for 562 days, making any evaluation of his performance difficult. His strategy was sound, his tactics were inconsistent, and his temperament ill-suited for such a highly sensitive task. His actions had little bearing on the outcome of the war, but the war played a role in shaping his diplomatic perspective.

Michael Polley

Additional Reading
Byrnes, James F., *Speaking Frankly* (1947).
Feis, Hubert, *Between War and Peace: The Potsdam Conference* (1960).

C

Cameron, Donald (1916–1961)

Royal Navy lieutenant. Cameron, born in Carluke, Scotland, on 18 March 1916, served as a Royal Naval Reserve officer during the war. On 22 September 1943, he commanded the midget submarine *X-6* on a raid against the German battleship *Tirpitz,* anchored at Alten Fjord (q.v.), in northern Norway. The *X-6* along with the *X-7* traveled more than 1,000 miles from their base, negotiated a minefield, dodged nets, gun defenses, and German listening posts to place their charges under the target. The mines went off an hour later, seriously damaging the *Tirpitz,* taking her out of action for several months. Cameron was captured by the Germans. He and the other submarine commander, Basil Place (q.v.), received the Victoria Cross. Cameron transferred to the Royal Navy after the war.

Carl O. Schuster

Additional Reading

Kennedy, Ludovic, *Floating Fortress* (1979).
MacIntyre, D., *The Naval War Against Hitler* (1971).
Piekalkiewicz, Janusz, *The Sea War; 1939–1945* (1980).

Campbell, John Charles (1894–1942)

British brigadier. One of the most dashing British leaders of the war in the desert, "Jock" Campbell was born in Thurso, Scotland, on 10 January 1894. He originally was commissioned in the Royal Horse Artillery. In the early stages of the campaign in North Africa, the British were numerically painfully weak. Under Campbell's command they developed a tactic of attacking in brigade-sized or smaller groups of tanks and infantry in trucks, supported by towed field guns. These so-called "Jock Columns" were highly mobile and ideally suited to hit-and-run warfare. On 21 November 1941, at Sidi Rezegh (q.v.), Campbell won the Victoria Cross while in command of the 7th Armoured Division. He was killed in action on 26 February 1942.

David T. Zabecki

Additional Reading

Bidwell, Shelford, and Dominick Graham, *Fire-Power: British Army Weapons and Theories of War 1904–1945* (1982).

Canaris, Wilhelm (1887–1945)

German admiral, director of the *Abwehr.* The son of a mine manager, Canaris joined the Imperial German Navy in 1905 and was commissioned three years later. After his ship, the cruiser *Dresden,* was scuttled in Chilean waters during World War I, he escaped from internment and made his way back to Germany. From November 1915 until October 1916, he was posted to Spain on an intelligence mission. In April 1918, he became a U-boat commander.

During the 1920s and early 1930s, Canaris held a number of executive and staff positions; he also gained further experience in intelligence work. Late in 1934, he was chosen to succeed Captain Konrad Patzig as head of the *Abwehr* (q.v.), the military intelligence and counterintelligence branches of the *Reichswehr.* Until his dismissal in February 1944, he directed and expanded the *Abwehr* for the benefit of the German armed forces. At the same time, however, he also protected a number of anti-Nazis on his staff and repeatedly helped victims of Nazi terror. He was promoted to the rank of full admiral in January 1940.

Following the attempt on Adolf Hitler's life in July 1944, Canaris was arrested and eventually transferred to the Flossenburg concentration camp in southern Germany. Along with his former chief associate, Major General Hans Oster (a dedicated and highly active anti-Nazi), Canaris was hanged by the SS on 9 April 1945. His role in the Third *Reich,* both before and during World War II, is still the subject of considerable scholarly controversy.

Ulrich Trumpener

Additional Reading
Abshagen, K.H., *Canaris* (1956).
Höhne, Heinz, *Canaris: Hitler's Master Spy* (1976).
Kahn, David, *Hitler's Spies: German Military Intelligence in World War II* (1978).

Carol II (1893–1953)

King of Romania. In the interwar years, Carol II was in exile in southern France with his lover, a divorcee. The affair created political turmoil because Carol's wife, Helen, princess of Greece, was well liked. When Carol's father, Ferdinand, died in 1927, Carol's five-year-old son, Michael, gained the throne and ruled under a regency. In June 1930, Carol returned secretly, disbanded the regency, and resumed the throne. The Romanians considered him dictatorial and anti-democratic.

Carol thwarted Nazi attempts to force a Romanian alliance and stifled opposition from Corneliu Codreanu, a Fascist leader later imprisoned. Proclaiming neutrality, Carol attempted to improve relations with Romania's neighbors as well as Britain and France. Unfortunately, the Allies were uninterested.

Carol visited Adolf Hitler (q.v.), who demanded an alliance between Germany and Romania as well as the release of Codreanu. He was prepared to oppose Hitler, but he desperately sought Western allies. Britain and France offered rhetorical guarantees against aggression and minimal credit for defense. He ordered the construction of fortifications on the borders.

The Soviet Union demanded portions of Bessarabia and Bukovina, which Carol, fearing retaliation, surrendered while also attempting to appease Germany. In 1940, he abdicated the throne in favor of his son, but Michael (q.v.) was soon dominated by dictator General Ion Antonescu (q.v.) who brought Romania into the war against the Soviet Union. In August 1944, Michael regained control, and severed ties with Germany.

Carol, meanwhile, fled to Portugal, where his great-grandparents had been the reigning monarchs. He later settled in Mexico where he devised a Free Romania movement and unsuccessfully sought aid from various allies. In 1944, he wrote *Orbit of Satan,* analyzing the history of Europe since the end of World War I and stressing the evils of Nazism and Stalinism. He died in Portugal on 3 April 1953 of a heart attack.

Elizabeth D. Schafer

Additional Reading
Popescy-Putrie, I., *La Roumanie pendant la Deuxième Guerre Mondiale* (1964).
Hillgruber, A., *Hitler, König Carol und Marschal Antonescu* (1954).
Lungu, Dov B., *Romania and the Great Powers, 1933–1940* (1989).

Carré, Mathilde Lily (1908–1971)

Abwehr (q.v.) double agent from France. Carré, known to the resistance and SOE (q.v.) by her code name "La Chatte" (The Cat), was responsible for the betrayal of occupied France's 120–member INTERALLIE intelligence network to the *Abwehr.* Later, as the mistress of *Abwehr* Sergeant Hugo Bleicher (q.v.), she collaborated with German intelligence in a deception operation, passing false information to the SOE. Convicted of treason at war's end, she was sentenced to life in prison, only to be released in 1954. She promptly disappeared from public view, surfacing to write her memoirs in an attempt to justify her actions. Her book was published in French in 1959 and in English in 1960.

Mark Rummage

Additional Reading
Howarth, Patrick, *Undercover: The Men and Women of Special Operations Executive* (1980).
Young, Gordon, *The Cat with Two Faces* (1957).

Carton de Wiart, Adrian (1880–1963)

British lieutenant general. Sir Adrian Carton de Wiart was born on 5 May 1880 in Brussels, Belgium, and educated in Britain. He perhaps is most famous for his suicidal leadership style and for being wounded in nearly every campaign in which he participated—beginning with the Boer War in 1899. His most serious injuries occurred in November 1914, where he lost an eye in Somaliland in action against the Dervishes, and in May 1915 at Ypres, Belgium, where he lost a hand. Reckless though he was, he earned the Victoria Cross in 1916, was promoted to brigadier general in 1917, commanded three brigades, and caught the attention of Winston S. Churchill (q.v.).

After World War I, Carton de Wiart was assigned to the British Military Mission to Poland. He left the army in 1924 and remained in Poland. In the days immediately prior to the outbreak of World War II, he was recalled to the active army list and made head of the British Military Mission in Poland.

When Germany invaded Poland in September 1939, Carton de Wiart offered to fight on the side of the Poles. His differences with Polish commander in chief Marshal Edward Śmigły-Rydz (q.v.), however, convinced him to return to Britain. The impact of the German *Luftwaffe* on Polish morale also made a deep impression on Carton de Wiart.

In April 1940, Carton de Wiart commanded the Central Norwegian Expeditionary Force for Operation MAURICE. His mission was to secure the Trondheim area. With German naval and air barrages continuously hammering British positions, the normally aggressive Carton de Wiart called for an evacuation in late April, which the Royal Navy executed on 2 May.

In April 1941, he was appointed head of the British Military Mission in Yugoslavia. He subsequently was shot down over the Mediterranean, captured by the Italians, and held as a POW for more than two years. In March 1943, the sixty-three-year-old Carton di Wiart and Lieutenant General Richard O'Connor (q.v.) escaped through a tunnel. They remained at large for eight days before being recaptured. Finally, in August 1943, Carton de Wiart was released as a goodwill gesture by Italy in hopes of laying the groundwork for an armistice.

In October 1943, Carton de Wiart was appointed as Churchill's representative to China's Chiang Kai-shek, acting as liaison between Chiang and Lord Louis Mountbatten (q.v.). Carton de Wiart retired in 1946 and published his memoirs in 1950. He died in County Cork, Ireland, on 5 June 1963.

William H. Van Husen

Additional Reading

Carton de Wiart, Adrian, *Happy Odyssey* (1950).
Derry, T.K., *The Campaign in Norway* (1952).
Lord Ismay, *The Memoirs of Lord Ismay* (1960).
Zaloga, S., and V. Madej, *The Polish Campaign 1939* (1985).

Čatloš, Ferdinand (1896–1972)

Slovakian general, commander in chief of the Slovak Army. From 1939 to 1944, Čatloš was commander in chief and minister of war of Slovakia, an "independent country under German auspices." The Slovak Army participated in the 1939 invasion of Poland, and the 1941 invasion of the Soviet Union. The Slovak Army, staffed by many officers who supported Eduard Beneš (q.v.), was the organizational center of the 1944 Slovak Rising, during which Čatloš disarmed the German garrison in Bratislava.

Andrzej Suchcitz

Additional Reading

Grant-Duff, Sheila, *German Protectorate: The Czechs Under Nazi Rule* (1942).
Korbel, Josef, *The Communist Subversion of Czechoslovakia* (1959).
Mastny, Vojtech, *The Czechs Under Nazi Rule* (1971).

Cavallero, Ugo (1880–1943)

Italian marshal, chief of the Italian Supreme General Staff, 1940–1943. Cavallero served with distinction in World War I and was promoted to brigadier general. He was undersecretary of war from 1925 until he fell out with Pietro Badoglio (q.v.) in 1928. Badoglio would not allow him to participate in the Ethiopia campaign (q.v.), but Cavallero subsequently commanded Italy's forces in East Africa from November 1937 until May 1939, when he was dismissed by his superior, Amadeo di Savoia (q.v.) the duke of Aosta.

On 6 December 1940, Cavallero succeeded Badoglio as chief of the supreme general staff, and he assumed command in Albania, where he prevented complete defeat. His direction of Italy's military was hampered by Benito Mussolini's (q.v.) interference. Cavallero also recognized Italy's ultimate military success was tied to Germany, and therefore, he acquiesced to the strategic demands of the Germans. The ten divisions and additional artillery he sent to Russia deprived Italy's forces in North Africa of essential reinforcements.

On 31 January 1943, as the North African front was collapsing, Cavallero was dismissed by Mussolini. After the fall of Mussolini, Badoglio ordered his arrest. Released by the Germans, Cavallero refused their demand that he lead Italian forces against the Allies. On 14 September 1943, he was found shot, either by his own hand or by the Germans.

Bernard A. Cook

Additional Reading

Cavallero, Ugo, *Comando Supremo, Diario 1940–1943 del Capo di S.M.G.* (1948).

Ceva, Lucio, *La Condotta Italiana della Guerra: Cavallero e il Comando Supremo 1941–1942* (1975).

Chaffee, Adna R. (1884–1941)

American major general. Chaffee was born in Junction City, Kansas, on 23 September 1884, and graduated from West Point in 1906. Although a cavalryman and a horseman, he was an early admirer of the tank and its potentials. He spent years trying to sell the concept of a separate armored force to the leadership of the U.S. Army.

In 1934, Chaffee led an armored force in maneuvers at Fort Riley, Kansas. The few tanks the army had in those days normally were assigned to infantry units; but during the maneuvers Chaffee mustered a purely armored force, which confounded and surpassed infantry and mounted cavalry. Chaffee's results, however, still did not convince army leaders, who were fighting for every defense dollar in a Depression-strapped federal budget.

It wasn't until the German invasion of Poland in September 1939 that the U.S. Army awakened to the potential of an armored division. The subsequent German invasion of Western Europe in early 1940, combined with the successful *Blitzkrieg*-style tactics employed by U.S. forces in maneuvers in 1940, finally convinced the army of the necessity of having an armored force. The 1940 maneuvers involved mechanized troops from the 7th Cavalry Brigade, and the Provisional Tank Brigade, all led by Chaffee.

The Armored Force was formed on 10 July 1940 and Chaffee was appointed its commander. Initially, it was composed of the 7th Cavalry Brigade (Mechanized), the 6th Infantry (Armored), and the Provisional Tank Brigade at Fort Benning. The following month Chaffee organized the I Armored Corps, consisting of the 1st Armored Division (7th Cavalry renamed) at Fort Knox and the 2nd Armored Division (Provisional Tank Brigade renamed). The Armored Force of 1940 numbered only 464 tanks, a minute force should the U.S. find itself in a confrontation with Germany. One division required more than 1,000 combat-type vehicles, and equipment shortfalls would not ease until 1943.

Chaffee never had a chance to see his Armored Force built to its potential. He succumbed to illness on 22 August 1941. He was succeeded by Major General Jacob Devers (q.v.) as the Armored Force commander. Chaffee has been called the "Father of the Armored Force." Like his contemporaries, Heinz Guderian of Germany, Charles de Gaulle of France, and Percy Hobart of Britain (qq.v.), he had a profound influence on the evolution of the mobile tactics of World War II.

William H. Van Husen

Additional Reading

Kelly, Orr, *King of the Killing Zone* (1989).

Stubbs, Mary Lee, Stanley Russell Connor, and Janice E. McKenney, *Army Lineage Series: Armor-Cavalry, Part II* (1972).

Chamberlain, Houston Stewart (1855–1927)

Racial ideologue. Although born a British subject, Chamberlain later became a German citizen. The leading proponent of the supremacy of the "Aryan" race, he also viewed Judaism as a threat to the German nation, the only extant representative of the Aryan race and the sole rightful rulers of the world. Because of his anti-Semetic ideology and his pro-German sympathies, as exemplified in his book, *The Foundation of the 20th Century* (1899), his racial theories were readily adopted by the Nazis, including Alfred Rosenberg (q.v.), who based some of his own theories and writings on Chamberlain's.

Steven B. Rogers

Additional Reading

Toland, John, *Adolf Hitler* (1976).

Chamberlain, Neville (1869–1940)

British prime minister 1937–1940. The son of Joseph Chamberlain and the step-brother of Austen Chamberlain, Neville felt great pressure to succeed. Ironically, it was Neville who attained the office that eluded his father and step-brother. Without the personal magnetism, oratorical skills, and humor of Winston S. Churchill (q.v.), or the good looks and youth of Anthony Eden (q.v.), or the affability of his predecessor, Stanley Baldwin, Chamberlain was consistently at a disadvantage in politics. He entered politics at age fifty, after a relatively unsuccessful career as a businessman. He proved adept as minster of health and imaginative on issues of social reform. He rose steadily within the Conservative Party because of his industriousness, thoroughness, and methodical manner.

Chamberlain is best known for his policy of

appeasement (q.v.). His programs and conduct from 1937 to 1940 have come under much criticism, and his critics charged that had he stood firm in the face of Adolf Hitler and Benito Mussolini (qq.v.) in 1937, World War II could have been avoided. Recently, however, his policy of appeasement has been reappraised. To Chamberlain, as well as most European politicians of the day, appeasement signified an attempt to bring about the general pacification of European tension through negotiation of outstanding issues and grievances on Germany's part, and in this way to remove the possibility of the recourse to war. He wanted, at all costs, to avoid another conflagration like World War I.

Chamberlain is most often criticized for his conduct at the Munich Conference in September 1938. He flew to Hitler's mountain retreat in Bavaria and became convinced that Hitler could be trusted, and that Czechoslovakia must part with the Sudetenland (q.v.). He met with Hitler a second time only to learn that Hitler wanted all of Czechoslovakia. Later that same month, Hitler and Chamberlain met at Munich, where they, along with Mussolini and Édouard Daladier (q.v.), agreed to the original German demands for the Sudetenland. Chamberlain returned home feeling like a conquering hero for avoiding war and saving Czechoslovakia. He declared that he had achieved "peace in our time." Many cheered the prime minister for his diplomatic triumph, though a few, like Churchill, referred to the agreement as a total and unmitigated defeat. Churchill's prophecy came true when, in March 1939, the Nazis broke the treaty and invaded the rest of Czechoslovakia. Chamberlain was guilty of misreading Hitler. The prime minister believed Hitler was a practical man, like himself, interested only in redressing the legitimate wrongs done to Germany after World War I. Chamberlain was not alone.

After Hitler broke the Munich agreement, Chamberlain abandoned appeasement. Throughout 1939, he worked to rearm Britain. He was reproached, however, for not pursuing more seriously a treaty with the Soviet Union. He fundamentally distrusted the USSR and only made facile attempts at an anti-Fascist pact. He was also faulted for his lack of leadership during the war. He miscalculated Germany's strategy, doubting the Nazis would attack in the West. He resigned in May 1940, after Norway fell. He turned the reins of government over to his nemesis, Winston Churchill, and died six months later.

Glenn R. Sharfman

Additional Reading
Feiling, Keith, *The Life of Neville Chamberlain* (1946).
Fuchser, Larry W., *Neville Chamberlain and Appeasement: A Study in the Politics of History* (1982).
Rock, William R., *Neville Chamberlain* (1969).

Chernyakovsky, Ivan Danilovich (1906–1945)

Soviet general, commander of the 3rd Byelorussian Front (army group). The Soviet Army entered World War II with the youngest general officer corps of all the Allies. Chernyakovsky, the son of a railroad worker, was the youngest of the young. He first joined the Red Army in 1924, graduated from the Kiev Artillery School in 1928, and the Mechanization and Motorization Academy a decade later. His broad combat arms training prepared him for the variety of command positions he held during World War II.

As commander of the Sixtieth Army, he recaptured Voronezh and Kursk (qq.v.) in 1943. His talents were recognized by Georgy Zhukov (q.v.), who recommended him for command of the 3rd Byelorussian Front. In the Byelorussian offensive his forces participated in the capture of Minsk, moved through Latvia, and took Vilna. The 3rd Byelorussian Front then continued its westward

General Ivan Chernyakovsky. (IWM RR 2172)

movement, eventually capturing Königsberg. He, however, did not live to see the capture of the city and its subsequent renaming to Kaliningrad. He was killed by an artillery shell near Mehlsack in February 1945.

Chernyakovsky is nearly unique among the Soviet generals of the war. He had not participated in World War I, the revolution, or the civil war. He was one of the few Soviet generals who did not attend the Frunze Military Academy, and he was a Jew. Nonetheless, at the time of his death, he was recognized by his contemporaries in the Soviet military as a brilliant field commander.

Thomas Cagley

Additional Reading
Bialer, Seweryn, *Stalin and His Generals* (1984).

Cherwell, Lord
See LINDEMANN, FREDERICK

Cheshire, Leonard (1917–1992)
Royal Air Force group captain, bomber pilot. Cheshire joined the Oxford University Air Squadron in 1936 and was commissioned in the RAF Volunteer Reserve in 1937. He began operations

Group Captain Leonard Cheshire, VC, DSO, and 2 Bars, DFC. (IWM CH 12667)

in Whitleys and in June 1940, and joined Number 102 Squadron. He quickly demonstrated competence and leadership ability. In October 1943, he became commanding officer of Number 617 (Pathfinder) Squadron and pioneered new methods of low-level target marking that greatly improved RAF night bombing techniques (*see* Pathfinder Technique). Between 1940 and 1944 he completed 100 bombing missions, an incredible figure considering the extremely high mortality rate of Allied bomber crews.

Transferred to the Far East in late 1944, Cheshire was the official British observer in the camera aircraft at the bombing of Nagasaki. He won the Distinguished Service Order three times, and in October 1944 he was awarded the Victoria Cross. After the war, he left the RAF and founded the Cheshire Foundation Homes and Mission for the Relief of Suffering, an important private charity in Britain.

Wes Wilson

Additional Reading
Cheshire, Leonard, *Bomber Pilot* (1943).
Harris, Sir Arthur, *Bomber Offensive* (1947).

Choltitz, Dietrich von (1894–1966)
German general, German commander of occupied Paris. Scion of a newly ennobled family, von Choltitz was commissioned in a Saxon infantry regiment at the beginning of World War I. After long service in a cavalry unit during the 1920s and early 1930s, he transferred to the air transportable 16th Infantry Regiment and eventually became its commander.

In August 1942, von Choltitz commanded the 260th Infantry Division. He briefly served as an acting corps commander during the winter battles in the eastern Ukraine, and he participated in the ensuing German withdrawals as commander of the 11th *Panzer* Division and interim commander of XLVIII *Panzer Korps*. Posted to Italy in 1944, he was moved to France in June, where he took command of the LXXXIV *Korps* after its commander, General Erich Marcks, was killed near St. Lô.

As German resistance in Normandy began to crumble, von Choltitz was entrusted by Adolf Hitler (q.v.) with the defense of Paris, receiving strict orders to hold the city to the bitter end. Despite these orders, von Choltitz conducted the defense in a fairly restrained fashion, established contacts with the French resistance, neutral diplomats, and the Red Cross. On 25 August 1944, he disregarded

Hitler's orders to destroy Paris, and surrendered the city and its garrison to General Philippe Leclerc (q.v.). He was released from captivity in April 1947.

Ulrich Trumpener

Additional Reading
Collins, Larry, and Dominique Lapierre, *Is Paris Burning?* (1965).
Humble, Richard, *Hitler's Generals* (1974).
Pryce-Jones, David, *Paris and the Third Reich: A History of the German Occupation,* 1940–1944 (1981).

Christian X (1870–1947)
King of Denmark. Christian X pursued a policy of limited collaboration to protect his people from the severity of German occupation during World War II. He successfully maintained Danish neutrality during World War I and wrongly believed this option was possible in 1940. When Germany invaded Denmark on 9 April 1940, German bombers, streaming over Copenhagen, convinced him to capitulate. He called on his people to remain neutral and appointed pro-German Erik Scavenius as foreign minister. Christian refused, however, to name members of the Danish Nazi Party to his government. He continued to show himself in public as a constant reminder of Danish independence and opposition to Nazi philosophy. In November 1941, Adolf Hitler (q.v.) forced him to join the Anti-Comintern Pact (q.v.) and to appoint Scavenius as premier. Christian remained king until his death in 1947.

Justin D. Murphy

Additional Reading
Outze, Borge (ed.), *Denmark During the German Occupation* (1946).
Petrow, Richard, *The Bitter Years: The Invasion and Occupation of Demark and Norway, April 1940–May 1945* (1974).

Chuikov, Vasily Ivanovich (1900–1982)
Marshal of the Soviet Union, commander of the Sixty-second Army. Chuikov started his working career as a bellhop and apprentice. He joined the Red Army in 1918 and became a regimental commander at the age of nineteen. He served in the Russo-Polish War (q.v.) and later attended the Frunze Military Academy. He then served for many years with the Eastern Department. He was stationed in China from 1926 to 1937 as Soviet military attache and military advisor to Chiang Kai-shek. On his return from the east he was selected by Georgy Zhukov (q.v.) for future high command.

At the time of the German offensive against Stalingrad (q.v.), Chuikov was the deputy commander and then commander of the First Reserve Army (later renamed the Sixty-fourth Army). In September 1942, he took command of the Sixty-second Army on the west bank of the Volga. Through sheer perseverance, he held the Germans for nearly seventy days, and by so doing bought time for the Soviets to prepare their counteroffensive.

Chuikov survived Stalingrad and led his army, renamed the Eighth Guards Army, into Berlin. After the war, he served as the supreme commander of Soviet troops in Germany, and was the senior inspector general in the Ministry of Defense.

Thomas Cagley

Additional Reading
Bialer, Seweryn (ed.), *Stalin and His Generals* (1984).
Chuikov, Vasily, *The Battle of Stalingrad* (1963).
Shukman, Harold (ed.), *Stalin's Generals* (1993).

Churchill, Peter (1909–1972)
British Army officer and SOE agent. Churchill was a British Army officer who served in the Special Operations Executive (SOE) (q.v.) during World War II. He parachuted behind enemy lines several times, and assisted in organizing resistance in occupied France. The Germans captured him in 1943 and he spent the rest of the war in prison. The Germans could have legally put him to death for espionage, but refrained because they thought he was a relative of British Prime Minister Winston S. Churchill (q.v.). He was not.

Paul Rose

Additional Reading
Churchill, Peter, *Duel of Wits* (1953).
———, *Of Their Own Choice* (1952).
Deacon, Richard, *A History of the British Secret Services* (1980).

Churchill, Winston Spencer Leonard (1874–1965)
British prime minister. Winston S. Churchill was one of Britain's greatest sons and a titan of the twentieth century. Descended from the great military leader the duke of Marlborough, Churchill was born at Blenheim Palace on 30 November 1874, to

an American mother (Jennie Jerome) and English father (Lord Randolph Churchill). He was sent off to boarding school shortly before his eighth birthday. As a boy he was difficult and often disobedient, and he was a mediocre student at Harrow and also at the Royal Military College, Sandhurst.

Commissioned a lieutenant in the cavalry in 1895, the year of his father's death, Churchill served as an army officer and war correspondent in five major wars. Between 1895 and 1900, he had military assignments in Cuba, India, and the Sudan. Ever ambitious and lusting for fame, Churchill, at age twenty-four, resigned his commission and became a war correspondent in the Boer War. In 1899, he was captured by the Boers but escaped. Something of a hero, he returned to Britain and in 1901, a year after losing his first parliamentary bid, won a seat in the House of Commons as a Conservative.

In politics, Churchill was a maverick, even a parliamentary outlaw. He was characterized by egocentricity and boyish enthusiasm. In 1904, he broke with the Conservatives and joined the Liberal Party. He held a number of increasingly important posts under Prime Ministers Henry Campbell-Bannerman and Herbert Asquith, including undersecretary of state for the colonies (1905–1908), president of the Board of Trade (1908–1910), and home secretary (1910–1911). In 1908, he married Clementine Hozier.

In 1911, at age thirty-six, Churchill became first lord of the Admiralty. He worked with zeal over the next two years to assure that the Royal Navy was ready for a general European war. He converted the fleet from coal to oil, carried out modernization and expansion, and cleared out deadwood. On the outbreak of war, he ordered the fleet to sea on his own responsibility.

Shortly after the beginning of World War I, Churchill became deeply involved in the defense of Antwerp. He traveled there and actively directed military operations. In the process, he drew considerable criticism. Always interested in new ideas, he pushed development of the tank through the Landships Committee established at the Admiralty in February 1915.

Churchill was also the chief advocate of the 1915 Dardanelles campaign. The plan was to secure the straits, provide easy direct access to Russia, and drive Turkey out of the war. Success might also enlist the support of several Balkan states against the Central Powers. The plan appealed to Churchill's desire for action, but it was poorly thought out. Allied military operations in the eastern Mediterranean ended in disappointment and failure, largely because he insisted (despite his disclaimers at the time and later) that the Dardanelles could be forced by ships alone and that naval gunfire could silence the Turkish shore batteries (in this, as would often be the case, Churchill ignored expert military advice). When troops were brought in the Gallipoli campaign, they were too few and too late. In the storm of political debate that followed, Asquith brought in Conservatives and Labour MPs to a new coalition government and carried out a ministerial reshuffle. Churchill, though ardently defending his plan in the Dardanelles, resigned from the Admiralty, thinking his political career ended.

By November 1915, Churchill had joined the army on the western front to get a firsthand look at trench warfare. In less than two months, he received command of a battalion. By May 1916, he was back in Britain. For more than a year, rumors of his return to the cabinet circulated in London, but Conservative Party opposition and lingering public suspicions over the Dardanelles campaign kept Churchill from office.

Finally, in July 1917, his friend and the new prime minister, Lloyd George, named him minister of munitions. For the next fifteen months, until the war ended, he concentrated on increasing the manufacture of ammunition in British factories and helped to create a shell surplus. He also frequently visited troops in France and met with Allied leaders there.

Churchill was secretary for war and air minister from 1918 to 1921, at the Colonial Office (1921–1922), and chancellor of the exchequer (1924–1929). In the latter post, he helped pare the military and naval budgets. In 1924, he rejoined the Conservative Party. As one astute observer noted, he was a Democrat "to the very bone and imbued with a deep reverence for Parliament and a strong sense of human rights, but he was never quite a liberal." He never had the liberal reluctance to use force in solving problems. "And though he revelled in discussion he was by temperament an intellectual autocrat. He never liked having to go other people's way. He infinitely preferred his own."

For the next eleven years from 1929, Churchill was in the political wilderness. Known for his belligerent opposition to Communism (some hold that this was the one constant in his foreign policy views), he was nonetheless discouraged. Adolf Hitler's (q.v.) rise gave him a cause and purpose. The British people in the early 1930s were absorbed by domestic affairs and he was one of the few who sensed the dangers of Nazism. Although he was a

Prime Minister Winston Churchill (center), flanked by General Władysław Sikorski (left) and General Charles de Gaulle (right). (IWM A 7233)

champion of military preparedness, it should be noted that, had the bombers Churchill proposed in the mid-1930s actually been built, in 1940, they would have been obsolete and, in any case, the wrong kind of aircraft. Not well known is that Churchill was an early admirer of Italy's Benito Mussolini (q.v.). Also, he was late in breaking with Prime Minister Neville Chamberlain (q.v.), even congratulating him after the September 1938 Munich Agreement (q.v.) with Hitler.

Despite this, by the outbreak of World War II in September 1939, Churchill's views about Hitler were proven correct and those of Chamberlain proven wrong. On 1 September, Chamberlain found it prudent to invite Churchill back into the cabinet and, two days later, he offered him his old World War I post as first lord of the Admiralty. A signal was promptly flashed to the fleet: "Winston is back."

Ironically, Churchill's plans helped topple Chamberlain from power. Churchill pushed for mining both German waterways and Norwegian coastal waters. The latter plan, designed to provoke German retaliation as an excuse for British intervention in Norway, was a disaster. The Germans anticipated the British move and struck in great force. The Norwegian fiasco and the subsequent successful German invasion of France and

the Low Countries, caused Chamberlain's removal from office. The two choices to succeed him were Edward Wood (q.v.), the earl of Halifax, who believed the war lost and that an honorable peace with Hitler might be achieved, and Churchill, who wanted to fight on despite what appeared to be long odds. Although he was never popular with his colleagues, Churchill became prime minister, in part because he was known for being decisive, something Halifax was not.

For the next five years, Prime Minister Churchill proved a decisive and forceful wartime leader. More than anything else, he was successful in mobilizing public support for the war against Germany. His courage, resilience, and stubbornness all set an example for the nation, much as Georges Clemenceau had done for France in World War I. Churchill was a brilliant speaker and writer. His leadership and obstinacy impressed the Americans, many of whom doubted Britain's ability to continue the struggle after the defeat of France.

In contrast to U.S. President Franklin D. Roosevelt (q.v.), Churchill directed strategy and made major military decisions in the fashion of Hitler and Soviet premier Josef Stalin (q.v.). Churchill's approach to military affairs was reflected in what Field Marshal Alan Brooke (q.v.) termed his "passion for the offensive." He was willing to take risks, and he believed that generals always overestimate enemy strength and underestimate their own. Overcaution was equated with defeatism, and the one sin was inaction. The result was a series of precipitous decisions, a number of which had unfortunate consequences.

Churchill did not shrink from hard decisions, such as the sinking of units of the French fleet in 1940 or, at the height of the Battle of Britain (q.v.), sending military supplies to the Suez, but he also made mistakes. His decision to reinforce the big naval base at Singapore proved unsound, as did sending out England's newest battleship, the HMS *Prince of Wales,* without carrier protection. His decision to intervene militarily in Greece in 1941 was a major blunder as it halted the British drive in North Africa just as the British were on the verge of victory against the Italians. He was also wrong in his decision to support only the partisans in Yugoslavia (thus ensuring a Communist victory there). He was preoccupied with the Mediterranean theater of war and incorrect in his assessment of the Balkans as "the soft underbelly of Europe." Indeed, Churchill opposed plans for a cross-channel invasion of France until almost the eve of the invasion.

Churchill worked hard on the relationship with Roosevelt to bring the United States into the war. The resulting coalition was as close as any in history between two sovereign states. British resources were strained to the maximum, and American influence in decision making grew in proportion to gains in military strength. Early on, the British had their way, but by 1944, they were junior partners in the alliance.

Despite his hatred of Communism, Churchill extended a hand to the Soviet Union. Unlike Roosevelt and the Americans, who wanted to win the war at the cheapest cost in human life, Churchill thought in terms of geopolitical advantage. During a meeting in Moscow in 1944, he struck a bargain with Stalin regarding spheres of influence in Eastern Europe. Certainly he understood Stalin much better than Roosevelt, who believed he could charm the Soviet dictator into reasonableness.

Churchill doubted cooperation with the Russians was possible. He pointed out to Roosevelt, and to his successor, Harry S Truman (q.v.), that the Soviets were not living up to their pledges made at the Teheran and Yalta Conferences (*see* Conferences, Allied). He told Truman that he wanted "to shake hands with the Russians as far

east as possible." He hoped that Allied troops might race the Soviets to Berlin and Prague, and he tried to convince the American president not to withdraw American troops from Saxony and Thuringia in Germany until the Soviets honored their pledges.

Churchill also thought in nineteenth-century terms regarding empire. He announced at one point that he had "not become prime minister to preside over the death of the British Empire," and he opposed independence for India.

After Germany's surrender in May 1945, Churchill called for elections that July. The leader of the Labour Party and deputy prime minister, Clement Attlee (q.v.), wanted to wait until the Japanese defeat, but Churchill was adamant. The British people were weary of sacrifice and ready for domestic change. In what was one of the most stunning victories in British electoral history, a Labour majority returned to Parliament and Attlee became prime minister.

Although out of power, Churchill used his formidable influence to rally the West against the Soviet Union. He was certainly a key figure in the coming of the Cold War, and his 1946 speech at Fulton, Missouri, popularized the term, "Iron Curtain." During the same speech, he called for an alliance of Britain and the United States against the Soviet Union.

On the defeat of Labour in the 1951 elections, Churchill returned to office as prime minister. Ill health forced him to step aside in 1955, and it fell to his successor, Anthony Eden (q.v.), to deal with the Suez crisis of 1956 and show how weak Britain had really become. Churchill was always extremely conscious of his place in history, even to the point of attempting to alter it. His widely read multi-volume memoirs of both World War I and World War II contain frequent distortions of fact.

Churchill died in London on 24 January 1965, and is buried beside his parents and brother in the churchyard at Bladon, a short distance from Blenheim Palace. He is remembered as one of the great statesmen of the twentieth century.

Spencer C. Tucker

Additional Reading

Brendon, Piers, *Winston Churchill: A Biography* (1984).
Charmley, John, *Churchill, the End of Glory: A Political Biography* (1993).
Gilbert, Martin, *Winston S. Churchill,* Vol. 7: *Road to Victory, 1941–1945* (1986).
Lamb, Richard, *Churchill As War Leader* (1991).

Lewin, Ronald. *Churchill As Warlord* (1982).
Manchester, William. *The Last Lion: Winston Spencer Churchill, Visions of Glory: 1874–1932* (1983).

Ciano, Count Galeazzo (1903–1944)

Foreign minister of Italy. Ciano parlayed his position as Benito Mussolini's (q.v.) son-in-law into appointments as propaganda minister in 1934 and foreign minister in 1936. He was a capable and intelligent diplomat, but his unabated ambition put Italy on a course for disaster. His first task was to gain acceptance of the conquest of Ethiopia (q.v.). Meeting with Adolf Hitler (q.v.) in October 1936, he gained Germany's recognition of the Italian Empire, which led to the Axis Pact (q.v.) and the Anti-Comintern Pact. Ciano supported the April 1939 invasion of Albania to counter Germany's acquisition of Austria and Czechoslovakia.

On 22 May 1939, Ciano signed the Pact of Steel on the understanding that Germany would refrain from war for at least three more years. When Hitler revealed his plans to invade Poland, Ciano urged Mussolini to remain neutral. After Italy entered the war on 10 June 1940, Ciano advocated the Italian invasion of Greece (q.v.) to counter German penetration into the Balkans. As the war turned against Italy, he increasingly professed anti-German sentiments and was dismissed as foreign minister on 6 February 1943. Appointed ambassador to the Vatican, he played a leading role in the conspiracy that toppled Mussolini from power on 26 July 1943. At Hitler's demand, Ciano was executed on 11 January 1944.

Justin D. Murphy

Additional Reading
Ciano, Count Galeazzo, *Ciano's Diary* (1947).
Villari, Luigi, *Italian Foreign Policy Under Mussolini* (1956).

Clark, Mark Wayne (1896–1984)

American general, commander, U.S. Fifth Army. The son of a military officer, Clark entered the U.S. Military Academy at West Point in 1913. There, he befriended many men who later became prominent military and political leaders. These contacts would benefit him during World War II. He graduated in 1917 and served in the 11th Infantry Regiment in France during World War I. He was wounded and classified unfit to return to combat. Frustrated, he spent the remainder of the war supervising ration shipments.

After the war, Clark was posted to various stations, including Fort Benning and the Presidio. He studied at the Fort Leavenworth Command and General Staff College and the Army War College. Shortly after World War II began, he was assigned to a staff job in Washington, D.C.

Clark received rapid promotions, and the criticism of his peers in the process. In August 1940, he was promoted to lieutenant colonel, and one year later he was a temporary brigadier general. In March 1942, he became acting chief of staff of U.S. Army Ground Forces. In April, he was promoted to major general and appointed commander of II Corps in June. By July of 1942, he was the nominal commander of all U.S. ground forces in Europe, headquartered in London.

To prepare for Operation TORCH in the fall of 1942, Clark secretly traveled by submarine to Algeria to negotiate with French leaders. He urged them to support the Allied landings in Africa. The French leadership in North Africa was factional. His decision to deal with Admiral Jean François Darlan (q.v.), who had German connections, was controversial. Clark justified his choice by stating that Darlan was the only leader Clark thought had control and could negotiate an armistice.

After Clark was promoted to lieutenant general, he pressured General Dwight D. Eisenhower (q.v.) for a command position. In January 1943 Clark assumed command of the U.S. Fifth Army, and held that position throughout the Italian campaign. During this campaign, he was criticized as being egotistic and self-serving, being promoted too fast as compared to his peers, and seeking publicity. Many military leaders, soldiers, and citizens thought that he unnecessarily risked soldier's lives in an erratic campaign that was waged primarily to secure his selfish objectives.

On 1 October 1943, the Fifth Army captured Naples and Adolf Hitler (q.v.) ordered German forces to reinforce Rome and its surrounding territory. Clark, seeking American and personal success, was anxious to get to Rome before the British. The competition with British forces often motivated him to make decisions based on momentary developments and situations in the field without conferring with his staff or subordinate commanders. The Allied advance north in the winter was tedious and often static.

In January 1944, Clark was selected for command of the Seventh Army for the upcoming invasion of southern France, Operation ANVIL. He was, however, eager to capture Rome with the Fifth Army, with which he believed the public identified him. He stated that Operation ANVIL was a mistake, and thought the Allies should continue the strong drive through Italy. Afraid that another officer would be assigned command of the Fifth Army, he asked to be relieved of the Seventh Army assignment.

On 22 January 1944, in Italy, Operation SHINGLE began with Clark's U.S. VI Corps landing at Anzio (q.v.). Meanwhile, his 36th Division, fighting its way toward Cassino, tried to cross the Rapido River (q.v.), where it suffered heavy losses at the hands of the Germans. Clark was criticized for the carnage, accused of improper leadership, and pressured to accept the Seventh Army command. He insisted he stay in Italy to capture Rome. Clark's wife, meanwhile, lectured in the U.S. about his military successes, which raised questions among other military officers about his true motivations and intentions. Clark stated that his only ambition was to command an American army in combat victoriously, and he reassured his superiors that he was acting solely for American and Allied interests, not his own.

During the attacks on Cassino, Clark initially objected to the bombing of Monte Cassino (q.v.), the Benedictine abbey, but he acquiesced to other officers who feared the Germans would use the building for cover. On 15 February 1944, the abbey was bombed to rubble. Within a month, the city of Cassino was also destroyed.

In April, Clark traveled to the U.S. for a brief furlough. He returned to Italy hoping to capture Rome before the D-Day invasion, thereby maintaining his spot in the limelight. General Sir Harold Alexander (q.v.), the Allied commander in Italy, wanted the British Eighth and U.S. Fifth Armies to push toward Rome together, while the U.S. VI Corps broke out of the Anzio beachhead to seize Valmontone, a town astride the German line of communications. This would position VI Corps to cut off a large portion of the German armies to the south. Clark, however, unsure about the plan, told VI Corps to be flexible for a change of orders to what actions he considered most appropriate at the time of combat. Alexander insisted his plan be executed, and Clark ordered VI Corps to attack as Alexander ordered. Then Clark changed the orders and sent VI Corps to attack Rome directly. He did not inform Alexander of the change until after the attack had started.

Rome, in Clark's opinion, symbolized success and personal prestige for him and his troops. He felt that because his men had endured the frustrating winter struggle, they, more than the British, deserved the honor of liberating Rome. Also, he realized that the capture of Rome would earn him

C

Lieutenant General Mark W. Clark, at the link-up point of the Anzio break-out, 25 May 1944. (IWM NA 15394)

public accolades and recognition of his military leadership.

Clark believed the enemy was reduced in strength with minimal reserves, grossly underestimating their true resources. He divided the forces so they could attack both northwest and northeast, planning to move toward Rome quickly while cutting the enemy's major communication line. Unfortunately, because of Clark's change in troop location, the decentralized forces, both British and American, were unable to achieve their immediate operational goals. As a result, the Germans launched a vigorous counterattack, and Allied maneuvers became more defensive than offensive.

Finally, after a week of fighting, the Allied troops unexpectedly breached the line. On 5 June 1944, Clark's troops captured Rome, but many of the German troops escaped north in the process. Clark then wanted to continue movement northeast through the Balkans to meet the Soviets, which he considered vital for establishing the basis for Soviet-American postwar relations. The Allied leadership, however, considered southern France a more important objective, and Clark's Fifth Army stopped on 30 October outside Bologna.

In December 1944, Clark assumed command of the Allied 15th Army Group in Italy. His troops were a polyglot of nationalities, including British, Americans, Poles, Brazilians, and Indians. In March 1945, he was promoted to general. In April, his troops occupied the Po Valley and Bologna. Clark accepted the German surrender in Italy in May. He traveled briefly to the U.S., then returned to Europe.

Clark helped liberate Austria and was commander of U.S. occupation forces in Austria in July 1945. He expunged Nazi influences, rebuilt housing, supplied food, and assisted refugees. He prevented Soviet domination while trying to secure an independent, democratic Austria. In the U.S., meanwhile, Texas veterans of the 36th Division blamed Clark for the tragedy at the Rapido River. Congressional military committees later held hearings, exonerating Clark.

In 1947, Clark was first commander of the Sixth Army at the Presidio, and then commander of U.S. Army Field Forces at Fort Monroe, Virginia. During the Korean War, he served as commander in chief of the U.N. Command, and then U.S. commander in chief of the Far East from May 1952 to July 1953. He signed the armistice at Panmunjon on 27 July 1953. He retired the following October. By the time of his retirement, he had collected numerous American and foreign decorations for his military service in Europe and Asia.

After his retirement, Clark accepted the position as president of the Citadel military college in Charleston, South Carolina. He retired from that post in July 1965. He spent his latter years inspecting war memorials as chairman of the American Battle Monuments Commission, traveling to familiar World War II sites. Clark died in Charleston on 17 April 1984. The Citadel named Mark Clark Hall in his honor.

Clark's command of the Fifth Army and his decisions concerning the liberation of Rome have been the focus of contemporary and historical criticism. Many of his peers, including Eisenhower and Patton, frequently doubted his ability and judgment because of his seemingly selfish actions in Italy. Clark also had many ardent supporters such as British prime minister Winston S. Churchill (q.v.), who called him the "American Eagle." Clark's motivations and actions made him a controversial, yet an ultimately effective, Allied leader in Europe.

Elizabeth D. Schafer

Additional Reading
Blumenson, Martin, *Mark Clark* (1984).

Clark, Mark, *Calculated Risk* (1949).
Mathews, Sidney, T., *General Clark's Decision to Drive on Rome* (1990).

Clarke, Bruce C. (1901–1988)

American brigadier general. Although originally commissioned in the Corps of Engineers, Clarke was one of America's best armored commanders. He graduated from West Point in 1925. As a colonel, Clarke commanded Combat Command A (CCA) of Major General John S. Wood's (q.v.) 4th Armored Division. During Operation COBRA, the breakout from Normandy (q.v.), Clarke earned a Distinguished Service Cross. He then led CCA as the 4th Armored Division spearheaded the drive of General George S. Patton's (q.v.) U.S. Third Army across France. During the battle for Nancy (q.v.), Clarke sent his 37th Tank Battalion, commanded by Lieutenant Colonel Creighton Abrams (q.v.), on a wide sweep north of the city, completing its encirclement and cutting off the German defenders.

Promoted to brigadier general, Clarke assumed command of Combat Command B (CCB) of the 7th Armored Division shortly before the start of the German Ardennes offensive (q.v.). On 17 December 1944, Clarke led CCB into St. Vith (q.v.) and kept the Germans out of the vital crossroads town for several days. Clarke was forced to conduct a fighting withdrawal on 21 December, but by that time CCB had contributed significantly to disrupting the north wing of the German attack.

After World War II Clarke rose to the rank of full general. His last assignment was commander in chief of the United States Army in Europe. He retired from the army in 1962.

David T. Zabecki

Additional Reading
Cole, Hugh M., *The Ardennes: Battle of the Bulge* (1965).
———, *The Lorraine Campaign* (1950).
Weigley, Russell F., *Eisenhower's Lieutenants: The Campaigns of France and Germany, 1944–1945* (1981).

Clay, Lucius D. (1897–1978)

American general, commander of U.S. occupation forces in Germany. The son of a U.S. senator, Clay was born in Marietta, Georgia. He graduated from the U.S. Military Academy at West Point in 1918, then studied civil engineering at the Engineer Officers' Training Camp. In the 1920s, he was assistant professor of military science and tactics at the Alabama Polytechnic Institute in Auburn. He also prepared training regulations and taught at the U.S. Military Academy. During the 1930s, he participated in several military engineering projects from the Panama Canal Zone to the Philippines, where he was on the staff of General Douglas MacArthur.

When war broke out in Europe, Clay became secretary of the Airport Approval Board and assistant to the administrator on civil aeronautics. Here he organized and directed the defense airport programs for the expansion of 277 airports and the construction of 197 new ones in the United States, Alaska, and several Pacific Islands. When the United States entered World War II, General Clay became deputy chief of staff for requirements and resources at Headquarters, Services of Supply. In July 1942, he was assistant chief of staff of materiel with the army service forces. In this post, he supervised production and procurement programs for the army.

In November 1944, General Dwight D. Eisenhower (q.v.) called Clay to France to command the Normandy base section, European Theater of Operations, and the port of Cherbourg. It was during this command that Clay made his greatest contribution to the war effort. He was able to clear up a shipping tangle that had delayed the movement of supplies to Allied forces invading Europe. He doubled the rate of movement in a single day.

The following month, Clay returned to the United States to serve in the Office of War Mobilization, where he oversaw the coordination of all government agencies in the exercise of their war production responsibilities. In April 1945, he was back in Europe as an assistant to Eisenhower. His official title was deputy military governor and U.S. representative on the coordinating committee for Germany. In March 1947, he became commander in chief of U.S. forces of occupation in Germany and U.S. forces in Europe, as well as military governor of the U.S. zone in Germany. In this position, he was famous for coordinating the Berlin Airlift (q.v.) in 1948. He retired from the army in 1949 and died in Chatham, Massachusetts, on 16 April 1978.

Robert F. Pace

Additional Reading

Ziemke, Earl F., *The U.S. Army in the Occupation of Germany, 1944–1946* (1975).

Cochran, Jacquelin (1906?-1980)

Director of Women's Air Service Pilots (WASPs) (q.v.). America's greatest woman pilot was born into poverty, probably in 1906, though her origins remain obscure. She worked in mill towns as a child and moved about with her foster family until she left to work as a beautician. After training to be a nurse, she returned to the beauty business in a fashionable New York salon. A chance meeting with industrialist Floyd B. Odlum resulted in her taking flying lessons at New York's Roosevelt Field in 1932, an endeavor conceived to facilitate her growing interest in establishing a cosmetics firm. Within three weeks, she was a licensed pilot.

In 1938, Cochran won the transcontinental Bendix Air Race, becoming one of the world's preeminent fliers. Encouraged by General Henry H. "Hap" Arnold (q.v.) shortly after congressional approval of Lend-Lease (q.v.) in March 1941, Cochran flew a Lockheed bomber across the Atlantic to Prestwick, Scotland, in June. Continuing on to London, she met with British Air Transport Auxiliary officials to devise a program to train women fliers for service with the U.S. Army Air Forces. In July 1943, she was appointed director of the Women's Air Service Pilots. It was an organization she protected fiercely, though one she exposed to the obvious dangers of target towing for air-to-air and ground-to-air gunnery training.

Cochran's political savvy was incapable of maintaining the WASPs beyond December 1944. The program was deactivated due to the inability of the women to be militarized, and through a persuasive campaign to garner sympathy for unemployed male pilots.

When the war ended, she became a foreign correspondent in the Pacific theater. In 1953, she became the first woman to fly faster than the speed of sound. She continued setting and resetting records through the 1960s when she piloted a Lockheed F-104 fighter at a record 1,429.3 mph.

William Camp

Additional Reading

Boles, Antoinette, *Women in Khaki* (1953).
Wood, Winifred, *We Were WASPs* (1946).

Collins, J. Lawton (1896–1987)

American lieutenant general, commander, U.S. VII Corps. Joseph Lawton Collins graduated from the U.S. Military Academy at West Point in 1917 as an infantry lieutenant. Just missing service in World War I, he spent two years in Germany with the American occupation forces. He returned to student assignments at Forts Benning and Sill, and then as instructor at the military academy. The variety of his postings gave him broad experience in various combat arms that later served him well. At the start of World War II, Collins was the commander of the 25th Infantry Division in Hawaii, taking the division to Guadalcanal and New Georgia. His aggressive command style in these early Pacific battles earned him the nickname "Lightning Joe."

In late 1943, Collins was assigned as commander of VII Corps in preparation for the upcoming invasion of Normandy (q.v.). One of his units, the 4th Infantry Division, successfully landed at UTAH Beach on 6 June 1944. He led three infantry divisions in an attack on the port of Cherbourg that the Allies wanted to bring in supplies. He captured it twenty days after D-Day, but the Germans blew up the port before surrendering, rendering it useless for several months. When Operation COBRA broke out from the Normandy beachhead in late July, it was the VII Corps that led the way. After his troops narrowly missed closing the Falaise gap in August, VII Corps units pursued the retreating Germans across France and Belgium. During the Ardennes offensive (q.v.), VII Corps played a major role in halting the northern half of the German attack.

In April 1945, Collins returned to the United States as deputy commanding general of Army Ground Forces. Following the war, he became a full general. He was army chief of staff in 1949, serving in that position for most of the Korean War.

Randy Papadopoulos

Additional Reading

Collins, J. Lawton, *Lightning Joe: An Autobiography* (1979).
Karolevitz, Robert F. (ed.), *The 25th Infantry Division in World War II* (1946).
U.S. Center of Military History, *Utah Beach to Cherbourg 6 June–27 June 1944* (1948).
Weigley, Russell, *Eisenhower's Lieutenants: The Campaigns of France and Germany, 1944–1945* (1981).

Coningham, Arthur (1895–1948)

British air marshal, commander of the Desert Air Force and the Allied Second Tactical Air Force. Considered by his peers and historians to be one of the very best tactical air commanders of World War II, Sir Arthur Coningham was one of the original architects of tactical air support. He was born in Brisbane, Australia, on 19 January 1895. His father was a noted Australian sportsman who moved the family to New Zealand, where Arthur

was educated at Wellington College. He served in a New Zealand regiment in World War I, transferring to the Royal Flying Corps in the summer of 1916. His service with New Zealand troops earned him the nickname "Mary," a distortion of the native Maori. Late that same year, he was in France as a fighter pilot.

Coningham's reputation as a pilot was enhanced during the next two decades in Egypt and Iraq. When war began in Europe in 1939, he was promoted to air commodore and given command of a night bombing group based in Yorkshire. For the next two years, he commanded bombing missions and developed his philosophy of tactical airpower. He was convinced of the necessity of aircraft support for ground and naval forces.

In July 1941, Coningham was selected to command the Desert Air Force in North Africa. There he applied the principles of tactical airpower to the war. His tactics were successful in support of General Bernard L. Montgomery's (q.v.) Eighth Army at El Alamein (q.v.). In return, Montgomery supported the contention that the air force remain independent. Coningham contended that speed and flexibility of airpower were the major advantages of the air forces, and Montgomery agreed.

For the next two years, Coningham commanded air support for the Allied armies in Tunisia, the capture of Sicily, and finally the invasion of southern Italy (qq.v.). In January 1944, he returned to England to command the Allied Second Tactical Air Force in the Normandy (q.v.) invasion. After the initial invasion, his operation moved to France, where he remained until war's end. In the last months of the war, he commanded more than 100,000 men and 1,800 airplanes spread over Western Europe. Ironically, differences with Montgomery led to a bitter dispute between the two. Coningham's biographer, Vincent Orange of the University of Canterbury in Christ Church, concluded this was a quarrel he could not win against the popular "Monty," and Coningham's reputation suffered.

When the war ended, Coningham accepted the less than prestigious position of commander at the Flying Training Center. Knighted in 1946, he was then asked to retire in 1947, the victim of a lack of service on the air staff. In January 1948, he died in an air accident in the Atlantic.

An outstanding air commander, Coningham spent his entire thirty-one-year career as an active pilot. His lasting contribution to tactical air support is legendary in the continuing history of airpower.

Boyd Childress

Additional Reading

Fenwick-Owen, Roderic, *Desert Air Force* (1948).

Orange, Vincent, *Coningham: A Biography of Air Marshal Sir Arthur Coningham, KCB, KBE, DSO, MC, DFC, AFC* (1990).

Terraine, John, *A Time for Courage: The Royal Air Force in the European War, 1939–1945* (1985).

Cooper, Peter Duff (1890–1945)

British politician and opponent of appeasement. Cooper served in the British War Office from 1935 to 1937 and later became first lord of the Admiralty in Neville Chamberlain's (q.v.) government. He saw World War II as inevitable and sought to modernize the Royal Navy. He failed to get Chamberlain to support his effort. Cooper's early faith in the League of Nations (q.v.) faded and he called for Britain to return to balance of power politics by opposing any European power that sought to dominate the Continent. After the 1938 Munich crisis (q.v.), he denounced Chamberlain's appeasement (q.v.) policy in the House of Commons and resigned from government.

For a while, Cooper wrote a weekly column for the *Evening Standard* newspaper, and in 1939–1940, he made an extended tour of the United States. He served as minister of information in 1940, and 1941, became chancellor to the Duchy of Lancaster. After Pearl Harbor, he became resident cabinet minister in Singapore and established a war council. He returned to Britain after the fall of the city.

As an admirer of Charles de Gaulle (q.v.), Cooper served as British representative on the Gaullist-established French Committee of National Liberation, and he sought to heal the rift with France left by the war. In 1944, he became British ambassador to France.

Paul Rose

Additional Reading

Eden, Anthony, *Facing the Dictators* (1962).

Namier, Lewis B., *Diplomatic Prelude 1938–39* (1948).

Cota, Norman (1893–1971)

American major general. Cota was a big, blustery New Englander known as "Dutch." He was the first U.S. general officer ashore on OMAHA Beach on D-Day, as assistant division commander of the 29th Infantry Division. He later served as com-

mander of the 28th Infantry (Keystone) Division, which he led through Paris in a liberation parade in August 1944. His presence in Paris was part of an American show of force in support of Charles de Gaulle (q.v.) to prevent a possible Communist takeover. Cota led the 28th Division in the attack on the Siegfried Line (q.v.) near St. Vith, saw heavy combat in the Hürtgen Forest (q.v.), and played a key role in repulsing the German Ardennes offensive (q.v.).

Paul J. Rose

Additional Reading

Ambrose, Stephen E., *D-Day June 6, 1944: The Climactic Battle of World War II* (1994).

MacDonald, Charles B., *A Time for Trumpets: The Untold Story of the Battle of the Bulge* (1985).

Toland, John B., *The Story of the Bulge* (1959).

Crerar, Henry Duncan Graham (1888–1965)

Canadian general, commander of the Canadian First Army. Crerar was born in Hamilton, Ontario. On his graduation from the Royal Military College in 1909, he joined the 4th Battery, a Hamilton militia artillery unit. He served as an artillery officer in World War I, winning the Distinguished

Brigadier General (later General) Henry D.G. Crerar. (IWM HU 60904)

C

Service Order in 1915 and gaining distinction as a staff officer in counter-battery work. He transferred to the permanent force after the war and was attached to the British War Office for several years. He returned to Canada in 1927 and was assigned to the Department of National Defense where he worked for the chief of the general staff, General A.G.L. McNaughton (q.v.). Crerar's administrative abilities were an important asset in the resource-starved interwar Canadian Army. The combination of ability and connections served him well, and he became director of military intelligence and operations in 1935.

In October 1939, Crerar was sent to Britain where he established the Canadian Military Headquarters, a forward echelon of the Department of National Defense. He largely defined the lines of communication that existed between the minister in Canada and the Canadian Army overseas. His ambition was to obtain a field command, but he was appointed chief of the general staff in 1940. There he developed the program of expansion that turned the Active Service Force into the Canadian First Army, and was responsible for the dispatch of Canadian troops to Hong Kong. He assumed command of the Canadian I Corps in 1942 and quickly intensified the training regimen, calling for a stricter adherence to regulations. He impressed his British superior, General Bernard L. Montgomery (q.v.), but their relations were soured by Crerar's rigid interpretation of the Canadian Army's autonomy.

The publicity-shy Crerar sought combat experience throughout 1943, but he had not led a large formation in battle when he replaced McNaughton as army commander in 1944. Crerar was not directly involved in the Normandy (q.v.) invasion, but as the senior combatant officer in the Canadian Army, he was responsible to the government for all Canadian troops in Europe, a responsibility he took very seriously.

Crerar's main operational task after the establishment of his army headquarters in July 1944 was the difficult struggle to close the Falaise gap. He led the Canadian Army in its successful operations against the Channel ports, operations characterized by massive artillery preparations and methodical assaults. He was later criticized for his cautious approach, but he was assigned multiple tasks and given little logistical support. He was invalided to Britain in late September 1944 during the Scheldt (q.v.) operation, and did not return until 7 November.

Crerar controlled a greatly expanded Canadian Army in the Rhineland (q.v.) offensive in the winter of 1945. The offensive was a feat of logistical and administrative organization, but it soon became a grinding battle of attrition. He was respected for abilities displayed in the operation, but this respect did not translate into affection. The retiring Crerar was never well known by his own troops. He was considered cold and aloof by some subordinates and was an exacting commander.

Crerar retired from the army immediately after the war and was soon lost from the public eye. He died having received very little recognition for his services.

Paul Dickson

Additional Reading

Canada, Department of Defense, *The Canadian Army in World War II, 1939–1945,* 3 vols. (1945–1946).

Stacey, C.P., *Arms, Men and Governments: The War Policies of Canada 1939–1945* (1970).

———, *Six Years of War* (1955).

Cripps, Richard Stafford (1889–1952)

British ambassador to the Soviet Union and member of the War Cabinet. Sir Richard Cripps was the son of the Labour foreign minister, Lord Parmoor, and Beatrice Webb's sister, Theresa—a political activist and author of the late nineteenth and early twentieth centuries. A brilliant but sickly young man, he carved out an enviable academic record at University College London before World War I. During the war, poor health confined him to work in the British munitions industry.

After the war, Cripps became a very successful barrister as well as a radical socialist. He was one of the most influential members of the Independent Labour Party in the 1930s. His sincerity and Christian idealism made him a powerful figure on the radical fringes of the Labour Party prior to the war. In the late 1930s, he advocated a popular front program to oppose Nazism. At the outbreak of the war, he made himself available for government service. Prime Minister Winston S. Churchill (q.v.) named him ambassador to the Soviet Union in June 1940 to help sway Josef Stalin from Adolf Hitler (qq.v.), a "lunatic in the land of lunatics" it was said. Although unsuccessful during his twenty months in Moscow, Cripps found himself a popular hero in Britain following Hitler's attack on the Soviet Union.

Churchill recognized Cripps's power and influence, bringing him into the War Cabinet and making him leader of the House of Commons in February 1942. Cripps served for sixteen months, resigning from the war cabinet in order to take over as a highly successful minister of aircraft, where his talents for organization served him well.

After the war, Cripps was one of the dominant figures in Clement Attlee's (q.v.) Labour ministry as president of the Board of Trade, minister for economic affairs, and finally as chancellor of the exchequer. For many, Cripps personified the strengths and weaknesses of the postwar austerity. Poor health forced his resignation in October 1950 and he died eighteen months later.

John P. Rossi

Additional Reading
Cooke, Colin, *The Life of Sir Richard Stafford Cripps* (1957).

Cunningham, Alan (1887–1983)
British lieutenant general, commander of British forces in Ethiopia. Sir Alan Cunningham was born in 1887 in Edinburgh, where his father was a professor of anatomy. His elder brother Andrew (q.v.) became an admiral, and the two brothers were to achieve the pinnacles of their careers against the same enemy at the same time, the Italians in 1940 and 1941.

Educated at Cheltenham and the Royal Military Academy at Woolwich, Cunningham was commissioned into the Royal Artillery in 1906. He spent World War I on the western front, winning a Distinguished Service Order. Between the wars, he attended both the Royal Navy Staff College and the Imperial Defence College. The early stages of World War II found him commanding an infantry division.

In 1940, Cunningham was chosen to command British forces in Kenya. Under the overall command of Archibald Wavell (q.v.), his forces, in conjunction with those of General Sir William Platt operating from Sudan, were ordered to liberate Ethiopia and to defeat all Italian forces in East Africa. The campaign, which started in January 1941, was a brilliant success. He entered Addis Ababa on 5 April, having advanced 1,700 miles and capturing 400,000 square miles of enemy-held territory and 50,000 prisoners. His forces suffered only 500 casualties. Then, in conjunction with Platt, he advanced on Amba Alagi, where the Italian commander, Amadeo di Savoia (q.v.), the duke of Aosta, surrendered on 16 May.

In June 1941, Cunningham took command of the Eighth Army in North Africa. German General Erwin Rommel and his *Afrika Korps* (qq.v.) were tougher opponents than the Italians,

and Cunningham could not repeat his Ethiopian success. During Operation CRUSADER, British armor was outfought by Rommel's greater tactical ability and superior tanks. With his tank losses increasing and German armor operating in his rear, Cunningham asked permission to break off the engagement. General Claude Auchinleck (q.v.), judging that Rommel would soon outrun his supplies, and that Cunningham had lost his nerve, replaced him with Neil Ritchie (q.v.) and ordered the offensive continued. It is probable that poor health was a factor in Cunningham's performance.

Cunningham played no further active part in the war. In 1945, he became British high commissioner in Palestine. He retired when the British mandate ended in 1948. He died in Kent in 1983 at the age of ninety-five.

Philip Green

Additional Reading
Crawford, Robert J., *I Was an Eighth Army Soldier* (1944).
Guingand, Francis de, *Generals at War* (1964).
Tucker, Sir Francis J.S., *Approach to Battle: A Commentary; Eighth Army, 1941–1943* (1963).

Cunningham, Andrew (1883–1963)
British admiral of the fleet, Allied naval commander Mediterranean. Cunningham was born in Dublin in 1883. After graduation from the Edinburgh Academy, he entered the Royal Navy in 1897 via the training ship *Britannia*. Throughout World War I, he was a destroyer captain, seeing action in the Dardanelles and the Dover Straits and at the amphibious raid on Zeebrugge. He was noticeable both for his gallantry (winning three Distinguished Service Orders) and his demanding standards. He sacked a large number of officers who failed to meet his requirements.

Between the wars, his career, spent almost entirely at sea, progressed steadily. By 1939, he was an admiral and acting commander in chief of the Mediterranean Fleet. The summer of 1940 saw the fall of France and the entry of Italy into the war. For the next three years, the conflict in the Mediterranean theater was mainly one between Britain and Italy, especially at sea. His first task was to immobilize the French Fleet at Alexandria to prevent it from falling into Axis hands. This he achieved with his French counterpart, Admiral René-Emile Godfroy, in contrast to the bloodshed at Mers el-Kébir (q.v.).

Cunningham's mission was to control the

Admiral of the Fleet Sir Andrew Cunningham, DSO and 2 Bars, on the bridge of the HMS Arethusa *with Air Chief Marshal Sir Charles Portal, DSO, MC. (IWM A 24197)*

Mediterranean against hostile ships and aircraft, and thus keep the lines of communication open from the Middle East back to Britain via Gibraltar. Defeat could have led to the loss of Malta, Egypt, and the Suez Canal, with disastrous consequences for the British. The Italian Fleet was modern and well trained, and it outnumbered Cunningham's.

Though his task was far from easy, his policy was resolutely offensive, and within a year, two victories won at almost no cost, virtually eliminated the Italian surface fleet. In November 1940, his carrier-borne Swordfish biplanes launched a night torpedo attack on the enemy fleet in Taranto (q.v.) harbor. Half the Italian battleships were put out of action and the remainder were forced to shelter in Naples. In March 1941, off Cape Matapan (q.v.), in the first use of radar at sea in any significant engagement, three British battleships opened fire at night on the unsuspecting Italians with 15-inch guns at a range of two miles. Three heavy cruisers and two destroyers were sunk.

Not all of Cunningham's successes were so easily gained. In the confined waters of the Mediterranean, British warships were rarely out of range of shore-based Axis aircraft. Convoys from Gibraltar, used to relieve the besieged island of Malta, came under attack from airfields from Sicily, only sixty miles away. Additionally, the evacuation of British and Commonwealth troops from Greece and Crete (qq.v.) resulted in heavy losses in British ships and men.

One story from the Crete episode illustrates his determination and strength of character. To a staff officer who quite properly pointed out the losses to date and the risk of worse to come if Cunningham continued with the operation under constant Axis attack, he replied, "It takes the Navy three years to build a ship, but 300 years to build a tradition; we must not let the Army down." The evacuation went on and the losses mounted, but thousands of British, Australian, and New Zealand troops were saved to fight another day.

After a short spell in Washington in 1942 leading the British naval team on the Combined Chiefs of Staff (q.v.), Cunningham returned to the Mediterranean as Allied naval commander. Here he was responsible for the naval contribution to three successful Allied landings: the Operation TORCH landings in North Africa in 1942, and the invasions of Sicily and Salerno (qq.v.) the following year. When Italy negotiated an armistice after the overthrow of Benito Mussolini (q.v.) in 1943, Cunningham had the satisfaction of accepting the surrender of the Italian fleet in Malta. "Be pleased to inform their Lordships," ran his stately signal to London, "that the Italian battle fleet has surrendered and now lies at anchor beneath the guns of the fortress of Malta. God save the King!"

Later that year, Cunningham returned to Britain to become first sea lord, the professional head of the Royal Navy. He remained in that office until the end of the war. For his war services, he was created Viscount Cunningham of Hyndhope.

A thorough professional in the traditions of the Royal Navy, Cunningham had the ability to cope with shortages in the early years of the war and to handle the plentiful resources of the later years. Despite having started his service in the nineteenth century, he understood modern technology, and his two most complete victories were owed to naval aviation and radar, respectively. He was of implacable and resolute spirit, and a man of humor and warmth. Moreover, he could cooperate with allies and other services, a quality not shared by every high commander of World War II. It has been said that throughout World War II, he never took an unwise action. When he died in 1963, Field Marshal Lord Harold Alexander (q.v.) called him, "one of the great sea commanders of our island race."

In retirement, Cunningham was lord high commissioner of the general assembly of the Church of Scotland, and for three years, lord rector of Edinburgh University.

Philip Green

C

Additional Reading
Chatterton, Edward K., and Kenneth Edwards, *The Royal Navy: From September 1939 to September 1945,* 5 vols. (1942–47).
Cunningham, Andrew, *A Sailor's Odyssey* (1951).

Czuma, Walerian (1890–1962)

Polish major general, commander of the Warsaw garrison in 1939. Czuma's energetic organization of Warsaw's defenses thwarted the initial German attempt to capture the city on 9 September. For three weeks, he coordinated the resistance against artillery and air bombardments and attempts to storm the city. Following Warsaw's surrender on 27 September 1939, he became a POW until the end of the war.

Andrzej Suchcitz

Additional Reading
Mazur, Tadeusz, et al. (eds.), *We Have Not Forgotten, 1939–1945* (1960).
Norwid-Neugebauer, Mieczusław, *Defense of Poland, 1939* (1942).
Zaloga, Steven, and Victor Madej, *The Polish Campaign, 1939* (1985).

D

Daladier, Édouard (1884–1970)

Prime minister of France on the outbreak of World War II. First elected to the Chamber of Deputies in 1919, Daladier was a protege of Radical Socialist leader Édouard Herriot and was party leader himself in 1927. Daladier held a succession of cabinet posts before becoming premier in 1933, and again briefly in 1934. He helped bring the radicals into the popular front with the Socialists and Communists in January 1936, but soon lost enthusiasm for collaboration with the Communists. On the collapse of the popular front in 1938, he again became prime minister.

During his two-year tenure as prime minister, Daladier was preoccupied with foreign policy and national defense, although he took steps to reinvigorate the economy. He was one of the signatories to the Munich Agreement (q.v.), although he held no illusions about it. He was shocked by the Molotov-Ribbentrop Pact (q.v.) of August 1939. At the outbreak of war, he reacted by outlawing the Communist Party and ordering its leaders arrested. After the German defeat of Poland, he resisted intense pressure to withdraw France from the war.

Daladier's problems were complicated by Franco-British disagreements over the conduct of the war and parliamentary factionalism. A cabinet crisis occurred in March 1940, and he was ousted on 20 March, partly because he failed to aid Finland against the Soviets. He was replaced by Paul Reynaud (q.v.) but remained in the government as war minister.

On 21 June 1940, Daladier and other parliamentary leaders sailed from Bordeaux for Casablanca to set up a government-in-exile. General Henri Pétain (q.v.) ordered them arrested. Daladier was among those tried at Riom in 1942 on charges of being responsible for the French defeat. Although the trial was suspended, he remained in confinement until liberated in 1945.

Spencer Tucker

Additional Reading

Chapman, Guy, *Why France Fell: The Defeat of the French Army in 1940* (1969).

Horne, Alistair, *To Lose a Battle: France 1940* (1969).

Reynaud, Paul, *In the Thick of the Fight* (1955).

Daluege, Kurt (1897–1946)

Commander of the German Order Police. Born in Upper Silesia, Daluege was trained as an engineer. He served in World War I and was later a leader in the Rossbach *Freikorps*. He joined the NSDAP and the SA (qq.v.) in 1922 and later transferred to the SS (q.v.). Appointed by Hermann Göring (q.v.) as the commander of the Prussian police in 1933, Daluege infiltrated this organization with reliable SS men and purged all anti-Nazi elements. He was later appointed Prussian state counselor and served in the *Reichstag*. In 1936, he was appointed commander of the Order Police and was responsible for its complete militarization. He became protector of Bohemia and Moravia in 1942 after Heydrich's (q.v.) assassination and was responsible for the destruction of Lidiče (q.v.). Daluege was hanged by the Czechs in 1946.

Steven B. Rogers

Additional Reading

Daluege, Kurt, *Tag der Deutschen Polizei—1934* (1935).

Grant Duff, Sheila, *German Protectorate: The Czechs Under Nazi Rule* (1942).

Dankers, Oskar (1883–1965)

General and first general director of Latvia. Dankers was a retired Latvian general appointed by the Germans in 1941 to lead the Latvian "self-administration." He served until the Germans retreated from Latvia during the summer of 1944. He later sought German approval for a new Latvian national council under his leadership as a vanguard for renewed Latvian independence.

Steven B. Rogers

Additional Reading

Bilmanis, A., *A History of Latvia* (1951).
Dankers, Oskar, *Lai Vesture Spriez Tiesu [Let History Judge It]* (1956).
Misiunas, Romuald J., and Rein Taagepera, *The Baltic States. Years of Dependence, 1940–1980* (1983).

Darby, William Orlando (1911–1945)

American brigadier general, founder of the U.S. Rangers (q.v.). Originally assigned to the field artillery branch, Darby was a curious choice to command an elite infantry unit styled after the American rangers commanded by Robert Rogers during the French and Indian Wars of the eighteenth century. After a brief tour as aide-de-camp to the commander of the 34th U.S. Infantry Division (one of the first U.S. units in the European theater), Darby was selected to organize the ranger program in June 1942. He set upon his new task with zeal, beginning the organization and training of the new force at Achnacarry, Scotland, under the tutelage of the British commandos (q.v.). He was said to have been a born leader, personally fearless, and an adherent of the "lead by example" school of combat leadership.

Officially, Darby commanded only the 1st Ranger Battalion; but from their inception until December 1943, he created, organized, trained, and led the 1st, 3rd, and 4th Ranger Battalions, which were known throughout the war as "Darby's Rangers." In December 1943, he was promoted to colonel and given official command of all three battalions.

After 1st and 3rd Battalions were destroyed near Anzio (q.v.) in January 1944 (through no fault of his), Darby commanded the 179th Infantry Regiment. In April 1944, he returned to the U.S. to join the Operations Division of the War Department's general staff. By April 1945, he was assistant division commander of the U.S. 10th Mountain Division.

One of the first Americans to enter the European theater, Darby was also one of the last to be killed in it, by a stray artillery round on 30 April 1945 in Italy. He was posthumously promoted to brigadier general.

John D. Beatty

Additional Reading

Darby, William O., *We Led the Way* (1945).
King, Michael J., *William Orlando Darby: A Military Biography* (1981).

Darlan, Jean François (1881–1942)

French admiral and politician. Nicknamed the "kowtowing admiral" *(l'amiral courbette)* and referred to by some as the greatest string-puller in the French Navy, Darlan was an ambitious opportunist. He was also an anglophobe, particularly after Mers el-Kébir (q.v.). He served as naval minister almost continuously between 1926 and 1939, and as the French Navy's executive head between 1933 and 1940, during which time he nurtured it to its prewar apogee.

Darlan continued as minister of the navy under the Vichy regime between 9 February 1941 and 18 April 1942. As General Henri Pétain's (q.v.) nominated *dauphin,* or successor, he served as "prime minister" with additional ministerial responsibilities of internal affairs, foreign affairs, information, and defense. It was here that Darlan sought closer collaboration with the Germans hoping to win better conditions for the French. Darlan's second meeting with Adolf Hitler (q.v.) at Berchtesgarden in May 1941 led to the signing of the "Paris Protocols," which resulted in the offer of logistical support to the Germans and the opening of the ports of Bizerte, Casablanca, and Dakar to the German *Kriegsmarine* (Navy). Darlan also permitted the transport of war materials through French Tunisia to help German general Erwin Rommel (q.v.) in his North African campaign. In return for these concessions, the Germans freed 100,000 French POWs and allowed the rearming of a dozen French warships. Darlan, however, gave too much away, winning little in return for Vichy France, which became effectively allied with Germany in the Mediterranean theater. Darlan was in Algiers on the eve of the Allied invasion of North Africa on 8 November 1942. After initially opposing the Allied landings, he suddenly reversed course and claimed that he was sent to Algeria by Pétain to strike a bargain with the Allies. Attempting to prevent other French factions from taking power, Darlan agreed to cooperate with the Allies in return for their recognition of his authority. He signed the cease-fire (the "Darlan Deal") with

General Mark W. Clark (q.v.) and Ambassador Robert Murphy on 11 November.

On 24 December 1942, Darlan was assassinated in Algiers under mysterious circumstances by Fernand Bonnier de la Chapelle, a young fanatic linked with the French royalists. There has been some suggestion that this was financed by the British Secret Intelligence Service (q.v.).

Robert C. Hudson

Additional Reading

Huddleston, Sisley, *France: The Tragic Years* (1954).
Montmorency, Alec de, *The Enigma of Admiral Darlan* (1943).
Tompkins, Peter, *The Murder of Admiral Darlan: A Study in Conspiracy* (1965).

Darnand, Joseph (1897–1945)

French collaborationist. Darnand was one of France's most highly decorated NCOs in World War I. He saw action in 1940 as well. With the creation of the Vichy (q.v.) regime, he became a key figure in its security system, eventually heading the feared *Milice Française* (q.v.). He led the *Milice* in a vicious war with the resistance, for which he was executed in October 1945.

Stephen M. Cullen

Additional Reading

Dank, Milton, *The French Against the French: Collaboration and Resistance* (1974).
Littlejohn, David, *The Patriotic Traitors* (1972).

Davis, Benjamin O., Sr. (1880–1970)

America's first black general officer. Davis began his fifty-year military career as an officer of volunteers during the Spanish-American War. His contributions and persistent advocacy within an army still influenced by racial prejudice allowed him to advance in rank, despite significant obstacles. The administration of President Franklin D. Roosevelt (q.v.) selected Davis for promotion to brigadier general on 26 October 1940, recognizing the need for a black general officer, the need for support of the black community prior to the 1940 election, and the coming mobilization for World War II.

When Davis reached the then mandatory retirement age of sixty-four, chief of staff of the army General George C. Marshall (q.v.) ordered him returned to active duty status on 28 June 1941. Davis was assigned as the head of a special section within the army's inspector general office to tackle the problems of racial segregation in an expanding wartime army.

Davis's World War II service focused on mitigating the severe problems created by segregation policies both on and off army posts throughout the United States. Davis worked to change the leadership climate within the segregated black units. (*See* Black Units in the U.S. Military.) He conducted tours of Army posts, investigating racial incidents and defusing these problems.

At the request of General Dwight D. Eisenhower (q.v.), who desperately needed to solve racial problems in the U.S. Army in Europe, Davis made a trip to the European Theater of Operations (ETO) in 1942. Working closely with Major General John C.H. Lee, Eisenhower's chief of services of supply, Davis proposed various solutions. These included increasing the number of black officers by selecting qualified individuals for Officer Candidate School, improving the overall quality of leadership within black units, and providing black American history training for all U.S. soldiers.

Upon his return to the United States, Davis continued to prod policy makers, through the Secretary of War's Advisory Committee, to improve a racial climate detrimental to the war effort. One of his efforts was the 1943 film, *The Negro Soldier,* which was widely distributed and used as a teaching tool.

Davis returned to Europe in 1944, and at Lee's request, continued to work to improve racial policies. Davis also continued documenting on film black units in combat. Late in 1944, high American infantry casualties forced a change in policy that allowed black soldiers to volunteer as infantry replacements. Davis's activities through 1945 focused on the training, morale, and combat deployment of black infantry replacement platoons within the ETO.

Despite his efforts, Davis was unable to make major changes in U.S. Army racial policies during his own career. But his ability to work within the army system, his educational activities, and his persistence in reducing the worst aspects of military segregation laid the foundation for the fully-integrated U.S. Army that followed a few years after the end of World War II.

Keith Wooster

Additional Reading

Fletcher, Marvin E. *America's First Black General: Benjamin O. Davis, Sr., 1880-1970* (1989).
Lee, Ulysses, *The Employment of Negro Troops* (1966).

Davis, Benjamin O., Jr. (1912–)

American colonel, commander of the U.S. 332nd Fighter Group. The 332nd Fighter Group was the only all-black combat air group ever organized by the U.S. Army Air Forces. As a captain, Davis was the leader of an initial cadre of thirteen black airmen that entered flight training in August 1941 at Tuskegee Army Air Field, Alabama. He and four others graduated on 7 March 1942, and they were the first of approximately 1,000 black airmen who would graduate from the Tuskegee facility. They formed the nucleus of the newly created 99th Pursuit Squadron.

Lieutenant Colonel Davis led the squadron of twenty-six pilots and 300 enlisted men in its first action in North Africa, while assigned as part of the 33rd Fighter Group based at Fordjouna, Tunisia. In September 1943, three months after the 99th Pursuit Squadron entered combat, a hostile internal army report claimed Davis's pilots lacked air discipline and aggressiveness.

Davis fought these calumnies by testifying before the War Department's advisory committee on Negro troop policies. He stressed the very real handicaps his unit had to work under: an absence of experienced formation and element leaders, dependence on outdated P-40 fighter aircraft, and manning shortfalls 20–30 percent below white fighter squadrons. Despite these problems, 99th Pursuit Squadron pilots flew up to six sorties a day, and stood their ground against enemy fighter counterattacks, which they encountered 80 per-cent of the time. As a result of Davis's testimony, the advisory committee voted against withdrawing the squadron from combat operations and thus gave it precious time to gain experience.

Future success came quickly. On 27–28 January 1944, Davis's pilots shot down thirteen German fighters. Subsequent successes set the stage for the formation of the 332nd Fighter Group, which, under Colonel Davis's command, absorbed the 99th Pursuit Squadron in June 1944. Eventually, the four-squadron group flew P-51 Mustangs in the European theater with great success. The 332nd Fighter Group performed 15,000 sorties and 1,500 missions, 200 of which involved bomber escort. Davis's pilots shot down 111 enemy aircraft, nearly all of which were fighters. They destroyed 150 airplanes on the ground and demolished more than 600 railroad boxcars and other rolling stock. Most significantly, the 332nd Fighter Group never lost a friendly bomber to an enemy fighter in all the bomber escort missions it performed.

Under the leadership of Benjamin O. Davis, Jr., who later became the first black general officer in the United States Air Force, the 332nd Fighter Group won two significant battles during World War II, the fight for air supremacy over the skies of Europe, and the fight for respect and equality in the segregated U.S. Army Air Forces.

Peter R. Faber

Additional Reading

Francis, Charles E., *The Tuskegee Airmen: The Story of the Negro in the U.S. Air Force* (1956).
Furr, Arthur, *Democracy's Negroes: A Book of Facts Concerning the Activities of Negroes in World War II* (1947).
Osur, Alan M., *Blacks in the Army Air Forces During World War II* (1977).
Wilson, Ruth, *Jim Crow Joins Up: A Study of Negroes in the Armed Forces of the United States* (1944).

Dean, William Frishe (1899–1981)

American major general, commander, 44th Infantry Division. A native of Illinois, Dean graduated from the University of California at Berkeley in 1922 and received his commission in 1923. At the beginning of World War II, Lieutenant Colonel Dean was assistant secretary of the War Department's general staff. In mid-1944, Dean became assistant commander of the 44th Infantry Division, part of General Alexander Patch's (q.v.) Seventh Army. In January 1945, Dean became the division commander.

Colonel Benjamin O. Davis, Jr. (IWM EA 35890)

After the war, Dean commanded first the 7th, and then the 24th Infantry Divisions, stationed in Japan. On 21 July 1950, he disappeared while fighting a rear-guard action at Taejon, Korea. He was awarded the Medal of Honor for the action, although he was not confirmed as a POW until December 1951. He was released in September 1953.

Randy Papadopoulos

Additional Reading
Dean, William F., and W.L. Worden, *General Dean's Story* (1954).

Degrelle, Léon (1906–1993)

Belgian Fascist, *Waffen-SS* commander. In the 1930s Degrelle was a founder of the Rexists, the Fascist party in Belgium. During the war he formed the Wallon Legion. That unit later became integrated into the *Waffen-SS* (q.v.) order of battle as the 28th SS Division, although it was never larger than regimental strength. Degrelle commanded the unit in Russia. He received the Knight's Cross with Oak Leaves, making him the highest decorated foreigner in German service. Adolf Hitler (q.v.) once told him, "If I had a son, I would have liked him to be like you." After the war Degrelle was condemned by a Belgian court. He escaped to Spain, where he lived in exile until his death at age eighty-seven. To the very end Degrelle continued to proclaim Hitler as "the greatest genius of all time."

David T. Zabecki

Additional Reading
Keegan, John, *Waffen SS: The Asphalt Soldiers* (1970).

Degtiarev, Vasily Alekseevich (1880–1949)

Soviet major general of the Engineer Artillery Service, and small arms designer. Degtiarev was one of the twentieth century's premier designers of military weapons. He headed the Soviet Union's first design bureau for the development of small arms. In 1934 he developed a submachine gun, which in its 1940 modification, became the widely used PPD. He also designed the PTRD antitank rifle, and co-designed the 12.7mm DShK antiaircraft machine gun. He was made a Hero of Socialist Labor and received three Orders of Lenin for his work.

David T. Zabecki

Additional Reading
Union of Soviet Socialist Republics, *The Great Soviet Encyclopedia,* English translation of the 3rd edition (1975), Vol. 8., p. 92.

Dempsey, Miles Christopher (1896–1969)

British lieutenant general, commander of the British Second Army. Sir Miles Dempsey commanded an infantry company during World War I at age nineteen. After the war, he toured Europe's battlefields, compiling a collection of carefully indexed and annotated maps, drawing many himself. Montgomery (q.v.) later said Dempsey could "describe foreign terrain so vividly from a map that it [became] almost a pictorial reality to listeners."

Dempsey returned to Europe in 1940, commanding the British Expeditionary Force's 13th Infantry Brigade, which he skillfully led in a three-day holding battle during the evacuation from Dunkirk (q.v.). He subsequently helped train the new armies being raised against the anticipated German invasion of Britain. In June 1941, his exceptional organizational skills earned him the task of forming and commanding a new armored division, as well as a promotion to major general.

After El Alamein (q.v.), General Bernard L. Montgomery requested Dempsey's transfer from Britain to command XIII Corps as a lieutenant general. From January to April 1943, Dempsey was chief of staff of Montgomery's planning headquarters for Operation HUSKY. He then returned to XIII Corps to lead the eastern assault on Sicily.

Lieutenant General Sir Miles Dempsey, DSO, MC. (IWM H 21064)

During Operation HUSKY, XIII Corps seized Syracuse and Augusta, then moved into the strategic town of Catania, where he maintained diversionary pressure while British XXX Corps outflanked the Axis defensive line.

Following Allied victory in Sicily, Dempsey's corps crossed the Strait of Messina and landed at Calabria in another secondary action in support of the Salerno (q.v.) landings. This corps then pushed northward, spearheading British Eighth Army operations for the rest of the year.

In January 1944, Montgomery assumed command of 21st Army Group in Britain, choosing Dempsey to lead the unbloodied British Second Army, the only change of senior commanders for Operation OVERLORD that Montgomery requested. "I had the greatest admiration for Dempsey, whom I had known for many years. He took the Second Army right through to the end of the war and amply justified this confidence in his ability and courage," Montgomery later wrote.

At the Normandy (q.v.) beachhead, the Germans concentrated their tanks against Second Army, respecting British military prowess above American. Montgomery's operational plans, therefore, were based on Second Army drawing the bulk of the German combat power. Through July 1944, Dempsey tied down up to nine *Panzer* divisions, enabling General Omar N. Bradley's (q.v.) U.S. First Army to make the main Allied breakout at St. Lô (q.v.).

Following the breaching of the Seine, Second Army sprinted northward, liberating Brussels and Antwerp (q.v.). Dempsey recommended against the subsequent Operation MARKET-GARDEN, favoring an Anglo-American assault near Wesel. Unlike Montgomery, he believed the reports of massed armor near Arnhem, and felt the Second Army was not ready for the operation. Montgomery overruled those objections.

After the Arnhem (q.v.) debacle, Dempsey cleared the enemy from south and west of the Maas, on one occasion trucking in two divisions to plug a gap in the front. Second Army was then picked for the main attack over the Rhine River in Operation PLUNDER. He withdrew two divisions from combat in February 1945 to train on the Maas in river crossing techniques, fine-tuning his plan from lessons observed. He also helped persuade Montgomery to allocate the U.S. Ninth Army an independent assault zone in the operation, rather than relegate it to the reserve, soothing ruffled American egos.

Across the Rhine, the Second Army drove to the Baltic, taking the major northwest German ports and blocking any Soviet advance on Denmark. After the German surrender, Dempsey was appointed commander in chief, Allied land forces Southeast Asia. In 1946, he was promoted to general and appointed commander in chief of the Middle East.

He chose retirement in 1947, confiding to a friend, "I have spent too much of my life smashing things up. I would like to do some construction work before I am too old." He became chairman of a brewery and chairman of the Racecourse Betting Control Board, a fitting post for an officer who frequently bet on the course of wartime operations.

Unassuming and retiring, Dempsey nonetheless impressed with quiet command of his tasks. Montgomery's chief of staff, General Francis de Guingand (q.v.), called him "a most able and cooperative colleague." Dempsey kept his subordinates firmly under control without engendering enmity.

As a staff officer, Dempsey helped shape the forces that liberated Europe. As a commander, he was often chosen to spearhead operations. His greatest contribution to Allied success, however, was his ability to subordinate his ego, "without jealousy or anger," as Bradley observed, repeatedly accepting the task of holding down enemy forces while other commanders took the glory. In this role, Dempsey facilitated Allied victory in Sicily, Italy, and above all, Normandy.

For his contributions, King George VI (q.v.) knighted Dempsey, together with de Guingand, during a visit to the 21st Army Group in Holland; the first knighting of soldiers in the field since Agincourt. Sir Miles Dempsey died at his home in Berkshire on the twenty-fifth anniversary of Operation OVERLORD.

Sidney Dean

Additional Reading

Essame, Hubert, *The Battle for Germany* (1969).
Guingand, Francis de, *Generals at War* (1964).
Hastings, Max, *Overlord* (1984).
Montgomery, Bernard L., *Memoirs* (1958).

Dentz, Henri-Fernand (1881–1945)

French general. As military governor of Paris, General Dentz was obliged to surrender the French capital to the Germans in June 1940. Dentz, however, is better known for the role he played as Vichy governor of Syria, and his assistance to the Germans in staging pro-Nazi coups in both Syria and Iraq in April 1941. Dentz granted the *Luftwaffe* the use of Aleppo as a refueling point, enabling the

Axis forces to come within bombing range of the Suez Canal zone and the Iraqi oil fields. Syrian ports, roads, and railways were also made available for the transportation of German equipment to Iraq, and Dentz supplied Iraqi rebels with French war material as well as transmitting all information concerning British forces in the Near East to the German high command.

Dentz's collaboration with the Germans in Syria seriously menaced areas then vital to British interests, and broke communications between Palestine and Iraq. The Allies first offered to support Dentz if he came over to their side and resisted the German landing. Dentz refused, and conforming strictly to his instructions from the Vichy government, he opposed the subsequent Allied invasion force made up of Austrian and Free French troops. Deprived of any logistic support, Dentz finally was forced to ask for an armistice on 12 July 1941.

At the end of the war, Dentz was one of the few French generals to be punished for pro-Vichy activities. Condemned to death in 1945, his sentence was commuted to forced labor for life. He died a short time afterward in Fresnes Prison.

Robert C. Hudson

Additional Reading

Aron, Robert, *The Vichy Regime, 1940–1944* (1958).

Farmer, P., *The Vichy Political Dilemma* (1955).

Devers, Jacob Loucks (1887–1979)

American general, commander of Allied 6th Army Group. Devers was born in York, Pennsylvania, on 8 September 1887, and graduated from the U.S. Military Academy at West Point, where he was an outstanding athlete, in the class of 1909. Commissioned into the artillery, he spent World War I at the School of Fire at Fort Sill, Oklahoma. He was convinced that his career was ruined by not seeing combat duty in France. Until 1936, when he returned to West Point, he spent the interwar years in a series of artillery training assignments at Fort Sill and staff positions in Washington, D.C. These tours were broken by attendance at the Command and General Staff College (1924–1925), and the Army War College (1932–1933).

Devers's abilities were noticed by General George C. Marshall (q.v.), and in June 1939, Devers was named chief of staff of the Panama Canal Department, the first of three key prewar assignments he received from Marshall. While in Panama, Devers was jumped over 474 other colonels and promoted to brigadier general. In July

1940, Devers was back in Washington, D.C., and was senior army member of the board that selected the bases in the Destroyers for Bases Deal (q.v.) with Great Britain. A few months later, he took command of the 9th Infantry Division at Fort Bragg, North Carolina. During his nine months there, he supervised the rapid expansion (300 percent) of Fort Bragg into one of the army's largest and most active training bases, and he received his second star there.

Finally, in July 1941, Marshall sent Devers to Fort Knox, Kentucky, as chief of the Armored Force, supervising the development of the U.S. Army's growing mechanized capability. Although he had spent over two decades in artillery, Devers quickly became an advocate of mobile combined arms warfare, featuring close cooperation between air and ground elements. He also helped spur the development of heavier tanks with greater firepower, correctly predicting that greater hitting power and improved survivability of heavier tanks would be as important as the greater mobility of light armored vehicles. On 6 September 1942, he received his third star.

Devers's desire for an operational command came about in May 1943, when he was named overall commander of the European Theater of Operations (ETO) after Lieutenant General Frank Andrews (q.v.) was killed in a plane crash. Devers oversaw the buildup of American land and air forces in Great Britain during the rest of 1943, and he was responsible for much of the training for the planned cross-channel attack. He hoped to lead that attack, clearly destined to be the centerpiece of the American wartime effort in Europe.

Instead, Devers was sent to the Mediterranean theater of operations as deputy supreme Allied commander at the end of 1943, when General Dwight D. Eisenhower (q.v.) returned to the ETO. Devers finally received his long-sought combat command in September 1944, when he was named commander of the 6th Army Group after the invasion of southern France (q.v.) in Operation DRAGOON.

As 6th Army Group commander, Devers was the equal of Field Marshal Bernard L. Montgomery and General Omar N. Bradley (qq.v.) under Eisenhower. During the campaign in France, it became apparent, however, that Devers was not part of Eisenhower's (or Bradley's) inner circle. His 6th Army Group included the U.S. Seventh Army and the French First Army, under General Jean de Lattre de Tassigny (q.v.), which in turn meant dealing with General de Gaulle (q.v.). Devers's well-deserved reputation for diplomacy was often tested by this relationship, as during the imbroglio over the Colmar pocket (q.v.) and the German threat to Strasburg in December 1944 and early January 1945.

On 26 March 1945, three weeks after he received his fourth star, Devers's forces crossed the Rhine River and drove across southern Germany and into Austria. On 6 May, Devers, representing the Allies, accepted the surrender of all German forces in the region.

For four years after the war, Devers served as commander of the U.S. Army Ground Forces, until his retirement in September 1949. For most of the 1950s, he was associated with the Fairchild Engine and Airplane Corporation in Washington, D.C., where he lived until his death on 15 October 1979.

Daniel T. Kuehl

Additional Reading

Clarke, Jeffrey J., and Robert Ross Smith, *Riviera to the Rhine: The United States Army in World War II* (1993).
Eisenhower, Dwight D., *Crusade in Europe* (1948).
Weigley, Russell, *Eisenhower's Lieutenants: The Campaigns of France and Germany, 1944–1945* (1981).
Wilt, Alan F., *The French Riviera Campaign* (1981).

Dietl, Eduard Wolfram (1890–1944)

German colonel general, alpine commander. Dietl was born in Bad Aibling, Germany, on 21 July 1890. In 1909, he entered military service with the 5th Infantry Regiment as a cadet, receiving his commission two years later. During World War I he was wounded several times, and earned the Iron Cross First Class. Dietl remained in the *Reichswehr* following the war, and by 1938 was a major general in command of the 8th Mountain Division.

After serving in the Polish campaign in 1939, Dietl and his mountain troops were sent to Norway in 1940. Outnumbered by British, French, and Polish forces, Dietl managed to hold out at Narvik (q.v.) by drafting as infantrymen sailors from ships that had been sunk during the initial invasion. He also salvaged much-needed ammunition, food, and weapons from sunken ships in the town's harbor. His skillful defense earned him the nickname, "The Hero of Narvik." He later remarked: "I'm the Hero of Narvik. Had the British stayed two more hours, I would have left!"

In May, 1940 Dietl was promoted to lieutenant general and awarded the Knight's Cross by Adolf Hitler (q.v.). Two months later, he received

General of Infantry Eduard Dietl, during the Norwegian Campaign. (IWM HU 1796)

the Oak Leaves to the Knight's Cross. Dietl then assumed command of the 20th Mountain Army, fighting for the next four years in Finland and Lapland. During that time he was promoted to colonel general. After visiting Hitler at the Obersalzberg, Dietl planned to return to Norway, but was killed on 23 June 1944 when his plane crashed into a fog-shrouded mountain. Hitler posthumously awarded him the Swords to the Knight's Cross on 1 July.

Mark Conrad

Additional Reading

Brett-Smith, Richard, *Hitler's Generals* (1977).
Lucas, J., *Alpine Elite* (1980).

Dietrich, Josef ("Sepp") (1892–1966)

German SS *Panzer* general. *Oberstgruppenführer* "Sepp" Dietrich was the illegitimate child of a Bavarian maidservant. He became one of the most recognizable figures of the *Waffen-SS* (q.v.). He was little educated and a butcher by trade. He served in the regular German Army from 1911 to 1918, ending the war as a sergeant, a stature permanently affixed in the minds of many *Wehrmacht* and fellow *Waffen-SS* officers. After World War I, he joined the *Freikorps* (q.v.), fighting Communists in the streets.

Dietrich joined the Nazi Party in 1923, gaining Adolf Hitler's (q.v.) attention by his burly toughness. For many years, he was Hitler's personal chauffeur and bodyguard. Hitler assigned Dietrich to establish his private guard. By 9 November 1933, the *Stabswache* grew and became the *Liebstandarte Adolf Hitler* (LAH). On 30 June 1934, he led the LAH against Ernst Röhm and the SA during the "Night of the Long Knives" (qq.v.).

As a favorite of Hitler, Dietrich enjoyed an independence like no other SS officer, often to Heinrich Himmler's (q.v.) disgust. Under Dietrich's tutelage, the LAH expanded and organized as a motorized infantry regiment, participating in the campaigns in Poland and France. The LAH fought in Greece as a full division even though it was only at brigade strength.

In June 1941, Dietrich commanded his well-equipped LAH during Operation BARBAROSSA and the invasion of the Soviet Union. During this time, the Soviets accused Dietrich of personally ordering the execution of 4,000 prisoners in retaliation for the murder of several SS men. In July 1942, the LAH was transferred to occupied Vichy France (q.v.), but by December 1942, the unit was sent back to the Russian front as part of the SS *Panzerkorps*.

In July 1943, Dietrich and his division transferred to Italy to bolster Benito Mussolini's (q.v.) crumbling government. On 27 July, he became commander of the I SS *Panzer Korps;* and by October, he was back to the Russian front. In spring 1944, he transferred to Normandy in time for the D-Day invasion. He attempted to discuss the war situation with Hitler, who refused to listen. Thus, by fall 1944, Dietrich was becoming disillusioned with Hitler.

In October 1944, Dietrich was appointed commander of the new Sixth *Panzer* Army, consisting of reconstituted *Panzer* divisions and hastily formed infantry divisions. The new unit's mission was to spearhead the December Ardennes offensive (q.v.). He had little confidence in the plan. Much to Hitler's chagrin, the Sixth *Panzer* Army was halted by numerically inferior American forces at Monshau, Elsenborn Ridge, and along the Ambleve River. It was during this campaign that Dietrich was implicated in a series of atrocities against American soldiers and Belgian civilians, including the Malmedy massacre (q.v.).

In early 1945, the Sixth *Panzer* Army transferred to Hungary to take part in the failed Lake Balaton counteroffensive. Unable to relieve Budapest (q.v.) and defend Vienna, Hitler became enraged with Dietrich.

After the war, Dietrich was tried by the Americans for his involvement in the Malmedy massacre and sentenced to life in prison. His sentence was later reduced, and he was released in October 1955. He was later tried by a Munich court for his involvement in the "Night of the Long Knives" incident and served an additional eighteen months. He was released in February 1959, and died in Ludwigsburg on 21 April 1966.

Dietrich was overly fond of alcohol, courageous, ruthless, and barely competent at division command. Above division level, he required able assistants, like Fritz Krämer, for detailed planning and operations.

Samuel J. Doss

Additional Reading

Messenger, Charles, *Hitler's Gladiator* (1988).
Quarrie, Bruce, *Hitler's Samurai: The Waffen SS in Action* (1986).

Dill, John Greer (1881–1944)

British field marshal, chief of the British Joint Staff Mission. Sir John Dill was born in County Armagh, Ireland, on 25 December 1881. He was educated at Cheltenham College and the Royal Military College at Sandhurst, and commissioned into the Leinster Regiment on 8 May 1901. He joined his regiment in South Africa where he served until the end of the Boer War.

At the outbreak of World War I, Dill was a student at the Staff College at Camberley. In October 1914, he was appointed brigade major of the 25th Brigade, 8th Division. In 1916, he was appointed to the staff of the Canadian Corps and promoted to major. In 1917, he saw action on the staff of 37th Division at Arres and Ypres. He was regarded as having a talent for military affairs and a strong sense of duty. As a staff officer, he was considered to have exceptional ability. He was transferred to the operations branch general headquarters, and in March 1918, he became chief of the branch with the temporary rank of brigadier general. During the war, he was wounded, mentioned in dispatches eight times, awarded the Distinguished Service Order in 1915, and appointed Commander of the Order of St. Michael and St. George in 1918.

Dill served in a variety of posts in the postwar years. In 1930, he was given accelerated promotion to major general, and in January 1931, he became the commandant of the Staff College. In 1934, he moved to the War Office and took over as director of military operations and intelligence.

Other staff appointments followed until the outbreak of World War II, when much to his disappointment, he was given command of the British I Corps instead of a War Office appointment.

Dill's corps was stationed along the frontier of Belgium, but in April 1940, he was recalled to the War Office to take the post of vice chief of the Imperial General Staff. Shortly after, he became the chief, but with events such as the fall of France and the losses in the Middle East, he urged caution. In pursuing this course, Dill came into conflict with Prime Minister Winston S. Churchill (q.v.). As one difference followed another, Churchill gradually came to believe that Dill was overcautious and even obstructive. Long hours of work, and the long illness of his wife, who died in 1940, caused a deterioration of Dill's own health. His health later improved, but he continued to advise extreme caution and eventually Churchill decided to relieve him. On 18 November 1941, it was announced that Dill would retire on reaching the age of sixty. In recognition of his services, the king conferred the rank of field marshal and Dill was appointed governor-designate of Bombay, India.

With the entry of Japan into the war, Churchill visited the United States and was accompanied by Dill as acting head of the British Joint Staff Mission. Following the initial success of the mission, Dill's appointment became permanent. In January 1943, he attended the Casablanca Conference (*see* Conferences, Allied), where his tact proved invaluable. He later visited Brazil and attended conferences in India, China, and Canada, as well as the Teheran Conference.

In the United States, Dill won the confidence and trust of President Franklin D. Roosevelt (q.v.) and became a personal friend of General George C. Marshall and Admiral Ernest J. King (qq.v.). In January 1944, he received the Howard Memorial Prize from Yale University and an honorary doctorate of law from the College of William and Mary, as well as degrees from Princeton and the University of Toronto. Late in 1944, Dill became ill again and died in a hospital in Washington, D.C., on 4 November. He was buried in Arlington National Cemetery, where a monument was erected in his honor. He is the only non-American soldier so honored. A posthumous award of the American Distinguished Service Medal was conferred by President Roosevelt, who commented that Dill was "the most important figure in the remarkable accord which has been developed in the combined operations of our two countries."

Alan Harfield

Additional Reading
Bryant, Sir Arthur, *The Turn of the Tide, 1939–43* (1957).

Dodd, William E. (1869–1939)

U.S. ambassador to Germany. Dodd, an academic by profession and a historian by training, was appointed U.S. ambassador to Germany in 1933. Nazi Germany was a key post that needed a professional diplomat; he was a patronage appointment whose good intentions and hard work never compensated for his lack of foreign policy expertise. While in Germany, he chose to associate mainly with the handful of liberal-minded Germans still in circulation, and as a result overestimated the extent of German opposition to Hitler. His dispatches to Washington concerning the churches' reaction to Nazism are a model of American naivete concerning German church-state relations. His personal boycott of the 1936 Berlin Olympics was understandable, but caused embarrassment to the Roosevelt administration.

Despite professional shortcomings, Dodd deserves credit as an early and prominent voice in American politics that pointed out the aggressive nature of Nazi Germany. Although difficult to prove, his observations may have had an impact on President Franklin D. Roosevelt (q.v.). Although his death shortly after recall from Berlin occurred in the wake of a fatal hit-and-run car accident, he was fortunate that he did not live long enough to be labeled a "premature anti-Fascist" after World War II.

Michael Polley

Additional Reading
Dallek, Robert, *Democrat and Diplomat* (1974).
Dodd, Martha, *Ambassador Dodd's Story* (1941).
Dodd, William E., *My Years in Germany* (1939).

Dollfuss, Engelbert (1892–1934).

Austrian chancellor, 1932–1934. Dollfuss led the authoritarian Christian Social Party, which maintained a hard line against other Austrian political parties. It refused to enter into coalition with the Socialists even though this might have curbed the growing influence of the Austrian Nazis. He came to power in May 1932 and dismantled parliamentary democracy in Austria by the following March, creating a one-party state. Supported by Benito Mussolini (q.v.), he banned the Nazis in June 1933. During the violent suppression of the Socialists in 1934, Austrian authorities massacred hundreds of innocent people in Vienna's working-class neighborhoods. Dolfuss was assassinated by the Nazis during an aborted coup on 25 July 1934 and was succeeded by Kurt von Schuschnigg (q.v.).

Steven B. Rogers

Additional Reading
Jagschitz, Gerhard, *Der Putsch* (1976).
Maass, Walter B., *Assassination in Vienna* (1972).

Dönitz, Karl (1891–1980)

German grand admiral. Germany's last grand admiral was born in Gruenau-bei-Berlin on 16 September 1891, the second son of an engineer who specialized in optics. Dönitz was an excellent student with a quick mind and a great capacity for study and hard work. In his later career, he showed a talent for innovation, fostering development of the special forces and technologies his predecessor, Grand Admiral Erich Raeder (q.v.), had opposed. These, however, came too late to change the naval situation in World War II.

Dönitz's active participation in Adolf Hitler's (q.v.) strategic deliberations, as well as his aggressive professions of loyalty to the Third *Reich,* did little to improve Germany's strategic direction and compromised his postwar efforts to distance himself from the regime's unsavory policies. Nonetheless, his accomplishments as commander of the German U-boat arm mark him as one of the outstanding operational naval commanders of the war. Twice he nearly defeated Great Britain in World War II, but both times he failed.

Dönitz entered the Imperial German Navy in 1910 and was commissioned *Leutnant zur See* three years later. His first posting was to the light cruiser *Breslau,* which accompanied the battle cruiser *Goeben* into Constantinople and brought the Ottoman Empire into World War I. In the Black Sea, he earned the Iron Cross and a reputation for initiative under fire. He transferred to the U-boat Command in 1916. One year later, he reported to his first U-boat, *U-39,* commanded by Germany's leading ace of that war, *Kapitänleutnant* Walter Forstmann. It was there that Dönitz learned submarine tactics from a master. In the Mediterranean in 1917, Germany's U-boats were at the peak of their World War I effectiveness.

Dönitz served under Forstmann for less than a year. He moved on to command two U-boats in the war's final year, *UC-25* and *UB-68.* It was in the latter boat that he was captured by the British while attacking an Allied convoy near Malta on 4 October 1918. He was released from captivity after the war and accepted into the new *Reichsmarine* in 1919.

Serving in a navy denied submarines, Dönitz was assigned to torpedo boats and was promoted to *Kapitänleutnant* in 1921. From there, he served in a variety of posts, including tours of duty in the *Marineleitung,* which conducted both the clandestine rearmament program and the suppression of Communism within the navy. Among those with whom he worked were such later German naval leaders as Wilhelm Canaris, Wilhelm Marschall (qq.v.), and Erich Raeder. Dönitz was promoted to *Korvettenkapitän* (Lieutenant Commander) in 1929, and assumed command of the 4th Torpedo Boat Half-Flotilla. He used that post to perfect the "group tactics" he learned in the Mediterranean and would later employ as commander of the U-boats.

Dönitz spent the next three years in the Admiralty Office, working on, among other things, the clandestine U-boat program. It was there that he was promoted to *Frigattekapitan* (Commander). He became the resurrected U-boat arm's first chief in 1935, following a one-year tour as commander of the light cruiser *Emden.* As U-boat chief, he oversaw the rapid deployment of nearly 300 U-boats by 1943. The early years were marked by detailed progress in training and production. Starting with a small force of 250-ton Type II coastal U-boats, he refined his force into a highly trained elite. It was, however, as much a period of frustration as triumph.

Germany lacked the resources to give all the services what they wanted and the *Kriegsmarine* (as the German Navy was renamed in the Third *Reich*) had the lowest priority. Moreover, navy chief Admiral Raeder preferred large ships. As a result, Germany entered the war with only fifty-seven operational U-boats in service and six under construction. More than half of those in service were the small coastal boats Dönitz had intended for training use only.

It was not an auspicious beginning, but Dönitz's U-boats gave a good account of themselves, even penetrating the British base at Scapa Flow (q.v.) to sink the battleship HMS *Royal Oak.* That triumph put the U-boat force and its chief firmly in the public's eye and led to his promotion to *Konteradmiral* (Rear Admiral). The U-boat force still faced significant problems.

German torpedoes proved unreliable and several boats were lost because of a fault in the Type VIIA's exhaust system. This problem was easily solved, but the "Torpedo Scandal" took more than two years to fix. Also, Germany's economic shortfalls affected U-boat construction, and Dönitz's command had little influence over U-boat modifications and future designs. Interservice rivalry with the *Luftwaffe* limited the air support he received, and unbeknownst to Dönitz, the Allies began to read his operational codes by mid-1941. They retained that ability, with few but critical interruptions, for the remainder of the war.

Despite these difficulties and disadvantages, Dönitz and his wolf pack tactics nearly brought Great Britain to its knees twice during the war; once in 1941 and again in the spring of 1943. Assuming overall command of the *Kriegsmarine* on 31 January 1943, he immediately tried to both rationalize the German U-boat program with Germany's overall economy, and accelerate development of the latest U-boat designs and equipment, including radar. It was too little, too late. Still, he continued to press the U-boat program and took an active part in Hitler's strategic deliberations in an effort to increase the navy's share of resources. Dönitz did manage to save the big ships that Hitler ordered scrapped, but otherwise he contributed little to improve Germany's strategic situation.

Impressed with Dönitz's integrity and loyalty, and as a slap against the leadership of the army and air force, Hitler appointed him successor to the crumbling Third *Reich*. After Hitler's suicide, he became the *Reich's* president on 30 April 1945, and Martin Bormann (q.v.) became the new chancellor.

As president, Dönitz continued the evacuation of personnel from the east while attempting to negotiate a separate peace with the Western Allies. Finally convinced of the futility of that course, he surrendered Germany on 7 May 1945. Taken into custody fifteen days later, he subsequently was convicted as a war criminal and spent eleven and a half years in prison. Released in 1956, he wrote three sets of memoirs and retired to a quiet life in Aumühle, West Germany, where he died in his sleep on Christmas Eve 1980.

Carl O. Schuster

Additional Reading

Dönitz, Karl, *Memoirs: Ten Years and Twenty Days* (1959).

Padfield, Peter, *Dönitz: The Last Führer* (1984).

Thompson, Harold Keith, and Henry Strutz (eds.), *Dönitz at Nuremberg: A Re-appraisal* (1976).

Donovan, William Joseph (1883–1959)

American major general, director of the Office of Strategic Services (OSS) (q.v.). "Wild Bill" Donovan was born in Buffalo, New York, and educated at Columbia University. He entered law practice in 1912, and he also became active as a National Guard officer. He served on the Mexican border in 1916 and in World War I as the colonel of the 165th Infantry Regiment, the former "Fighting 69th." He was wounded three times and won numerous decorations, including the Medal of Honor. After the war, he served briefly as a U.S. military observer in Asia.

Donovan was the architect of centralized intelligence in World War II. On the eve of the war, American intelligence was a fragmented enterprise. As President Franklin D. Roosevelt's (q.v.) private envoy to Great Britain during 1940 and early 1941, he studied the British intelligence system, and later lobbied at home for the creation of a civilian agency charged with coordinating U.S. intelligence efforts.

On 26 April 1941, Donovan first presented his recommendations to Roosevelt. The proposed agency would carry sole responsibility for overseas intelligence work and be subordinated directly to the president. On 11 July 1941, Donovan was appointed to the new post of Coordinator of Information (COI), with a mandate to implement his proposals and act as the president's chief intelligence officer. He envisaged his new agency not only as the focus of centralized intelligence collection and analysis, but also as the executor of paramilitary and clandestine warfare.

In persuading the president to create COI, Donovan temporarily outmaneuvered both the military and the civilian bureaucratic claimants to intelligence primacy. Politically, however, he soon overextended himself. He tried to expand the scope of operations. In so doing, he caused jurisdictional disputes with rival agencies. By early 1942, the stage in Washington was set for a broad bureaucratic offensive to dismember COI. The Joint Chiefs of Staff (JCS) then unexpectedly offered Donovan a lifeline. Primarily in order to acquire control over paramilitary special operations, the JCS proposed to incorporate his apparatus under the JCS aegis.

For his part, Donovan was anxious to protect his organization and integrate it into the central war machinery. By an executive order of 13 June 1942, the COI was reorganized under the JCS as the Office of Strategic Services with Donovan as director. The OSS preserved its charter for espionage, special operations, covert action, and intelligence analysis. Indeed, JCS control was nominal, and the OSS operated substantially outside of traditional military hierarchy.

Donovan's organization proved to be a flexible instrument, constantly adapting to the "roaring flux" of wartime demands. By 1945, he had ". . . lifted intelligence out of its military rut," and expanded the application of collection and analysis across the spectrum of international political, economic, cultural, and geographic factors that now confronted the U.S. The overall influence of OSS special operations on the military outcome of the war is questionable. The most unique and enduring aspect of the OSS resulted from his emphasis on intelligence analysis. In a larger sense, Donovan's unprecedented accomplishment was in establishing a centralized U.S. intelligence structure.

General Douglas MacArthur would not allow the OSS to operate under his command in the Pacific. It operated in the European theater of operations and in the Indian-Burma campaign. The OSS was disbanded by President Harry S Truman (q.v.) on 1 October 1945. Donovan subsequently was given no role in the formulation of the National Security Act of 1947, which created the Central Intelligence Agency (CIA). The CIA, however, was conceived directly from the Donovan proposal of November 1944 for a peacetime strategic intelligence agency. After a brief stint as U.S. ambassador to Thailand in 1953–1954, he retired from government service to his New York law firm. He died in Washington, D.C., on 8 February 1959.

Stephen Donahue

Additional Reading
Brown, Anthony Cave, *Bodyguard of Lies* (1975).
Casey, William, *The Secret War Against Hitler* (1988).
Ford, Corey, *Donovan of OSS* (1970).
Ranalagh, John, *The Agency: The Rise and Decline of the CIA from Wild Bill Donovan to William Casey* (1986).

Doolittle, James H. (1896–1993)
American lieutenant general, commander of the U.S. Eighth Air Force. "Jimmy" Doolittle was one of the top American combat air commanders of the war. During the interwar years, he gained an international reputation as a racing pilot and an aeronautical engineer. The first man credited with performing an outside loop in 1929, he was also the first to take off and land totally under instrument control. Leaving the Army Air Corps to pursue a business career with Shell Oil Company, he was instrumental in the development of the high-octane gasoline essential for high-performance combat aircraft.

Recalled to active duty in 1941, Doolittle was selected by General Henry H. "Hap" Arnold (q.v.) to lead the famed Tokyo raid consisting of sixteen B-25 medium bombers that took off from an aircraft carrier. Although little physical damage was caused by the air strike, the psychological effects of the mission were enormous, and Doolittle was awarded the Medal of Honor.

Promoted to brigadier general, Doolittle was selected to command the Twelfth Air Force for the invasion of North Africa. Although he experienced early difficulties with his commander, General Dwight D. Eisenhower (q.v.), Doolittle proved an effective air leader. Promoted to major general, he was then given command of the Fifteenth Air Force for the Italian campaign. Once again he impressed his superiors, and when Eisenhower was appointed supreme Allied commander for Operation OVERLORD, he asked that Doolittle accompany him to Britain to command the Eighth Air Force.

Realizing that air superiority was essential in order for the invasion to succeed, Doolittle directed his escort fighters to be more aggressive and to seek out the *Luftwaffe* interceptors rather than stay close to the bomber stream in a defensive posture. Considering this his most important decision of the war, the new tactics were successful. In February 1944, the *Luftwaffe* began to break, and by D-Day the Allies had air supremacy over the beaches. Lieutenant General Doolittle led the Eighth Air Force until the end of the European war. His command was then refitted with B-29s and sent to the Pacific, but before he could take them into combat against Japan, the war ended.

Doolittle led three numbered air forces during the war. Eisenhower stated he had grown and matured as a combat leader more than anyone else under his command. Following the war, Doolittle returned to Shell Oil. In 1985, he was promoted to general on the retired list by President Ronald Reagan for his outstanding service during and after World War II.

Phillip S. Meilinger

Additional Reading
Doolittle, James H., *I Could Never Be So Lucky Again* (1991).
Freeman, Roger A., *The Mighty Eighth: Units, Men, and Machines: A History of the U.S. Eighth Army Air Force* (1970).
Glines, Carroll V., *Jimmy Doolittle, Master of the Calculated Risk* (1980).

Thomas, Lowell, and Edward Jablonski,
Doolittle: A Biography (1976).

Dorman-Smith, Eric (1895–1969)

British major general. Eric Dorman-Smith was one of the first British officers to grasp the importance of the revolution in armored mobile warfare. Serving in the 1930s as part of the War Office's SD-2 Section, he was one of the innovators charged with developing an armored warfare doctrine for the infant Royal Tank Corps. After a period with the Indian Army, Dorman-Smith was transferred in 1940 to the Middle East Staff College in Haifa.

When the Italian Tenth Army crossed the Libyan frontier to invade British-controlled Egypt in September 1940, Dorman-Smith was posted to Egypt, where he served as a staff officer under General Sir Richard O'Connor (q.v.). Dorman-Smith played a major role in the planning of O'Connor's victory at Beda Fomm (q.v.) in February 1942. As General Sir Claude Auchinleck's (q.v.) chief of staff, Dorman-Smith was the principal planner of the British victory at Alam el Halfa (q.v.) in July 1942. Dorman-Smith's main contribution was the emphasis on mobile warfare, which he had championed since his days at the War Office.

When Prime Minister Winston S. Churchill (q.v.) sacked Auchinleck, Dorman-Smith was relieved too, ostensibly on the grounds that he had abandoned the strategically worthless position of Tobruk. After the war, Dorman-Smith successfully sued Churchill for libel when the former prime minister wrote in his memoirs that the British troops had lost confidence in Auchinleck and Dorman-Smith. Churchill was compelled to revise his account of the North African campaign (q.v.).

John F. Murphy, Jr.

Additional Reading

Barnett, Corelli, *The Desert Generals* (1982).
Bidwell, Shelford, and Dominick Graham, *Fire-Power: British Army Weapons and Theories of War 1904–1945* (1982).

Dornberger, Walter (1895–1980)

German major general, head of the V-2 project. Born in Giessen in 1895, Dornberger served in the artillery in World War I. A hardworking, studious, and intelligent individual, the *Reichswehr* retained him after the war. While still on active duty, he graduated with distinction from the Berlin Technical Institute in 1929. In 1930, he became the deputy of the army's ballistic weapons department. Here he recruited Wernher von Braun (q.v.). These two became the nucleus for the German rocket team that ultimately developed the dreaded V-2 rocket, the genesis of all modern ballistic missile and space launching systems.

Colonel Dornberger assumed command of the new Peenemünde research facility in 1937. In May 1943, he was promoted to major general as the new V-2s were entering mass production. He lost operational control over the rocket program in August 1944. On 12 January 1945, he was appointed head of *Arbeitsstab Dornberger* (Working Staff Dornberger) tasked to develop air defense missile systems.

Dornberger surrendered to the Americans in May 1945. Imprisoned for two years in Britain, he emigrated to the U.S. in 1947 and became a consultant to the U.S. Air Force on rocket programs. He joined Bell Aircraft Corporation in 1950 and was active in early U.S. spacecraft design. He died in the United States in 1980.

Carl O. Schuster

Additional Reading

Collier, Basil, *The Battle of the V-Weapons, 1944–1945* (1964).
Dornberger, Walter, *V-2* (1954).
Klee, Ernst, and Otto Merk, *The Birth of Missile: The Secrets of Peenemünde* (1965).

Douglas, William Sholto (1893–1969)

British air marshal, chief of Royal Air Force Fighter Command and later Coastal Command. Born at Oxford on 23 December 1893, Sir William Douglas grew up in London, attended Lincoln College, Oxford, and joined the army when World War I began. He volunteered for the Royal Flying Corps and soon trained as a pilot. Between the wars, he was an active flyer, both commercial and military. When World War II began, he was deputy chief of the air staff with responsibility for training and equipment. His philosophy centered on the use of new aircraft, the advantages of radar, and air support for army and naval forces. He favored a large defensive air force to oppose German bombing attacks. In November 1940, he was promoted to air marshal, and he was knighted in 1941.

Near the end of the Battle of Britain (q.v.), Douglas succeeded Air Chief Marshal Sir Hugh Dowding (q.v.) as head of Fighter Command, where he sought to initiate offensive operations against the Germans. In January 1943, Douglas was transferred to the Middle East Command. A year later, he returned to Britain as head of Coastal Command, where he helped plan operations for the Normandy (q.v.) invasion.

After the war, Douglas became military governor of the British occupation zone in Germany. When he retired in 1948, he was raised to a peerage and served on the boards of both the British Overseas Airways Corporation and British European Airways. He died in Northampton on 29 October 1969.

Boyd Childress

Additional Reading
Douglas, William Sholto, *Years of Command: The First Volume of the Autobiography of Sholto Douglas* (1963).
———, *Years of Combat: The Second Volume of the Autobiography of Sholto Douglas* (1966).
Wykeham, Peter, *Fighter Command: A Study of Air Defense, 1914–1960* (1960).

Douhet, Giulio (1869–1930)

Italian general, pioneer airpower theorist. By 1909, Douhet, a career officer in the Italian Army, began to evolve novel theories about the application of mechanized forces in warfare. Though neither an engineer nor an aviation pilot, he expressed in his writings the concept of an aerial battlefield requiring an independent service distinct from the army and the navy. He was regarded contemptuously by his military peers, and he received a reprimand for inappropriately consenting to the construction of three-engine Caproni bombers. The rout of Italian forces at Capretto in 1917 served to vindicate his scathing and publicly expressed indictments of the high command, remarks that earned him a court-martial and a prison sentence.

On his release, Douhet was made head of Italy's Central Division of Aviation. His further inability to influence planning and policy eventually led to his 1921 book, *The Command of the Air,* an essay to delineate the concept of total war waged by an independent air arm to break completely the will of the enemy, including the morale of civilians. Alexander P. de Seversky (q.v.) praised the 1942 English translation as "marking America's coming of age in the matter of aviation thinking." He excused Douhet's mistaken notions as those of a theorist working without complete technical knowledge. What came to be known as the Douhet Doctrine (q.v.) had a significant impact on the conduct of the air campaign in World War II.

William Camp

Additional Reading
Douhet, Giulio, *The Command of the Air* (1921).

Dowding, Hugh Caswall Tremenheere (1882–1970)

British air chief marshal, commander of Fighter Command during the Battle of Britain (q.v.). Sir Hugh Dowding was born at Dumfriesshire on 24 April 1882, the son of a school teacher. He was educated at Winchester and on completion, chose a career in the military. After attending the Royal Military Academy, he was stationed in Gibraltar, Ceylon, and Hong Kong before serving six years in India. He developed an interest in flying after his return to Britain and learned to fly at a school run by the manufacturer Vickers. While stationed at the Staff College at Camberly, he picked up the nickname "Stuffy," due to his habit of avoiding many of the antics of his fellow officers.

When war broke out in 1914, Dowding was an experienced flyer with the Royal Flying Corps, where his duties included those of observer, pilot, and flight commander. In 1917, he rose to the rank of brigadier general. In 1919, he was assigned to the newly created Royal Air Force (RAF). In 1926, he became director of training at the Air Ministry. His continued successes were rewarded with increasing influence over British air policy. He was knighted in 1933.

Dowding's training and experience as an aviator ran parallel with continuing developments in aircraft design and equipment. From the Air Council, he oversaw the use of fighters such as the Spitfire and Hurricane, and heavy bombers such as the Stirling. He also championed radar. His ideas were based on trial and error; he valued imagination and utilization of proven research on aircraft, equipment, supply, and personnel. Although his thinking countered prevailing views on the use of air forces, he remained convinced the future of air war depended on new ideas and applications.

In 1936, Dowding was appointed to head the newly formed Fighter Command, where he worked diligently to establish British air defense. Because he was well over fifty, many thought the World War I flyer too old for such intense duty.

From late summer 1938 to August 1940, there were five rumors of his replacement; but the pugnacious Dowding endured, stressing the need to maintain the fighter defenses at home. He appeared at a cabinet meeting in May 1940, to oppose the removal of more fighters from Britain to cover operations on the Continent. His pilots had

Just as Dowding reached the zenith of his career, he was replaced at Fighter Command by Air Marshal William Sholto Douglas (q.v.) in late November 1940. Dowding's removal, and the set of circumstances surrounding it, presents a case of intrigue and jealousy within the Royal Air Force. A constant critic of Dowding and his valued supporter Keith Park (q.v.), was Trafford Leigh-Mallory (q.v.), who resented playing second-string behind Park. During the initial stages of the Battle of Britain, the air staff urged Dowding to meet German attacks with large formations and superior numbers, what Leigh-Mallory called "Big Wings." Another prominent fighter pilot, Douglas Bader (q.v.), was the proponent of the "Big Wing" theory and a Leigh-Mallory supporter.

When Dowding resisted, Leigh-Mallory bristled and turned to the air staff for support. By November 1940, he convinced the air staff that Dowding had mismanaged the air battle. On 16 November, Dowding and Park were unceremoniously replaced by Leigh-Mallory and Bader, respectively. As one contemporary summarized it, while Dowding and Park won the Battle of Britain, they lost the war of words.

Although age was against him, Dowding was still a popular figure at home. He traveled to the still neutral United States for the Ministry of Aircraft Production, where his views ran counter to those of the British diplomatic corps. When he returned home in June 1941, he set to writing his account of the Battle of Britain, which he completed that October. He had intended to retire, but Prime Minister Winston S. Churchill (q.v.) urged him to delay his departure and accept a position inspecting Royal Air Force establishments. Dowding's differences with the Air Ministry resurfaced and he finally retired in July of 1942. *Twelve Legions of Angels,* his resulting book, was not published until 1946 due to wartime censorship. He contended the small volume would absolve his strategy, but he considered the book a failure due to the five-year delay in printing.

In retirement, Dowding turned to lecturing and writing, producing four books and countless newspaper essays. He studied spiritualism and theosophy and became virtually obsessed with the occult. His heroic leadership during the Battle of Britain made him a legend after the war. He died on 15 February 1970 at age eighty-eight.

Boyd Childress

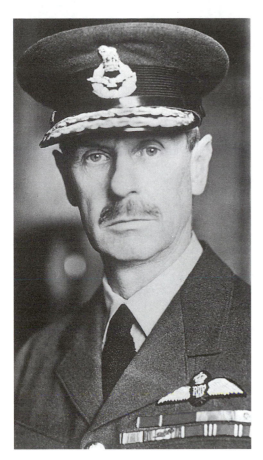

Air Chief Marshal Sir Hugh C.T. Dowding. (IWM D 1417)

gained much-needed experience providing air cover for the withdrawal from Dunkirk (q.v.), but the Battle of Britain would be the real proving ground for Dowding's force; he had only 600 fighters at his disposal.

In 1940, Dowding was fifty-eight years old, but still a relentless air commander. While he was grounded as a pilot due to his age during the crucial months of August to November 1940, he nevertheless deployed his forces, provided the necessary relief for personnel, and replaced pilots (whom he referred to affectionately as his "chicks") and aircraft. His strategy was to use smaller fighter formations, ideally suited for flexibility and able to respond quickly to unwarned attacks. His command during the Battle of Britain showed the dedication and energies of a much younger man. During these months, he maintained awareness of the use of radar aboard airplanes to oppose the potential threat of night bombing missions. With the success of Britain's air arm against seemingly German superiority, he emerged as the nation's first air hero.

Additional Reading
Dowding, Hugh Caswell Tremenheere, *Twelve Legions of Angels* (1946).

Richards, Denis, *Royal Air Force, 1939–1945,* 3 vol. (1953–1954).

Terraine, John, *A Time for Courage: The Royal Air Force in the European War, 1939–1945* (1985).

Wright, Robert, *Dowding and the Battle of Britain* (1969).

Wykeham, Peter, *Fighter Command: A Study in Air Defense, 1914–1960* (1960).

Drabik, Alex (1911–1993)

American sergeant, first U.S. soldier to cross the Rhine. Drabik, a second-generation Polish American, was a former butcher from Toledo, Ohio. At age thirty-two he was the third-oldest man in his company. On the afternoon of 7 March 1945, First Lieutenant Karl Timmerman of A Company, 27th Armored Infantry Battalion, Combat Command B, 9th U.S. Armored Division, ordered his men over the span of the Ludendorff Bridge at Remagen (q.v.). Sergeant Drabik led his squad across, and became the first soldier since Julius Caesar to force his way across the defended Rhine. As soon as he reached the other side, a German soldier rose and pointed his rifle almost point-blank at Drabik's chest. Drabik later said, "He had me cold, but he didn't fire." The German lowered his rifle and surrendered. Following closely behind Drabik, Timmerman was the first officer across. Later they were both among the thirteen soldiers to receive the Distinguished Service Cross for the action at Remagen.

Samuel J. Doss

Additional Reading

MacDonald, Charles B., *The Last Offensive* (1984).

Reichelt, Walter E., *Phantom Nine, The 9th Armored (Remagen) Division, 1942–1945* (1987).

Reichley, John, "The First Since Caesar," *Military Review* (March 1988), pp. 62–63.

Dulles, Allen Welsh (1983–1969)

OSS (q.v.) station chief in Switzerland. In October 1941, Dulles was enlisted into the infant U.S. intelligence organization, the Office of the Coordinator of Information (COI), directed by William Donovan (q.v.). Dulles was one of the few Americans with espionage experience. From 1917 to 1919, he served as a Foreign Service officer running intelligence operations against the Central Powers from the U.S. legation in Berne, Switzerland. When the COI was superseded by the Office of Strategic Services (OSS) in June 1942, Dulles requested a return assignment to Switzerland. In November 1942, he arrived in Berne with a suitcase, two crumpled suits, and a $1 million letter of credit with which to set up and run an operation that, according to the official OSS postwar report, had the ". . . best OSS intelligence record of the war."

Because of its political neutrality and central geographical position in Nazi-dominated Europe, Switzerland was the crossroads of espionage and intrigue by the belligerent powers. The OSS Berne mission was a small, belated entry into a field already crowded with agents, double agents, informants, mountebanks, and refugees representing a host of nationalities and causes.

Dulles expanded his initial two-man staff to include a dozen operatives, and established safe houses in Basel, Zurich, Lugano, Ascona, and Geneva. From Lugano and the nearby Italian enclave of Campione, intelligence networks into northern Italy were organized along with support for the unified Italian partisan movement, CLNAI, based in Milan. OSS suboffices in Geneva, and later the French border town of Annemasse, directed networks into southern France and aid to the French resistance. By 1945, Dulles controlled from his office at Herrengasse 23, Berne, a well-financed U.S. espionage apparatus that ranged from London to Prague.

A German Foreign Ministry official in Berlin, Fritz Kolbe, and the vice-consul of the German consulate general in Zurich, Hans Bernd Gisevius, were the principal agents recruited by Dulles. Between March 1943 and May 1944, Gisevius provided a critical window into the *Schwarze Kapelle* (Black Orchestra), the anti-Nazi conspiracy among German military and government officials. Code named BRAKERS by Dulles, the conspiracy finally collapsed with the failed attempt to assassinate Adolf Hitler on 20 July 1944.

In August 1943, Kolbe walked into Herrengasse 23 after being rejected by the British MI-6 (q.v.) station chief in Berne as a German deception agent. Dulles recruited Kolbe immediately and assigned him the cover name of "George Woods." The issue of Kolbe's bona fides sparked a contentious debate within Anglo-American intelligence circles, but on balance Kolbe proved a genuine source. Until his escape to Switzerland in April 1945, Kolbe furnished OSS Berne with a steady stream of material regarding German military and air attache reports from Japan, and German espionage activities in Spain, Sweden, Switzerland,

Britain, and Turkey. Magnanimous in its own blunder, MI-6 later described Kolbe as the "prize intelligence source of the war."

Between February and May 1945, Dulles conducted Operation SUNRISE, the negotiations with SS General Karl Wolff (q.v.). resulting in the surrender of all German and Italian forces in Italy on 2 May 1945. Following the war, the so-called Dulles Report of January 1949, commissioned by President Harry S Truman (q.v.), became the blueprint for the organization and operation of the fledgling Central Intelligence Agency (CIA). Dulles served as director of central intelligence from 10 February 1953 to 29 November 1961, the longest to serve in that post. His brother, John Foster Dulles, was the secretary of state during much of that period. Allen Dulles died in Washington, D.C., on 29 January 1969.

Stephen Donahue

Additional Reading
Ranalagh, John, *The Agency: The Rise and Decline of the CIA from Wild Bill Donovan to William Casey* (1986).

Winks, Robin W., *Cloak and Gown: Scholars in the Secret War, 1939–1961* (1987).

Dumitrescu, Petre (1882–1948)

Romanian colonel general, commander of Romanian Forces in the Soviet Union. Dumitrescu led the Romanian Third Army from 1941 to 1944, participating in operations in Bessarabia and the Soviet Union. In the Crimea, his forces captured Krasnodar and Maikop. During the battle of Stalingrad (q.v.), his forces protected the German Sixth Army's left flank. His Third Army was shattered and sent reeling back by the Soviet counteroffensive. In 1944, he became the commander in chief of Army Group Dumitrescu.

Andrzej Suchcitz

Additional Reading
Cretziany, Alexandre, *The Lost Opportunity* (1957).
Ileana (Princess of Romania), *I Live Again* (1952).

D

Eaker, Ira Clarence (1896–1987)

American general, commander of the U.S. Eighth Air Force, commander of the Mediterranean Allied Air Forces. When the United States entered the European war in 1942, it was Brigadier General Eaker who commanded the first American bombing effort against Western Europe. After 1944, he shifted to the air war in the Mediterranean. He was a major figure in the gradual movement of the Army Air Force to a separate U.S. Air Force, and later became a leading proponent of American airpower.

Eaker was born in Texas in 1896, and after graduating from Southeastern Normal College (Oklahoma), he entered the army in 1917. He joined the air corps and gained extensive flying experience. In 1929, he was one of four young pilots to set an endurance flying record. In 1936, he flew the first transcontinental instrument flight. In the air corps, he held several administrative posts, attended army schools at Maxwell Air Force Base and Fort Leavenworth, and received a degree in journalism from the University of Southern California in 1933.

This educational background apparently served Eaker well. He and General Henry H. "Hap" Arnold (q.v.) published three books together on airpower and preparedness. In 1936, the two published *This Flying Game,* a popular aviation history. *Winged Warfare* (1941), and *Army Flyer* (1942) followed, and again they supported American mobilization for the war effort. As American involvement in World War II moved toward reality, Eaker traveled to Britain to observe the Royal Air Force (RAF).

In February 1942, Eaker and a small staff arrived in Britain to establish the U.S. Eighth Air Force. When planes began to arrive in May, he and his staff assimilated RAF tactics and proposed the

Lieutenant General Ira C. Eaker receiving the Distinguished Service Medal from Lieutenant General Jacob L. Devers. (IWM NA 14101)

use of B-17s for daylight bombing, suggesting that his crews were trained and the aircraft were equipped for day missions. In spite of the fact that this thinking ran counter to the British procedure of night attacks, daylight raids were approved. Eaker flew an aircraft on the first American bombing attack on northern France in August—his philosophy being to lead by example.

American bombing efforts continued into late 1942, but British and American leaders wished for more effective results. Prime Minister Winston S. Churchill (q.v.) wanted Eaker to consider night raids, but at the Casablanca Conference (*see* Conferences, Allied) in January 1943, Eaker was able to persuade Churchill to agree to daylight bombing. For his leadership in commanding these bombing efforts, Eaker was decorated with the Silver Star in 1942.

After the Casablanca Conference, U.S.

bomber strength improved in Britain and air attacks were increased. In February 1943, Eaker was named commander of the Eighth Air Force. By mid-1943, the British and American air arms formed the Combined Bomber Offensive (*see* Strategic Bombing). Eaker was able to coordinate difficulties with the need for fighter escorts on bombing raids. He also stressed the need for the most advanced technology available.

In late 1943, his old friend, General Arnold, selected Eaker to assume command of the Mediterranean Allied Air Forces. This post proved more difficult than the European command, as he first moved operations from North Africa to Italy. An even more imposing task was coordinating raids against German targets from the Mediterranean as well as bases in Britain. These targets included rail lines and oil reservoirs in Germany and Austria. He also coped with the demand for air support for ground forces on the Italian front and in Yugoslavia. The liberation campaign in the south of France also called for air support, and he capably handled the constantly shifting demands on airpower. Finally, as commander of the Mediterranean Allied Air Forces, he was responsible for maintaining open shipping lanes in the Mediterranean, thus ensuring the continuity of supply.

Eaker played an important administrative and strategic role in American air superiority in Europe after the summer of 1942. As the end of the war approached, he was appointed to deputy commander of the Army Air Forces and returned to the United States in the spring of 1945. From his position in Washington, he was one of the guiding forces advocating a separate air force. Along with old friends Carl Spaatz (q.v.) and "Hap" Arnold, Eaker helped establish the air branch of the services in 1947. That achieved, Eaker retired at age fifty-one. He continued to advocate airpower through writings and public appearances. He served as an executive for both the Hughes and the Douglas aircraft companies. In August of 1987, Eaker died at the age of ninety-one.

Boyd Childress

Additional Reading

Freeman, Roger A., *The Mighty Eighth: Units, Men, and Machines: A History of the U.S. Eighth Army Air Force* (1970).
Parton, James, *"Air Force Spoken Here": General Ira Eaker and the Command of the Air* (1986).

Ebert, Friedrich (1871–1925)

First president of the Weimar Republic. Born in Heidelberg, Ebert initially learned the trade of saddler. It was on a walking tour through Germany as a young man that he first became aware of the widespread poor conditions of the working class. In Bremen, he founded an organization to provide social and legal support to workers. He eventually became member of the central committee of the Social Democratic Party (SPD), and in 1912, he was elected to the *Reichstag*. He pushed for the improvement of the workers' conditions by parliamentary measures rather than revolutionary means. As SPD chairman and floor leader, he fought for the integration of the proletariat into the political system of the monarchy.

During World War I, the old structures of Germany began to dissolve and the Social Democrats' power increased. After the abdication of Kaiser Wilhelm II, Ebert became chancellor of the *Reich* and successfully managed to direct the revolution of November 1918 along legal lines. Elected president of the new Weimar Republic (q.v.) in 1919, he was confronted with a rising conservative opposition against the SPD and himself. In November 1923, Adolf Hitler (q.v.) and his comrades attempted to overthrow the republic, but the *putsch* failed because of Ebert's firm control of the reins of government.

Ebert died of appendicitis in 1925. His great contribution was the foundation of the Weimar Republic and the preservation of its unity during the six stormy years of his presidency.

Wolfgang Terhörst

Additional Reading

Ebert, Friedrich, *Kämpfe und Ziele* (1927).
Maser, Werner, *Friedrich Ebert, der erste deutsche Reichspräsident: Eine politische Biographie* (1987).

Eddy, Manton S. (1892–1962)

American major general, U.S. XII Corps commander. Eddy established his reputation as a capable frontline commander, consistently defeating the enemy with outflanking and enveloping maneuvers. In June 1942, he took command of the 9th Infantry Division. He led the division throughout the North African campaign and captured Bizerte (q.v.) on 7 May 1943. In August, the 9th Division fought in Sicily (q.v.). On 10 June 1944, Eddy led the 9th Division ashore in the U.S. VII Corps sector of Normandy (q.v.). He attacked westward and cut off the Cotentin peninsula on 17 June. He received the Distinguished Service Cross for "repeated acts of bravery" in the capture of

Cherbourg. In July, the 9th Infantry Division took part in the Operation COBRA breakout at St. Lô (q.v.).

August 1944, Eddy assumed command of XII Corps, part of General George S. Patton's (q.v.) Third Army. Eddy distinguished himself repeatedly in the Lorraine campaign (q.v.). On 20 December 1944, his corps executed a 90-degree change in direction, moving north of Luxembourg City, in order to attack the southern shoulder of the German Ardennes offensive (q.v.). XII Corps then attacked northeasterly into the Eifel, continuing the Third Army's offensive. At 2200 hours on 22 March 1945, elements of Eddy's 5th Infantry Division crossed the Rhine at Oppenheim. XII Corps then continued its sweep to the Elbe. In April 1945, illness forced Eddy to return to the United States. In 1948 he was promoted to lieutenant general, and in the 1950s, he commanded the Seventh Army and U.S. Army Europe.

Samuel J. Doss

Additional Reading

Blumenson, Martin, *Breakout and Pursuit* (1961).
Cole, Hugh M., *The Lorraine Campaign* (1950).

Eden, Anthony (1897–1977)

British foreign secretary. Virtually Sir Anthony Eden's entire career was spent in formulating and implementing British foreign policy. He served on the western front during World War I as the youngest brigade major in the British Army. After the war he studied Arabic and Persian at Christ Church, Oxford. In 1923, Eden won election as a Conservative member of Parliament (MP). For the next two decades, he held numerous posts in the Foreign Office: secretary to Austen Chamberlain, undersecretary for foreign affairs, minister for the League of Nations (q.v.), foreign secretary (three separate times), and war secretary.

Eden finally acceded to the prime minister's office in 1955. He was brought down by a combination of a foreign policy blunder in committing Britain to an ill-conceived Suez War against Egypt, and from ill health that plagued him most of his adult life. The impetus for Eden's determination to stop Egyptian leader Gamal Abdel Nasser came from Eden's experience in the 1930s. In 1935, he visited Benito Mussolini (q.v.) in Rome in order to work out an agreement on Ethiopia. The Italian dictator rebuked him, and thereafter, he became determined to halt Italian aggression. While not willing to appease Mussolini, he seemed to be less forceful when confronting Adolf Hitler (q.v.). Eden came away impressed with Hitler after their meeting in Germany in 1935. Eden's resolve to halt Italian colonial claims, his dislike of Prime Minister Neville Chamberlain's (q.v.) personal diplomacy, and his disagreement with Chamberlain's rejection of America's overture to help maintain the balance of power in Europe led him to resign from the Foreign Office in 1938. Chamberlain had tried to placate Mussolini by acquiescing to Italy's annexation of Ethiopia without consulting Eden.

Eden was replaced by Lord Halifax, Edward Wood (q.v.), who, like Chamberlain, believed that appeasement (q.v.) was Britain's wisest course of action. Both Hitler and Mussolini were delighted to see Eden go and even took some credit for his downfall. After the war began, Eden returned to government briefly as dominions secretary under Chamberlain, and then as minister of war and foreign secretary under Winston S. Churchill (q.v.). He adroitly supervised the rebuilding of the British Army, but always had to live under Churchill's shadow.

Eden's role in British foreign policy during the 1930s is controversial. He saw himself as an anti-appeaser in the mold of Churchill. In reality, Eden's firm stance against Italy had more to do with the foreign secretary's personal animosity toward Mussolini than a firm belief in standing up to dictators. Like most British politicians of the period, he was determined to avoid war with Germany at almost any cost. He had lost two brothers in World War I, and would lose a son in World War II. He believed nations cannot be expected to incur automatic military obligations, except for areas where vital interests are concerned. To Eden, Austria, Spain, and Czechoslovakia did not appear vital areas to British interests. His criticism of the Munich Agreement (q.v.) was much less vehement than Churchill's. In 1956, however, Eden deemed the Suez a vital region, and he acted accordingly. While Eden proved to be an unsuccessful prime minister, his integrity and devotion to his work are beyond reproach.

Glenn R. Sharfman

Additional Reading

Eden, Anthony, *Memoirs,* 2 vols. (1965).
James, Robert Rhodes, *Anthony Eden* (1986).
Peters, Anthony R., *Anthony Eden at the Foreign Office, 1931–1938* (1986).

Eichmann, Adolf (1906–1962)

German SS lieutenant colonel. Born in the

Rhineland, Eichmann's family moved to Linz, Austria, in 1914. There he came under the influence of the Austrian National Socialist movement. In early 1932, he became a member of the SS (q.v.), but fled to Germany the following year when the Austrian Nazis were outlawed. He trained with the Austrian SS legion near Passau until he was transferred to Dachau in 1934 for additional military training.

Eichmann was sent to Berlin in September 1934, joined the Security Service (SD) (q.v.) and was assigned to its newly established Jewish Affairs Department. His early duties included negotiations with Zionists concerning the emigration of German Jews to Palestine, which he visited in late 1937.

After the German-Austrian *Anschluss* (q.v.) in March 1938 and the establishment of the *Reich* Protectorate of Bohemia and Moravia (q.v.) in early 1939, Eichmann supervised Jewish affairs in these areas and arranged for the emigration of Jews from Vienna and Prague. The outbreak of the war in September 1939 halted Germany's efforts to send Jews to British-controlled Palestine. Occupied Poland was now selected as the destination for deported Jews.

Eichmann transferred to the RSHA (q.v.), and created the Central Emigration Office. That was combined with the Jewish Affairs Department to create Department IV B4. He also participated in the Wannsee Conference (*see* Final Solution) in January 1942 where the mass extermination of the European Jews was planned. Over the next two years, he was responsible for arranging and scheduling the transport of Jews to death camps in the east.

Eichmann went to Hungary in early 1944 in order to expedite the deportation of Hungarian Jews. A former ally, Hungary had yet to deport its Jews, and fearing the Hungarians might soon withdraw from the alliance, Germany occupied Hungary in March 1944.

After the war, Eichmann assumed a number of aliases and lived in various places in Germany until escaping to Argentina in 1950. He was apprehended by Israeli intelligence in 1960 and tried as a war criminal the following year. He was convicted and subsequently hanged in 1962.

Steven B. Rogers

Additional Reading

Arendt, Hannah, *Eichmann in Jerusalem* (1963).
Clarke, Comer, *Eichmann: The Man and His Crimes* (1960).
Donovan, John, *Eichmann: Man of Slaughter* (1960).
Lang, Jochen von (ed.), *Eichmann Interrogated* (1983).
Linze, Dervy A., *The Trial of Adolf Eichmann* (1961).
Reitlinger, Gerald, *The Final Solution* (1953).
Zeiger, Henry A. (ed.), *The Case Against Adolf Eichmann* (1960).

Eicke, Theodor (1892–1943)

German inspector of the concentration camps and *Waffen-SS* (q.v.) division commander. A career policeman during the Weimar Republic (q.v.), Eicke eventually lost his job as a result of his anti-republican activities. He joined the NSDAP and the SA in 1928 and transferred to the SS (qq.v.) in 1930. He fled to Italy in 1932 after being convicted of a political bombing. He returned to Germany after the Nazis took power in 1933 and was appointed by Heinrich Himmler (q.v.) as commandant of the Dachau concentration camp in June 1933.

In 1934, Eicke was appointed inspector of concentration camps and commander of the SS Death's Head guard units. He was responsible for the reorganization of the camp system and the drafting of the instructions and regulations governing the behavior of the guards and the treatment of camp inmates. He was appointed commander of the SS Death's Head Division in 1939 and saw action in Poland, France, and the Soviet Union. He was killed in action on the eastern front in 1943.

Steven B. Rogers

Additional Reading

Sydnor, Charles W., *Soldiers of Destruction* (1977).

Einstein, Albert (1879–1955)

German-American physicist. In 1921, Einstein won the Nobel Prize for his accomplishments in theoretical physics. Adolf Hitler's (q.v.) rise to power caused Einstein, a Jew, to renounce his German citizenship and settle in the United States to work at the Institute for Advanced Study in Princeton, New Jersey. During the 1920s and 1930s, European physicists produced significant scientific breakthroughs leading to the conclusion that bombarding uranium-235 with neutrons would set off a chain reaction releasing tremendous amounts of energy.

In the spring of 1939, a group of physicists, many of them refugees from Nazism, approached Einstein about writing a letter to President Franklin D. Roosevelt (q.v.) outlining the implications of the recent discoveries. Einstein's letter explained that through nuclear fission, "extremely powerful bombs of a new type may thus be constructed." Einstein's announcement, and the danger of Nazi Germany devoting its resources to the creation of such a bomb, provided the catalyst for the American government's sponsorship of the MANHATTAN Project (q.v.). Ironically, Einstein was barred from working on the atomic bomb project because he was considered a security risk.

Susanne Teepe Gaskins

Additional Reading

Baker, Paul R., *The Atomic Bomb: The Great Decision* (1968).
Gigon, Fernand, *Formula E=MC²* (1958).
Pais, Abraham, *"Subtle Is the Lord—": The Science and the Life of Albert Einstein* (1982).

Eisenhower, Dwight David (1890–1969)

American General of the Army, supreme Allied commander in Europe. Eisenhower was commander of the Allied armies in North Africa, Italy, France, and Germany from 1942 to 1945. Devoted to service to the U.S. Army and his country, skilled as a manager and strategist, masterful at public relations, committed to Allied solidarity, and concerned with the morale and well-being of his troops, "Ike" was a wise and eminently successful general.

Born in Denison, Texas, Eisenhower spent his childhood in Abilene, Kansas, before attending West Point. He was commissioned second lieutenant of infantry in 1915 but never reached France during World War I. Between 1915 and 1922, he held a variety of training assignments. From 1922 to 1925, he served in Panama as a staff officer to General Fox Conner, who acted as a mentor in strategic and political thinking. Eisenhower later called his Panama experience "a sort of graduate school in military affairs and the humanities." Conner arranged Eisenhower's admission to the Command and General Staff College at Fort Leavenworth, where Eisenhower finished first in his 1926 class. He helped General John J. Pershing write a guidebook to World War I battlefields, served on the Battle Monuments Commission, and graduated from the Army War College in 1928.

In 1929, Eisenhower joined the office of the assistant secretary of war, responsible for contingency mobilization planning. His superlative work impressed General Douglas MacArthur, who, when he became chief of staff of the U.S. Army, named

Eisenhower his military aide in February 1933. Eisenhower accompanied MacArthur to Manila in 1935 to establish a Filipino army. He came to dislike MacArthur, but remained a loyal aide.

On 1 July 1916, Eisenhower married Mary Geneva (Mamie) Doud, a devoted army wife who turned her life to her husband and his career. They endured thirty-five household moves in the first twenty-five years of marriage, residence in inhospitable climates, and repeated and prolonged separations. Their first son, Doud Dwight (Icky), died of scarlet fever at age three in 1921. A second son, John Sheldon Doud, born in 1922, graduated from West Point in 1944.

When World War II began, Eisenhower became a regimental executive officer at Fort Lewis, Washington, and by June 1941, he was promoted to chief of staff of the Third Army at Fort Sam Houston, Texas. He studied the training, equipment, and logistics problems that beset the army, won heavily publicized army war games in Louisiana in the summer of 1941, and became a brigadier general that September.

On 12 December 1941, army chief of staff General George C. Marshall (q.v.) summoned Eisenhower to the War Plans Division in Washington to advise on MacArthur's imperilled garrison in the Philippines. Eisenhower concluded that although the islands would fall, the army must defend them to preserve its prestige and honor, that Australia ought to be developed as an alternative base in the Pacific, and that the army should concentrate on Europe. At the Arcadia Conference (*see* Conferences, Allied), Eisenhower distinguished himself by cooperating with the British and suggesting means to integrate theater and strategic commands. Convinced that Eisenhower was the army's best staff officer, Marshall appointed him chief of the War Plans Division (later the Operations Division) in February 1942. The next month, Eisenhower was promoted to major general and named Marshall's special aide.

As head of the War Plans Division, Eisenhower endorsed Marshall's demand for an early Allied invasion of France to avoid a Soviet defeat. This idea was opposed by the navy, which demanded initiatives in the Pacific, and by the British, who wanted to avoid trench warfare in France, protect their Middle East empire, and have the Americans gain experience in North Africa before undertaking operations in France. Eisenhower and Marshall rejoined that action in North Africa in 1942 would prevent an invasion of France the next year. In May–July 1942, Marshall sent Eisenhower to London to promote an early cross-channel assault, named him commander of the European Theater of Operations, and promoted him to lieutenant general. Impressed by Eisenhower's skill and devotion to the alliance, the British endorsed his appointment but rejected his argument that the Allies invade France in September.

Because President Franklin D. Roosevelt (q.v.) sided with the British, Eisenhower lost his battle over where to attack, but won a personal war in late July 1942 when the Combined Chiefs of Staff (q.v.) named him commander of Operation TORCH, the invasion of Northwest Africa. Despite Eisenhower's advocacy of daring operations in France, ironically, Operation TORCH demonstrated his military caution and political inexperience. He limited landings to Casablanca, Oran, and Algiers to avoid engaging German troops. Prior to the attack, he failed to negotiate a truce with Vichy French troops, who inflicted 1,800 Allied casualties before a cease-fire deal was negotiated. That deal recognized Admiral Jean François Darlan (q.v.), an avowed Fascist, as high commissioner of North Africa and drew harsh press criticism and calls for Eisenhower's dismissal. Because of delays, Eisenhower lost some tactical authority to British subordinates in January 1943. At the battle of Kasserine Pass (q.v.) Eisenhower first engaged German field marshal Erwin Rommel (q.v.), who demonstrated a superior hand, inflicted great losses on the U.S. units, and withdrew only when his supplies ran thin.

In these gray clouds there were silver linings. Eisenhower's friends defended the "Darlan deal" as a step that saved American lives. His command was preserved and he earned his fourth star in February 1943. Military setbacks impelled Eisenhower and others to fight harder. In spring 1943, the Allied offensive intensified, and Axis forces in Africa surrendered in May.

That success renewed the debate on when to invade France, and the Combined Chiefs of Staff authorized Eisenhower to decide where to attack next. Because a cross-channel assault had to wait until 1944, Ike decided to attack Sicily and Italy in the interim. Again, he proved a cautious commander. During the invasion of Sicily (q.v.), Eisenhower spent much time arbitrating tactical disputes between his rival subordinates, Generals Bernard L. Montgomery and George S. Patton (qq.v.). In September, Eisenhower rejected suggestions for amphibious attacks near Rome and ordered landings in the south and a march up the peninsula. That route was less risky but long and arduous. Rome would not be liberated until June 1944.

Eisenhower also practiced reserved diplomacy. After Benito Mussolini's (q.v.) fall in July 1943, Eisenhower wanted to entice Marshal Pietro Badoglio (q.v.) to surrender and turn against the Germans. Burned by the Darlan deal, he sought approval from the Combined Chiefs of Staff, which delayed several weeks, during which Hitler sent nineteen divisions to reinforce northern Italy. Eisenhower and Badoglio planned joint operations to capture Rome, but the Italians' wavering compelled Eisenhower to abandon the plan at the last minute. Although Italy's army disintegrated when Allied units attacked, Germans entrenched in northern Italy resisted tenaciously.

In December 1943, Roosevelt appointed Eisenhower to command Operation OVERLORD, the invasion of France, the most prestigious Allied military appointment of the entire war. Eisenhower proved a master at planning and execution. Although his forces suffered setbacks on D-Day (6 June 1944) (*see* Normandy), and in the ensuing campaigns in Western Europe, they eventually liberated occupied territory, gained momentum, and crushed Axis power in France and western and southern Germany in late 1944 and early 1945. On 16 December 1944, Eisenhower was promoted to the five-star rank of general of the army.

Allied crossings of the Rhine River in March 1945 forced Eisenhower to make a decision, still shrouded in controversy, regarding the targets of the Western offensive. He rejected suggestions to launch a concentrated push for Berlin, and decided to maintain a broad offensive, although that approach would allow the Soviets the honor of liberating the German capital. Eisenhower argued that the Soviet Army would win a race to Berlin; that the city lay within the occupation zone assigned to Moscow; that Western units needed to secure mountainous southern Germany to deny it to diehard Nazis; that German Army units, rocket sites, and atomic research facilities were more important military targets than Berlin; that a race to Berlin would outreach fighter support and cost heavy casualties; that the Soviets might react by occupying northern Germany and Denmark; and that a push to Berlin would undermine the Grand Alliance.

Similarly, Eisenhower ordered Patton to halt his drive at the Czechoslovak border, even though the road to Prague lay open. Although many Westerners regretted that Soviet troops captured Berlin, Eisenhower's cautious but unrelenting approach contributed significantly to the collapse of German resistance.

When World War II ended, Eisenhower considered retirement, but duty and opportunity compelled him to remain active in national and global developments. In May 1945, he became head of the American occupation zone in Germany. Eisenhower was a devoted de-Nazifier, but he abandoned plans to deindustrialize Germany. He disdained the use of the atomic bomb as needlessly provocative to the Soviets and visited Moscow in August to promote East-West friendship.

Named chief of staff of the U.S. Army in November 1945, Eisenhower endorsed several losing causes, such as the complete integration of the armed services, universal military training, international control of atomic weapons, amity with the Soviets, and military preparedness. In February 1948, he retired from military service to write his memoirs, *Crusade in Europe,* and three months later he accepted the presidency of Columbia University. In 1949, he returned to the Pentagon as a consultant and in October 1950, became supreme Allied commander, Europe, to shore up NATO during the Korean War.

In the late 1940s, Eisenhower became politically active, established personal contacts with wealthy supporters, and polished his public image. Courted by both major political parties, he resigned from NATO in July 1952 to seek the Republican nomination for president and won the presidential elections of 1952 and 1956. As president, he proved to be a fiscal conservative, skilled manager, practitioner of containment and counterrevolution abroad, and an inactive leader on domestic matters.

After 1961, Eisenhower enjoyed a quiet retirement of bridge and golf. Following a series of heart attacks, he died on 28 March 1969 and was laid to rest in Abilene, Kansas.

Peter L. Hahn

Additional Reading

Ambrose, Stephen E., *Eisenhower: Soldier, General of the Army, President-Elect, 1890–1952* (1983).
———, *The Supreme Commander: The War Years of General Dwight D. Eisenhower* (1970).
Eisenhower, David, *Eisenhower: At War, 1943–1945* (1986).
Eisenhower, Dwight D., *Crusade in Europe* (1948).
———, *Papers,* Vol. III (1970).

Ellsberg, Edward (1891–1983)

U.S. Navy captain, salvage expert. Ellsberg graduated from the U.S. Naval Academy in 1914. He was salvage officer in 1925 for the recovery of the submarine *S-51* lost off Block Island, New York. He resigned from the navy in 1926 and went to work for private industry. He took part in the salvage operation of the submarine *S-4* in 1927. In December 1941, he volunteered to return to active duty in the navy. His first assignment, in early 1942, was a salvage officer for raising sunken ships destroyed at the port of Massawa, Eritrea. In November 1942, he was sent to Oran, Algeria, to help clear and rehabilitate that port. He returned to the United States in February 1943 due to sickness. In 1944, he was ordered to Great Britain to assist in the preparations for the Normandy landing. He took part in the assembly and building of MULBERRY, an artificial harbor (q.v.), and in salvage operations at the beachhead. After the war, he returned to private salvage work and a literary career. He wrote numerous books on the sea and a trilogy on his World War II experiences.

Charles H. Bogart

Additional Reading

Ellsberg, Edward, *The Far Shore* (1961).
———, *No Banners, No Bugles* (1949).
———, *Under the Red Sea Sun* (1946).

Epp, Franz Xaver *Ritter* von (1868–1947)

German *Freikorps* (q.v.) leader. Von Epp was a volunteer in the German expedition to China, and a company commander in the 1904–1906 colonial war against the Hereros and Hottentots in German Southwest Africa. During World War I, he commanded a Bavarian infantry regiment. In 1919, he established the *Freikorps Epp* in Thuringia with the full support of the *Reichswehr.* This private army helped to smash the People's Republic of Bavaria in Munich and suppressed the Communist revolt in the Ruhr. Through his chief of staff, Ernst Röhm (q.v.), von Epp made contact with Adolf Hitler (q.v.), whom he supported with 60,000 marks of *Reichswehr* funds by buying the Nazi Party's newspaper, the *Völkischer Beobachter.*

When the SA (q.v.) was reorganized in 1926, von Epp took over command of the Munich district. He joined the NSDAP (q.v.) in 1928 and became the Nazi deputy for Oberbayern-Schwaben in the *Reichstag.* After the Nazi takeover, he was appointed governor of Bavaria. In 1936, he became head of the Colonial Office. After the suppression of the SA, von Epp's influence waned because he objected to what happened during the

Night of the Long Knives (q.v.). He died on 31 January 1947 in American custody.

Franz Seidler

Additional Reading
Mitchell, David, *1919 Red Mirage* (1970).
Watt, Richard M., *The Kings Depart* (1968).

Estienne, Jean Baptiste (1860–1936)

French general. Trained as an artillery officer, Estienne is best known as the father of the French tank, and as a theorist of tank warfare. In 1916, supported by Marshal Joseph-Jacques-Césaire Joffre and working independently of the British, Estienne introduced the first French tanks, the St. Chamond and the Schneider. To overcome their design faults, he advocated the mass production of light tanks (Renault FTs) that could be employed in large numbers, relying on British heavy tank support when needed.

After World War I, Estienne's idea of an independent armored force was rejected, and in 1920, light tank units were permanently allocated to infantry formations in the French Army. Nevertheless, his ideas continued to be developed by Colonel Charles de Gaulle (q.v.) and others in the 1930s. The success of German tanks in the Spanish civil war (q.v.) cast doubts on the static defense policy of the Maginot Line (q.v.). Despite the rush to replace the antiquated Renault FTs by modern light and medium tanks, little time remained to organize and train French armored crews to the conditions of *Blitzkrieg* (q.v.) warfare.

Robert C. Hudson

Additional Reading
Gerard, Robert M., *Tank-Fighter Team* (1942).
Piekles, Dorothy M., *France Between the Republics* (1946).
White, B.T., *Tanks and Other AFVs of the Blitzkrieg Era* (1972).

E

F

Falkenhausen, Alexander von (1878–1966)
German general. A professional soldier of the old school, Falkenhausen served as military governor of occupied Belgium and northern France from 1940–1944. Born in Blumenthal on 29 October 1878, he served with the Turkish Army in Palestine during World War I. Retained by the *Reichswehr* after the war, he headed the German military mission to China from 1934 to 1938. He was recalled to active duty in 1939 and appointed military governor in September 1940.

Suspected of involvement with the German opposition to Adolf Hitler (q.v.), he was arrested in July 1944. He was sent to Dachau concentration camp, where he was liberated by U.S. forces at the end of the war. On 7 March 1951, he was convicted by a Belgian military tribunal of executing hostages and deporting 25,000 Jews. Sentenced to 12 years' imprisonment, he was released after only three weeks, in recognition of his other wartime efforts to thwart SS (q.v.) actions against Jews. He died in Nassau, Germany, on 31 July 1966.

Carl O. Schuster

Additional Reading
Graml, Herbert, et al., *The German Resistance to Hitler* (1970).
Humble, Richard, *Hitler's Generals* (1974).

Falkenhorst, Nikolaus von (1885–1968)
German colonel general, commander in Norway. Nikolaus von Jastrzembski was commissioned in a West Prussian infantry regiment in 1904. Seven years later, his family name was officially changed to "von Falkenhorst." After long service on the western front, he participated as a staff officer in the German expedition to Finland in 1918. From 1933 to 1935, Colonel von Falkenhorst served as military attache at Prague, Belgrade, and Bucharest. He subsequently commanded a division and was elevated to a corps command on the eve of World War II.

In February 1940, primarily because of his prior experience in amphibious operations in northern Europe, General von Falkenhorst was chosen to prepare and carry out Operation *WESERÜBUNG,* the seizure of Norway and Denmark. After the successful completion of that mission, he was promoted to colonel general and served as the *Wehrmacht* commander in Norway until December 1944. In 1946, a British-Norwegian court sentenced him to death, but the verdict was subsequently commuted to life imprisonment. He was released from Werl prison in July 1953.

Ulrich Trumpener

Additional Reading
Falkenhorst, Nikolaus von, *The Trial of Nikolaus von Falkenhorst, Formerly Generaloberst in the German Army* (1949).
Rich, Norman, *Hitler's War Aims,* 2 vols. (1973–1974).
Ziemke, Earl F., *The German Northern Theater of Operations* (1959).

Farūq I (1920–1965)
King of Egypt, 1936–1952. In 1939, Egypt severed relations with the Axis nations. Although following British advice and declaring neutrality, Egypt became the Allies' primary base in the Middle East. Farūq, seeking to improve his domestic position, vacillated between nationalist and pro-British wartime policies.

In 1942, Britain forced Farūq, suspected of harboring Nazi sympathies, to appoint pro-Allied Mustafa Nahas as prime minister. In 1944, Farūq ousted Nahas, but in February 1945, declared war on the Axis in order to participate in the peace settlements. His postwar nationalist aspirations led to conflict with Britain. A coup ousted Farūq in 1952.

Sidney Dean

Additional Reading

Georges-Picot, Jacques, *The Real Suez Crisis* (1975).

Faulhaber, Michael von (1869–1952)

Cardinal and principal author of the papal encyclical *Mit brennender Sorge*. Faulhaber was archbishop of Munich and Freising from 1917 to 1952 and in 1921 was named cardinal. He first praised Adolf Hitler (q.v.) for his concordat with the Vatican. In 1933, however, he gave four advent sermons defending the Old Testament and condemning Nazi racial policy, thus becoming the first important Catholic leader to publicly criticize the religious policy of National Socialism.

Alfred Rosenberg (q.v.) attacked Faulhaber's belief that veneration of race and blood would lead to a denial of Christianity in his 1935 work *To the Dark Men of Our Age*. In 1937, Faulhaber drafted the papal encyclical *Mit brennender Sorge* (With Burning Sorrow) for Pope Pius XII. This dealt strongly with the position of the Catholic Church in Germany and was read from all pulpits in the *Reich* on 21 March. On 6 November 1940, he sent a letter protesting the euthanasia program to Franz Gürtner, *Reichsminister* of the interior, writing: "I cannot remain silent when maintenance of moral foundations is at stake."

Susan Pentlin

Additional Reading

Friedlander, S., *Puis XII and the Third Reich* (1966).
Hoffmann, Peter, *The History of the German Resistance 1933–1945* (1977).
Rhodes, Anthony, *The Vatican in the Age of Dictators, 1922–1945* (1973).

Fleischer, Carl (1883–1942)

Norwegian major general, commander in chief of the Norwegian army-in-exile. In 1940, Fleischer was the commander of the Norwegian 6th Infantry Division. His energy and ability led to the containment of the Germans in the Narvik (q.v.) area. Later, he participated in the recapture of the town. He was suspicious of the Allies, especially after they evacuated from Norway. From 1940 to 1942, he was commander in chief of the Norwegian army-in-exile. In 1942, he was sent to Canada as military attache.

Andrzej Suchcitz

Additional Reading

Ash, Bernard, *Norway 1940* (1964).
Curtis, Monica (ed.), *Norway and the War: September 1939–December 1940* (1941).
Lehmkuhl, Dik, *Journey to London: The Story of the Norwegian Government at War* (1946).
MacIntyre, Donald, *Narvik* (1971).

Fleming, Ian Lancaster (1908–1964)

Royal Naval volunteer reserve officer (Special Branch). Fleming, celebrated creator of James Bond, was himself for a time an integral part of the British Admiralty's Naval Intelligence Division. Personally recruited in 1939 by Director of Naval Intelligence John Godfrey (q.v.), he left his job as a stockbroker to act as Godfrey's personal assistant and was charged with handling the actual day-to-day running of naval intelligence. While he discharged his duties with a combination of tact and imagination that won him praise, Fleming continually sought a more active role, and often traveled as Godfrey's personal emissary.

In 1942, Fleming spearheaded the creation of 30 Assault Unit, a squad of Royal Marines who acted as "intelligence commandos," targeting classified Axis technology and documents. The unit's greatest triumph was the capture of the entire German naval archives at Tambach near war's end.

Despite a promising intelligence career, Fleming left the Admiralty in November 1945. He was awarded the Commander's Cross of the Danish Order of the Danneborg.

Mark Rummage

Additional Reading

Hampshire, Cecil A., *The Secret Navies* (1978).
Pearson, John, *The Life of Ian Fleming* (1966).

Forbes, Charles Morton (1880–1960)

British admiral of the fleet, commander of the Home Fleet. Born in Colombo, Sri Lanka, Sir Charles Forbes had the misfortune of being commander in chief of the Home Fleet during a period of German aerial and intelligence supremacy. Although his fleet was ready for combat when the war started in September 1939, its bases, lacking both antisubmarine and antiaircraft defenses, were not.

Moreover, Forbes was the last major Allied

naval commander to fight the Germans without the benefit of ULTRA (q.v.) intelligence and before the full effects of massed airpower were understood. German intelligence was reading 50 percent of his operational traffic while the *Luftwaffe* was conducting reconnaissance against his bases.

Forbes commanded his forces well despite these disadvantages and constant interference from higher authority. Having earned Prime Minister Winston S. Churchill's (q.v.) enmity during the Norwegian campaign, Forbes was replaced as commander in chief, Home Fleet, on 2 December 1940. He became flag officer, Portsmouth, a position he held until August 1943. He died in London on 28 August 1960.

Carl O. Schuster

Additional Reading

Hough, Richard, *The Longest Battle* (1986).
James, William M., *The British Navies in the Second World War* (1946).
MacIntyre, Donald, *Narvik* (1971).

Forrestal, James Vincent (1892–1949)

American secretary of the navy. Born in Matteawan, New York, Forrestal worked as a reporter, attended Dartmouth College and Princeton University, sold bonds, and served as an aviator in the United States Navy in 1917–1918. An ambitious and tireless worker, he earned a reputation as the "boy wonder of Wall Street" by arranging shrewd and profitable financial deals and became a partner in his firm in 1923, vice president in 1926, and president in 1938.

Compelled by a sense of service to his country, Forrestal accepted appointments as special assistant to the president (June 1940), undersecretary of the navy (August 1940), and secretary of the navy (May 1944). His navy offices were nerve centers of the war effort in Washington. A master administrator, he excelled at reorganizing the Navy Department, marshalling private industry to meet military needs, procuring and allocating precious resources, and coordinating production efforts across government. Although navy officers resented his recruitment of civilians as top aides, he brilliantly facilitated the navy's wartime buildup.

As secretary of the navy, Forrestal advocated postwar military preparedness, strategic planning on a global scale, and coordination of military, diplomatic, and economic policies. He formulated key provisions of the National Security Act of 1947 and vigorously promoted the policy of containment. Appointed the first secretary of defense in July 1947,

he soon succumbed to the stress of his service. Diagnosed with involutional melancholia, a mental illness, he resigned from government in March 1949 and committed suicide on 22 May 1949.

Peter L. Hahn

Additional Reading

Millis, Walter (ed.), *The Forrestal Diaries* (1951).
Rogow, Arnold A., *James Forrestal: A Study of Personality, Politics, and Policy* (1963).

Foulkes, Charles C.C. (1903–1969)

Canadian lieutenant general, commander of Canadian I Corps. Foulkes came to Canada from Britain at an early age. His army career began when he joined the Royal Canadian Regiment in 1926. He was a general staff officer in the Permanent Force and a graduate of the British Staff College at Camberley when Canada declared war on Germany. He went overseas with the Canadian 1st Division as a brigade major in November of 1939. He impressed his superiors with his abilities as a staff officer, was rapidly promoted, and received the Commander of the British Empire award for his staff work in Britain. He held various staff and operational appointments until assuming command of the Canadian 2nd Division in January 1944.

Foulkes's first battle during the Normandy (q.v.) campaign was unsuccessful, and he was heavily censured by the Canadian II Corps commander, General Guy Simonds (q.v.), for his inadequate control and high losses. Foulkes later was awarded the Distinguished Service Order in France. He continued to command the 2nd Division as it fought its costly battles in Normandy and cleared the Scheldt (q.v.) estuary. He took over temporary command of the Canadian II Corps when Simonds became acting army commander.

Foulkes earned a reputation as a driving commander with a stubborn propensity for unimaginative frontal assaults. He was promoted to lieutenant general and sent to Italy in November 1944 to command Canadian I Corps. He impressed the commander of the British Eighth Army in Italy, quickly adapting to the problems of the terrain. He was not well liked by his subordinates, however, many of whom considered him a "cold fish" and too politically oriented.

Foulkes returned to Holland when his corps was transferred to the Canadian First Army in the spring of 1945. He served as the Canadian Army's first postwar chief of the general staff until 1951.

He was the chairman of the chiefs of staff until his retirement in 1960. He died largely unheralded for his achievements during the war.

Paul Dickson

Additional Reading
Foster, Tony, *Meeting of Generals* (1986).
Stacey, C.P., *The Victory Campaign* (1960).

Foulois, Benjamin D. (1879–1967)

American major general, aviation pioneer. Foulois was one of America's leading advocates of military airpower during the interwar years. He was born in Connecticut and enlisted in the army during the Spanish-American War. He quickly rose to the rank of first sergeant, and then received a commission directly from the ranks. In 1908 Foulois became one of the first officers detailed to the new Aeronautical Division of the Signal Corps. In 1909 he flew as Orville Wright's passenger during the army's final acceptance test of the Wright Flyer.

Foulois served for a time as the Chief of the Air Service of the American Expeditionary Force in France during World War I. During the 1920s he held various air and ground assignments. In 1931, Foulois became the chief of the U.S. Army Air Corps, with the rank of major general. His four years in office were marked by controversy and almost constant battling with the War Department and the General Staff. In 1934 he testified before the House Military Affairs Committee that the army was incapable of managing and developing the nation's air assets.

Foulois retired in 1935 under a cloud. His constant agitating for an independent air force, however, forced the army to reorganize its air arm under a General Headquarters (GHQ) Air Force, which became the organizational model for the Army Air Forces in World War II. For the first time, all the army's air assets came under a single commander. That commander was Major General Frank Andrews (q.v.), who became the chief of GHQ Air Force when it was created about the time of Foulois' retirement. When Foulois took office in 1931, the speed, range, and payload of the U.S. bomber force were little different than they had been in World War I. By the time he left office, the Army Air Corps was already starting to purchase the B-17 bomber.

David T. Zabecki

Additional Reading
Foulois, Benjamin D., and Carroll V. Glines, *From the Wright Brothers to the Astronauts:*

The Memoirs of Major General Benjamin D. Foulois (1968).
McClendon, R. Earl, *The Question of Autonomy for the U.S. Air Arm* (1950).

Four Chaplains

Heroes of the SS *Dorchester* sinking. On 3 February 1943, the SS *Dorchester*, a U.S. troop transport ship, was torpedoed and sunk off the coast of Greenland. In what the U.S. War Department later described as "one of the most noble deeds of the war," four army chaplains courageously gave away their own life jackets so the maximum number of troops could be saved. All four chaplains, Lieutenants Clark V. Poling (1910–1943), John P. Washington (1908–1943), Alexander D. Goode (1911–1943), and George L. Fox (1900–1943), went down with the ship.

Survivors of the disaster reported the chaplains went among the panic-stricken men, many of whom believed a plunge in the icy water would mean certain death, and encouraged them to abandon the ship. The chaplains distributed life jackets until all were issued, and then gave up their own. They were last seen by the survivors praying together with their arms linked as the ship went down.

The chaplains represented all three of the major Western religions. Poling and Fox were Protestants, Washington was Catholic, and Goode was Jewish. In the postwar years, their combined act often was held up as a shining example of interfaith action. They posthumously were awarded Distinguished Service Crosses in a special ceremony in Washington on 19 December 1943.

Kevin Dougherty

Additional Reading
Gushwa, Robert, *The Best and Worst of Times: The United States Army Chaplaincy: 1920–1945* (1977).
Thornton, Francis B., *Sea of Glory: The Magnificent Story of the Four Chaplains* (1953).

Fourcade, Marie-Madeleine (1911–1989)

French resistance leader. Fourcade was the only woman to head a major resistance network in France during World War II. She organized and ran the ALLIANCE, a network of thousands of agents with clandestine radio receivers, airfields, arms caches, and dead drops. Historian David Schoenbrun wrote of the organization: "At the risk of torture and death they sabotaged Nazi communications, published propaganda tracts and journals, spied on Hitler's military installations, and sent the intelligence back to London."

Mother of two small children, Fourcade was not only a successful spymaster, but also a beautiful one, "with raven's black hair parted in the middle and brushed sleekly down the side of her head, framing her large, deep brown eyes and firmly chiseled features and full lips."

Fourcade made many secret and dangerous trips back and forth to Britain. Once she nearly froze to death in a winter crossing of the Pyrenees to Portugal doubled up in a mail sack. Twice she was arrested and twice she escaped. The *Gestapo* (q.v.) called her network NOAH'S ARK, because members used animal names as aliases. Her alias was HEDGEHOG.

Paul Rose

Additional Reading

Fourcade, Marie-Madeleine, *Noah's Ark* (1968).
Nogueres, Henri, *Histoire de la Resistance en France* (1969).
Schoenbrun, David, *Soldiers of the Night: The Story of French Resistance* (1980).

Franco, Francisco Bahamonde (1892–1975)

Spanish general and dictator. Franco was born in 1892 and became a career Spanish Army officer. He gained a reputation as a calculating and ambitious military leader while serving as a field commander during the Morocco rebellion in 1921. He eventually rose to the rank of army chief of staff and held that position until he took over as commander in chief of the military forces of the Spanish insurgency led by General Emilio Mola (q.v.).

In 1930, the once-popular constitutional Spanish monarchy and the conservative authoritarian dictatorship of General Miguel Primo de Rivera y Orbaneja was in serious disarray due their inability to quell internal disorder or address serious economic and political pressures. This led to the establishment of the Spanish Republic in 1931, and the ascendancy in 1932 of new right-wing reactionary and conservative monarchist forces opposed to the republic.

The republic alienated the Spanish military by reducing the officers corps and the military budget. Many of the leading Spanish generals also had strong ties to the former monarchy and the Catholic Church, other targets of the republic. An attempted military coup in August 1932 failed miserably. Republican attempts over the next two

years to bring conservative and clerical elements into the government were openly opposed by the parliamentary left and actually led to a leftist rebellion in October 1934. It too, failed. The republic was firmly in control and a new popular front government was elected in 1936. It became clear that only a strong and coordinated military coup would be able to topple it. The Spanish generals, including Chief of Staff Franco, refused to move against the government on their own authority since there appeared to be no threat of an openly leftist takeover.

When the popular front began to falter during the summer of 1936, Mola led an army conspiracy. Franco finally threw his support to the insurgency when he was selected to serve as commander in chief of the Insurgent (also called Nationalist) military forces. He quickly consolidated his power and had himself declared head of the Spanish state in October 1936.

Nazi Germany and Italy were Franco's chief military and economic benefactors during the Spanish civil war (q.v.). Germany supplied a large number of "volunteers" to Franco's army. German and Italian aircraft conducted combat and transport operations in support of Franco's Army of Africa returning to the Spanish mainland in the summer of 1936. Additional units of the *Luftwaffe*, including the *Kondor Legion* (q.v.), were later sent to Spain.

Despite German and Italian support for Franco during the Spanish civil war, and his openly pro-German sentiments, Spain remained neutral and never formally joined the Axis. Even after the war began, he maintained conciliatory relations with Great Britain and France. After a long civil war, the Spanish military was not in a position to participate in a larger European conflict. With the collapse of France in 1940, however, Franco moved Spain closer to Germany in order to gain territorial concessions in North Africa and Gibraltar. In 1941, Franco sent the Spanish "Blue Division" in the German invasion of the Soviet Union.

Because of Spain's neutrality, Franco retained power after the war and continue to serve as the country's paramount leader until his death in 1975. A king was not restored to the Spanish throne until after Franco's death.

Steven B. Rogers

Additional Reading

Crozier, Brian, *Franco* (1967).
Dundas, Lawrence, *Behind the Spanish Mask* (1943).
Feis, Herbert, *The Spanish Story: Franco and the Nation at War* (1948).

Hayes, Carlton J.H., *Wartime Mission in Spain, 1942–1945* (1945).

Frank, Anne (1929–1945)

Holocaust victim. Annelies Marie Frank was the second daughter of Otto Frank, a German Jewish merchant, and Edith Holländer. She was born on 12 June 1929, in Frankfurt am Main, Germany. Because of the growing persecution of the Jews by the Nazis, the Frank family emigrated to Amsterdam, Holland, in 1934. There Anne attended kindergarten and elementary school. In July 1942, two years after the German invasion of Holland, the family went underground. The Franks and four others lived in a secret annex to a warehouse on the Prinsengracht Canal. On 4 August 1944, the hiding place was betrayed to the *Gestapo* (q.v.) and all inhabitants were deported. Anne was sent to the Bergen-Belsen concentration camp, where she died in March 1945 of typhoid fever. Her father was the only member of the family to survive.

After their deportation, Anne's personal diary was found among other papers left behind. She kept her diary between June 1942 and August 1944. With great insight, she described the problems and conflicts between the eight people cramped into small living quarters, existing under constant fear of discovery and death. She wrote movingly about her dreams, hopes, and feelings in the difficult position of being the youngest person in the hiding place and simultaneously going through adolescence.

Anne's diary was published first in Dutch in 1947. Since its original publication, the diary has been translated into more than fifty languages and dramatized by Frances Goodrich and Albert Hackett in the play, *The Diary of Anne Frank* (1956). It was also produced as a movie in 1959.

Antje Richter

Additional Reading

Frank, Anne, *The Diary of a Young Girl* (1952).
Frank, Otto, *The Works of Anne Frank* (1959).
Schnabel, Ernst, *Anne Frank: A Portrait in Courage* (1958).
Warmbrunn, Werner, *The Dutch Under German Occupation, 1940–1945* (1963).
Woerden, Peter van, *In the Secret Place: A Story of the Dutch Underground* (1954).

Frank, Hans (1900–1946)

Nazi jurist and governor-general of occupied Po-

Hans Frank, Governor-General of Occupied Poland. (IWM HU 6253)

land. Frank joined the German Workers' Party in 1919 and took part as a *Freikorps* (q.v.) member in the 1923 "Beer Hall *Putsch*" (q.v.). He fled following its failure, but returned to Munich after completing his law degree. He claimed that his formal entry into the Nazi Party occurred in 1928. In 1929, he became head of the Nazi Party's legal department. In September 1930, he entered the *Reichstag* as a Nazi delegate. In March 1933, he became the minister of justice of Bavaria, and on 22 April 1933, *Reich* commissioner of justice. On 31 December 1934, he was appointed minister without portfolio in Adolf Hitler's (q.v.) government.

On 19 September 1939, Frank became chief administrator for occupied Poland, and on 12 October 1939, Adolf Hitler appointed him governor-general of German-occupied Poland, that part not directly incorporated into Germany. Known as the General Government (q.v.), he brutally governed this territory from Wavel Castle in Krakow.

Through a reign of terror, he pursued the destruction of Polish national identity and the exploitation of the inhabitants and resources of the General Government for the benefit of Germany. He ordered a systematic extermination of the Polish intelligentsia and put such a drastic levy on Polish agricultural production that famine and epidemic followed. He deported approximately one million slave laborers to Germany, and he supported the extermination of the Polish Jewish community.

Frank was tried with the other principal Nazi leaders at Nuremberg (*see* International Military Tribunal). In an emotional statement, he expressed his feeling of guilt for atrocities committed during his administration in Poland. He attempted to exonerate himself, however, by blaming them on the excesses of subordinates or claiming that they were the work of other components of the Nazi administration, directed by Heinrich Himmler and Fritz Sauckel (qq.v.), over which he had no control. Frank was, nevertheless, found guilty of war crimes and crimes against humanity, condemned to death, and hanged in October 1946.

Bernard A. Cook

Additional Reading

Davidson, Eugene, *The Trial of the Germans— An Account of the Twenty-Two Defendants Before the International Military Tribunal at Nuremberg* (1966).
Piotrowski, Stanislaw, *Hans Frank's Diary* (1961).
Posner, Gerald L., *Hitler's Children: Sons and Daughters of Third Reich Leaders Talk About Themselves and Their Fathers* (1991).

František, Jósef (1912–1940)

Czech ace, RAF sergeant. František was the top-scoring Czech ace of World War II. He was a member of the Czech Air Force at the time Germany took over Czechoslovakia. František escaped to Poland and in March 1939 he enlisted in the Polish Air Force. During the September 1939 campaign, František shot down two German aircraft.

When Poland collapsed, František escaped to Romania, where he was interned. He escaped from the internment camp and made his way through the Balkans to Syria. In May 1940 he arrived in France and joined the French Air Force. During the May 1940 campaign, František shot down an additional nine German aircraft.

With the fall of France in June 1940, František escaped to Britain where he joined the RAF and was posted to the primarily Polish Number 303 Squadron, Flying Hurricanes. František quickly became one of the best Battle of Britain fighter pilots.

František died in an accident on 8 October 1940, while making a seemingly routine landing. At the time of his death, he was the top-scoring ace of RAF's Fighter Command.

David T. Zabecki

Additional Reading

Baker, E.C.R., *The Fighter Aces of the R.A.F.* (1962).

Fraser, Bruce (1888–1981)

British admiral, commander in chief of the British Home Fleet. The son of a general in the Royal Engineers, Sir Bruce Fraser was born in London and educated at Bradfield and aboard the HMS *Britannia*. He saw action in the Dardanelles in 1916 and was captured by the Bolsheviks at Baku in 1920 while on a mission to the White Russian Navy. Most of the interwar years were spent at sea, specializing in gunnery.

In the first three years of the war, Fraser was third sea lord (with the rank of vice admiral), responsible for ship construction and repair. His efforts played a prominent part in the building of escorts for the Atlantic convoys and in developing radar. In 1943, he replaced Admiral John Tovey (q.v.) as commander in chief of the Home Fleet. His main task was escorting Allied convoys to Murmansk, and a major threat to their safety was the German capital ships in northern Norway.

After Fraser's midget submarines crippled the *Tirpitz* at its own base in September 1943 (*see*

Admiral Sir Bruce Fraser, GCB, KBE. (IWM A 30245)

Alten Fjord Raid), he led a task force to engage a German attack on Convoys RA-55A and JW-55B in January 1944. In the ensuing battle of North Cape (q.v.), the only battleship action in European waters during the war, he made brilliant use of ULTRA (q.v.) intercepts and radar to outwit his opponent, Admiral Eric Bey. The destruction of the battleship *Scharnhorst* completely removed the surface threat to the Murmansk convoys for the remainder of the war.

Fraser later commanded the small British fleet in the Pacific, and he signed the Japanese surrender document on Great Britain's behalf in Tokyo Bay in September 1945. He was promoted to admiral of the fleet and became first sea lord in 1948. He retired in 1952.

Fraser was a bluff sea dog of the old school. Though he had no reputation as an intellectual, he had a thorough grasp of the application of modern technology to add to the traditional professional skills of the Royal Navy.

Phillip Green

Additional Reading

Chatterton, Edward K., and Kenneth Edwards, *The Royal Navy: From September 1939 to September 1945,* 5 vols. (1942–1947).

Humble, Richard, *Fraser of North Cape* (1983).

Fraser, Simon Christopher (Lord Lovat) (1911–1995)

British brigadier, commando leader at Dieppe and Normandy. Lord Lovat graduated from Oxford University and was commissioned into the Scots Guards in 1934. He served there until he left the army three years later. In 1939, as war seemed imminent, he joined the Lovat Scouts, a yeomanry (volunteer cavalry) unit his father had formed during the Boer War. Leaving the scouts, he joined the newly formed commandos (q.v.) and participated in early shakeout missions, as they gained experience and reputation.

In 1942, Lovat led Number 4 Commando in the Dieppe raid (q.v.), where his force was the only one to accomplish its assigned mission. Following Dieppe, he conducted commando training and was then selected to command the 1st Special Service Brigade, which consisted of Number 3, 4, 6, and 45 (Royal Marine) commandos. During the Normandy (q.v.) landings, Lovat's brigade had the mission of securing the Allied eastern flank. On D-Day, he led his troops onto SWORD Beach with his personal bagpipers playing. Severely wounded six days later, he was evacuated.

Following the war, Lovat served as undersecretary of state for foreign affairs and became known as a lecturer and agronomist. He was the seventeenth baron of Lovat, as well as the twenty-fifth chief of Clan Fraser.

Steven D. Cage

Additional Reading

Lovat, Simon (Lord), *March Past* (1978).

Fredendall, Lloyd Ralston (1883–1963)

American major general, commander U.S. II Corps. Dismissed from West Point in 1903 for his low grade-point average, Fredendall transferred to the Massachusetts Institute of Technology. In 1907, he won, via a written test, a direct commission in the U.S. Army. During World War I, he commanded an officer training school in France. Between the wars, he graduated from the Command and General Staff College and served on the inspector general staff.

In October 1940, he assumed command of the U.S. Army's first motorized division, the 4th Infantry Division. Owing to his excellence as a trainer of men, he was given command of the II Corps in July 1941 and led it during the Carolina maneuvers. In June 1942, he took command of XI Corps. Shortly after, Fredendall returned to command II Corps and led it ashore at Oran in the invasion of North Africa. Receiving high marks for the initial operations of II Corps, he was promoted to lieutenant general. In February 1943, II Corps was defeated by the *Afrika Korps* (q.v.) at the battle of Kasserine Pass (q.v.). As a result of this defeat, he was relieved of his command by General Dwight D. Eisenhower (q.v.).

Back in the United States, Fredendall became commanding general of the Second Army. He held this position for the rest of the war, doing an excellent job of preparing U.S. Army troops for combat.

Charles A. Bogart

Additional Reading

Harmon, Ernest N., *Combat Commander* (1970).

Howe, George, *Northwest Africa: Seizing the Initiative in the West* (1957).

Frederick, Robert T. (1907–1970)

American major general, commander of the 1st Special Services Force. Frederick was the first commander of the elite U.S.-Canadian 1st Special Services Force (q.v.), which was the antecedent of

Major General Robert T. Frederick receiving the Distinguished Service Order from Field Marshal Montgomery, 26 June 1945. (IWM BU 8375)

today's U.S. Special Forces. He was commissioned in the Coast Artillery in 1928 from the U.S. Military Academy. His service prior to World War II included tours of duty in Hawaii and Panama.

As a staff officer in the War Plans Division during the early part of the war, Frederick recommended against a British proposal to create a joint U.S.-Canadian special fighting force. The proposal was adopted anyway and in 1942, he was selected to activate and command what became known as the "Force." As commander, he led by example to ensure the Force was fit and proficient. The Force embodied these goals and trained to operated at night, in mountains, as amphibious soldiers, and as paratroopers. Their first test came in the Aleutians, but the Japanese evacuated before the Force arrived. Late in 1943, the Force was sent to Italy where its special skills and leadership succeeded in breaking a long-standing stalemate. The Force was also used at Anzio (q.v.) and other areas in straight infantry roles.

Throughout its combat service in World War II, the Force was never defeated. Frederick left the Force in 1944 to serve as commander of the 1st Airborne Task Force in the invasion of southern France. He finished the war as commander of the 45th Infantry Division. Following the war, he commanded the 4th and 6th Infantry Divisions and was the chief of the Military Assistance Group in Greece in 1951. He retired as major general in 1952, having earned two Distinguished Service

Crosses, two Distinguished Service Medals, the Silver Star, two Legions of Merit, the Bronze Star, the Combat Infantryman's Badge, and eight Purple Hearts. He was wounded in action more than any other American general officer in World War II.

Steven D. Cage

Additional Reading

Adleman, Robert, and George Walton, *The Devil's Brigade* (1966).
Packe, M., *First Airborne* (1948).
Warren, John C., *Airborne Operations in World War II* (1956).

Freisler, Roland (1893–1945)

Nazi jurist, president of the People's Court. Freisler was born in Celle. During World War I he was captured by the Russians and spent five years imprisoned in Siberia where he learned to speak fluent Russian and developed a passionate hatred for communism.

After returning to Germany in 1920, Freisler studied law at Jena. He joined the Nazi Party in 1925 and steadily rose within its ranks. In 1932 he became the director of personnel at the Prussian Ministry of Justice. In 1934 he was appointed a state secretary with the special duty of combating sabotage. On 20 January 1942, Freisler participated in the Wannsee Conference, at which the Final Solution (q.v.) to the "Jewish Problem" was posed.

In 1942 Freisler became the president of the dreaded People's Court *(Volksgericht),* a kangaroo tribunal set up to quickly dispose of traitors and enemies of the *Reich.* Freisler was notorious for berating and demeaning defendants, and for handing out death sentences. He was especially vindictive toward the accused members of the July Plot (*see* Opposition to Hitler) against Adolf Hitler's (q.v.) life.

On 3 February 1945, Freisler was presiding over the treason trial of Fabian von Schlabrendorff (q.v.). Just as von Schlabrendorff was being led into the court, the building was bombed in a U.S. air raid. Freisler, clutching von Schlabrendorff's file, died in the attack. Von Schlabrendorff survived both the bombing and the war.

David T. Zabecki

Additional Reading

Buchheit, G., *Richter in roter Robe* (1968).
Kramer, Gerhard F., *The Influence of National Socialism on the Courts of Justice and the Police in the Third Reich* (1955).

Wagner, W., *Der Volkgerichtshof in nationalsozialistischen Staat* (1974).

Freyberg, Bernard (1889–1963)

New Zealand lieutenant general, corps commander. Born in London, Sir Bernard Freyberg grew up as a New Zealander. He first saw combat service during World War I with the Royal Naval Volunteer Reserve at Antwerp, Belgium. His bravery was quickly apparent. He won the first of his four Distinguished Service Orders (DSO) at Gallipoli and the Victoria Cross on the Somme in 1916 while serving as a temporary lieutenant colonel attached to the Royal Naval Division. Given this success it was no surprise that he made the military his career. By the early 1930s, he was a high-flyer at the British War Office.

After a brief spell as a civilian due to illness, he rejoined the military at the start of World War II and was given command of New Zealand forces overseas, thus renewing his attachment to that country. His men resisted the German advance on Athens in 1941, but they were forced to withdraw to Crete (q.v.). There, despite material shortages, his troops inflicted serious casualties on General Kurt Student's (q.v.) XI Air Corps.

Freyberg again was forced to withdraw, this time to Egypt and the North African theater with the British Eighth Army. There he had a personality clash with General Claude Auchinleck (q.v.), which affected his command. By 1943, however, both he and his men were revitalized and staged the assaults leading to Allied victory on the Mareth Line (q.v.).

In Italy, under the U.S. Fifth Army, came the action at Monte Cassino (q.v.) for which Freyberg was often criticized. As a corps commander, he argued for the bombing of the monastery, thereby creating mountains of rubble to assist the German defenders, taking a heavy toll of New Zealand and other Allied lives. Nonetheless, he was awarded one of the bars to his DSO and not long after, led his troops triumphantly into Trieste.

Freyberg was an imposing individual with great all-around abilities. His multiple wounds in both world wars bear witness to his physical power and bravery. He went on to successful postwar service, gaining many honors of state, and becoming governor-general of his beloved New Zealand. He was highly respected by German general Erwin Rommel (q.v.), a tribute most military commanders would envy.

Chris Westhorp

Additional Reading

Baker, John, *The New Zealand People at War* (1965).
New Zealand Department of Interior Affairs, *New Zealand in the Second World War, 1939–1945* (1949).

Lieutenant General Sir Bernard Freyberg, VC, DSO and 3 Bars. (IWM NA 10630)

Frick, Wilhelm (1877–1946)

German interior minister. Frick studied law at Göttingen, Munich, Berlin, and Heidelberg between 1896 and 1901. He entered the Bavarian civil service in 1904 and by 1909, he was leader of the political police in Bavaria. Here he often supported right-wing groups like the Nazis. He took part in the 1923 "Beer Hall *Putsch*" (q.v.) and was sentenced to fifteen months in prison. He did not serve the time because in 1924, he was elected to the *Reichstag* as a deputy of the National Socialist Freedom Movement, which replaced the temporarily banned NSDAP (*see* National Socialist German Workers' Party).

In January 1930, Frick took over the post of people's education minister in the province of Thuringia. There he led a campaign against "Negro and jazz music." Additionally, he issued prayer instructions for schools, secured a professorship for a "race researcher" at the university of Jena, and

F

pushed civil servants who were loyal to the Weimar Republic (q.v.) out of police and government.

On 30 January 1933, Adolf Hitler (q.v.) named Frick *Reichsminister* of the interior for the new government. Under Frick's leadership, some of the most decisive measures for the establishment of the National Socialist state were taken and the German civil service was purged of Communists and Social Democrats. He also took part in enacting the Nuremberg Laws (q.v.) in 1935. He could not persecute his own political opponents, however, because Hermann Göring in Prussia and Heinrich Himmler (qq.v.) in the rest of Germany were in firm control of the police.

Frick's influence diminished during the war. In August 1943, Himmler took over the Interior Ministry, and Frick became governor of the protectorate of Bohemia and Moravia (q.v.). At the Nuremberg trials (*see* International Military Tribunal), Frick was convicted of crimes against humanity, war crimes, and participation in planning a war of aggression. He was hanged on 1 October 1946.

Franz Seidler

Additional Reading

Davidson, Eugene, *The Trial of the Germans* (1966).
Gallagher, Richard, *Nuremberg: The Third Reich on Trial* (1961).
Keller, Douglas, *22 Cells in Nuremberg: A Psychiatrist Examines the Nazi Criminals* (1947).
Lunau, Heinz, *The Germans on Trial* (1948).

Friedeburg, Hans Georg von (1895–1945)

German admiral, U-boat commander. "A particularly gifted organizer and a man endowed with an exceptional capacity for work." Thus did Grand Admiral Karl Dönitz (q.v.) describe von Friedeburg, a career naval officer, who up to 1938 was mainly involved with surface vessels. That year, however, the successful captain became head of the organizational section of the submarine forces. His work centered about training, personnel, technical issues, and weapons procurement.

Hard work and a harmonious relation with Dönitz resulted in promotions to admiral, and by 1943, von Friedeburg followed Dönitz as commander of Germany's U-Boats. Despite this position, Friedeburg is better remembered as the man who, in May 1945, negotiated the preliminary surrender of northwestern Europe to British General Bernard L. Montgomery (q.v.) and signed the declaration of unconditional surrender with U.S.

General Dwight D. Eisenhower (q.v.) on 7 May in Rheims, and a day later, with Soviet Marshal Georgy Zhukov (q.v.) in Berlin. Distraught at the complete collapse of Germany, von Friedeburg committed suicide a few days later.

John Dunn

Additional Reading

Dönitz, Karl, *Memoirs: Ten Years and Twenty Days* (1959).

Friessner, Johannes (1892–1971)

German colonel general, army group commander. The son of a construction engineer, Friessner was one of the few Saxons to attain a high position in the *Wehrmacht*. After serving as inspector of the army educational system, he became a divisional commander on the eastern front in 1942, took over a corps in 1943, and assumed responsibility for defending the Narva sector in 1944. Promoted to colonel general, he briefly commanded Army Group North and was then sent to Moldavia as head of Army Group *Südukraine*.

Composed of two German and two Romanian armies, Army Group *Südukraine* was hit by a major Soviet offensive in August 1944. Within a few days, the Romanians switched over to the Allied side, and most of Friessner's German divisions were trapped and eventually wiped out. After retreating into Hungary with the remnants of his troops, he restored a semblance of stability at his front but was dismissed by Adolf Hitler (q.v.) on 22 December 1944. In 1951, Friessner briefly served as chairman of the *Verband Deutscher Soldaten,* the German Federal Republic's largest veterans' organization.

Ulrich Trumpener

Additional Reading

Ceaugescu, Ilie, Florin Constantiniu, and Mihail E. Ionescu, *A Turning Point in World War II: 23 August 1944 in Romania* (1985).
Kurowski, Franz, *Deutsche Offiziere in Staat, Wirtschaft und Wissenschaft* (1967).

Fritsch, Werner von (1880–1939)

German colonel general, commander in chief of the German Army. Von Fritsch entered the German Army when he was eighteen. At the age of twenty-one, he was transferred to the War Academy in Berlin. Ten years later, he was appointed to a coveted position on the German General Staff (q.v.). He served in World War I. In the 1920s he

Colonel General Werner Freiherr *von Fritsch. (IWM MH 13142)*

ated Fritsch, but Hitler refused to reinstate him, successfully ridding himself of the last representative of conservatism in a high position. On 22 September 1939, von Fritsch was killed in Poland in a small-unit action, after being recalled to the army in an honorary position as colonel in chief of his old regiment, the 12th Artillery. His death is widely considered a suicide. (*See* also Blomberg-Fritsch Crisis.)

Robert F. Pace

Additional Reading

Humble, Richard, *Hitler's Generals* (1974).
Rothfels, Hans, *The German Opposition to Hitler: An Appraisal* (1948).
Taylor, Telford, *Sword and Swastika: Generals and Nazis in the Third Reich* (1952).

Fritzsche, Hans (1900–1953)

German chief of radio broadcasting. Fritzsche studied history and philosophy. In 1924, he became an editor at the *Telegraphen Union* and the *Presse Nachrichten Dienst,* which both belonged to the press group of Alfred Hugenberg. In 1923, Fritzsche joined the German National People's Party, a right-wing group similar to the Nazis. By 1932, he was the head of the wireless service of the central news agency of German radio. When on 1 May 1933, the wireless service came under the *Reich* Ministry for People's Education and Propaganda, he became the leader of communications in the press department. That same day, he joined the Nazi Party.

Fritzsche was in the position to authorize all the news broadcasts and control everything written in the German press, and all the information for foreign consumption. In 1938, he became the head of the press department and in November 1942, he headed the radio department of the ministry with the rank of ministerial director. He became widely known for his radio broadcasts ("This is Hans Fritzsche speaking"), which at first seemed objective, but which always followed the Nazi Party line. Toward the end of the war, his broadcasts lapsed into pure propaganda.

In May 1945, after many of the Nazi elite had committed suicide, Fritzsche was left as one of the highest-ranking government officials to take part in the capitulation negotiations. He identified for the Red Army the corpses of his former boss Joseph Goebbels (q.v.) and his family. Fritzsche was a defendant in the first Nuremberg trials (*see* International Military Tribunal), but was acquitted and released on 1 October 1946. In 1947, a Ger-

was promoted to lieutenant colonel and headed a department in the *Reichwehr* Ministry. In 1930, his hard work and ability led to his promotion to major general and command of a cavalry division. In February 1934, President Paul von Hindenburg (q.v.), who liked his traditionalism, named him chief of the high command of the army. In May 1935, he was promoted to commander in chief of the German Army.

Von Fritsch never disguised his contempt for the Nazi Party and the SS (q.v.). He confronted Adolf Hitler (q.v.) upon learning of his plan to use force against Austria and Czechoslovakia, arguing that Germany was not militarily prepared for such enterprises. Early in 1938, von Fritsch fell victim to a plot to discredit him engineered by Heinrich Himmler and Hermann Göring (qq.v.). They accused him of paying blackmail to an ex-convict to cover up homosexual offenses, and they paid a man to testify to that effect. On 4 February, Hitler announced that von Fritsch had resigned for health reasons.

On 18 March 1938, a military court exoner-

F

man de-Nazification court sentenced him to nine years in a work camp. He was released in September 1950 and died three years later in Cologne.

Franz Seidler

Additional Reading
Bramstead, Ernest K., *Goebbels and National Socialist Propaganda, 1925–1945* (1965).
Childs, Harwood L., and J.B. Whitton (eds.), *Propaganda by Short Wave* (1942).
Fritzsche, Hans, *The Sword in the Scales* (1953).
Zeaman, Zbynek, *Nazi Propaganda* (1964).

Fromm, Friedrich (1888–1945)

German colonel general. Born in Berlin on 8 October 1888, Fromm was Germany's chief of army equipment and commander of the Reserve Army for most of World War II. A World War I veteran, he was appointed to his wartime posts in September 1939 following service in a variety of primarily staff posts in the *Reichswehr*. A weak and vacillating man, he is best remembered for his participation in and subsequent betrayal of the July plot to assassinate Adolf Hitler (q.v.). Despite his efforts to hide his involvement, Fromm was convicted by a "people's court" and executed by firing squad on 19 March 1945.

Carl O. Schuster

Additional Reading
Manvell, Roger, *The Conspirators: 20th July 1944* (1971).
Mitcham, Samuel W., Jr., *Hitler's Field Marshals and Their Battles* (1988).
Schlabrendorff, Fabian von, *They Almost Killed Hitler* (1947).

Frost, John Dutton (1912–1993)

British lieutenant colonel, parachute battalion commander. Born into an army family, Frost joined the army himself and became one of Britain's first airborne soldiers. He served as commanding officer of the 2nd Battalion of the newly formed Parachute Regiment and was to remain so throughout the war. In February 1942, as a major, he led C Company on a daring and very successful raid against the German radar site at Bruneval (q.v.) in northern France.

Frost is remembered principally for the central role he played in the heroic stand made by the 1st Parachute Brigade at the bridge at Arnhem (q.v.) in September 1944. His 600-strong force was decimated in resisting the attacks of overwhelm-

ing German forces for four consecutive nights. He was wounded in the action and taken prisoner. He later received the Military Cross. After the war, he continued in his military career and retired as major general in 1968. In 1977, the people of Arnhem honored Frost by renaming the bridge after him.

Chris Westhorp

Additional Reading
Farrar-Hockley, Anthony, *Operation Market-Garden* (1970).
Guingand, Sir Francis de, *Generals at War* (1964).
Ryan, Cornelius, *A Bridge Too Far* (1974).

Fuller, John Frederick Charles (1878–1966)

British major general, military historian and theorist. J.F.C. Fuller developed the idea of using tanks as offensive weapons en masse and heavily influenced the German ideas of *Blitzkrieg* (q.v.) warfare. Educated at Sandhurst, he joined the army in 1898 and served in the Boer War.

A general staff officer at the outbreak of World War I, Fuller soon realized the offensive capabilities of the tank to overcome trench warfare. In December 1916, he received command of the Heavy Branch of the Machine Gun Corps (actually the new tank corps). Using his ideas of the tank as an offensive weapon, he planned the attack on Cambrai in 1917, in which tanks were first used en masse. His subsequent PLAN 19 called for a coordinated attack of tanks and airplanes to win the war by striking for the enemy's command centers. The war ended before the plan could be implemented.

After the war, Fuller, in his *Lectures on Field Service Regulations III*, pushed for the creation of a totally mechanized army coordinated with airplanes, but his ideas went ignored in Britain. His condescending attitude and sharp tongue created many enemies. Given command of a new tank brigade in 1926, he argued himself out of the position because of philosophical reasons. Promoted to major general in 1930, he remained in the army until 1933 when he was retired.

On retirement, Fuller became a special correspondent for the *Daily Mail* in Ethiopia in 1935, and made several trips to Germany. In *Towards Armageddon* (1937), he prophesied much that would occur in Europe. He warned that if Adolf Hitler (q.v.) went to war, he would throw himself at his enemies "like a flash of lightning in the night."

With the beginning of World War II, many of Fuller's ideas became reality. Although the British military refused to listen to him, the Germans were attentive. Their *Blitzkrieg* incorporated much of Fuller's writings.

After the war, Fuller continued to study history and write, publishing his magnum opus, *Military History of the Western World,* in the 1950s. His ideas on the future of war and technology and his tank tactics heavily influenced Sir Basil H. Liddell Hart (q.v.) and others who helped revolu-tionize warfare in the later 1930s and World War II.

Laura Matysek Wood

Additional Reading

Fuller, J.F.C., *Memoirs of an Unconventional Soldier* (1936).

———, *Towards Armageddon* (1937).

Reid, Brian H., *J.F.C. Fuller: Military Thinker* (1987).

Trythall, Anthony John, *Boney Fuller* (1977).

F

G

Gabreski, Francis (1919–)

American lieutenant colonel, pilot. Born to Polish immigrant parents in Oil City, Pennsylvania, "Gabby" Gabreski nearly washed out of flight school, in which he had enlisted as an aviator cadet in July 1940. Commissioned in March 1941, he was assigned to the 45th Fighter Squadron, 15th Fighter Group, Wheeler Field, Hawaii.

An eyewitness to the December 7 Japanese assault on Pearl Harbor, Gabreski was unable to get airborne until two hours after the attack. Even then, he and eleven other pilots were dispersed by friendly antiaircraft fire. He stayed with the 15th Fighter Group for about a year, then transferred to Britain, where his fluent Polish and limited Czech language capabilities were of use as an interpreter of intelligence.

Anxious to see some action, however, Gabreski finagled an assignment to RAF Ferry Command, Prestwick, Scotland, which gave him the opportunity to fly all types of aircraft. Soon bored again, he wrangled a temporary duty assignment as a liaison officer to the Polish Air Force. Assigned to Number 315 RAF Squadron in London, he gained valuable experience flying twenty combat missions in Spitfires.

When the 56th Fighter Group, also known as the "Wolf Pack" was formed, Gabreski volunteered and soon became the operations officer. Assigned to the 61st Squadron, he used the radio call sign "Keyworth Blue Leader." By the summer of 1944, Lieutenant Colonel Gabreski had thirty-one kills, making him the top-scoring U.S. ace in Europe. The result of what one observer described as "cocky aggressiveness combined with superior flying skill." After his twenty-eighth aerial kill on 5 July 1944, he was awarded the Polish Cross of Valor by General Władysław Sikorski (q.v.), the prime minister of the Polish government-in-exile.

On 20 July 1944, on what ironically was supposed to be his last mission, Gabreski flew low to escape ground fire while strafing an airfield near Coblenz, Germany. His plane's propeller dug into the sod, causing him to crash-land. He evaded German patrols for five days before being captured.

Taken to a nearby *Luftwaffe* station for interrogation, he was greeted by the intelligence officer with the words, "Hello, Gabby, we've been waiting for you for a long time!" The most prominent member of the 56th Fighter Group's "Terrible Three" (including Hubert Zemke [q.v.] and David Schilling) ended the war as a POW at *Stalag Luft I* in Barth, Pomerania.

David A. Foy

Additional Reading
Gabreski, Francis, and Carl Molesworth, *Gabby: A Fighter Pilot's Life* (1991).
Ward, Edward, *Time Out: American Airmen at Stalag Luft I* (1951).

Gaffey, Hugh J. (1895–1946)

American major general, commander U.S. XII Corps. Gaffey was born in Hartford, Connecticut, and entered the army as a lieutenant of field artillery on 15 August 1917. During the early years of World War II, he commanded the 2nd Armored Division in North Africa. In April 1943, he was promoted to major general, and the following year, he became chief of staff of General George S. Patton's (q.v.) Third Army.

During the relief of Bastogne (q.v.), Gaffey commanded the 4th Armored Division, and led that unit into Germany. In the last months of the war, he assumed command of XII Corps. He was one of the army's premier experts on armored warfare, and one of Patton's most trusted subordinates.

He died in a plane crash shortly after the end of the war.

A. Gregory Gutgsell, Jr.

Additional Reading
Farago, Ladislas, *Patton: Ordeal and Triumph* (1964).
Patton, George S., Jr., *War As I Knew It* (1947).

Gale, Humphrey Myddelton (1890–1971)

British lieutenant general. Sir Humphrey Gale was a specialist in logistics and administration. He served as the administrative officer to home forces commander in chief, General Sir Alan Brooke (q.v.) for two years before assuming the same post with U.S. General Dwight D. Eisenhower (q.v.) when the latter was commander of Allied forces in the Mediterranean. He served with Eisenhower until transferring to SHEAF (q.v.) as Ike's chief administrative officer in 1944.

Paul Rose

Additional Reading
Guingand, Sir Francis de, *Generals at War* (1964).
Tollemache, Edward, *The British Army at War* (1941).

Gale, Richard Nelson (1896–1982)

British lieutenant general, commander of the British 6th Airborne Division. Born 25 July 1896, Richard Gale lived most of his early life in Australia. During World War I, he served with the Machine Gun Corps in France, finishing as a company commander with a Military Cross. He spent most of the interwar years in India, including fifteen years as lieutenant, an indication of the stagnation in the British Army at the time. By 1940, he was the commander of a territorial army battalion.

In 1941, at age forty-five, Gale was selected to form Britain's first parachute brigade. Before he could take the new force into action, he was appointed director of airborne forces at the British War Office. By 1944, he was back in active command with the 6th Airborne Division, which he led during its jump on D-Day. He spent the final months of the war commanding the British I Airborne Corps.

In his postwar assignments, Gale served as commander in chief of the British Army of the Rhine and as NATO's deputy supreme Allied commander, Europe. He was one of the small group of determined professional soldiers who introduced the airborne concept to the British Army. It is perhaps appropriate that he died in July 1982, just at the conclusion of the Falklands campaign, during which the British Parachute Regiment gained further recognition.

Phillip Green

Additional Reading
Bliven, Bruce, *The Story of D-Day, June 6, 1944* (1956).
Gale, Richard, *With the 6th Airborne Division in Normandy* (1952).
Gregory, Barry, *British Airborne Troops* (1974).
Norton, Geoffrey G., *The Red Devils: The Story of the British Airborne Forces* (1971).

Galland, Adolf (1912–1996)

German general, *Luftwaffe* ace. Galland joined the *Luftwaffe* in 1932 and flew with the *Kondor Legion* in the Spanish civil war (qq.v.). He later commanded a close air transport squadron during the invasion of Poland. Transferred to fight-

General of Fighters Adolf Galland. (IWM MH 6038)

G

ers just before the invasion of France, he achieved his first air-to-air victory over Belgium in May 1940. He took part in the Battle of Britain (q.v.), was promoted to lieutenant colonel and commanded Fighter Group JG-26 by the end of 1940. A superb pilot and born hunter, he championed offensive tactics that would free his fighters from bomber escort and enable them to win control of the air.

Following Ernst Udet's (q.v.) suicide, Galland was promoted to lieutenant general and appointed general of the fighters. As the tempo of the Allied air war against Germany increased, he again championed an aggressive strategy designed to mass the *Luftwaffe*'s available fighter strength against enemy bomber formations. Although this strategy did achieve initial successes against the Allied bomber offensive, his efforts were complicated by interference from Hermann Göring (q.v.) who favored a dispersed perimeter defense. Galland became the scapegoat for the *Luftwaffe*'s failure to keep control of the air over Germany, and in January 1945, he was relieved as general of fighters. Yet, his reputation was such that he was personally ordered by Adolf Hitler (q.v.) to command the elite fighter squadron *Jagdverband* 44, which flew Me-262 jets in the final defense of Germany. During the war, Galland scored a total of 104 air-to-air victories.

Budd A.R. Jones

Additional Reading
Galland, Adolf, *The First and the Last* (1957).
Grey, Charles G., *Luftwaffe* (1944).
Johnen, Wilhelm, *Duel Under the Stars: A German Night Fighter Pilot in the Second World War* (1957).
Killen, John, *The Luftwaffe: A History* (1967).

Gallery, Daniel V. (1901–1977)
American rear admiral, antisubmarine expert. Gallery was the first U.S. naval officer since 1815 to capture an enemy ship on the high seas. He was born in Chicago and graduated from the U.S. Naval Academy in 1920. Following early surface service, he became an aviator in 1927 and served as an instructor until 1932. After further training, he joined and later commanded a scouting squadron. Later, he was posted as chief of the Bureau of Ordnance's aviation section until 1941, when he was selected for embassy duty in London.

Gallery then commanded the fleet air base at Reykjavik, Iceland, conducting aerial antisubmarine and convoy patrols. Assuming command of a submarine hunter-killer task group in 1943, he

made plans to capture a German U-boat. In June 1944, his group captured the *U-505* after it surfaced and was abandoned by its crew. Although the boat was booby-trapped, the mission was a success, and it provided information on German codes and torpedoes. In 1945, Gallery transferred to the Pacific Ocean where he finished the war and was promoted to rear admiral.

After the war, Gallery was assistant chief of naval operations, commander of a carrier division in the Mediterranean, and commander of a fleet hunter-killer (antisubmarine) force in the Atlantic. Returning to the Chicago area, he was chief of naval air reserve training and commander of the Ninth Naval District. His final assignment was commanding the naval district in Puerto Rico. After retiring, he continued to write navy-oriented books begun earlier in his career.

Steven D. Cage

Additional Reading
Blair, Clay, Jr., *Silent Victory: The U.S. Submarine War Against Japan* (1978).
Roscoe, Theodore, *United States Submarine Operations in World War II* (1949).

Gamelin, Maurice Gustave (1872–1958)
French general, commander in chief of the Allied armies on the outbreak of World War II. Gamelin was a graduate of the French Military Academy at St. Cyr. In World War I, he was on the staff of general Joseph-Jacques-Césaire Joffre; later he commanded a division. He became chief of the general staff of the French Army in 1931, and its commander in chief in 1935. He was much criticized for lack of action in the early months of World War II. Scholarly and publicity-shy, he prided himself on his abilities as a planner, but he was sadly out of touch with the new realities of war.

Gamelin's plan for relieving Poland required a two-week delay to bring French artillery out of storage and call up reservists. Operation SAAR, the limited French offensive between the Moselle and the Rhine, went badly. Poland was already collapsing and the offensive was canceled. More resolute action might have carried the French to the Rhine.

Gamelin subsequently yielded the initiative to the Germans, waiting for them to attack or for Allied strength to be so great that the Allies could overwhelm them. His Plan "D," endorsed by the Allied supreme council in mid-November, played into German hands. It called for the Allies to send most of their mobile units into Belgium when the Germans struck west. They were to push as far toward the Ruhr as possible. But the deeper the Allied units deployed, the more likely they were to be cut off by the German thrust into the Ardennes.

Gamelin was removed from command on 19 May and replaced by General Maxime Weygand (q.v.). He was arrested by the Vichy government. One of the defendants at the Riom Trials in 1942, he was later imprisoned by the Germans and liberated in 1945.

Spencer Tucker

Additional Reading

Chapman, Guy, *Why France Fell; The Defeat of the French Army in 1940* (1969).

Gamelin, Maurice-Gustave, *Servir,* 3 vols. (1946–1947).

Horne, Alistair, *To Lose a Battle: France 1940* (1969).

Werth, Alexander, *France 1940–1945* (1956).

Garand, John Cantius (1888–1974)

American ordnance engineer, inventor of the U.S. semiautomatic rifle M-l, "the Garand." Born in Quebec, Canada, Garand moved to the U.S. in 1899. At age thirteen, he received the first of many patents. He submitted his first firearm design to the U.S. government in 1916. He was recruited to join the engineering department of the Springfield Armory in 1919. There he was assigned the task of developing a semiautomatic rifle to replace the M-1903 Springfield rifle. The model that was adopted by the U.S. Army in 1936 increased the firepower of an infantry company fivefold over the bolt action 1903 rifle.

In 1944, the U.S. government awarded Garand the Medal for Merit for "exceptionally meritorious service." The M-1 rifle performed so well during the battle of Bataan in 1942 that General Douglas MacArthur praised its "outstanding performance." General George S. Patton (q.v.) said; "I consider the M-l the greatest weapon ever made." More than six million "Garands" were produced. It saw action in both the European and Pacific theaters of World War II. Subsequently, it saw extensive action in Korea and Vietnam.

Garand so enjoyed ice-skating that he once flooded the parlor in his house in winter and allowed it to freeze, thus creating an indoor skating rink. A photograph of him ice-skating in his parlor is on display at the Springfield Armory museum.

Richard J. Smith

Additional Reading

Canfield, Bruce N., *A Collector's Guide to the M1 Garand and the M1 Carbine* (1988).

Dvarecka, Chris, *Springfield Armory: Pointless Sacrifice* (1968).

G

Gaulle, Charles Joseph de (1890–1970)

French brigadier general, leader of the Free French. De Gaulle was one of the titans of the twentieth century whose contributions rank him as one of the greatest of French statesmen. Throughout his life he manifested a rebellious streak in pursuit of his goals. A cold and aloof leader, he often found himself alone, a situation that suited him.

De Gaulle was born in 1890 into a family with an intellectual, monarchist, and Catholic background. He graduated from the French Military Academy at St. Cyr, and was a captain in World War I. Wounded several times, he was captured by the Germans at Verdun. His attempts to escape were thwarted by his conspicuous six-foot, five-inch height. Classmates at St. Cyr called him the "asparagus." After the war, he returned to the military academy as a professor of history. In 1920, he went to Warsaw with the French military mission, then studied and taught at the *École de Guerre*. For a time he was aide-de-camp to Marshal Henri Pétain (q.v.). In 1932, he was promoted to lieutenant colonel.

De Gaulle was a man of formidable intelligence and a brilliant military thinker. His writings angered many in the French Army, for he strongly advocated the new theories of armored warfare. In 1934, he published *Vers l'Armee de Métier (The Army of the Future)*. In it, he called for the formation within the French Army of six divisions (100,000 men), entirely motorized, tracked, and partially armored. Each would have its own attached air support and would consist of one brigade each of infantry, armor, and artillery.

De Gaulle's views went largely unheeded in his own country, even though Deputy Paul Reynaud (q.v.) tried unsuccessfully to introduce his program into the 1935 defense budget. The Left distrusted a professional army, and the French Army leaders preferred to rely on defense and massive numbers, as in World War I.

In 1937, de Gaulle was promoted to colonel and later that year, commanded the 507th Tank Regiment at Metz. He continued to urge the French Army to change its doctrine on the employment of tanks. The French high command ignored his memorandum on the lessons of the German victory over Poland. The first French tank divisions did not assemble for training until January 1940, and that conversion was only half complete by the time the Germans invaded. Rather than massed employment, most French tanks remained split up in small units of ten or fewer tanks supporting infantry units.

On 10 May 1940, German forces struck. The next day, de Gaulle was given command of the 4th Armored Division, which was in the process of organizing; only one of its battalions had ever been on maneuvers. There was also insufficient infantry support, and no artillery or antiaircraft. Despite these shortcomings, de Gaulle's division was able to achieve one of the few French military successes against the Germans near Laon in 1940.

On 5 June, Premier Reynaud appointed de Gaulle to the cabinet as undersecretary of state for national defense. The next day, de Gaulle called on General Maxime Weygand, Maurice Gamelin's (qq.v.) replacement as commander of the French Army. Weygand asked him how to deploy the 1,200 tanks still available. De Gaulle urged independent operation as the Germans were doing. The next day, he recommended the formation of a corps of three tank divisions with himself as commander. Weygand did not act on the suggestion.

De Gaulle tried to hold Reynaud to a plan to withdraw French forces onto the Brittany peninsula, where they could be supported from Britain. When the French cabinet voted to sue for peace, de Gaulle, on 17 June, flew from Bordeaux with the British liaison group. The following night, he spoke over the BBC to his countrymen and told them France had lost a battle but not the war. They must continue to resist the Germans.

There would not have been a French resistance without de Gaulle. Although at the time he was virtually unknown in France, no other high-ranking official had escaped, and so the role of leader fell to him, a task for which he believed himself suited. Most Frenchmen thought him reckless, even mad. Germany had for all practical purposes won the war, and for the indefinite future Europe would be under a *Pax Germanica*. France should, therefore, ingratiate itself with Germany to secure a role in the new Europe. This was certainly the view of the new Vichy (q.v.) government headed by Pétain.

De Gaulle's movement became known as the Free French. He met British prime minister Winston S. Churchill (q.v.) for the first time on 9 June 1940, but the British leader was much taken by him. Without Churchill's support in the months that followed, all his efforts would have been in vain. Even when Churchill ceased to be a friend,

de Gaulle never forgot his early support. By 1943, thanks largely to his control over the distribution of Allied money and arms into France, de Gaulle was the unchallenged leader of those French resisting the Germans.

Determined to restore France to greatness, de Gaulle insisted other leaders treat him as an equal. He was often in collision with the British and Americans, who did not want France to return to a major role in world affairs.

The early euphoria between de Gaulle and Churchill soon soured. The general was both haughty and highly suspicious. His first military venture was mounted in September 1940. It was a joint Anglo–Free French expedition against Dakar (q.v.) in West Africa, and it was a disaster. Rather unfairly, de Gaulle received the brunt of the blame. It dashed hopes of an early rallying of West and North Africa and discouraged Frenchmen elsewhere from joining the general's cause. In Britain, many came to feel the Free French were unreliable and that indiscretions compromised the operation. This was untrue but was used by the British and Americans as an excuse to justify excluding the French from other Allied operations.

De Gaulle was convinced the British were out to undermine France. Most upsetting was the British failure to support Free French operations against Vichy-controlled Syria in 1941. He saw this as a British plot to take over the French position in the Levant. He was angry for not being informed of the invasions of Madagascar and North Africa ahead of time; nor was he taken into the planning for the Normandy (q.v.) invasion.

If the relationship with Churchill was rocky, that with U.S. president Franklin D. Roosevelt (q.v.) was tempestuous. It was also more important, since Churchill followed Roosevelt's lead regarding French policy. Roosevelt had a negative attitude toward de Gaulle and the French role in the world. He also was convinced, unjustly, that de Gaulle had Fascist or dictatorial leanings. Although at first ambiguous, de Gaulle's position became clear by 1942 when he spoke of a return to France's traditional liberties and the need for a Fourth Republic.

Roosevelt's attitude reflected the fact that only a few of the influential French exiles in the United States backed de Gaulle, and that the U.S. State Department wanted favorable relations with the Vichy regime. This was to prevent further collaboration between France and Nazi Germany, to have a listening post in Europe, and to neutralize the French Navy. The Vichy-controlled navy was a particular concern after the destruction of the U.S. Pacific fleet at Pearl Harbor.

Roosevelt was therefore enraged when, a week after Pearl Harbor and without informing the United States beforehand, de Gaulle ordered Free French forces to seize the two Vichy-controlled fishing islands of St. Pierre and Miquelon west of Newfoundland. His policies and modus operandi were bound to cause friction, but the U.S. also made mistakes, including Roosevelt's misguided attempt at the Casablanca Conference (*see* Conferences, Allied) to replace de Gaulle with General Henri Giraud (q.v.). It was Roosevelt's decision that delayed recognition of the French Committee of National Liberation until October 1944, well after the Normandy invasion and two months after the liberation of Paris. De Gaulle remembered these actions and they poisoned relations between the two Anglo-Saxon powers and France for years.

In 1946, de Gaulle abruptly resigned as provisional president and retired to write his memoirs. He returned to power in 1958, in the midst of a crisis over Algeria, to establish the Fifth Republic, and was elected its president. He finally retired in 1969. The belief that de Gaulle was antidemocratic is ironic, because his greatest legacy to France lay in the realm of restoring and revitalizing democratic processes.

Thanks to de Gaulle's effort, France was present at the surrenders of Germany and Japan. France also received occupation zones in both Germany and Austria, and gained permanent membership in the United Nations Security Council. Not a bad performance for a country crushed as France was in 1940.

Spencer Tucker

Additional Reading

Aglion, Raoul, *Roosevelt and De Gaulle* (1988).
Aron, Robert, *De Gaulle Before Paris* (1962).
———, *De Gaulle Triumphant* (1964).
Cook, Don, *Charles De Gaulle: A Biography* (1983).
Funk, Arthur, *Charles De Gaulle: The Crucial Years* (1959).
Kersaudy, François, *Churchill and De Gaulle* (1982).

Gavin, James M. (1907–1990)

American major general, commander of the 82nd Airborne Division. Gavin established a reputation for extreme courage, a general officer who made decisions based on personal reconnaissance and frontline familiarity. He profoundly influenced Allied airborne forces doctrine, stressing the necessity of jumping close to objectives to facilitate their immediate capture.

Gavin graduated from West Point in 1929 as an infantry officer. During World War II, his promotions were meteoric. In July 1942, he became the first commander of the 505th Parachute Infantry Regiment, which in March 1943 was attached to the 82nd Airborne Division commanded by Major General Matthew B. Ridgway (q.v.). On the night of 9 July 1943, Gavin's regimental combat team spearheaded the Sicily invasion. Elements of his command fought a critical engagement on the Biazza Ridge on 11 July, facing a large element of the Hermann Göring *Panzer* Division. On 1 October 1943, his regiment assisted in the capture of Naples.

On 10 October 1943, at the very young age of thirty-six, Gavin became a brigadier general and assistant division commander of the 82nd. From November 1943 to February 1944, he was the senior airborne advisor to the Operation OVERLORD planners. He wrote the standard operating procedures used by all British and American airborne troops and supporting airlift forces in Normandy. On 6 June 1944, he commanded Task Force A, the parachute assault element of the 82nd Airborne Division's jump to support the lodgment of U.S. VII Corps. On 15 August, he assumed command of the 82nd.

During Operation MARKET-GARDEN, the 82nd's missions were to seize bridges over the Maas and Waal Rivers, the Maas-Waal Canal, and the high ground at Groesbeek, Holland. Although Gavin fractured two vertebrae during his parachute landing, he continued on his feet, his division winning every tactical engagement they fought.

In October 1944, Gavin became the youngest major general in the U.S. Army. During the German Ardennes offensive (q.v.) the 82nd moved into blocking positions in the vicinity of Trois Ponts-Vielsalm. Its front extended more than twenty-five miles, with units spread out over an area of 100 square miles. The 82nd fought significant battles with the 1st, 2nd, and 9th SS *Panzer* Divisions and the 62nd *Volksgrenadier* Division. In early February 1945, Gavin's division captured Schmidt in the Hürtgen Forest (q.v.).

While attached to the British Second Army, the 82nd made an assault crossing of the Elbe River on 30 April 1945. On 2 May, Gavin accepted the surrender of 125,000 prisoners. In July 1945, the 82nd assumed occupation duties in Berlin, with Gavin as the U.S. representative on the city *Kommandatura*.

Later in his career, Gavin served as chief of staff, Fifth Army; chief of staff, Allied Forces South; commander VII Corps; and deputy chief of staff for operations, Department of the Army. He was promoted to lieutenant general in March 1955, the rank at which he retired in 1958. During the Eisenhower administration, Gavin was army chief of research and development. He came to oppose then current U.S. defense policy, which stressed an overwhelming emphasis on strategic nuclear retaliation at the expense of conventional capabilities. Gavin later served as ambassador to France for part of the Kennedy administration.

Samuel J. Doss

Additional Reading
Gavin, James M., *On to Berlin: Battles of an Airborne Commander, 1943–1946* (1978).
Marshall, S.L.A., *Night Drop* (1962).

Gehlen, Reinhard (1902–1979)
German major general, intelligence officer. The son of a publishing house manager, Gehlen joined the *Reichswehr* in 1920, was commissioned in the artillery three years later, and eventually qualified as a general staff officer. After lengthy service in a variety of staff positions, Gehlen took over the "Eastern Group" in the operations branch of the general staff. When the results of German intelligence work against the Soviet Union became increasingly disappointing, the head of the 12th Branch (Foreign Armies East), Colonel Eberhard Kinzel, was removed in April 1942, and Gehlen was appointed in his stead.

Traditionally, the 12th Branch was concerned primarily with the evaluation of intelligence data. Under Gehlen, though, the Branch gradually absorbed key personnel of the *Abwehr's* (q.v.) intelligence-gathering and counterintelligence services, vastly increasing the scope of its activities. There is general agreement that under Gehlen's management the 12th Branch produced estimates of widely varying quality. On 9 April 1945, Major General Gehlen was forced to step down and subsequently went into hiding in the Bavarian Alps. He surrendered to the U.S. Army two weeks after V-E Day and eventually convinced them that he and his associates could be of great value to the West. He was taken to Washington for consultation with U.S. intelligence officials.

Released from captivity in July 1946, Gehlen created an intelligence organization in West Germany that kept track of developments in Soviet-dominated Eastern Europe and the Soviet Union

itself. In 1956, this U.S.-sponsored "Gehlen Organization," was officially transformed into the *Bundesnachrichtendienst* (BND), the CIA of the Federal Republic of Germany. Gehlen remained in charge of the BND until April 1968 and was succeeded by one of his senior wartime associates, General Gerhard Wessel.

Ulrich Trumpener

Additional Reading
Gehlen, Reinhard, *Der Dienst: Erinnerungen 1942 bis 1971* (1971).
Kahn, David, *Hitler's Spies: German Military Intelligence in World War II* (1978).
Whiting, Charles, *Gehlen: Germany's Master Spy* (1972).

George II (1899–1947)
King of Greece. George II was intensely disliked by many of his subjects because of his lack of opposition to the interwar rule of the Greek dictator Ioannis Metaxas (q.v.). When Italy invaded in 1940, Metaxas rallied the country, but the war only served to unleash violent forces for change. In 1941, circumstances led to the king himself assuming the premiership. He asked Britain for aid. He had very strong support in British establishment circles, but he could not stop the Germans. He then fled and established a government-in-exile based on Crete. He actually lived there very little, preferring life in London, a fact that did little to endear him to his fellow Greeks.

In Greece, meanwhile, civil war was about to erupt. The Communists were a very powerful force and the king promised to hold a plebiscite on the monarchy after the war. Support for this institution was severely strained by the fact that collaborators with the Germans were often monarchists, fearing the Communist Greeks more than the Nazis. The British proved crucial in stabilizing the situation at the war's end. With their guidance, the Communists were defeated. In 1946, the Greeks voted for the king to return. One year later, he died.

Chris Westhorp

Additional Reading
Heckstall-Smith, Anthony, and H. Baille-Gohman, *Greek Tragedy* (1961).
Kousoulas, Dimitrios G., *The Price of Freedom: Greece in World Affairs, 1939–1953* (1953).

George VI (1895–1952)
King of Great Britain and constitutional head of

the British Empire. The second son of George V, the future king was educated at the Royal Naval College at Dartmouth and Trinity College, Cambridge. Following family tradition, he served in the Royal Navy, seeing action at the Battle of Jutland in 1916. Later, as duke of York, he was instrumental in setting up summer camps aimed at getting young men from industrial slums out into the countryside. He played tennis well enough to take part in the 1926 Wimbledon matches.

The abdication of his elder brother, Edward VIII, brought him unexpectedly to the throne. One of his first significant acts was to visit the United States, the first British monarch to do so. It was a clear indication that British leaders knew they would need American help in the trials to come.

As a constitutional monarch, George VI had no effective powers, despite the fact that every one of the millions of servicemen and women in the empire swore allegiance to him, that every order was issued in his name, that every medal bore his profile. He was, though, an important figurehead and his role set the example of an empire involved in total war.

Motivated by a strong sense of duty and actively supported by his wife, Queen Elizabeth, he remained in London even when Buckingham Palace was hit by German bombs. He made constant morale-raising visits to armaments factories, blitzed cities, and his troops in many theaters of war. Overcoming a bad speech impediment, he broadcast messages of quiet hope across the world. Within the British constitutional system, and given Britain's adherence to traditional values, his sense of duty provided an excellent complement to Prime Minister Winston S. Churchill's (q.v.) pugnacious political leadership.

George VI lived to see the start of the breakup of the empire over which he had reigned, particularly the independence of India in 1947. On his death in 1952, he was succeeded by his eldest daughter, who became Queen Elizabeth II.

Philip Green

Additional Reading
Judd, D., *King George VI* (1982).
Kendal, Alan, *Their Finest Hour: An Evocative Memoir of the British People in Wartime, 1939–1945* (1972).
Roberson, Ben, *The Royal Family in Wartime* (1945).

Georges, Alphonse Joseph (1875–1951)

French general. The son of a *gendarme*, Georges had a distinguished military career before World War II. Seriously wounded in 1914, he served on the French General Staff in Salonika in 1915, and headed Marshal Ferdinand Foch's bureau of operations in 1918. He commanded a regiment in the Rhineland in 1923, and between 1925 and 1926, he headed Marshal Henri Pétain's (q.v.) headquarters staff in Morocco during the war against the Rif. Georges was wounded badly at Marseilles on 9 October 1934, during the assassination of King Alexander of Yugoslavia.

At the start of World War II in January 1940, Georges was commander in chief, Allied forces, northeastern front. Poor relations existed between Georges and his superior, General Maurice Gamelin (q.v.), complicating inter-Allied communications. For example, it was never clear whether ultimate responsibility for the British Expeditionary Force rested with Gamelin or Georges.

In 1940, Georges feared the Allies would be trapped by a German diversion in the Low Countries, which he did not believe would be the decisive theater of operations. He was also concerned that no joint planning between the Allies, the Belgians, and the Dutch developed. He therefore voiced reservations about Gamelin's Plan "D" directive to advance into neutral Belgium and establish a defensive line on the River Dyle. The events of May 1940 ultimately proved him right. His supporters, including British prime minister Winston S. Churchill (q.v.), claimed that he did not have sufficient freedom of action to direct the battle of 1940. His detractors argued that his judgment was affected by his poor health resulting from injuries received in 1934. Unfortunately, unlike Gamelin and Maxime Weygand (q.v.), Georges left no memoirs to argue his case.

Robert C. Hudson

Additional Reading
Beaufre, André, *1940: The Fall of France* (1967).
Bond, Brian, *France and Belgium, 1939–1945* (1975).
Goutard, Adolphe, *The Battle of France* (1958).
Greenwell, Harry J., *Why France Fell* (1958).
Horne, Alistair, *To Lose a Battle, France 1940* (1969).

Gerow, Leonard Townsend (1888–1972)

American lieutenant general, commander, U.S. V Corps and Fifteenth Army. Gerow attended the Virginia Military Institute and graduated with distinction in 1911. As an infantry officer, he served in a variety of posts in the U.S. In 1918,

Lieutenant Colonel Gerow went to France to command the purchasing office of the Army Signal Corps.

In the interwar years, Gerow attended the Infantry School, where he was the top student in the class that included Omar N. Bradley (q.v.). Gerow also attended the Command and General Staff and War Colleges. After overseas service in China and the Philippines, Gerow served in the War Plans Division of the army general staff, chaired an army tactical doctrine board, and served as chief of staff of the 2nd Infantry Division. In December 1940, he became chief of the War Plans Division in Washington, D.C. He relinquished that position to Dwight D. Eisenhower (q.v.) in February 1942 to take command of the 29th Infantry Division.

Gerow assumed command of U.S. V Corps in July 1943. He led his corps from the Normandy (q.v.) landings, through Paris (he was the first American general to enter the liberated city), northeast France, and Belgium, and into the grueling Hürtgen Forest and Ardennes offensive (qq.v.) battles. His talents as an operational commander earned his promotion to lieutenant general and command of the Fifteenth Army in January 1945.

Randy Papadopoulos

Additional Reading

Ewing, Joseph, *Let's Go: A History of the 29th Infantry Division in World War II* (1948).
Roy, Claude, *Eight Days That Freed Paris* (1945).
Weigley, Russell F., *Eisenhower's Lieutenants: The Campaigns of France and Germany, 1944–1945* (1981).

Gibbs, William Francis (1886–1967)

American naval architect. As designer of the Liberty ship (q.v.), Gibbs played a critical role in maintaining the flow of war materiel from the United States to Europe during World War II. Born in New York City on 24 August 1886, into a wealthy family, he pursued a career in engineering and ship design, even though his college degrees were in law and economics.

When the United States entered World War I, he was appointed naval architect to the Shipping Control Commission. In 1922, he and his brother, Frederick, organized Gibbs Brothers, Inc., which, after its merger into Gibbs & Cox, became the largest ship design firm in the United States. As a designer, Gibbs made ships that were almost unsinkable by increasing the number of watertight compartments in the hold.

In 1940, the United States Maritime Commission asked Gibbs, who by then had become the principal designer of U.S. naval vessels, to design a cargo vessel for mass production. The product was the famous "Liberty ship," which, by reducing the types of engines, gears, and parts, and by introducing assembly line techniques, cut production time from four years to three weeks. Appointed controller of shipbuilding when the United States entered the war, he introduced these same techniques to increase production of naval vessels by 700 percent. After the war, he received several honors and awards for his war service. He designed the passenger liner *United States.* He died in New York on 6 September 1967.

Justin Murphy

Additional Reading

Funne, Richard (ed.), *Main Ship: The History of a Wartime Shipyard* (1947).
Sawyer, L.A., and W.H. Mitchell, *Victory Ships and Tankers* (1974).

Gibson, Guy Penrose (1918–1944)

Royal Air Force wing commander, commander of the Ruhr Dams raid. Gibson was born in Simla, India, on 12 August 1919, the younger son of Alexander James Gibson of the Indian Forest Service. He was educated at St. Edwards School, Oxford, and during his time at school, showed that he was strong-minded, determined, and physically strong. He left school early and was commissioned in the Royal Air Force in November 1936.

Gibson joined Bomber Command's Number 83 Squadron after training, and took part in the first air attack on Germany, the bombing of the Kiel Canal. In July 1940, he was awarded the Distinguished Flying Cross. Following the Battle of Britain (q.v.), he transferred to Fighter Command as a night-fighter pilot. He completed ninety-nine missions and shot down six enemy aircraft, after which he returned to Bomber Command and completed three operational tours of duty. He requested to remain in operations.

Gibson was selected to command Number 617 Squadron, organized to attack the Ruhr dams (q.v.) on the Mohne and Eder Rivers. On the night of 16–17 May 1943, he led the attack and, having dropped his bombs first, he continued to circle over the target to draw German antiaircraft fire. Both dams were destroyed, but eight of the sixteen aircraft on the mission were lost. Thirty-three officers and men were decorated for this difficult mission and Gibson was awarded the Victoria Cross.

Following the "Dambusters" attack, Gibson flew on only two further operational missions. On 19 September 1944, he was shot down and killed over Rheydt, Holland.

Alan Harfield

Additional Reading
Gibson, Guy, *Enemy Coast Ahead* (1946).

Gillars, Mildred Elizabeth (1900–1988)
Nazi propagandist. In 1948, "Axis Sally" was convicted of treason for broadcasting enemy propaganda during the war. Originally from Maine, Gillars briefly studied drama at Ohio Wesleyan University. Failing in her career as an actress, she traveled to France in 1929. Within five years, she moved to Nazi Germany, and by 1940, she began broadcasting for Radio Berlin, which was managed by her lover, Max Otto Koischwitz.

Gillars went to prisoner-of-war camps in France, Germany, and Holland and posed as a Red Cross representative, soliciting messages she told prisoners would be relayed to their families. Instead, the recordings were embellished and broadcast in order to destroy soldier morale. Earning 3,000 marks per month, she also broadcasted anti-Semitic messages.

Gillars was arrested in 1945 but released. In August 1948, the U.S. Justice Department brought her to Washington, D.C., and her trial began on 25 January 1949. For six weeks, the jury heard her recordings, including "Vision of an Invasion," a pre-D-Day broadcast, testimony from war prisoners, and her admission that she was pressured by Koischwitz and her emotions for him, the *Gestapo* (q.v.), and economic demands to broadcast the propaganda. On 10 March 1949, the jury sentenced her to ten to thirty years in prison for violating Overt Act X. She was released in 1961 and died on 25 June 1988.

Elizabeth D. Schafer

Additional Reading
Edwards, Charles C., *Berlin Calling: American Broadcasters in Service to the Third Reich* (1991).
Gombrick, Ernst H., *Myth and Reality in German War-Time Broadcasts* (1970).

Giraud, Henri (1874–1949)
French general. Appointed commander of the French Seventh Army in 1939, Giraud ordered French troops into Belgium on 10 May 1940, following Germany's invasion of that country. After the German breakthrough on the Meuse on 15 May, Giraud replaced General André-Georges Corap as commander of the French Ninth Army. Shortly after, Giraud was captured by the Germans and sent to a prison camp in Saxony. This reflected his earlier career in World War I, when he was captured in 1914 and later escaped to fight brilliantly at Malmaison in 1917.

In April 1942, Giraud escaped from the Germans once again. He arrived in Algiers in November 1942, where he rallied to the Allied cause. Following Admiral Jean François Darlan's (q.v.) assassination in December 1942, Giraud was appointed commander in chief in French North Africa. In May 1943, he became co-president, with General Charles de Gaulle (q.v.), of the French Committee for National Liberation. Politics not being Giraud's forte, there followed a series of stormy confrontations with de Gaulle. Giraud resigned in November 1943, and went on to play an important role in the liberation of Corsica in April 1944.

Robert C. Hudson

Additional Reading
Gallager, Wesley, *Back Door to Berlin: The Full Story of the American Coup in North Africa* (1943).
Horne, Alistair, *To Lose a Battle, France 1940* (1969).
McVane, John, *Journey into War: War and Diplomacy in North Africa* (1943).
Price, G. Ward, *Giraud and the North African Scene* (1944).

Godfrey, John Henry (1888–1971)
British admiral, director of British naval intelligence. Appointed to head the Admiralty's intelligence division in February 1939, Godfrey brought to his post a wealth of experience in both staff and operational commands dating back to 1903. From the start, he undertook to reform his division for greater effectiveness.

Godfrey's most notable achievements as DNI included strengthening the Admiralty's operational intelligence center and the creation of the Joint Intelligence Committee to promote the sharing of information between civilian and military intelligence organizations.

Godfrey was also among the first to see the value of ULTRA (q.v.), and the opportunity for deception afforded by the XX Committee (q.v.). While staffers as varied as Ian Fleming and Ewen

Montagu (qq.v.) gave him their undivided loyalty, Godfrey's abrasive style and personal inflexibility led to his relief as DNI in 1942. He subsequently commanded the Indian Navy. The only naval officer of his rank to receive no recognition for his wartime services, Godfrey retired in 1946.

Mark Rummage

Additional Reading

Beesly, Patrick, *Very Special Admiral: The Life of Admiral J.H. Godfrey, C.B.* (1980).

McLachlan, Donald, *Room 39: A Study in Naval Intelligence* (1968).

Goebbels, Paul Joseph (1897–1945)

German minister of propaganda. Goebbels was born the son of a bookkeeper and grew up in a deeply Catholic environment. During his childhood, he suffered from several severe health problems, which left him with a slight physical stature and a club-foot on his right leg. His physical deformities resulted in a sense of inferiority, which he tried to overcome through academic achievements. He attended universities in five different cities, although he actually could not afford it. His financial dependency on his father and his girlfriend further fired his ambition to excel at something,

but he had no real idea what it was he wanted to do. Like many other Germans of the period, the loss of the war and collapse of the monarchy in 1918 left him in a social and political vacuum. He couldn't identify with the liberal system of the Weimar Republic (q.v.), and he came to view both Germany's national disgrace and his own hopeless situation as the victims of international capitalism.

In 1921, Goebbels graduated with a doctorate in the history of literature and made a fruitless attempt to earn his living as a writer. In 1922, he temporarily worked in a bank. In later years, he indicated that his contact with several rich and influential Jews convinced him of the validity of his extreme anti-Semitism (q.v.). Once more out of work, he experienced a political awakening at a convention of the Nazi Party (*see* National Socialism) in 1924.

All of Goebbels's extreme and obscure opinions seemed to be confirmed by the National Socialist ideology. He immediately joined the party and established a local chapter in Gladbach. From then on, his sense of aimlessness was over. In 1925, he became party secretary of the North Rhineland district, and took over the editorship of several party publications. He later edited the Nazi Party's *Der Angriff.* "The Little Doctor," as he was called, quickly recognized his exceptional talent for affect-

German Propaganda Chief Josef Goebbels (left) and Interior Minister Wilhelm Frick (right). (IWM MH 9219)

ing people with his speeches. He found he enjoyed controlling a crowd only with his words.

In his early days with the party, Goebbels supported Adolf Hitler's (q.v.) internal rival, Gregor Strasser. When it became clear that Strasser would lose the power struggle, Goebbels changed sides without hesitation. Hitler recognized Goebbels's extraordinary abilities and sent him to Berlin as *Gauleiter*, with the mission of reorganizing the fractured party structure there. To win over new followers, Goebbels combined skillful rhetoric with brutal violence. He ordered the SA (q.v.) to bully political opponents in the streets, while he promised the people peace and order from the Nazi Party. As he once said, "It is of no consequence that propaganda has a high level, only that it succeeds."

By 1930, Goebbels helped turn the NSDAP into the second strongest party in Germany. Hitler owed a large measure of his success in January 1933 to Goebbels. In his propaganda, he continually invented catchy new slogans and myths that stuck deeply in people's minds. Perhaps the most significant was the *"Führermythos,"* the myth that Hitler was the one and only savior of the German nation. Hitler rewarded Goebbels on 13 March 1933 with the post of minister of propaganda.

Ironically, the more Goebbels succeeded in strengthening the Nazis' position, the less they needed his eloquence. His numerous extramarital affairs were a source of embarrassment that weakened his position within the leading clique. Only the coming of the war reversed the Little Doctor's declining influence. Once again he was needed, this time to bolster the staying power of the German people. His shameless prophecies of the "final victory" culminated in the infamous Berlin speech in February 1943, in which he invoked the specter of "total war."

Appointed plenipotentiary for total war in July 1944, Goebbels extended working hours, conscripted women, and reduced education and entertainment. He continued to tell the German people lies about "wonder weapons," and called on them to make more and more sacrifices. When it became obvious that Germany could not win the war, his last propaganda campaign was aimed at salvaging the Nazis' world and his own position. But it was all in vain. In the end, the man who virtually created the *Führer* simply ignored the political testament of Hitler, who intended Goebbels to succeed him as chancellor of the *Reich* after his own suicide. On 1 May 1945, at Hitler's bunker in besieged Berlin, Goebbels and his wife, Magda, followed their idol into death, after they first poisoned their six small children. Goebbels was one of the most influential men of the Third *Reich*, but he could only exist in a house of lies. His life was a reflection of his motto: "Propaganda has nothing to do with truth!"

Wolfgang Terhörst

Additional Reading
Ebermayer, Erich, and Hans Meissner, *Evil Genius* (1954).
Heiber, Helmut, *Goebbels: A Biography* (1983).
Herzstein, Robert E., *The War That Hitler Won: Goebbels and the Nazi Media Campaign* (1986).
Lochner, Louis P., *The Goebbels Diaries* (1948).
Riess, Curt, *Joseph Goebbels: A Biography* (1949).

Goerdeler, Carl Friedrich (1884–1945)

German opposition leader. Born in a small town in Pomerania, Goerdeler started his career in municipal administration. He served as an officer in World War I, and in 1930 he became the lord mayor of Leipzig. Educated on the basis of the value system of prewar Prusso-German society, he remained firmly attached to the traditional views of the authoritarian state, believing in the rule of law and order, scientific expertise, and strong government.

Originally cooperating with the National Socialist regime, Goerdeler soon opposed the racist and antireligious tendencies in its ideology. After his resignation in 1937, he made several attempts to create a nationwide political opposition. As the final course of World War II became more obvious for Germany, he aimed at replacing National Socialism (q.v.) with a strong national-conservative government under his leadership. He also tried to win Allied support for this undertaking.

Owing to the internal weakness of the civil opposition, the actual leadership of the German opposition movement passed to a group of dissident army leaders. After the unsuccessful *putsch* of 20 July 1944, Goerdeler, who was to be chancellor in the new government, was sentenced to death. He was executed in Berlin on 2 February 1945.

Goerdeler and his fellow conspirators embodied the ambitions and weaknesses of the conservative civil-military opposition to Adolf Hitler (q.v.). The opposition's historical heritage, however, played an essential role in the political and moral legitimacy of the postwar West German state.

Georgi Verbeeck

Additional Reading
Fitzgibbon, Constantine, *To Kill Hitler* (1972).

Graml, Hebert, et al., *The German Resistance to Hitler* (1970).

Ritter, Gerhard, *Carl Goerdeler und die deutsche Widerstandsbewegung* (1951).

———, *The German Resistance: Carl Goerdeler's Struggle Against Tyranny* (1958).

Golikov, Filip Ivanovich (1900–1980)

Soviet colonel general, commander of the Voronezh Front (army group). Golikov, like so many of his Soviet military contemporaries, came from a peasant background. He joined both the Communist Party and the Red Army in 1918 and served in the civil war. Between the civil war and World War II, he spent nearly a decade in party activities, mixed in with attendance at military schools, including the Frunze Military Academy. He held various command assignments during the 1930s, including command of the Sixth Army. Although he had no experience in intelligence work, Golikov in July was appointed head of Soviet military intelligence, the GRU. Many historians, as well as many of his peers within the Soviet military, blamed him for the failure to correctly evaluate German intentions prior to the launching of Operation BARBAROSSA.

Soviet Premier Josef Stalin (q.v.) apparently did not hold this failure against Golikov, since his assessments of the Germans had conformed with Stalin's own preconceived notions. After the start World War II, Golikov commanded the Tenth Army, and then the Fourth Shock Army. In 1942, he assumed command of the Briansk Front, and then the Voronezh Front. This second position would have proved the undoing of a politically less well-placed general. The Voronezh Front did not just collapse in the face of the German attack, it was a complete rout. At Voronezh (q.v.), Golikov's armor actually outnumbered the attacking Germans, but he lacked both disciplined soldiers and air superiority, and his advantage was lost. Although his forces had the Germans in a virtual trap at Voronezh, the Germans were able to break out onto the open steppes. His defenses then collapsed and his soldiers went into full retreat. In Golikov's defense, it must be noted that although he had armored superiority, his soldiers were hastily assembled into a unit, and they had limited practice or training. In effect, they were little more than bodies that could be thrown in front of the Germans in a desperate effort to slow the advance.

Golikov was replaced by Konstantin Rokossovsky (q.v.), but remained in Stalin's favor. He was given further positions of responsibility, but not in combat. For the remainder of the war, he served as chief of the Main Directorate of Cadres. Immediately following the war, he was a delegate on the Repatriation Affairs Council of the Soviet Union.

In the later years following the war, Golikov again was given command assignments, and he went on to head the Military Academy of Armored Troops in 1956. From 1958 to 1962, he was the chief of the Main Political Directorate of the Soviet Army and Navy.

Thomas Cagley

Additional Reading
Bialer, Seweryn (ed.), *Stalin and His Generals* (1984).

Seaton, Albert and Joan, *The Soviet Army: 1918 to the Present* (1987).

Shukman, Harold (ed.), *Stalin's Generals* (1993).

Göring, Hermann (1893–1946)

German *Reichsmarschall,* commander in chief of the *Luftwaffe,* number two leader of the Nazi Party. Göring was born on 12 January 1893 in Rosenheim, the son of a judge who was *Reichskommissar* to South West Africa under Otto von Bismarck in 1885. He entered the army in 1914 as a lieutenant of infantry, but through political connections he transferred to the air force. His distinguished flying career included the award of the Iron Cross First Class, as well as Germany's highest decoration for bravery, the *Pour le Mérite* (the "Blue Max"). He ended the war as commander of the famed Richthofen Squadron and an air ace with twenty-two victories.

After the war, Göring flew in air shows in Denmark and Sweden. It was in the latter country were he met his first wife, Baroness Karin von Fock-Kantzow, whom he married in Munich in 1922. His World War I fame and aristocratic background made him an excellent propaganda tool for the nascent Nazi Party he had just joined. Because of his leadership qualities, Göring was named commander of the SA by Adolf Hitler (qq.v.). As its head, Göring marched with other Nazis in the failed Beer Hall *Putsch* (q.v.) of November 1923. Receiving serious wounds, Göring was spirited off to Austria, Italy, and finally Sweden by his wife, where he recuperated. As a result, he acquired a morphine addiction that lasted until his capture by the Allies in 1945.

With the general amnesty granted to all participants of the Beer Hall *Putsch,* Göring returned to Germany in 1927, rejoined the Nazi Party, and the following year, was elected to the *Reichstag* as one of the NSDAP's first deputies. Over the next five years, Göring's contacts with industry, political conservatives, and the military proved indispensable in Hitler's climb to power. With the victory the NSDAP obtained in the election of 31 July 1932, Göring became president of the *Reichstag.*

Subsequent to Hitler being named chancellor on 30 January 1933, Göring became Prussian minister of the interior, commander in chief of the Prussian police and *Gestapo* (q.v.), and commissioner of aviation. Once in control of the police force, he, along with Heinrich Himmler and Reinhard Heydrich (qq.v.), was able to purge the Prussian police of non-Nazis and replace them with SA and SS men. They also rounded up all political opponents (Communists, Social Democrats, etc.) and interned them in concentration camps. This was prosecuted with great fervor following the *Reichstag* fire (q.v.) of 27 February 1933.

Göring's wife, Karin, died of tuberculosis in October 1931. In 1935, he married corpulent German actress Emmy Sonnemann in a wedding ceremony that was the premier social event of the Third *Reich*. At their lavishly furnished estate, Karinhall (named after his former wife), he was able to live the life of a country squire surrounded by priceless art treasures and vast hunting grounds.

On 1 March 1935, Göring was named commander in chief of the newly created *Luftwaffe* and given the task of building up the number of planes and pilots. His powers grew when, the following year, he was appointed commissioner plenipotentiary for the four-year plan. In November 1937, he replaced Hjalmar Schacht (q.v.) as minister of the economy, and subsequently became the founder of the *Reichswerke Hermann Göring*, a state-owned enterprise producing steel. That position gave him the opportunity to completely oversee the growing German economy, as well as to enrich himself.

A popular figure with the German people, Göring was not only respected as a highly decorated World War I veteran, but he also was viewed as Hitler's successor. His flamboyance and jocularity in public were matched by his cold and calculating demeanor when it came to brutally striking out against political rivals. This was exemplified by his role in the trumped-up charges levied against Field Marshal Werner von Blomberg and General Werner von Fritsch (qq.v.) in February 1938. Promoted to field marshal following the Blomberg-Fritsch Affair (q.v.), Göring hoped to assume their powers over the military.

In internal state affairs, Göring played a primary role against the Jews, first during *Kristallnacht* (q.v.) when he levied a fine against them of one billion marks, followed up with measures barring Jews from pursuing employment, education, and recreation. On 31 July 1941, he instructed Heydrich to proceed with the "Final Solution" (q.v.) to the "Jewish problem" in the occupied territories.

Göring also played a major role in Germany's foreign policy in the late 1930s. He was instrumental in the *Anschluss* (q.v.) of Austria and the takeover of Czechoslovakia. As war loomed on the horizon, he was named *Reich* council chairman for national defense on 30 August 1939, and that was followed by his official appointment as Hitler's successor on 1 September.

Göring personally supervised the *Luftwaffe's* air campaigns in Poland, Norway, Belgium and Flanders, and France (qq.v.). With victory in the French campaign, he was promoted to the exclusive rank of *Reichsmarschall.* That period was the zenith of Göring's career. Following the failure of the *Luftwaffe* in the Battle of Britain (q.v.), the indefinite postponement of Operation SEA LION, and the aerial bombardment of Germany itself by the Allies, his standing and prestige both among the people and the party hierarchy began to plummet. Failure to supply the beleaguered Sixth Army at Stalingrad (q.v.) and to protect German cities and factories from Allied bombing added to his descent in popularity. He was supplanted by Goebbels, Speer, Bormann, and Himmler (qq.v.) in the eyes of Hitler. Göring retreated into his own fantasy world and the security of Karinhall.

The end for Göring came when he left the Berlin *Führer* Bunker on 20 April 1945 for Bavaria. Hitler, under the influence of Bormann, was made to believe that Göring tried to wrest power away from him, prompting Hitler to expel Göring from the party and to order his arrest for treason. On 9 May, he was taken into custody by elements of the U.S. 36th Infantry Division. He was placed on trial in Nuremberg (*see* International Military Tribunal) in 1946. There he was found guilty on all counts and condemned to death. Göring cheated the hangman by swallowing cyanide on the day before his execution.

José E. Alvarez

Additional Reading

Göring, Emmy, *My Life with Göring* (1972).

Lee, Asher, *Göring, Air Leader* (1972).

Manvell, Roger, *Göring* (1962).

Mitcham, Samuel W., Jr., *Hitler's Field Marshals and Their Battles* (1988).

Mosley, Leonard, *The Reich Marshal: A Biography of Hermann Göring* (1974).

Overy, R.J., *Göring, The "Iron Man,"* (1984).

Gorshkov, Sergei Georgievich (1910–1988)

Soviet admiral, commander of the Azov and Danube Flotillas. The son of a teacher, and born too late to participate in either the revolution or civil war, Gorshkov was one of the beneficiaries of the military purges (q.v.) of the 1930s. He attended the Frunze Naval School, followed by specialized training to prepare him for command of torpedo boats. He initially served in the Black Sea Fleet, followed by several years in the Pacific Fleet. In 1939, he commanded a brigade of cruisers. Pacific service kept him well away from Moscow and the purges that were eliminating his superiors. As a result, by age thirty-one, he was admiral in command of the Azov Flotilla.

After the start of the war, Gorshkov left the Azov Flotilla and became deputy commander of the Novorossiisk Defense Area, where he found himself in the unusual position of being a naval officer in command of the Fourty-seventh Army during the defense of the Caucasus (q.v.). He then returned to command the Azov Flotilla and led the naval forces in the liberation of the Taman peninsula and the entire Crimea (q.v.).

Gorshkov next moved on to command the Danube Flotilla and played a key role in all the military actions throughout the countries bordering the Danube and its tributaries. He was active in the recapture of the Ukraine, and the Soviet moves into Romania, Bulgaria, Hungary, and Austria (qq.v.), culminating in the liberation of Vienna and Linz. His actions brought him to the favorable attention of two future Soviet leaders, Nikita Khrushchev (q.v.) and Leonid Brezhnev. In the final days of the war, Gorshkov commanded a squadron in the Black Sea Fleet.

After the war, Gorshkov served in various increasingly important positions. He was chief of staff and then commander of the Black Sea Fleet from 1945 through 1955. In 1955, he became deputy commander in chief of the Soviet Navy and commander in chief the next year. He held that position until 1985, when Mikhail Gorbachev quietly removed him.

Thomas Cagley

Additional Reading

Golovko, Arsenic G., *With the Red Fleet: The War Memoirs of the Late Admiral Arsenic G. Golovko* (1965).

Gort, John (1886–1946)

British field marshal, commander in chief of the British Expeditionary Force in France. An aristocrat and a guards officer, Lord Gort earned the Victoria Cross and other awards for bravery in World War I, together with an unrivaled reputation as a fighting battalion commander. Between the wars, he commanded a brigade and rose meteorically from major general to general between 1937 and 1939. Appointed commander in chief of the British Expeditionary Force (BEF) on the outbreak of World War II, he had no real experience in high command. He moved to France with four divisions, subsequently increased to thirteen, and was placed by his government under the command of the French. On 10 May 1940, the German *Blitzkrieg* (q.v.) tactics and overwhelming superiority of modern equipment led to immediate French withdrawals, with which Gort conformed.

On 27 May, Gort was ordered to provide two divisions to support a last-throw counterattack by the French. British Prime Minister Winston S. Churchill (q.v.) urgently supported this planned offensive. Certain it would fail and the front disintegrate, and suspecting the imminent surrender of the Belgians on his left, Gort disregarded his French superiors and Churchill, used the two divisions to secure his left flank, and on his own initiative directed the BEF toward the coast at Dunkirk (q.v.). Defending a contracting perimeter and sustaining constant attack from the air, an evacuation was successfully completed and 250,000 troops, including many of the future leaders of the British Army, reached Britain.

Gort was later governor of Malta (q.v.) during the siege, but was never again employed in high command. The quintessence of a regimental soldier, his virtues of leadership, loyalty, inspiration, and unquestioning obedience were, to an extent, his failings in high command. Both his corps commanders, Lieutenant Generals John Dill and Alan Brooke (qq.v.), were highly critical of Gort as commander in chief. Brooke said of Gort in his published diaries, "I had no confidence in his leadership when it came to handling large forces. He seemed incapable of seeing the wood for the trees." For his own part, Gort thought Brooke a pessimist and considered sacking him.

History was less than fair to Gort. In retrospect, many consider that his decision to march to the sea saved the British Army. The verdict of General Bernard L. Montgomery (q.v.), a division commander in the BEF, was "Gort saw clearly that he must get the men of the BEF back to England. For this I give him full marks."

B.K. Warner

Additional Reading
Beckles, Gordon, *Dunkirk and After, May 10th– June 17th, 1940* (1940).
Collier, Richard, *The Sands of Dunkirk* (1961).
Divine, Arthur D., *Dunkirk* (1945).
Horne, Alistair, *To Lose a Battle, 1940* (1969).

Gott, William Henry Ewart (1897–1942)

British lieutenant general. Sir William Gott was born on 13 August 1897, and was educated at Harrow and Sandhurst. He was commissioned in February 1915 into the King's Royal Rifle Corps and joined the 2nd Battalion in France. In July 1917, he was wounded in the arm and leg. While he was at the casualty clearing station in the headquarters area, a withdrawal was ordered. Gott and another wounded officer were left to be taken prisoners. It was while he was a POW that he received his nickname "Strafer" from the German prayer *Gott Strafe England,* and it was by this name that he was known affectionately for the rest of his life. He made three unsuccessful attempts to escape, reaching the Dutch border in one attempt.

During the years between 1919 and 1939, Gott served twice in India, and in the autumn of 1938, he was promoted to lieutenant colonel and given a command of the 1st Battalion Kings Royal Rifle Corps, which was marked for conversion to a motorized battalion.

After four years of continuous service in Egypt and Libya, including two years campaigning in the difficult desert terrain, Gott rose to the command of the British Eighth Army. His appointment was unanimously welcomed throughout the Middle East, such was his reputation as an officer and soldier. On 7 August 1942, as he was flying to Cairo for a few days' leave, the bomber in which he was traveling was attacked by two German Bf-109s. The plane was raked from end to end and landed by the wounded pilot, but Gott, along with other passengers, was killed during the attack.

The obituaries all treated the death of Gott as a disaster to the country, the army, and most of all to the Eighth Army. One young officer wrote ". . . 'Strafer' has been killed. To most of us out here if it had been the death of our own father it could hardly have come as a greater shock." Gott was replaced as commander of the Eighth Army by Lieutenant General Bernard L. Montgomery (q.v.).

Alan G. Harfield

Additional Reading
Barnett, Correlli, *The Desert Generals* (1982).
Pitt, Barrie, *The Crucible of War: The Year of Alamein 1942* (1982).
Tucker, Francis I.S., *Approach to Battle: A Commentary; Eighth Army, November 1941 to May 1943* (1963).

Govorov, Leonid Aleksandrovich (1897–1955)

Marshal of the Soviet Union, commander of the Soviet Leningrad Front (army group). Born into a peasant family, Govorov attended the Konstanin Artillery School in 1917 and entered the tsar's army as a lieutenant. In 1919, he joined the Red Army, and during the civil war, he commanded an artillery battalion. Following the civil war, he attended advanced artillery schools, the Frunze Military Academy, and the General Staff Academy. He was chief of staff of artillery of the Seventh Army during the Finnish Winter War (q.v.). During the purges (q.v.), he was investigated by the NKVD (q.v.), but by the start of World War II, he was chief of the Dzerzhinsky Artillery Academy.

Shortly after Germany's invasion, Govorov was appointed chief of artillery for the western front. In October 1941, he assumed command of the Fifth Army, and participated in the defense of Moscow (q.v.), including the December 1941 counterattack. From April 1942–May 1945, he commanded the Leningrad Front. He broke the German siege of Leningrad (q.v.) by pushing a corridor from Lake Ladoga to Schlüsselburg. When the Germans pulled back, his front followed them through the Baltic states.

After the war, Govorov became commander in chief of the national air defense forces, as well as deputy minister of defense in 1954. His son, Vladimir Leonidovich Govorov, also served in the war and became a general. Such occurrences were very rare in the Soviet Union.

Thomas Cagley

Additional Reading
Bialer, Seweryn, *Stalin and His Generals: Soviet Military Memoirs of World War II* (1969).
Seaton, Albert and Joan, *The Soviet Army: 1918 to the Present* (1987).

Graziani, Rodolfo (1882–1955)

Italian marshal, chief of staff of the Italian Army, 1939–1941. Graziani became Italy's youngest colonel in World War I. As commander in Tripolitania

G

Marshal Rodolfo Graziani in Allied captivity, 30 April 1945. (IWM NA 24747)

and then as vice-governor of Cyrenaica, he brutally pacified Libya by 1932. Subsequently, as governor of Somalia, he won for the southern front a much greater role in Ethiopia (q.v.) than originally planned by Pietro Badoglio (q.v.). Graziani decisively defeated the army of Ras Desta at Ganale Doria in January 1936. His seizure of Harar on 8 May after an offensive through the Ogaden Desert won for him the rank of marshal and the office of viceroy of Ethiopia.

By February 1937, Graziani had crushed the remnants of Ethiopia's army. Following an attempt on his life in Addis Ababa on 19 February 1937, he adopted a brutal policy of reprisals, which provoked widespread insurgency. When further brutality, including the use of poison gas, did not quell the rising, he was replaced in November 1937 as viceroy by Amedeo di Savoia (q.v.), the duke of Aosta.

On 31 October 1939, Graziani succeeded Alberto Parini as chief of staff of the Italian Army. He prepared the army for war but realized its limitations. On 28 June 1940, Graziani, while retaining his post as chief of staff, was appointed commander in Libya. Complaining of inadequate

support, he was compelled by Benito Mussolini (q.v.) to invade Egypt. In September, his forces cautiously penetrated fifty miles to Sidi Barrani (q.v.), eighty miles from the British railhead at Mersa Matruh. There he deployed his forces in ten (too widely dispersed) camps.

The British, with two divisions, counterattacked Graziani's ten divisions on 9 December 1940. After his forward units were overrun, he wasted his forces in a series of poorly conceived and poorly executed attempts to stabilize the front. With the defeat of his remaining forces at Beda Fomm (q.v.) on 5–7 February 1941, Graziani, claiming to be on the verge of nervous collapse, was relieved of his command and allowed to return to civilian life in Italy. Later, he was censured by a court of inquiry, at which he was attacked by Badoglio for incompetence and cowardice. He was not punished, however. Despite his military shortcomings, he benefited from his loyalty to Mussolini and the Fascist movement.

After King Victor Emmanuel (q.v.) and Badoglio agreed to an armistice, Graziani became the minister of defense and chief of staff for

Mussolini's Italian Social Republic. Here he directed the effort against the resistance in northern Italy. After the war, the Italian Military Tribunal sentenced him to nineteen years of solitary confinement for collaboration, but he was released from prison on 3 May 1950.

Bernard A. Cook

Additional Reading

Archer, Jules, *Twentieth Century Caesar: Benito Mussolini* (1964).

Deakin, Frederick W., *The Brutal Friendship: Mussolini, Hitler, and the Fall of Italian Fascism,* 1966).

Graziani, Rodolfo, *Ho Difeso la Patria* (1947).

MacGregor-Hastie, Roy, *The Day of the Lion: The Life and Death of Fascist Italy, 1922–1945* (1963).

Grechko, Andrei Antonovich (1903–1976)

Soviet general, commander of the Soviet First Guards Army. Grechko, the son of a peasant family, was too young for World War I. He saw his first service as a volunteer with the Red Army in 1919. He displayed an uncanny ability in cavalry tactics. Unlike many of his contemporaries, there is little evidence of his party activities in the years prior to World War II. He did attend the Cavalry Officer School, the Frunze Military Academy, and the Academy of the General Staff. Most of his troop duty during this period was with cavalry units.

In 1941, Grechko commanded the 34th Cavalry Division. In January 1942, he assumed command of the V Cavalry Corps on the southern front. A few months later, he commanded the Twelfth Army in the northern Caucasus, which stood between the Germans and the oil supplies both sides needed so badly. In 1943, he became deputy commander of the 1st Ukrainian Front (army group) and fought at Kiev. Later that year, he took command of the First Guards Army and led it through Czechoslovakia (q.v.) in 1945.

After the war, Grechko continued to serve in various command positions. From 1960 to 1967, he was commander in chief of the Warsaw Pact armies. In 1967, he became minister of defense, and held that position until his death.

Thomas Cagley

Additional Reading

Bialer, Seweryn (ed.), *Stalin and His Generals* (1984).

Seaton, Albert and Joan, *The Soviet Army: 1918 to the Present* (1987).

Greim, Robert von (1892–1945)

German field marshal, last commander in chief of the *Luftwaffe.* The son of a Bavarian police officer, von Greim began his military career as a gunnery officer. During World War I, he transferred to the flying corps and became a successful fighter pilot, which earned him both a Bavarian patent of nobility and the Prussian *Pour le Mérite* (the "Blue Max"). Between 1919 and 1934, he held a variety of aviation jobs and spent three years in China.

Upon his military reactivation, von Greim rose rapidly in rank and was in charge of the 5th Air Division when World War II broke out. From October 1939 to April 1942, he commanded the V Air Corps in various theaters of war. He became head of *Luftwaffe* Command East (renamed the Sixth Air Force) in May 1943, with which he supported various army groups on the eastern front.

For his accomplishments, von Greim was promoted to colonel general in 1943 and received several high decorations from Adolf Hitler (q.v.). Increasingly dissatisfied with Hermann Göring's (q.v.) performance, the *Führer* in 1944 toyed with the idea of making von Greim the de facto commander of the *Luftwaffe,* but von Greim's scruples, along with other factors, led to abandonment of this plan.

During the final days of the Third *Reich,* on 26 April 1945, Hitler summoned Greim to Berlin. During his flight into the embattled capital, he was wounded in the leg. Hitler appointed Greim supreme commander of the *Luftwaffe* and promoted him to field marshal—the last German promoted to that rank. Greim spent two days in the Chancellery bunker and was then flown out of the burning city center. After a stopover in Schleswig-Holstein, he was flown to Bohemia and eventually transferred to a hospital in Austria. On 24 May 1945, he committed suicide in Salzburg.

Ulrich Trumpener

Additional Reading

Grey, Charles, *Luftwaffe* (1944).

Killen, John, *The Luftwaffe: A History* (1967).

March, Cyril (ed.), *The Rise and Fall of the German Air Force 1933–1945* (1983).

Groves, Leslie R. (1896–1970)

American lieutenant general, director of the MANHATTAN Project. In September 1942, Groves, a colonel in the U.S. Army Corps of Engineers, found himself promoted to brigadier general and assigned to command the top-secret

MANHATTAN (Engineer District) Project (q.v.), the Allied effort to produce the first atomic bomb. He assembled the scientific, technical, and administrative staff to get the job done, supervising 125,000 people, a secret $2 billion budget, and the construction of several facilities vital to the effort, including the Los Alamos Laboratory in New Mexico.

Groves coordinated the scientists and security for a project that was of the highest secrecy and greatest urgency. Through his forceful leadership and single-minded drive, he provided the whole project with organization, motivation, and discipline. He managed to keep a wide variety of "long hairs and crackpots," as he allegedly referred to his team of scientists, happy. Toward the end of the war, he assisted in the selection of possible atomic bomb targets in Japan, and after V-J Day, he worked as an advisor on atomic policy to President Harry S Truman.

Susanne Teepe Gaskins

Additional Reading
Groves, Leslie R., *Now It Can Be Told: The Story of the Manhattan Project* (1962).
Lawren, William, *The General and the Bomb: A Biography of General Leslie R. Groves, Director of the Manhattan Project* (1988).

Grynszpan, Herschel (1921–1940?)

Assassin of a German diplomat whose act was used as a pretext for *Kristallnacht*. Grynszpan came from a family of Polish-Russian Jews who fled anti-Semitism in Russia prior to World War I. Born in Hannover in 1921, Grynszpan left Germany in 1936. He intended to emigrate to Palestine, but ended up in Paris instead. There he led an apparently aimless existence.

In late 1938, Grynszpan received a letter from his sister saying that his whole family, along with all other Polish Jews living in Hannover, had been arrested without warning and were being deported to Poland. Grynszpan obtained a pistol, and as an act of revenge, he went to the German Embassy in Paris on 7 November 1938 and killed Ernst vom Rath, a junior diplomat. The Nazi propaganda organs inside Germany seized upon Rath's death to whip up an anti-Jewish frenzy. The result was *Kristallnacht* (q.v.), the "Night of Broken Glass," on 9 November 1938.

Grynszpan was tried for murder in France, but legal maneuvering dragged his case out. After the fall of France in 1940, German authorities took Grynszpan back to the *Reich*. He was imprisoned at the Sachsenhausen concentration camp. He disappeared in Nazi custody in late 1940.

David T. Zabecki

Additional Reading
Thalmann, Rita, and Emmanuel Feinermann, *Crystal Night* (1974).

Guderian, Heinz (1888–1954)

German colonel general, *Panzer* expert. Guderian, known as *"Schneller* Heinz" (Fast-moving Heinz), was the father of the German operational concept known as *Blitzkrieg* (q.v.). He was born on 17 June 1888, to a military family. His father, an officer from a solid Prussian family, was an open supporter of tactical and technological change within the army, and this would have a lifelong impact on his son. Following in his father's footsteps, he opted for a career in the army and became a lieutenant in 1908. In 1912, on the advice of his father, he opted for instruction in signal communication and came into contact with a major innovation in technology—radio. It was a decision that would shape his life from that time on.

Possessed with an analytical mind capable of rapid decisions, Guderian mastered both French and English and entered the German War Academy as the youngest officer ever to attend. When war was declared in August 1914, he was assigned to a wireless unit attached to a cavalry division within the Second Army. This was a sobering experience. He realized quickly that many of the conservative generals on the general staff neither appreciated nor understood the tools they had at their command. Breakdowns and miscommunications were the order of the day, and this left a definite impression on the young Guderian.

Guderian was crushed by the German defeat of 1918 and the Treaty of Versailles (q.v.) of 1919. He was retained in the Weimar's 100,000-man army and became a part of the inspectorate of motorized troops in 1921. While working with this new technology, he had time to read the works of J.F.C. Fuller and Basil H. Liddell Hart (qq.v.) on tank and mechanized warfare. By the end of the 1920s, he was organizing maneuvers using combined arms troops with motorized vehicles and radios.

When Adolf Hitler (q.v.) came to power in 1933, Guderian was enthusiastic. Hating the Versailles Treaty and aware of Hitler's unorthodox approach to military matters, Guderian hoped the *Führer* would be a willing listener to plans for an armored force. In 1934, the *Panzertruppe* was created with Colonel Guderian as its chief of staff.

General of Panzer *Troops Heinz Guderian in France, May 1940. (IWM MH 9239)*

was personally decorated by Hitler with the Knights Cross of the Iron Cross, he had a special place of honor at dinner with the *Führer*.

In 1940, Guderian went into action in France with his XIX Korps under General Ewald von Kleist (q.v.), and even though his *Panzers* made spectacular gains, he and von Kleist bitterly quarreled. On 20 May, Guderian, now under the protection of General Gerd von Rundstedt (q.v.), reached the English Channel. In a rapid move three days later, his troops entered Boulogne.

During the Russian campaign in 1941, Guderian's *Panzertruppe* performed remarkably, driving to within 200 miles of Moscow. Working with von Kleist again in the south of Russia, Guderian's troops participated in the encirclement and surrender of four full Soviet armies.

Guderian had a monumental temper and a gargantuan ego. In December 1941, he dared to contradict Hitler when the *Führer* ordered all German forces to maintain their advanced positions during the severe Soviet winter. In December 1941, Guderian was dismissed from active command on the orders of Hitler, much to the relief of a number of fellow generals. He remained in eclipse until February 1943, when he was recalled to active service as inspector general of *Panzer* forces. *Schneller* Heinz became disillusioned with Hitler, whom he had once seen as a savior of Germany, but he never entered into any of the various plots against Hitler. Quite reasonably, Guderian, once Hitler's star, was not trusted by fellow officers who were planning an attempt on the *Führer's* life.

Following the 20 July 1944 plot against Hitler, Guderian was investigated but was found to be uninvolved with the plotters. His feelings about the plot remain vague, but what is certain was that he was totally committed to salvaging the German Army. The memories of the 1919 Versailles *Diktat* remained in his mind. He continually argued with Hitler, even to the point of both men screaming at each other until they fell silent from exhaustion. After the 20 July plot, Guderian was made chief of staff of the army high command, but the bad blood between Hitler and Guderian reached a crescendo on 21 March 1945, when Hitler sacked him for the last time.

Those who knew Guderian realized that his heart was weakening under the strain of the last year of the war. Hitler knew it too, using it as an excuse to remove him. On 10 May, as his beloved German Army lay in ruins, Guderian was captured by the Americans in southern Germany. After being held prisoner for two years, he was released in

There was opposition within the army to Guderian's concepts of combined arms operations directed by commanders at the front, using radio to orchestrate operations. But it was this concept that appealed to Hitler, and Guderian's star began to rise.

Before the outbreak of war in 1939, General Guderian continued to build his combined arms armored force, and during the Polish campaign he commanded the XIX Korps in General Günther von Kluge's (q.v.) Fourth Army. Guderian's tanks were the mailed fist that smashed Polish resistance in the Danzig Corridor. He served in the lead with the 3rd *Panzer* Division, in a specially built armored vehicle with the best radio equipment. As the Polish campaign ended, he felt that his years of fighting for a combined arms armored force with radio communications were totally vindicated. The rising star of the *Panzer* force had entree to Hitler since the mid-1930s, and when he

June 1947, and devoted the remainder of his life to the writing of *Panzer Leader,* which was published in 1952. On 14 May 1954, his heart weakened, his health in decline, the father of *Blitzkrieg* warfare died.

Guderian's place in military history is that of a practical innovator rather than a chair-bound theoretician. From his youth and his World War I experience, he quickly saw that radio could give a commander immediate contact with the entire battlefield. Decisions came in minutes rather than hours. He was also interested in motorization. The tank, but more vitally the combined arms team of infantry, armor, and artillery, increased the speed of battle to an intensity unknown in previous conflicts. He was not an original thinker, but he was a superb synthesizer of what he read and observed. He knew that the modern battlefield was three-dimensional, with air making a vital contribution to victory. His great distinction lay in extending the battlefield rapidly, coupled with the shock action of combined arms warfare.

James Cooke

Additional Reading
Barnett, Correlli (ed.), *Hitler's Generals* (1989).
Guderian, Heinz, *Panzer Leader* (1952).
Keegan, John, *Guderian* (1973).
Macksey, Kenneth, *Guderian: Creator of the Blitzkrieg* (1976).
Mellenthin, F.W. von, *German Generals of World War II: As I Saw Them* (1977).

Guingand, Francis de (1900–1979)

British lieutenant general, Montgomery's chief of staff. Sir Francis "Freddie" de Guingand rose from major to major general between 1939 and 1945 by serving in a series of high-level and demanding staff posts, without ever commanding troops or personally being involved in combat. Born in London of French Catholic descent, educated at Ampleforth and Sandhurst, he was commissioned in 1919. After service in India and Ireland, and five years on secondment to the King's African Rifles, he entered the Staff College in 1935. There his contemporaries and his superiors noted his quick analytical intelligence, along with his lifelong interest in wine, women, and gambling.

The start of World War II found de Guingand, still only a major, as military assistant to Leslie Hore-Belisha (q.v.), the British war minister, a post at the center of military and political affairs. When Hore-Belisha resigned in 1940, de Guingand went to the Middle East, filling a num-

ber of staff posts at GHQ and Eighth Army. By the time Bernard L. Montgomery (q.v.) arrived in August 1942, de Guingand was a brigadier, heading the Eighth Army's operations staff. The two served together three times briefly before the war, and each respected the other. Montgomery's first act was to appoint de Guingand his chief of staff, a nonexistent post in the British Army at that time.

De Guingand served Montgomery in this capacity until the end of the war, first in the Eighth Army, then in the 21st Army Group. Together they planned and executed the battle of El Alamein, the 1,500-mile advance to Tunisia, and the invasions of Sicily and Italy (qq.v.). Returning to Britain in 1944, the partnership served in northwest Europe from D-Day to V-E Day. They made a perfect team, the flair, quick intelligence, and loyalty of the one, complementing the dour and methodical professionalism of the other. De Guingand's tact and diplomacy were used increasingly, as the European campaign progressed, to counteract his commander's abrasive attitude toward superiors and Allies.

Although he was rewarded for his achievements by a knighthood and many British and foreign decorations, the end of de Guingand's military career was sad. With his health damaged by his strenuous wartime efforts, and embittered that Montgomery could not find him a suitable job in the postwar army, he resigned in 1946. Following the war, he made a second career for himself in business in South Africa.

Philip Green

Additional Reading
Guingand, Frederick de, *Generals at War* (1964).
———, *Operation Victory* (1960).
Moorehead, Alan, *Montgomery* (1946).
Richardson, C., *Send for Freddie* (1987).

Guryevich, Mikhail Iosifovich (1892–1976)

Soviet aircraft designer. Born in Kharkov in 1892, Guryevich was the son of a distiller. A brilliant mathematics student, he received a scholarship to Kharkov University in 1913, only to be expelled for revolutionary activity. He fled to France and continued his studies at Montpellier University and returned to Russia after the October Revolution in 1917. He resumed his studies at the Kharkov Technological Institute, and formed the first aviation studies program there. His first work was in glider design.

Guryevich first met Artem I. Mikoyan (q.v.),

after joining the Polikarpov Design Bureau in 1938. In 1939, they formed the Mikoyan-Guryevich (abbreviated MiG) Design Bureau, producing their first fighter, the MiG-1, in 1940. In 1941, they brought out the MiG-3, the most widely used Soviet fighter aircraft of World War II. The MiG Bureau continued to design the top-of-the-line Soviet fighters for more than forty-five years following the war.

Guryevich was the design genius of the team. A somber, modest introvert, he had a brilliant mind that easily and quickly formulated preliminary designs. He had, however, little patience for the development and production process. Thus he and Mikoyan were a perfect complement to each other; one the intellectual visionary, the other the pragmatic problem solver. Guryevich received four Orders of Lenin for his work, and in 1957 he was made a Hero of Socialist Labor.

Carl O. Schuster

Additional Reading

Belyakov, R.A., and J. Marmain, *MiG: Fifty Years of Secret Aircraft Design* (1994).

Butowski, Piotr, and Jay Miller, *OKB MiG: A History of the Design Bureau and Its Aircraft* (1994).

H

Haakon VII (1872–1957)

King of Norway. In 1905, Norway declared its independence from Sweden and elected Prince Carl of Denmark as King Haakon VII. At the beginning of World War II, he hoped Norway could remain neutral, but the German invasion of 8 April 1940 forced him to choose between submission or resistance. To Adolf Hitler's (q.v.) surprise, Haakon refused to appoint Vidkun Quisling (q.v.) prime minister and advocated that Norway fight to maintain its independence. Forced into exile on 7 June 1940, after the Allies evacuated Narvik (q.v.), he organized a government-in-exile in London. He returned to Norway on 7 June 1946, and reigned until his death on 21 September 1957.

Justin D. Murphy

Additional Reading

Michael, Maurice, *Haakon: King of Norway* (1958).
Petrow, Richard, *The Bitter Years: The Invasion and Occupation of Denmark and Norway, April 1940–May 1945* (1974).

Hackett, John Winthrop (1910–)

British colonel, commander of the 4th Parachute Brigade. Hackett was born in Australia and was schooled at Oxford. Commissioned in 1931, he served much of his early career in the Mideast. In 1942, he became an operations officer in North Africa, later serving as the senior staff officer of the raiding forces. Selected as commander of the 4th Parachute Brigade in 1943, he led it in Italy and at Arnhem (q.v.).

Following the war, Hackett commanded an armored brigade, an armored division, and troops in Trans-Jordan and Northern Ireland. He was wounded and decorated for bravery three times.

He served on the general and Imperial General Staffs, and concluded a second tour with the British Army of the Rhine as its commanding general. After retiring, Hackett became an author and lecturer of classics and military history.

Steven D. Cage

Additional Reading

Ryan, Cornelius, *A Bridge Too Far* (1974).

Halder, Franz (1884–1972)

German colonel general, chief of the German army staff. Halder was born into a Roman Catholic officer's family on 30 June 1884 in Würzburg. He came from a long line of soldiers, and at age eighteen, joined the 3rd Royal Bavarian Field Artillery Regiment. In 1911, he was admitted to the Bavarian *Kriegsakadamie* in Munich, and in 1914 received the much-sought-after admission to the general staff. He served in ever-higher staff positions throughout the war, from divisional through army group level. In 1919, he was selected as one of the elite few officers in the postwar 100,000-man *Reichswehr*. Between 1921 and 1930, he served in a variety of regimental and staff appointments, including tactics instructor and battery commander.

In the 1930s, Halder rose rapidly as German rearmament took effect. He was promoted to colonel in 1931, major general in July 1934, and between October 1935 and October 1936, he commanded the 7th Division. In August 1936, he was promoted to lieutenant general, and two months later moved to the general staff in Berlin, where he remained until his sacking in 1942.

Halder's close-cropped hair and *pince-nez* gave him the appearance of a pedant, but he actually had a lively personality and a first-rate mind

Colonel General Franz Halder. (IWM GER 1279)

and was generally regarded as the brains of the general staff. He held a series of general staff positions between 1936 and 1938, culminating in his being named as the chief of the *Oberkommando des Heersleitungs* (OKH, or Army General Staff) in late August 1938, after General Ludwig Beck (q.v.) resigned to protest Adolf Hitler's (q.v.) actions leading up to the Czech crisis.

Although Halder intensely disliked and mistrusted Hitler, he carried out his duties as chief of OKH brilliantly. Planning for the Polish and French campaigns demonstrated his mental agility and his understanding of the new style of rapid mobile warfare being advanced by *Panzer* generals like Heinz Guderian and Erich von Manstein (qq.v.). During the 1940 campaign in France, Halder's diaries clearly revealed his impatience with Hitler's nervousness and meddling, and documented the deteriorating relations between the two.

Promoted to colonel general at the end of the French campaign, Halder's planning for Operation BARBAROSSA, the invasion of the Soviet Union in June 1941, featured sweeping pincer movements on a huge scale, exploiting the superior mobility and command-control capabilities of the *Panzer* forces. Even while they were encircling

Soviet forces by the hundreds of thousands, however, he had to endure increasingly virulent diatribes from Hitler. During the 1942 campaign in Russia, they clashed almost constantly until Hitler dismissed him on 24 September. He played no further role in the war.

Right from the start, Halder actively opposed Hitler. Virtually as soon as he assumed the position of chief of OKH, he began plotting the overthrow of Hitler, whom he saw as leading Germany into a new European war. The Anglo-French appeasement at Munich, however, negated the war fear in Germany and removed the necessary conditions for a successful *putsch*. During the winter following the Polish campaign, Halder again tried to engineer a move against Hitler, the so-called Zossen *Putsch,* but was forced to call it off midway. Although Halder had no active contact with the July 1944 plot, he was arrested and sent to a concentration camp until the end of the war. After the war, he was engaged in the writing of various histories of the war. His 1950 book, *Hitler As Warlord,* overstated the case against Hitler and inflated his own. His most important contribution to the historiography of the war was the publication of his OKH diaries, *The Halder Diaries: The Private War Journals of Colonel General Franz Halder,* which provide a detailed picture of the daily workings of OKH. Halder died 2 April 1972 at age eighty-seven, in Aschau, Upper Bavaria.

Daniel T. Kuehl

Additional Reading

Barnett, Correlli (ed.), *Hitler's Generals* (1989).
Halder, Franz, *The Halder Diaries: The Private War Journals of Colonel General Franz Halder* (1976).
———, *Hitler As Warlord* (1950).
Liddell Hart, Basil H., *The German Generals Talk* (1948).

Halifax, Lord

See WOOD, EDWARD

Hall, John (1891–1978)

American rear admiral, U.S. amphibious force commander. At the beginning of World War II, Captain Hall was head of the strategy department at the U.S. Naval War College. When the United States became a combatant, he was promoted to rear admiral and became acting chief of staff of Rear Admiral Henry Kent Hewitt's (q.v.) amphibious force of the Atlantic Fleet. Involved in Operation TORCH, Hall's advance base unit landed on the beaches of Morocco on 8 November 1942. On 19 November, he became commander of sea frontier forces, Western Task Force, whose objective was to secure Casablanca. His base unit functioned smoothly with French cooperation, and his forces patrolled and escorted ships through the protective minefields stretching northwestward from Casablanca for twenty-two miles.

In 1943, when preparations were being made for the invasion of France, Hall was given command of XI Amphibious Force (XI 'Phib) and Force "O" (for OMAHA Beach). His duties were the most varied of any attack force commander because he had more experience in amphibious assault than anyone in the European theater. He supervised training for the invasion of Force "U," as well as his own Assault Force "O." All U.S. fire support ships reported to him and conducted exercises under his direction. He exuded confidence, exclaiming, "I do not expect to be repulsed on any beach."

When the invasion came in June 1944, Assault Force "O" achieved success on the Normandy (q.v.) beachhead, owing largely to Hall's training exercises. With the operation successful, he was relieved on 27 June, but remained commander of XI 'Phib. He organized Operation SWORDHILT in August to secure a landing for part of General George S. Patton's (q.v.) Third Army on the Brest peninsula. In November, Hall transferred to the Pacific theater, commanding the Southern Assault Force at Okinawa, where deploying troops and supplies ran smoothly under his direction. Hall died in 1978.

Robert F. Pace

Additional Reading

Cant, Gilbert, *America's Navy in World War II* (1945).
Jones, Vincent, *Operation TORCH* (1972).

Hallaren, Mary Agnes (1907–)

American lieutenant colonel, staff director, Women's Army Auxiliary Corps (WAAC) (q.v.). Hallaren was a member of the first WAAC Officer Candidate School class in August 1942. In December 1942, she became the assistant WAAC commandant at the 2nd WAAC Training Center in Daytona Beach, Florida. While there, she trained and later led the 1st WAAC Separate Battalion to Britain, arriving there on 16 July 1943. The battalion, consisting of 555 enlisted and nineteen officers, was so anxious to go to Britain, that there

was no recorded case of anyone going absent without leave (AWOL) prior to departure. Once they reached Britain, the battalion was divided into companies and assigned to jobs at various army air force stations.

From July 1943 to June 1945, Lieutenant Colonel Hallaren served as the WAAC staff director attached to the U.S. Eighth Air Force. From June 1945 to June 1946, she was the WAAC staff director at headquarters, European Theater of Operations (ETO). Hallaren felt that she could speak for the enlisted women serving under her command. She did her best to get the ETO policy of not allowing enlisted WAACs to date officers, American or foreign, reversed, but to no avail.

Hallaren became the deputy director of the Women's Army Corps (WAC) in June 1946. Later, with her promotion to colonel, she was appointed the third WAC director, serving from May 1947 to May 1953. When the WAC became a component of the regular army on 12 June 1948, she became the first woman to receive a regular army commission. She retired from active duty in 1960.

Marjorie D. Kemp

Additional Reading

Ross, Mary S., *American Women in Uniform* (1943).
Treadwell, Mary, *The U.S. Army in World War II: Special Studies: The Women's Army Corps* (1954).

Hancock, Joy Bright (1898–1986)

American navy captain, director of the WAVES. During World War I, Hancock served as a female auxiliary yeoman in the U.S. Navy. Between the wars she worked for the navy as a civilian. In October 1942, she was appointed lieutenant in the newly organized WAVES (q.v.). During the war, she had a major role in developing the policies used governing the employment of women in the navy. In the spring of 1946, she participated in the successful congressional fight to retain the WAVES as part of the peacetime navy. In July 1946, she became director of the WAVES and fought successfully for the WAVES to become part of the regular navy. In October 1948, she became the first woman to be a regular officer in the navy. Hancock retired from the navy in July 1953.

Charles H. Bogart

Additional Reading

Hancock, Joy B., *Lady in the Navy* (1972).
Hodges, J.H., et al., *Women at War* (1944).

Harmon, Ernest Nason (1894–1979)

American major general, commander U.S. XXII Corps. Harmon was born in Massachusetts and graduated from the U.S. Military Academy at West Point in 1917. He served in World War I in the Meuse-Argonne offensive, and was wounded in action. Between wars, he attended the Command and General Staff College and the Army War College. In July 1940, he became assistant chief of staff of the I Armored Corps, under the newly organized Armored Force. In November 1941, he became chief of staff of the Armored Force.

Harmon assumed command of the 2nd Armored Division ("Hell on Wheels") in July 1942, and led the division in French Morocco and Tunisia (q.v.). In April 1943, he took command of the 1st Armored Division, which fought at Salerno (q.v.). In May 1944, the 1st Armored Division led the breakout from the Anzio (q.v.) beachhead and was the first division to cross the Tiber River. He returned to the United States briefly in the summer of 1944, but that September, he returned to command the 2nd Armored Division again. During the Ardennes offensive (q.v.) in December 1944, Harmon's division defeated the German spearhead short of the Meuse River.

Harmon finished the war as commander of XXII Corps. After the war, he took command of VI Corps in Germany and developed it into the U.S. Constabulary. After retiring from the army, he became president of Norwich University. Widely regarded as one of the best U.S. divisional commanders, his memoir, *Combat Commander,* is a minor classic.

Randy Papadopoulos

Additional Reading

Harmon, Ernest N., *Combat Commander* (1970).
Houston, Donald E., *Hell on Wheels* (1977).

Harpe, Josef (1887–1968)

German colonel general, commander of Army Group A. Harpe began his career in the infantry, but after World War I, he became increasingly interested in mechanized warfare. From 1931 until Adolf Hitler's (q.v.) rise to power, he was in charge of the *Reichswehr's* secret tank training center in the Soviet Union.

After leading the 12th *Panzer* Division during the invasion of Russia, Harpe took over XLI *Korps* in 1942. In November 1943, he took command of the Ninth Army in the central sector of the eastern front. Promoted to colonel general in April 1944, he briefly headed the Fourth *Panzer* Army in the Ukraine and was then appointed commander of Army Group North Ukraine (later Army Group A), with which he retreated to the upper Vistula. In mid-January 1945, the Red Army rapidly smashed through his lines, and he was immediately relieved of his command.

Unlike most of his colleagues in similar circumstances, Harpe eventually received another field command. In March 1945, he was sent to the western front to take over the remnants of the Fifth *Panzer* Army. Trapped with his troops in the Ruhr pocket (q.v.), he tried to escaped but was captured by soldiers of the U.S. 17th Airborne Division on 17 April.

Ulrich Trumpener

Additional Reading

Bradford, George, *Great Tank Battles of World War II* (1970).
Humble, Richard, *Hitler's Generals* (1974).
Westphal, Siegfried, *The German Army in the West* (1952).

Harriman, W. Averell (1891–1986)

U.S. diplomatic envoy. Born in New York City, the son of a wealthy financier and railroad builder, Harriman graduated from Yale University in 1913. During World War I, he organized the Merchant Shipbuilding Corporation, which soon controlled the largest merchant fleet under the American flag. During the 1920s, he built his investment banking firm into one of the largest in New York. President Franklin D. Roosevelt (q.v.) appointed him administrative officer of the National Recovery Administration (NRA) in 1934.

Before the U.S. entered World War II, Roosevelt called Harriman to Washington to work with the National Defense Advisory Commission. A trusted adviser to Roosevelt, he was made an envoy to London in 1941 to expedite Lend-Lease (q.v.) aid and other aspects of U.S. wartime support for Great Britain. He reported directly to the White House, bypassing the State Department. He was present at the formulation of the Atlantic Charter (q.v.), and in September, Roosevelt sent him to Moscow with the rank of ambassador to arrange war aid to the Soviet Union.

Harriman subsequently attended all Allied war strategy meetings, including the 1945 Potsdam Conference (*see* Conferences, Allied). He was Roosevelt's personal representative at the August 1942 meeting of British prime minister Winston S. Churchill and Soviet premier Josef Stalin (qq.v.)

in Moscow, and in October 1943, Roosevelt appointed him ambassador to the Soviet Union. He remained at this post until the end of the war. Harriman had a long and successful association with the government after the war. He died in 1986.

Robert F. Pace

Additional Reading

Dobson, Alan P., *U.S. Wartime Aid to Britain, 1940–1946* (1986).

Jones, Robert H., *The Roads to Russia: U.S. Lend-Lease to the Soviet Union* (1969).

Kennan, George, *Memoirs 1925–1950* (1967).

Harris, Arthur Travers (1892–1984)

British air chief marshal, commander in chief of Royal Air Force Bomber Command. Sir Arthus Harris was born on 13 April 1892. His father was an engineer in the Indian Civil Service, and the young Harris was educated in Britain while his parents were in India. In 1899, the independent-minded Harris moved to Rhodesia, where he joined a Rhodesian regiment when World War I broke out. In 1915, he joined the Royal Flying Corps. During World War I, he saw action as a night pilot and commanded a night training squadron. This experience had considerable impact on Harris and his role in World War II.

In the period between the global conflicts, Harris was commissioned a squadron leader in the Royal Air Force, commanded a training school, served an assignment in India, and held a command in Iraq. He completed the Army Staff College in 1929, and then returned to the Middle East. From 1933 to 1937, he held several posts at the Air Ministry; the last of which was deputy director of planning, where he supported the development of new heavy bombers.

When Harris was named to command Number 5 Bomber Group in 1939, there was little indication that he would become the most controversial RAF figure of World War II, perhaps of all time. The Hampden aircraft his unit used were more suited to night bombing, and he was successful against German airfields and naval vessels. Under his command, the British mined German waters, a tactic used to greater advantage later in the war. In November 1940, Charles Portal (q.v.), chief of air staff, appointed Harris to his staff and sent him to the United States to coordinate the purchase of aircraft and equipment. There, Harris developed excellent relations with the Americans. In 1942, Portal named him to head Bomber Command.

Air Chief Marshal Sir Arthur T. Harris, DFC. (IWM CH 5493)

Harris had complete confidence in heavy bombers. His priorities for conduct of the war were simple: recall all bombers from the Middle East, obtain as many aircraft as possible from the United States, and increase British production of bombers. He was intractable about diverting bombers to other assignments and had a ruthless contempt for opposing views.

In May 1942, the RAF conducted a Harris-conceived attack on Cologne (q.v.), code named MILLENNIUM. His idea focused on a 1,000-bomber night attack to surprise and overwhelm any resistance. While the attack created considerable destruction in Cologne, the overall impact was not as extensive as damage reports indicated. The British were not aware of this at the time, however, and MILLENNIUM was considered successful. Its real lasting impact was psychological for both sides.

As a result, Harris created greater support for Bomber Command and the concept of area bombing (*see* Strategic Bombing). Two more 1,000-bomber attacks were launched, against Essen (1–2 June 1942) and Bremen (25–26 June 1942). Success, however, was only moderate. Nevertheless, Bomber Command remained a powerful weapon of war under the leadership of "Bomber" Harris. He was knighted in 1942.

The bombing of German industry created havoc with the enemy war machine and its ability to replenish military equipment. Especially important were the targets of Germany's petroleum producing capability, although he was not a strong advocate of attacking oil supplies. He saw U-boat bases and construction yards as more advantageous targets. In fall 1943, Harris told Churchill that a combined British and American bombing of Berlin would cost the Allies about 400 or 500 aircraft but would cost the enemy the war.

Bomber Command was significantly active during Operation OVERLORD. Harris initially opposed relaxing the bombing of German cities to support the Normandy (q.v.) campaign, but Bomber Command nevertheless did its share by destroying German railroad and coastal targets. The bombing helped pave the way for the Allied invasion, as well as preventing the Germans from reinforcing their forward units.

In February 1945, a combined British and American attack dropped 3,500 tons of bombs on Dresden (q.v.). The results were devastating, but the firestorm that engulfed the city created another at home. One German estimate put the dead at 135,000, causing Churchill to cease the operation designed to bring Germany to its collective knees by rendering the German cities wastelands. But by the time of the German surrender in May 1945, there was little damage left to be done by bombing the German cities. Bomber Command had achieved the goals set by Harris.

While Harris should have been given considerable credit for the war ending when it did, he was instead vilified by many as "Butcher" Harris for area bombing and for the total devastation of targets like Dresden. His strategy and tactics were condemned and public opinion generally questioned much of the bombing. He retired in September 1945, openly perplexed at the public's perception of his actions. That same year, he wrote *Bomber Offensive* to record the accomplishments of Bomber Command and justify its role. The book was not published until 1948, with an extensive rebuttal by the Air Ministry.

Controversy followed Harris into retirement and beyond. He moved to South Africa where he ran the South African Marine Corporation until 1953. He then returned to Britain into permanent retirement until his death on 5 April 1984. The storm of controversy followed Harris long after his death. In 1992, the Bomber Command Association erected a "private" statue of Harris in London, in the face of widespread public protest in Germany and Britain.

Boyd Childress

H

Additional Reading

Harris, Arthur Travers, *Bomber Offensive* (1948).

Hastings, Max, *Bomber Command* (1979).

Messenger, Charles, *"Bomber" Harris and the Strategic Bombing Offensive, 1939–1945* (1984).

Saward, Dudley, *Bomber Harris: The Story of Marshal of the Royal Air Force* (1985).

Terraine, John, *A Time for Courage: The Royal Air Force in the European War, 1939–1945* (1985).

Webster, Charles Kingsley, *The Strategic Air Offensive Against Germany, 1939–1945* (1961).

Hartmann, Erich (1922–1993)

Luftwaffe major, German ace. Hartmann was a fighter pilot credited with shooting down 352 enemy aircraft, the highest total in the history of aerial warfare. He was the sixth *Luftwaffe* pilot to receive the Knight's Cross of the Iron Cross with Swords, Oak Leaves, and Diamonds. He spent the majority of the war fighting on the eastern front, was captured by the Soviets at the war's end, and remained ten years in prison before being released. He retired as a colonel from the West German *Bundesluftwaffe* in 1973.

Max Mulholland

Additional Reading

Obermaier, Ernst, *Fighter Pilots, 1939–1945* (1966).

Toliver and Constable, *Blond Knight of Germany* (1970).

Hausser, Paul (1880–1972)

Waffen-SS colonel general, commander of Army Group G. The son of a Prussian army officer, Hausser was commissioned in the infantry in 1899, held a variety of staff and command positions before, during, and after World War I, and retired from the *Reichswehr* as a major general in 1932. Two years later, he joined the SS (q.v.) and eventually became the inspector of its combat units.

In October 1939, Hausser was commander of one of the new combat divisions formed by the SS. Two years later, while leading his division (known as *Das Reich*) toward Moscow, Hausser was badly wounded. Though blinded in one eye, he returned to active duty the following June as commander of the newly formed SS *Panzer Korps,* which he led with great distinction during the next two years.

On 29 June 1944, Hausser transferred to the western front and took over the German Seventh Army, whose previous commander, Colonel General Friedrich Dollmann, had succumbed to a heart attack. On 20 August, Hausser was wounded once again, but managed to escape from the Falaise pocket (q.v.). After his recovery, he was promoted to *SS-Oberstgruppenführer,* and on 28 January 1945, he was sent to the southern sector of the western front as commander of Army Group G. Long known for his independence of spirit vis-à-vis Adolf Hitler and Heinrich Himmler (qq.v.) (he repeatedly defied orders in crisis situations), Hausser was dismissed on 2 April and eventually placed at the disposal of the German supreme commander in Italy.

After spending four years in POW and labor camps, Hausser became active in West German veterans affairs and wrote several accounts about the *Waffen-SS* (q.v.). There is general agreement today that he was the ablest of the senior *Waffen-SS* commanders, and that his devotion to Nazi ideas was relatively limited. It is also clear that he was fully aware of various plots against the regime but kept quiet. He died at age ninety-two at Ludwigsburg in Swabia.

Ulrich Trumpener

Additional Reading

Hausser, Paul, *Soldaten wie andere auch: Der Weg der Waffen-SS* (1966).
Stein, George H., *The Waffen SS: Hitler's Elite Guard at War* (1966).

Heinrichs, Axel Erik (1890–1965)

Finnish lieutenant general, chief of staff of the Finnish armed forces. As Finnish III Corps commander during the 1939–1940 Finnish Winter War (q.v.), Heinrichs successfully resisted Soviet attacks on the Taipale area. From February to March 1940, he was commanding general of the Kannas Army, holding the Soviet advance to a minimum. During the Continuation War (*see* Finland), he was commanding general of the Karelian Army, liberating the Karelia-Ladoga region. Later, he was chief of the general staff. After Finland joined the Allies, he became commander in chief of the Finnish armed forces.

Andrzej Suchcitz

Additional Reading

Chew, Allen F., *The White Death: The Epic of the Soviet-Finnish Winter War* (1971).
Coats, William P., and Z.K. Coats, *Soviet-Finnish Campaign, Military and Political, 1939–1940* (1942).
Condon, Richard W., *The Winter War: Russia Against Finland* (1972).
Jacobson, Max, *The Diplomacy of the Winter War: An Account of the Russo-Finnish War, 1939–1940* (1961).

Heinrici, Gotthard (1886–1961)

German colonel general, commander Army Group Vistula in the 1945 defense of Berlin. Born in Gumbinnen, East Prussia, Gotthard Heinrici was a cousin of Gerd von Rundstedt (q.v.). Heinrici entered the Prussian Army in 1911 and served as an infantry officer in World War I. He rose to the rank of colonel in the interwar *Reichswehr,* and served as an assistant to Colonel General Werner von Fritsch (q.v.), then commander of the Berlin Military District.

At the outbreak of World War II, Heinrici was a major general in command of the 16th Infantry Division. He commanded that unit in the 1939 Polish campaign, then took command of XII *Korps* for the 1940 campaign in France. At the start of Operation BARBAROSSA he commanded XLIII *Korps,* and later took over the Fourth Army, a part of Army Group Center. Throughout 1942, 1943, and the first half of 1944, Colonel General Heinrici's forces fought in the long series of Soviet offensives designed to push German forces back from Moscow. In the processes of parrying these numerous thrusts, Heinrici came to be recognized by his peers as Germany's premier defensive commander. During the course of the war Heinrici received the Knight's Cross with Oak Leaves and Swords.

Illness forced Heinrici's relief in early June 1944. Thus he missed the Soviet's Byelorussia (q.v.) offensive that annihilated his old unit. Returning to duty in August 1944, Heinrici commanded the First *Panzer* Army in Poland and then Army Group Vistula in the defense of Berlin (q.v.) in March and April 1945. Condemned by Adolf Hitler and General Wilhelm Keitel (qq.v.) for retreating in the face of overwhelming odds, Heinrici surrendered to the Western Allies in 1945.

Randy Papadopoulos

Additional Reading

Ryan, Cornelius, *The Last Battle* (1966).
Ziemke, Earl F., *Stalingrad to Berlin* (1966).

Henderson, Nevile (1882–1942)

British ambassador to Germany. Sir Nevile Henderson joined the British Foreign Office in 1905, served as ambassador to Argentina (1935–1937), and then ambassador to Germany (1937–1939). In 1932, Henderson was knighted, and then made a privy councilor in 1937. While serving in Germany, he became especially friendly with the Nazi leadership, most particularly with Hermann Göring (q.v.). Henderson became an outspoken supporter of National Socialist policy and seemed to firmly believe Adolf Hitler's (q.v.) vows and promises. Henderson is generally regarded as one of the principle architects of the policy of appeasement (q.v.), and is said to have used all his power and influence to force its implementation. Due to failing health, he returned to Britain in 1939 and died on 30 December 1942.

Rob Nadeau

Additional Reading

Great Britain Foreign Office, *British War Blue Book: Documents Concerning German-Polish Relations and the Outbreak of Hostilities Between Great Britain and Germany on September 3, 1939* (1949).

Woodward, Sir Llewellyn, *British Foreign Policy in the Second World War*, 3 vols. (1962–1971).

Hermann, Hajo (1913–)

Luftwaffe major, night fighter ace. Hermann began the war as a bomber pilot, sinking twelve Allied ships before being chosen to lead an experimental night-fighter squadron designed to counter British bombing attacks. Employing his "Wild Boar" tactics, he scored impressive results in the summer of 1943, doing much to blunt the RAF's Berlin offensive. Consequently, the night-fighter program received renewed emphasis and three wings of the *Luftwaffe* were organized for this duty. Hermann eventually became inspector of German air defenses. He advocated massed fighter defenses, but promoted the Me-262 jet as a high-speed bomber. He was captured by the Soviets in 1945 and imprisoned until 1955.

Donald Frazier

Additional Reading

Murray, Williamson, *Strategy for Defeat: The Luftwaffe, 1933–1945* (1983).

Williams, Eric, *Great Air Battles: An Outline of War in the Air with Fourteen First Hand Accounts by Airmen Who Took Part* (1971).

Hershey, Lewis Blaine (1893–1977)

American general, director of the Selective Service System (SSS). Hershey was born in Jamestown, Indiana, and enlisted as a private in the field artillery in 1911. Ultimately, he completed sixty-two years of active military duty. In 1936, he was appointed to the joint Army-Navy Selective Service Committee and was made director of the SSS in 1940, administering conscription in America. During World War II, the SSS classified all males between the ages of eighteen and sixty-five and ultimately drafted 10 million. He remained the head of the SSS until the draft ended in 1973. During the Vietnam War, he became something of a personal target for the antiwar movement.

A. Gregory Gutgsell, Jr.

Additional Reading

Flynn, George Q., *Lewis B. Hershey, Mr. Selective Service* (1985).

Harris, Marc (pseud.), *The U.S. in the Second World War* (1946).

Hess, Rudolf (1894–1987)

Deputy *Führer* of Germany. Hess lived in Egypt until age fourteen. He was forced by a domineering father to attend business schools in Germany and Switzerland. When World War I broke out, the technically gifted Hess volunteered for the army to escape his father's control. The end of the war left him adrift, but he was soon attracted to the rightist Thule Society in Munich. He eagerly accepted the organization's anti-Semitic explanations of Germany's misfortunes. Professor Karl Haushofer's geopolitical thesis of a people's *Lebensraum* (q.v.) also fascinated him.

Hess increasingly became convinced that Germany could only be saved by a new and strong leader. In May 1920, he found that leader in Adolf Hitler (q.v.). It became like a religious fixation for him, who regarded Hitler as not only the coming savior of Germany, but also as a modern Messiah. Though only five years older, Hitler became an absolutely dominating father figure for Hess. He joined the Nazi Party as member number 16, and even left the university to become Hitler's private secretary.

As a result of the 1923 Beer Hall *Putsch* (q.v.), Hess spent seven months with Hitler in Landsberg prison. There he edited the manuscript for *Mein Kampf* (q.v.), and suggested to Hitler his own vision of Germany's *Lebensraum* in the east. Hess never criticized any of his leader's views or decisions. Even his marriage to Ilse Pröhl was instigated

Deputy Führer *Rudolf Hess. (IWM MH 7430)*

At the International Military Tribunal (q.v.) in Nuremberg, Hess received a life sentence for crimes against peace. His real influence in the Third *Reich* was largely overstated. Of the several defendants who received life sentences at Nuremberg, only Hess remained in prison for the rest of his life. Several times in later years, the Western Allies wanted to release him on humanitarian grounds, but the Soviets vetoed it. During his forty-one years in Berlin's Spandau Prison, he never expressed regret for the Third *Reich*. At the age of ninety-three, he committed suicide. His son, Wolf Rüdiger, maintained his father was murdered by British agents. Hess remained an enigma to the end.

Wolfgang Terhörst

Additional Reading

Douglas-Hamilton, James, *Motive for a Mission: The Story Behind Rudolf Hess's Flight to Britain* (1986).
Hess, Rudolf, *Prisoner of Peace* (1954).
Hutton, Joseph B., *Hess: The Man and His Mission* (1970).
Manvell, Roger, and Heinrich Fränkel, *Hess* (1971).

by Hitler. For him, Hitler was "simply the incarnate of pure reason." Through this blind belief in Hitler, Hess laid the foundations of the later *Führer* cult.

Hess's unconditional loyalty was rewarded on 21 April 1933 with the post of deputy *Führer* of the NSDAP. But with the growing strength of National Socialism, Joseph Goebbels, Hermann Göring, Martin Bormann (qq.v.) and others increasingly displaced Hess from Hitler's inner circle. Hess wasn't interested in power, only the *Führer's* favor. He sank into apathy and began suffering from several imaginary diseases. Nevertheless, Hitler officially nominated his old companion as his second successor (after Göring) shortly before the German invasion of Poland.

Yet Hess still felt himself continuously slipping out of the inner circle. He tried to redeem himself with his bizarre flight to Scotland on 10 May 1941. He tried, according to his story, to negotiate peace between Germany and Great Britain as "related northern states." All the evidence indicates that Hitler had no previous knowledge of his action. The British imprisoned him, Hitler disclaimed him and said he was crazy, and Hess suddenly suffered from amnesia and symptoms of hysterical persecution mania.

Hewitt, Henry Kent (1887–1972)

American vice admiral, commander of amphibious forces, U.S. Atlantic Fleet. Between U.S. Naval Academy graduation in 1907 and Pearl Harbor, Hewitt rose to rear admiral. During World War II, he led naval forces in key amphibious assaults on North Africa and in the Mediterranean. He trained and led the U.S. Western Naval Task Force in the Allied invasion of North Africa in November 1942. Since the Royal Navy had primary responsibility for the Mediterranean, he served under the British. As a vice admiral, he commanded U.S. naval forces in northwest African waters and the U.S. Eighth Fleet when it became operational in March 1943.

Hewitt successfully directed American naval participation in landings at Sicily and Salerno (qq.v.) in July and September 1943. Those offensives provided footholds for the Allied thrust through Italy. A strong proponent of both daylight landings and extensive pre-assault bombardment, he used his accumulated experience to capably lead the assault on southern France (q.v.) in 1944. He also assisted in the Pearl Harbor investigation.

Hewitt managed to successfully balance interservice, internation, and strategic concerns within an Allied command structure. Admiral Sir

Andrew Cunningham (q.v.), his superior, graphically summed up his ability to be both an American and an Allied naval officer: "I never wholly like a man until I have had a fight with him, and now that Hewitt has had it out with me, I love and respect him.'"

Promoted to admiral in 1946, Hewitt replaced Admiral Harold Stark (q.v.) as commander of U.S. Naval Forces Europe and served in that post until September 1946. He retired in 1949.

Edward J. Sheehy

Additional Reading

Hewitt, H. Kent, *The Reminiscences of Admiral H. Kent Hewitt,* 2 vols. (1962).

Morison, Samuel E., *History of United States Naval Operations in World War II,* 15 vols. (1947–1962).

Heydrich, Reinhard (1904–1942)

Chief of the German security police and the SD. Born in Halle/Saale to a middle-class Catholic family that firmly believed in the "Stab-in-the-Back" myth (q.v.) and the betrayal of Germany by the Jews, Heydrich was raised in an environment in which anti-Semitism (q.v.) and sympathy for right-wing and nationalist organizations were encouraged. As a youth Heydrich was a member of a local *Freikorps* (q.v.) unit and later belonged to the violent *Deutscher Schutz- und Trutzbund.*

Heydrich entered the German Navy as a cadet in 1922 and planned to make his career as a military officer. But he served only until 1931, when he was judged unfit for service as a result of an indiscretion with another officer's daughter. Unemployed during the chaotic final years of the Weimar Republic (q.v.), Heydrich joined the NSDAP and was active in the SA (q.v.) in Hamburg.

Heydrich's cool logic, management abilities, and almost ideal Germanic appearance soon brought him to the attention of Heinrich Himmler (q.v.), who appointed him to head the SS Security Service (SD) (q.v.). Himmler later considered dismissing Heydrich from the SS because of pervasive rumors about his Jewish ancestry. Yet Himmler recognized in his young lieutenant abilities that he himself did not possess, and these talents would make it possible for the German police to evolve out of the SS.

Taking control of the Munich police in 1933 following Adolf Hitler's (q.v.) appointment as chancellor, Heydrich gradually assumed responsibility for the Bavarian police and various state branches of the political police. Heydrich was also appointed head of the Prussian police and the *Gestapo* (q.v.) in 1934 and was instrumental in assuring the primacy of the SS through the elimination of Ernst Röhm and the SA during the Night of the Long Knives (qq.v.) in June 1934.

Heydrich gained control of the criminal police after Himmler was appointed chief of the German Police in July 1936. Given his domination of a large sector of Nazi Germany's security and intelligence apparati, Heydrich created the *Reich Security Main Office* (RSHA) (q.v.) in 1939 to consolidate these operations within a single agency. Heydrich and the RSHA assumed responsibility for implementing the *Reich*'s aggressive racial and political policies against German Jews and Germany's neighbors. Heydrich's police played a key role in *Kristallnacht* (q.v.) and other anti-Jewish actions. He also planned the 1939 Gleiwitz raid (q.v.) that the *Reich* used as an excuse to attack Poland, thereby precipitating World War II. The RSHA also assumed a greater role in intelligence operations, which brought it and Heydrich into direct conflict with the *Wehrmacht's* intelligence organization, the *Abwehr,* headed by Admiral Wilhelm Canaris (qq.v.).

Following the invasion of Poland, Heydrich used *Einsatzgruppen* (q.v.), mobile detachments of

SS Obergruppenführer *Reinhard Heydrich. (IWM STT 773)*

the security police and the SD, to carry out the consolidation and ghettoization of the Polish Jews. These *Einsatzgruppen* also participated in the invasion of the Soviet Union in June 1941, carrying out mass murders of Jews and Communists.

In July 1941, Heydrich was charged by Hermann Göring (q.v.) with responsibility for the "final solution of the Jewish problem" in Europe (*see* Final Solution). It was Heydrich who drafted the mass extermination plans that were discussed and approved at the January 1942 Wannsee Conference in Berlin. Now the SS, police, and other ministerial agencies within the *Reich* would coordinate their activities to insure that the Final Solution was realized.

In late 1941, Himmler sent Heydrich to Prague as the *Reich* protector of Bohemia and Moravia although he still retained his titles as chief of the security police and the SD. Once again Heydrich used his skills and talents in an attempt to pacify the Czechs. Heydrich's tenure in Prague was cut short when Czech agents blew up his car in May 1942. Heydrich died of his wounds in early June. As an act of retribution, the Nazis completely destroyed the Czech village of Lidiče (q.v.) and murdered its male inhabitants.

Heydrich was one of the cruelest and most ruthless leaders of the Third *Reich*. Full of cynicism and contempt, he demonstrated an almost total lack of human compassion. Heydrich's lack of humanity, coupled with his management abilities, made is possible for him to rise through the ranks of the Nazi hierarchy and assume a key role in the implementation of the Nazi Germany's genocidal policies.

Steven B. Rogers

Additional Reading

Fest, Joachim C., *The Face of the Third Reich* (1970).
MacDonald, Callum, *The Killing of SS Obergruppenführer Reinhard Heydrich* (1989).
Reitlinger, Gerald, *The Final Solution: The Attempt to Exterminate the Jews of Europe* (1953).
Wighton, Charles, *Heydrich: Hiltler's Most Evil Henchman* (1962).

Hill, Roderic Maxwell (1894–1954)

British chief marshal, air defense commander. Sir Roderic Hill was born 1 March 1894 in Hampstead, the oldest child of a mathematics professor at University College, London. He demonstrated a serious interest in science from an early age. He studied architecture at University College but also was consumed by flying. When war began in 1914, he enlisted, entering the Royal Flying Corps in 1916. He was a highly decorated flyer who was among the earliest test pilots.

Between the wars, Hill continued as a test pilot and instructor at the RAF Staff College. He was also instrumental in improving aircraft repair and maintenance. He served in the Middle East, and when war once again broke out in 1939, he was sent to Canada and the United States representing the British Purchasing Mission.

Moving constantly between the U.S. and Britain, Hill became director of research and development, occupied with improving the offensive firepower of the Spitfire fighter. In 1941, he returned to the U.S. to work with American manufacturers equipping RAF airplanes. Here his technical and scientific background was crucial for British interests in the armament of heavy bombers. He finally returned to Britain in 1942 as commandant of the RAF Staff College and was given command of a fighter group in July 1943.

Hill's success was rewarded with the promotion to air marshal for air defense of Great Britain, charged with defending against German air assaults. He devised defensive measures to cope with German flying V-1 buzz bombs (*see* V-1/V-2 Offensive). These menacing aerial attacks began on 13 June 1944, and while his defenses were innovative, the German offensive was costly. In the mid-July, he made a bold decision on his own to redeploy defenses, moving ground guns to the coastal area and having fighters operate in advance and to the rear of the coastal guns. Although the Air Ministry voiced its disapproval, the redeployment was a success, and his measures saved London from more severe damage. His overstepping of authority was forgiven and he was knighted in 1944.

Following the defense of London, Hill assumed control of Fighter Command, a post he held until the German surrender. Following his retirement in 1948, he became rector of the Imperial College of Science and Technology, where his technical knowledge and military reputation helped him to expand the institution. He resigned in 1954 and died in London on 6 October.

Boyd Childress

Additional Reading

Bolitho, Hector, *The Penguin in the Eyrie: An RAF Diary, 1939–1945* (1974).
Hill, Prudence, *To Know the Sky: The Life of Air Chief Marshal Sir Roderic Hill* (1962).

MacMillan, Norman, *The Royal Air Force in the World War,* 4 vols. (1942–1950).

Himmler, Heinrich (1900–1945)

Reichsführer of the SS. Among the most feared leaders of the Third *Reich,* Himmler ruled the SS, a vast empire of police forces, concentration camps, economic enterprises, and combat troops. To many who knew him, he was vacillating and insecure. But throughout his career, he remained loyal and committed to Adolf Hitler (q.v.), and Hitler clearly depended upon him.

Himmler was born on 7 October 1900 in Munich, where his father was a school teacher. Caught up in the excitement of World War I, he left school to enlist. He was too late, however, to see any combat. After the war, he became active in anti-democratic paramilitary organizations, which claimed to be fighting against forces out to destroy the fatherland. He later returned to school, studying agriculture and expecting to emigrate from Germany.

He joined the Nazi Party after hearing Hitler speak on 24 February 1924. He held some party offices in Bavaria before Hitler appointed him deputy *Reich* leader of the SS in 1927, and *Reich* leader of the SS on 6 January 1929. Here he was subordinate to Ernst Röhm's SA (qq.v.), and he commanded only about 300 men. Himmler was determined to build his organization, to create an elite order based on the Nazi ideology. His abilities as an organizer quickly became apparent. By 1933, the SS grew to more than 50,000 members.

When the Nazis seized power, Himmler's only appointment was that of police chief in Munich, a relatively minor position. But from that base, he and his deputy, Reinhard Heydrich (q.v.), systematically gained control over the political police throughout Germany. Another important move came when Himmler sided against Röhm. It was SS troops that arrested and shot many of the SA leaders on 30 June 1934, an action that decimated the SA. A major obstacle to Himmler and the independence of the SS was thereby removed.

Himmler steadily expanded his domain. He strengthened the police after being appointed chief of the German police on 17 June 1936, and consolidated the rapidly growing concentration camp system around three major sites: Dachau, Sachsenhausen, and Buchenwald (*see* Concentration Camps). In addition, he built the prestige of the SS and assumed new titles. On 7 October 1939, he was appointed *Reich* commissioner for the strengthening of Germandom, a position that

Reichsführer SS *Heinrich Himmler, surrounded by members of his staff. (IWM PIC 65669)*

made him a central figure in the occupation and population policies affecting Eastern Europe.

The outbreak of war provided Himmler with new opportunities and less competition from other party organizations. SS agencies spread rapidly into the occupied areas where, for example, senior SS and police commanders (HSSPF), gained enormous power. He directed the security police and security service, agencies instrumental in the occupation and pacification of occupied Europe that also played a predominant role in the annihilation of Jews and political opponents. The SS increasingly became a state within the state that he envisioned as ruling the *Reich* after the war. He continued to assume additional duties, including *Reich* minister of the interior (23 August 1943), and commander of the Replacement Army and chief of military armament (21 July 1944).

Himmler also directed the expansion of the concentration camp system when it became a source of vast power and wealth, as it spread through the occupied areas, especially Eastern Europe. Many prisoners were assigned first to work details, usually related to the armaments industry. Often they were worked to death. The concentration camps were also the major instruments of mass murder in the Final Solution (q.v.).

In the last months of the war, Himmler attempted to broker a separate peace with the Western Allies. His efforts were unsuccessful, and when Hitler learned of them he turned against his "loyal Heinrich." With the collapse of Nazi Germany,

Himmler and several aides disguised themselves and fled to northwestern Germany where they were taken into custody by British troops. During his interrogation on 21 May 1945, he identified himself and then bit into a cyanide pill hidden in his mouth. He died instantly.

Robert G. Waite

Additional Reading

Breitman, Richard, T*he Architect of Genocide: Heinrich Himmler and the Final Solution* (1990).
Frischauer, Willi, *Himmler: The Evil Genius of the Third Reich* (1953).
Höhne, Heinz, *The Order of the Death's Head: The Story of Hitler's SS* (1969).
Padfield, Peter, *Himmler, Reichsführer SS* (1990).
Speer, Albert, *Infiltration* (1981).

Hindenburg, Paul von (1847–1934)

German field marshal, president of the Weimar Republic (1925–1934). As chief of staff of the German Army during World War I and as second president of the Weimar Republic (q.v.), Paul von Hindenburg provided Germans with the father figure they needed during the turbulent war and postwar years. His aristocratic leanings and military bearing, however, ultimately worked against democracy and played a major role in Adolf Hitler's (q.v.) rise to power.

Born in Posen on 2 October 1847, into an old Prussian *Junker* family, von Hindenburg entered the army as a cadet at age eleven and served in the Seven Weeks' War and the Franco-Prussian War. Although a general at his retirement in 1911, he was not noted as a great military leader.

In August 1914, von Hindenburg was recalled to active service as nominal commander over the eastern front, where he was to supervise Erich Ludendorff (q.v.) in pushing back the Russian invasion. While Ludendorff was chiefly responsible for the German victories at Tannenberg and Masurian Lakes, von Hindenburg received the credit and was promoted to field marshal. With fighting on the western front bogged down in trench warfare, the successes of von Hindenburg and Ludendorff on the eastern front brought them even greater prestige.

Finally, on 29 August 1916, Kaiser Wilhelm II appointed von Hindenburg chief of staff, with Ludendorff as his deputy. Together, they established a virtual military dictatorship over Germany. Although Ludendorff was the real military genius directing the German war machine, von Hinden-burg captured the popular imagination as the firm authoritarian figure Germans needed.

Despite Germany's defeat in the autumn of 1918, von Hindenburg escaped public blame, partly because he allowed Ludendorff to present the army's demand for a negotiated settlement. More important, he added the force of his prestige to the "stab-in-the-back myth" (q.v.) by publicly testifying that the army had been forced to capitulate because of the revolution at home.

Retiring again in the summer of 1919, von Hindenburg tried to cultivate an image of political nonpartisanship. However, when Friedrich Ebert (q.v.), the first president of the Weimar Republic, died in 1925, the German Nationalist Party and other conservatives placed the seventy-seven-year-old von Hindenburg on the second ballot, after their candidate was defeated in the first ballot. Because of his immense prestige as Germany's wartime leader, von Hindenburg was elected.

Although a monarchist at heart, von Hindenburg sincerely tried to carry out his duties as president. Disdainful of the sharp divisions within the *Reichstag*, in 1930, he appointed a "presidential government" under Chancellor Heinrich Brüning (q.v.). Lacking the support of a parliamentary majority, Brüning governed through the emergency powers given the president in Article 48 of the Weimar Constitution.

Despite this abuse of presidential power, the republican parties supported von Hindenburg's reelection in the 1932 presidential elections, because he was the only candidate who could defeat Hitler. Many of von Hindenburg's advisors, especially Major General Kurt von Schleicher (q.v.), believed Hitler could be controlled and urged von Hindenburg to bring him into the government in order to provide popular support for an authoritarian regime. On 30 January 1933, therefore, von Hindenburg named Hitler chancellor. Increasingly senile, he was in no position to prevent Hitler from consolidating dictatorial power in his own hands. When he died on 2 August 1934, Hitler assumed the powers of president as well.

Justin Murphy

Additional Reading

Bracher, Karl D., *The German Dictatorship* (1970).
Wheeler-Bennett, John W., *Hindenburg: The Wooden Titan* (1967).

Hitler, Adolf (1889–1945)

Führer of the German Third *Reich*. Hitler was born on 20 April 1889 in Braunau in Upper Austria at the German frontier. His father, Alois, a customs officer, was the illegitimate child of Maria Anna Schicklegruber. Hitler's grandfather was, in all probability, one of the "Hiedler" brothers. Alois was legitimized, after the fact, in 1877, when his baptismal record was corrected to indicate that Johann Georg Hiedler, who subsequently married Anna, had fathered him.

Hitler's relations with his father were strained, and he seemingly nurtured a baseless suspicion that his grandmother had been impregnated by a Jewish businessman for whom she had worked as a maid. Hitler's animosity toward his father and fear of polluted blood became intermeshed with his excessive attachment for his mother, Klara Pölzl, at least a first cousin, if not a niece, of Alois. His egotistical and arrogant desire to dominate, his belief that he was elected by fate for greatness, his obsession with Germany, and his pathological hatred for the Jews all seem to be rooted in a deeply disturbed personality.

In 1905, two years after his father's death, Hitler, who was raised in the Linz area, ended his unsatisfactory performance in secondary school without a diploma. After a year and a half of idle fantasizing, he went to Vienna expecting to excel at the Academy of Fine Arts. His failure to gain entry and his mother's death from cancer were devastating experiences. He was never able to accept responsibility for his failures. Instead of ascribing his rejection at the academy to his own shortcomings, he found a convenient explanation in a Jewish conspiracy to thwart German artistic expression.

In Vienna, despite an orphan's pension and an inheritance, Hitler lived on the margins of society in settlement houses. There his anti-Semitism and brutal social Darwinism grew exponentially. He was influenced by the proponents of hyper-nationalist anti-Semitism that was rampant in prewar Vienna. Karl Lueger, the anti-Semitic populist, became for Hitler an inspiring model.

In 1913, Hitler left Vienna for Munich to avoid induction into the army of, what he regarded to be, the racially destructive Austro-Hungarian regime. He was plying his trade as a painter of scenes and advertisements, when to his delight, World War I erupted. Though an Austrian citizen, he immediately volunteered for the Bavarian branch of the Imperial German Army. He served as a runner *(Meldegänger)* in the 1st Company of the 16th Bavarian Reserve Infantry Regiment, or List Regiment. As part of the 6th Bavarian Division of Bavarian Crown Prince Rupprecht's Sixth Army, Hitler and his regiment fought in the fierce first battle of Ypres. In four days of fighting between Becelaere and Gheluvelt, Hitler's unit was reduced from 3,500 to 600 men.

Hitler, who was eventually promoted to lance corporal, participated in hard fighting at Neuve Chapelle, the Somme in 1916, Bapaume, Arras, and, again, at Ypres in 1917. His military performance seems to have been exemplary. He was awarded the Iron Cross Second Class in 1914, and the Iron Cross First Class in 1918. Reputedly, he single-handedly took a number of prisoners. He was wounded in late 1916, and was recovering from a gassing on 14 October 1918, which temporarily blinded him, when the armistice was signed. His experiences with largely static trench fighting would later dispose him to intense, rapidly moving, and rapidly terminated engagements. He did not wish to see his forces bogged down in a war of attrition. He also recognized the central importance of psychological warfare and the necessity of maintaining morale and the will to fight on the home front.

Hitler was appalled by the armistice, the Treaty of Versailles, and the Weimar Republic (qq.v.). He believed that Germany's degradation was the work of traitors, specifically Jews and Marxists. Amid the chaos that gripped Germany, and his own personal turmoil, he sought to remain in the military, which provided the first degree of stability and meaning to his adult life. He was eventually employed as a political lecturer and spy by the army in Munich.

Sent to investigate the German Workers' Party on 12 September 1919, Hitler was attracted by the tenor of the organization. He so impressed the party's leaders with an impromptu speech that they invited him to become a member not only of the party, but also of its executive board. In April 1920, he became chairman of this minuscule party, which was renamed the National Socialist German Workers' Party (q.v.). By 1921, he was its uncontested *Führer* (Leader).

During the great inflation and political turmoil of 1923, Hitler attempted to gain power by force in the unsuccessful Beer Hall *Putsch* (q.v.). To avoid placing himself again in opposition to the army, he decided henceforth to use the political system to gain control of the government. The Great Depression provided the opportunity. The Nazi vote rose from 2.6 percent in 1928 to 18.3 percent in September 1930, and 37.4 percent in July 1932.

Unable to form a stable government of the Right without the Nazis, traditional conservatives, led by Franz von Papen (q.v.), persuaded President Paul von Hindenburg (q.v.) to offer Hitler the chancellorship. Hitler became chancellor on 30 January 1933, but traditional conservatives dominated his original cabinet. He thwarted their hope to control and use him. He received emergency powers following the *Reichstag* fire (q.v.), and a pliable *Reichstag* vote on 23 March gave him, through the Enabling Act (q.v.), the power to rule by decree for four years.

By 14 July 1933, he outlawed all political parties in Germany other than his own Nazi Party. When von Hindenburg died on 2 August 1934, Hitler combined the offices of chancellor and president. There was now no individual or institution with the legal power to remove him. The army accepted the consolidation of his power and the alteration of its oath of loyalty to a personal oath of fealty to Hitler. Its acquiescence was rooted in Hitler's elimination of the threat that the army might be absorbed by the larger paramilitary SA *(Sturmabteilung)* by having its leader, Ernst Röhm (qq.v.) and several hundred other SA leaders and political opponents murdered during the Night of the Long Knives (q.v.) in 1934.

In 1934, Hitler, in title, became the supreme commander of the German armed forces. In February 1938, he became the effective leader. After Field Marshal Werner von Blomberg (q.v.), the minister of war and commander in chief of the armed forces, and General Werner von Fritsch (q.v.), the commander in chief of the army, expressed reservations when Hitler bared his aggressive intent at the 5 November 1937 *Reichs* Chancellery, or Hossbach Conference, Hitler humiliated and removed both of them from their posts. On 4 February, the more pliable General Walther von Brauchitsch (q.v.) was made commander in chief of the army. Hitler, however, became his own minister of war. He did not want anyone in that post who might counter his desires.

The task of the War Ministry was now assumed by the new *Oberkommando der Wehrmacht* (High Command of the Armed Forces, or OKW) (q.v.), which was effectively Hitler's personal military staff. It was headed by General Wilhelm Keitel (q.v.), whose character is indicated by the name his colleagues in the military derisively used behind his back, *Lakaitel* (Lackey). The subordination of the military was capped off in 1941 when Hitler removed von Brauchitsch and personally assumed the title commander in chief of the army.

Hitler, who welcomed neither counsel nor opposition, did not permit the OKW and its operational staff to function as strategic advisors. They merely translated his decisions into orders. Hitler was not an incapable strategist. He had a keen instinct for surprise. He realized the key importance of psychology to strategy and was a master at placing his forces in a psychological advantage over his adversaries. He had foreseen, in the face of his generals' skepticism, the possibility of reasserting German military control over the Rhineland (q.v.) in March 1936, the *Anchluss* of Austria (q.v.) in March 1938, and occupation of the Sudetenland (q.v.), with the acquiescence of the British and French, and indeed, taking the remainder of Czechoslovakia in March 1939 without combat. His forte was to undermine possible resistance in advance.

Hitler's 23 August 1939 Molotov-Ribbentrop Nonaggression Pact (q.v.) with the Soviet Union, though it failed to deter Britain and France from declaring war, kept Russia out of the early phases of the war. It greatly facilitated the German victories in Poland and the west. Hitler, to the dismay of the general staff, wished to complement the rapid defeat of Poland with a precipitous attack against France. Weather prevented this and provided Hitler with the opportunity to mandate a new plan of attack.

In the west, Hitler demonstrated a flair for originality and daring. Hitler adopted General Erich von Manstein's (q.v.) plan for an attack through the Ardennes toward Abbeville as an alternative to the broad encirclement advocated by the general staff. He also deserves credit for the daring conception of the 1940 Norway campaign (q.v.), which preceded the attack against France by a month. He did, however, rein in his armor, and prevented a complete defeat of the enemy at Dunkirk (q.v.). Here he demonstrated a willingness, which would become increasingly disastrous, to override the battlefield judgments of his commanders.

The overall correctness of Hitler's assessments, however, confounded the professionals. His apparent infallibility clouded his judgment and weakened the self-confidence of his generals. His earlier successes persuaded him to dismiss the objections of field commanders when their expertise should have been utilized. He increasingly underestimated the enemy and overextended his forces. The prelude to disaster was his decision to invade the Soviet Union. He had long been obsessed with expansion to the east, but his military had deep reservations about the campaign. Hitler asserted that the issue had to be decided by the time the Dneiper was reached; but, when that was not accomplished, he made the decision to continue.

Hitler replicated the not uncommon military failing of pressing attacks that were increasingly hopeless. While his decision in December 1941 to forbid a general withdrawal before Moscow perhaps prevented a rout, his sacrifice of the Sixth Army at Stalingrad (q.v.) was inexcusable. This disaster was followed shortly by the surrender of the *Afrika Korps* (q.v.) in May 1943. With his single-minded obsession with Russia, he failed to provide General Erwin Rommel (q.v.) with the adequate support needed to take the Suez Canal.

Hitler increasingly intervened in operational questions and minute tactical details to enforce his belief that voluntary withdrawals could never be countenanced. His unwillingness to approve strategic withdrawals lost to Germany the possibility of establishing defensive and defendable lines in Russia. Hitler, based upon the inability of the German military in 1917 to implement in a slower fashion its planned withdrawal to the Hindenburg Line, did not believe that men would fight to retain a position if defensive works were prepared to its rear. The German collapse in Russia as well as in France were hastened by this prohibition against strategic withdrawals.

Hitler's central command and technical ability to communicate directly with the front commanders made his ill-considered rigidity much more intrusive than it could have been in World War I. Thus field commanders were deprived of the essentially important ability to react instantaneously to changing conditions. Hitler and his command headquarters were handicapped by distance from and alienation of the front. The gap between the reality of the front and the high command intensified with the loss of control of the air. Increasingly, Hitler's orders and countermeasures presumed conditions that no longer existed.

He overestimated his own forces, not taking into consideration their demoralization and weakening, and underestimated those of his opponents. Through his grasp of minutiae and the force of his will, he pushed his opinion forward with increasingly disastrous results. Thus dismissing the cautions of the general staff, based on the inadequacy of German strength, he assigned unreasonably ambitious objectives as in the 1944 Ardennes offensive (q.v.) to forces inadequate in manpower, material, and fuel.

To maintain his undisputed dominance, Hitler deliberately divided and pitted party leaders and branches of the political administration against one another. This was true of the military as well. He deliberately fostered antagonism between the general staff of the army (OKH), which was assigned responsibility for the eastern front, and the OKW which was responsible for other fronts. He appointed and removed a series of commanders on the eastern and western fronts for the impertinence of independent assessment and as scapegoats for failure.

Hitler rejected realistic estimates and lost sight of the possible, and criminally prolonged an irretrievably lost war beyond reason. He brusquely dismissed Rommel's implicit call for an armistice after the Allies established themselves on the Normandy coast. To the very end, he was ordering men and units to meaningless slaughter. It was finally to save Germany that a number of high-ranking military men joined in the ill-fated conspiracy of 20 July 1944 to kill Hitler and negotiate an end to the war. It was as though having determined he would not survive the war, he wished to bring down as much of Germany with him as he could.

On 16 April 1945, Hitler told the commander in chief of Army Group Kurland, General Karl Hilpert, that "if the German people lose this war, they will have proven themselves unworthy of me." He also commanded Albert Speer (q.v.) to carry out what Speer described as an effort to ". . . systematically destroy the foundations of our national existence." Having kept the death and destruction going to the bitter end, and without remorse or the acceptance of responsibility, Hitler killed himself on 30 April 1945.

Bernard A. Cook

Additional Reading

Bullock, Alan, *Hitler: A Study in Tyranny* (1963).
Fest, Joachim C., *Hitler* (1974).
Halder, Franz, *Hitler As War Lord* (1950).
Hitler, Adolf, *Mein Kampf* (1942).
Kubizek, August, *The Young Hitler* (1954).
Lewin, Ronald, *Hitler's Mistakes* (1984).
Liddell Hart, Basil H., *The German Generals Talk* (1948).
Toland, John, *Adolf Hitler* (1976).
Waite, Robert G.L., *Hitler: The Psychopathic God* (1978).

Hlinka, Andrej (1864–1938)

Slovak cleric and nationalist leader. Born to a Catholic family in northern Slovakia, Hlinka became an ordained priest and an ardent Slovak nationalist who fought for minority rights in the Austro-Hungarian Empire. The authorities arrested him and stripped him of his clerical powers. Although many Slovaks sought independence, he advocated Slovak autonomy within a united

H

Czechoslovakia. Disappointment with the new state's separation of church and state led him to reestablish the Slovak Peoples' Party and press for still greater Slovak autonomy. After his death in 1938, the party renamed itself in Hlinka's honor and was transformed into a right-wing party that governed the Slovak puppet state created by the Nazi occupation in 1939.

Steven B. Rogers

Additional Reading
Beneš, Eduard, *From Munich to New War and New Victory* (1954).
Mastny, Vojtech, *The Czechs Under Nazi Rule: The Failure of National Resistance, 1939–1942* (1971).

Hobart, Percy (1885–1957)

British major general, tank expert. Born in India, Sir Percy Hobart graduated from the Royal Military Academy at Woolwich in 1904, ranking high enough to fill a rare vacancy in the Royal Engineers. Serving in India, he was part of the Indian Expeditionary Force that made its way to the western front in 1915, then to Mesopotamia the following year. Remarking that the next war would be won by the tank, he joined the Royal Tank Corps in 1923, eventually rising to command the 1st Army Tank Brigade in 1934. In 1938, he raised the formation that eventually became the 7th Armoured Division. He retired in 1939.

In 1941, he was serving as a colonel in the Home Guard (q.v.) when recalled by Prime Minister Winston S. Churchill (q.v.) to command first the 11th Armoured Division and then the 79th Armoured Division. The latter, a specialized formation that trained and provided units for mine-clearing and other armor/engineer tasks, thus giving Hobart full scope for his innovative thinking. The most famous equipment items in the division's inventory were tanks able to clear lanes through minefields with chains rotating around a powered drum (the Flail), a floating tank for assaulting beaches (the Valentine duplex drive), and a flame-thrower tank (the Crocodile), among others. His special tanks were known as "Hobby's Funnies."

Hobart retained command of the 79th Armoured Division, operating directly under 21st Army Group, through campaigns in northwest Europe from D-Day to Germany's surrender. After the war, he was lieutenant governor of the Royal Hospital from 1945 to 1953. He died on 19 February 1957.

William Rawling

Additional Reading
Macksey, Kenneth, *Armored Crusader: A Biography of Major-General Sir Percy Hobart* (1967).
Martel, Giffard le Q., *An Outspoken Soldier* (1949).

Hobby, Oveta Culp (1905–1996)

American colonel, director of the Women's Army Corps. In August 1941, President Franklin D. Roosevelt appointed Hobby, a Texas lawyer, to head the Women's Division of the U.S. War Department's Bureau of Public Relations. In May 1942, she became commander of the new Women's Auxiliary Army Corps (WAAC) (q.v.).

Colonel Oveta Culp Hobby, Chief of the WAAC. (IWM CH 7608)

Hobby was commissioned a colonel in September 1943, one of only two female colonels in the U.S. Army during the war. Nicknamed "Miss Spark Plug," she resigned in July 1945. On 11 April 1953, she became secretary of the new Department of Health, Education, and Welfare, but resigned in 1955 to return as editor of the Houston *Post,* published by her husband, former Texas Governor William Hobby. She became chairman of the board on her husband's death in 1965.

Laura Matysek Wood

Additional Reading
Boles, Antoinette, *Women in Khaki* (1953).
Shea, Nancy B., *The WAACS* (1943).
Treadwell, Mattie, *The Women's Army Corps* (1954).

Hodges, Courtney Hicks (1887–1966)

American lieutenant general, commander U.S. First Army. A native of Perry, Georgia, Hodges attended the U.S. Military Academy at West Point but failed to graduate because of poor academic grades. In 1906, he enlisted in the U.S. Army as a private, and was commissioned a second lieutenant in 1909. In 1916, he served with General John J. Pershing's expedition to Mexico. During World War I, he was promoted to lieutenant colonel and received the Distinguished Service Cross.

In the interwar years, Hodges served as an instructor at West Point and the Infantry School at Fort Benning. In 1940, Brigadier General Hodges returned as commandant of the Infantry School, where he launched a series of reforms to improve the school's curriculum. He was succeeded at the Infantry School by General Omar N. Bradley (q.v.). Hodges's final post before World War II was chief of infantry, where he used his influence to support the army's adoption of the "bazooka" antitank weapon (*see* Infantry Weapons U.S.), the jeep (q.v.), the M-1 carbine, and the use of airborne troops. His enthusiastic interest in organizing and training soldiers fundamentally shaped the American military that fought and won World War II.

In the first years of the war, Hodges headed the Army Ground Forces school system and commanded X Corps, preparing the troops for overseas combat. In February 1943, he was promoted to lieutenant general and took the U.S. Third Army to Britain. In January 1944, he became deputy to General Bradley, then commander of the U.S. First Army. When Bradley became commander of the 12th Army Group, Hodges assumed command of First Army. He led the First Army through northern France, into Belgium for the bitter Ardennes offensive (q.v.), and from there into Germany and the link up with Soviet forces on the Elbe River in March 1945.

Hodges was a talented logistician and administrator who worked to ensure a unified and cohesive army staff. He was also a competent operational commander who tended to be methodical in his planning. While he was not an aggressive general, Hodges was quite willing to replace subordinates who failed to perform, and his willingness to do so provided the First Army with a set of very talented leaders. He gave the First Army the firm guiding force that allowed its aggressive corps and division commanders to defeat the *Wehrmacht*.

Randy Papadopoulos

Additional Reading
Bradley, Omar N., *A Soldier's Story* (1951).
Snyder, Louis L., *The War: A Concise History, 1939–1945* (1962).
Weigley, Russell F., *Eisenhower's Lieutenants: The Campaigns of France and Germany, 1944–1945* (1981).

Lieutenant General Courtney H. Hodges. (IWM NYP 29397)

Hoepner, Erich (1886–1944)

German colonel general, *Panzer* commander, member of the opposition against Adolf Hitler (q.v.). Born at Frankfurt/Oder on 14 September 1886, Hoepner was never a Nazi supporter. As a division commander in Thuringia, he refused to hang a Hitler portrait in his office. He joined other *Wehrmacht* officers in opposition to the planned Nazi invasion of Czechoslovakia in 1938. He would have been responsible for the neutralization of the SS should it have attempted to prevent the *Wehrmacht's* removal of Hitler. No such attempt was ever made.

Hoepner, a protege of Heinz Guderian (q.v.), assumed command of armored *Wehrmacht* units during the campaigns against Poland, France, and the Soviet Union. His 1939 advance on Warsaw covered 140 miles in seven days. Contempt for the SS was manifested in his dispute with Theodor Eicke (q.v.) and his Death's Head Division, which came under Hoepner's command during the German advance on Dunkirk (q.v.) in 1940. At one point, he called for an investigation of an SS atrocity and threatened action against anyone who killed prisoners of war. Despite this attitude, he later ordered his men to carry out Hitler's Commissar Order (q.v.) during the Soviet campaign.

Hoepner received command of the Fourth *Panzergruppe* prior to the invasion of the Soviet Union in June 1941. Assigned to Army Group North, his armored and mechanized divisions were the mainstay of the German advance on Leningrad (q.v.). Bogged down on the city's outskirts as a result of Hitler's meddling in strategic planning, the Fourth *Panzergruppe* was transferred to the central front in September 1941 to assist in the attack on Moscow (q.v.). He ordered his men to retreat in December 1941, a contravention of Hitler's direct order, and was removed from duty.

In July 1944, Hoepner participated in the abortive attempt on Hitler's life and was hanged at Berlin's Plötzensee prison on 8 August 1944.

Steven B. Rogers

Additional Reading

Humble, Richard, *Hitler's Generals* (1974).
Lunau, Heinz, *The Germans of Trial* (1948).
Manvell, Roger, *The Conspirators: 20th July 1944* (1971).
Scheibert, Horst, *Panzers in Russia* (1974).

Holland, Lancelot (1887–1941)

British vice admiral, commander of the 3rd Battle Cruiser Squadron. Holland led the battle cruiser HMS *Hood* and the new battleship HMS *Prince of Wales* into combat against the German battleship *Bismarck* (q.v.) south of Iceland on 24 May 1941. A well-respected officer, he had commanded a battleship squadron against the Italians at Sparviento the previous year. He died when a German shell ignited an ammunition magazine aboard his flagship, the *Hood.* The resulting explosion destroyed the ship instantly. There were only three survivors.

Carl O. Schuster

Additional Reading

Roskill, Stephen W., *The War at Sea 1939–1945: The Defensive* (1954).
Smith, Bertie W., *War at Sea, 1941–1943* (1944).

Hoover, J. Edgar (1895–1972)

Director of U.S. Federal Bureau of Investigation (FBI). Hoover dominated American domestic intelligence investigations in World War II. He became FBI director in 1924 and implemented scientific and progressive measures in law enforcement. When World War II began, he fielded counterespionage and intelligence-gathering systems. The FBI inspected industrial plants that produced critical war supplies in order to prevent sabotage.

Hoover provided daily communiques to President Franklin D. Roosevelt, who ardently supported his activities. He also established the General Intelligence Section for political information and the custodial detention program for custody of enemy aliens. Domestically, he was unpopular for his reliance on wiretapping to obtain information and his order for the arrest of several Spanish civil war (q.v.) veterans, whom he associated with Communist threats to domestic security.

Hoover wanted to eliminate domestic hysteria resulting from fears of spies and saboteurs. He helped produce movies and magazine articles designed to reassure the public that the FBI was preventing infiltration of dangerous foreign elements. Roosevelt allowed Hoover to have sole control of domestic intelligence. Foreign intelligence was placed under the jurisdiction of William Donovan and the Office of Strategic Services (qq.v.), greatly upsetting Hoover. When Roosevelt died, Hoover lacked confidence in President Harry S Truman (q.v.) and joined with anti-Communist legislative factions in launching attacks against the Truman administration.

Elizabeth D. Schafer

Additional Reading

Powers, Richard G., *Secrecy and Power: The Life of J. Edgar Hoover* (1987).

Hope, Bob (1903–)

American entertainer, humanitarian. Leslie Townes Hope was born in England and immigrated with his family to Cleveland, Ohio, in 1907. After a short career as a professional boxer, he entered show business, performing in vaudeville, the Ziegfeld Follies, radio, television, and movies.

Hope started performing for U.S. and Allied troops in "Victory Caravan" in January 1942. He continued performing for American troops, wherever they were stationed, for the next fifty years. He took his shows to where the troops were, at camps, ships, hospitals, and the battlefronts. His annual Christmas shows in Korea and Vietnam have become part of the enduring legends of those wars as well.

Hope received many awards and honorary degrees in recognition of his work, including the Presidential Medal of Freedom and Honorary Commander of the Order of the British Empire. In March 1995, the U.S. Navy launched USNS *Bob Hope,* the first of a new class of fast sealift ships.

A. Gregory Gutgsell, Jr.

Additional Reading
Hope, Bob, *Don't Shoot, It's Only Me* (1990).

Hopkins, Harry Lloyd (1890–1946)
Advisor to President Franklin D. Roosevelt (q.v.). Hopkins, born in Sioux City, Iowa, started his career in the public welfare sector. He served as general director of the American Red Cross during World War I. In President Roosevelt's New Deal, Hopkins headed the Federal Emergency Relief Administration and then the Works Progress Administration. In 1938, Roosevelt appointed him secretary of commerce.

After the 1939, invasion of Poland (q.v.), Roosevelt turned increasingly to Hopkins for advice. Hopkins resigned his cabinet position and moved into the White House to be close to the president. In December 1940, he went to London as Roosevelt's personal representative to ascertain British war needs. He returned with information that helped push the Lend-Lease Act (q.v.) through Congress. Roosevelt placed him in charge of aid to Britain, Greece, and China.

Hopkins participated in other administrative actions regarding the war. He took part in negotiations leading to U.S. Navy patrols in the western Atlantic, to naval escorts for British shipping, and to stationing American marines on Greenland and Iceland. In July 1941, his conferences with Soviet Premier Josef Stalin (q.v.) led to Lend-Lease aid for the Soviet Union.

When the United States became an active belligerent, Hopkins remained one of Roosevelt's closest aides. He continued to handle Lend-Lease issues and chaired the Munitions Assignment Board. He accompanied Roosevelt to all major war councils, and he continued to travel to London on special assignments.

Following Roosevelt's death, Hopkins remained for a short time as President Harry S Truman's (q.v.) advisor. His last mission was negotiating with Stalin over procedural issues regarding the Security Council of the United Nations (q.v.).

His success in these meetings helped to secure the agreement on the organization of the United Nations. After retiring from government service, Hopkins died on 29 January 1946.

Robert F. Pace

Additional Reading
Charles, Searle F., *Minister of Relief: Harry Hopkins and the Depression* (1963).
McJimsey, George, *Harry Hopkins: Ally of the Poor and Defender of Democracy* (1987).
Sherwood, Robert E., *Roosevelt and Hopkins* (1948).

Hore-Belisha, Leslie (1893–1957)
British secretary of state for war. During World War I, Hore-Belisha served as a major in the Royal Army Service Corps. He was a Liberal politician in a Tory-dominated government, but Neville Chamberlain (q.v.) gave him an opportunity in the ministry of transport, where he did well. In 1937, Chamberlain made Hore-Belisha secretary of state for war, considering him a safe choice who would support the current policy of rearming the Royal Air Force and Royal Navy at the expense of modernizing the army.

Once in office, Hore-Belisha turned into a zealous and ruthless reformer, intent on dragging the British Army kicking and screaming into the twentieth century. He immediately alienated many in the military establishment by turning to Basil H. Liddell Hart (q.v.), the outspoken military correspondent for *The Times,* as an unofficial advisor.

During his tenure in office, Hore-Belisha improved the terms of service and living conditions of the common British soldier. He doubled the size of the territorial army and he forced a reluctant Chamberlain to introduce conscription. Next, Hore-Belisha radically overhauled the antiquated career system for officers, earning him much animosity among the upper ranks. He also reorganized Britain's antiaircraft defenses.

Perhaps Hore-Belisha's greatest contribution was the creation of a modern field army capable of fighting on the Continent. After the Munich crisis (q.v.), he started campaigning in Whitehall for the priority and funding necessary to create such a force. Thanks largely to his efforts, Britain's five-division British Expeditionary Force (BEF) was one of history's first fully motorized forces, and it was ready to deploy to France as soon as the war started.

Hore-Belisha's missionary zeal and blunt

manner earned him many enemies, especially among the highest-ranking commanders. After a visit to France in 1939, he vocally criticized the rate of construction of field fortifications. This enraged the generals even more, who finally enlisted the support of the king to have him removed. Bowing to pressure from all sides, Chamberlain in January 1940 offered Hore-Belisha a different position in the government. He chose instead to resign.

Hore-Belisha was later raised to the peerage, but he never again played a significant role in British public life. Despite his removal from office early in the war, he was one of Britain's great military reformers and his initiatives came not a minute too soon for a British Army about to lunge into history's greatest war.

David T. Zabecki

Additional Reading

Bond, Brian, *British Military Policy Between the Two World Wars* (1980).

Liddell Hart, Basil H., *Memoirs,* 2 vols. (1965).

Minney, R.J. (ed.), *The Private Papers of Hore-Belisha* (1991).

Lieutenant General Sir Brian Horrocks, DSO, MC. (IWM B 9302)

Horrocks, Brian (1895–1980)

British lieutenant general, commander of XXX Corps. Sir Brian Horrocks took command of a machine gun battalion in the British Expeditionary Force (BEF) on 13 May 1940, the day the Germans invaded Western Europe. In the ensuing days, he made a strong impression on General Bernard L. Montgomery (q.v.), his divisional commander. After Dunkirk (q.v.), Horrocks was promoted to brigade commander on 17 June, and a year later made a division commander.

Within a few days of taking over the Eighth Army in the desert, Montgomery sent for Horrocks to fill a corps commander vacancy. Two weeks later, his corps was the main instrument in winning the battle of Alam Halfa (q.v.). It was also German General Erwin Rommel's (q.v.) first defeat. Horrocks then commanded an armored corps for the battles of the Mareth Line (q.v.) and Tunis. While rehearsing for the Salerno (q.v.) landing in Italy, he was severely wounded.

Recovered by August 1944, Horrocks commanded XXX Corps in 21st Army Group in Normandy and northern France (qq.v.) and stayed in that appointment for the rest of the war. Arguably the most experienced corps commander in the British Army, he was tall and lean with an imposing presence. Montgomery was his mentor; he fought all his battles under Monty's command and was his faithful disciple.

B.K. Warner

Additional Reading

Darby, Hugh, and Marcus Cunliffe, *A Short Story of 21st Army Group* (1949).

Horrocks, Brian, *Corps Commander* (1978).

North, John, *Northwest Europe 1944–45: The Achievement of the 21st Army Group* (1953).

Horst, Katie ter (1907–1992)

"The Angel of Arnhem." Katie ter Horst of Oosterbeek, Holland, won undying fame during Operation MARKET-GARDEN in September 1944 when, at great personal risk, she ministered medically and spiritually to hundreds of wounded British paratroopers. Her husband, Jan ter Horst, was in the resistance when the battles for Arnhem (q.v.) began. Left with five children, she opened her home to the wounded of the British 1st Airborne Division. Knowing that the Germans might execute her for assisting the enemy, she continued to assist British and local doctors. After the battle, she and her children left their battered home, returning only after the war. At the age of eighty-five, while walking with her husband in Oosterbeek, the Angel of Arnhem was killed and her husband seriously injured by a car that swerved off the road and struck them.

James J. Cooke

Additional Reading
Chatterton, George S., *The Wings of Pegasus* (1962).
Ryan, Cornelius, *A Bridge Too Far* (1974).
Whiting, Charles, *A Bridge at Arnhem* (1974).

Horthy, Miklós (1868–1956)

Hungarian admiral, regent of Hungary. Horthy, Hungary's regent from 1920 until 1944, was one of the most notable figures in Hungarian history. His successes during World War I, as an Austro-Hungarian admiral and in overthrowing the Hungarian Communist government in 1919, induced his appointment as regent. His governing reflected monarchical leadership, militarism, anti-Communism, anti-Semitism (q.v.), and fervent irredentism.

Throughout World War II, Horthy practiced a twofold diplomatic policy. Horthy, the opportunist, allied with Germany to regain territories lost after World War I. Also, Germany's economic aid and military puissance seduced him to its side. However, recognizing the probability of an Allied victory, he attempted to maintain Western contacts. He delayed direct military involvement until Hungary declared war on the Soviet Union in 1941. Additionally, he refused to deport Jews to avoid repercussions for cooperating with the Axis. On 15 October 1944, the Germans imprisoned Horthy and installed a puppet regime. After the war, he retired to Portugal, where he died in 1956.

Judith Podlipnik

Additional Reading
Horthy, Miklós, *Memoirs* (1956).
Kertesz, Stephen D., *Diplomacy in a Whirlpool* (1953).

Horton, Max Kennedy (1883–1951)

British vice admiral, antisubmarine commander. Born in 1883, Sir Max Horton entered the Royal Navy in September 1898. He was an early pioneer in submarines, gaining his first submarine command, the *A-1,* in 1905. He was Britain's foremost submarine commander in World War I, rising to command a submarine flotilla by war's end. He is best known as commander of the western approaches from 1942 to 1945. There he commanded the Allied anti-submarine warfare (q.v.) effort at the height of the Battle of the Atlantic (q.v.).

Horton commanded a variety of seagoing units during the interwar period, rising to the rank of vice admiral in 1937. As commander of the reserve fleet in August 1939, he mobilized 12,000 reservists and 133 ships within a week; a phenomenal performance. He then served a brief tour as commander, northern patrol before moving up to flag officer, submarines, in 1940. His greatest challenge came in November 1942 with his appointment as commander, western approaches.

Resolute, courageous, bold, and charismatic, Horton commanded the forces which defeated the U-boat threat during that fateful spring of 1943, when German Admiral Karl Dönitz's (q.v.) wolf packs came closest to victory. Facing 385 operational U-boats and rising Allied shipping losses, Horton proved a brilliant commander who used his intelligence support, including ULTRA (q.v.), to best deploy his forces. He skillfully used convoys (q.v.) to defeat the wolf packs at their peak. His efforts were critical to the Allied victory—there would have been no D-Day had he lost his struggle with Dönitz. Horton retired in August 1945 and died on 30 July 1951.

Carl O. Schuster

Additional Reading
Howarth, Stephen (ed.), *Men of War: Great Naval Leaders of World War II* (1993).
Roskill, Stephen W., *The War at Sea 1939–1945,* 4 vols. (1954–1961).

Höss, Rudolf (1900–1947)

German SS commandant of Auschwitz. Höss was born 25 November 1900 in Baden-Baden. In late 1914, he joined the kaiser's army and served on the Turkish front where he was injured in combat. After the war, he gravitated toward conservative and right-wing groups. In 1923, he was convicted of complicity in the murder of a teacher and served five years in Landsberg prison. It was there Höss met Adolf Hitler (q.v.) and recorded much of Part I of *Mein Kampf* (q.v.). After his release in 1928, Höss joined the Nazi Party and later became a member of the SS (q.v.).

In 1934, Höss, as a corporal, was posted at Dachau concentration camp. By 1940, he moved up to the rank of SS captain and was given the new position of camp commandant of Auschwitz, at Oswiecim in occupied Poland. There he carried out the systematic extermination of 2.5 million Jews and other "undesirables"—Gypsies, Jehovah's Witnesses, eastern Europeans, and other non-Aryans.

Höss's methods were cruelly efficient. He had a gas chamber built to contain 2,000 people at a time. Originally, carbon monoxide was used for gassing, but that used too much fuel and was not very efficient. He used a form of cyanide gas called *Zyklon* B (q.v.) which proved gruesomely effective. Heinrich Himmler (q.v.) was so impressed during a visit in July 1942, that he promoted Höss to SS major. In 1945, Höss became deputy inspector for all concentration camps.

Höss was tried by a Polish court in 1946 and sentenced to death. Death was by hanging and the sentence was carried out on 15 April 1947 at the very site of his atrocities—Auschwitz.

William H. Van Husen

Additional Reading
Höss, Rudolph, *Commandant of Auschwitz: Autobiography of Rudolph Höss* (1953).
Kraus, Ota, and Erich Kulka, *The Death Camp: Documents on Auschwitz* (1966).

Hossbach, Friedrich (1894–1980)
German lieutenant general, Adolf Hitler's (q.v.) adjutant. Hossbach is remembered primarily for what became known in history as the Hossbach Protocol (q.v.), which contained notes of a key Hitler conference on the topic of Germany's need for *Lebensraum* (q.v.).

Hossbach entered the German Army in 1913 as a career officer. In 1934, he became chief of the central section of the general staff, as well as the *Führer's* adjutant. During the 5 November 1937 conference between Hitler and his key military leaders, Hossbach took careful notes and turned them into a secret document five days later. That memorandum later became one of the key pieces of evidence at the Nuremberg trials (*see* International Military Tribunal).

During the Blomberg-Fritsch crisis (q.v.) in 1938, Hossbach defied Hitler's order of secrecy and warned General Werner von Fritsch (q.v.) of the charges pending against him. Shortly thereafter, Hossbach was dismissed from his post as adjutant. When the war started, he was restored to the general staff. As a *General der Infantrie,* he commanded the XVI *Panzer Korps* in 1943. He later took command of the Fourth Army on the Rus-

sian front, but was again dismissed by Hitler on 30 January 1945 for withdrawing his troops into East Prussia contrary to orders.

Paul J. Rose

Additional Reading
Hossbach, Friedrich, *Zwischen Wehrmacht und Hitler, 1934–1938* (1949).
Liddell Hart, Basil H., *History of the Second World War* (1970).

Hoth, Hermann (1885–1971)
German colonel general, *Panzer* army commander. The son of an army surgeon, Hoth joined a Thuringian infantry regiment in 1904. From 1910 to 1913, he attended the Prussian War Academy and became an intelligence officer. Holding many staff positions both during and after World War I, he eventually became a specialist in armored warfare.

Appointed commander of XV Corps in November 1938, Hoth distinguished himself during the western campaign and was promoted to colonel general in July 1940. Four months later, he took charge of the Third *Panzergruppe*. After leading that unit into central Russia, he was appointed commander of the Seventeenth Army in the Ukraine in October 1941. In preparation for the great summer offensive, he was switched to the Fourth *Panzer* Army in June 1942, leading it first across the Don toward the Caucasus and then toward the lower Volga.

After failing to break the ring around the Axis forces in Stalingrad (q.v.) (Operation *WINTERGEWITTER),* Hoth played an important role in the gradual restoration of the German lines in the eastern Ukraine and in the ensuing battle of Kursk (q.v.) in July 1943. Four months later, Adolf Hitler (q.v.) dismissed him, complaining especially about his alleged "pessimism" and "defeatist attitude." Actually, he was a very capable field commander, unflappable and well-liked by his troops.

Like many other senior *Wehrmacht* figures, Hoth was tried by an American military court (the OKW Case) and sentenced to fifteen years' imprisonment (*see* American Military Tribunals). After his release from Landsberg prison in 1954, he published a didactic piece on armored warfare based on the experiences of his *Panzer* group during the opening months of Operation BARBAROSSA.

Ulrich Trumpener

Additional Reading
Brett-Smith, Richard, *Hitler's Generals* (1976).

Hoth, Hermann, *Panzer-Operationen: Die Pan-zergruppe 3 und der operative Gedanke der deutschen Führung, Sommer 1941* (1956).
Mellenthin, F.W. von, *Panzer Battles* (1956).

Hoxha, Enver (1908–1984)

Albanian partisan leader. Born to a middle-class Muslim family in southern Albania, Hoxha studied in France from 1930 to 1936, and then returned home to teach French in a secondary school. Because of his experiences in France, he became involved in the nascent Communist movement that was part of the anti-Italian resistance beginning in early 1941. Later that year Tito (q.v.) helped the Albanian Communists establish a formal party based on the Yugoslav model and under Hoxha's leadership.

Hoxha established a Communist-dominated popular front in September 1942. He also created an army of national liberation in March 1943 and it defeated the Italians by September. Although Germans troops replaced the Italians, Hoxha formed the Anti-Fascist Council of National Liberation in May 1944, which established a provisional government as the German forces withdrew. Hoxha quickly took complete control of Albania and eliminated all opposition to Communist rule. He remained absolute ruler of Albania until his death in 1984.

Steven B. Rogers

Additional Reading
Amery, Julian, *Sons of the Eagle* (1948).
Skendi, Stavro (ed.), *Albania* (1956).

Huebner, Clarence R. (1888–1972)

American major general. Huebner enlisted in the U.S. Army in 1910. His administrative skills caught the attention of his superiors and through their encouragement, he was commissioned second lieutenant in 1916. During World War I, he served in various positions and commands, finishing the war as a lieutenant colonel. When the U.S. entered World War II, Brigadier General Huebner was director of the training division of Army Service Forces in Washington, D.C. In March 1943, he was promoted to major general and posted as deputy chief of staff to British General Sir Harold Alexander (q.v.) in North Africa.

In late July 1943, during the Sicily (q.v.) campaign, General Omar N. Bradley relieved Major General Terry Allen and Brigadier General Theodore Roosevelt, Jr. (qq.v.) of command of the U.S.

1st Infantry Division (ID). The 1st ID was having discipline problems. On the battlefield they were superb, but their behavior between battles left a lot to be desired. Huebner was assigned command of the division with orders "to get the division under control." To instill discipline, he went back to the basics with close order drill, calisthenics, field training, conditioning marches, and weapons practice.

After Sicily, the 1st Infantry Division went to Britain to prepare for the cross-channel invasion. On 6 June 1944, they hit OMAHA Beach and were pinned down on the beachhead. At 1600 hours that day, Huebner landed and personally commanded the expansion and eventual breakout of the beachhead. After the Normandy breakout, 1st ID moved into Belgium and trapped a large German force at Mons. They fought in the battle for Aachen and later in the Hürtgen Forest (qq.v.).

In January 1945, Huebner was given command of U.S. V Corps. His first accomplishment was seizing the Roer dams. Afterwards, he crossed the Rhine River and moved toward the Elbe River. In late April, V Corps came under General George S. Patton's (q.v.) Third Army. Patton immediately ordered Huebner to take Pilsen, Czechoslovakia, the last battle of the war for V Corps.

After the war, Huebner moved V Corps back to the United States where they prepared to ship out to the Pacific. Huebner, however, remained in America and became G-3 of Army Ground Forces. In 1946, he became chief of staff, ground forces, European theater. In 1947, he received his third star and became military governor of Germany (homeland of his grandfather) and commander in chief, United States Army Europe until his retirement in 1950. Huebner died on 23 September 1972.

William H. Van Husen

Additional Reading
Blumenson, Martin, and James L. Stokesbury, *Masters of the Art of Command* (1975).
Hoyt, Edwin P., *The GI's War* (1988).

Hull, Cordell (1871–1955)

American secretary of state. Hull served as U.S. secretary of state from March 1933 to November 1944. A southern internationalist with a distinguished legislative background, Hull's accomplishments included his role in the Lend-Lease (q.v.) program and the establishment of the United Nations (q.v.). His weaknesses included frequent preoccupation with bureaucratic infighting and his reluctance to delegate authority within the State Department.

Despite his background and legislative expertise, Hull preferred a cautious American response to Axis and Japanese aggression until 1941. Once war began, he worked energetically to secure bipartisan support of U.S. foreign policy. A notable example was the absence of debate of foreign policy during the 1944 presidential elections. His actual input into the shaping of foreign policy was not negligible, but it was limited, since President Franklin D. Roosevelt (q.v.) made the major decisions and neglected to take Hull along to the wartime conferences in Teheran and Cairo (*see* Conferences, Allied). Hull spent much of his time trying to limit the influence of others.

Among Hull's rivals in the jostling for foreign policy influence were Vice President Henry Wallace, Treasury Secretary Henry Morgenthau (q.v.), and Sumner Welles. Hull objected strenuously to the proliferation of wartime agencies that tackled issues traditionally handled by the State Department. The truth was that State was sluggish, understaffed, and incapable of fulfilling its wartime obligations. When Hull blocked the Morgenthau Plan (q.v.) in 1944, his influence was positive. In blocking Henry Wallace's request to become secretary of state in 1944 and his sabotaging of Sumner Welles's career, Hull showed his petty side and acted to the detriment of American policy.

The undisputed high point of Hull's tenure was his lobbying for a postwar international organization. From a later perspective, the United Nations may seem to have fallen far short of its original goals, but in 1945 it was a source of optimism for a world desperately in need of that commodity. Hull was subordinate to Roosevelt, but it was doubtful any secretary of state could have been more independent given Roosevelt's zest for personal diplomacy. If secretaries of state were classified the way presidents are, Hull would be considered one of the "near greats."

Michael Polley

Additional Reading
Hull, Cordell, *The Memoirs of Cordell Hull,* 2 vols. (1948).
Smith, Gaddis, *American Diplomacy During the Second World War, 1941–1945* (1965).

Hume, Edgar Erskine (1889–1952)
American brigadier general, medical officer. Hume received an M.D. from Johns Hopkins University and joined the army in 1917. He served in Italy and France during World War I. Following the war, he established himself as a leading public health official. He was instrumental in stemming the typhus epidemic in Serbia in 1919. During World War II, Hume headed the Allied occupation government in the Fifth Army region, 1943–1945, and reestablished city governments in Naples, Rome, and Florence. Promoted to major general in 1949, he was appointed chief surgeon of the Far East command. He retired in 1951.

Hume probably was the most decorated medical officer in the history of the U.S. Army, receiving over the course of his career three Distinguished Service Medals, four Silver Stars, the Soldier's Medal, the Legion of Merit, four Bronze Stars, two Air Medals, four Purple Hearts, and high decorations from forty-two other countries.

Roger Tuller

Additional Reading
Andrus, Edwin, et al. (eds.), *Advances in Military Medicine* (1948).
Fishbein, Morris (ed.), *Doctors at War* (1945).

Husseini, Amin el (1897–1974)
Mufti of Jerusalem. Amin el Husseini (Husayni), born in Jerusalem in 1897, was the mufti of Jerusalem, and a strong Palestinian Arab nationalist who led the resistance against Zionists in Palestine. In 1910, he received a commission in the Turkish artillery after studying in Jerusalem, Cairo, and Istanbul. Sir Herbert Samuel, the first British governor of the Palestine Mandate, appointed him president of the Supreme Muslim Council. From that position, and later as mufti of Jerusalem, he organized the opposition to the British mandate and any further Jewish immigration. He encouraged anti-Jewish passions that resulted in rioting in August leaving 133 Jews dead at the hands of Arab mobs.

In 1936, the various Palestinian nationalist factions coalesced into the Arab High Committee, under the leadership of Husseini. The committee demanded a stop to Jewish immigration and an end to transfers of land from Arabs to Jews, who were then coming to Palestine in record numbers as they fled Nazi persecution in Europe. A general strike led to an Arab uprising that finally forced the British to abandon the idea of any Jewish state in Palestine. The committee wanted Jewish immigration restricted for five years, and then contingent on Arab consent. Still implacable, the mufti went to Lebanon in 1937, where he encouraged anti-British feeling in Iraq and Syria just before World War II.

During the war, Husseini spent most of his time in Germany, encouraging Palestinians and other Arabs to join the Muslim unit of the German Army. He made radio broadcasts from Berlin and did everything he could to help the German cause.

In 1945 he fled to Egypt. Husseini died on 4 July 1974 in Beirut, Lebanon.

Richard A. Voeltz

Additional Reading

Bethell, Nicholas, *The Palestinian Triangle* (1978).
Gilmour, David, *Dispossessed—the Palestinians, 1917–1980* (1980).

H

I

Iachino, Angelo (1889–1976)

Italian admiral, commander of Italy's main battle fleet. Born on 24 April 1889, Iachino served in a variety of seagoing assignments during World War I. A brilliant and decisive junior officer, he finished the war as a gunnery specialist, and remained one throughout his career. He was a fluent English-speaker who served as the Italian naval attache to Great Britain from 1931 to 1934. When Italy entered the war on 10 June 1940, Iachino was the commander of the 2nd Cruiser Squadron.

As a result of the reorganization of the fleet on 10 December 1940, Iachino was promoted to commander of Italy's main battle fleet. He proved a decisive tactical commander but his operational plans were hampered by the Italian Navy's tactical shortcomings, fuel shortages, and overly-restrictive strategic instructions from the main naval staff. He tried to develop a sea-based naval arm, but Italy left the war before the aircraft carriers could be completed (*see* Aircraft Carriers, German and Italian).

Iachino retired to Rome after the war, eschewing a postwar career in politics or writing. He died on 3 December 1976.

Carl O. Schuster

Additional Reading
Bragadin, Marco, *The Italian Navy in World War II* (1957).
Pack, S.W.C., *The Battle of Sirte* (1972).

Ibn Saud, Abd'al Aziz (1880–1953)

King of Saudi Arabia, 1927–1953. Overall, Ibn Saud favored the Allies in World War II, but he kept his options open until declaring war on Germany in early 1945. He courted the Axis in 1939, simultaneously promising Britain "undying loyalty." As the war progressed, he skillfully played off Britain against the United States. A massive aid package convinced him that the United States should supplant Britain as the dominant Western power in the region. Saudi Arabia participated in no war actions, but as a formal belligerent, sat as a founding member of the United Nations (q.v.).

Sidney Dean

Additional Reading
Lacey, Robert, *The Kingdom: Arabia and the House of Sa'ud* (1981).

Ilyushin, Sergey Vladimirovich (1894–1977)

Soviet colonel general of the engineer service, and aircraft designer. Ilyushin started working as an aircraft mechanic in 1916. In 1919 he joined the Red Army. After a brief stint as a military commissar, he commanded an aircraft maintenance unit during the civil war. He graduated from the Zhukovsky Air Force Engineering Academy in 1926, and in 1931 became chief of the Central Design Office. Under his direction that organization developed the Il-2, which was one of the most successful ground-attack aircraft in history. The Germans called it the "Black Death."

After the war Ilyushin developed the Il-40, one of the first jet ground-attack planes; the Il-28, the Soviet's first jet bomber; and in 1962, the Il-62, a turbofan transcontinental passenger plane that became the flagship of *Aeroflot*. Ilyushin was twice a Hero of Socialist Labor, and received seven Orders of Lenin.

David T. Zabecki

Additional Reading
Union of Soviet Socialist Republics, *The Great Soviet Encyclopedia,* English translation of the 3rd edition (1975), Vol. 10., p. 147.

Inayat-Khan, Noor ("Madeleine") (1914–1944)

British SOE agent. Raised in France, Inayat-Khan fled to Britain in June 1940, and in February 1943, joined the SOE (q.v.). On 16 June 1943, she became the first woman agent airdropped into France. There, she was a radio operator for the Paris-based underground network PROSPER. When the *Gestapo* (q.v.) broke PROSPER, she was described as sure to be caught because she was "so beautiful" that she would attract German agents as honey attracts flies. "Madeleine" declined rescue and continued transmitting until arrested on 13 October 1943.

SOE Agent Noor Inayat-Khan, GC, MBE. (IWM HU 28683)

After five weeks of interrogation at Paris *Gestapo* headquarters and two escape attempts, Noor was sent to Pforzheim prison and kept shackled in isolation until her 12 September 1944 execution at Dachau concentration camp. Noor was posthumously awarded the George Cross and *Croix de Guerre.*

Clayton D. Laurie

Additional Reading

Fuller, Jean Overton, *Madeleine: The Story of Noor Inayat-Khan* (1952).
Hoeling, Adolph A., *Women Who Spied* (1967).

Ingersoll, Royal Eason (1883–1976)

American admiral, commander of the U.S. Atlantic Fleet, 1942–1944. A 1905 graduate of the U.S. Naval Academy, Ingersoll served in both World War I and II. From 1916 to 1918, he was assigned to the navy's communication office. In 1918–1919, he was communications officer for the U.S. delegation to the peace conference at Versailles. Promoted to captain in 1927, he served until 1938 on various high-level operations staffs. In addition, he commanded two heavy cruisers. In 1938, he was promoted to rear admiral and assumed command of Cruiser Division 6. In 1940, he became assistant to the chief of naval operations.

In 1942, Ingersoll took command of the Atlantic Fleet and was promoted to vice admiral and then admiral. As commander Atlantic Fleet, he was responsible for convoy protection, antisubmarine warfare (until the formation of the Tenth Fleet), overseeing training of all new construction on the east coast, and the seaward defense of the Western Hemisphere. His command covered the Atlantic Ocean from the ice packs of Greenland to the shores of Antarctica.

The U.S. Navy's participation in the Northwest Africa invasion was under Ingersoll's overall command and he was deeply involved in the Normandy (q.v.) landings. In November 1944, he relinquished command of the Atlantic Fleet to assume command of the Western Sea Frontier. His responsibility was to ensure the flow of men, supplies, and equipment to the Pacific Fleet. He retired in 1946.

Charles Bogart

Additional Reading

Cant, Gilbert, *America's Navy in World War II* (1942).
Morison, Samuel Eliot, *History of U.S. Naval Operations in World War II,* 15 vols. (1947–1962).

Iňgr, Sergej (1894–1956)

Czech lieutenant general, commander in chief of the Czechoslovak army-in-exile. Iňgr was a corps commander during the Sudetenland crisis. From 1940 to 1945, he was commander in chief of the Czechoslovak army-in-exile, and he also held the post of minister of defense until 1944. He organized a Czech division in France in 1940; a battalion in North Africa that fought at Tobruk and El Alamein (qq.v.); and a brigade that fought on the European mainland in 1944–1945. He unsuccessfully tried to obtain British assistance for the Slovak Rising in the autumn of 1944. He was dismissed from the Czech government under Soviet pressure.

Andrzej Suchcitz

Additional Reading
Beneš, Eduard, *From Munich to New War and New Victory* (1954).
Mastny, Vojtech, *The Czechs Under Nazi Rule* (1971).
Moravec, Frantisek, *Master of Spies: The Memoirs of General Frantisek Moravec* (1975).
Toman, Peter, *Round the World to Britain* (1946).

Ingram, Jonas Howard (1886–1952)

American admiral, commander in chief, U.S. Atlantic Fleet. Ingram graduated from the United States Naval Academy in 1907. While at the academy, he was known for his outstanding athletic abilities. In 1906, he caught the first forward pass thrown in an Army-Navy game, scoring a touchdown with the catch. He later served as head football coach at the Naval Academy from 1915 to 1917. During the action at Vera Cruz in 1915, Ingram was awarded the Medal of Honor.

After the outbreak of World War II, Ingram commanded U.S. naval patrol operations in the South Atlantic. He was charged with protecting shipping from German surface raiders and U-boats and with securing permission for the establishment of American support facilities and naval and air bases in Brazil. His efforts paved the way for full Brazilian-American cooperation in the Atlantic Campaign (q.v.). During the early years of the war, his cruisers and destroyers sank or captured six German blockade runners. In the summer of 1943, his aircraft smashed a German U-boat attack, sinking eight submarines, and successfully closing the Atlantic narrows to the Germans.

In recognition of his success in the South Atlantic, Ingram was promoted to admiral and made commander in chief of the Atlantic Fleet in November 1944. In early 1945, he warned of the possibility that German U-boats might launch a missile attack on New York City. Although the German Navy lacked the technology, it did send a pack of six conventional U-boats to operate off the East Coast of the United States. He deployed his hunter-killer groups as mobile ocean barriers. His ships and planes sank five of the U-boats in the last large-scale operation in the Battle of the Atlantic.

After forty-four years of service, Ingram retired on 1 April 1947. In retirement, he became commissioner of the newly formed All-American Football Conference from 1947 to 1949.

Donnie O. Lord

Additional Reading
Cant, Gilbert, *America's Navy in World War II* (1945).
Morison, Samuel Eliot, *History of U.S. Naval Operations in World War II,* 15 vols. (1947–1962).

Ironside, Edmund (1880–1959)

British field marshal, chief of the Imperial General Staff 1939–1940. The son of a military surgeon, Sir Edmund Ironside was born in Edinburgh. After education at Tonbridge and the Royal Military Academy at Woolwich, he was commissioned into the Royal Artillery in 1899 in time to serve in the Boer War. Disguised as a Boer wagon driver, his intelligence activities set the pattern for his future, for in parallel with his orthodox career, he became an interpreter in seven languages and served in a wide variety of intelligence and semi-diplomatic posts. He also found time to play rugby for Scotland.

After graduating from the Staff College in 1913, Ironside spent World War I in France, serving with a Canadian division at Vimy and Passchendaele. He ended the war as a brigade commander with a Distinguished Service Order. Immediately after the war, he commanded the Allied force in Archangel sent to help the White Russians. Between the wars, he held various appointments in India, was Commandant of the Staff College, and commander in chief at Gibraltar.

The start of World War II found Ironside chief of the Imperial General Staff (CIGS), the professional head of the British Army. He was, however, "bitterly disappointed not to command an army in the field." This frustration was made worse by his difficult relationship with Leslie Hore-Belisha (q.v.), the zealous and reforming war minister. After Dunkirk (q.v.), he was replaced by John Dill (q.v.) as CIGS. Ironside became the commander in chief of the Home Forces.

"Tiny" Ironside was outspoken but highly intelligent and inventive. Although his military experience stretched back to the nineteenth century, he was a strong advocate of air-land cooperation and he well understood the potential of armored warfare. His misfortune was that at age sixty, despite his gallant service in two previous wars, he was considered too old and too conservative to play a major part in World War II.

Philip Green

Additional Reading
Chatterton Edward K., and Kenneth Edwards, *The Royal Navy: From September 1939 to September 1945,* 5 vols. (1942–1947).
Ironside, Sir Edmund, *The Ironside Diaries; 1937–1940* (1962).

Ismay, Hastings (1887–1965)

British general, Churchill's chief of staff. During World War II, Winston S. Churchill (q.v.) was not only prime minister, but British defense minister as well. In this second capacity, he was served by General Sir Hastings "Pug" Ismay as his chief staff officer. His position was similar to that of Admiral William Leahy (q.v.), chief of staff to President Franklin D. Roosevelt (q.v.).

Ismay was born in India in 1887, the son of a judge. He was educated at Charterhouse and Sandhurst before being commissioned into the Indian Army in 1905. He saw action on the Northwest Frontier and spent the whole of World War I in minor campaigns in Africa. Although he was awarded a Distinguished Service Order, his lack of experience on a major battlefront, in contrast to his contemporaries, led him to choose a staff career.

After attending the Indian Staff College, he spent the interwar years in high staff assignments in London and Delhi. In 1936, he passed up an opportunity to command a cavalry brigade to remain in his present assignment on the influential Committee of Imperial Defence. Major General Ismay became Churchill's chief staff officer when the latter became prime minister in May 1940.

Ismay's essential task was to act as liaison between Churchill and the chiefs of staff, and later with the Americans. "I spent the whole war in the middle of a web," he later wrote. He commanded Churchill's absolute trust and confidence, and showed great diplomatic skills in averting friction and smoothing over personal clashes. He was a loyal subordinate, but no docile "yes"man. Churchill could use him as a sounding board for his plans, and get an honest and blunt appraisal in return. Ismay was promoted to general in 1944.

In 1946, Ismay retired from the army and was raised to the peerage as a baron, but his service to the state was by no means over. In 1947, he went to India as Lord Louis Mountbatten's (q.v.) chief of staff during the independence and partition period. In 1952, Ismay became the first secretary-general of the fledgling NATO. He retired from that post in 1957. Ismay was at the center of world affairs for some twenty years. He was a man without personal ambition, motivated primarily by the old-fashioned idea of service to his country.

Philip Green

Additional Reading
Ismay, Hastings, *Memoirs of General the Lord Ismay* (1960).
Wingate, Ronald, *Lord Ismay* (1970).

J

Jackson, Robert H. (1892–1954)

U.S. chief prosecutor at the Nuremberg trials. A former U.S. attorney general and associate justice of the Supreme Court, Jackson took leave of the court on his appointment by President Harry S Truman to be the U.S. chief of counsel to the International Military Tribunal (q.v.) at Nuremberg. He was foremost in establishing the organization, jurisdiction, and conduct of trial procedures. His cross-examination of Hermann Göring (q.v.) was one of the most notable events of the trial. The tribunal ruled that defendants were allowed to give full answers to questions as they deemed appropriate. Although Jackson demonstrated Göring's direct participation in the worst Nazi crimes, Göring attempted what Jackson specifically wanted to avoid, propagandizing of the proceedings by defendants' justification of the Nazi cause.

Samuel J. Doss

Additional Reading

Davidson, Eugene, *The Trial of the Germans* (1966).
Maser, Werner, *Nuremberg: A Nation on Trial* (1979).
Tusa, Ann, and John Tusa, *The Nuremberg Trial* (1984).

James, M.E. Clifton (1897–1963)

British actor, General Bernard L. Montgomery's (q.v.) double. A minor actor and a wartime army lieutenant, James, in the spring of 1944, impersonated General Montgomery, whom he closely resembled in physical appearance. Operation COPPERHEAD sought to mislead the Germans about D-Day by having "Montgomery" visit Mediterranean bases in late May. Berlin thought the trip a deception, but the man really was Montgomery.

Richard Wires

Additional Reading

James, Clifton, *I Was Monty's Double* (1954).

Jány, Gusztav (1883–1947)

Hungarian colonel general, commander of the Hungarian Second Army. Jány commanded the Second Army in operations in the Soviet Union. The army participated in offensive operations in the Ukraine toward the Don River, where his forces dug in south of Voronezh. In January 1943, the Hungarian Second Army's lines were smashed by a Soviet offensive, despite his attempts to rally his forces by flying from unit to unit.

Andrzej Suchcitz

Additional Reading

Czebe, Jeno, and Tibor Petho, *Hungary in World War II* (1946).
Kallay, Nicholas, *Hungarian Premier: A Personal Account of a Nation's Struggle in the Second World War* (1954).

Jeschonnek, Hans (1899–1943)

German colonel general, chief of staff of the *Luftwaffe*. Jeschonnek was a German pilot in World War I with two air victories. In 1923, he became active in the secret rebuilding of the *Luftwaffe*. He received general staff training and became Erhard Milch's (q.v.) adjutant at the Aviation Ministry in 1933. A bright young officer, he was promoted rapidly after 1934, achieving the rank of colonel general by 1942.

As chief of the general staff of the *Luftwaffe* from February 1939 to August 1943, Jeschonnek participated in general planning and military campaigns. Convinced that the war would be short, he sacrificed long-term planning for short-term goals. He favored the invasion of the Soviet Union. He concentrated on a tactical air force with dive bombers and committed flight instruction crews to combat. He became Hermann Göring's (q.v.) scapegoat for *Luftwaffe* failures. After successful RAF raids on Hamburg and Peenemünde (qq.v.) in July–August 1943, Jeschonnek took his own life on 18 August.

Laura Matysek Wood

Additional Reading

Irving, David, *The Rise and Fall of the Luftwaffe: The Life of Field Marshal Erhard Milch* (1973).

Mitcham, Samuel W., Jr., *Men of the Luftwaffe* (1988).

Jodl, Alfred (1890–1946)

German colonel general, chief of OKW operations. Jodl headed the group of younger senior general staff officers who advocated unwavering application of the *Führerprinzip* (q.v.) within the armed forces. Under Wilhelm Keitel's (q.v.) tutelage, Jodl became head of the *Wehrmacht's* department of national defense in 1935, which Jodl developed into a highly effective operations department. His ultimate goal was to make it into a "Super General Staff" with authority over the individual service general staffs.

After Adolf Hitler (q.v.) assumed direct control over the *Wehrmacht,* Jodl's department became, as Hitler's personal military staff, a semi-political organ to supply Hitler with information and to circulate and supervise his orders. With the outbreak of war, the organization was redesignated *Wehrmachtsführungsstab* (Wehrmacht Operational Staff). Jodl, who had returned to his old service arm for an artillery command, was recalled to take over the *Wehrmachtsführungsstab* on 23 August 1939.

A brilliant organizer, Jodl actually ran the *Oberkommando der Wehrmacht* (OKW) (q.v.) during World War II, while the *Wehrmacht's* nominal chief of staff, Keitel, served primarily as Hitler's military mouthpiece. Although both men were slavishly devoted to Hitler, Jodl enjoyed the *Führer's* confidence to a much greater extent. He was considered pathologically ambitious by his peers, but his devotion to Hitler was genuine and lasted beyond the *Führer's* death.

In private, Jodl spoke freely with Hitler as few others could, protesting when the *Führer's* military decisions made no sense. To the outside, however, Jodl always backed Hitler and his policies, and tried to protect him from anything unpleasant. When General Johannes Blaskowitz (q.v.), the military governor of Poland, sent a detailed report of SS atrocities to the OKW in 1940, Jodl not only did not pass it on to Hitler, but even refused to read it himself, considering Blaskowitz's action "uncalled for."

On 7 November 1943, Jodl addressed the *Reich's Gauleiters* to rally them in light of the collapsing eastern front, stressing that a political solution was a coward's solution. He considered himself a faithful, apolitical soldier. He developed his own philosophy, according to which war was "the basic element in politics, the prime mover of things, and thus an end in itself," as he later related to Basil H. Liddell Hart (q.v.).

In April 1945, Jodl devised a plan to turn the entire western front (later amended to the northern portion of the western front) to fight the Soviets, signaling to the Western powers that Germany's real battle was against Communism. As the Allies closed in on the *Reich,* he fled with Keitel and the OKW staff into the Mecklenburg forests. He set his last hopes on the relief of Berlin by General Walther Wenck's army in coordination with the turned western front. Wenck was stopped by the Soviets on 27 April, and the remaining German armies surrendered in early May.

On 8 May 1945, Jodl signed the instrument of capitulation with the Western powers. He was condemned as a war criminal at Nuremberg (*see* International Military Tribunal) in October 1946 and hanged. A German de-Nazification court exonerated him posthumously in 1953.

Sidney Dean

Additional Reading

Barnett, Correlli (ed.), *Hitler's Generals* (1989).

Görlitz, Walter, *History of the German General Staff* (1953).

Jodl, Luise, *Jenseits des Endes* (1976).

Shirer, William L., *The Nightmare Years: 1930–1940* (1984).

Johnson, John E. (1915–)

British ace. Born in 1915, "Johnnie" Johnson qualified to be a civil engineer in 1938 and joined the Royal Air Force Volunteer Reserve in 1939. Mobilized that year, he began flying with Number 616 Squadron soon after the Battle of Britain (q.v.). His long list of victories began in January 1941, when he damaged a Do-17. By the end of the war he was credited with thirty-eight enemy aircraft destroyed, making him the highest-scoring RAF ace.

Not only a good pilot and accomplished shot, Johnson demonstrated excellent leadership abilities, first commanding Number 610 Squadron before taking over various RCAF wings between March 1943 and March 1945, when he became station commander for Number 125 Wing. His combined skills as flyer and leader earned him the Distinguished Service Order and two Bars, the Distinguished Flying Cross and Bar, and the American Distinguished Flying Cross. After World War II, Johnson served as an exchange officer with the U.S. Air Force and served in the Korean War, where he was further awarded the U.S. Legion of Merit. Johnson retired as an RAF air vice marshal.

Bill Rawling

Additional Reading

Cosgrove, Edmund, *Canada's Fighting Pilots* (1965).
Coughlin, Tom, *The Dangerous Sky: Canadian Airmen in World War II* (1968).
Johnson, J.E., *Wing Leader* (1957).

Joyce, William (1906–1946)

British propaganda broadcaster for the Germans. Throughout the war, Joyce broadcast English-language propaganda on Radio Hamburg. With his assumed upper-class accent and obvious falsehoods, he aroused amusement and ridicule in Britain, where he was known contemptuously as "Lord Haw Haw." His propaganda efforts on behalf of his Nazi masters were of no value, indeed probably counterproductive; nor was he successful in his attempts to seduce British POWs of Irish birth from their loyalty to the Crown.

Joyce was born in the United States of Irish parents, and lived there and in southern Ireland until emigrating to Britain in 1922. He joined Oswald Mosley's (q.v.) Union of Fascists, and when they expelled him, he set up his own fanatical British Nazi Party before finally fleeing to Germany in September 1939. Having used a British passport (obtained by falsely claiming to have been born in Ireland), he was found guilty of treason at the Old Bailey in 1945 and executed the next year.

Philip J. Green

Additional Reading

Gombrich, Ernst H., *Myth and Reality in German War-Time Broadcasts* (1970).
West, Rebecca, *The Meaning of Treason* (1949).

Juin, Alphonse Pierre (1888–1967)

French general, commander in North Africa 1941–1943, and Italy 1943–1944. Juin was born in Algeria and graduated with Charles de Gaulle (q.v.) from Saint Cyr. During World War I, Juin was captain in the Moroccan Division. By 1940, he was divisional commander. He was captured by the Germans and imprisoned at Königstein, but Marshal Henri Pétain (q.v.) arranged his release in 1941, contingent on an oath not to take arms against Germany.

Juin was named commander of the Vichy troops in Morocco and subsequently ordered resistance to the Allied landings of November 1942. He then joined the Allies and became commander in chief of French forces in North Africa, but the stigma of Vichy clung to him until 1943, when he led the French into Italy with the Allies. At the Garigliano, Juin outflanked the Germans, enabling a breakthrough at Monte Cassino (q.v.) on 12 May 1944. Marshal Albert Kesselring (q.v.) held Juin in high regard as a military opponent.

Juin became army chief of staff in postwar France and remained active in territorial affairs until his retirement in 1962. He was named Marshal of France posthumously.

Mary Anne Pagliasotti

William Joyce, a.k.a. "Lord Haw-Haw." (IWM PL 68682)

Additional Reading

Aron, Robert, *France Reborn* (1964).
Goutard, Adolphe, *The Battle of France* (1940).
Tournoux, Jean R., *Pétain and De Gaulle* (1966).

K

Kaiser, Henry J. (1882–1967)

American industrialist and ship builder. Kaiser is a typical case study in the American image of the self-made man. He began as a civil engineer, building highways in the American West from 1914 to 1929, and in Cuba in 1930. He moved on to dams and bridges from 1933 to 1943. In 1940, he acquired a number of shipyards in California and Oregon, and began construction of aluminum plants.

When the war broke out and there was great demand for cargo ships, Kaiser adapted mass production techniques for the construction. By 1944, a Kaiser-designed shipyard could launch a new Liberty ship (q.v.) hull every four days. This compares with pre-Kaiser construction of similar capacity (about 4,000 tons displacement) vessels constructed in fourteen months. He also designed and built the versatile jeep (q.v.) utility vehicle and the "jeep carrier," small escort aircraft carriers (CVE) intended primarily for convoy escort and antisubmarine duties. The latter were built on Liberty ship hulls.

After the war, Kaiser turned his hand to steel and aluminum manufacturing, founding the Kaiser Aluminum and Metals Corporation. He also briefly manufactured automobiles along with the jeep.

John D. Beatty

Additional Reading

Connery, Robert H., *The Navy and the Industrial Mobilization in World War II* (1951).
Walton, Francis, *The Miracle of Victory of World War II: How American Industry Made Victory Possible* (1956).

Kaltenbrunner, Ernst (1903–1946)

Chief of the *Reich* Security Main Office. A fanatical Nazi, Kaltenbrunner rose rapidly through the party and police ranks to become head of the *Reich* Security Main Office (RSHA) (q.v.), and one of the most powerful individuals in Nazi Germany. He was born on 4 October 1903 in Austria. As a law student, he organized anti-Jewish and anti-Catholic actions and adopted the racist ideology popular then.

In 1930, Kaltenbrunner joined the Austrian Nazi Party and entered the SS (q.v.) the following year. He was active in the Austrian Nazi Party, and Heinrich Himmler (q.v.) rewarded him with an appointment as head of the Austrian SS in January 1937. After *Anschluss* (q.v.) of Nazi Germany and Austria, he became the chief of security for the higher SS and police leader in Vienna. He was intensely loyal to Himmler, an absolute true believer in Nazi ideology, and an effective policeman.

After the assassination of Reinhard Heydrich (q.v.), Himmler appointed Kaltenbrunner chief of

RSHA *Chief Ernst Kaltenbrunner in the dock at Nuremberg, 1946. (IWM MH 17454)*

the RSHA on 30 January 1943. This organization united the various police forces and controlled the concentration camps. To a large degree, he continued the established Nazi policies, especially the murderous pursuit and systematic annihilation of Jews, Communists, POWs, Slavs, and political dissenters. As a result of these activities, he was prosecuted at the Nuremberg trials (*see* International Military Tribunal) and convicted of war crimes and crimes against humanity. He was sentenced to death and executed on 16 October 1946.

Robert G. Waite

Additional Reading

Appleman, John A., *Military Tribunals and International Crimes* (1954).

Black, Peter, *Ernst Kaltenbrunner: Ideological Soldier of the Third Reich* (1984).

Davidson, Eugene, *The Trial of the Germans* (1966).

Weil, Joe (ed.), *The Bloody Record of Nazi Atrocities* (1944).

Kammhuber, Josef (1908–1986)

Luftwaffe lieutenant general, commander of the German night-fighter force. Born in Burgkirchen-Oberhagen on 19 August 1908, Josef Kammhuber entered the Bavarian Pioneers (combat engineers) just as World War I began in August 1914. He qualified as a pilot in 1919, but he remained a member of the *Pioniere Korps* until 1930, when he assumed command of the *Reichwehr*'s secret pilot training school in Lipetsk, in the Soviet Union. From there he served in a variety of technical development and command positions, including command of bomber and night-fighter groups.

Kammhuber assumed command of all German night-fighter units in September 1943, just at the height of the British night bombing campaign. A technocrat as well as a commander, it was Kammhuber who developed the system of radar sites and fighter control stations called the Kammhuber Line, which inflicted heavy losses on the British bomber "streams" as they entered German airspace. His system's effectiveness declined, however, as Allied numbers and technical superiority grew. He finished the war as chairman of a special task force assigned to develop equipment and tactics to defeat Allied bombing.

After the war Kammhuber was one of the first officers to enter the newly formed *Bundesluftwaffe* (West German Air Force) in 1956. He rose to the rank of full general as the *Luftwaffe*'s inspector general. He died in Munich on 25 January 1986.

Carl O. Schuster

Additional Reading

Price, Alfred, *Luftwaffe: Birth, Life, and Death of an Air Force* (1969).

Suchenwirth, Richard, *Command and Leadership in the German Air Force* (1969).

Keitel, Wilhelm (1882–1946)

German field marshal, chief of staff of the OKW. Keitel was convinced Adolf Hitler's (q.v.) accession to power constituted the "greatest revolution in all world history." Keitel became chief of the *Wehrmachtsamt* in October 1935, serving as deputy to the war minister and de facto commander in chief of the armed forces. In February 1938, Hitler eliminated the War Ministry and transformed the *Wehrmachtsamt* into the *Oberkommando der Wehrmacht* (q.v.) (Armed Forces High Command) (OKW), assuming direct personal control of the combined armed forces.

A sensitive, emotional man, Keitel wept over the downfall of War Minister Werner von Blomberg (q.v.), a relative by marriage. His shock did not prevent him from accepting the proffered appointment to OKW chief of staff. Awed by what he perceived as Hitler's military genius, he became a willing puppet whose primary function was serving as the *Führer*'s military spokesman and chief military advisor.

Keitel believed modern warfare was no longer merely a question of strategy, but largely a matter of economics and propaganda. The proper exploitation of human potential was more decisive than deployment plans, necessitating the existence of the OKW's operational staff under General Alfred Jodl (q.v.) as a politico-military "Super General Staff" over the service general staffs.

After the fall of France, Hitler tasked Keitel with pressing home the German demands in the June 1940 armistice "negotiations." Prohibited from departing one iota from Hitler's instructions, Keitel dictated terms "brutally and arrogantly," as American correspondent William L. Shirer (q.v.) observed. As a result, he was promoted field marshal in July.

Despite his personality faults, Keitel was a competent staff officer. His estimates of Soviet strength preceding Operation BARBAROSSA proved extremely accurate. He agreed with other senior officers in December 1941 that the offensive should be halted in favor of secure winter quarters. Because of this, he had a major falling out with Hitler. Jodl had to talk Keitel out of suicide over the *Führer*'s apparent lack of faith in him. Reconciled, Keitel promptly signed and dis-

Field Marshal Wilhelm Keitel prepares to sign the instrument of surrender in Berlin, 9 May 1945. He is flanked by General Admiral Hans von Friedeburg (right) and Colonel General Paul Stumpff (left). (IWM FRA 203385)

tributed Hitler's *"Nacht und Nebel"* order (q.v.). Keitel also sat on the "court of honor" that expelled Claus von Stauffenberg's (q.v.) surviving coconspirators from the military, subjecting them to prosecution before the Nazi "People's Court" rather than a court-martial.

Keitel retained his faith in Hitler to the end. He encouraged the *Führer's* illusions about a last-ditch defense, and attempted to shield Hitler from negative reports by field commanders. In April 1945, Keitel took the OKW staff into the forests while Hitler stayed in Berlin. He and Jodl tried to coordinate an abortive last-minute relief of Berlin by General Wenck's three-division army. Keitel ordered all other units to "stop the enemy" and open the way for Wenck, stressing no commander had authority to modify these orders, under penalty of death. As Wenck was stopped and the remaining operational forces surrendered, Keitel signed the capitulation agreement with the Soviets on 8 May.

At Nuremberg (*see* International Military Tribunal), Keitel claimed to have been merely a soldier performing his duty. He was condemned on 1 October 1946 and shortly after hanged as a war criminal.

Sidney Dean

Additional Reading

Barnett, Corelli (ed.), *Hitler's Generals* (1989).
Görlitz, Walter, *History of the German General Staff* (1953).
Keitel, Wilhelm, *The Memoirs of Field Marshal Keitel* (1966).
Liddell Hart, Basil H., *The German Generals Talk* (1948).
Mitcham, Samuel M., Jr., *Hitler's Field Marshals and Their Battles* (1988).

Kennan, George Frost (1904–)

Kennan was born on 16 February 1904 in Milwaukee, Wisconsin. He attended St. John's Military Academy, then Princeton University, graduating in 1926. After school, he joined the Foreign Service and soon acquired an appreciation for languages. After his first postings in Geneva and Hamburg, he decided to specialize in the study of Russian culture, which he began in 1928.

Since the United States had no relations with the Soviet Union at that time, Kennan studied in the Baltic cities of Tallinn, Riga, and Kovno. His first assignment was vice consul in Tallinn; from there, he transferred to Riga. In the summer of 1929, he was sent to Berlin to study academic Russian. After his third year, he was sent back to

Riga where he was assigned to the Russian section of the legation. Riga was the nearest he could get to a Russian assignment as the United States and the Soviet Union were still two years away from diplomatic relations.

In 1934, Kennan accompanied William C. Bullitt, Washington's first ambassador to Moscow, as his interpreter. An appointment as a diplomatic secretary to Moscow followed. In the next few years, he witnessed Stalin's purges (q.v.), and he wrote analytical dispatches on the entire process. He saw the Soviet Union as a great nation ruled by an evil man.

In the summer of 1937, Kennan went to Washington to serve for a year at the Russian desk. After Washington, he went to Prague where he worked for Wilbur J. Carr, minister to Czechoslovakia. Just as Kennan arrived in Prague, the Munich crisis (q.v.) occurred, and the American legation closed. Kennan subsequently was posted to the American embassy in Berlin.

The staff of the American embassy took over the interests of France and Great Britain as well as the duties of the consular offices of various German cities, which now were closed. Kennan worked for the charge d'affairs, Alexander Kirk, as an administrative officer. With America's entry in World War II in December 1941, Kennan, along with the rest of the staff, was evicted from Germany. Before leaving Germany, however, they were taken prisoners by the *Gestapo* (q.v.) and held in a building near Bad Nauheim for five months. They finally were released and sent out through Spain and Portugal in exchange for a party of Germans.

Kennan returned to work in August 1942 and was assigned a desk in the personnel section; by Labor Day that year, however, he was posted to Portugal and assigned as counselor of legation. His superior, Bert Fish, died, and Kennan became chargé d'affaires. He was instrumental in obtaining from the Portuguese government facilities in the Azores permitting the U.S. to fly land-based aircraft to Europe, via the archipelago.

On 14 January 1944, Kennan left Lisbon for London as counselor of the embassy and political advisor to Ambassador John G. Winant. The newly established European Advisory Commission (EAC) was set up in London. The EAC was formed to establish terms of surrender and divide Germany into occupied zones. Kennan and Winant found themselves in the dark over most matters, as they were not allowed to do anything without instructions from the United States.

Kennan's next assignment was to Moscow in July 1944 as minister-counselor, primarily an administrative position. He saw the Yalta Declaration as a shady deal in which the United States should have taken no part. He viewed any dealings with the Soviet leaders with great skepticism. He did not agree with the alliance with the Soviet Union because he believed the Soviets would only respond to force. The forming of the United Nations was then in progress, but Kennan felt an international organization for the preservation of peace and security could not take the place of a well-conceived and realistic foreign policy. Several weeks working in Moscow during the summer of 1944 was enough to convince him that not only U.S. policy toward the Soviet Union, but also U.S. plans and commitments for the shaping of the postwar world were based on a dangerous misreading of the personality, intentions, and politics of Soviet leaders.

Kennan wrote an essay entitled *Russia—Seven Years Later*. In it he wrote what he thought about Russia generally and Josef Stalin's (q.v.) Russia in particular. He explained his view of Soviet foreign policy and the Stalin era. He assessed the situation in which the Soviet leaders found themselves at the time, and forecast in general terms their reaction and behavior in the immediate postwar period. At that time, Kennan advocated a prompt and clear recognition of the division of Europe into spheres of influence and of a policy based on such a division.

As a realist, Kennan viewed the Potsdam Conference with skepticism. He felt the principles of joint quadripartite control were unreal and unworkable. His seventeen years of experience with Russian affairs made him doubt that the Soviets would follow any democratic practices.

The handling of war criminals was another policy with which Kennan disagreed. He felt that any man responsible for atrocities, once apprehended, should be executed immediately. Kennan strongly felt that it was a mockery of justice to conduct trials, using Soviet judges who represented the cruel and repressive regime that carried out the purges, as well as all the brutalities and atrocities against the Poles and the Baltic peoples.

Kennan was convinced that any economic aid to the Soviet government would lead to problems at a later date. He now was "acting ambassador" in the Soviet Union. At the time, the Treasury Department asked why the Soviets were unwilling to adhere to the rules of the World Bank and International Monetary Fund. This gave Kennan the opportunity to explain Soviet policy in detail. His answer, in the form of an 8,000-word telegram, dealt with the basic features of the Soviet postwar outlook, the background of that outlook, its projection on the level of official and unofficial policy, and the inherent implications of American policy. The effect of the telegram in Washington was sensational. It changed Kennan's career overnight.

Kennan immediately became a candidate for many different positions. In April 1946, he was transferred to Washington and assigned as the "first deputy for foreign affairs" at the newly established National War College. His duty was to devise and direct the political portions of the combined military-political course of instruction. Here he toured the country delivering speeches on Russia and Communism. He wrote no prepared speeches and spoke with enthusiasm from memory and an assortment of scribbles. He lectured at the Army, Naval and Air War Colleges, the Naval Academy, Yale, Virginia, Williams, and Princeton Universities, and at various private and semi-private groups around the East Coast. Apart from lecturing, he wrote numerous articles.

Kennan was still at the National War College in 1947 when the British government abandoned its support for Greece. He was part of a committee established to study the problem of assistance to Greece and Turkey. From the problems of Greece and Turkey, the committee moved to the subject of the Middle East. During this time, President Harry S Truman (q.v.) presented his famous Truman Doctrine message. Kennan felt that the sweeping language of the message might be subject to misinterpretation. He felt that no distinction was given to areas vital to U.S. security.

On 28 April 1947, Secretary of State George C. Marshall (q.v.) returned from Moscow and asked Kennan to go to the State Department and immediately set up the policy planning staff. Marshall ordered Kennan to assemble a staff to examine Europe's problems and how the United States could help. The staff was established on 5 May 1947 and included Joseph E. Johnson, Colonel Charles Hatwell Bonesteel III, Jacques Reinstein, Ware Adams, and Carleton Savage. On 23 May, they gave their recommendations to Marshall. The outcome was the Marshall Plan (q.v.).

During Kennan's service at the National War College, the secretary of the navy, James Forrestal (q.v.), sent him a paper on the subject of Marxism and Soviet power and asked for comments. Instead of commenting, Kennan wrote his own paper on the same subject. The editor of *Foreign Affairs* magazine also asked him for some writings on the same theme. Kennan then submitted the same paper for clearance to the Committee on Unofficial Publication, with the understanding that it would be published anonymously. The article appeared in the June 1947 issue of *Foreign Affairs* entitled "The Sources of Soviet Conduct."

The article, known as the "X Article," first spelled out the principles of "containment," and came to be identified with the foreign policy of the Truman administration. Kennan realized there were some serious deficiencies in the article. He had failed to mention the satellite states of Eastern Europe. A second deficiency was his failure to clarify what he meant by containment of Soviet power. He did not mean the containment by military means of a military threat, but the political containment of a political threat. A third deficiency was the failure to distinguish between various geographic areas, and to clarify that the containment he was speaking of was not something that he thought the United States could do everywhere successfully. In his own mind, he distinguished between areas he thought were vital to U.S. security and ones that were not.

Kennan left Washington, D.C., in August 1950 and took a position at Princeton University at the Institute of Advanced Study, where he exercised his great creative ability. In later years, he took exception to the anti-Communist emphasis and Cold War rhetoric that marked the U.S. attitude toward the Soviet Union. In 1957, he proposed a mutual withdrawal of Soviet and U.S. forces from central Europe and the unification and neutralization of East and West Germany. Additionally, he opposed the nuclear arming of NATO. Over the years, he continued to publish books frequently on U.S.-Soviet relations and European diplomacy.

Vivian Stacey

Additional Reading
Combs, Jerald A., *The History of American Foreign Policy* (1986).
Kennan, George F., *Memoirs 1925–1950* (1967).
———, *Russia and the West Under Lenin and Stalin* (1960).

Kesselring, Albert (1885–1960)

Luftwaffe field marshal, commander of Army Group C. In 1933, artillery Colonel Kesselring was chosen by Hermann Göring (q.v.) to become *Luftwaffe* chief of administration. There he served as military assistant to *Luftwaffe* State Secretary Erhard Milch (q.v.) during the covert air force expansion program. In June 1936, Major General Kesselring became *Luftwaffe* chief of staff. During the invasion of Poland, Colonel General Kesselring commanded the

Field Marshal Albert Kesselring. (IWM HU 51040)

First *Luftflotte* (Air Fleet), with twenty groups of fighters and bombers. In 1940, he led the Second *Luftflotte* on the western front, executing precision strikes on selected targets in Rotterdam (q.v.), and later bombarding Dunkirk (q.v.). He was promoted to field marshal in July 1940.

The Second *Luftflotte* participated successfully in the Battle of Britain (q.v.) until Kesselring advised Adolf Hitler (q.v.) that the bombing campaign could be redirected against London. Impatient with the rate of progress achieved attacking British airfields and industry, Kesselring wanted to lure the RAF up to destroy it in the air.

In 1941, with its losses against the RAF more than replaced, the Second *Luftflotte* had 1,000 aircraft and was the largest air fleet committed against the Soviet Union. According to Soviet records, Kesselring's force destroyed 738 aircraft on the first day of the fighting. Having secured air superiority in his sector, he then concentrated on providing ground support for Army Group Center, inflicting heavy losses on Soviet armor and infantry, especially in the various "cauldrons" of encircled and trapped formations.

In November 1941, Kesselring, with his staff and one of his two air corps, was transferred to Italy. As commander in chief south, his primary mission was interdiction of British operations from Malta, which had virtually cut off the *Afrika Korps'* (q.v.) supply lines. By May 1942, Malta's military infrastructure lay in ruins, as the *Luftwaffe* continued to inflict serious losses on British ships in the Mediterranean. Together with Admiral Erich Raeder (q.v.), Kesselring urged Hitler to approve Operation HERCULES, the occupation of the island. After General Erwin Rommel (q.v.), supported by Kesselring's air corps, took Tobruk (q.v.) in June 1942, Hitler dropped the plan.

Kesselring believed Rommel's decision to pursue the retreating British into Egypt to be "madness" as long as the RAF retained intact bases there. Hitler, nonetheless, ordered Kesselring to provide Rommel with full support. While he had no operational control over Rommel, Kesselring did support and co-direct the North African campaign until the Axis defeat in May 1943.

When the Allies landed in Sicily (q.v.) on 10 July 1943, Kesselring ordered delaying actions while supervising the masterful six-day evacuation of 100,000 Axis troops and 10,000 vehicles to the Italian mainland. When the Allies landed in Italy proper in September, he had only eight German divisions with which to defend the central and southern peninsula. (northern Italy was covered by Rommel's army group, still outside Kesselring's authority.) He needed two of his divisions around Rome to disarm the now unreliable Italian forces. With the remainder, he stalled the Allied advance while awaiting reinforcements.

In November 1943, Rommel's army group was dissolved. Kesselring was given authority over all German forces in Italy. This expanded command was redesignated Army Group C. He held the Allies from Rome for eight months after their landing. Vacating the Gustav Line in May 1944, Kesselring declared Rome an open city rather than risk its destruction. He conducted a ten-week fighting retreat to the Gothic Line (q.v.), where the Allies were again held until April 1945.

Injured in an automobile accident in October 1944, Kesselring returned to his command in January 1945. In March, he was ordered to assume command of the western front from Field Marshal von Rundstedt (q.v.). With typical dry humor, he greeted his new staff with the words, "Well, Gentlemen, I am the new V-3"—a sardonic reference to Hitler's faith in the new "wonder weapons." With Kesselring's forces depleted and low on resources, he could only slow the enemy's advance.

On 15 April 1945, Hitler, his long-term distrust of the army generals at its peak, devised a desperate final defense plan. He divided the remaining *Reich* into two defensive zones. He appointed Admiral Karl Dönitz (q.v.) to command the north and Kesselring the south. On 7 May, Kesselring surrendered his forces to the Western Allies.

Kesselring's 1947 death sentence by a British tribunal for shooting Italian hostages was commuted to life; he was released in October 1952. As chief of administration, Kesselring deserves much of the credit for building the *Luftwaffe* into a formidable force, handicapped by the requirement to perform much of this secretly. Under his command, the Second *Luftflotte* was the most effective large unit of the *Luftwaffe,* contributing significantly to *Blitzkrieg* success. He masterfully directed operations against the British in the Mediterranean, then delayed full Allied conquest of Italy by one and one half years. His record was marred by his misjudgment in the Battle of Britain, which cost Germany dearly.

Sidney Dean

Additional Reading

Barnett, Correlli (ed.), *Hitler's Generals* (1989).

Bekker, Cajus, *The Luftwaffe War Diaries* (1969).

Görlitz, Walter, *History of the German General Staff* (1953).

Kesselring, Albert, *A Soldier's Record* (1954).

Macksy, Kenneth, *Kesselring: German Master Strategist of the Second World War* (1996).

Mason, Herbert, *The Rise of the Luftwaffe* (1973).

Keyes, Geoffrey Charles Tasker (1917–1941)

British lieutenant colonel, commando leader. Keyes, the son of Admiral of the Fleet Sir Roger Keyes (q.v.), was born in Aberdour, Scotland, on 18 May 1917. He was the youngest colonel serving in the British Army when he led elements of Number 11 Scottish Commando in an attack on German general Erwin Rommel's (q.v.) headquarters on 17–18 November at Beda Littoria, Libya. Landing from submarines 250 miles behind German lines, Keyes led his force without guides to the building they believed housed Rommel. Keyes was killed in the attack. Ironically, Rommel was nowhere near the building at the time. Rommel later sent his own personal chaplain to conduct the funeral service for Keyes, and the Germans buried him with full military honors. Keyes was awarded the Victoria Cross posthumously.

David T. Zabecki

Additional Reading

Keyes, Elizabeth, *Geoffery Keyes, V.C. of the Rommel Raid* (1956).

Keyes, Roger (1872–1945)

British admiral of the fleet, director of Combined Operations, 1940–1941. Like General Bernard L. Montgomery (q.v.), Sir Roger Keyes could proudly claim to have served the British Crown for more than fifty years. Remarkably for a senior officer of World War II, he first saw action in the nineteenth century. He joined the Royal Navy at age fifteen and served against slave traders and in the Boxer Rebellion. In World War I, he served at the Dardanelles and commanded the amphibious raid on the German submarine base at Zeebrugge in 1918. In 1930, he was promoted to admiral of the fleet.

In 1940, Keyes was recalled from retirement to become the first head of the new Amphibious Warfare (later Combined Operations) Directorate. As such, he was responsible for the formation and early activities of the commandos (q.v.) and the initial planning for the eventual return to the European mainland. His previous amphibious experience made him a wise choice, but in October 1941, Prime Minister Winston S. Churchill (q.v.) replaced him with the youthful and dynamic Louis Mountbatten (q.v.). Keyes then served as liaison officer to the Belgian forces in Britain until his death in 1945.

On 18 November 1941, his son, Lieutenant Colonel Geoffery Keyes (q.v.), was killed leading a commando raid on Rommel's (q.v.) headquarters on the Libyan coast. For his courage and leadership, the younger Keyes was awarded the Victoria Cross, posthumously. A plaque commemorating the services of the Keyes, father and son, stands in London's St. Paul's Cathedral.

Philip Green

Additional Reading

Chatterton, Edward K., and Kenneth Edwards, *The Royal Navy: From September 1939 to September 1945,* 5 vols. (1942–47).

Keyes, Sir Roger, *Amphibious Warfare and Combined Operations* (1943).

Khrushchev, Nikita Sergeevich (1894–1973)

Military commissar and Communist Party chief of the Ukraine. Born in the Ukraine, the son of a poor peasant, Khrushchev's early life gave him a firsthand understanding of the poor living conditions of the working classes in Russia. In 1918, he joined the Bolshevik Party and served as military commissar in the Red Army. As a delegate to the fourteenth Party Convention in 1925, he became a strong supporter of Josef Stalin's (q.v.) hard line. After proving his worth as a loyal party agitator, Khrushchev was chosen for higher functions within the party.

Khrushchev was no theorist, but a man of action with great organizing ability. Protected by Stalin, he had a rapid rise through the political ranks of the Soviet Union. He directed the construction of the Moscow subway. As the party chief of the Ukraine, he supervised the 1939 annexation of eastern Poland under the Molotov-Ribbentrop Pact (q.v.). Despite his influence, however, he was not appointed to Stalin's State Defense Committee in 1941. Stung by the slight, he started to dissociate himself from Stalin.

Khrushchev served as Marshal Seymon Budenny's (q.v.) political commissar of the Southwestern Front (army group). To prevent vital industrial capacity from falling into German hands, he supervised its dismantling and removal to east of the Urals. He also blew up the Dnieper Dam to further disrupt industrial activity in the Ukraine. After Budenny's dismissal, he continued as commissar of the Southwest Front, and participated in the battles for Stalingrad and Kursk (qq.v.).

On 6 November 1943, Khrushchev entered the liberated Ukranian capital of Kiev with the Soviet troops. In 1944, he served with the 1st Ukranian Front, and undertook a series of purges that allowed him to build a secure political power base in the Ukraine.

After Stalin's death in 1953, Khrushchev emerged from an internal power struggle as the ruler of the Soviet Union. During his decade in power, he ended the Stalin cult, opened the Soviet Union to the west, and initiated numerous internal reforms. His inconsistency and his irritable character, however, caused problems at home and abroad. He lost prestige as the result of the Berlin and Cuban missile crises. In 1964, he was deposed for being a "hare-brained schemer" and sent into retirement.

Wolfgang Terhörst

Additional Reading

Ebon, Martin, *Nikita Khrushchev* (1986).
Khrushchev, Sergei, *Khrushchev on Khrushchev: An Inside Account of the Man and His Era, by His Son* (1990).
Snow, Edgar, *The Pattern of Soviet Power* (1945).
Werth, Alexander, *Russia at War, 1941–1945* (1964).
White, William L., *Report on the Russians* (1945).

King, Ernest Joseph (1878–1956)

American fleet admiral, commander in chief of the U.S. Fleet. Born in Cleveland on 23 November 1878, King rose to command the world's largest navy, totaling more than 8,000 ships and 24,000 aircraft manned by more than three million people. A blunt and forceful man, he guided the U.S. Navy through World War II, often shaping Allied strategy in the navy's favor by sheer force of will. An Anglophobe, he fought any proposal that detracted from what he saw as America's primary theater of war, the Pacific. Although his obstinance often interfered with overall Allied strategy, that same stubbornness enabled him to overcome obstacles inhibiting the construction of the ships, submarines, and aircraft needed to support a worldwide war effort. As such, he stands out as one of the major figures of the war.

Accepted into the U.S. Naval Academy in 1897, King first saw action aboard the cruiser USS *Indianapolis* during the Spanish-American War. Graduating in 1901, he first served as navigator aboard the survey ship USS *Eagle* before moving on to the new battleship USS *Illinois* for its European show-the-flag cruise of 1902. It was aboard that ship that he was commissioned in 1903. An aggressive and forthright officer, he seemed destined for greatness except for two weaknesses that his superiors noted: drinking, and arrogance that almost bordered on insubordination. The former he corrected, at least publicly. The latter stayed with him to his grave.

King served in a variety of sea tours in weapons, administration, and engineering between 1903 and 1909, including a brief stint as an instructor at the Naval Academy. He went from there to a tour as flag secretary to the commander of the Atlantic Fleet, Admiral Hugo Osterhaus. That tour was followed by successive postings at the Naval Academy, as commander of two destroyers, and as commander of a destroyer squadron.

In 1915, King was appointed engineering officer on the staff of Admiral Henry Mayo and remained with him when Admiral Mayo became commander of the Atlantic Fleet later that year. Mayo subsequently took the Atlantic Fleet across to Europe when America entered the war in 1917. It was a profound experience for King, attending planning conferences and dealing with the Washington and Royal Navy bureaucracies. He came away from it with a deep appreciation for the difficulties of commanding a fleet at war, and an even deeper contempt for bureaucracies.

King found himself in command of a refrigerator ship after the war. He then qualified on submarines, and took command of the submarine station in New London, Connecticut, in 1923. There he leaped into national prominence, raising the submarine *S-51* some five months after it sank. Still unable to get a surface command, Captain King jumped at the opportunity to command an aviation unit, the seaplane tender USS *Wright*. He thus qualified as a pilot in 1927, followed by a brief tour as assistant head of the aeronautics bureau, and then command of the aircraft carrier USS *Lexington* in June 1930.

In August 1932, Rear Admiral King took charge of the Aeronautics Board just at the lowest point of the Great Depression. It was a difficult time, but King quickly learned how to lobby Congress for funding in aviation programs. Many of the aircraft he fostered provided great service in the war.

In 1938, Vice Admiral King took command of aviation forces and bases, a post that gave him command of five aircraft carriers and all Pacific Fleet shore-based aircraft. Here he recommended detachment of the faster aircraft carriers away from the battleships to conduct independent strikes, escorted only by destroyers and fast cruisers. Unfortunately, it was an idea beyond the vision of the navy's leadership at the time.

King moved to the navy's General (advisory) Board as a rear admiral in 1939 and appeared to be headed for retirement. He was saved in 1940 by a chance selection to accompany the secretary of the navy on a fact-finding mission. Impressed by King's vision and drive, Secretary Charles A. Edison urged President Franklin D. Roosevelt (q.v.) to appoint King as commander of the Atlantic Fleet, a position King assumed as admiral in February 1941.

On 17 December 1941, King was appointed commander in chief of the U.S. Fleet, which gave him authority over all navy bureaus and departments. There he was answerable directly to the president. He became one of the primary members of the combined Allied staff for the prosecution of the war. He further went on to become chief of naval operations in March 1942, replacing Admiral Harold Stark (q.v.) who became commander, U.S. Naval Forces, Europe.

A strong advocate of the Pacific campaign, King alternately supported and opposed General

Fleet Admiral Ernest J. King. (IWM NYF 21633)

George C. Marshall's (q.v.) second front plans in order to gain the most resources he could to fight Japan. King supported the invasion of Sicily but opposed the Salerno (qq.v.) landings. He fought General Douglas MacArthur's views on Pacific strategy with equal energy, opposing the assault on the Philippines. He was just as forceful with the civilian bureaus and companies that built his ships and supplied his fleet.

King retired as five-star fleet admiral in December 1945 and began work on his memoirs. He died following a series of strokes on 25 June 1956. Tough, combative, and parochial to a fault, he nonetheless was the strongest leader the U.S. Navy has ever known. He forced the navy to develop the fleet train concept so vital to the Pacific campaign (enabling ships to be supplied and repaired without returning to homebase). His crowning achievement in the war, however, was his influence on

K

naval doctrine and tactics. He was the author of the carrier–air strike tactics used so effectively in the Pacific. He also established the operational evaluation group that continues to evaluate the navy's tactics and operations to this day. No other officer has had such complete authority over the navy and its institutions, and few could have wielded it so well.

Carl O. Schuster

Additional Reading

Buell, Thomas B., *Master of Sea Power: A Biography of Fleet Admiral Ernest J. King* (1980).

Howarth, Stephen, *Men of War* (1992).

King, Ernest J., and W.M. Whitehall, *Fleet Admiral King* (1952).

Larrabee, Eric, *Commander in Chief: Franklin Delano Roosevelt, His Lieutenants, and Their War* (1987).

King, William Lyon Mackenzie (1874–1950)

Prime minister of Canada. A trained economist who studied at the University of Toronto, the University of Chicago, and at Harvard, King entered the Canadian parliament in 1908 and the following year, was appointed minister of labour in the cabinet of Wilfried Laurier. He was named head of the Liberal Party in 1919 and assumed the role of leader of the opposition. Following the Liberal electoral victory in 1921, he became prime minister, an office he held from 1921 to 1930, and again from 1935 to 1948.

The Liberal government under King did not openly oppose Nazi Germany's expansionist policies. Despite its claim of autonomy in international affairs, the Canadian parliament supported Britain's policy of appeasement (q.v.). Canada also followed Britain's lead in declaring war on Germany in September 1939, although King's government, in deference to the French Canadian population, did not support the drafting of Canadian troops for wartime service overseas. Conscription for home defense was finally approved in 1940.

King's cabinet stressed the importance of supporting Britain's war effort, especially after the British retreat from Dunkirk (q.v.). In late 1941, British Prime Minister Winston S. Churchill (q.v.) traveled to Ottawa and urged greater involvement in the war. King assigned some home defense units to Britain and they participated in the Normandy (q.v.) invasion. As a result of decreased enlistments and a growing number of casualties, the Canadian parliament finally approved conscription for overseas service in 1944.

King remained prime minister until his retirement in 1948. He and his government played only a minor role in the immediate postwar changes in Europe and the world.

Steven B. Rogers

Additional Reading

Churchill, Winston S., *The Second World War*, 6 vols. (1948–1953).

Robertson, Terence, *Dieppe: The Shame and the Glory* (1962).

Kirk, Alan Goodrich (1888–1963)

American admiral, commander of U.S. Amphibious Forces, Atlantic Fleet. A graduate of the U.S. Naval Academy, Kirk served in World War I as an engineer at the Dahlgren Naval Proving Grounds. After the war, he served on the presidential yacht *Mayflower*, as a naval aid at the White House, as commander of a destroyer, and on several key staff assignments. He was promoted to captain in 1938 and sent to London as naval attache in 1939. In March 1941, he returned to the United States as rear admiral to head naval intelligence. The following March, he returned to London as naval attache and chief of staff to Admiral Harold Stark (q.v.), commander of U.S. naval forces in Europe.

In February 1943, Kirk assumed command of Amphibious Forces, Atlantic Fleet. He took part in the landings in Sicily and Normandy (qq.v.). In 1944, Kirk took command of U.S. naval forces in France, and he commanded naval forces involved in the crossing the Rhine River. Promoted to vice admiral in 1945, he was assigned to the navy General Board.

Kirk retired in 1946 as a full admiral and became ambassador to Belgium. From April 1949 to October 1951, he was ambassador to the Soviet Union. For the next ten years, he was involved in the operation of radio broadcasts to Eastern Europe. In 1962, he was envoy to the Congo, and from 1962 to 1963, ambassador to the Republic of China.

Charles A. Bogart

Additional Reading

Mason, James T. (ed.), *The Atlantic War Remembered* (1990).

Morison, Samuel Eliot, *History of U.S. Naval Operations in World War II,* 15 vols. (1947–1962).

Kleeberg, Franciszek (1888–1941)

Polish major general, commander of the Polesie Operational Group during the Polish campaign. During the 1939 Polish campaign, Kleeberg was commander of the Brzesc Military District. He defended Brzesc from 10 to 14 September, and recaptured Kobryn for a brief period. As commander of the independent Polesie Operational Group, he conducted operations against the Soviet Army. Then his group fought against the German XIV Motorized Corps at the battle of Kock from 2 to 6 October, which brought the Polish campaign to an end. He was forced to surrender due to lack of ammunition. He died in a German POW camp.

Andrzej Suchcitz

Additional Reading

Bethel, Nicholas, *The War Hitler Won, September 1939* (1972).
Kennedy, Robert M., *The German Campaign in Poland, 1939* (1956).
Norwid-Neugebauer, Mieczusław, *Defense of Poland, September 1939* (1942).
Wroblewski, Jan, *Samodzielna Grupa Operacyjra Polesie 1939* (1989).

Kleist, Paul Ludwig Ewald von (1881–1954)

German field marshal, commander Army Group A. Ewald von Kleist was among the many German generals forced to retire, ostensibly for medical reasons, during Adolf Hitler's (q.v.) 1938 purge of the officers corps, but he was recalled to duty in 1939. Formerly a skeptic of armor, he commanded the Fourteenth Army's *Panzer Korps* during the invasion of Poland.

In the campaign against France, he commanded army-strength *Panzergruppe* Kleist, which spearheaded Army Group A's thrust through the Ardennes. On 13 May 1940, his units crossed the Meuse without waiting for infantry or artillery support to catch up, contributing greatly to the *Blitzkrieg* success of the operation by cutting off the Allied forces in Belgium. By 24 May, he was poised to take Dunkirk (q.v.) before the retreating BEF could reach the city; but he was restrained by direct orders from Hitler.

In March 1941, Colonel General von Kleist's *Panzergruppe* assembled in Bulgaria for the invasion of Yugoslavia. His units smashed through the Yugoslav defenses on the first day of operations, boldly thrusting forward, ignoring threatening enemy forces on the flanks. He took Belgrade on 13 April.

Field Marshal Paul Ewald von Kleist. (IWM GER 1269)

After the Balkans, von Kleist commanded the First *Panzergruppe* Army as the spearhead for Army Group South in Operation BARBAROSSA. First *Panzergruppe* Army had only 600 tanks available; the rest of the allocated force was still in transit from Greece or being refurbished. His deep penetration destabilized Soviet resistance in the Ukraine, and established a bridgehead west of Rostov.

First *Panzergruppe* Army executed the decisive counterstrike against the Soviet armies during the first battle of Kharkov (q.v.) in May 1942, then led Army Group A's 1942 drive on the Caucasus (q.v.). Von Kleist reached the Maikop oil fields in August, but short on fuel and with his army cannibalized to support the forces at Stalingrad (q.v.), he was unable to cross the mountains.

In November 1942, von Kleist became Army Group A commander. In January 1943, he began the orderly withdrawal from the Caucasus to a bridgehead east of Kerch, earning promotion to field marshal. During the 1943 Soviet assault on the Kuban bridgehead, he defended with limited German and Romanian resources before completing his fighting retreat from the Crimean peninsula that October.

By April 1944, von Kleist's force, redesignated Army Group Southern Ukraine, was forced to retreat into Romania, whereupon he relinquished command to Field Marshal Ferdinand Schörner (q.v.) and retired from the army. In 1948, von Kleist was extradited by the Western Allies to the Soviet Union, where he died a POW in 1954.

Von Kleist was a superb product of the old general staff school. He demonstrated repeatedly in Russia the value of elastic defense, successfully fighting prolonged holding actions against vastly superior odds. Earlier, in France, his initiative in advancing without support to seize the opportunity of the moment in true cavalier manner accelerated Germany's victory. His contribution would have been even greater had Hitler not restrained him before Dunkirk.

Von Kleist left his political legacy with the words spoken to historian Basil H. Liddell Hart: "The German mistake was to think that military success could solve political problems. Indeed, under the Nazis we tended to reverse Clausewitz's dictum and to regard peace as an interruption of war."

Sidney Dean

Additional Reading

Barnett, Correlli (ed.), *Hitler's Generals* (1989).
Görlitz, Walter, *History of the German General Staff* (1953).
Kleist, P., *Zwischen Hitler und Stalin, 1939–1945* (1950).
Liddell Hart, Basil H., *The German Generals Talk* (1948).
Mellenthin, F.W. von, *Panzer Battles* (1956).

Kluge, Günther von (1882–1944)

German field marshal, commander in chief west. General Günther von Kluge commanded the Fourth Army during the invasions of Poland and France, and was made a field marshal in July 1940. In 1941, his Fourth Army controlled two armored groups, spearheading Army Group Center's advance into the Soviet Union. He assumed command of Army Group Center that December and wove a sturdy defensive network against subsequent Soviet counter-assaults.

Injured in October 1943, von Kluge returned to active status in July 1944, when Adolf Hitler (q.v.) appointed him commander in chief west in the hope he could work a defensive miracle in Normandy. On 17 July, he assumed the additional command of Army Group B.

Von Kluge's initial optimism quickly faded. As his underequipped *Panzer* divisions failed in the 6 August 1944 Avranche counterattack, the German forces on the western front collapsed. On 17

Field Marshal Günther von Kluge. (IWM MH 6058)

August, Field Marshal Walther Model (q.v.) appeared with orders to relieve von Kluge. Choosing to drive back to Germany, he took poison on 19 August 1944, near Metz. In his suicide letter he professed shame over failing his mission, and ended with affirmations of loyalty to Hitler.

In fact, von Kluge knew his dismissal was connected to Hitler's distrust of him after the 20 July assassination attempt. Documents found with the conspirators showed von Kluge was aware of the plot and while refusing to participate, made no report. Hitler also suspected him of negotiating with the Allies. He preferred cyanide to a trial, but even in death, he could not violate the oath of fealty to the man he knew was the ruin of the nation he aspired to serve.

Sidney Dean

Additional Reading

Barnett, Correlli (ed.), *Hitler's Generals* (1989).
Görlitz, Walter, *History of the German General Staff* (1953).
Liddell Hart, Basil H., *The German Generals Talk* (1948).

Knox, Frank (1874–1944)

American secretary of the navy. Knox, a journalist, politician, vice presidential candidate, and Republican, was appointed secretary of the navy in July 1940 by Democratic president Franklin D. Roosevelt (q.v.) to achieve a measure of bipartisanship during World War II. Knox's experience as a politician and administrator was helpful in prosecuting the war. He was successful in modernizing the U.S. Navy and particularly in keeping the Pacific war effort supplied. He died in 1944 while still in office.

Paul J. Rose

Additional Reading

Larrabee, Eric, *Commander in Chief Franklin Delano Roosevelt: His Lieutenants and Their War* (1987).
Prange, Gordon, *Pearl Harbor: The Verdict of History* (1986).

Knox, Jean Marcia (1908–)

Director of the British Auxiliary Territorial Service. Born on 14 August 1908, the daughter of G.G. Leith-Marshall, Knox served as a nursing sister and married RAF Squadron Leader G.R.M. Knox. With the threat of war in 1938 the Auxiliary Territorial Service (ATS) (q.v.) was formed on 9 September of that year.

Mrs. Knox volunteered for military service and was commissioned as a subaltern. Because of her former service she was promoted on 29 September 1938 to the rank of senior commander (company commander), which equated to the rank of major. She was appointed senior controller (brigadier) of the service, and then on 30 May 1941, became chief controller and director (major general) of the ATS, a post she held for two years.

During that time she also served as a member of the Army Sports Control Board at the War Office, where she represented the many service women then serving in the British Army. During her two years as the chief controller she had the responsibility of increasing the strength of the service, and by September 1943 she had 212,475 service women under her command. Jean Knox was appointed Commander of the British Empire in 1943. In 1945 she married, for the second time, to Stuart Montague, Baron Swaythling, and became Lady Jean Swaythling.

Alan G. Harfleid

Additional Reading

Bidwell, Shelford, *The Women's Royal Army Corps* (1977).
Priestly, John B., *British Women Go to War* (1943).

Knudsen, William S. (1879–1948)

American lieutenant general, director of the Office of Production Management. Born in Copenhagen, Knudsen was the president of Chevrolet Motor Car Company, 1924–1937; president of General Motors Corporation, 1937–1940; director of industrial production for the National Defense Research Council (NDRC), 1940–1941; director of Office of Production Management, 1941; and from 1942 to 1945, lieutenant general in charge of production for the U.S. War Department.

Knudsen immigrated to the U.S. in 1899 and worked for the Ford Motor Company, supervising plant construction until World War I. During World War I, he supervised the construction of Eagle boats (small submarine chasers) for Ford. Appointed by President Franklin D. Roosevelt (q.v.) to the NDRC, Knudsen's organizational skills and technical background made him a success in the business world and helped to make the U.S. a success in World War II. Each of his posts (all were essentially the same job) had direct responsibility for production of armaments, supplies, and materiel. His willingness to forgo management of one of the world's largest corporations to help his adopted country fight the war was typical of the kinds of sacrifices many business people in the United States were willing to make.

John D. Beatty

Additional Reading

Fairchild, Bryon, and Jonathan Grossman, *The Army and Industrial Manpower* (1959).
Greenfield, Kent R., et al., *The Organization of Ground Combat Troops* (1947).

Koenig, Pierre (1898–1970)

French general. Before World War II Pierre Koenig served in the French Foreign Legion during the Rif campaign (1920–1926). As a captain he fought in the Norway (q.v.) campaign in 1940, and with the fall of France rallied to General Charles de Gaulle (q.v.) in London, along with several other lower-ranking officers. Koenig fought at Bir Hacheim (q.v.) in July 1942, where the Free French forces distinguished themselves in a fifteen-day holding action against repeated assaults from German General Erwin Rommel's *Afrika Korps* (qq.v.). This action, which cost a quarter of Koenig's troops, allowed the British to withdraw into Egypt.

Koenig was appointed commander in chief of the Free French forces in Britain, and following the Allied landings in Europe, he was nominated as commander in chief for the French Forces of the

Interior (*Forces Françaises de l'interieur,* or FFI). Although not taken seriously at first by the Anglo-American Allies, the FFI made a considerable contribution to the war effort by tying down substantial German forces in Brittany, and dislocating German rail transport throughout the greater part of France.

On the liberation of Paris (q.v.) in August 1944, Koenig was appointed military governor of Paris. Then, despite being the hero of Bir Hacheim, Koenig was shunted off to the relatively unimportant job of commanding the French occupation zone in Germany until 1949. Ironically, this was typical of the French Army at the end of World War II. It was the Vichy Armistice Army that provided the most of France's top postwar generals (such as de Lattre de Tassigny [q.v.]), rather than those loyal to de Gaulle, who had served in the Free French Army.

Robert C. Hudson

Additional Reading

Gaulle, Charles de, *Memoires de Guerre,* 2 vols. (1956).

Horne, Alistair, *The French Army and Politics* (1984).

Konev, Ivan Stepanovich (1897–1973)

Marshal of the Soviet Union, commander of the Soviet 1st and 2nd Ukranian Fronts (army groups). The son of farmers, Konev originally served as a draftee in the tsar's army in 1916 and was promoted for bravery under fire. He joined the Red Army in 1918 and saw considerable action in the far eastern republics. He graduated from the Frunze Military Academy in 1926. His political acumen helped him to survive the purges (q.v.) of the 1930s.

In 1942, Konev commanded the Kalinin Front in the defense of Moscow, and in 1943, he stopped the German advance at Kursk (q.v.). In late 1943 and 1944, he commanded the Steppe Front (later redesignated the 2nd Ukranian Front). During the fight to retake the Ukraine, he encircled ten German divisions at Korsun-Sevchenovsky. The Germans managed to break out, but only at a loss of some 20,000 troops. He then led the 1st Ukrainian Front in the liberation of Lwów.

In the final days of World War II, Konev's actions had more of an impact on the Western Allies. Both Konev and Georgy Zhukov (qq.v.) were in a position to strike at Berlin. Josef Stalin (q.v.), fearing the Americans would reach the city first, ordered Zhukov's force, which was closer, to press the attack. Stalin ordered Konev to drive on the Elbe River, effectively cutting the Allies off from what became East Germany. Konev then turned south, and entered Prague in May 1945.

Konev became the commander in chief of Warsaw Pact forces from 1955 to 1960, and then inspector general of the Soviet Ministry of Defense until his death in 1973.

Thomas Cagley

Additional Reading

Bialer, Seweryn (ed.), *Stalin and His Generals* (1984).

Guillaume, Augustin L., *Soviet Arms and Soviet Power: The Secret of Russian Might* (1949).

Shukman, Harold (ed.), *Stalin's Generals* (1993).

Kopański, Stanisław (1895–1976)

Polish lieutenant general, chief of the general staff, Polish army-in-exile. In 1939, Kopański was the chief of operations of the Polish Army. Between 1940 and 1942, he commanded the Independent Carpathian Rifle Brigade, taking a prominent part in the 1941 defense of Tobruk and the 1942 battle of Gazala (qq.v.). After a brief spell as commanding general of the 3rd Carpathian Rifle Division, Kopański was appointed chief of the Polish General Staff in 1943.

Andrzej Suchcitz

Additional Reading

Garliński, Józef, *Poland, S.O.E., and the Allies* (1969).

Mikołayczyk, Stanisław, *The Rape of Poland* (1947).

Kozhedub, Ivan N. (1920–1991)

Soviet ace and major general. Kozhedub was the son of a Ukrainian peasant. In 1940 he completed chemical engineering school and immediately entered the Soviet Air Force. Kozhedub graduated from the Aviation School for Pilots in 1941, and then served through the end of 1942 as a pilot instructor.

From March 1943 until the end of the war Kozhedub flew as an operational pilot assigned to the Voronezh, Steppe, 2nd Ukrainian, and 1st Byelorussian Fronts. He flew a total of 330 combat missions and scored 62 air-to-air kills, making him the leading Soviet ace of the war. He received the Hero of the Soviet Union award three times.

Kozhedub remained in the Soviet Air Force

after World War II. In 1956 he graduated from the Military Academy of the General Staff. In 1964 he was assigned as First Deputy Commander of Aviation for the Moscow Military District, with the rank of colonel general of aviation. In 1992 Kozhedub was a marshal of aviation serving as the military advisor to the group of general inspectors.

David T. Zabecki

Additional Reading
Kozhedub, Ivan N., *I Serve the Homeland* (1949).

Kramer, Josef (1906–1945)

SS commandant of Bergen-Belsen. Kramer was one of the most notorious concentration camp commandants. An early SS member, Kramer joined the concentration camp service in 1934, and served at numerous camps (including Auschwitz) prior to becoming the last commandant at Bergen-Belsen. Unrepentant and sadistic, Kramer

Bergen-Belsen Camp Commandant Josef Kramer under Allied arrest, 18 April 1945. (IWM BU 3751)

was condemned as a war criminal and executed by the Allies in November 1945.

Max Mulholland

Additional Reading
Gilbert, Martin, *The Holocaust* (1985).
Kramer, Josef, *The Trial of Josef Kramer and Forty-Four Others: The Belsen Trial* (1949).
Manvell, Roger, *S.S. and Gestapo Rule by Terror* (1969).

Krancke, Theodor (1893–1973)

German admiral. Krancke was born in Magdeburg on 3 March 1893. At the outbreak of World War II he was the chief of staff to the commander of German coastal defenses on the North Sea. In late 1940, Krancke assumed command of the *Admiral Scheer*. In that position, he also was chief of staff to the commander of German naval forces in Norway. From January 1942 to March 1943, Krancke served as the naval representative at Adolf Hitler's (q.v.) headquarters. During the Allied landings at Normandy (q.v.), Krancke commanded the German naval forces defending the coastal waters of France outside the Mediterranean. He finished the war as the commander in chief of the German naval command in Norway.

Carl O. Schuster

Additional Reading
Carell, Paul, *Invasion: They're Coming* (1964).
Ryan, Cornelius, *The Longest Day* (1964).
Showell, Jak P., *The German Navy in World War Two* (1979).

Krebs, Hans (1898–1945)

German general, last chief of the German General Staff. The son of a Hanoverian schoolmaster, Hans Krebs joined the army in September 1914 and was a regimental adjutant by war's end. He subsequently married a wine merchant's daughter and served in several line regiments. By 1930, his superior intelligence and other talents were finally recognized, and he spent the remainder of his life in staff positions, including several postings to Moscow as an assistant or deputy military attache (1933–1934, 1939, and 1941).

Colonel Krebs served two years as chief of staff in the Bavarian VII Corps. In early 1942, he was subsequently made chief of staff of the Ninth Army in the central sector of the Russian front. A year later, he became Field Marshal Günther von Kluge's (q.v.) chief of staff at Army Group Center,

K

and continued in that position under Field Marshals Ernst Busch and Walther Model (qq.v.). After Model's transfer to the western front in mid-August 1944, Krebs, now lieutenant general, followed him there as chief of staff. He thus became directly involved in the eventual stabilization of the German front and the Ardennes offensive (q.v.).

In mid-February 1945, General Krebs was assigned to the German Army high command (OKH). In March, Adolf Hitler (q.v.) chose him to succeed Colonel General Heinz Guderian (q.v.) as "interim" chief of the general staff. Although Krebs was at times depicted as a Nazi toady, he was actually a man of moderate views and highly respected by most who knew him. After Hitler's suicide, Krebs personally negotiated with General Vasily Chuikov (q.v.) regarding the surrender of Berlin's garrison. He then returned to the Chancellery bunker and shot himself.

Ulrich Trumpener

Additional Reading
Herwarth, Hans von, *Against Two Evils* (1981).
Humble, Richard, *Hitler's Generals* (1974).

Kretschmer, Otto (1912–)
German naval officer, U-Boat commander. Germany's leading U-boat ace to survive World War II, Lieutenant Commander Otto Kretschmer was born on 1 May 1912 in Ober-Heiden, Germany. The son of a schoolmaster, he was an excellent student and passed the entrance exam for naval officer's training at the age of seventeen. Too young to enter service that year, he spent the intervening twelve months studying in France and Italy before entering the naval training class of 1930. In many ways, his outside studies and studious nature proved his strongest attributes both in combat and during the postwar period.

Kretschmer believed in loyalty to the government but eschewed Nazi efforts to glorify his successes through propaganda. He was a free thinker who employed daring and innovative tactics to achieve success, becoming the first U-boat commander to sink 250,000 tons of shipping in World War II. More importantly, he had a genuine concern for the training and welfare of his men, and they adored him in return.

Kretschmer is best known for his exploits in *U-99,* the submarine he commanded at the time he was captured on 8 March 1941. Released in 1947, Kretschmer joined the new *Bundesmarine* in 1955 and rose to the rank of rear admiral before retiring in 1970. His courage and intelligence

served him well throughout his long and distinguished military career, which included a postwar tour as the chief of staff to NATO's commander, Baltic approaches.

Carl O. Schuster

Additional Reading
Frank, Wolfgang, *The Seawolves* (1964).
Hoyt, Edwin, *The Warriors* (1989).

Krupp von Bohlen und Halbach, Alfried (1907–1967)
German industrialist. The oldest son of Berta Krupp and Gustav von Bohlen und Halbach, Alfried inherited one of the largest manufacturing dynasties in central Europe. By 1943 after taking over the Brno works in Czechoslovakia, the Cruesot and Schnider works in France, and practically every other steel manufactory in occupied Europe, he had assembled by far the largest dynasty.

Krupp plants built small arms, artillery, submarines, railroad rolling stock, tanks, mines, fuzes, and heavy manufacturing equipment for Germany during the entire war. Krupp also controlled nearly every iron and coal mine in Europe, European Russia, and South America.

Alfried was found guilty by the Nuremburg tribunal of using Nazi-supplied slave labor and sentenced to ten years' imprisonment. He was restored to the directorship of the Krupp works in 1951 (after his father's death), and controlled the works until his own death. He was the last Krupp to control the business as a family concern.

John D. Beatty

Additional Reading
Homze, Edward L., *Foreign Labor in Nazi Germany* (1967).
Manchester, William, *The Arms of Krupp* (1968).

Krupp von Bohlen und Halbach, Gustav (1870–1950)
German industrialist. Gustav was the husband of Berta Krupp (the eldest of two daughters of Alfred Krupp), and was trained as a diplomat before he was matched to Berta to provide an heir for the Krupp dynasty. Gustav supported Adolf Hitler (q.v.) in his early days, as did many German industrialists, wrongfully thinking they could control him. He became disillusioned with the Nazis and by 1939, gave control of the Krupp Works to his oldest son Alfried (q.v.). One of his other four sons was killed in Russia during the war.

After his dismissal by the Nuremberg trials (*see* International Military Tribunal) and his de-Nazification, Gustav was allowed to act as caretaker for the concern from 1945 to 1950 while Alfried was in prison for using Nazi-supplied slave labor during the war.

John D. Beatty

Additional Reading
Manchester, William, *The Arms of Krupp* (1968).
Seydewitz, Max, *Civil Life in Wartime Germany: The Story of the Home Front* (1945).

Kubiliunas, Petras (1894–1946).

General and first general counselor of Lithuania. Before the war, Kubiliunas was chief of the general staff of the Lithuanian Army under General Stasys Raštikis. Imprisoned and sentenced to death for his role in a 1934 coup attempt, he was freed by the Germans and appointed to head the Lithuanian self-administration in August 1941.

Steven B. Rogers

Additional Reading
Ivinskis, Zenonas, "Lithuania During the War" in V. Stanley Vardys (ed.) *Lithuania Under the Soviets, 1940–1964* (1965), pp. 61–84.
Misiunas, Romuald J., and Rein Taagepera, *The Baltic States. Years of Dependence, 1940–1980* (1983).

Kutrzeba, Tadeusz (1886–1947)

Polish lietenant general, commander of the Polish Army "Poznann." On 9 September 1939, Kutrzeba launched his Army "Poznann" in a counteroffensive against the Germans that led to the battle of Bzura, the single largest fight of the Polish campaign. The attack, aimed against the left flank of the Eighth Army racing to Warsaw, shattered one German division. Despite initial success, Kutrzeba's forces were overwhelmed by German reinforcements. After his defeat, remnants of his army group made their way to Warsaw. From 20 to 27 September, Kutrzeba was deputy commander of Army "Warazawa." He led the surrender negotiations for the capital, and following the defeat of Poland, he was a POW until 1945.

Andrzej Suchcitz

Additional Reading
Kennedy, Robert M., *The German Campaign in Poland, 1939* (1955).
Zaloga, Steven, and Victor Madej, *The Polish Campaign 1939* (1985).

Kuznetsov, Nikolai Gerasimovich (1902–1974)

Soviet admiral of the fleet and commander in chief of the Soviet Navy. Kuznetsov was born of poor peasants and joined the Red Navy in 1919. He participated in the civil war as a sailor in the Dvina Flotilla. After the war, he attended the Naval Academy, and was appointed commander of a cruiser. During the Spanish civil war (q.v.), he was naval attache to Spain and directed Soviet volunteer sailors. From 1937 to 1939, he was deputy commander and then commander of the Pacific Fleet. Following the military purges (q.v.), he became the commissar of the navy at the age of thirty-seven, and two years later, commander in chief.

In 1941, Kuznetsov organized a series of alerts and exercises to prepare the navy for what he saw was the coming conflict. Based on the sudden departure of German ships from Soviet ports, he actually placed the fleet on combat alert before the Germans attacked, thus preventing the destructive surprise suffered by the army.

Kuznetsov enjoyed Josef Stalin's (q.v.) confidence and was a member of the *Stavka* (q.v.). Throughout the war, he mustered needed armaments and supplies to keep Soviet flotillas and fleets in combat and to provide needed shore and coastal support to both defensive and offensive operations. He took part in the Yalta and Potsdam Conferences (*see* Conferences, Allied). After the war, he fell into disfavor and was demoted, but he eventually became a deputy minister of defense in 1953.

Thomas Cagley

Additional Reading
Bialer, Seweryn (ed.), *Stalin and His Generals* (1984).
Isakov, Ivan S., *The Red Fleet in the Second World War* (1947).
Shukman, Harold (ed.), *Stalin's Generals* (1993).

L

Lacey, James H. "Ginger" (1917–1989)

Royal Air Force sergeant and pilot. The top-scoring surviving British fighter pilot of the Battle of Britain (q.v.), Sergeant J.H. Lacey was the son of a Yorkshire cattle dealer. He learned to fly in his late teens. In the summer of 1940, while serving with No. 501 Squadron, he shot down twenty-seven German aircraft, (including the He-111 that bombed Buckingham Palace). Between August and October 1940, Lacey was credited with eighteen enemy aircraft destroyed, six damaged, and four probables.

In 1941, Lacey was commissioned and served briefly with No. 501 Squadron as an officer. In 1942, he was posted to No. 602 Squadron, then transferred to non-operational postings (including India in 1943), but he did not resume operational flying until the final months of the war. In February 1945, while commanding No. 17 Squadron in Burma, Lacey shot down a Japanese fighter, his twenty-eighth and final confirmed victory.

Wes Wilson

Additional Reading

Baker, E.C.R., *The Fighter Aces of the R.A.F.: 1939–1945* (1962).

Lyall, Gavin, *The War in the Air, 1939–1945: An Anthology of Personal Experiences* (1968).

Laidoner, Johan (1884–1953)

Estonian general, commander in chief of the Estonian armed forces. Laidoner was commander in chief of the Estonian armed forces during the 1918–1920 war of independence. He remained commander in chief at the time of the Soviet invasion in June 1940. He informed his government that the army could put up a brief resistance, but only at the cost of the destruction of the nation. In July 1940, Laidoner was deported to the Soviet Union, where he died.

Andrzej Suchcitz

Additional Reading

Meiksins, Gregory, *Baltic Riddle: Finland, Estonia, Latvia, Lithuania—Key Points of European Peace* (1943).

Nodel, Emmanuel, *Estonia: Nation on the Anvil* (1963).

Suabe, Arveds, *Genocide in the Baltic States* (1952).

Langsdorff, Hans (1894–1939)

German naval captain, commanding officer of the *Graf Spee.* Langsdorff joined the Imperial German Navy in 1912 as a cadet and commissioned in 1915 at the head of his class. During World War I, he served on a variety of different surface vessels and was decorated several times for his skilled handling of minesweeping ships in combat. Langsdorff served in a variety of posts in the interwar *Reichsmarine,* and in 1938 was given the great honor of being selected as captain of the armored cruiser *Graf Spee,* then the fleet flagship. Quiet and reserved, Langsdorff was a consummately professional naval officer. Following the outbreak of hostilities in 1939, the *Graf Spee* conducted a tremendously successful commerce-raiding campaign in the South Atlantic before being run aground. Langsdorff, ashamed at his poor performance, and humiliated by his defeat in battle by a British cruiser squadron off of the Platte River (q.v.) shot himself in his hotel room in Montevideo, Uruguay, following the ordered scuttling of his ship.

Max Mulholland

Additional Reading

Hough, Richard, *Death of a Battleship* (1963).

Raeder, Erich, *Struggle for the Sea* (1959).
Rasenack, F.W., *Panzerschiff Admiral Graf Spee* (1957).

Lassen, Anders (1921–1945)

Danish commando leader. As a Danish volunteer serving with the British Eighth Army, Major Lassen led numerous successful raids against German targets in the eastern Mediterranean and in Italy. He was killed at age twenty-four while leading a diversionary attack near Lake Comacchio in northern Italy. He was the only foreigner to receive Britain's Victoria Cross during the war.

Steven B. Rogers

Additional Reading
Rying, Bent, *Denmark History: Danish in the South and North* (1981).
Werstein, Irvine, *That Denmark Might Live* (1967).

Lattre de Tassigny, Jean de (1889–1952)

French general, commander of the French First Army. Jean de Lattre de Tassigny had a fascinating politico-military career. An anti-Bolshevik before the war, with possible connections with extreme right-wing political organizations, he became a Pétainist, then a Gaullist, and he might even have had links with the Communists at the end of the war. He was an opportunist who nevertheless became the French soldier-hero of World War II and later rose to the rank of marshal.

Wounded four times in World War I and yet again during the 1920–1926 Rif campaign, de Lattre was an opponent of the popular front. He was the contact between General Maxime Weygand (q.v.) and the members of several French right-wing organizations, such as the monarchist *Camelots du Roi,* the anti-Communist *Jeunesse Patriote,* and the war veteran organization *Croix de Fer.* By September 1939, he was a general and chief of the headquarters staff of the French Fifth Army in Alsace. Between April and June 1940, he commanded the French 14th Infantry Division, acquitting himself with distinction in May 1940 by holding up the Germans for many days at Rethel on the River Aisne.

In 1941, de Lattre, now a committed Pétainist and commander of the Vichy forces in Tunisia, was transferred to the Seventeenth Military District at Montpellier. By this time, the Vichy Armistice Army had drawn completely within itself, and for want of weapons had become a hollow force.

General Jean de Lattre de Tassigny signs the Four-Power Document for France in Berlin, 5 June 1945. (IWM AP 69738)

Emphasis was placed on ideology, carrying out public works, and parading; a reflection, perhaps, of his penchant for spit and polish. Given that relatively few French Army officers left France to join the Gaullists in London, de Lattre, ever the pragmatist, was not alone in sharing the same wait-and-see attitude of other senior officers, including Weygand, Alphonse Juin, and Alphonse Georges (qq.v.). In November 1942, the Germans invaded the Vichy zone. Refusing to obey orders and stay confined to barracks, de Lattre resisted and took to the hills with several hundred men. He was the only senior commander to disobey the Vichy government. He was subsequently arrested and sentenced to ten years' imprisonment. Escaping to Algiers in September 1943, he joined the Free French cause. It was there, in French North Africa, that the future French Army was formed, even though only 10 percent of the officers were Gaullists.

De Lattre, the former Pétainist, went on to lead the French First Army in 1944. Landing at Saint-Tropez on 16 August, his army liberated Toulon, Marseilles, Lyons, Dijon, Belfort, Colmar (q.v.), and Alsace. France's top soldier at the time of the liberation, de Lattre led his victorious troops into Karlsruhe, Freiburg, Ulm, and Constance, Germany. On 8 May 1945, de Lattre was the French signatory to the German surrender in Berlin. One German general commented with acerbity: "Even the French are here." Interestingly, some historians suggested that at the end of the war, de Lattre might have momentarily flirted with French Communists and Soviet Army officers with the intention of becoming head of a French people's army.

Known affectionately to his men as "King John," de Lattre later became one of the few successful generals in the French Indochina war. He combined the roles of commander in chief of the French Expeditionary Corps as well as high commissioner in Hanoi. He was one of the few commanders ever to beat North Vietnam's General Vo Nguyên Giap on the battlefield. De Lattre returned to France and died of cancer in early 1952. On his deathbed, he was awarded his marshal's baton.

Robert C. Hudson

Additional Reading

Horne, Alistair, *The French Army and Politics, 1870–1970* (1984).

Lattre de Tassigny, Jean de, *The History of the First French Army* (1952).

Paxton, Robert O., *Parades and Politics at Vichy: The French Officer Corps Under Marshal Pétain* (1966).

Laval, Pierre (1883–1945)

Foreign minister and deputy head of state of Vichy France. Laval was prominent in international affairs in the 1930s. As foreign minister of the Third Republic, he made a secret agreement with the British to surrender Ethiopian territory to Italy. As soon as World War II started, he became convinced of a rapid and conclusive German victory. He urged that France conclude an armistice with Germany in order to establish a viable political position in Adolf Hitler's (q.v.) new Europe.

Laval was instrumental in having the national assembly vote Marshal Henri Pétain (q.v.) emergency powers, and Laval became the foreign minister and deputy head of state of the new collaborationist government established at Vichy. Laval, however, advocated a far more active form of collaboration and was dismissed by the old marshal in December 1940. Reinstated in April 1942, largely at German insistence, Laval continued to assert that France must bargain hard with Germany. The Germans used Laval to obtain better supplies of French workers for Germany and greater security for their western front, while Germany's main energies were directed against the Soviet Union.

As German difficulties in the war increased, Laval developed a wait-and-see policy toward responding to Hitler's increased demands for French assistance. He walked a political tightrope between Germany and the resistance movements and the Free French. By the beginning of 1944, civil war was rapidly unfolding throughout France. The Vichy regime was spent. Laval did not represent France, and if the Germans thought that through him they could continue gaining French assistance, they were grossly mistaken.

In August 1944, Laval was carried off by the retreating Germans. He returned to France in 1945 from Spain to stand trial for treason. Laval was sentenced to death and was shot on 15 October 1945.

Cederic Fry

Additional Reading

Thomson, *David, Pierre Laval and Charles de Gaulle* (1951).

Tissier, Pierre, *I Worked with Laval* (1942).

Warner, Geoffrey, *Pierre Laval and the Eclipse of France* (1968).

Werth, Alexander, *France, 1940–1955* (1956).

Laycock, Robert E. (1907–1968)

British major general, commando leader. Sir Robert Laycock graduated from the Royal Military College at Sandhurst in 1927 and was assigned to the Royal Horse Guards. He progressed through regimental and instructional assignments until 1939 when he was assigned to the British Expeditionary Force (BEF). After returning to Britain, he volunteered for the newly formed commandos (q.v.). He became the commander of Number 8 Commando and made his reputation as a trainer.

As lieutenant colonel in 1941, he commanded a five-commando element known as Layforce. In April 1941, he led a raid against Bardia (q.v.) (off Libya) to divert German forces in the Mediterranean. After a subsequent mission to assist in the evacuation of Crete (q.v.), Layforce was disbanded because of high casualties. In November 1941, Laycock commanded a small force in Libya with the mission of capturing German general Erwin Rommel (q.v.). The attempt failed and Laycock, one of only two survivors of the British force, successfully evaded Germans and Italians in the desert for forty-two days before he reached British lines.

Returning to Britain, Laycock became commander of the Special Service Brigade, which conducted training for all commandos. In 1943, he returned to action, leading commandos in both Sicily and Italy. In October, as Britain's youngest major general, he succeeded Lord Louis Mountbatten (q.v.) as chief of Combined Operations (q.v.), remaining in that post until 1947. In 1954, he retired as major general and later served as governor of Malta.

Steven D. Cage

Additional Reading
Ladd, James, *Commandos and Rangers of World War II* (1978).
Young, Peter, *Commando* (1969).

Leahy, William D. (1875–1959)

American fleet admiral, President Franklin D. Roosevelt's (q.v.) chief of staff. Leahy graduated from the U.S. Naval Academy at Annapolis, Maryland, in 1897 and first served during the Spanish American War. He also served in the Boxer Rebellion, the Philippines Insurrection, the Punitive Expedition in Mexico, and in various American operations in Haiti and Nicaragua. During World War I he commanded the secretary of the navy's boat, where he first met Assistant Navy Secretary Franklin D. Roosevelt. Leahy also commanded a liner that was used to trap enemy vessels.

Admiral William D. Leahy and General Henri Giraud. (IWM NY 143)

Following World War I, he commanded two cruisers and a battleship, and served as chief of navy Bureaus of Navigation and Ordnance. Promoted to flag rank in 1927, he eventually rose to the rank of admiral and served as the chief of naval operations from 1937 to 1939. After retiring from the navy, he was appointed governor of Puerto Rico by President Roosevelt. In 1941, he served as ambassador to Vichy France.

In 1942, Leahy was recalled by Roosevelt to become his chief of staff. Later that year, he became the first chairman of the new (yet informal) U.S. Joint Chiefs of Staff. In these capacities, he was privy to all major conferences and decisions of the war. In 1944, he became the U.S. Navy's first fleet (five-star) admiral. Following the death of Roosevelt, Leahy continued until 1949 to serve as chief of staff to President Harry S Truman.

Steven D. Cage

Additional Reading
Larrabee, Eric, *Commander in Chief Franklin Delano Roosevelt: His Lieutenants and Their War* (1987).
Leahy, William, *I Was There* (1950).
Pfannes, Charles E., and Victor Salamone, *The Great Admirals of World War II*, Vol. 1 (1983).

Leclerc, Philippe (1902–1947)

French lieutenant general, commander of the French 2nd Armored Division. Leclerc was a *nom de guerre* adopted to protect his family in France. His real name was Phillipe François Marie Leclerc de Hautecloque. In 1940 he was captured as a captain at Lille. He escaped, was captured again, and escaped again to join Charles de Gaulle (q.v.) in Britain. Leclerc was sent to Africa as military governor of Chad and Cameroun. In December 1942, he led a Free French force across the Sahara to join the British Eighth Army in Lybia. His force later fought in Tunisia (q.v.).

During the Normandy (q.v.) invasion, Leclerc was given command of the French 2nd Armored Division. When Paris was recaptured in August 1944, he was given the honor of being the first to enter the city, and receiving the German surrender. Later in the war, his division fought in Alsace and finally penetrated into Bavaria as far as Berchtesgaden.

In August 1945, Leclerc was sent to Indochina, where he took Hanoi and received the surrender of the Japanese. He was the French representative aboard the battleship USS *Missouri* during the Japanese surrender ceremony. In July

1946, he became inspector of French North African forces. Shortly thereafter, he was killed in a plane crash. In 1952, Leclerc was posthumously promoted to marshal of France.

Cederic Fry

Additional Reading

Deporte, A.W., *De Gaulle's Foreign Policy, 1944–46* (1968).

Maule, Henry, *Out of the Sand: The Epic Story of General Leclerc and the Fighting French* (1966).

Leeb, Wilhelm von (1876–1956)

German field marshal, commander of Army Group C (France) and Army Group North (Soviet Union). Wilhelm *Ritter* von Leeb was one of the highest-ranking generals to oppose the Nazi regime. In 1923, he commanded Bavarian artillery units that put down the Nazis in the Beer Hall *Putsch* (q.v.). As commander of army units in Bavaria when Nazis overthrew the Bavarian state government in March 1933, he asked the Defense Ministry in Berlin for permission to crush the coup, but was ordered not to get involved.

Field Marshal Wilhelm Ritter *von Leeb. (IWM GER 1271)*

A devout Catholic, von Leeb came into conflict with Nazi authorities who did not want to retain army chaplains. In January 1938, Adolf Hitler (q.v.) relieved him of his command when Werner von Blomberg and Werner von Fritsch (qq.v.) were dismissed. In March 1939, he was recalled to lead army units in the invasion of Czechoslovakia.

Because von Leeb was the German Army's leading expert on defensive strategy, he was placed in charge of forces along the West Wall to prevent a French invasion of Germany while German troops attacked Poland. As early as October 1939, he urged diplomatic negotiations to end the war. After being named commander of Army Group C for the invasion of France, he was unable to get the other army group commanders, Fedor von Bock and Gerd von Rundstedt (qq.v.), to refuse to carry out Hitler's orders. As a result, von Leeb was under constant *Gestapo* (q.v.) surveillance. During the French campaign he sealed off the French forces within the Maginot Line (q.v.). On 19 July 1940 he was promoted to field marshal.

During the invasion of the Soviet Union, von Leeb commanded Army Group North and protested Hitler's orders for the liquidation of Red Army commissars. On 20 October 1941, he was halted by Hitler's orders when he might have taken Leningrad (q.v.). With the approach of winter, von Leeb favored a withdrawal into Poland to regroup. He planned to renew the offensive the following spring, but his plans never materialized because Hitler assumed complete command of the German Army and forced von Leeb's retirement.

In 1948, von Leeb was sentenced to three years' imprisonment by the American Military Tribunals (q.v.) but was released for time served awaiting trial.

Justin D. Murphy

Additional Reading

Görlitz, Walter, *History of the German General Staff, 1657–1945* (1953).

Mitcham, Samuel W., Jr., *Hitler's Field Marshals and Their Battles* (1988).

Wheeler-Bennett, John W., *The Nemesis of Power: The German Army in Politics, 1918–1945* (1961).

Leese, Oliver W.H. (1894–1978)

British general, commander of the Eighth Army. Commissioned in the Coldstream Guards, Sir Oliver Leese fought in Flanders in World War I, and between 1918 and 1939, he advanced steadily in rank. In 1940, he was the deputy chief of staff

Lieutenant General Sir Oliver Leese, DSO, walking through Casino, 16 May 1944. (IWM NA 15096)

of the British Expeditionary Force (BEF), and was evacuated from Dunkirk (q.v.). In 1941, as a tank warfare expert, he commanded the Guards Armored Division. In 1942, at General Sir Bernard L. Montgomery's (q.v.) request, Leese took over the XXX Corps of the Eighth Army. Lieutenant General Leese led it through the El Alamein (q.v.) victory and into the Italian campaign. On Montgomery's transfer and recommendation, Leese commanded the Eighth Army in Italy from January to September 1944. Leese, however, was constantly under criticism for his leadership style, which included isolation from his subordinates and methodical slowness—apparently in emulation of his mentor.

In May 1945, Leese became the commander of Allied Land Forces, Southeast Asia. There he exercised extremely poor judgment in relieving the commander of the Fourteenth Army, General Sir William Slim, one of the best British commanders of the war. In reaction to the resulting uproar,

Leese himself was relieved and replaced with Slim in August 1945. Leese went home as commander in chief of the Eastern Command and retired in 1946.

Richard Wires

Additional Reading

Samwell, H.P., *An Infantry Officer with the Eighth Army* (1945).

Tucker, Sir Francis, *Approach to Battle: A Commentary; Eighth Army, November 1941 to May 1943* (1963).

Leigh-Mallory, Trafford (1892–1944)

British air chief marshal, commander in chief Allied air forces for Operation OVERLORD. Sir Trafford Leigh-Mallory was born at Cheshire on 11 July 1892, the son of an Anglican minister. He was educated at Magdalene College, Cambridge, and joined the army in 1914. He joined the Royal Fly-

Air Marshal Sir Trafford Leigh-Mallory, KCB, DSO and Bar, with Lieutenant General Lewis H. Brereton. (IWM EA 15106)

ing Corps in 1916 and served in France. When the Royal Air Force (RAF) was formed in 1918, he resigned from the army to accept an RAF commission. Between the two world wars, he attended the RAF Staff College and the Imperial Defence College, and served as an air instructor at the Army Staff College. After a brief posting to Iraq, he was promoted to air commodore in 1936, and air vice marshal in 1938. When World War II began, he was commanding Number 12 Fighter Group, the same command he held during the crucial months of the Battle of Britain (q.v.).

Leigh-Mallory's Number 12 Fighter Group provided air defense for Britain's industrial centers and the shipping routes of the British east coast. In early 1940, he clashed personally with the head of Fighter Command, Hugh Dowding (q.v.). Leigh-Mallory resented playing second fiddle to Keith Park's (q.v.) Number 11 Group and was an early critic of Park's strategy. He openly bragged he would see Dowding removed and had nothing but contempt for his commander. His actions bordered on insubordination and Leigh-Mallory consistently challenged Dowding's orders.

Dowding's biggest mistake was not forcing his two group commanders to reconcile their differences. Leigh-Mallory's idea was the "Big Wing" theory, promoted by air ace Douglas Bader (q.v.). The Big Wing formation called for RAF fighters to attack in large groups to mass airpower against enemy bombers. Dowding and Park resisted until Leigh-Mallory convinced the air staff of the Big

Wing's superiority. William Douglas (q.v.) replaced Dowding and Leigh-Mallory assumed control of Park's Number 11 Group in the middle of November. Historians agree that Dowding and Park won the Battle of Britain but lost the war of words with Leigh-Mallory.

For the remainder of his command of Number 11 Group, Leigh-Mallory advocated the Big Wings, and mass formation of fighters accompanying bombers—operations called "circuses." Another tactic of Fighter Command was the "rhubarb," or air sweep of massed fighters. These offensive moves against the *Luftwaffe* were only marginally effective and shifted the advantages gained by Fighter Command in the Battle of Britain. Leigh-Mallory's concepts generally sacrificed the element of surprise. While he claimed 437 German fighters destroyed and another 182 possibly lost or damaged between June and September 1941, actual losses were closer to 128 aircraft destroyed and seventy-six more damaged. Leigh-Mallory apparently saw inflated enemy losses as necessary justification for his fighter tactics.

Despite the criticisms of his air tactics, Leigh-Mallory did realize some military success. His sorties into Europe by day and night utilizing cloud cover as well as support for Arthur Harris's (q.v.) light bombers and raids on coastal France were generally a success. He also provided air support for the army and navy in the Dieppe (q.v.) raid in August, 1942.

In July 1942, Leigh-Mallory was promoted to acting air marshall, and in November, he became commander of Fighter Command. Here again he advocated an offensive posture, with an eye to the inevitable European invasion. Fighter Command under Leigh-Mallory was broadly successful, all but eliminating the sight of German aircraft near the British coast. His efforts were recognized in 1943 with the appointment as air commander in chief–designate for the invasion of Europe. Britain's tactical air forces worked closely with the U.S. Army Air Forces, and Leigh-Mallory managed the operational command of these massed units. He was knighted in 1943.

As he was during the trying months of the Battle of Britain in 1940, Leigh-Mallory remained a controversial figure. In January 1944, Air Marshal Arthur Coningham (q.v.) was appointed to command the Allied Second Tactical Air Force under Leigh-Mallory. The two clashed almost immediately and Coningham thought his new superior was out of his element and incapable of coordinating air efforts with the Americans. Leigh-Mallory also ran afoul of General Bernard L.

Montgomery (q.v.). Once the Normandy (q.v.) invasion was fully under way, he stressed the need for Montgomery to take and hold advantageous airfields, a task the British commander could not accomplish rapidly enough to satisfy Leigh-Mallory.

Montgomery initially doubted the convictions of Leigh-Mallory, whom he considered too much of a "safety first" man. As events developed, however, Montgomery's opinion appeared unwarranted. It was at Leigh-Mallory's urging that Bomber Command was first used in tactical support of ground forces. Although he clashed with Air Marshal Arthur Harris and U.S. General Carl Spaatz (q.v.), he pushed for control of all strategic aircraft supporting ground operations in France. Perhaps his greatest contribution to Operation OVERLORD was his "Transportation Plan" (q.v.), concentrated attacks on German communications in France prior to the D-Day landings. At the height of the European invasion he commanded more than 9,000 Allied aircraft.

In the November 1944, when Allied victory was in sight, Leigh-Mallory was reassigned as Allied air commander in Southeast Asia. But when he left London on 14 November with his wife, his plane was lost. Several months later their deaths were confirmed by the discovery of the aircraft wreckage in the mountains of France.

Boyd Childress

Additional Reading
Bowyer, Michael J.F., *2 Group RAF: A Complete History 1936–1945* (1974).
Bryant, Arthur, *The Turn of the Tide* (1957).
MacMillian, Norman, *The Royal Air Force in the World War* (1950).
Morgan, F.E., *Overture to Overlord* (1950).
Newton Dunn, Bill, *Big Wing: The Biography of Air Marshal Sir Trafford Leigh-Mallory, KCB, DSO, and Bar* (1992).

LeMay, Curtis E. (1906–1990)
American major general, bomber commander. Considered one of the greatest American air commanders of World War II, Curtis LeMay was bomber commander in both the European and Asian theaters. After the war, he was architect of the postwar U.S. Strategic Air Command. He was born on 15 November 1906, in Columbus, Ohio. He received a degree from Ohio State University, entered the National Guard, and eventually qualified as a military aviator.

When America entered the war, LeMay was made commander of the 305th Bomb Group, one of the first U.S. air units in Britain. In the early days of daylight bombing, bombers did not have fighter escorts. He developed defensive tactics with flights of aircraft flying at staggered heights. He led many of the raids himself. In June 1943, he was given command of the 3rd Air Division. His emphasis on tough training for his aircrews earned him the nickname "Iron Ass."

After August 1944, LeMay was transferred to the China-Burma-India Theater where he led bombing missions on Japanese targets inside China. The atomic bombing missions against Hiroshima and Nagasaki were carried out by LeMay's XX Bomber Command. After the war, he was involved in the Berlin Airlift (q.v.), built the Strategic Air Command, and finished his military career in 1964 as chief of staff of the U.S. Air Force. In 1968, LeMay was Independent candidate George Wallace's running mate in the presidential election. He was also a trustee of the National Geographic Society. He died on 1 October 1990.

Boyd Childress

Additional Reading
Coffee, Thomas E., *Iron Eagle: The Turbulent Life of General Curtis LaMay* (1986).
LeMay, Curtis, *Mission with LeMay* (1965).

Lemnitzer, Lyman L. (1899–1988)
American brigadier general, military-political officer. Known primarily as a post–World War II figure, Lemnitzer's career was energized by his World War II performance. Commissioned into the Coast Artillery in 1920 from the U.S. Military Academy, Lemnitzer progressed through normal duties and schools. After graduating from the U.S. Army War College in 1940, he was assigned to the War Department's War Plans Division. In August 1942 he went to Britain to join General Dwight D. Eisenhower's (q.v.) Allied force headquarters. There Lemnitzer worked on the final plans for Operation TORCH. In October 1942, he accompanied General Mark Clark (q.v.) on his secret mission to gain French support for the TORCH landings. Later in the war, Lemnitzer served as the commander of an antiaircraft artillery brigade, then as deputy chief of staff to General Sir Harold Alexander (q.v.).

After the war Lemnitzer commanded two divisions and eventually became army vice chief of staff (1957–1959), chief of staff (1959–1960), and chairman of the Joint Chiefs of Staff (1960–1962). He was also Allied commander in chief in the Far East (1955–1957) and supreme Allied commander, Europe (1963–1969). He held more top-level military positions than any U.S. officer before or since.

Steven D. Cage

Additional Reading

Bell, William Gardner, *Commanding Generals and Chiefs of Staff, 1775–1983* (1983).

Webb, Willard J., and Ronald Cole, *The Chairmen of the Joint Chiefs of Staff* (1989).

Léopold III (1901–1983)

King of Belgium. Léopold III succeeded his father, King Albert, in 1934. Léopold was heavily influenced by the German invasion of his country in World War I and was determined to remain neutral in the event of another Franco-German conflict. After the German remilitarization of the Rhineland (q.v.), he withdrew Belgium from its military alliance with France.

When war erupted in September 1939, Léopold rejected French and British proposals to discuss war plans for fear of giving Adolf Hitler (q.v.) a pretext to invade Belgium. When Germany invaded Belgium in May 1940 and France began to collapse, Léopold ordered his army to lay down its arms. Although he authorized his cabinet to establish a government-in-exile in London, he chose to remain in Belgium.

Léopold's popularity declined after his second marriage to a commoner. After he traveled to Berchtesgaden to gain concessions from Hitler, Belgians branded Léopold a collaborator. Opposition to him was so great that he was forced to abdicate in 1951 in favor of his eldest son, Baudouin.

Justin D. Murphy

Additional Reading

Cammaerts, Emile, *Prisoner at Laeken: King Leopold* (1941).

Goffin, Robert, *Was Leopold a Traitor?* (1941).

Goris, Johannes A. (ed.), *Belgium in Bondage* (1943).

Wright, Gordon, *The Ordeal of Total War, 1939–1945* (1970).

Ley, Robert (1890–1945)

Director of the German Labor Front *(Deutsche Arbeitsfront)*. Robert Ley, an air force veteran with a doctorate in chemistry, joined the Nazi Party in 1924. He was appointed *Gauleiter* in the Rhineland (q.v.) in 1925, and joined the Nazi representatives in the Prussian *Landestag* in 1928 and the *Reichstag* in 1930. In April 1931, he was assigned to party headquarters in Munich to provide order for the chaotic party organization. He succeeded and, in December 1932, replaced Gregor Strasser as chief of party organization.

In May 1933, Adolf Hitler (q.v.) placed Ley at the head of the German Labor Front. Ley presided over the suppression of the independent labor unions and organized the *Kraft durch Freude* (Strength through Joy) program to win the support of workers through sports, theatricals, concerts, outings, and vacations. He also promoted the production of *Kraft-durch-Freude-Wagens* (or Volkswagens) as proof of the new order's "socialization of comfort." Under his direction, the Labor Front opened three schools to prepare new leaders for the party. During the war, he directed first the recruiting and then the impressment of workers from the occupied countries for labor in Germany.

The breadth of his plans and ambitions brought him into conflict with other party leaders. At the best of times violent and uncouth, Ley's unsavoriness was accentuated by heavy drinking. Ley was captured by members of the 101st Airborne Division near Berchtesgarten on 16 May 1945. On 25 October 1945, while awaiting trial at Nuremberg, Ley hanged himself in his cell.

Bernard A. Cook

Additional Reading

Fest, Joachim, *The Face of the Third Reich* (1970).

Ley, Robert, *Wir alle helfen dem Führer* (1937).

Liddell Hart, Basil H. (1895–1970)

British military historian and theorist. Sir Basil H. Liddell Hart helped lead the fight for a mechanized army in Britain in the years before World War II. The outbreak of World War I cut short his schooling at Cambridge and he joined the army, becoming a lieutenant in the infantry in December 1914. During the Somme offensive of 1916, he was gassed and spent the rest of the war in Britain training infantrymen.

After the war, Liddell Hart began a long and distinguished writing career. In 1920, he wrote the British Army's official *Infantry Training* manual, which included his "expanding torrent" concept that evolved out of World War I German infiltration tactics. He was heavily influenced by the writing of J.F.C. Fuller (q.v.) on mechanized warfare and the use of airpower and soon became a leading advocate through his "indirect approach" aimed at dislocating the enemy and reducing the means of resistance.

Liddell Hart remained in the army until 1924

when he was mustered out due to a heart problem; he retired as a captain in 1927.

In 1925, Liddell Hart became a military correspondent for the *Daily Telegraph* and in 1935, he moved to *The Times* of London as a military advisor. Throughout the 1920s and 1930s, he published extensively on strategy and tactics and soon developed a great reputation as a military expert.

Liddell Hart's reputation brought him access to government officials. He strongly advocated a defensive strategy for Britain and spoke against raising a large army to fight in France. In 1937, Leslie Hore-Belisha (q.v.) became secretary of state for war in Neville Chamberlain's (q.v.) government, and Liddell Hart became Hore-Belisha's personal adviser. During the crucial year of 1937, Liddell Hart helped shape important British strategic decisions. However, his ideas to mechanize the army with tanks and antiaircraft forces were strongly resisted. After the German defeat of France, Liddell Hart's reputation declined dramatically, as his predictions failed to unfold and cost the British greatly in 1940. He became a correspondent for the *Daily Mail,* but his reputation suffered further as he repeatedly called for a negotiated settlement with Adolf Hitler (q.v.). During the rest of the war, he remained on the sidelines.

Liddell Hart's reputation bounced back during the 1950s, and by the 1960s, he shined again as a brilliant military thinker. He wrote extensively on military affairs as well as military theory, including infantry tactics and armored operations. During the 1950s, he criticized nuclear deterrence theory and the idea of massive retaliation. His influence also grew through the many young historians who studied and worked with him and who spread his ideas. Liddell Hart was knighted by Queen Elizabeth in 1966.

He remains a controversial figure in military history. Many criticize his actions and theories, which contributed to the British disaster at the beginning of World War II. Also, Liddell Hart actively worked to restore his reputation after the war and employed surviving German generals to help in this effort. His post–World War II writings often contradicted what he said before the war, and seemed to show him as the lone figure warning against the German danger. His great volume of research and writing established a strong reputation that was difficult to question, but recent scholarship has been chipping away at this well-known British historian and strategist.

Laura Matysel Wood

Additional Reading
Bond, Brian, *Liddell Hart: A Study of His Military Thought* (1977).
Liddell Hart, Sir Basil H., *Memoirs* (1965).
Mearsheimer, John J., *Liddell Hart and the Weight of History* (1988).

Lindemann, Frederick Alexander (Lord Cherwell) (1886–1957)

Winston S. Churchill's (q.v.) scientific advisor. Lindemann was born in Germany of a British father and American mother. He was trained in science and worked under Professor Walther Hermann Nernst of Berlin, receiving his doctorate in 1910. Exceptional work in practical and theoretical physics brought him the directorship of Oxford's Clarendon Laboratory, which he turned into an outstanding research facility.

Lindemann came to Churchill's attention in the 1920s, serving as his key scientific advisor for the rest of his life. In the mid-1930s, Lindemann backed development of radar (q.v.) and served on various committees to study ways of improving Britain's defenses. During the war, he joined Churchill as interpreter of scientific matters. "The Prof," as Churchill always called him, made significant contributions to the war effort, especially in explosives and analyzing material for the prime minister. He was stubborn, often wrong-headed, but also frequently correct, as when he showed that the RAF was exaggerating the effectiveness of mass bombing.

In 1942, Churchill brought Lindemann into the government as paymaster-general, a post he held for the duration of the war. For his services, Churchill raised Lindemann to the peerage as 1st Viscount Cherwell. Lindemann was an odd character by any measure. A bachelor, vegetarian, superb tennis player, and doggedly loyal to Churchill, he was something of a loner and an ascetic, but he had his defenders. Sir John Colville, Churchill's private secretary, called him "good company," "never boastful," and an "acquired but pleasing taste." Lindemann died in 1957.

John P. Rossi

Additional Reading
Birkenhead, Lord, *A Prof in Two Worlds* (1961).

Linton, John W. (1905–1943)

British naval commander, submarine captain. John W. Linton was born in England in 1905. A star rugby player in his earlier years, he became the commander of the submarine HMS *Pandora* in 1940, and the HMS *Turbulent* in 1941. Linton guided the HMS *Turbulent* in an aggressive manner, inflicting high casualties on the Axis. Under his command the HMS *Turbulent* destroyed more than twenty Axis vessels and 100,000 tons of shipping. Roaming the waters of the Mediterranean, the HMS *Turbulent* attacked the Italian coastline regularly. Through these coastal engagements the HMS *Turbulent* destroyed Italian trains and truck depots. Linton had great success disrupting Axis supply convoys en route to North Africa.

On 12 February 1943, the HMS *Turbulent* was sunk by the Italians. On 3 May 1943, the Admiralty officially announced that Linton and the HMS *Turbulent* were presumed lost at sea. On 25 May 1943 Linton was awarded the Victoria Cross posthumously for his actions during the war. He also held the Distinguished Service Cross and the Distinguished Service Order.

Brian J. Sullivan

Additional Reading

Casey, Robert J., *Battle Below: The War of the Submarine* (1945).
Great Britain Admiralty, *His Majesty's Submarines* (1945).

List, Wilhelm (1880–1971)

German field marshal, commander Army Group A. Born on 14 May 1880, in Oberkirchberg, Wilhelm List served with the Bavarian General Staff and in the Balkans in World War I. He entered the *Reichswehr* in 1923 and rose rapidly in rank while serving in a variety of staff and command positions. He commanded the Fourteenth Army as a colonel general in the Polish campaign, and the Twelfth Army in France. He earned his field marshal's baton in July 1940.

List commanded the German forces in the Balkan campaign, retaining that command until October 1941. From there, he went to Norway inspecting defenses before assuming command of Army Group A in southern Russia on 7 June 1942.

An underrated but effective commander, List was dismissed unfairly by Adolf Hitler (q.v.) in September 1942 for his failure to break through Soviet defenses in the Caucasus. In reality, the problem was Hitler's division of forces to go after two different objectives, Stalingrad and the Caucasus (qq.v.). List never served in a high command position again.

At Nuremberg in 1948, he was sentenced to life imprisonment. Pardoned and released in 1952, List died in Garmisch on 18 June 1971.

Carl O. Schuster

Additional Reading

Barnett, Correlli (ed.), *Hitler's Generals* (1989).
Görlitz, Walter, *History of the German General Staff* (1953).
Micham, Samuel W., Jr., *Hitler's Field Marshals and Their Battles* (1988).

Litvak, Lilly (1922?–1943)

Top-scoring female ace of World War II. In 1941, after the German invasion of the Soviet Union, the famous Soviet female aviator, Marina Raskova, organized several women's regiments for the Red Air Force. One of the volunteers was Lilly Litvak, who had learned to fly before the war at the Moscow Flying Club. After training, she was assigned to the 586th Interceptor Regiment, and then transferred to the 758th Fighter Regiment, defending Saratov north of Stalingrad. In her Yak-1, she shared victories against a German Ju-88 and several Do-17s.

In January 1943, Litvak was transferred to the 73rd Fighter Regiment of the elite Guards Air Division of the Eighth Air Army. In February, she and her friend, pilot Katya Budanova, were commissioned and awarded the Order of the Red Banner. In March, Lieutenant Litvak participated in fierce air battles in the vicinity of Belgograd, Orel, and Kharkov and was wounded. She was awarded a second Order of the Red Banner for shooting down a German observation balloon. In July, she was wounded again. Shortly afterward, she was forced to bail out when she and her wing commander were attacked by ten German Bf-109s.

On 1 August 1943, Litvak's Yak, "Yellow 44," was last seen chasing three Bf-109s. She was credited with a total of twelve victories, making her the leading woman ace of all time.

Dennis A. Bartels

Additional Reading

Lee, Asher, *The Soviet Air Force* (1950).
Myles, Bruce, *Night Witches: The Amazing Story of Russia's Women Pilots in World War II* (1995).
Wagner, Ray (ed.), *The Soviet Air Force in World War II* (1973).

Löhr, Alexander (1885–1947)

German colonel general, commander of Army

Group E. The son of an Austrian ship's captain and a Russian-born nurse, Löhr began his military career in a Hungarian infantry regiment. After service in World War I, he continued in the Austrian *Bundesheer* and eventually became commander of its aviation branch. In 1938, he transferred to the German *Luftwaffe* and a year later was appointed head of its Fourth *Luftflotte* (Air Fleet). There he participated in the Polish, Balkan, and Russian campaigns.

In 1942, Colonel General Löhr, like other veterans of the Hapsburg army, was assigned to the Balkan theater, first as commander of the Twelfth Army and then as commander in chief of Army Group E. From January to August 1943, and again from March 1945 on, Löhr and his staff, which included Lieutenant Kurt Waldheim (q.v.), constituted the top echelon of the *Wehrmacht* in southeastern Europe. During much of this period, Löhr's authority was restricted to Greece and the Aegean islands.

In 1944–1945, Löhr presided over the gradual withdrawal of German troops from the Balkan peninsula. In Yugoslav captivity from 11 May 1945, he was tried and executed in February 1947.

Ulrich Trumpener

Additional Reading

Diakow, Jaromir, *Generaloberst Alexander Löhr: Ein Lebensbild* (1964).

Douglas-Smith, Aubrey E., *Guilty Germans* (1942).

Gisevius, Hans B., *To the Bitter End* (1947).

Humble, Richard, *Hitler's Generals* (1974).

Lord Haw Haw

See JOYCE, WILLIAM

Lovat, Lord

See FRASER, SIMON

Low, David (1891–1963)

British political cartoonist. David Low was born in Dunedin, New Zealand, in April 1891. His first cartoon was published when he was only eleven years old. Early in his career he worked as a police-court sketcher. From 1911 to 1927, he worked as a political cartoonist in Australia. In 1927, he moved to London, where he worked for the *Evening Standard* until 1950.

Some critics consider Low to be the greatest English-language cartoonist of the twentieth century. His brilliant caricatures of Adolf Hitler, Benito Mussolini, Winston Churchill, Josef Stalin (qq.v.), and other world leaders made him famous. Low was an early and ardent opponent of Nazism. When Hitler became chancellor in 1933, Low's cartoons were banned in Germany. He also made enemies at home for his relentless opposition to the British government's policy of appeasement (q.v.).

Low's cartoons captured the spirit of the British people during the war, and many of those cartoons are reproduced in modern history books. He unflinchingly portrayed all sides of the British character, however, and his most famous creation was the bombastic and reactionary Colonel Blimp (q.v.).

Low had turned down a knighthood in the 1930s. He finally accepted one the year before he died. During his lifetime more than thirty collections of his drawings were published. A major retrospective of his work opened in his native New Zealand in 1996.

David T. Zabecki

Additional Reading

Seymour-Ure, Colin, and Jim Schoff, *David Low* (1985).

Lucas, John Porter (1890–1954)

American major general, commander, U.S. VI Corps. John Lucas, a native of West Virginia, graduated from the U.S. Military Academy at West Point as a cavalryman in 1911. Prior to U.S. entry into World War I, he saw service in the Philippines, and also in General John J. Pershing's 1916 expedition into northern Mexico. Lucas was wounded in action in World War I while serving as the commander of the 108th Signal Battalion.

Between the world wars, Lucas attended the Field Artillery School, the Command and General Staff College, and the Army War College. He also taught at the Artillery School, served as a Reserve Officer Training Corps instructor at several universities, commanded a variety of field artillery units, and served at the War Department in Washington, D.C.

By the start of World War II, Lucas was a major general in command of the 3rd Infantry Division. Later he succeeded Omar N. Bradley (q.v.) as commander of U.S. II Corps in Sicily, and then he commanded VI Corps in both the Salerno and Anzio (qq.v.) landings of 1943 and 1944. Because of both the vagueness of General Mark Clark's (q.v.) orders to VI Corps and Lucas's own excessive caution, the Allied force at Anzio failed to break out of its beachhead. Anzio became a bloody impasse that trapped the sorely needed VI Corps in the small pocket and, more importantly, failed to envelop the German defenses in the Liri Valley.

An introspective general and an uninspired operational commander, Lucas bore the bulk of the blame for the failure at Anzio. He was succeeded by Major General Lucian Truscott (q.v.) as VI Corps commander in May 1944. Lucas was transferred back to the United States and commanded the Fourth Army in Houston, Texas, until the war's end.

Randy Papadopoulos

Additional Reading
Blumenson, Martin, *Anzio* (1963).
———, *Salerno to Cassino* (1969).
Trevelyan, Raleigh, *Rome '44* (1981).

Ludendorff, Erich (1865–1937)

German general, political reactionary. Having served as *Quartiermeistergeneral* (Deputy Chief of Staff) of the German Army during the last two years of World War I, Erich Ludendorff played a leading role in spreading the "stab-in-the-back" myth (q.v.), which undermined the Weimar Republic (q.v.). Born at Kruszewnia (near Pozan) on 9 April 1865, Ludendorff entered the German Army in 1883. Noticed for his brilliant military mind, he was promoted to the general staff in 1895, on which he served as chief of the mobilization section from 1908 to 1913. A colonel when World War I began, Ludendorff won promotion to general officer rank after leading the successful assault on Liege (5–16 August 1914), an action for which he also received the coveted *Pour le Mérite*.

Transferred to the eastern front to serve as chief of staff for Field Marshal Paul von Hindenburg (q.v.), Ludendorff planned the great German victories at Tannenberg and Masurian Lakes in 1914. When Hindenburg became chief of staff of the German Army on 29 August 1916, Ludendorff accompanied him as his deputy, through which position he virtually controlled German political and military affairs until the end of the war. After his five spring offensives of 1918 failed, Ludendorff stunned Kaiser Wilhelm II by announcing that the war was lost and demanding the formation of a popular government that could negotiate a favorable peace with the Allies. When it became clear that the terms would

be harsh, Ludendorff reversed course and demanded a continuation of the war. When the kaiser and Chancellor Max (Prince of Baden) refused, Ludendorff resigned in protest on 26 October 1918. During the November revolution he fled to Sweden.

By his actions at the close of the war, Ludendorff not only escaped personal responsibility for Germany's surrender, but also helped establish the stab-in-the-back myth. Returning to Germany in 1919, Ludendorff joined the far-right opposition to the Weimar Republic and participated in both the Kapp *Putsch* and Adolf Hitler's Beer Hall *Putsch* (qq.v.) of 1923. By participating in the Beer Hall *Putsch,* and later standing trial alongside Hitler, Ludendorff lent considerable credibility and respectability to the Nazis early in their movement. He served as a Nazi delegate to the *Reichstag* from 1924 to 1928 and unsuccessfully challenged von Hindenburg in the presidential elections of 1925. After breaking with Hitler and the Nazis, Ludendorff spent the 1930s advocating a return to the worship of pagan Nordic gods, denouncing Freemasons, and writing his theories of total war. He died at Tutzing on 20 December 1937.

Justin Murphy

Additional Reading
Bracher, Karl Dietrich, *The German Dictatorship* (1970).
Goodspeed, D.J., *Ludendorff* (1966).
Ludendorff, Erich, *Ludendorff's Own Story* (1919).

Lütjens, Günther (1889–1941)

German admiral, commander High Seas Fleet. Lütjens was born in Wiesbaden in May 1889. A stern, determined officer, he entered the Imperial German Navy as a cadet in 1907, and spent most of his naval career in torpedo boats. His last pre–World War II position was flag officer, torpedo boats, from October 1937 to October 1939. From there he was promoted to admiral and made commander in chief, reconnaissance forces on 1 January 1940.

On 9 July 1940, Lütjens replaced Admiral Wilhelm Marschall (q.v.) as fleet commander and was posted aboard the battleship *Bismarck* (q.v.). Determined not to repeat Admiral Marschall's mistakes as fleet commander, Lütjens communicated frequently with naval headquarters during the *Bismarck* sortie in May 1941. Ultimately, that may have been the most critical factor in his death

Admiral Günther Lütjens. (IWM MH 6067)

because it enabled Allied forces to track down the *Bismarck* and destroy it on 27 May 1941.

Carl O. Schuster

Additional Reading

Diamond, Walker Dew, *Memoirs of Ships and Men* (1964).

Hildebrand, Hans H., and Ernst Henriot, *Deutschlands Admirale 1849–1945* (1989).

Masters, David, *In Peril on the Seas: War Exploits of Allied Seamen* (1960).

Lutze, Viktor (1890–1943)

Chief of staff of the SA. Viktor Lutze was born in Bevergen, Westphalia, on 28 December 1890. In World War I, he served in Infantry Regiment 369 and Reserve Infantry Regiment 15 of the German Army, was wounded, and decorated with the Iron Cross, First and Second Class.

In 1922, Lutze joined the Nazi Party and served in the SA (q.v.). After Adolf Hitler (q.v.) came to power in 1933, Lutze, a high-ranking SA commander, was appointed police president of Hanover. In March 1934, he was elevated to prefect of Hanover. He remained loyal to Hitler during the "Night of the Long Knives" (q.v.), the June 1934 purge of the SA. He took part in the arrest of key SA leaders.

As a reward for his loyalty, Hitler appointed Lutze chief of staff of the SA, succeeding the executed Ernst Röhm (q.v.). Lutze was responsible for holding the SA together after the 1934 purges. He remained SA chief of staff until his death. In May 1943, Lutze and his daughter were killed in an accident. He was succeeded by Wilhelm Schepmann as SA chief of staff.

Stephen L. Frost

Additional Reading

Fest, Joachim, *The Face of the Third Reich* (1970).

Gallo, Max, *The Night of the Long Knives* (1972).

Lynn, Vera Margaret (1917–)

British entertainer. Vera Lynn was born on 20 March 1917, the daughter of a plumber from East Ham. She first performed as a singer in 1924 and sang with the Ambrose Orchestra from 1937 to 1940. In 1939 she was named the "Forces Sweetheart," and from 1941 to 1947 she broadcast her own radio show, *Sincerely Yours*. During the war years she was a tireless entertainer of British troops throughout the world. Her signature song was *We'll Meet Again*. She is perhaps best remembered for popularizing *The White Cliffs of Dover*, which became one of the Allied anthems of the era and enjoyed great popularity with American audiences.

Vera Lynn was awarded the Order of the British Empire in 1969. In 1975, she was created a Dame of the British Empire for her charitable work and long association with the entertainment business.

Alan Harfield

Additional Reading

Lynn, Vera, *We'll Meet Again* (1989).

M

McAfee, Mildred (1900–)

American naval captain, director of the WAVES. In August 1942, Mildred McAfee was in her sixth year as president of Wellesley College when she accepted a commission as lieutenant commander in the U.S. Navy Reserve (USNR) and became director of the WAVES (q.v.). From nothing she built the WAVES into a force of 86,000 officers and enlisted women, performing all types of jobs previously considered unsuitable for women.

They undertook those jobs both inside and outside of the United States. In 1943, McAfee pressured Congress to pass a law making WAVES eligible for all benefits and allowances available to U.S. Navy men. In November 1943, she became the first woman to hold the rank of captain in the U.S. Navy. In all, some 150,000 women served in the WAVES during the war. Captain McAfee left the navy in February 1946 and returned to the academic world.

Charles H. Bogart

Additional Reading
Mason, John T., *The Atlantic War Remembered* (1990).
Ross, Mary S., *American Women in Uniform* (1943).

McAuliffe, Anthony C. (1898–1975)

American brigadier general, assistant division commander 101st Airborne Division. McAuliffe was born in Washington, D.C., and graduated from the U.S. Military Academy at West Point in 1918. Trained as an artillery officer, he was a reliable and resourceful officer. His principal wartime service was with the 101st Airborne Division.

The 101st was commanded by Maxwell Taylor (q.v.), with Gerald Higgins as assistant division commander. McAuliffe was the divisional artillery commander and parachuted into Normandy (q.v.) during the D-Day invasion. Subsequently, the 101st participated in action in Holland and then was assigned in a less active sector in the Ardennes. In December 1944, Taylor was called to Washington on a special mission, and Higgins was in Britain attending a series of lectures on lessons learned

Major General Anthony B. McAuliffe and General Maurice Gamelin in Austria at the end of the war. (IWM KY 66092)

in the Holland action. Thus McAuliffe was in temporary command of the 101st at Bastogne when the Germans launched the Ardennes offensive (q.v.). When the 101st became surrounded, McAuliffe received the German surrender ultimatum and became famous for his succinct but poignant answer: "Nuts!"

McAuliffe had more than sheer bravado backing up his curt answer. First, airborne soldiers and units were trained to operate behind enemy lines; thus being surrounded by the enemy was the operational norm. Second, Allied intelligence was convinced that the Germans did not have the forces left to sustain attacks. McAuliffe and his staff believed that with sufficient airdropped supplies, they could hold out.

Following the relief of the 101st Airborne Division, McAuliffe was awarded the Distinguished Service Cross, promoted to major general, and given command of the 103rd Infantry Division. After the war, McAuliffe served in a variety of assignments until his retirement in Washington, D.C., were he lived until his death in 1975.

Thomas Cagley

Additional Reading
Marshall, S.L.A., *Bastogne* (1946).
Pallud, Jean Paul, *The Battle of the Bulge: Then and Now* (1984).
Weigley, Russell F., *Eisenhower's Lieutenants* (1980).

McCreery, Richard (1898–1967)
British general, commander of the Eighth Army, 1944–1945. Although trained as an old-fashioned cavalry man, Sir Richard McCreery fully understood modern armored tactics. The fortunes of war, however, denied him the chance of displaying this talent to the fullest. Educated at Eton and Sandhurst, he was commissioned into the 12th Lancers in 1915. He served in France during World War I, was wounded, and was awarded a Military Cross. Apart from attending the Staff College, he spent the interwar years with his regiment.

For his command of a mechanized brigade during the retreat to Dunkirk (q.v.), McCreery was awarded the DSO. After two years commanding an armored division in Britain, he went to the Middle East as chief of staff to Harold Alexander (q.v.). There, remote from the action, he had no chance to shine, but he was observed closely. In 1959, he wrote an article that aroused great interest and controversy by criticizing General Bernard Montgomery's handling of armor at El Alamein (qq.v.) and his subsequent pursuit of General Erwin Rommel (q.v.).

In 1943, McCreery took over British X Corps, commanding it in the slugging match at Salerno (q.v.) and in the slow advance through Italy—a series of infantry battles in difficult terrain and not a theater where he could make use of his flair for modern armored warfare.

In November 1944, he took command of the Eighth Army for the final stage of its epic march from Egypt to Austria. At the end of the war, he became commander of British troops in Austria. There he inevitably was involved in the political complications caused by the ending of World War II and the repatriation of alleged Nazi collaborators to Yugoslavia and the Soviet Union. McCreery's last military assignment was commander in chief of the British Army of the Rhine from 1946 to 1948.

Philip Green

Additional Reading
Linklater, Eric, *The Campaign in Italy* (1951).
Samwell, H.P., *An Infantry Officer with the Eighth Army* (1945).
Tucker, Sir Francis (IS), *An Approach to Battle: A Commentary: Eighth Army, November 1941 to May 1943* (1963).

McGrigor, Rhoderick (1893–1959)
British rear admiral, commander of the 1st Cruiser Squadron. McGrigor commanded the battle cruiser HMS *Renown* of Force H protecting the Malta convoys (q.v.) and took part in the pursuit of the *Bismarck* (q.v.). From 1941 to 1943, he was assistant chief of the naval staff (weapons). In 1943, he commanded the naval assault on the island of Pantellaria, and the assault force on BARK SOUTH Beach in the invasion of Sicily (q.v.).

In March 1944, he commanded 1st Cruiser Squadron and aircraft carriers of the Home Fleet, carrying out convoy duties in the Arctic and successfully harassing enemy shipping in the North Sea. In one sortie, his forces destroyed ten ships of an eleven-ship enemy convoy.

Andrzej Suchcitz

Additional Reading
Batimeus (pseud.), *East of Malta, West of Suez: The Official Admiralty Account of the Mediterranean Fleet, 1939–1943* (1944).
Belot, Raymond de, *The Struggle for the Mediterranean, 1939–1945* (1951).

McIndoe, Archibald Hector (1900–1960)

Pioneering British plastic surgeon. Sir Archibald McIndoe was born in Dunedin, New Zealand, on 4 May 1900. He was educated at Otago High School and University, qualifying in 1924 and winning the junior medicine and senior clinical surgery prizes. He left for the United States to continue his career at the Mayo Clinic where he was considered one of the most promising surgeons. He arrived in Britain in 1930 and specialized in abdominal surgery before moving on and adapting his skills to the meticulous requirements of plastic surgery. In 1932, he was appointed a general surgeon to the Hospital of Tropical Diseases.

At the time of the outbreak of war, in 1939, McIndoe was already a plastic surgeon of great promise and was appointed as a consultant in plastic surgery to the Royal Air Force. He also became involved in treating casualties with facial injuries and burns from London air raids. He built up the tiny Queen Victoria Hospital to become a model for the treatment and care of RAF personnel who had been severely burned. Not only did he act as their specialist but fought to get the injured better pay and conditions until they were rehabilitated. He refused to be "put into uniform" because as a civilian, he was able to go directly to the air staff without having to go through channels.

McIndoe was a first-class surgeon and a superb administrator, which, added to his powerful personality, made him the ideal man for the difficult task he had to carry out. He was appointed Commander of the British Empire in 1944 and knighted in 1947. He died in London on 12 April 1960, and his ashes were buried in the RAF Church of St. Clement Danes, in the Strand—a rare honor for a civilian doctor, but one highly regarded by his combatant colleagues.

Alan G. Harfield

Additional Reading

McLeave, Hugh, *McIndoe: Plastic Surgeon* (1962).
Mosley, Leonard, *Faces from the Fire* (1962).

McLain, Raymond Stallings (1890–1954)

American major general, commander US XIX Corps. Raymond McLain grew up in Oklahoma and joined the state's National Guard as an enlisted man in 1912. Commissioned a lieutenant of infantry in the guard in 1914, McLain was called to active duty on the Mexican border in 1916 and then again for World War I in 1917. In World War I, he commanded a machine gun company of the 36th Infantry Division in both the Champagne-Marne and Meuse-Argonne battles.

After the armistice, McLain left the military and returned to his banking career. In 1921, he returned to duty with the Oklahoma guard as the operations officer in the 179th Infantry Regiment, and later operations officer in the 45th Infantry Division. McLain attended the U.S. Army Command and General Staff College in 1938, and continued to serve with the Oklahoma National Guard until the outbreak of World War II.

During World War II, Brigadier General McLain served as divisional artillery commander of the 45th Infantry Division in Sicily (q.v.) and Italy, including the Anzio (q.v.) landings. In April 1944, he transferred to the 30th Infantry Division. After the Normandy (q.v.) landings he commanded the 90th Infantry Division, winning the Distinguished Service Cross. In October 1944, he assumed command of XIX Corps. His forces crossed the Elbe River at Magdeburg just prior to war's end.

After World War II, McLain remained in the army, serving as comptroller of the Department of the Army, and retiring as a lieutenant general in 1953. He was one of the few National Guard officers to command a division and the only one to command a corps in World War II.

Randy Papadopoulos

Additional Reading

Robinson, Don, *News of the Forty-Fifth* (1946).

McNair, Lesley James (1883–1944)

American general, commander, U.S. Army Ground Forces. A native of Minnesota, "Whitney" McNair attended the U.S. Military Academy at West Point and graduated as an artillery officer in 1904. His assignments prior to World War I included a variety of positions of the Ordnance Corps and a period as an observer of French artillery techniques. He served in the 1914 expedition to Vera Cruz and with General John J. Pershing in northern Mexico in 1916. In 1917, McNair was a major with the 1st Division of the American Expeditionary Force (AEF) in France. He acquired the reputation as a highly talented gunner, developing techniques for infantry-artillery cooperation. He was promoted to temporary brigadier general at age thirty-five, the youngest general officer in the AEF.

Following World War I, McNair reverted to his permanent rank of major. He served as an instructor at the General Service School and then as a professor of military science and tactics at Purdue University. After completing the Army War College in 1929, McNair served at the Field Artillery School, with the Civilian Conservation Corps, as commandant of the Command and General Staff College at Fort Leavenworth, and as chief of staff of Army General Headquarters in Washington, D.C.

In the use of armor in warfare, McNair regarded tanks as simply mechanized cavalry that could only pursue and exploit a defeated enemy. He assigned little value to using tanks in an assault, and preferred the more traditional infantry-artillery team. Nevertheless, he was instrumental in beginning the reform of the Command and General Staff College, a process that made it the crucial educational institution for senior American officers in World War II.

In March 1942, Lieutenant General McNair assumed command of Army Ground Forces. He supervised the mobilization and training of the rapidly growing United States Army during World War II. Given the gigantic task of integrating personnel of the Regular Army, National Guard, Army Reserve and conscripts, McNair controlled the activities of the many schools and training facilities in the United States. At their peak strength, these facilities trained more than 1.5 million soldiers at a time.

Although holding largely administrative positions throughout the war, McNair took every opportunity to get up to the front to see for himself. In Tunisia (q.v.) in 1943 he was wounded by an enemy artillery shell. He continually pushed his boss, General George C. Marshall (q.v.) to let him have a field command. In June 1944, McNair relinquished command of Army Ground Forces and went to Britain as commander of the nonexistent and diversionary 1st Army Group. On 25 July, he was at the front with the 30th Infantry Division, observing the preparation for the St. Lô (q.v.) breakout, when U.S. Army Air Force bombs accidentally fell on their positions, killing McNair. Some weeks later, his son, an artillery colonel, was killed in action in the Pacific. Lesley McNair was the highest-ranking American officer ever killed in action. In 1945, he was promoted posthumously to the grade of full general, the only American officer to receive such a distinction.

McNair deserves great credit for building the United States Army into the force instrumental in defeating the Axis powers. Appropriately dubbed "the maker of armies" by his chief of staff, James G. Christiansen, McNair turned the small constabulary force of the 1930s into the most powerful American military force ever.

Randy Papadopoulos

Additional Reading

Greenfield, Kent R., Robert R. Palmer, and Bell I. Wiley, *The Organization of Ground Combat Troops* (1947).

Kahn, E.J., Jr., *McNair: Educator of an Army* (1945).

Palmer, Robert R., Bell I. Wiley, and William R. Keast, *The Procurement and Training of Ground Combat Troops* (1948).

McNaughton, Andrew G.L. (1887–1966)

Canadian general. McNaughton was an electrical engineer who as a Royal Canadian Artillery officer in World War I pioneered scientific techniques in gunnery. He remained in the Canadian Army after the war, and in 1929, he became the chief of the Canadian General Staff. In 1935 he became president of the National Research Council.

McNaughton was commander in chief of Canadian troops in Europe from December 1939 to December 1943. He fought hard to keep his Canadian forces together, and protested the piecemeal assignment of some Canadian units to the Italian campaign. His position was not supported by the Canadian minister of national defence, Layton Ralston. McNaughton later resigned when British chief of the Imperial General Staff, General

General Andrew McNaughton (left) with Field Marshal Lord Gort, VC, GCB, DSO and 2 Bars. France, 1940. (IWM HU 69236)

Sir Alan Brooke (q.v.), decided he was unsuitable for a field command.

McNaughton returned to Canada and retired from the army in October 1944. The following month he became minister of national defence in the cabinet of Prime Minister Mackenzie King (q.v.). Despite his best efforts, Canada was forced to introduce limited conscription, and McNaughton was blamed by Canadian voters. He was forced to resign from the cabinet in August 1945.

David T. Zabecki

Additional Reading
Nicholson, G.W.L., *The Gunners of Canada* (1967).
Stacey, C.P., *The Canadian Army, 1939–1945: An Official Historical Summary* (1948).

Mackensen, Eberhard von (1889–1969)
German colonel general, commander of the First *Panzer* and Fourteenth Armies. The son of a famous Prussian field marshal, Eberhard von Mackensen was commissioned in the cavalry in 1908, and eventually became a general staff officer. At the beginning of World War II, he served as chief of staff to General Wilhelm List (q.v.).

In January 1941, von Mackensen was made commander of III Corps. He led III Corps in the Ukraine and the Caucasus (q.v.) until November 1942. During the next eleven months, he led the First *Panzer* Army back to the Dnieper River. He was then sent to Italy to take charge of the newly created Fourteenth Army. After containing the Allies for more than four months in the Anzio (q.v.) beachhead, he was blamed for German setbacks and the fall of Rome and lost his command on 5 June 1944.

After the war, Colonel General von Mackensen was sentenced to death in connection with the Ardeatine Caves massacre (q.v.), but the penalty was subsequently commuted to life imprisonment. He was released from Werl Prison in October 1952.

Ulrich Trumpener

Additional Reading
Mackensen, Eberhard von, *Vom Bug zum Kaukasus: Das III. Panzerkorps im Feldzug gegen Sowjetrussland 1941–42* (1967).
Ziemke, Earl F., *Stalingrad to Berlin: The German Defeat in the East* (1968).

Maczek, Stanisław (1892–1994)
Polish lieutenant general, commander of the Pol-

ish 1st Armored Division. During the Polish campaign, Maczek was commander of the Polish 10th Motorized Cavalry Brigade and fought against General Paul von Kleist's (q.v.) XXII *Panzer Korps.* In France in 1940, Maczek commanded a motorized brigade at the battle of Montbard. During the fighting in northwest Europe in 1944–1945, he led the Polish 1st Armored Division, attached to the Canadian First Army. It was Maczek's units that finally closed the Falaise (q.v.) gap on 20 August 1944. He went on to liberate Breda in October 1944. In May 1945, his division occupied the German naval base at Wilhelmshaven.

Andrzej Suchcitz

Additional Reading
Keegan, John, *Six Armies in Normandy* (1982).
Mikolayczyk, Stanisław, *The Rape of Poland* (1947).

Mae, Hjalmar (1901–1978)
First director of the Estonian County Directorate. Dr. Hjalmar Mae participated in a failed pro-Fascist Estonian coup in 1935 and was imprisoned. In 1938, he contacted the Germans concerning future relations should the Fascists assume power in Estonia. The Germans appointed Mae to head the Estonian "self-administration" in September 1941. He was decidedly more pro-German than his Latvian and Lithuanian counterparts.

Steven B. Rogers

Additional Reading
Misiunas, Romuald J., and Rein Taagepera, *The Baltic States: Years of Dependence, 1940–1980* (1983).
Nodel, Emanuel, *Estonia: Nation on the Anvil* (1963).

Maginot, André (1877–1932)
French minister of war, established the Maginot Line. Maginot was one of the primary sponsors of the Maginot Line (q.v.) and the doctrine of defensive tactics adopted by the French military in the interwar years. Maginot served as an infantry private during World War I, and he rose to the rank of sergeant and lost a leg at Verdun. Since he personally knew the horrors of blood, mud, and barbed wire, he hoped the massive defensive line would prevent heavy losses in any future conflict. Maginot's very name became a symbol of the belief in the elaborate fixed defenses.

Cederic Fry

Additional Reading

Beaufre, André, *1940: The Fall of France* (1967).

Goutard, Adolphe, *The Battle of France, 1940* (1958).

Rowe, Vivian, *The Great Wall of France: The Triumph of the Maginot Line* (1959).

Malenkov, Georgy Maksimilianovich (1902–1983)

Political commissar, member of the Soviet State Defense Committee. Malenkov was born into a middle-class family and actively participated in the revolution. His early years centered on political activism, including service in the Red Army during the civil war. He served in several different military units, but always as a political worker, rather than a military leader.

Malenkov rose rapidly to positions of trust and influence. He was a confidant of Josef Stalin's (q.v.) and was in charge of carrying out the purges during the 1930s in Byelorussia and Armenia. During World War II, Malenkov was a member of Stalin's five-member State Defense Committee. He was responsible for supplying the Soviet Army with equipment and the Soviet Air Force with aircraft and engines. During the first years of the war, he was also political commissar on a number of different Fronts (army groups). From 1943 to 1945, he was the chairman of the Committee for the Restoration of the Economy.

After the war, Malenkov became deputy chairman of the Council of Ministers. He briefly took power after Stalin's death, but was ousted by Nikita Khrushchev (q.v.).

Thomas Cagley

Additional Reading

Snow, Edgar, *The Pattern of Soviet Power* (1945).

Werth, Alexander, *Russia At War, 1941–1945* (1964).

Malinovsky, Rodion Yakovlevich (1898–1967)

Marshal of the Soviet Union, commander of the Soviet 2nd and 3rd Ukrainian Fronts (army groups). Malinovsky was a soldier in the tsarist army and joined the Red Army in 1919. He joined the Communist Party in 1926 and attended the Frunze Military Academy. He was also a military advisor during the Spanish civil war (q.v.). After two years in Spain, he returned to Frunze as an instructor. On the eve of World War II, he was the commander of the XLVIII Rifle Corps on the Romanian border.

Malinkovsky's first assignment in the war was commander of the Sixth Army in the Ukraine. In December 1941, he took command of the South-western Front. One year later, at Stalingrad (q.v.), he prevented Erich von Manstein (q.v.) from reaching the encircled German Sixth Army. When the Soviets went on the offensive in 1943, he commanded the 3rd Ukrainian Front. On line with Ivan Konev and Georgy Zhukov (qq.v.), they swept across the Ukraine from south to north, driving the Germans from the Ukraine and sealing off the Crimea (q.v.).

After securing the Black Sea Coast, Malinkovsky, then in command of the 2nd Ukrainian Front, drove first into Romania and then into Hungary. He took Budapest (q.v.) in February 1945, and liberated Slovakia that April. His forces gained a reputation for ruthless and savage behavior, particularly in Hungary. After his men captured Budapest, they went on a binge of rape and plunder.

After the defeat of Germany, Malinovsky was sent to Manchuria, where he participated in the waning days of the war against Japan. In 1957, he became the Soviet minister of defense.

Thomas Cagley

Additional Reading

Bialer, Seweryn (ed.), *Stalin and His Generals* (1984).

Kerr, Walter B., *The Russian Army: Its Men, Its Leaders, and Its Battles* (1944).

Shukman, Harold (ed.), *Stalin's Generals* (1993).

Malraux, Georges André (1901–1976)

French resistance leader, writer. During the Spanish civil war (q.v.) (which served as the setting for his novel, *Man's Hope*), Malraux organized an international air squadron. In 1940 he served in the French tank corps. He was captured, escaped from a German prisoner-of-war camp, and joined the underground in 1943. Malraux was the commander of a French underground unit in the Correze. Using the *nom de guerre* "Colonel Berger," he also led a brigade in Alsace-Lorraine during the last few months of the war. He served as Charles de Gaulle's (q.v.) propaganda chief from 1945 to 1946. A noted novelist as well as an avid collector and connoisseur of art, Malraux was French minister of cultural affairs under de Gaulle from 1958 to 1968.

L. Lee Baker

Additional Reading

Hewitt, James, *André Malraux* (1978).

Malraux, André, *Anti-Memoirs* (1968).

Mannerheim, Carl Gustav Emil (1867–1951)

Finnish field marshal, commander of the Finnish armed forces. As an officer of the Imperial Russian Army, Mannerheim served as lieutenant colonel in the Russo-Japanese War and as general in the 12th Cavalry Division in World War I. After the Bolshevik Revolution of 1917, he returned to his native Finland were he led the local "Whites" to victory in the Finnish civil war (January–May 1918) and later served as the regent of Finland (November 1918–July 1919).

In 1931, Marshal Mannerheim became supreme commander of the Finnish armed forces. Between 1939 and 1944, he led the Finns in two different wars against the Soviet Union. First, in the famous Winter War (q.v.) of 1939–1940, Mannerheim's forces successfully held back the advances of more numerous Soviets. For four months, the Finns caused Josef Stalin considerable embarrassment by revealing Red Army weaknesses.

From 1941 to 1944, Mannerheim led the Finnish Army in a second war against the Soviets, known as the Continuation War. Although collaborating in Germany's Operation BARBAROSSA, Mannerheim insisted his army was fighting a separate war and was merely a cobelligerent of Germany. Accordingly, after a rapid advance on the ports of Leningrad in the fall of 1941, Mannerheim rejected a combined Finno-German attack against the city itself. In 1943, he argued in favor of a separate peace agreement between Finland and the Soviet Union.

As a politician, his antipathies toward Germany and connections to many Western leaders were well-known. Mannerheim was elected president of Finland in 1944. He quickly led the Finns out of the war, and a separate peace treaty between Finland and the Soviet Union was signed in Moscow in September 1944. As part of that treaty, the Finns drove the German forces out of northern Finland in the 1944–1945 War of Lapland (q.v.).

Mannerheim was a master of defensive warfare. His performance during World War II, especially in the Winter War, catapulted him to the status of national hero in Finland. He resigned from public life in 1946, and spent his remaining years in Switzerland where he died in Lausanne on 28 January 1951.

Jussi Hanhimaki

Additional Reading

Condon, Richard W., *The Winter War: Russia Against Finland* (1972).
Erfurt, W., *Der Finnische Krieg, 1941–1944* (1950).
Jagerskiold, Stig, *Mannerheim: Marshal of Finland* (1986).
Mannerheim, Carl, *The Memoirs of Marshal Mannerheim* (1954).

Manstein, Erich von (1887–1973)

German field marshal, commander of Army Group South. Erich von Lewinski was born in Berlin on 24 November 1887. An aunt, Frau von Manstein, adopted him at an early age. Young von Manstein entered the Royal Prussian Cadet Corps in 1900. At age twenty, he received a commission in the 3rd Foot Guards. The future field marshal had an unspectacular career in World War I, serving at the Masurian Lakes in 1914, Poland and Serbia in 1915, and Verdun in 1916 in both line and staff positions.

In 1929, von Manstein became a general staff officer. As colonel and chief of staff of Military District III in 1934, he was ordered to dismiss Jewish officers serving under him. He refused to obey, and in fact openly criticized the high command for cowardice by surrendering to the Nazis. General Werner von Fritsch (q.v.), commander in chief of the army, protected his promising young staff officer.

As a major general, von Manstein left von Fritsch in 1938 to command the 18th Infantry Division. That same year, he was chief of staff to General Wilhelm von Leeb's (q.v.) army during the occupation of Czechoslovakia. During the Polish campaign, he served as chief of staff to General Gerd von Rundstedt's (q.v.) Army Group South. By the second week of the war, von Manstein had masterminded the decisive battle of the campaign at the Bzura River. By turning the *Panzer* divisions away from Warsaw, nine divisions of Army Poznan (one-quarter of the Polish Army) were encircled.

That autumn and winter saw von Manstein with von Rundstedt's army group preparing for the invasion of Western Europe. With General Heinz Guderian (q.v.), von Manstein planned the brilliant *Sichelschnitt* (sickle cut) maneuver, the war-winning alternative to the unimaginative repetition of the Schlieffen Plan (q.v.) of World War I. The army high command stifled this plan until one of Hitler's personal adjutants brought it to the *Führer's* attention. After discussing the plan with von Manstein, Hitler ordered the adoption of the plan the next day. Von Manstein was given command of the XXXVIII Corps during the subsequent campaign.

During Operation BARBAROSSA, von Manstein led the LVI Panzer Corps, part of the

Field Marshal Erich von Manstein in the Crimea, talking with Colonel (later Lieutenant General) Dietrich von Choltitz. (IWM MH 2104)

Fourth *Panzer* Group, which sliced through the Baltic states. Despite starting very fast and capturing the Dvina River bridges intact at Dvinsk, he indecisively halted his corps at that city "waiting for orders." This mistake contributed directly to the Germans' failure to take Leningrad (q.v.).

In September 1941, von Manstein took over the Eleventh Army fighting in the Crimea (q.v.). After a nine-month seesaw battle, the Germans prevailed. His forces captured the fortress of Sevastopol (q.v.) and 100,000 Soviet troops on 3 July 1942. Hitler promoted him to field marshal the same day.

As part of the general German defensive following Soviet Operation URANUS in late 1942, von Manstein commanded Army Group Don. Holding in some places while counterattacking in others with General Hermann Hoth (q.v.), von Manstein tried in vain to relieve his comrades encircled at Stalingrad (q.v.). His masterful withdrawal from the Caucasus (q.v.) that winter thwarted a Soviet attempt to trap the First *Panzer* Army.

In the spring of 1943, the Soviets sought to finish off Army Group South. They achieved a deep penetration and took Kharkov (q.v.) but in the end suffered a significant setback. During this time, Hitler gave von Manstein a degree of operational freedom unheard of at this late stage in the war. Executing his "Backhand Blow" maneuver, he proved the value of husbanding reserves, sidestepping the enemy, then hitting him at the right moment. He also demonstrated the importance of mobility when defending against the Soviets. All these lessons, however, were lost on the *Führer*.

During the ill-fated Operation CITADEL (launched over the objections of von Manstein and others), he led the southern pincer. Throughout the remainder of 1943, Army Group South fought westward from the Don, to the Dnieper River, to the western Ukraine. Shackled by orders from above, the army group never retreated when sound military doctrine dictated. Von Manstein was given permission to move only when it was too late, when forced to do so by the enemy, or when actually falling back. By early 1944, Hitler lost faith in his abilities and dedication, and on 30 March, he replaced von Manstein with Field Marshal Walther Model (q.v.).

Von Manstein retired to his estate, and at the end of the war, he surrendered to the British Army. He went on trial for war crimes in mid-1949, and was tried on seventeen charges, including making war and following the Commissar Order (q.v.). In 1951, the British convicted him of less than one-half of these charges, and sentenced him to eighteen years' imprisonment. They released him after two and one half years. Historian Basil H. Liddell Hart (q.v.) called von Manstein "the ablest of the German generals."

Robert Kirchubel

Additional Reading

Barnett, Correlli (ed.), *Hitler's Generals* (1989).
Manstein, Erich von, *Lost Victories* (1958).
Mellinthin, F.W. von, *German Generals of World War Two: As I Saw Them* (1977).
Mitcham, Samuel W., Jr., *Hitler's Field Marshals and Their Battles* (1988).

Manteuffel, Hasso Eccard von (1897–1978)

German general, commander Third and Fifth *Panzer* Armies. Born in Potsdam of an old, aristocratic, and famous Prussian military family, the aggressive "Little *Panzer* General" was among Germany's best field commanders. Never intimidated by Adolf Hitler (q.v.), Manteuffel often appeared personally before him, giving Hitler realistic briefings without regard for the *Führer's* wrath at hearing the unpleasant truth.

Short in stature and slight in build, *Freiherr* von Manteuffel was nonetheless an Olympic equestrian athlete. He saw action as a cavalry officer in France in 1916–1918. He remained in the regular army during the Weimar Republic. In 1934, he transferred to the *Panzer* troops, later holding a variety of staff and inspectorate positions under General Heinz Guderian (q.v.). Manteuffel distinguished himself as a battalion and regimental commander in the 7th *Panzer* Division during Operation BARBAROSSA in 1941. In November, he brought his *Kampfgruppe* to within twenty-two miles of Moscow (q.v.), and on 31 December he was awarded the Knight's Cross of the Iron Cross.

In July 1942 Manteuffel was posted in North Africa. A collection of units were put under his command and were called "Division Manteuffel." Against numerically superior forces, his division fought until boxed in at Bizerte (q.v.) in April 1943. On 30 April he collapsed from exhaustion and was transferred from Africa via hospital ship. In May 1943, Manteuffel was promoted to major general. That June he was named to command the 7th *Panzer* Division, then hotly engaged in the Soviet Union. On 1 August he assumed command and was wounded three days later. In November, his division distinguished itself at Zhitomir, and as a result, Hitler awarded him the Oak Leaves to the Knight's Cross.

In February 1944, Manteuffel was awarded the Swords to the Knight's Cross and assumed command of the *Grossdeutschland* Division. That March the Soviets surrounded the division, but Manteuffel maneuvered out of the trap without abandoning a single weapon. In May, the division stopped a Soviet offensive near Ploesti, Romania. On 1 September 1944, Hitler promoted Manteuffel to *General der Panzertruppe* and gave him command of the Fifth *Panzer* Army, which conducted limited counterattacks against General George S. Patton's (q.v.) U.S. Third Army in Lorraine (q.v.) that September.

On 3 November, Manteuffel was briefed on the Fifth *Panzer* Army's supporting role to Josef "Sepp" Dietrich's (q.v.) Sixth *Panzer* Army for the Ardennes offensive (q.v.). Manteuffel strongly endorsed Model's (q.v.) "Small Solution," but Hitler refused. In the first few days, Manteuffel's army was slowed down by fierce American resistance at St. Vith (q.v.) and Clervaux, then halted at Bastogne (q.v.). He had no choice but to surround Bastogne and continue his drive to the Meuse River. During the offensive, the Fifth *Panzer* Army was far more successful than the Sixth SS *Panzer*.

On 28 February, Hitler awarded Manteuffel the Diamonds to the Knight's Cross. Two days later Manteuffel took command of the tattered Third *Panzer* Army in the east, defending along the Oder River. On 3 May he managed to surrender what remained of his army to the Western Allies, avoiding Soviet capture. After the war, he lectured senior American military officers at the U.S. Army War College, and served in the German *Bundestag*. He died in Diessen on Ammersee.

Samuel J. Doss

Additional Reading

Kurowski, Franz, "Dietrich and Manteuffel" in *Hitler's Generals,* Correlli Barnett (ed.) (1989).

MacDonald, Charles B., *A Time for Trumpets: The Untold Story of the Battle of the Bulge* (1985).

Marschall, Wilhelm (1886–1976)

German general admiral, commander of the High Seas Fleet. Born in Augsburg, Germany, on 30 September 1886, Wilhelm Marschall ended World War II as one of Germany's top three admirals. As chief of operational staff during the immediate prewar period, he was responsible for formulating the *Kriegsmarine's* wartime strategy and operational doctrine. Marschall also served as commander of the German naval forces off Spain from 1937 to 1938. He assumed command of the fleet's operational forces in October 1939, but in June 1940, he was relieved by Admiral Erich Raeder (q.v.) for not rigidly following instructions during the Narvik (q.v.) campaign.

Marschall subsequently served in a variety of shore-based posts. He was promoted to general admiral on 1 February 1943, one of the few German officers to ever hold that rank. Although not a daring officer, he had great organizational skill and personal courage, earning the *Pour le Mérite,* Germany's highest decoration, as a U-boat commander in World War I. He died in Munich on 20 March 1976.

Carl O. Schuster

Additional Reading

Hildebrand, Hans H., and Ernst Henriot, *Deutschlands Admirale 1849–1945* (1989).

Humble, Richard, *Hitler's High Seas Fleet* (1971).

Von Der Porten, Edward P., *The German Navy in World War II* (1969).

Marseille, Hans-Joachim (1919–1942)

Luftwaffe captain, ace. As a fighter pilot, Marseille was acclaimed Germany's most deadly aerial marksman. He flew exclusively against the Western Allies, and received his greatest reputation while flying Bf-109s in the Libyan desert. His 158 victories earned him the sobriquet "Star of Africa," as well as the Swords, Oak Leaves, and Diamonds to the Knight's Cross of the Iron Cross. He was killed bailing out of a stricken plane.

Max Mulholland

Additional Reading
Grey, Charles G., *Luftwaffe* (1944).
Killen, John, *The Luftwaffe: A History* (1967).
Toliver, Raymond F., and Trevor J. Constable, *Fighter Aces of the Luftwaffe* (1977).

Marshall, George Catlett (1880–1959)

American General of the Army, U.S. Army chief of staff. George C. Marshall served as U.S. Army chief of staff from 1939 to 1945. His authority over the army's wartime activities was unprecedented. He was responsible for the army's size, organization, equipment, training, and strategy. His talents in orchestrating these varied programs prompted British Prime Minister Winston S. Churchill (q.v.) to call Marshall "the true organizer of victory."

Marshall's military background suited him well for the position of chief of staff. He served in France during World War I and in the Far East before and after the war. This experience gave him a global view of events. At various times, he served as aide to three generals, including General of the Armies John J. Pershing when he was chief of staff. Through these positions, Marshall gained insights into the decision-making process of the army's hierarchy.

As assistant commandant of the Infantry School, Marshall greatly influenced the interwar development of infantry doctrine and he selected, served with, and helped develop many of the men who would lead the major combat units during World War II. He also had several assignments in the plans and operations area, giving him a firm understanding of strategic thought. Thus when Marshall took the oath of office on 1 September 1939 (the same day Germany invaded Poland), he was well-prepared for the tasks that lay ahead.

World War II was the first time in the history of the U.S. Army that the chief of staff exercised full control over all the army's worldwide wartime activities, and Marshall faced far broader responsibilities than his World War I predecessors. Accordingly, he delegated wide authority to his major field commanders and relied greatly on their individual initiative. For the most part, Marshall exercised command from Washington, where he maintained effective control over the army's zone of the interior programs. To keep abreast of the worldwide situation, Marshall transformed the War Plans Division into the Operations Division, which served as his Washington command post. From the Operations Division, he was able to direct the strategic activities of U.S. Army commands in all theaters, while still remaining responsive to the needs of the rapidly expanding force at home.

Under Marshall's supervision, the army and air corps (then still part of the army) increased in size from about 200,000 to nearly eight million men. When Marshall became chief of staff, he noted "continuous paring of appropriations had reduced the army virtually to the status of a third-rate power." Actually, when Holland was defeated by Germany in 1940, the U.S. replaced Holland as the number-ten military power in the world. Expansion was essential, but many factors had to be considered. At first, President Franklin D. Roosevelt (q.v.) was hesitant to declare an emergency mobilization because he believed a small expansion was all the American public was ready to accept.

Marshall was very selective in his employment of the initially authorized 17,000-man expansion. The bulk of the new troops were assigned to infantry units. Here the old "square" divisions were reconfigured into smaller but more mobile "triangular" divisions capable of deploying en masse or as three separate infantry-artillery teams. Additional funds went for transportation assets to create "motorized" divisions, capable of long-range truck movement. He envisioned a mobile war and reorganized the army accordingly.

In April 1940, as the war in Europe escalated and the U.S. public became less isolationist, Marshall urged the secretary of war to continue the buildup. On 31 May, Roosevelt placed a military appropriations bill before Congress that Marshall felt was adequate in terms of materiel, but not in manpower.

At the same time, Marshall did not push for the establishment of a draft. He felt such a move would force the army to break up its few trained units in order to provide cadres for the influx of recruits. Civilian leaders, particularly Henry

Stimson (q.v.), did push for a draft, and on 12 July, Marshall finally endorsed their program as a necessary adjunct to federalizing National Guard units. Marshall, however, remained adamant that mobilization be orderly and well-planned, rather than superficial and hasty.

A crucial item on Marshall's agenda was unity of command. He described this principle of war (q.v.) as "the very keystone of successful military operations." He pressed for all air, ground, and naval forces in a given theater to come under the command of a single officer. Interservice rivalries made this no easy task to accomplish. In matters concerning the army and navy, he directed that "coordination shall be effected by the method of mutual cooperation." The unified command of joint army-navy operations would be determined by the character of the specific operation. Generally, this approach worked well.

Relationships with the Army Air Corps (later the Army Air Forces) were a little more difficult. Most army aviators became very vocal in their demands for air autonomy. Marshall wanted to move gradually in this matter in order to prevent the air corps' separation from the army at a critical juncture in the war. At the same time, Marshall hoped to gain the largest possible amount of air-ground cooperation within the reorganized army. Before he assumed office, Marshall toured U.S. air stations and aircraft factories with General Frank Andrews (q.v.) of the air corps, in order to gain a better appreciation of the air element's needs. This knowledge allowed Marshall to channel the energies of air officers into programs that approximated aviation objectives while still serving the needs of ground force commanders.

In November 1940, Marshall firmly stated his view that the primary American strategic objective in any future war was the defeat of Germany. Accordingly, the primary theater of operations would be the Atlantic. Throughout 1941, Marshall continued to stress that "collapse in the Atlantic would be fatal; collapse in the Far East would be serious but not fatal." Likewise, he confirmed that the Philippines would be defended, but in such a way as not to jeopardize any major efforts in the Atlantic. His prewar service in China and the Philippines freed him of any charges of parochialism on this point. By establishing priority of effort to the Atlantic, he concentrated combat power where it was most needed, while conducting economy of force operations elsewhere.

Once the Atlantic was confirmed as the principal theater, Marshall set out to persuade the Allies of the necessity of the cross-channel invasion that would become Operation OVERLORD. He presented his case at all the major Allied conferences (see Conferences, Allied). At Casablanca in January 1943, he argued that a cross-channel invasion should be launched from Great Britain. In opposition, the British continued to push for operations in the Mediterranean. At the Washington Conference in May 1943, he warned that operations in the Mediterranean would consume men and landing craft needed for Operation OVERLORD.

The string of offensives at Sicily, Salerno, and Anzio (qq.v.) led Marshall to suspect that General Dwight D. Eisenhower (q.v.) was becoming unduly influenced by the British. He cautioned Eisenhower against falling victim to "localities" and pressure from the British. In the end, Marshall's genius lay in his ability to steer the Allied focus toward OVERLORD while at the same time placating Churchill and his insistence on the Mediterranean. He summed up his own contribution when he said, "I doubt if I did anything better in the war than to keep Churchill on the main point." Churchill himself praised Marshall for his "balance of mind" in the strategic debate. Marshall's diplomacy and ability to establish and adhere to priorities allowed the Allies to make the most of limited resources and occasionally conflicting strategies.

George Marshall retired as army chief of staff on 20 November 1945. He was then named by President Harry S Truman (q.v.) to head a special mission to China. That was the beginning of a distinguished second career as a statesman. His key postwar accomplishment came during his tenure as secretary of state from 1947 to 1949, when he developed a plan for European recovery known as the Marshall Plan (q.v.). In 1950, he became secretary of defense. In 1953, he became the first military man to receive the Nobel Peace Prize for his contributions to the postwar recovery of Europe. This, perhaps, was his crowning achievement. The man who organized the Allied victory also organized the rebuilding of what the war had destroyed. Marshall died on 16 October 1959, after living a life that his biographer Forrest Pogue described as the "perfect blend of soldier and civilian."

Kevin Dougherty

Additional Reading

Cline, Ray S., *The War Department: Washington Command Post: The Operations Division* (1951).

Pogue, Forrest C., *George C. Marshall,* 3 vols. (1973).

Watson, Mark Skinner, *Chief of Staff: Prewar Plans and Preparations* (1950).

Marshall, Samuel L.A. (1900–1977)

American colonel, chief historian of the European Theater of Operations. A newspaperman by training and experience, S.L.A. Marshall (known universally as "Slam") was one of the most influential military historians of World War II. Marshall spent his entire military career as a reservist, first receiving his commission from the ranks during World War I at the age of seventeen. For the next sixty years, he pursued parallel careers as a reserve officer and as a journalist and writer. As a reporter, he covered most of the world's major wars during that period.

During World War II, Marshall was the chief historian of the U.S. European Theater of Operations. He recruited many of the historians and initiated the work that led to the widely respected *U.S. Army in World War II* series. Marshall also emphasized conducting direct interviews with participants of combat actions as soon as possible after the event. As a result of these interviews, Marshall wrote *Men Against Fire* in 1947.

The book was a penetrating analysis of the American infantryman and small unit cohesion and effectiveness. Marshall pointed out many problems with American combat performance, and offered recommendations to correct them. The U.S. Army adopted many of his recommendations. In recent years, some historians have criticized Marshall's work by exposing flaws and inconsistencies in his data. Almost all veterans of infantry combat continue to agree, however, that regardless of the flaws in Marshall's data or data collection methods, his conclusions in *Men Against Fire* are right.

Marshall wrote more than thirty books about war, many of them from first-hand experience. After World War II he was promoted to brigadier general in the U.S. Army Reserve. S.L.A. Marshall was the only American to serve in uniform in World War I, World War II, Korea, and Vietnam.

David T. Zabecki

Additional Reading

Marshall, S.L.A., *Men Against Fire* (1947).
———, *Bringing Up the Rear: A Memoir* (1979).

Martel, Giffard le Quesne (1889–1958)

British lieutenant general, commander of British Armoured Corps. Born in Millbrook, Southampton, on 10 October 1889, Martel was educated at Wellington and the Royal Military Academy at Woolwich. He was commissioned into the Royal Engineers in 1909. In August 1914, he went to France for two years, returning in the summer of 1916 to design a practice battlefield in Norfolk where tank crews could be trained. He returned to France on the staff of the newly formed Tank Corps and remained serving with tanks until November 1918. Shortly before the end World War I he was given command of a tank-bridging battalion of the Royal Engineers.

In the years between the wars Martel continued to take a great interest in tank development and warfare. On the outbreak of war in 1939, he was given command of a motorized division of the Territorial Army—the 50th Northumbrian Division. During the German breakthrough on the Meuse in May 1940, Martel's division was rushed forward to counterattack, hitting the flank of General Erwin Rommel's (q.v.) 7th *Panzer* Division and causing the German high command to consider suspending their drive to the Channel. Due to the small size of his force, Martel was unable to keep up the pressure on the German division and he eventually had to withdraw.

Following the fall of France, the need for a single chief for the British armored forces was put to the Army Council, a move that was fully supported by Prime Minister Winston S. Churchill (q.v.). In December 1940, Martel was appointed commander of the Royal Armoured Corps. He held the post for nearly two years, but with the creation of the so-called Tank Parliament, where various armored divisional commanders and other tank experts could meet, he felt that his overall control was weakened. He was extremely unhappy with the interference with his authority. With this conflict unresolved, he departed in September 1942 on an extended tour of units in India and Burma. In his absence, the post of commander, Royal Armoured Corps was abolished.

On Martel's return to the United Kingdom he was appointed head of the military mission in Moscow. He returned to Britain in February 1944 and soon after lost an eye during the bombing of the Army and Navy Club in London. He was placed on retired pay in 1945 and devoted himself to writing, which included a controversial book, *Our Armoured Forces.*

He was promoted to lieutenant general in 1942, and in 1943 was appointed Knight Commander of the British Empire. He was made a Knight Commander of the Bath in 1944 on his return from Moscow. Sir Giffard Martel died at Camberley on 3 September 1958.

Alan G. Harfield

Additional Reading

Clay, Ewart W., *The Path of the 50th Northumbrian Division in the Second World War, 1939–1945* (1950).

Martel, Giffard, *An Outspoken Soldier* (1949).

Martin, William ("1907–1943")

Royal Marine major, "The Man Who Never Was." "Major William Martin," Royal Marines, was an identity created as part of Operation MINCEMEAT (q.v.). An anonymous male corpse with official identification and forged letters designed to mislead the Axis was put overboard from a British submarine on 30 April 1943. He was made to seem the victim of an aircraft accident off Huelva, Spain, the known residence of an active German *Abwehr* (q.v.) agent.

The corpse, that of a young man whose death from exposure and pneumonia mimicked death at sea, was procured from a Picadilly morgue in the fall of 1942 and kept in dry ice. The name, "William Martin," was chosen for its commonplaceness. The props planted on the body included a photo of and letters from his fiancee, "Pam"; a bill for an engagement ring; ticket stubs and a club bill, dated to reinforce the "crash-date"; and for extra realism, an overdraft from Lloyd's Bank.

The false materials were copied and pronounced genuine by the *Abwehr*. "Martin" was buried in Huelva with full military honors. At the request of the dead man's real family, his actual identity remains secret. "Martin's" creator, Ewen Montagu (q.v.) said of this man who had died uncared-for in London, "In life, he had done little for his country; but in death he did more than most could achieve in a lifetime of service."

Sidney Dean

Additional Reading

Montagu, Ewen, *The Man Who Never Was* (1953).

Reit, Seymour, *Masquerade: The Amazing Camouflage Deceptions of World War II* (1978).

Masaryk, Tomáš (1850–1937)

First president of Czechoslovakia. Tomáš Masaryk was a well-known philosopher before becoming active in politics. He was born to a Slovak family near Hodonin, Moravia, on 7 March 1850. Because of his father's low social status, Masaryk's education began slowly. He studied in Vienna and Leipzig before receiving a doctorate in philosophy. In 1882, Masaryk became professor of philosophy at the Czech University in Prague. He became increasingly more active in contemporary issues and political affairs, especially the Czech national movement. He concluded that for the nationalist movement to prosper, it had to operate on a "scientific" basis and be led by people like himself.

Masaryk continued to work for reform within the Hapsburg Empire, and only after the outbreak of war in 1914 did he advocate independence for Czechoslovakia. He launched a campaign to achieve that goal and traveled abroad in support of independence. With Allied support, he proclaimed the independence of Czechoslovakia on 14 October 1918. He was elected the new state's first president a month later.

A serious domestic problem of the 1920s was the need to reconcile the desire of Czechs to run their own state and the need to provide minority rights to the Germans and other ethnic groups. In foreign policy, Masaryk allied Czechoslovakia with France in 1924 and joined with Romania and Yugoslavia to form the "Little Entente." He remained president of Czechoslovakia until failing health forced his retirement in December 1935. He died on 14 September 1937.

John David Waite

Additional Reading

Ludwig, Emil, *Defender of Democracy: Masaryk of Czechoslovakia* (1936).

Zemen, Zbynek, *The Masaryks: The Making of Czechoslovakia* (1976).

Mascarenhas de Morais, João Batista (1883–1955)

Brazilian major general, commander in chief of the Brazilian Expeditionary Force. Mascarenhas de Morais commanded the 25,000-man Brazilian force that fought in the Italian campaign. The Brazilian force was under the operation control of the U.S. Fifth Army and took part in the capture of Monte Cassino (q.v.) in May 1945.

Andrzej Suchcitz

Additional Reading

McCann, Frank D., *The Brazilian-American Alliance in World War II, 1937–1945* (1973).

Masterman, John C. (1891–1977)

Chairman of the British XX Committee. By late 1940, Britain needed to coordinate information supplied to captured enemy agents being used to feed false reports to German intelligence. Sir John Masterman chaired the Twenty (XX) Committee (q.v.), formed in January 1941, to plan Britain's leaks. British security forces arrested all known German agents in Britain and the XX Committee under Masterman's direction used them to send false intelligence to the Germans. The highly successful "double-cross" operation took its name from the group's Roman numerals.

Richard Wires

Additional Reading

Farago, Ladislas, *The Game of Foxes: The Untold Story of German Espionage in the United States and Great Britain During World War II* (1971).

Masterman, John C., *The Double-Cross System in the War of 1939–1945* (1972).

Mauldin, William (1921–)

American journalist and cartoonist. Born in Mountain Park, New Mexico, Bill Mauldin attended the Chicago Institute of Fine Arts and then entered the army in 1942. He joined the staff of the *45th Division News* as a cartoonist, inventing his most famous characters, "Willie and Joe" (q.v.).

He soon joined the staff of *Stars and Stripes,* where his often irreverent tribute to the common soldier delighted and inspired a large audience, prompting newspapers all over the United States to publish his cartoons. His cartoons, however, irritated some high-ranking army officers, most notably General George S. Patton (q.v.). Mauldin published *Up Front* and *Star Spangled Banter,* two cartoon-filled books about his army experiences. In 1945, he received the Pulitzer Prize for his Willie and Joe drawings.

Robert Pace

Additional Reading

Mauldin, Bill, *Back Home* (1947).

———, *Up Front* (1945).

May, Geraldine Pratt (1895–)

American colonel, first director of the Women's Air Force. Geraldine Pratt May was born on 21 April 1895, and graduated from the University of California at Berkeley in 1920. In July 1942, she enlisted in the Women's Army Auxiliary Corps (WAAC) (q.v.). She was commissioned a second lieutenant after graduating from the first WAAC officer's training school.

May was assigned to the Army Air Forces, and in March 1943, she became WAAC staff director for the Air Transport Command, coordinating WAAC personnel at more than forty bases spanning the globe. Promoted to lieutenant colonel in May 1945, she assumed progressively more responsible positions, finally being appointed the first director of the Women's Air Force in June 1948, with the rank of colonel.

Boyd Childress

Additional Reading

Ross, Mary S., *American Women in Uniform* (1943).

Treadwell, Mattie E., *The Women's Army Corps* (1954).

Mellenthin, Friedrich-Wilhelm von (1904–1997)

German major general, general staff officer. The son of a Prussian gunnery officer, von Mellenthin joined the *Reichswehr* in 1924, received his commission in the cavalry four years later, and attended the War Academy from 1935 to 1937. Thereafter, he served almost exclusively in general staff positions, including nearly five years as the senior intelligence officer at various corps and army headquarters.

After fifteen months on General Erwin Rommel's (q.v.) staff in North Africa, von Mellenthin was hospitalized for amoebic dysentery and then sent to the eastern front. As chief of staff of XLVIII *Panzer Korps,* he witnessed the Axis debacle at Stalingrad (q.v.) and the eventual German retreat from the Ukraine. When his commanding general, Hermann Balck (q.v.), took over the Fourth *Panzer* Army in August 1944, Colonel von Mellenthin moved with him as chief of staff. Four weeks later, he and Balck were transferred to Lorraine where they took charge of Army Group G. A run-in with the army high command in November 1944 led to Mellenthin's recall and eventual assignment to the front as a regimental commander.

Early in March 1945, by now major general, von Mellenthin was once again given a chief of staff posting, this time with the Fifth *Panzer* Army. Following the demise of that army in the Ruhr pocket (q.v.), he and some other staff officers tried to escape but were captured on 3 May.

After two years in American captivity, von

Mellenthin became a businessman, and in 1950, he emigrated to South Africa. His postwar publications include a widely read account of his wartime observations, entitled *Panzer Battles,* a book about German generals, and a commentary on NATO's chances against the Soviet armed forces.

Ulrich Trumpener

Additional Reading

Carlson, Verner R., "Portrait of a German General Staff Officer," *Military Review* (April 1990), pp. 69–81. Humble, Richard, *Hitler's Generals* (1974).

Mellenthin, F.W. von, *German Generals of World War II: As I Saw Them* (1977).

———, *Panzer Battles: A Study of the Employment of Armor in the Second World War* (1956).

Mengele, Josef (1911–1979)

German SS doctor. In June 1985, a team of sixteen forensic experts assembled from the United States, Brazil, and West Germany announced to the world that they had positively identified the remains of Dr. Josef Mengele, one of the most hated Nazis of World War II. Mengele, also known as the "Angel of Death," presided over the slaughter of some 400,000 innocents as chief doctor at the Auschwitz-Birkenau concentration camp.

Mengele was born 16 March 1911, in Gunzburg, Germany. During the 1920s, he studied philosophy in Munich, where he was exposed to the racial theories of Alfred Rosenberg (q.v.). Mengele went on to earn a medical degree at the University of Frankfurt am Main, and subsequently, in 1943, joined the research staff of the Institute for Hereditary Biology and Racial Hygiene. In the early months of World War II, he served as a medical officer in France and Russia. In 1943, Heinrich Himmler (q.v.) appointed him chief doctor at Auschwitz, where he performed thousands of medical experiments on camp inmates. He was particularly interested in genetics and the problems of increasing human reproduction. In the name of medical science, Mengele injected serum into the eyes of infants to change their eye color, sewed twins together to simulate Siamese twins, and allowed newborn infants to starve to death to see how long it would take.

Mengele fled Auschwitz on Christmas Eve 1944, in the face of the approaching Red Army. From 1944 until 1949, he worked as a farmhand in Germany. At one point in 1947, he was arrested by U.S. Army Intelligence, but was released because his name did not appear on any of the wanted lists. In 1949, with a Red Cross passport, Mengele fled to South America, living initially in Argentina. In subsequent years he moved frequently between Uruguay, Paraguay, and Argentina before settling in Brazil in 1961. He assumed the name of an acquaintance and avid Nazi, Wolfgang Gerhard. In 1979, while on an outing to the beach, he suffered a stroke and drowned. He remained unrepentant to the end. In 1977, during a visit with his son, Mengele claimed to have had no regrets and nothing to be sorry for.

Richard E. James

Additional Reading

Levy, Alan, *Wanted! Nazi Criminals at Large* (1962).

Mitscherlich, Alexander, and Fred Mielke, *Doctors of Infamy: The Story of the Nazi Medical Crimes* (1949).

Menzies, Stewart G. (1890–1968)

Chief of the British Secret Intelligence Service. Sir Stewart Menzies led the British Secret Intelligence Service, or MI-6 (q.v.), an element of the Foreign Office, for most of World War II, having become its head late in 1939. Although he was involved in many types of operations, his most critical role was his supervision of the system for gathering information by reading coded German messages sent through Enigma (q.v.) cypher machines. His stature was considerably enhanced by his almost daily conferences with Prime Minister Winston S. Churchill (q.v.) about the latest ULTRA (q.v.) data (taken from Enigma transmissions) on German intentions and capabilities. ULTRA information reduced the Allies' dependence on agents in Axis-held territory, although agents also played an important part in the intelligence effort.

Relations between Menzies and William J. Donovan (q.v.), director of the United States Office of Strategic Services (OSS) (q.v.), were initially cordial. Gradually, however, relations between the two men and their agencies deteriorated, although not to the extent that Allied interests were seriously harmed. In many ways, Menzies was a traditionalist in the handling of intelligence operations, but he clearly appreciated the impact of technology in his field. He exploited cryptography (q.v.) to the fullest, thereby significantly influencing the Allied conduct of World War II in Europe.

Benjamine R. Beede

Additional Reading

Brown, Anthony Cave, *"C": The Secret Life of Sir Stewart Menzies, Spymaster to Winston Churchill* (1987).

Winterbotham, Frederick W., *The Ultra Secret* (1974).

Meretskov, Kirill Afanasievich (1897–1968)

Soviet marshal. Born in 1897 to a poor peasant family near Moscow, Meretskov managed to avoid military service during World War I. He joined the Communist Party on 1 May 1917 and was made military head of his local soviet. Wounded twice in the civil war, he decided to make the army a career. In the interwar years he attended the Frunze Military Academy and held a variety of posts, including a tour in Czechoslovakia in 1935, followed by a ten-month tour as an advisor to Spain during its civil war.

Meretskov was bright and he impressed many of his superiors, including Josef Stalin (q.v.). His bright star, however, would soon dim in battle. During the Finnish Winter War (q.v.) of 1939–1940, Meretskov's forces failed to breach the Mannerheim Line (q.v.), and repeated attacks produced high Soviet casualties. Frustrated, Stalin appointed Major General Semen Timoshenko (q.v.) over Meretskov on 7 January 1940. Timoshenko eventually breached the Mannerheim Line and pushed the Finns back to Vyborg in early March, forcing an armistice.

After the Winter War, Meretskov was posted to combat training assignments. In late 1940, he was named chief of the general staff, but soon was dismissed for his lackluster presentation at a major command and staff exercise and his open disagreement with Marshal Boris Shaposhnikov (q.v.). Meretskov resumed his position as head of combat training, where he developed plans for a large armor and mechanized force patterned after the German *Panzer* units.

Shortly after the outbreak of Operation BARBAROSSA, Meretskov was arrested and accused of anti-Soviet conspiracies. He was cleared in September 1940 and posted to Leningrad. On 12 December, he commanded the Volkhov Front consisting of four field armies. His mission was to lift the siege of Leningrad (q.v.). After he failed to lift the siege, his Volkhov Front was absorbed by General M.S. Khozin's Leningrad Front on 23 April 1942. Meretskov was downgraded to command of the Thirty-Third Army.

Khozin fared no better at relieving Leningrad,

Marshal Kirill Meretskov superceded Zhukov as chief of the Soviet General Staff. (IWM RR 2104)

and on 8 July 1942, Stalin reestablished the Volkhov Front and reinstated Meretskov. He managed to open supply gaps into Leningrad, but the relief was temporary, arriving in bits and pieces. The final lifting of the siege did not occur until January 1944. In the meantime, Meretskov was ordered to mount an attack at Mga in coordination with the counteroffensive at Kursk (q.v.).

After Leningrad, Stalin assigned Meretskov to the Karelian Front, which had been relatively quiet since 1941. His first task was to get Marshal Carl Mannerheim (q.v.) and Finland out of the war. This was accomplished on 25 August 1944. That October, in coordination with the Soviet Northern Fleet, Meretskov pushed the German Arctic forces from Finland into Norway, where Norwegian resistance groups captured the remaining German troops. On 26 October, Stalin promoted Meretskov to marshal.

Meretskov finished the war as commander of the 1st Far Eastern Front, which forced the surrender of the Japanese Kwantung Army on 17 August 1945. Meretskov died on 30 December 1968.

William H. Van Husen

Additional Reading

Shukman, Harold (ed.), *Stalin's Generals* (1993).

Vitukhin, Igor, *Soviet Generals Recall World War II* (1981).

Ziemke, Earl F., *Stalin to Berlin: The German Defeat in the East* (1968).

Ziemke, Earl F., and Magna E. Bauer, *Moscow to Stalingrad: Decision in the East* (1987).

Messerschmitt, Willy (1898–1978)

German aviation engineer. After studying engineering at the Technical University of Munich, Willy Messerschmitt founded the Messerschmitt Aircraft Construction Company in Augsburg in 1923. At first, the company only built sport planes. In 1926, it produced the first German all-metal plane, the M-17. In 1930, the Munich Technical University awarded him an honorary professorship in aircraft design.

Messerschmitt was a major force in the buildup of the German Air Force. His most famous and most successful design was the Bf-109, built in 1935. It became the standard German fighter in World War II and was built in a number of different models. The Me-209 set a speed record of 755 kilometers per hour (about 468 mph) for piston-engine planes that stood until 1969. During the war, he developed other models, like the Me-163 rocket fighter, and the first jet fighter, the Me-262 *Schwalbe*. For his accomplishments, he received numerous titles and honors.

In 1948, Messerschmitt was classified a Nazi supporter by a de-Nazification board. His postwar work involved the design of cockpit rollers. Starting in 1956, he once again started designing jets for NATO and the German Air Force. In 1969, he became an associate of the group Messerschmitt Bölkow-Blom, GmbH. He died in 1978 in Munich.

Franz Seidler

Additional Reading

Caidin, Martin, *Me-109: Willy Messerschmitt's Peerless Fighter* (1969).

Smith, John R., and A.L. Kay, *German Aircraft of the Second World War* (1972).

Messervy, Frank Walter (1893–1974)

British major general, commander of the 1st and 7th Armored Divisions. Sandhurst-educated and commissioned in 1913 into the Indian Army, Sir Frank Messervy served in World War I and then India. In 1940, he joined British forces fighting the Italians in East Africa. Between 1941 and 1943, he commanded various divisions in Egypt and Libya.

In November 1941, he held the Indian 4th Division's surrounded headquarters near Sidi Omar for seven days before repelling the Germans. Taking over the British 1st Armored Division just before its destruction in January 1942, Messervy was unfairly relieved. He was then assigned command of the 7th Armored Division.

In May 1942, he was captured when the *Afrika Korps* (q.v.) overran his headquarters, but soon escaped. After postings in Cairo with Indian units, he went to general headquarters in India in 1943 and served in the Burma campaign in 1944–1945. He retired as lieutenant general in 1948. Considered an inspiring leader, he won many distinctions, including the Distinguished Service Order.

Richard Wires

Additional Reading

Essame, Hubert, *The 43rd Wessex Division at War, 1944–1945* (1952).

Tucker, Sir Francis, *Approach to Battle: A Commentary, Eighth Army, November 1941 to May 1943* (1963).

Metaxas, Ioannis (1871–1941)

Greek general, dictator. Metaxas became an officer in 1890. Following service in the 1897 Greco-Turkish War, he studied in Germany, returning to serve on the Greek General Staff during the Balkan War of 1912–1913. Becoming chief of staff in 1913, his monarchist views were no secret and he resigned when the king was deposed in 1917.

During subsequent monarchies, Metaxas served in key positions. As premier in 1936, he proclaimed a dictatorship to avert a Communist strike. When Benito Mussolini (q.v.) invaded Greece (q.v.) in October 1940, Metaxas mobilized his reserves and repelled the Italians. By November, the Greeks had the upper hand and occupied half of Albania. Metaxas died in office prior to the German invasion of Greece in support of Italy.

Steven D. Cage

Additional Reading

MacKenzie, Compton, *Wind of Freedom: The History of the Invasion of Greece by the Axis Powers, 1940–1941* (1943).

Papagos, Alexandros, *The Battle of Greece, 1940–1941* (1949).

Meyer, John (1919–1975)

American lieutenant colonel, leading ace of the

U.S. Eighth Air Force. John Charles Meyer was born on 3 April 1919, in Brooklyn, and attended public schools in Queens, the Peekskill Military Academy, and Dartmouth. He joined the army air force in 1940 and trained as a fighter pilot. In 1943, he was assigned to the Eighth Air Force in Britain. Flying a P-51 Mustang, he shot down twenty-four German aircraft and destroyed thirteen more enemy planes on the ground, making him the Eighth Air Force's top ace.

After the war, Meyer returned to Dartmouth and graduated in 1947. Promoted to colonel in 1951, he served as a fighter pilot in Korea. A highly decorated officer, he retired as a major general in 1970. He died in Bethesda, Maryland, on 2 December 1975.

Boyd Childress

Additional Reading

Freeman, Roger A., *The Mighty Eighth: Units, Men, and Machines of the Eighth Army Air Force* (1970).

Gurney, Gene, *Five Down and Glory: A History of the American Air Ace* (1958).

Meyer, Kurt (1911–1954)

German SS major general, commander of the 12th SS *"Hitlerjugend" Panzer* Division. Kurt *"Panzer"* Meyer was a resolute, courageous, and fanatical commander. He joined the SS in 1933, fought in Poland in 1939, and Holland and France in 1940. In April 1941, commanding a reconnaissance battalion in Greece, he and a detachment were trapped in an exposed position at the Klisura Pass. Meyer tossed a grenade at his men's heels to get them moving. The Greeks broke and Meyer took more than 1,000 prisoners, losing six killed and nine wounded. Next day, he earned the Knight's Cross to the Iron Cross by capturing Kastoria, bagging 11,000 prisoners and supplies.

Meyer was a brilliant regimental commander in Russia for three years. In Normandy in June 1944, he became Germany's youngest major general (SS-*Gruppenführer*) and division commander. His 12th SS *Panzer* Division stopped the British VIII Corps during Operation EPSOM and halted Operation TOTALIZE north of Falaise on 9 August, allowing much of the German Seventh Army to escape.

After the war, a Canadian tribunal sentenced Meyer to death (later commuted to life) for the mid-June 1944 execution of forty Canadian prisoners at Chateau Audrieu *(see Waffen-SS)*.

Released because of ill health in 1954, he died shortly thereafter.

Samuel J. Doss

Additional Reading

Meyer, Kurt, *Grenadiers* (1983).

Quarrie, Bruce, *Hitler's Samurai: The Waffen SS in Action* (1984).

Michael I (1921–)

King of Romania. From 1927 to 1930, Michael was king of Romania under a regency. He was deposed by his father, Carol II (q.v.). When Carol abdicated in 1940, Michael regained a much-reduced kingdom, partially annexed by Hungary, Bulgaria, and the Soviet Union. Until 1944, Michael acted merely as head of state, with the political power resting in the hands of Marshal Ion Antonescu (q.v.).

In the autumn of 1943, Michael silently backed efforts at secret negotiations with the Allies for Romania to switch sides. With military defeat looming, he was instrumental in removing the Antonescu government on 23 August 1944, and placing Romania on the side of the Allies. Up to end of the war, Romanian forces operated alongside the Red Army. On 30 December 1947, the Communists forced Michael's abdication.

Andrzej Suchcitz

Additional Reading

Cretzianu, Alexandre, *The Lost Opportunity* (1957).

Pavel, Pavel, *Why Rumania Failed* (1944).

Popescy-Putrie, I, *La Roumanie pendant la Deuxième Guerre Mondiale* (1964).

Middleton, Troy Houston (1889–1976)

American lieutenant general, commander U.S. VIII Corps. Troy Middleton graduated from Mississippi Agricultural and Mechanical College in 1909. He enlisted in the army in 1910 and was commissioned in 1912. He participated in the Mexican Punitive Expedition in 1916, and during World War I he rose to the command of both the 39th and 47th Infantry Regiments.

Interwar service for Middleton consisted of both attendance and teaching at the Infantry School and the Command and General Staff College and troop duty in the Philippines. In 1937, he retired from the army to become Dean at Louisiana State University. He returned to active duty in 1941.

M

During World War II, Middleton commanded the 45th Infantry Division, leading that unit in Sicily and Italy. In northwest Europe he commanded VIII Corps. He was best known as the "soldier's soldier." He demonstrated his talent for coolness and reliability in the Ardennes offensive (q.v.), when his corps was struck fiercely by two of the three attacking German armies. His crucial decision to defend the vital road junctions of the Ardennes, including Bastogne, proved instrumental in blunting the German attack. Middleton was one of the most effective U.S. Army corps commanders in the European theater.

Randy Papadopoulos

Additional Reading
Price, Frank J., *Troy H. Middleton: A Biography* (1974).
Weigley, Russell F., *Eisenhower's Lieutenants: The Campaigns of France and Germany, 1944–1945* (1981).

Mihailović, Draža (1893–1946)

Yugoslav *Četnik* leader. When the Germans invaded in 1941, the Yugoslav Royal Army (q.v.) rapidly collapsed. As a member of the operation bureau of the general staff, Draža Mihailović formed the remnants into a resistance army based in Serbia. He pledged support for the monarchist government-in-exile, of which he became war minister in 1942.

The conservative politics of Mihailović's movement, its desire to restore the old regime unaltered, was not popular with the majority of Yugoslavs, who saw the war as an opportunity both to drive out the invader and fight for a better way of life. To this end, they lent their support to the Communist guerrilla forces of the man who became popularly known as Tito (q.v.). Another factor undermining Mihailović's *Četnik* (q.v.) forces was their relative inactivity in the face of a very bitter and hard-fought war being waged by Tito's Yugoslav National Army of Liberation.

Mihailović explained away this lethargy by insisting that his people wanted to avoid civilian reprisals. This inactivity led to greater support for Tito's forces. The stronger they became, the greater became Mihailović's tendency to collaboration with the Germans. He was motivated by a rivalry bordering on hatred for Tito, combined with a fierce opposition to Communism. Eventually, the British transferred their support to Tito. By acting as he did, Mihailović hoped to eliminate Tito and secure a place of power for himself in a German-aligned Yugoslavia. His acts succeeded in getting him dismissed from his ministerial post in 1944 and resulted in his execution immediately after the war by the triumphant Communist-dominated coalition led by Tito.

Chris Westhorp

Additional Reading
Brown, Alec, *Mihailović and Yugoslav Resistance* (1943).
Martin, David, *Ally Betrayed: The Uncensored Story of Tito and Mihailović* (1946).
Milazzo, Matteo J., *The Cetnik Movement and the Yugoslav Resistance* (1975).
Seitz, Albert, *Mihailović: Hoax or Hero* (1953).

Mihov, Nikola (1891–1945)

Bulgarian lieutenant general and minister of war. Mihov commanded the Bulgarian Fifth Army in the 1941 occupation of Yugoslavia. The main mission of his troops was fighting Yugoslav resistance in Macedonia. In 1942, Mihov became Bulgarian minister of war. Following the death of Tsar Boris III (q.v.), Mihov was appointed one of the regents for the minority of Tsar Simeon II. In 1945, Mihov was executed by the Bulgarian Communist government.

Andrzej Suchcitz

Additional Reading
Miller, Marshall L., *Bulgaria During the Second World War* (1975).

Mikołajczyk, Stanisław (1901–1966)

Prime minister of the Polish government-in-exile. Born in 1901, Mikołajczyk was one of the central figures in Polish populist politics. He was a prominent figure in the moderate-right faction of the complex populist mosaic of interwar Poland. He fought in the September 1939 campaign, was briefly interned in Hungary, and eventually reached France. There he assumed the leadership of the Populist Party abroad and was a vice premier of the Polish government-in-exile led by General Władysław Sikorski (q.v.). On Sikorski's death on 14 July 1943, Mikołajczyk became premier.

Hardly the commanding, charismatic figure who preceded him, Mikołajczyk inherited an increasingly desperate political situation. The 1943 Teheran Conference emphasized the West's disinterest in protecting Poland against Soviet demands (*see* Conferences, Allied), a fact made brutally clear during the tragic Warsaw Rising (q.v.). Pressured for political and territorial compromises by Josef Stalin (q.v.), largely abandoned by the West, and presiding over an increasingly frustrated and fractious government, Mikołajczyk resigned on 24 November 1944, and was replaced by the relatively obscure Tomasz Arciszewski (q.v.).

Mikołajczyk's departure coincided with the demise of the Polish government-in-exile as a serious factor in international affairs. Acting independently, Mikołajczyk accepted the Yalta accords regarding Poland and joined the Communist-dominated postwar Polish government in 1945. It was a controversial effort to retain some link between Poland and the West by preserving the populist movement and hence the pluralistic political system in Poland. His efforts were to no avail and he was forced to flee in 1947. Mikołajczyk died in exile in 1966.

M.B. Biskupski

Additional Reading
Miklołajczyk, Stanislaw, *The Rape of Poland* (1948).
Raczński, Edward, *In Allied London* (1963).
Salter, Cedric, *Flight from Poland* (1940).

Mikoyan, Artem Ivanovich (1905–1970)

Soviet colonel general of the technical service, and aircraft designer. Mikoyan, the son of a carpenter, was born in a small village in Armenia. With little formal education, he began working as a lathe operator in 1923. He acquired a love of flying during his period of national service in the Red Army from 1928 to 1930. In 1931, he entered the Soviet Air Force Academy, and graduated from the Zhukovsky Air Force Engineering Academy in 1936. From there he joined the Polikarpov Design Bureau, working on the Chaika Team. In that post he gained Josef Stalin's (q.v.) attention as an effective production-line organizer.

In November 1939, Stalin appointed Mikoyan to head a design team to develop the Soviet Union's new fighters for the next decade. Mikoyan accepted the position, asking only that his friend, Mikhail Guryevich (q.v.) join him as his assistant. That team became the foundation of the Mikoyan-Guryevich (abbreviated MiG) Design Bureau, which over the next fifty years produced an outstanding line of fighter aircraft that dominated Soviet fighter production and Western intelligence threat assessments during the Cold War.

In 1940 the MiG Bureau produced its first fighter, the MiG-1. It was a fast but unstable aircraft that quickly was replaced by the MiG-3, the most widely used Soviet fighter aircraft of World War II. MiG efforts to develop a long-range fighter escort were interrupted by the German invasion. In the resulting reorientation of Soviet industry, the MiG team came to specialize on interceptors. At the end of the war, the MiG team was in the best position to exploit the first captured turbojets and German research. The result was the MiG-9, the first Soviet jet fighter.

Mikoyan retired in 1969 after suffering a stroke. He died the following year of heart problems. A kind and considerate man, he was not a good designer himself, but he was an innovative and efficient organizer who could solve production problems quickly. This talent and his affable nature made him the perfect facilitator for a design team filled with brilliant minds and passionate personalities. Mikoyan was twice a Hero of Socialist Labor, and he received six Orders of Lenin for his work.

Carl O. Schuster

Additional Reading
Belyakov, R.A., and J. Marmain, *MiG: Fifty Years of Secret Aircraft Design* (1994).
Butowski, Piotr, and Jay Miller, *OKB MiG: A History of the Design Bureau and Its Aircraft* (1994).

Milch, Erhard (1892–1972)

German field marshal, inspector general of the *Luftwaffe*, inspector general, state secretary for the Aviation Ministry, and director of air armament. During the Third *Reich*, Milch's mother was suspected of being a Jew. Nonetheless, he became the managing director of Adolf Hitler's (q.v.) *Luftwaffe* in World War II. A man of vision, irreverence, and personal courage, he had great abilities as an organizer and administrator. After serving in a fighter group in World War I, he left the military in 1921 to join the civilian air industry. As chief executive of *Lufthansa* in 1929, he worked behind the scenes to help re-create a German air force. After his introduction to Hitler in 1932, Milch became state secretary for the Air Ministry. Hermann Göring (q.v.) allowed him to direct personally the *Luftwaffe*'s development. He transformed the German aircraft industry into a huge enterprise producing the world's largest air force by 1939.

At the beginning of the war, Göring named Milch inspector general of the *Luftwaffe*. In 1940, Milch took charge of the German Air Force in Norway, his only field command, and received the Knight's Cross. On 19 July 1940, he was promoted

Field Marshal Erhard Milch. (IWM STT 809)

to field marshal. After the death of Ernst Udet (q.v.) in 1941, Milch became director of air armament and led a revival of the *Luftwaffe* by reorganizing the industry and greatly increasing production. In April 1942, he and Albert Speer (q.v.) were made dictators of transportation in Germany. Once the Allied air raids on Germany began, Milch stressed that the key to German air defense was an umbrella of fighters to protect the armaments industry; Göring and Hitler failed to grasp this concept.

Milch was responsible for the development of the V-1 flying bomb, and pressed for its rapid implementation. In January 1943, he commanded the airlift at Stalingrad (q.v.), but failed to save the Sixth Army. He continually pushed the development of the Me-262 jet as a fighter, against the wishes of Hitler, who saw it as a bomber. On 20 June 1944, Milch was removed from most of his posts.

At the Nuremberg trials (*see* International Military Tribunal) he acted as a defense witness for Göring. Milch was later tried, and on 17 April 1947, although acquitted of one charge of experimentation on humans, he was sentenced to life in prison as a war criminal. On 31 January 1952, the American high commissioner commuted his sentence to fifteen years, and in 1955, he was released. He worked as an industrial consultant in Dusseldorf until his death on 25 January 1972.

Laura Matysek Wood

Additional Reading

Bartz, Karl, *Swastika in the Air: The Struggle and Defeat of the German Air Force, 1939–1945* (1956).

Irving, David, *The Rise and Fall of the Luftwaffe: The Life of Field Marshal Erhard Milch* (1973).

Mitcham, Samuel W., Jr., *Hitler's Field Marshals and Their Battles* (1988).

———, *Men of the Luftwaffe* (1988).

Miller, Glenn (1904–1944)

U.S. Army Air Force band leader. Alton Glenn Miller was born in Clarinda, Iowa. He was a trombonist, composer, and band leader who worked with such big band era greats as Ben Pollack, Red Nichols, Ray Noble, and the Dorsey brothers. In the five years prior to the war, Miller perfected a unique sound featuring the reed section, making his dance band the most popular in America.

In 1942 he enlisted in the Army Air Forces Technical Training Command and organized a soldier band that played at thousands of morale-boosting events for U.S. and Allied service personnel.

At approximately 1335 hours on 15 December 1944, a C-64A transport aircraft carrying Major Miller and others en route from Britain to Paris was lost over the English Channel. His band continued into 1945 under the co-leadership of Sergeant Jerry Gray and Technical Sergeant Ray McKinley.

A. Gregory Gutgsell, Jr.

Additional Reading

McCarthy, Albert, *The Dance Band Era* (1971).

Mitchell, William Lendrum (1879–1936)

American brigadier general, airpower theorist. Although he died before the start of World War II, "Billy" Mitchell had a profound influence on U.S. Army Air Force doctrine and organization. During his tenure with the American Expeditionary Force (AEF) in World War I as a brigadier general, he learned three basic principles from European airmen. First, the French convinced him that fighter and bomber aircraft achieved superior results when assigned to large combat organizations.

Such an arrangement not only enabled airmen to conduct independent operations throughout the western front, it also prevented local ground force commanders from hoarding precious aircraft. Second, Major General Hugh Trenchard (q.v.), the commander of the Royal Flying Corps in France, taught his American colleague that offensive air operations were indispensable for military success. Third, Mitchell assimilated the precepts of Colonel Giulio Douhet (q.v.), an Italian theorist who advocated the large-scale use of strategic bombers to destroy the "vital centers" of an enemy nation.

Subsequent to his famous court-martial in December 1925, the iconoclastic Mitchell wrote approximately 100 newspaper and magazine articles and two books, all of which popularized and refined the three basic concepts he learned in Europe. His writings also received wide dissemination by influential organizations such as the Air Corps Tactical School and the office of the chief of the air corps. As a result, future army air force leaders like Henry H. "Hap" Arnold and Carl Spaatz (qq.v.) readily embraced Mitchell's principles. They assumed, for example, that future wars would be sharp, short, and cheap.

As Mitchell observed in *Winged Defense,* written in 1925, wars of attrition pitting one army against another were now *passe.* Future conflicts, as Douhet had predicted, would feature strategic bombardment attacks against an enemy nation's vital centers. These centers, as Mitchell further observed in *Skyways,* written in 1930, included civilian populations, transportation hubs, and industrial facilities. Any large-scale disruption of these targets would incapacitate an enemy nation and quickly demoralize its civilian population. Strategic airpower was thus at the forefront of a nation's offensive and defensive might. It enabled a state to exert its will with relative impunity.

To realize the global potential of airpower, Mitchell concluded that a reorganization of the American military was necessary. Operational autonomy for the air arm was no longer enough. Mitchell advocated the creation of a Department of Defense with coequal service branches. Only a consolidated air force, operating as a full partner with land and sea forces, could realize its full offensive potential.

Mitchell's speaking out earned him the enmity of the senior military leadership of the 1920s and an eventual court-martial. After his conviction and suspension from the army, Mitchell now had the freedom to effectively promote his vision of airpower. By the mid-1930s, Mitchell the polemicist had largely succeeded. Army Air Corps lead-ers by that time advocated doctrinal and organizational autonomy. Lieutenant Colonel Harold L. George, for example, formalized U.S. strategic bombing doctrine in his capacity as the director of the Air Corps Tactical School's Department of Air Strategy and Tactics. The main features of this doctrine then reappeared in AWPD-1, "the air plan that defeated Hitler." General Benjamin Foulois (q.v.), in turn, was one among many who agitated for organizational reform. As a result, in 1935, the army created the relatively unconstrained General Headquarters, Air Force. It then yielded to large semi-autonomous organizations like the Eighth and Fifteenth Air Forces in World War II; and their successes paved the way for the creation of the U.S. Air Force in 1947.

Billy Mitchell was the key to all these developments. Although all of his assumptions and predictions were not borne out completely by the course of the war, Mitchell provided the critical link between the revolutionary ideas introduced by European airmen in World War I and the unfettered strategic operations performed by U.S. Army Air Forces in World War II.

In belated and posthumous recognition of his contributions to U.S. airpower, the B-25 bomber was named after him; and after World War II, the U.S. Congress awarded Mitchell the Medal of Honor.

Peter R. Faber

Additional Reading
Hurley, Alfred F., *Billy Mitchell: Crusader for Air Power* (1975).
Mitchell, William L., *Skyways* (1930).

Mitford, Unity Valkyrie (1914–1948)
British Nazi sympathizer. A member of the British upper class, Unity Mitford was one of four sisters well known in British political and literary circles between the wars. One sister, Diana, married Sir Oswald Mosley (q.v.), leader of the British Union of Fascists. Unity was a firm believer in the Nazi creed and infatuated with its leaders. She was on close terms with many of them. She remained in Germany after the war started, but was returned to Britain in 1940 with an accidental gunshot wound. Her activities and sympathies were harmless enough. What little significance that she and her small circle of friends might have had was to influence German leaders to believe, mistakenly, that their views were supported by the British upper class.

Philip Green

Additional Reading
Pryce-Jones, D., *Unity Mitford, A Quest* (1976).

Model, Walther (1891–1945)

German field marshal, commander of Army Group B. Walther Model came to Adolf Hitler's (q.v.) attention early and rose quickly, serving as chief of staff of the IV Corps during the assault on Poland, and chief of staff of the Sixteenth Army during the invasion of France. His performance was rewarded with command of 3rd *Panzer* Division in Operation BARBAROSSA, with promotion to commander of the III *Panzer Korps* in 1941. In 1942, he assumed command of the Ninth Army, where he pioneered the use of dug-in tanks as mobile "hedgehogs," demonstrating the defensive value of armor. During four weeks of fierce winter fighting he destroyed one Soviet army and decimated another.

Model persuaded Hitler to postpone the 1943 attack on the Kursk (q.v.) salient, stressing that the German forces needed additional tanks for the operation, but the Soviets prepared defenses before these arrived. Thus, Operation CITADEL, begun in July 1943 with Model commanding the northern arm, quickly faltered, and was cancelled by Hitler in the face of the Allied landing in Italy.

Field Marshal Walther Model. (IWM MH 12850)

In the ensuing period, Model again displayed his skill in defensive operations. In October 1943, he was chosen to command Army Group North, which he withdrew in good order from Leningrad (q.v.) in January 1944, stabilizing the front between Narva and Pskov. In April 1944, he was promoted to field marshal and replaced Erich von Manstein (q.v.) as commander of Army Group South (renamed Army Group Northern Ukraine). He resisted the Soviet thrust toward the Carpathian passes, but was pushed back into eastern Galicia and Bessarabia. As Army Group Center collapsed in June under the Soviet Byelorussian offensive (q.v.), Model replaced Ernst Busch (q.v.) as Army Group Center Commander while retaining Army Group Northern Ukraine. He stopped the Soviets along the Vistula. He was then sent to the western front to relieve Günther von Kluge (q.v.) as commander in chief west and Army Group B commander on 16 August 1944.

Model rallied and regrouped his forces. In September 1944, Gerd von Rundstedt (q.v.) was appointed commander in chief west, while Model retained Army Group B. Model bore primary responsibility for delaying the British-American advance into Germany until spring 1945. He ignored Hitler's order to destroy what remained of the Ruhr infrastructure, and made arrangements to secure the basic needs of the civilian population.

On 2 April Army Group B was surrounded. Model dissolved his force, released the majority of his soldiers from service, and, with volunteers, attempted an armed breakout. Disillusioned over Hitler's failure to provide the promised last-minute relief via "miracle weapons," Model shot himself on 17 April 1945.

A leader with an iron hand, Model was not always popular with his men or with the senior *Wehrmacht* leadership; but he retained Hitler's favor to the end, just as he retained faith in the *Führer*. Model was the first field commander to denounce the 20 July 1944 assassination plot against Hitler and proclaim his fidelity. His excellent organizational skills, especially when on the defensive, enabled him to scrape together human and material resources and forge them, first in the east, then in the west, into functional forces that could not stop, but did significantly delay, the Allied advance.

Sidney Dean

Additional Reading
Barnett, Correlli (ed.), *Hitler's Generals* (1989).
Görlitz, Walter, *History of the German General Staff* (1953).

Liddell Hart, Basil H., *The German Generals Talk* (1948).

Mellenthin, F.W. von, *Panzer Battles* (1956).

Mitcham, Samuel W., Jr., *Hitler's Field Marshals and Their Battles* (1988).

Mola Vidal, Emilio (1887–1937)

Spanish general, Nationalist commander. Emilio Mola Vidal was born in Placetas, Cuba, in 1887, the son of a civil guard captain. He attended the Spanish Military Academy in Toledo and in 1909, joined the army in Morocco. Through his actions in combat, he rose to the rank of colonel by 1926 and became brigadier general after the pacification of Morocco in 1927. He was appointed director of state security under King Alfonso XIII. Ruthless and cunning, he was feared and despised by the populace. In 1936, he was appointed military commander of Pamplona.

From Pamplona, Mola became the principal organizer of the July uprising and took command of all Nationalist forces in the northern zone of Spain. He made his mark on history when he was asked with which of his four columns he thought he would seize the Spanish capital. He responded with the "Fifth Column," made up of Nationalist supporters inside the city. Failing to take Madrid, he turned his attention to a successful campaign in the North. He was killed on 3 June 1937 while flying from Burgos to Salamanca.

José Alvarez

Additional Reading

Feis, Herbert, *The Spanish Story: Franco and the Nations at War* (1948).

Vigon, J., *General Mola: El Conspirador* (1957).

Mölders, Werner (1913–1941)

German general, *Luftwaffe* inspector general of fighters. Werner Mölders joined the *Luftwaffe* in 1935 and saw combat with the *Kondor Legion* (q.v.) in 1936 in Spain. As leader of III *Staffel* of *Jagdgruppe* JG-88, he led all German pilots with fourteen victories. Not only a skilled fighter pilot but a masterful tactician, he developed the *Schwarm* "Finger Four" flying formation used by both the *Luftwaffe,* and later by the RAF. In the Battle of France, he commanded *Gruppe* III of JG-53, before being shot down. He survived and went on to achieve fifty-eight air-to-air kills during the Battle of Britain (q.v.). In the Soviet Union, he led JG-51 and scored an additional thirty-three kills.

He was the first of only twenty-six German officers to be awarded the Knight's Cross of the Iron Cross with Oak Leaves, Swords, and Diamonds. He also was the first combat pilot in history to score more than 100 victories. Promoted to the rank of general of fighters and appointed inspector general of the fighter arm, he directed air operations over the Crimea when recalled to Berlin for the funeral of Ernst Udet (q.v.). On 21 November 1941, the He-111 he flew to Berlin crashed in fog and rain at Breslau. *"Vati"* (Daddy) Mölders died instantly, having achieved 115 air victories at age twenty-eight.

José Alvarez

Additional Reading

Obermaier, Ernst, *Luftwaffe Holders of the Knight's Cross* (1966).

Toliver, Raymond F., and Trevor J. Constable, *Fighter Aces of the Luftwaffe* (1977).

Molotov, Vyacheslav Michailovich (1890–1986)

Soviet foreign minister. Molotov was the son of Michail Scriabine, a liberal shopkeeper, who influenced his son's appreciation for the existing social tensions of turn of the century Russia. The younger Scriabine's unusual intellect led him to the works of Marx and Engels. There he found the theoretical basis for his aim of overcoming tsarist society.

He joined the Bolshevik Party as early as 1906 and changed his name to Molotov (from the Russian for hammer, *molot*). During his underground party work in St. Petersburg and Moscow, he maintained an active correspondence with the exiled Lenin. Molotov himself was arrested and banished several times. After the revolution in 1917, he took his place in the upper ranks of new Communist leadership.

Like Josef Stalin (q.v.), Molotov was an advocate of a pure doctrine that allowed no deviation. Because of his great analytic and organizing abilities, he quickly made himself indispensable to the party. From 1921 to 1957, he was permanent member of the Central Committee of the Communist Party, and from 1926 to 1952, he was a member of the Politburo. Having been appointed Soviet premier in 1930, he bears some responsibility for the ruthless elimination of opposition in the following years. He became known as "the closest friend and companion of comrade Stalin," and one of his daughters married Stalin's son.

With the intensification of international tension in the late 1930s, Stalin needed somebody he could absolutely trust to represent the interests of the Soviet Union abroad. As a result, Molotov became foreign minister in 1939. He tried to keep the Soviet Union out of war by all means. On 23 August 1939, he signed the nonaggression treaty, the Molotov-Ribbentrop Pact (q.v.), with Germany. A secret provision of that treaty led to the partition of east central Europe between the Nazis and the Soviets after Adolf Hitler's (q.v.) invasion of Poland. Less than two years later, the Germans violated the pact by their activities in Finland and Romania. Molotov confronted the Germans, negotiations broke down, and the German invasion followed.

During the war, Stalin assumed the premiership from Molotov, who remained foreign minister and became a member of the State Defense Committee. Molotov concluded war alliances with Great Britain and the United States, and during his negotiations with Winston S. Churchill and Franklin D. Roosevelt (qq.v.), he obstinately insisted on the opening of a second front in Europe. In June 1943, he engaged in secret negotiations through intermediaries with Joachim von Ribbentrop (q.v.). The talks broke down, but the news reached the Western Allies that the Soviets were trying to reach a separate peace.

At Stalin's side, Molotov took part in all of the great conferences during and after the war. As "Mister *Njet*," he played his part in the beginning of the Cold War by blocking progress during the postwar conferences of 1945 and 1946. After Stalin's death in 1953, Molotov fell into disfavor with the new strong man, Nikita Khrushchev (q.v.). Molotov was able to hold on for a few more years, but he finally was sent into retirement in 1961. When he died in 1986, his funeral was virtually ignored by the Communist Party because of his long and close association with Stalin.

Wolfgang Terhörst

Additional Reading

Bromage, Bernard, *Molotov: The Story of an Era* (1956).

Dallin, D.J., *Soviet Russia's Foreign, 1939–1942* (1942).

Lauterbach, Richard F., *These Are the Russians* (1945).

Snow, Edgar, *The Pattern of Soviet Power* (1945).

Moltke, Helmuth James von (1907–1945)

German jurist, Christian intellectual, and opposition leader. Helmuth James *Graf* von Moltke was born on his family's estate in Kreisau, Silesia (now

Krzyżowa, Poland). He was the great-grandnephew of Field Marshal Helmuth von Moltke. Before the Nazis came to power, von Moltke practiced as an international lawyer in Berlin.

Von Moltke opposed the Nazi regime from the beginning. As early as 1933, he formed a small group of intellectuals, professionals, and military officers into the Kreisau Circle (q.v.), a group dedicated to planning a post-Hitler Germany.

During the war, von Moltke held a post as a legal advisor in the foreign branch of the German High Command *(see Oberkommando der Wehrmacht)*. From that position he helped many prisoners of war, hostages, and forced laborers.

In January 1944, von Moltke was taken into custody on suspicion of having warned a colleague of his own impending arrest. After the 1944 July Plot (*see* Opposition to Hitler), von Moltke was tried for treason before Judge Roland Freisler's (q.v.) dreaded People's Court. Condemned to death, von Moltke was hanged at Berlin's Plötzensee Prison on 23 January 1945.

David T. Zabecki

Additional Reading

Balfour, Michael, and Julian Frisby, *Helmuth von Moltke: A Leader Against Hitler* (1972).

Moltke, Helmuth J. von, *Letters to Freye 1939-1945* (1990).

Monnet, Jean (1888–1979)

French expert on military procurement. Monnet was an important but little-known problem solver who usually worked behind the scenes. Often, others took the credit for his ideas. Declared unfit for military service in World War I, he served as a member of the Civil Supplies Service, where his ideas led to the creation of an Allied Planning Board.

After the war, Monnet served for a time as the deputy secretary-general of the League of Nations (q.v.). When war again threatened, he was convinced that Allied victory rested on superiority of armaments. Appalled by his country's lack of preparedness, he headed a mission to secure arms from the United States. This achieved little before the fall of France.

In June 1940, Monnet rejected an invitation to join General Charles de Gaulle's (q.v.) government-in-exile. He believed victory rested on British survival and the production capacity of the United States. He returned to Washington as a member of the British Purchasing Mission.

Surprisingly, Monnet had considerable influence in Washington. He suggested the phrase "Arsenal of Democracy," (q.v.) and the Lend-Lease (q.v.) program was in part his conception. He also perceived early the need for extremely high levels of arms production in the United States and was able to convince President Franklin D. Roosevelt (q.v.) of this.

With peace, Monnet went to work reviving the French economy. The "Monnet Plan" was a model for democratic economic planning. Often known as "Mister Europe," he was the driving force behind the European Common Market, based on the concept of avoiding war through economic and political integration.

Spencer Tucker

Additional Reading
Monnet, Jean, *Memoirs* (1978).

Montagu, Ewen E.S. (1901–1985)
British lieutenant commander, naval intelligence officer. A barrister and amateur yachtsman, perhaps best remembered as the architect of Operation MINCEMEAT (q.v.), Montagu joined Britain's Royal Naval Volunteer Reserve in 1938. On 16 November 1940, at the urging of Naval Intelligence Director Admiral J.H. Godfrey (q.v.), he transferred to London to oversee NID 17M, the Admiralty subsection concerned with nonoperational ULTRA (q.v.) decrypts.

NID 17M arose from Admiral Godfrey's early realization that nonoperational "special intelligence," mostly *Abwehr* (q.v.) traffic, produced by Bletchley Park (q.v.) could be used to strategic advantage. Montagu was charged with collating this information and turning it back on the enemy. This latter responsibility led to his involvement with the W-Board and its working group, the Twenty (XX) Committee (q.v.).

Montagu was required to prepare daily Orange Summaries of ULTRA intelligence for Admiralty use in addition to his "double-cross work" for the Twenty Committee. Working from the cramped basement of the Admiralty or the Twenty Committee's offices in St. James Street, Montagu participated in a number of deception plans, including FORTITUDE, while aiding in the creation of plausible "chicken-feed" for double agents to pass on to their *Abwehr* masters.

Following the war, Montagu returned to his law practice, eventually becoming judge advocate of the fleet and chairman of the Quarter Sessions for Middlesex. He was honored with the Order of the British Empire for his part in MINCEMEAT.

He died on 19 July 1985, after a distinguished legal career.

Mark Rummage

Additional Reading
Howard, Michael, *British Intelligence in the Second World War,* Vol. 5: *Strategic Deception* (1990).
McLachlan, Donald, *Room 39: A Study in Naval Intelligence* (1968).
Montagu, Ewen, *Beyond Top Secret Ultra* (1977).

Montgomery, Bernard Law (1887–1976)
British field marshal, commander of the 21st Army Group. Sir Bernard Law Montgomery was born at St. Mark's Vicarage, Kensington Oval, London, on 17 November 1887, and was educated at St. Paul's. His early life was dominated by a tyrannical mother whose stern method of upbringing caused him to rebel continually, and no doubt, molded his character with a confidence and determination that drove him throughout his life. He became a gentleman cadet at the Royal Military College, Sandhurst, at the age of nineteen. He quickly became a lance corporal within the college, and after a difficult period, he eventually passed out thirtieth on the list of 150 cadets.

Montgomery joined the Royal Warwickshire Regiment in 1908 and moved to India with the regiment's 1st Battalion stationed at Peshawar. During the next two years, he devoted his time to learning his profession in a dedicated manner. Following the outbreak of World War I, he saw action and was awarded the Distinguished Service Order, mentioned in dispatches, promoted to brevet major, and severely wounded.

In 1923, Montgomery was posted to the 49th West Riding Division in Yorkshire. There, he was completely absorbed in his military career and even conducted private military classes of his own for junior officers. He was determined to study and teach the theory of warfare and to show that war had progressed beyond trench warfare and that a battle was a precise and technical operation. He believed every possible risk must be examined and provided for before a battle commenced. He also believed attack was the key, and with good and determined planning the attack should always succeed.

Following a period of eleven years in staff appointments, Montgomery returned to his parent regiment, where his determined manner and progressive ideas were not entirely to the liking of other regimental officers. In 1925, at the age of thirty-eight, and after many years as a confirmed bachelor soldier, Montgomery decided it was time to get married. He was on leave in Switzerland when he met his future wife, Betty Carver. She was the daughter of an Indian civil servant and a widow with two small sons. Her husband had been killed at Gallipoli. While on holiday, Montgomery spent time teaching the two boys skating and other games, and continued to see the family after their return to Britain.

In January 1926, Montgomery was appointed to a job completely to his liking. He was sent to the British Army Staff College at Camberley as an instructor. He enjoyed his three-year tour there. On 27 July 1927, he married Betty Carver and set up home at Camberley. Despite his marriage, he continued to be utterly dedicated to the army. It is recorded that following his marriage "the staff and the students did not find much change in him." He was an uncompromising instructor and remained so during the remainder of his time at Camberley.

Montgomery became a lieutenant colonel in 1931 and assumed command of his battalion. Right from the start, he was determined to run his unit his way. At Alexandria, Egypt, he found his men were unhappy with the Sunday church parades. He ordered that in the future, the Sunday service could be attended in civilian clothes, and he personally read the lesson. This brought the

inevitable reprimand from headquarters in Cairo, but Montgomery insisted on his rights as commanding officer and won.

In 1934, Montgomery was promoted to colonel and appointed senior instructor at the Military Staff College at Quetta, India. It was a time of great contentment, with his military career advanced and his employment at the Staff College ideal for his temperament and beliefs. With him was his wife and their son David, born in 1928. It was during this tour of duty that Quetta was devastated by an earthquake in May 1935, with the loss of more than 30,000 people. Montgomery was involved in the rescue operation, which was carried out by the British garrison troops who, based outside the town, missed the worst of the devastation.

Following the tour of duty at Quetta, Montgomery returned to the United Kingdom in the early summer of 1937 and took command of the 9th Infantry Brigade at Portsmouth. He was promoted to the rank of brigadier. One biographer of Montgomery comments that he "had left England six years before, an untried and rather unpromising commander of a battalion. Now he was coming home, a man of influence, an acknowledged mentor in the Army." With the assumption of command, Montgomery was allocated official quarters at Ravelin House. While preparations were under way for the family to reunite at Ports-

Field Marshal Sir Bernard Law Montgomery (later Viscount Montgomery), flanked by Major General J. Lawton Collins (left) and Major General Matthew B. Ridgway (right). (IWM B 13174)

mouth, he was called away on maneuvers with his new brigade.

Montgomery and his wife agreed that she would go to Burnham-on-Sea with their son David. While on the beach, Betty was bitten on the leg by an unknown insect. When she returned to their rooms, she was weak and faint, and a doctor was called. Montgomery was informed and he immediately went to the hospital at Burnham-on-Sea, where he found his wife much worse and with the infection spreading. Despite amputation, the infection continued to spread and on 19 December 1937, Betty died.

Montgomery went back to the empty house at Portsmouth with his son. He engaged a male servant, and no woman was allowed to enter the house. For the next five months, he lived as a recluse except for his work, which he performed each day. He said nothing of his loss to his staff and years later he commented, "My married life was absolute bliss. The death of my wife was a shattering blow from which I recovered with great difficulty, and very slowly."

With the buildup of the British Army prior to the outbreak of the war, Montgomery was promoted to major general in 1938 and given command of the 3rd Division, which he took to France. He brought the 3rd Division back from Dunkirk (q.v.), one of the last officers to leave the beach. In 1939, he moved on to command the British V Corps, followed by a move to XII Corps in 1941 and to South-Eastern Command in 1942.

Montgomery received the news that he was to take over the command of the British Eighth Army in North Africa following the unexpected death of General William H. Gott (q.v.). Lieutenant General Montgomery landed at Cairo on 12 August 1942, ready to take command of an army low in morale. He was always notorious in military circles as a law unto himself, and his new appointment brought no change. He was often more feared by the senior officers on his staff than by the junior ones. He had the knack of encouraging younger officers to talk, and he listened to what they had to say. He was described as being "just a bit mad and likes showing off. And he's always causing trouble." Whatever other officers thought of him, he was without a doubt "the Commander." He believed that to be weak was to lose, and he had no intention of losing.

Having assumed command of the Eighth Army, he carried out a successful campaign in North Africa, including his famous victory at El Alamein (q.v.). He provided a popular image, wearing a Royal Tank Regiment black beret with the regimental badge, along with his general officer's badge. It was quite irregular, but it made him a "character" and he was seen as such by the men of his command. His unorthodox dress, military bearing, and manner of speech made him a popular figure with the press. To the civilian population of the United Kingdom, who suffered constant air raids and news of defeats and setbacks, he was a successful and colorful general, and he immediately became a popular figure. The press played a great part in fostering his image and he soon became known to the army and civilians alike as "Monty."

Following the campaign in North Africa, Montgomery was involved in successful campaigns throughout Italy (q.v.). He then returned to Britain to take part in Operation OVERLORD (*see* Normandy). He was the overall ground forces commander during the D-Day landings on 6 June 1944. After the formation of the U.S. First Army, Montgomery commanded the British Second Army.

After the successful Allied landings, the British advance was halted at Caen (q.v.) by a superior German force. The supreme Allied commander, General Dwight D. Eisenhower (q.v.), pressed Montgomery to break out; but despite attack after attack, gallantly conducted and heavily supported by artillery and air strikes, the German line held. Montgomery's Second Army was constantly faced with far larger tank concentrations. It was part of the plan for the British forces to attract the bulk of the German armor and artillery to the north of the beachhead so that the U.S. First Army could break through to the south. There were those on the British General Staff who failed to realize this fact and who looked for advances so that place names could be used to show just how effective the Allied advance was progressing.

With the delay, pressure, mainly by British officers on the general staff, caused a deepening rift between Montgomery and Eisenhower. At that time, it was not generally known that the German strategy demanded that the British advance be stopped at all costs. For Montgomery, the situation became critical, but an agreement over the conduct of the campaign was reached with General Eisenhower, and Montgomery continued to play a key role in the battle for Europe.

Montgomery was appointed commander of the mostly British Commonwealth 21st Army Group in 1944. On 23–24 March 1945, his army group crossed the Rhine and advanced into the German industrial area of the Ruhr. At Lüneburger Heide, at 1830 hours on 4 May 1945, the German high command signed an instrument of unconditional surrender, to Montgomery, for all the German armed forces in Holland and in northwest Germany and Denmark.

Following the end of the war in Europe, Montgomery held a number of appointments, including commander of the British Army of the Rhine, chief of the Imperial General Staff, and finally deputy supreme Allied commander Europe from 1951 to 1958. He was appointed Knight Grand Cross of the Order of the Bath in 1945 and Knight of the Order of the Garter in 1946. He was also elevated to the peerage, as 1st Viscount Montgomery of Alamein, in recognition of his contributions to the British war effort. Montgomery died at his home on 24 March 1976. He was given a state funeral at St. George's Chapel in Windsor Castle.

Alan Harfield

Additional Reading

Hamilton Nigel, *Monty: The Making of a General, 1887–1942* (1981).
———, *Monty: Master of the Battlefield, 1942–1944* (1983).
———, *Monty: The Field Marshal, 1944–1976* (1986).
Lewin, Ronald, *Montgomery As a Military Commander* (1971).
Montgomery, Bernard L., *The Memoirs of Field Marshal the Viscount Montgomery of Alamein, KG* (1958).

Morgan, Frederick E. (1894–1967)

British lieutenant general, principal planner of Operation OVERLORD. Sir Frederick Morgan was born in 1894 and graduated from the Royal Military Academy in 1913. During World War I, he spent four years at the front where he was twice mentioned in dispatches and suffered from shell shock. In 1938, he was named commander, support forces, for the British 1st Armoured Division. He fought with them during the 1940 campaign in France. Various staff appointments followed until, in March 1943, he was named chief of staff to the supreme Allied commander (COSSAC), with specific orders to draft plans for the invasion of France.

Morgan's eventual plan chose Normandy as the site for the invasion, limited the number of troops to three divisions on a front of twenty-five miles, and recommended the creation of an artificial harbor to provide port facilities. Almost immediately, his plan came under attack. General George C. Marshall (q.v.) believed it unimaginative because it "would draw German mobile reserves like a magnet." More damaging were General Bernard L. Montgomery's (q.v.) criticisms, which argued that Morgan had come under General Dwight D. Eisenhower's (q.v.) spell and thus could not be trusted. Montgomery called for an expansion to five divisions and the front widened to fifty miles. In 1944, Morgan was "kicked upstairs" to become deputy chief of staff to Eisenhower. He played little role during the rest of the war.

Morgan's role in the war was obscured by Montgomery's hostility toward him. Still, it was Morgan's general plan that was followed by the Allies in the greatest combined amphibious assault in history. After the war, he served briefly and unhappily as director of the United Nations Relief and Recovery Administration in Germany. From 1951 to 1956, he played a prominent role in the development of the British atomic energy program. He died in 1967.

John P. Rossi

Additional Reading

Morgan, Frederick E., *COSSAC's Memoirs: Overture to Overlord* (1951).
———, *Peace and War: A Soldier's Life* (1961).

Morgenthau, Henry J., Jr. (1881–1967)

U.S. treasury secretary, 1934–1945. The son of a self-made millionaire immigrant, Henry Morgenthau, Jr., became a gentleman farmer following his graduation from Cornell. He was a close friend of Franklin D. Roosevelt (q.v.), whose estate was near Morgenthau's farm. Morgenthau became secretary of the treasury in 1934. Although fiscally conservative, Morgenthau followed Roosevelt's policy of massive deficit spending to overcome the Depression, and later, to finance the war. Morgenthau participated from the beginning in developing the Lend-Lease (q.v.) program, which he stressed as vital to keeping America out of the war.

U.S. defense spending rose as the likelihood of entry into the war increased. To minimize the threat of inflation, Morgenthau vastly expanded the savings bond program, which he had initiated in 1935 to help finance the New Deal. Although best remembered as the author of the Morgenthau Plan (q.v.), he also was a driving force behind establishing the International Monetary Fund and the World Bank. During his eleven-and-a-half-year tenure as treasury secretary, Morgenthau helped carry the American economy through the Depression and World War II.

Sidney Dean

Additional Reading

Beard, Charles A., *President Roosevelt and the Coming of the War* (1948).

Morshead, Leslie James (1889–1959)

Australian lieutenant general, commander of the Australian 9th Division and the Tobruk garrison. Sir Leslie Morshead served with Australian forces in Europe during World War I. In the 1930s, he commanded various infantry units. Between 1939–1941, he commanded the Australian 18th Infantry Brigade in the Middle East. In early 1941, he assumed command of the Australian 9th Division.

When German general Erwin Rommel's (q.v.) forces drove the British out of Cyrenaica in the spring of 1941, Morshead headed the large garrison in besieged Tobruk (q.v.). General Archibald Wavell (q.v.) told him, "the defense of Egypt now depends largely on you," and "I know I can count on you to hold Tobruk to the end." Morshead defended the vital port against repeated attacks. He received key replacements and supplies by sea but could never drive back the Axis forces. Australia finally insisted that the 9th Division be relieved during September–October 1941. The 9th Division moved to El Alamein (q.v.) where Morshead continued as its commander. He also served as commander in chief of Australian Forces, Middle East.

An effective champion of his dominion's forces, Morshead opposed removal of units from his divisions, a fragmenting practice often pressed by his superiors, and the overuse of Australians as shock troops. He did, however, welcome decisive actions against the enemy. In 1943, Morshead returned to Australia and held successive major commands; the Australian II Corps (1943–1944), New Guinea Force (1944), Australian Second Army (1944), and Borneo Force (1945). A highly respected leader and concerned about his troops' well-being and morale, he always inspired confidence. His honors included the KBE, *Legion d'Honneur,* and the U.S. Medal of Freedom.

Richard Wires

Additional Reading

Maughan, Barton, *Tobruk and El Alamein* (1966).

Miller, Ward A., *The 9th Australian Division Versus the Afrika Korps* (1987).

Moskalenko, Kirill Semenovich (1902–1985)

Soviet colonel general. Moskalenko was born on 11 May 1902. After primary school in his home town of Grishino in the Ukraine, he attended agricultural school. In 1920, he joined an armed detachment fighting in the civil war. Through various military schools, Moskalenko gravitated toward cavalry-artillery. He rose steadily through the ranks, and by 1935, he commanded the 23rd Mechanized Brigade in the Far East. It was there he made the transition from cavalry to tanks.

In 1936, Moskalenko moved back west to Kiev and commanded the 133rd Mechanized Brigade. When the Finnish Winter War (q.v.) broke out, he was an artillery commander in the 51st Perekop Rifle Division. He emerged from that war as a brigadier general, and by June 1940, he was a major general commanding the XXXV Rifle Corps in the Bessarabian campaign.

When Germany launched Operation BARBAROSSA, Moskalenko was in command of the 1st Artillery Antitank Brigade in Kiev. His unit came up against Field Marshal Gerd von Rundstedt's (q.v.) Army Group South. In September 1941, Moskalenko took command of the XV Rifle Corps and broke out of the ring surrounding Kiev (q.v.). In early 1942, he commanded Thirty-Eighth Army, part of the Northern Attack Group on the north Donets River. That summer, Moskalenko assumed command of the First Tank Army, which at the time was only partially formed. In August, he took over First Guards Army and launched an offensive between the Don and Volga Rivers to hold off the German thrust on Stalingrad (q.v.). At the end of September, Josef Stalin (q.v.) ordered him to assume command of the Fortieth Army of the Voronezh Front—Moskalenko's fourth command in as many months.

In January 1943, the *Stavka* ordered Voronezh Front to attack the Kharkov and Kursk axes. That summer, at the Kursk salient, Moskalenko was ordered to hold any German attempt to break through. At the end of August, he was once again on the outskirts of Kiev, this time advancing toward the Dnieper and crossing it under fire on 23 September. It was here he earned his first Hero of the Soviet Union award.

The end of October 1943 found Colonel General Moskalenko once again at the helm of Thirty-Eighth Army, this time moving in on Kiev, which finally was liberated on 4 November. Continuous hammering by Marshal Georgy Zhukov's (q.v.) 1st Ukrainian Front succeeded in smashing German Army Group South in April 1944, with Moskalenko pushing the Germans to the southern Bug River.

In September 1944, Moskalenko drove

through the Carpathians. His objective was Dukla Pass, connecting Poland with Slovakia. He secured that objective on 6 October. He then moved through southern Poland and back into Czechoslovakia. For Moskalenko, the war ended with Thirty-Eighth Army converging on Prague.

After the war, Moskalenko took command of the Moscow Air Defense District. Of notable postwar interest was his involvement in the arrest, trial, and execution of Lavrenty Beria, head of the NKVD (qq.v.). Moskalenko made the initial arrest and was one of the members of Beria's tribunal. For six months after Beria's 23 December 1953 execution, Moskalenko and Marshal Sergei Rudenko conducted an (after the fact) investigation into the Beria case. As a result of his loyalty to Nikita Khrushchev (q.v.), Moskalenko was promoted to marshal of the Soviet Union in 1955. In 1978, he was awarded his second Hero of the Soviet Union.

William H. Van Husen

Additional Reading

Shukman, Harold (ed.), *Stalin's Generals* (1993).
Vitukhin, Igor, *Soviet Generals Recall World War II* (1981).
Ziemke, Earl F., and Magna E. Bauer, *Moscow to Stalingrad: Decision in the East* (1987).

Mosley, Oswald (1896–1980)

British Fascist leader. Sir Oswald Mosley, World War I veteran and former government minister, founded the British Union of Fascists (BUF) in 1932. A striking and youthful Fascist leader, he demanded that Britain concern itself solely with its Empire. Consequently, the BUF advanced a foreign policy based on the slogan, "Mind Britain's Business." With the outbreak of war, his Fascists campaigned for peace along those lines. In 1940, fears of a fifth column (unfounded as they were), led the British government to intern around 1,000 Fascists, including Mosley. That ended BUF activity, but Mosley reemerged after the war with the slogan: "Europe a Nation."

Stephen M. Cullen

Additional Reading

Mosley, Sir Oswald, *My Life* (1966).
Skidelsky, Robert, *Oswald Mosley* (1981).

Moulin, Jean (1899–1943)

French resistance leader. A member of the radical Left and often described as a crypto-Communist, Jean Moulin became the martyr of the French resistance. As prefect for Chartres in June 1940, he was arrested and tortured by the *Gestapo* (q.v.) for refusing to sign a document that falsely accused black French soldiers of committing atrocities. He later escaped to Britain and rallied to General de Gaulle (q.v.) in London.

Holding ministerial rank in the Free French government, Moulin was parachuted into the south of France in January 1942. As de Gaulle's personal representative, he had the difficult task of uniting the different resistance factions under de Gaulle and of forming a secret army. His efforts resulted in the creation of the United Resistance Movement (MUR) and the National Council of the Resistance (CNR). The aims of the MUR and CNR were to fight against the occupying powers, overthrow the home-grown dictatorship, and win France's liberty.

Moulin's mission was extremely important for de Gaulle on the international scene, since the leader of the Free French had to strengthen his position by convincing the American and British governments that he alone had the French resistance (q.v.) behind him. This need was clearly demonstrated in November 1942 when, following the Allied invasion of Northwest Africa (q.v.), the Anglo-American Allies showed a preference for General Henri Giraud (q.v.) as an alternative to de Gaulle in the French leadership struggle.

Working incognito and answering to the aliases of Jacques Martel, Max, Rex, and Regis, Moulin remained in the south of France where he organized and administered the resistance on Gaullist lines. Eventually his luck ran out. On 21 June 1943, while attending a secret resistance meeting in Caluaire near Lyons, he was arrested by the *Gestapo*. There is little doubt that he was betrayed by a member of the resistance. He also failed to post guards to warn of the approaching *Gestapo* agents. He was interrogated and tortured by SS *Obersturmführer* Klaus Barbie (q.v.) at *Gestapo* headquarters in Lyons. He then was deported to Germany where he died in transit.

In postwar years, Jean Moulin's memory was transmogrified by some into the Gaullist symbol of heroic patriotism, particularly when his ashes were transferred to the *Pantheon* in December 1964. Despite this, his obvious betrayal by a member of the resistance lies at the very heart of a seemingly never-ending controversy *(les guerres franco-françaises)* that continues to rock the conscience of French society.

Robert C. Hudson

Additional Reading

Calef, H., *Jean Moulin* (1980).

Ehrlich, Blake, *The Resistance: France 1940–45* (1965).

Michel, H., *Jean Moulin L'Unificateur* (1964).

Werth, Alexander, *France 1940–1955* (1957).

Mountbatten, Louis (1900–1979)

British vice admiral, chief of Combined Operations, supreme Allied commander Southwest Asia. Lord Louis Mountbatten descended from German aristocracy and was related to the British Royal Family, but he rose to Admiral of the Fleet (after World War II) by his own ability and strength of character. He was born at Windsor in 1900. While still a naval cadet at Dartmouth in 1914, his father was forced to resign as Britain's first sea lord because of his German birth, despite anglicizing the family name from Battenburg to Mountbatten. Whatever other effect this might have had on young Louis, it seems to have implanted in him a determination to succeed by reaching the pinnacles of the British establishment.

During World War I, Mountbatten served on battleships. Afterward, following a year at Cambridge, he accompanied his cousin the Prince of Wales (later King Edward VIII) on royal tours of Australia, India, and Japan. Though he and his wife earned reputations as members of the polo-playing playboy set, between the wars his career progressed steadily. One of his commanding officers reported: "this officer's heart and soul are in the Navy."

Mountbatten's service between 1939 and 1945 can be divided into three phases. For the first two years, he was constantly in action as captain of the 5th Destroyer Flotilla, particularly during the evacuations of Norway and Crete (qq.v.), where he survived the loss of his own ship, the HMS *Kelly*. His standards of seamanship were sometimes suspect, but never his courage or leadership. In 1942, he was promoted to vice admiral and filled the new post of chief of Combined Operations (q.v.). As such, he was responsible for planning the highly successful commando attack on Saint-Nazaire, and the costly failure of the Canadian raid on Dieppe (qq.v.). He was also involved in the early planning stages for Operation OVERLORD.

Taken by Prime Minister Winston S. Churchill (q.v.) to the Quebec Conference in 1943 (*see* Conferences, Allied), Mountbatten was appointed supreme Allied commander Southeast Asia. Though his appointment was not entirely welcome by some of his subordinates, by August 1945, Allied forces had reconquered Burma and were poised to invade Malaya. After accepting the Japanese surrender in Singapore, he dealt successfully with the problems of restoring civil government in the vast areas handed back by the enemy. For his services in this theater, the son of a German aristocrat was granted a British title, making him Earl Mountbatten of Burma.

At the end of 1946, Prime Minister Clement Attlee (q.v.) persuaded Mountbatten to become the last British viceroy of India. He returned to the Royal Navy in 1949, and by 1955, he rose to hold his father's 1914 post of first sea lord. He then went one step farther to become the first chief of the defense staff, a tri-service post designed to coordinate all defense activity.

After Mountbatten's retirement in 1965, he continued to play a prominent part in public affairs. His life of service to Britain and on the international scene came to a tragic end in 1979. Along with two other members of his family and a young Irish bystander, he fell victim to an attack by Irish terrorists at Sligo, in the Republic of Ireland.

Philip Green

Additional Reading

Mountbatten, Lord Louis, *Report to the Combined Chiefs of Staff from the Supreme Commander, Southeast Asia* (1951).

Ziegler, Philip, *Mountbatten* (1985).

Müller, Heinrich (1900–1945?)

Head of the *Gestapo*. Heinrich Müller shaped the *Gestapo* (q.v.) into a terrorizing police force that prevented effective opposition to the Nazis in Germany. After having served on the eastern front during World War I, for which he received the Iron Cross First Class, Müller became a Bavarian policeman and at first worked against the Nazis. Reinhard Heydrich (q.v.), intrigued by Müller's blind obedience and professional competence, chose him as second in command of the *Gestapo* in 1933. Müller was denied admission to the NSDAP (q.v.) until 1939 because of his earlier work against the Nazis, but this roadblock only served to make him work harder to please his masters.

This rather unintelligent, stubborn bureaucrat effectively controlled dissent within the Third *Reich* by appearing to put everyone under constant surveillance. He rose rapidly making SS colonel in 1937 and SS lieutenant general on 9 November 1941. He had played a key role in providing information, which led to the dismissal of Generals Werner von Blomberg and Werner von Fritsch (qq.v.), and he staged the border incidents that were a prelude to the invasion of Poland. He personally signed the order requiring immediate delivery to Auschwitz of 45,000 Jews by 31 January 1943. His subordinate, Adolf Eichmann, directed the Final Solution (qq.v.).

In March 1944, Müller ordered the execution of British officers who escaped detention from a camp near Breslau. He was last seen on 28 April 1945, in the *Führer*'s bunker in Berlin, where he was called upon to interrogate Hermann Fegelein, Eva Braun's (q.v.) brother-in-law, for the crime of trying to escape from the bunker. Müller then disappeared. A burial was recorded for him on 17 May 1945, but when the grave was exhumed in 1963, it held three unidentifiable bodies. Rumors circulated that the *Gestapo* chief, who had reduced murder to a problem of administration, defected to the Soviet Union. Other rumors placed him among other German exiles in Brazil and Argentina. In 1973, he was placed on the list of most-wanted Nazis.

Laura Matysek Wood

Additional Reading

Crankshaw, Edward, *Gestapo: Instrument of Tyranny* (1956).

Delarue, Jacques, *The Gestapo: A History of Horror* (1964).
Douglas, Gregory, *Gestapo Chief: The 1948 Interrogation of Heinrich Müller* (1996).
Manvell, Roger, *SS and Gestapo: Rule by Terror* (1969).

Murphy, Audie L. (1924–1971)

American lieutenant. Audie L. Murphy was the most highly decorated American soldier of World War II. He was born near Kingston, Texas, and grew up in poverty and a broken home. After first being rejected by the navy and the Marine Corps because of his short stature, he enlisted in the army in June 1942. He spent the entire war in the 3rd Infantry Division, serving in Tunisia, Sicily, Anzio, and the landing in southern France (q.v.). He received a battlefield commission on 15 October 1944.

At Holtzwihr, France, on 26 January 1945, Second Lieutenant Murphy was the commander of B Company, 15th Infantry. Under heavy German attack, Murphy ordered a withdrawal of his unit while he stayed behind. As a lone forward observer and nearly encircled by the enemy, he engaged in close combat with 250 infantry troops and six tanks. He killed at least fifty men and forced an enemy retreat, although wounded in the process. As the result of that action he was awarded

Major General John W. O'Daniel presenting the Medal of Honor to Lieutenant Audie L. Murphy. (IWM AP 69087)

the Medal of Honor a few days before his 21st birthday.

After the war Murphy acted in forty motion pictures, including his autobiographical film *To Hell and Back*. Other movies include *The Red Badge of Courage* and various Westerns, which netted more than $2 million. Failed business dealings forced him into bankruptcy in 1968. While on a business trip on 28 May 1971, Murphy died in a plane crash near Roanoke, Virginia. In addition to the Medal of Honor, his twenty-eight decorations included the Distinguished Service Cross, two Silver Stars, the Legion of Merit, two Bronze Stars, three Purple Hearts, the French Legion of Honor, the French *Croix de Guerre,* and the Belgian *Croix de Guerre*.

A. Gregory Gutgsell, Jr.

Additional Reading

Murphy, Audie L., *To Hell and Back* (1949).
Spiller, Roger, "The Price of Valor," *MHQ: The Quarterly Journal of Military History* (spring 1993), pp. 100–110.

Murrow, Edward R. (1908–1965)

American radio journalist. By 1937, Murrow was working for CBS (Columbia Broadcasting System) as its European director of programs in London. He witnessed firsthand the growing tensions in Europe in the late 1930s. He broadcasted directly from Vienna the German completion of their *Anschluss* with Austria (q.v.). The broadcasts made by Murrow during the Munich crisis (q.v.) were among the first overseas broadcasts from CBS.

Murrow made reports from London during the Battle of Britain (q.v.), often coolly broadcasting from the city's rooftops during Germany's nightly bombing raids against Britain and describing the arduous conditions the people lived under. Always the sober observer, he possessed a talent for making the events occurring across the Atlantic come alive for people huddled around their radios in America. "This—is London," became his opening trademark for his wartime broadcasts and the signature by which he was known throughout the United States.

After the war, Murrow returned to the United States and became vice president in charge of news, education, and discussion programs for CBS. He soon returned to the air to produce and narrate the show *Hear It Now* in 1947. In 1951, he brought the show to television as *See It Now*. On this show in 1954 he attacked Senator Joseph McCarthy and

McCarthyism for its infringement on civil liberties. The show was instrumental in bringing about the downfall of McCarthy. Murrow continued with *See It Now* until 1959. In 1961, he left CBS to become director of the U.S. Information Agency until 1964. Murrow died of cancer in 1965.

Susanne Tepe Gaskins

Additional Reading

Murrow, Edward R., *This Is London* (1967).
Persico, Joseph E., *Edward R. Murrow: An American Original* (1988).

Mussolini, Benito (1883–1945)

Fascist leader of Italy. Benito Mussolini was the Italian leader who plunged Italy into World War II. He was born on 29 July 1883, near the village of Predappio in the Romagna. His father, Alessandro, was a blacksmith who worked only intermittently, and his mother Rosa was the village schoolteacher. They named him for Benito Juárez, the Mexican revolutionary and president. Young Benito was fed a steady diet of radical politics. His mother wanted him to be a schoolteacher, and he gave it a try, but found it too boring.

Mussolini's ambition and talent enabled him to rise from obscurity. As an adolescent, he joined the revolutionary or syndicalist section of the Italian Social Democratic Party. Throughout early manhood, he played the agitator, founding unions and fomenting strikes. He also found time to indulge in frequent love affairs, invariably conducted without the usual preliminaries. From his youth, he seems to have been a violent person. At age eighteen, he took as mistress the young wife of a soldier away on station. He mistreated her and at one point stabbed her with a pocket knife. His frequent love affairs continued even after marriage. Strangely, his wife and family pictured him as devoted husband and family man.

Mussolini was not always a militarist. At age nineteen, he fled Italy to escape compulsory military service. He lived in Switzerland for three years doing odd jobs and relying in part on money his mother sent. He occasionally attended university lectures, but his radical socialist views caused him to be expelled from one Swiss canton after another, and he served time in prison. From this experience Mussolini considered himself well-versed in foreign affairs.

An amnesty for criminals allowed Mussolini to return to Italy. He submitted to compulsory military service and then resumed the agitator's role, supplementing it with radical journalism. His work was such that in 1912, he was named editor of *Avanti*, the official journal of the Socialist Party.

Mussolini was soon arrested for antimilitarist activities and imprisoned for five months. When World War I began, he revealed his opportunism by supporting Italian participation on the Allied side, so that the country might gain "unredeemed" lands in the Tirol and along the Adriatic. He founded his own newspaper, *Il Popolo d'Italia (The People of Italy)*, to promote this end. He wrote, "Neutrals have never dominated events. . . . It is blood that moves the wheels of history." This interventionist stance led to Mussolini's expulsion from the Socialist Party.

Italy entered the war on the Allied side in 1915, not because of popular demand but from a cynical bargain (the secret Treaty of London) by its leaders for territorial gains at the expense of Austria-Hungary. He volunteered for war service and fought at the front until 1917 when, as a corporal, he was wounded and discharged.

On the return of peace the Socialists resumed their agitation. Mussolini's reaction came in March 1919 when he organized demobilized ex-soldiers into his first *Fascio di Combattimento* or combat bands. The word *fascio* recalled the bundle of rods carried by the lictors of ancient Rome as the symbol of state power. It became the emblem of Fascist Italy.

Postwar Italy suffered from serious problems, one of which was profound disillusionment over the results of the war. Italy had 600,000 men killed, drained its treasury, and accumulated a large debt. It gained from the breakup of the Austro-Hungarian Empire, but this also weakened claims for territory that included non-Italian populations. Although Italy did secure the southern Tirol (Trentino) and part of the Dalmatian coast including Trieste, Italians felt their role in the war had been belittled. There was widespread unemployment and rampant inflation. At the same time the country suffered from weak government: some two dozen political parties paralyzed the country, and there was widespread corruption. Mussolini came to power in large part as a result of these circumstances.

Meanwhile, Mussolini carefully built the Fascist organization. His first attention went to the Black Shirt (q.v.) squads, militia supported with financial contributions (not always voluntary) from businessmen and landlords. They were distinguished by their black shirts and Roman salute. By the summer of 1919, the Black Shirts clashed with Socialists and Communist groups.

By 1921–1922, a veritable civil war raged the length of the Italian peninsula. Mussolini's approach was to meet all violence with greater violence.

From the beginning, the Fascists had little program beyond a devotion to their leader *(Il Duce)*, Italian nationalism, "law and order," and opposition to Communism. For years after they came to power, the Fascists claimed to have saved Italy from Communism, even though there was little support for that conclusion. Certainly Mussolini exploited middle- and upper-class fears of Socialism and Communism. It was only after the Fascists were in power that they developed their own program.

In the 1921 elections, the Fascists gained less than 10 percent of the vote, but the size of the organization (300,000 members by the end of September 1922) forced a possible route to power. By September, Mussolini was demanding he be named premier, and in late October some 10,000 of his followers converged on Rome (although Mussolini remained safe in Milan until he was informed that the "March on Rome" had succeeded).

When King Victor Emmanuel III (q.v.) refused to authorize martial law, Premier Luigi Facta resigned and on 29 October 1922, the king called upon Mussolini to be premier. It was all quite legal, or almost so. On 25 November, threatened with new elections held under Fascist supervision, the Parliament conceded Mussolini full power for one year; he kept it for twenty years and plunged Italy into ruin in the process.

While historians have shown a tendency in recent years toward revisionism on leaders of World War II, there has been no such effort with Mussolini, apart from memoirs of his immediate family. Mussolini believed Fascism was the way of the future. He felt Western democracies were incapable of bold and quick decisions. His own style of government was "divide and rule." Once in power, he rearranged Italy into a corporate structure in which all power flowed downward. *Il Duce* held all key government ministries himself and insisted on making even the most minute decisions. His memory may have been prodigious but it was filled with trivia; rarely did he see the grand design. His focus was always on appearances rather than substance.

Mussolini was unable to deliver on his pledge of economic security, for which the Italian people yielded their liberty. Despite propaganda to the contrary, Italian trains did not run on time. He did achieve more in education and a campaign to wipe out illiteracy. His most significant early domestic achievement was the 1929

Lateran Treaty (q.v.) ending the nearly sixty-year-old feud with the papacy.

In foreign affairs, Mussolini was obsessed with maintaining a balance of power in central Europe, leaving Italy free for expansion in the Mediterranean and Africa. He saw Italy as the dominant military power in the region and the "fulcrum" of European politics. Toward this end, he would not shrink from force. "Words are beautiful things," he said, "but muskets and machine guns are even more beautiful." He had little sympathy with the niceties of diplomacy. Like Adolf Hitler (q.v.), he opted for quick solutions and did not shrink from the use of force, although initially he had no desire to involve Italy in war with a major power.

For Mussolini, appearances were everything. He built his career on bluster and sham. He told the Italian people that their military was perfectly organized with the best equipment, which was complete fabrication. He boasted of tank divisions that did not exist, and he referred to clouds of airplanes that would "blot out the sun." His generals knew the truth. When he was appointed chief of staff of the army in 1939, Marshal Rodolfo Graziani (q.v.) complained that Italy's military was as obsolete as the ancient Macedonian phalanx.

Mussolini's dominant motivations were personal vanity and a desire for adulation; not surprisingly, flattery was a key factor in his undoing. He became captivated by his own myth of the invincible leader. Ultimately, he came to believe his own propaganda, that only he could be trusted to make the right decisions and that his intuition was always right. Serious study and discussion were not Mussolini's style. He loved to make snap decisions, often with unfortunate results. On top of this, he changed his mind frequently and precipitously, and he was totally inept as a war leader. He ordered military campaigns begun on short notice with no thought to the need for detailed planning. The hallmarks of the Italian state and military under Mussolini were administrative confusion and incompetence.

In the early 1930s, Mussolini aligned Italy with France and Britain. Italy was then the dominant military power in central Europe. In 1934, when the Nazi Party of Austria attempted a *putsch* in Vienna, he rushed troops to the Brenner Pass.

In October 1935, the Italian military invaded and subsequently defeated Ethiopia (q.v.). This drove a wedge between Italy and the Western democracies. Italy's subsequent involvement in the Spanish civil war (q.v.) on the Nationalist side led to further isolation from the West. Through nego-

tiations, and with some reluctance, Mussolini worked out a partnership with Hitler. The Axis Pact (q.v.) was made public in November 1936. Mussolini played a key role in convincing Hitler to meet with Western leaders at Munich in September 1938.

In April 1939, Italy took over Albania (q.v.). Mussolini was fearful Germany would lose a new world war, and he refused to join Hitler in the invasion of Poland, forcing less than a week's delay in the start of the German offensive. Mussolini preferred to wait until there was no longer any doubt about a German victory. Hitler's string of successes finally goaded him into action. In June 1940, Mussolini sent the Italian Army into southeastern France (Roosevelt called it the "stab in the back" [q.v.]) and ordered an attack on British possessions in Africa. Repeatedly he scattered Italy's meager resources, insisting, for example, that the Italian Air Force participate in the Battle of Britain (q.v.). The Germans correctly thought Italy's resources would be better utilized in North Africa, but he insisted on waging "parallel war."

In October 1940, after scant preparation, Mussolini ordered the invasion of Greece (q.v.). This seemed to have been decided on in a moment of pique to pay back Hitler for his failure to inform him of the date for the invasion of France. When the Greeks pushed Italian troops back and began their own counter-invasion of Albania, Hitler came to Mussolini's rescue. This digression wasted German resources and may have fatally delayed the invasion of the Soviet Union. Mussolini also insisted on sending Italian "motorized" divisions to the fight against the Soviet Union.

In July 1943, the Fascist Grand Council voted to depose Mussolini. Hitler ordered him rescued by German commandos. Mussolini was installed as nominal leader of a puppet state in northern Italy under complete German control. As the end of the war approached in April 1945, he and his mistress, Clara Petacci, sought to flee Italy with a German convoy. Partisans captured them on 28 April and shot both that same day; their bodies were taken to Milan. The violence taken by crowds against the bodies was so great that they were strung up, upside down. "Poor Mussolini," someone said, "He was always upside down."

Mussolini never accepted responsibility for his failures. Like Hitler, he blamed others, such as his generals, when he alone was responsible. He claimed the Italian people were not worthy of him and said he was prepared to fight "to the last Italian." He may have been the least brutal of the major dictators of World War II, but he was bad enough. Certainly his dictatorship served his own interests and not those of the Italian people. To the end, his chief motivation was personal power.

Spencer C. Tucker

Additional Reading

Deakin, Frederick W., *The Brutal Friendship: Mussolini, Hitler and the Fall of Italian Fascism* (1966).

Kirkpatrick, Ivone, *Mussolini: A Study in Power* (1964).

Mussolini, Benito, *La Fascisme, Doctrine, Institutions* (1933).

Smith, Denis Mack, *Mussolini* (1981).

Taylor, A.J.P., *The War Lords* (1978).

N

Nassau-Weilburg, Charlotte von (1895–1985)

Grand duchess of Luxembourg. Charlotte von Nassau-Weilburg became grand duchess at age twenty-three in January 1919. The people of Luxembourg demanded annulment of the republic and abdication of Charlotte's sister. Charlotte was a popular, democratic monarch who stabilized the country, and as a result, the dynasty was retained.

Although Luxembourg had declared neutrality in May 1940, Germany, nevertheless, invaded and absorbed the territory into the Third *Reich*. On 10 May 1940, while Nazi troops parachuted into her country, Charlotte fled Luxembourg. Initially, Luxembourg citizens considered Charlotte's abrupt departure a betrayal, but they soon realized she could negotiate with the Allies and defend Luxembourg's independence. She established a Luxembourg Relief Fund in London, then moved to the United States, seeking Allied support. In September 1944, her husband, Felix, and son, Jean, arrived with Allied forces and liberated Luxembourg. Her contemporaries credited her with preserving her country's sovereignty during World War II.

In the postwar era, under Charlotte's leadership, Luxembourg rescinded its neutrality with a constitutional amendment (1948). It joined the United Nations, Benelux, North Atlantic Treaty Organization, Brussels Treaty Organization, and European Recovery Program. Charlotte abdicated in November 1964, and was succeeded by her son, Prince Jean.

Elizabeth D. Schafer

Additional Reading

Newcomer, James, *The Grand Duchy of Luxembourg: The Evolution of Nationhood 963 A.D. to 1983* (1984).

Nebe, Arthur (1896–1945)

Chief of the German criminal police. A noted criminologist before the war, Nebe joined the Nazi Party in 1929. From May to November 1941 he served as the commander of *Einsatzgruppe* B in Russia. Implicated in the 20 July 1944 plot to assassinate Adolf Hitler (q.v.), he was arrested and subsequently executed. It was alleged at the Nuremberg trials (*see* International Military Tribunal) that Nebe was responsible for the murder of innocent civilians in Byelorussia.

Steven B. Rogers

Additional Reading

Hilberg, Raul, *The Destruction of the European Jews,* 3 vols. (1985).
Manvell, Roger, and Heinrich Fränkel, *The July Plot: The Attempt in 1944 on Hitler's Life and the Men Behind It* (1964).

Neurath, Konstantin von (1873–1956)

German foreign minister, Appointed in 1939 *Reichsprotector* of Bohemia and Moravia. *Freiherr* von Neurath was born into a noble Württemberg family and entered the German foreign service in 1901. In 1916, he accepted an appointment as *Kabinettschef* to the king of Württemberg. An ambitious man, he returned to the foreign service during the Weimar Republic (q.v.) and was ambassador to Italy and Great Britain. In 1932, he became the foreign minister in Franz von Papen's (q.v.) cabinet. When Adolf Hitler (q.v.) became chancellor, Neurath continued to serve in this capacity until 1938. In 1939, he was appointed *Reich* Protector for Bohemia and Moravia (q.v.).

In Czechoslovakia, he frequently came into conflict with state secretary Karl Hermann Frank. When Hitler sent Reinhard Heydrich (q.v.) to suppress Czech resistance and speed up the deportation of Czech Jews, von Neurath left Prague. Hitler did not accept his resignation until 1943. Neurath returned to Württemberg, convinced the war would end in Germany's defeat.

Neurath had contact with the German opposition through Karl Strölin, mayor of Stuttgart, but he opposed plans for Hitler's assassination. When his niece told him about a concentration camp with Jewish prisoners near his Leinfelderhof estate and begged him for help, he replied: "Leave me in peace." Tried at Nuremberg and found guilty on all four counts of the indictment, von Neurath spent seven years in Spandau prison. He died in 1956.

Susan Pentlin

Additional Reading

Davidson, Eugene, *The Trial of the Germans* (1966).

Fest, Joachim C., *The Face of the Third Reich* (1970).

Niemöller, Martin (1892–1984)

German clergyman. Martin Niemöller was born in the western German town of Lippstadt, the son of a Lutheran pastor. After military service during World War I and theological studies at the University of Münster, he became a pastor in Berlin-Dahlem in 1931. Being a convinced conservative and patriot, Niemöller originally welcomed the National Socialist revolution, but soon attacked its antireligious tendencies and interference in internal church affairs. As the leader of the Pastors' Emergency Union *(Pfarrernotbund)* and the Confessing Church *(Bekennende Kirche),* he became one of the most important representatives of the religious opposition to the National Socialist regime. After his arrest in 1937, he was confined in concentration camps until the end of the war.

After World War II, Niemöller played an essential though controversial role in the international church community. His personal authority inspired the Stuttgart Declaration of Guilt, which openly stated that the German Protestant churches had been morally responsible for failing to resist National Socialism. His personal role expressed the often contradictory political and ideological attitude of the German churches to the National Socialist regime.

Georgi Verbeek

Additional Reading

Bentley, James, *Martin Niemöller* (1984).

Deutsch, Harold C., *The Conspiracy Against Hitler in the Twilight War* (1968).

Niven, James David Graham (1910–1983)

David Niven was born on 1 March 1910 in Kirriemuir, Scotland. He attended the Royal Military College at Sandhurst and was commissioned second lieutenant in the Highland Light Infantry in 1929. He served in Malta and Dover before resigning his commission in 1932. For a short time he served as a military advisor to a group of Cuban revolutionaries, but he was forced to leave the country when the insurgents were defeated. Niven then made his way to California, where he started his acting career in 1935 by landing bit parts in Hollywood films.

When war broke out in Europe in 1939, Niven returned to Britain and was commissioned a lieutenant in the Rifle Brigade. He served in France and participated in the evacuation from Dunkirk (q.v.). Shortly after the fall of France, he was promoted to major and assigned to the secretive Phantom Reconnaissance Regiment. He later served in the British Army's intelligence branch, where he participated in the planning of various deception operations. In one such operation, Niven arranged for Lieutenant M.E. Clifton James (q.v.), an actor closely resembling General Bernard L. Montgomery (q.v.), to impersonate the general to mislead German intelligence.

In early 1944, Niven went on leave to appear in the war film *The Way Ahead.* On D-Day, Lieutenant Colonel Niven landed at Normandy (q.v.) with the U.S. 1st Infantry Division, and stayed with that unit until it reached the Rhine River. He received the Legion of Merit from the U.S. Army. Near the end of the war, he became chief of the Allied Forces Radio Network in Belgium, Holland, and eventually Germany. One of his accomplishments was establishing programming according to the needs and desires of ordinary soldiers. He remained on the Continent until August 1945, when he once again resigned his army commission.

Under contract with Samuel Goldwyn, Niven went on to star in over eighty films and several stage productions. He won the Academy Award for Best Actor in 1958 for the film *Separate Tables.* David Niven died on 29 July 1983 of amyotropic lateral sclerosis, commonly known as "Lou Gehrig's disease."

William Van Husen

Additional Reading

Buckley, William F., "David Niven, RIP," *National Review* (19 August 1983).

Niven, David, *The Moon's a Balloon* (1972).
———, *Bring on the Empty Horses* (1975).
Pace, Eric, "David Niven Dead at 73: Witty Actor Won Oscar," *New York Times* (30 July 1983).
Pryor, Thomas M., "Mr. Niven Is Given a Ribbon," *New York Times* (23 December 1945).

Norden, Carl Lukas (1880–1965)

American inventor, developer of the Norden bombsight. Born in the Netherlands in 1880, Norden emigrated to the United States in 1904. In 1911, he went to work for Elmar Sperry on the research and development staff for Sperry Gyroscope Company. His research helped bring the gyroscope from the embryonic stage of development to a reliability sufficient for the navy. Beginning in 1918, Norden embarked upon a long career of working closely with the navy that would last throughout World War II. He initially concentrated on designing a stable gun platform and radio-controlled aircraft to serve as flying bombs. Norden succeeded in developing radio control to fly aircraft, and the device reached the stage of production, but was never used in combat because naval officials considered it an inhuman and undiscriminating weapon. Its controls, however, were the forerunner of the automatic pilot mechanism that became an integral part of the Norden bombsight used during World War II.

After World War I, the Naval Bureau of Ordnance asked Norden to design a device for dropping bombs from aircraft onto moving ships. While working on the sight, Norden was assisted by Theodore H. Barth and Frederick I. Entwhistle. Together they succeeded in designing the Norden bombsight (q.v.), which was used extensively over Europe and Japan by the U.S. Army Air Force. It has been called one of the two major secret weapons of the American war effort.

Norden also designed numerous military devices. He developed catapults and arresting gear for the World War II aircraft carriers USS *Lexington* and USS *Saratoga;* the first hydraulically controlled landing gears; and a device that linked his bombsight with an automatic pilot, leaving crew members free to watch for enemy fighters while over target areas.

Donnie O. Lord

Additional Reading
Walton, Francis, *The Miracle of World War II: How American Industry Made Victory Possible* (1956).

Norstad, Lauris (1907–1988)

American major general, air force operational planner. Norstad spent his early career as a pilot in both fighter and bomber aircraft. A brilliant thinker, he was chosen in 1942 by General Henry H. "Hap" Arnold (q.v.) to serve on his special advisory council. Later that year, Norstad was appointed operations officer of the Twelfth Air Force for the Northwest African invasion. In March 1943, he was promoted to brigadier general, and after further duty in the Mediterranean theater, he returned to Washington and Arnold's staff. In August 1944, Norstad was appointed chief of staff of the Twentieth Air Force, whose B-29s were beginning a strategic air campaign against Japan. In an unusual combat arrangement designed to withhold control of the bombers from the theater commanders, Arnold himself commanded the Twentieth. Norstad actually directed the efforts of the B-29s and played a major role in planning the two atomic strikes.

Renowned as a deep and incisive thinker, Norstad also had a reputation as a ruthless trouble shooter and problem solver. After the war, he continued to rise in rank and responsibility, and in 1952, he received his fourth star at the age of forty-five. In 1956, he was appointed supreme Allied commander Europe, the only airman to date to ever hold that position. He retired in 1963.

Phillip S. Meilinger

Additional Reading
Craven, Wesley, and James L. Cate (eds.), *The Army Air Forces in World War II* (1948).
Jordan, Robert S. (ed.), *Generals in International Politics* (1987).
Morrison, Wilbur H., *Hellbirds: The Story of the B-29s in Combat* (1960).

Novikov, Alexsander Alexsandrovich (1900–1976)

Soviet colonel general, commander in chief of the Air Forces of the Soviet Army. Novikov joined the Red Army in 1919 and the Communist Party the following year. He fought in the civil war as an infantryman. Following the civil war, he attended the Higher Infantry School and the Frunze Military Academy. He was chief of staff of the air forces of the Leningrad Military District in the mid-1930s. He gained combat experience as the chief of staff of the air forces of the Karelian Front (army group) during the Soviet-Finnish Winter War (q.v.) in 1939.

In February 1942, Novikov became deputy commander of the Air Forces of the Soviet Army.

Marshal Alexsander Novikov, commander in chief of the Soviet Air Force. (IWM RR 2148)

After the defeat of Germany, Novikov directed air actions against the Japanese Kwantung Army in Manchuria. In the postwar years, he commanded long-range aviation units, and served briefly as deputy chief of the newly independent Soviet Air Force.

Thomas Cagley

Additional Reading
Shukman, Harold (ed.), *Stalin's Generals* (1993).
Werth, Alexander, *Russia at War, 1941–45* (1964).

Two months later, he became commander and held that position for the remainder of the war. He coordinated aviation support on several fronts. He was in charge of all air actions at Stalingrad, Kursk, and Byelorussia (qq.v.). Soviet airpower was used primarily in support of ground actions. Their aircraft were generally inferior to the *Luftwaffe,* but what the Soviets lacked in quality they made up for in quantity.

Nye, Archibald (1895–1967)

British lieutenant general, vice chief of the Imperial General Staff. Among the few top British officers commissioned directly from the ranks, Sir Archibald Nye fought in World War I, advanced steadily through the interwar period, and in 1940–1941, served as director of staff duties. With General Alan Brooke's (q.v.) appointment as chief of the Imperial General Staff in November 1941, Nye became vice-chief. He was the youngest vice-CIGS in British Army history. He was promoted to lieutenant general and held that rank until 1946. Highly respected for his abilities, especially skilled in execution of policy, he often represented Brooke at key meetings. Nye later served as high commissioner in India and in Canada between 1948 and 1956.

Richard Wires

Additional Reading
Bryant, Arthur, *The Turn of the Tide* (1957).
Morgan, F.E., *Overture to Overlord* (1950).

O'Connor, Richard (1889–1981)

British general. Commissioned from Sandhurst in 1909, Sir Richard O'Connor served with distinction in World War I, winning the Distinguished Service Order with Bar, and the Military Cross. In 1936 he was posted to India, where he commanded the Peshawar Brigade on the volatile northwest frontier. The start of World War II found O'Connor as commander of the British 7th Division and governor of Jerusalem, where he had dealt with the Arab Revolt.

As a lieutenant general in command of the Western Desert Force, O'Connor was responsible for countering the Italian invasion of Egypt in 1940. When the Italian advance bogged down, O'Connor used his time well in preparing a counterstroke. On 9 December 1940, O'Connor opened Operation COMPASS. Within two days, O'Connor's forces smashed Italian resistance at the battle of Sidi Barrani (q.v.). In spite of the withdrawal of the Indian 4th Division by the British high command, O'Connor pushed the Italians back into Libya. In January 1941, O'Connor reorganized the Western Desert Force and launched a sharp blow on the Italian fortress of Bardia (q.v.). The fortress fell in two days. Next, O'Connor captured Tobruk (q.v.) on 21 January 1941. Finally, O'Connor's forces captured some 20,000 Italians at Beda Fomm (q.v.) in February 1941. The British and Australians suffered only nine killed and fifteen wounded in that battle. In a period of ten weeks O'Connor's forces captured some 130,000 Italian and Libyan troops, and nearly 400 tanks.

In a sense, O'Connor's victories led to his own undoing. The collapse of the Italian Tenth Army in Libya forced Adolf Hitler to come to Benito Mussolini's (qq.v.) aid. Thus the first elements of the *Afrika Korps* (q.v.) arrived in Libya in February 1941. On 31 March, General Erwin Rommel

(q.v.) launched his counterattack, striking at the British position at El Aghiela. Rommel's task was made easier by the fact that the Western Desert Force had been stripped of many of its units, sent off to prop up the doomed situation in Greece.

While reconnoitering forward, O'Connor was captured by a German patrol in April 1941. In September 1943, he escaped from an Italian prisoner-of-war camp and made his way back to Britain. During the Allied operations on the Continent in 1944 and 1945, O'Connor commanded the British VIII Corps in France. In early 1945 he was promoted to full general, and returned to India to take over the eastern and northwestern commands.

John F. Murphy, Jr.

Additional Reading

Barnett, Corelli, *The Desert Generals* (1982).
Baynes, John, *The Forgotten Victor: General Sir Richard O'Connor, KT, GCB, DSO, MC* (1989).
Keegan, John (ed.), *Churchill's Generals* (1991).

O'Daniel, John W. (1894–1975)

American major general, commander of the 3rd Infantry Division. "Iron Mike" O'Daniel began his career as an infantry officer in World War I, where he received the Distinguished Service Cross for action at St. Mihiel. It was there he received his nickname as a result of wounds received while serving in the infantry company commanded by Mark Clark (q.v.). In December 1941, O'Daniel was promoted to colonel and in July 1942 he commanded the American Invasion Training School in Great Britain. During Operation TORCH O'Daniel commanded the 168th Infantry Regiment that captured Algiers. In December 1942, as a brigadier general, O'Daniel organized the Fifth

Army Invasion Training Center for the upcoming landings in Sicily.

In June 1943, O'Daniel became deputy commander of 3rd Infantry Division, one of the U.S. Army's best in World War II. The following February at Anzio (q.v.) he assumed command of the division from Major General Lucian Truscott (q.v.). In August 1944, O'Daniel led his division into southern France (q.v.), and then drove up the Rhone Valley. His troops fought in the Colmar pocket (q.v.), entered the West Wall near Zweibrücken, crossed the Rhine River in March 1945, and participated in the capture of Nürnberg, Augsburg, Munich, Salzburg, and Berchtesgaden. In May, O'Daniel received Field Marshal Albert Kesselring's (q.v.) surrender.

After the war, O'Daniel became U.S. military attache in Moscow. In July 1951, he commanded I Corps in Korea. That same year, he was promoted to lieutenant general, and in 1952, appointed commander, U.S. Army forces, Pacific. In 1954, he became chief, Military Assistance Advisory Group for Indochina, thus becoming America's first commander in Vietnam.

Samuel J. Doss

Additional Reading

Taggart, Donald G. (ed.), *History of the Third Infantry Division in World War II* (1987).

Oesch, Karl (1892–1978)

Finnish lieutenant general, chief of the general staff. Oesch was chief of the Finnish General Staff during the Finnish Winter War (q.v.). At the war's end, he was commanding general of the Coastal Group that threw the Soviets back across the frozen Gulf of Viipuri. In 1941, he assumed command of IV Corps, and retook Viipuri. In 1944, he was commanding general of the Karelian Isthmus Force. Under Soviet pressure, he was forced to give up Viipuri, but he did manage to prevent his own force from disintegrating.

Andrzej Suchcitz

Additional Reading

Coates, William, and Z.K. Coates, *Soviet-Finnish Campaign, Military and Political* (1939–1940).

Erfurth, W., *Der Finnische Krieg 1941–1944* (1950).

Okulicki, Leopold (1898–1946)

Polish major general, last commander in chief of the Home Army. In 1939, Okulicki commanded a battalion in the defense of Warsaw. In 1940, he became chief of staff of the Resistance Army in the Soviet zone of occupation. He was captured and imprisoned in Lubianka prison. Later, Okulicki was the commander of the Polish 7th Infantry Division in the Soviet Union and then in the Middle East. In 1944, he parachuted back into Poland on orders of the London-based government-in-exile. He became the last commander of the Home Army *(Armia Krajowa)* (q.v.) following the failure of the Warsaw Rising (q.v.). In March 1945, he was abducted by the Soviets, put on show trial, and sentenced to ten years' imprisonment.

Andrzej Suchcitz

Additional Reading

Garliński, Józef, *Poland in the Second World War* (1985).

Hollingworth, Clare, *Three Weeks' War In Poland* (1940).

Mikołajczyk, Stanisław, *The Rape of Poland* (1947).

Olbricht, Friedrich (1888–1944)

German general, member of the opposition to Hitler. The son of a schoolmaster, Friedrich Olbricht joined the Royal Saxon Army in 1907. He served as a regimental adjutant and as a staff officer during World War I. During the next two decades, he held a variety of command and staff positions, including a long term (1926–1931) in the army's intelligence branch (T-3).

Commander of the 24th Infantry Division from November 1938, Olbricht distinguished himself during the invasion of Poland and was among the first to receive the newly created Knight's Cross to the Iron Cross from Adolf Hitler (q.v.). Olbricht, however, had long been critical of the Nazi system, and during the war years, he became increasingly active in opposing it.

Reassigned to the army high command in February 1940 as head of its general army office, Olbricht used his administrative position to encourage and abet various civilian and military figures plotting Hitler's overthrow. He played a key role, in collaboration with Claus von Stauffenberg (q.v.) (his chief of staff from October 1943 to June 1944), in tailoring the VALKYRIE Plan (a scheme originally designed to crush domestic unrest) to the needs of the anti-Nazi plotters.

Following Stauffenberg's attempt on Hitler's life on 20 July 1944, Olbricht tried to set off the VALKYRIE measures, but was only partially successful. Along with Stauffenberg and two other officers, Olbricht was shot that evening. He is generally regarded as one of the most principled of the German generals who turned against Hitler during the war. Today, he is honored by a memorial plaque in the *Bundeswehr*'s army office at Cologne.

Ulrich Trumpener

Additional Reading
Balfour, Michael, *Withstanding Hitler in Germany, 1933–1945* (1988).
Fitzgibbon, Constantine, *To Kill Hitler* (1972).
Schmadecke, Jürgen, and Peter Steinbach (eds.), *Der Widerstand gegen den Nationalsozialismus* (1985).

Oppenheimer, J. Robert (1902–1967)

Scientific director of the MANHATTAN Project (q.v.) from October 1942 to October 1945. He was the only American scientist willing and able to manage the project that many of the refugee scientists in the project agreed to work under. His opposition to the actual use of nuclear weapons and other security concerns caused him to be removed from his post shortly after the war ended.

John D. Beatty

Additional Reading
Lamont, Lansing, *Day of Trinity* (1985).
Rhodes, Richard, *The Making of the Atomic Bomb* (1986).

O

Österman, Hugo (1892–1972)

Finnish lieutenant general, military representative to the German high command. During the Finnish Winter War (q.v.), Österman was commanding general of the Finnish Kannas Army, defending the Karelian isthmus. His unit fought the Soviets to a halt at the Mannerheim Line in February 1940, but the weight of the Red Army finally breached the position. During the War of Continuation, Österman was inspector general of infantry. Briefly in 1944, he was the Finnish representative at the German OKW (q.v.).

Andrzej Suchcitz

Additional Reading
Condon, Richard, *The Winter War: Russia Against Finland* (1972).
Erfurth, W., *Der Finische Krieg, 1941–1944* (1950).

P

Paget, Bernard Charles Tolver (1887–1961)

British general, commander in chief Home Forces. Paget was born on 15 September 1887, the third son of Francis Paget, bishop of Oxford. He was educated at Shrewsbury and the Royal Military College, Sandhurst, and commissioned into the Oxfordshire and Buckinghamshire Light Infantry in 1907. During World War I, he saw service on the western front with his regiment and was wounded twice, once severely, leaving his left arm practically useless for the rest of his life. He also served on the staff of Sir Douglas Haig at GHQ.

Following Paget's graduation from Staff College in 1920, he held three instructional posts where his teaching ability was fully exercised. By ill fortune he was only to serve in action for seven days during the whole of World War II. In that eventful week, however, he accomplished an outstanding feat of arms. Given command of British forces in Norway in 1940, he found the troops ill-equipped for fighting in the narrow valleys and snow-covered hills. Despite this, and the loss of his artillery and transport when the ship carrying this equipment was sunk, he used his small force to the best advantage. The Germans had air superiority and outnumbered the small British task force. Paget requested reinforcements only three days after his arrival to take command; nonetheless, he was ordered to extricate his troops and evacuate Norway. He succeeded in achieving this after fighting five very skillful rear-guard actions and inflicting heavy damage on the German forces. His skill and determination during this short campaign brought high praise from the prime minister in the House of Commons.

Paget was then appointed chief of staff, Home Forces, and later commander of South-Eastern command. His appointment was a short one, since he was promoted to commander in chief, Home Forces, a post he held until June 1943. He then was given command of 21st Army Group, consisting of fifteen divisions, and remained in command until he handed over to General Bernard L. Montgomery (q.v.) at the end of 1943. Paget then was appointed commander in chief, Middle East forces, where he served until 1946.

Paget revolutionized the British Army's training organization, introduced divisional battle schools, and set up a school of infantry. While he was an extremely effective commander of training, his failing of being too rigid, sometimes to the point of obstinacy, precluded him from obtaining another combat command.

Alan G. Harfield

Additional Reading

Ash, Bernard, *Norway 1940* (1964).
Harvey, Maurice, *Scandinavian Misadventure: The Campaign in Norway, 1940* (1990).

Papagos, Alexandros (1883–1955)

Greek general, commander in chief of the Greek armed forces. Papagos assumed command of the Greek armed forces on 28 October 1940 and successfully halted the Italian invasion. He went over to the offensive, attacking at the Metzovan Pass, forcing the Italians to retreat. In the general offensive begun on 14 November, the Greek forces at Koritsa broke through Mount Morava, defeated the Italian Ninth Army, and advanced into Italian-held Albania.

Papagos kept operations confined to the mountains where the Italians could not take advantage of their technical superiority. On 9 March 1941, Papagos halted a new Italian offensive in its tracks. His late withdrawal into the Aliakom defense line did not really affect the outcome of the German invasion, begun on 6 April. Papagos, however, maintained a stubborn resistance. He was captured by the Germans and imprisoned at Dachau.

Andrzej Suchcitz

Additional Reading
Myers, E., *Greek Entanglement* (1955).
Pyromaglou, C., *La Résistance Grecque* (1948).

Papandreou, Georgios (1888–1968)
Premier of the Greek government in exile. Papandreou became a lawyer in Athens following studies there and in Germany. He began his political career in 1915 as prefect, later serving as governor of the Aegean Islands, minister of the interior, and minister of education. Throughout his political career, he was known as anti-authoritarian and anti-monarchist. He was exiled by the Metaxas (q.v.) government in 1935 after founding an opposition political party.

Known as an anti-Axis agitator, Papandreou was imprisoned by the Germans (1942–1944) and later escaped to Cairo. From there he founded the Greek government in exile, resigning later because of the civil war. He was recalled as Premier in 1945. After that term in office, he continued in Greek politics until his final election as premier in 1963. He was dismissed by the king in 1965.

Steven D. Cage

Additional Reading
Myers, E., *Greek Entanglement* (1955).
Papandreou, Georgios, *La Libération de La Grèce* (1948).

Papen, Franz von (1879–1969)
German politician and vice chancellor. Born to an aristocratic Catholic family in Westphalia, von Papen had a distinguished military career. He was appointed captain on the *Reichswehr* General Staff in 1913 and served as the German military attache in Mexico City and Washington. He was expelled from the United States in 1916 after being accused of participating in seditious activities. During World War I, he served in France, Turkey, and Palestine.

Following the war, von Papen became a leader of the conservative Catholic Center Party and served in the Prussian legislature from 1920 until 1932. He was never sympathetic to the republican cause and supported the aristocracy's call for a return of the monarchy. In turn, he was supported by the upper class, business leaders, and the military.

With the support of General Kurt von Schleicher (q.v.), a key member of the defense ministry, von Papen was appointed to replace Heinrich Brüning (q.v.) as chancellor in June 1932. Although he did not enjoy a strong majority in the *Reichstag*, he appointed a number of right-wing nationalists to crucial government positions and thereby began the dismantling of the Weimar Republic (q.v.). He deposed the Social Democratic government of Prussia and assumed direct control of the province as *Reich* commissar. He remained chancellor until December 1932, when General Schleicher pressured President Paul von Hindenburg (q.v.) to appoint him chancellor.

After General Schleicher's appointment, von Papen allied himself with Adolf Hitler (q.v.) and together they urged President von Hindenburg to appoint a Nazi/conservative coalition. Hindenburg acquiesced, and in January 1933, Hitler was appointed chancellor with von Papen as his vice chancellor. By the time the Nazis consolidated their control of the government in mid-1934, von Papen realized he served no purpose in a Nazi-dominated government. Once again he began to call for a return of the monarchy, an action that outraged Hitler who targeted von Papen for death during the Röhm purges (*see* Night of the Long Knives). Von Papen was spared only through the good offices of Hermann Göring (q.v.) and resigned as vice chancellor. He somehow managed to remain on good terms with the Nazis and subsequently was appointed special minister and later ambassador to Vienna, where he played a key role in the *Anschluss* (q.v.). During the war, he later served as German ambassador to Turkey.

Von Papen was tried and acquitted of war crimes at Nuremberg (*see* International Military Tribunal), but he was later tried and convicted by a German de-Nazification court and sentenced to two years in prison.

Steven B. Rogers

Additional Reading
Papen, Franz von, *Memoirs* (1953).
Wheaton, Eliot B., *Prelude to Calamity: The Nazi Revolution 1933–1945* (1968).

Park, Keith Rodney (1892–1975)
British air marshal, commander of Number 11 Fighter Group during the Battle of Britain. Sir Keith Rodney Park was born at Thames, New Zealand, on 15 June 1892. His father was a col-

lege professor. The younger Park was educated locally, studying mining at Otago University. He first went to sea; but in 1914, he joined the New Zealand Expeditionary Force, gained a commission in the New Zealand Artillery, saw service in France, and was seriously wounded at the Somme. He volunteered for the Royal Flying Corps and when the Royal Air Force was formed in 1918, he was promoted to captain. Following World War I, he was a flying instructor, fighter station commander, assigned to duty in Argentina, and by 1938, attached to Fighter Command as a senior staff officer.

By 1940, Park was senior air staff officer to Air Marshall Sir Hugh Dowding (q.v.) for two years. His loyalty to Dowding was well established. In April, Park was appointed to command Fighter Group Number 11, and that July, he was promoted to air vice marshal.

Park was responsible for fighter protection during the British evacuation of Dunkirk (q.v.), during which he flew a Hurricane in order to directly observe the operation. He was convinced the air cover his fighters provided was crucial to the success of the Dunkirk evacuation. Also, he realized the importance of the experience of the air war over France. This May-to-June experience was crucial for the British pilots who would see action in the next months over Britain. He wanted to double the number of squadrons to four in the air at one time—from twenty-four to forty-eight aircraft. Much to his dismay, Dowding refused and Park's overextended pilots faced extremely difficult odds. The Hurricane and Spitfire aircraft also had small fuel capacities, and the necessity of having to refuel added to the dilemma. The result was severe criticism of the RAF by the exhausted troops of the British Expeditionary Force. Dowding accepted the criticism unmovingly, and Park's loyalty remained unchanged.

The Battle of Britain (q.v.) was the most significant period in the nation's air history and Park's career. He commanded Fighter Group Number 11, charged with the most important region to patrol and defend, from Southampton to Norwich, including London. The weight of the assignment led him to visit his squadrons and ground crews on a regular basis. As he had done earlier in the Dunkirk evacuation, he flew his own Hurricane to evaluate the men and aircraft, their performance and morale, and to inspire his pilots on the crucial role they played. He spent long hours on the job and relentlessly advocated support for his flyers.

The Battle of Britain was the culmination of the Dowding-Park working relationship, but not of Park's career. His strategy was to disrupt enemy formations before they could bomb their targets, utilizing radar to determine potential German attack patterns. At no time did Park enjoy numerical advantage, causing him to avoid fighter-to-fighter combat. He focused his fighters instead on the enemy bombers. Dowding and Park did not try to fool themselves; they were keenly aware of the difficult odds. Pilots and ground crews were overtaxed and British efforts often depended on the Women's Auxiliary Air Force (WAAF). Their work at airfields, forward radar installations, and Dowding's headquarters drew the highest praise from both Dowding and Park.

During the Battle of Britain, Park supported by Dowding, resisted the "Big Wing" theory advocated by Number 12 Group commander Trafford Leigh-Mallory (q.v.). The "Big Wing" formation would concentrate more aircraft against enemy assaults, thus enabling the British to inflict greater losses on German forces. However, this required more time for all of the aircraft to become airborne and assemble. In the face of intense German bombing of London in late August, Leigh-Mallory reacted slowly to Park's request for support, which heightened the feud between the two. Park criticized him publicly. As their personal battle simmered, the British lost 466 fighters between 24 August and 6 September. London came under heavier attacks; but in the face of these numbing difficulties, Park's fighters persisted. Dowding continued to resist change and by the middle of September the tide had turned in favor of the British, thanks primarily to Dowding and Park.

Leigh-Mallory continued to insist that the "Big Wing" was more effective than Park's strategy. By the middle of November, the air staff agreed. William Sholto Douglas (q.v.) replaced Dowding and Leigh-Mallory replaced Park in command of Number 11 Group. Park accepted an assignment to command a training group, a swift fall for one of the true heros of the defense of Britain against the feared German *Luftwaffe*.

Park resurfaced in January 1942 in Malta (q.v.). Air defenses on Malta were much like those in the Battle of Britain but on a smaller scale. By bottling up German air forces over Malta, Park assisted in the North African campaign (q.v.) of the Allied armies in the desert. His fighters launched merciless attacks on German air bases on Sicily and played havoc with German supply lines. His forces also provided air support for the Allied invasion of Sicily (q.v.).

In early 1944, Park was made supreme air commander in the Middle East. When the emphasis shifted to the European theater, he was sent to Southeast Asia to support the conquest of Burma. He was knighted in 1945, as the war ended. He retired in 1946 to his native New Zealand. He died at Auckland on 5 February 1975.

Boyd Childress

Additional Reading
Bryant, Arthur, *The Turn of the Tide* (1957).
Mitchell, Alan W., *New Zealanders in the Air War* (1945).
Morgan, F.E., *Overture to Overlord* (1950).

Patch, Alexander M. (1889–1945)

American lieutenant general, commander of U.S. Seventh Army. Patch was commissioned as an infantry lieutenant from the U.S. Military Academy at West Point in 1913. He served in routine regimental assignments on the U.S. western frontier and participated in the Mexican Punitive Expedition prior to the start of World War I. He then served in combat with the American Expeditionary Force (AEF) in France, ending the war as an expert on the machine gun and having served as a battalion commander.

Between the wars, Patch served three tours of duty as an instructor of military science at the Staunton (Virginia) Military Academy. He served as an advisor/instructor to the Alabama National Guard, and he completed both the Command and General Staff College and the Army War College. He served on the Infantry Board during the organization and testing of what would become the army's triangular division of World War II.

All of Patch's experience in training paid off. When World War II started, he became a regimental commander. He was promoted to major general in 1942 and was sent to the Pacific where he activated and commanded the American Division. He later commanded the XIV Corps on Guadalcanal. After a year, he left the Pacific for health reasons and returned to the United States, where he commanded the IV Corps and the Desert Training Center.

Patch was promoted to lieutenant general in 1944 and given command of the Seventh Army, which he led during the invasion of southern France (q.v.) in August. His army helped form the pincer that closed on Germany from the south. The Seventh Army captured Munich and Nuremberg, and on 5 May 1945, Patch accepted the surrender of Army Group G. After V-E Day, Patch was given command of the Fourth Army in the United States in preparation for fighting in the Pacific. When the war ended, he was tasked to study the army's organization for the future. He died before the end of the year and was posthumously promoted to general in 1954.

Steven D. Cage

Additional Reading
Clarke, Jeffery J., and Robert Ross Smith, *Riviera to the Rhine* (1993).
Wyant, William K., *Sandy Patch: A Biography of Lt. Gen. Alexander M. Patch* (1991).

Pattle, Marmaduke Thomas St. John (1913–1941)

British ace, RAF squadron leader. Pattle is the "forgotten" ace of the RAF. His actual score of confirmed air-to-air victories is unknown because his flight records were lost. Estimates of his confirmed score range from thirty-four to forty-one. If the latter estimate is correct, Pattle would be the RAF's leading ace of World War II. His number of probable victories also exceeded forty.

Pattle was born in Cape Province, South Africa, in 1913. After he completed college, he joined the South African Air Force as a cadet, but transferred to the Royal Air Force in 1936. When the war broke out in North Africa, Pattle was serving in the RAF's Number 80 Squadron, flying obsolete Gladiator biplane fighters against the Italian Air Force. In November 1940, Number 80 Squadron was sent to Greece, and in February 1941 they finally were equipped with modern Hurricanes.

Pattle's score climbed quickly throughout the Greek campaign. On 28 February 1941, Squadrons 80 and 33 shot down twenty-seven Italian aircraft, with Pattle accounting for three. It was not the only time he achieved three victories in one day. In March 1941 Pattle assumed command of Number 33 Squadron.

On 20 April, Pattle led the fifteen remaining operational RAF Hurricanes on Greece in a desperate attack against a wave of German *Stuka* dive bombers escorted by almost one hundred Bf-109 and Bf-110 fighters headed for Athens. In the ensuing fight, Pattle was shot down and crashed in Eleusis Bay. The RAF's second highest, and possibly highest, scoring ace never received a decoration higher than the Distinguished Flying Cross and Bar.

David T. Zabecki

Additional Reading
Baker, E.C.R., *The Fighter Aces of the R.A.F.* (1962).

Patton, George S., Jr. (1885–1945)

American general, commander of the U.S. Third Army. The most colorful and controversial American general in the European theater of World War II, Patton captured the imagination of the American public. Bold, dashing, aggressive, pugnacious, and a brilliant tactician, he and his Third Army led the Allied drive across Western Europe, moving faster and farther than any other army in history.

Patton's wealthy family had a proud military heritage. Patton's grandfather and six great-uncles fought with distinction as Confederate officers in the American Civil War. Earning the pride of his doting family and upholding the reputation of his gallant soldier-ancestors was the source of Patton's drive and fueled his vision of himself as a man destined to rank as a great captain.

Patton entered Virginia Military Institute in 1903, like his father and grandfather before him. He completed a year there and then entered the U.S. Military Academy at West Point. He graduated in 1909, choosing cavalry as his branch. The following year, he married Beatrice Banning Ayer, a Boston heiress who devoted her life to supporting his egocentricity.

Patton energetically strove to outshine his peers in the small peacetime army. He placed fifth in the modern pentathlon in the 1912 Olympics, became the army's first master of the sword, excelled as an equestrian, became a Washington, D.C., socialite, and learned to use his personal wealth to promote his career. He began a lifetime study of military affairs and cultivated relationships with important men, some of whom would support him as his career faltered during World War II.

In 1916, Patton joined General John J. Pershing on the Mexican Punitive Expedition to capture Pancho Villa. Patton gained fame when he killed two of Villa's men in a gunfight and returned to Pershing's headquarters with the bodies strapped to the hood of an automobile, claiming that he led the first motorized attack in history. Thus began both his reputation as a sanguinary and bold combat leader and his fateful association with mechanized warfare.

In 1917, Pershing took Patton to France and World War I. In November, Patton became the first member of the U.S. Army's Tank Corps and organized the American Tank School in France. In September 1918, Lieutenant Colonel Patton led his 304th Tank Brigade in the St. Mihiel and Meuse-Argonne offensives, was wounded, earned a promotion to colonel, and awarded the Distinguished Service Cross for valor. His fearless front-line leadership, aggressive drive, and willingness to exceed orders became legendary and would be his hallmark in the next world war.

Following Armistice Day, Patton assumed command of the 304th Tank Brigade at Ft. Meade, Maryland, and began an enduring friendship with his deputy, Major Dwight D. Eisenhower (q.v.). Patton experimented with armored vehicle developments, funding some personally. When the National Defense Act of 1920 eliminated the Tank Corps, Patton returned to the cavalry and spent the next twenty years in a variety of command and staff assignments. That he survived the small peacetime army, hit hard by the Great Depression, can only be attributed to his burning desire to fulfill his destiny.

Patton continued his studies and published numerous articles in military journals. Still infatuated with armored warfare, he was careful not to alienate his less-forward-looking cavalry superiors—a difficult challenge for such a tenacious man. The German *Blitzkriegs* (q.v.) of 1939 and 1940 were the type of warfare for which Patton longed. When the new chief of staff of the army, General George C. Marshall (q.v.), created the U.S. Armored Force in July 1940, he appointed Patton to command a brigade of the new 2nd Armored Division at Fort Benning, Georgia. Patton was promoted to brigadier general in October, assumed command of the division in January 1941, and received his second star three months later.

During large-scale maneuvers in the summer of 1941, Patton and his "Hell on Wheels" division stole center stage with their élan. A *Life* magazine cover story symbolized him as the flamboyant American tanker. Following the Japanese attack on Pearl Harbor, he accepted command of the I Armored Corps with its 1st and 2nd Armored Divisions. In July 1942, Patton, a long-time student of amphibious operations, went to Washington, D.C., to plan an invasion of Northwest Africa (q.v.).

Patton led the Western Task Force in an amphibious assault into Morocco on 8 November 1942 as part of Operation TORCH. In March 1943, following the tragic battle of Kasserine Pass (q.v.), Eisenhower gave Patton command of the demoralized II Corps and secured his promotion to lieutenant general. Patton quickly whipped the corps into an effective fighting force and launched an offensive in Tunisia (q.v.).

By mid-April Patton was preparing to lead the Seventh Army in the amphibious invasion of Sicily (q.v.) that July. Dissatisfied with his mission of securing the British left flank while General Bernard L. Montgomery's (q.v.) Eighth Army attacked

Lieutenant General George S. Patton, Jr., flanked by Major General Manton S. Eddy (left) and Major General Horace McBride, 22 November 1944. (IWM EA 44643)

north to seize Messina, Patton drove his army hard, conducted three amphibious end-around operations along Sicily's northern coast, and marched into Messina ahead of Montgomery on 16 August. Patton thus restored the respect of the U.S. Army and placed himself at the forefront of American combat commanders.

Patton's hopes for even greater opportunities were dashed when it was publicized that he had slapped two soldiers suffering from battle fatigue while visiting hospitals in Sicily. Reprimanded by Eisenhower in August for the incidents, Patton watched helplessly as the choice combat assignments eluded him. His career might have ended had it not been for the friendship of Eisenhower, Marshall, and Secretary of War Henry L. Stimson (q.v.).

In January 1944, Eisenhower gave Patton command of the fledgling Third Army in Britain, but Patton was stung to learn that he would not participate in Operation OVERLORD. Instead, he would be a key figure in the most pervasive Allied deception effort of the war, Operation FORTITUDE (q.v.), designed to deceive the German leadership as to the actual timing and location of the main invasion. Fascinated with his fighting ability, the Germans kept an entire army in Calais to counter what they believed would be the main invasion led by the Allies' master of amphibious

warfare. As a result, German forces in Normandy were unable to stop the main invasion force in June 1944. Though Patton did not attack on D-Day, his was a significant role in ensuring the success of the invasion.

Upon the Third Army's activation in France on 1 August 1944, Patton immediately thrust through a gap created by Operation COBRA and unleashed his personal version of *Blitzkrieg*. In an unequalled dash across France toward the Siegfried Line (q.v.), the Third Army drove back the German defenders 600 miles in thirty days.

Patton's Third Army was a three-corps war machine of nearly 350,000 soldiers, 669 tanks, and fifty-one field artillery battalions and had the cooperation of the XIX Tactical Air Command. By September, however, the Third Army had outpaced Allied efforts to keep it resupplied, and Patton was forced to conduct a frustrating battle against stubborn German fortifications around Metz (q.v.). Patton stockpiled enough supplies by 9 November to sustain operations and resumed the offensive, capturing Metz on 22 November. He then prepared to renew operations against the Saar region in December.

By 24 November, Patton suspected a major German attack through the Ardennes (q.v.) and initiated contingency plans for the Third Army's role. Patton was the only senior Allied commander who anticipated and was prepared for the major German offensive on 16 December. Wheeling his army 90 degrees to the north, Third Army drove nearly 100 miles in the dead of winter into the German left flank, and relieved the encircled U.S. 101st Airborne Division at Bastogne (q.v.) on 26 December 1945. In January, the Third Army closed the base of the German penetration, linking up with the U.S. First Army near Houffalize, cutting off the remnants of the German forces. Patton's anticipation of and reaction to the German Ardennes offensive was his greatest moment.

Resuming the offensive in late January, Patton captured Trier on 1 March, crossed the Rhine on 22 March, and drove through the heart of Germany, advancing thirty miles a day. At war's end, Third Army was on the outskirts of Prague.

In September 1945, Eisenhower relieved Patton due to his willingness to use former Nazis as civil administrators, and placed him in command of the Fifteenth Army, chartered to begin writing the U.S. Army's official history of the war. On 21 December 1945, Patton died in his sleep, not from the "last bullet of the last war" as he believed a warrior should, but from complications resulting from an automobile accident near Mannheim on 9 December.

Steven Dietrich

Additional Reading

Blumenson, Martin (ed.), *The Patton Papers, 1885–1940,* and *1940–1945,* 2 vols. (1972, 1974).

D'Este, Carlo, *Patton: A Genius for War* (1996).

Essame, H., *Patton: A Study in Command* (1974).

Farago, Ladislas, *Patton: Ordeal and Triumph* (1963).

Patton, George S., Jr., *War As I Knew It* (1947).

Paulus, Friedrich (1890–1957)

German field marshal, commander of the German Sixth Army at Stalingrad. Friedrich Paulus was born on 23 September 1890, at Breitenau in Hesse to a middle-class family. He very much wanted to join the Imperial Navy but was rejected because of his social background. In 1910, he joined the 111th Infantry Regiment as an officer cadet and made second lieutenant in 1911. In 1912, he married a Romanian aristocrat, Elena Rosetti-Solescu.

Paulus participated in many of the biggest battles of World War I, from the Marne to Verdun and ended the war as a captain in the *Alpenkorps*

stationed in Serbia. He managed to retain a position in the *Reichswehr* and served as a company commander of the 13th Infantry Regiment at Stuttgart from 1919 to 1921. His real capabilities lay in staff work. He held a variety of staff posts from 1921 to 1933, where he developed a reputation for studying every situation minutely and then drawing up orders in explicit detail. He was promoted to lieutenant colonel in 1933 and in 1934–1935 commanded a new motorized battalion. He became chief of staff for a new *Panzer* corps in 1935.

Promoted to major general in 1939, Paulus served as chief of staff for the Tenth (later Sixth) Army under General Walther von Reichenau (q.v.) and saw action in the invasion of Poland. The deliberate and detailed Paulus made an ideal chief of staff for the ruthless and impatient Reichenau. In May 1940, Paulus moved with the newly renumbered Sixth Army into Holland on the western front. From August to September 1940, he worked on the plans for Operation SEA LION (q.v.), which came to naught. In late summer of 1940, Paulus was made *Oberquartiermeister,* or director of operations at the general headquarters of the army where he helped develop Operation BARBAROSSA.

In the spring of 1941, he traveled to Romania

Field Marshal Friedrich Paulus. (IWM HU 1961)

to negotiate with Germany's new allies and to help ease the move into the Balkans. Paulus visited General Erwin Rommel (q.v.) in North Africa in 1941 to assess the action in that theater. Paulus concluded that Rommel was too aggressive and could jeopardize BARBAROSSA by pulling away vital resources needed for the attack on Russia. With the invasion of the Soviet Union in June 1941, Paulus oversaw operations from army headquarters.

In January 1942, Paulus replaced Reichenau as commander of the Sixth Army in Russia. In his new command, he quickly faced a tough test when he barely managed to defeat a Soviet offensive at the first battle of Kharkov in February 1942. With the German Army on the move in the summer of 1942, his Sixth Army drove deep into southern Russia. By late August, they had reached the outskirts of Stalingrad (q.v.) where they met fierce opposition from General Vasily Chuikov's (q.v.) Sixty-second Army. In late October, Paulus held all but one-tenth of the city, but he was hampered by overextended supply lines, bad weather, and a lack of reinforcements. The Soviets, on the other hand, poured men and equipment into the Stalingrad front.

A Soviet counteroffensive on 19–23 November smashed through the weak Romanian sectors of the Axis front to the north and south of the city and quickly threatened to engulf the Sixth Army. Paulus was slow to react to the Soviet threat and was overwhelmed by its swiftness. He lacked transport for his army, which made any counterattack or escape extremely difficult. General Erich von Manstein's (q.v.) XLVIII *Panzer* Corps attempted to reach the beleaguered and besieged Sixth Army in Stalingrad, but Paulus, hampered by his transport problems, took little action to help the relief effort. Manstein was stopped by 19 December, and Paulus, under orders from Adolf Hitler to stay and fight, decided his army had to stand its ground in order to prevent collapse along the entire German front. *Reichsmarschall* Hermann Göring (q.v.) assured Hitler that the *Luftwaffe* could resupply the Sixth Army by air, but this soon proved impossible.

On 15 January 1943, Hitler promoted Paulus to field marshal and awarded him Oak Leaves to the Knight's Cross. No German field marshal had ever surrendered, and Hitler believed Paulus would fight to the end with his army or commit suicide. The last of the wounded Germans were evacuated from Stalingrad on 24 January. With his army starving and freezing, Field Marshal Paulus surrendered his remaining 91,000 men to the Soviets on 2 February 1943.

After the unsuccessful plot against Hitler in July 1944 and the execution of many of his former friends in the aftermath, Paulus joined the anti-Hitler group among the POWs in Russia. He remained in the Soviet Union as a prisoner of war with the survivors of Stalingrad until 1953. Upon his return from captivity, he was forced to remain in East Germany. His wife had died in 1949, but his son lived in West Germany. Paulus was diagnosed with a degenerative neuromuscular disorder in 1953, and after a long and painful fight, he died on 1 February 1957 in a Dresden clinic. As the defeated German commander at the most crucial battle of World War II in Europe, Paulus had been much criticized for his actions in obeying Hitler's orders to stand and fight.

Laura Matysek Wood

Additional Reading
Barnett, Correlli (ed.), *Hitler's Generals* (1989).
Görlitz, Walter, *Paulus and Stalingrad* (1963).
Mellenthin, F.W. von, *German Generals of World War II As I Saw Them* (1977).
Mitcham, Samuel W., Jr., *Hitler's Field Marshals and Their Battles* (1988).
Werth, Alexander, *The Year of Stalingrad* (1966).

Pavelić, Ante (1889–1959)
Croatian separatist, leader of the *Ustaša*. Pavelić was born in Bradina, Bosnia-Herzegovina. In 1920 he was elected to the *Skupstina*, the Yugoslav Parliament. Believing that violence and terrorism were legitimate means to achieve political power, Pavelic formed the *Ustaša* (q.v.) movement.

Pavelić was forced to leave Yugoslavia when King Alexander dispensed with the Constitution in 1929. Pavelić settled in Sophia, Bulgaria, where he signed a cooperation pact with the members of the Macedonian separatist movement. In reaction, the Yugoslavian government tried Pavelić *in absentia* and sentenced him to death. Pavelić was given asylum in both Hungary and Italy, countries that saw in his movement an opportunity to weaken from within and exploit the fragile Yugoslav government.

In 1934 a *Ustaša* agent assassinated King Alexander in Marseilles, France. Pavelić again was sentenced to death *in absentia*, this time by the French government. Pavelić, however, continued to receive protection from German, Hungarian, and Italian authorities.

After the Axis powers swept through the Balkans (q.v.) in 1941, Pavelić returned to Yugoslavia. With German support, he seized absolute power and proclaimed himself *Poglavnik*, the dic-

P

tator of the Independent State of Croatia. Ultra nationalist, militantly Catholic, and fiercely anti-Serb, Pavelić used the *Ustaša* to maintain his power throughout Croatia and the annexed portions of Bosnia.

In 1945 Pavelić escaped from the Balkans as the Soviet forces moved in. He first made his way to Austria, and then to Argentina. He later returned to Europe and settled in Spain, which offered him protection from Allied justice and the revenge of Yugoslav leader Tito (q.v.). Pavelić died in Madrid in 1959.

Francesco Fatutta

Additional Reading

Djilas, Milovan, *Wartime* (1977).
Roberts, Walter R., *Tito, Mihailović and the Allies, 1941–1945* (1973).
Singleton, Fred, *Twentieth Century Yugoslavia* (1976).

Pavlov, Dimitry G. (1893–1941)

Soviet general, commander of the Soviet Western Front. Pavlov had a brief and undistinguished career in both world wars. As a member of the tsar's army, he was captured by the Germans. After joining the Red Army in 1918, he attended a variety of cavalry and armored schools. He served as chief of Soviet armored personnel sent to fight in the Spanish civil war, which brought him to Josef Stalin's (q.v.) attention. Thanks largely to his political loyalty, Pavlov enjoyed a rapid rise through the ranks. His training and ability, however, often were not commensurate with his positions.

When Pavlov became commander of the Western Front in June 1941, he was ill-prepared to deal with the German attack. Relying entirely on directions from Moscow, and ignoring his own intelligence sources, he did not place his soldiers on alert at the first signs of German movement. In tune with the mood in Moscow, he did not want to react to the incursions across the Soviet borders for fear of provoking the Germans. When the Germans rolled over the border in force, Pavlov's troops retreated in droves.

Following the crushing defeat of Pavlov's front (army group), he, his chief of staff, and the Fourth Army commander were executed. Ironically, Pavlov had achieved his position because of the 1937 military purges (q.v.), only to be executed himself because he did not measure up to the required standards.

Thomas Cagley

Additional Reading

Bialer, Seweryn (ed.), *Stalin and His Generals* (1984).
Kerr, Walter B., *The Russian Army: Its Men and Its Battles* (1944).

Peiper, Joachim (1915–1976?)

German *Waffen-SS* lieutenant colonel. As the commander of *Kampfgruppe-Peiper* during the Ardennes offensive (q.v.), Peiper led the abortive mission to seize bridges over the Meuse River within seventy-two hours of the start of the German attack. During World War II, Peiper commanded *Waffen-SS* (q.v.) units responsible for at least two wartime atrocities. The first took place in September 1943 in northern Italy. There he ordered the destruction of the town of Boves and the mass execution of its inhabitants. The second was the murder of seventy-one American prisoners of war at Malmedy (q.v.) on 17 December 1944, during the German Ardennes offensive. For their actions at Malmedy, Peiper and sixty-nine others were tried before an American military tribunal at Dachau in the spring of 1946. The tribunal, on 16 July 1946, condemned Peiper and forty-three others to death, but the sentences were later commuted to life imprisonment. Peiper was later released. In 1976, his house in France burned under mysterious circumstances. Peiper's body was not recovered, but he was declared dead.

Michael G. Mahon

Additional Reading

Pallud, Jean-Paul, *Ardennes 1944: Peiper and Skorzeny* (1987).
Reitlinger, Gerald, *The SS, Alibi of a Nation, 1922–1945* (1981).
Reynolds, Michael, *The Devil's Adjutant: Joachim Peiper, Panzer Leader* (1995).
Whiting, Charles, *Massacre at Malmedy: The Story of Joachim Peiper's Battle Group, Ardennes, 1944* (1981).

Peniakoff, Vladimir ("Popski") (1897–1952)

British lieutenant colonel, commander of "Popski's Private Army." Born in Belgium to Russian parents, Peniakoff attended Cambridge and served as a French artilleryman during World War I. After the war, he moved to Egypt, where he became enthralled with the desert and its lore. Commissioned as a British army lieutenant in 1941, Peniakoff's knowledge of the desert proved useful in limited raids to disrupt Axis operations. The British reinforced his individual success by authorizing a unit of five officers and eighteen others to do more damage. "Popski's Private Army" was self-contained in U.S. jeeps (q.v.). They conducted raids and reconnaissance behind Axis lines in Africa and Italy from its activation in 1942 until the end of the war. It was the smallest independent unit of the British Army in World War II.

Steven D. Cage

Additional Reading

Peniakoff, Vladimir, *Popski's Private Army* (1950).

Warner, Philip, *Secret Forces of World War II* (1991).

Willet, John, *Popski: A Life of Vladimir Peniakoff* (1954).

Pétain, Henri Philippe (1856–1951)

French marshal, chief of state of Vichy France. Pétain came from the Artois where he was remembered during his school days as *Pétain-le-Bref* because he spoke so little. He entered the Saint-Cyr military academy in 1876. In the official journal he was listed in the order of merit as number 403 of 412. In 1890, he graduated from the *École Supérieure de Guerre*. An early fitness report described Pétain as: "Cold. Worth getting to know, perhaps not entirely developed, will be a good officer."

In 1895, Captain Pétain moved to Paris to serve on the general military staff of the governor of Paris. This was the period of the infamous Dreyfus Affair. Pétain's feelings on that situation are unknown, even though he was the aide-de-camp to General Emile Zurlinden, who was involved in the attempts to cover up the case. In 1900, Pétain was promoted to major. In 1942, writer Emile Laure described Pétain's early military career as, ". . . almost inferior to the normal, guaranteeing him against envy and jealousy." Yet Pétain was continuously studying recent battles and developing theories on modern warfare.

Pétain's star shined brilliantly during the first year of World War I. His use of troops, artillery, and firepower at the Marne and in the Artois offensive of 1915 earned his rapid promotion to corps commander. His high point came during the 1916 battle of Verdun, where his theories of defensive warfare came into full play. He ended World War I as commander of the French Army and was presented his marshal's Baton in November 1918.

In the interwar years, as vice president of the French General Staff, and later in 1934 as minister of war, Pétain was instrumental in developing the doctrine that France should not wage offensive war. He was one of the primary supporters of the Maginot Line (q.v.).

In 1940, Pétain was serving as ambassador to Spain when Germany invaded. He was recalled by Paul Reynaud (q.v.) to act as deputy prime minister. He rejected Reynaud's proposal to continue the resistance against Germany in an alliance with Britain. Reynaud resigned on 16 June and Pétain replaced him. He offered the Germans an armistice on 22 June 1940. On 10 July, the National Assembly under the leadership of Pierre Laval (q.v.) voted him emergency powers that he used to proclaim himself head of the French state. He set up his capital at Vichy in the zone left unoccupied by the Germans. The Germans allowed him to retain a 10,000-man military force.

In October 1940, Pétain met with Adolf Hitler (q.v.) at Montoire to offer France's cooperation. Pétain consistently attempted to trade his government's cooperation, materiel, and workers to Germany in order to protect France and its colonies. He did, however, resist the more active collaboration policy of Laval, who advocated that France enter the war on the side of the Germans. In December 1940, Pétain dismissed Laval as Vichy's deputy head of state, but was forced by the Germans to reinstate him in April 1942.

When the Allies invaded French Northwest Africa (q.v.) in November 1942, the Germans occupied the remainder of France, and Pétain's government became powerless. Nonetheless, he continued to advocate a blind neutrality, even ordering the French not to assist the Allied liberators after the Normandy (q.v.) landings. Along with many members of the hollow Vichy government, Pétain was removed to Germany in August 1944.

In April 1945, Pétain voluntarily returned to France to defend his Vichy government policies. He was put on trial for treason, convicted, and sentenced to death on 15 August. The sentence, however, was commuted to life imprisonment by Charles de Gaulle (q.v.), who had served in Pétain's regiment at the start of World War I. Pétain died in exile on the Ile d'Yeu off the Brittany coast on 23 July 1951.

Pétain's place in French history is mixed. On 29 May 1966, President Charles de Gaulle presided over the fiftieth anniversary observance of the Verdun battle. Concerning the glory and shame of Pétain he said, "If by misfortune, in another time, in the extreme winter of his life, and at a time of extraordinary events, the attrition of age led Marshal Pétain to failures deserving of blame, the glory which he won at Verdun twenty-five years earlier cannot be contested, nor forgotten by the nation."

Today, there is a movement in France to re-instate Pétain and have him buried at Verdun with the men he commanded. But for political reasons, the French government will not allow it.

Cederic Fry

Additional Reading

Aron, Robert, *The Vichy Regime 1940–1944* (1958).

Griffiths, Richard, *Marshal Pétain* (1970).

Paxton, Robert, *Vichy France: Old Guard and New Order* (1972).

Roy, Jules, *The Trial of Marshal Pétain* (1968).

Peter II (1923–1970)

King of Yugoslavia. Peter became king after the 1934 assassination of his father, Alexander I. Up until 1941, the effective control of the government rested with Prince Paul, the regent. Peter took effective power after a coup on 27 March 1941. Following the rapid German advance into Yugoslavia, the king and his cabinet withdrew to Greece, Palestine, and eventually London, where they established a government-in-exile.

In October 1943, Peter moved the seat of the government to Cairo. He was pressured by the British to drop his minister of war, General Draža Mihailović in favor of Tito (qq.v.). Though forced to accept the Subasić-Tito agreement on the future of postwar Yugoslavia, Peter was opposed to it. It forced the king to set up a regency council to represent him in Yugoslavia. Tito broke the agreements and deposed the king in November 1945.

Andrzej Suchcitz

Additional Reading

Jukić, Ilija, *The Fall of Yugoslavia* (1974).

Ristić, Dragisha, *Yugoslavia's Revolution of 1941* (1966).

Petrov, Ivan Efimovich (1896–1958)

Soviet general, commander of the Soviet 2nd Byelorussian and 4th Ukrainian Fronts (army groups). Petrov was the son of a shoemaker. He received the normal schooling for children of his class and became a junior officer in the tsar's army. In 1918, he quickly switched allegiances, and became a Communist Party member. He did not have a particularly distinguished interwar career, serving as much time as a political commissar as he did in command. His experiences centered around

King Peter II of Yugoslavia with General Dusan Simović (left) and Court Minister M. Knezević. (IWM H 10922)

cavalry and rifle units. He headed the Tashkent Military Infantry School in the mid-1930s, and commanded a rifle division in 1940.

During World War II, Petrov spent most of his time with units in the southern regions of the Soviet Union. He commanded at various times the Forty-fourth Army, the Black Sea Group of Forces of the Transcaucasus Front, the Thirty-third Army of the Western Front, the 2nd Byelorussian Front, and the 4th Ukrainian Front. He played significant roles in the defenses of Odessa and Sevastopol (q.v.), and was commander during an unsuccessful landing operation (by the Maritime Operational Group) in the Crimea (q.v.). In April 1945, he was removed from command of the 4th Ukrainian Front because of the failure of the offensive in the Carpathians. He was demoted, but continued to serve. At the war's end, he was the chief of staff of the 1st Ukrainian Front.

After the war, Petrov held a variety of positions, including deputy chief inspector of the army, deputy commander in chief of ground forces and, in his last position before his death, chief scientific consultant for the deputy minister of defense.

Thomas Cagley

Additional Reading
Bialer, Seweryn (ed.), *Stalin and His Generals* (1984).
Kournakoff, Sergi N., *Russia's Fighting Forces* (1942).

Piłsudski, Józef Klemens (1867–1935)

Polish marshal and political leader. Charasmatic revolutionary and successful general, Marshal Jósef Piłsudski was the *de facto* leader of Poland from 1926 until his death in 1935. While most state functions were of slight interest to him, he maintained tight control over military and foreign affairs. These special interests were the result of his views of the nature of Polish relations with the Soviet Union and Germany. Both countries surrendered territories to his nation as a result of the treaties of Versailles (q.v.) and Riga. The Weimar/Nazi and Soviet leaderships never accepted these as final, so tensions were often high. He argued war with either neighbor was probable, and thus gave most of his attention to that problem.

Poland's survival, he reasoned, depended on strong alliances, a fast-acting military, and some degree of self-sufficiency. While directing the nation's foreign policy with an eye for peace, Piłsudski made every effort to obtain defensive understandings with potential enemies and victims of Germany and the Soviet Union. The most significant of these was an alliance with France that called for joint actions against German aggression. In 1933, Piłsudski attempted to stretch this treaty and launch a "preventive war" against the newly empowered regime of Adolf Hitler (q.v.). France balked. This, combined with previous disappointments, caused Piłsudski to negotiate a nonaggression pact with Germany.

The treaty, according to Piłsudski, removed Poland "from Germany's hors d'oeuvres to her dessert." He warned his subordinates that it, along with a similar Polish-Soviet pact, merely gained time. The aging marshal urged Poland's leaders to make use of this time to build up the military and strengthen alliances.

While Piłsudski's efforts failed to prevent the conquest of Poland in 1939, many would claim his character, prestige, and legacy allowed Poland to survive the savage trial of World War II.

John Dunn

Additional Reading
Jedrzejewicz, Wacław, *Piłsudski: A Life for Poland* (1982).
Mazur, Tadeusz, *We Have Not Forgotten, 1939–1945* (1960).
Mikołajczyk, Stanisław, *The Rape of Poland* (1947).

Pius XII, Pope (1876–1958)

Roman Catholic spiritual leader. Eugenio Pacelli served as pope of the Roman Catholic Church from 1939 to 1958. His World War II leadership of the Vatican has been subjected to severe criticism. Critics charge that he gave his blessing to Benito Mussolini's invasion of Ethiopia (qq.v.), supported Francisco Franco (q.v.), did not denounce Adolf Hitler's (q.v.) invasion of Western Europe in 1940, signed a concordat with Hitler, and did not take a strong stand against the extermination of six million Jews. Many believe a pope could do no less than oppose Hitlerism with every fiber of his being and urge his followers to do the same. Diplomatic niceties were not enough. If there was ever a just cause, this was it.

Having spent twelve years as Nuncio in Germany after 1917, where he learned German, Pius XII often expressed his affection for the German people, whom he came to know well. His critics took this to mean that he was pro-Nazi. This criticism is unjust; he detested the Nazis and all they represented. He did appear to have been a prudent, perhaps even a timid man, who preferred not to provoke the Nazis unnecessarily. His reticence can be attributed in part to his desire to maintain close relations with 30 million German Catholics.

Rolf Hochhuth's play, *The Deputy,* sensationally portrayed the pope as cynical, money-minded, and callous, particularly regarding Nazi prosecution of the Jews. Hochhuth, however, availed himself freely of poetic license. He may have written an excellent play, but is it historically accurate? Anthony Rhodes, among other historians, pointed out that Hochhuth often confused fact with fiction.

The Italian Fascists and the German Nazis both opposed Pacelli's candidacy to the papacy in March 1939; the former warned him not to repeat the aggressive practices of his predecessor, Pius XI. He was cautioned to be a *homo novus* to all nations. This appears to be the line he chose to follow.

In April 1939, a confidential memorandum from the German Foreign Ministry stated the early Nazi view of the new pope:

> At first he seems pro-German. His excellent knowledge of our language is significant, and he has frequently advocated good relations between the Church and Italian Fascism: and during the Abyssinian war, he supported and furthered the patriotic attitude of the Italian clergy . . . but his championship of an orthodox Church policy frequently led him into basic differences with National Socialism.

The pope's many defenders argue that his options were limited; his position was weak; he had few opportunities to influence the course of events; and he urged Catholic bishops to speak out and to transcend race, faiths, and nationalities. Yet, in a 1943 letter to Monsignor Preysing in Berlin, he took a contrary position, saying,

> We leave to local pastors the care of weighing the extent of the danger of reprisals and the possible means of pressure in episcopal declarations, or to remain silent where the duration and atmosphere of the war make it advisable, *ad maiori mala vitanda.*

Today, with the benefit of hindsight, what could the pope have done differently? The answer, much, if he had been willing to accept the risk involved. He could have used his position as a spiritual leader to arouse righteous indignation toward the Nazis. The moral authority of a pope speaking in the name of hundreds of millions of devoted Catholic followers, plus his not inconsiderable influence among other religious groups, should not be minimized when directed toward Christian Europe. If he had put aside all tactical, political, and diplomatic considerations, and taken a firm and unbending moral position that ignored all risks to himself and his followers, who knows what could have been achieved? Large-scale passive resistance, which has proven to be a powerful weapon against despotic forces, was never tried.

The Nazis were not indifferent to public outrage when massively expressed. The historical record clearly shows that the degree of severity of Nazi repression varied by country depending upon the attitude of the local population. In countries like Poland, and to a lesser degree France, where anti-Semitism was rife, severe measures were taken against the Jews, using local anti-Semites as auxiliary policemen. But in countries like Denmark, where the population turned out *en masse* in support of their Jews, the Nazis retreated. In Germany, while individual members of the clergy were persecuted, the Nazis drew back from taking on entire Christian churches while engaged in a total war. They chose their targets carefully.

However, openly condemning Nazi murders was risky at best, and involved a delicate judgement on just how Hitler would personally react. Hitler had plans at one time to kidnap the pope and imprison him in Wartberg, Upper Saxony.

Any *ex cathedra* condemnation of Nazi atrocities certainly would have been dangerous. If sufficiently provoked, it is likely that Hitler would have carried out his plans to have the pope kidnapped. Some of the efforts in opposition to the Nazis did, in fact, backfire. In the Netherlands, for example, the Catholic Church together with the Reformed Church of Holland threatened to protest publicly unless deportation of the Jews stopped. Nazi authorities promised to spare "baptized Jews" if the matter was dropped. The Reformed Church agreed, but the Catholic archbishop of Utrecht refused and issued a pastoral letter condemning the persecutions. The Nazis promptly arrested the converted Catholic Jews and deported them to the death camps, sparing the converted Protestant Jews.

Pius XII clearly understood the dangers of strong official condemnation from the church. Anthony Rhodes quoted Don Pisso Scavizzi reporting the Pope as saying at the time:

> I have often considered excommunication to castigate in the eyes of the entire world the fearful crime of genocide. But after much praying and many tears, I realize that my con-

demnation would not only fail to help the Jews, it might even worsen their situation. . . . No doubt a protest would have gained me the praise and respect of the civilized world, but it would have submitted the poor Jews to an even worse persecution.

He seems to have agonized long and hard over what could be done and come to the conclusion that any strong condemnation would be counterproductive.

What then are the facts in the case? One cannot honestly conclude that Pope Pius XII approved of Fascism, Nazism, or Franco. Nor did the Vatican endorse the Italian campaign in Ethiopia, although certain Italian bishops did. As did most Western leaders, the pope initially preferred Fascism and Nazism to Communism, which was always cited at the nondemocratic alternative. By his own admission he could have taken a stronger stand on behalf of the Jews, but considered it unwise to do so. We know now that appeasing the dictators was a mistake, but was that lesson so clear at the time?

What will be the historical judgment of Pope Pius XII? This is still a potential minefield in which a contemporary historian should fear to tread. In the field of faith and morals, the successor to the first bishop of Rome is held by the church he leads to be infallible and deserves to be judged by his own ecclesiastical peers. Perhaps the final judgment on the place in history of Pius XII would best be left to the writings of future Catholic theologians.

Paul Rose

Additional Reading

Bull, G., *Vatican Politics* (1966).
Halecki, Oscar, *Pius XII* (1953).
Rhodes, Anthony, *The Vatican in the Age of the Dictators (1922–1945)* (1973).

Place, Basil (1921–1994)

Royal navy lieutenant. Place was born in Worcestershire, England, on 19 July 1921. On 22 September 1943 he commanded the midget submarine *X-7* on a raid against the German battleship *Tirpitz,* anchored at Alten Fjord (q.v.), in northern Norway. The *X-7* along with the *X-6* traveled more than 1,000 miles from their base, negotiated a minefield, dodged nets, gun defenses, and German listening posts, to place their charges under the target. The mines went off an hour later, seriously damaging the *Tirpitz,* taking her out of action for several months. He and the other submarine commander, Donald Cameron (q.v.), received the Victoria Cross. Place remained in the Royal Navy after the war, retiring as a rear admiral.

Carl O. Schuster

Additional Reading

Kennedy, L., *Floating Fortress* (1979).
MacIntyre, D., *The Naval War Against Hitler* (1971).
Piekalkiewicz, J., *Sea War: 1939–1945* (1980).
Roskill, S.W., *The War at Sea 1939–1945,* 4 vols. (1954–1961).

Pohl, Oswald (1892–1951)

SS-Obergruppenführer. Pohl was born in Duisburg on 30 June 1892. He joined the Nazi Party in 1926. While serving as a naval officer in 1929, he joined the SA (q.v.). In 1934, after Adolf Hitler (q.v.) had come to power, Pohl quit his post as senior paymaster of the German Navy to become the chief administrative officer of the RSHA (q.v.).

From 1942 to 1945, Pohl was the chief of the *Wirtschafts-und Verwaltungshauptamt* (WVHA), the economic and administrative central office of the SS. In that position he was responsible for the administration of all concentration camps (q.v.) and all SS works projects. The functionaries of the WVHA also ensured that all valuables confiscated from Jewish inmates were sent to Germany, and they supervised the melting down of gold teeth taken from the inmates. The WVHA's primary focus was the exploitation of slave labor, and in 1943 Pohl's "economic experts" organized Eastern Industries, Ltd., to consolidate the few Jewish businesses that remained in the ghettos.

During the last years of the war Pohl also held honorary rank as a general in the *Waffen-SS* (q.v.). He went into hiding when the war ended. In May 1946 he was arrested disguised as a farm worker. On 3 November 1947, he and other SS officers involved in operating the concentration camps went on trial before an American Military Tribunal (q.v.). Pohl was convicted and hanged at Landsberg prison on 8 June 1951.

David T. Zabecki

Additional Reading

Höhne, Heinz, *The Order of the Death's Head* (1970).
Kogon, Eugen, *The Theory and Practice of Hell* (1960).

Popov, Markian Mikhailovich (1902–1969)

Soviet colonel general, commander of the Soviet

Bryansk and 2nd Baltic Fronts (army groups). Popov, the son of a peasant, graduated from a teachers' seminary in 1913. In 1916, he became an ensign in the tsar's army. He joined the Red Army in 1919 and served as a division chief of staff during the civil war. In the interwar years he attended various military schools, graduating from the Military Political Academy in 1931. Between 1931 and 1941, his most significant position was command of a rifle corps in the Finnish Winter War (q.v.). He was a corps commander in the early days of World War II, moving to deputy commander of rear services in 1941.

In 1942, Popov became commander of the Bryansk Front, located on Konstantin Rokossovsky's (q.v.) right flank north of the Kursk (q.v.) salient. When the German Operation CITADEL started in July 1943, Popov's armies played a major role in repulsing Günther von Kluge's (q.v.) Army Group Center. Popov's troops, in concert with Vasily Sokolovsky's (q.v.) on his right flank, liberated Orel and Bryansk on 20 July 1943. Shortly after Kursk, the Bryansk Front was reduced in size, redesignated the 2nd Baltic Front, and moved into position opposite the German Sixteenth Army south of Leningrad (q.v.).

Although Leningrad was eventually liberated, Popov came under criticism for moving too slowly. After his front failed to take Riga, he was relieved of his command and replaced by Andrei Yeremenko (q.v.). Popov became deputy commander of the 1st Byelorussian Front, and subsequently commanded the Seventieth Army in the 1st and 2nd Byelorussian Fronts in 1944–1945.

Popov was a competent but cautious leader. He was never really trusted by Josef Stalin (q.v.). Following the war, Popov became the head of advanced training courses at the Frunze Military Academy, and retired in 1959.

Thomas Cagley

Additional Reading

Bialer, Seweryn (ed.), *Stalin and His Generals* (1984).
Werth, Alexander, *Russia at War, 1941–1945* (1964).

Portal, Charles Frederick Algernon (1893–1971)

British marshal of the Royal Air Force, chief of the air staff. Sir Charles Portal was an accomplished administrator, whose supervision and guidance of the British Royal Air Force during World War II included a strategy of aggressive bombing, and whose coordination with American air forces earned him the respect of other Allied commanders.

Portal was born into a well-to-do family on 21 May 1893, near Hungerford. He was an excellent athlete and sportsman as a youth, and he was educated at Christ Church, Oxford, where he also qualified for the bar. When the European war broke out in August 1914, he enlisted in the Royal Engineers. He was assigned as a motorcycle dispatch rider, but in the summer of 1915, he joined the Royal Flying Corps. He first flew as an observer, and later qualified as a pilot. Promoted several times by war's end, he flew more than 900 missions.

In 1919, Portal was promoted to major. Like many other prominent World War I airmen, he was next employed as a flying instructor. His instincts for flying were matched by his planning abilities, and he moved rapidly through the ranks of command. In 1934, he commanded the British forces in Aden (in present-day Saudi Arabia). He returned to Britain in 1935, just as Benito Mussolini (q.v.) began advancing on Ethiopia (q.v.). Two years later, Portal was assigned to the Air Ministry, heading up organizational activities, a position closely suited to his skills. From this vantage, he developed training and expansion of airfields, both essential aspects of British air defense. When World War II began, he was promoted to air marshal.

In April 1940, Portal was reassigned to Bomber Command, a difficult operational post that demanded all of his abilities to employ the bombers to the best strategic advantage. His problems included the need for fighter escorts on day raids, ineffective night bombing, and later, the German invasion of France, which necessitated an abrupt change in tactics. As the ground war against the Allies intensified, he recommended attacking targets inside Germany, a view shared by Prime Minister Winston S. Churchill (q.v.). Although lacking effectiveness, these area assaults did cause the Germans to redirect their own air strategy. Portal also advocated bombing Germany's industrial capacity.

In October 1940, Portal became chief of the air staff. He pushed himself relentlessly, becoming involved with all aspects of the command. His most significant accomplishment was maintaining the independence of the air forces. He argued successfully that ground and naval efforts could be coordinated with air support. The experience of the North African campaign provided support for his position, and centralized airpower continued.

While Portal benefited from Churchill's support, he nevertheless had some bitter differences with the prime minister. One such issue was Portal's support of Arthur Tedder's (q.v.) command in North Africa. He also appointed the controversial Arthur Harris (q.v.) to Bomber Command. Another conflict ensued over the American decision to attack German targets by day, a policy Churchill opposed. Portal supported the Americans. His strategic air offensive drew criticism during and after the war, but the controversial strategy did serious damage to Germany's industrial war effort. Despite their differences, Churchill once called Portal "the accepted star of the Royal Air Force."

The end of the war was not the end of Portal's military career. Almost immediately, he accepted a position in the effort to develop atomic energy. Although his role was minimal, his organizational skills and the respect he commanded aided the development of the British atomic bomb by 1951. In the ensuing years, Portal held several posts in industry, the last as chairman of British Aircraft Corporation (1960–1968).

Highly decorated during the war, he was knighted in 1940. He died in April 1971. Admirers and even some historians have judged Portal's contribution to British survival and eventual victory in World War II as more vital than even Churchill's. Without doubt, his strategic air offensive was a significant factor in both shortening and ending the war in Europe.

Boyd Childress

Additional Reading

Bryant, Athur, *The Turn of the Tide* (1957).
MacMillian, Norman, *The Royal Air Force in World War II* (1950).
Probert, Henry, *High Commanders of the Royal Air Force* (1991).
Richards, Denis, *Portal of Hungerford: The Life of Marshal of the Royal Air Force Viscount Portal of Hungerford, KG, GCB, OM, DSO, MC* (1977).

Pound, Alfred Dudley Pickman Rogers (1877–1943)

British admiral of the fleet and first sea lord. An officer of the line in the tradition of the old Royal Navy, Sir Alfred Dudley Pound distinguished himself early in his career by his performance in the World War I battle of Jutland, and his role in founding the Admiralty's plans division. Tutelage in the art of command from such officers as Sir William Fisher and Roger Keyes (q.v.) enabled him

Admiral of the Fleet Sir Alfred Dudley Pickman Rogers Pound. (IWM A 20791)

to rise rapidly through the ranks in the interwar period. When the office of first sea lord became vacant in 1939, Pound's combination of operational and staff experience singled him out as an ideal candidate.

Pound assumed the duties of first sea lord and chief of naval staff in June 1939; a month later he was promoted to the rank of admiral of the fleet. Sixty-two years of age and in failing health, he displayed a remarkable fortitude of will in coping with the strain through four years of war. A perfectionist who set high standards for himself and his commanders, he was resented by the Admiralty for his micro-management of naval operations, a practice that at times stretched his command ability too thin. He also came under criticism for the Royal Navy's initial failure to interdict the U-boat menace in the North Atlantic. Only later was it realized that much of the success of German admiral Karl Dönitz's (q.v.) wolf packs lay in the ability of the *Kriegsmarine's B-Dienst* to decipher British convoy codes.

Pound's unwillingness to risk his fleet during the ill-fated 1940 invasion of Norway (q.v.) brought him under further attack. Despite these blots on his reputation, he was the principal organizer of British naval strategy in the first years of the war, and the architect of most of the Royal Navy's early triumphs. Laid to his credit are the sinking of the *Bismarck* (q.v.), the scuttling of the *Graf Spee,* the successful Allied landing in Northwest Africa (q.v.), the invasion of Sicily (q.v.), and British domination of the Mediterranean. Beginning in January 1943, he was able to report successes in the Battle of the Atlantic (q.v.) as well. By September of that year, with ultimate victory in sight, the combined strains of ill health and his wife's death forced Pound to resign his command. He died less than a month later, ironically, on 21 October, Trafalgar Day.

Mark Rummage

Additional Reading

Howarth, Stephen (ed.), *Men of War: Great Naval Leaders of World War II* (1993).

Roskill, Stephen W., *The War at Sea 1939–1945,* 4 vols. (1954–1961).

Previsi, Prenk (? – ?)

Albanian general, commander in chief of the German-controlled Albanian Army. In 1939, Previsi was Albania's military attache in Rome. Between 1943 and 1944, he was the commander in chief of the Albanian Army under German control. He successfully prevented the raising of an Albanian SS Division. He later joined the Zogist resistance army, fighting both the Germans and the Communists. In 1944, he provided protection for the British Military Mission.

Andrzej Suchcitz

Additional Reading

Amery, Julian, *Sons of the Eagle* (1948).

Prien, Günther (1908–1941)

German naval commander, U-boat captain. Commander Günther Prien is best known for sinking the British battleship HMS *Royal Oak* in Scapa Flow (q.v.). In a daring feat of seamanship, *U-47* penetrated the anchorage at night during 13–14 October 1939 and torpedoed the *Royal Oak,* which sank with heavy loss of life. Although the battleship was an old, unimproved type of World

War I vintage, the skillful attack was a propaganda coup. Prien was lionized in Germany as "the Bull of Scapa Flow" and his memoirs were published. He became the first U-boat ace to sink 50,000 tons of Allied shipping and amassed more than 170,000 tons before *U-47* was destroyed in March 1941.

Robert C. Fisher

Additional Reading

Frank, Wolfgang, *Enemy Submarine: The Story of Günther Prien* (1954).

van der Vat, Dan, "Commander Günther Prien," in Stephen Howarth (ed.), *Men of War: Great Naval Leaders of World War II,* pp. 394–404 (1993).

Prior, Willem (1876–1946)

Danish general, commander in chief of the Danish Army. Prior was one of the more determined Danish leaders. He favored continuing the fight after Germany's invasion on 9 April 1940. His efforts to prolong Danish resistance ended when the king and government decided to capitulate after a campaign lasting only four hours. Danish casualties were thirteen killed and twenty-three wounded. The Germans sustained twenty killed and wounded.

Andrzej Suchcitz

Additional Reading

Outze, Borge (ed.), *Denmark During the German Occupation* (1946).

Petrow, Richard, *The Bitter Years: The Invasion and Occupation of Denmark and Norway, 1940–1945* (1974).

Pyle, Ernest Taylor (1900–1945)

American war correspondent. Columnist "Ernie" Pyle became one of the most beloved American figures of the war. After attending Indiana University, he worked as a journalist. As a syndicated columnist for the Washington *Daily News* in 1935, he toured the United States by automobile with his wife. During the war, he witnessed the bombing of London and covered campaigns in North Africa, Sicily, Italy, France, and the Pacific. His informal and personal stories of the average GI, which used real names and hometowns, made him very popular.

Pyle helped implement the six months overseas service stripe and the $10.00 per month raise for combat soldiers. His columns were collected into several books, including *Here Is Your War* and

Brave Men, and he won the Pulitzer Prize in 1944. On 17 April 1945, while covering the U.S. assault of Ie Shima in the Pacific, Pyle was killed by a Japanese sniper.

Laura Matysek Wood

Additional Reading

Miller, Lee G., *The Story of Ernie Pyle* (1950).

Pyle, Ernest Taylor, *Brave Men* (1944).

P

Quesada, Elwood R. (1904–1993)

American lieutenant general, commander of U.S. IX Tactical Air Command. "Pete" Quesada was one of America's foremost tactical air commanders of World War II. He was known as a tireless worker, devoted to mission accomplishment without being parochial, and proved to be enormously innovative. He was one of the architects of the modern tactical air support system for ground combat operations.

As a 1st Lieutenant, Quesada was selected by Ira Eaker and Carl Spaatz (qq.v.) to be a pilot in the seven-day aerial refueling test conducted in 1929. Flying a modified Fokker, Spaatz, Eaker, and Quesada set a world record with more than 150 hours of continuous flight in the "Question Mark," an allusion to the wind-curved refueling hose that connected two aircraft in the air. The flight proved air refueling could increase substantially the range and loiter time of combat aircraft.

During the interwar period, Quesada held various flying and high-level staff assignments. This exposed him to a broader perspective on airpower issues, and helped him to better understand the need to integrate airpower with ground forces. While working for General Frank Andrews (q.v.), Quesada helped create the organization of the new general headquarters staff of the army air corps. Later, as an aide to General Henry H. "Hap" Arnold (q.v.), Quesada established the criteria for the new Lend-Lease (q.v.) shipments of aircraft and munitions to Great Britain. In these jobs, he proved himself to be an adroit leader who possessed superb communication and organizational skills. These traits would serve him well during the war.

In 1942, Quesada was promoted to brigadier general. In 1943, he went to North Africa where he commanded the XII Fighter Command and was deputy commander of the Northwest African Coastal Command, whose mission was to interdict Axis shipping and protect Allied convoys operating in the Mediterranean. After the North African campaign, he moved to Britain to head the IX Fighter Command. In April 1944, he was promoted to major general and took over the IX Tactical Air Command. In that position, he organized, equipped, and trained pilots to provide air support for Allied forces in the Normandy (q.v.) invasion.

In order to eliminate the training deficiencies that caused airmen so much trouble in North Africa, Quesada developed a program to "crossflow" combat experiences from the Italian theater into his own organization. Each pilot was trained to conduct escort, interdiction, and fighter sweep missions. Each commander attended crossflow programs taught by the best commanders in the European Theater of Operations. Every pilot was encouraged to use his initiative, creativity, and aggressiveness to develop new tactics, which could further exploit the advantages of airpower.

When Quesada decided his forces lacked adequate communications, he sent a sergeant to New York to buy FM radio equipment. After proving this equipment worked better than AM radios, Quesada worked with the Quartermaster Corps to procure these radios en masse for all his fighter units. He also suggested to General Omar N. Bradley (q.v.) that such radios be put into the lead tanks of ground units so they could communicate directly with his aircraft. Flying over U.S. armored units, the IX Tactical Air Command crews protected the forces, swept potential bottlenecks from the battlefield, and contributed greatly to the U.S. ability to finally break out of the hedgerows of Normandy. This integrated air-ground team, employing armored column cover tactics, proved immensely effective in the campaign for northern France.

Perhaps Quesada's greatest challenge of the war came during the German Ardennes offensive (q.v.). He was responsible for all air operations over the Bulge. Despite bad weather, which initially constrained the use of airpower, he and his crews used blind bombing techniques and their finely honed close support tactics to protect Allied units in the Bulge.

After V-E Day, Quesada returned to the United States to become chief of air intelligence for the remainder of the war. In the postwar period, Quesada became the first commander of the Tactical Air Command (TAC). He was also the military director of the Eniwetok hydrogen bomb tests. After retiring in 1951, he worked for Olin Industries, established the missile and space division at Lockheed, and served as a special assistant to President Dwight D. Eisenhower (q.v.). In January 1959, he became the first administrator of the newly organized Federal Aviation Administration.

Michael L. Wolfert

Vidkun Quisling. (IWM MISC 17436)

Additional Reading

Blumenson, Martin, *Breakout and Pursuit* (1961).

Hughes. Thomas, *OVERLORD: Pete Quesada and the Triumph of Tactical Air Power in World War II* (1995).

Pallud, Jean Paul, *The Battle of the Bulge* (1984).

Quisling, Vidkun (1887–1945)

Norwegian National Socialist leader and collaborationist. Quisling was, in many ways, a tragic figure. He was a brilliant soldier, linguist, relief worker, one-time government minister, and staunch patriot. Yet his name became a universal synonym for traitor, and his wartime government of Norway degenerated into oppression and ineffectiveness.

Quisling started his career as a professional soldier by completing the Norwegian Military Academy as cadet of honor, a student so brilliant he was personally received by the king. From 1918, he held a series of military-diplomatic posts in Russia where he helped to provide League of Nations (q.v.) relief during the civil war. His organizational skills were such that Leon Trotsky (q.v.) offered him a post on the Red Army's General Staff. Returning from Russia in the early 1920s, he

was, at first, attracted to the Communists, but he quickly followed his pro-peasant inclinations and eventually became minister of defense in the Agrarian Party government of 1931. It was in that post, however, that he showed the first signs of political ineptitude and heavy-handedness.

Increasingly attracted by the example of German Nazism, Quisling founded his *Nasjonal Samling* (NS) in 1933. However, his party was never able to achieve more than 2 percent of the vote in Norway, although, at local level, it did manage 10 percent. The 1930s didn't produce any real success for Quisling, and from 1936, his party went into a decline that was interrupted only in the early years of the occupation.

Increasingly forgotten at home, Quisling turned to Germany, and made several trips there in 1939 to discuss a possible NS coup in Norway. His chance came in April 1940 when, during the confusion of the German occupation of Oslo, Quisling declared himself prime minister. The Germans, however, had other ideas, and it was not until September 1940 that Quisling formed a government.

He attempted to build on the newfound, if limited, popularity of *Nasjonal Samling,* and tried to create his ideal Norway, based on the principles of land and folk. As usual, the Germans were unwilling to leave a home-grown national socialist to his own devices. The continued German interference, as much as any resistance, greatly hampered Quisling.

By the time of Norway's liberation in May 1945, the minister-president was an isolated figure. At his trial, Quisling maintained that all he had done was in the interests of Norway. He was shot at Oslo's Akershus Castle on 24 October 1945.

Stephen M. Cullen

Additional Reading

Hayes, Paul M., *Quisling* (1971).

Hewins, Ralph, *Quisling: Prophet Without Honor* (1965).

Knudsen, Harold F., *I Was Quisling's Secretary* (1967).

R

Raczkiewicz, Władysław (1885–1947)

President of Poland in exile. Raczkiewicz was appointed president of the Republic of Poland on 30 September 1939 and led the Polish nation through the war. In many ways he formed a counterbalance to General Władysław Sikorski (q.v.). Raczkiewicz was critical of the handling of the evacuation of Polish troops from France and unsuccessfully tried to dismiss Sikorski. He opposed the final draft of the Polish-Soviet Agreement of 1941, which left the question of Poland's eastern frontier open. A much respected politician, he represented the highest symbol of Poland's fight for full sovereignty and territorial integrity.

Andrzej Suchcitz

Additional Reading

Garliński, Józef, *Poland in the Second World War* (1985).
Mikołajczyk, Stanisław, *The Rape of Poland* (1947).

Raczyński, Edward (1891–1993)

Polish ambassador to Britain from 1934 to 1945. Raczyński negotiated many of the Anglo-Polish agreements of the period, including the Mutual Assistance Alliance of 1939, and the August 1940 Armed Forces Treaty. From 1941 to 1943, he was also director of the Polish Foreign Ministry. He was president of the anti-Communist Polish government-in-exile in London from 1976 to 1986.

Andrzej Suchcitz

Additional Reading

Garliński, Józef, *Poland in the Second World War* (1985).
Raczyński, Edward, *In Allied London* (1962).

Raeder, Erich (1876–1960)

German grand admiral, commander in chief of the navy. *Grossadmiral* Erich Raeder dominated German naval thinking and strategy for nearly twenty years. He commanded the *Kriegsmarine* from 1935 until January 1943. A conservative officer whose strategic vision was firmly planted in the previous war, he opposed development of German naval special warfare forces, placed a low priority on radar and electronic systems development, and continued to emphasize surface gun batteries in aircraft carrier designs long after events at sea demonstrated the primacy of the carrier's air wing. Nonetheless, he supervised the development of a fleet that, although heavily outnumbered, fought well against overwhelming odds and very nearly won the war at sea.

Born in Wandsbek (near Hamburg) on 24 April 1876, Raeder joined the Imperial German Navy in 1894 and was commissioned as an officer three years later. He served in a variety of staff and fleet positions during World War I, ending his war service as the communications officer to Admiral Franz von Hipper, commander of the Imperial High Seas Fleet. Accepted into the *Reichsmarine* after the war, his initial postwar duties included preparation of historical records from World War I for the naval archives. This position enabled him to study the actions and lessons from the war. It had a profound effect on his view of naval tactics and strategy.

Between 1920 and 1922, Raeder wrote two volumes of the official history of the Imperial German Navy in World War I. The volume on the operations conducted by the deployed German cruiser squadrons achieved high acclaim both in Germany and abroad. More significantly, the project secured his belief that large-scale "raiding squadrons" offered Germany its best chance of

Grand Admiral Erich Raeder, in his cell at Nuremberg. (IWM DEU 503412)

ing squadrons. A worldwide supply and support organization was established in various neutral countries and remote island areas. His raiders would not have to search the world and pray for luck to get their supplies. He had a network in place that could be activated in time of war.

Raeder also pushed for technological developments to support his strategy. He successfully advocated the *Deutschland*-class (pocket battleship) design for the Weimar Republic (q.v.) in 1928 and then, as head of the *Kriegsmarine,* he directed the design of long-range diesel-powered surface units. He also pressured his designers to develop special high pressure steam boilers so his combatants could achieve higher fuel efficiency and power density. The *Kriegsmarine* rushed the new system into service without adequate testing. As a result, German destroyer readiness suffered during the war. Often up to 20 percent of the destroyer force was sidelined for propulsion system problems. His views also affected aircraft carrier designs and contributed to Germany's failure to produce one during the war.

War broke out before Raeder could implement the Plan Z, but he positioned the *Kriegsmarine* to make the most of what he had. The *Deutschland* class units and most of the U-boats were at sea by September 1939. Other than the navy's small size, the only negative factors were the loss of the naval air arm to the *Luftwaffe* in 1938 and the shortage of naval mines. Neither of these factors appeared critical in the war's initial stages. The *Luftwaffe* seemed cooperative and German submarines and surface raiders enjoyed significant successes, sinking large numbers of merchant ships and even penetrating Scapa Flow (q.v.) to sink the battleship HMS *Royal Oak.* U-boat losses were higher than expected but did not seem alarming. Meanwhile, Soviet assistance enabled Germany to escape the worst effects of the Allied blockade and fuel was not in short supply. This advantage changed rapidly, however.

The *Graf Spee* was cornered off Montevideo and scuttled in December 1939. Steel and labor shortages forced a reduction in the fleet construction program and torpedo failures blunted the U-boat campaign. Then came the successful but costly Norway campaign (q.v.) in April 1940, which Raeder advocated to gain bases and outflank Great Britain. More than half of the German destroyer and cruiser force was sunk. The next year saw the *Bismarck* (q.v.), Germany's largest battleship, go down, and subsequently, Hitler's first direct interference in naval operations. Raeder also suffered a loss of prestige and influence that year.

winning a war at sea. In his view, all other elements of the navy (submarines, aircraft, etc.) were merely supporting arms to assist these squadrons. A vice admiral by 1925, he was promoted to admiral and chief of the naval command in 1928, a post that enabled him to formulate the navy's strategy and tactics.

Appointed commander in chief of the *Kriegsmarine* in 1935, Raeder took a gradual, balanced approach to fleet expansion. Despite his preference for surface raiding groups, he recognized the submarine's role. Clandestine design bureaus were formed and construction of the submarine (U-boat) arm were begun. Still, he wanted to avoid antagonizing Great Britain, instead seeing France and the Soviet Union as Germany's primary future foes. He pushed Adolf Hitler (q.v.) to gain British acceptance of Germany's naval expansion plans. The resulting Anglo-German Naval Agreement of 1935 (q.v.) achieved this goal, giving Germany the right to build a fleet equal to approximately 35 percent of the Royal Navy's strength.

Hitler's activities in Eastern Europe forced a change in plans, however, and Raeder was directed to develop a fleet that would deter British "interference" until 1942 and be ready for war by 1943–1944. The resulting Plan Z (q.v.) was developed in January 1939, and it reflected Raeder's strategic view. On 1 April 1939, he was promoted to *Grossadmiral* (grand admiral).

Raeder's new fleet would be centered on raid-

He had urged Hitler not to invade the Soviet Union until Britain was defeated, but Hitler ignored his advice.

What followed was two years of fuel shortages inhibiting ship deployments. The Allies also broke Germany's naval codes. Forewarned of German naval plans, the Allies generally were able to prevent Germany's surface squadrons from gaining the advantage. With the exception of the U-boat command, the *Kriegsmarine* was relegated to a "fleet-in-being." Hitler's restrictive rules of employment combined with fuel shortages and Allied naval and air supremacy prevented the effective employment of the major surface units. Then came the disastrous battle of the Barents Sea (q.v.) in January 1943, after which Hitler ordered the scrapping of all major surface combatants. Raeder refused and offered his resignation, which Hitler accepted on 30 January 1943. Raeder spent the rest of the war in retirement. Admiral Karl Dönitz (q.v.) was appointed his successor.

Raeder never lost faith in surface raiding groups, even though it was Dönitz's innovative submarine tactics, not surface raiders, which nearly won the Battle of the Atlantic (q.v.). Raeder blamed the surface raiders' disappointing results on poor execution, the lack of units, or the failure of supporting elements such as the *Luftwaffe*. Arrested after the war, he was tried and convicted as a war criminal at Nuremberg (*see* International Military Tribunal) and sentenced to twenty years in prison. He was released on 26 September 1955, and wrote his memoirs in 1959. He died in Kiel, Germany, on 6 November 1960.

Carl O. Schuster

Additional Reading

Martienssen, Anthony K., *Hitler and His Admirals* (1949).

Raeder, Erich, *My Life* (1960).

Thomas, Charles, *The German Navy in the Nazi Era* (1990).

Rall, Günther (1918–)

Luftwaffe major, commander of *Jagdgeschwader* 300. Günther Rall, destined to become World War II's third highest ace, joined the German military as a cadet in 1936. A friend at the Dresden *Luftwaffe* Officer's School convinced him to become a pilot. He joined the famed *Jagdgeschwader* (JG) 52 in 1939, and scored his first kill against a French P-36 on 12 May 1940. Due to heavy losses during the Battle of Britain (q.v.), he rose quickly to the rank of major. He was then posted to the Balkans to

guard the Romanian oil fields and Danube River bridges and to fly against the RAF on Crete (q.v.). He flew in support of Army Group South during Operation BARBAROSSA. In late 1941, he was shot down. Temporarily paralyzed as a result of the crash, he required nine months to recover.

Rall returned to action with JG 52 and received the Knight's Cross in September 1942, the Oak Leaves on the occasion of his 101st victory two months later, and the Swords in September 1943 for shooting down 200 enemy aircraft. Downed himself eight times during the war, he spent another six months in a hospital in 1944. Toward the end of the war, he commanded the elite JG 300 in Salzburg, where his tally reached 275 kills. He flew a total of 621 missions during his career. In 1956, he joined the West German *Bundeswehr*. He retired as a lieutenant general.

Robert Kirchubel

Additional Reading

Mitcham, Samuel W., Jr., *Men of the Luftwaffe* (1988).

Obermaier, Ernst, *Luftwaffe Holders of the Knight's Cross* (1966).

Ramsay, Bertram (1883–1945)

British admiral. Although he never commanded a major fleet, Sir Bertram Ramsay is recognized as one of the outstanding naval leaders of World War II. He was the European theater's undisputed master of amphibious warfare. The son of a calvary brigadier, he was born in January 1883 and joined the Royal Navy as a midshipman fifteen years later. An exceptionally bright officer, he commanded both a monitor and a destroyer during World War I. He was promoted to captain in 1923. From there, he went on to command several cruisers and the battleship HMS *Royal Sovereign* before his promotion to rear admiral in 1935. He then resigned his appointment as chief of staff, Home Fleet and was placed on half pay. He retired as a vice admiral in early 1939.

As a retired flag officer, Ramsay had the mobilization post of flag officer, Dover. It thus fell to him to plan and conduct Operation DYNAMO, the evacuation of the British Expeditionary Force (BEF) from Dunkirk (q.v.). His masterful planning, fast thinking, and ability to improvise saved the British Army.

In March 1942, Ramsay was selected to plan the Allies' first major amphibious assault, Operation TORCH. He was also chief planner for Operation HUSKY, the assault on Sicily (q.v.). The success of those operations led to his promotion to admiral and assignment as commander in chief of Allied naval forces for Operation OVERLORD. The resulting naval segment of that assault, Operation NEPTUNE, was his crowning achievement, but it was not his final amphibious assault.

Faced with the need to open Antwerp to facilitate the Allied advance into Germany, Ramsay conducted the assault on the Scheldt (q.v.), which controlled the port's approaches. His success solved the severe logistics logjam that plagued the Allies in Western Europe. That was his last operation. He was killed in a plane crash on 2 January 1945. Although not as heralded as those who fought major fleet actions, his was a unique and critical contribution to the Allied victory.

Carl O. Schuster

Additional Reading
Chatterton, Edward K., and Kenneth Edwards, *The Royal Navy: From September 1939 to September 1945* (1947).
Howarth, Stephen (ed.), *Men of War: Great Naval Leaders of World War II* (1993).

Raštikis, Stasys (1896–1980)
Lithuanian general, commander in chief of the Lithuanian Army. As commander in chief of the Lithuanian Army in 1939, Raštikis supported a policy of neutrality toward the conflict in Poland. In 1939, forces under his command occupied the Wilno district of Poland. He was dismissed in 1940. After the Soviet invasion of Lithuania, he fled to Berlin. He became the defense minister in Colonel Kazys Skirpa's (q.v.) government, but he refused senior military appointments under German command.

Andrzej Suchcitz

Additional Reading
Harrison, Ernest, *Lithuania's Fight for Freedom* (1952).
Norem, Owen J., *Timeless Lithuania* (1945).

Reichenau, Walther von (1884–1942)
German field marshal, commander of the German Sixth Army. Walther von Reichenau was one of the first important military experts to place himself at Adolf Hitler's (q.v.) service. He believed it was essential that the army associate itself with a party that best aroused patriotism and therefore turned to the Nazis. He especially adopted the Nazi idea of the *Volksheer* (People's Army), and he broke long-standing Prussian military traditions by staying in close contact with his troops and even regularly participating in physical training exercises with his men.

Von Reichenau served as Werner von Blomberg's (q.v.) chief of staff in Königsberg and used his contacts with Hitler to secure von Blomberg's appointment as defense minister. When General Kurt Hammerstein resigned as commander in chief of the German Army in January 1934, von Blomberg and Hitler recommended von Reichenau to fill the position. President Paul von Hindenberg chose General Werner Fritsch (qq.v.) instead, because von Reichenau broke vaunted Prussian traditions by associating with his troops. Hitler, not yet prepared to challenge the army, instead named von Reichenau as second in charge at the Defense Ministry. After Fritsch was dismissed in January 1938, Hitler again tried to name von Reichenau commander in chief of the army, but backed down under strong opposition from senior officers.

During World War II, von Reichenau held many important field commands. During the Polish campaign, his Tenth Army (later redesignated the Sixth Army) captured Warsaw. During the Battle of France, he led the Sixth Army through Holland and northern Belgium, diverting British and French attention from the Ardennes. On 14 June 1940, his forces occupied Paris. He was promoted to field marshal the next month.

In Operation BARBAROSSA, von Reichenau led the Sixth Army in its advance through the Ukraine. He wholeheartedly endorsed Hitler's orders to exterminate the Red Army commissars. In early January 1942, von Reichenau replaced Field Marshal Gerd von Rundstedt (q.v.) as commander of Army Group South, but he died of a heart attack a few weeks later.

Justin D. Murphy

Additional Reading
Görlitz, Walter, *History of the German General Staff, 1657–1945* (1953).
Mellenthin, F.W. von, *German Generals of World War II As I Saw Them* (1977).
Mitcham, Samuel W., Jr., *Hitler's Field Marshals and Their Battles* (1988).

Reinhardt, Georg-Hans (1887–1963)
German colonel general, commander of Army Group Center. Like Johannes Friessner (q.v.), Reinhardt began his military career as a subaltern in the Royal Saxon infantry. After World War I,

he held a number of staff positions and took a training course at the *Reichswehr*'s secret armored warfare school in the Soviet Union. From 1938 to early 1940, he was in command of the 4th *Panzer* Division. He then took over XLI *Panzer Korps,* whose mechanized units distinguished themselves during the western campaign, the invasion of Yugoslavia, and the opening phases of Operation BARBAROSSA.

In October 1941, Reinhardt succeeded Colonel General Hermann Hoth (q.v.) as commander of *Panzer* Group Three (soon to be redesignated Third *Panzer* Army), which he led until August 1944. In late 1941, during the battle of Moscow (q.v.), Reinhardt was the only senior commander to counsel against further retreats by the embattled units of Army Group Center. In the summer of 1944, following the catastrophic collapse of Army Group Center in Byelorussia (q.v.), Reinhardt succeeded Field Marshal Walther Model (q.v.) as its commander, and presided over its fighting retreat into East Prussia. On 26 January 1945, Hitler fired Reinhardt for insubordination.

Along with several other senior generals, Reinhardt was tried by an American Military Tribunal (q.v.) (the OKW case) and sentenced to fifteen years' imprisonment. He secured an early release and published extensively on his wartime experiences.

Ulrich Trumpener

Additional Reading

Reinhardt, Hans, *Panzer-Gruppe 3 in der Schlacht von Moskau und ihre Erfahrungen im Rückzug* (1953).

Ziemke, Earl F., *Stalingrad to Berlin: The German Defeat in the East* (1968).

Reitsch, Hanna (1912–1979)

German test pilot. Hanna Reitsch is best known as the leading woman test pilot of Nazi Germany. Together with General Robert *Ritter* von Greim (q.v.), she flew in and out of Berlin under heavy Soviet fire at the end of April 1945. A passionate follower of Adolf Hitler (q.v.), she wanted to stay in the *Führerbunker* to await the end there but was ordered to leave. She repeatedly set world records as a woman glider pilot in the 1930s, the 1950s, and in 1970. Appointed flight captain in 1937, she performed test flights for the *Luftwaffe* with all kinds of planes from helicopters to jets. After a fifteen-month internment following the end of the war, she eventually served as pilot and flight instructor in several countries, including India and Ghana. She came to hold a more critical attitude toward the Nazi regime in her memoirs.

George P. Blum

Additional Reading

March, Cyril (ed.), *The Rise and Fall of the German Air Force, 1933–1945* (1983).

Reitsch, Hanna, *Flying Is My Life* (1945).

Remarque, Erich Maria (1898–1970)

German writer. A German soldier during World War I, Remarque's experiences served as the basis for his 1929 best-seller, *All Quiet on the Western Front.* This classic antiwar novel portrays in graphic detail the devastating impact of war on an entire generation of Germans whose youthful optimism and belief in their country was shattered by the war. The Nazis, who idolized war, denounced the novel as a betrayal of the German soldier and his noble mission. They organized protests against the book and the subsequent 1930 film adaptation. Both the novel and the film were banned, and in 1933, Remarque was stripped of his citizenship. He continued to write from exile in Switzerland and the United States. *All Quiet on the Western Front* has been translated into forty-five languages and has sold over 50 million copies world-wide.

Steven B. Rogers

Additional Reading

Pfeiler, William K., *War and the German Mind* (1941).

Remarque, Erich Maria, *All Quiet On the Western Front* (1929).

Rendulic, Lothar (1887–1971)

Austrian colonel general, commander of German Army Group North. Scion of an old Austrian military family, Rendulic was undoubtedly one of Adolf Hitler's (q.v.) most capable senior commanders. Commissioned in the Habsburg Army in 1910, he served on both the Russian and the Italian fronts during World War I, earned a doctorate in law, and eventually was sent to Paris as Austrian military attache. Because of his membership in the Nazi Party, he was forced into retirement in 1936 but resumed active service after the *Anschluss* (q.v.).

Following stints as a divisional and a corps commander in Russia, Rendulic was sent to the Balkans where he led the Second *Panzer* Army against Tito's (q.v.) partisans from August 1943 until June 1944. He then transferred to Finland and subsequently presided over the successful withdrawal of the Twentieth Mountain Army into northern Norway. Early in 1945, he took over Army Group North (in East Prussia), later served briefly as commander of Army Group Kurland, and ultimately was sent to his native Austria to direct the operations of Army Group South *(Ostmark)*. He surrendered to U.S. forces on 7 May 1945.

Rendulic was sentenced to twenty years imprisonment by an American military tribunal (q.v.), but he was released from Landsberg prison in December 1951.

Ulrich Trumpener

Additional Reading
Kennedy, Robert M., *German Antiguerrilla Operations in the Balkans,* 1941–1944 (1954).
Rendulic, Lothar, *Gekämpft, Gesiegt, Geschlagen* (1952).

Reynaud, Paul (1878–1966)

Prime minister of France at the time of the German invasion. Reynaud was one of the few French politicians who, in the mid-1930s, saw the need to modernize the French military and free the army from its World War I mind-set. He advocated armored forces and sought unsuccessfully to implement Charles de Gaulle's (q.v.) plans for a modern, armored striking force. On the collapse of the popular front in 1938, Premier Édouard Daladier (q.v.) appointed Reynaud finance minister, with responsibility for the domestic economy. He sought to reinvigorate the economy by removing restrictions and inequities.

On 21 March 1940, Daladier was voted out and Reynaud became premier. Reynaud was dominated by his mistress, the Countess Helene de Portes, and she often acted in his place while he was indisposed. The countess and Daladier's mistress, Marquise Jeanne de Crussol, fueled a bitter rivalry between the two men. Reynaud did not control military policy, as Daladier was minister of national defense until 19 May.

Fundamentally an Anglophile, Reynaud nonetheless criticized the British for failure to contribute substantial resources to France. Later, he shared the French Army view that the British "always made for harbors." When he finally replaced Maurice Gamelin (q.v.) as commander in chief, he pledged to continue the fight against the Germans, but on 16 June, a majority of the cabinet voted to ask Hitler for terms.

Reynaud was one of the defendants at the Riom Trials in 1942. After the Germans took over the unoccupied Vichy zone, he was imprisoned. He was liberated in 1945.

Spencer Tucker

Additional Reading
Chapman, Guy, *Why France Fell: The Defeat of the French Army in 1940* (1969).
Horne, Alistair, *To Lose a Battle: France 1940* (1969).
Reynaud, Paul, *In the Thick of the Fight* (1955).
Werth, Alexander, *France 1940–1955* (1956).

Ribbentrop, Joachim von (1893–1946)

German foreign minister. Although von Ribbentrop came from a traditional officer family, he never intended to follow a military career. As a boy, he learned to speak English and French fluently, and at age seventeen, he left Germany to become a businessman in Canada. With the outbreak of World War I, von Ribbentrop returned to Germany and fought with the German Army on various fronts. He rose to the rank of first lieutenant and had his first diplomatic experience as an aide-de-camp during the armistice negotiations in 1918.

After the war, von Ribbentrop turned again to business. As a wine importer, he met Otto Henkell, the rich German champagne producer, whose daughter, Annelies, he married in July 1920. It was for von Ribbentrop a major step into the upper circles of German society. His nearly pathological vanity and ambition even led him to pay his noble aunt to adopt him in 1925, so he could assume the aristocratic *von* in his name.

Like many of his generation, von Ribbentrop viewed the conditions of the Versailles Treaty (q.v.) as a national shame, and he feared the rising Communist influence in Germany. During the final stages of the Weimar Republic (q.v.), he dove into politics by arranging secret meetings at his Berlin villa with Adolf Hitler and Chancellor Franz von Papen (qq.v.). Von Ribbentrop, sensing opportunity, quickly joined the Nazi Party and from their first meeting in August 1932, he did not budge from Hitler's side. The *Führer* appreciated von Ribbentrop's command of foreign languages, his social connections, and his international experiences. Hitler made him his consultant on foreign policy and encouraged him to establish the "Bureau Ribbentrop" in direct competition with the German Foreign Ministry. Von Ribbentrop secured a sensational success in 1935 with the signing of the Anglo-German Naval Agreement (q.v.).

German Foreign Minister Joachim von Ribbentrop, in an SS uniform. (IWM NYT 68692)

During the following two years as ambassador in London, he tried unsuccessfully to cement a political alliance with Great Britain to counter Communism and to establish a continental German hegemony. Quite the contrary, he expanded the Berlin-Rome Axis to include Japan, making it in effect an international anti-British pact.

Appointed foreign minister in February 1938, von Ribbentrop obstinately encouraged Hitler to follow a brutal imperialist policy leading to war. His last great triumph was the Ribbentrop-Molotov Pact (q.v.) of August 1939, which was supposed to definitively isolate Great Britain. For Hitler, of course, the agreement with Josef Stalin (q.v.) was only a tactical maneuver in his dynamic annihilation policy.

During the war, von Ribbentrop tried in vain to reverse his increasing loss of importance by posing as a rigorous "Jew-hunter." Because of his obvious incompetence, his arrogance, and his total lack of humor, he alienated everybody and finally even lost Hitler's esteem.

Even after the total collapse of the Third *Reich,* von Ribbentrop could not leave his diplomatic world of dreams. Without betraying a single sign of insight into his crimes, he was sentenced to death at Nuremberg (*see* International Military Tribunal) and was hanged on 16 October 1946. A humiliating product of National Socialism, he was best characterized by one of its leading figures, Joseph Goebbels (q.v.): "He bought his name, he married his money, and he obtained his post by trickery."

Wolfgang Terhörst

Additional Reading

Davidson, Eugene, *The Trial of the Germans* (1966).
Ribbentrop, Joachim von, *The Ribbentrop Memoirs* (1953).
Weitz, John, *Hitler's Diplomat: The Life and Times of Joachim von Ribbentrop* (1992).

Richthofen, Wolfram von (1895–1945)

Luftwaffe field marshal, commander of the *Kondor Legion.* Von Richthofen joined the German Air Force in 1917 and served for a short time with his cousin Manfred, the famous Red Baron. In 1938, Wolfram von Richthofen commanded the *Kondor Legion* (q.v.) in Spain, where he developed the tactics of close ground support by aircraft. Von Richthofen led an air corps against France in May 1940, and shortly afterward was promoted to general of fliers. In May and June 1941, he commanded the VIII Air Corps during the battle for Crete (q.v.). In 1942, he commanded the Fourth Air Fleet on the Russian front, and in February 1943, he was promoted to field marshal. From June 1943 to November 1944, Richthofen commanded the Second Air Fleet in Italy. Ill health forced his retirement and he died in Austria on 12 July 1945.

Michael Mahon

Additional Reading

Mitcham, Samuel W., Jr., *Hitler's Field Marshals and Their Battles* (1988).
———, *Men of the Luftwaffe* (1988).

Ridgway, Matthew Bunker (1895–1993)

Americal lieutenant general, commander XVII Airborne Corps. Matthew B. Ridgway was born at Fort Monroe, Virginia. He graduated from the U.S. Military Academy at West Point in 1917 and received advanced training as an infantry officer. In addition to the normal assignments for officers during the interwar period, he accompanied General George C. Marshall (q.v.) on a special mission to South America in 1939. Following that mission, Ridgway was assigned to the Operations Division of the War Department, a post General Dwight D. Eisenhower (q.v.) particularly wanted him in. In 1942, Ridgway became the commander of the 82nd Infantry Division, and guided that unit's conversion to an airborne division. He commanded the 82nd during its combat jumps into Sicily (q.v.) and jumped with his men into Normandy (q.v.).

Prior to the landings in Sicily, Ridgway established himself as a general who would not mince words, particularly if it involved unsound tactical decisions. Also, as the leader of the U.S. Army's first airborne division, he played a far greater role in operational and tactical planning than was normal for one of his rank. This was particularly evident in the early days of the war, especially prior to the landings in Sicily.

Some leaders had a distorted vision of the capabilities of airborne soldiers, and tended to forget that they were supposed to operate without heavy weapons, heavy artillery, and in many instances, air cover. Thanks to his intervention, and logical objections, several dubious airborne operations were cancelled, doubtlessly saving thousands of lives.

Another characteristic of Ridgway was his enviable ability to quickly cut to the core of a problem, ignoring side issues and focusing on how to best achieve the solution. He established the pattern for use of airborne forces as a complement to, not a replacement for, conventional ground forces. Like General George S. Patton (q.v.), Ridgway had his difficulties with some of the Allies, particularly British commanders. Arguments generally centered over who would receive the bulk of the transport assets, or which units would lead the assaults and which would follow on to mop up.

Ridgway commanded the XVIII Airborne Corps during the unsuccessful Operation MARKET-GARDEN and also during the German Ardennes Offensive (q.v.). In November 1945, he assumed command of the Mediterranean Theater of Operations. After the war, he served in a variety of high-level positions, culminating in command of the U.S. Eighth Army in Korea in 1950–1951. He finished his career as chief of staff of the U.S. Army from 1953 to 1955. In 1986, he was awarded the U.S. Presidential Medal of Freedom.

Thomas Cagley

Additional Reading
Cole, Hugh M., *The Ardennes: Battle of the Bulge* (1965).
Marshall, S.L.A., *Night Drop: The American Airborne Invasion of Normandy* (1962).

Ridgway, Matthew B., *Soldier: The Memoirs of Matthew B. Ridgway* (1956).

Riefenstahl, Leni Bertha Helene Amalia (1902–)

German filmmaker. Born in Berlin, Leni Riefenstahl attended the Academy of Arts with the hopes of becoming a professional dancer. She had some initial success in solo appearances until an injury ended her dancing career in 1924. Inspired by the movie *Mountain of Fate,* she switched to acting. Soon, however, she realized her true ambitions lay in the field of directing. Her first movie, *The Blue Light,* showed her strong empathy for the aesthetics of nature. It enjoyed great success in Germany.

Although Nazi propaganda chief Joseph Goebbels (q.v.) constantly hindered her work because she once rejected his advances and because he wanted control of all the information media, Adolf Hitler (q.v.) selected her to film the Nazi Party rallies in 1933 and 1934. Her *Triumph of the Will* is considered one of the great documentary and alleged classics of propaganda film. Hitler also urged her to make a film about the 1936 Olympic games in Berlin. The *Berlin Olympiad* is also considered a great documentary. She was the first film director to make movies outside of a studio and the first to film underwater Olympic action.

Riefenstahl was a brilliant director who did not care about politics. She associated with many high-level Nazis and today is still accused of having abused interned Gypsies for her movie *Lowland.* After the war, she was arrested by the Allies, but was finally cleared of all Nazi incriminations. Nevertheless, Riefenstahl had to abandon her very promising directing career, with the result that the world has been denied the benefits of her directing genius. She turned to photography and established another reputation as a leading photographer. At age eighty-five, she published her memoirs.

Wolfgang Terhörst

Additional Reading
Ford, Charles, *Leni Riefenstahl: Schauspielerin, Regisseurin und Fotografin* (1982).
Riefenstahl, Leni, *Memoiren* (1987).

Ritchie, Neil Methuen (1897–1983)

British lieutenant general. Sir Neil Ritchie served with distinction during World War I, winning the Distinguished Service Order and the Military Cross. In 1941 he was the deputy chief of staff of General Sir Claude Auchinleck's (q.v.) Middle East

Command. In November 1941, right in the middle of Operation CRUSADER, Auchinleck decided to remove General Sir Alan Cunningham (q.v.) as commander of the Eighth Army. He chose Ritchie to replace Cunningham, bypassing the more experienced desert generals, Willoughby Norris and A.R. Godwin-Austen.

At first fortune seemed to smile on Ritchie. After a grim slugging match, German General Erwin Rommel (q.v.) was forced on the night of 7–8 December to retreat before British pressure, bringing a successful end to Operation CRU-SADER. Auchinleck, however, had remained at Eighth Army headquarters in virtual command for the first ten days of Ritchie's tenure. After a short pause, Rommel went back on the offensive, pushing the British back and taking Benghazi on Christmas Eve. On 26 May 1942, Rommel struck at Gazala (q.v.), retaking the fortress of Tobruk (q.v.) on 21 June, and pushing the Eighth Army back to the borders of Egypt. Auchinleck removed Ritchie on 25 June 1942.

Ritchie returned to Britain and later commanded British XII Corps in Europe in 1944. He was promoted to full general in 1946, and he retired in 1951.

John F. Murphy, Jr.

Additional Reading
Barnett, Corelli, *The Desert Generals* (1982).
Keegan, John (ed.), *Churchill's Generals* (1991).

Rogge, Bernhard (1899–1982)

German vice admiral. Born in Schleswig, Bernhard Rogge served in the German merchant marine during World War I and in the interwar period. In early 1939, he was appointed commander of the sail training ship *Albert Leo Schlagter*. In July of that year he was promoted to the rank of captain *(Kapitan zur See)* and given command of the vessel that would become the commerce raiding auxiliary warship *Atlantis*. It was in that post that he became famous as Germany's most successful surface commerce raider, sinking twenty-two ships displacing 145,968 tons. He also set a record for sea endurance, spending 622 continuous days at sea and sailing more than 102,000 nautical miles in the process (*see Atlantis* Raids).

Rogge survived the sinking of the *Atlantis* and made it back to Germany, where he was awarded the Oak Leaves to the Knight's Cross of the Iron Cross. In 1942 he was appointed inspector general of training establishments inspectorate, and the commander of fleet training formations. Promoted to rear admiral *(Konteradmiral)* on March 1943, he was given command of *Kampfgruppe* Rogge. Two years later he was promoted to vice admiral *(Vizeadmiral)*.

Because of his chivalrous conduct as captain of the *Atlantis,* Rogge was not brought to trial by the Allies. In 1955, he was accepted into the new West German *Bundesmarine,* and rose to the rank of vice admiral. His last post was as commander of the 1st Defense Area, Kiel. He died in 1982 and was buried with full state honors.

Carl O. Schuster

Additional Reading
Frank, Wolfgang, and Bernhard Rogge, *The German Raider Atlantis* (1956).
Schmalbach, Paul, *German Raiders* (1977).

Röhm, Ernst (1887–1934)

Chief of the Nazi Party's *Sturmabteilung* (SA) (q.v.). It is hard to be objective about Ernst Röhm. On the one hand, he was a tough, courageous army officer, wounded and decorated in World War I, a gifted organizer, and a leader of men. On the other, he was arrogant, "bull-headed," overconfident, utterly contemptuous of society's laws and mores, and a militant homosexual at a time when homosexuality was both illegal and condemned by the accepted standards of German society.

Röhm had few friends in the Nazi Party. Ironically, Adolf Hitler (q.v.) was one of them. Hitler probably had a good deal of genuine admiration for him. He was deeply indebted to Röhm for the assistance he, and through him the *Reichswehr,* gave the Nazi Party in its early years. Röhm participated in the 1923 Beer Hall *Putsch* (q.v.). He was one of very few party comrades with whom Hitler used the familiar *Du* in speaking, instead of the formal *Sie.* Röhm for his part was not awed by Hitler. He never fell under Hitler's spell, never fell victim to his arresting personality, or his "charisma." In this respect, Röhm was virtually unique.

Röhm was born to soldier: he loved the military life and the camaraderie associated with it. Convinced the Treaty of Versailles (q.v.) was profoundly unjust, he devoted his great energies after 1918 to its abolition. Therefore, he supported the Nazi Party and virtually any other militantly nationalist formation in postwar Germany. When he became leader of the SA in 1924 and again in 1931, he set about transforming it into a militia that could be used to throw off the shackles of Versailles. But time and again Röhm ran into Hitler's greatly differing conception of the role of the SA.

Eventually this led to the Night of the Long Knives (q.v.). From 30 June to 2 July 1934, Hitler authorized a purge eliminating persons threatening his dictatorship. More than 200 people (Rudolf Pechel, an informed and reliable source, places this figure at 922) were killed in this bloodbath, including Nazi Party official Gregor Strasser (q.v.), former chancellor General Kurt von Schleicher, Franz von Papen's secretary Edgar Jung, and Ernst Röhm. With one stroke, Hitler eliminated any potential opposition and consolidated his power.

Jon Moulton

Additional Reading

Gallo, Max, *The Night of the Long Knives* (1972).
Pinson, Koppel S., *Modern Germany* (1966).
Tolstoy, Nikolai, *Night of the Long Knives* (1972).

Rokossovsky, Konstantin Konstantinovich (1896–1968)

Marshal of the Soviet Union, commander of the Soviet Don, Central, and 1st and 2nd Byelorussian Fronts (army groups). Rokossovsky was the son of middle-class parents. His father was Polish. His parents died just before he was drafted into the tsar's army, where he served as an NCO during World War I. In 1917, he joined the Red Army, and gained valuable command and combat experience during the civil war. During that period, he served in cavalry units. When he attended the Frunze Military Academy, he concentrated on cavalry tactics.

In the late 1930s, Rokossovsky commanded a corps in Manchuria. That assignment nearly proved the end of him. The NKVD (q.v.) accused him of being a spy for China, and he was tortured and imprisoned. Although he was still in prison, he managed to survive the mass executions of the senior officer corps during the military purges (q.v.). It was from a prison camp that General Georgy Zhukov (q.v.) selected Rokossovsky for frontline command in 1941.

Rokossovsky led the Soviet's first tank counterattack in the Ukraine, and his inexperienced XI Mechanized Corps temporarily halted the German *Panzer* forces. He then transferred to the north, where he help organize the breakout of surrounded Soviet units at Smolensk (q.v.) in August 1941. He was then given command of the Sixteenth Army, and participated in the successful defense of Moscow (q.v.). The defense held and a Soviet counterattack pushed Field Marshal Walther Model (q.v.)

Marshal Konstantin Rokossovsky. (IWM PIC 71331)

back, but Rokossovsky had a major clash with Zhukov in the process. Rokossovsky appealed what he thought was an unwise order to the chief of the general staff. He received permission for an alternate action, but Zhukov, on hearing of the new order, revoked it with a tersely worded message that the units in question were in his command, and he would establish the line of defense.

Following the defense of Moscow, Rokossovsky commanded the Don Front at Stalingrad (q.v.), where his troops broke through the Italian and Romanian forces, allowing the Soviets to encircle General Freiderich Paulus's (q.v.) Sixth Army. In 1943, Rokossovsky commanded the Central Front, which blunted and held Model's thrust at Kursk (q.v.). In October the Central Front was redesignated the Byelorussian Front and spearheaded the Soviet drive into Poland. He took Lublin and Brest-Litovsk and trapped two German *Panzer* corps. He was held east of Warsaw by Model, and failed to relieve the city during the Warsaw Rising (q.v.). Since he was a Pole himself, this caused a great deal of later resentment among the Poles.

The Soviets reorganized their fronts in January 1945. Rokossovsky took command of the 2nd Byelorussian Front and took Warsaw. He then swept through northern Poland to take Danzig on

30 March. That trapped the German armies in East Prussia against the Baltic, and neutralized the German force that had prevented the final assault on Berlin. As a result, Zhukov's right flank was protected by Rokossovsky's force, and Zhukov was then free to concentrate on Berlin.

Rokossovsky's contribution to the Soviet Union in World War II was in his use of armored forces. At one point, he was fighting with regiments reduced to less than 200 men, yet was able to successfully delay or defeat German forces. As a result of Rokossovsky being in Poland at the war's end, his troops became the occupying force in that country. After the war, he was the commander of the Northern Group of Forces, and eventually served as Poland's minister of national defense. He later returned to the Soviet Union and served in a variety of positions within the Soviet Ministry of Defense until his death.

Thomas Cagley

Additional Reading

Bialer, Seweryn (ed.), *Stalin and His Generals* (1984).
Rokossovsky, Konstantin, *A Soldier's Duty* (1985).
Shukman, Harold (ed.), *Stalin's Generals* (1993).

Rommel, Erwin (1891–1944)

German field marshal, commander of the *Afrika Korps*. One of the acknowledged operational and tactical geniuses of World War II, Rommel won undying fame as the "Desert Fox" in North Africa and as the defender of Normandy in 1944. He was not of the *Junker* class, nor was he born into a military family.

Born on 15 November 1891, in Ulm, in the German state of Württemberg, Rommel was the son of a mathematics teacher and a middle-class mother. He was also the product of a German *Reich* which was formed only twenty years prior to his birth. It was a world of patriotism and middle-class intellectual values that shaped Rommel. He considered a career in engineering, but in 1910, he joined the army as an officer cadet in a Württemberg regiment. A middle-class urge for security overrode the uncertainty of engineering, and in January 1911, he was commissioned a subaltern in his regiment.

Rommel performed his duties in a steady but unspectacular manner, but the outbreak of war in 1914 changed this colorless young soldier dramatically. He ended the war as a captain, and with Germany's highest decoration for bravery, the *Pour le Mérite*. As an infantry officer in France, Roma-

nia, and the Italian front, Rommel displayed dash, courage, and a sound grasp of infantry tactics, especially at the platoon and company level. The young Rommel, while transformed into a warrior, still displayed no penchant for higher command.

Like many of his brother officers, Rommel was aghast at the restrictive military provisions of the 1919 Versailles Treaty (q.v.), but was retained by the 100,000-man Weimar Army. He seemed oblivious to politics, although he regarded Adolf Hitler (q.v.) as a German patriot who might very well reverse the economic conditions of Germany and undo much of the hated Treaty of Versailles. In the late 1920s, while teaching infantry tactics, Rommel recorded his experiences in the Great War in a book entitled *Infanterie greift an (Infantry Attacks),* which Hitler read, taking great interest in what Rommel had written.

Throughout the Polish campaign, Rommel, a newly promoted major general, commanded Hitler's personal bodyguard. He asked Hitler for the command of a *Panzer* division, which he was given despite opposition from the army staff. On 15 February 1940, with no real tank experience, he assumed command of the 7th *Panzer* Division.

During the 1940 France campaign, Rommel proved to be an able, daring commander. Like General Heinz Guderian (q.v.), he preferred to command from the front, being personally involved with every aspect of combat action. So successful and so rapid was his division's actions, the 7th became known as the "Ghost Division." From his rapid crossing of the Meuse River on 13 May to his receiving the British surrender at St. Valery on 17 June, Rommel's Ghosts outdistanced other *Panzer* forces. He again attracted the *Führer's* attention.

On 9 January 1941, Hitler decided to send a German force to North Africa to salvage the military situation there, the Italians having suffered a humiliating defeat. Rommel landed in Tripoli on 12 February, ahead of his *Panzer* force. He did not get along well with the Italians, who continually failed to keep his force supplied. By the end of March, his *Afrika Korps* (q.v.) was on the move, and the war in the desert changed. From April 1941 to March 1942, the British were driven from Libya into Egypt. Rommel was denied pursuit of the routed British, and by the time he was ready to resume the offensive in the spring of 1942, the British had revitalized.

After a series of victories, Rommel was promoted to field marshal on 21 June 1942. Throughout the summer, he fought a series of battles around El Alamein (q.v.). Denied victory and then stalemated, by October it was clear the *Afrika Korps*

Field Marshal Erwin Rommel and the pilot of his observation plane. (IWM HU 5590)

would have to retreat back into Libya. Against the expressed orders of the *Führer,* Rommel ordered the move to save what was left of the depleted *Panzer* force.

On 9 March 1943, Rommel, sick and dispirited, boarded a plane in Tunis and left Africa for Germany. However, he had accomplished near-miracles on the desert. He understood that desert warfare was almost limitless as far as space was concerned and constant maneuver was the key to victory. The desert was like an ocean with no key terrain features, no real identifiable avenues of approach, and the flanks of the enemy had to be found with relentless reconnaissance.

Water and fuel were vital to an armored force, but just as important were greases, oils, and repair parts. Desert warfare is extremely hard on tanks and armored vehicles, and a system of ceaseless maintenance is required. Rommel lost the logistics battle, and with it the campaign. He slowly lost the battle for the air, and the air component of the desert warfare is vital in reconnaissance, interdiction, and bombardment. British airpower grew increasingly bolder and more numerous, and the *Afrika Korps* became a target in an environment where there was no place to hide. With the war raging in Russia, there were no reinforcements to send, and even replacements slowed to a trickle.

North Africa, for the *Führer* and the army staff, became merely a sideshow.

In November 1943, Rommel was appointed to prepare the defenses on the Atlantic in preparation for the inevitable cross-channel invasion. What he found depressed him. The Atlantic Wall was almost nonexistent and there were no real combat troops to defeat the Allies on the beaches where he knew they had to be stopped. Serving under Field Marshal Gerd von Rundstedt (q.v.), Rommel made vast improvements along the Channel coast. By June 1944, Rommel succeeded in building a half-million obstacles that would seriously impede the Allied landings on 6 June. Rommel, however, still could not convince army planners to prepare for decisive battle on the beaches.

Due to a series of masterful deception plans, it was unclear where the actual Allied force would land, and, consequently, when the invasion began on 6 June 1944, Rommel could not get the troops necessary to halt the invasion on the beaches. On 17 July, he was seriously wounded when his staff car was strafed by an Allied aircraft.

On 20 July 1944, three days after Rommel was wounded, there was an attempt on Hitler's life. Rommel was on the periphery of the plot to kill Hitler. Certainly by late 1943, he was aware of the monstrous nature of the Nazi regime and knew that Germany was losing the war. Implicated slightly in the July plot, Rommel was placed under surveillance. On 14 October, he was given a choice: commit suicide and receive a state funeral, with assurances that his family would be safe; or face the certain outcome of a Nazi-rigged people's court. Rommel chose to die by his own hand.

Field Marshal Erwin Rommel, "the Desert Fox," emerged from World War II as a commander of near-mythic proportions. His command in the desert was a masterpiece of understanding speed, reconnaissance, and maintenance. The very nature of the desert supply lines, the stiffening resolve of the British, and the constant pounding from the air cost Rommel his campaign. He certainly knew that stopping the Allies on the Channel beaches swiftly was the key to possible victory, but he was never given the opportunity to test his concept. His involvement in the various plots against Hitler still remains shrouded in controversy. He was, however, a masterful planner, superb commander, and a genius in the operational arts in a desert environment.

James Cooke

Additional Reading

Barnett, Correlli (ed.), *Hitler's Generals* (1989).
Douglas-Home, Charles, *Rommel* (1973).
Fraser, David, *Knight's Cross: A Life of Field Marshal Erwin Rommel* (1993).
Irving, David, *The Trial of the Fox* (1977).
Liddel Hart, Basil H. (ed.), *The Rommel Papers* (1953).
Mitcham, Samuel W., Jr., *Hitler's Field Marshals and Their Battles* (1988).
Young, Desmond, *Rommel, the Desert Fox* (1950).

Roosevelt, Franklin Delano (1882–1945)

President of the United States (1933–1945). Elected an unprecedented four times, Roosevelt served during the Great Depression and World War II. A victim of poliomyelitis in 1922, his charismatic personality and optimistic outlook helped to keep up the faith and confidence of the American people during the great economic crisis of the 1930s and World War II.

Roosevelt was born on 30 January 1882, at the family home in Hyde Park, New York. His father, James, was descended from a long line of Roosevelts who had emigrated from Holland in the early seventeenth century and established the well-known Hudson River aristocracy. Mother Sara Delano, a sixth cousin of James Roosevelt,

belonged to this same aristocracy. At twenty-six, she was exactly half of James's age when they were married in 1880. Fear of becoming an old maid had caused her to marry an older man against her family's objections. She accepted James only long enough to produce a child, Franklin. From that time all conjugal relations ceased, and she devoted her life to being a loving, admiring, and doting mother.

As an only child, Franklin was tutored at home until age fourteen to permit his independently wealthy family to make frequent European trips. They went at least annually, and sometimes more often, to Germany, Britain, France, Italy, and Belgium to hobnob with the upper crust of Europe and America, while enjoying Europe's famous spas and vacation spots. When traveling in the United States, they traveled in their private railway car, which provided living, sleeping, and dining facilities, as well as space for the servants who always accompanied them.

At fourteen years of age, young Franklin entered Groton, a school patterned after the great English public schools. There he associated with wealthy youth of his own class and background. In 1900, he enrolled at Harvard. His diverse extracurricular activities and active social life detracted from his studies, resulting in a lackluster academic record. Roosevelt's worldview was influenced by the progressive and moderated *laissez-faire* economic theories taught by some of his professors. Theodore Roosevelt, his fifth cousin and twenty-sixth president of the United States, also had a progressive and liberalizing influence on the young Franklin. His admiration for "Uncle Teddy" inspired him to enter politics.

During his last year at Harvard, Franklin became engaged to Eleanor Roosevelt, Theodore's niece and his own fifth cousin. In the close-knit Roosevelt clan, marrying distant cousins was common practice. It was Eleanor who made Roosevelt aware of the suffering of the underprivileged classes then living in America's slums and rural areas. She also influenced his turning away from the racist and anti-Semitic views often expressed by his parents. Her very positive and dynamic influence on Franklin's life, political views, and subsequent policies cannot be overstressed.

After graduation from Harvard, Franklin and Eleanor lived for five years in New York while he attended law school. After passing the bar exam, he quit law school and served briefly as a law clerk with the distinguished law firm of Carter, Ledwards, and Milburn. At the age of twenty-eight he was elected to the New York State Senate where

R

he gained national attention by opposing Tammany Hall, the New York City Democratic Party political machine. He championed the needs of upstate farmers, while learning the political game from such proven tacticians as Robert Wagner and Al Smith.

Roosevelt supported the presidential campaign of Woodrow Wilson in 1912 and served as Wilson's assistant secretary of the navy for seven years. In that position he learned well the politics of the federal government and the ways of Washington, D.C. His efforts to reform the navy along modern, more efficient lines met with limited success. In 1918, he made an extended tour of World War I battlefields and naval bases in Europe to see firsthand how the war was going. As assistant naval secretary, he acquired knowledge and learned skills and techniques that served him well as commander in chief during World War II. Out of his naval experience he became a strong advocate of military preparedness.

Roosevelt ran as a vice-presidential candidate on the democratic ticket in 1920 with James M. Cox. He campaigned vigorously for the ticket, while advocating Senate ratification of the Treaty of Versailles (q.v.), which would have put the United States in the League of Nations (q.v.). The ticket was defeated soundly by Republicans Warren G. Harding and Calvin Coolidge.

After the election, Roosevelt tried his hand briefly in business until felled by poliomyelitis in August 1921. He remained paralyzed from the hips down for the remainder of his life. Through the loyal support of Louis Howe and Eleanor, who traveled the state and spoke on his behalf, he stayed in contact and involved with state and national politics while recuperating.

Except for the inability to use his legs, Roosevelt achieved a robust recovery, and made the nominating address for Governor Al Smith in 1928. He was elected governor of New York the same year, with the strong support of Smith, the outgoing governor, who had hoped to control and manipulate the relatively inexperienced Roosevelt. Roosevelt's insistence on being his own man created a lifelong split with his former supporter and mentor. As Herbert Hoover swept the country for the Republicans in 1928, Roosevelt was elected governor of New York by 25,000 votes.

During his first term as governor, Roosevelt provided tax relief to farmers and achieved a program providing low-cost public utilities to state consumers. Except for the utility issue, his policies did not differ greatly from those of conservative Republican President Herbert Hoover, who would

be his presidential opponent in 1932. Roosevelt's widespread appeal led to his renomination in 1930, by which time he was being widely discussed as a presidential candidate. The Republicans hoped to defeat him in New York to avoid facing him nationally in 1932. Hoover sent in some of the big guns of his cabinet, including Secretary of State Henry Stimson, Secretary of the Treasury Ogden L. Mills, and Secretary of War Patrick Hurley to campaign against Roosevelt. Their efforts were in vain. The popularity of Roosevelt's program, plus the ever-deepening Depression, led to his reelection by a margin of 725,000 votes.

During his second term as governor (1930–1932), Roosevelt battled with the Republican-controlled legislature for his progressive measures to alleviate the effects of the Depression. These interparty fights helped prepare him to promote and defend his New Deal program as president. These measures included state-supported old-age pensions, unemployment insurance, regulated working hours for women and children, and publicly developed electric power—all measures he would enact as president. He became the first governor to establish a state relief administration. In a series of "fireside chats" (a communication technique he would continue to use as president), he proved an effective speaker using the relatively new medium of radio. His administration was made up of many notable people, including James Farley, Francis Perkins, Samuel Rosenman, and Harry Hopkins (q.v.), all of whom later played major roles in the Roosevelt presidency.

As the Depression tightened its grip on the entire country, Roosevelt sought new ways of aiding the disadvantaged. To assist him in responding to the unprecedented economic, social, and political challenges, he enlisted the aid of a "brain trust" of professors from Columbia University. Acting on their suggestions, he promoted programs designed to provide relief to suffering New Yorkers. The "brain trust" included Adolf Berle, Raymond Mosley, and Rex Tugwell, all of whom also played leading roles in the subsequent Roosevelt presidency. His policies, practices, and successes made Roosevelt stand out as the most imaginative and dynamic prospect for the presidency in 1932. He was seen as the hope for the poor and the downtrodden of Depression-ridden America.

Winning the Democratic nomination in 1932 was more difficult than defeating the Republicans. The mood of the time was summed up by the slogan "anybody but Hoover." Since anyone apparently could defeat Hoover, many Democrats insisted on trying. But first they had to stop

Roosevelt. The "two-thirds" rule then practiced at Democratic nominating conventions made it easy for a relatively small faction to block a frontrunner on the early ballots. Roosevelt's main opposition came from such stalwarts as John Nance Garner of Texas, former Secretary of War Newton D. Baker of Ohio, and the party's 1928 presidential candidate, Al Smith. Roosevelt held a strong early lead, but could not breach the two-thirds mark until a deal was struck with Garner releasing the Texas delegates in return for the vice-presidential nomination. In his acceptance speech, Roosevelt told the convention, "I pledge you, I pledge myself, to a New Deal for the American people."

During the campaign Roosevelt discussed some of what he meant by a "New Deal." He favored curbing agriculture overproduction that depressed farm prices. He urged an old-age pension program, conservation, public power, unemployment insurance, regulation of the stock exchange, and the repeal of Prohibition. He said little about foreign policy, economic reforms, or job creation. To win, little was required except to denounce Hoover who, like George Bush exactly sixty years later, was unwilling, for philosophical reasons, to use the executive powers of his office to deal with economic and social problems.

Roosevelt swept the nation, winning 22 million votes to Hoover's 15 million, and 472 electoral votes to Hoover's 59. The resultant political realignment and the legacy of Franklin Roosevelt made the Democrats the majority party in America up through the end of the twentieth century.

When Roosevelt took office on 4 March 1933, many banks across the country had closed, industrial production stood at 56 percent of what it had been in 1929, 25 percent of the workforce was unemployed, and farmers were in dire straits. In his inaugural address he told America he would take prompt and decisive action to bring relief. His own unshakable self-confidence made his promise believable. Even the U.S. Congress was so dismayed by the general situation they gave him what almost amounted to a blank check during his first "One Hundred Days," thus allowing a broad array of relief measures to be enacted.

Roosevelt first sought measures for quick recovery and then reforms of the system intended to bring long-term relief. His cabinet was chosen with a view toward establishing a consensus. It included both liberals and conservatives, three Republicans, and for the first time, a woman, Francis Perkins, as secretary of labor. There was something in his program for everyone. He sought to reassure business leaders by supporting banking reform and introducing a program to promote government economy. He never became, however, a disciple of Keynesian economics, as often charged.

Roosevelt provided funds for relief of the suffering and pushed through Congress authorization for the Federal Emergency Relief Administration (FERA), the Civilian Conservation Corps (CCC), the Home Owner's Loan Corporation (HOLC), and the Public Works Administration (PWA). Millions of farmers and homeowners were aided by a mortgage relief program. The Reconstruction Finance Corporation (RFC), established by the Hoover administration, was broadened and liberalized to offer loans to small as well as large businesses.

Many other programs, too numerous to include here, were developed in an effort to stimulate the economy while providing immediate relief. New Deal innovations such as the Tennessee Valley Authority (TVA), Social Security, and the Securities and Exchange Commission (SEC) are now accepted as permanent functions of the federal government. Roosevelt felt that experimentation was necessary to see what would work. If it does not work, he once stated frankly, "let's abandon it and try something else, . . . but let's do something."

This attitude and the programs he established clearly showed that Roosevelt was flexible and would use the executive powers of his office to push needed programs through Congress. He used frequent speeches, press conferences, and his famous "fireside chats" to project the power of his extraordinary charisma to reassure and bolster the people's confidence. He earned the people's gratitude for himself and his party by halting the frightening slide of 1932 and 1933.

While reassuring many people and bringing a limited degree of recovery—full economic recovery would only come with the war—Roosevelt frightened many conservatives and businessmen who felt he was going too far and was a "traitor to his class." The truth is, this practical political leader, using moderate economic measures, probably saved capitalism by correcting some of its worst abuses and by restoring the people's faith in their economy and country. The masses remained Roosevelt's supporters, but the middle class that supported him in 1932 and 1936 subsequently returned to the Republican Party. One of his most controversial schemes, the so-called "court-packing" plan, had the long-range and unintended result of moving the orientation of the U.S. Supreme Court away from support of the establishment and big business toward a position, where it remained throughout the rest of the twentieth century, of supporting civil rights and antimonopoly measures.

R

Roosevelt had an unusual talent for governing. He filled any political office with natural ease and skill. He had been born to the purple, and directing, or even manipulating, the activities of others came naturally to him. Both by training and instinct he was a natural leader. He knew how to make part of a loaf sound like a royal feast, and he felt instinctively those things that could not be intellectually explained. He was imaginative, dynamic, and jaunty to the point of annoying his enemies while delighting his friends and supporters. He was devoted to public service and saw his own life as history, from which he drew lessons as he tackled political, economic, and social problems. Such thinking came naturally to a man who saw his own life as almost synonymous with that of the nation.

With his election to an unprecedented third term in 1940, Roosevelt began the second phase of his presidential career, involving principally his role as commander in chief during World War II. He took this role more seriously than any other president, except perhaps Abraham Lincoln. Eric Larrabee in his classic book, *Commander in Chief,* writes "in practice he intervened more often and to better effect in military affairs than did even his battle-worn contemporaries like Churchill or Stalin." Mark S. Watson, an official U.S. Army historian believes Roosevelt "was the real and not merely a nominal commander-in-chief." While possessing the same constitutional authority as all other presidents, Roosevelt was more willing to exercise every aspect of it than were the others.

Roosevelt was slow in reacting to the threat posed by the European dictators Adolf Hitler and Benito Mussolini (qq.v.). So also were the population and the Congress, who overwhelmingly opposed any U.S. involvement in another European war. But when war started in Europe in 1939, Roosevelt used his executive powers to help Britain, and later the Soviet Union, despite strong Congressional and public opposition. He pushed through Congress authorization for the Lend-Lease (q.v.) program for aid to Britain and the initial funds to finance the American arms buildup. He had to battle strong antiwar opposition until the Japanese attack on Pearl Harbor unified the country in favor of all-out war.

Roosevelt arranged with the British to have the Allied alliance directed from Washington, which meant from the White House. He followed the progress of the war closely and received daily briefings on every campaign. He was not merely a dilettante in military matters. He was an active and knowledgeable commander in chief. His in-

terest in military matters had started at the age of fifteen, when he was given a copy of Alfred Thayer Mahan's *The Influence of Sea Power upon History.* Roosevelt had worked hard to discern its meaning. As assistant navy secretary, he had absorbed the lessons of World War I.

Roosevelt defined the American World War II involvement as a protracted one in pursuit of high principle. He emphasized it was the Allies who held the high moral ground and fought for a just cause. He, and not the Axis leaders, politicized the confrontation as a supreme effort involving "total war," and he made early preparations for a long struggle. It was the democracies, especially Britain and America, rather than the dictators, that organized themselves at the beginning for a total war fought for total objectives.

Ironically, despite their head start in war preparation, it was 1943 before either the Japanese or the Germans reached full economic and industrial mobilization—and by then their efforts were too little and too late. The United States, in Roosevelt's words, became the "Arsenal of Democracy" (q.v.), as the Americans fed, clothed, and armed themselves and their allies. American industrial production assured Allied victory. To Roosevelt, the war was much like the Depression—a straight-line continuum ran from one to the other. In his thinking the war required a concerted effort similar to that of the Depression to rally the nation to meet a great national challenge. Even the early defeats of the war were compared to the bankruptcy, impoverishment, and hunger he dealt with in 1933.

One of Roosevelt's major tasks was to put together a coalition of U.S. political leaders, both Democratic and Republican, to win the war. He reached out to Republicans Henry Stimson and Frank Knox (qq.v.) as secretaries of war and navy, respectively. To him this was like any other major political effort. He needed to select qualified assistants and military commanders and unify the country, while liberating the "generous energies" of the American people. He well understood the "inter-dynamics of American strength" and how to mobilize it. Once these strengths were mobilized they needed only to be steered, not driven. This great dynamic force then moved forward under its own momentum and accomplished the enormous task of winning the war.

The military leaders he assembled (some feel they drifted into place) to run the war represented a remarkable achievement. He resisted advice to form an American General Staff and instead built his own informal organization. That group of key leaders included General George C. Marshall (q.v.), who ran the army; Admiral Ernest J. King (q.v.), who rebuilt and reanimated the navy; General Henry H. "Hap" Arnold (q.v.), who invented and led the army air forces; General Douglas MacArthur, who symbolized American determination in the Pacific; General Dwight D. Eisenhower (q.v.), who led the great Anglo-American Alliance; and Roosevelt's personal chief of staff, Admiral William D. Leahy (q.v.), who, because of his seniority, chaired the Joint Chiefs of Staff (JCS). Roosevelt molded this group into an effective and cohesive high command, which was led to believe it was in charge, when in fact Roosevelt was.

Most of these men possessed a personal magnetism similar to that of Roosevelt himself. In their presence men could sense the influence of these dynamic personalities that challenged them to excel. Thus the World War II Joint Chiefs of Staff came into being in a very casual manner, without an official charter or formal operating procedures. This loose and irregular organization shocked the straight-laced British, who saw it as a throwback to George Washington's times. Roosevelt denied King's request for a "piece of paper" that would make them legal by insisting it "would provide no benefit and might in some way impair flexibility." As Larrabee points out, he meant his "flexibility," not theirs. He felt his word was all the authorization they would need. He was the undisputed leader and they were the analytical minds with the mission of executing his orders.

It is an understatement to say that Roosevelt's wartime policies were controversial. Critics blamed him for the brilliantly planned and executed Japanese attack on Pearl Harbor. It is true that poor communications between Hawaii and Washington, plus the lack of a centralized intelligence agency to evaluate the threat, helped the Japanese achieve surprise. But extremists to this day claim, without the slightest evidence, that he invited and welcomed the attack. He was assailed for delaying the D-Day landing in Normandy (q.v.) until 1944, although it is clear these landings could not have been made earlier because of the lack of shipping, specialized landing barges, and control of the vital Atlantic shipping lanes. His unconditional surrender policy (q.v.) was criticized, with some justification, for discouraging the anti-Hitler opposition in Germany. Also, Roosevelt has been criticized with some justification for not taking stronger measures while the war was in progress to ensure U.S. and Western political interests vis-à-vis the Soviet Union.

It is easy, with the benefit of hindsight, to second-guess and exaggerate the failings of Roosevelt as a political and military leader. What is clear, however, is that he led the American people successfully through their greatest economic crisis and their largest military challenge ever. Despite his failings, and he had many, he was a decent, strong, and highly popular president who ranks as one of the two or three outstanding presidents in American history.

Like Lincoln eighty years before, Franklin D. Roosevelt did not live to see the end of his war. Roosevelt died in office on 12 April 1945, just as the Allied armies were closing in on Berlin from both the east and the west. He was succeeded by his vice president, Harry S Truman (q.v.), to whom fell the task of concluding World War II.

Paul J. Rose

Additional Reading

Burns, James M., *Roosevelt: The Soldier of Freedom* (1970).

Larrabee, Eric, *Commander in Chief: Franklin Delano Roosevelt, His Lieutenants, and Their War* (1987).

Lash, Joseph P., *Roosevelt and Churchill: The Partnership That Saved the West* (1976).

Morgan, Ted, *F.D.R.: A Biography* (1985).

Roosevelt, Theodore, Jr. (1887–1944)

American brigadier general, assistant division commander, U.S. 1st and 4th Infantry Divisions. The son of President Theodore Roosevelt, Theodore Jr. graduated from Harvard University in 1908, and volunteered for service in World War I. While serving as a major in the St. Mihiel offensive in the 26th Infantry Regiment, 1st Infantry Division, Roosevelt was wounded in action and received the Distinguished Service Cross. After the war, he helped create the American Legion, served as assistant secretary of the navy, governor of Puerto Rico, and governor-general of the Philippines. He also authored or coauthored nine books.

In World War II, Roosevelt was recalled to active service with his old regiment, this time as its colonel. Later assigned as assistant division commander of the 1st Infantry Division under Major General Terry de la Mesa Allen (q.v.), Roosevelt served with the "The Big Red One," in Northwest Africa and Sicily (qq.v.). While in Sicily, Allen and Roosevelt attracted the displeasure of Major General Omar N. Bradley (q.v.), their corps commander, for their impulsive command style. Bradley relieved both men, ostensibly for their inability to make speedy progress in the drive to Messina.

Roosevelt subsequently became a liaison officer for the U.S. Fifth Army. In 1944, he was assigned to headquarters, U.S. First Army, and then as assistant division commander of the 4th Infantry Division for the Normandy (q.v.) landings. Despite fragile health and a severe case of arthritis that caused him to limp with a cane, he repeatedly requested permission to go ashore with the first wave. He finally won his case when he put the request in writing. He was the only general officer to land in the first wave on UTAH Beach; and at the age of fifty-seven, one of the oldest soldiers there. On the beach he repeatedly led groups over the seawall and established them inland, being under constant enemy fire the entire day. Roosevelt died suddenly of a heart attack on 12 July, undoubtedly aggravated by the battle stress of 6 June. He died the same day he was scheduled to assume command of the 90th Infantry Division. Bradley later commented that Roosevelt's conduct on UTAH Beach was the bravest act he had ever known in over forty years of military service.

Roosevelt was awarded the Medal of Honor posthumously. His younger brother, Quinten, had been killed in World War I and buried at Chateau-Thierry in France. After World War II, his remains were moved to the World War II American cemetery at Colleville-sur-Mer, Normandy. These two sons of President Theodore Roosevelt are buried there, along with 9,386 other American war dead.

Randy Papadopoulos

Additional Reading

Ambrose, Stephen, *D-Day June 6, 1944: The Climactic Battle of World War II* (1994).
Roosevelt, Eleanor Butler Alexander, *Day Before Yesterday: The Reminiscences of Mrs. Theodore Roosevelt, Jr.* (1959).

Rosenberg, Alfred (1893–1946)

Nazi ideologue. Born to an expatriate ethnic German family from Tallinn, Estonia, Rosenberg studied art and architecture in Moscow. In 1918, he escaped the Russian Revolution and fled to Munich, where he held a number of jobs and was attracted to right-wing and anti-Semitic groups. It was there he met Adolf Hitler (q.v.) and joined the Nazi Party. It was to serve as a forum through which he could express his virulent hatred of Jews and Communists. He also became a leading theorist and a strong advocate of the Nazi's pan-Germanic theory of *Lebensraum* (q.v.).

National Socialism, according to Rosenberg, was the noblest of ideals and he urged all Germans to strive for its perfection. He attempted to intellectualize and define these ideals, and during the early 1920s, he authored a number of obscure political and ideological tracts condemning Jews, Communists, and Freemasons. As the party's only true ideologue, he also served as an editor of the *Völkischer Beobachter*. In 1930, he published *The Myth of the Twentieth Century,* which attempted to explain historical events through an analysis of racial differences.

Although Rosenberg was never considered part of Hitler's inner circle, he served in a number of party and state leadership roles. The nominal party chief during Hitler's imprisonment after the 1923 Beer Hall *Putsch* (q.v.), he also headed the party's foreign affairs department. When the Nazis assumed power in 1933, he was disappointed that he was not appointed foreign minister. He continued to quarrel with the foreign ministry, arguing that ideology should be considered when making foreign policy decisions. He was outraged when Germany signed the 1939 accord with the Soviet Union. He believed ideology was sacrificed for purely political considerations.

After the invasion of the Soviet Union in 1941, Rosenberg was given the formal title of *Reich* minister for the eastern occupied territories, but he nevertheless remained outside the decision-making process. He eventually resigned that position in late 1944. After the war, Rosenberg was tried for war crimes at Nuremberg (*see* International Military Tribunal) and executed.

Steven B. Rogers

Additional Reading

Cecil, Robert, *The Myth of the Master Race: Alfred Rosenberg and Nazi Ideology* (1972).
Chandler, Albert R., *Rosenberg's Nazi's Myth* (1968).
Nova, Fritz, *Alfred Rosenberg* (1986).

Rotmistrov, Pavel Alekseevich (1901–1982)

Soviet general, commander of the Fifth Guards Tank Army. Rotmistrov, too young to serve in the tsar's army, followed the same path as many of the other Soviet officers of the era; he joined the Red Army at an early age, and later received his formal military education at the Frunze Military Academy.

At the start of World War II, Rotmistrov was the chief of staff of the III Mechanized Corps. His abilities to plan for operational uses of tanks, coupled with a willingness to study the tactics of other armies, made him not just unusual in the

Soviet military, but allowed for a fair comparison to America's foremost tank commander. Like General George S. Patton (q.v.), Rotmistrov studied past tank battles closely. He firmly believed in the use of armor as an operational weapon, and he demonstrated his tactical abilities at Kursk (q.v.) where he commanded the Fifth Guards Tank Army, the reserve of Marshal Ivan Konev's (q.v.) Steppe Front (army group).

Rotmistrov knew his T-34 tanks were outgunned by the 88mm main guns of the German *Panzers*. When the Soviet high command was forced to commit Rotmistrov's force, he instructed his tank crews to close with the enemy before engaging. That led to devastating destruction on both sides, but it neutralized the firepower of the German tanks. Since his tanks could be easily replaced, this tactic was instrumental in destroying the German armored forces, and also destroyed the myth of German superiority in armored operations.

Thomas Cagley

Additional Reading

Bialer, Seweryn, ed., *Stalin and His Generals* (1984).

Rowecki, Stefan (1895–1944)

Polish lieutenant general, commander in chief of the Polish Home Army. During the 1939 Polish campaign, Rowecki was commander of the Warsaw Armored-Motorized Brigade, defending the middle Vistula. From 1940 to 1943, he was the commander in chief of the Home Army *(Armia Krajowa)*. He built it up into one of the most formidable of the Allied underground armies. It carried out sabotage and intelligence-collecting operations, and disrupted German lines of communications and war production. He was arrested by the *Gestapo* (q.v.) in 1943. On Heinrich Himmler's (q.v.) orders, he was shot in the first days of the Warsaw Rising (q.v.).

Andrzej Suchcitz

Additional Reading

Garliński, Józef, *Poland in the Second World War* (1985).
Mikołłayczyk, Stanisław, *The Rape of Poland* (1947).

Rudel, Hans-Ulrich (1916–1982)

Luftwaffe colonel, legendary German "tank buster," highest decorated *Luftwaffe* pilot of the war. Rudel joined the *Luftwaffe* in 1936 and trained as a dive-bomber pilot. Flying on the eastern front from the opening days of Operation BARBAROSSA, he took part in the destruction of the Soviet fleet at Kronstadt and is credited with sinking the battleship *Marat*. A pilot of incredible determination and courage, he flew despite fatigue, jaundice, and wounds (including amputation of his right foot), and completed an incredible 2,530 sorties with eleven air-to-air victories.

Rudel introduced the 37mm cannon armed Ju-87G *Stuka* to the eastern front in April 1943, and flying this type, he destroyed 532 tanks in the last two years of the war. In March 1944, he was shot down, evaded capture by the Soviets, and made it back to German lines.

Repeatedly decorated for valor, Rudel was the sole recipient of the Golden Oak Leaves to the Knight's Cross of the Iron Cross. Following the war, he went into self-imposed exile in Argentina. He returned to Germany in 1953 and involved himself in nationalist and right-wing politics.

Budd A.R. Jones

Additional Reading

Rudel, Hans Ulrich, *Stuka Pilot* (1979).
Smith, Peter C., *The Stuka at War* (1971).

Ruge, Otto (1882–1961)

Norwegian general, commander in chief of the Norwegian Army. Ruge was appointed commander in chief of the Norwegian Army in April 1940. His main objective, during the Norway (q.v.) campaign, was to prevent the Germans from making headway northward. He held successive defensive positions, stalling the enemy and at the same time avoiding having his own forces overwhelmed. Largely due to his determination, it took the Germans two months to conquer Norway.

Andrzej Suchcitz

Additional Reading

Ash, Bernard, *Norway, 1940* (1964).
Koht, Halvdan, *Norway Neutral and Invaded* (1941).
Ruge, Fredrich "The Invasion of Norway" in H.A. Jacobsen and J. Rohwer, *Decisive Battles of World War II: The German View* (1965).

Rundstedt, Gerd von (1875–1953)

German field marshal, commander in chief west. Gerd von Rundstedt was born on 12 December 1875, at Achersleben in the Harz. He entered the

Lichterfelde Cadet Academy in 1893, and received his commission in 1900. During World War I, he held staff positions in the west in 1914, on the eastern front from 1915–1917, and returned to the west in 1918.

During the Weimar Republic (q.v.), he commanded the 18th Infantry Regiment and the 2nd Cavalry Division. From 1932–1938, he commanded Group I (six divisions) in Berlin. Throughout this time, he frequently requested release from service. This concession was finally granted and he retired in early 1939.

Von Rundstedt's retirement lasted only a few months, however. In the summer of 1939, Adolf Hitler (q.v.) called on him to lead Army Group South in the invasion of Poland. His forces, consisting of the Eighth, Tenth, and Fourteenth Armies (the latter including Paul von Kleist's [q.v.] *Panzer Korps*) represented the *Wehrmacht's* main thrust. During the crisis caused by the Lodz Army's attack on his northern flank, von Rundstedt temporarily abandoned his loose command style and flew to the Eighth's headquarters to personally issue the necessary orders. For him, and the newly expanded German military, the Polish campaign was a baptism under fire in a new form of warfare.

After the Polish campaign, von Rundstedt and his staff transferred to Koblenz to prepare for war in the west. Army Group A initially had a secondary role. But on the initiative of his chief of staff, Erich von Manstein (q.v.), the planned *Schwerpunkt* (center of gravity) shifted to his army group. Von Rundstedt championed the new plan until, through a number fortuitous consequences, Hitler ordered its implementation. Army Group A now included the Fourth, Twelfth, and Sixteenth Armies. Once again, von Kleist commanded von Rundstedt's (and the bulk of Germany's) *Panzers.*

In one of the war's best-known episodes, Army Group A raced across northern France, trapping the mass of the Allied forces against the channel coast. During the Battle for France, the army group attacked down the Rhone Valley to Marseilles. Von Rundstedt's reward was promotion to field marshal in July 1941. He was earmarked to lead Operation SEA LION, the abortive invasion of Britain.

During Operation BARBAROSSA, von Rundstedt commanded Army Group South (Sixth and Seventh Armies and the First *Panzer* Group) aimed at Kiev and the Donets industrial region. Also under his command were the Eleventh Army and the Romanian Third and Fourth Armies. Army Group South trapped 100,000 Soviet troops at Uman and made up the southern pincer during the great encirclement battle at Kiev (q.v.). Von Rundstedt lead his army to Rostov in November 1941, but then he suffered a heart attack and once again retired.

In March 1942, von Rundstedt returned to active duty as commander in chief west. There he used his diplomatic skills, to coordinate the efforts of army, navy, and *Luftwaffe* units, the Italian Fourth Army, the Vichy French, the French railway, and *Organization Todt* (q.v.). For the next two years, with second rate units and equipment, he fought the French resistance, defeated the Canadian landing at Dieppe (q.v.), and reinforced the German occupation of Italy. Additionally, he planned to throw back the Allied invasion he knew would soon come. He tried to anticipate the exact location of the landings, dealt with Allied air superiority and placement of his sparse *Panzer* reserves, and operated within a convoluted command structure that occupied much of his time.

At Normandy (q.v.), von Rundstedt was handicapped by the twin factors of Hitler's "stand fast" orders and belief in a second landing farther north. Von Rundstedt knew it was only a matter of time before the Americans broke out of Normandy and overran the slower defenders; a repeat of his own maneuver four years earlier. Eleven days after D-day, he and his principal sub-

Field Marshal Gerd von Rundstedt. (IWM MH 10132)

ordinate, Field Marshal Erwin Rommel (q.v.), met with Hitler to try and convince the *Führer* to adopt a mobile defense to halt the Allies. Hitler used the deteriorating situation as an excuse to relieve von Rundstedt two weeks later.

Hitler recalled von Rundstedt one last time on 5 September 1944, to once again take over as commander in chief west. His first task was to stabilize the front. This he accomplished, no thanks to Hitler, but instead due to the Allies' distraction with Operation MARKET-GARDEN. Starting in mid-October, von Rundstedt began preparations for the last German offensive in the west. The Ardennes offensive (q.v.), Hitler's idea, accomplished very little in the end. On 9 March 1945, von Rundstedt retired for good during the battle for Germany proper.

The field marshal surrendered to the Americans at the end of the war. He was one of the few strategic thinkers among the Germany's generals, and was universally respected by friend and foe alike.

Robert Kirchubel

Additional Reading

Barnett, Correlli (ed.), *Hitler's Generals* (1989).

Blumentritt, Günther, *Von Rundstedt: The Soldier and the Man* (1952).

Messenger, Charles, *The Last Prussian: A Biography of Field Marshal Gerd von Rundstedt, 1875–1953* (1991).

Mitcham, Samuel W., Jr., *Hitler's Field Marshals and Their Battles* (1988).

R

S

Sad Sack

American cartoon figure. Just as Charlie Chaplin's little tramp immortalized in film the little man who was overwhelmed by the world, the comic strip hero Sad Sack did the same for the average American in uniform during World War II. The luckless character was created and drawn by Sergeant George Baker (q.v.), and appeared in *Yank* magazine. After the war, the comic strip went into commercial syndication. Sad Sack tried to make it in life, and in the army, but lack of luck and intelligence always plagued him. Never able to get it quite right, he often found himself at the mercy of others who deceived or cheated him at will. The name comes from a colorful army slang expression, a "sad sack of shit."

Richard A. Voeltz

Additional Reading

Baker, George, *The Sad Sack: His Biography in 115 Cartoons from the Pages of* Yank *Magazine* (1944).
Hess, Stephan, and Milton Kaplan, *The Ungentlemanly Art: A History of American Political Cartoons* (1968).

Sansom, Odette (1912–1995)

British SOE agent. This Frenchwoman was the mother of three children, living in Britain when the war started. Her desire to help her native country led to her recruitment by the newly formed Special Operations Executive (q.v.) in 1942. Together with other women of binational background, she was infiltrated into France where she helped resistance circuits to function. She was not particularly effective and was arrested in 1943. Her stoicism in the face of fourteen brutal torture and interrogation sessions at the hands of the *Gestapo* (q.v.) led to her fame. She was placed in Ravensbrück concentration camp and survived to become the first woman awarded the George Cross, Britain's highest decoration for noncombatant heroism.

Chris Westhorp

Additional Reading

Fourcade, Marie-Madeleine, *Noah's Ark* (1973).
Schoenbrun, David, *Soldiers of the Night: The Story of French Resistance* (1980).

Sauckel, Fritz (1894–1946)

German plenipotentiary general for the utilization of labor. Sauckel, who was a French prisoner of war from 1914 until November 1919, joined the Nazi Party in 1923. In 1924, he was appointed party business manager in Thuringia, and in 1927, *Gauleiter* for Thuringia. From 1927 to 1933, he was Nazi representative in the Thuringian parliament, and on 26 August 1932, he became interior minister of the state of Thuringia. On 5 May 1933, Adolf Hitler (q.v.) appointed him governor of Thuringia.

At the beginning of the war, Sauckel, who became an *SS-Obergruppenführer* without function, became *Reich* defense administrator for the Kassel area. On 21 March 1942, he was appointed plenipotentiary general for the utilization of labor. He provided slave labor for Germany by imposing compulsory labor service on occupied territories. Of the five million foreign workers obtained by Sauckel's program, he estimated only 200,000 came voluntarily. He disclaimed responsibility for the manner in which many workers were obtained, transported, and treated once in Germany. Nonetheless, Sauckel bore the ultimate responsibility, and he specifically supported the ruthless manner in which many workers were obtained. At the

Nuremberg trial (*see* International Military Tribunal), he was convicted of war crimes and crimes against humanity. He was hanged on 16 October 1946.

Bernard A. Cook

Additional Reading

Bracher, Karl D., *The German Dictatorship* (1970).
David, Claude, *Hitler's Germany* (1963).
Davidson, Eugene, *The Trial of the Germans* (1966).
Homze, Edward L., *Foreign Labor in Nazi Germany* (1967).

Savoia, Amadeo di (1898–1942)

Italian viceroy in Ethiopia, 1937–1941. Di Savoia, a cousin of King Victor Emmanuel (q.v.), deserted his military post in Africa to return to Italy during Benito Mussolini's (q.v.) 1922 march on Rome. He subsequently was pardoned and stationed in Libya between 1925 and 1931. The king prevented his cousin from participating in the 1936 Ethiopia campaign (q.v.), but di Savoia, now the Duke of Aosta, was appointed viceroy for Italian East Africa in November 1937. Despite clashes with Mussolini's undersecretary for Italian Africa, Attilio Teruzzi, and his own military subordinates, Ugo Cavallero (q.v.) and Enrico Cerulli, Aosta, after May 1939, with the assistance of Guglielmo Nasi, largely pacified Ethiopia.

When Italy declared war on Great Britain, Aosta was cut off from reinforcements and supplies by British control of the Red Sea. Although in August 1940 he defeated the British at Tug Argan and occupied British Somaliland, he realized the futility of attempting to attack Egypt. Two-thirds of his soldiers were natives, and many of these were of questionable loyalty. Faced with growing insurgency, he decided to concentrate on the defense of key positions against the British. On 27 March 1941, Keren Pass, the western gateway to Eritrea, fell to the British after eight weeks of dogged Italian resistance. On 6 April, Italian civil authorities in Addis Adaba, plagued by the breakdown of civil order, welcomed the arrival of British forces from the south. Aosta concentrated his forces, which had fallen back from Keren Pass at Amba Alagi, a fortified position that blocked the main pass between the capital and Eritrea. There, after a siege of two weeks, he surrendered to the British on May 19. His fragile health was further undermined by the campaign, and he died in Nairobi on 3 May 1942.

Bernard A. Cook

Additional Reading

Berretta, Alfio, *Amedeo d'Aosta* (1956).
Rogari, Sandro, "Savoia, Amedeo di, Duke of Aosta," *Historical Dictionary of Fascist Italy* (1982), pp. 488–489.

Schacht, Hjalmar Horace Greeley (1877–1970)

President of the *Reichsbank* and German minister of economics. Schacht, a prominent banker with a doctorate in economics, was appointed director of currency on 17 March 1923 and president of the *Reichsbank* on 22 December 1923. He held these posts until 1930, and was reappointed president of the *Reichsbank* by Adolf Hitler (q.v.) on 17 March 1933. Schacht supported Hitler's rearmament effort by floating long-term loans and devising a system of five-year notes to obtain large sums of short-term money. In August 1934, he was appointed minister of economics, and in May 1935, plenipotentiary general for war economy. In those capacities, he planned the industrial mobilization of Germany and began the stockpiling of raw materials.

As a result of Schacht's opposition to Hermann Göring's (q.v.) plans to increase the production of synthetics and to mobilize the entire economy for war, Hitler attacked Schacht's conservatism as an impediment to the rearmament program. On 5 September 1937, Schacht went on leave from the Ministry of Economics and resigned that post on 16 November 1937. On 20 January 1939, Hitler dismissed him as president of the *Reichsbank* for his continued advocacy of drastic cuts in military expenditures. Since resigning from the Ministry of Economics, Schacht held the post of minister without portfolio, but Hitler removed him from that office on 22 January 1943 because of his "attitude."

On 23 July 1944, Schacht was arrested and imprisoned following the attempt on Hitler's life. Seized by the Allies, he was charged with crimes against peace and conspiring to wage wars of aggression, but was acquitted at Nuremberg on 1 October 1946. In May, 1947, he was condemned to eight years' imprisonment by a Stuttgart deNazification court. Released from custody in November 1950, he died in 1970.

Bernard A. Cook

Additional Reading

Peterson, Edward N., *Hjalmar Schacht: For and Against Hitler: A Politico-economic Study of Germany, 1923–1945* (1954).

Schacht, Hjalmar, *Accounts Settled* (1948).

———, *Confessions of the Old Wizard* (1956).

Simpson, Amos E., *Hjalmar Schacht in Perspective* (1969).

Schellenberg, Walther (1910–1952)

Chief of *Gestapo* intelligence. Born in Saarbrücken, Schellenberg attended law school in Bonn and was fluent in several languages. He joined the Nazi Party in 1934 and served as aide to both Reinhard Heydrich and Heinrich Himmler (qq.v.). Schellenberg was instrumental in the creation of the *Einsatzgruppen* (q.v.), first deployed in Czechoslovakia in 1938, and later in Poland and along the eastern front. He was also involved in the Venlo incident, a counterintelligence operation against British agents in Holland in November 1939.

Between 1939 and 1942, Schellenberg was deputy chief of Department VI in the RSHA (q.v.) responsible for *Gestapo* activities outside the *Reich*. In 1941, Himmler appointed him to negotiate the cooperation between the *Wehrmacht* and the RSHA in the upcoming Soviet campaign, negotiations ensuring the *Einsatzgruppen* would operate in frontline areas.

Schellenberg was appointed chief of Department VI in 1942. After the arrest of Admiral Wilhelm Canaris (q.v.) and the dismantling of the *Abwehr* (q.v.) in 1944, Schellenberg was appointed chief of combined secret services. He was later instrumental in assisting Himmler's negotiations for a separate armistice with the Western Allies.

Steven B. Rogers

Additional Reading

Manvell, Roger, *SS and Gestapo: Rule by Terror* (1969).

Schellenberg, Walther, *The Labyrinth* (1956).

———, *The Schellenberg Papers* (1956).

Schindler, Oskar (1908–1974)

Famed for Steven Spielberg's depiction of him in the 1993 Academy Award–winning movie, *Schindler's List,* Oskar Schindler was born to a German Catholic family in the Sudeten region of Czechoslovakia on 28 April 1908. He married in 1928; however, his reputation as a womanizer was verified by his wife, Emilia, who claimed that in their twenty-nine years of marriage, he had no less than nineteen lovers.

Initially, Schindler was an opportunist. He moved to Krakow, Poland, shortly after the Nazi occupation began, bought an enamel factory, and manned it with Jewish forced labor from the Plaszow concentration camp. His opportunism soon turned to horror on witnessing the hatred and violence directed toward the Jews by the Nazis.

Schindler ran his factory until war's end, but he spent millions of dollars keeping his Jewish workers alive. Figures indicate that he saved some 1,200 Jews from certain death by housing and feeding them in his factory and in his home. He provided a safe haven for the Jews until 1944 when the Germans closed Plaszow and moved the remaining prisoners to Auschwitz.

After the war, Schindler tried to reestablish a business in Allied-occupied Germany but failed. In 1949, he and his wife moved to Argentina. Eight years later, with his marriage in ruins, he left his wife and returned to Germany. Schindler died in Frankfurt on 9 October 1974, at the age of sixty-six. At his request, he was buried in Jerusalem.

William H. Van Husen

Additional Reading

Keneally, Thomas, *Schindler's List* (1982).

Robinson, Gail, "Widow's Dissent," *World Press Review,* May 1994.

Silver, Eric, "A Crook, a Womanizer, and a Hero," *MacLean's,* 17 January 1994.

Schirach, Baldur von (1907–1974)

German Nazi youth leader. Von Schirach met Adolf Hitler (q.v.) in 1925 and immediately joined the Nazi Party. While von Schirach was studying German and art history in Munich in 1927, he started to organize the National Socialist German Student Association and became its leader in 1928. Because of his organizational skills, Hitler made him the youth leader *(Jugendführer)* of the Nazi Party in October 1931. In this function, he also supervised the Hitler Youth (q.v.), the National Socialist Student Association *(Schülerbund),* the *Bund Deutscher Mädel,* and the *Jungvolk.* After the Nazis came to power, he became *Jugendführer* of the German *Reich.*

According to the 1936 youth law, von Schirach was in charge of total youth education outside of the classroom. With his unconditional adoration for Hitler, and with the emotional style of his speeches and poems, he knew how to thrill young people. His goal was to teach hardness and militarism, qualities he represented neither in his looks nor in his attitude. In numerous pamphlets like *Die Hitlerjugend* in 1934, or *The Revolution of Education* in 1939, he swore to the ideals of fighting and the spread of anti-Semitic catchwords. He dedicated himself and his organization to his idol, Hitler.

In the long run, von Schirach was unable to cope with the power struggle and the intrigues within the Nazi heirarchy. In 1940, he lost his position to his rival, Artur Axmann. After a short voluntary assignment in France as an infantry officer, von Schirach became *Gauleiter* and *Reichsstatthalter* in Vienna in August 1940, where he stayed until the end of the war. There were intrigues against him there because of his progressive cultural politics. He finally lost all influence when, during a 1943 visit to Hitler at the Berghof, he criticized German occupation policies and the deportation of Jews. He did that because of the high death rates, even though he, himself, approved of the deportation of 185,000 Jews from Austria to the east. In 1942, he still praised the deportations in a speech as a "contribution to European culture."

Von Schirach was tried at the first Nuremberg trials (*see* International Military Tribunal) where he admitted his guilt. He "educated the German youth for a million-times-murder." He was sentenced to twenty years' imprisonment, which he served in Berlin's Spandau prison. He died in August 1974.

Franz Seidler

Additional Reading

Davidson, Eugene, *The Trial of the Germans* (1967).
Schirach, Baldur von, *Ich Glaubte an Hitler* (1967).
Schirach, Henriette, *Der Preis der Herrlichkeit* (1956).

Schlabrendorff, Fabian von (1907–1980)

German diplomat, Leading anti-Nazi. After completing legal training, von Schlabrendorff entered the Foreign Ministry in 1938. "A silent and unassuming young man," he never doubted where Nazism would lead. In the summer of 1939, the German resistance sent him to London to inform Winston S. Churchill of Adolf Hitler's (qq.v.) determination to invade Poland.

From early 1941, von Schlabrendorff served as an ordnance officer on the staff of General Henning von Tresckow (q.v.), Army Group Center. Von Schlabrendorff frequently carried messages between resistance leaders on the Russian front and the Home Army in Berlin and was in almost constant contact with Carl Goerdeler and Ludwig Beck (qq.v.). In 1943, he armed a British-made bomb disguised as bottles of Cointreau and had it placed in Hitler's plane as he boarded for a flight to East Prussia. Although the firing pin released, the detonator failed to ignite. The next day, von Schlabrendorff flew to Hitler's headquarters at Rastenburg and successfully retrieved the bomb.

Later, he attempted to persuade Hitler to visit Army Group Center headquarters where he planned to shoot him. Arrested after the attempted coup in July 1944, he was brought before the People's Court in February 1945. Ironically, Judge Roland Freisler (q.v.) was killed in an air raid, clutching von Schlabrendorff's files in his hand. He was acquitted of the charges, but immediately arrested by the *Gestapo* (q.v.) again and sent to Dachau and latter Flossenbürg. The U.S. Army liberated him south of the Brenner Pass in May 1945.

In 1967 von Schlabrendorff became a justice of the Supreme Court of the Federal Republic of Germany and served until his retirement in 1975.

Gerhardt B. Thamm
Susan Pentlin

Additional Reading

Hoffmann, Peter, *The History of the German Resistance 1933–1945* (1977).
Schlabrendorff, Fabian von, *Revolt Against Hitler: The Personal Account of Fabian von Schlabrendorff* (1948).

Schleicher, Kurt von (1882–1934)

German general and chancellor in Weimar Republic. Born to a wealthy Brandenburg family, von Schleicher began his military career in 1900 and served in Paul von Hindenburg's (q.v.) former regiment along with the field marshal's son, Oskar. Schleicher, who was a vain and unscrupulous man, ingratiated himself with the important military leaders of the time, quickly moved through the ranks, and was chosen to serve on the German General Staff (q.v.). Von Schleicher saw only limited combat on the eastern front during World War I, and for that he was awarded the Iron Cross.

Von Schleicher's penchant for power and intrigue served him well, and he seldom was far from the center of power, especially in the formative years of the Weimar Republic (q.v.). He assisted in the formation of the *Freikorps* (q.v.), although he refused to be a part of the Kapp *Putsch* (q.v.). Following General Hans von Seeckt's (q.v.) appointment as commander in chief of the *Reichswehr,* von Schleicher became one of his chief confidants, charged with the supervision of the Black *Reichswehr* (q.v.), a secret military force. Like von Seeckt, von Schleicher favored the army over the state and had little use for the democratic institutions of the Weimar Republic. When Seeckt fell from grace following von Hindenburg's election as *Reich* president in 1925, von Schleicher abandoned his former sponsor.

Von Schleicher remained a key member of the Defense Ministry. In early 1928, von Hindenburg decided that the minister of defense should be a general, and it was von Schleicher who advocated the appointment of Wilhelm Gröner, the man whose trust and support von Schleicher had enjoyed since 1918, when Gröner appointed him quartermaster general, and whose world view was most similar to his own. Despite widespread opposition to this choice, von Schleicher's influence was strong and Gröner received the appointment. In return, he appointed von Schleicher to a senior position in the ministry that gave the latter de facto control over the *Reichswehr*. When Gröner became acting chancellor during Chancellor Hermann Müller's illness, he relied on von Schleicher to guide him through the cabinet's political minefields. Not only did von Schleicher influence the affairs of state through Gröner, he used his association with Oskar von Hindenburg to gain direct access to his father, the president. Von Schleicher hoped this influence would result in the *Reichswehr*'s direct subordination to the president, thereby giving von Schleicher ultimate political power.

Von Schleicher found another ally of sorts in Heinrich Brüning (q.v.), whom von Hindenburg asked to form a new cabinet in 1930. A decorated war hero, Chancellor Brüning acquiesced in the face of von Schleicher's attempts to reverse von Seeckt's earlier attempt to depoliticize the *Reichswehr*. This further destabilized the few remaining democratic institutions of the Weimar Republic. Faced with the growing political power of Hitler's Nazi Party and its attempt to gain the support of the *Reichswehr* for a coup d'etat, von Schleicher unilaterally sought to cooperate with the Nazis in order to strengthen the power of the *Reichswehr* and to ensure that the SA (q.v.) remained under army control. Von Schleicher, like his superiors, had no intention of allowing Adolf Hitler (q.v.) to gain control of the *Reich*.

Von Schleicher realized, however, that Chancellor Brüning was not strong enough to keep the Nazis in check, nor could he be replaced until von Hindenburg's reelection as president was assured. Once this was accomplished, von Schleicher gave his support to Franz von Papen (q.v.), the leader of the conservative Catholic Center Party, who was appointed chancellor in June 1932. Von Schleicher replaced Gröner as minister of defense and emerged as the dominant force in the new cabinet. But von Schleicher was uncomfortable with von Papen's inability to form a stable government in the face of Nazi opposition, and soon withdrew his support of the conservative chancellor. Without the support of the army and key cabinet ministers, von Hindenburg was forced to replace Papen, and von Schleicher was appointed chancellor in early December 1932—while retaining the Defense Ministry portfolio.

The years of constant intrigue and mechanizations were costly and von Schleicher was never able to gather the support he needed to govern in the face of mounting Nazi opposition. Von Schleicher was unable to secure a parliamentary majority, and Papen allied himself with Hitler and urged Hindenburg to appoint a Nazi/conservative coalition to replace von Schleicher. These efforts ultimately proved effective. Von Schleicher tendered his resignation on 30 January 1933, and Hitler was appointed chancellor. Von Schleicher remained a critic of the new Nazi-dominated government, and Hitler was certain that von Schleicher was conspiring with the SA against him. On orders from Hitler, von Schleicher was murdered on 30 June 1934, the "Night of the Long Knives" (q.v.), when the Nazis settled their score with their opponents.

Steven B. Rogers

Additional Reading

Gay, Peter, *Weimar Culture: The Outsider As Insider* (1968).

Marcon, Helmut, *Arbeitsbeschaffungspolitik der Regierungen Papen und Schleicher: Grundsteinlegung für die Beschäftigungspolitik im Dritten Reich* (1974).

Morris, Warren B., *The Weimar Republic and Nazi Germany* (1982).

Scheele, Godfrey, *The Weimar Republic: Overture to the Third Reich* (1975).

Schildt, Axel, *Militärdiktatur mit Massenbasis? Die Ouerfrontkonzeption der Reichswehrführung um General von Schleicher am Ende der Weimarer Republik* (1981).

Wheeler-Bennett, J.W., *The Nemesis of Power: The German Army in Politics, 1918–1945* (1964).

Schörner, Ferdinand (1892–1973)

German field marshal, commander Army Groups North and A. One of Adolf Hitler's (q.v.) most controversial generals, Ferdinand Schörner was born in

1892, the son of a Munich policeman. He commanded a regiment in Poland, and a mountain division in the campaigns against France and Greece. He fought in the Soviet Union on the Murmansk front from autumn 1941 until October 1943, when he was transferred to southern Russia to command Army Detachment Nikopol. In March 1944, after approximately two months as head of the National Socialist Guidance Officer Corps, he became commander of Army Group South Ukraine. In July, he received command of Army Group North, and in mid-January 1945, Hitler sent him to Army Group A, whose forces he kept relatively intact until Germany's surrender.

On 9 May 1945, Schörner flew to Tyrolia in civilian clothing. His critics charge that he abandoned his men to the Soviets, but his supporters claim he was following orders to assume command of the mythical National Redoubt (q.v.).

Schörner earned his reputation for tenacity on the defense. His methods were effective but brutal; he ordered soldiers executed for cowardice. His credo was that a soldier's fear of his commander should exceed his fear of the enemy. When stationed on the Murmansk front, on receiving reports that Arctic conditions were damaging morale, he issued an order stating: "The Arctic doesn't exist!"

Howard D. Grier

Additional Reading

Mellenthin, Friedrich von, *German Generals of World War II As I Saw Them* (1977).

Mitcham, Samuel W., Jr., *Hitler's Field Marshals and Their Battles* (1988).

Taylor, Telford, *Sword & Swastika: Generals and Nazis in the Third Reich* (1952).

Scholl, Hans (1918–1943)
Scholl, Sophie (1921–1943)

Leaders of the White Rose German opposition movement. Hans and Sophie Scholl were student leaders of the opposition group called the White Rose (q.v.) at the University of Munich in 1942–1943. They were children of an anti-Nazi small-town mayor in Württemberg. After Adolf Hitler's seizure of power in 1933, Hans became an enthusiastic member and leader of the Hitler Youth (q.v.). Sophie also joined the *Bund Deutscher Mädel* and rose to a leadership position. By 1937, however, the young Scholls' fascination with Nazism waned and several of the Scholl children were, in fact, arrested by the *Gestapo* (q.v.) for their contacts with banned youth groups of the pre-Hitler era.

Hans and Sophie, nonconformists at heart, continued to read forbidden books.

While a medical student, Hans served as an orderly during the French campaign of 1940 and later on the Russian front. These experiences, as well as deepening Christian convictions, reinforced his inclination to become a resister. As a student at Munich University, he was influenced by the ideas of the elderly Catholic publicist Carl Muth, whose journal, *Hochland,* was banned by the Nazis.

Together with Alexander Schmorell, Christoph Probst, and Willi Graf, all fellow medical students, Hans formed the circle of the White Rose in the spring of 1942. He was soon joined by his sister Sophie, a student of biology and philosophy. She attended the popular philosophy lectures of Professor Kurt Huber, a conservative nationalist and anti-Nazi, and facilitated his contact with Hans and the White Rose.

During the spring term of 1942, and again after November, following frontline duty in Russia, Hans initiated the drafting of a series of six leaflets, the last two of which were either revised or authored by Huber. In increasingly more passionate language, the leaflets branded the actions of the Nazi regime as crimes, and called for its overthrow. All youthful members of the White Rose assiduously distributed the leaflets in Munich and other cities. Hans and Sophie were among the most daring in the writing and distribution of leaflets. At Munich University, 18 February 1943, they were observed and arrested. Four days later they were tried by a people's court and executed. In the face of their trial and execution they showed extraordinary courage and dignity, leaving an inspiring example of students who spoke out against Nazi tyranny while others remained silent.

George P. Blum

Additional Reading

Jens, Inge (ed.), *At the Heart of the White Rose: Letters and Diaries of Hans and Sophie Scholl* (1987).

Scholl, Inge, *La Rose Blanche* (1965).

Vinke, Hermann, *The Short Life of Sophie Scholl* (1984).

Schuschnigg, Kurt von (1897–1977)

Chancellor of Austria. Von Schuschnigg was born on 14 December 1897, at Riva on Lake Garda, where his father, an Austrian army officer, was stationed. In 1915, he graduated early from the renowned Jesuit school, Stella Matutina, in Feldkirch, Austria, and joined the Austrian Army.

For the remainder of World War I, he served on the Italian front.

After the war, von Schuschnigg studied law and set up a legal practice. In 1927, he was elected Tyrolean deputy to the Viennese parliament. Politically conservative, a devout Roman Catholic, and a monarchist, he became identified with that faction of the Christian Social Party headed by Ignaz Seipel, the priest/politician.

In the 1930s, von Schuschnigg was minister of justice, and then minister of education in the government of Dr. Engelbert Dollfuss (q.v.). At Dollfuss's behest, von Schuschnigg undertook a number of important assignments, including negotiations with the German *Reich*. Following Dollfuss's assassination in 1934, von Schuschnigg became chancellor and minister of defense and foreign affairs.

In an increasingly radicalized situation, von Schuschnigg managed to frustrate Nazi attempts to seize power, but at the cost of making his government progressively more authoritarian. Like Dollfuss, he relied mainly on Benito Mussolini (q.v.) to counter overt German aggression. But after the League of Nations (q.v.) imposed sanctions on Italy for its invasion of Ethiopia (q.v.) in 1935, Italian support eroded as Adolf Hitler (q.v.) and Mussolini found common ground in the Spanish civil war (q.v.).

In the spring of 1938, renewed Nazi violence within Austria led to threats of direct action by the *Reich*. On 12 February 1938, von Schuschnigg met Hitler at Berchtesgaden, where Hitler demanded amnesty for jailed Austrian Nazis and the inclusion of pro-Nazis in the Austrian cabinet.

On returning to Vienna, von Schuschnigg made the necessary changes, but he refused to abandon the idea of Austrian independence and planned a plebiscite on the issue. Hitler demanded the cancellation of the plebiscite and von Schuschnigg's resignation. After diplomatic calls for help failed to win international support, he announced to the country that he was calling off the plebiscite and resigning under the threat of armed German intervention. The *Anschluss* (q.v.) followed on 11 March 1938. Von Schuschnigg was seized by Nazi officials, placed under arrest, and remained in various concentration camps until May 1945.

After the war, von Schuschnigg was not allowed back into Austria by the Soviets and the socialist government in Vienna. He emigrated to the United States where he became professor of political science and history at St. Louis University. In 1967, he returned to Austria, where he lived in quiet retirement near Innsbruck until his death in 1977.

Throughout his life, von Schuschnigg felt constrained to defend his government's actions. Jewish and socialist groups charged that his government prepared the way for a Nazi takeover, which left them vulnerable to Nazi terror. He claimed that internal and international situations left him few options.

Robert Gerlich

Additional Reading

Schuschnigg, Kurt von, *Austrian Requiem* (1946).
———, *Brutal Takeover* (1971).
Sheridon, R.K., *Kurt von Schuschnigg: A Tribute* (1942).

Seeckt, Hans von (1860–1936)

German colonel general, commander in chief of the German *Reichswehr*. The son of a German general from Silesia, von Seeckt served in the Prussian Army, rising to a position on the general staff in 1899. He served in key military positions for the Central Powers during World War I, including commander of the Austro-Hungarian Twelfth Army, and later chief of staff of the Turkish Army. Following the war, he was a member of the German delegation to the treaty negotiations at Versailles.

Von Seeckt was an aristocrat and a strong supporter of the German monarchy. He had little sympathy for the new Weimar Republic (q.v.) even though he was appointed commander in chief of the army command of the *Reichswehr* in 1920. In that position, he sought to develop an army independent of the state; his allegiance was to his soldiers, not the government. He sanctioned the creation of a secret and illegal military force, the so-called Black *Reichswehr* (q.v.), which exceeded the 100,000 troops permitted under the Versailles Treaty (q.v.). He also violated this treaty by permitting German units to train in the Soviet Union.

A strong supporter of right-wing conservative nationalism, von Seeckt employed the army to suppress Communist insurgencies throughout Germany. He also ordered the army to suppress the Nazi coup in Bavaria in November 1923, thereby gaining the enmity of Adolf Hitler (q.v.), who also condemned him for having a Jewish wife.

Von Seeckt was replaced as commander in chief of the *Reichswehr* in 1926. He remained politically active and was elected to the *Reichstag* in 1930. He later reconciled himself with Hitler and the Nazis and was appointed senior military advisor to the Chinese army of Chiang Kai-shek in 1934–1935. He died in Berlin in 1936.

Steven B. Rogers

Additional Reading

Mellenthin, Friedrich von, *German Generals of World War II As I Saw Them* (1977).

Taylor, Telford, *Sword & Swastika: Generals and Nazis in the Third Reich* (1952).

Wheeler-Bennett, John, *Nemesis of Power: The German Army in Politics* (1953).

Selassie, Haile (1891–1975)

Emperor of Ethiopia. Although Haile Selassie played only a small direct part in World War II, within his lifetime Ethiopia (also known as Abyssinia) experienced, in compressed form, all the stages of recent African history: old traditional ways, European conquest and colonialism, independence, and finally a post-independence coup. When he was born in 1891 as Prince Ras Tufari, Ethiopia, an ancient Christian monarchy, was one of only two African countries free from European control (the other being Liberia). In 1916, after leading a successful rebellion, he became regent and effectively head of the government before being crowned emperor in 1930.

In 1935, Ethiopia (q.v.) was invaded by Fascist Italy, an episode that cruelly emphasized the weakness of the League of Nations (q.v.) as World War II approached. However much its members protested, it was clearly unable to take any effective action. By 1936, the Italian conquest was complete, and Ethiopia became part of Benito Mussolini's (q.v.) "new Roman Empire." Selassie found refuge in Great Britain.

After Italian entry into the war in 1940, British forces under General Alan Cunningham (q.v.) invaded Ethiopia and Italian Somaliland from Kenya, and after a short campaign secured the Italian surrender. Ethiopian guerrillas, led by British officer Orde Wingate (q.v.), played a significant part in liberating their country. Selassie returned in triumph to Addis Ababa, his capital. British troops remained in Ethiopia until the end of the war, but he made it quite clear that despite his country's friendly attitude toward the British, their presence was not to be regarded as permanent.

On the postwar international scene, Selassie played a prominent part in the founding of the Organization of African Unity as more African states gained their independence. Internally, he pursued a policy of bringing his country into the modern world, at the same time trying not to upset it's traditional religious and cultural values.

Progress moved too slowly for the more impatient younger element, and after a disastrous famine in 1973, he was deposed in 1974. Despite charges of corruption, he was held in such high esteem for his leadership against the Italians during World War II that he was permitted to remain in his palace until his death the following year.

Philip Green

Additional Reading

Barker, Arthur J., *Eritrea 1941* (1966).

Dower, Kenneth C., *Abyssinian Patchwork: An Anthology* (1949).

Lockot, C., *The Mission: Life, Reign, and Character of Haile Selassie* (1989).

Steer, George L., *Sealed and Delivered: A Book on the Abyssinian Campaign* (1942).

Senger und Etterlin, Frido von (1891–1963)

German lieutenant general, defender of Cassino. Frido von Senger und Etterlin was born in southern Germany. In 1912, he was one of six German students selected to attend Oxford as Rhodes scholars. During World War I he served in the army as an infantry officer. After the war, he stayed in the *Reichswehr* as a cavalry officer. Senger had a quiet and uneventful life until World War II. In 1940, he commanded a motorized unit during the invasion of France, managing to capture Cherbourg just ahead of Rommel (q.v.). After France surrendered, Senger remained there for occupation duties until he was transferred to Turin as chief liaison officer of the Franco-Italian Armistice Commission.

In 1942, Senger was transferred to the eastern front, taking part in the attempt to relieve the Sixth Army at Stalingrad (q.v.). After that failed, he became convinced Germany could not win the war. In November 1943, he was placed in command of the XIV *Panzer Korps,* tasked with stopping the Allied advance on Rome. Senger had the abbey of Monte Cassino (q.v.) within his area of operations, and took precautions to protect it from destruction. He evacuated the monks and works of art and ensured German forces did not occupy the building. Despite this, the Allies bombed it into rubble, which German paratroopers then occupied and held until 18 May 1944.

Surrendering to General Mark Clark (q.v.) in 1945, Senger was a prisoner of war in Wales until 1947. He then returned to Germany, working as a schoolmaster. In 1960, his book, *Krieg in Europa (War in Europe)*, was published in Germany, and again in 1964 as *Neither Fear nor Hope* in the United States.

Mark Conrad

Additional Reading

Hapgood, D., *Monte Cassino: The True Story of the Most Controversial Battle of World War II* (1986).

Senger und Etterlin, Frido von, *Neither Fear nor Hope* (1964).

Seversky, Alexander P. de (1894–1974)

Russian-American aviation theorist and aeronautical engineer. The innovative and provocative de Seversky had already amassed considerable aviation and military experience by the time he arrived in the United States in 1918. Born in Russia, he held the rank of lieutenant in the Imperial Russian Navy. He was shot down during a night bombing mission in July 1915, and suffered the loss of his right leg. Perseverance enabled him to return to active duty, eventually claiming thirteen German aircraft. He devised techniques in formation flying and aerial refueling and invented a novel bombsight.

In 1918, de Seversky was part of the naval aviation mission sent to the United States by the provisional revolutionary government. He volunteered his services to the U.S. War Department when the Russian embassy was closed. Further development of his bombsight netted seed money for his initial American aeronautical endeavors, and he continued to flight test as a civilian pilot. He became a U.S. citizen in 1927 and was commissioned major in the Air Corps Specialists Reserve.

During the 1930s, Seversky Aircraft Corporation pioneered in the construction of sleek and speedy all-metal, cantilever-wing monoplane fighters for the U.S. Army Air Corps. Along with fellow Russian émigré Alexander Kartveli, de Seversky designed and built the first fighter with an air-cooled engine supercharged for high altitude combat, a development that culminated in the extensively produced P-47 Thunderbolt escort fighter-bomber. By this time, he left the firm he had founded and embarked upon a rigorous campaign to enlighten the American public to the efficacy of airpower and the critical need to apply effectively a doctrine of strategic bombardment.

De Seversky's 1942 *Victory Through Airpower* was widely popularized by an animated Disney film. Twice the winner of the Harmon Trophy, bestowed by Presidents Franklin D. Roosevelt and Harry S Truman (qq.v.), de Seversky continued his exhortations in the name of airpower while articulating the need for a dominant air service in order to contain the ever-threatening Soviet Union. His public proclamations about the conduct of the air war during World War II proved prescient, though his postwar claims tended to be less accurate. He was disregarded during later U.S. administrations, and instead sought technical solutions to non-aviation matters like air pollution.

William Camp

Additional Reading

Seversky, Alexander P. de, *Victory Through Air Power* (1942).

Walton, Francis, *The Miracle of World War II: How American Industry Made Victory Possible* (1956).

Seyss-Inquart, Arthur (1892–1946)

Reich governor of Austria and *Reich* commissar of the Netherlands. Born in Stammern, Austria, Seyss-Inquart studied law in Vienna and was an early member of the illegal Austrian Nazi Party. A strong advocate of union with the *Reich,* he was appointed state councilor in May 1937 and pressured chancellor Kurt von Schuschnigg (q.v.) to be more accommodating to German demands. Seyss-Inquart was appointed Austrian minister of the interior in February 1938, with responsibility for the police and internal security, and Austrian chancellor in March 1938.

The day after his appointment, German troops entered Austria and Seyss-Inquart played a principal role in the *Anschluss* (q.v.). He remained in Vienna as the *Reich* governor for the newly established *Ostmark* until October 1939, when he was appointed deputy governor of the General Government of Poland (q.v.), the non-annexed portion of the country.

Appointment as *Reich* commissar of the Netherlands followed in May 1941. Employing other Austrian Nazis at the exclusion of local Dutch Nazis, Seyss-Inquart's ruthless administration is credited with completely subordinating the Dutch economy and local political administration to the necessities of the German war effort. Hundreds of thousands of Dutch workers were employed as forced laborers in German-controlled industry. He also supervised the deportation of more than 100,000 Dutch Jews to concentration camps in Germany and Poland. He was captured by the Allies after the war and tried and executed at Nuremberg (*see* International Military Tribunal) for crimes against humanity.

Steven B. Rogers

Additional Reading

DeJong, L., *The German Fifth Column and the Second World War* (1956).

Rosar, Wolfgang, *Deutsche Gemeinschaft: Seyss-Inquart und der Anschluss* (1971).

Watson, Ann, *They Came in Peace* (1972).

Shaposhnikov, Boris Mikhailovich (1882–1945)

Marshal of the Soviet Union, chief of the Soviet General Staff. Shaposhnikov was the second-oldest Soviet military commander of World War II. The son of a white-collar worker, he joined the Russian Army in 1901. He attended the Moscow Military School and the Tsarist Academy of the General Staff.

During World War I, he initially served in staff positions, but assumed command of a regiment in 1917. He joined the Red Army in 1918, and served in a variety of staff positions, including chief of the intelligence section of the revolutionary military council's field staff. From 1925 to 1937, he was the commander of various military districts, and also military commissar of the Frunze Military Academy. He served on the investigative board that conducted the purges (q.v.) of the military in 1937. Shaposhnikov apparently was uncomfortable in that assignment, but he held his council and continued to work within the inner circle of trusted Stalinist leaders.

In 1940, Shaposhnikov was the chief of the Soviet General Staff and head of the *Stavka* with Georgy Zhukov (qq.v.) as his deputy. Shaposhnikov advised Josef Stalin (q.v.) to abandon the forward Soviet troop dispositions in eastern Poland and consolidate behind the Stalin Line along the old borders. He was dismissed for making that suggestion. In July 1941, after the German attack, Stalin reorganized the *Stavka* and reinstated Shaposhnikov, who continued to council withdrawal and strategic defense.

In November 1941, Shaposhnikov became ill, and was replaced by General Aleksandr Vasilevsky (q.v.). Despite his illness, he helped plan the defense of Moscow (q.v.) and the subsequent counterattack. In June 1942, he advised against the Soviet attack at Kharkov, which he considered premature. Still ill, he was appointed deputy commissar of defense. In June 1943, he became the commandant of the Voroshilov Military Academy, and held that post until his death in 1945.

Thomas Cagley

Additional Reading

Bialer, Seweryn (ed.), *Stalin and His Generals* (1984).

Shukman, Harold (ed.), *Stalin's Generals* (1993).

Werth, Alexander, *Russia at War, 1941–1945* (1964).

Shirer, William L. (1904–1993)

American journalist. Shirer traveled to Europe in the 1920s as a *Chicago Tribune* correspondent. He became a pioneer radio broadcaster for the Columbia Broadcasting System (CBS) in Berlin before World War II. Fluent in German and married to a Viennese woman, he had access to many high-ranking Nazis, conversing with them and witnessing the political, military, and cultural changes Adolf Hitler (q.v.) was implementing.

Shirer's broadcasts were contemporary accounts of the evolving worldwide crisis. He tried to warn Western officials of the danger Hitler represented, but his pleas, regarded as unbelievable, went unheeded. Shirer attempted to portray the European situation as truthfully as possible, noting the populace's lack of enthusiasm for the impending war. He used secret sources and endured Nazi surveillance, being followed and wiretapped.

After covering the early campaigns and remarking on how the Germans revolutionized warfare techniques, Shirer departed Germany in December 1940. He returned in 1945 and attended the Nuremberg trials (*see* International Military Tribunal). Despite his renown for his portrayals of the Third *Reich,* he was criticized by journalist peers in the United States during the 1950s as being sympathetic to liberal politics and was subsequently blacklisted from the profession. He regained his professional credibility and standing when he published *The Rise and Fall of the Third Reich: A History of Nazi Germany* in 1960.

Elizabeth D. Schafer

Additional Reading

Shirer, William L., *Berlin Diary: The Journal of a Foreign Correspondent, 1934–1941* (1941).

——, *The Rise and Fall of the Third Reich: A History of Nazi Germany* (1960).

Shtemenko, Sergei Matveevich (1907–1976)

Soviet colonel general, chief of the operations directorate of the Soviet General Staff. The son of a peasant, Shtemenko joined the Red Army in 1926 and the Communist Party in 1930. He spent the late 1920s and 1930s attending various military schools, capped by the General Staff Academy in 1940. He was one of the rare Soviet generals who never commanded in the field during the war. In the interwar years, he had not served in any capacity that would have "blooded" him in battle, being too young for the tsar's forces or the civil war, and in school during the Spanish civil war (q.v.).

From 1941 through early 1943, Shtemenko was in the Axis section of the operations directorate of the general staff. In April 1943, he was appointed chief of the operations directorate, and remained in that position until the end of the war. Shtemenko organized the military operations of the Transcaucasus Front (army group) in 1942. Those operations were successful, and he was assigned to similar tasks for the Black Sea and Northern Fronts. All of those operations were given to him while he was in the Axis section. After he moved up to chief of the operations directorate, he continued to work from the supreme headquarters, planning operations for nearly all of the fronts at one time or another. He played a key role in planning for the final assault on Berlin (q.v.).

Shtemenko was a consummate staff officer and a prolific writer. He left a number of documents behind that recorded, through his eyes, the command and control of the Soviet General Staff, including Josef Stalin's (q.v.) involvement in specific operations.

Following the war, Shtemenko served in the general staff, both as deputy and chief. He was the Soviet deputy prime minister from 1948 through 1952. After Stalin's death, Shtemenko was demoted and dropped out of sight for a few years. He returned to public life in 1959, and finished his career as chief of staff of the Warsaw Pact forces in 1968.

Thomas Cagley

Additional Reading

Bialer, Seweryn (ed.), *Stalin and His Generals* (1984).
Shukman, Harold (ed.), *Stalin's Generals* (1993).
Werth, Alexander, *Russia at War, 1941–1945* (1964).

Shumilov, Mikhail Stepanovich (1895–1975)

Soviet colonel general, commander of the Seventh Guards Army. The son of a peasant, Shumilov attended military school under the tsar and served as an ensign during World War I. He joined the Red Army and the Communist Party in 1918 and served

in the civil war as the commander of a rifle regiment. After the civil war, Shumilov attended the Higher Infantry School in 1929. During the Finnish Winter War (q.v.), he commanded a rifle corps.

At the start of World War II, Shumilov commanded a rifle corps, but he quickly became deputy commander of the Fifty-fourth Army in the Leningrad Front (army group). In 1942, he became the commander of the Sixty-fourth Army at Stalingrad (q.v.). That unit was one of three reserve armies thrown into the battle to stop the German Sixth Army. The three armies totaled thirty-eight divisions, but fourteen of them numbered less than 1,000 men each. Although the Sixty-second Army bore the brunt of the fighting, the three armies combined to defeat the Germans. After Stalingrad, the Sixty-fourth Army was reorganized as the Seventh Guards Army, which in 1944 was placed under Marshal Ivan Konev's (q.v.) 2nd Ukrainian Front. During the battle for the Ukraine (q.v.), Shumilov's forces attacked the German Eighth Army's left flank, helping to encircle that pocket of German resistance.

Following the war, Shumilov commanded various military districts. After a brief retirement, he became a military consultant to the group of inspectors general of the Soviet Ministry of Defense.

Thomas Cagley

Additional Reading

Bialer, Seweryn (ed.), *Stalin and His Generals* (1984).

Sikorski, Władysław E. (1881–1943)

Polish general, prime minister and commander in chief of the Polish government-in-exile. Born near Kraków in Austrian Poland, Sikorski was early involved in Polish patriotic and paramilitary activities. During World War I, he rose to the rank of colonel commanding Polish units serving with the Austrians. Joining the army of reborn Poland, he played a brilliant role in the 1919–1921 Russo-Polish War (q.v.) and was made chief of the general staff. He thereafter held a number of posts, including briefly prime minister in 1922–1923.

When Józef Piłsudski (q.v.) returned to power in 1926 via a coup, Sikorski's career was derailed. He was a leading opponent of the Piłsudski regime (1926–1935) and of its successor (1935–1939). During this time, he published a number of important books, including the prophetic *The Future War*, in 1934.

Sikorski was not given a command in the 1939 September campaign, but instead went to

France. With the fall of Poland, its government fled to Romania and was interned. Seizing the moment, he was instrumental in creating an exile government in Paris on 30 September 1939, where he held the combined posts of prime minister and commander in chief.

When France fell in June 1940, the Polish government moved to London. There Sikorski began to rebuild a Polish military-in-exile and conducted vigorous diplomacy, notably in regard to a future Polish-Czechoslovakian confederation.

When the Germans invaded the Soviet Union in June 1941, Sikorski signed the Sikorski-Maisky Agreement with the Soviets on 30 July 1941, which reestablished Polish-Soviet relations severed since the Soviet attack in September 1939. That important, yet controversial, step allowed for the formation of a Polish Army in the Soviet Union from Polish POWs captured in 1939.

Sikorski showed imagination and flexibility in his diplomacy and carried on far-reaching negotiations in both Washington and Moscow. In April 1943, however, the discovery of the mass graves at Katyń (q.v.) provoked a crisis in Polish-Soviet relations. Because both Washington and London attached great significance to smooth relations with Josef Stalin (q.v.), the Polish-Soviet imbroglio weakened Poland's standing with the West. In the midst of this crisis, Sikorski was killed in an airplane crash off Gibraltar on 4 July 1943. The circumstances of the accident remain mysterious and have given rise to considerable speculation.

After Sikorski's death, the Polish government-in-exile was succeeded by less able and far less prepossessing men. Ultimately, however, it was not Sikorski's death, but the West's decision to discount Poland in order to pursue harmony with Stalin. This led to the rapid demise of the Polish London government.

M.B. Biskupski

Additional Reading

Sword, Keith (ed.), *Sikorski: Soldier and Statesman* (1990).
Meiklejohn, Terry, *Poland's Place in Europe: General Sikorski and the Origins of the Oder-Neisse Line, 1939–1943* (1983).

Sikorsky, Igor (1889–1972)

Russian-American aircraft inventor. An aircraft designer of great skill, Sikorsky produced the first successful American helicopter (q.v.). A Russian emigrant who already had an impressive reputation as designer of the large World War I Ilya Moroments

bomber aircraft, he found a niche in the American aviation industry by producing seaplanes.

Sikorsky experimented with vertical flight. By early 1942, he perfected a single-main-rotor helicopter that provided the best compromise between hovering capability, horizontal speed, and precise control. The U.S. air arms recognized the usefulness of Sikorsky's work and during the war ordered three distinct models; R-4, R-5, and R-6. His helicopters operated in noncombat roles, but they provided a solid base for future military applications.

Michael E. Unsworth

Additional Reading

Cochrane, Dorothy, *The Aviation Careers of Igor Sikorsky* (1989).

Simonds, Guy Granville (1903–1974)

Canadian lieutenant general, commander of Canadian II Corps. Simonds, born in Suffolk, England, came to Canada in 1912. He was a "Sword of Honour" graduate of the Royal Military College of Canada, taking a commission in the Royal Canadian Artillery. He was posted to various batteries throughout Canada, attending the British Staff College at Camberley in 1936–1937.

Simonds proceeded overseas in 1939 as the general staff officer 2 of Canadian 1st Division, where recognition of his tactical and staff abilities led to rapid promotion. He established a Canadian staff college in 1941 and by 1943, he was given divisional command. He was highly praised for his handling of the Canadian 1st Division in Sicily (q.v.); and he came to be considered a protege of General Bernard L. Montgomery (q.v.), a man whom he greatly admired. Simonds's ability brought him the command of the Canadian II Corps, but his temperamental and high-strung nature led to personality conflicts with his superior, General Henry Crerar (q.v.), while in the Mediterranean.

Simonds's II Corps entered the line in Normandy (q.v.) on 11 July 1944. His innovative solution for cracking the German defenses involved the use of the first Allied armored personnel carriers. His complicated plans for Operations TRACTABLE and TOTALIZE provided the initial Allied breakthrough, but stiff German resistance was soon encountered. As a result, he had a number of senior officers who failed to meet his exacting standards removed. In September, with some reservations, he deployed his strung-out forces to both invest the Channel ports and to clear the Scheldt (q.v.) estuary.

As acting commander of Canadian First Army from 26 September, Simonds was praised by all for his handling of the army during the difficult operations in October; especially his attack on Walcheren Island. His confidence and energy were mirrored by the army headquarters staff, and while his cold personality did not engender affection, he was universally respected.

Simonds returned to command of II Corps in November, conducting bitter operations in the Rhineland (q.v.) in 1945. At the end of the war, he was acknowledged as the best tactician produced by the Canadian Army, and he was called the best corps commander in the Allied armies.

After the war, passed over for the post of chief of the general staff, Simonds unsuccessfully sought a commission in the British Army. He held appointments at the Imperial and Canadian National Defense Colleges before being appointed chief of the general staff in 1951, a post he held until 1956. He was largely responsible for producing one of the finest peacetime armies in Canadian history.

Paul Dickson

Additional Reading

Copp, Terry, and Robert Vogel, *Maple Leaf Route: Scheldt* (1985).

English, John A., *The Canadian Army and the Normandy Campaign* (1991).

Graham, Dominick, *The Price of Command: A Biography of General Guy Simonds* (1994).

Whitaker, Dennis, and Shelagh Whitaker, *Tug of War: The Canadian Victory That Opened Antwerp* (1984).

Simović, Dušan (1882–1962)

Yugoslavian general, prime minister of Yugoslavia. Simović served in the Balkan wars and in World War I. During the interwar years, he served as the commandant of the Officers' Military School, chief of the general staff, and chief of the air staff. When Germany invaded Yugoslavia on 6 April 1941, he was simultaneously prime minister and chief of the supreme command. He took over the premiership on 27 March, following the coup that overthrew the rule of the regency under Prince Paul. The coup was precipitated by Yugoslavia joining the Tripartite Pact on 25 March, and it was directed against the perceived policy of surrender to Germany. He was more of a figurehead than otherwise. The real moving spirit in the coup was air force General Borivoje Mirković. Although Simović mobilized the Yugoslav military, the complicated call-up system, plus the desire not to pro-

voke Germany, meant the army was far from ready when the invasion began.

Simović divided his forces into three army groups. His intention was to fight a delaying action on the borders, withdrawing to the south, and even into Greece, if necessary. His main task was to prevent the enemy from driving a wedge between his forces and the Greek Army, while at the same time keeping a close watch on Bulgaria. He was optimistic up until the Germans captured Skopje on 10 April, and split the Yugoslav from the Greek Army. At the same time, the individual Yugoslav armies became operationally isolated. That evening, he issued the orders for all army groups and armies to fight independently, whenever in contact with the enemy.

Belgrade (q.v.) fell on 13 April. Faced with total defeat, Simović resigned as chief of the supreme command, and charged his successor to sue for an armistice. Together with King Peter II (q.v.), he went into exile. Simović retained the premiership until 10 January 1942, but his leadership was weak and ineffective. He appointed General Draža Mihailović (q.v.) commander of the resistance forces, and initiated military cooperation with the Polish military-in-exile.

By 1942, Simović had alienated the Serbs, the Croats, and the royal court. After his resignation, he held no other government posts, although in 1944 from retirement, he urged the Yugoslav people to support Tito (q.v.). In February 1945, Peter named him member of the proposed regency council, but Tito opposed the nomination.

Andrzej Suchcitz

Additional Reading

Calder-Marshall, Arthur, *Watershed* (1947).

Fotitch, Constantin, *The War We Lost: Yugoslavia's Tragedy and the Failure of the West* (1948).

Singleton, Fred, *Twentieth-Century Yugoslavia* (1976).

Sudjić, Milivoj, J., *Yugoslavia in Arms* (1942).

Simpson, William Hood (1888–1980)

American lieutenant general, commander, U.S. Ninth Army. William "Texas Bill" Simpson graduated from the U.S. Military Academy at West Point in 1909 and served in the Philippines and in the 1916 Mexican Punitive Expedition in pursuit of Pancho Villa. In World War I, Simpson served as a staff officer in the 33rd Infantry Division. In the interwar years, Simpson completed the usual series of school assignments, fully mastering the skills needed to coordinate the operations of a high-level headquarters.

At the start of World War II, Simpson commanded the 35th and the 30th Infantry Divisions in training, and then the XII Corps. In October 1943, he assumed command of the Fourth Army in California. In May 1944, Simpson and most of his staff went to Britain to organize the Eighth Army, which shortly after was redesignated the Ninth Army. In September 1944, the Ninth Army captured the port of Brest (q.v.), France, then advanced into Holland. Ninth Army troops were first to cross the Rhine River in Operation GRENADE and advanced the farthest of any American army into the Third *Reich* before halting to meet the Soviets at the Elbe River.

A low-key personality who strove to build a strong and unified army staff, Simpson granted his subordinates full latitude to run their own commands. Consequently, Simpson worked closely with his long-time chief of staff, Brigadier General James E. Moore, who executed Simpson's ideas. When asked about Simpson after World War II, General Dwight D. Eisenhower (q.v.) stated that Simpson "was the type of leader American soldiers deserve," a fitting testament to a highly competent officer. Simpson was promoted to full general on the retired list in August 1954.

Randy Papadopoulos

Additional Reading
MacDonald, Charles, *The Siegfried Line Campaign* (1963).
Weigley, Russell F., *Eisenhower's Lieutenants: The Campaigns of France and Germany, 1944–1945* (1981).

Skalski, Stanisław (1915–)

Polish ace, RAF wing commander. Skalski was born in Kodyma, Russia, but his family moved to Poland when he was still a baby. In 1936 he entered the Polish Air Force. Flying an obsolete P-11 fighter, Skalski scored his first air-to-air victory on 1 September 1939, the first day of World War II. Before Poland fell, Skalski shot down four more German aircraft.

Like many Polish airmen, Skalski made his way to Britain and entered the RAF. In the spring of 1941 he joined the all-Polish Number 303 Squadron—the RAF's top scoring squadron. In April 1942 he assumed command of the all-Polish Number 317 Squadron. Later that year he was selected to form a unit of veteran Polish fighter pilots. Operating as a part of Number 145 Squad-

ron in North Africa, "Skalski's Circus" scored twenty-five victories in its first few weeks in action.

On 8 May 1943, Skalski assumed command of Number 601 Auxiliary Squadron, making him the first Polish pilot to lead an English squadron. In April 1944 he took command of Number 2 (Polish) Fighter Wing, flying P-51 Mustangs deep into France and the Low Countries. Skalski ended the war with 17.5 confirmed kills with the RAF, added to his five with the Polish Air Force. He received the Distinguished Service Order, and the Distinguished Flying Cross and Two Bars.

After World War II, Skalski turned down job offers from the RAF and the USAAF. He returned to Poland and helped build its air force. In 1948 he was accused of being a British spy and was interrogated, tortured, and condemned to death. His sentence later was commuted to life in prison. He was released in 1956, but forced back into the Polish military. He finally retired from the Polish Air Force as a major general.

David T. Zabecki

Additional Reading
Baker, E.C.R., *The Fighter Aces of the R.A.F.* (1962).
Zamoyski, Adam, *The Forgotten Few: The Polish Air Force in the Second World War* (1995).

Skirpa, Kazys (1895–1979)

Lithuanian colonel and military attache in Berlin. Skirpa was founder of the Lithuanian Activist Front, which coordinated underground resistance against the Soviet occupation of Lithuania, 1940–1941. He drew up plans for an armed revolt and proposed a new provisional government in which he would serve as prime minister. The Germans placed him under house arrest in 1941 and prohibited him from returning to Lithuania.

Steven B. Rogers

Additional Reading
Kaslas, Bronis J., *The USSR-German Aggression Against Lithuania* (1973).
Misiunas, Ronuald J., and Rein Taagepera, *The Baltic States: Years of Dependence 1940–1980* (1983).

Skorzeny, Otto (1908–1975)

German SS commando leader. Otto "Scarface" Skorzeny was the war's best-known commando. His methods were brilliant, often accomplishing his mission with minimal enemy and friendly ca-

SS-Standartenführer *Otto Skorzeny. (IWM HU 46178)*

sualties. By late 1944, Allied intelligence experts labeled him "the most dangerous man in Europe."

Born in Vienna, Skorzeny studied engineering at Vienna University. As a junior officer, he served with the *SS Leibstandarte* Adolf Hitler (later 1st SS *Panzer* Division) in the Low Countries in 1940, and the Balkans and Soviet Union in 1941–1942. He was badly wounded in Russia. On 18 April 1943, he was placed in command of the Friedenthal *Jägergruppen,* a collection of volunteers from all services. He organized two battalions, trained in unconventional operations with Allied weapons, and organized special groups according to foreign language proficiency.

Skorzeny gained worldwide attention when he rescued Benito Mussolini (q.v.) from captivity at Gran Sasso (q.v.) in the Italian Alps. Skorzeny's seventy-man glider force landed on the plateau, rushed the hotel, and freed Mussolini within five minutes, all without firing their weapons and without casualties. Mussolini's rescue bolstered Fascist resolve in northern Italy against the new Badoglio government and the Allies.

In the fall of 1944, Adolf Hitler (q.v.) feared Hungary's defection to the Soviets. On 15 October, Skorzeny kidnapped Milos Horthy, son of the regent of Hungary, Admiral Miklós Horthy (q.v.).

The next day, Skorzeny captured the regent himself, and a pro-Nazi government took over.

On 22 October, Hitler personally promoted Skorzeny to lieutenant colonel in the *Waffen-SS,* then ordered him to organize a special formation and undertake extensive covert operations for the upcoming Ardennes offensive (q.v.). Commanding the 150th *Panzer* Brigade, his mission (code named Operation *GREIF)* was to capture bridges over the Meuse River, commit sabotage, and create havoc behind Allied lines. By 16 December, with insufficient preparation time, he assembled 2,500 volunteers and a motley collection of American uniforms, equipment, and a few vehicles. A handful of special troops in American uniforms and jeeps, some speaking English, managed to penetrate American lines. Their exploits were largely unsuccessful, but wild rumors (i.e., Eisenhower was to be assassinated) spread tremendous suspicion among American troops. On 21 December, Skorzeny's brigade conducted a conventional attack at Malmedy and was soundly defeated. In January 1945 the brigade was disbanded.

From January to March, Skorzeny commanded a large force of troops and defended a bridge over the Oder River. In March 1945, men with demolitions from his Danube frogmen group attempted to destroy the American-captured Remagen Bridge (q.v.); but none reached it. At the end of the war, Skorzeny was organizing troops to defend the National Redoubt (q.v.) in southern Bavaria. He surrendered in Salzburg on 19 May 1945.

When he was tried at Dachau for war crimes, several British commando officers testified in Skorzeny's behalf. He was acquitted of all charges, but not released. He escaped on 27 July 1947, moved to Spain, married a wealthy Spanish countess, and established a highly prosperous engineering business. He also operated an underground network assisting former SS men escaping to South and North America. Illness and resulting spinal surgery in 1970 paralyzed him from the waist down, but he taught himself to walk again within three months. He died in Madrid five years later.

Samuel J. Doss

Additional Reading

Infield, Glenn B., *Skorzeny: Hitler's Commando* (1981).
Pallud, Jean-Paul, *Ardennes 1944: Peiper and Skorzeny* (1987).
Skorzeny, Otto, *Skorzeny's Secret Missions* (1951).
Whiting, Charles, *Skorzeny* (1972).

Slessor, John (1897–1979)

British air marshal, commander of RAF Coastal Command. The son of an army officer, Sir John Slessor was crippled by polio as a child. Despite lameness in both legs, family connections helped him secure a commission in the Royal Flying Corps during World War I. In the 1930s, he worked in the plans branch of the Air Ministry. When World War II broke out, he was director of plans branch. He recognized the numerical superiority of the enemy and advocated the use of initiative as a countermeasure.

A strong advocate of aerial attack, Slessor was responsible for drafting the proposal at the Casablanca Conference that allowed for continued operations in the Pacific and the Far East (sought by the United States), while simultaneously focusing the Allies' main efforts on Germany (sought by the French and British).

In 1943, Slessor became the head of RAF Coastal Command. His intensive use of shore-based aircraft against the German U-boats operating out of French ports was a crucial factor in the Allies' final victory in the Atlantic.

In 1944, he moved to the Mediterranean as deputy commander in chief of Allied air forces. There he was involved in supporting the landings in southern France (q.v.). After World War II, he became chief of the British air staff.

Thomas Cagley

Additional Reading

Bryant, Athur, *The Turn of the Tide* (1957).
Slessor, John, *The Central Blue: The Autobiography of Sir John Slessor, Marshal of the RAF* (1957).

Slovik, Edward D. (1920–1945)

American private. The only U.S. soldier shot for desertion since the Civil War. Eddie Slovik was found guilty of desertion in the face of the enemy and put to death on 31 January 1945, the first such execution since the American Civil War. In August 1944, Slovik landed in Normandy and became petrified the first time he found himself in combat. When the prospect of combat confronted him again, he ran away, later giving himself up and making a full confession. On 11 November, he was tried by court-martial, unanimously found guilty, and sentenced to death. He was tried, not by combat-experienced officers, but mostly by medical and dental officers, who convicted him, but who expressed shock that he had actually been executed. The army made an example of him, in part

to atone for the mass desertions during the Ardennes Offensive (q.v.). He died before a twelve-man firing squad at the age of twenty-five. The army sentenced forty-nine men to death for deserting under fire, but only Slovik was executed.

Susanne Teepe Gaskins

Additional Reading

Huie, William Bradford, *The Execution of Private Slovik* (1954).

Śmigły-Rydz, Edward (1886–1941)

Polish marshal, military dictator of Poland. A protege of Józef Piłsudski (q.v.), Śmigły-Rydz was a successful army group commander during the 1919–1920 Russo-Polish War (q.v.). Following Piłsudski's death, Śmigły-Rydz, nominally the supreme commander of the armed forces, became the real political power in the country. In 1935, he set about modernizing the Polish military. In March 1939, he ordered a partial mobilization, and initiated detailed defensive preparations. His strongly centralized system of command proved tragic for the Poles in 1939.

Śmigły-Rydz's primary intention was to fight a delaying action from the borders, withdrawing to the Vistula and, if necessary, southeastward toward the border with allied Romania. He saw the Polish campaign as only the first stage in a European war in which his main task was to prevent his forces from being destroyed before France and Britain could attack Germany from the west, in accordance with their treaty obligations. When Germany invaded Poland on 1 September 1939, only some 75 percent of the Polish military was mobilized.

On the second day of the war, Śmigły-Rydz sanctioned the withdrawal of Army Krakow, which was to have been the lynch pin of the southeastward maneuver. On 6 September, he ordered a withdrawal to the Vistula, but that line was soon breached, leading to further retreat. Abandoned by his allies, Śmigły-Rydz had no doubts about the final outcome of the campaign. The Soviet invasion on 17 September eliminated any operational sense of defending the Romanian bridgehead.

Together with the Polish government, Śmigły-Rydz crossed into Romania with the aim of reaching France and re-creating the Polish Army to continue the struggle. Instead he was interned. In 1940, he escaped to Hungary and made his way back to Warsaw. He died there under an assumed name.

Andrzej Suchcitz

Additional Reading

Garliński, Józef, *Poland in the Second World War* (1985).

Zaloga, Steven, and Victor Madej, *The Polish Campaign 1939* (1985).

Smith, Ian (1919–)

British fighter pilot and later prime minister of Rhodesia. Smith was born in Seluwke, Rhodesia, on 8 April 1919. Educated locally, he attended Rhodes University in South Africa but left in 1939 to join the Royal Air Force. As a fighter pilot with a Rhodesian unit, he was shot down twice. After the first time, he had facial plastic surgery. The second time he was shot down in Italy and joined a band of Italian partisans for five months before reaching Allied forces. He returned to action and served with another RAF squadron when the war ended.

Following the war, Smith entered politics and was elected to the Rhodesian parliament. In 1964, he became prime minister of Rhodesia, a position he held until 1979. Under his leadership, the nation struck for independence in 1965 and the Smith-led government maintained white rule until his unseating in 1979. He remained on the political scene in opposition to the new government as Rhodesia was renamed Zimbabwe in 1980.

Boyd Childress

Additional Reading

MacDonald, John F., *The War History of Southern Rhodesia*, 2 vols. (1947–50).

Smith, Walter Bedell (1895–1961)

American lieutenant general, Dwight D. Eisenhower's chief of staff. Smith was born in Indianapolis, Indiana, to a middle-class family in the heart of middle America. Both his parents were buyers for a dry-goods firm. In 1910, while attending high school, he enlisted in the Indiana National Guard and six years later, served with General John J. Pershing's expedition into Mexico.

After briefly enrolling at Butler University in Indiana, Smith returned to active duty in 1917 and was commissioned a second lieutenant. He was wounded by shrapnel during the American attack along the Marne in 1918. On his return home, he decided to pursue a career in the regular army. He joined as first lieutenant in 1920.

Although he never completed college, during the interwar years Smith established a reputation as a superb military administrator. He carved out a distinguished record at both the Infantry School at Fort Benning and the Command and General Staff College at Fort Leavenworth. He came to the attention of General George C. Marshall, who, along with "Ike" Eisenhower (qq.v.) was to become his patron.

Marshall brought Smith to Washington in October 1939 to begin preparations for the expansion of the army. During his early career promotions were slow for Smith, but within two years he rose from major to brigadier general under Marshall's tutelage. Smith was appointed U.S. secretary of the Combined Chiefs of Staff (q.v.) and served in that capacity until September 1942. Eisenhower specifically asked for him as his chief of staff when he took over as Allied commander for the invasion of Northwest Africa (q.v.). Smith served in that capacity for the duration of the war. The two men formed an almost perfect relationship complementing each other's strengths. Eisenhower called Smith "a master of detail with the clear comprehension of main issues . . ." Smith often stood in for Eisenhower at various Allied military functions, including the surrender of Italy.

An aloof, quick-tempered officer with no tolerance for incompetence, Smith smoothed Eisenhower's difficult task of coordinating U.S. and British cooperation. Known as Ike's protector, he saw that Eisenhower concentrated on important issues by taking on most routine staff matters himself.

Smith's diplomatic skills came to the fore after the war. President Harry S Truman (q.v.) appointed him ambassador to the Soviet Union, where he served from 1946 to 1949. He guided U.S. policy in Moscow during the formative years of the Cold War. While suspicious of Josef Stalin's (q.v.) expansionist policies, Smith rejected the concept of monolithic Communism. For example, he counseled the cultivation of Tito's (q.v.) deviationist tendencies in Yugoslavia.

In 1950, at the outbreak of the Korean War, Truman named Smith director of the CIA. He served there until Eisenhower's election as president, when he was picked as assistant secretary of state to John Foster Dulles. Thus he was one of the few men to serve both Truman and Eisenhower at the highest levels. Smith's diplomatic skills served him best during the complex negotiations at the 1954 Geneva Conference, following the French collapse in Indochina. Allied leaders, especially the British, preferred him to the more prickly Dulles.

Promoted to full general in 1951, Smith retired in 1954 due to poor health (he suffered from stomach ulcers for years). He died seven years later.

Eisenhower provided the perfect epitaph: Smith was, "one of the great staff chiefs of history, worthy to rank with Gneisenau."

John P. Rossi

Additional Reading
Crosswell, D.K.R., *The Chief of Staff: The Military Career of General Walter Bedell Smith* (1991).
Eisenhower, Dwight D., *Crusade in Europe* (1948).
Smith, Walter B., *My Three Years in Moscow* (1950).

Smuts, Jan Christiaan (1870–1950)

South African statesman and military leader. Prior to the outbreak of the war, Smuts and his Union Party served in a coalition government headed by Prime Minister James B.M. Hertzog, the leader of the National Party. The coalition collapsed after the German invasion of Poland and Smuts called for South Africa to declare war on Germany. Having served as a member of the British War Cabinet during World War I, Prime Minister Smuts and his government were steadfast supporters of Winston S. Churchill (q.v.) and the British war effort, which included the deployment of South African troops in the European and North African theaters.

Steven B. Rogers

Additional Reading
Cockram, Ben, *General Smuts and South African Diplomacy* (1970).
Ingham, Kenneth, *Jan Christiaan Smuts* (1986).

Sokolovsky, Vasily Danilovich (1897–1968)

Marshal of the Soviet Union, commander of the Soviet Western Front (army group) and deputy commander of the 1st Byelorussian Front. Sokolovsky grew up in poor peasant surroundings, escaping from his poverty by joining the Red Army in 1918. He held company, regimental, and brigade-level command positions in the civil war. After the civil war he attended the Military Academy of the Workers' and Peasants' Army. From there he was posted to Central Asia to serve as deputy chief of the operations division of the general staff. Prior to World War II, he served as chief of staff of a division and corps, division commander, deputy chief of staff of the Volga Military District, and chief of staff of the Urals and Moscow Military Districts.

In February 1941, Sokolovsky was appointed deputy chief of the general staff. By mid-summer 1941, he was the chief of staff of General Ivan Konev's (q.v.) Western Front, responsible for organizing the defense of Moscow (q.v.). Sokolovsky commanded the Western Front at Kursk (q.v.) and in the liberation of Smolensk in September 1943. In early 1944, he became chief of staff of the 1st Ukrainian Front. That February he was held responsible for the failure to advance north from the Pripet marshes. Nonetheless, he then became deputy commander of Marshal Georgy Zhukov's (q.v.) 1st Byelorussian Front during the final assault on Berlin (q.v.).

After the war, Sokolovsky was the commander in chief of the Soviet Group of Forces in Germany. He also was the Soviet military governor of Berlin; and when he walked out on the four-power talks, it signaled the start of the Cold War. In later years Sokolovsky became one of the most respected military theorists in the Soviet Union. His 1961 book, *Soviet Military Strategy,* became the foundation of Soviet nuclear war-fighting strategy.

Thomas Cagley

Additional Reading
Bialer, Seweryn (ed.), *Stalin and His Generals* (1984).
Werth, Alexander, *Russia at War, 1941–1945* (1964).

Somervell, Brehon B. (1892–1955)

American lieutenant general, commander of U.S. Army Service Forces. A 1914 West Point graduate, engineer, World War I divisional G-4 (logistics) officer, and WPA administrator, Somervell commanded the U.S. Army Service Forces and was General George C. Marshall's (q.v.) chief logistics advisor between 1942–1945. Somervell's first war-related command was the construction division of the Quartermaster Corps, which he reorganized in 1940–1941 to meet increased army base and housing needs. In December 1941, he became assistant chief of staff, G-4, War Department general staff, and played a key role in developing mobilization, munitions, and shipping production programs.

Following the U.S. War Department reorganization in March 1942, Somervell commanded the Services of Supply (SOS), renamed the Army Service Forces (ASF) in 1943. The SOS consisted of administrative agencies, corps areas, and technical services that supplied, supported, and managed the army at home and abroad. He wanted to revamp the SOS to make "the U.S. Army the best-equipped, the best-fed, the most mobile Army on the face of the earth." While not fully successful, Marshall praised Somervell's efficiency and the ASF, which received recruits, fed, clothed, housed, and transported them, ran and maintained communications, and procured the ships, munitions, and supplies vital to victory.

During his military career, Somervell earned the Distinguished Service Medal with two oak leaf clusters and two Legions of Merit. He retired in 1946.

Clayton D. Laurei

Additional Reading

Millet, John D., *The Organization and Role of the Army Service Corps* (1954).

Morris, R.B., and J. Woodress, *Global Conflict: The United States in World War II: 1937–1946* (1962).

Somerville, James (1882–1949)

British admiral of the fleet. Born in Somerset on 17 July 1882, Sir James Somerville joined the Royal Navy in 1897. He earned the Distinguished Service Order in 1915 in the Dardanelles. During World War II, he commanded Force H during the successful pursuit of the *Bismarck* (q.v.) in May 1941. A technocrat and staff officer by background, he proved a solid, if not spectacular commander.

Somerville did well during the prewar period, but ill health led to his retirement as a vice admiral on 31 July 1939. His most significant prewar contribution was the development of radar (q.v.) for the Royal Navy. The research and development organization he established gave the Royal Navy the technical edge it needed to defeat its Axis counterparts.

Recalled to active duty upon mobilization, he participated in Operation DYNAMO before assuming command of Force H, based in Gibraltar, on 27 June 1940. His first operation was the controversial attacks on the French fleet at Mers el-Kébir (q.v.) and Oran. His subsequent activities were directed against the Axis, primarily the escorting of convoys to Malta (q.v.) throughout the North Africa campaign (q.v.).

After the *Bismarck* episode, Somerville went on to command the British Eastern Fleet in the Indian Ocean, remaining there until he was appointed to represent the Admiralty in Washington, D.C., in 1944. He was promoted to admiral of the fleet on 8 May 1945, and supervised the return of Lend-Lease (q.v.) materials to the United States. He died in Britain on 19 March 1949.

Carl O. Schuster

Additional Reading

Chatterton, Edward K., and K. Edwards, *The Royal Navy: From September 1939 to September 1945,* 5 vols. (1942–47).

Howarth, Stephan (ed.), *Men of War: Great Naval Leaders of World War II* (1993).

Sönsteby, Gunnar Fridtjof Thurman (1918–)

Norwegian resistance fighter. An obscure accountant before the war, Sönsteby was galvanized by the German occupation of Norway into joining the resistance. After SOE (q.v.) training, he returned to his homeland to found the Oslo Gang, a daring band of saboteurs whose exploits were a thorn in the side of General Nikolaus von Falkenhorst's (q.v.) occupation forces. Near the war's end, the Oslo Gang stole the archives of the Department of Justice and National Police Headquarters, securing the principal evidence that led to the conviction of Vidkun Quisling (q.v.) and his fellow collaborators.

Mark Rummage

Additional Reading

Cruickshank, Charles, *SOE in Scandinavia* (1986).

Sönsteby, Gunnar, *Report from No. 24* (1965).

Sorge, Richard (1895–1944)

German-Soviet double agent. Sorge was a German journalist, based in Japan, who was also a highly placed Soviet agent and head of a very successful spy ring. Masquerading as a loyal German correspondent, he fed detailed information to Moscow on Japan's military capabilities and intentions. Four months prior to the German invasion of the Soviet Union in June 1941, Sorge is supposed to have informed the Soviets of German intentions. He told Josef Stalin that Japan was preparing to attack the United States. This knowledge allowed the Soviets to move their alpine divisions from Siberia in late 1941 to help in the defense of Moscow.

He was arrested in Tokyo on 16 October 1941, and reported hanged on 7 November 1944. There was some doubt, however, as to his actual death. His body was exhumed after the war. His size, a hip bone broken in World War I, plus his gold teeth convinced those who knew him of his identity. His executioner also testified as to his identity.

Max Mulholland

Additional Reading

Deakin, F.W., and G.R. Story, *The Case of Richard Sorge* (1966).

Sosabowski, Stanisław (1892–1967)

Polish major general, commander of the Polish 1st Independent Parachute Brigade. Sosabowski was the commander of the 21st Infantry Regiment in the defense of Warsaw during the 1939 Polish campaign. In 1944, he commanded the Polish 1st Independent Parachute Brigade at Arnhem (q.v.), where it was dropped late and in the wrong position, at Driel. His attempts to cross the Rhine to reinforce the British 1st Airborne Division failed. Sosabowski's deep skepticism about Operation MARKET-GARDEN right from the start, had proved correct.

Andrzej Suchcitz

Additional Reading

Garliński, Józef, *Poland in the Second World War* (1985).
Ryan, Cornelius, *A Bridge Too Far* (1974).
Sosabowski, Stanisław, *Freely I Served* (1982).

Sosnkowski, Kazimierz (1885–1969)

Polish general, commander in chief of the Polish armed forces. During the 1939 Polish campaign, Sosnkowski was commander of the southern front, and delivered one of the Polish Army's few tactical successes at Lwów on 14–16 September. After the fall and partition of Poland, Sosnkowski escaped to France where he was appointed commander in chief of the resistance army. He held that position until 1940, when the post was transferred to commanders in occupied Warsaw. He was also minister of state, a cabinet post he resigned from following the Polish-Soviet Agreement of 1941.

Sosnkowski became commander in chief of the Polish armed forces on 8 July 1943, and held that post until the end of September 1944. He unsuccessfully tried to ensure an adequate flow of supplies to the Polish Home Army. Sosnkowski opposed an uprising in Warsaw outside the framework of Operation *BURZA*. His strong stance with Poland's allies in demanding practical assistance and in opposing Soviet attempts to dominate Poland, led to his enforced resignation as a result of Soviet pressure on Britain for his removal.

Andrzej Suchcitz

Additional Reading

Garliński, Józef, *Poland in the Second World War* (1985).
Mikolayczyk, Stanislaw, *The Rape of Poland* (1947).

Spaak, Paul-Henri (1899–1972)

Foreign minister of the Belgian government-in-exile. Born in an upper-middle-class family, Spaak was educated as a lawyer at the University of Brussels. In 1932, he started a long career as member of parliament for the Belgian Labour Party. Entering the cabinet in 1935, he became Belgium's prime minister in 1938–1939, and again in 1946 and in 1947–1949. He also was minister of foreign affairs in 1936–1938, 1947–1949, 1954–1957, and in 1961–1966.

During World War II, Spaak served as foreign minister of the Belgian government-in-exile in London. After the war, he played important roles in different international organizations, such as the United Nations (q.v.) and the European Economic Community. He became one of the main advocates of the economic recovery and political unity of postwar Western Europe. He also served as secretary-general of NATO from 1957 to 1961.

During World War II, Spaak was the main promoter of an active war policy in favor of the Western Allied forces. Among the members of the government-in-exile, criticism arose against the attitude of King Leopold III (q.v.), still in Belgium, who was accused of favoring an appeasement policy toward the Germans.

After World War II, Spaak played a decisive role in the broad political alliance of the Communist, Socialist, and Liberal Parties to prevent the restoration of Leopold's kingdom, which led to an open constitutional crisis in 1950. During the 1950s and 1960s, Spaak voiced a moderate and conservative mainstream line within the Western Social Democratic Parties. On the international scene, he was strongly in favor of thorough Atlantic-European cooperation.

Georgi Verbeek

Additional Reading

Huizinga, J.H., *Mr. Europe: A Political Biography of Paul-Henri Spaak* (1961).
Motz, Roger, *Belgium Unvanquished* (1942).
Raven, Helene J., *Without Frontiers* (1960).

Spaatz, Carl (1891–1974)

American general, commander of U.S. Army Air Forces in Europe, first chief of staff of the U.S. Air Force. Spaatz was born in rural Boyertown, Pennsylvania, on 28 June 1891. In 1914, he graduated from the U.S. Military Academy at West Point, where he picked up the nickname "Tooey," and became one of the army's first pilots. In May 1917, he was promoted to captain and commanded the 31st Aero Squadron in France. He organized an aviation training school and flew a handful of combat missions with three downed German aircraft to his credit.

Spaatz was promoted to major in 1920 and held commands in California, Texas, and Michigan. In January 1929, he, Captain Ira Eaker, and 1st Lieutenant Elwood Quesada (qq.v.) established a flight endurance record, with in-flight refueling, as part of a series of publicity flights designed to bring attention to the developing field of aviation.

Much of Spaatz's career was influenced by General William L. "Billy" Mitchell (q.v.), the prime advocate of airpower in the U.S. Army. Because of his unpopular views in support of Mitchell, Spaatz spent fifteen years as a major. He was a defense witness when Mitchell was court-martialed for excessive criticism of the U.S. military's aviation policies. In 1935, Spaatz was promoted to lieutenant colonel, and in 1936, he graduated from the Command and General Staff College at Fort Leavenworth.

In 1940, Spaatz accompanied an observation team to Britain. In July 1941, he was appointed chief of staff to General Henry H. "Hap" Arnold (q.v.), the chief of the U.S. Army Air Forces. Now a brigadier general, Spaatz was fully involved in the American air effort in Europe.

In May 1942, Spaatz was named commander of the U.S. Eighth Air Force, and a few months later he was appointed head of the Air Force Combat Command. In the fall of 1942, he went to North Africa to command the Allied air forces under General Dwight D. Eisenhower (q.v.) and remained throughout Operation TORCH. Spaatz demonstrated the ability to get along well with British commanders, which led to his return to Europe in 1944.

In January 1944, Spaatz was named to command the U.S. Strategic Air Forces. Here he clashed with the British air strategy being carried out under

Lieutenant General Carl Spaatz (second from left) and Major General James Doolittle (second from right) visiting a heavy bombardment wing in England. (IWM EA 13381)

Arthur Harris (q.v.), the head of the Royal Air Force Bomber Command. Spaatz favored targeting the German transportation system and oil production sites, while Harris opted for attack against Germany's industrial machine using area bombing. During the summer of 1944, Allied bombing of oil and transportation targets proved dramatically successful and significantly hampered the resupply of German ground forces. Spaatz and Harris did share one belief—airpower had the potential to eliminate the need for major land operations.

After the war in Europe, Spaatz assumed command of the strategic air forces in the Pacific. Following the war, he succeeded Arnold as chief of the U.S. Army Air Force, and later became the first U.S. Air Force chief of staff when that branch of service was formed in 1947.

Spaatz retired in July 1948. He held several civilian positions after retirement, including national security affairs correspondent for *Newsweek* magazine, and chairman of the Civil Air Patrol (q.v.). He also served on the committee selecting Colorado Springs as the location for the new U.S. Air Force Academy. Following his death on 14 July 1974, he was buried at the Colorado site.

Boyd Childress

Additional Reading

Davis, Richard G., *Carl A. Spaatz and the Air War in Europe* (1993).
Freeman, Roger A., *The Mighty Eighth: Units, Men and Machines: A History of the Eighth Army Air Force* (1970).
Mets, David R., *Master of Airpower, General Carl A. Spaatz* (1988).

Speer, Albert (1905–1981)

German architect and minister of armaments. Born to a prosperous Mannheim family, Speer grew up in Heidelberg, and later studied architecture in Karlsruhe, Munich, and Berlin. While in Berlin in the early 1930s, Speer recognized the growing influence of the Nazis and viewed Adolf Hitler (q.v.) as savior of a shattered Germany. He joined the Nazi Party in 1931, more out of fascination for Hitler, than for the prospect of doing architectural work.

Speer's 1932 design of a party headquarters building in Berlin impressed Hitler so much that he was invited to build and furnish other new party buildings in Berlin and Nuremberg. In 1933, Speer handled the technical arrangements for the party rally at Berlin's Tempelhof airport and was also called on to assist in refurbishing Hitler's official residence and chancellery offices. Through their mutual love of architecture, Speer soon became part of Hitler's inner circle, even though his education and training set him apart from Hitler's normal coterie of henchmen.

Speer became a protege through whom Hitler could realize his architectural visions for a New Germany. One of Speer's first major assignments in 1934–1935 was the rebuilding of the Nuremberg stadium to be used for future party rallies. This project was followed in 1936 with Hitler's order of design plans for the rebuilding of Berlin.

In 1937, Speer was appointed inspector general of buildings for Berlin, but he had no institutional power and his position was due to his close personal relationship to Hitler. In 1938, Hitler gave Speer a year to complete the new *Reich* Chancellery. His completion of this task on time proved Speer's ability to meet short deadlines.

Preparing drawings for the rebuilding of Berlin kept Speer busy until 1943. Hitler placed great political importance on these plans and ordered Speer to continue his designs for the new German capital, even after the war began. As the war progressed, however, Speer was forced to divert his attention to the designing and building of military facilities and assisting in the construction armaments factories.

In February 1942, Fritz Todt (q.v.), the minister for armaments and munitions, died in a mysterious plane crash, and Speer was appointed as his replacement. He immediately began to rebuild factories, bridges, and transportation links. He toured the front to observe the performance of equipment and various weapon systems, something he knew very little about.

Speer restructured the ministry and introduced industrial self-responsibility. He urged standardization and division of labor and converted industry to mass production for better efficiency. The ministry remained a "steering organization" to manage overall production quotas, while technicians from leading firms were made responsible for separate areas of armaments production. This restructuring led to a rapid rise in production. By mid-1942, wartime demands forced Hitler to suspend all major building projects, with the exception of a few special ones. Speer could now focus his attention on armaments production.

Speer recommended to Hitler that construction and armaments production remain in his ministry, a stand that placed him at odds with Hermann Göring (q.v.), who hoped to bring armaments production under the jurisdiction of his

Reichsminister *Albert Speer (left), Grand Admiral Karl Dönitz (center), and Colonel General Alfred Jodl,* shown after their arrest in May 1945. (IWM AP 69125)

four-year plan. Speer also tried to present a realistic appraisal of the German economy, but the Nazi leadership, for the most part, refused to accept his findings. Even Hitler did not agree with Speer's proposed austerity programs planned to assist in the revitalization of armaments production. Hitler failed to understand the problems facing armaments production and the need for an overall plan for Germany's war economy; he was more concerned with pressing military matters.

In April 1942, a central planning authority was created within Göring's four-year plan. Speer asked Hitler again to place all war-related production under his control, thereby permitting him to transform factories geared for the production of consumer goods into armaments plants. As Germany's industrial reserves dwindled throughout 1942 and 1943, Speer looked to the industrial potential of other countries under German domination. Factories in these countries could produce consumer goods while German factories were converted to armaments production. Hitler eventually acquiesced and Speer was subsequently appointed *Reich* minister for armaments and war production.

Air raids in 1943 and early 1944 exacted a high price on German industry and armaments production, yet Speer managed to meet production quotas through decentralization. At his urging, important factories were moved to outlying areas. Despite the increasing frequency of air raids, the transportation network remained operational and industrial production actually increased until the summer of 1944. In June 1944, Speer's ministry gained responsibility for air armaments.

By late summer 1944, armaments production could no longer meet military requirements. Shortly thereafter, Speer fell into disfavor with Hitler, and they often quarreled. Speer would later circumvent Hitler's planned scorched earth policy. Speer believed it would lead to the annihilation of the German people and would hamper postwar reconstruction.

After the war, Speer was captured and tried for crimes against humanity at Nuremberg (*see* International Military Tribunal). He was the only defendant to admit complicity in Nazi crimes and received a twenty-year sentence. Speer was released from Spandau prison in 1966, and returned to Heidelberg to work on his memoirs.

Steven B. Rogers

Additional Reading

Reif, Adelbert (ed.), *Albert Speer: Kontroversen um ein deutsches Phänomen* (1978).
Schmidt, Matthais, *Albert Speer: The End of the Myth* (1984).
Sereny, Gitta, *Albert Speer: His Battle with Truth* (1995).

Speer, Albert, *Inside the Third Reich: Memoirs* (1970).

———, *Spandau: The Secret Diaries* (1976).

Zilbert, E.R., *Albert Speer and the Nazi Ministry of Arms* (1981).

Speidel, Hans (1897–1987)

German lieutenant general. Speidel, chief of staff for General Erwin Rommel (q.v.) on the western front in 1944 and one of the plotters against Adolf Hitler, helped establish the postwar West German military apparatus. Born in Metzingen on 28 October 1897, Speidel became an officer cadet in 1914 and served throughout World War I. In 1925, he attained his Ph.D. Assigned to the general staff of the 3rd Division in 1930, he became the assistant to the military attache in Paris in 1933. In 1935, he headed the western intelligence division of the German General Staff.

He returned to general staff work with the outbreak of World War II. In June 1940, as chief of staff for the military governor in France, General Karl Heinrich von Stülpnagel (q.v.), Speidel drafted the surrender imposed on the French. Reassigned to the eastern front in 1942–1943, as chief of staff for an army group, Major General Speidel's anti-Hitler opinions hardened, and he became an active member of the resistance group in the army.

As the Germans prepared for a possible Allied invasion in January 1944, Lieutenant General Speidel served as Rommel's chief of staff for Army Group B. Speidel, who believed the war was lost, tried to convince the army command in Berlin to negotiate with the Allies. When his efforts were ignored, he worked to overthrow Hitler and arranged for Stülpnagel to meet Rommel and try to convince him to join the plot; Rommel apparently gave his conditional support.

After the July 20th plot to kill Hitler failed, Speidel escaped implication, but was arrested by the *Gestapo* (q.v.) when he refused to destroy Paris rather than let it fall to the advancing Allies. Imprisoned in Berlin and extensively interrogated, he was acquitted by a court of honor in September 1944. He remained in detention but escaped in early 1945 and went into hiding. Liberated by the French, he became a witness for the prosecution at the Nuremberg trials (*see* International Military Tribunal).

Returning to academic pursuits, Speidel taught contemporary history at the University of Tübingen, 1949–1950. As an advisor on military affairs to Chancellor Konrad Adenauer (q.v.), Speidel helped plan a new German Army. From 1951 to 1954, Speidel served as the chief German military delegate at the conference on foundations of a European defense association. In 1955, Lieutenant General Speidel of the *Bundeswehr* became chief of the department of the joint armed forces, a "separate but equal" department parallel to the three service departments, responsible for joint and common issues. Promoted to general, he subsequently was appointed commander of NATO's Allied Land Forces, Central Europe, Fontainebleau, France, where he served from 1957 to 1963.

After his retirement from the military in 1964, Speidel headed the *Stiftung Wissenschaft und Politik* research foundation, from 1964 to 1978. Speidel, the only principal postwar survivor of the army plots against Hitler, died at Bad Honnef on 28 November 1987.

Laura Matysek Wood

Additional Reading

Barnett, Correlli (ed.), *Hitler's Generals* (1989).

Speidel, Hans, *Invasion 1944* (1950).

———, *We Defended Normandy* (1951).

Sperrle, Hugo (1885–1953)

Luftwaffe field marshal, commander of the *Kondor Legion* and the German Third Air Fleet. Sperrle served in the German Air Force during World War

Field Marshal Hugo Sperrle. (IWM MH 6096)

I and by 1934, he became one of the major leaders of the secret German Air Force. He was promoted to major general the following year and in 1936, he became the first commander of the *Kondor Legion* (q.v.) in Spain. He directed the Third Air Fleet during the 1940 invasion of France, and in July, he was promoted to field marshal.

During the Battle of Britain (q.v.), Sperrle stressed the need to destroy the Royal Air Force if German bombers were to be successful. By June 1944, Sperrle's Third Air Fleet was reduced to less than 500 operational aircraft, and it had no success against the Allied invasion. This failure led Hitler to relieve Sperrle of his command on 19 August 1944. The Allies later tried Sperrle for war crimes, but he was acquitted of all charges. He died in Munich on 2 April 1953.

Michael G. Mahon

Additional Reading
Mitcham, Samuel W., Jr., *Hitler's Field Marshals and Their Battles* (1988).
———, *Men of the Luftwaffe* (1988).

Stalin, Josef (1879–1953)

Dictator of the Soviet Union and commander in chief of Soviet military forces. A Georgian and Soviet political leader, Stalin was absolute dictator of the Soviet Union between 1929 and his death in 1953. His major political accomplishment was to convert Communism in the Soviet Union from what had been a relatively egalitarian, revolutionary movement into an authoritarian, repressive, and bureaucratic political system. He established an industrial system that enabled the Soviet Union to defeat Adolf Hitler (q.v.). In accomplishing these ends, he institutionalized terror to a degree seldom seen in world history. It is estimated that he had as many as 20 million Soviet citizens murdered in the process.

Stalin, whose real name was Iosif Vissarionovich Dzhugashvili, was born in Gori, Georgia, the son of a shoemaker. In 1899, he became a professional revolutionary, and was first arrested in 1902. During the Russian civil war, he served as a high-level political commissar with the Red forces in the field. From 1917 to 1923, he was the commissar of the people for the nationalities of Russia in the first Soviet government.

In April 1922, Stalin was appointed secretary general of the Central Committee of the Communist Party of the USSR, which marked the start of his rise to power. After Lenin's death, he consolidated his power, driving all of his political rivals out of the party. When he succeeded in expelling Leon Trotsky (q.v.) from the Soviet Union in 1929, Stalin's position became virtually unassailable.

Through a series of brutal five-year plans that enforced collectivism and industrialization, Stalin changed the Soviet Union from a backward agrarian country into a modern industrialized state. During the 1930s, he continued to tighten his grasp on the reins of power by eliminating internal enemies through a series of treason trials and purges (q.v.).

In the years before World War II, Stalin's foreign policy was aimed at defending the Soviet Union from the openly expansionist policies of Nazi Germany. When he concluded that a series of treaties negotiated with France and Czechoslovakia would not achieve this objective, he decided to deal with Germany directly. The result was the Molotov-Ribbentrop Pact (q.v.) of 1939, which in a secret protocol agreed to the division of Poland and the placing of the Baltic states (q.v.) under the Soviet sphere of influence. The subsequent Finnish Winter War (q.v.) also gave Stalin more leverage in dealing with the Germans; but the Finns fought back much harder than anyone expected, revealing serious weaknesses in the Soviet military apparatus.

When the German leviathan steamrolled across the Soviet frontier and the Red Army on 22 June 1941, Stalin was dumbstruck. For days he dithered in a melancholic daze as the sheer scale of the catastrophe, largely of his own making, became apparent. On 30 June, his psychological paralysis began to lift as he approved the creation of the overarching State Defense Committee (GoKo), with himself at its head. He quickly regained his merciless composure, executing failed Red Army commanders and placing the government on a total war footing. In the meantime, his belief in his own mastery of military affairs and strategy revived—with ominous consequences for Red Army operations.

Stalin injected total dominance into military planning. He fostered a deeply held belief, dating from the civil war, that any dedicated Bolshevik could master strategy and tactics in a matter of days. Initially, this resulted in a myriad of orders from Stalin to defend untenable lines or counterattack, orders that meant little to the shattered and encircled forces that received them. His appointment to senior commands of incompetent cronies from his civil war days, Semyon Budenny and Kliment Voroshilov (qq.v.) chief among them, exacerbated the spiraling crisis.

In September 1941, the disastrous giant encirclement of 650,000 Soviet troops at Kiev (q.v.) resulted after Stalin refused to approve a timely retreat. In May 1942, he dismissed the objections of his general staff, mainly Boris Shaposhnikov and Georgy Zhukov (qq.v.), and committed to the premature Kharkov (q.v.) counteroffensive. The result was the annihilation of the Red Army's Southwestern Front (army group) which, in turn, cleared the way for the wide *Wehrmacht* sweep to Stalingrad and the Caucasus oil fields.

By mid-1942, Stalin learned to adopt a more cautious tack in his personal interventions into combat operations. In September, he endorsed a proposal by Zhukov and Aleksandr Vasilevsky (q.v.) for the double envelopment of the German forces at Stalingrad (q.v.). This plan succeeded in cutting off Friedrich Paulus's (q.v.) Sixth Army in November and led to its surrender in February 1943.

The battle of Stalingrad ended the myth of German invincibility, and the summer campaign of 1943—and history's greatest tank battle at Kursk (q.v.)—verified that the war had reached its strategic turning point. Despite some early vacillation, Stalin subdued his impulse for a frontal assault and accepted the entrenched, defensive posture advocated by his commanders, who had possession of detailed intelligence regarding the imminent German attack, Operation *ZITADELLE*. When the attack came, the German *Panzer* echelons broke against the prepared Soviet positions in what was a decisive defensive victory. The resulting counterattack then permanently shifted the strategic initiative to the Soviets. By the end of November, the Red Army had established three bridgeheads across the Dnieper River (q.v.), and was poised for the advance into Eastern Europe and the Balkans.

With Soviet success, however, Stalin returned to his previous single-minded insistence on continuous offensives on broad fronts, instead of the closer assault frontages to spearhead the advance desired by the field commanders. This led to many ill-prepared attacks and resulted in high Red Army casualties in the otherwise successful race to Berlin.

Stalin's role as a military commander in 1941 and 1942 was marked by disastrous defeats and enormous battlefield losses, to which he apparently was completely indifferent. Indeed, Zhukov considered Stalin's worth as a commander primarily in that "he excelled above all as a military economist who knew how to collect reserves even while the front was consuming manpower in gargantuan mouthfuls," while also deploying those reserves to decisive effect—such as the Soviet counteroffensive at Kursk. Otherwise, the main point in Stalin's military performance was that by September 1942, he finally learned to listen to his experts. Militarily, this is probably the biggest difference between Stalin and Adolf Hitler, who never did quite grasp this vital lesson.

Stalin was an uncertain military commander, but his deficiencies in the military realm were overridden by two primary considerations. The first was his absolute mastery over the apparatus of the Soviet state. The second was his keen, overriding feel for grand strategy; the geopolitical, diplomatic, economic, and industrial factors that defined his wartime and postwar objectives.

Some Soviet allies expected that after World War II, the USSR, which emerged from the war as a truly great power, would feel sufficiently secure to give up the despotic system, or at least temper its earlier institutional rigidities. Instead, the harsh prewar system was restored in the USSR, and the conquered countries of Eastern Europe were molded into the same system and placed under harsh Moscow rule. Stalin seemed convinced that his large army was not adequate defense against the industrial and military superiority of the United States and a soon-to-be-revived Western Europe.

By 1950, the Soviets recovered sufficiently to appear as a serious threat to Western Europe. These fears prompted Europe and the United States to form the North Atlantic Treaty Organization (NATO) as an anti-Soviet defense alliance. In response, the Soviets created the Warsaw Pact and the Cold War hardened along military lines.

After Stalin's death in March 1953, Nikita Khrushchev (q.v.) began a "de-Stalinization" campaign at the Twentieth Party Conference in 1956 by denouncing Stalin and Stalinism. Turmoil followed in the Communist Bloc as rebellions broke out in East Germany, Poland, and Hungary. Subsequently, increased efforts at independence in Yugoslavia, Czechoslovakia, and China made it clear that the earlier Western view of Communism as a monolithic entity was inaccurate. By 1960, astute observers of Communism were convinced that polycentrism better described developments in the splintering international Communist movement. By this time, those flaws and crevices, which would ultimately bring down the Communist system, were clearly evident.

Stalin will most likely be remembered as one of the greatest mass murderers of all time.

Stephen Donahue

Additional Reading

Conquest, Robert, *Stalin: Breaker of Nations* (1992).

Erickson, John, *The Soviet High Command: A Military-Political History 1918–1941* (1962).

Kennan, George F., *Russia and the West Under Lenin and Stalin* (1960).

Tremain, Rose, *Stalin* (1975).

Ulam, Adam B., *Stalin: The Man and His Era* (1973).

Stangl, Franz (1908–1971)

Austrian SS officer, commandant of the Treblinka concentration camp. Born in Austria, Stangl joined the Austrian police in 1931 and the illegal Austrian Nazi Party in 1936. As a lieutenant in the German police after the *Anschluss* (q.v.), he was appointed superintendent of the Euthanasia Institute at Schloss Hartheim in November 1940, and assumed responsibility for the murder of hundreds of physically and mentally disadvantaged inmates.

In March 1942, Stangl was transferred to Lublin and was appointed to command the Sobibor concentration camp, one of three camps erected in eastern Poland in late 1941 and early 1942 in preparation for the extermination of the Polish Jews. He remained at Sobibor until September 1942, a period during which 100,000 Jews were killed. He was reassigned as commandant of Treblinka and there supervised the murder of 800,000 Jews before the camp was closed in the autumn of 1943.

After the war, Stangl fled to Syria and later to South America. In 1967, he was extradited to West Germany, tried and sentenced in 1970 to life imprisonment. He died in prison the following year.

Steven B. Rogers

Additional Reading

Hassman, Jan, *The Brown Heart: The Concentration Camp, Europe Under the Rule of Hitler* (1948).

Sereny, Getta, *Into That Darkness* (1974).

Steiner, Jean F., *Treblinka* (1967).

Stark, Harold Raynsford (1880–1972)

American admiral, commander, U.S. Naval Forces, Europe. As chief of naval operations (CNO) from 1939–1942, Stark played an important role in American preparations for war. As conflict neared, he helped provide the groundwork for a strengthened "two-ocean" navy. A guiding force behind joint Anglo-American discussions on war planning prior to Pearl Harbor, he concluded that Allied strategy should focus on defeating Germany. Like other American leaders in 1941, he expected a Japanese move in the Pacific, but not necessarily against Hawaii. However, his late November "war warning" to Pacific commanders became a source of controversy and debate during hearings after the attack.

Within days of Pearl Harbor, President Franklin D. Roosevelt selected Admiral Ernest King (qq.v.) as commander in chief, U.S. Fleet. The posts of CNO and CinC overlapped however; so Roosevelt, in March 1942, gave King sweeping powers by combining both positions. Stark then went to London as commander, U.S. Naval Forces Europe (COMNAVEUR), an office he held until 1945. No stranger to Britain, he had served as aide to Admiral William Sims during World War I, and learned the necessity of close cooperation with the British.

Stark's primary function in Britain centered on administration rather than operations. Thus, in early 1943, while he served as commander, Twelfth Fleet, he participated in planning for the invasion of France. The British thought highly of Stark, and he worked well as a sailor/diplomat in wartime Britain. He also served as naval advisor to the European Advisory Commission studying provisions for Nazi surrender. Replaced by Admiral H. Kent Hewitt (q.v.) as COMNAVEUR in 1945, Stark retired from the navy in 1946.

Between 1944 and 1946, Stark testified before both naval and congressional investigations into Pearl Harbor. The navy inquiry first faulted Stark for failing to be clear in warning naval commands of potential Japanese hostilities. The later congressional examination was more favorable, however, and Admiral King changed his negative appraisal of Stark's role, a decision supported by Secretary of the Navy John L. Sullivan.

Known as "Betty" to close friends because of a Naval Academy nickname revolving around a Revolutionary War hero, Stark had a reputation for kindness and gentleness, and as a man who "looked more like a bishop than a sailor." He not only helped prepare the U.S. Navy for World War II, but also provided an important liaison with Allies during the conflict.

Edward J. Sheehy

Additional Reading

Morrison, Samuel Eliot, *History of U.S. Naval Operations in World War II,* 15 vols. (1947–1962).

Simpson, B. Mitchell, III, *Admiral Harold R. Stark: Architect of Victory, 1939–1945* (1989).

Stauffenberg, Claus von (1907–1944)

German colonel, leader of the German opposition to Adolf Hitler (q.v.). Claus Schenk *Graf* von Stauffenberg, a distinguished staff officer, was a major leader of the conspiracy against Hitler in World War II. He attempted to assassinate the *Führer* by placing a bomb at his headquarters in Rastenburg, East Prussia, on 20 July 1944. Born in 1907, von Stauffenberg came from a notable south German aristocratic family. His mother was the granddaughter of the Prussian general August Gneisenau. Though brought up a devout Catholic, he also was taught to respect his mother's Lutheran faith. Through his twin brothers, he came into contact with the poet Stefan George, who frowned on materialist and bourgeois society and sought to inspire German youth to develop a new nobility of spiritual beauty.

Despite poor health, von Stauffenberg opted for a military career. He was commissioned second lieutenant in 1930, and quickly achieved a reputation as a skilled technician and a leader with wide interests. After attending the War Academy in Berlin and now a captain, he became a logistics officer in 1938, and was posted to the German General Staff in 1940.

Von Stauffenberg served in the occupation of the Rhineland (q.v.) and subsequently in the Polish and French (qq.v.) campaigns. Though approving of the remilitarization of the Rhineland and the Austrian *Anschluss* (q.v.), he became disturbed by the Blomberg-Fritsch affair and *Kristallnacht* (qq.v.). In the spring of 1939, he exclaimed of Hitler: "The fool is going to war!" Although he had doubts about Hitler's war strategies and was especially critical of Nazi policies in the Soviet Union, he did not formally joined the conspiracy against Hitler until 1943, after he recovered from grave wounds suffered during the North African campaign. The force of his personality and his moderate conservative views, including appreciation for the role of workers in society, appealed to a broad spectrum of the anti-Nazi opposition and enabled him to assume a prominent role in the conspiracy.

On 1 July 1944, Colonel von Stauffenberg was appointed chief of staff to General Friedrich Fromm (q.v.), the commander of the Reserve Army. In this capacity, he gained direct access to Hitler's staff conferences. As a severely disabled war hero he was spared the routine search of persons admitted to Hitler's presence. He carried a bomb in his briefcase on three different occasions in July 1944, hoping to kill not only Hitler but also Hermann Göring and Heinrich Himmler (qq.v.). Even though the latter were not present on 20 July, von Stauffenberg activated the time bomb and after the explosion bluffed his way out of Hitler's complex, believing that the *Führer* was dead.

Delays in implementing the plans of the conspiracy to take over the government, which might have failed even under more favorable circumstances, and the fact that Hitler survived, thwarted any effective action by the conspirators against the Nazi forces. Von Stauffenberg and several of his associates were overpowered in the evening of 20 July, court-martialed, and shot in the courtyard of the Berlin War Ministry. Today, von Stauffenberg is regarded as the spiritual mentor of the modern German Army *(Bundeswehr)*.

George P. Blum

Additional Reading
Berben, P., *L'Attentat Contre Hitler* (1962).
Graber, Gerry S., *Stauffenberg* (1973).
Kramarz, Joachim, *Stauffenberg* (1967).
Manvell, Roger, *The Conspirators: 20 July 1944* (1971).

Steflea, Ilia (1887–1945)

Romanian colonel general, chief of the Romanian General Staff from 1942 to 1944. Steflea's attempts to obtain badly needed military supplies for the Romanian Army on the eastern front fell on deaf German ears. With failures mounting, he pressed for the withdrawal of the Romanian Army. From August 1944, he commanded the Romanian Fourth Army, facing the Soviets on the Prut and Siretul Rivers.

Andrzej Suchcitz

Additional Reading
Cretzianu, Alexandre, *The Lost Opportunity* (1957).
Pavel, Pavel, *Why Rumania Failed* (1944).
Popescy-Putrie, I, *La Roumanie pendant la Deuxième Guerre Mondiale* (1964).

Steinhoff, Johannes (1913–1994)

Luftwaffe colonel, commander of the first all-jet fighter wing. "Mackey" Steinhoff was one of the few *Luftwaffe* aces whose career began with biplanes and ended with jets. He saw combat on all the major fronts of World War II; the Battle of Britain with JG-26, the eastern front with JG-52, North Africa and Italy with JG-77, and finally the defense of the *Reich* with JG-7 and JV-44. He accumulated 993 combat missions and 176 aerial victories, was shot down twelve times, and was decorated with the Knight's Cross of the Iron Cross with Oak Leaves and Swords.

Steinhoff began his military career in the German Navy in 1934. His passion for flying left no doubt the *Luftwaffe* would be his branch of service, to which he transferred in 1936. After his distinguished war service in piston-engine fighters, he was selected in November 1944 to command JG-7, the first all-jet fighter wing. He was removed from that command because of his involvement with other senior officers in a conspiracy to remove Hermann Göring (q.v.). Steinhoff was later assigned to Adolf Galland's (q.v.) JV-44, called the "Squadron of Experts." On 18 April 1945, the war ended for Steinhoff when his Me-262 jet fighter crashed and burst into flames during a takeoff. He was burned badly and disfigured, but he survived.

When the West German *Bundeswehr* was established in the mid-1950s, he became one of the founding commanders of the new *Luftwaffe*. He was still on flight status and qualified on all the *Luftwaffe's* jets at the age of fifty-three. He commanded Allied Air Forces, Central Europe, at Fontainebleau, France, during the mid-1960s. He retired in 1972 as a full general, and inspector general of the *Luftwaffe*.

José Alvarez

Additional Reading
Steinhoff, Johannes, *The Final Hours* (1985).
Toliver, Raymond F., and Trevor J. Constable, *Fighter Aces of the Luftwaffe* (1977).

Stephenson, William (1896–1989)

Chief of British security coordination in North America. Sir William Stephenson, "The Man Called 'Intrepid,'" was born on 11 January 1896 in Canada. He was seriously wounded in World War I and later became an important industrialist. During World War II, he was appointed by Winston S. Churchill (q.v.) to head the British security coordination in North America. Known as "Little Bill," he worked with U.S. General William Donovan (q.v.), "Big Bill," to establish America's first intelligence service, the Office of Strategic Services (OSS) (q.v.).

Paul J. Rose

Additional Reading
Hyde, A. Montgomery, *The Quiet Canadian: The Secret Service Story of Sir William Stephenson* (1964).
Stevenson, William, *Intrepid's Last Case* (1984).
———, *A Man Called INTREPID* (1976).

Stettinius, Edward Reilly (1900–1949)

U.S. secretary of state. As secretary of state from November 1944 to July 1945, Stettinius brought extensive organizational skills to that office. Unfortunately, his leadership abilities were much more modest. President Franklin D. Roosevelt (q.v.) was resolved to conduct on his own all major diplomacy at the end of the war.

The State Department was badly in need of reorganization. Due to the amorphous nature of diplomatic tasks, State had difficulty turning back bureaucratic raids by other agencies. Within the department, contested authority and personality clashes had taken their toll. Stettinius possessed an impressive background in management perfectly suited for the task. Although his achievements were substantial, they were not the sort of work that wins public accolades.

Stettinius found his appointment viewed with consternation by liberal opinion-makers. The State Department seemed to be slipping into the hands of conservative power brokers; he was not considered a match for them. Key issues such as refugees, decolonization, and U.S.-Soviet relations would be handled by foes of liberalism. He was seen as a malleable leader with no contribution to make if a liberal peace was to be forged.

Despite such obstacles, Stettinius worked hard to improve the public image of the State Department. His impact on wartime policies was slight, but he played a major role in laying the foundations for a Department of State at last capable of dealing with the continual crises of the twentieth century.

Michael Polly

Additional Reading
Rose, Lisle A., *After Yalta* (1973).
Stettinius, Edward R., *Roosevelt and the Russians* (1949).

Stewart, James M. (1908–1997)

U.S. Army Air Force colonel, film actor. Jimmy Stewart was born in Indiana, Pennsylvania. He graduated from Princeton University in 1932 with a degree in architecture. That same year he started his acting career, appearing on stage in New York City. By the start of World War II, Stewart had appeared in several now-classic films, including *It's a Wonderful Life, Mr. Smith Goes to Washington,* and *The Philadelphia Story,* for which he won an Oscar.

Stewart entered the U.S. Army Air Force in 1942 and qualified as a bomber pilot. He was assigned to the 445th Bomb Group, stationed at Tibenham, in Norfolk, England. On 7 January 1944, as a major, Stewart led forty-eight B-24s in a mission on Ludwigshaven. After the completion of the bombing run, he noticed that the 389th Bomb Group, the lead group in the mission, was heading back to Britain on a wrong bearing that would take them directly over *Luftwaffe* fighter fields in France. With communications out, Stewart elected to follow with his group to provide fire cover. As a result, the 389th lost only eight bombers on the return trip. Stewart brought all of his own back.

Stewart flew a total of twenty missions, including Bremen, Münster, and Berlin, earning a Distinguished Flying Cross with Oak Leaf Cluster, and the Air Medal with three Oak Leaf Clusters. He finished the war as a colonel. After the war Stewart resumed what became one of the most distinguished acting careers in film history. He also remained in the U.S. Air Force Reserve, becoming a brigadier general in 1959.

David T. Zabecki

Additional Reading
"*Life* Comes Home with Jimmy Stewart," *LIFE,* 24 September 1945, pp. 126–128.

Stimson, Henry Lewis (1867–1950)

U.S. secretary of war. Stimson was a Republican of patrician upbringing and lifestyle, and a lawyer by training and occupation. He served as a colonel in the artillery during World War I. He held high office in two Republican administrations, as secretary of war (1911–1913) under President William Howard Taft, and secretary of state (1929–1933) under President Herbert C. Hoover, before being appointed secretary of war by Democratic President Franklin D. Roosevelt (q.v.) (FDR) in June 1940.

In the early twentieth century, Stimson was associated with a group of American expansionists led by President Theodore Roosevelt, who believed it was the right and destiny of the United States to become a dominant world power. He was loyal to those views, even in the isolationist 1920s and 1930s. He spoke out as a lone voice in favor of American action to check the rise of the Axis powers after 1937. This was one of the main reasons FDR wanted him in his cabinet in the summer of 1940, a time when the international situation was deteriorating sharply.

Stimson became an effective administrator of the War Department. He earned respect and loyalty from those who worked for him, and established good relations with the press and Congress. This was necessary for the promotion of the various war preparations measures he deemed essential to the national security of the United States. The most important of these, the passing of an unprecedented peacetime draft law by Congress on 14 September 1940, was a great personal triumph for him. He was almost alone in the Roosevelt administration in pushing for it, although toward the end of the lobbying campaign, he did obtain some useful support from FDR. Without this measure, the United States would have taken far longer to mobilize when war came than was the case, and the defeat of the Axis powers inevitably would have been delayed.

After the United States declared war on Germany and Japan in December 1941, Stimson found himself increasingly excluded from major policy decisions regarding the war effort. In part this was because Roosevelt, as commander in chief of the armed forces, preferred to deal with the army chief of staff, General George C. Marshall (q.v.), directly, instead of through the secretary of war, as was the normal practice. Another cause of Stimson's exclusion was he was too aristocratic to have much of a political base, although that probably contributed to Roosevelt's appointment of him in the first place.

Despite his lack of influence, Stimson did not resign, and he continued to serve the United States government loyally and capably, as befitted his character and principles. Never afraid to speak his mind, the crusty war secretary was one of the few in the administration who could tell Roosevelt exactly what he thought. On one occasion, Stimson put the phone down on FDR when the latter was in the midst of a particularly tedious and frivolous monologue on foreign policy.

David Walker

Additional Reading
Hodgson, Godfrey, *The Colonel: The Life and Wars of Henry Stimson, 1867–1950* (1990).
Stimson, Henry L., and McGeorge Bundy, *On Active Service in Peace and War* (1947).

Stirling, Archibald David (1915–1990)

British colonel, founder of the Special Air Service (SAS) (q.v.). The son of a brigadier general in the Scots Guards, Sir David Stirling was born in 1915 and educated at Cambridge University. When World War II broke out, he was training in the Rockies for an attempt on Mount Everest. After a short spell in his father's regiment, Stirling transferred to Number 3 Commando in the Middle East. It was there, with the approval of General Claude Auchinleck (q.v.), that Stirling recruited and trained sixty-six men for parachute raids on the German airfields in Libya. This team was known as L Detachment, Special Air Service Brigade (although there were no other detachments). It marks the beginning of the famous SAS. Their first attack was defeated by high winds and sandstorms, and only twenty-two of the sixty-six survived.

With the assistance of the Long-Range Desert Group (q.v.), Stirling switched from parachutes to specially equipped vehicles as the mode of transport. The basic SAS tactic was to cover the final miles on foot, raid the objective, and then withdraw deeper into enemy territory, rather than back toward British lines. In the eighteen remaining months of the desert campaign, the SAS destroyed some 350 aircraft, mined roads, derailed trains, blew up ammunition and fuel dumps, and killed many times their own number. Their most spectacular feat was a jeep-borne raid on Sidi Haneish airfield near Benghazi, in which forty German aircraft were destroyed, including many of the latest Bf-109Fs.

The Germans were forced to divert units from frontline duty to guard their rear areas. With grudging admiration, they accorded Stirling the nickname, "The Phantom Major." He finally was captured in Tunisia (q.v.). Although he escaped five times, his six-foot, five-inch frame always gave him away, and he was recaptured. He ended the war in Colditz (q.v.). The SAS—"his" regiment—continued to harass the Germans for the rest of the war. Today, it is recognized as one of the world's leading counterinsurgency forces, with spectacular successes in Malaya, Oman, and the Falklands to its credit.

After the war, Stirling played a leading role in promoting racial harmony in Africa, and helped set up an organization dedicated to frustrating terrorism. He was typical of a breed of British officers who excelled at irregular warfare. He was awarded the DSO for his wartime exploits, and knighted shortly before his death in 1990.

Philip Green

Additional Reading

James, Malcomb, *Born of the Desert* (1991).
Young, Peter, *Storm from the Sea* (1958).

Stratton, Dorothy C. (1899–)

American Coast Guard captain, director of the SPARS. In 1942, while she was the dean of women at Purdue University, Stratton took a leave of absence to join the U.S. Navy's WAVES (q.v.). In November 1942, when the U.S. Coast Guard formed its women reserves, known as the SPARS, she resigned from the navy to become director of the SPARS with the rank of lieutenant commander. In 1946, Stratton left the SPARS with the rank of captain and returned to Purdue. A first for the U.S. Coast Guard, as a result of Captain Stratton's insistence, was that, from the beginning, all officers, whether male or female, trained together. Maximum strength of the SPARS during the war was 8,300 officers and enlisted.

Charles H. Bogart

Additional Reading

Banning, M., *Women for Defense* (1942).
Mason, John T. (ed.), *The Atlantic War Remembered* (1990).

Strauss, Franz Josef (1915–1988)

First defense minister of postwar West Germany. Strauss grew up in a Bavarian Catholic family. He was a brilliant student who never accepted Nazi ideology. As an artilleryman, Strauss participated in the 1940 campaign in France, and then joined the Sixth Army on its way to Stalingrad (q.v.). Commissioned as a second lieutenant, he repeatedly managed to change commands in order to save the lives of his troops. He suffered severe frostbite on his feet in 1942, was sent home, and became instructor at an air defense school.

During his impressive postwar political career, Strauss was a federal cabinet minister several times, and prime minister of Bavaria for ten years. Perhaps his greatest contribution came as the nation's first defense minister in 1956, and the formation of the West German *Bundeswehr*. He was primarily responsible for instilling the new German military with the very democratic principles that were alien to the old German military.

Wolfgang Terhörst

Additional Reading

Scharnagl, Wilfried, *Bayern und Strauss: Lebenswerk und Abschied* (1989).

Streeter, Ruth Cheney (1895–1990)

U.S. Marine Corps colonel, director of the U.S. Marine Corps Women's Reserve. In 1940, Streeter bought an airplane, began to learn to fly, and joined the Civil Air Patrol (q.v.) in an effort to promote war preparedness. In August 1943, with the formation of the U.S. Marine Corps Women Reserves (USMC-WR), she was named director of the WR with the rank of major. In November 1943, she was promoted to lieutenant colonel and in 1945, to colonel. Under her direction the USMC-WR grew to a peak strength of 19,000 officers and enlisted marines. That freed enough men to form the 6th Marine Division. The USMC-WR were employed in the United States in all types of noncombat assignments. Streeter retired from the Marine Corps in December 1945.

Charles H. Bogart

Additional Reading

Stremlow, Mary V., *A History of the Women Marines, 1946–1977* (1986).

Streicher, Julius (1885–1946)

German publisher of the anti-Semitic newspaper *Der Stürmer, Gauleiter* of Franconia. Streicher led the Jew baiters in Germany through his newspaper *Der Stürmer.* An elementary school teacher, he received an Iron Cross First Class for his actions in World War I. In 1919, he founded the anti-Semitic *Deutsche-Soziale Partei,* which merged with the NSDAP in 1921. He became a personal friend of Adolf Hitler (q.v.). In 1925, Streicher was appointed *Gauleiter* (District Leader of the Nazi Party) for Franconia with headquarters in Nuremberg. His attacks on the Weimar (q.v.) government led to his dismissal from his teaching post in 1928, but in 1929 he was elected to the Bavarian legislature as a Nazi delegate.

Streicher's political influence centered on his newspaper *Der Stürmer,* which he founded in 1923. The paper became the best-known anti-Semitic publication in the world, reaching millions of Germans with its coarse style and lurid pictures, aimed at goading the population into action against the Jews.

The paper's impact was helped by a system of display cases in public places throughout the country. *Der Stürmer* led the campaign for the Nuremberg Laws (q.v.) of 1935. Hitler claimed it was the only paper he read entirely, and he seemed attracted by Streicher's crudeness and vulgarity, often protecting him from enemies within the Nazi Party.

In 1933, Hitler made Streicher director of the Central Committee for the Defense Against Jewish Atrocity and Boycott Propaganda. Streicher became a member of the *Reichstag* in 1933 and in 1934 was promoted to *SA-Gruppenführer.* With *Der Stürmer's* circulation as high as 500,000 in 1937, he received an ample income, supplemented by other newspapers and expropriated Jewish property.

Streicher made many enemies within the party, who despised his wealth and lewd style. After he alleged that Hermann Göring (q.v.) was impotent and that his daughter was conceived through artificial insemination, Göring had Streicher's businesses and personal life examined, leading to his removal from all party posts—although Streicher was allowed to continue publishing *Der Stürmer.*

Streicher was captured by the Allies at the end of the war and put on trial. The International Military Tribunal (q.v.) found him guilty of incitement to murder of the Jews, and he was sentenced to die. Loyal to Hitler and his anti-Semitic beliefs to the end, Streicher was hanged on 16 October 1946.

Laura Matysek Wood

Additional Reading

Bytwerk, Randall L., *Julius Streicher* (1983).
Lunau, Heinz, *The Germans on Trial* (1948).
Varga, William, *The Number One Nazi Jew Baiter* (1981).

Stresemann, Gustav (1878–1929)

Foreign minister of Weimar Germany. During the French occupation of the Ruhr (q.v.) and the hyperinflation of 1923, Stresemann emerged as Germany's most prominent leader. As foreign minister for the next six years, he pursued a policy of fulfillment that met Germany's obligations under the Versailles Treaty (q.v.) and gained its concessions. The Dawes Plan of 1924 provided Germany with foreign loans and rescheduled reparation payments.

As a consequence of the 1925 Locarno Pact (q.v.), Germany gained admission to the League of Nations (q.v.), and Stresemann shared the 1926 Nobel Peace Prize with French Foreign Minister Aristide Briand. In 1927, Stresemann obtained the abolition of the Inter-Allied Military Control Commission. Shortly before his death on 3 October 1929, he won acceptance of the Young Plan (q.v.) and the evacuation of the Rhineland (q.v.) five years ahead of schedule. Although some historians have questioned his sincerity, Stresemann used only peaceful means to achieve German interests. Unfortunately, his achievements left Adolf Hitler (q.v.) in a better position to launch Germany along the path of conquest.

Justin D. Murphy

Additional Reading

Eyck, Erich, *A History of the Weimar Republic,* 2 vols. (1970).

Sontag, Raymond J., *A Broken World, 1919–1939* (1971).

Stresemann, Gustav, *His Diaries, Letters, and Papers,* 3 vols. (1935–1940).

Stroop, Jürgen (1895–1951)

German SS general. Stroop joined the SS (q.v.) in 1934, and by 1939 was an *SS-Brigadeführer.* Considered by many in the Nazi leadership as an expert in the pacification of civilians, he was given the assignment in April 1943 of putting down the Jewish uprising in the Warsaw Ghetto (q.v.). With 2,000 men, Stroop planned to remove the 56,000 Jews in three days. The task took almost three weeks. Thousands of Jews were killed or sent to Treblinka and Lublin. Stroop was later appointed higher SS and police leader in Greece. He was tried by the Americans after the war for killing U.S. aviators in Greece. He was extradited to Poland where he was retried and hanged in Warsaw in 1951.

Steven B. Rogers

Additional Reading

Moczarski, Kazimierz, *Conversations with an Executioner* (1981).

Stroop, Jürgen, *The Stroop Report* (1979).

Strydonck de Burkel, Viktor van (1876–1961)

Belgian lieutenant general, commander in chief of the Belgian army-in-exile. Van Strydonck de Burkel was commander of the I Military District (Brussels) during the 1940 Belgium and Flanders (q.v.) campaign. From 1940 to 1944, he was commander of the Belgian army-in-exile. Its main operational force was a brigade-sized unit that fought in northwest Europe. On the liberation of Belgium, he was appointed chief of the Belgian Military Mission to SHAEF (q.v.).

Andrzej Suchcitz

Additional Reading

Motz, Roger, *Belgium Unvanquished* (1942).

Rigby, Françoise, *In Defiance* (1960).

Student, Kurt (1890–1978)

German colonel general, airborne commander, commander of Army Group H. Born in Neumark, Brandenburg, in Prussia to a family of the minor nobility, Kurt Student was commissioned in the *Yorkschen Jäger* Regiment in 1911. He underwent pilot training in 1913, and during World War I, he commanded *Jagdstaffel* (Fighter Squadron) 9 in France. In 1917 he was wounded in air-to-air combat.

Immediately after the war Student was assigned to the *Reichswehr*'s illegal aviation organization, the *Fliegerzentrale,* and secretly trained in the Soviet Union. With the German preparations for open rearmament in 1933, Lieutenant Colonel Student was selected as director of the air ministry's technical schools. In early 1938 as a major general, Student took command of the *Luftwaffe*'s newly formed 7th *Fliegerdivision* (Air Division—paratroopers and glider-borne infantry). He also became inspector of airborne forces.

One battalion of Student's paratroopers participated in the invasions of Denmark and Norway (qq.v.). The paratroopers' most notable successes came during the attacks on Belgium, when another battalion captured several bridges over the Albert Canal and took the Belgian fortress of Eben Emael (q.v.) at low cost. In the German conquest of Holland, Student was again wounded and subsequently promoted to lieutenant general.

Student turned his attention to possible airborne operations against Gibraltar and Malta in 1941; but it was on the island of Crete (q.v.), in Operation *MERKUR,* that his troops met their most severe test of the war. Landing on 20 May 1941, *Fliegerdivision* 7 succeeded in capturing the island in two weeks, but at a cost too prohibitive of its highly trained and specialized troops. Nonetheless, Student received the Knight's Cross of the Iron Cross. At the same time, however, Adolf Hitler (q.v.) prohibited further large-scale airborne operations, only allowing the use of paratroopers for Otto Skorzeny's (q.v.) rescue of Benito Mussolini (q.v.) from the Gran Sasso (q.v.) in 1943.

The remainder of the war saw German paratroopers fighting as high-quality infantry, although Student expanded the airborne branch to more than 160,000 troops. A creative officer, albeit one prone to single-minded persistence in pursuit of his objectives, regardless of the cost, Student commanded the German First Parachute Army in the defense of Holland against Allied paratroopers in 1944. His envy of Allied airborne capabilities in Operation MARKET-GARDEN was quite clear and ironic in view of his own successes earlier in

Colonel General Kurt Student. (IWM MH 6100)

the war. Student finished World War II as commander of Army Group H. He was charged and convicted of war crimes, although his sentence was not confirmed and he served no time in prison. He died in the West German town of Lemgo in 1978.

Randy Papadopoulos

Additional Reading
Barnett, Correlli, *Hitler's Generals* (1989).
Farrar-Hockley, A.H., *Student* (1973).

Stülpnagel, Karl Heinrich von (1886–1944)

German general, military governor of France, conspirator against Adolf Hitler. Von Stülpnagel, born in Darmstadt, was a professional soldier of the old school. Although he disapproved of the Nazi regime, he held the post of quartermaster general on the German General Staff (q.v.) from November 1938 to June 1940. He next commanded the Seventeenth Army in Russia until October 1941; but his most significant role was as military governor of France, beginning in March 1942. During his

tenure, more than 29,000 French hostages were executed in an attempt to deter further civilian resistance.

Stülpnagel feared a successful Allied invasion of France and joined the anti-Hitler conspiracy. During the July 1944 assassination attempt on Hitler, he effected the only successful overthrow of Nazi power with the arrest of all 1,200 SS and SD (qq.v.) personnel in Paris. Upon discovering the assassination had not occurred, he ignored warnings that he should go into hiding and left by car to drive to Berlin. He stopped at Verdun, where he had commanded troops in World War I, and shot himself. Only blinded by the suicide attempt, he was taken to Berlin, where he went before the People's Court. He was tortured and hanged in Ploetzensee prison on 30 August.

Robert F. Pace

Additional Reading
Rothfels, Hans, *The German Opposition to Hitler: An Appraisal* (1948).
Taylor, Telford, *Sword and Swastika: Generals and Nazis in the Third Reich* (1952).

Świrski, Jerzy (1882–1959)

Polish vice admiral, commander in chief of the Polish Navy. Świrski was commander in chief of the Polish Navy from 1925 to 1947. On his initiative, three destroyers left for Britain before the outbreak of the war, thus forming the nucleus of the Polish navy-in-exile. During the war, the Polish Navy under his command sank 100,000 tons of enemy shipping and took part in the battles of Norway, the Atlantic, the Mediterranean, the D-Day landings, the sinking of the *Bismarck* (qq.v.), and the Murmansk convoys.

Andrzej Suchcitz

Additional Reading
Garliński, Józef, *Poland in the Second World War* (1985).
Peszke, Michael A., *The Polish Navy in the Second World War* (1989).

Szabo, Violette (1921–1945)

British SOE agent. The daughter of an English father and a French mother, Violette Bushell met and married a Free French officer named Szabo in London in 1941. She joined SOE as a French language expert in 1943, and was trained in espionage and parachute jumping. Code named "CORINNE," from her cover name, Corinne Reine Leroy, she flew

SOE Agent Violette Szabo, GC. (IWM HU 16541)

into France in April 1944 on a scouting mission for D-Day and came out in early June. On 7 June 1944, she returned to France, parachuting into the

Limoges region. She was wounded in a shoot-out with SS troops, taken to Paris *Gestapo* (q.v.) headquarters, and then sent to the Ravensbrück concentration camp. She was shot at Ravensbrück in January 1945. Posthumously awarded the George Cross, she was immortalized in the film and book, *Carve Her Name with Pride.*

Stephen L. Frost

Additional Reading
Minney, Rubeigh J., *Carve Her Name with Pride* (1956).

Szylling, Antoni (1884–1971)

Polish lieutenant general, commander of Army Krakow in the Polish campaign. Szylling commanded Army Krakow, the pivot of the Polish operational plan in 1939. Defending Polish Silesia, he thrice extricated his army from German pincers, preventing its destruction. He successively withdrew to the rivers Nida, Dunajec, and San, keeping the pincers open. He spent the remainder of the war as a POW in Germany.

Andrzej Suchcitz

Additional Reading
Garliński, Józef, *Poland in the Second World War* (1985).
Zaloga, Steven, and Victor Madej, *The Polish Campaign 1939* (1985).

T

Tank, Kurt (1898–1985)

Chief engineer and test pilot for Focke-Wulf. After working for the Rohrbach engine plant from 1924 to 1930, Tank moved to the famous aircraft manufactory called Focke-Wulf, where he was responsible for all their designs throughout the war. They included the FW-58 twin-engine transport, the FW-200 *Kondor* (originally an airliner but adapted to maritime bombing and reconnaissance duties), the FW-190 fighter/bomber/interceptor family and its high-performance variant, the TA-312, and the TA-152 high altitude fighter. After the war, Tank designed aircraft in India and Argentina.

John D. Beatty

Additional Reading

Killen, John, *A History of the Luftwaffe* (1968).
Schliephake, Hanfried, *The Birth of the Luftwaffe* (1971).

Taylor, Maxwell D. (1901–1987)

U.S. Army lieutenant general Taylor set his course early in life when, at the age of five, he declared his intent to go to the U.S. Military Academy at West Point. He held to his goal and became one of the most respected officers of his generation. During the years after his graduation from West Point in 1922, advancement was slow. By 1941, he was a major in command of an artillery battalion, when he was sent to Washington to serve on the general staff. Subsequent advancement came rapidly, and by 1942, Taylor became brigadier general and assumed command of divisional artillery in the 82nd Airborne Division.

The 82nd Airborne participated in actions in Sicily (q.v.) and Italy. In 1943, Taylor volunteered for a mission behind enemy lines to reach an ac-

cord with dissident Italian officers and to receive their terms for surrender. Following that dangerous mission, he assumed command of the 101st Airborne Division. The 101st Airborne parachuted into Normandy (q.v.) on D-Day, with Taylor becoming the first U.S. general to reach French soil during the war. In 1944, Taylor was still in command of the 101st Airborne when it jumped during Operation MARKET-GARDEN. He was wounded slightly during that action.

The 101st Airborne was sent to the Ardennes in late 1944, and Taylor was called to Washington for a special conference. Thus he was not present during the division's heroic stand at Bastogne (q.v.) during the Ardennes offensive (q.v.). Afterward, he resumed direct command and led the 101st Airborne throughout the remainder of World War II.

In 1945, Taylor was appointed superintendent of West Point. There he altered the curriculum to reflect his belief that military leaders should be mentally as well as physically fit. He placed more emphasis on liberal arts, and while still demanding fitness, lessened the focus on sports competitions.

Taylor served as chief of staff of the U.S. Army from 1955 to 1959. During this assignment, he championed the concept of limited response, but his ideas were not widely accepted within the Eisenhower administration. Taylor retired in 1959. In 1961, he became presidential advisor to John F. Kennedy. In October 1962, President Kennedy recalled Taylor to active duty and appointed him chairman of the Joint Chiefs of Staff. After retiring a second time in 1964, Taylor served as U.S. ambassador to the Republic of Vietnam. He resigned in mid-1965.

Thomas Cagley

Additional Reading

Kinnard, Douglas, *The Certain Trumpet: Maxwell Taylor and the American Experience in Vietnam* (1991).

Marshall, S.L.A., *Night Drop: The American Airborne Invasion of Normandy* (1962).

Ryan, Cornelius, *A Bridge Too Far* (1974).

Taylor, John M., *General Maxwell Taylor: The Sword and the Pen* (1991).

Taylor, Telford (1908–1998)

U.S. prosecutor at Nuremberg. Taylor was a lawyer, writer, and officer in the U.S. Army Intelligence Service in World War II. He directed the American processing of information from Bletchley Park (q.v.), the British ULTRA (q.v.) exploitation center.

After the war, Taylor was U.S. counsel for the prosecution at the Nuremberg trials (*see* International Military Tribunal). He supervised the compilation of OSS studies on war crimes and was responsible for war crimes and crimes against humanity in the east. He prepared a plan to bring more than 200 more Nazi leaders to trial before other tribunals at various locations in Germany.

On 17 October 1946, the day after the execution of top Nazi leaders, President Harry S Truman (q.v.) appointed him to succeed Justice Robert Jackson (q.v.) as chief U.S. counsel. Taylor later taught at Harvard and Yale Law Schools and wrote several books, including *Nuremberg and Vietnam: An American Tragedy.*

Paul J. Rose

Additional Reading

Maser, Werner, *Nuremberg: A Nation on Trial* (1979).

Taylor, Telford, *Sword & Swastika; Generals and Nazis in the Third Reich* (1952).

———. *War Crimes and International Law* (1949).

Tedder, Arthur (1890–1967)

British air chief marshal, Allied deputy supreme commander for Operation OVERLORD. Unquestionably the force behind the theory and organization of British airpower during World War II, Sir Arthur Tedder was the acknowledged head of Allied air forces for Operation OVERLORD. Tedder was born at Glenguin in Scotland on 11 July 1890, the son of a civil servant. He was educated in London when his family moved there and he graduated from Magdalene College, Cambridge. His military career began unspectacularly in Fiji, and he joined the Royal Flying Corps (RFC) in 1916. During World War I, he flew bombing and reconnaissance missions in France, where his abilities caught the eye of Hugh Trenchard (q.v.), then a major general in the RFC. Tedder later served in Egypt, and by the end of the war, became a training expert.

Between the wars, Tedder increased his reputation for training, serving in the air ministry and as an instructor at the Royal Air Force Staff College from 1929 to 1931. He served in the Far East from 1936 to 1938, when he returned to the air ministry as director of research and development. From this vantage, he was now in a position to influence the future of British airpower and its role in the impending global conflict. This included developments in bombers, radar, navigation, and weaponry.

Tedder moved to the Middle East soon after war began, and in June 1941, he was named commander in chief of the Middle East Air Force. As a result of the loss of Tobruk (q.v.), Winston S. Churchill (q.v.) attempted to remove Tedder, but he backed down when chief of air staff Charles Portal (q.v.) intervened.

Tedder's strategy was to provide his squadrons with technical support, a continuing attack on Axis supply lines through the Mediterranean, and air support of the ground forces. All this time, he staunchly opposed both army and navy attempts to incorporate air forces. His steadfast tactics proved significant to British strategy and the decisive victory at El Alamein (q.v.) in November 1942. In February 1943, Tedder was named commander in chief of the Mediterranean Allied Air Forces under Allied supreme commander Dwight D. Eisenhower (q.v.). The Axis surrender in Tunisia (q.v.) in May 1943 brought recognition of Tedder's skills from his earlier critic, Churchill.

Tedder's style of command was an admirable combination of composure and diplomatic presence. He parlayed these qualities into a system of effective coordination with Britain's allies. When planning for the invasion of Normandy (q.v.) reached the critical stage, he returned to London with Eisenhower, where he was named deputy supreme commander, enjoying the confidence of both Churchill, Portal, and Eisenhower.

Tedder's subtle skills of command and diplomacy were instrumental in Operation OVERLORD. His air strategy was to isolate enemy land forces with major bombing offensives, labeled the "Tedder Carpet." A staunch advocate of airpower, Tedder continued to plan and implement air attacks on German forces in France and Germany as the war in Europe ground to its destructive end. It was in large part due to Tedder's insistence that bombing continued through 1944 and into the early campaigns of 1945.

In May 1945, Tedder was in Berlin to sign a surrender agreement, after which he briefly assumed a planning role in the campaign against Japan. He returned home to a promotion to marshal of the Royal Air Force in September. He was later appointed chief of the air staff in January of 1946 where he was also knighted.

The immediate postwar period found Tedder in administrative command positions. He published *Air Power in War* in 1948, and went to Washington to represent the British in the formation of the North Atlantic Treaty Organization (NATO). He retired from the service in 1951, and worked at Cambridge University and the British Broadcasting Corporation (BBC). From 1954 to 1960, he was chairman of the Standard Motor Company. He published his memoirs *With Prejudice* in 1966. He died the following year.

Tedder joined the British air forces during the infant stages of the service and was responsible for World War II strategy in North Africa, and later France and Germany. An expert in training, organization, and diplomacy, he was a key player in the success of British airpower and the defeat of Germany.

Boyd Childress

Additional Reading
Morgan, Frederick E., *COSSAC'S Memoirs: Overture to Overlord* (1951).
Tedder, Arthur, *Air Power in War* (1948).
———, *With Prejudice: The War Memoirs of Marshal of the Royal Air Force Lord Tedder* (1966).
Weigley, Russell F., *Eisenhower's Lieutenants: The Campaigns of France and Germany, 1944–45* (1981).

Templer, Gerald (1898–1979)
British lieutenant general, commander of British 6th Armoured Division. Although belonging to a generation of British officers who saw extensive frontline duty in 1914–1918 and then held senior posts in 1939–1945, Sir Gerald Templer's fame rests mainly on his Cold War achievements in Malaya. Born in Britain in 1898 and educated at Wellington and Sandhurst, Templer served with the Royal Irish Fusiliers in France in World War I. Between the wars, he served in Iran, Iraq, Egypt, and Palestine, where he won the DSO during the

1936 Arab rebellion, an exceptionally high award for a company commander in a minor campaign.

Templer returned to France in 1939, this time on the intelligence staff of the British Expeditionary Force (BEF). Evacuated through Dunkirk (q.v.), he held a series of staff appointments in Britain, reaching the rank of lieutenant general by 1943. In that year, he reverted to major general at his own request in order to obtain a combat assignment. He commanded first the 56th Division in North Africa, and then the 6th Armoured Division in Italy, including a hectic period on the Anzio (q.v.) beachhead. His combat service ended when he was severely wounded by a mine in 1944.

After his recovery, Templer became the director of civil affairs and military government in the British occupation zone of Germany. In that capacity, he dismissed Konrad Adenauer (q.v.), then the Mayor of Cologne and later chancellor of West Germany, for paying too much attention to politics and not enough to the living conditions of the population. Adenauer appears to have borne no grudge, for in later years he often visited Templer whenever he was in London.

From 1952 to 1954, Templer was both high commissioner and commander in chief in Malaya. In this dual role, he was responsible for all civilian and military matters. By a combination of ruthless military action and a "hearts and minds" political campaign, he broke the back of the rebellion and set Malaya on the road to independence. He finished his career as chief of the Imperial General Staff from 1955 to 1958.

Philip Green

Additional Reading
Clutterbuck, Richard, *The Long War: The Emergency in Malaya 1948–1960* (1967).

Terboven, Josef (1898–1945)
German commissioner for Norway. Terboven served in World War I, finishing the war with the rank of lieutenant. After the war, he returned to school to complete his study of economics and to become a banking accountant. In Munich, he joined the fledgling Nazi Party in 1923 and participated in the Beer Hall *Putsch* (q.v.). Later in Essen, he organized the local SA (q.v.) and became the party *Gauleiter* in 1928. In February 1935, after the Nazis were in power, Adolf Hitler (q.v.) appointed Terboven president of the Rhein province. In September 1939, he became *Reich* defense commissioner of Military District VI.

On 24 April 1940, Terboven became

Reichskommissar for Norway. In this position, he was the head of the German occupation government. Under his control, the Norwegian economy was subordinated exclusively to German interests. He promoted collaboration among the Norwegians, but at the same time, he held down Vidkun Quisling (q.v.). Terboven suppressed any kind of opposition and planned for the integration of Norway into the "Greater German *Reich*." On 11 May 1945, after the German surrender, Terboven committed suicide in Oslo.

Franz Seidler

Additional Reading

Ash, Bernard, *Norway 1940* (1964).
Johnson, Amanda, *Norway—Her Invasion and Occupation* (1948).

Thoma, Wilhelm von (1892–1948)

German general, commander of the *Afrika Korps.* Von Thoma was a leading German expert on armored warfare. As a major, he commanded the first German tanks in the Spanish civil war (q.v.). In September 1940, von Thoma took command of the elite 3rd *Panzer* Division. On 24 October 1942, General Georg Stumme, temporary commander of the German and Italian troops in Africa, died of a heart attack at El Alamein (q.v.) and command of the *Afrika Korps* (q.v.) fell to von Thoma. Adolf Hitler (q.v.) ordered Erwin Rommel (q.v.), who was in Germany on sick leave, to return to El Alamein. On Rommel's arrival he chastised von Thoma for not shelling the British. On 2 November, British General Bernard L. Montgomery (q.v.) began his all-out offensive against German positions. Von Thoma was slightly injured in an artillery attack on his headquarters. He reported that only thirty-five tanks remained, and Rommel decided to withdraw.

Hitler countermanded this and ordered the troops to remain in place and fight to the death if necessary. With his few remaining tanks, von Thoma fought throughout the evening of 3 November. The next day, lamenting that Hitler's order was "absolute madness," von Thoma donned a clean uniform, put on his medals, and drove his tank into the middle of the battle. He was taken prisoner standing at attention by his burning tank. That evening, he dined with Montgomery, but declined to discuss German strategy. Rommel, however, believed von Thoma had turned traitor, commenting that he never did like him. Von Thoma died as a prisoner of war in 1948.

Robert F. Pace

Additional Reading

Hamilton, Nigel, *Monty: The Making of a General, 1887–1942* (1981).
Lewin, Ronald, *Rommel As a Military Commander* (1968).

Thyssen, Fritz (1873–1951)

German industrialist. Thyssen was an early Nazi Party member and industrialist who, like the Krupps (q.v.), initially backed Adolf Hitler (q.v.) and the Nazis in their rise to power, and convinced several other industrialists to do the same. Thyssen became virtual economic dictator of the heavy industrial heartland of Germany in the Ruhr River valley while maintaining his control of a major Krupp competitor in steel production. Like Gustav Krupp, Thyssen became disillusioned with the Nazis and their draconian policies, and frightened when he discovered they were not about to be controlled by their industrial backers. But unlike most other industrialists, he spoke his mind about it.

By 1939, Thyssen was forced to flee to Switzerland. Enticed back to Germany by promises of power and no arrest, he was imprisoned by the Nazis in 1941, where he spent the rest of the war. Tried by a German de-Nazification court in 1948, he was declared a minor Nazi for his pre-1939 activities and fined.

John D. Beatty

Additional Reading

Homze, Edward I., *Foreign Labor in Germany* (1967).
Prittle, Terence, *Germans Against Hitler* (1964).

Tillich, Paul (1886–1965)

German theologian and socialist leader. Tillich was one of the most influential theologians of the twentieth century. After becoming a Lutheran minister and serving with distinction in World War I, he devoted his life to teaching and writing theology and philosophy at numerous German universities in the 1920s. He became a staunch opponent of the Nazis, and in May 1933 "won the honor," as he put it, of being the first non-Jewish faculty member to be dismissed for being "politically unreliable." Shortly after, he emigrated to the United States, where he continued his teaching career.

Tillich drew the wrath of the Nazis by his association with the Social Democratic Party (SPD), his editing of the *Neue Blätter für den*

Sozialismus, and his book, *The Socialist Decision.* He found Hitler uncivilized and dangerous and, he cautioned, "Should political romanticism and war-like nationalism become victorious, the self-destruction of the European peoples is assured. The task of rescuing European society from a return to barbarism is given into the hands of Socialism." Tillich opposed both Communism and Nazism as romantic panaceas, and he blamed capitalism as the source of all social ills. He was one of the few Protestant theologians who chose to disavow himself from Nazism rather than trying to seek accommodation.

Glenn R. Sharfman

Additional Reading
Pauck, Marion, and Wilhelm Pauck, *Paul Tillich: His Life and Thought* (1976).

Timoshenko, Semen Konstantinovich (1895–1970)

Marshal of the Soviet Union, commander of the Soviet Western and Southwestern Fronts (army groups). Timoshenko grew up in peasant surroundings and was drafted into the tsar's army in 1915. He served in World War I as a machine gunner in the enlisted ranks. In 1918, he joined the Red Army and participated in actions against the White Guards in the Crimea. During these campaigns, he served with Josef Stalin, Semyon Budenny, and Georgy Zhukov (qq.v.). Those early connections helped Timoshenko in the future, particularly during the military purges (q.v.) of the 1930s. He attended various advanced cavalry courses in the 1920s and the Lenin Military Political Academy in 1930. He spent the decade before World War II as a troop commander in various military districts.

Of all the Soviet commanders of World War II, Timoshenko had one of the least successful records. Yet he not only survived, he went on to hold distinguished positions after the war. Prior the start of World War II, he was the commissar of defense and chairman of the *Stavka* (q.v.). As commander of the Western Front in 1941, he would not give permission for the commanders being attacked by the Germans to return fire. When the German attack along a 420-kilometer front centered on Smolensk (q.v.), he sent eleven armies against the enemy, costing the Soviets 300,000 prisoners. Actually, he had wanted to break off the counterattack, but Stalin refused. Timoshenko did, however, manage to get 500,000 soldiers disengaged and into defensive positions around Moscow.

In September 1941, Timoshenko was transferred to the command of the Southwestern Front, where he failed to prevent the German breakthrough to the Crimea (q.v.). In May 1942, he mounted an offensive at Kharkov (q.v.), where his units collapsed after five days of intense fighting. Soviet losses amounted to two armies, and another 240,000 prisoners. For the remainder of the war, he served in lesser assignments on a variety of fronts. Variously, he coordinated operations for the Leningrad, Northern Caucasus, 2nd and 3rd Baltic, and the 2nd, 3rd, and 4th Ukrainian Fronts.

Following the war, Timoshenko commanded troops in several military districts. From 1961 until his death in 1970, he was chairman of the Soviet Committee for War Veterans.

Thomas Cagley

Additional Reading
Bialer, Seweryn (ed.), *Stalin and His Generals* (1984).
Guillaume, Augustin L., *Soviet Arms and Soviet Power* (1949).
Shukman, Harold (ed.), *Stalin's Generals* (1993).

Tiso, Josef (1887–1947)

President of the German-controlled Republic of Slovakia (q.v.). Tiso was a Slovak Catholic priest who was active in nationalistic politics. In 1938, he became the chairman of the Slovak People's Party. From October 1938 to March 1939, he was premier of Slovakia in the federal Czecho-Slovakia. He was removed from office by the federal government in Prague, but he was reinstated the same month when Slovakia became "independent" under German domination.

Under Tiso, Slovakia participated alongside Germany in the 1939 invasion of Poland, and the 1941 invasion of the Soviet Union. Tiso was elected president of the republic in October 1939. He retained that post until 1945 when Slovakian statehood ended. After the war, Tiso was tried and executed by Czechoslovak authorities.

Andrzej Suchcitz

Additional Reading
Lettrich, Josef, *History of Modern Slovakia* (1955).
Mastny, Vojtech, *The Czechs Under Nazi Rule* (1971).

Tito (born Broz, Josip) (1892–1980)

Leader of the Communist resistance forces in occupied Yugoslavia. In the second half of World War II, Tito became world famous as the leader of the Yugoslav partisans, the largest resistance movement in occupied Europe. He is equally famous for his postwar defiance of Josef Stalin (q.v.). Yet before 1939, he was unknown outside Yugoslavia, except to the staff of the Comintern (q.v.). Any assessment of his wartime role demands a study of his experiences in the first fifty years of his life, and these conveniently can be divided into three phases: his youth; World War I and the Russian Revolution; and the interwar period.

He was born Josip Broz in 1892 at Kumroveć, a remote village in Croatia, then part of the Austro-Hungarian Empire. He was the seventh of fifteen children of a peasant farmer. He adopted the *nom de guerre* Tito later in life for security reasons, and was known officially by this name during and after the war. One story holds that the name derives from the Serbo-Croatian phrase, "*ti to*," an imperative meaning "you, do this," but Tito always denied it. An extremely intelligent youth, he wanted to emigrate to America but could not afford the fare. Instead, at the age of fifteen, he was apprenticed to a mechanic. Once qualified, he plied his trade around central Europe—Trieste, Munich, Plzen, and Vienna—learning German and Czech and improving his technical skills. When he was conscripted in 1913, he worked as a test driver for Daimler.

Whether as a Croat Tito felt any loyalty toward the Austro-Hungarian Empire is doubtful, but he was intelligent, fit, skilled at his trade, and his travels matured him. He made an excellent soldier, and by the start of World War I, he was already a sergeant major commanding a platoon in his Croatian regiment. He soon was in action against the Russians in Carpathia, but on Easter Day 1915, he was severely wounded and captured. He appears to have been well-treated by the Russians, possibly because he was a fellow Slav. He learned Russian and on recovery, was put to work as a mechanic.

In the chaos of the 1917 revolution, Tito's POW status became meaningless. From the start, he sided with the revolutionaries and became an enthusiastic Bolshevik. He joined the Red Guard, fighting with them for three years around Omsk. This experience had a decisive effect on Tito, still only in his mid-twenties. He had seen, indeed, had played a part in, the triumph of the working class and the establishment of the Soviet state.

When he returned home after seven years, Tito acquired a definite purpose in life; he was henceforth a dedicated Communist, determined to spread the revolution to his own country as soon as possible. His own country was now Yugoslavia (literally the country of the South Slavs). A monarchy and one of the successor states to the Austro-Hungarian Empire, it was a confederation of Serbs, Croatians, Bosnians, and Slovenes, united more by hatred of past oppressors like Austria and Turkey than by any love for each other. Tito joined the Communist Party, but after an attempt on the Prince Regent's life, it was declared illegal and its Central Committee was forced to operate from Vienna. Between the wars, he rose steadily in the hierarchy, with several key episodes standing out.

In 1928, Tito was arrested and charged with membership in an illegal organization. He made no attempt to defend himself, but instead questioned the legality of the state and its court, and strongly asserted that the future lay with Communism. He spent six years in prison, but his outspoken stand won excellent publicity for both the party and himself. He then spent a year on the Comintern staff in Moscow. This gave him a wider world view of Communist activity that was to stand him in good stead in years to come. Returning clandestinely to Yugoslavia, he was responsible for the recruitment and dispatch of left-wing volunteers to the Spanish civil war (q.v.).

In 1937, Tito suddenly was summoned to Moscow. This being the height of Stalin's purges (q.v.), Tito had every reason to feel alarmed. He was promoted rather than purged, becoming, at the age of forty-five, secretary general of the Yugoslav Communist Party. His first step was to move its headquarters back from Vienna. "It is impossible," he wrote, "to expect a worker's democratic movement to succeed if its leaders are far from the scene of the struggle. . . . Moreover, life in exile causes men to decay, whatever their political talents." He replaced those who had decayed in exile with younger, more practical revolutionaries, and vigorously extended the party's networks into the more remote areas of the country.

Tito's formative years were now over. To his native intelligence and ruthlessness were added four years of battle, a dedication to the cause of Communism, twenty years of underground work, plus an inside knowledge of the Comintern. It is hard to imagine a better training for the trials to come.

Initially, Tito saw World War II as a conflict between two imperialist camps, and he hoped Yugoslavia could stay neutral. So too, for different reasons, did the legitimate government. Despite signing a treaty of friendship with the Axis, Yugoslavia was invaded in April 1941, and occupied within ten days. The royal government fled to London, and the country was split into three puppet states, Croatia, Serbia, and Montenegro, under German and Italian suzerainty.

Once Germany invaded the Soviet Union later that year, the war was transformed for Tito into one of national liberation and revolution. He now saw his chance of not merely evicting the Germans, but of building a new socialist Yugoslavia. Events in Yugoslavia in World War II, and in particular Tito's actions, can only be understood against that background. Further, it must be remembered that the conflict was three-sided: Germans and Italians; Tito's Communist partisans; and Yugoslavs loyal to the old royal government.

The royalist resistance, the Četniks (q.v.), was led by Colonel Draža Mihailović (q.v.), a regular officer. He was supported by Britain, which sent arms and liaison officers. Initially, Britain was not even aware of Tito's existence. At first, the two movements cooperated, particularly at the local level. The two leaders met twice, but were unable to agree on full cooperation. Their aims were too far apart, and moreover, Mihailović was a cautious man, concerned about German reprisals on civilians. By 1942, the two movements were fighting each other.

In October 1943, Tito set up a new government with himself as the head and commander in chief. He was officially recognized by Winston S. Churchill, Stalin, and Franklin D. Roosevelt (qq.v.) at Teheran (see Conferences, Allied). Henceforth, Tito received massive Allied (mainly British) logistic support, amounting to some 40,000 tons in eighteen months. Tito's movement grew from a collection of guerrilla bands into a full-scale army of 250,000 (eventually 800,000) men and women, albeit lightly equipped by World War II standards. Mihailović and his Četniks sat out the rest of the war, even on occasions joining the Italians and Germans in anti-Communist operations. (In fairness, it must be said that many British officers who fought with the Četniks claim this was usually in response to Communist provocations.)

The Yugoslav War of Liberation (q.v.) was fought with great cruelty and bitterness on both sides; casualties were heavy, discipline harsh, conditions even harsher. Tito spent most of the war in the field with his partisans. Whenever they were faced with defeat, the partisans moved to a new area, usually in the mountains. They pinned down some thirty Axis divisions that otherwise could have fought elsewhere.

As each area was liberated, Communist government was set up, and by the end of the war, Tito was in full control of Yugoslavia. He had, moreover, met with and been treated as a head of government by Churchill, and successfully insisted to Stalin that the Red Army seek his permission before entering Yugoslavia in pursuit of the Germans. Tito soon consolidated his grip. All internal political and religious enemies were ruthlessly eliminated. Ljubo Sirč, an ex-partisan who later became a professor at Glasgow University, estimated that 300,000 perished at this time. Milovan Djilas, one of Tito's closest associates, alleges that Tito only ordered the killings to stop because "no one fears death anymore."

In the autumn of 1945, single-party elections were held and Tito became president of the new republic, a position he held until his death. In the early postwar years, he was solidly in the Communist camp; at loggerheads with the West over Trieste, and giving active support to the Communist rebellion in Greece (q.v.). He soon came to realize, however, that the Soviet Union had no interest in helping Yugoslavia develop into a self-contained industrial state, but regarded it as a raw-material-producing colony. This was not what he and his partisans had fought to achieve for four bitter years. Relations between Tito and Stalin deteriorated steadily. In June 1948, Yugoslavia was expelled from the Cominform (postwar successor to the Comintern), and the breach was complete.

Stalin once said: "I will shake my little finger and there will be no more Tito"; but Stalin was completely wrong. Tito and his independent socialist republic survived by cleverly playing off East against West and by taking advantage of Yugoslavia's strategic position in the Cold War. Tito now moved onto the world stage as one of the leaders of the nonaligned states, their first conference being held in Belgrade in 1957.

Born the son of simple peasants and receiving little formal education, Tito was one of the most fascinating characters of the twentieth century, and without a doubt one of the heroic figures of World War II. The key to his achievements was that, while he was both an ardent patriot and a fervent Communist, whenever the two conflicted, he chose patriotism. Had he lived to see the events of 1989 and 1990, he would have rejoiced in the reassertion of national independence by the East European countries; but he would have been saddened by their simultaneous rejection of revolutionary socialism.

Communism arrived in most of Eastern Europe on the backs of Soviet tanks, and was upheld by those tanks for forty years. In contrast, the

Yugoslavs under Tito set up their own Communist state unaided, and they developed it their own way. Their Communism, Tito claimed, "was not something imported from Moscow, but had its origins in the forests and mountains of Yugoslavia." Many of his own countrymen acknowledged that Tito was the only true Yugoslav. During his lifetime, there frequently was speculation as to whether anyone but he could hold together the fractious, multiethnic Yugoslav federation. By 1995, fifteen years after his death, the answer clearly was no.

Philip Green

Additional Reading

Dedijer, Vladimir, *Tito Speaks* (1953).
Jones, William, *Twelve Months with Tito's Partisans* (1946).
MacLean, Fitzroy, *Disputed Barricade* (1957).
Padev, Michael, *Marshal Tito* (1944).
Ulam, Adam B., *Titoism and the Cominform* (1952).
Wolf, Robert Lee, *The Balkans in Our Time* (1956).

Tizard, Henry (1885–1959)

British scientist. Born in Kent, Sir Henry Tizard studied mathematics (1905) and chemistry (1908) at Oxford and established his reputation with papers on color changes of indicators in 1911. In World War I he served as an experimental equipment officer for the Royal Flying Corps. In 1922 he joined the Department of Scientific and Industrial Research, but left in 1929 to become rector of the Imperial College in 1929. He continued, however, to work on defense projects as chair of a subcommittee of the Committee of Imperial Defence, which came to be called the Tizard Committee. It was in this capacity that Tizard made his contribution to the war effort, encouraging the development of radar (q.v.) and, perhaps more importantly, forming scientific ties with the United States in 1940, in what came to be called the Tizard Mission.

Although Tizard lacked any marked scientific originality, Tizard was quick to see the practical applications of new discoveries and could foresee fields in which research was most needed. He continued to advise his government, as well as others of the commonwealth, into the postwar period. Retiring in 1952, he took an active interest in scientific and educational affairs until his death in 1959.

William Rawling

Additional Reading

Clark, Ronald W., *The Rise of the Boffins* (1962).
———, *Tizard* (1965).
Zimmerman, David, *Top Secret Exchange: The Tizard Mission and the Scientific War* (1996).

Todt, Fritz (1891–1942)

German minister of armaments and head of *Organisation Todt* (q.v.). Todt was a famous civil engineer and administrator who served the Third *Reich* in a variety of different posts, lastly as *Reich* minister for armaments and munitions (1940–1942). His most famous accomplishments were the construction of the *Autobahnen* (high-speed motorways), and the West Wall (q.v.), a series of defenses known to the Allies as the Siegfried Line.

Todt was born to a prosperous middle-class family in southern Germany and was a student at the Munich College of Technology when war broke out in 1914. He served in both the infantry and the flying corps, and was severely wounded in combat. Continuing his studies after his war service, Todt finished his degree at the University of Karlsruhe, and then began a career as a rather unassuming engineer. It was during this time that he first became exposed to National Socialist politics. A highly educated man, he was more entranced and intrigued by the personality of Adolf Hitler (q.v.) than he was swayed by the radical racist ideas of the Nazi Party.

Todt was one of the earliest members of the Nazi Party. He joined in 1922 and rose to the honorary rank of colonel in the SS. Following the accession of Hitler as chancellor in 1933, Todt was named head of the German road and highway department. It was in that capacity that he demonstrated his exceptional engineering skills and administrative talent. His ability to deliver high-priority prestige projects on time resulted in more and more responsibility being assigned to him. Quiet, modest, and reserved, Todt was head of a massive construction and public works agency called, in his honor, the *Organisation Todt*.

Todt's proven brilliance was well-exploited by Hitler, and Todt was granted extraordinary independence and leeway in the completion of the myriad tasks he was assigned. Ever the modest technocrat, his power and lack of true party commitment rankled other more staunch Nazi Party leaders; yet his abilities and indispensability were grudgingly acknowledged. By 1938, he ruled over a huge administration responsible for roads and highways, the entire construction industry, water-

Reichsminister *Dr. Fritz Todt. (IWM MH 6101)*

ways and power plants, and the building of military fortifications.

In order to complete the defensive positions in the last hectic year before the outbreak of war, Todt was allowed to commandeer not only labor battalions of the *Reich* Labor Service, but also active-duty army units as well. He was appointed minister of armaments and munitions in 1940 (in addition to his other titles), a post coveted by Hermann Göring (q.v.), who was head of the four-year plan. The bizarre division and overlapping of offices resulted in numerous clashes between these two powerful men.

As the war spread, Todt's workload continued to increase. He supervised the initial stages of the Atlantic Wall construction, and also planned the building of the string of gigantic concrete U-boat pens along the French and Norwegian coastlines. He was promoted to honorary SS general and, to provide manpower to complete the stupendous construction projects carried out under his aegis, he reluctantly agreed to use slave labor in his building crews.

The stress of his positions began to affect his physical and mental health. Nominally apolitical,

Todt suffered a crisis of conscience and by late 1941, began to harbor doubts about Germany's ability to win the war. His inspection trips to various fronts convinced him that the huge gap between Germany's resources and commitments was insurmountable. Increasingly pessimistic, his mood became ever more despairing. The horrible conditions the troops on the eastern front were fighting under particularly unnerved him. His negative appraisal of Germany's strategic position became increasingly well known. Todt, a loyal servant of the state, if not of the party, may have fallen victim to a Nazi Party intrigue to oust him. He died under mysterious circumstances when his plane crashed on takeoff in February 1942. His many positions were then assumed by Todt's young assistant, Albert Speer (q.v.), who was more amenable to the Nazi elite.

Max Mulholland

Additional Reading

Homze, Edward L., *Foreign Labor in Germany* (1967).
Raleigh, John M., *Behind the Nazi Front* (1940).
Seidler, Franz, *Fritz Todt: Baumeister des Dritten Reiches* (1986).

Tokarev, Fedor Vasilevich (1871–1968)

Soviet small arms designer. Tokarev graduated from the Cossack Cadet School in 1900 and served several years in cossack regiments. In 1907, while a student at the Officers' Infantry School, he modified the bolt-action M-1891 Mosin rifle, converting it to a semiautomatic. After the October 1917 revolution, Tokarev went to work at the Tula Arms Factory. His many successful small arms designs included the Model TT semiautomatic pistol in 1930, and the SVT semiautomatic rifle in 1938. Tokarev was made a Hero of Socialist Labor in 1940, and received four Orders of Lenin.

David T. Zabecki

Additional Reading

Union of Soviet Socialist Republics, *The Great Soviet Encyclopedia,* English translation of the 3rd edition (1975), Vol. 26., p. 203.

Tolbukhin, Fedor Ivanovich (1894–1949)

Marshal of the Soviet Union, commander of the Soviet Southern Front (army group). Tolbukhin grew up in a peasant family. He was drafted into the tsar's army and was captain by the end of World War I. In 1918, he joined the Red Army and served

Marshal Fedor Tolbukhin. (IWM NA 22647)

in the civil war as divisional chief of staff. After the civil war, he attended various service schools. In 1934, he graduated from the Frunze Military Academy. During the 1930s, he was chief of staff of a division and a corps. In 1938, he became the chief of staff of the Transcaucasian Military District. That same year, he joined the Communist Party.

When World War II started, the Transcaucasian District became the Transcaucasus Front, and Tolbukhin continued to serve as chief of staff. Over a sixteen-month period starting in late 1941, he served successively as chief of staff of the Caucasus Front and the Crimea Front, deputy commander of the Stalingrad Military District, commander of the Sixty-eighth Army, and commander of the Fifty-seventh Army defending Stalingrad (q.v.). In 1943, he assumed command of the Southern Front.

In April 1944, Tolbukhin, in conjunction with Andrei Yeremenko (q.v.), led the offensive that recaptured the Crimea (q.v.). Attacking with nearly a 500,000-man advantage and heavy aerial bombardment, Tolbukhin moved swiftly down the peninsula, taking 25,000 German prisoners in the process. His forces also drove the Crimean Tartars from the area, sending half a million of them into exile deep inside the Soviet Union. The Tartars, many of whom collaborated with the Germans, were given no quarter by Tolbukhin.

After the Crimea, Tolbukhin commanded the armies that liberated the Ukraine, Romania, Bulgaria, Yugoslavia, Hungary, and Austria. At the end of the war, he became supreme commander of the southern group of forces in Bulgaria and Romania.

His final assignment was commander of the Transcaucasian Military District, the same position he held at the start of World War II.

Thomas Cagley

Additional Reading

Bialer, Seweryn (ed.), *Stalin and His Generals* (1984).

Heisler, J.B., *Russia's Fighting Men* (1945).

Kerr, Walter B., *The Russian Army: Its Men, Its Leaders and Its Battles* (1944).

Touvier, Paul (1915–1996)

Regional militia chief, Vichy France. Touvier was the first French citizen tried under a 1964 statute for World War II–era crimes against humanity. The trial concluded in 1994. In April of that year the seventy-nine-year-old Touvier was sentenced to life in prison. His earlier death sentence in absentia from a 1947 trial had been pardoned secretly in 1971 by then president Georges Pompidou.

Touvier, by his own admission, ordered the execution of seven Jews in June 1944, in reprisal for the assassination of a collaborationist minister in Paris. Since he "spared" ninety-three of the 100 Jews ordered executed by the Nazis, he felt exonerated.

Touvier's case, and that of Maurice Papon in 1998, may well be France's last war crimes trials. In the words of Shimon Samuels, European director of the Simon Wiesenthal Center, "biologically we are reaching the end and psychologically the will is evaporating." More importantly, fewer witnesses can be found to testify in such cases as the years pass.

Patricia K. Rose

Additional Reading

Dank, Milton, *French Against the French: Collaboration and Resistance* (1974).

Huddleston, Sisley, *France: The Tragic Years: An Eye Witness Account of War, Occupation and Liberation* (1954).

Tovey, John Cronyn (1885–1971)

British admiral, commander in chief of the British Home Fleet. Sir John Tovey, son of an army officer, joined the Royal Navy in 1900. His first command was a destroyer in World War I. By the start of World War II, he was an admiral. Tovey fought a number of actions against the Italians in the Mediterranean before being recalled to London in 1940, to become commander in chief of the Home Fleet. It was in that command that he led one of the most successful British sea exploits in World War II, the sinking of the *Bismarck* (q.v.) in 1941. He earned Winston S. Churchill's (q.v.) disfavor, however, by complaining about the lack of air support to British convoys. Tovey left his command, just prior to the D-Day invasion. He retired after giving up his command, serving the remainder of his life in minor Church of England functions.

Thomas R. Cagley

Additional Reading
Chatterton, Edward K., and K. Edwards, *The Royal Navy: From September 1939 to September 1945,* 5 vols. (1942–47).
Fuller, J.F.C., *The Second World War, 1939–1945: A Strategical and Tactical History* (1949).
Roskill, Stephen W., *The War at Sea, 1939–1945,* 3 vols. (1954–1960).

Townsend, Peter W. (1914–1995)

Royal Air Force group captain. Born in Rangoon, Burma, Townsend showed an early passion for adventure and first flew in a Bristol fighter biplane when he was only fourteen years old. From 1933 to 1935, he trained at the RAF College and thereafter served as a flight commander with Number 1 and Number 43 Fighter Squadrons. He has the distinction of being the pilot who shot down the first German aircraft over Britain during World War II—an He-111 on 3 February 1940.

In May 1940, he became squadron leader of Number 85 Squadron, which he strengthened with battle-tested veterans of the Battle of France. He personally led his Hurricanes into attacks against Messerschmitt escorts on many occasions. His combat leadership led to his being awarded the Distinguished Service Order and two Distinguished Flying Crosses. His squadron went on to become one of the most effective night fighter units in the RAF. Townsend served as equerry to King George VI (q.v.) from 1944 until the king died in 1952.

Chris Westhorp

Additional Reading
Lyall, Gavin, *War in the Air, 1939–1945: An Anthology of Personal Experience* (1968).
Townsend, Peter, *The Odds Against Us: Memoirs of Aerial Combat at Night During the Battle of Britain* (1987).

Trenchard, Hugh Montague (1873–1956)

Marshal of the Royal Air Force, first chief of the RAF. Although not a major direct participant in World War II, Sir Hugh Trenchard built the Royal Air Force and fashioned it into one of the principal instruments of Germany's defeat. He was born on 3 February 1873 at Taunton, England. The son of a lawyer, he was educated erratically until finally entering the military in 1893. His early military career in India and South Africa was undistinguished. After the Boer War, his next assignment was in Nigeria, where he spent seven more unremarkable years. In 1912, at the age of thirty-nine, he took up flying.

Trenchard was assigned to the Royal Flying Corps almost immediately. With his considerable military experience, he became an instructor and administrator and helped to define the new art of flying. A large man with a thunderous voice and presence, he picked up a permanent nickname— "Boom." At an age when many contemplated military retirement, Trenchard was just beginning his aviator's career.

When war broke out in 1914, Trenchard was an established advocate of airpower. In the spring of 1915, the British began an aggressive bombing offensive from the air. When new aircraft became available in 1916, he led the effort to provide air support for the battle on land. He insisted on a philosophy of aggressive air attack, and by 1918, he was able to form an independent bombing force designed to deliver strategic bombing inside Germany. The war came to an end before the concept crystallized, yet he made his point. He was highly decorated for his service and was knighted in 1918.

Trenchard not only faced the German menace during the Great War, he also waged a domestic battle to create an air corps independent of the army and navy, and in April 1918, the Royal Air Force was created. In 1919, Trenchard became chief of the air staff, a post he held until 1929. After Trenchard retired from the military, he was picked to head the metropolitan police in 1931.

When World War II broke out in 1939, Trenchard, at age sixty-six, once more entered his country's service. In truth, he could do very little other than lend his considerable reputation and stature as a proponent of airpower. He served as an official advisor and consultant and maintained a constant dialogue with Winston S. Churchill (q.v.)—naturally advocating air offense. Trenchard cited the lack of effective night bombing against Germany, and suggested unrestricted bombing attacks, but the British strategy focused on a more conservative air war.

After the war, Trenchard continued to advocate airpower. He served in the House of Lords and received numerous honors and awards in his later years. He died in London in February 1956. Trenchard was the single instrumental figure in the establishment of the Royal Air Force. From 1912 to 1929, he was the driving force behind British airpower, and historians credit Trenchard as the inspiration of future national air forces. His role in World War II was limited, but the British successes in the air can be attributed to his efforts in the evolutionary years of the Royal Air Force.

Boyd Childress

Additional Reading
Boyle, Andrew, *Trenchard* (1962).
Bryant, Arthur, *The Turn of the Tide* (1957).
MacMillan, Norman, *The Royal Air Force in the World War,* 4 vols. (1950).
Morgan, F.E., *Overture to Overlord* (1950).

Trepper, Leopold (1904–1982)
Soviet espionage agent. A Polish Jew and a shop-keeper's son, Trepper was orphaned early and knew poverty firsthand. For lack of money, he dropped out of Kraków University where he was studying history and literature. Hard times working as a mason, miner, and locksmith led him into politics and the Polish Communist Party. Harassed by the police for being a Communist and a Jew, he left for Palestine and worked as a farmhand on a kibbutz. Disliking the "parched strip of desert known as Palestine," he went to France and received clandestine instructions under the famous Isala Bir, known as "Phantomas."

Forced to leave France, Trepper went to Berlin and joined the *Razvedupr* (Soviet secret police). After training in Moscow, he replaced Walter Krivitsky, who had defected to the United States, as Soviet resident director for Western Europe. Trepper's cover was a Canadian businessman, Adam Mikler, using Canadian passport number 43 671, taken from a Canadian killed in the Spanish civil war. As a major general in the GRU (Soviet military intelligence), he directed the famous Red Orchestra (q.v.) during World War II. Speaking French, Russian, Polish, and German, Trepper ran what historian David Dallin called an organization that was "remarkable and unique." He was a major figure in World War II espionage and deserves to be remembered as perhaps the greatest spy master of all time.

Paul J. Rose

Additional Reading
Dallin, David, *Soviet Espionage* (1957).

Höhne, Heinz, *CODE-WORD: DIRECTOR, The Story of the Red Orchestra* (1970).
Perault, Giles, *The Red Orchestra* (1967).

Tresckow, Henning von (1901–1944)
German major general, member of the opposition to Adolf Hitler (q.v.). The son of a Prussian general and married to the daughter of World War I chief of staff General Erich von Falkenhayn, von Tresckow began his military career during World War I in the prestigious 1st Foot Guards, but quit the army in 1920. After studying law and economics, he worked for a while in a bank and as a factory manager. In 1926, he was readmitted to the *Reichswehr* and eventually graduated at the top of his class from the War Academy. From 1936 until his death, he served almost exclusively in staff positions.

From December 1940, von Tresckow was posted to Army Group B (later Army Group Center) as a principal general staff officer, which brought him into frequent contact with Field Marshal Fedor von Bock and his successor, Günther von Kluge (qq.v.). Outraged by the brutalities of the Nazi regime, von Tresckow became increasingly involved in organizing resistance to that regime. By the time he was transferred from Army Group Center in the summer of 1943, he had recruited a large number of officers to the cause.

After a brief stint as a regimental commander at the front, Colonel von Tresckow was appointed chief of staff to the commander of the Second Army. Promoted to major general in January 1944, he continued his efforts to recruit supporters for action against Hitler, but he had only limited success. A few hours after Claus von Stauffenberg's (q.v.) failed assassination attempt on Hitler, von Tresckow is reported to have said: "Now everyone will turn upon us and cover us with abuse. But my conviction remains unshaken—we have done the right thing. Hitler is not only the arch-enemy of Germany, he is the arch-enemy of the whole world." The next day, 21 July 1944, von Tresckow shot himself.

Ulrich Trumpener

Additional Reading
Balfour, Michael, *Withstanding Hitler in Germany 1933–45* (1988).
Scheurig, Bodo, *Henning von Tresckow: Eine Biographie* (1973).

Trotsky, Leon (1879–1940)
Leading Bolshevik revolutionary, Soviet commis-

sar of war (1918–1925). Trotsky, whose real name was Lev Davidovitch Bronstein, was the founder and organizer of the Red Army. He was born in Kherson Province, Ukraine. He was a brilliant Marxist theoretician and organizer who, by mid-1917, had achieved a position in the Bolshevik hierarchy second only to Lenin. Trotsky masterminded the Bolshevik *Putsch* in October 1917. As the regime's first foreign affairs commissar, Trotsky introduced the "neither war nor peace" policy at the Brest-Litovsk peace negotiations—although he later was overruled by Lenin and forced to agree to German territorial demands in return for a formal treaty withdrawing Russia from World War I.

In March 1918, Trotsky was appointed Bolshevik war commissar and president of the Supreme War Council. Trotsky had his most far-reaching effect in this office. He built the Red Army from its foundations during a time when the shaky Bolshevik reign was faced with the enormous challenges of civil war, economic chaos, and the (even more desperate) attempt to impose its will on the Russian population.

Trotsky forced an iron discipline and a centralized authority upon the ragtag, infant Red Army. Compulsory military service was decreed in May 1918. Discipline was enforced by the bullet—Trotsky believing that only the most brutal methods could rally the dispirited ranks. Significantly for a Marxist theorist, he rejected as patently absurd the dogma of the "Marxist-Proletarian Strategy," which, for example, extolled the fighting virtues of worker and peasant militia over regular troops—a belief advocated by Josef Stalin (q.v.). Thus Trotsky staffed 75 percent of the Red Army officer corps with "experts"—professional soldiers of the former tsarist army. At the same time, he introduced the political commissar system to ensure constant indoctrination, and to keep a ruthless watch on the ideological loyalty of troops and officers alike. By the end of the civil war in November 1920, the legacy of Trotsky's military reforms was evident—the Red Army had grown to five million soldiers; universal military training of reserves had been systematized, and resulted in pool of a further one million men; and more than 100 new military schools were churning out urgently needed officers. In short, Trotsky's organizational genius and stern strategic direction won the civil war and ensured the survival of Bolshevik power.

Yet while Trotsky was in large measure the regime's saviour, he also became its most prominent victim. Long-standing acrimony with Stalin resulted first in Trotsky's dismissal as war commissar in 1925, and then his expulsion from the So-

viet Union in 1929. During his nomadic exile through Turkey, France, and Norway, he continued to rail—in articles and lectures—against the monolithic cult of Stalin. Landing in Mexico City in January 1937, Trotsky founded an anemic opposition movement, the Fourth International. Since his deportation from the Soviet Union, however, he had been stalked continually by Stalin's secret police, the NKVD (q.v.). At his Mexico City villa, Trotsky was finally silenced by an assassin's ice pick to his skull in August 1940.

Stephen Donahue

Additional Reading

Erickson, John, *The Soviet High Command: A Military-Political History 1918–1941* (1962).

Lincoln, W. Bruce, *Red Victory: A History of the Russian Civil War* (1989).

White, D. Fedotoff, *The Growth of the Red Army* (1944).

Truman, Harry S (1884–1972)

President of the United States. Truman was a combat veteran of World War I, serving in France as an artillery battery commander. As a U.S. Senator, he gained national acclaim in 1941, as chairman of the Committee to Investigate the National Defense Program, eliminating millions of dollars in defense contracting waste and abuse. His efforts ensured the United States a viable defense industry on the eve of its entry into World War II.

Elected vice president in 1944, he was unprepared to become president upon Franklin Roosevelt's (q.v.) death on 12 April 1945. Roosevelt had failed to share with Truman significant details concerning the war. Truman was unaware of the MANHATTAN Project (q.v.), among other things, until after he became president and was informed by Secretary of War Henry Stimson (q.v.).

Truman supported the San Francisco Conference of Nations establishing the United Nations (q.v.), and garnered bipartisan and popular support for the U.N. He hoped this would help sell a postwar internationalist foreign policy to a traditionally isolationist America.

On Germany's surrender on 7 May 1945, Truman appointed General Dwight D. Eisenhower (q.v.) head of the American occupation zone and supported de-Nazification and war crimes prosecution. He opposed, however, the Morgenthau Plan (q.v.), fearing such a policy would leave Germany open to Communist conquest. At the Potsdam Conference, he built on the agreements of Yalta to establish with Josef Stalin, Winston S. Churchill, and Clement Attlee (qq.v.), the conditions of the Four-Power occupation of Germany and the peace treaties with Germany's allies and cobelligerents.

Soviet actions contrary to the Yalta Declaration documented the need for a firm Anglo-American stand to prevent Soviet domination of Europe. Popularly mandated demobilization stripped American military strength in Europe to 391,000 in 1946; Soviet demobilization retained 2.8 million troops. Truman used economic means and the American nuclear monopoly (he quickly decided against international control of nuclear weapons) to control Soviet aspirations in postwar Europe. He also decided to deny the Soviets a role in the occupation of Japan.

In 1945, Stalin proceeded cautiously, wary of provoking Western military action. In 1946, he withdrew from Iran under Anglo-American pressure. By 1947, however, he felt secure enough to place the defense and police establishments of the Eastern European states in the hands of local Communists. He dropped all pretense in 1948 with the Communist coup in Czechoslovakia and the Berlin Blockade (q.v.).

Truman likewise first proceeded cautiously, not only wary of Soviet conventional superiority in Europe, but also hoping a change in Moscow's policies would allow the wartime friendship to continue, which he considered vital for a viable U.N. Eventually, however, a dynamic policy of containment crystallized, characterized by three landmark decisions: the Truman Doctrine, the Marshall Plan (q.v.), and the establishment of NATO.

On 12 March 1947, Truman articulated the Truman Doctrine in a speech before Congress, summarized in the sentence: "I believe that it must be the policy of the United States to support free peoples who are resisting attempted subjugation by armed minorities or by outside pressures." Congress approved Truman's request for $400 million in economic aid, military supplies, and military advisory missions to Greece, ravaged by Communist-instigated civil war, and Turkey, pressured by Moscow over control of the Dardanelles, keeping this gateway to the Middle East outside the Soviet sphere.

The Marshall Plan provided $12 billion for economic recovery in Europe between 1947 and 1951 to prevent Communism benefiting from economic chaos. Significantly, the western part of Germany benefited most from this aid. Truman also offered aid to the Soviets and Eastern Europe, but Stalin refused in July 1947, forcing the East

Europeans to follow suit. This aid to the Eastern bloc was insincerely offered hoping that Stalin would refuse it.

Stalin's rejection of the Marshall Plan heralded an escalation phase of the Cold War. In addition to the Marshall Plan was the Brussels Pact (the cornerstone of the Western European Union) formed with American backing, in March 1948, by Britain, France, and the Benelux. The Berlin Blockade and Airlift (q.v.) demonstrated the West's resolve to stop the spread of Communism. The formation of NATO, 4 April 1949, was offset the same year by the East's economic bloc, COMECON, and in 1955 by the Warsaw Pact. On Truman's initiative, in light of Soviet intransigence regarding democratic reunification of Germany, came the creation of the Federal Republic of Germany out of the Western occupation zones in May 1949, followed by the proclamation of the German Democratic Republic in the east. Soviet testing of a nuclear bomb in September 1949 ended America's nuclear monopoly and initiated the postwar arms race, which included rearmament and subsequent inclusion of the German states into their respective alliances. All these events brought about the end of the anti-Axis alliance and helped escalate tensions in post-World War II Europe.

Truman also reorganized the American defense and intelligence establishments for the postwar era. His administration created the National Security Council, the Department of Defense, the United States Air Force, and the Central Intelligence Agency.

By the end of his second term, Truman saw a European order that would remain basically unchanged until the late 1980s. His policies rebuilt Western Europe, integrated the greater part of Germany into the West, and in Europe, prevented the spread of Communism outside the Soviet occupation zone.

Sidney Dean

Additional Reading
McCullough, David, *Truman* (1992).
Robbins, Jhan, *Bess and Harry* (1980).
Truman, Harry S, *Years of Decision* (1955).

Truscott, Lucian King, Jr. (1895–1965)
American lieutenant general, commander, U.S. Fifth Army. A native of Oklahoma, Lucian Truscott started out as a schoolteacher and enlisted in the U.S. Army during World War I. Selected for officer training, he served as a cavalry lieutenant on the Mexican border. His interwar assignments in-

cluded troop duty in Hawaii and Texas and attendance at various army schools, including the Command and General Staff College. He was an instructor at that institution just prior to World War II.

As a brigadier general in 1942, Truscott served as the American liaison officer to the British commando forces, where he suggested that the U.S. Army's projected equivalent force be named "Rangers" (q.v.). In November 1942, he led a special task force in the capture of Port Lyautey, French Morocco, during the Allied invasion of Northwest Africa (q.v.). In March 1943, Truscott assumed command of the famous 3rd Infantry Division (Rock of the Marne) and led it in the capture of Messina and Palermo in Sicily (q.v.). The 3rd Infantry Division also landed at Salerno and Anzio (qq.v.) under Truscott's command.

Truscott's toughest challenge came in 1944 when he relieved Lieutenant General John Lucas (q.v.) as commander of VI Corps at the Anzio beachhead. Leading the May breakout from the Anzio perimeter, Truscott's VI Corps entered Rome on 4 June. The VI Corps then participated in the ANVIL-DRAGOON landings in southern France (q.v.). Truscott propelled his corps in the Allied advance up the Rhone River valley in late summer 1944, scoring one of his most significant tactical successes at Montelimar.

In December 1944, Truscott returned to Italy to assume command of Fifth Army from General Mark Clark (q.v.). In spring 1945, Truscott led Fifth Army in the drive across the Po Valley (q.v.), taking Bologna on 21 April. When Fifth Army was inactivated in October 1945, Truscott succeeded General George S. Patton (q.v.) as commander of the Third Army, in occupation duty in Bavaria. In July 1954, Truscott was promoted to full general on the retired list.

Randy Papadopoulos

Additional Reading

Clarke, Jeffrey J., and Robert Ross Smith, *Riviera to the Rhine* (1993).

Graham, Dominick, and Shelford Bidwell, *Tug of War: The Battle for Italy, 1943–1945* (1986).

Truscott, Lucian K., *Command Missions* (1954).

Tukhachevsky, Mikhail Nikolaevich (1893–1937)

Marshal of the Soviet Union, Soviet military and tactical theorist. Tukhachevsky is widely considered the most brilliant product of the Red Army during the interwar period. Despite falling victim to Stalin's purges (q.v.) in 1937, Tukhachevsky's conceptual legacy had a defining influence on Soviet military operations during World War II, and since.

Born in Penza to a family of indigent means but aristocratic pedigree, Tukhachevsky completed Imperial Cadet Corps training in 1912. Months prior to the outbreak of the war in August 1914, he graduated from the Aleksandrov Military Academy as a junior lieutenant, whereupon he was posted to the Imperial Guard. Taken prisoner and sent to Germany in February 1915, he later escaped and returned to Russia via Switzerland in October 1917. Tukhachevsky set to work training troops in the Moscow vicinity, a task that rapidly gained him the approving eye of Leon Trotsky (q.v.).

Under Trotsky's political patronage, Tukhachevsky became a member of the Bolshevik Party in April 1918, and months later took command of the First Red Army, deployed against the Czechoslovak Legion on the eastern front. A series of spectacular battlefield victories ensued for Tukhachevsky during the Russian civil war against White Russian forces on the eastern and Caucasian fronts. In April 1920, at age twenty-seven, Tukhachevsky was given command of the Western Front (army group) in the war against Poland. Following a successful spring offensive that year, Tukhachevsky's forces were repulsed in front of Warsaw by a daring Polish counterattack in August.

By 1926, Tukhachevsky had become the Red Army chief of staff. Within two years, he ran afoul of Josef Stalin (q.v.) for proposing the rapid development of air and armored forces—a concept denounced as "nonsense" by Stalin. Tukhachevsky was exiled to the military district command in Leningrad. Despite this temporary eclipse, he returned to Moscow in 1931, as deputy commissar for military and naval affairs, and later, chief of ordnance, responsible for weapons development. In 1935, he was created a marshal of the Soviet Union.

As the whirlwind of Stalin's terror swept through the nation in the late 1930s, Tukhachevsky was branded by charges—fabricated on Stalin's order—of leading a "military-Trotskyist organization" and conspiring with German Army circles to overthrow the Soviet state. Demoted to the command of the Volga Military District in May 1937, he was seized en route by the NKVD (q.v.), tortured, and summarily shot on 12 June.

Tukhachevsky was the driving force behind

Soviet military modernization during the 1920s and 1930s. An early advocate of armor and aircraft, he introduced widespread doctrinal reform to the Red Army. Reported to be an admirer of Napoleon, Tukhachevsky adapted the essence of Napoleonic formulas for combined arms operations to exploit the emerging technologies of mechanized warfare. His theories centered on the idea of a mobile shock army, spearheaded by large tank and motorized infantry formations, and supported by heavy artillery and tactical aviation, achieving the decisive breakthrough on the enemy's front and flanks. Coordinated with this firestorm assault, parachute troops, or "air-landing corps," would attack the enemy in his rear area depth, disrupting reserves and supplies.

The military purges, which commenced with Tukhachevsky's execution, were followed by the disbandment of the Red Army tank corps created by him, and the discrediting of his doctrinal ideas. The arrival of the Nazi *Blitzkrieg* on Soviet soil in June 1941, however, brutally vindicated Tukhachevsky's vision. The abortive experiments by Tukhachevsky in forming shock groups, deploying artillery and tanks *en masse,* and in overall combined arms operations, were urgently resurrected by the Kremlin starting in late 1941, and became the hallmark of the Soviet war-fighting doctrine for the remainder of the life of the Soviet Union.

Stephen Donahue

Additional Reading

Butson, Thomas G., *The Tsar's Lieutenant: The Soviet Marshal* (1984).

Erickson, John, *The Soviet High Command: A Military-Political History 1918–1941* (1962).

Shukman, Harold (ed.), *Stalin's Generals* (1993).

Tucker, Robert C., *Stalin in Power: The Revolution from Above, 1928–1941* (1990).

Twining, Nathan F. (1897–1982)

American general, commander of U.S. and Allied air forces in the Mediterranean and Pacific theaters. As a major, Twining first worked in the office of the chief of the air corps from August 1940 through May 1942. In quick succession, he was chief of technical inspection in the operations division, an assistant executive to General Henry H.

"Hap" Arnold (q.v.), and the director of war organization and movements.

In July 1942, Brigadier General Twining left Washington, D.C., and became chief of staff to Major General Millard F. Harmon, Jr., commander of U.S. Army Air Forces in the South Pacific. Subsequently, Twining became commander of Thirteenth Air Force in January 1943. On 27 January 1943, the B-17 carrying him plummeted into the sea between Guadalcanal and Espiritu Santo. He drifted in a rubber raft for six days and was so badly sunburned that he required skin treatments for months after his rescue.

With Twining recovered, Admiral William Halsey gave him tactical control of all army, navy, marine, and Allied air forces in the South Pacific. As COMAIRSOLS (Commander Air Solomons), Twining provided air support for, among others, the landings on Treasury Islands and Bougainville.

Twining then succeeded General James H. Doolittle (q.v.) as commander of Fifteenth Air Force operating out of Italy. Between January 1944 and July 1945, he oversaw the costly bombing attacks against the Ploeşti (q.v.) oil fields in Romania, and his units attacked the Messerschmitt works at Regensburg (q.v.), Germany. Such attacks illustrated his unqualified faith in daily strategic bombing and in enduring the costs associated with such a strategy.

Twining carried out the ultimate air attack against an enemy's heartland, the atomic attacks on Hiroshima and Nagasaki, when he assumed command of the Twentieth Air Force from Curtis E. LeMay (q.v.) on 2 August 1945. The attacks brought to a close Twining's wartime role as a senior operational commander of tactical and strategic air forces. He vigorously supported America's massive retaliation doctrine during his tenure as chairman of the Joint Chiefs of Staff from 1957 to 1960.

Peter R. Faber

Additional Reading

Craven, Wesley F., and James L Cate (eds.), *The Army Air Forces in World War II,* 7 vols. (1948–1958).

Puryear, Edgar F., *Stars in Flight* (1981).

Twining, Nathan, *Neither Liberty nor Safety* (1966).

Webb, Willard J., and Ronald Cole, *The Chairmen of the Joint Chiefs of Staff* (1989).

U

Udet, Ernst (1896–1941)

Luftwaffe lieutenant general, director general of equipment. Udet is one of the more tragic figures of the *Luftwaffe*. The second-ranking German ace in World War I with sixty-two victories, he was a well-known figure in the postwar demilitarized aviation scene, thanks to his appearances at numerous air shows and in several adventure films. With the 1934 reestablishment of German military aviation, his old friend Hermann Göring (q.v.) placed him in increasingly more important positions. He ultimately became director general of equipment.

Udet was influential in establishing the operational and tactical characteristics of warplanes, selecting the ultimate designs that fulfilled these parameters, and organizing their production. He was particularly enamored with the dive-bombing concept and championed its acceptance by the *Luftwaffe*. While a dazzling pilot, he woefully lacked administrative and organizational skills. Ultimately, he squandered much of the German aviation industry's resources.

Realizing by late 1941 that Germany was in an inferior strategic position, and that his past actions contributed to a serious lack of replacement aircraft, Udet took his life on 17 November 1941. His death was reported as an accident in the line of duty, and he was given a hero's funeral by the Third *Reich*.

Michael E. Unsworth

Additional Reading

Galland, Adolf, *The First and the Last* (1957).
Ishoven, Armand van, *The Fall of an Eagle: The Life of Fighter Ace Ernst Udet* (1979).
Johnen, Wilhelm, *Duel Under the Stars: A German Night Fighter Pilot in the Second World War* (1957).
Killen, John, *The Luftwaffe: A History* (1967).

Ujejski, Stanisław (1891–1981)

Polish major general, commander in chief of the Polish Air Force. In 1939, Ujejski was the chief of the army air staff. Between 1940 and 1943, as commander in chief of the Polish Air Force, he laid the foundations of its organization, and built it up to a level of sixteen squadrons. Two of those units distinguished themselves in the Battle of Britain (q.v.). He was somewhat unpopular with his younger pilots, due to a lack of combat experience.

Andrzej Suchcitz

Additional Reading

Cynk, Jerzy, *History of the Polish Air Force* (1972).
Garliński, Józef, *Poland in the Second World War* (1985).
Norwid-Neugebauer, M., *Defense of Poland* (1942).

Unrug, Józef (1884–1973)

Polish vice admiral, commander in chief of the Polish Navy. Unrug commanded the Polish Navy from 1925 to 1939. During the invasion of Poland, he commanded Coastal Defense, and directed operations in the Baltic. He ordered Poland's submarine squadron to operate as long as possible, then make for Sweden or Britain. After the destruction of the navy, he commanded the defense of the Hel peninsula, surrendering on 1 October 1939. From 1939 to 1945, he was held in various POW camps, including Colditz (q.v.).

Andrzej Suchcitz

Additional Reading

Garliński, Jósef, *Poland in the Second World War* (1985).
Peszke, Michael A., *The Polish Navy in the Second World War* (1989).

Upham, Charles Hazlitt (1908–1994)

New Zealand officer, two-time winner of the Victoria Cross. Upham was a second lieutenant in the 20th Battalion, 2nd New Zealand Expeditionary Force, when he won his first VC on Crete (q.v.) for actions between 22 and 30 May 1941. Twice wounded by mortar rounds, he refused medical evacuation and carried a wounded man to safety when his company was forced to withdraw. On 30 May he fought off a German attack at Sphakia, killing twenty-two Germans in the process.

Second Lieutenant (later Captain) Charles H. Upham, VC and Bar, in North Africa, 16 October 1941. (IWM E 6067)

Upham won the Bar to the VC at Ruweisat Ridge (q.v.) in the Western Desert on 14–15 July 1942. A captain by then, he was wounded twice, but insisted on remaining with his men. Just before dawn he led his company in an attack, during which he personally destroyed a German tank and several guns with hand grenades. His arm was broken by machine gun fire, but he continued in command until he collapsed from loss of blood.

David T. Zabecki

Additional Reading

Beshara Press Ltd., *The Register of the Victoria Cross* (1988).
Pringle, Dave J.C., and W.A. Glue, *20th Battalion and Armoured Regiment* (1957).

Urbanowicz, Witold (1906-1996)

Polish ace, RAF wing commander. Urbanowicz joined the Polish Air Force on his eighteenth birthday. When the Germans invaded Poland in 1939, he was an instructor pilot at the Air Training School at Dęblin. With fifty aviation cadets, he escaped to Romania and eventually made his way to France, and then Britain.

Urbanowicz scored the first of his seventeen victories with the RAF on 15 August 1940. When the legendary, all-Polish Number 303 Squadron was formed at the end of August 1940, Urbanowicz was given command of A Flight. After the commander of Number 303 Squadron was killed, Urbanowicz succeeded him.

In April 1941, Urbanowicz became the commander of the first all-Polish fighter wing in the RAF. Shortly thereafter he was sent to Washington as an assistant air attaché. He made a series of lecture tours at USAAF flight schools, but Urbanowicz chafed to get back into combat. As the result of a chance meeting in Washington with Major General Claire L. Chennault, Urbanowicz managed to secure a temporary assignment to Chennault's Fourteenth Air Force in China.

Flying P-40s in China, Urbanowicz shot down three Japanese aircraft. At the conclusion of his assignment in China, Urbanowicz returned briefly to Britain, and then to Washington again, this time as full air attaché. When Washington withdrew its recognition from the London-based Polish government-in-exile, Urbanowicz was out of a job.

After the war, Urbanowicz remained in the United States. He became an American citizen and worked for various U.S. airlines. He never returned to Poland until after the fall of the communist government. On the day that he returned to a democratic Poland, he was promoted to the rank of general in the Polish Air Force by President Lech Wałęsa.

David T. Zabecki

Additional Reading

Baker, E.C.R., *The Fighter Aces of the R.A.F.* (1962).
Zamoyski, Adam, *The Forgotten Few: The Polish Air Force in the Second World War* (1995).

Urquhart, Robert Elliott (1901–1988)

British major general. Urquhart served as an infantry officer in North Africa in 1941, and in Sicily and Italy in 1942–1943. In 1944 he assumed command of the British 1st Airborne Division—known as the while his staff assumed him dead or captured. After resisting German counterattacks for a week, Urquhart withdrew his forces across the Rhine on orders from General Sir Bernard L. Montgomery (q.v.). Urquhart was one of the last British troops to withdraw. He returned with only 2,400 of the 10,000 men he started with.

On 10 May 1945, Urquhart landed in Oslo at the head of British and Norwegian airborne troops. After the war he became a company director in Scotland.

John F. Murphy, Jr.

Additional Reading

Baynes, John, *Urquhart of Arnhem: The Life and Times of Major General R.E. Urquhart, CB, DSO* (1994).

Ryan, Cornelius, *A Bridge Too Far* (1974).

Major General Robert Urquhart, DSO and Bar, outside Arnhem, 22 September 1944. (IWM BU 1136)

"Red Devils." It was his first assignment with airborne troops.

Urquhart commanded the "Red Devils" during Operation MARKET-GARDEN, the September 1944 Allied attempted to seize bridges over the Rhine. The attack culminated at Arnhem (q.v.) in the Netherlands, which was the objective of the 1st Airborne Division. Not parachute-qualified himself, Urquhart and his immediate staff landed by glider some miles short of Arnhem. MARKET-GARDEN failed for a wide range of operational and strategic reasons, all of them beyond Urquhart's control.

Urquhart was an aggressive commander who believed in leading from the front. When radio communications broke down, he went up to the forward areas to see what was happening for himself. He was cut off in the process, and for a

Ustinov, Dmitry Fedorovich (1908–1984)

Soviet minister of armaments. Ustinov was born on 30 October 1908, to a working class family from Samara (now Kuibyshev) on the Volga River. He finished vocational school in 1927 and graduated from the Institute of Military Mechanical Engineering in 1934.

Ustinov worked as a design engineer at the Bolshevik plant in Leningrad and became its director in 1937. The plant was geographically close to the Finnish Winter War (q.v.) arena, and it produced armaments for the Soviet forces operating in Finland. His efficient methods in running the plant drew the attention of Josef Stalin (q.v.), who elevated Ustinov to commissar of armaments (later changed to minister of armaments) in June 1941, just days after the German invasion.

As armaments minister, Ustinov quickly increased production of tanks and other materiel vital in slowing the German advance in the early months of the war. His success garnered him the award of Hero of Socialist Labor in 1942. In 1944, he was given the military rank of colonel general of army engineers. After the war, he remained colonel general in the reserves, continuing as minister of armaments until 1957.

An early advocate of the space program, Ustinov was instrumental in successfully launching the first man in space, Yuri Gagarin, in 1961. For this, Ustinov earned his second Hero of Socialist Labor. In 1976, Premier Leonid Brezhnev elevated Ustinov to minister of defense, a break from the tradition of having a career military man at the top Soviet defense post. That same year, Ustinov was made marshal, then marshal of the Soviet

Union to give him equal rank with his top military leaders. In 1978, he was awarded the Hero of the Soviet Union. As defense minister, Ustinov was responsible for sending more than 115,000 troops to Afghanistan, beginning in 1979. He remained minister of defense until his death on 20 December 1984, after a long illness.

William H. Van Husen

Additional Reading

Pace, Eric, "Ustinov Had Key Roles in Military and Politics," *New York Times,* 22 December 1984, p. 6.

Schmemann, Serge, "Defense Minister of Soviet Union Is Dead at Age 76," *New York Times,* 22 December 1984, p. 1.

Vitukhin, Igor, *Soviet Generals Recall World War II* (1981).

V

Vandenberg, Hoyt S. (1899–1954)

American lieutenant general, commander of the U.S. Ninth Air Force. One of the most accomplished planners, staff officers, and commanders in the U.S. Army Air Forces during World War II, Vandenberg served in the air staff plans division from 1939 to 1942. He was then appointed air planner for the Northwest African invasion, later becoming chief of staff of the Twelfth Air Force during Operation TORCH. In 1943, he became an air planner for Operation OVERLORD and in February 1944, was named deputy commander, Allied Expeditionary Air Forces. This difficult position found him caught between his superior, Air Chief Marshal Sir Trafford Leigh-Mallory (q.v.), and his American mentor, Lieutenant General Carl Spaatz (q.v.), commander of the U.S. Strategic Air Forces.

Vandenberg was extremely successful in this role, and in September 1944, he was given command of the Ninth Air Force, the largest tactical air unit in history. In that position, he provided air support to General Omar N. Bradley's (q.v.) 12th Army Group. Vandenberg was especially active during the German Ardennes offensive (q.v.), earning Bradley's praise, as well as a third star. According to captured intelligence reports, the Germans considered Vandenberg the most brilliant American air planner of the war.

With the German surrender, Vandenberg returned to the air staff in Washington. In 1947, he was promoted to general, and the following year, he became chief of staff of the U.S. Air Force, serving until his retirement in June 1953. He died of cancer in April 1954.

Phillip S. Meilinger

Additional Reading

Frisbee, John L. (ed.), *Makers of the Modern Air Force* (1987).

Meillinger, Phillip S., *Hoyt S. Vandenberg: The Life of a General* (1989).
Puryear, Edgar F., Jr., *Stars in Flight: A Study in Air Force Character and Leadership* (1981).

Van Fleet, James Alward (1892–1992)

American major general, commander U.S. III Corps. A native of New Jersey, James Van Fleet graduated from West Point as an infantryman in 1915. He served in World War I as a machine gun battalion commander and was wounded in France. His interwar service included assignments as a Reserve Officer Training Corps instructor at Florida and Kansas State Universities, attendance at the Infantry School, and command of infantry units in Panama and the United States.

An aggressive combat leader, Van Fleet trained and commanded the 8th Infantry Regiment of the 4th Infantry Division from 1941 to 1944. He led that regiment ashore in Normandy (q.v.) on 6 June 1944. Over the course of the next nine months, Van Fleet became assistant division commander of the 2nd Infantry Division, commander of the 90th Infantry Division, and commander of XXIII Corps in Britain. In March 1945, he assumed command of III Corps, which spearheaded the First Army's advance from the Reamagen bridgehead across Germany.

After World War II, Van Fleet succeeded General Matthew B. Ridgway (q.v.) as commander of the U.S. Eighth Army during the Korean War. In 1953 he retired from the army as a full general. Van Fleet was the only American soldier to earn three Distinguished Service Crosses during World War II.

Randy Papadopoulos

Additional Reading
Weigley, Russel F., *Eisenhower's Lieutenants: The Campaigns of France and Germany, 1944–1945* (1981).

Vasilevsky, Aleksandr Mikhailovich (1895–1977)

Marshal of the Soviet Union, chief of the Soviet General Staff. Vasilevsky was educated in a theological seminary. He entered the tsar's army and reached the rank of captain by the end of World War I. He joined the Red Army in 1919 and served as a regimental commander during the civil war. After the civil war, he served as chief of a divisional school. Although he did not receive the same military education as his contemporaries, he did attend the General Staff Academy in 1937. Coincidentally, he emerged on the higher military scene at the same time the purges (q.v.) were creating a number of vacancies at the top echelons of command. After serving for a period as regimental commander, he became a member of the general staff in Moscow.

Vasilevsky had an impressive ability to examine an issue thoroughly and follow through with lucid assessment of the situation. He became recognized as an excellent staff officer and was assigned to the department of combat training of the general staff. Immediately prior to World War II, he was deputy, and then chief, of operations.

Vasilevsky replaced Marshal Boris Shaposhnikov (q.v.) as chief of the general staff in June 1942, and remained in that position until nearly the end of the war. His masterpiece of operational planning was the coordination of three fronts (army groups) at Stalingrad (q.v.). At Kursk (q.v.), he personally supervised the Red Army's defensive preparations, and he vetoed the suggestion of General Nikolai Vatutin and Nikita Khrushchev (qq.v.) that the Soviets should attack first. From 1944, Vasilevsky was responsible for coordinating the operations of the 2nd and 3rd Byelorussian Fronts in Byelorussia and East Prussia. In the last few months of the war, he assumed personal command of the 3rd Byelorussian Front after General Ivan Chernyakovsky (q.v.) was killed.

After Germany's surrender, Josef Stalin sent Vasilevsky to the Far East in August 1945 in an unsuccessful attempt to gain equal footing with the Western Allies in the victory over Japan. Stalin even proposed that Vasilevsky share postwar occupation power on an equal basis with General Douglas MacArthur.

Vasilevsky's contribution to World War II can be measured by the success of the operations he planned. He very often was physically present on the front lines. Of the thirty-four months he served as chief of staff, he spent twenty-two months at the front. Following the war, he served in various defense positions, culminating as first deputy minister of defense.

Thomas Cagley

Marshal Aleksandr Vasilevsky. (IWM PIC 58818)

Additional Reading
Bialer, Seweryn (ed.), *Stalin and His Generals* (1984).
Shukman, Harold (ed.), *Stalin's Generals* (1993).
Vasilevsky, Alexander, *A Lifelong Cause* (1981).

Vatutin, Nikolai Fedorovich (1901–1944)

Soviet general, commander of the Soviet Southwestern and 1st Ukrainian Fronts (army groups). Vatutin was born to a peasant family in Kursk province. He was too young for World War I, but he joined the Red Army in 1920 and fought in the civil war. He became a member of the Communist Party in 1921, but there is little evidence of his party activities other than membership. Prior to World War II, he attended the Poltava Infantry School, the Frunze Military Academy, and the General Staff Academy. He served in various staff positions, including chief of the operations divi-

General Nikolai Vatutin. (IWM RUS 4740)

sion of the general staff. His strengths were in staff and operational work.

At the start of the war, Vatutin was chief of staff of the Northwestern Front. In 1942, he became deputy chief of the general staff. Later that year, he assumed command of the Voronezh Front. In November 1942, he commanded the Southwestern Front at Stalingrad (q.v.). In conjunction with Generals Konstantin Rokossovsky and Andrei Yeremenko (qq.v.), he cut off the German Sixth Army. At Kursk (q.v.) in July 1943, Vatutin halted Field Marshal Erich von Manstein's (q.v.) attack, and then counterattacked, taking Kharkov.

In late 1943, Vatutin commanded the 1st Ukrainian Front. He liberated Kiev in January 1944, and then linked up with General Ivan Konev's (q.v.) 2nd Ukrainian Front to seal off the Germans in the Korsun pocket, south of Kiev. Vatutin did not live to see the success of the 1944 offensive. Insurgent Ukrainians, freed from fighting the Germans, turned their weapons on the Soviets. He was seriously wounded in a Ukrainian ambush, and died in March 1944.

Thomas Cagley

Additional Reading

Bialer, Seweryn (ed.), *Stalin and His Generals* (1984).

Shukman, Harold (ed.), *Stalin's Generals* (1993).

Vessey, John William (1922–)

American lieutenant. John Vessey enlisted in the Minnesota National Guard in 1939. He served as an artillery sergeant in the 34th Infantry Division in North Africa and Italy. In May 1944, while serving as a battery first sergeant, Vessey earned a Bronze Star and received a battlefield commission while fighting at the Anzio (q.v.) beachhead.

In the years following World War II, Vessey remained in the army and rose to hold the highest position in his profession. He commanded a field artillery battalion during the Vietnam War, earning a Distinguished Service Cross for the defense of Fire Support Base GOLD in March 1967. From 1982 to 1985, he served as chairman of the Joint Chiefs of Staff. Following his retirement at the rank of full general, Vessey served as the Bush administration's negotiator with Hanoi on POW/MIA issues.

Randy Papadopoulos

Additional Reading

Houghen, John H., *The Story of the Famous 34th Infantry Division* (1949).

Webb, Willard J., and Ronald Cole, *The Chairmen of the Joint Chiefs of Staff* (1989).

Vian, Phillip (1894–1968)

British rear admiral. Sir Phillip Vian was born on 15 June 1894. He is best known as the commander of the mission in which 299 British prisoners of war were rescued from the *Graf Spee's* supply ship, the *Altmark,* in Jossing Fjord. It was a daring operation that characterized his approach to combat, and also earned him the Distinguished Service Order (DSO).

Following his 1911 graduation from the Royal Naval College at Dartmouth, Vian served aboard destroyers in World War I. He progressed through a variety of command and staff assignments before assuming command of a reserve destroyer flotilla in Plymouth in September 1939. That December he was given command of the 4th Destroyer Flotilla in Rosyth. In was in that post that he conducted the *Altmark* Raid (q.v.) on 16 February 1940.

In October 1940, Vian earned a bar to his DSO for his actions in destroying a German convoy off Norway. He earned a second bar to his DSO for his actions in attacking the *Bismarck* (q.v.) in May 1941. Two months later he was promoted to rear admiral, at the age of forty-seven.

Vian spent much of the remainder of the war as a task group commander, first in the Norwegian

Rear Admiral Phillip Vian, DSO and 2 Bars, on the bridge of the HMS Cossack. *(IWM A 1595)*

Sea, and then in the Mediterranean. He could be found in the thick of the fighting wherever he served. As commander of the short-lived Force K, he attacked German facilities in the Arctic and evacuated Soviet and Norwegian citizens from Spitzbergen (q.v.). In September 1941 he assumed command of the 15th Cruiser Squadron in the Mediterranean, where he led a Royal Navy task force in the first battle of Sirte (q.v.).

Vian commanded an amphibious landing unit at Salerno (q.v.), a combined carrier-cruiser task force at Normandy (q.v.), and the British Carrier Task Force in the Pacific during the battle for Okinawa. Unfortunately, his actions in the Pacific campaign revealed that he had little appreciation for the importance or nature of carrier air operations. Nonetheless, he gave a characteristically solid and aggressive performance.

A modest man, he was one of Britain's most aggressive and effective wartime naval leaders. Always in the thick of the action, he participated in most of the major naval engagements of the war in Europe. During his postwar career he served as fifth sea lord of the Admiralty (in charge of naval aviation) and commander in chief of the Home Fleet, reaching the rank of admiral of the fleet. Retiring in 1952, be became a director of Britain's Midland Bank and a major insurance company. He died in Ashford Hill, England, on 22 May 1968.

Carl O. Schuster

Additional Reading

Howarth, Stephen (ed.), *Men of War: Great Naval Leaders of World War II* (1993).

Vian, Phillip, *Action This Day* (1960).
Wiggan, Richard, *Hunt the Altmark* (1990).

Victor Emmanuel III (1869–1947)

King of Italy. Victor Emmanuel was born in Naples on 11 November 1869, the son of King Umberto I and Margherita of Savoy-Genoa. He received a military education and entered the army. On 24 October 1896, he married Princess Elena, daughter of the first and only king of Montenegro. The couple had four daughters and one son.

He succeeded to the Italian throne on 29 July 1900, with the assassination of his father by an anarchist in Manza. During the early years of Victor Emmanuel's reign, Italy fought in wars against Turkey (1911) and against Austria-Hungary in World War I. In the fall of 1922, the Fascist Party came into political power when the king invited Benito Mussolini (q.v.) to form a government. In 1929, a concordat between the Italian government and the papacy defined the position of the Catholic Church in the Fascist state.

Mussolini championed a vigorous foreign policy of expansion. On 9 May 1936, Mussolini proclaimed the annexation of Ethiopia (q.v.) and gave the king an imperial title. In 1939, Albania (q.v.) was subjugated and Victor Emmanuel III became the king of that country. The king, however, was mainly a figurehead during the period of Mussolini's dictatorship.

Italy entered World War II as a result of the close collaboration between Mussolini and Adolf Hitler (q.v.). In July 1943, after some disastrous military reverses, the king asserted himself by having Mussolini arrested and replaced by Marshal Pietro Badoglio (q.v.), the military leader who conducted the Ethiopian campaign.

The Italian attempt to switch sides in World War II was not successful. After the Allied liberation of Rome on 4 June 1944, the king was forced to turn over royal authority to his son, Crown Prince Umberto, the lieutenant general of the realm. On 9 May 1946, the king formally abdicated his throne and went into exile in Egypt. King Umberto II had a very brief reign, however. In a plebiscite held in June 1946 to determine Italy's future, the majority of the voters decided for a republic. Victor Emmanuel III died in Alexandria, Egypt, on 28 December 1947.

Bernard Weber

Additional Reading

Collier, Richard, *Duce: The Rise and Fall of Benito Mussolini* (1971).

Denkin, Frederick W., *The Last Days of Mussolini* (1966).

Smith, Denis M., *Italy and Its Monarchy* (1989).

Vietinghoff genannt Scheel, Heinrich von (1887–1952)

German colonel general, army group commander. The scion of an old noble family, von Vietinghoff was commissioned in the Prussian guards in 1907 and later became a staff officer. At the beginning of World War II, he was in command of the 5th *Panzer* Division. After two and a half years of distinguished service as a corps commander, he led the Ninth Army in Russia on an interim basis, and was then sent to the Channel coast as commander of the Fifteenth Army.

Following the Allied conquest of Sicily (q.v.) in August 1943, von Vietinghoff was transferred to Italy to take over the newly created German Tenth Army. When the supreme commander of the southwest theater, Field Marshal Albert Kesselring (q.v.), was injured in October 1944, Colonel General von Vietinghoff served as his replacement until January 1945. He then flew to Latvia to assume command of Army Group Kurland. His subsequent attempts to secure the evacuation of the Kurland pocket were in vain.

On 10 March 1945, von Vietinghoff was ordered back to Italy and officially became Kesselring's successor. Despite considerable difficulties, he successfully surrendered the remnants of his troops to the Allies on 2 May 1945.

Ulrich Trumpener

Additional Reading
Jackson, W.G.F., *The Battle for Italy* (1967).
Smith, Bradley F., and Elena Agarossi, *Operation Sunrise: The Secret Surrender* (1979).

Vlasov, Andrei Andreievich (1900–1946)

Soviet lieutenant general, commander of the Russian Liberation Army. Born on 1 September 1900 into a peasant household in Nizhnii-Novgorod province, Vlasov began his military career in 1919 after joining the Red Army during the height of the Russian civil war, foreign intervention, and the Allied economic blockade against Soviet Russia. He distinguished himself on the southern front against White Generals Anton Ivanovich Denikin and P.N. Wrangell, and advanced in rank and assignments. This career pattern continued, despite his family background, seminary training, and late membership in the Communist Party. He

survived Stalin's purges (q.v.) of the Soviet military leadership in the late 1930s, perhaps only because he was posted to China as advisor to Chiang Kai-shek.

In the opening phases of World War II, Vlasov, commanding the IV Mechanized Corps in Lwów and the Thirty-seventh Army in Kiev, eluded German encirclement. He helped defend Moscow (q.v.) in December 1941, and distinguished himself as commander of the new Twentieth Shock Army in the counterattack that forced the Germans to retreat with heavy losses. He was one of the heroes of that first turning point in the war. In January 1942, he was promoted to lieutenant general and awarded highest military honors.

Vlasov came to grief in attempting to discharge his next assignment, the relief of besieged Leningrad (q.v.) from the Volkhov Front (army group) on Josef Stalin's (q.v.) orders. In March 1942, Vlasov assumed command of a battered and encircled army. Stalin's permission to withdraw through a still-existent small gap came too late. The bulk of the army was captured or killed. Vlasov chose to remain with his troops, thus ensuring death or capture. The latter occurred in July 1942. In captivity, his latent and hidden antagonisms toward Stalin and his ruinous policies coalesced into his decision to attempt the overthrow of Stalin's regime.

Thus began Vlasov's final, tragic, and excruciating ordeal. He collaborated with and was exploited by the Nazi regime, a relationship entered into reluctantly by both parties. Vlasov became head of the Russian Liberation Army (ROA) (q.v.), eventually reaching three-division strength. He wanted to create a national Russian army that, opposed to Stalin and Communism, would fight along with Germany and liberate Russia, with a view to forming a new Russian national state.

The Russian National Committee, formed in late 1942, proposed not only the eradication of Stalinism, but a program of reform, including the return of land to the peasants, reestablishment of private trade and industry, and civil rights. The history of that movement was caught between the Nazis' ethnic paranoia in a lethal ideological war, and the German Army's need to cope with an increasingly difficult military situation. Adolf Hitler (q.v.) always considered the Slavs "subhuman," incapable of governing themselves. No independent state was to emerge in Eastern Europe, Germany's future *Lebensraum* (q.v.). Hitler's racial policies ensured his defeat.

Hitler's and Vlasov's positions were irreconcilable. Yet hundreds of thousands of Russians and

V

members of other Soviet ethnic groups served mostly in German uniforms as national legionnaires, or *Hilfswillige,* supporting the *Wehrmacht* on and behind the front. They were motivated by anti-Stalinism, fear, or deprivation. All in all, these were massive indications of discontent. As defeat loomed larger in 1944, more German officials came to support the Russian Liberation Army and the Committee for the Liberation of Russia's Peoples, established in November 1944 in Prague. Encouragement even came from Heinrich Himmler (q.v.), head of the SS. After a brief stint on the Oder front in April 1945, the ROA, on its own, deployed to Czechoslovakia and aided in the liberation of Prague. Vlasov, like so many others, believed a military clash between the West and the Soviet Union was very likely after the defeat of Nazi Germany. In May 1945, Vlasov was captured in Czechoslovakia by a detachment of Soviet troops while actually in American custody. In Moscow, he was indicted, along with his closest associates, on charges of treason, sabotage, and collaboration with the enemy. He was tried, convicted, and hanged in 1946.

Important questions remain. Was Vlasov a traditional traitor, or a Russian patriot whose anti-Stalinism emerged fully in captivity, and who saw in collaboration, however naively conceived, the chance to defeat Stalin? Most interpretations tend toward the latter. What if the Nazi regime had radically modified its policies? Was Vlasov an exemplar of the emerging opposition to Stalin's destructive policies? Apart from the related tragic story of the forced "repatriation" of Soviet citizens after 1945, was Vlasov a reformer, tragically fixed in a complex vortex somewhere between the Kronstadt rebels of 1921 and Mikhail Gorbachev? Although revisionism is in full swing in the former Soviet Union, no one has yet proposed a radical review of the "Vlasov Phenomenon."

Norbert H. Gaworek

Additional Reading

Fröhlich, Sergej, *General Wlassow: Russen und Deutsche zwischen Hitler und Stalin* (1987).

Hoffmann, Joachim, *Die Geschichte der Wlassow-Armee* (1986).

Shukman, Harold (ed.), *Stalin's Generals* (1993).

Thorwald, Jürgen, *The Illusion: Soviet Soldiers in Hitler's Armies* (1975).

Voronov, Nikolai Nikolaevich (1899–1968)

Marshal of the Soviet Union, chief of artillery of the Soviet Army. Voronov was born in St. Petersburg, where his father was a clerk. He joined the Red Army in 1918 and served in the civil war as an artillery battery commander. After the civil war, he held a wide variety of artillery assignments, including battalion and regimental command. He attended the Frunze Military Academy, and in

Marshal of Artillery Nikolai Voronov, one of the principal planners of the Stalingrad Offensive. (IWM RUS 5125)

1934, became director of the Leningrad Artillery School. He was an advisor during the Spanish civil war (q.v.) and was chief of artillery of a front during the Finnish Winter War (q.v.). At the start of World War II, Voronov was the chief of artillery of the Soviet Army, deputy commander of the main artillery directorate, and commander of the national air defense forces. Although his titles changed, he basically remained the chief of artillery throughout the war. In that position, he played a major planning and operational role in nearly every major campaign. From his experiences in Spain and Finland, he understood the value of concentrating artillery, rather than scattering firing units among divisions and regiments. By retaining centralized control of firepower, the Soviets were able to achieve maximum effect from their artillery.

Voronov supervised the transition from horse-drawn to mechanized power for the guns. He introduced the artillery division into the Soviet military structure, as well as the heavy artillery brigade for the assault divisions. His fire planning masterpiece probably was Stalingrad (q.v.), where 2,000 guns pounded the Germans prior to the Soviet attack. Josef Stalin (q.v.) later called the Soviet artillery the "God of War."

Following World War II, Voronov continued to push for advances in artillery technology, including missiles. From 1950 to 1953, he was president of the Academy of Artillery Sciences, the organization responsible for developing strategic nuclear weapons. In 1965, he was made a Hero of the Soviet Union.

Thomas Cagley

Additional Reading
Bellamy, Chris, *Red God of War* (1986).
Bialer, Seweryn (ed.), *Stalin and His Generals* (1984).

Vörös, Janos (1891–1968)

Hungarian colonel general, chief of the general staff of the Hungarian Army. On Hungary's entry into the war, Vörös commanded the 2nd Motor Car Brigade. In 1944, he became chief of the general staff. He opposed resistance to the German occupation of Hungary. He also deserted Admiral Miklós Horthy (q.v.) under pressure from the Germans. Next, Vörös crossed over to the Soviets, becoming minister of national defense in the Soviet-backed provisional national government.

Andrzej Suchcitz

Additional Reading
Czebe, Jeno, and Tibor Petho, *Hungary in World War II* (1946).
McCartney, Carlile A., *A History of Hungary 1929–1945*, 2 vols. (1956–57).

Voroshilov, Kliment Yefremovich (1881–1969)

Marshal of the Soviet Union, commander of the Soviet Northwestern Front (army group). Voroshilov was the oldest Soviet military figure of World War II. He was one of the earliest Bolsheviks, joining the party in 1904. He was an active participant in the early revolutionary activities, and during the civil war, he developed partisan tactics that were to emerge again during World War II. In the civil war, he served with Josef Stalin and Semyon Budenny (qq.v.) in the Red First Cavalry Army. Voroshilov commanded the Red forces at Tsaritsyn in 1918 when they achieved a significant victory over the Whites. His political commissar was Stalin.

In 1924, Voroshilov was appointed commander of the Moscow garrison, and he replaced Frunze (after his death) as commissar in Moscow in 1925. Although Trotsky once said he ". . . lacked military and administrative ability," Voroshilov nonetheless reached the rank of marshal of the So-

Marshal of the Soviet Union Kliment Voroshilov. (IWM RUS 393)

viet Union and commissar of defense by 1935. When the military purges (q.v.) started in 1937, he was one of two marshals (out of five) to survive.

In May 1940, Voroshilov became the deputy chairman of the defense committee. He also was given command of the Northwestern Front, but he failed to stop the Germans or prevent the encirclement of Leningrad (q.v.). He was replaced by Georgy Zhukov (q.v.) and assigned to staff positions for the rest of the war. He remained a close ally of Stalin, and he attended the Teheran Conference in November 1943. He also negotiated with the British over the stationing of an Anglo-American air force in the Transcaucasus, but the plan was rejected by the Soviets.

After the war, Voroshilov was chairman of the Allied Control Commission in Hungary. In 1953, he became chairman of the Presidium of the Supreme Soviet. In 1960, however, he fell into disfavor with Nikita Khrushchev (q.v.), and was removed from all official positions.

Thomas Cagley

Additional Reading

Bialer, Seweryn (ed.), *Stalin and His Generals* (1984).

Kerr, Walter B., *The Russian Army: Its Men, Its Leaders, and Its Battles* (1944).

Shukman, Harold (ed.), *Stalin's Generals* (1993).

Waesche, Russell R. (1886–1946)

American admiral, commandant of the U.S. Coast Guard. Graduating from the Coast Guard Academy in 1906, Waesche worked his way up through the Coast Guard ranks to become its chief ordnance officer in 1928. President Franklin D. Roosevelt (q.v.) appointed him commandant of the Coast Guard in 1936, with the rank of rear admiral. As commandant, he established the Coast Guard Institute and Correspondence School, integrated the Lighthouse Service into the Coast Guard, and increased the number of commissioned officers. Roosevelt reappointed him to another term in 1940.

During World War II, the Coast Guard was under the operational control of the navy, and Waesche presided over the largest expansion of Coast Guard services in American history. Enlistment increased by more than fifteenfold under his direction, and the Coast Guard participated in every major invasion of the war. In addition to its traditional duties, the Coast Guard maintained the security of ports, patrolled the Greenland coastal waters, escorted convoys, took part in antisubmarine patrols, rescued survivors of sunken merchant vessels, and even captured two German saboteurs who landed in Florida and on Long Island. Waesche, promoted to vice admiral in 1942, had command over these operations.

After being reappointed to a third term in 1944, Waesche was promoted to admiral in April 1945, the first Coast Guard officer to attain that rank. That December, he retired from active service. In 1946, he received the navy's Distinguished Service Medal, and President Harry S Truman (q.v.) named him as one of only ten admirals and generals to retain their wartime ranks permanently. Waesche died on 17 October 1946, in Bethesda, Maryland.

Robert F. Pace

Additional Reading

Grove, Arch A., and Lee Grove (eds.), *Sea, Surf, and Hell: The U.S. Coast Guard in World War II* (1945).

Willoughby, Malcolm F., *The U.S. Coast Guard in World War II* (1957).

Waldheim, Kurt (1918–)

Austrian lieutenant, intelligence officer in the German Army. The military career of Waldheim during World War II has become the subject of intense international research and debate since 1986. A past secretary general of the United Nations, he was elected president of Austria that year. During the campaign, allegations accusing him of participation in Nazi wartime atrocities surfaced and were seriously investigated.

Waldheim, a career diplomat, always admitted fighting with the German Army, first in France and then on the eastern front in 1941. A slight foot injury caused him to return to his native Austria. In most later accounts, he contended that his military career ended at that point. Actually, he recovered and was attached to various German Army units in Yugoslavia and Greece from 1942 to 1945. Serving primarily as an interpreter and intelligence officer, he was stationed first with German Army headquarters in Belgrade, and later with General Alexander Löhr's (q.v.) army group in Greece and Yugoslavia.

Waldheim held no command positions. Although he undoubtedly knew of reprisal actions against partisans in the Balkans and of deportations of civilians, including Jews, his military position offered him few opportunities to oppose the German Army's policies directly. Gradually the debate surrounding him shifted from the question of legally defined criminal acts to his moral responsibility as a witness to the brutal German campaigns in the Balkans.

William D. Bowman

Additional Reading

Gruber, Karl (ed.), *Kurt Waldheim's Wartime Years: A Documentation* (1987).
Palumbo, Michael, *The Waldheim Files: Myth and Reality* (1988).

Walker, Frederick John (1896–1944)

Royal Navy captain, ASW expert. The son of a naval officer, Frederick Walker entered the Royal Navy (RN) in 1909 and served in a variety of seagoing assignments during World War I. He acquired an interest in antisubmarine warfare (ASW) and by 1921 was considered a specialist in the field. In 1934 he assumed command of the HMS *Fleetwood,* the yacht of the commander in chief of the Far East Fleet. While in that post, and as executive officer of the HMS *Valiant,* his outspoken views on ASW and the fleet's overreliance on sonar (q.v.) got him into trouble with his superiors. As a result, he was passed over for promotion to captain in 1938. That same year, he assumed command of the RN's ASW training school in Portland. It was in that post that he developed the tactics and procedures that would make him the war's leading ASW commander.

When the war started, Walker was the operations officer on the staff of Vice Admiral Bertram Ramsay (q.v.) at Dover. Walker prepared the initial plans for the protection of British shipping that carried the British Expeditionary Force (BEF) to France, and for Operation DYNAMO (q.v.), the Dunkirk evacuation. In 1941, Walker assumed command of the sloop HMS *Stork,* which also made him the senior officer of the 36th Escort Group. In that position he established his reputation as a preeminent ASW commander when he commanded the escort for Convoy HG-76, during the Convoy Battle off Portugal (q.v.) on 14–23 December 1941. Walker's aggressiveness led to the sinking of four U-boats at a cost of one escort carrier, a sloop, and two merchant ships. Most other convoys during that period were being devastated, while inflicting virtually no losses on their U-boat attackers.

His successes as an escort commander should have given Walker exceptional credibility during a major conference on ASW held in January 1942, but his views were largely rejected by his peers. Walker, however, stuck to developing his own tactics, believing that they ultimately would be validated by his record. He was right. In July 1942, his successes finally won him a belated promotion to captain. Three months later he was appointed captain in charge of escort groups in the Western Approaches Command.

Vice Admiral Max Horton (q.v.), the commander of the Western Approaches Command, believed Walker could accomplish more out at sea. In February 1943, Horton allowed Walker to train and direct aggressive "hunter-killer" groups to concentrate against the U-boat wolf packs threatening the convoys within the command's area. Walker was given command of the first such unit, the 2nd Escort Group, which consisted of five sloops. After initial training in Walker's new tactics (*see* Submarine and Antisubmarine Warfare), the group deployed to the mid-Atlantic gap in May 1943. Walker's technique of "creeping attack" exploited with deadly effect the new forward-throwing ASW weapons (Squid, Hedgehog) that had entered service in 1942.

Walker increasingly found his services in demand. Unfortunately, the strain of constantly being at sea and training new personnel and ship crews began to take their toll on his health. Complaining of giddiness while ashore to discuss a forthcoming operation, he was rushed to the Royal Naval Hospital, Seaforth, where he died of a cerebral thrombosis on 9 July 1944.

Walker was an aggressive and brilliant ASW tactician who earned three Distinguished Service Orders (DSOs) during the war. Although his outspoken views cost him promotion to captain in the prewar period and probably prevented him from reaching flag rank, few naval officers of the modern era have had so much of an impact on naval operations. His tactics formed the cornerstone of western ASW doctrine until the late 1970s, and remain a significant influence today. It is very likely that he will continue to influence ASW tactics well into the next century.

Carl O. Schuster

Additional Reading

Hackam, Willem, *Seek and Strike: Sonar and Anti-Submarine Warfare and the Royal Navy 1914–1954* (1984).
Howarth, Stephen (ed.), *Men of War: Great Naval Leaders of World War II* (1993).
MacIntyre, Donald, *Battle of the Atlantic* (1968).
Robertson, Terence, *Walker, R.N.: The Story of Captain Frederic John Walker* (1956).

Walker, Walton Harris (1889–1950)

American lieutenant general, commander of U.S.

XX Corps. Walker was born in Belton, Texas, and graduated from the U.S. Military Academy at West Point in 1912. During World War I, he served with 5th Infantry Division in France, seeing action in the St. Mihiel and Meuse-Argonne offensives. By January 1942, Walker was a major general and commander of the IV Armored Corps at Camp Young, California. There, Walker established the Desert Training Center, responsible for training armored units for desert warfare in North Africa. In February 1944, his corps was redesignated XX Corps and ordered to Britain. Walker's corps was committed in Normandy (q.v.) in July (D+48) and became part of General George S. Patton's (q.v.) Third Army.

The XX Corps earned its nickname "Ghost Corps" for the speed of its advance. Pushing into France from the Loire River to the Moselle, Walker ran out of gas and was forced to pause before the fortifications at Metz (q.v.). In August 1944, units of XX Corps took the historic French town of Chartres (without damaging the cathedral) in a brief, well-organized assault. Walker's greatest challenge came during the Ardennes offensive (q.v.) when Patton swung the bulk of the Third Army north to force a corridor into Bastogne (q.v.). Walker's XX Corps was left to cover the front that had been held by an entire field army. Walker accomplished the task with vigorous reconnaissance combined with the use of extensive minefields.

During February and March 1945, Walker led XX Corps through the Siegfried Line (q.v.). On 13 March, the 31 artillery battalions of the corps opened a barrage on German positions at the apex of the Saar-Moselle triangle, seventy-five miles west of the Rhine. Nine days later, XX Corps crossed the Rhine at Mainz and pushed through Kassel, Jena, and Regensburg. On 9 April, Walker's units liberated the Buchenwald concentration camp near Weimar. By May 1945, Walker's units reached Linz, Austria, the farthest advance east of any of Patton's elements.

Walker finished World War II as the commander of the 8th Service Command in Dallas, Texas. In September 1948, he assumed command of the Eighth Army in Japan. During the first months of the Korean War, Walker took command of Korean and other U.N. ground forces in Korea. In August and September, he conducted one of history's most skillful defensive battles at the "Pusan Perimeter." Later that year, on 23 December 1950, Walker was killed in a jeep accident on the road between Seoul and the front. He had been promoted to full general just three days earlier. Nicknamed "Johnny Walker" for his fondness for drinking and eating, Walker was less a brilliant tactician than an energetic, no-nonsense commander who believed in leading from the front.

David S. Foy

Additional Reading

Allen, Robert S., *Lucky Forward: The History of Patton's Third U.S. Army* (1947).
Blumenson, Martin, *Breakout and Pursuit* (1961).
Cole, Hugh M., *The Lorraine Campaign* (1950).
Weigley, Russell F., *Eisenhower's Lieutenants: The Campaigns of France and Germany, 1944–1945* (1981).

Wallenberg, Raoul (1912–1947?)

Swedish special diplomatic envoy to Hungary. Born to a prominent business and diplomatic family in Stockholm, Wallenberg lived a life of privilege; he was well-traveled and multilingual. A man of many interests, he studied architecture at the University of Michigan and graduated in 1935. After graduation, he went to work for a Dutch bank in Haifa, Palestine, where he met Jewish refugees fleeing Nazi-occupied Europe. Recognizing the plight of the Jews, he was sent as a special envoy to the Swedish legation in Budapest in July 1944, a position funded by the U.S. War Refugee Board and the American Jewish Joint Committee. He met and negotiated with Nazi officials, including Adolf Eichmann (q.v.), as he attempted to secure the freedom of Hungarian Jews.

Wallenberg was eventually responsible for rescuing hundreds of thousands of Jews from certain death and deportation by issuing them Swedish passports and housing them in buildings protected by the Swedish flag. As the Red Army approached Budapest in the spring of 1945, he went to meet Soviet officers at Debrecen, Hungary. He and his driver were never seen again. Although the Soviets long denied any responsibility for Wallenberg's disappearance, they later admitted that he had died in Siberia in 1947. Rumors, however, continued to circulate up through the 1990s that he might still be alive. The United States made Wallenberg an honorary citizen in 1981, thereby permitting the State Department to press the issue of his release.

Steven B. Rogers

Additional Reading

Adachi, Agnes, *Child of the Winds: My Mission with Raoul Wallenberg* (1989).
Anger, Per, *With Raoul Wallenberg in Budapest* (1981).

Bierman, Joseph, *Righteous Gentile: The Story of Raoul Wallenberg* (1981).

Rosenfeld, Harvey, *Raoul Wallenberg: Angel of Rescue* (1982).

Wallis, Barnes Neville (1887–1979)

British aeronautical engineer. A brilliant, innovative aeronautical engineer during the prewar period, Wallis used geodetic construction in the design of the R100 airship. During World War II, he turned his abilities to bomb development and subsequently was responsible for some of the most famous and effective munitions produced.

Wallis believed fully in the strategic bombing doctrine. He was an early advocate of large bombers carrying large loads in an attempt to obtain the most economic and destructive offensive firepower. He once envisioned a high altitude "Victory" aircraft that would carry a ten-ton load and deliver an earthquake, shock-type effect of immense destructive power capable of winning the war.

The Victory aircraft never flew, but Wallis did receive considerable official help over a number of years with the development of his "bouncing bomb" (in fact, a revolving depth charge). His dogged determination carried his team through to success with the development of the weapon and the method of delivery. It was used to good effect on the famous 1943 Ruhr Dams raid (q.v.).

British Air Chief Marshal Sir Arthur Harris (q.v.) described Wallis as a "Wizard Boffin." His later research returned to the big, deep penetration bomb idea in a more modified form with his subsequent Tallboy and Grand Slam designs. They were used against shipping, V-weapon launch sites, and the German infrastructure. His wartime efforts brought him knighthood.

Chris Westhorp

Additional Reading

Great Britain Air Ministry, *Bomber Command* (1945).

———, *The Origins and Development of Operational Research in the Royal Air Force* (1963).

Munson, K.G., *ABC British Aircraft of World War II* (1961).

Warlimont, Walther (1894–1976)

German general, deputy chief of the OKW operations staff. Warlimont began his military career as a lieutenant of foot artillery in June 1914. During World War I, he commanded batteries on both the western and Italian fronts. After the war, he was attached to General Ludwig Maercker's *Freikorps* before transfer to the *Reichswehr* as an artillery officer. He qualified for general staff training and was later sent to Britain for language studies. After further duty with the general staff and the foreign armies intelligence section, he went to the United States in 1929 to study industrial mobilization.

In 1936, Warlimont traveled to Spain as the German military attache to General Francisco Franco (q.v.). He believed the Spanish civil war (q.v.) would be prolonged and opposed direct German intervention. In 1938, Warlimont headed the home defense section and became acting chief of the OKW (q.v.) operations section. His overseas experience, knowledge of industrial affairs, and pragmatic world view uniquely positioned him among German officers to function effectively on the operations staff. His influence was muted by his natural reserve and cautious nature. Furthermore, Adolf Hitler (q.v.) did not trust him.

From 1939 to 1944, Warlimont was deputy chief of the OKW operations section under Alfred Jodl (q.v.). He thus was present on 20 July 1944, when the assassination attempt was made on Hitler. Because of injuries he sustained, he was medically retired in September 1944. Arrested by the Allies in 1945, he was sentenced at Nuremberg to life imprisonment. After his release in 1957, he pursued historical studies of the war and eventually published *Inside Hitler's Headquarters* in 1964.

Philip Bechtel

Additional Reading

Görlitz, Walter, "Keitel, Jodl, and Warlimont," in *Hitler's Generals,* Correlli, Barnett (ed.), (1989).

Warlimont, Walther, *Inside Hitler's Headquarters* (1962).

Watson-Watt, Robert Alexander (1892–1973)

British scientist, developer of radar. Born in 1892 and acquiring his bachelor of science degree from the University of St. Andrews in 1912, Sir Robert Watson-Watt made many contributions to meteorology. He is best remembered for his work in radio direction finding, later called radar (q.v.). A trial on 26 February 1935 demonstrated the possibility of locating flying aircraft by bouncing electromagnetic waves off them. After many trials and tribulations a workable system, called CHAIN

HOME (q.v.) was installed along the east coast of Great Britain in 1938. This achievement was as much due to Watson-Watt's determination and administrative skills as to his abilities as a scientist.

Further work brought CHAIN HOME LOW radar to detect aircraft flying below CHAIN HOME's horizon; as well as AI (airborne interception) sets that could be installed in aircraft; ASV (air to surface vessel) devices to allow aircraft to locate ships at sea; specialized equipment for controlling antiaircraft artillery, differentiating between friendly and enemy aircraft; and radio-navigation for bombers. Watson-Watt's role in all this was as team leader, gathering expert personnel, ensuring that projects stayed on track, and keeping the red tape at bay. For his work, Watt was knighted in 1942. He died on 5 December 1973.

William Rawling

Additional Reading
Guerlac, Henry E., *Radar in World War II* (1987).
Jones, R.V., *The Wizard War* (1978).
Watson-Watt, Robert, *The Pulse of Radar: An Autobiography* (1959).

Wavell, Archibald (1883–1950)
British field marshal, commander in chief Middle East 1939–1941, commander in chief India 1941–1943. In 1939, Sir Archibald Wavell's reputation was high. He was an innovative and imaginative trainer, a commander inspiring confidence, a military writer of distinction, and a reader of the classics and poetry. As British commander in chief in the Middle East, he carried enormous responsibilities covering Egypt, Sudan, East Africa, Palestine, Jordan, and Iraq. In 1940, he faced a threat on two fronts, from 200,000 Italian and native troops in Libya, and 300,000 troops in East Africa, mainly in Ethiopia. By arithmetic comparison, he was greatly outnumbered in troops, equipment, and aircraft.

Between December 1940 and February 1941, a force of two British divisions defeated an Italian invasion of Egypt, advanced into Libya, and killed or captured 150,000 troops, 400 tanks, and 800 guns. Wavell was not in tactical command of this success, his part as commander in chief was setting objectives and providing forces. Between November 1940 and May 1941, he led a two-pronged advance from Kenya in the south and the Sudan in the north, forcing the vastly superior Italian forces in East Africa (q.v.) to surrender.

Two brilliant and widely separated campaigns under Wavell's direction virtually eliminated the Italian Army from the Middle East by early 1941. But a succession of events nearly swamped his sparse forces. German general Erwin Rommel and the *Afrika Korps* (qq.v.) arrived, advanced to the Egyptian frontier, and besieged Tobruk (q.v.); four British divisions were sent to Greece to help stem the German invasion; action was taken against the pro-Vichy French forces in Syria; and troops were

General Sir Archibald Wavell, KCB (later Field Marshal Earl Wavell). (IWM E 450)

sent to Iraq where a pro-German coup threatened British bases and oil supplies. Success was achieved in Syria and Iraq, but the intervention in Greece was disastrous, and with the loss of Crete (q.v.) that followed, some 30,000 British troops were lost.

At the time, it was thought that political considerations overruled Wavell's military judgement, but in a published statement in 1950, he insisted his judgment at the time was that, despite the dangers, there was a reasonable chance of success in Greece. In May 1941, at his direction, a British force of about two and a half divisions launched an offensive against Rommel's forces to evict them from Egypt and relieve Tobruk—Operation BATTLEAXE. In signals to Prime Minister Winston S. Churchill (q.v.), Wavell displayed a lack of confidence in this operation, and by 17 June, British losses, particularly armour, were so heavy that the force was withdrawn. In July, Wavell was relieved and appointed commander in chief in India.

Immediately after Pearl Harbor, Wavell was appointed (at the urging of U.S. General George C. Marshall [q.v.]), supreme commander of Allied forces in the Far East. For seven weeks, Wavell was in command of what was known as ABDA forces (America, British, Dutch, and Australian) in an area embracing Burma, Malaya, the Philippines, and the Dutch East Indies. No general was assigned to a more hopeless situation. Air and sea supremacy were already lost, and in the ensuing few months, the Japanese occupied all British, American, and Dutch possessions in Southeast Asia. Before the final Japanese success, he left Allied supreme command and reverted to commander in chief in India. There he remained responsible for the Burmese front until mid-1943, when he was appointed viceroy of India.

Wavell was an enigma; a brilliant mind and a great military thinker, yet inarticulate to the point of appearing withdrawn and diffident. He described himself as "slow of thought and sparing of speech." As a result, his relations with politicians, particularly Churchill, were arid. But within the army, despite his inability to communicate and a shunning of any form of publicity, he was regarded with great confidence and respect.

A thick-set man with total integrity, in adversity Wavell appeared to all as a rock. Yet despite this and his reputation at the beginning of the war, it must be said he did not live up to his promise. In some instances, particularly in the Middle East, his actions appear, with hindsight, to have been ill considered. Intervention in Greece, misjudgment of the timing of Rommel's first advance into Egypt, and subsequent direction of the abortive Operation BATTLEAXE are cases in point. He also seems, from his reports as ABDA commander, to have seriously underestimated the Japanese.

Nonetheless, in successive appointments with vast responsibilities, Wavell carried an enormous burden and faced great difficulties. Above all else, he held the Middle East and dealt the Italian Army a crushing defeat from which they never recovered.

B.K. Warner

Additional Reading

Connell, John, *Wavell, Scholar and Soldier* (1964).

———, *Wavell, Supreme Commander 1941–1943* (1969).

Wavell, Archiblad P., *Speaking Generally* (1946).

Wedemeyer, Albert Coady (1897–1993)

American lieutenant general, key Allied strategist. Wedemeyer graduated from the U.S. Military Academy at West Point in 1919 and was posted to Georgia, China, the Philippines and Washington, D.C., over the course of the next sixteen years. From 1936 to 1938, he studied at the *Kriegsakademie* in Germany, the first American officer to do so since World War I.

The start of World War II found Wedemeyer assigned to strategic planning, working with Dwight D. Eisenhower and George C. Marshall (qq.v.). In July 1942, Wedemeyer was promoted to brigadier general and served on the Joint Strategic Committee and later as chief of the strategy and policy group. He participated in the principal joint and combined strategy conferences as an aide to or representative of General Marshall. In the early years of the war, Wedemeyer was one of America's most influential framers of military strategy, and was the principal author of the Victory Program, the initial plan for the total mobilization of the U.S. military.

In October 1943, Wedemeyer became chief of staff to Lord Louis Mountbatten (q.v.) in Southeast Asia. When General Joseph Stillwell was relieved in October 1944, the China-Burma-India command was split in two with Wedemeyer assuming command of the China portion. At age forty-seven, he was the youngest Allied theater commander of World War II.

After the war Wedemeyer commanded the U.S. Sixth Army in the United States. He retired in 1951 and was promoted to full general on the retired list in 1954. Although principally remembered for his role in China, Wedemeyer's major contribution to World War II was as one of the guiding lights in the early formulation of American and Allied strategy.

Michael Polly

Additional Reading
Wedemeyer, Albert C., *Wedemeyer Reports* (1958).
Weigley, Russell F., *The American Way of War* (1973).

Weichs, Maximilian von (1881–1954)

German field marshal, Army Group B commander. The scion of an old established Roman Catholic family, *Freiherr* von Weichs entered a Bavarian cavalry regiment in 1900. After attending the Bavarian War Academy in Munich, he held a variety of staff and command positions during and after World War I. As commander of the 3rd Cavalry Division in 1935, he presided over its transformation into the 1st *Panzer* Division. Two years later, he took over the XIII Corps in Nuremberg.

Following the 1939 Poland campaign (q.v.), von Weichs was given command of the newly created Second Army, with which he participated in the 1940 campaign and the invasion of Yugoslavia. In July 1941, he and his staff were sent to Byelorussia. During the ensuing operations of his Second Army in the central sector of the eastern front, he became ill and spent the critical period between November 1941 and January 1942 on sick leave.

In preparation for the great 1942 summer offensive in the south, von Weichs was entrusted with command of the newly formed Army Group B, which initially included the Sixth Army thrusting toward Stalingrad. His role in the ensuing Axis disasters along the Don River and around Stalingrad (q.v.) is still a matter of controversy.

In August 1943, Field Marshal von Weichs was sent to Belgrade to serve as German supreme commander in southeastern Europe. He was relieved of that command on 25 March 1945. After the war, he was indicted for war crimes but was deemed too ill to stand trial. Released in 1948, he died six years later.

Ulrich Trumpener

Additional Reading
Blau, George E., *The German Campaigns in the Balkans (Spring 1941)* (1953).
Mitcham, Samuel W., Jr., *Hitler's Field Marshals and Their Battles* (1987).
Ziemke, Earl F., and Magna E. Bauer, *Moscow to Stalingrad: Decision in the East* (1987).

Weizsäcker, Ernst von (1882–1951)

German diplomat. Ernst *Freiherr* von Weizsäcker was born in Stuttgart on 12 May 1882. During World War I he served in the German Navy, reaching the rank of commander. In 1920, he entered the foreign service and served in increasingly important consular and diplomatic posts. He was ambassador to Norway from 1931 to 1933, and ambassador to Switzerland from 1933 to 1936. When Joachim von Ribbentrop (q.v.) became foreign minister in 1938, von Weizsäcker became state secretary of the Foreign Ministry. From 1943 to 1945, von Weizsäcker was German ambassador to the Vatican.

As a high-ranking Foreign Ministry official, von Weizsäcker was arrested by the Allies and tried as a war criminal before an American Military Tribunal (q.v.) in Nuremberg. In his defense, von Weizsäcker insisted that he always had resisted Adolf Hitler's (q.v.) foreign policy and had made every effort to keep high-ranking Nazis out of the foreign service. He claimed that he had accepted Nazi Party membership and honorary SS rank only "for decorative reasons."

In April 1949, von Weizsäcker was convicted of complicity in the crimes of the Nazi regime and sentenced to seven years' imprisonment. His sentence later was commuted to five years. In 1950 he was released under a general amnesty.

During Ernst von Weizsäcker's trial, one of his defense counsels was his own son, Richard von Weizsäcker, who, on 1 July 1984, became the president of the Federal Republic of Germany. During his ten years in office, Richard von Weizsäcker won international respect and admiration for his unflinching stand that Germans should squarely face the crimes of the Nazi era.

David T. Zabecki

Additional Reading
Weizsäcker Ernst von, *Memoirs* (1951).

Westmoreland, William Childs (1914–)

American colonel, chief of staff, U.S. 9th Infantry Division. Westmoreland, who as a full general commanded U.S. forces in Vietnam from 1964 to 1968, and was chief of staff of the U.S. Army from 1968 to 1972, learned his trade on the battlefields of World War II. A 1936 graduate of the U.S. Military Academy at West Point, he originally wanted to become a pilot, but could not qualify because of eye problems. He was commissioned in the field artillery and assigned to one of the U.S. Army's last horse-drawn units.

During World War II Westmoreland served in North Africa, including the battle of Kasserine Pass (q.v.), as an artillery battalion commander in the 9th Infantry Division (Old Reliables). After the capture of Tunisia (q.v.), he saw action in Sicily (q.v.) and in northwest Europe. He finished the war as divisional chief of staff.

Randy Papadopoulos

Additional Reading

Blumenson, Martin, *Rommel's Last Victory: The Battle of Kasserine Pass* (1968).

Mittelman, Joseph B., *Eight Stars to Victory: A History of the Ninth U.S. Infantry Division* (1948).

Westmoreland, William C., *A Soldier Reports* (1976).

Westphal, Siegfried (1902–1982)

German general. In November 1941, Lieutenant Colonel Westphal was the operations officer of General Erwin Rommel's (q.v.) *Panzergruppe Afrika.* In January 1944, Westphal became chief of staff to Field Marshal Albert Kesselring (q.v.), commander of Army Group C in Italy. Though devoted to Kesselring, Westphal was disgusted with German efforts in Italy, which he described as a "poor man's war." Like many of his contemporaries, Westphal firmly believed in the divorce of politics from professional soldiering and steadfastly refused all attempts at being entangled in National Socialist ideology. Stung by criticism that the German Army's senior leaders had failed to restrain Adolf Hitler (q.v.), Westphal's response was that the army's senior leadership did not have the political acumen necessary to do so.

In September 1944, as a lieutenant general, Westphal became chief of staff to Field Marshal Gerd von Rundstedt (q.v.), the *OB West* (commander in chief, west). The change displeased von Rundstedt since Westphal had replaced the field marshal's favorite staff officer, Günther Blumentritt. Westphal, however, played a key role in the planning for the Ardennes offensive (q.v.). In early March 1945, Westphal returned to his previous post as chief of staff to Kesselring. After the war, Westphal wrote one of the first important insider's accounts of the German Army in the war.

David A. Foy

Additional Reading

Cooper, Matthew, *The German Army, 1933–1945: Its Political and Military Failure* (1978).

Westphal, Siegfried, *The German Army in the West* (1951).

Wever, Walther (1887–1936)

German major general, first chief of the German Air Command Office. On 1 September 1933, Wever was appointed chief of the air command office, in effect making him the first chief of the *Luftwaffe* general staff. As *Luftwaffe* chief, he worked tirelessly to make the *Luftwaffe* the equal of the other military services. He readily embraced modern technology and was a strong advocate for the development of a four-engine bomber. One of his main attributes was his ability to get along with his superiors, especially Hermann Göring (q.v.). Wever's enthusiasm also inspired subordinates with an ardent devotion to duty. His death, a result of a plane crash near Dresden on 3 May 1936, was a severe loss to the *Luftwaffe* high command and to Germany.

Michael G. Mahon

Additional Reading

Killen, John, *The Luftwaffe: A History* (1967).

Mason, Herbert M., Jr., *The Rise of the Luftwaffe* (1973).

Weygand, Maxime (1867–1965)

French general, last commander in chief of the French Third Republic. Weygand was born in Brussels, but his origins remain obscure. Among others, his father was rumored to be King Léopold II of the Belgians. Weygand was allowed to enter the French Army, and during World War I he was chief of staff to Marshal Ferdinand Foch. Weygand retired in 1935, but in 1939, he was recalled by Premier Paul Reynaud (q.v.), who named him commander of French forces in Lebanon and Syria. At the height of the Battle of France, Reynaud summoned him home to replace Maurice Gamelin (q.v.) as Allied supreme commander.

Weygand arrived in France on 20 May, far too late to reverse the situation; yet he still attempted to mount a viable resistance along the Weygand Line behind the Somme River. When that line crumbled, he informed the government on 11 June of the need to sign an armistice. For him, it was the only solution to saving French Africa and rebuilding military forces for a later attack against Germany. On 17 June, he accepted the position of minister of defense in Marshal Henri Pétain's (q.v.) Vichy government, and then delegate general in North Africa. In that position, he signed an agreement with Robert Murphy, President Franklin D. Roosevelt's (q.v.) personal representative to French Africa, that provided the Americans with raw materials, and, more importantly, prepared the way for the Allied landing of November 1942.

Weygand's actions made him suspect to the Germans, who after obtaining his recall, was arrested by the *Gestapo* (q.v.) and deported to Germany. Liberated by the Americans in May 1945, he was soon arrested on the orders of Charles de Gaulle's (q.v.) government, but the charges were dismissed in 1948. Weygand was a brave and competent general, tasked with the impossible in 1940.

Cederic Fry

Additional Reading
Goutard, Adolphe, *The Battle of France, 1940* (1958).
Werth, Alexander, *France 1940–1955* (1956).
Weygand, Maxime, *Recall to Service: The Memoirs of General Maxime Weygard* (1952).
Weygand, Maxime, and J. Weygand, *The Role of General Weygand* (1948).

Wheeler, Earle Gilmore (1908–1975)

American colonel, chief of staff, U.S. 63rd Infantry Division. The man who as a full general was chairman of the Joint Chiefs of Staff (1964–1970) for a major period of the Vietnam War, learned his trade on the battlefields of World War II. Born in Washington, D.C., Earle Wheeler graduated from the U.S. Military Academy at West Point as an infantry officer in 1932. He served in Tientsin, China, with the 15th Infantry Regiment before World War II. In 1942, Wheeler commanded an infantry battalion in the United States. In December 1944, he became chief of staff of the 63rd Infantry Division, which saw action in France and Germany. Wheeler was selected to lead a special assault regiment against Adolf Hitler's (q.v.) mountain fortress in the Bavarian Alps, but Germany surrendered just before the operation was scheduled to begin.

Randy Papadopoulos

Additional Reading
Webb, Willard J., and Ronald Cole, *The Chairmen of the Joint Chiefs of Staff* (1989).
Wheeler, Earl G., *Addresses* (1970).

White, Isaac Davis (1901–1991)

American major general, commander of the U.S. 2nd Armored Division. "I.D." White was an aggressive and generally successful leader of the 2nd Ar-

mored Division. He was immensely popular with officers and enlisted men alike. From October 1940 to January 1941, White commanded the 2nd Armored Reconnaissance Battalion, and he later commanded one of the division's armored regiments. In early 1943, White became commander of the division's Combat Command B, leading it in Northwest Africa, Sicily, and northern France (qq.v.).

In Normandy, White was promoted to brigadier general. During the Ardennes offensive (q.v.) Combat Command B surrounded and destroyed a large part of the 2nd *Panzer* Division at Celles (q.v.). On 19 January 1945, White took command of 2nd Armored Division from Major General Ernest Harmon (q.v.). Shortly after V-E Day, White was sent to command the Cavalry School at Fort Riley, Kansas. He later achieved the rank of full general.

Samuel J. Doss

Additional Reading
Houston, Donald E., *Hell on Wheels* (1977).

Wilhelmina (1880–1962)

Queen of the Netherlands. Wilhelmina Helena Pauline Maria was born 31 August 1880 in the Hague, the daughter of King William III and of his second wife, Emma of Waldeck-Pyrmont. On her father's death on 21 November 1890, she became queen of the Netherlands, her mother serving as regent until 1898. She was married to Duke Henry of Mecklenburg-Schwerin in February 1901 and had a daughter in April 1909.

During World War I, Wilhelmina played a significant role in the maintenance of her country's neutrality. With the invasion of the Netherlands by the Germans in World War II, she fled to Britain with her family and members of her cabinet. She was noted for her radio broadcasts from London encouraging Dutch resistance to the German occupation. In 1942, she visited both Canada and the United States.

With the end of the German occupation of the Netherlands in 1945, Queen Wilhelmina was welcomed back enthusiastically to her native land. In September 1946, she abdicated the throne in favor of her daughter, Juliana, and took the title of princess of the Netherlands. She died 28 November 1962 in the palace of Het Loo.

Bernard Weber

Additional Reading
Ashton, H.S. (pseud.), *The Netherlands at War* (1941).

Maass, Walter B., *The Netherlands at War 1940–1945* (1970).

Wilhelmina, *Lonely but Not Alone* (1960).

Willie and Joe

American cartoon figures. There may be no more indelible image of the American infantryman in Europe during World War II than that created by Willie and Joe, the cartoon characters who appeared in the army newspaper *Stars and Stripes.* These two scruffy, sweating, swearing, knights of combat sprang from the imagination of a twenty-one-year-old GI named Bill Mauldin (q.v.).

Through the hilarious adventures of his two heroes, Willie and Joe, Mauldin became the most famous American war cartoonist. He captured the grim humor and fatalism of combat, the utter absurdity of war, that made his two characters so appealing to enlisted men, who could immediately identify with the plight of Willie and Joe: let's do our duty, although we may complain about it; let's get the war over with, and let's go home in one piece. Officers might not have been as enthusiastic about Willie and Joe, however.

After the war, "still sound in limb and spirit," Mauldin published *Up Front,* which included his best wartime cartoons, and a text to match. He warned his readers from the very beginning, "my business is drawing, not writing." He explained, "I've used Willie and Joe in my cartoons because riflemen like them are the basic guys and the most important guys in a war."

In *Back Home,* Mauldin followed his two heroes through the comedy of adjustment to civilian life. Mauldin went on to have a successful career as a political cartoonist, but for a generation of Americans, he will always be linked to those two war weary fighters with cigarette butts dangling from their mouths, who needed a shave and a hot bath, and maybe a stiff drink—Willie and Joe.

Richard A. Voeltz

Additional Reading
Mauldin, Bill, *Back Home* (1947).
———, *Up Front* (1945).

Wilson, Henry Maitland (1881–1964)

British field marshal, Allied commander in the Middle East. When the war began, Sir Henry Wilson commanded British troops in Egypt and contributed to General Richard O'Connor's (q.v.) successful 1940–1941 Western Desert operations against the Italians. As part of General Archibald

Wavell's (q.v.) Middle East Command, Wilson was also the chief planning officer for General Alan Cunningham's (q.v.) victorious Ethiopian campaign. Wilson lead the ill-fated British expedition to Greece (q.v.) in February 1941, but was responsible for the skillful May retreat that saved Allied forces from disaster. Immediately thereafter, he suppressed a pro-Axis revolt in Iraq and occupied the Vichy French colony of Syria. He commanded Allied forces in Palestine, Transjordan, Lebanon, and Syria until assuming the Persia-Iraq command in late summer 1942.

When General Harold Alexander (q.v.) left to serve as Dwight D. Eisenhower's deputy in 1943, Wilson succeeded him as commander in chief, Middle East. In January 1944, Wilson was named supreme Allied commander, Mediterranean. By this time, tactical control of operations passed to General Mark Clark (q.v.) and Alexander. Wilson took charge of administration, policy, and strategy questions, always maintaining excellent Anglo-American relations. On the death of General John Dill (q.v.) in November 1944, Wilson became head of the British Joint Staff Mission in Washington and participated in the Yalta and Potsdam Conferences (*see* Conferences, Allied). He represented the British Army on the Combined Chiefs of Staff (q.v.) until April 1946.

Known as "Jumbo" because of his physique and gait, Wilson possessed a strong, forceful character and direct manner. Despite the lack of combat posts, he was considered an astute strategist and sound tactician.

Clayton D. Laurie

Additional Reading
Dewar, Michael, "Wilson," in *Churchill's Generals,* John Keegan (ed.) (1991).
Wilson, Sir Henry M., *Eight Years Overseas, 1939–1947* (1949).
Wilson, Sir Henry M., *His Life and Diaries* (1927).

Wingate, Orde Charles (1903–1944)

British major general, pioneer in unconventional warfare. An advocate of small force warfare, Wingate acquired his irregular warfare skills in the Sudan halting Arab attacks on the oil pipelines. He made his name by putting radical ideas into practice, something that did not endear him to the British Army establishment. He pioneered the concept of counter-gangs, exemplified by his highly effective special night squads that operated, often preemptively, in Palestine to defend Jewish settlements in the 1930s. Politically, he was a Zionist.

When World War II broke out, Wingate was able to employ his expertise with well-trained, well-motivated groups. His Gideon Force was instrumental in capturing Italian-held installations in Ethiopia in 1940. Devoted to carrying the war into the enemy's territory, he contributed greatly to early theories of counterinsurgency. His most famous innovation was probably his least effective, the long-range penetration groups that fought the Japanese in Burma and were known as the Chindits. Wingate died in a jungle plane crash late in the war. His legacy lives on today in the Israeli Defense Force, one of the world's most effective armies.

Chris Westhorp

Additional Reading
Sykes, Christopher, *Orde Wingate* (1959).
Tulloch, Derek, *Wingate in Peace and War* (1972).

Winkelman, Henri Gerard (1876–1952)

Dutch general, commander in chief of the Dutch armed forces. In 1940, Winkelman's Dutch Army consisted of nine divisions. They resisted the German invasion along the Peel and Grebbe Lines, but were overwhelmed by superior force. Winkelman surrendered the forces under his direct command on 14 May 1940, after a four-day campaign and following the bombing of Rotterdam (q.v.). He remained a POW until 1945.

Andrzej Suchcitz

Additional Reading
Maass, Walter B., *The Netherlands at War* (1970).
Warmbrunn, Werner, *The Dutch Under German Occupation, 1940–1945* (1963).

Wittmann, Michael (1914–1944)

Waffen-SS captain, tank commander. Michael Wittmann most likely was the greatest armored fighting vehicle commander of the war. Commanding a PzKpfw VI Tiger, he personally destroyed more than 100 Soviet tanks and armored assault guns between March 1943 and January 1944. Transferred to the western front, Wittmann commanded a tank company of the *Panzer Lehr* Division in the fighting at Normandy (q.v.). On 14 June 1944, Wittmann led a counterattack against elements of the British 7th Armoured Division. In roughly one half hour of fighting,

Wittmann personally destroyed at least twenty-one British tanks and twenty-eight armored vehicles. Later that day Wittmann's tank was knocked out, but he and his crew escaped unharmed. Wittmann received the Swords and Oak Leaves to the Knight's Cross for the action. On 8 August Wittmann was leading an element of four Tigers when they were engaged by a single Sherman Firefly tank of 1st Northamptonshire Yeomanry. Within a period of twelve minutes the Firefly destroyed three of the German tanks, including Wittmann's. There were no survivors.

David T. Zabecki

Additional Reading
Agte, Patrick, *Michael Wittmann and the Tiger Commanders of the Leibstandarte* (1996).
Simpson, Gary L., *Tiger Ace: The Life Story of Panzer Commander Michael Wittmann* (1996).

Witzleben, Erwin von (1881–1944)

German field marshal, conspirator against Adolf Hitler (q.v.). Von Witzleben, born in Breslau to an old Prussian family, had great regard for the traditions of the German officer corps. Although essen-

Field Marshal Erwin von Witzleben. (IWM HU 17282)

tially nonpolitical, he became involved in the conspiracy against Hitler as early as 1934. Ulrich von Hassell wrote: "I had a good feeling about him—a man of clear purpose and good perception."

As commander of the Third Military District in Berlin, Witzleben drew up military plans to arrest Hitler in 1938. After the Munich Agreement (q.v.) of 1938, Witzleben became commander of the First Army of Army Group C. He was promoted to field marshal in 1940, but in 1942 he was relieved as army commander in chief, west and forced into retirement.

On 20 July 1944, in the brief period of time the conspirators believed they had succeeded in assassinating Hitler, von Witzleben assumed the post of supreme commander of the army. In orders declaring a state of emergency, he explained: "The German soldier is confronted with a historic task. The salvation of Germany will depend on his energy and morale." Von Witzleben was tried by the People's Court and executed on 8 August 1944.

Susan Pentlin

Additional Reading

Deutsch, Harold C., *The Conspiracy Against Hitler in the Twilight War* (1968).
Galante, Pierre, *Operation Valkyrie: The German Generals Plot Against Hitler* (1981).

Wöhler, Otto (1894–1987)

German general, Army Group South commander. Wöhler began his career in 1913 as an officer candidate in the 167th (Alsatian) Infantry Regiment. After frontline service during World War I, he qualified as a staff officer. In April 1938, he was posted to Vienna as a principal general staff officer of the newly created Army Group 5, which became an army command in 1939 under Colonel General Wilhelm List (q.v.).

In December 1939, Colonel Wöhler was appointed chief of staff of XVII *Korps*. In 1940, he moved in the same capacity to the Eleventh Army where he eventually served as Erich von Manstein's (q.v.) right hand. In April 1942, Wöhler became Günther von Kluge's (q.v.) chief of staff at Army Group Center.

Having already gained some direct combat experience as interim leader of a special battle group, Wöhler received a corps command in northern Russia in April 1943. Four months later, he took over a group of divisions in the Ukraine that were later transformed into the Eighth Army. The following year, he was also given supervisory

authority over the Romanian Fourth Army (until August 1944), and later, over the Hungarian First Army.

Two days before Christmas, Wöhler was appointed commander of Army Group South, replacing Colonel General Johannes Friessner (q.v.). Wöhler thus became responsible for a major section of the eastern front, centered on Hungary. Following a futile counteroffensive by *Waffen-SS* (q.v.) divisions in March 1945, he presided over the retreat of his army group into Austria. He was then removed from his command on 7 April.

A capable staff officer and field commander, Wöhler was, for reasons unknown, never promoted beyond general. After the war, he was tried by the American Military Tribunal (q.v.) (the OKW case) and sentenced to eight years.

Ulrich Trumpener

Additional Reading

Haupt, Werner, *Heeresgruppe Mitte, 1941–1945* (1968).
Ziemke, Earl F., *Stalingrad to Berlin: The German Defeat in the East* (1968).

Wolff, Karl (1900–1984)

German SS colonel general, military governor of northern Italy. Wolff served as an officer in World War I. He joined the Nazi Party and rose rapidly within that organization. In January 1939, he was promoted to lieutenant general of the *Waffen-SS* (q.v.). In 1941, he became Heinrich Himmler's (q.v.) chief of staff and was his primary liaison officer with Adolf Hitler (q.v.). Two years later, Wolff was named German military governor of northern Italy and plenipotentiary to Benito Mussolini (q.v.). In February 1945, believing Allied victory imminent, he initiated unauthorized negotiations with Allen Dulles of the U.S. Office of Strategic Services (OSS) (qq.v.). His representative secretly met Dulles in Zurich and their negotiations led to an early surrender of the German forces in Italy. Not tried at Nuremburg, Wolff testified as a prosecution witness.

In 1961, Wolff published his memoirs, revealing his role in Himmler's inner circle and how he played a major part in building the SS state. He was arrested in January 1962 and the Munich State Court convicted Wolff on charges of sending at least 300,000 people, mostly Jews, to the Treblinka death camp; obtaining additional railroad cars to deport Jews from ghettos; overseeing SS participation in slave labor programs at major German companies; and being a willing participant (albeit in an advisory capacity) in the "Final Solution" (q.v.). In 1964, Wolff was sentenced to fifteen years in prison. He was released in 1971.

Robert F. Pace

Additional Reading

Reitlinger, Gerald R., *The SS: Alibi of a Nation, 1922–1945* (1956).

Simpson, Christopher, *Blowback: America's Recruitment of Nazis and Its Effects on the Cold War* (1988).

Wood, Edward Frederick Lindley (Lord Halifax) (1881–1959)

British foreign secretary and ambassador to the United States. Lord Halifax, a British diplomat, was foreign secretary from 1938 until posted as ambassador to the United States in 1941. He attended the first sessions of the United Nations (q.v.). While operating between the Foreign Office and the office of the prime minister, Halifax conducted negotiations with the respective parties during the Ethiopian crisis and other international crises. He aligned himself with Prime Minister Neville Chamberlain (q.v.), who believed in ideals such as personal contact among state leaders and the ability to resolve problems face to face as reasonable men. Unfortunately, those ideals resulted in the policy of peace at any price. Halifax had a ". . . realistic contempt for the pacifist attitude." He once said: "What matters most is the motive on which resort to the use of force is had." Halifax retired as ambassador to the United States in 1946. He died on 23 December 1959.

Rob Nadeau

Additional Reading

Colvin, Ian, *The Chamberlain Cabinet* (1971).

Wood, Edward F.L., *American Speeches of the Earl of Halifax* (1947).

Woodward, Llewellyn, *British Foreign Policy in the Second World War*, 2 vols. (1962–71).

Wood, John Shirley (1888–1966)

American major general, commander of the U.S. 4th Armored Division. Wood, called an American Rommel, led the 4th Armored Division in France in July 1944, to achievements General George S. Patton (q.v.) described as "unequalled . . . in the history of warfare." Wood was born in Arkansas and graduated from the U.S. Military Academy at West Point in 1912. He served in France during World War I, and in varied assignments between the wars. As part of Patton's Third Army, he quickly proved to be a master of mobile armored

British Ambassador to the United States, Lord Halifax, with Foreign Secretary Anthony Eden. (IWM NY

combat. Wood's strong character and fine mind marked his command style. He was original, bold, skilled, and relentless. He was also compassionate and devoted to his men.

Wood was relieved of command on 3 December 1944, officially for health reasons. The real reason was that he clashed with the U.S. XII Corps commander, Major General Manton Eddy (q.v.), who saw him as far too willful and independent.

Wood served at Fort Knox for the remainder of the war. Despite his relief, he was one of the best divisional commanders the U.S. Army ever produced.

Edward Steele

Additional Reading
Koyen, Kenneth A., *The Fourth Armored Division: From the Beach to Bavaria* (1946).

Y

Yeager, Charles Edward (1923–)
American major, fighter pilot, and test pilot. "Chuck" Yeager was born on 13 February 1923, in Myra, West Virginia. In September 1941, after graduating from high school, he enlisted in the army. Assigned to the army air corps, he completed aviation training and was commissioned a reserve flight officer in March 1943. In November 1943, he arrived in Britain as a fighter pilot with the Eighth Air Force. He flew sixty-four missions over Europe, downed thirteen enemy aircraft, and was shot down himself.

After the war, Yeager became a prominent test pilot. On 14 October 1947, he became the first man to break the sound barrier in the experimental aircraft X-1. In 1953, he established a world speed record in an X-1A. By 1952, he was a colonel, commanding the Aerospace Research Pilot School at Edwards Air Force Base. He retired from the air force in 1975 with the rank of brigadier general and became a familiar figure endorsing consumer products on television advertisements.

Boyd Childress

Additional Reading
Lundgren, William R., *Across the High Frontier: The Story of a Test Pilot, Major Charles E. Yeager, USAF* (1955).
Yeager, Chuck, *Yeager, an Autobiography* (1985).

Yeo-Thomas, Forest Fredric (1902–1964)
British wing commander, SOE operative. "Tommy" Yeo-Thomas was born in Britain and raised near Dieppe, France. In 1920, he escaped from the fighting in Poland. After joining the RAF in 1939, he was commissioned in 1941. He joined the Special Operations Executive (SOE) (q.v.) in 1942; his code name was "White Rabbit." He acted as a liaison/troubleshooter between the SOE and the Free French Forces of the Interior (q.v.). He convinced Prime Minister Winston S. Churchill (q.v.) to step up supply airdrops to the resistance after an inspection tour in November 1943. Yeo-Thomas was arrested by the German SD (q.v.) in Paris in 1944 and was taken to Buchenwald concentration camp, from which he managed to escape.

John D. Beatty

Additional Reading
Asprey, Robert B., *War in the Shadows* (1975).
Cookridge, Edward H., *Inside S.O.E: The Story of Special Operations in Western Europe 1940–1945* (1966).
Foot, Michael R.D., *S.O.E. in France* (1966).

Yeremenko, Andrei Ivanovich (1892–1970)
Soviet marshal, front (army group) commander. Yeremenko's parents were Ukrainian peasants. He was drafted into the tsar's army in 1913 and promoted for bravery in battle during World War I. He joined the Red Army in 1918, and served as a calvary officer during the civil war. He led a reconnaissance unit, and then became chief of staff and later deputy commander of a cavalry regiment. Following the civil war, he attended various military and political schools. He completed the advanced command courses, the Military Political Academy, and the Frunze Military Academy in 1935. After graduating from Frunze, he commanded a cavalry division from 1935 to 1938, and then assumed command of the VI Cossack Corps. That unit took part in the occupation of Poland in September 1939.

When the war started, Yeremenko was posted in the Far East. He was recalled by Josef Stalin (q.v.)

and given command of the Western Front. Between August 1941 and May 1945, Yeremenko commanded eight different fronts and two armies. In his first assignment of the war, he was able to restore stability to the deteriorated situation brought about by the German advance against the hapless Dimitry Pavlov (q.v.). Later in August 1941, Yeremenko took command of the Bryansk Front. He was severely wounded in October and out of action for several months.

Recovering from his wounds, Yeremenko was given command of the Fourth Shock Army and participated in the defense of Moscow (q.v.). Georgy Zhukov (q.v.) recognized his abilities, and assigned him to command of the Southeastern Front at Stalingrad (q.v.). In this role, he was one of three generals personally chosen by Zhukov to defend and eventually liberate Stalingrad.

In 1943, Yeremenko participated in the advance on Smolensk. He then took command of the Independent (Black Sea) Maritime Front, with orders to clear the Crimea (q.v.). In 1944, he led the 2nd Baltic Front in the capture of Dvinsk in Latvia. His final wartime assignment was command of the Carpathian Front.

Yeremenko was an outstanding tactician. He thoroughly understood the concept of using airpower to soften an enemy, following up with as much armor as could be massed on an objective, and mopping up with infantry. He made judicious use of reserves and had the ability to locate and exploit any enemy weaknesses. Following the war, he commanded various military districts until 1958, when he became inspector general of the Ministry of Defense of the Soviet Union. He held that position until his death in 1970.

Thomas Cagley

Additional Reading

Bialer, Seweryn (ed.), *Stalin and His Generals* (1984).
Lucas, James (ed.), *Command: A Historical Dictionary of Military Leaders* (1988).

Z

Zaleski, August (1883–1972)

Polish foreign minister. Zaleski was foreign minister in the government-in-exile of General Władysław Sikorski (q.v.) from 1939 to 1941. He resigned over his opposition to the imprecise wording of the Polish-Soviet Agreement, which left open the question of Poland's eastern frontier. From 1943 until the end of the war, he was head of the civil chancellery of the president of the Polish Republic.

Andrzej Suchcitz

Additional Reading

General Sikorski Historical Institute, *Documents on Polish-Soviet Relations 1939–1945* (1961).

Kaiski, Jan, *The Great Powers and Poland 1919–1946* (1985).

Lumas, Richard C., *Forgotten Holocaust: The Poles Under German Occupation, 1939–1944* (1986).

Zeitzler, Kurt (1895–1958)

German general of *Panzer* troops, chief of the general staff 1942–1944. Kurt Zeitzler was born in Brandenburg in 1895. He joined the 4th Thuringian Infantry Regiment just before World War I. During the war he commanded the 72nd Infantry Regiment. Between the wars, Zeitzler completed staff training through the *Reichwehr*'s general staff in disguise, the *Truppenamt*. After brief service in the new *Panzer* army, Zeitzler participated in the planning of the 1939 invasion of Czechoslovakia. Early in World War II, he held a combat command in the Polish campaign and a staff post during the conquest of France in 1940.

Zeitzler was widely regarded as an efficient and enthusiastic officer. His rapid rise was due to both his organizational competence and his personal acquaintance with and loyalty to Adolf Hitler (q.v.). In 1942, Zeitzler rose three grades to the rank of lieutenant general and became chief of the general staff.

Throughout his service as the senior staff officer of the German Army, Zeitzler frequently clashed with Hitler, who asserted increasingly greater control over military operations. Much of Zeitzler's efforts, especially during the Stalingrad (q.v.) campaign, focused on diverting Hitler from intervening in military decisions. Zeitzler's efforts often succeeded, but he failed to gain the degree of autonomy the German generals desired, especially the authority to conduct strategic withdrawals. When his disagreements with Hitler erupted into violent arguments, Zeitzler would attempt to quit his post, but Hitler refused to accept his resignation. Finally, following the bomb plot of 20 July 1944, Zeitzler went on sick leave and was replaced by General Heinz Guderian (q.v.) as chief of staff.

Randy Papadopoulos

Additional Reading

Liddell Hart, Basil H., *The German Generals Talk* (1979).

Mellenthin, Frederick W. von, *Panzer Battles, 1939–1945* (1950).

Zemke, Hubert (1914–1994)

American colonel, air group commander. Zemke made his reputation with the 56th Fighter Group of the Eighth Air Force based in Britain. He was an outstanding commander, combining brilliance as a combat pilot with inspirational leadership and sound tactical knowledge. The group he led became the premier American fighter unit in the European theater. He accomplished this by instilling his men with air discipline and an aggressive spirit.

Zemke's tactical awareness was most apparent in the way he devised means of playing on the strengths of the new P-47 Thunderbolt fighter, which looked like a poor aircraft in its initial outings. He forced his pilots to exploit its advantages of weight, firepower, and high altitude capability, and to nullify its weaknesses.

Zemke continued to improvise and devise new tactics as the war progressed. One such tactic was the "Zemke Fan," essentially an adoption of German U-boat naval tactics for air warfare. The "Fan" would find the enemy by ranging and seeking, then contact friendlies, and close for the kill. Little wonder the 56th became known as "Zemke's Wolf Pack."

Zemke was a leading ace of the 56th Fighter Group. In August 1944, he was transferred to the 479th Fighter Group, the newest in the Eighth Air Force. On his very last scheduled combat mission his P-51 shed a wing in a storm and he became a POW. The fighter groups he molded, taught, and led were a testament to his skill. The 56th Fighter Group was unchallenged in terms of absolute kills; its victory-to-loss ratio was superb; and it produced six of the top ten U.S. aces in Europe, including the top two.

Chris Westhorp

Additional Reading

Gurney, Gene, *Five Down and Glory: A History of the American Air Aces* (1958).

Peaslee, Budd J., *Heritage of Valor: The 8th Air Force in World War II* (1963).

Zemke, Hubert, *Zemke's Stalag: The Final Days of World War II* (1991).

Zhukov, Georgy Konstantinovich (1896–1974)

Marshal of the Soviet Union. Zhukov was the son of a shoemaker in the small village of Strelkovka. In his memoirs, he described his home life as poor, but not unpleasant. As was the custom, when he reached his early teens, he was apprenticed—to a furrier in Moscow. It was from there he was drafted into the tsar's army in 1915. He served with distinction, earning two St. George Crosses for valor as a junior noncommissioned officer. He was wounded in action, and received his discharge in 1918. After being discharged, he joined the Red Army and the Communist Party in 1919.

Although most major Soviet military figures were members of the party, few realized the rewards of party membership as much as Zhukov. In one of his early battles during the civil war, he fought the Whites across the same terrain on which he would twenty years later fight the Germans. He was a member of a cavalry brigade under the command of Semyon Budenny (q.v.). Josef Stalin (q.v.), present as a senior party official, was impressed with the ruthless pursuit of the enemy displayed by Budenny, Semen Timoshenko (q.v.), and Zhukov. All were destined to become Marshals. More importantly, when Stalin purged the military in the mid-1930s, these three not only survived, but their careers noticeably improved.

During the 1920s, Zhukov attended various cavalry courses, graduating from the advanced course in 1925. Although the records were destroyed and it was denied by some, there is evidence that Zhukov also attended a *Reichswehr*-sponsored leadership course in Germany during the late 1920s. In any event, his formal military education was completed by the obligatory attendance at the Frunze Military Academy in 1930. Subsequent to his military education, Zhukov commanded a variety of cavalry units, from brigade through corps.

In addition to command, Zhukov served as a military advisor in Spain and in China. Following his advisory roles, he served with some distinction in the Far East in the late 1930s. Under his command, his corps proved superior in combat and reflected his abilities as a leader, trainer, and disciplinarian. He played a key role in the defeat of the Japanese in Mongolia in 1939.

Zhukov's service in the Far East was more than an "out of sight, out of mind" situation. He and other prominent purge (q.v.) survivors of the 1930s served in the "Cavalry Clique." He's been described as ruthless, a bully, arrogant, and demanding. These traits, while not bringing comfort (although they would be fully understood, respected and, to an extent, tolerated) to a dictator such as Stalin, would well serve the needs of a country reeling under enemy attack.

After Zhukov's service against the Japanese in 1939, he was sent to Kiev to command a special military district in 1940. In January 1941, Stalin named him chief of the general staff and deputy commissar of defense. Although fully qualified for those roles, the positions were not appealing to Zhukov, as he felt he was far more effective and comfortable as a commander of troops than as a shuffler of paper.

Zhukov was not without an innate sense of tactical knowledge, and demonstrated that ability on several occasions prior to his selection as chief

Marshal of the Soviet Union Georgy Zuhkov (right) and Air Chief Marshal Sir Arthur Tedder sign the instrument of surrender for the Allies in Berlin, 9 May 1945. (IWM FRA 203380)

of staff. In war games held in early 1941, he defeated the armies led by the incumbent chief of staff. Stalin was so angry at the defeat of his favored forces, that he replaced the "incompetent" chief of staff with Zhukov. While not a marriage made in heaven, the selection meant that Zhukov would produce needed war plans for Stalin's approval, therefore satisfying Zhukov's need to be in charge of military operations. On the other hand, Stalin had a habit of issuing military plans as his own creations, thereby improving his credibility among the Soviet armed forces. Thus, Stalin was to enjoy the successes of Zhukov's military genius, while simultaneously avoiding having Zhukov become a popular folk hero—or so he thought.

Stalin appointed himself generalissimo of the Soviet armed forces, and selected Zhukov as his deputy. This arrangement played to Zhukov's strengths, as he was able to focus all of his abilities on developing strategy, organizing units, and bringing discipline to the Soviet military.

With the rapid collapse of the Soviet armies at the onset of the German offensive in June 1941, Stalin quickly sent his military strategist to the Smolensk (q.v.) salient, as commander of the reserve army group. But Zhukov was not to enjoy the time needed to develop his defenses at Smolensk. General Kliment Voroshilov (q.v.) was besieged at Leningrad (q.v.), and Stalin ordered his deputy there to prevent the collapse of that city.

Zhukov's strength and confidence, overshadowed only slightly by demands on his subordinates, proved to be the tonic needed to shift the course of the battle. Granted, he did assume command nearly simultaneously with the German offensive's peak, but he had no way of knowing the enemy would not continue to maintain pressure on the defenders.

Zhukov knew only one way to keep units and soldiers on line, and that was through threat of death. He relieved commanders at all levels, and promised that any who left the battle would be shot on the spot. When Zhukov sensed, or learned through intelligence sources, that the German offensive was faltering, he quickly ordered troops from the defense into the offense, and was able to repel the enemy from Leningrad. He was to enjoy no respite, however, as his leadership was soon needed elsewhere.

At the time Stalin ordered him to Leningrad, Zhukov was preparing to go on the offensive against the Germans at Yelnya. Not as a result of his departure, but coincident with it, the Germans picked that axis for their long-anticipated attack on Moscow (q.v.). The Germans massed three infantry armies, fourteen armored and nine motorized divisions for the attack, which opened on 30 September 1941. The Soviets had eighty rifle, two motorized infantry, one tank, and nine cavalry divisions, plus thirteen tank brigades. These forces were organized into three fronts (army groups). The Germans attacked with expected ferocity and, although fighting gallantly, the Soviets were outmaneuvered and slowly fell back toward the Moscow suburbs. The Germans paid a terrible price, however, particularly in tank battles, as the Soviet T-34 proved its value as a fighting vehicle.

The Germans pushed forward, and by 6 October, were within firing range of Moscow. Two significant events occurred that day: the first snow of winter fell, and Stalin recalled Zhukov from Leningrad to take over defense of the capital. Zhukov immediately took charge, displaying the same harshness and decisiveness he had displayed at Leningrad. He combined two of the fronts into a unified command, replaced seemingly weak commanders at will, and through his personality, combined with his well-known rage, brought about the resolve that was required to save the city. Weather and geography, of course, also played important roles in Zhukov's success. As the Germans advanced, they had more and more territory to protect, thereby weakening their flanks. Although Russian winters are famous for their harshness, the winter of 1941 was particularly brutal, and wore heavily on the attackers, who were too long in the field.

From analyses of previous battles, Zhukov knew the Germans invariably attacked with well-trained and disciplined German soldiers, positioning their less reliable Axis allies on the flanks. Trading space for time, he allowed the Germans to push forward, thus providing his own forces the opportunity to attack the less disciplined units on the flanks. After the German advance was stopped, he brought forward rested reserve forces and smashed through the German lines, turning the Soviet defense into a counterattack.

Throughout the war, Zhukov continually was used in this manner by Stalin. His strength and confidence were used again to thwart the Germans at Stalingrad (q.v.) in 1942. He also was involved in the German defeat at Kursk (q.v.) in 1943. From there, Zhukov directed the Soviet sweep across the Ukraine, replacing Nikolai Vatutin (q.v.) in command of the 1st Ukrainian Front. In June 1944, Zhukov commanded all of the Soviet fronts in the breakthrough against German Army Group Center in Byelorussia (q.v.). He continued the Soviet push across Poland, halting short of Warsaw (q.v.) in August 1944. With the resumption of the offensive in January 1945, his forces advanced across Prussia at the rate of 100 miles per week. He crossed the Oder River on 16 April, and launched the final assault on Berlin (q.v.) on 2 May. On 8 May 1945, Zhukov accepted the German surrender in Berlin.

Zhukov was an exceptionally talented commander, without a doubt the Soviets' best. Although his strong personality traits contributed to his success, another trait, one seen in few other Soviet officers, was more important: he dared to stand up to Stalin—and he survived. Although a member of the Communist Party, Zhukov did not deceive himself nor his soldiers about the realities of war, nor did he pontificate on Socialist doctrine or placate party officials. He was first and foremost, a soldier. He fought to protect a political system in which he believed, but he clearly understood wars are won not with words, but with weapons.

Shortly after the war, in 1946, Zhukov fell into Stalin's disfavor, primarily because of his heroic image and popularity. He was shifted into near-oblivion, and did not return to public view until after Stalin's death. Nikita Khrushchev (q.v.) brought Zhukov back into the public eye when he made him minister of defense in 1955. He was relieved of that post in 1957, and again slipped into obscurity by being assigned to meaningless positions well out of sight. Shortly thereafter, he retired from public life, returning only briefly in 1965 to receive the Order of Lenin. He lived in comfortable retirement, writing his memoirs, until his death in 1974.

Thomas Cagley

Additional Reading

Bialer, Seweryn (ed.), *Stalin and His Generals* (1984).

Chaney, Otto Preston, Jr., *Zhukov* (1971).

Moynahan, Brian, *Claws of the Bear: The History of the Red Army from the Revolution to the Present* (1989).

Seaton, Albert, *Stalin As Military Commander* (1976).

Shukman, Harold (ed.), *Stalin's Generals* (1993).

Spahr, William J., *Zhukov: The Rise and Fall of a Great Captain* (1995).

Zhukov, Georgy, *The Memoirs of Marshal Zhukov* (1971).

Zuckerman Itzhak (1915–1981)

Deputy commander of the Warsaw Ghetto uprising. Zuckerman was appalled by the passivity and even cooperation of the local Jewish councils and militia with the Nazi authorities in putting into practice a systematic program of annihilation of the Polish Jews. As early as March 1942, he urged the creation, training, and arming of underground

Jewish fighting squads patterned after the similar units of the Polish resistance (q.v.).

Initially, he encountered the strong opposition of many leaders of the Jewish community who believed such steps would only exacerbate the Nazi extermination policies. Only at the end of July 1942, when the daily trainloads of some 5,000 Jews began leaving the Warsaw Ghetto for Treblinka to be gassed, were his views accepted by some in the Jewish community. The Jewish Fighting Organization *(Żydowska Organizacja Bojowa—ŻOB* for short) was formed with Mordecai Anielewicz (q.v.) as its leader and Zuckerman as one of his deputies.

Zuckerman established the first contact with the commander of the Polish Home Army (Armia Krajowa-AK), General Stefan Rowecki (qq.v.) and obtained from him a few rifles, pistols, grenades, and some explosives. During the Warsaw Ghetto (q.v.) uprising from 18 January to 16 May 1943, Zuckerman was one of Anielewicz's deputies and his liaison officer with the Home Army. After Anielewicz's suicide, he took over the command of a small group of the surviving insurgents and led them through the sewers to the "Aryan" side of Warsaw, where they joined the Polish resistance forces to continue the struggle. Zuckerman died in 1981 in Tel Aviv, Israel.

M.K. Dziewanowski

Additional Reading

Bruce, George, *The Warsaw Uprising, 1 August–2 October 1944* (1972).

Tushnet, Leonard, *To Die with Honor: The Uprising of Jews in the Warsaw Ghetto* (1965).

Zuckerman, Itzhak, *A Surplus of Memory: Chronicle of the Warsaw Ghetto Uprising* (1991).

Zukerman, Isaac, and Moshe Basak (eds.), *The Fighting Ghettos* (1962).

Zylberberg, Michael, *A Warsaw Diary, 1939–1945* (1969).

Z

Units and Organizations

A

Abwehr (German Military Intelligence)

The *Abwehr* was the German high command's unified, all-services branch for strategic espionage, sabotage, and counterespionage. The individual services retained their own intelligence sections for operational and tactical intelligence. The *Abwehr* was created in the late 1920s but had predecessors going back to Frederick the Great. In the Third *Reich,* the *Abwehr* was initially led by Navy Captain Conrad Patzig. When Navy Captain (later Admiral) Wilhelm Canaris (q.v.) became head of the *Abwehr* in 1935, the agency was "in shambles." By 1941, however, Canaris had revitalized it. According to Michael Geyer, the *Abwehr* "commanded its own sprawling apparatus, its own field organization in Germany and abroad, and also a small police force . . ., several intelligence field units, and . . . specialized combat units for sabotage and commando operations."

After 1936, the *Abwehr* was organized into three main sections corresponding to its three major tasks, plus two other less important bureaus. *Abwehr I* was responsible for espionage. It collected military, political, economic, and social information on foreign powers.

Abwehr II engaged in sabotage and subversion, including commando raids in wartime. Sometimes called "covert operations" or "special duties," this was the most controversial of the agency's three main functions. Höhne gives several examples of *Abwehr II* in action. It was used by the *Wehrmacht* high command in the 1938 Sudetenland crisis to instigate acts of sabotage. Later, a commando unit called the *Brandenburgers* (q.v.) thrusted deep into Poland, Belgium, Holland, and Russia simultaneously with the *Wehrmacht's* attacks on those countries in 1939–1941. Its goal was to secure strategic bridges, forts, and other installations before they could be destroyed by the defend-

ers. In 1940–1941, *Abwehr II* was given a disinformation task, namely misleading the Soviet Union, then Germany's friend, into thinking that the military buildup prior to Operation BARBAROSSA was actually directed at Great Britain rather than at the Soviets.

Counterespionage *(Abwehr III)* involved protecting the German armed forces from enemy spies, including possible German traitors. It therefore included domestic surveillance. This was the least controversial of the *Abwehr's* activities.

In addition to the above three main branches, the *Abwehr* had other bureaus responsible for administration (Section Z) and for collecting military and political information. The latter went under the name *Abteilung Ausland* (later *Amtsgruppe Ausland*)—"Foreign Branch." Headed by Leopold Burkner, it collated foreign political material of military interest from overt sources (attache reports, the foreign press and radio, Foreign Office sources, etc.), as well as from clandestine sources." *Abteilung Ausland* appears to have been considerably less important than *Abwehr I, II,* or *III.*

From the beginning of the Third *Reich,* the relationship between the *Abwehr* and the *Gestapo* (q.v.) was especially critical. In 1933–1934, Patzig welcomed the *Gestapo's* creation and its efficient dealing with the regime's opponents. In fact, the two intelligence agencies cooperated with one another. Although there was no systematic coordination of military intelligence between them, there was plenty of informal cooperation. There was also competition.

Between 1935 and 1943, the *Abwehr* entered into several agreements with the SS (q.v.) in order to delimit spheres of influence. One of these treaties was the famous "Ten Commandments" of 26 December 1936, an attempt to resolve some of the jurisdictional disputes between Canaris and Reinhard Heydrich (q.v.), the head of the Security Police. Yet this agreement failed to settle the conflicts and the competition continued. Friction also arose between the *Abwehr* and *Gestapo* over the execution of the *Abwehr's* orders. The *Abwehr* was at a disadvantage here as it had no executive arm of its own and was therefore dependent for internal executive action on the *Gestapo*. The underlying problem was that Heydrich and Walter Schellenberg (q.v.) had designs on the *Abwehr*. Their goal was a unified German intelligence service under SS control. They achieved that goal in mid-1944.

One feature distinguishes the *Abwehr* from virtually every other central agency in the Nazi government: several of its top officers were opposed to Adolf Hitler's (q.v.) military goals and criminal activities. The main dissidents within the *Abwehr* were Admiral Canaris himself, a conservative nationalist whose role in the opposition to Hitler was often ambiguous and fluctuated with events; Hans Oster, Canaris's chief of staff; and Hans von Dohnanyi, head of the foreign policy reports desk in the central administrative office. All three had access to information about the criminal activities of the Nazi regime, such as the murder of Poles, Jews, and others, that was kept from the average German citizen. They also had a perfect cover from which to operate against the regime.

Headquartered in Berlin's government district, *Abwehr* officers regularly traveled to foreign countries on official business where they made contacts and promoted their cause. They also communicated with foreigners and fellow conspirators inside Germany. As a consequence, they could and did work quite openly (some would say too openly) against Hitler both inside and outside Germany.

According to Höhne, some of the stories regarding Admiral Canaris, for example that he was a superb intelligence administrator, are myths. By 1943–1944, the *Abwehr* was characterized by inefficiency, corruption, nepotism, over-staffing, incompetence, and red tape—presumably due to Canaris's leadership. Following a series of agency blunders, Hitler dismissed Canaris as chief of the *Abwehr* on 11 February 1944. The next day, the SS descended on the *Abwehr* and began to distribute its sections to the SD and RSHA (qq.v.). The *Abwehr* was finished. Canaris himself was initially placed under house arrest, later released, and then rearrested following the 20 July 1944 attempt on Hitler's life. On 9 April 1945, he was hanged by the Nazis for high treason. Ironically, he had nothing to do with Claus von Stauffenberg's (q.v.) assassination plot.

Jon Moulton

Additional Reading

Geyer, Michael, "National Socialist Germany: The Politics of Information," in Ernest R. May (ed.), *Knowing One's Enemies: Intelligence Assessment before the Two World Wars* (1984).

Höhne, Heinz, *Canaris: Hitler's Master Spy* (1979).

Kahn, David, *Hitler's Spies: German Military Intelligence in World War II* (1978).

Aces

The consensus definition of an ace is the fighter pilot credited with five or more air-to-air victories. The derivation of the word *ace* is from the French colloquial *as,* or athletic champion. During World War I, the French labeled any pilot who shot down ten or more enemy aircraft an ace. The Germans applied the term *experter* (expert) to the fighter ace. Initially, the British refused to designate a pilot as an ace. Instead, they felt the concept of teamwork within their air force was more essential. Partially to improve morale among British pilots in World War I, Air Marshal Hugh Trenchard (q.v.) changed his attitude.

When the Americans entered the war in 1917, they adopted the system but reduced the required number of kills to five. The leading air aces of World War I were Germans *Rittmeister* Manfred *Freiherr* von Richthofen ("Red Baron") with eighty kills, and Lieutenant Ernst Udet (q.v.) with sixty-two kills; French Captain René Fonck, with seventy-five kills; Canadian Major William Bishop with seventy-two kills; British Major Edward C. Mannock with seventy-three kills; and American Captain Edward "Eddie" Rickenbacker with twenty-six kills.

The five victories defining an ace became widely accepted in World War II, although the various national air forces used different methods to credit kills. The Germans, for example, used one kill for each aircraft downed. The Royal Air Force, United States Army Air Forces, and U.S. Navy pilots divided aerial victories into fractions if pilots shared the kill. The Soviets and Italians counted each aircraft destroyed separately. The U.S. Eighth Air Force even awarded its pilots credit for air-to-ground kills. Of course, the statistical problem arose when two or more fighter pilots shared in the same kill. In the German Air Force each pilot received full credit, which is one of the reasons the *Luftwaffe* had a large number of high-scoring aces.

In World War II, the leading *Luftwaffe* ace was Major Erich Hartmann (q.v.) with an incredible 352 kills—all but seven against Soviet aircraft. *Luftwaffe* pilot Gerhard Barkhorn (q.v.) had 301 kills. Hartmann and Barkhorn are the highest-scoring aces of all time. Given the nature of modern aerial combat, it is very unlikely their records will ever be matched. The RAF's official leading ace was Group Captain John E. Johnson (q.v.) with thirty-eight kills. The actual leader, however, may have been fabled Squadron Leader Marmaduke Thomas St. John Pattle (q.v.), whose service was in North Africa and Greece but whose records of aerial combat were lost. The top U.S. ace of the war was Major Richard Bong, whose forty kills came in the Pacific theater. The leading USAAF aces in Europe were Colonel Francis S. Gabreski (q.v.) with thirty-one kills, and Major Robert S. Johnson with twenty-eight kills. At least two German pilots were aces in both World Wars. Hilmer von Bülow-Bothkamp had six kills in World War I, and eighteen in World War II; Theodor Osterkamp shot down thirty-two enemy aircraft in World War I, and six in World War II.

Perhaps the definition of an air ace is nowhere better summarized than in the words of USAAF General James Doolittle (q.v.), who thought an ace must have uncommon eyesight, strength and agility, maintain his cool and have a calculated recklessness, be courageous, and occasionally lucky.

Boyd Childress

Leading World War II Aces in Europe and North Africa

Name	Rank	Kills	Remarks
American			
Francis S. Gabreski	Colonel	31	
Robert S. Johnson	Major	28	
George E. Preddy	Major	26	KIA Plus 5 Ground
Lance C. Wade	Wing Commander	25	RAF
John C. Meyer	Colonel	24	Plus 13 Ground
Raymond S. Wetmore	Major	22.5	Plus 2 Ground
David C. Shilling	Colonel	22.5	KIA Plus 10.5 Ground
Don S. Gentile	Captain	22	2 with RAF Plus 7 Ground
Frederick J. Christensen, Jr.	Major	21.5	
John J. Voll	Major	21	
Walker M. Mahurin	Lt. Colonel	21	
Donald D. Gentile	Captain	20	KIA
French			
Pierre H. Clostermann	Squadron Leader	33	RAF
Marcel Albert	Captain	23	Soviet Air Force
Jean E.F. Demozay	Wing Commander	21	RAF
Pierre Le Gloan	Lieutenant	18	KIA
Roland de la Poype	Captain	17	
Jacques Andre	Lieutenant	16	
Louis Delfino	Cadet	16	
Edmond Marin la Meslee	Captain	15	KIA
British			
J.E. Johnson	Group Captain	38	
J.R.D. Braham	Wing Commander	29	19 Night Fighter
R.R.S. Tuck	Wing Commander	29	
N.F. Duke	Squadron Leader	28	

(continued next page)

Name	Rank	Kills	Remarks
British *(continued)*			
J.H. Lacey	Squadron Leader	27	
E.S. Lock	Flight Lieutenant	26	KIA
B. Drake	Wing Commander	24.5	
W. Vale	Squadron Leader	24	
G. Allard	Flight Lieutenant	24	KIA
D.R.S. Bader	Wing Commander	23	
R.F. Boyd	Wing Commander	22.5	
D.E. Kingaby	Wing Commander	22.5	
H.M. Stephen	Squadron Leader	22.5	
M.N. Crossley	Squadron Leader	22	
M.M. Stephens	Wing Commander	22	
H.J.L. Hallowes	Wing Commander	21.5	
B.A. Burbridge	Wing Commander	21	21 Night Fighter
G.K. Gilroy	Group Captain	21	
E.W.F. Hewett	Squadron Leader	21	
A.A. McKellar	Squadron Leader	21	KIA
J.E. Rankin	Air Commodore	21	
R.H. Harries	Wing Commander	21	KIA
J. Cunningham	Group Captain	20	19 Night Fighter
W.D. David	Group Captain	20	
Australian			
C.R. Caldwell	Group Captain	28.5	8 in Australia
Canadian			
G.F. Beurling	Flight Lieutenant	31.3	
V.C. Woodward	Squadron Leader	22	
H.W. McLeod	Squadron Leader	21	KIA
New Zealander			
C.F. Gray	Wing Commander	27.5	
A.C. Deere	Wing Commander	22	
E.D. Mackie	Wing Commander	22	
W.V. Crawford-Compton	Wing Commander	21.5	
R.B. Hesselyn	Flight Lieutetant	21.5	
South African			
Pattle, M.T. St.J.	Squadron Leader	34	40+ Probables KIA
A.G. Malan	Group Captain	35	
J.J. LeRoux	Squadron Leader	23.5	KIA
P.H. Hugo	Group Captain	22	
Irish			
B. Finucane	Wing Commander	32	RAF KIA
Czech			
J. František	Sergeant	28	2 Polish Air Force 9 French Air Force 17 RAF KIA

(continued next page)

Name	Rank	Kills	Remarks
	Polish		
Stanisław F. Skalski	Wing Commander	22.5	5 Polish AF
			17.5 RAF
Witold Urbanowicz	Wing Commander	20	17 RAF
			3 USAAF in China
Michal Gladych	Major	18.5	Polish AF
Eugeniusz Horbaczewski	Squadron Leader	16.5	RAF
			KIA
Marian Pisarek	Wing Commander	12.5	RAF
			KIA
Jan Zumbach	Squadron Leader	12.5	RAF
Antoni Głowacki	Squadron Leader	11.5	RAF
Michal K. Macieiowski	Pilot Officer	10.5	RAF
Henryk Szczęsny	Wing Commander	10.3	RAF
	Soviet		
Ivan N. Kozhedub	Major General	62	
Alexsandr I. Pokryshkin	Guards Colonel	59	
Grigori A. Rechkalov	Captain	58	
Nikolai D. Gulaev	Major	57	4 prior to
			June 1941
Arseny V. Vorozheikin	Major	52	6 in Mongolia
			1939
Kirill A. Yevstigneyev	Colonel	52	
Dimitri B. Glinka	Major	50	
Alexsandr Klubov	Captain	50	
	Romanian		
Constantino Cantacuzino		60	
	Finnish		
Hans H. Wind	Captain	75	
	Italian		
Adriano Visconti	Major	26	KIA
Teresio Martinoli	Sergeant	23	KIA
Franco Lucchini	Captain	21	KIA
Leonardo Ferruli	Lieutenant	21	KIA
Mario Visentini	Captain	20	KIA
Franco Bordoni Bisleri	Captain	19	
Luigi Gorrini	Sergeant	19	
Furio Lauri	Lt. Colonel	18	
Ugo Drago	Captain	16	
	Spanish–Blue Squadron		
Gonzalo Hevia Alvarez-Quiñones	Capitan	12	
Mariano Cuadra Medina	Comandante	10	
Fernando Sánchez-Arjona y Courtoy	Teniente	9	KIA
José Ramón Gavilán y Ponce de León	Capitan	9	
Vicente Aldecoa Lecando	Alferez	8	
Angel Salas Larrazábal	Comandante	7	
José Arango López	Capitan	7	
Bernardo Meneses Orozco	Teniente	6	

A

(continued next page)

Name	Rank	Kills	Remarks
Spanish–Blue Squadron *(continued)*			
Luis Azqueta Brunét	Teniente	6	
Lorenzo Lucas Fernández-Peña	Teniente	6	
Francisco Valiente Zarraga	Teniente	6	
Manuel Sánchez-Tabernero de Prada	Teniente	6	
Antonio Alós Herrero	Capitan	5	
German–Eastern Front			
Erich Hartmann	Major	352	
Gerhard Barkhorn	Major	301	
Günther Rall	Major	275	4 in the West
Otto Kittel	Lieutenant	267	KIA
Walter Nowotny	Major	258	3 in the West KIA
Wilhelm Batz	Major	237	
Erich Rudorffer	Major	222	86 in the West
Hermann Graf	Colonel	212	10 in the West
Theodor Weissenberger	Major	208	33 in the West
Hans Philipp	Lt. Colonel	206	29 in the West KIA
Walter Schuck	Lieutenant	206	
Heinrich Ehrler	Major	204	KIA
Anton Hafner	Lieutenant	204	20 in the West KIA
Helmut Lipfert	Captain	203	
German–Western Front			
Heinrich Bär	Lt. Colonel	220	96 in the East
Hans-Joachim Marseille	Captain	158	KIA
Joachim Müncheberg	Major	135	33 in the East KIA
Werner Schroer	Major	114	12 in the East
Kurt Bühligen	Lt. Colonel	112	
Adolf Galland	Lt. General	104	
Egon Mayer	Lt. Colonel	102	KIA
Josef Priller	Colonel	101	
German–Night Fighters			
Heinz-Wolfgang Schnaufer	Major	121	
Helmut Lent	Colonel	110	KIA
Heinrich zu Sayn-Wittgenstein	Major	83	
Werner Streib	Colonel	66	
Manfred Meurer	Captain	65	
German–Jet Fighters			
Heinrich Bär	Lt. Colonel	16	220 Total
Franz Schall	Captain	14	137 Total
Hermann Buchner	Master Sergeant	12	
Georg-Peter Eder	Major	12	78 Total
Erich Rudorffer	Major	12	
Karl Schnarrer	Lieutenant	11	

Table compiled by Boyd Childress, Dennis Bartles, and José Alvarez.

Additional Reading

Baker, E.C.R., *The Fighter Aces of the R.A.F.* (1962).

Shores, Christopher, *Air Aces* (1983).

Toliver, Raymond F., and Trevor J. Constable, *Fighter Aces of the Luftwaffe* (1977).

Afrika Korps

The *Deutsches Afrika Korps* (*DAK*) officially came into existence in mid-February 1941, when Lieutenant General Erwin Rommel (q.v.) was given command of various German army units sent to Libya to support the Italians. The transportation of the requisite personnel and their equipment to North Africa took many weeks, and it was only in April that the transfer of the 5th Light Division was completed. This division, initially commanded by Major General Johannes Streich, was subsequently beefed up in strength and in mid-August 1941 became the 21st *Panzer* Division.

Starting in early April elements of the 15th *Panzer* Division arrived in Libya as well, and by the middle of the year the *DAK* evolved into a two-divisional mobile strike force. A third German division, the 90th Light Division, under Major General Max Sümmermann, appeared in Libya in the fall of 1941, but like several other German divisions transferred to Africa in 1942–

1943, it did not become an integral part of the *DAK*.

In August 1941, the command structure in North Africa was modified by the appointment of Rommel as head of Panzer Group Africa, renamed *Panzer-Armee-Afrika* in early 1942. With Rommel's appointment, General Ludwig Crüwell assumed command of the *DAK* in October 1941. In May 1942, even before Crüwell was shot down in his observation plane and captured, Lieutenant General Walther Nehring assumed command of the *DAK*. Three months later, Nehring was wounded in the battle of Alam el Halfa (q.v.) and was evacuated. On 4 November, his successor, General Wilhelm von Thoma (q.v.), surrendered to the British during the battle of El Alamein (q.v.).

The retreat of the *DAK*, or what was left of it, was initially directed by the surviving chief of staff, Colonel Fritz Bayerlein (q.v.), but on 13 November 1942, an official successor to von Thoma was appointed, General Gustav Fehn. Flown in from the Caucasus front, Fehn arrived in Libya ten days later and was placed in charge of the entire *Panzer-Armee* while Rommel hurried off to Germany. After very unpleasant meetings with Adolf Hitler, Hermann Göring, and Albert Kesselring (qq.v.), Rommel returned to Africa on 2 December 1942.

Fehn's command of the *DAK* ended in mid-

A group of Afrika Korps *troops being vaccinated at an oasis in the desert, 31 May 1942. (IWM MH 5838)*

January 1943, when he was wounded. Fehn's command was temporarily held by Major General Kurt von Liebenstein followed by Lieutenant General Heinz Ziegler, the latter having previously served as "permanent deputy" for Colonel General Hans-Jürgen von Arnim (q.v.), commander of Fifth *Panzer* Army in northern Tunisia. These interim arrangements ended early in March, when Lieutenant General Hans Cramer was officially installed as commander of the *DAK*. A veteran of Rommel's earlier campaigns (commanding the 8th *Panzer* Regiment from October 1941 to March 1942), Cramer presided over the decline and eventual capitulation of the *DAK*.

During its two years in Africa, the composition and strength of the *DAK* underwent numerous changes. While its basic two-divisional structure remained in effect until the very end, the *DAK* was augmented occasionally by other units (both German and Italian) for particular missions. As for the strength of the *DAK*, it started in April 1941 with 9,300 men and 130 tanks. Its armored component rose to 150 tanks by mid-June, and to 260 by mid-November 1941. By the time Rommel drove into Egypt in June 1942, the *DAK*'s tank strength had dwindled to ninety, but it rose again in subsequent weeks and stood at 230 by late August. After the battle of El Alamein, only a handful of tanks remained. Thanks to both replacements and repairs, the *DAK* had fifty-five tanks at its disposal when it settled down in the Mersa el Brega position, but was down again to twenty-three by the end of 1942.

Throughout its campaigns in Libya and Egypt, the *DAK* reported directly to Rommel. Once his forces were pushed back into Tunisia, the *DAK* was temporarily split. In mid-February 1943, the *DAK* was assigned to the newly created Italian First Army, commanded by General Giovanni Messe. The *DAK* remained part of Messe's army until the general Axis surrender in Tunisia (q.v.), 12–13 May 1943.

Ulrich Trumpener

Additional Reading
Cortesi, Lawrence, *Rommel's Last Stand* (1984).
Irving, David, *The Trail of the Fox: The Life of Field Marshal Erwin Rommel* (1977).
Liddell Hart, Basil H., *History of the Second World War* (1970).

Air Force, Belgian
The Belgian Air Force was formed on 1 March 1920 as part of the Belgian Army. It was plagued from its inception to outbreak of the war by shortages of modern aircraft. Belgium did develop its own fighter aircraft, the Renard R-36, but relied on the United States and Great Britain for most of the aircraft it flew.

The Belgian Air Force consisted of three regiments: an observation and army cooperation unit, a fighter regiment, and a reconnaissance and bombing regiment. The fighter regiment had six squadrons and seventy-nine aircraft, and in addition each squadron had its own antiaircraft squadron.

When the Germans invaded Belgium, only 180 of the 234 aircraft available were operational, and most of these 234 aircraft were obsolete. The Belgian Air Force deployed during the German offense in May of 1940. As part of the Belgian forces-in-exile, the Belgian Air Force participated in the Battle of Britain (q.v.) in 1940 and 1941 and in the western front campaigns of 1944 and 1945.

Thomas A. Cardwell, III

Additional Reading
Mollo, Andrew, *The Armed Forces of World War II* (1981).

Air Force, British
The Royal Air Force (RAF) was originally established in April 1918, when the Royal Flying Corps and the Royal Naval Air Service merged into an independent air force. Both services were active in World War I, but during the interwar period, the RAF had to fight to maintain its independent status. During the postwar period, the RAF first developed as a strategic bombing force. It expanded in the 1930s to insure comparable strength with the German *Luftwaffe* both in numbers and in modern aircraft. Under the leadership of airmen like Hugh Trenchard (q.v.) and Edward Ellington, the RAF increased its dedication to long-range bombing, and aircraft were designed with this strategy in mind. During World War II, the RAF was the mainstay in Britain against the powerful *Luftwaffe*. That both the RAF and the nation survived is, in large part, a tribute to the RAF and its superb air and ground crews.

In 1939, the RAF was under the command of the Air Council, whose members included political as well as military figures. The chief of the air staff at the outbreak of World War II was Sir Cyril Newall, who was succeeded by Air Chief Marshal Sir Charles Portal (q.v.) in October 1940. The RAF was organized into seven home commands and seven foreign commands in 1939. Home commands included Bomber Command,

Fighter Command, and Coastal Command, supported by the Balloon, Reserve, Training, and Maintenance Commands. Overseas commands were located in the Middle East, the Mediterranean, and India. While the command structure of the RAF changed during the first several years of the war, the basic form of the three operational commands remained.

Bomber Command was the largest of the three. In 1939, it had fifty-five squadrons and 920 aircraft, although as few as 350 were first-rate bombers. Fighter Command was composed of thirty-nine squadrons with approximately 600 aircraft, although many fighters lacked recent technological innovations. Most of these aircraft were committed to the defense of Britain. Coastal Command possessed a paltry ninety-six aircraft, most of which were obsolete. In September 1939, total RAF strength was 3,609 serviceable aircraft, up from 2,542 only a year before. Personnel numbered 11,519 officers and 162,439 enlisted men, with fewer than 1,750 in the Women's Auxiliary Air Force (WAAF). These numbers doubled a year later, and at maximum strength, the RAF counted more than one million personnel.

During the initial months of the war, the RAF did not fare well against the *Luftwaffe*. Due to a lack of operational aircraft and trained aircrews, the British forces simply reacted to the Nazi onslaught. During the final four months of 1939, Bomber Command flew only 591 sorties and lost forty aircraft. On the defensive from the start, Fighter Command was forced to react to German advances in France. Generally, the RAF targeted the German Navy and shipping.

Initial British strategy called for the RAF to conduct long-range daylight bombing missions without escort aircraft—a strategy that proved suicidal against superior German fighters. At this early stage of hostilities, night attacks were out of the question. Bomber Command redirected its efforts to minelaying and to the support of ground operations in France in 1940.

In 1940, the RAF faced grave difficulties with the diversion of its forces to the Mediterranean, North Africa, and the Far East. Germany intended to win the European war by the fall of 1940, and the Battle of Britain (q.v.) was the culmination of the *Luftwaffe*'s design to gain air superiority over the RAF. Before Fighter Command's heroic stand during August through October 1940, however, the RAF's bombers and fighters were assigned to the defense of France. Between the Dunkirk (q.v.) evacuation in late May and the fall of France in June, Bomber Command delivered almost 2,000 tons of bombs against the Germans. By the end of the year, they had dropped more than 13,000 tons. Targets included German transportation lines, naval targets, airfields, and aircraft factories. The RAF also targeted German oil reserves, including refineries, a strategy the United States Army Air Forces (USAAF) would assume with a vengeance after 1942.

The most decisive air battle of the war was the Battle of Britain. Initially, the *Luftwaffe* targeted British naval bases and shipping, using large formations of bombers escorted by fighters. In the first ten days (8–18 August), the Germans lost 697 aircraft. They then shifted targets to include airfields and industry, using smaller bomber groups but increased fighter escorts. Losses were again heavy for the *Luftwaffe*—562 aircraft from 19 August to 5 September. Finally, London was targeted and German bombers attacked by night, with fighters using their speed to bomb by day.

The day, however, belonged to the RAF and Air Chief Marshal Hugh Dowding (q.v.) and his "chicks," the pilots of Fighter Command. Dowding had already lost nearly one-quarter of his frontline pilots in the battle for France and at Dunkirk, but Fighter Command responded with incredible bravery and courage. In the Battle of Britain, the RAF lost 375 pilots, with an additional 358 wounded, many of whom were inexperienced and reserve pilots.

Especially critical to RAF success was the role of Fighter Command's Number 11 Group, under the command of Keith Park (q.v.), whose aircraft bore the brunt of *Luftwaffe* attacks. Number 11 Group had the primary responsibility of the defense of London, and despite the losses of aircraft, pilots, and civilian life, his pilots held firm. Dowding was also quick to credit radar (q.v.) as an early warning system against incoming German air attacks.

As the Battle of Britain ended, the feud between Dowding and his critics also came to a head. Both Air Marshal Sholto Douglas and Air Vice-Marshal Trafford Leigh-Mallory (qq.v.), commanding Fighter Command's Number 12 Group, were highly critical of Dowding and Park, insisting the "big wing" theory of air defense would be more effective against the *Luftwaffe* raids. The "big wing" concept, which required fighter aircraft to mass before attacking incoming German formations, was the idea of Wing Commander Douglas Bader (q.v.). The result of the volatile dispute was Douglas replacing Dowding and Leigh-Mallory taking command of Park's Number 11 group.

For the record, Germany lost 2,375 aircraft,

and Dowding was credited with winning the Battle of Britain—however narrow a margin Fighter Command achieved. During 1940, Fighter Command flew 121,079 sorties and lost 1,186 aircraft; Bomber Command flew 22,473 sorties, dropped 13,033 tons of bombs, and lost 509 aircraft. In the Mediterranean and Middle East, RAF losses were considerably less (133 aircraft).

The Empire Air Training Scheme was implemented in 1940. Later known as the British Commonwealth Air Training Plan, the idea was conceived to train pilots from British dominions—Canada, Australia, South Africa, Southern Rhodesia, and India—as well as volunteers from the United States. At peak strength, there were 333 flying schools, with 153 in Britain and ninety-two in Canada. The rest were distributed throughout the nations of the British Commonwealth. While the benefits from the Empire Training Scheme were not really felt until after late in 1943, the plan provided training for more than 300,000 airmen. The scheme also promoted the creation of national air forces in the countries where the schools operated.

Another mission of enormous proportion for the RAF was the Battle of the Atlantic (q.v.). German U-boats, often traveling in wolf packs, preyed on Allied shipping, disrupting supplies and transportation. RAF Coastal Command had inadequate aircraft for the mission, and Fighter Command and Bomber Command presented more pressing demands on RAF resources. It was not until 1943, when the United States Army Air Force entered the Battle of the Atlantic, that the course of battle turned. Coastal Command was able to use American manufactured long-range aircraft. Along with aircraft from the convoy escort carriers, the U-boat menace finally was beaten back.

During the war, the RAF also benefited from the industrial expansion at home and in the United States to mass manufacture aircraft of all types. Many American aircraft designs were first used in combat by RAF pilots, and giant aeronautics firms like Boeing, Republic, and North American learned from the RAF's experience with their airplanes. These manufacturers revised and improved aircraft to accommodate the demands of the European air war. The Republic P-51 Mustang and the Consolidated Vultee B-24 Liberator were two aircraft first introduced in combat by the RAF; both were improved in later models due, in large part, to RAF experiences.

The RAF also benefited from aircraft supplied by the Americans through the Lend-Lease (q.v.) program. In all, Lend-Lease provided the British with more than $6 billion in aircraft and aeronautical equipment, but the British also produced many dependable aircraft of their own. Beginning in late 1940, British fighter production was intense. Hurricane production reached 13,080 in Britain by Hawker, Gloster, and Austin Motors; 23,330 Spitfires were manufactured by 1947. These two were the most successful RAF fighters. A third RAF fighter was the Gloster Typhoon. Although not built at the remarkable rate as the Hurricanes and Spitfires, 3,270 Typhoons were built. The first became operational in 1943.

The most successful RAF bomber was the Avro Lancaster, the champion long-range heavy of Bomber Command. Capable of speeds of 287 miles per hour with a range of 2,530 miles and a bombload of 18,000 pounds, the Lancaster was built in large numbers (7,377 total manufactured). In all, Lancasters flew 156,000 sorties and dropped 608,612 tons of bombs, all in the European campaign.

With Fighter Command and Coastal Command generally occupied with the defense of London and Britain, it initially fell to Bomber Command to carry the Allied offensive—especially before USAAF entrance into the war after June 1942.

As chief of the air staff, Portal was a strong advocate of long-range bombing, yet the RAF's bombers were not capable of such operations early in the war. Bomber Command's losses were heavy and the raids were ineffective. The RAF strategy shifted to night bombing missions, because its fighters were not capable of the long-range escorts so vital for daylight bombing. Night bombing, however, was not consistently effective because of the inaccuracy of bomb aiming technology.

In February 1942, Arthur T. Harris (q.v.) assumed command of Bomber Command. Nicknamed "Bomber" by many and "Butcher" by others, Harris was the most controversial air leader of the war. Under Harris, Bomber Command's strategy did not change, it just intensified. The rate of sorties and the tonnage of bombs dropped quadrupled by the end of the war but so did the number of aircraft lost. In 1942 alone, the RAF dropped 31,704 tons of bombs on German targets.

On the night of 30 May 1942, the RAF launched the first of the "thousand-bomber" raids. Heralded as the largest air attack ever made, the first of these night raids sent 1,130 bombers of all types at the German industrial city of Cologne (q.v.). The RAF flew only British-built bombers, including Handley-Page Halifaxes and Hampdens, Avro Manchesters and Lancasters, Vickers-

Armstrong Wellingtons, Armstrong Whitworth Whitleys, and Short Stirlings. These aircraft dropped 1,500 tons of bombs in less than two hours with a loss of only forty-four aircraft. The effect was devastating—more than 250 factories and an estimated one-third of the city's population were lost.

On the night of 1 June, 1,036 bombers attacked Essen; and on 25 June, a third raid took place on Bremen (this time with the support of U.S. bombers). Aircraft from Coastal Command and Fighter Command also joined the bombers on these raids.

By 1943, Bomber Command had more Avro Lancasters with improved navigational aids, as well as better escort aircraft. The final key to the formula was the USAAF strategy of daylight bombing, using B-17s and B-24s escorted by the war's best fighter, the P-51 Mustang. This split strategy, the Combined Bomber Offensive (q.v.), eventually brought Germany and its industries to their collective knees. The USAAF targeted petroleum resources from the start of its role in the air war. The objective was to deprive the Germans of oil to run their war machine.

In the final months of 1943, the Allied Expeditionary Air Forces (AEAF) was formed to provide a tactical air arm for the pending Allied invasion of Europe. The three components of the AEAF were the U.S. Ninth Air Force, RAF Fighter Command, and the newly formed Allied Second Tactical Air Force. Air Chief Marshal Arthur Coningham (q.v.), a proven commander from the North African campaign, was given command of the Second TAF. Air Chief Marshall Trafford Leigh-Mallory became commander in chief of the AEAF, as well as being named second in command of the entire invasion force under U.S. general Dwight D. Eisenhower (q.v.). The operational concept of the AEAF called for Fighter Command to function as a defensive force, while the Ninth Air Force and Second TAF were to be the offensive arms.

During the first three months of 1944, the AEAF constantly bombed German forward positions in Europe. In April, the attacks were further intensified with an emphasis on transportation networks. The attacks were widely spread in order to confuse the German command as to where the eventual invasion would come ashore. By 6 June, the AEAF had flown more than 80,000 sorties and dropped more than 10,000 tons of ordnance to soften up the enemy. The Ninth Air Force provided the close air support for the invading ground forces while the Second TAF responded to specific

British Air Order of Battle 1 September 1939	
Modern Twin-Engine Medium Bombers	194
Obsolete Twin-Engine Medium Bombers	96
Twin-Engine Light Bombers	292
Obsolete Single-Engine Light Bombers	160
Single-Engine Monoplane Fighters	798
Single-Engine Biplane Fighters	148
Twin-Engine Fighters	54
Reconnaissance Aircraft	113
Monoplane Carrier-Based Fighters[1]	21
Biplane Carrier-Based Fighters[1]	12
Carrier-Based Torpedo Aircraft[1]	127
Seaplanes and Floatplanes[1]	123
Transport Aircraft	18
Training Aircraft (all types)	982
Reserve Aircraft (all types)[2]	2,200

Notes:
1. Royal Navy, Fleet Air Arm
2. On mobilization, the RAF converted half of its active aircraft to training or reserve units in order to facilitate expansion and also to have a ready reserve to replace expected losses. Those aircraft are included in this figure.

calls for air strikes. During the first month after D-Day, AEAF aircraft flew over 150,000 sorties with losses of less than 1 percent. More than 3,600 German aircraft were destroyed by AEAF units from 6 June through the middle of September. Allied losses totaled 2,959 aircraft.

Fighter Command, meanwhile, was the designated air defense of Great Britain and destroyed 250 *Luftwaffe* aircraft during air attacks. When German V-1 flying bombs were launched against London and the southeastern region of England, Fighter Command was allocated to Operation DIVER (q.v.) to counter the threat. Fighter Command also provided support for Second TAF bombers. In June 1944, Fighter Command flew 21,000 sorties over Normandy. During 1944, Fighter Command destroyed a total of 700 *Luftwaffe* aircraft, some 500 in night operations. The AEAF was the largest air task force ever formed, and it achieved its goal beyond expectations. RAF contributions were considerable, but perhaps even more remarkable was the cooperation between the various elements of the AEAF.

Right from their entry into the war, the USAAF was sensitive to indiscriminate bombing, responding to political and moral pressure to bomb military and war industry targets and avoid civilian casualties as much as possible. The RAF, however, armed with short memories of *Luftwaffe* attacks on London and the "Blitz," was not so deeply concerned. "Bomber" Harris earned his nickname, as RAF bombers continually attacked urban areas in Germany. The British pounded cities such as Berlin, Essen, Cologne, and Hamburg. They dropped 36,000 tons of ordnance on Essen and nearly 35,000 tons on Cologne. In one of the more controversial attacks of the war, RAF and USAAF bombers caused the infamous firestorm at Dresden (q.v.) on 13–14 February 1945. The shock of the Dresden firestorm led British prime minister Winston S. Churchill (q.v.) to call a halt on such attacks on German cities. Despite extensive criticisms aimed directly at Harris, he felt he had achieved the goal he had set for the RAF—to destroy German industry and Germany's will to fight. Postwar analysis, however, showed Germany's will had, in fact, hardened.

For the entire war, the total tonnage of RAF bombing in Europe was immense—955,044 tons. German industrial cities were the targets for nearly half of that ordnance (430,747 tons). The RAF also laid 47,307 mines, totaling 33,263 more tons of explosives. During the war, Fighter Command flew 700,226 sorties; Bomber Command flew 392,137; and Coastal Command flew 235,749.

On the negative side, RAF aircraft and personnel losses were heavy. Bomber Command alone lost 9,120 aircraft, while Fighter Command suffered 3,558 destroyed. Coastal Command lost 1,579 assorted aircraft. Added to the loss of more than 14,000 aircraft was a total of 70,253 aircrewmen. Of that total, 47,293 were from Bomber Command.

The total strength of the RAF during World War II was 1,208,843 men and women, of whom 185,595 were aircrew. These numbers include personnel from the various Commonwealth nations—more than 130,000 from the Commonwealth fought with either the RAF or the air forces of their nations.

The history of the RAF in World War II was one of heroism yet not without harsh criticism. The Battle of Britain brought out the best in Fighter Command, but the firestorm at Dresden in February 1945 drew biting attacks on Bomber Command's strategy. Churchill concluded early in the war that victory would be gained in the air. After the Battle of Britain, Churchill uttered his memorable tribute to RAF pilots who held off the continuous *Luftwaffe* attacks. The RAF did not win the war alone, of course, but in the fateful summer of 1940, British airpower forestalled an early—and catastrophic—end to the war in Europe.

Boyd Childress

Additional Reading

Baker, E.C.R., *The Fighter Aces of the R.A.F.* (1962).

Delve, Ken, *The Source Book of the RAF* (1994).

Morrison, Wilbur H., *Fortress Without a Roof: The Allied Bombing of the Third Reich* (1982).

Richards, Denis, and Hillary St. G. Saunders, *The Royal Air Force, 1939–1945,* 3 vols. (1953–1954).

Terraine, John, *A Time for Courage: The Royal Air Force in the European War, 1939–1945* (1985).

Wood, Derek, *The Narrow Margin: The Battle of Britain and the Rise of Air Power 1930–40* (1961).

Air Force, Canadian

During World War I, numerous Canadian airmen played important roles in the British Royal Flying Corps. The Royal Canadian Air Force (RCAF) did not become an independent branch of the Canadian military until 1938. An air force was formed under the direction of the Canadian Army in 1922–1923. The air contingent was greatly limited in its scope and by economic restraints. The primary role of the RCAF was forest patrolling, firefighting, surveying, aerial photography, exploration, emergency medical and police flights, and even crop and forest dusting. The potential of aviation also served to open up previously inaccessible areas of Canada. The RCAF served a civil aviation function before German aggression in Europe brought an end to world stability.

When World War II began, the RCAF generally assumed a defensive posture, but before the war was over, it would make significant contributions in training, transportation of aircraft to Britain, and antisubmarine warfare in the North Atlantic. In 1939, the RCAF was undermanned, with few active aircraft. In September 1939, there were 4,153 active officers and airmen, although the RCAF was authorized 7,259 personnel. RCAF could count on only fifty-five aircraft, many obsolete, and other civilian aircraft adapted to military use. In addition, the outbreak of the war threatened to limit aircraft supply from the United States because of its initial neutral status.

As war loomed on the European horizon, the British Commonwealth Air Training Plan (BCATP) was conceived by the Royal Air Force (RAF). BCATP was designed to train pilots and crewmen for the RAF and Britain's allies. Canada was a logical selection because of its geographical distance from the war in Europe. From 1940 to 1945, training schools were set up for pilots, aircrews, air observers, navigators, communications personnel, bombardiers and gunners, flight engineers, and ground crews. Approximately 360 schools were established across Canada, many of which were originally RAF training centers. All were absorbed and operated by the RCAF.

By war's end, BCATP schools were given considerable credit for the steady improvement in aircrew performance. When the plan ended in March 1945, the schools had graduated 131,553 trainees, including 72,835 RCAF graduates. These included 25,747 pilots, 12,855 navigators, 6,659 bombardiers, 12,917 gunners, and 1,913 flight engineers. The remainder of the graduates included RAF personnel as well as 9,606 Australians and 7,002 New Zealanders. Some of those trained were Americans who chose to circumvent their nation's neutrality during the early years of the war.

Another important RCAF contribution was the work of its Ferry Command, whose job was to transport aircraft across the Atlantic to the RAF. After the initial stages of the air battles of 1940, the British Air Ministry had a desperate need for airplanes. By the summer of 1940, British orders for aircraft in the United States numbered 26,000, with a delivery schedule of 1,000 per month. When American industrial productivity increased, those figures grew. To implement delivery, RCAF established the Ferry Command in November 1940. Between late 1940 and 1945, RCAF pilots, as well as pilots of other nations, flew thousands of airplanes across the North Atlantic to Britain and to sites in North Africa. In 1942 alone, 1,900 aircraft were delivered. Efforts increased the following year with British pilots ferrying aircraft back to Britain along with RCAF pilots. By the end of the war, Ferry Command organized the delivery of 9,027 aircraft to all theaters of the war. This represented more than 25 percent of the aircraft supplied to the British and Allies.

On the Canadian home front, RCAF was responsible for the defense of the nation against both the Germans on the eastern frontier and possible Japanese attacks on the West Coast. Those missions came under the control of the Home War Establishment (HWE), which coordinated the air defenses of Canada, divided into the Eastern Air Command (headquartered at Halifax) and Western Air Command (headquartered at Vancouver, 1939, and 1943 to 1945, and at Victoria, 1939 to 1942). RCAF was also responsible for the security of the St. Lawrence. On 8 May 1942, a German U-boat penetrated the Gulf of the St. Lawrence. By the end of the year, two waves of German submarines had sunk twenty-one ships, and RCAF was forced to provide air escorts along with the convoy escorts of the Royal Canadian Navy. As U-boat activity increased in the North Atlantic, RCAF was required to provide more air cover.

Between November 1942, and May 1943, Allied shipping losses increased. The intensified Allied air efforts contributed significantly to the decline in shipping losses, from 124 in 1943, to only seventeen in 1944. For their part, RCAF accounted for or contributed to the destruction of twenty-one U-boats, more than 10 percent of the losses attributed to the combined air forces of the Commonwealth nations.

RCAF also contributed to the European air war with individual pilots and units. Number 1 Fighter Squadron was active in the Battle of Britain (q.v.) and Number 6 Group in Bomber Command was made up of RCAF pilots and crews. The leading ace of the RCAF was Flight Lieutenant George F. Beurling (q.v.), who scored thirty-one and one-third kills. Beurling was most active in the air battles for Malta (q.v.). Other leading aces were squadron leaders Wally McLean and Vernon Woodward.

RCAF squadrons increased steadily during the war from fourteen home-based squadrons in 1939, to forty-eight in late 1941 (twenty-one overseas, seventeen in Canada), to seventy-seven by the beginning of 1944 (thirty-eight overseas, thirty-nine in Canada). In real numbers, operational aircraft increased from 160 in December 1941, to a high of 380 in December 1943.

In December 1944, RCAF counted 200 operational aircraft. RCAF squadron strength diminished after the end of 1944 but there were still forty-six in Europe and twenty-four in Canada in early 1945. During the entire war, the RCAF suffered between 13,036 and 17,101 dead (different sources report different casualty figures) and approximately 10,000 wounded, taken prisoner, or missing. A total of 95,000 RCAF personnel served overseas, with 28,505 attached directly to the RAF. RCAF pilots saw combat duty in ten countries.

Boyd Childress

Additional Reading

Douglas, W.A.B., *The Creation of a National Air Force* (1986).

Roberts, Leslie, *There Shall Be Wings: A History of the Royal Canadian Air Force* (1959).

Wise, S.F., *The Official History of the Royal Canadian Air Force* (1980).

A

Air Force, Danish

The Danish Defense Act of 1937 established an army air force consisting of two air battalions. One was based on Jutland and the other on Sjaelland. In 1940, the Danish Air Force had three squadrons consisting approximately of twenty-one interceptors, twenty-seven reconnaissance aircraft, and nineteen trainers.

The Germans occupied Denmark but allowed the Danish military forces to exist up to 1943. In August 1943, the Germans disbanded the Danish armed forces and made the military prisoners of war. Following the disbandment, several Danish pilots made their way to Sweden, where they trained on Swedish Saab B-17s. They planned to establish a Danish Brigade in Sweden but that never came about.

Thomas A Cardwell, III

Additional Reading
Outze, Borge (ed.), *Denmark During the German Occupation* (1946).
Palmer, Paul, *Denmark in Nazi Chains* (1942).

Air Force, Dutch

Prior to the Dutch surrender in 1940, the air force of the Netherlands was an independent branch of service made up of naval and army forces. The Army Air Service was under the command of the Air Defense Headquarters, and included one air brigade with three regiments (twenty-four squadrons) and had 124 frontline aircraft. A number of Dutch Army Air Service pilots left the Netherlands after the Dutch surrender. Members of the air force who managed to reach Britain after the fall of France were from August 1942 to June 1943 a part of "A" Flight, Number 167 Squadron, RAF. In June 1943, the unit became all-Dutch, and was renumbered 322 Squadron. The Dutch Army Air Service participated in the German offensive of 1940, the Battle of the Atlantic, the Battle of Britain (qq.v.), and also served in the Pacific.

Thomas A. Cardwell, III

Additional Reading
Maass, Walter B., *The Netherlands at War: 1940–1945* (1970).
Mollo, Andrew, *The Armed Forces of World War II* (1981).

Air Force, Finnish

The Finnish Air Force was never a formidable or deciding factor in the Finno-Soviet conflicts between 1939 and 1944. Nevertheless, it did play its own important role in Finnish defensive fighting of the Winter War (q.v.), as well as during the Finno-Soviet War of 1941–1944 (q.v.). Throughout World War II, however, the Finnish Air Force remained a miniature power compared to the air forces of the two big contenders in northeast Europe, the Soviet Union and Germany.

Traditionally, the Finnish Air Force was subordinate to both the ground forces and the navy. This was evident in the military development program of the 1930s, which focused primarily on strengthening the ground forces, especially the defense of Finland's eastern border, the Mannerheim Line. Thus, by the outbreak of the Winter War in late 1939, the Finnish Air Force had only 145 planes, of which 114 were operational. Most were obsolete. They were greatly outnumbered by the Soviet Air Force, which had approximately 1,000 fighters in the Isthmus of Karelia in December 1939 and January 1940. Despite the air arm's numerical inferiority, however, most major Finnish cities were too far inland for Soviet bombers to inflict serious damage. The Finns were also quite successful in securing most of their supply routes.

During and after the Winter War, Finland acquired a number of new planes from Great Britain, the United States, Italy, France, and Sweden. However, most of the buildup of the Finnish Air Force was the result of Finland's closer ties with Germany. By July 1941, when the Finns effectively began their cooperation with the Germans, the Finnish Air Force had 307 planes. Of these, 230 were fighters, but of seventeen different models. As the war dragged on, the Finns could get spare parts only for the German models, another factor that made Finland more dependent on Germany.

With German help, the Finnish Air Force was able to dominate the air space in Karelia during the 1941 offensives and cause damage to the Soviet supply lines. No major air offensives were conducted during the subsequent years of static warfare (late 1941–early 1944). Most air actions were limited to attacking the Murmansk railroad, which proved unsuccessful, and successfully preventing the enemy from bombing Helsinki or other major Finnish cities. The Soviet offensive of 1944 again proved the relative ineffectiveness of the Finnish Air Force, which was unable to hinder the Soviet advance in any way.

In summary, the Finnish Air Force played a minor role in the Finno-Soviet conflicts between 1939 and 1944. This was due to the fact that air warfare in general played only a minor role, and that the bulk of operations took place on the ground, especially in the Isthmus of Karelia. The Finnish Air Force's most significant roles came in securing the supply routes of the ground forces and providing intelligence on enemy troop movements.

Jussi Hanhimaki

Additional Reading

Coats, William, and Z.K. Coats, *Soviet-Finnish Campaign: Military and Political, 1939–1940* (1942).

Luukkaneh, Eino A., *Fighter over Finland: Memoirs of a Fighter Pilot* (1963).

Air Force, French

Throughout the interwar period, military aviation in France was closely tied up with the operational plans of the French Army and Navy. Strategic planning emphasized the defense of the "national skies" and the maintenance of communications with the French colonies. Contrary to the theories developed by Hugh Trenchard and Giulio Douhet (qq.v.), which stressed the offensive roles of bomber forces, the French Air Force (*Armée de l'Air*) played a defensive rather than an offensive role. As such, the *Armée de l'Air* relied upon fighter and reconnaissance aircraft at the expense of the bomber. This is clearly demonstrated by the makeup of its frontline aircraft, with 637 fighters, 489 reconnaissance aircraft, and 242 bombers. By comparison, the German *Luftwaffe* played an offensive role, employing 1,680 bombers, 1,210 fighters, and 640 reconnaissance planes.

To compound the situation, French generals refused to organize and develop joint operations between ground troops and aircraft in their mistaken belief that air forces would not play an important role in modern war. Attempts to improve the relationship between the two services failed on practical grounds at the time of the German attack in May 1940. The army continued to rely on telephone rather than radio communications, rendering any attempt at joint operations impossible in the face of continued German attack.

Toward the end of the May–June 1940 campaign, the army general staff progressively lost control of its combat units. As the French retreated, disorganization increased. Eventually, the *Armée de l'Air* was obliged to abandon frontline airfields, putting greater pressure on the overworked airfields farther south. Had the *Luftwaffe* profited from the situation by bombing these airfields, French losses would have been greater.

As it was, the losses were severe. On the eve of the German invasion, 77,500 men were serving in the *Armée de l'Air*, of whom 5,600 were aircrew. During the fighting in May and June, 40 percent of the officers and 20 percent of the enlisted men were killed in action. Lost were 410 aircraft in air combat and 432 from other causes. Despite almost impossible odds, the French still managed to down 733 enemy aircraft.

After the French armistice with Germany and despite air force casualties, the general staff of the French Army, especially Generals Maurice Gamelin, Maxime Weygand, and Alphonse Georges (qq.v.), heavily criticized the *Armée de l'Air* as a major contributor to the loss of northern France. They based their criticism on perceived combat failure and its concomitant effect on the morale of French ground forces, who were constantly under attack from German aircraft in apparently undefended skies.

Air Force General François d'Astier de la Vigerie countered the general staff criticism with the claim that the *Armée de l'Air* was made scapegoat by army generals who were trying to save their own reputations in the aftermath of defeat. It was not the actual fighting abilities of French aircrews that were at fault, but rather the whole support system that broke down.

The key to the *Armée de l'Air*'s problem was, therefore, logistical. In May 1940, 70 percent of French aircraft were unavailable for combat, either because of mechanical failure or because they were inadequately armed. Numerous contemporary accounts bear witness to the stockpiles of new aircraft held in the rear, while those used in combat were so few. For example, 120 propellerless Potez 63s and Bloch MB-152s were stored at Chateaudun. Likewise, dozens of Bréguet 693 bombers

French Air Order of Battle 1 September 1939	
Modern Twin-Engine Medium Bombers	8
Obsolescent Twin-Engine Medium Bombers	690
Modern Single-Engine Fighters	425
Single-Engine Biplane Fighters	75
Twin-Engine Fighters	90
Reconnaissance Aircraft	296
Biplane Carrier-Based Fighters	24
Biplane Carrier-Based Bomber\Torpedo Planes	20
Seaplanes and Floatplanes	218
Transport Aircraft	24
Autogiros	8
Training Aircraft (all types)	1,000
Reserve Aircraft (all types)	1,600

were sent to frontline squadrons without their bombsights. Few French aircraft were equipped with radio, and further confusion was caused by having a command system in which orders came independently from General Têtu, chief of Air Cooperation Forces Command, General Joseph Vuillemin of the Air High Command, numerous local commands, and commanders of local land forces.

Furthermore, instead of maintaining a corps of transport pilots to shuttle aircraft from the factories to frontline squadrons, the French resorted to combat pilots to do the job, taking them out of action for three or four days at a time. During the Phony War (q.v.), the aircraft industry continued to work at a peacetime tempo. There are accounts of how aircraft engineers and fitters worked only daytime shifts in the factories. In September 1939, only sixty aircraft were produced in all of France, and throughout 1939, the aircraft industry manufactured 600 airplanes compared to the German annual production of nearly 3,000. Writer André Maurois later remarked how in October 1939, then minister of finance Paul Reynaud (q.v.) took an after-dinner tour around some of the armament factories in Paris only to find, to his amazement, they were closed. To try and make up for this lost time, the French government resorted to buying a number of Curtiss Hawks from the United States.

Compounding the logistical problem was the failure of successive French governments to provide a solid rearmament program in the late 1930s, due to both a lack of consistency in policy and the considerable power that different aircraft constructors were able to wield in the political lobbies. The result meant numerous orders on an uneconomical variety and small numbers of airplanes that were hand-built in small workshops rather than employing mass production methods. Production was both slow and expensive; for example, each Morane-Saulnier MS-406 fighter required 18,000 man-hours of labor as opposed to 5,000 for the German Messerschmitt Bf-109. The *Armée de l'Air* was supplied with a varied range of equipment. Although this included the excellent Dewoitine 520 single-seat fighter, which was comparable to the British Spitfire, only seventy-nine were in service when the Germans invaded France. Furthermore, the *Armée de l'Air* was burdened with aircraft such as the outdated and slow MS-406, and obsolete aircraft such as the outclassed Amiot 143 bomber.

Following the French armistice, some French aircrews escaped to fight with distinction either with the Royal Air Force, or after 1942, on the eastern front with the Soviet-equipped Normandie-Nieman Fighter Regiment.

Robert C. Hudson

Additional Reading
Deighton, Len, *Blitzkrieg: From the Rise of Hitler to the Fall of Dunkirk* (1979).
Horne, Alistair, *To Lose a Battle: France 1940* (1969).
Saint-Exupéry, Antoine de, *Flight to Arras* (1942).

Air Force, German

The German Air Force, or *Luftwaffe*, enjoyed a phoenix-like existence. Rising up from almost nothing in 1933, it had grown into the world's most powerful air force by 1939, only to end the war as a spent, broken force of a only few hundred aircraft grounded by lack of fuel. The intervening years were ones of struggle and triumph. Throughout it all, its pilots and ground crews endeavored to fulfill the changing and growing requirements placed on them by Germany's expanding list of opponents. Losses grew, replacements dwindled, and fuel became increasingly scarce. Pilots and planes both declined in quality as the war progressed, even as the numbers and quality of their opponents improved. The end was inevitable, and as the *Luftwaffe*'s fortunes declined, so did Germany's.

The *Luftwaffe*'s rapid growth was largely the result of preparations made during the years immediately following World War I. Although the Versailles Treaty (q.v.) prohibited Germany from having combat aircraft, a small nucleus of former flying corps officers was retained in the interwar *Reichswehr*. Those officers began planning the rebirth of German airpower as early as 1920. From 1922 on, they had the active covert assistance of Europe's other pariah state, the Soviet Union. Pilot training and tactical air combat development was conducted clandestinely at Lipetsk Airfield southeast of Moscow. The graduates of Lipetsk and other air-trained officers were secreted into key staff positions within Germany's small 100,000-man army. Most of these officers would later command the *Luftwaffe*'s formations in World War II. Commercial air activities and research were subsidized by the state to provide a pool of pilots and ground crews to sustain the aircraft industry.

By 1926, Germany was the most air-minded nation in Europe. Membership in gliding clubs exceeded 50,000. These clubs, secretly subsidized by the defense ministry of the Weimar Republic (q.v.), enabled Germany to expand its pool of potential pilot candidates. Military officers were released from active duty to fly for *Lufthansa*, the German national airline. By 1933, Germany had nearly 2,500 pilots in uniform and another 5,000 in reserve. The nucleus of the *Luftwaffe* was already formed. All it needed was aircraft.

Adolf Hitler's (q.v.) rise to power in 1933 brought Hermann Göring (q.v.) into the government, making him, among other things, air minister. His deputy, Erhard Milch (q.v.), was also head of *Lufthansa*. Milch's first action was to expand the airline and its related training schools. He also ordered the construction of new aircraft factories and funded engine research. At that time, Germany's aircraft engines lagged behind British and American-built units in power output and density, and in fuel efficiency. Airfields and maintenance facilities were also expanded. He also initiated a series of "exploratory air route" flights. These flights not only opened new air routes for *Lufthansa*, but also provided cover for a covert air reconnaissance program. Many of the targets hit by the *Luftwaffe* in 1939 and 1940 were photographed initially by one of these flights.

The first military aircraft entered production in 1934. Most were biplanes, but the Ju-87 and He-111 prototypes appeared as well. Publicly advertised as new sport planes or high-speed airliners, these new aircraft became the *Luftwaffe's* first operational combat planes. Early production was dominated by the need for training aircraft. The infrastructure and foundations of the new force had to be built first, yet it had to be strong enough to deter an attack on Germany the moment its existence became known.

The preparations paid off. The *Luftwaffe* had 1,888 aircraft of all types in service when Hitler announced its existence in March 1935. All the concealed air units and flying clubs, even police observation planes, were suddenly turned over to the new military organization. Within days, the *Luftwaffe* rose from nothing to a force of more than 20,000 officers and men. It was this group that constituted the foundations on which the *Luftwaffe* organized itself into the world's most powerful air force by 1939.

After it went public, the *Luftwaffe* began to improve its aircraft and test them in competitions all over Europe. An air war college was established and the new leaders began to refine the tactics and procedures that would guide the *Luftwaffe* through the coming war. Great stress was placed on unit mobility and rapid response times. The flying units

Luftwaffe Strength in World War II

	Total 1 Sept 1939	France 10 May 1940	Russia 22 June 1941
Reece Aircraft	604	640	710
Heavy Bombers	0	0	0
Medium Bombers	1,180	1,300	775
Dive Bombers	366	380	310
Ground-attack	40	46	0
Fighters, 1 engine	1,125	860	830
Fighters, 2 engines	195	350	90
Coastal Aircraft	240	0	55
Transport Aircraft	552	475	30

and their ground staffs were viewed as Germany's "fire brigades," rushing wherever needed on short notice. They had to be able to operate from temporary landing fields within twenty-four hours of arrival. It required great organization, preparation, and coordination. Through 1941, the *Luftwaffe* remained the best air force in the world at executing such operations. Other countries' air forces copied these techniques and used them against the *Luftwaffe* in the war's later years.

The *Luftwaffe* also began to develop a doctrine. One of the prevailing myths of World War II is that the *Luftwaffe* entered and fought the war with a doctrine directed purely toward supporting the army. In fact, nothing could be further from the truth. From the very beginning, the *Luftwaffe's* leadership saw the service as an independent force with a strategic mission. They saw supporting army operations as an adjunct to fulfilling that mission. Within that context, the Luftwaffe saw its operations in three phases: (1) destruction of the enemy's air force and its supporting infrastructure; (2) destruction of the enemy's reserves and logistics base in the rear; and (3) destruction of the enemy's industrial capacity and morale. Each phase was integrated into the requirements of the overall military situation. The destruction of the enemy air forces would enable the *Luftwaffe* to attack the enemy's rear, thereby facilitating the army's ground advance. That in turn would provide the forward bases from which the *Luftwaffe* could then break the enemy's will to resist.

This sequence of operations was intended to reduce the likelihood of Germany fighting the sort of costly final offensives that broke the country's morale in World War I. Germany's air operations before 1941 can only be understood when viewed from this context. The Polish, Scandinavian, and western campaigns of 1939–1940 all followed this sequence.

The Battle of Britain (q.v.) should have followed this sequence, but Hitler's order to hit London was a major deviation from *Luftwaffe* doctrine. Britain's air defenses had not been defeated at that point, and the change in *Luftwaffe* bombing operations came just as those defenses were nearing collapse. Had the first phase of the battle been followed through to completion, then the second phase, the invasion of Britain (*see* SEA LION, Operation), might have become practical. Once the army was ashore and pushing on the enemy capital, the *Luftwaffe* could then have shifted to the third phase. In any event, Hitler's decision to bomb London was an attempted shortcut, skipping a vital phase in the campaign. It was a catastrophic error that cost Germany the battle and possibly the war. Given a respite from attacks on its forces and infrastructure, the RAF recovered enough to ultimately defeat the *Luftwaffe* over Great Britain.

The *Luftwaffe* also was a pioneer in airborne operations which fit, doctrinally, into the second phase of the air operation. The *Luftwaffe* was unique in World War II in that it was the only air force that owned both the air transport units and the airborne forces they dropped. One advantage this had was that both the transporters and the transported shared the same views on how to conduct an airborne operation. For this reason, the *Luftwaffe* expended more effort ensuring an accurate drop than did its opponents during the war. Unfortunately for its airborne troops, the *Luftwaffe's* airborne doctrine called for those troops to be dropped nearly on top of their objective.

The airborne force commander, General Kurt Student (q.v.), also believed in an "oil drop" approach to airborne landings. He felt that a series of small drops would prevent mutual interference between units, stretch out the enemy's forces, and enable his airborne forces to seize a large area of territory quickly. That approach proved costly in Crete (q.v.).

The *Luftwaffe* viewed airborne operations in two primary categories: tactical and operational. Tactical drops took place within fifty kilometers of the front, employed limited forces, and had limited objectives. A tactical force was expected to be relieved by conventional ground forces within twenty-four hours of landing. An operational-level landing involved a deeper drop, beyond fifty kilometers from the front, a larger landing force, and was directed at an objective that supported the conduct of a campaign. These units were expected to be relieved within forty-eight to seventy-two hours of landing.

The only changes the *Luftwaffe* made to its doctrine came as a result of experience in the Spanish civil war (q.v.). The German intervention there began in August 1936 and eventually grew into a major operation. The *Luftwaffe's* contingent was designated the *Kondor Legion* (q.v.). The *Luftwaffe's* experiences in Spain had a major influence on its equipment, strategy, doctrine, and tactics in World War II. Inadequacies of Germany's biplane fighters became apparent. Strategic bombing was "proven," and refinements were made in communications and aerial reconnaissance.

The most significant impact on the *Luftwaffe* came from the Legion's experiences in aerial combat and in providing "close air support" to army operations. Prewar tactics called for pilots to fly in tight three-plane formations, where all followed the formation leader. Fighting against superior Soviet aircraft demonstrated the fallacy of those tactics. Instead, the Germans adopted the more flexible two-plane wingman and leader formation used by all modern air forces to this day. The *Kondor Legion* also proved the efficacy of fighter sweeps, which, freed from the need to escort bombers, ranged out far and wide to destroy enemy fighter formations before they could intercept German bombers. It was a tactic that served the Germans well until Göring ordered its abandonment in the Battle of Britain.

The best known of the tactical innovations to come out of Spain was the development of close air support tactics. Developed by the Legion's commander, Wolfram von Richthofen (q.v.), the new tactics called for dive bombers and light attack aircraft to strike enemy ground formations in close contact with friendly forces. Although not a new concept and one opposed by the *Luftwaffe's* senior leadership, he revolutionized it by adding the new variation of providing such support during the mobile phases of ground combat.

Heretofore, air forces avoided joining in fluid ground combat situations because of the potential for hitting friendly forces by mistake. Von Richthofen solved the problem by assigning *Luftwaffe* officers in ground unit headquarters to coordinate the close air support and guide planes into target areas. It was a major innovation that only was partially assimilated by the *Luftwaffe* by the time of the 1939 Poland (q.v.) campaign. Close air support tactics were perfected over the next two years and became an almost defining element of German ground operations by 1941.

Little attention was given to maritime operations in the *Luftwaffe's* early years. That changed when the German Navy's aircraft were transferred to the *Luftwaffe* in January 1939. Basically, the *Luftwaffe* adopted the navy's doctrine as its own, but made three changes—two correct and one critically wrong. First, Göring threw out the navy's designs for its carrier aircraft, replacing their biplanes with top of the line *Luftwaffe* aircraft, carrier-based versions of the Bf-109 fighter and Ju-87 dive bomber. The air wing was combat-ready before war broke out, but Admiral Erich Raeder (q.v.) failed to complete construction of the aircraft carrier and the planes reverted to regular *Luftwaffe* service in 1940. Second, the *Luftwaffe* differed in its approach to mine warfare (q.v.). In keeping with the *Luftwaffe*'s preference for massed attacks, it ordered mines laid in dense fields by large bomber formations. This was a far superior tactic than the small-scale drops used by Raeder during the war's early months.

In the third tactical change the *Luftwaffe* made a serious mistake. Believing bombing alone to be a sufficient system for attacking ships, the *Luftwaffe* canceled development of aerial-delivered torpedoes. As a result, the German naval air wings fought the first two years of the war without these effective antiship weapons. In some areas, they borrowed torpedoes from nearby Italian units, but that was only a stop-gap measure. There also was little emphasis on training for antishipping strikes. Although it inflicted heavy losses on naval ships and merchant shipping when employed en masse, the *Luftwaffe*'s antiship operations were not as effective as they could have been.

The *Luftwaffe*'s doctrine recognized three basic types of aerial reconnaissance: tactical, operational, and strategic. Tactical reconnaissance was done almost exclusively in support of the army and involved mostly direct observation and reporting within the tactical zone (within fifty kilometers of the front lines). Reconnaissance in the operational zone could involve either photographic collection against enemy facilities, airfields, and units affecting current or future military operations, or direct observation and reporting of enemy units beyond the tactical zone. It also could include forward reconnaissance ahead of the army's axis of advance.

One lesson the *Luftwaffe* learned from Spain was that tactical and operational reconnaissance was most effective when the results were disseminated to ground commanders quickly. Thus, Germany's photographic intelligence primarily relied on monoscopic photography, which could be developed and analyzed quickly. Although this accelerated the reporting process, it had unexpected consequences later in the war (*see* Intelligence Operations).

Strategic reconnaissance was purely a *Luftwaffe* concern. Directed against the enemy's industrial and communications centers, it was intended to facilitate strategic planning and bombing. The *Luftwaffe* assigned operational and strategic reconnaissance missions to its "long-range" reconnaissance squadrons. The *Luftwaffe* generally used stereoscopic photography only in its strategic collection operations. The only true strategic reconnaissance conducted by the *Luftwaffe* during World War II took place on the Russian front.

The *Luftwaffe* also established a fairly significant signals intelligence (q.v.) organization. Intended to provide warning of enemy air movements, the *Luftwaffe*'s signals intelligence units fell into two categories: permanent stations that supported the high command, and mobile stations assigned in support of each *Luftflotte* (Air Fleet). The former came under the *Forschungsamt* (Research Office), which intercepted and tried to decrypt foreign diplomatic and strategic communications. It achieved some major successes before the war, monitoring embassy telephone lines, naval and air force command nets, and diplomatic traffic.

Mobile stations were organized into regiments, which typically moved with and operated near the *Luftflotte* headquarters. Their decryption activities were limited to low-level tactical codes, but they proved particularly adept at providing advanced warning of enemy air raid activities. Fortunately for the Allies, the *Luftwaffe* only integrated signals and photographic intelligence at the *Luftflotte* level and never established a system of correlating reporting and analysis between such headquarters until mid-1944. By then it was too late.

These doctrinal roots guided the force that Milch built. His efforts, however, were constantly undermined by Hitler's ever-changing strategic requirements. Originally ordered to build a large deterrence force, Milch concentrated on small, easily manufactured units that required few resources. He never lost sight of the need to build a balanced force, and he built the infrastructure and industrial base to support one. He finally was freed to establish a balanced force in 1938. Hitler's guidance was that Milch should prepare the *Luftwaffe* for war by 1942–1944.

With that in mind, Milch developed a construction program that called for a *Luftwaffe* of 5,000 firstline aircraft by 1942, including heavy as well as medium and light bombers. The war started before his program had any hope of reaching fruition. Moreover, Göring's jealousy of Milch's rapport with Hitler led him to undermine Milch's authority and slowly push him into the background. Robbed of his organizational abilities and rational policies, the *Luftwaffe* entered World War II a formidable force with very little sustaining power. Its reserves, training, research programs, and logistics infrastructure were all inadequate for fighting a prolonged war. More significantly, the *Luftwaffe* lacked the leadership to correct flaws. Göring replaced competent technical managers in the support structure with cronies who lacked the expertise and temperament to detect problems, much less solve them.

This then, was the force that went to war on 1 September 1939. Its aircraft and support structures were superior to that of any of its European opponents. Its operational strength also was unequaled, with a small reserve of between 10 and 25 percent of firstline strength, depending on aircraft type. It was a force organized along functional lines. The former naval strike wings were placed under the operational control of the *Kriegsmarine,* while tactical reconnaissance units were placed under the army's operational control. The *Luftwaffe* was a force ready for war, and its early operational successes seemed to support this.

In the Polish campaign, the *Luftwaffe* destroyed significant numbers of Polish aircraft on the ground during the first three days of the assault. It then shifted into a ground interdiction role, destroying Polish troop concentrations, logistics, and communications facilities and fortifications. Von Richthofen's air group employed close air support effectively, greatly facilitating General Heinz Guderian's (q.v.) *Panzer* advance. Within two weeks, the Polish Army ceased to be a coordinated fighting force. The *Luftwaffe* then shifted into the third phase of its operations, breaking the Polish will to resist. The mass bombing of Warsaw (q.v.) commenced on 25 September 1939. The city surrendered two days later.

The *Luftwaffe* spent the months between the Polish campaign and the western offensive re-equipping some units, forming new units, and absorbing the lessons of the early fighting. One thing stood out—air reconnaissance units suffered disproportionate losses during the campaign. Otherwise, in the euphoria of victory, several other significant problems were ignored. Intelligence missed the dispersal of the Polish Air Force in the days before the war broke out. Communications security was poor, and maintenance organization began to falter in the campaign's closing days. The *Luftwaffe*'s leadership, however, concentrated on what went well. They further refined close air sup-

port procedures and trained additional units for that mission.

The Scandinavian and western campaigns went very well for the Germans, both tactically and operationally. German paratroopers suffered heavily in Holland, but the assault on the Belgian fort at Eben Emael (q.v.) went perfectly. Norway, Denmark, Holland, Belgium, and France all fell. The *Luftwaffe* seemed unstoppable.

Then came the Battle of Britain (q.v.) where the *Luftwaffe*'s organizational and equipment shortcomings came home to roost. The *Stuka* dive bombers, the Bf-110 twin-engine fighter, and all the medium bombers except the Ju-88 proved unsuitable for combat against a modern air force. The intelligence service's faults precluded German air commanders from having an even partially accurate picture of the RAF's structure, status, weaknesses, or intentions. Göring's and Hitler's interference turned an already serious situation into a disaster. The Germans had already lost the Battle of Britain when the *Luftwaffe* was shifted eastward to participate in Operation BARBAROSSA.

The *Luftwaffe* that entered Russia was a force past its peak. Its strength dispersed across the depth and breadth of Europe, it went into Russia with only 80 percent of the forces it had had in France the year before. The campaign in Crete decimated its airborne and air transport units, and the decision to use navigational training units to support that operation depleted the training program at a time when the *Luftwaffe* was trying to expand. Aircraft serviceability was down to less than 65 percent in some units. More seriously, fuel reserves were at their lowest ebb since the war began. The air war in the east (q.v.) bled the *Luftwaffe*'s tactical units for three years. Yet it was there that the *Luftwaffe* actually conducted the sort of strategic bombing its creators envisioned.

The *Luftwaffe* found itself stretched further and further as the war went on. The *Kriegsmarine* wanted it to support the Battle of the Atlantic (q.v.), while the army used it as a "fire brigade" in North Africa (q.v.) and Russia. Hitler wanted it to defend France, Norway, and Romania. Meanwhile, its technical and procurements branches were crippled by incompetent leadership and neglect. The *Luftwaffe* was not ready to face the growing air threat from the West.

The *Luftwaffe*'s final death knell was delivered by the Allied bombing campaign. With the RAF bombing at night and the Americans by day, the *Luftwaffe* found itself drawing more and more of its resources home. The technical supremacy it enjoyed when the war started slowly eroded even as its opponents grew in numerical strength. Technically, Germany's airborne radars simply could not compete. Pilot training programs had to be cut as fuel supplies continued to dwindle. The quality and quantity of *Luftwaffe* aircraft and aircrews declined steadily.

By 1944, the *Luftwaffe* was outnumbered, outgunned, and fighting from a position of technological and intelligence inferiority. The introduction of new jet and rocket fighters simply could not stem the tide. Whatever hope the Germans had of restoring the balance evaporated with Göring's ill-considered Operation *BODEN-PLATTE* (q.v.) on 1 January 1945. Two months later, putting more than a dozen planes into the air was a major operation for the *Luftwaffe.*

The *Luftwaffe's* failures in World War II can be traced to its lack of competent technical and strategic leadership. Göring simply was incapable of long-term planning, and he established a high command of competing agencies unable to work together. The technical requirements and procurement branches were incompetently led before 1942. As a result, Germany fought the last two years of the war with the same basic aircraft and equipment with which it had entered the war. The newer jet aircraft and "secret weapons" systems could have been available up to six months earlier had the *Luftwaffe's* research and development program been run with any degree of consistency and competence. Ultimately, however, the *Luftwaffe* failed because it was asked to do too much. Germany did not have the resources to defeat the entire world.

Carl O. Schuster

Additional Reading
Bekker, Cajus, *Angriffshöhe 4000: Ein Kriegstagebuch der Deutschen Luftwaffe 1939–1945* (1964).
Her Majesty's Stationery Office, *The Rise and Fall of the German Air Force* (1948).
Irving, David, *The Forschungsamt* (1969).
———. *The Rise and Fall of the Luftwaffe* (1973).
Killen, John, *A History of the Luftwaffe* (1964).
Miller, Richard, *The German Air War in Russia* (1992).
Murray, Williamson, *Luftwaffe* (1985).
Nielsen, Andreas, *The German Air Force General Staff* (1959).

Air Force, Greek

The Greeks had no separate or independent air force as such. The Greek Air Ministry was responsible for all air services maintained by the army and navy. The Greek Army Air Service was small, with about 250 officers and 3,000 enlisted personnel. The air service had forty-four fighters, forty-six bombers/reconnaissance planes, sixteen general purpose aircraft, and twenty flying boats. When the Germans invaded in April 1941, only forty-one combat aircraft were operational. The primary purpose of the Army Air Service was to provide air support for land forces.

In the wake of the invasion of Greece by the Germans and the subsequent occupation, some Greek Air Force personnel evacuated to the Near East, where they formed two fighter groups and one bomber group. Those units flew with the RAF for the remainder of the war.

Thomas A. Cardwell III

Additional Reading
McNeil, William H., *The Greek Dilemma: War and Aftermath* (1947).
Sarafis, Stefanos, *Greek Resistance Army: The Story of ELAS* (1951).

Air Force, Italian

The Italians were at the forefront of the military use of aircraft early in the twentieth century, pioneering their use in reconnaissance and other military operations under army auspices rather than as an independent arm. They formed the first air group, the *Flottiglia Aeroplani,* and it was the Italians who, in 1911, dropped bombs and grenades on Turkish targets near Tripoli in North Africa. This act initiated a new era in which warfare gained an extra dimension.

New techniques spawned theorists, and one such was the Italian General Giulio Douhet (q.v.) who attracted the attention of Benito Mussolini (q.v.) and was made commissioner of air for the newly independent air arm, the *Regia Aeronautica* (RA), in 1923. Mussolini largely overrode Douhet and preferred to develop a range of colonial bombers with which to expand Italy's empire into Africa. It was a costly decision, for it meant that the RA was neglected in terms of the technology then available and that its capabilities were irrelevant to a future war in Europe against the better-equipped powers.

Italian aircraft designers tended to ignore the need for speed and defensive armament when they were creating planes for use against primitive enemies who could not threaten them. Even so, in June 1940 when it entered the war, Italy looked to have a powerful force with 1,000 bombers, several

**Italian Air Order of Battle
1 September 1939**

Modern Twin- and Tri-Engine Medium Bombers	62
Obsolescent Twin- and Tri-Engine Medium Bombers	1,046
Obsolete Twin-Engined Light Bombers	69
Obsolete Single-Engine Light Bombers	116
Obsolescent Single-Engine Monoplane Fighters	163
Obsolete Single-Engine Biplane Fighters	629
Reconnaissance Aircraft	465
Seaplanes and Floatplanes	302
Transport Aircraft	87
Training Aircraft (all types)	2,450
Reserve Aircraft (all types)	400

thousand fighters and trainers, and more than 750 other aircraft.

Italy did have capable designers (its success with car engines revealed the depth of Italy's technological skill), but it lacked good direction and management. Good aircraft designs tended to be the exception rather than the rule, and even then a lack of materials and uncoordinated production meant they appeared in limited numbers. Several companies operated in Italian airplane manufacture: Savoia-Marchetti (SM), Fiat, Società Italiana Caproni (Ca), Cantieri Riuniti dell'Adriatico (Cant), and Officine Meccàniche Reggiane (MC), to name several of the more prominent.

During the war, Italy fielded some 2,000 biplanes fighters in frontline service, a reflection of the conservatism of its pilots and of the poor state of the RA in comparison to rival air forces. The Italian pilots clung to the old ways at a time when the world of aviation was changing quickly around them. They preferred the open cockpit and the biplane, believing skill and maneuverability ranked above speed and firepower. They held back Italian design at a time when technology was giving other countries the edge.

Mussolini's role in the story of the RA failure is a crucial one. He failed badly both in the strategic application of his available airpower and in the future types that should be developed. His control and interference were such that the accusation has to be leveled at him personally. He persisted with the idea of the bomber and he continued to use land-based aircraft to "dominate" the Mediterranean, because he scoffed at the idea of aircraft carriers. He also neglected specialist aircraft types and interfered with dispositions so much that assets were wasted.

The Italians failed to coordinate their efforts properly. Their paper strength was never fulfilled. They had some good aircraft, but many were inadequate and the backup was poor. Bad training and maintenance also played their parts and it is noticeable that the RA's attrition rate was very high. Of the 7,000 or so aircraft they put into action, only 500 remained by 1943 when the Italian forces split, and a rump calling itself *Aviazione della Repubblica Sociale Italiana* continued to fight alongside the *Luftwaffe*. These figures tell their own story and illustrate the nature of the threat the RA posed to opposing air forces in practice.

Chris Westhorp

Additional Reading
Bonciani, Carlo, *F Squadron* (1948).
Jackson, William G.J., *The Battle for Italy* (1967).
Overy, R.J., *The Air War 1939–1945* (1980).

Air Force, Norwegian
The Royal Norwegian Air Force was divided into army and naval air forces. From 1941, steps were taken to unify the Norwegian Army and Naval Air Force into the Royal Norwegian Air Force. This was accomplished in exile in August 1944.

When the Germans occupied Norway, air force personnel came to Britain to fight with the Allies. In 1940, a Norwegian training facility was established in Canada. On 25 April 1941, the first Norwegian squadron, Number 330, became operational and served with the RAF Coastal Command. On 21 July 1941, the first Norwegian fighter squadron, Number 331, was formed. In January 1942, a second fighter squadron, Number 332, became operational. At that time there were about 200 officers and 1,400 enlisted personnel serving with the RAF. By January 1945, the Royal Norwegian Air Force had eighty operational aircraft in five squadrons.

Thomas A. Cardwell III

Additional Reading
Moulton, James L., *The Norwegian Campaign of 1940: A Study of Warfare in Three Dimensions* (1966).
Wright, Myrtle, *Norwegian Diary, 1940–45* (1974).

Air Force, Polish
Relative to its size, the Polish Air Force (PAF) played a disproportionately significant role in

World War II. The complex saga of the PAF has three major headings: the September campaign of 1939, the reconstituted PAF that fought in the West, and the little-known story of Polish air units on the eastern front.

When Germany invaded on 1 September 1939, the PAF numbered 397 combat aircraft: 159 fighters, 154 bombers, and eighty-four reconnaissance craft. Oft-repeated figures crediting the Poles with much larger numbers are in error and probably derive from faulty German intelligence reports. In accordance with prewar plans, all aircraft were moved to secret bases immediately before hostilities. As a result, the *Luftwaffe* destroyed far fewer Polish aircraft on the ground than the established legend would have it. Flying obsolete machines (principally the PZL P-11 and the still older PZL P-7) and outnumbered by more than four to one, the PAF inflicted striking damage on the *Luftwaffe,* which lost almost 600 aircraft over Poland, about one-quarter through aerial combat. PAF losses totaled 327, about seventy in aerial combat.

Whereas this testifies to the skill and tenacity of the PAF, its efforts were poorly coordinated with the ground forces and it was excessively dispersed, grievously limiting its strategic and tactical effectiveness. Bombers were not well utilized, and scored only isolated tactical success. When the Soviets invaded on 17 September, the remnants of the PAF evacuated to Romania or Hungary, thus ending the air war.

After the fall of Poland, the PAF was reconstituted in France and Britain under General Władysław Sikorski's (q.v.) Polish government-in-exile. By June 1940, the PAF had almost 7,000 men in France, but was inadequately equipped due to French dilatoriness. Nonetheless, Polish pilots scored an impressive fifty-six aerial kills in the losing effort of 1940. With France's fall, the bulk of the PAF reassembled in Britain, where some of its units were being refitted. Relations with the British initially were awkward as London insensitively demanded the Poles take loyalty oaths to the king and wear RAF uniforms. Nonetheless, the PAF's performance in the 1940 air war over Britain has become legendary. Number 303 Squadron, for example, outperformed every RAF unit.

Approximately 15 percent of all Allied pilots at the height of the Battle of Britain (q.v.) were Polish. Polish pilots destroyed enemy craft at an astounding seven-to-one ratio. As PAF squadrons multiplied so did their achievements. Throughout 1941, Poles scored 26 percent of all RAF kills. In addition to its fighter component, the PAF raised four bomber squadrons, which also made a significant contribution to RAF Bomber Command. The PAF in Britain eventually counted 20,000 men in fourteen squadrons and played a role in every major air action: the Battle for the Atlantic, the Dieppe Raid, D-Day, and tragic bomber missions to aid their homeland during the 1944 Warsaw Rising (qq.v.). Historian Jerzy Cynk calculated the PAF flew almost 90,000 sorties, destroyed more than 500 enemy planes, and almost 200 V-1 flying bombs. The PAF also flew 16,000 transport sorties.

In the summer of 1943, Polish air units were created in the Soviet Union to serve with the Polish ground units established by Moscow. It grew slowly over the next year and by the autumn of 1944, the Polish 1st Composite Air Division included almost 600 men and about 100 aircraft.

PAF personnel on the eastern front, Soviet equipped and trained, began combat operations on 23 April 1944, largely in ground-attack roles as part of Soviet operations along the Polish front. The eastern front PAF's reconnaissance and attack assignments were performed in close conjunction with Polish ground units serving with the Red Army. Eastern front PAF units participated in all of the operations in the following months, reaching the 400 aircraft level by the spring of 1945. During the Berlin offensive (q.v.), Polish airmen accounted for almost 5 percent of the Soviet Air Force. By war's end in May 1945, eastern front PAF pilots downed 20 German planes and completed almost 19,000 sorties.

M.B. Biskupski

Additional Reading

Arct, Bohdan, *Polish Wings in the West* (1971).
Cynk, Jerzy B., *History of the Polish Air Force, 1918–1968* (1971).
Zamoyski, Adam, *The Forgotten Few: The Polish Air Force in the Second World War.* (1995).

Air Force, Soviet

In a speech delivered in 1931, three years into the first Soviet five-year plan for rapid industrialization, Josef Stalin (q.v.) declared, "We are fifty or a hundred years behind the advanced countries. We must make good this distance in ten years. Either we do it, or they crush us!" This view lay behind vigorous efforts to develop a modern Soviet aircraft industry, which began in 1918 with the establishment of the Central Aerodynamic State Institute (TsAGI) by Lenin's Bolshevik government.

Effective ground support for anti-Bolshevik

White forces fighting on the Tsaritsyn front had been provided by Number 47 Squadron of the British Royal Air Force during the Russian civil war. (Later, Tsaritsyn was renamed Stalingrad). Stalin, Semyon Budenny, and Leon Trotsky (qq.v.), who commanded Red forces on that front, thus came to understand the importance of airpower. They took a keen interest in the rapid development of Soviet military aviation.

In the 1930s, Soviet designers like N.N. Polikarpov, Andrei N. Tupolev, P.O. Sukhoi, Aleksandr S. Yakovlev, Serngey V. Ilyushin (q.v.), V.M. Petliakov, and others, produced world-class machines, initially powered by license-built aero engines from the West. Soviet aircraft captured several international records. V.F. Chkalov, V.K. Kokkinaki, Mikhail Gromov, and other pilots achieved international notoriety for their record-breaking flights. Soviet aviators were portrayed by the Soviet press as combining the technological-scientific knowledge, dynamism, and political consciousness that would typify the "New Man" of socialist society.

The Soviets led the world in starting mass production of fighter and bomber monoplanes with enclosed cockpits and retractable undercarriages. These saw service in the Spanish civil war (q.v.) against Franco's German and Italian allies, and in China against the Japanese. During the fighting between the Soviets and Japanese in 1939, at the point where the Khalka River formed the border between Mongolia and Japanese-controlled Manchuria, the Soviet Air Force (*Voenno-Vozhdusnis Sili*, or VVS) struggled for air superiority with the Japanese Army Air Force, while the Soviets manhandled the Japanese on the ground. Air-to-air rockets, used for the first time in history, were mounted on Soviet fighter biplanes. Strikes by four-engine Tb-3 bombers helped push Japanese forces out of Mongolia.

In the Russo-Finnish Winter War (q.v.), the small Finnish Air Force inflicted heavy losses on second-line VVS units. (The best VVS units were kept in the Soviet Union to counter a possible German attack.) In response to the poor performance of the VVS in Finland, a major reorganization program was undertaken.

In early 1939, at a meeting in the Kremlin, Stalin, Vyacheslav Molotov (q.v.), L.M. Kaganovich, and other Soviet leaders instructed aircraft and aircraft engine manufacturers to produce new military aircraft of all types. By this time, aircraft engine designers like Vladimir Klimov, Aleksandr Mikulin, and Arkady Shvetsov were producing much-improved versions of Western engines, such

as the Klimov 1,050 hp M-105, which was based on the French Hispano-Suiza 12Y. Soviet aircraft armament designers Nudelmann, Suranov, Yartsev, and M.I. Volkov, were producing world-class cannons and machine guns. These engines and weapons were incorporated into the new fighter designs by Aleksandr Yakovlev and S.A. Lavochkin. The resulting series of Yakovlev (Yak) and Lavochkin (La) fighters became mainstays of the Soviet Air Force during World War II.

General Semen Timoshenko (q.v.), who, after the initial Soviet setbacks, had been appointed to bring a speedy Soviet victory in Finland, was given the task of reorganizing the Soviet armed forces, including the VVS. In 1940, he replaced the basic VVS tactical unit of twenty- to thirty-plane squadrons, grouped into air brigades assigned to military districts, with regiments of forty to sixty planes. Three to five regiments made up an air division, which replaced the air brigades. The air divisions were assigned to military districts, or grouped into air corps that could be independently assigned. Some regiments had a single function— for example, ground attack—while composite regiments consisted of fighters, bombers, and ground-attack aircraft. Composite regiments were more common.

Timoshenko also reorganized the VVS command structure into frontal aviation, army aviation, long-range bomber aviation, and corps aviation. A frontal aviation unit normally consisted of three or four bomber, attack, or fighter air divisions, each with 200 to 300 planes, and assigned to a front. Army aviation units consisted of one or two composite air divisions attached directly to an army. Corps aviation squadrons were assigned liaison duties with rifle, mechanized, or cavalry corps, and were subordinate to the corps commander. Rear services were also reorganized. In 1941, air base regions were created, each airfield having maintenance battalions whose sizes varied with the number and types of aircraft based at the field.

Despite the international role of Soviet airpower in the late 1930s, Soviet military aircraft were still relatively unknown in the West. Soviet aircraft observed in Spain were sometimes described by Western commentators as mere copies of Western machines. The Soviet-Japanese clash on the Mongolian border was overshadowed in the West by the German invasion of Poland. Western accounts of Finns fighting against overwhelming odds were more common in the Western press than sober assessments of the capabilities of Soviet military aircraft. It was also widely assumed in the

West that Stalin's purges (q.v.) of the Soviet officer corps had crippled Soviet military capabilities.

VVS reorganization and reequipping programs were devastated by the German invasion on 22 June 1941. Command and control structures had to be totally rebuilt. On 29 June, Stalin and the *Stavka* (q.v.) appointed General P.F. Zhigarev as VVS commander. Despite tremendous losses, special *Stavka* VVS reserve units were created. Units of this force were assigned to the different fronts as the need arose. In order to improve control and concentration of airpower, each air division was reduced in size to two regiments, and regimental strength was cut from sixty aircraft to twenty-two. In a move to increase mobility, rear services were no longer tied to particular units or airfields.

VVS ability to resist the *Luftwaffe* improved in November 1941, when four air divisions were transferred to western Russia from the far east of the Soviet Union. In early December, VVS units that distinguished themselves in combat were given the title of "Guards." This practice continued throughout the war, and guards units received the best equipment and personnel.

Despite the experience gained in the Spanish civil war, Soviet Air Force fighter tactics at the time of the German invasion were based on the theory that fast, heavily armed monoplane fighters could force the enemy into combat with lightly armed maneuverable biplane fighters. Consequently, Soviet fighter tactics were based on close collaboration of large formations. In 1941–1942, these tactics proved ineffective. Soviet fighters, on encountering Axis fighters, would usually form a defensive circle, or "snake" toward Soviet lines at low altitude.

Like other air forces, the VVS eventually adopted the two-plane element as the basic tactical unit for fighter aircraft, with the element leader protected by his wingman. Four planes, usually flying in stepped formation, made up a group. After 1942, offensive sweeps by Soviet fighters usually involved a group, composed of three or four pairs of aircraft, which covered a particular sector of the front. Another group held back in reserve. After the battle of Stalingrad (q.v.), single pairs of "free hunters" were often allowed to seek out the enemy.

Ground-attack tactics were improved by Major General I.S. Folbin and other combat fliers, who pioneered use of the twin-engine Petlyakov Pe-2 as a dive bomber. Leading Soviet ground-attack pilots developed techniques for subjecting *Wehrmacht* armored vehicles—especially tanks—to surprise and continuous attack against their most vulnerable points. Six-plane groups with pairs as basic elements were used for ground attack. Line formations replaced V-formations after 1942.

In 1942, General Zhigarev was replaced by General A.A. Novikov (q.v.). Another major reor-

Soviet Air Order of Battle

	1 Sept 1939	22 June 1941[1]
Obsolete Four-Engine Bombers	369	43[2]
Modern Twin-Engine Medium Bombers	230	241
Obsolescent Twin-Engine Bombers	1,614	1,946
Twin-Engine Torpedo Bombers	540	683
Modern Single-Engine Ground Attack Planes	0	100
Obsolete Single-Engine Light Bombers	1,280	4,100
Modern Single-Engine Fighters	120	1,000
Obsolescent Single-Engine Fighters	3,900	4,400
Single-Engine Biplane Fighters	7,389	4,200
Reconnaissance Aircraft	687	1,100
Seaplanes and Floatplanes	300	360
Transport Aircraft	2,000	3,100[3]
Autogiros	1	7
Training Aircraft (all types)	5,000	6,000
Reserve Aircraft (all types)	6,000	5,000

Notes:
1. Out of a total inventory of 32,100 aircraft on 22 June 1941, 2,541 were assigned to the Soviet Navy.
2. Most of these were converted into transports, but were used occasionally as night harassment bombers during the war.
3. These figures also include Aeroflot aircraft, which were immediately available to the military when requested.

ganization of the VVS was undertaken, which involved combining frontal and army aviation units into air armies attached directly to ground units. Commanders of air armies were subordinated to the commanding general of a particular front. By November 1942, thirteen air armies were formed. In addition, the *Stavka's* VVS reserve was expanded and used to reinforce the air armies on active fronts. The strength of fighter and ground attack regiments increased from twenty-two to thirty-two aircraft. In 1942–1943, the average air army had 900 to 1,000 planes; in 1943–1944, this increased to 1,500; by 1945, each air army had 2,500 to 3,000 aircraft. These changes, coupled with improved quality and quantity of fighter and ground-attack aircraft, allowed greater mobility and concentration of airpower where it was most needed.

Guards Colonel A.I. Pokryshkin (fifty-nine victories) was one of the leading Soviet air commanders. His formula, "altitude, speed, maneuver, fire," was the basis for successful Soviet fighter tactics. Use of the first Soviet fighter-control radar was pioneered by Pokryshkin's squadron in the Black Sea region in 1944.

The Soviet Air Force included combat flyers from the Soviet Asian republics, and from several of the smaller Soviet nationalities, including the Eskimos of northeastern Siberia. Lilly Litvak (q.v.), one of the women fighter pilots of the VVS, scored twelve victories before she disappeared during a combat mission in August 1943. The highest-scoring Soviet ace, Major General Ivan N. Kozhedub, (q.v.), finished the war with sixty-two victories.

Like all other major air forces in World War II, the VVS had to solve the problem of providing effective fighter escorts for bombers. Experience showed that when escorting fighters stayed close to bombers, they could not prevent attacking fighters from breaking up bomber formations. In the Kuban air battles of 1943, Pokryshkin and others solved this problem with stepped formations. Groups of fighters, flying 1,500 to 3,000 feet above a bomber formation, were supposed to break up attacking groups of enemy fighters. Other fighters, flying close to the bombers, dealt with any enemy fighters that penetrated the top cover. A pair of radio-equipped fighters flew ahead of the bomber formation to warn of approaching enemy fighters. (Not all Soviet fighters were radio-equipped.) These tactics proved to be so effective that they were copied by the *Luftwaffe* in 1943 and were used by the Soviet Air Force long after World War II.

The Soviet Air Force of World War II was almost exclusively a tactical air arm, whose main task was support of ground forces. Early proponents of strategic bombing, like Marshal Mikhail Tukhachevsky (q.v.) and air force chiefs Iakov Alksnis and Vasily Khripin, were victims of the prewar purges. After the German invasion, relocation of the Soviet aircraft industry to Novosibirsk, Komsomolsk, Irkutsk, and other cities east of the Urals, coupled with priority production of fighters and ground attack aircraft, precluded the creation of a large force of strategic bombers.

Despite the relative lack of strategic bombers, a long-range aviation branch (ADD) of the VVS was formed in March 1942 under the command of Major General A.E. Golovanov. It was intended as a strategic force but proved more useful in a tactical role. ADD was redesignated Eighteenth Air Army in 1944 and used to support Soviet offensives in Poland, East Prussia, and Berlin (qq.v.).

Unsophisticated production techniques and lack of advanced materials like duralumin meant that Soviet aircraft were relatively simple. Wood composites were widely used for spars and ribs. Nevertheless, the relatively simple Soviet production and maintenance techniques allowed VVS aircraft to operate in extreme cold and on rough fields that sometimes grounded their more sophisticated *Luftwaffe* opponents. When the Soviets used more advanced materials in engines and airframes, their planes, with a few exceptions, matched those of the Western Allies in range and performance.

Although aircraft from the U.S. and Britain were used by the VVS, their total number of 18,800 was small in comparison to the approximately 137,000 aircraft produced by the Soviets between 1941 and the end of the European war. American deliveries of aluminum and other materials for aircraft construction were, perhaps, more important to the Soviet war effort than deliveries of aircraft.

In comparison to the Soviets, Nazi Germany produced approximately 100,700 aircraft between 1941 and May 1945. After the German conquest of the western Soviet Union in 1941, Soviet aircraft production fell by 50 percent, as entire aircraft plants were evacuated. By spring 1942, Soviet aircraft production returned to the prewar level of 1,000 per month. By the end of 1942, the Soviets had produced 25,436 aircraft to Germany's 15,409. Despite Albert Speer's (q.v.) reorganization of aircraft production in 1944, the German aircraft industry never caught up.

After the disastrous Soviet defeats that followed the initial German invasion, Western commentators predicted a speedy Nazi victory. Soviet defeats were attributed to the purges and to the supposedly negative influence of political commissars on Soviet command decisions. It was also widely assumed that a socialist society was incapable of producing advanced military technology. The performance of the VVS and the Soviet aircraft industry during World War II showed this assumption to be false.

Dennis A. Bartels

Additional Reading

Boyd, Alexander, *The Soviet Air Force Since 1918* (1977).

Hardesty, Von, *Red Phoenix, The Rise of Soviet Air Power, 1941–45* (1991).

Jackson, Robert, *The Red Falcons: The Soviet Air Force in Action, 1919–1969* (1970).

Lee, Asher, *The Soviet Air Force* (1950).

Wagner, Ray (ed.), *The Soviet Air Force in World War II: The Official History* (1973).

Air Force, Spanish

In 1936, when the Spanish civil war (q.v.) began, the Spanish Air Force found itself at a critical moment in its history. Its principal fighters, bombers, and reconnaissance aircraft possessed poor firepower and were obsolete. The decision was made to modernize the air force with some of the latest models from Europe.

The uprising in July 1936 dramatically changed the situation. The Republican government had approximately 200 military airplanes, while the Nationalists gained control of about 100. According to the authors of *Crónica De La Aviación Espanola,* had the Republican government moved quickly and decisively with its larger air force, it could have prevented General Francisco Franco's (q.v.) Army of Africa from reaching the southern shores of the Iberian Peninsula in what was history's first large-scale military airlift. It is possible that the revolt could have been crushed in its infancy.

On 18 July 1936, the Spanish Air Force split in two. The Republicans received additional aircraft and pilots from France, as well as Soviet and mercenary aviators from various nations. The Nationalists acquired invaluable assistance from Italy and Germany. Germany's *Kondor Legion* (q.v.) and Italy's fighters and bombers gave the Nationalists the needed air support for their offensives against the government. Spanish pilots flew on both sides of the conflict and several became aces. Many pilots who remained loyal to the govern-

ment received their training in the Soviet Union, and some even flew with the Soviet Air Force during World War II.

When Germany invaded the Soviet Union in 1941 and Franco sent the Blue Division, the Spanish Air Force also sent a contingent of fighter pilots, which became known as the Spanish Expeditionary Air Squadron (*La Escuadrilla azul da Caza*) or the Blue Squadron. Five squadrons alternated on the line and were led by five different commanders: Majors Salas, Larrazábal Salvador, Ferrandis, Medina Cuadra, and Murcia. Each squadron was composed of seventeen pilots and eighty men for the ground crews. While the Blue Division was attached to German Army Group North, Blue Squadron was assigned to support Army Group Center under Field Marshal Albert Kesselring's (q.v.) Second *Luftflotte.*

At first, Blue Squadron was attached to *Jagdgeschwader* (Fighter Wing) 27, and was later assigned to JG-51. The primary role of the squadron was supporting ground forces. Sometimes it escorted German bombers. Piloting Messerschmitt Bf-109s (which they flew during the civil war), and later in 1943, the Focke-Wulf FW-190s, Spanish aviators participated in the push on Moscow (q.v.) and Kharkov, and in the battles of Kursk (q.v.) and Smolensk. Spanish fighter pilots were credited with shooting down more than 150 Soviet planes, and ten Spanish pilots became aces. Blue Squadron was recalled to Spain on 1 October 1943, having lost twenty-two members either dead or missing. One man, taken prisoner by the Soviets, returned in 1954.

José Alvarez

Additional Reading

Plocher, Hermann, *The German Air Force versus Russia, 1941* (1965).

Proctor, Raymond L., *Agony of a Neutral: La División Azul* (1974).

Air Force, Swiss

Neutral Switzerland, due to its geographical position between the two Axis powers of Italy and Germany, had its airspace violated many times by all sides during the course of World War II. The Swiss Air Force, part of its army, was active against all sides.

Early in the war, the Swiss shocked the *Luftwaffe* with the stout defense of their country. German aircraft received a mauling at the hands of the superb Swiss pilots who, befitting a mountainous people, made the best use of the topography to outwit the *Luftwaffe*. They skillfully used the mountain valleys and engaged in steep diving movements that confused the Germans. The Germans, thereafter, largely respected Swiss neutrality.

Beginning in late 1940, however, it was the Allies who were a problem for the Swiss. The Swiss were handicapped by not having radar (q.v.) or night fighters with which to stop or oppose bomber overflights. Swiss antiaircraft artillery was, however, very good and particularly strong, with more than 4,000 pieces at the war's end. These *Flak* guns claimed many victims, although the desire to down Allied aircraft was not always keenly held.

In 1940, the Swiss Air Force had Morane D-3801 and German Messerschmitt Bf-109 aircraft operational as fighters, and they went on to claim twenty kills against the Axis and Allies. The entire 300-strong force (including non-fighters) was organized into three regiments, with five *Abteilungen* (groups) and twenty-one *Kompanien* (flights). Their ninety Bf-109's were mainly E-models, but some were D-models. Other types in service were obsolete Federal Factory C-35 biplanes used for observation, and some Dewoitine D-27's and Fokker CV's. The Morane was a useful intermediate fighter that played a key part in making the Swiss Air Force an effective combat unit.

The major weakness of the Swiss was the poor state of their communications systems. On the other hand, they had a 3,000-strong spotter corps manning a nationwide chain of observation posts that watched the skies and reported any violations. This relatively primitive system managed to direct the tenacious Swiss fighters into battle.

The Swiss had very strict rules of engagement. It was these rules, together with a fear of becoming more embroiled in a wider conflict, that resulted in rare air-to-air clashes. As the war went on, air defense was handled virtually by the antiaircraft guns alone, and Swiss aircraft stayed in the background.

Chris Westhorp

Additional Reading
Dupuy, Trevor N., *The Air War in the West, September 1939–May 1941* (1963).
Fodor, Denis J., *The Neutrals* (1982).

Air Force, U.S.
The United States Air Force, the definitive airpower in the world today, was established in 1947, though the origins of the air force began in 1920. In that year, the U.S. Army established its Army Air Service. In 1921, the U.S. Navy organized its Bureau of Aeronautics. Though neither force was particularly strong, each branch was adding improved aircraft, and there were calls to create an independent air force.

The next pivotal step came in 1940 when Robert Lovett, a World War I navy flyer and prominent banker, was appointed as special assistant to the secretary of war in December, and then assistant secretary of war for air in April 1941. It fell to Lovett to organize the air forces and improve aircraft production. On 20 June 1941, the U.S. Army's Air Corps and its Air Force Combat Command were unified under the single command of General Henry H. "Hap" Arnold (q.v.) as the U.S. Army Air Forces (USAAF). Although complete autonomy as an independent branch of the military services was delayed until 1947, the USAAF operated in World War II virtually as a separate entity.

When the United States was drawn into the war, the USAAF was a relatively small force, with only 4,000 aircraft and 25,000 personnel. Lend-Lease (q.v.), however, created the industrial base from which to increase aircraft production. By the end of 1942, the number of aircraft available tripled. More importantly, aircraft models produced were equal to, and in some cases superior to, those of the enemies. As the war continued, the industrial war machine produced aircraft in remarkable numbers. Between 1940 and August 1945, the USAAF received 229,554 additional aircraft, a prodigious increase over the size of the force at the time of Pearl Harbor.

Japanese victories in early 1942 dictated reorganization of the USAAF. The major fighting commands of the USAAF were the numbered air forces. During the initial stages of World War II, they were primarily active in the Pacific. The Fifth, Seventh, Tenth, Eleventh, Thirteenth, and Fourteenth Air Forces operated in the Far East.

In January 1942, Major General Carl Spaatz's (q.v.) Eighth Air Force was activated. In May, it absorbed Brigadier General Ira Eaker's (q.v.) VIII Bomber Command. From its inception, the Eighth Air Force was designed for the strategic bombing of Germany and German-held territory in Europe. With its headquarters at High Wycombe near London, the Eighth Air Force was organized into bomber, fighter, service, and training commands. Projections called for the Eighth Air Force to include 137 combat groups—seventy-four bomber groups, thirty-one fighter groups, twelve observation groups, fifteen transport groups, four photography groups, and one mapping group. The British provided 127 installations for use by Spaatz's command.

The Ninth Air Force was created in 1942 from elements of the Eighth Air Force as the Middle East Air Forces, under Major General Lewis H. Brereton (q.v.). Consisting primarily of heavy bombers, the Ninth Air Force saw extensive duty in North Africa against the Germans. By the fall of 1942, additional medium bombers and fighters joined the Ninth Air Force to support the British campaign at El Alamein (q.v.). Brereton's units were later assigned to the campaigns in Italy and Sicily (q.v.) and eventually rejoined the Eighth Air Force in Europe.

The Twelfth Air Force was established in Washington on 20 August 1942 under the command of Major General James H. Doolittle (q.v.) and was first active in North Africa. In February 1943, the Twelfth Air Force joined Royal Air Force (RAF) units of the Northwest African Air Forces. After the North African campaign (q.v.), the Twelfth Air Force saw duty in the Mediterranean with the invasions of Sicily and Italy, and bombed Monte Cassino (q.v.) in one of the more controversial air attacks of the war.

In November 1943, the Fifteenth Air Force was created to bomb German targets in southern Europe from captured bases in Italy. The Fifteenth Air Force was absorbed in early 1944 by the United States Strategic Air Forces in Europe under Spaatz and Doolittle.

From the arrival of the USAAF in Britain in early 1942, the role of the Americans in relationship to the RAF was critical. While the Eighth Air Force was anxious to flex its airborne muscle, the questions of control and target selection and the issue of day versus night bombing had to be addressed with the RAF leaders. The RAF used night bombing raids in its area bombing strategy, but initially approved the USAAF's tactics of daylight bombing with RAF fighter escorts. Eventually, American fighters replaced the RAF escorts, but the question of day versus night bombing attacks surfaced continually and was not resolved until the Casablanca Conference in January 1943 (*see* Strategic Bombing).

During the war, the moral dilemma raised by target selection occupied the American political and military leadership as well as the USAAF. Aerial attacks on civilian targets caused genuine and lasting concern, especially considering the prospects for postwar Europe. While the British air staff felt any attacks on Germany justified, the Americans showed obvious reluctance. The area bombing strategy used by Ninth Air Force airplanes in Eastern Europe in 1943 proved the American point; the Americans lost any chance at

U.S. Army Air Forces Order of Battle

	1941	1943	1944
Fighters	2,170	11,875	17,198
Light Bombers	1,544	6,741	9,169
Heavy Bombers	288	8,118	13,790
Recce Aircraft	475	714	1,804
Transports	254	6,466	10,456

Note: Figures represent USAAF strength worldwide, including Europe, the Pacific, and the United States.

a political advantage to the Soviets, who did not create the devastation of American airpower. The USAAF staff, however, was trying to end the war and save American lives.

The initial USAAF involvement in European air attacks came in July 1942, when it joined selective strikes with RAF units. These were repeated in August and September. In October, the USAAF began to step up air attacks on enemy targets in France. On 7 November, USAAF bombers dropped almost 700 tons of bombs on Brest and attacks continued into December on shipping and rail targets in occupied France.

The RAF was still the dominant airpower during the first year of American involvement in the war over the skies of Europe. In January 1943, the USAAF made its first raid on Germany, bombing Hamburg at night. By March, USAAF bombing missions were on the increase, targeting U-boat bases and U-boat plants. In all, the Eighth Air Force dropped 1,666 tons of bombs during the month, with heavier attacks to come. In May, tonnage increased to 2,865. In comparison, the RAF in the Ruhr air campaign (q.v.) dropped 2,000 tons of bombs in one raid alone on Dortmund. The USAAF, still playing a subsidiary role, attacked German airfields in August, destroying 631 enemy aircraft, as well as aircraft and ball bearing plants.

It was also during August that the major flaw in USAAF air strategy became all too obvious—the lack of fighter cover for bombing missions. On 17 August 1943, 146 B-17s left British airfields to attack aircraft works in Regensburg and 230 bombers targeted the ball bearing works at Schweinfurt, Germany (qq.v.), all without fighter support. The results were disastrous: twenty-four bombers were lost at Regensberg and thirty-six at Schweinfurt. A total of 550 aircrewmen were lost, and the ball bearing factories were not totally destroyed. In September, U.S. airmen downed 262 enemy airplanes and bombed German air bases and railroad lines. By the fall, the daylight strategy suffered from fewer days of operation (five in October), but the USAAF was able to conduct ten major raids in December dropping 12,000 tons of bombs.

In the Mediterranean theater, the Ninth Air Force attacked elements of the Italian Navy on 11 August 1942, but most of the action of the USAAF was in support of the Allied forces in the Northwest Africa campaign. By May 1943, the Northwest African Air Forces (NAAF), composed of aircraft from the Ninth and Twelfth Air Forces, became more active in targeting sites in Sicily and Italy.

With a crumbling Italy as its main target, NAAF stepped up sorties in the summer of 1943 in preparation for the invasions of Sicily and later Italy. On 19 July, in the first air attack on Rome, 700 aircraft dropped 1,100 tons of bombs on the city. In both July and August, NAAF flew 20,000 sorties, primarily against Italian targets. In September, the air forces dropped 15,000 tons of bombs in Italy, all in preparation for the September Allied invasion. For the remainder of 1943, NAAF was primarily active in support of Allied ground operations.

In 1944, RAF and USAAF air activity increased, as the combined air forces pounded German targets in the occupied territories and cities of Germany. January saw the formation of the United States Strategic Air Forces in Europe when Fifteenth Air Force from the Mediterranean theater joined Eighth Air Force. Spaatz was the overall commander. That month, the RAF dropped 10,000 tons of bombs, but the Americans dropped 22,000 tons and destroyed 937 enemy aircraft.

The targets continued to be German industry, railroads, shipping, and U-boat yards, as well as airfields in occupied France. In February, the USAAF bombed seventeen major aircraft factories and twenty airfields. As Allied invasion plans continued to evolve, air attacks reached greater levels. During March, British and American air forces combined to drop almost 50,000 tons of bombs on enemy targets, 30,172 by the USAAF. The USAAF launched attacks on Berlin on 3, 4, 6, and 8 March and destroyed more than 1,000 enemy aircraft throughout the month. The bombing continued in April with the same types of targets. During the final month prior to Normandy (q.v.), the USAAF dropped 63,000 tons of bombs with 1,268 *Luftwaffe* planes downed. Berlin and oil targets were bombed extensively.

By D-Day, the USAAF pounded German targets with more than 180,000 tons of bombs during the first five months of 1944. As a result of USAAF supporting the Allied invasion on the coast of France, bombing operations continued on a smaller scale. Oil refineries in Germany, Hungary, Yugoslavia, and Austria were targeted. Just after midnight on 6 June 1944, the RAF sent 1,000 bombers against the Normandy coast, followed by another 1,000 USAAF bombers against the German air forces at daylight, driving the *Luftwaffe* back to Paris. These successes were not without losses and criticism.

During March and April 1944, bombing missions against the Balkans were costly and inflicted heavy civilian casualties. On 4 April, 300 heavy bombers of the USAAF targeted Sofia, Bulgaria, a military objective because of its rail yards. Eaker estimated the attack killed 12,000 people, half of them Romanian refugees. While the resulting public relations nightmare flamed at home and in Europe, Americans continued to target east European sites, including Yugoslavia and Romania.

The objective of war is to defeat the enemy. In order to do that, the Allied air forces were not only attacking the German military, but also destroying its industrial war machine. While the British seemed to show little reluctance in bombing civilians, American political leaders and military strategists adopted a policy of avoiding unnecessary civilian casualties. President Franklin D. Roosevelt (q.v.) approved the formation of a commission that attempted to preserve the architectural, artistic, and historical sites in Europe, and aircrews were given maps designating what to avoid. Rome, where Vatican City survived the attacks, was an example of the precision bombing of which the Americans were capable. Eventually, however, the tempo of the war made target selection more and more difficult, and many German cultural sites were all but obliterated by Allied bombing.

In the weeks and months following D-Day, the Allied air forces not only provided extensive support for ground force operations, but also continued to pound deeper into enemy territory. July and August saw increased bombing in Germany, as the USAAF stepped up attacks on German industries, bombing Kiel, Munich, Peenemünde, Schweinfurt, Regensburg, and Bremen among the major industrial targets. The *Luftwaffe* was virtually unable to mount a significant response.

The RAF and USAAF had to divert a large measure of their assets to the tactical air support of the advancing ground forces, thus making the number of bombing missions all the more impressive. If numbers are a yardstick, September provides proof positive of Allied air superiority over Europe. That month, the RAF dropped 52,400 tons of bombs and the USAAF 60,000 tons. On 11 September alone, USAAF fighters destroyed 116 German fighters, and the Americans targeted

German-held areas in Italy and the Balkans. For the remaining months of 1944, Allied successes continued unabated. In November, the USAAF destroyed another 723 German aircraft, many on the ground. On 24 December, 2,000 Eighth Air Force bombers attacked airfields, railroads, bridges, and supply centers. That was the largest American bomber effort yet in the war. USAAF fighter groups claimed seventy German aircraft downed.

The year 1944 marked the most impressive display of airpower ever as the RAF and USAAF flew daily missions against targets of all types. The American approach of hitting oil refineries and supplies was the unsung strategy of the war, and the one significant difference between the leaders of the two air forces. The British still pushed for their Allies to target German cities and thus civilians. For the most part, however, the Americans refused to comply with British wishes. The exceptions, mostly against oil targets in the Balkans, were nevertheless considered successful and necessary. Eaker approved of these raids and believed they were all within the stated American objectives.

During the final year of the war, the primary focus of the USAAF shifted to the Pacific. That in no way signaled a decrease in Allied bombing activity in Germany, either in tactical air support of ground troops or in the pattern of destroying German war industries. The RAF did most of the damage against targets in Germany while the USAAF provided tactical air support. The Eighth Air Force was instrumental in stopping the Ardennes offensive (q.v.) in January 1945. In February, the USAAF resumed heavy bomber missions, dropping the highest tonnage of the war (74,000 tons), sending up more than 1,000 bombers on fifteen of twenty operational days. American forces virtually matched that total in March. On 16 April, Spaatz announced only tactical air support requirements remained for the USAAF in Europe.

In addition to direct combat operations, the USAAF in World War II also had a global logistics mission. In 1932, the Army Air Corps established a temporary air transport group that became permanent in 1937. The system was still expanding when the Air Corps Ferrying Command was created in May of 1941 to deliver aircraft to Britain under the Lend-Lease program. In June 1942, the transportation network was renamed the Air Transport Command under Brigadier General Harold George. Cyrus Smith, then president of American Airlines, was made temporary colonel as George's chief of staff. Under their leadership, ATC

became a truly global system with almost 200,000 personnel and 3,700 aircraft.

Initially, civilian pilots were recruited, trained, and, in many instances, received military commissions. By the end of the war, all ATC staff were military. Commercial airlines assisted in training the army pilots and airmen. Prior to the strengthening of ATC, the airlines had done most of the War Department's air transport under contract. In 1942, 88 percent of the military's transport was contract work. That figure steadily decreased until only 19 percent was awarded by contract in 1945. The volume of cargo distributed by ATC during the war years is a tribute to the combined military-civilian effort. Covering a 40,000-mile network, ATC used C-46, C-47, and C-54s to carry troops and supplies to all theaters of war. The ATC was disbanded in September 1946.

From July 1940 to the end of August 1945, the USAAF accepted a total of 229,554 different aircraft: fighters, bombers, transports, and others. Peak strength was 75,000 aircraft. The entire USAAF numbered 2,411,294 personnel, 306,889 of whom were officers. Total casualties for the entire service were 115,382, with 52,173 dead.

The USAAF's role in the global war did not end in May 1945. Three months later, U.S. B-29s dropped atomic bombs on the Japanese cities of Hiroshima and Nagasaki, the ultimate expression of the military and airpower of the American nation.

Did airpower win the war? Not by itself, but the USAAF did supply a large measure of the vital force necessary for securing the final and total victory.

Boyd Childress

Additional Reading
Carter, Kit, *The Army Air Forces in World War II: Combat Chronology, 1941–1945* (1980).
Crane, Conrad C., *Bombs, Cities, and Civilians: American Airpower Strategy in World War II* (1993).
Craven, Wesley Frank, and James Lea Cate (eds.), *The Army Air Forces in World War II*, 7 vols. (1948–1958).
Schaffer, Ronald, *Wings of Judgment: American Bombing in World War II* (1985).

AK
See ARMIA KRAJOWA

ALSOS Mission
The ALSOS (Greek for "grove") Mission was the

Allied technical intelligence group in Europe from 1943 to 1945. It was initiated in 1943 by Brigadier General Leslie Groves (q.v.), the military commander of the MANHATTAN Project (q.v.). Its initial purpose was to determine the progress the Axis (specifically Germany) made in nuclear weapons development. It was assumed in the U.S. that Germany was far ahead of the Allies. The mission was unique because of its blend of military and civilian personnel cooperating in a common cause that actually worked without major problems. There was even a lack of friction when British civilian and military personnel joined the mission in late 1944.

The mission's civilian head was Dr. Samuel A. Goudsmit, a Dutch-born nuclear physicist. He was selected because he was one of the few major physicists who both worked on the MANHATTAN Project and worked with several German physicists thought to be involved with German nuclear weapons. The military commander was Lieutenant Colonel Boris T. Pash, a Russian-speaking, FBI-trained, army intelligence officer. Also in the group were a number of civilian and military personnel with backgrounds in science, mathematics, and engineering, many of whom spoke several European languages.

Their first foray into occupied Italy in 1943 yielded nothing. The mission entered Paris right after the first combat troops in August 1944, searching the Radium Institute and questioning staff members of the Joliot-Curie Laboratories for evidence of German progress. As they followed (and sometimes preceded) the Allied armies across Europe it became obvious that the Germans had made some erroneous calculations in 1941 and thus were at least four years behind the Allies in nuclear research.

By November 1944, based on interrogations and physical evidence, Goudsmit, Pash, and most of the mission were convinced Germany had no nuclear weapons; had little means of developing them; had less knowledge of how it was to be done; and had insufficient resources to construct them. Groves and others felt that until all the German scientists involved were captured, this conclusion was premature or perhaps planted. The mission continued to collect evidence until well after the surrender in May 1945. It stopped only when German scientists expressed their astonishment at the bombings of Hiroshima and Nagasaki.

The mission was not a failure, however. It did recover information on German high-pressure chemistry, synthetic petroleum and rubber production, hydrogen peroxide submarine propulsion

systems, rocket construction and guidance systems, and a number of other German wartime innovations.

John D. Beatty

Additional Reading

Gouldsmit, Samuel Abraham, *Alsos* (1947).
Rhodes, Richard, *The Making of the Atomic Bomb* (1986).

Armia Krajowa (AK)

The *Armia Krajowa* (AK) or Polish Home Army was formed in February 1942 from the military contingents of various political groups throughout Poland. Organized at the direction of the London-based Polish government-in-exile, the AK's first leader was General Stefan Rowecki (q.v.)—code named GROT. On 30 June 1943, Rowecki was arrested and subsequently executed by the *Gestapo* (q.v.). He was replaced by Lieutenant General Tadeusz Bór-Komorowski (q.v.). The AK reported directly to General Kazimierz Sosnkowski (q.v.), commander in chief of all Polish armed forces. In addition to the AK, the Polish armed forces included the Poland-based *Związek Walki Zbrojnej* (Union for Armed Struggle) and the regular Polish forces-in-exile fighting along side the Western Allies.

Sosnkowski divided Poland into six operational districts, each with its own underground military organization. The two principal districts were Warsaw, in the German occupation zone, and Lwów, in the zone occupied by the Soviet Union until June 1941. The Warsaw district also served as the overall headquarters for the AK. The Lwów district was commanded by Major General Michał Karaszewicz-Tokarzewski. The London-based government-in-exile sent Jan Stanisław Jankowski to Warsaw to serve as an intermediary between the London government and the AK. By June 1943, membership in the AK stood at about 300,000.

In its early months, the AK's operations concentrated on sabotage, intelligence gathering (with collected information fed to the Allies via the London government), small arms manufacturing, military training, unit mobilization exercises, and the printing of underground newspapers. Direct confrontation with the *Wehrmacht* was avoided. Initially, the London government wanted AK to remain a viable force. Once the Soviet Army had driven the Germans out of Poland, the AK was supposed to be strong enough to support the return of Polish sovereignty in the form of the London government.

On 5 April 1943, Moscow severed relations with the London government. Moscow's official reason for the break was the London government's accusations over the Soviet execution of Polish POW officers in the Katyń Forest (q.v.). Moscow, however, had additional reasons for the break. Soviet premier Josef Stalin (q.v.) had his own plans for Poland's postwar government that did not include the London Poles. Even after the break with Moscow, Sosnkowski initially directed the AK to coordinate with and fight alongside the Red Army.

Beginning in February 1944, as the Red Army was entering Poland, the AK launched Operation *BURZA* (TEMPEST) against the German Army. The first campaign was in Volhynia in eastern Poland, followed by one in Lwów in July. The Lwów campaign was conducted in coordination with Marshal Ivan Chernyakovsky's (q.v.) 3rd Byelorussian Front. But on 16 July at Wilno, Cherniakhovsky turned on the AK. He had the Polish officers arrested and he pressed nearly 6,000 AK soldiers into General Zygmunt Berling's (q.v.) Polish 1st Division of the Soviet Army.

Operation *BURZA* culminated with the Warsaw Rising (q.v.) from 1 August to 4 October 1944. While the Soviet forces of Marshal Konstantin Rokossovsky (q.v.) watched from the east bank of the Vistula River, the German Army systematically crushed the AK and destroyed the city. The Soviets refused to intervene for sixty-four days. The AK's casualties totalled 15,000 killed of its 40,000-strong Warsaw District. Some 150,000 civilians also were killed and 90 percent of the city was systematically destroyed. Operation *BURZA* ended with the defeat of the Rising. The AK was only a shadow force from that point on. The AK units that survived continued their struggle against the German Army at a drastically reduced level of operations.

Although Stalin used the AK to his advantage in coordination with the Red Army in its campaigns through Poland, he viewed the AK as criminals trying to seize power from what he considered as the rightful government-in-exile—the Lublin Committee. (The Lublin Committee also had a military arm called the *Armia Ludowa* or Polish People's Army). The Warsaw Rising ended with the Lublin Committee in a dominant political position, and the AK and Polish underground all but destroyed. Stalin's strategy, however, backfired in the long run. With the notoriously long historical memory of the Polish people, a bitter hostility existed between Poland and the Soviet Union throughout the Cold War years that followed World War II.

On 19 January 1945, the London government formally dissolved the AK. Many surviving AK soldiers went underground once more and joined the ultranationalist *Narodowe Siły Zbrojne* (National Armed Forces). They first fought against the Germans, and then against the Soviet-backed regime that took control as the Red Army moved through Poland. By the end of March 1945, the National Armed Forces disbanded. Its leaders were captured, sent to the Soviet Union for trial, and sentenced to prison terms.

For ten years after World War II, the AK and its members were branded as Nazi collaborators by Poland's communist government. As the events in Warsaw in August and September 1944 proved, nothing could have been further from the truth. In 1956, in the wake of the Soviet 20th Congress denouncing Stalin and his excesses, the AK was finally declared to have been patriotic. In Warsaw today there are more than one monument to those AK soldiers who fought in the Rising. At Warsaw's 1995 military ceremony commemorating the fiftieth anniversary of the end of World War II, many surviving *Armia Krajowa*, soldiers were among the honored guests in the reviewing stands.

William H. Van Husen

Additional Reading

Garliński, Józef, *Poland in the Second World War* (1985).

Hiscocks, Richard, *Poland: A Bridge for the Abyss* (1963).

Orpen, Neil D., *Airlift to Warsaw: The Rising of 1944* (1984).

Army, Australian

At the outbreak of the war, Australia did not have a standing army, only a militia some 35,000 strong. As in the United States, there was antipathy toward armies and soldiering, yet the Australians, having proven their excellence during World War I, were fine exponents of the art. Indeed, it could be said that Australia's national identity was forged in blood on the beaches of Gallipoli and in the trenches of the western front. They were dogged, determined, and full of fighting spirit.

Responding to the call of empire, Australia quickly formed a considerable number of men into an Australian Imperial Force (AIF) for overseas service, while a smaller Australian Military Force (AMF) was raised for local defense. Those who went abroad did so at the behest of British commanders, something that was to rankle the increasingly nationalistic Australians. Despite their reservations, the "Aussies," or "Diggers," served in incredible numbers: some 700,000 men out of an entire population of only seven million served. Of those, nearly 30,000 were killed, 40,000 wounded, and 30,000 captured.

What the AIF lacked was a policy. They wanted to be in the war but not absorbed by the British Army, and thereby have their identity lost. Yet, the Australian 6th Division, the first to go overseas, was offered to Britain without any clear direction given. Similarly, no thoughts were offered on how to defend against the Japanese. Therefore, when the Australians found themselves in the role of a fire brigade unit—rushing to Allied assistance in Greece, then Crete (qq.v.)—it was to a certain extent their own fault. The British attitude toward them often was contemptuous. It angered the AIF's commander in chief, General Sir Thomas Blamey (q.v.), that the order to withdraw from Greece was given without even consulting him.

The Australians always nurtured the belief that the British were using them as cannon fodder. The root cause of this was colonial tensions, no doubt, but it was a very real feeling exacerbated by the British establishment's dismissive attitude toward Australians (notably Prime Minister Winston S. Churchill's) and intensified by the fact that the AIF seldom served independently. As a result, the longer the war went on—especially after Japan's entry moved their focus from the European and North African theaters—the greater the strain on the Anglo-Australian relationship.

Shortly after the 6th Division deployed, it was joined by the 7th Division. They were used principally as infantry, serving in North Africa, Europe, and later Asia. They fought tenaciously and gallantly, securing nineteen Victoria Crosses, more than any other country of the empire. The Australians had a few armored units but suffered greatly from lack of equipment.

The first Australian troops to see action were those of the 6th Division, which played a crucial role in General Richard O'Connor's (q.v.) Western Desert Force victory at Beda Fomm (q.v.) in February 1941. This was the first British land success of the war. The Australians then found themselves diverted to Crete in a pointless action instigated by British commanders.

Perhaps the most famed Australian action came in 1941 at Tobruk (q.v.). By that time, Australia had three divisions in the Middle East under the command of its own General Leslie Morshead (q.v.) (nicknamed "Ming the Merciless" because of his resolution). At Tobruk, the 7th Division's 18th Brigade and the 20th, 24th, and 26th Brigades of the newly arrived and "green" 9th Division formed the defensive line against German General Erwin Rommel's battle-hardened *Afrika Korps* (qq.v.) offensive. The Australians held their positions for six months from April to November and thereby denied the Germans access to the vital port. This solid stand by the 15,000 Australians earned them the name "Rats of Tobruk." The action allowed the Allies subsequently to embark on the successful Operation CRUSADER. It also exacerbated political tensions, with many Australian politicians calling for "their boys" to be relieved and transferred back to Australia to deter the Japanese.

The 9th Division emerged from its baptism a toughened unit and became the epitome of Australian infantry. The division served with great distinction at El Alamein (q.v.), where German intelligence considered them the finest troops in the Eighth Army. In the later stages of the war, they returned to the Pacific theater to fight the Japanese.

Organized along British lines and generally equipped by the British and the Americans, the Australians displayed some inventiveness. They designed two 9mm submachine guns that were highly effective: the Owen and the Austen. The latter was an Australian version of the Sten, hence its name. They also produced a lightly armored scout-car, the Dingo, and a modification of the 25-pounder howitzer that was highly mobile in jungle and desert conditions.

The Australians remained concerned about the adequacy of the Allied forces in Singapore, a vital strategic point en route to Australia and the keystone to British power in Southeast Asia. The British constantly assured them, keen not to lose the Australians' vital force in the Middle East, but in February 1942, despite British assurances, Singapore fell, and with it Anglo-Australian tensions came to a head.

Having proven their ability, and with the Japanese on the offensive, the Australians demanded to go back home to face them. Equipment and material shortages still plagued their forces, but the men were fully confident. The British, however, remained scathing in private, even blaming the Australians for the loss of Singapore. They tried to delay any transfers, wanting to use the Australians elsewhere in the east more suitable to the defense of British interests. As the arguments escalated the Australians moved closer to the Americans. This relationship was to grow as the war went on.

Eventually, Australian divisions were transferred from the Middle East, but it was not until 1943 that the 9th Division returned to help secure the Allied victory in New Guinea. By that stage, all Australian efforts were focused on the Pacific campaign where they fought valiantly, often alongside the Americans, until the taking of Borneo in July 1945. The Australians had a say in the Pacific strategy, not to mention a vital interest, and they focused all their efforts toward the final victory.

Chris Westhorp

Additional Reading

Laffin, J., *Middle East Journey* (1958).
Maughan, B., *Australians at War* (1966).
Mollo, Andrew, *The Armed Forces of World War II* (1981).

Army, Belgian

Since Belgian independence and the creation of a multinational monarchy in 1830, Belgium maintained a policy of neutrality that was guaranteed internationally by the 1839 Treaty of London. Belgian neutrality was violated in August 1914 by German invasion. Despite subsequent German occupation, the remnants of the Belgian Army continued to fight bravely throughout World War I on the Yser front, a small strip of Belgian territory.

As one of the victorious powers in 1918, Belgium abandoned its traditional neutral policy between 1918 and 1936. Belgium maintained close military accords of mutual defense with France, and participated in occupying the Rhine and the Ruhr alongside the French Army. When the Germans entered the Rhineland (q.v.) in March 1936, at the time of the Ethiopian crisis, shock waves rippled throughout Europe. The ineffectiveness of the League of Nations (q.v.) was demonstrated to the world as war clouds began to gather over Europe.

In June 1936, under the influence of Foreign Minister Paul-Henri Spaak (q.v.), Belgium reaffirmed its neutrality and established an independent foreign policy. Despite a rearmament program and the extension of military service to seventeen months, Belgium's strategic position, as the smallest and most densely populated state in Europe, remained precariously weak, lying as it did on a traditional route of transit for European armies. The security of Belgium was further undermined by both the existence of an irredentist movement in the German-speaking sections of Eupen and Malmedy on the German-Belgium border, and the anti-French sentiment of Flemish nationalists. Despite the start of the war in September 1939, Belgium continued to maintain its neutrality throughout the "Phony War" (q.v.) period.

Because of Belgian neutrality since 1936, the Belgian Army did not participate in any joint exercises with the Allies, either before or during the Phony War period. Partly as a result, the eighteen-day Belgian campaign in 1940 was a total disaster for the Allied armies of Great Britain, Belgium, and France. The chaos was widespread. When British troops crossed the Belgian frontier on 11 May, in a bid to come to Belgium's aid, they were attacked by Belgian troops.

Despite having a mobilized strength of close to 550,000, the Belgian Army, which was divided into five regular and two reserve army corps, was inferior to friend and foe alike. Belgian soldiers were untrained, ill-equipped, poorly led, and totally inadequate to deal with the German onslaught they had to face.

The poor situation was worsened by an inadequate army air force and very little armored support. Belgium did not produce its own tanks and relied mainly on French and British equipment for its small mechanized force. The Belgian Army had a total of only forty-two obsolete light tanks, of which the light, two-man British-built Vickers-Carden-Lloyd was the principal weapon. Although an improved three-man version was to have been produced under license in Belgium, none were available before the German invasion.

Contemporary political opinion blamed the 28 May capitulation of Belgium for the continued retreat of the British and French armies, which led to the evacuation at Dunkirk (q.v.) and the eventual collapse of France. Although King Léopold III was vilified at the time by French Premier Paul Reynaud (qq.v.) and severely criticized by British prime minister Winston S. Churchill (q.v.), historical opinion has since established that Léopold's action alone was not the cause of German victory. Furthermore, Léopold's incitement to his army to continue fighting for two more days may have saved the French and British armies in their retreat into France.

Another argument shared by some historians is that the French and British allies should not have rallied to Belgium's aid on 11 May. Instead, they should have maintained their positions along the Maginot Line and the Franco-Belgian frontier, which was not fortified between Longwy and the coast. Such a deployment might have blunted the German tank thrust through the Ardennes at Sedan, and possibly could have prevented the early defeat of France.

Despite the deplorable situation, Belgian soldiers fought bravely. The Belgian Army fielded twenty-two divisions against German Army Group B. During the eighteen-day battle, 7,500 Belgian soldiers were killed and 15,850 were wounded. After the fall of Belgium and France, individual Belgian soldiers who made their way to Britain were eventually formed into the 1st Independent Belgian Brigade. That unit wore British uniforms and insignia, and operated under British control for the remainder of the war.

Robert C. Hudson

Additional Reading
Bitsch, Marie-Therese, *Histoire de la Belgique* (1992).
Bond, Brian, *France and Belgium, 1939–1940* (1975).
Mollo, Andrew, *The Armed Forces of World War II* (1981).

Army, Brazilian
On 26 October 1917, Brazil declared war on Germany because of U-boat attacks on its shipping. The Allies accepted Brazil's offer of naval ships but turned down its offer of troops. On 22 August 1942, again because of U-boat attacks on its shipping, Brazil declared war on Germany and Italy. The Allies immediately accepted Brazil's offer of its navy and air force for the war at sea but again turned down the offer of troops. The Brazilian Army once more found itself excluded from its nation's war effort.

During the 1930s, the Brazilian Army underwent a reorganization and modernization. In 1942, it consisted of mechanized, motorized, horse, and infantry units armed with British and German weapons. The supply of European weapons, however, ended in 1939 with the start of the war. Brazilian troop strength was 78,000 men with a reserve force of 200,000.

Determined to take an active part in the war, the Brazilian Army opened negotiations with the United States to upgrade troop armament and training for eventual commitment to battle. The United States was reluctant to create a modern army in Brazil, as they feared it would set off a new South American arms race. The United States finally agreed to equip, train, and transport one Brazilian infantry division to the Mediterranean theater.

On 9 August 1943, Brazil formed the 1st Expeditionary Infantry Division *(1a DIE)*. The new division consisted of the 1st, 6th, and 9th Infantry Regiments, three artillery regiments, and support troops. The commander was Major General João Baptista Mascarenhas de Morais (q.v.). The division table of organization and the equip-

ment was the same as a U.S. infantry division. The *1a DIE* sailed for Italy in a series of convoys between July and October 1944.

On arrival in Italy, the *1a DIE* was assigned to the U.S. Fifth Army's IV Corps. Elements of the *1a DIE* entered combat on 14 September 1944 along the Serchio River. That was the first occasion in which South American troops fought in Europe. As an entire unit, they entered combat in November 1944 in the Reno Valley. They were considered equal to a U.S. division in fighting ability. In the closing months of the war, the division advanced from Parma to Turin, during which the German 148th Division and other units were captured, totaling some 15,000 officers and men in all.

When the fighting ended on 2 May 1945, more than 25,000 Brazilians had served in Italy. The *1a DIE* suffered 11,617 wounded and 457 dead from a division strength of 15,000 during 239 days of combat. After a short period of occupation duty, the *1a DIE* returned to Brazil in the summer of 1945.

The *1a DIE* was supported in Italy by the 1st Brazilian Fighter Squadron flying P-47 Thunderbolt fighters. That unit saw action from October 1944 to May 1945 and lost nine pilots in combat.

Because of the refusal of the Allies to supply additional arms, the Brazilian Army was unable to expand to its planned strength of twenty divisions or to provide other troops to the Allies. Brazil did use some troops to guard Allied naval and air bases located on its territory, but Brazil's military manpower potential was never part of Allied plans.

Charles H. Bogart

Additional Reading
Fisher, Ernest F., *Cassino to the Alps* (1977).
Mascarenhas de Morais, João B., *The Brazilian Expeditionary Force* (1966).

Army, British
When World War I ended in 1918, the British Army was the largest it had ever been and one of the most efficient armies in the world. Old unit designations were all but lost in a bewildering array of battalions formed from still other cadres of battalions from various regiments. For example, the 14/2 Battalion, Middlesex Regiment, was the 14th Battalion formed from a cadre of the 2nd Battalion of the Middlesex Regiment; the 12/14 Battalion, Middlesex Regiment was the 12th Battalion formed from the 14th Battalion of the 2nd Battalion of the Middlesex Regiment. This phenomenon was characteristic of many regiments of

the British Army, with a wide variety of numerical designations, all associated with the enormous expansion of the army that took place throughout the war.

With the conclusion of the war, the huge British armies melted away with the general demobilization. Within a year, all that remained was a nominal regular army smaller than the prewar army. The organization of infantry regiments, though reduced to one or sometimes two battalions, remained the same, except for the addition of the Welsh Guards, raised in the second year of the war. In addition to its traditional role of policing the empire, the postwar British Army was involved with various international commitments. In the years immediately after 1918, the British Army (mainly its infantry units) was deployed in Russia, India, the Near and Far East, Ireland, and in the occupation of the Rhineland.

Allied victory in 1918 and the enormous price paid for it led to conflicting British military interpretations about the war. One school held that the war only could have been won using the methods actually employed; another believed it could have been won much more economically. Debate over tactical doctrine was a factor in the controversy. After the war, many still believed decisive victory was won by infantrymen with rifles and bayonets. Yet the machine gun and barbed wire had effectively stopped the foot soldier. Despite the introduction of many supporting arms that helped restore the infantryman's ability to advance, casualties remained high.

Two positions were advanced to overcome this problem. The first was to provide more support for the infantry in the form of artillery, aircraft, and tanks. The infantry then would move forward only when this support had neutralized enemy resistance. The other viewpoint was to increase the infantry's mobility and enhance it with a skillful combination of fire and maneuver. These two approaches, one emphasizing firepower, the other emphasizing maneuver, were the lines along which the debate raged between the wars.

The British Expeditionary Force (BEF) arrived in France in 1914 with just under 500 artillery pieces. By the end of the war, it had more than 6,000. As early as 1915, artillery had become vital to tactical success. In 1916, senior artillery officers at corps and army headquarters became more and more important in tactical planning, although many tradition-bound senior generals resisted this trend. By the battle of Cambrai in November 1917, techniques were adopted to enable artillery to fire effectively without disclosing their position in advance. After the war, artillerymen felt confident of their future role. In the postwar years, they concentrated on refining those aspects of their deployment that proved most effective during the war: centralized control, survey techniques, and counterbattery fire. They failed, however, to consider how to provide support in rapidly changing, fluid situations.

Machine guns and barbed wire stopped the mounted trooper even more effectively than they had the infantryman. The horse cavalry attempted to justify its continued existence by the few occasions it had performed useful functions on the western front and by its significant role in the Palestine campaign. As Archibald Wavell (q.v.) pointed out, mobility, not cavalry per se, was the key to the cavalry's successes. Motorized formations might have performed these tasks even more effectively. Resisting the argument that the horse was a relic on the battlefield, the British cavalry emphasized its traditional role rather than attempting to adapt to the needs of modern warfare.

The greatest controversy surrounded the past and future deployment of the tank. With the invention of tracked, gasoline-powered locomotion for farm vehicles, came the call for a motor-powered, tracked, armored vehicle able to advance under fire of machine guns and cross enemy earthworks. The resulting vehicle (called a "tank" for security reasons) was a concept pioneered by Lieutenant Colonel E.D. Swinton. Preliminary trials of the prototype tanks were held in Hatfield Park in January 1916. The trials were deemed a success but bureaucratic delays and skepticism prevented rapid development and deployment—foreshadowing an attitude that was to persist until 1940, when General Heinz Guderian (q.v.) demonstrated that the Germans had appreciated the ideas of British pioneers.

Disagreement over how tanks were to be employed resulted in further delays. In the event, General Sir Douglas Haig committed them prematurely and with only meager success on the Somme. By the end of the war, tanks were considered a significant element in British successes, and the newly formed Tank Corps had every reason to be enthusiastic about its potential. From a fragment of imagination, the tank grew to a force of twenty battalions and twelve armored car companies. Nevertheless, its future remained uncertain.

Few of the lessons of tank warfare were learned by the upper echelons of British military command. Proponents of the use of tanks in massed formations, J.F.C. Fuller, Percey Hobart, Basil Liddell Hart (qq.v.), among others, were not popular in upper military circles. A suggestion by Fuller that tanks might replace infantry and cavalry prompted the chief of the Imperial General Staff to withhold permission for him to publish his views in a book, because it might "disturb the minds of young officers." Interestingly, in 1920, a Royal Navy officer published an article about how the next war might be decided by a great tank raid on the enemy's communications. Fuller responded with a forecast of tank-carrying ships launching amphibious operations off the enemy's coast.

Lending to the uncertainty of the future of the tank in the British Army was the concept of "cooperation of all arms," which became a byword of postwar analyses. Haig felt that heavy artillery, machine guns, aircraft, tanks, and barbed wire played prominent parts in operations and, as a whole, had given a greater driving power to military operations. He did not, however, consider them able, in themselves, to obtain a decision. Their real function, Haig believed, was to assist the infantry to come to grips with the enemy. This sentiment was echoed by many high-ranking officers in the British Army, including Major General Hugh Elles, commander of the Tank Corps. The concept of cooperation of all arms, then, implied adjusting speed of supporting arms to the pace of the foot soldier, rather than accelerating the infantry rate of movement to that of the tank.

Debate in the interwar years was characterized on the one side by the traditional "how can we better fight the war next time?" approach, versus the proponents of reform who asked, "given developing technology, how can we fight future wars more rationally?" Reformers such as Fuller and Liddell Hart advanced sounder concepts of future warfare than the traditionalists, but there were flaws in the reformers' ideas. Fuller's main argument was that World War I showed separate corps of machine guns, tanks, and infantry did not tend toward efficient cooperation. Therefore, the army's main task was to reduce the various arms to that of the common denominator, the tank, which more than any other arm combined offensive and defensive power with mobility. The tank, he argued, was the best solution to the main problem of battle—how to "give blows without receiving them."

Fuller also believed that the primary land combat formations could ultimately be performed by three classes of mechanical vehicles: light, medium, and heavy tanks. Ultimately, they would replace the infantry and cavalry, and supplement the artillery, which would have to evolve into a type of tank anyway. Fuller's assumption was based partly on the analogy he made between sea and land warfare, in which the cross-country capacity of the tank liberated land combat from the constraints of fixed lines of communication. He felt that the tank introduced a means whereby naval conditions, which are mainly dynamic, could be superimposed on existing land conditions, which are more static, thereby evolving an entirely new theory of war on land. This analogy proved to be successful in circumstances characteristic of the World War II campaigns in the deserts of North Africa. As critics in the 1920s correctly pointed out, the analogy failed to account for mountains,

TABLE 1

British Army Divisional Strength

Division Type	No. of Troops	Automatic Weapons	Artillery (over 75mm)	AT Weapons	Motor Vehicles	Tracked Carriers	Tanks
Infantry c. 1939	13,860	700	72	75	1,710	140	28
Infantry c. 1942	18,000	867	72	48	2,158	256	223
Infantry c. 1944	18,350	1,352	54	492	2,142	595	0
Armored c. 1940	10,750	475	16	254	1,460	88	342
Armored c. 1942	15,000	872	48	220	1,468	361	290
Armored c. 1944	14,695	1,398	48	380	2,242	261	336
Airborne c. 1944	12,148	1,012	27	492	1,497	25	22

hills, ridges, woods, swamps, and other land features likely to be factors in future wars.

Liddell Hart supported Fuller's views to a great extent. He felt that the gasoline engine had revolutionized warfare, that the tank had to become the basic building block of the British Army, and that a new doctrine of swift penetration and envelopment had to replace the World War I doctrine of indecisive frontal attack. Liddell Hart proposed that success in future warfare would require the penetrating unit to move forward as long as it had a reserve behind it. Units that were held up would send their reserves to the flanks to widen the gaps. The main reserves would then pass through the gaps, and continue forward, thus widening the breach as the penetration deepened.

Essentially it was a simple concept, easy to grasp and apply, and it provided a rational basis for tactical instruction and practice. It did not incorporate the new mechanical technology, but a combination of Fuller's and Liddell Hart's ideas was feasible. Liddell Hart proposed a gradual transition into a "new model army" involving mechanization of divisional transport, battalion transport, artillery units, and infantry units.

There were key differences between Fuller's and Liddell Hart's mechanization plans. Liddell Hart described the progressive transition into the new army in greater detail than Fuller. He showed how each transport service could be mechanized, how much money would be required for each of the stages of the transition, and where he felt reductions could be made to obtain such funds. Another difference was his conception of the future of infantry in armored warfare.

Fuller advocated a division composed of twelve "infantry" battalions, each comprising two automatic rifle companies, one tank company, and one machine gun company. He recognized the need for infantry, but employed in a strictly auxiliary role. Liddell Hart advocated a division of three composite brigades, each with one battalion of heavy tanks, one battalion of medium tanks, one battalion of mechanized artillery, and three infantry battalions in armored carriers. The infantry would be used to clear land fortifications and hill defenses under cover of fire from the tanks. He did not consider a larger proportion of infantry necessary but, unlike Fuller, he envisaged tactical roles for it.

Both reformers saw the need for other changes in order to bring about the needed revolution the British Army's tactical doctrine. Both advocated reorganization of the War Office. Fuller wanted to abolish the Army Council and replace it with a commander in chief, assisted by a chief staff officer and a single staff of five departments, each consisting of a "think" section, a "liaison" section, and a "routine" section. Liddell Hart proposed the creation of a tactical research department, to help ensure tactics kept pace with technology. He also suggested amalgamation of the Royal Military Academy at Woolwich (which trained artillery and engineer officers) and the Royal Military College at Sandhurst (which trained infantry and cavalry officers) as a move to reduce the army's compartmentalization and to help prevent the loss of what he called "mental elasticity."

Strict economic constraints, the relaxation of European tensions, and accession of the Labour government in 1929 had a strong influence on British military planners. The year 1931 marked a significant turning point in the British Army between the wars. The army had not prospered between 1919 and 1931, but it had existed in a relatively stable environment. The War Office analyses of exercises held in 1929 reflected the opinion of the major commands. Debate about employment of the machine gun continued. Some proposed it be moved forward in close support of the rifle companies. Others that it be held back according to existing practice, but with units of armored carriers formed to move the machine guns ahead of an infantry assault.

Successes with tanks in the 1931 and 1932 maneuvers, and the extensive use of radios and signal flags led to the formation of a permanent tank brigade in 1934. In 1928, the first manual on mechanized warfare was published in Britain. The manual provided for vehicles to be divided into three classes: armored fighting vehicles (AFVs); armored carriers; and unarmored carriers, transport vehicles, and tractors. AFVs would enable an attacker to produce fire and movement, and at the same time, provide protection. Because emplaced artillery pieces would always be heavier and more accurate than those in movement, direct frontal assault on prepared positions would only be possible when supported by adequate covering artillery fire.

The years after 1931 were characterized by financial and political events in Britain and the world that caused major shifts. Military leaders were unsure how best to address difficulties of developing a new doctrine under circumstances marked by financial constraints, technological uncertainty, political unrest, and conflicting requirements of imperial defense and European commitment. Obligations levied on the army fol-

TABLE 2

British Army Order of Battle 1939–1945

	1939	1945
Divisions		
Infantry	21	18
Armored	1	7
Airborne	0	2
Totals	22	27
Brigades:		
Armored	3	10

lowing the war were primarily for infantry. Almost none of the prewar rank and file remained, very few of the experienced wartime troops had agreed to remain in service. British battalions, then, were composed largely of raw, untrained recruits. The remaining small cadre of officers and NCOs managed to train these young recruits to be soldiers, and they contributed greatly toward restoring the army's prewar standards of drill and discipline.

The peacetime establishment of the British Army, based on the 1920 plan, consisted of a Home Army of five divisions, mostly infantry, each of three brigades of four battalions, plus an artillery brigade, engineers, and transport units. There also were twelve cavalry regiments formed into two brigades. The five divisions of the Home Army accounted for a total of 141 infantry battalions.

Most of the line infantry battalions were organized on the establishment of 1920, which called for a battalion headquarters staff of nine officers and 129 soldiers and four rifle companies, each of six officers and 209 soldiers. Further breakdown remained essentially as it had before the war, but with the addition of two light machine gun sections to each platoon. Since the Machine Gun Corps was still in existence, the infantry battalion had no medium or heavy machine guns. In 1921, an additional headquarters "wing" was established to command and administer all the soldiers assigned to battalion headquarters—a move that replaced the old inefficient system of drawing men from the rifle companies to strengthen battalion command units.

The need for economy in the years following World War I prompted disbandment of the Machine Gun Corps. The infantry battalions thus were each allotted eight heavy machine guns, which became part of the headquarters wing. Some battalions also were equipped with mortar platoons for a brief period, but these were withdrawn soon after the addition of a close support regiment to the divisional artillery.

The British Army was further reduced in 1922 by the disbandment of five southern Irish regiments, brought about by the grant of Home Rule in Ireland. Net loss in personnel was mitigated somewhat by the decisions of many men to transfer to other regiments. The loss was further lightened by the decision to allow the Royal Inniskilling Fusiliers to give up its second battalion for disbandment in order to permit the Royal Irish Fusiliers (originally scheduled for disbandment) to remain in existence as a single battalion regiment.

In 1928, the battalion machine gun platoon was detached from the headquarters wing and became a company on its own. Its eight guns were increased to twelve, organized in three platoons of four, with provision for a fourth platoon on mobilization; but at the expense of one of the rifle companies. At the same time, the infantry battalions were given three Vickers-Carden-Lloyd carriers, small tracked vehicles armed with light machine guns and used mainly for reconnaissance.

In 1936, battalion support companies were strengthened by the addition of two 3-inch mortars per company. Some infantry battalions were earmarked for conversion to machine gun battalions to be used for divisional or corps troops, but this plan was not fully implemented until 1942. These battalions consisted of three machine gun companies, each of three platoons of four Vickers guns; and one antitank company of four platoons, each having four of the new 2-pounder antitank guns. By 1942, a company of 4.2-inch mortars, four platoons of four mortars each, was added. At that time the unit designation was changed from machine gun battalion to infantry support battalion. After 1945, these battalions reverted to normal infantry units.

The years immediately preceding World War II led to increases in infantry strength along with changes in battalion organizations. A number of the regiments had their second battalions restored. By 1939, a carrier platoon and a pioneer platoons were added to the infantry battalion. The fourth rifle company was restored, and each company retained its four platoons, but with the number of sections in each platoon reduced to three. Each section was equipped with Bren light machine guns, which greatly increased the company's firepower. Each infantry platoon also had a Boys antitank rifle and a light mortar. Thus, by the start of World War II, rifle company strength was almost the same as it had been in years past, but with greatly increased firepower.

While the new infantry training doctrine retained references to artillery barrages and the infantry–tank cooperation of World War I, new tactical concepts called for attacks to be made on wide fronts, with companies fighting their own way forward by fire and maneuver, making use of available supporting fires. Defense was to be established in depth, mindful of the need for concealment and mutual support, making maximum use of mortars, machine guns, and artillery for defensive fire.

The British Expeditionary Force (BEF) sent to France in September 1939 was ultimately built up to thirteen infantry divisions. In 1939, the British Army was the only completely motorized army in the world. Despite a doctrine based on high mobility, the *Wehrmacht* still continued to rely on the horse for 80 percent of its motive power. Nevertheless, the BEF was largely untrained and incompletely equipped. Initially Britain deployed more than 150,000 soldiers, 21,000 vehicles, and all the appropriate munitions to France. By April 1940, BEF strength stood at nearly 400,000, but this force was insufficient to stop the German *Blitzkrieg* when the "Phony War" (q.v.) turned into the "Hot War" in May 1940.

The BEF's only armored units, other than the divisional cavalry regiments, were two battalions of the Royal Tank Regiment assigned to the 1st Army Tank Brigade. The British 1st Armoured Division was still training at Salisbury Plain, and was not yet unprepared for combat. By 1945, the British had seven armored divisions deployed on various fronts.

From 1941 on, the British steadily built up their equipment, especially support weapons. In 1943, they added a support company to each battalion. The support company assumed many of the functions previously performed by the battalion's headquarters company. It consisted of a mortar platoon (increased to six mortars and transported in carriers), a carrier platoon (with an extra section of three carriers), and an antitank platoon with six 6-pounder guns (each towed by a carrier with an additional carrier for ammunition). In 1944, a section of Wasp flamethrowers mounted in carriers was added to the support company.

During the course of World War II, British rifle company armament was changed to replace the Boys antitank gun with the PIAT (Projector Infantry Antitank)—a difficult weapon to master, but much more efficient than its predecessor. A significant innovation in 1944 was the introduction of armored personnel carriers for infantry. The carriers were old Canadian Ram tanks with their turrets removed. Each could carry an infantry section, which added appreciably to the speed and flexibility of a combined armored/infantry attack. This was particularly useful in the latter, more fluid stages of the war in Europe.

During the war, the British Army, like its U.S. and Canadian counterparts, increased dramatically in size. In early 1939, the regular army had 227,000 troops, backed by 204,000 in the Territorial Army (reserve). By August 1939, the Territorial Army was expanded to 428,000. This force was organized into nine infantry divisions, one mobile division, and one cavalry brigade.

With the buildup, the British Territorial Army divided the United Kingdom into six geographical commands: Aldershot, Southern, Eastern, Northern, Western, and Scottish. The commands were divided into areas and zones, with troop strength dependent on the importance of the area. In addition to the commands, there were two districts: London and Northern Ireland. When hostilities began, the Territorial Army merged with the regular army, although throughout the war, conscripts enrolled in their respective territorial command or district.

During the war, peak strength of the British Army reached 2,920,000. Over the course of the war it committed seven armored, twenty-five infantry, and two airborne divisions to combat operations, plus sixteen armored brigades. (The separate armored brigades had the same tank strength as an armored division.) The vast majority of these units served in Europe, North Africa, and the Middle East.

The basic formation in 1944 was the infantry division. It was organized into into three infantry brigades of three battalions each, three field artillery regiments, and supporting units, for a total of 18,350 troops. The division was well equipped, particularly in artillery, with fifty-four 25-pounder gun/howitzers, and forty-eight 6- and 17-pounder antitank guns. The infantry battalion consisted of 821 officers and men, divided into four rifle companies. The battalion's headquarters company consisted of specialist platoons of signals, antiaircraft, mortars, carriers, pioneers, and administration.

In addition to the divisional field artillery regiments, the Royal Artillery also had medium and heavy artillery regiments. The medium artillery regiment consisted of 650 men, organized into two batteries, armed with either 6-inch howitzers or 60-pounder guns. The heavy artillery regiment consisted of 700 men, with one battery of 6-inch howitzers and three batteries of 8-inch or 9.2-inch howitzers.

The British armored division of 1944 had

14,695 troops. It consisted of an armored brigade, an infantry brigade, two field artillery regiments, and an antitank regiment. The armored brigade was organized into three armored regiments of 112 tanks each. The infantry brigade had three motorized infantry battalions.

All British airborne forces grew from the 1st Parachute Brigade, formed in September 1941. At the same time, the Glider Pilot Regiment, a part of the British Army Air Corps, also was organized. In December 1941, the glider pilots formed the core of the 1st Airlanding Brigade. Both brigades merged to form the 1st Airborne Division. The 4th Parachute Brigade was activated a year later to complete the division's structure. In May 1943, the British 6th Airborne Division was organized on a basis similar to the 1st Airborne Division—one airlanding and two parachute brigades. In late 1943, both divisions formed the 1st Airborne Corps under the command of Major General Frederick Browning (q.v.).

Wes Wilson
William H. Van Husen

Additional Reading
Bidwell, Shelford, and Dominick Graham, *Firepower: British Army Weapons and Theories of War 1904–1945* (1982).
Davis, Brian L., *British Army Uniforms & Insignia of World War II* (1983).
Gregory, Barry, *British Airborne Troops* (1974).
Howard, Michael (ed.), *The Theory and Practice of War* (1966).
Mollo, Andrew, *The Armed Forces of World War II* (1981).
Myatt, Frederick, *The British Infantry* (1983).
Reid, Brian Holden, *J.F.C. Fuller: Military Thinker* (1987).

Army, Bulgarian

Like the German Army, the Bulgarian Army was treaty-limited at the end of World War I. The Treaty of Neuilly restricted Bulgaria to an army of 1,000 officers and 19,000 troops, all of whom had to serve on twelve-year contracts. Although these provisions were intended to prevent Bulgaria from building up a large military reserve, they actually forced it to concentrate its limited defense funds on a small, highly trained, and reasonably well equipped professional force. This force was the most highly trained in the Balkans, and provided Bulgaria with the foundations for rapid expansion once the decision was made to abrogate the treaty in 1938. The nation's poor, primarily agrarian economy, however, limited the extent of the army's expansion.

Like Germany, Bulgaria circumvented the treaty's intent by a wide variety of ruses. It established a civilian labor corps that was military in organization and training but without weapons. The Bulgarian national police and frontier guards were also trained, equipped, and organized along military lines. Thus, Bulgaria's army was able to expand from eleven highly trained regiments to eleven fairly well trained but lightly equipped divisions in less than three years. Unfortunately, Bulgarian military equipment was of mixed origins (Czech, Italian, and German) and primarily obsolete. Little capital was available to buy first-rate weapons, especially antiaircraft guns and related fire control systems.

The Bulgarian Army structured itself along the German model. Each corps district was responsible for the recruitment, organization, training, and replacement of the units within its area, in much the same fashion as the German *Wehrkreis*. Bulgaria's General Staff, hidden before 1938, consisted of some seventy-nine officers who alternated between general staff and troop leadership assignments. Selection to the Bulgarian Military Academy (equivalent to U.S. Army Command and General Staff College) was on a competitive basis among officers in their fifth to seventh year of service. Technical and combat arms training was also provided to all officers prior to commissioning and at the mid-career point. Thus Bulgaria had a highly educated and trained officers corps.

The Bulgarian Army's expansion began in 1935 with the purchase of thirty-five Fait L.33 tankettes from Italy. The initial force increase was carried out in increments by expanding the army's infantry battalions into regiments and joining them with frontier guards battalions to form cadre training divisions. The expansion became more open with the abrogation of the Neuilly Treaty three years later, and voluntary recruitment was stepped up.

Universal conscription was enacted on 30 May 1940, requiring every physically able male under twenty to serve two years of military service. By the end of 1940, Bulgaria had thirteen infantry and two "rapid" divisions. The latter units were mixed cavalry and light mechanized units Bulgaria hoped would enable them to make the most of their limited motorized and mechanized equipment. It was an experiment they quickly abandoned.

The army grew again in 1941 as Bulgaria moved in behind the German advance to occupy what it saw as its national territories of Yugoslavian

"Macedonia" and Grecian Thrace. Germany facilitated this buildup by providing French tanks, trucks, and artillery captured in 1940. Several reserve divisions were later raised to garrison these territories. They were formed around one regular army regiment and carried a numerical designation of 10 plus the number of the regular division that provided the core regiment. These reserve divisions were generally poorly equipped and were formed for specific short-term operations. They were then dissolved and the core regiment returned to its parent division. Otherwise, the Bulgarian Army saw little combat until Bulgaria joined the Soviet Union (as Soviet troops approached Bulgaria's northern frontier) in driving German forces out of the Balkans after September 1944.

Bulgaria's officers and NCOs were well educated and well trained. Nonetheless, its limited economic base precluded it from building the modern mechanized army needed to survive in World War II's emerging multidimensional battlefield. It was an army short on mobility, antiaircraft armament, and long-range artillery. Although Germany mistook Bulgaria's tactical proficiency for political reliability and provided some modern weapons (including eighty-eight PzKpfw-IVh tanks) in 1943 and 1944, it was not enough to equip the entire army. Fortunately, Bulgaria's political leadership recognized the military's limitations and avoided actively committing it to the war.

Carl O. Schuster

Additional Reading

Madej, Victor, *Southeastern Europe Axis Armies Handbook* (1982).
Miller, Marshall L., *Bulgaria During the Second World War* (1975).

Army, Canadian

The wartime expansion and growth of the Canadian Army was a remarkable feat by any measure. The Permanent Active Militia, the unwieldy title given to Canada's professional full-time soldiers, had a strength of 4,261 all ranks in July 1939. The Non-permanent Active Militia, Canada's part-time soldiers, had a paper strength of 51,418 all ranks, the majority untrained. At its peak in June 1944, the renamed Canadian Army had a total strength of 495,073 all ranks. A training organization that could barely accommodate 30,000 troops for two weeks in 1938 churned out well over 730,000 men and women in uniform by 1945.

These men and women were organized into the Canadian First Army (an accurate historical as well as numerical title) and two corps consisting of three infantry divisions, two armored divisions, two armored brigades, two army artillery groups, plus ancillary headquarters troops, and the Canadian Women's Army Corps. In Canada, there were an additional three infantry divisions designated for home defense. The Canadian Army also was able to "loan" 673 officers to the manpower-starved British Army. In contrast to World War I, these Canadian formations were led and staffed almost exclusively by Canadians. An immense contribution from a nation of 11.5 million people, it was not achieved without cost.

Canada's initial mobilization plans for its ground forces were constrained by Prime Minister Mackenzie King's (q.v.) Liberal government desire to limit Canada's war effort to an industrial and agricultural contribution, to which, if events necessitated, might be added an air and naval component. The specter of the casualty lists of the army in World War I, and the politically divisive issue of conscription, loomed large in the minds of the government leaders. Strengthened by the government's fiscal conservatism, the constraints on the permanent militia's initial attempts at expansion were considerable. In contrast, the permanent force's mobilization plans for an overseas expeditionary force, Defence Scheme 3, envisioned an initial effort of a corps headquarters, two divisions and ancillary troops (to be expanded by four divisions if necessary), all of which would be volunteers. Designated "the Mobile Force," a sop to political concerns over the divisiveness of an expeditionary force, the overseas ground forces were to be organized, staffed, and concentrated under the auspices of this scheme.

On 1 September 1939, nine days before the formal Canadian declaration of war, the Canadian Active Service Force was authorized and the orders for mobilization sent across the country. Volunteer enlistments were brisk, if not spectacular, reflecting the mood of the country. By the end of September approximately 62,000 volunteers had come forward. Shortages of equipment and arms as well as fiscal restraints, however, prompted a suspension of recruiting by the end of the month. The government subsequently announced on 19 September that two divisions would be mobilized, one of which was available for overseas service.

The first Canadian Army troops arrived in Britain in October to establish an administrative link with National Defence Headquarters in Ottawa which became known as Canadian Military Headquarters (CMHQ). The first "flights" of the

Canadian 1st Division, commanded by Major General A.G.L. McNaughton (q.v.), sailed from Halifax in December.

By February 1940, there were approximately 23,000 half-trained and ill-equipped Canadian soldiers concentrated in Britain. Simultaneously, the senior officer at CMHQ, Brigadier H.D.G. Crerar (q.v.), anticipating a much larger army effort, created the administrative framework for a defense headquarters. Prompted by a government announcement in January that the Canadian 2nd Division would be sent overseas in the future, he also pressed for the early establishment of a Canadian corps. The fact, however, that the greatest policy dilemma in the fall and winter of 1939–1940 arose over whether the Canadian or British government should pay for the costs of Canadian ancillary troops illustrated the importance of fiscal constraints during the "Phony War" (q.v.).

The German invasion of Norway (q.v.) provided the first alterations to Canada's "limited liability" war policy; the fall of France destroyed it completely. On 17 May, the government decided to form a Canadian corps and mobilize a third infantry division for overseas service. At the end of May, a fourth division and a Veterans Home Guard were authorized. On 17 June, the National Resources Mobilization Act (NRMA) was drafted to register and mobilize all of Canada's human and material resources for home defense. An important provision of the act limited compulsory military service to service on Canadian soil and retained the voluntary nature of the overseas army.

Despite several alarms, and a brief excursion to southern France by units of the Canadian 1st Division, the Canadian Army saw no action during the battles of the spring and summer of 1940. Its main battles were fought in Ottawa, as Major General Crerar returned to Canada as chief of the general staff in July 1940 to bring a semblance of organization to the energetic but misdirected Canadian war effort. His 1941 and 1942 army programs secured government approval, after intense political maneuvering, for the Canadian 5th Armoured Division, an armored brigade, as well as the Canadian 6th Division for home defense. First Canadian Army Headquarters (FCA HQ) and Canadian II Corps headquarters were also established by these programs. By the end of 1940, the authorized strength of the army was approximately 178,000. By the end of 1942 the "ceiling" was 226,000 men and women. He also obtained government approval to change the title of the Permanent Active Militia to the Canadian Army.

In the summer of 1940, Canadian Army units were sent overseas only as they were equipped, a tortuously slow process as the Canadian industrial infrastructure also was being created from scratch. Training policy was standardized for both home defense army conscripts (NRMA men) and overseas "General Service" volunteers. Training was divided into basic and advanced categories. There were separate camps for each, as well as specialized training centers for the various arms and corps. Officer training was centered mainly at the Royal Military College of Canada.

Until 1943, a recruit could expect approximately eight weeks of basic training at one of forty basic training centers scattered across the country, and up to nine weeks at one of thirty-two advanced training centers. A volunteer recruit who showed a special aptitude would be sent to one of the specialized advanced training centers such as the Small Arms Training Center or the Canadian Signal Training Center. After mid-1943, he would join the reinforcement pool for the corps he was recruited into, such as the infantry or armored corps, and be sent into action as a replacement. At peak capacity in May 1943, 78,000 troops could be trained at any one time.

Formation and unit training in the Canadian Army followed the British model, as it did with operational doctrine, equipment, and organization. No formal training doctrine was established until 1942–1943 with the advent of battle drill schools, a regimental initiative rather than one from the top. This typified the fundamental problem of unit-level training in the Canadian Army—it was the purview of the commanding officer and depended almost entirely on the aptitude and experience of the unit's officers. This proved a serious problem, because the Canadian Army did not see any large-scale action until the Canadian 1st Division was employed in the invasion of Sicily (q.v.) in May 1943. Hong Kong and Dieppe (q.v.) were the only two actions before 1943 and both were disastrous, despite courageous showings by the Canadian troops. The lack of experience among the senior command was thus felt throughout the whole army.

The problems became apparent through the numerous exercises that dominated the Canadian Army's time in Britain. The army was slowly built up as divisions were sent overseas and entered the order of battle. Canadian I Corps was established in the fall of 1940; two more divisions joined the corps in 1941; by April 1942, FCA HQ was established. By mid-1943, the Canadian Active Service Force was complete with the addition of the Canadian 4th Armoured Division, 2nd Armoured Brigade, and formation of Headquarters, Canadian II Corps. The manpower ceiling for the army was approved at 232,100, a number later revised to 234,500. Manpower shortages, particularly of trained staff officers, and equipment shortages defined the pace of army expansion.

Equipment, whether built in Canada or Britain, differed little from that of the British Army. The main infantry weapon was the Lee-Enfield No. 4 and the Canadian-made 9mm Sten submachine gun. The 25-pounder formed the backbone of the artillery and the 6- and 17-pounders were the standard antitank guns. Until 1942, the Churchill and the Ram (the only Canadian developed tank of the war) stocked the armored regiments. From 1943, the Sherman, and variations thereof, was standard issue. The Canadian Army was the first to develop and use armored personnel carriers, called "Kangaroos," which were initially modified tanks or self-propelled guns. Most units did not receive their equipment until they arrived in Britain, further hampering training in Canada. The Canadian 4th Armoured Division, which was converted from an infantry division, was a notable exception.

From the fall of Dunkirk (q.v.) on, the Canadian Army formed one of the most coherent and well-equipped forces in Britain. The defense of Britain was its central role until early 1942, when it began training for its promised part in the return to the continent. Characterized as a "dagger pointed at the heart of Berlin," the Canadian Army nevertheless became increasingly marginal as the cross-channel invasion was postponed and the operational focus shifted to the Mediterranean.

The desire and necessity of obtaining combat experience for Canadian troops and officers became a divisive subject of debate among the senior army command, mainly because it undermined the hard-won World War I principle of maintaining the Canadian Army as a composite force in the face of British efforts to treat Canadian units as they would a British formation. Nevertheless, Crerar, the senior corps commander of Canadian I Corps, became an ardent advocate of sending a Canadian division or corps to the Mediterranean. This sentiment was shared by the Liberal government and the Canadian public. Canadian First Army commander Lieutenant General A.G.L. McNaughton fought a rear-guard action against breaking up the army. He was forced to concede the issue in April 1943 when the Canadian 1st Infantry Division, commanded by Major General Guy Simonds (q.v.), replaced a British division in the Sicily invasion force.

The years 1942 and 1943 proved difficult for the Canadian Army. Exercises in 1942 culled out the oldest and weakest of the senior divisional and unit commanders. The catastrophe at Dieppe (q.v.) prompted a renewed vigor in training and discipline, but by 1943, the senior command was concerned for morale and fearful lest the war end before the Canadians saw action. Sending Canadian troops to Italy also proved to be the first in a series of blows that toppled McNaughton from army command. A disastrous performance in Exercise SPARTAN in May 1943 provoked General Alan Brooke (q.v.), British chief of the Imperial General Staff, to approach the Canadian government regarding British concerns about McNaughton's suitability to command the Canadian First Army in operations. The dispatch of Canadian I Corps HQ and the 5th Armoured Division to Italy against McNaughton's express wishes sealed his fate. After several unpleasant confrontations with the British and the Canadian minister of national defense, McNaughton retired in December 1943 and was replaced by Crerar.

The inexperienced Crerar had not commanded Canadian I Corps in operations before he returned to Britain in March 1944 to take command of Canadian First Army. Canadian I Corps, was led by Lieutenant General E.L.M. Burns (q.v.) until October 1944, when personality conflicts with his British superiors prompted his removal. I Corps, however, fought with distinction in the Italian theater throughout 1944 and 1945. Dubbing themselves the "D-Day Dodgers," Canadian units in the Mediterranean were part of the British Eighth Army until they were reunited with the rest of the Canadian Army in April 1945.

Crerar's return to Britain marked the start of full Canadian involvement in operational planning for the D-Day invasion. The Canadian 3rd Infantry Division and 2nd Armoured Brigade were slated to land on JUNO Beach as part of the British Second Army. Canadian First Army would be activated under control of Field Marshal Bernard L. Montgomery's (q.v.) 21st Army Group when the Allies secured the necessary bridgehead. The Canadian 3rd Division landed in France on 6 June, pushing farther inland than any Allied unit, despite some control difficulties on the beaches. Despite the initial success, over the next three months the Canadian 2nd and 3rd Divisions had the highest casualty rates in the Anglo-American armies in the Normandy campaign (q.v.). This resulted from the combined effects of senior command difficulties, the Canadians' inexperience, and the strength of the German defenses they faced.

On 11 July, the Canadian II Corps became operational with Lieutenant General Simonds in command. Two weeks later, the Canadian First Army entered the theater under General Crerar and took operational control of Canadian II Corps and British I Corps. The Canadian Army played a predominant part in the battles that ended the fighting in Normandy and drove the Germans back up the coasts of Belgium and Holland. After fierce struggles to close the Falaise gap, the Canadian Army crossed the Seine, winding its way up the "long left flank" of the Allied armies.

Canada's "Cinderella" army, starved of supplies by Montgomery's ambitious drive to the Rhine, took the French and Belgium coastal ports in turn before slowing in the face of the German Army's determined defense of the Scheldt (q.v.) estuary, the key to the invaluable port of Antwerp. The Canadians' operations were characterized by methodical assaults supported by artillery and airpower. They took full advantage of the Allies' quantitative superiority to trade shells for lives.

The intensity of the Normandy and Scheldt battles resulted in a drastic shortage of trained infantry recruits for the Canadian Army—already stretched by its operations in two theaters. After a minor political crisis in Canada, a limited conscription was introduced in November 1944 to send NRMA personnel overseas. In total, only 16,000 conscripted "zombies," as they were termed, served in the Canadian Army. The reinforcement problem was resolved by the two-month quiet period following the Scheldt battles that allowed the Canadians to absorb new infantry recruits.

Canadian First Army's biggest tests were Operations VERITABLE and BLOCKBUSTER in February–March 1945. Both operations were designed to bring the 21st Army Group to the Rhine River. Nine British divisions came under Canadian command, as well as the Polish Division and Canadian II Corps. After several weeks of logistical miracles and bloody fighting in some of the worst conditions in the northwest European campaign, the Canadians cleared the region between the Maas and the Rhine Rivers of German troops. Reunited with Canadian I Corps in April, the Canadian Army was responsible for the relief of the starving Dutch population and the northern German ports. Lieutenant General Charles Foulkes (q.v.) commander of Canadian I Corps, accepted the local German surrender in May.

The Canadian Army now prepared to send a division of volunteers to the Pacific theater. Canadian Army involvement in the Pacific was limited to the brigade sent to Hong Kong in the fall of 1941 and an infantry brigade group deployed with the U.S. Army in the 1943 invasion of Kiska Island in the Aleutians. Several hundred officers and men also served as technical advisors to the Australian Army. The Canadian Army Pacific Force (CAPF), composed of approximately 17,800 officers and other ranks, all volunteers, began retraining in August 1945 to gain familiarity with U.S. Army organization and equipment. The Japanese surrendered before the CAPF was committed to combat operations.

The Canadian Army demobilized over the course of the next year. More than 730,000 men and women had enlisted; 24,000 were killed, and another 52,600 wounded. Many paid the price for trying to create an army from scratch. Inexperienced officers and men, a reliance on the British for operational doctrine and equipment, and equipment shortages all plagued the Canadian Army well into 1943. The strengths and weaknesses of the British Army were also those of the Canadian Army. Nevertheless, it was almost an entirely volunteer force, it fought with distinction in some of the toughest battles of the war, and its existence after twenty years of neglect was nothing short of miraculous.

Paul Dickson

Additional Reading
Copp, Terry, and Robert Vogel, *Maple Leaf Route*, 5 vols. (1983–86).
English, John A., *The Canadian Army and the Normandy Campaign: A Study of Failure in High Command* (1991).
Granatstein, J.L., *The Generals: The Canadian Army's Senior Commanders in the Second World War* (1993).
Stacey, C.P., *Arms, Men, and Governments: The War Policies of Canada, 1939–1945* (1970).

Army, Dutch

Holland had preserved its neutrality during World War I. Thus in the interwar period, the Dutch Army was starved of funds and largely neglected. The army was reduced to an 8,000-strong professional cadre, who trained the 60,000 conscripts between the ages of twenty and forty inducted annually. It was only in April 1940, in the face of mounting evidence of planned German aggression, that the Dutch Army mobilized.

On mobilization, the Dutch Army consisted of four corps, headquartered at Amsterdam, Arnhem, Breda, and Amersfoort. The army fielded a total of eight infantry divisions: a composite light brigade of cavalry, cyclists, armored cars, and horse-drawn artillery, and an antiaircraft brigade consisting of two regiments. They also had several independent heavy artillery regiments and reconnaissance battalions. The mobilized force totaled 114,000 troops and swelled to 270,000 with the call-up of reservists.

Forewarned by German officers who opposed invading a neutral country, the Dutch Army was on full alert on 10 May when the Germans struck. Overwhelmingly outnumbered, the Dutch were quickly overrun, formally capitulating four days later on 14 May 1940. Given that it was forewarned, the Dutch high command came under criticism after the war for failing to avert disaster. Despite offering stiff resistance, however, the Dutch Army simply lacked the establishment, equipment, training, and expertise necessary to stave off the German onslaught. Most significantly, the Dutch Army lacked the mechanized reserves, effective tactical airpower, and antitank weaponry necessary to stop German armor. Nonetheless, the German high command was impressed at the tenacity of the Dutch resistance.

After the capitulation, many Dutch troops eventually found their way to Britain where they were consolidated into Princess Irene's Motorized Brigade Group. Equipped and trained by the British, this Dutch brigade was assigned in 1944 to General Bernard L. Montgomery's (q.v.) 21st Army Group for Operation OVERLORD, the invasion of France. Landing in the latter stages of the campaign, after the initial bridgehead was established, the Dutch brigade fought in the Orne bridgehead on the extreme left flank of the Allied lodgment alongside the British 6th Airborne Division.

The brigade subsequently participated in the headlong advance across France and Belgium. After the abortive Allied airborne drop on Arnhem (q.v.), Princess Irene's Brigade crossed the Belgian-Dutch border on 30 September 1944 and took up watch at the important river crossing at Grave. On 25 April 1945, in the final days of the war, the brigade launched an attack across the Maas near Hedel in an abortive attempt to precipitate the capitulation of the German garrison cut off in northern Holland. After the final German surrender, the Princess Irene Brigade marched triumphantly into The Hague.

Russell Hart

Additional Reading
Maass, Walter B., *The Netherlands at War: 1940–1945* (1970).

Mollo, Andrew, *The Armed Forces of World War II* (1981).
Toland, John, *The Last 100 Days* (1956).

Army, Egyptian

Torn between a desire to stay clear of European squabbles and the hopes for complete independence from Great Britain, Egypt was the scene of considerable intrigue during the period 1939 to 1943. At the forefront of these efforts were influential members of the armed forces. Many resented the renewed British occupation, which, although legal by the 1936 Anglo-Egyptian Treaty, still rankled nationalists.

Egypt's military was fairly weak, consisting mainly of infantry battalions, light artillery, and a few antiaircraft units. The army was complemented by a minuscule air force and navy. A territorial militia was supposed to supplement these troops, but as Egyptian generals once told their sovereign, King Farūq (q.v.), the army could hold Cairo against the British for two hours, at best. Nonetheless, in the North African theater of 1940 to 1942, this tiny force could tip the scales. When Commonwealth forces were hard pressed by Italian or German troops, Egypt's forces might be able to strike from behind and cause irreparable harm.

From Britain's viewpoint, the most dangerous Egyptian military official was the commander in chief, General 'Aziz al-Masri. Having served with the Ottoman forces during World War I and being a staunch nationalist, he was suspect from the start. Unknown at the time, he was also an important member of the secret "Ring of Iron." This cabal, whose members included Gamal Abdul Nasser and Anwar al-Sadat, was willing to support Axis efforts against Great Britain.

In early 1941, al-Masri was forced to step down from his role as commander in chief, and Egyptian forces were ordered back from the Libyan frontier. That May, he was arrested while trying to fly to Iraq. He was released after announcing that he was working for British intelligence. In reality, he was a double agent, providing valuable information to Germany via radio. This, however, was not uncovered until August 1942, when he and Sadat were arrested for a second time. These arrests, combined with Britain's successful palace coup against King Farūq the previous February, and the disbanding of Egypt's royalist militia, brought an end to any chance of an armed revolt.

John Dunn

Additional Reading

Neguib, Mohammed, *Egypt's Destiny* (1955).

Sadat, Anwar, *In Search of Identity* (1978).

United States Egyptian Legation, *Egypt: Her Contribution to the War Effort* (1945).

Vatikiotis, P.J., *The Egyptian Army in Politics* (1961).

Army, Ethiopian

At the time of the Italian invasion in 1935, Ethiopia was virtually an unarmed country. The Ethiopian Army had 100,000 men, no tanks, no artillery, no combat airplanes, 125 machine guns, and 90 percent of the soldiers' weapons were remnants from the Boer War era. As a result, the Ethiopians conducted a guerrilla war, with limited success, compounded by a total lack of support from its allies. The French gave implicit approval to the Italians and the British and the Americans suspended arms shipments to the beleaguered country. The League of Nations (q.v.) dawdled and delayed in making any decisions until the issue was moot.

On 10 June 1940, Italy declared war on Britain and France. Two weeks later, Britain withdrew its recognition of the Italian conquest of Ethiopia and set about assisting its government-in-exile to return. General Archibald Wavell appointed British Colonel Orde Wingate (qq.v.) to serve on the Ethiopian emperor's staff and lead the combined Ethiopian-British-Sudanese forces in military operations against the Italians. Gideon Force, as it became known, consisted of fifty British officers, twenty British NCOs, 800 Ethiopian, and 800 Sudanese soldiers.

The force, put together in the Sudan, crossed over into Ethiopia in January 1941, its equipment and personnel carried not in modern vehicles of war, but on the backs of 25,000 camels. Simultaneous with Gideon Force entering Ethiopia, the British launched two attacks into the country. General Alan Cunningham (q.v.) set off for Addis Ababa from Kenya, and General William Platt headed for Kassala. General Cunningham was the first to reach Addis Ababa, and on 5 May 1941, the capital returned to Ethiopian control.

Thomas R. Cagley

Additional Reading

Spencer, John H., *Ethiopia at Bay: A Personal Account of the Haile Selassie Years* (1984).

Army, Finnish

With a population of less than four million, Finland had one of the smallest armies in Europe prior to World War II. It never exceeded 200,000 men in uniform, and was made up almost entirely of conscripts, who served for one or one-and-a-half years before passing into the reserves. They remained in the reserves until age sixty, and thereafter were required to serve in the militia.

Although there was enough manpower available for twelve infantry divisions, only nine divisions were operational, one from each of the country's nine military districts. Each military district was responsible for maintaining the supply depots and communication facilities required for mobilization in times of emergency. The Finnish Army, for the most part, lacked modern or sophisticated weapons, including tanks and heavy artillery, transports, and up-to-date communications facilities; most weapons were supplied by Britain and Sweden and were of World War I vintage. There was also very little standardization of weapon systems. Finland did not have an independent air force. The army maintained approximately 200 combat aircraft, only half of which were operational at the beginning of the war.

What the Finnish Army lacked in manpower and sophisticated weaponry it more than made up for in reconnaissance and knowledge of the country's sparsely populated forest and lake-covered topography. Well-equipped with skis and warm clothing, Finnish troops used the harsh northern climate to their advantage through the development of sophisticated winter warfare tactics. The individual soldier was determined to resist foreign aggression, and this was important because of the lengthy border with the Soviet Union.

Following the Russo-German conquest and partition of Poland in the autumn of 1939, Josef Stalin (q.v.) used his nonaggression treaty with Adolf Hitler (q.v.) to make territorial demands on Finland without fear of German intervention. The French and the British forces were not in a position to come to Finland's defense. The Finnish government refused to submit to Soviet demands to cede islands in the Gulf of Finland and territory on the Karelian isthmus, which the Soviets believed necessary for the proper defense of Leningrad, or to sell or lease land at Hango for a Soviet naval and air base. The government also mobilized the army.

The Soviet Union scrapped its nonaggression treaty with Finland, and the Red Army crossed the border on 30 November 1939, in an eight-prong attack stretching from the Karelian isthmus, between the Gulf of Finland and Lake Ladoga, all the way to the Arctic Ocean, where the Soviets also laid claim to Petsamo, Finland's only ice-free port in the north. The Soviet Air Force bombed Helsinki, as twelve Soviet divisions attempted to breach the heavily defended Mannerheim Line (q.v.), a series of defensive fortifications that extended across the Karelian isthmus. The determined Finnish defenders halted the Soviet advance.

Outnumbered almost four to one, and with only limited war materiel, the Finnish Army fought valiantly throughout December 1939 against a larger yet relatively ill-equipped and poorly trained Red Army, and it imposed heavy losses on the invaders. Staging a strategic thirty-mile retreat, the Finns lured the Soviet columns deep into the forests, where they often became stranded in deep snow. Camouflaged Finnish ski patrols, known among the Red Army ranks as "White Death," ambushed the Soviet units individually and annihilated them. The ski patrols also moved around the Soviet flanks and deep into the rear areas to sever vital supply lines.

By January 1940, Moscow realized it must alter its strategy—the Finnish Army had proven stronger than anticipated. The Finns knew they could not hold out against the numerically superior Soviet force, and that in the spring they would lose their strategic and tactical ability to pin down the Red Army. Stalin consolidated his forces along the Mannerheim Line in the south, and on 1 February 1940, the Soviet Air Force began a blanket bombing assault on the Finnish defensive positions along the Mannerheim Line as well as on the Finnish supply depots and railroad junctions located behind it. Heavy artillery pounded the Finnish fortifications day and night.

Both France and Great Britain desired to come to Finland's aid, but there was no way for an Allied expeditionary force to reach the besieged country through neutral Norway and Sweden. Volunteers from several countries, including Sweden, Norway, and other European countries, formed a battalion, but it never saw combat. After two weeks of intense fighting, the Red Army breached the Mannerheim Line. With more than one-third of its army killed or wounded during almost three months of bitter combat, and with supplies and ammunition virtually depleted, Finland sued for peace in March 1940. The Treaty of Moscow gave to the Soviet Union even larger territorial concessions than it had demanded prior to hostilities, including the entire Karelian isthmus and Petsamo.

Despite this treaty, threats of future Soviet aggression forced the Finns to seek foreign protection. The 1939–1940 Winter War (q.v.) proved that neither Britain nor France was in a position to come to Finland's assistance. It finally turned to Germany, which provided modern weaponry for a greatly expanded Finnish Army of nearly 500,000 mobilized troops (sixteen divisions and three independent brigades).

When the Germans invaded the Soviet Union in June 1941, Finland saw an opportunity to regain the territory it ceded to the Soviets, and to seize additional territory in the vicinity of the Soviet port at Murmansk. Finland declared war on the Soviet Union on 26 June 1941, and its army launched a major offensive against the Red Army east of Lake Ladoga in early July. By September, it had cut the supply lines to the northern sector of the front and had recaptured all Finnish territory within the pre-1940 boundaries.

When the German offensive stalled at the gates of Leningrad (q.v.) in January 1942, the Finnish Army, which had suffered an additional 75,000 casualties, consolidated its defensive positions on the Karelian isthmus and furloughed almost 100,000 troops. Honoring its 1918 treaty with the Soviet Union, Finland refused to use the Karelian isthmus to launch an attack against Leningrad. Should the Germans capture the city and continue to advance east of Lake Ladoga, the Finnish Army would once again take up arms against the Red Army. In the meantime, however, units of the Finnish Army, along with Estonian auxiliary units serving with the German Eighteenth Army, captured the Estonian islands of Suursaari, Lavansaari, and Tytärsaari in the Baltic Sea in March 1942.

Following the German surrender at Stalingrad (q.v.) in February 1943, Field Marshal Carl Mannerheim (q.v.) realized that Germany could no longer win the war and he demanded that all Finnish troops deployed with German units be returned to his command. Finland had achieved its wartime goals and wanted to cease hostilities against the Soviet Union as soon as possible. Germany, with the tide of the war turning against it, and with the Finnish Army pinning down more than 180,000 Red Army troops on the Karelian isthmus, could not afford for Finland to sue for a separate peace. Germany continued to maintain troops in the country, and it placed an embargo on military supplies to the Finnish Army to prevent them from falling into Soviet hands should Finland sign an armistice with the Soviet Union.

The Soviet Union called for territorial concessions similar to those of the 1940 Treaty of Moscow, and demanded heavy war reparations, the return of all Soviet prisoners of war, and at the very least a partial demobilization of the Finnish Army. Even while negotiations were conducted in Stockholm, the Soviets continued their bombardment of Finnish cities. The Finnish Army still controlled large tracts of Soviet territory, and it maintained its defensive positions, expecting that the Red Army might launch an offensive should Finland reject the Soviet terms for peace. Mannerheim also ordered the establishment of a defensive line behind the German units in the country, fearing they would withdraw.

The Stockholm negotiations reached an impasse in April 1944 and the Red Army launched a major offensive across the Karelian isthmus on 10 June 1944. The Finnish Army, numbering almost 270,00 men, equipped with 2,000 artillery pieces, 110 tanks, and 248 combat aircraft, was surprised by the scale of the attack and the size of the invading Soviet force. Once it regained territory lost in the Winter War, the Finnish Army had, for the most part, assumed a defensive posture, and it had been involved in almost no combat for more than four years. Now, nearly a half-million Soviet troops, supported by 10,000 artillery pieces, 800 tanks, and almost 1,600 combat aircraft overwhelmed the defenders.

By 15 June, the Red Army had breached the Mannerheim Line and reopened the vital rail link between Leningrad and Murmansk. The Finnish Army suffered 18,000 casualties in June 1944, a figure that rose to 32,000 by the middle of July. The Finnish Army offered to surrender unconditionally. The Soviet Union refused, believing it could finally win the war in the north and thereby free up troops needed on the central and southern sectors of the eastern front.

The Soviet offensive was able to accomplish what the Stockholm negotiations had failed to do. The Finnish Army was forced to abandon its territorial gains in the north in order to redeploy troops further to the south, near Lake Ladoga. Germany agreed to lift its embargo of military supplies, if the Finns agreed to stay in the war and demonstrate their willingness to support the German war effort. Finland agreed and soon German Army and *Luftwaffe* units were deployed along the eastern border, thereby permitting additional Finnish troops to move south to the Karelian isthmus.

Although the numerically superior Red Army had established an important bridgehead over the Vuoksi River, they soon realized that a final victory over Finland would require more troops and supplies than it was able to expend. The Karelian front on both sides of Lake Ladoga stabilized and, instead of penetrating further into the Finnish heartland, the Red Army began to garrison troops along the front. Other units were moved south and deployed against German Army Group North in the Baltic states.

Finland's war against the Soviet Union depended on the success or failure of Army Group North. When the tide turned against Germany in late July 1944, it began to withdraw its troops from Finland and vital supply routes across the Baltic Sea were severed. Facing insurmountable odds, and with casualties now numbering more than 60,000, the Finns knew they had to sue for peace. In early August 1944, Mannerheim was elevated to the presidency without a formality of an election or parliamentary approval.

Without official ties to the formal Finnish government, Mannerheim was not bound by any agreements with Germany. He also was free to negotiate with the Soviet Union, which indicated that it would agree to an armistice, if Finland severed diplomatic relations with Germany and ordered all German troops to leave the country by the middle of September 1944. The Finnish-Soviet armistice was signed on 19 September 1944. In late September and early October, the Finnish Army turned against those German units still in the country and eventually forced them to leave the country.

Steven B. Rogers

Additional Reading
Tanner, Väinö, *The Winter War; Finland Against Russia. 1939–1940* (1957).
Upton, Anthony F., *Finland, 1939–1940* (1979).
Ziemke, Earl F. and Magna E. Bauer, *Moscow to Stalingrad: Decision in the East* (1988).
———, *Stalingrad to Berlin: The German Defeat in the East* (1968).

Army, French
When war broke out, France was able to field an army of nearly five million soldiers throughout its empire. These were led by 37,000 career officers and 90,000 officers of the reserve. During the period of the *drôle de guerre* (Phony War, q.v.) the French Army was deployed in strength along the Maginot Line (q.v.) and along France's left flank facing northern Belgium. But for nearly 100 miles along the central Ardennes front there were only four light cavalry divisions, of mixed horse and tank units; supported by ten mediocre infantry divisions, and no reserves. When the Germans

launched their onslaught on Belgium, Luxembourg, and the Netherlands on 11 May 1940, the French Army retreated and eventually collapsed. The fall of France was due more to poor tactics, organization, and leadership, than to inadequate equipment or a shortage of tanks and aircraft, as had been claimed originally in the aftermath of the defeat.

To fully appreciate the state of the French Army in 1940 one has to take into account the effects of World War I on both French political life and public opinion—especially since the origins of the collapse of the French Army in the summer of 1940 can be traced back to the organizational policies that developed during the 1920s and 1930s. In 1940 the French Army was still employing the techniques of 1918, relying upon railways and horses, disregarding airpower, and resorting to communications by telephone, pigeon, and dispatch rider. Furthermore, since France had borne so much of the static fighting on the western front during World War I, and had suffered the highest mortality rate of all the combatant nations, a feeling pervaded France that Frenchmen would never again be able to fight in such slaughterhouses as the Marne or Verdun, where, respectively, 100,000 and 162,000 Frenchmen had been killed. Thus in complete contrast to the 1914 military doctrine of *attaque à l'outrance* (attack to the extreme), in which French soldiers were ordered continually to charge with élan against the enemy, French military doctrine had become defensive-minded, and the Maginot Line became the most obvious symbol of this.

Concomitant with this attitude was the extremist political climate that existed in France during the 1930s. This in turn led to errors in political judgment among the right-wing and traditionalist officer corps, for whom the Soviet Union and the spread of Communism posed a bigger threat to France than that presented by Nazi Germany. Yet, from a strategic point of view, any attempt to gain Soviet support in the east might have taken pressure off the west, as had been demonstrated repeatedly during World War I.

Changes in the strategic situation also applied to relations with France's neighbors, especially Belgium. A close ally of France since 1914, the Belgian government suddenly opted out of the alliance in 1936, preferring a return to neutrality following the German reoccupation of the Rhineland (q.v.). From that moment until May 1940, Belgium consistently refused to cooperate with France, even for its own defense. As a result, in May 1940 the French Army was forced to commit troops to the Belgian campaign without any recent experience of military collaboration and without a strategic reserve.

Many accounts of the period have argued that French governments were parsimonious in granting credits for military expenditure, particularly because of the great cost incurred by the construction of the Maginot Line. This interpretation is false, however, since government credits actually increased after 1936 with the introduction of a rearmament program. The problem was that money was not always used wisely by a general staff, which, between 1933 and 1935, spent no more than 50 percent of the annual credits that had been made available.

Before the rise of Adolf Hitler (q.v.) and the concomitant rearmament of Germany starting in 1934, French forces remained greatly superior to those of Germany. In fact, one of the great ironies of the 1940 campaign is that the French had more and better tanks than the Germans had—3,600 against 2,574, including 260 Somua 35s, which were considered to be the best tanks of their day. The problem confronting the French Army, however, was not the quality of its tanks, but rather the manner in which they were used. Instead of being concentrated in powerful "*Panzer*-style" divisions, they were deployed piecemeal throughout the army. The formation of the first French armored division came too late in 1939 and was further hindered by poor training and by a serious shortage of tank radios.

France had entered the 1930s relying on obsolete weapons left over from World War I—equipment such as the slow and lightly armed Renault FT tanks. This lack of modern equipment led to a new production program in 1935, but plans for the construction of the new Somua and Hotchkiss tanks were hampered by a lack of coordination between the army and the arms manufacturers. This was compounded by industrial unrest, linked to political hostility toward rearmament, which resulted in a serious reduction in the monthly production of tanks.

In March 1935, the French extended military service to two years, which allowed for the training of more NCOs and made up for the effects of the declining national birth rate that had been experienced throughout the period of World War I. In September 1936, a mechanization program started with the goal of establishing three light mechanized divisions (DLMs) and two armored divisions.

Despite the money made available, the French Army remained seriously short of much-needed

French Army Order of Battle

Divisions	May 1940	May 1945
Infantry	63	3
North African and		
Colonial Infantry	21	3
Armored	6	3
Light Mechanized	3	0
Motorized	9	1
Mountain	3	2
Light	10	0
Cavalry	5	0
Fortress	13	0
Total	133	12

weapons and equipment by the outbreak of war. They had no antitank mines, and few antitank and antiaircraft guns. In 1939, France had only five antiaircraft regiments compared to seventy-two in the German Army. Yet despite the shortages, France continued to export military equipment prior to May 1940.

In 1940, the typical French infantry division had 17,000 troops and 500 officers, organized into three infantry regiments, two artillery regiments, and a reconnaissance group of four squadrons. The division's antitank weapons consisted of only a company of 25mm antitank rifles and a battery of 47mm antitank guns. The infantry divisions were overwhelmingly dependent on horses for motive power. The 1940 French armored division consisted of two battalions of Char B tanks, two battalions of Hotchkiss light tanks, a battalion of motorized infantry, and a regiment of tractor-drawn artillery.

The French command structure was over-complicated and inefficient, often leaving field commanders uncertain of the parameters of their authority. This situation was further exacerbated by the rivalry between the commander in chief, General Maurice Gamelin (q.v.), and General Joseph Georges, who commanded the northeast front. Whereas the French command system might have sufficed for the type of static siege war experienced between 1914 and 1918, it was totally inadequate for the *Blitzkrieg* (q.v.) that was about to be launched against Belgium, the Netherlands, Luxembourg, and France. Communications between General J.E.A. Doumenc, the chief of staff, and Generals Gamelin and Georges, who all worked from separate headquarters, were further weakened by an archaic reliance on telephones, carrier pigeons, and dispatch riders, as opposed to the use of radio and teleprinters. The situation led one staff officer to comment that General Gamelin's

headquarters was, "like a submarine without a periscope."

Although crack units existed within the French Army, contemporary commentators commented more on the low morale that generally pervaded the army. This was especially true in the reservist units, where many of those called to the colors were unfit, middle-aged, poorly trained, and often ill-equipped. Many contemporary accounts have argued that French public opinion was dominated by pacifism between the wars, but this does not deny the fact that in September 1939, the general mobilization was carried out without any serious hitch. Although the enthusiasm of August 1914 was markedly absent, Frenchmen nevertheless joined their units with a grim determination to get the war over and done with. The only exception to this was the attitude of 300,000 members of the illegal Communist Party, who were totally bewildered by the recent Molotov-Ribbentrop Pact (q.v.).

It was not the outbreak of war itself, but rather eight months of inactivity during the *drôle de guerre* that undermined French morale, and this is borne out by numerous contemporary accounts of visits to the French trenches. Reservists often were unwilling to accept a return to military discipline. Furthermore, the winter of 1939 was the coldest in nearly fifty years and many soldiers resented that they had been obliged to relinquish their civilian occupations and their families for the trenches, while other men remained in the comfort of their own homes. The situation was exacerbated by poor army pay in contrast with civilian incomes, as well as a noticeable difference between the conditions of officers and those of the ordinary soldier.

The worst problem during this period was the *ennui* or boredom caused by inaction, which in turn led to indiscipline, drunkenness, alcoholism, and even incidents of pillaging and vandalism. As the *drôle de guerre* dragged on, more and more soldiers resorted to leaving their posts without permission on weekends *(filer à l'anglaise)*. Inexplicably, those in authority failed to utilize the eight-month respite to properly train the troops, especially the reservists. Once the Germans broke through the French lines at Sedan on 13–14 May 1940, panic, chaos, and disorder ensued. The French Army disintegrated, retreating along roads already blocked with fleeing refugees.

A foretaste of things to come had been indicated by the Allied experience in the ill-fated Norway campaign (q.v.) between April and June 1940. Following the German invasion of Norway, the

Allies deployed an expeditionary force made up of British, French, and Polish troops. Despite the ephemeral victory at Narvik (q.v.), all Allied troops were driven out of the country by 10 June.

The May–June campaign of 1940 was the worst defeat in French history. In six weeks of fighting between 10 May 1940 and 22 June, 92,000 French soldiers were killed and 200,000 were wounded. These were higher casualty figures than those suffered during the worst periods of fighting in 1914 and 1916. That may, in fact, suggest that despite the fact that French Army morale was very low during the eight-month-long *drôle de guerre,* once the Germans actually invaded France, the French soldier's determination to fight heroically came very much to the fore. There were examples of exceptional bravery, such as the fighting of the Saumur Cadets on the River Loire or the defense of Lyon by the 1st Regiment of Infantry.

Even in defeat there were some momentary successes, such as the French defense of its frontier with Italy. On 10 June, Benito Mussolini (q.v.), anxious to play his role in the French defeat, attacked France with an army of 500,000 troops. The Italians were met by General René Olry's 185,000-strong French Sixth Army, which was made up mostly of mountain troops—the *Chasseurs alpins* and *Chasseurs pyrénéens.* They defended a line from the Mediterranean coastal strip at Menton through the Maritime Alps into Dauphiné and Savoy up to the Swiss frontier.

During ten days of hard fighting, the Italians, despite an enormous superiority in men and materiel, failed to take any of the fortified peaks from Gorbio to the Swiss frontier, and only managed to advance a few kilometers to take Menton and Fontan. One account tells how, after the armistice, Mussolini visited the territory now occupied by the Italians. At Mont-Cenis on 30 June, he was greeted by the sight of a French tricolor flag still flying from a position held by two second lieutenants and fifty *Chasseurs alpins* and gunners who had refused to surrender. The following day they marched out of their positions fully armed and equipped to receive full military honors from the Italian company facing them.

Following the defeat of France in June 1940, two French armies came into existence: the Free French Forces (70,000 by June 1942), which originally were made up of exiled Frenchmen who rallied to General Charles de Gaulle (q.v.) in London; and the 120,000-strong Armistice Army of Vichy France (q.v.). For a period of four years France was divided. In the colonies, Frenchmen occasionally fought against Frenchmen, as demonstrated dur-

ing the attack on Dakar (q.v.) in September 1940. Likewise, in metropolitan France there were skirmishes between a variety of resistance groups and the paramilitary *Milice,* especially at the time of the Allied landings in June 1944.

Some Frenchmen, the *Malgré nous* from Alsace and Lorraine (q.v.), were incorporated into the ranks of the *Wehrmacht,* once those two regions had been integrated into Germany in 1940. Other Frenchmen, a handful, collaborated openly with the Germans by enlisting in the ranks of the LVF *(Légion des Volontaires Français).* The LVF was later incorporated into the *Waffen-SS* Charlemagne Division in 1943, which fought on the eastern front. The core of General Maxime Weygand's (q.v.) Armistice Army was stationed in North Africa, and after the German occupation of Vichy France in November 1942, it joined the Allied side, and was augmented by 12,000 Gaullist troops who had been fighting on the Allied side in the Ethiopian, Libyan, and Tunisian campaigns.

From 1943, eight French divisions, about 300,000 men, were equipped by the Allies. After the landings in Normandy (q.v.), this newly reconstituted French Army, supported by 120,000 French Forces of the Interior *(Forces Françaises de l'Intérieur)* (q.v.), fought in the campaigns of 1944–1945. On 16 August 1944, the four divisions of the French First Army, under the command of General Jean de Lattre de Tassigny (q.v.), landed on the Riviera coast near Saint-Tropez. Advancing northward, they liberated Toulon, Marseilles, Lyons, Dijon, Belfort, and Alsace, and then captured Stuttgart, Ulm, and Constance.

Meanwhile, General Philippe Leclerc's (q.v.) 2nd Armored Division landed in Normandy at the end of July 1944, liberated Le Mans and Alençon, and then spearheaded the liberation of Paris on 25 August. As part of the American Third Army, the French 2nd Armored Division fought in eastern France until the end of the year. In the spring of 1945, it pursued the Germans as far as Berchtesgaden, Hitler's mountain retreat in southern Bavaria.

The French Army made a considerable contribution to the liberation of France, and in French public opinion, the liberation of Strasbourg by French troops on 23 November 1944 effaced the humiliation of the summer of 1940. Heavily equipped by the Americans, the French Army at the end of the war was made up of 1,300,000 troops and 38,500 officers. They came from a variety of fighting units, including the Free French, the French Interior Forces, colonial troops, soldiers of the 1939–1940 campaign, returned prisoners of war, and the *naphtalinés,* those Armistice Army officers who were said to have taken their uniforms out of mothballs just in time for the celebration parades.

A purge of the French Army soon followed the end of the war. Seven hundred officers were immediately dismissed and the overall officer strength was gradually reduced to 22,000. Many officers who had joined de Gaulle between June 1942 and November 1942 were shunted into staff jobs at the end of the war. These included General Pierre Koenig, the hero of Bir Hakeim, and General Gaston Billotte (qq.v.). As for the 25,000–strong French Forces of the Interior (many of whom were suspected of Communist sympathies), only 4,000 remained in the French Army in 1946, and less than 2,000 in 1947.

The fighting, however, was not yet over for the French. The newly constituted French Army would go on to fight the bitter wars of decolonization in Indochina (1945–1954) and Algeria (1954–1962).

Robert C. Hudson

Additional Reading

Bond, Brian, *France and Belgium 1939–1940* (1975).

Deighton, Len, *Blitzkrieg: From the Rise of Hitler to the Fall of Dunkirk* (1979).

De La Gorce, P.-M., *The French Army* (1963).

Horne, Alistair, *To Lose a Battle, France 1940* (1969).

Army, German

More than any other organization in World War II, the German Army dominated the action on the ground, from the Channel Islands to the gates of Moscow, from the Arctic Circle to the sands of the Sahara. *Das Heer* of 1939–1945 was as fine a land army as Germany ever built, with organizational and operational traditions reaching back two centuries. It was responsible, in large part, for the spectacular successes of the Third *Reich* from 1938 to 1942. After the tide turned, the German Army doggedly defended Germany's borders and people from the onslaughts of the Soviets and the Western Allies, until it was overcome by sheer weight of numbers.

Although this is the conventional, and for the most part accurate, image of the World War II German Army, it overlooks some of the serious shortcomings of that organization, as well as its culpability in Germany's final downfall. Although it was a superb instrument of military power, it was not backed by a nation with the resources to support its operational needs. Furthermore, it was wasted by its own leadership in useless slugfests and pointless adventures. The German Army also was tied to strategic concepts dating back 200 years, slightly updated after World War I and given iron horses.

The German Army consisted of two principal subgroups—the field army *(Feldheer)* and the replacement army *(Ersatzheer)*. In 1939, this structure provided a field force in excess of two million men organized into roughly 120 divisions, and a force in training and transit of about 100,000. The proportion of replacements available never fully met frontline unit needs after 1942, when ground combat in the Soviet Union and North Africa became continuous. By 1944, the number of replacements and drafts in training and transit had fallen so far behind the increased demands that the practical availability of replacements dropped to zero.

Hitler was obsessed by numbers, primarily with the number of divisions. As the war dragged on and the strength of the army was sapped, additional draft waves were used to form new divisions rather than to reinforce existing formations. As the war continued, veteran units were bled

TABLE 1

German Army Infantry Divisions

Year	No. Divs. Formed	Remarks
1934–38	39	Active army.
1939	79	Reserve and *Landwehr.*
1940	67	Static and understrength units, most disbanded or converted by end of year.
1941	21	Weak and security units.
1942	12	All understrength or intended for service in Russia.
1943	20	Includes new regiments only. Nearly all from older divisions.
1944	96	Twelve waves, mostly reformed from destroyed units.
1945	20	Formed from remnants, schools, and the Labor Service.
Total	354	

TABLE 2

A

German Army Divisional Strength

Division Type	No. of Troops	Automatic Weapons	Artillery (over 75mm)	AT Weapons	Motor Vehicles	Horses	Tanks
Infantry c. 1940	17,200	1,238	74	105	942	5,375	0
Infantry c. 1944	12,352	2,022	82	108	615	4,656	0
Volksgrenadier c. 1944	9,069	2,159	92	248	426	3,002	0
Light/Motorized c. 1940	14,000	488	36	12	337	>1,500	28
Panzergrenadier c. 1944	13,833	2,542	54	120	2,637	>1,400	48
Panzer c. 1940	14,000	488	36	12	1,800	337	250
Panzer c. 1944	13,700	2,764	66	48	2,685	0	103

white by the constant transfer of their most experienced soldiers to form the cadres of the new units. This procedure broke up the personal bonds within units that are necessary to keep any combat army going. Thus, chronically understrength divisions were replaced and reinforced by chronically "green" formations. Table 1 shows the overall totals for infantry divisions.

The basic building block of the German Army was the infantry division *(Infanteriedivision)*. At the beginning of the war, there were a number of experimental motorized *(motorisierte Infanterie)* units of regiment size. By 1941, ten motorized infantry *(motorisierte Infanteriedivision)* or light infantry *(leichte Infanteriedivision)* divisions were formed. These units later were redesignated as armored infantry *(Panzergrenadier)* divisions. These divisions were organized along similar lines as the standard infantry division, but they had more vehicles and greater firepower, including an attached tank regiment. During the war a total of twenty-two motorized/armored infantry divisions were formed. Most were established at full strength, but were never maintained at that level.

Other forms of infantry divisions were variations on the base model. Mountain divisions *(Gebirgsjägerdivision)* were slightly smaller than the infantry division and with fewer motor vehicles. The security divisions *(Sicherungsdivision)* guarded lines of communication and conducted anti-partisan operations. The so-called peoples' grenadier divisions *(Volksgrenadierdivision)* were raised late in the war, and although numerically weaker, they were armed with a high proportion of auto-matic and antitank weapons. The fortress divisions *(Festungsdivision)*, were essentially stationary garrisons of little more than regiment or brigade strength.

The German Army's other principal type of division was the armored, or *Panzer* division. The first *Panzer* divisions were raised as entirely new units in 1937. Thereafter they were formed by converting light or other infantry divisions, or by breaking up other major formations. The *Panzer* division was the mailed fist of the German offensive. Theoretically it was an overwhelming powerful organization. In practice, however, the *Panzer* divisions quickly became worn down by attrition, and the lack of replacements and spare parts left them chronically weak. Because less than thirty-five *Panzer* divisions (including *Waffen-SS* (q.v.) were formed, they were almost constantly in action after 1941. Often, shattered *Panzer* divisions were reconstituted by stripping other divisions and even *Luftwaffe* units.

German divisions basically were triangular organizations, with three infantry or armored regiments, an artillery regiment, a reconnaissance battalion, an engineer battalion, signals, and divisional trains. Both the infantry and the *Panzer* divisions had smaller variants—two-regiment infantry divisions and *Panzer* divisions with no organic tanks. The structure for the variant divisions varied widely. Some had no signals, or no organic artillery, or no engineers, or no reconnaissance.

Table 2 shows the rough strengths of various division organizations at different stages during the war. The table states the authorized strength, which often was not achieved in practice. The 1944 *Panzer* division has only approximate figures because various sources do not agree. Antitank weapons included both guns and rocket launchers, but not tank main guns.

Above the divisional level, the corps *(Armee-Korps)* consisted of at least two (usually more) divisions, plus additional corps support troops and artillery. The XCI Korps was the highest-numbered corps. The next higher echelon was the field army *(Armee),* which consisted of two or more corps. The field army controlled additional artillery assets (such as railway guns), heavy tank units, and other nondivisional support units. Although field armies usually were designated by numbers, some were given a name. More than 100 field army organizations were formed during the war, although some in fact were little more than reinforced divisions.

The army group *(Heeresgruppe)* was the German Army's largest operational unit, controlling a number of field armies or corps directly. The army groups controlled the zones of communication in the rear of the fighting front and were responsible for the logistical needs of the entire region. Army groups were designated by either their location, their commander's name, or a letter.

The Germans also created a wide array of various ad hoc formations. These were sometimes called *ersatz* (replacement or substitute) units, or battle groups *(Kampfgruppe).* Ranging in sizes equivalent from a battalion up to a division, such units were formed according to local needs and to conform to local conditions with the troops available. They often gave good account of themselves and were dissolved as soon as they were no longer needed.

The German Army had the same types of technical and administrative units (engineer, postal, medical, etc.) as any other Western army, and in about the same proportion. There were, however, some small units operating in the German rear that had no equivalent in any other World War II army—death camp units. Such units were primarily formed and operated by the *Waffen-SS,* but the German Army had a few (probably no more than a dozen) operating in the Soviet Union. Both Germany and the Soviet Union also created penal units of incompetents and miscreants. These units were used for extremely hazardous duties, such as sweeping mines and leading assaults on heavily fortified positions.

The German Army had a number of elite units that were designated by name only. *Grossdeutschland* (Greater Germany), called "The Bodyguard of the German People," began in 1938 as a ceremonial

battalion. It expanded to regimental size in 1939, and to divisional size in June 1942. By spring 1945, it was *Panzerarmee Grossdeutschland,* consisting of five divisions in two corps. *Grossdeutschland* served mostly on the eastern front, suffering huge losses. The *Panzer-Lehr* Division was formed in the winter of 1943–1944 from instructors and school troops of the German *Panzer* schools. Commanded by Lieutenant General Fritz Bayerlein (q.v.), the *Panzer-Lehr* was the most powerful armored division in the German Army at the time of the Normandy landings. The *Panzer-Lehr* also suffered heavy losses, mostly from Allied airpower. Like the *Panzer-Lehr* Division, the *Infantrie-Lehr* Regiment was formed from instructors and elite school troops. In 1944, Hitler personally ordered the *Infantrie-Lehr* to the Anzio beachhead.

Command and control in the German Army suffered from confusion in the upper echelons. Three different command headquarters, the *Oberkommando das Heer* (Army High Command or OKH), the *Oberkommando der Wehrmacht* (Armed Forces High Command or OKW) (qq.v.), and the supreme commander (Hitler) and his staff often were not in agreement, and sometimes were in direct competition. At any given time, field units could receive entirely contradictory orders from all three headquarters. In practice, the OKH stood on the sidelines after 1941, and the OKW was largely irrelevant for most of the war, except for planning, supply, and administrative services. Hitler's *Führerhauptquartier* (q.v.) issued all the key orders of a strategic nature.

The real strength of the German Army lay in the ability of its field commanders to give orders, knowing that they would be carried out if humanly possible. As the result of intense training, German officers never had to worry much that their orders would be misunderstood, or that soldiers or units would refuse to carry them out. Contrary to the popular stereotype, however, German military officers were not all martinets and micro-managers. German military orders tended to focus on *what* was to be done, and *when* it was to be done. To a far greater degree than in the Western armies—and most certainly the Soviet Army—German officers let their subordinates decide *how* the mission would be accomplished. The Germans called this method of command *Auftragstaktik*—or Mission Orders. Many modern Western armies (including the U.S. Army) have attempted to adopt this philosophy, which is much easier to state than it is to practice.

During the course of the war, Hitler himself subverted the military command and control

TABLE 3

German Army Order of Battle 1939–1944

Divisions	1939	1944
Infantry	99	226
Panzer	9	26
SS Panzer	0	7
Panzergrenadier	4	11
SS Panzergrenadier	2	7
Cavalry	1	4
Jäger (Light)	0	12
Mountain	3	13
Parachute	2	11
Artillery	0	1
Luftwaffe Field	0	19
Totals	120	337

structure. Right from the start Adolf Hitler (q.v.) distrusted his generals, and they him. Unfortunately, in the early stages of the war, Hitler was "cursed" with extremely good luck and inept opponents. Hitler and his true believers took the largely political results of the Rhineland, Austria, and Czechoslovakia as conclusive proof of Hitler's intuitive genius in all strategic matters. Many generals, however, were only too aware that Hitler's successes up until late 1941 had been due to sheer bluff and luck. They thus tried to dissuade him from his more harebrained schemes, pointing out the deficiencies in the military structure and in the plans themselves. This only caused Hitler to lose patience and confidence in his military commanders.

In late 1941, General Walther von Brauchitsch (q.v.), army commander in chief, suffered a heart attack and submitted his resignation. Hitler took the opportunity to assume direct command of the army. After that point the OKH and OKW became mere appendages of Hitler, who began to issue orders directly to field commanders as low as the corps level. The generals in Berlin increasingly became high-ranking clerks and messengers.

The German Army was steeped in its own Prussian legends and origins. Those traditions, however, were formed in an era when armies only needed to win battles six months out of the year and to remain alive the other six. The armies of World War II, on the other hand, had to sustain themselves and operate continuously, and the German Army of 1939–1945 eventually proved incapable of doing so against determined resistance.

The principal operational technique of the German Army was based on the concept of the *Kesselschlacht*—the "cauldron battle" of encirclement by fast-marching infantry divisions, sup-ported on the wings by cavalry and strengthened by artillery. This concept came into its own during the Franco-Prussian War, with General Helmuth von Moltke's principles of "Fix, Encircle, Destroy"—*Umfassen, Einschliessen, Vernichten.*

Things changed between the nineteenth century and the twentieth. When the mobile tactics of the nineteenth century ran headlong into the firepower technology of the twentieth in World War I, the concept of the *Kesselschlacht* was abandoned in the hell of the trenches. After 1918, Germany's small (but highly professional) 100,000-man *Reichswehr* felt free to discard the operational concepts that had dominated World War I and search for new ideas. Many of those new ideas came from within its own ranks.

Colonel (later Colonel General) Heinz Guderian (q.v.) emerged as a strong advocate of armored warfare. His ideas were similar to those being advocated in Britain by J.F.C. Fuller, Basil Liddell Hart, and Percy Hobart (qq.v.); in France by Charles de Gaulle (q.v.); and in the United States by Adna R. Chaffee (q.v.). Guderian believed that a heavily armored, highly mobile force could pierce the enemy lines at a weak point and drive for the enemy's vitals. The Germans had attempted much the same sort of thing during their five great offensives in 1918, but the Stormtroop (*Stosstruppen*) units that spearheaded those attacks were all foot troops, without the ability to drive deep enough, fast enough.

During World War I, the trenches and barbed wire had turned the forward fighting zones into a morass. The tank never quite developed to the point where it could function as the steel equivalent of cavalry, and Germany lagged far behind the Allies in armored vehicle development. By the late 1920s, however, the German military had developed several promising tank designs secretly, in violation of the Versailles Treaty (q.v.). Within a few years after Hitler became chancellor in 1933, the Versailles restrictions were violated openly, and Germany's rearmament program went into high gear.

Guderian and the other armored theorists combined the American ideas of dive-bombing and close air support, the Soviet notion of glider and parachute-borne attacks, and the World War I lesson of closely coordinated infantry and artillery to produce what appeared to be a revolutionary breakthrough in ground combat methods. The resulting system came to be known as "Lightning War"—*Blitzkrieg* (q.v.). The weak link in the German system, however, was conventional field artillery. Ironically, the Germans had led the world in artillery fire techniques in the last year of World

War I. But by the middle of World War II, German artillery was hopelessly outmatched by the sheer numbers of Soviet artillery, and the technical sophistication and accuracy of British and American artillery.

As a survivor of four years in the mud and trenches of World War I, Hitler was very impressed with the military developments underway at the time he became chancellor. Enthusiastically, he endorsed the formation of the first *Panzer* divisions in 1937. But Hitler, and even many of the more tradition-minded German generals, misunderstood Guderian's entire theory. The principal idea was to use the breakthrough force to drive into the enemy's vital areas, completely ignoring military targets in their path, and concentrate on striking at the sources of industry and communications deep in the enemy's heartland. (This was exactly the strategic role the Allied air forces intended for precision bombing.) Instead, most German operational level commanders (with a few exceptions) spent most of World War II using the *Panzer* units as the primary tools to apply von Moltke's operational principles—breakthrough to encirclement. Although this approach was highly successful against the unwary and unschooled, it was not quite as revolutionary as it seemed at the time.

Perhaps the German Army's greatest strength lay in its proud heritage, and in the image of the near-invincibility that it gained as a result of the successful campaigns of 1939 and 1940. The flaws in the German Army were, however, greater than its considerable strengths. Hitler's personal direction of the day-to-day ground operations; the inability of the General Staff (q.v.) to stop the constant meddling; the military's own strict obedience to a code of conduct that Hitler and the Nazi Party publicly scorned; and Hitler's almost pathological insistence that nearly impossible operations could be performed—with the generals knowing full well that they were impractical at best and suicidal at worst—combined to cripple the German Army from the top down.

The German Army also was hobbled with external deficiencies that were beyond it's ability to control. Germany was chronically short of almost every vital resource for modern warfare—except enemies (both internal and external) and raw courage. When the war began, the *Panzer* divisions still relied on nearly 2,000 horses, and throughout the war, only 10 percent of the army was ever motorized. *OKH* planners calculated that the invasion of the Low Countries and France in 1940, as well as garrisoning Norway, Poland, and other areas, would require a force of 210 divisions—twenty more than were actually available. The chronic shortage of manpower and mechanized transport never really improved, even after the full mobilization of German industry to war production in 1944. By that time, it was too late.

Without a doubt, the combat operations of the German Army in World War II produced some of the most stunning victories in the annals of military history. That army probably was the only military force ever assembled that could have saved Germany from a much earlier defeat than was actually the case. Only the German Army of 1939–1945 could have held back for so long the combined forces of the Soviet Union, the British Commonwealth, and the United States.

The tremendous fighting power of the German Army derived in part from a powerful emotional bond formed between the men in the fighting units, and the ruthless efficiency they displayed in carrying out their orders. With infantry units formed around a light machine gun that could fire twenty rounds per second, and tank guns that could penetrate nearly any enemy armor at 25 percent greater ranges than their opponents, the Germans had great confidence in their equipment. Their deeply held traditions, passed on by the officers who were steeped in the ancient *Junker* values all throughout their training, were part of the glue that held them together.

The other part was the firmly held belief that they were surrounded by enemies, and that Germany always had been surrounded by enemies. A much smaller percentage of the German Army really believed the anti-Semitic and Nazi "supermen" propaganda that was regular fare in the *Waffen-SS.* Some in the German Army did buy this nonsense, of course, but they all believed very strongly in the cause of the preservation of Germany and its cultural heritage.

By the end of World War II, the German Army was diluted by *Volksgrenadier* units consisting of troops as young as twelve and as old as eighty, and by "stomach" and "ear" battalions of disabled veterans. It remained, however, a potent force until the end. The Ardennes offensive (q.v.) of December 1944 and the fanatical defense of Berlin were not carried out solely by Nazi fanatics or by ordinary Germans with pistols to their heads. These final actions were carried out by ordinary German soldiers committed to their cause—to Germany and to the German Army.

John Beatty

Additional Reading
Cecil, Robert (ed.), *Hitler's War Machine* (1975).

Cooper, Matthew, *The German Army: 1933–45: Its Political and Military Failure* (1984).

Djakov, Yuri L., and Tatjana S. Bushuyeva, *The Red Army and the Wehrmacht: How the Soviets Militarized Germany, 1923–33, and Paved the Way for Fascism* (1955).

Her Majesty's Stationery Office, *German Order of Battle 1944,* reprinted (1994).

Keegan, John, *Six Armies in Normandy* (1982).

Lucas, James, *The Last Year of the German Army: May 1944–May 1945* (1994).

Madej, Victor (ed.), *German Army Order of Battle 1939–45* (1978).

McLean, Donald B. (ed.), *Company Officer's Handbook of the German Army* (1975).

U.S. War Department, *TM-E 30–451 Handbook on German Military Forces,* reprinted (1990).

Army, Greek

During the interwar years, the Greek Army experienced a severe shortage of modern weapons and motorized transportation. In 1922, it suffered a humiliating defeat at the hands of Turkish troops led by Mustafa Kemal. That ended modern Greece's imperial ambitions. Defensively, however, the Greeks enjoyed the advantages of a mountainous frontier and experienced soldiers.

The Greek armed forces, under the command of General Alexandros Papagos (q.v.), included a general headquarters and five army corps areas. The army numbered about 430,000 soldiers and was organized into two army groups, each consisting of six general headquarters, six infantry divisions, nine mountain divisions, one cavalry division, and four mountain brigades. The mountain divisions, the central elements of the Greek Army, were organized along the lines of the infantry divisions, with three infantry regiments, one divisional artillery regiment, and other support units. Infantry divisions, however, had more artillery.

The Greek soldier's main weapon was the Mannlicher-Schoenauer M-1903/14 rifle. Support weapons included the Hotchkiss 8mm light machine gun, the St. Etienne M-1907 heavy machine gun, 81mm mortars, and 65mm mountain guns. Artillery in the mountain division consisted of four batteries of 75mm mountain guns and two batteries of 105mm guns, while the infantry division had nine batteries of 75mm field guns. The elite of the Greek Army was the Royal Guard, or *Evzones,* established during the war for independence.

Greek Army uniforms were largely based on British models. Officers wore uniforms that differed little from their British counterparts. Soldiers wore khaki uniforms, which also included side cap, tunic, single-breasted greatcoat, and pantaloons. The *Evzones* wore traditional dress—white full-sleeved shirt, waistcoat, pleated kilt, and red-tasseled cap. In combat, they donned khaki frock coats and breeches.

Greece mobilized its armed forces in 1940, just prior to Italy's 28 October invasion. Outnumbered, the Greeks fought valiantly and managed to push the invading forces out of Greece and back into Albania. Euphoria swept through Greece, and news of the Axis setback moved quickly through Europe. The success was temporary. Greek Army leaders hoped to avoid conflict with the Germans, knowing that defeat would be inevitable.

German forces invaded from Yugoslavia on 6 April 1941, and moved steadily forward, crushing the Greek Army. On 20 April, the Greek *Epirus* Army surrendered, and two days later, Allied forces (primarily British) began their evacuation. The first German troops reached Athens on 27 April. Some Greek forces did escape or were evacuated and formed two units under British command in North Africa.

The Greek 3rd Mountain Brigade participated in the battle of El Alamein (q.v.) and later returned to Egypt for additional training. This brigade went to Italy in August 1944 and was active until that November. It then returned to Greece to put down a Communist uprising.

A second unit, organized in August 1942 and known as the Sacred Company, was composed largely of officers from the *Evzones.* From an initial force of 500 men, it grew in strength to battalion size. It fought with the Free French in North Africa, and with New Zealand troops in Tunisia.

Robert G. Waite

Additional Reading

Fleischer, Hagan, *Im Kreuzschatten der Mächte: Griechenland 1941–1944,* vols. 1 and 2 (1986).

Mazower, Mark, *Inside Hitler's Greece: The Experience of Occupation, 1941–1944* (1993).

Mollo, Andrew, *The Armed Forces of World War II* (1981).

Army, Greenland

In May 1941, Greenland formed the smallest army to see combat in World War II. Formed by its Danish colonial governor, Eske Brun, the Greenland Army initially numbered fifteen men. Having no trained military personnel among Greenland's population of 22,000, Governor Brun recruited his force by calling for volunteers from the island's hunters and guides. Brun wanted the force to patrol Greenland's forbidding eastern seaboard, looking for German weather parties and any other evidence of German intrusion into the colony.

The patrol area stretched from just south of Scoresby Sound, Greenland's northernmost settlement, to the farthest limit of Greenland's navigable waters—far above 77 degrees north latitude. Drawing its name from the patrol area, the force was first called the Northeast Greenland Sledge Patrol. During the course of the war its members saw action against German weather parties. The Sledge Patrol made a significant contribution to the conduct of the Weather War (q.v.)—the battle for the Arctic weather stations that was so critical to weather prediction in those pre-satellite days.

Governor Brun's decision to form the sledge patrol was technically a violation of King Christian X's (q.v.) order that all Danes submit to German authority. Believing the king's order to have given under duress, Brun approached the American government for protection. The Americans agreed in May 1941, extending U.S. Coast Guard patrols to the waters off eastern Greenland and further agreeing to supply the colony's seaboard settlements and the Sledge Patrol. They also agreed to cooperate with the sledge patrol's commander, Ib Poulsen, the senior radioman at Eskimones, the northernmost Danish weather station in Greenland.

There was a reason why Brun chose to form his defense force in coordination with the Americans rather than the much closer Canadians. In the 1930s, Northeastern Greenland had been awarded to Denmark by an international court, following a dispute with Norway. More significantly, the colony originally had belonged to Norway and had been awarded to Denmark in 1821. Brun knew there were many Norwegians in Canada and Great Britain who would be willing to help defend Greenland—and in so doing, might lead to renewed Norwegian claims after the war. He therefore felt it was essential that Greenland be defended by a Danish/Greenland force supported by a disinterested party—the United States.

The Sledge Patrol's first action came on 13 March 1943, when a German weather party surprised one of its patrols near Sabine Island and killed the leader. Losing their equipment, the Greenlanders retreated back to Eskimones to warn Poulsen, who then requested further orders and automatic weapons. Governor Brun passed that request along to the Americans and appointed Poulsen commander of the Greenland Army, with the rank

of captain. Brun also changed the name of the force from the Northeast Greeland Sledge Patrol to the Army of Greenland, effective 15 March 1943. The Germans struck Eskimones before the automatic weapons arrived, seizing the station on 23 March. The Greenlanders escaped without injury, but had to make the perilous 400-mile trip to Ella Island without sleds, food, or equipment.

During the remainder of the war, the Greenland Army fought two more engagements with German weather parties, suffering two dead and four wounded during the war. Thus the Greenland Army's casualty rate of 40 percent was the highest of any army in World War II. In the end, the Greenland Army, supported by the U.S. Coast Guard and U.S. Army Air Forces, captured or forced the evacuation of all German weather parties from Greenland by October 1944. Formed to preempt Canadian or Norwegian forces from undertaking the defense of northeastern Greenland, the Greenland Army made a contribution to the Allied war effort far out of proportion to its size.

Carl O. Schuster

Additional Reading
Howarth, David, *The Sledge Patrol* (1957).
Willoughby, Malcome, F. *The U.S. Coast Guard in World War II* (1989).

Army, Hungarian

The 1920 Treaty of Trianon limited Hungary to a regular army of only 35,000 men and prohibited it from having tanks, airplanes, and heavy artillery. The resulting seven mixed brigades supported by a Danube River flotilla consisted almost entirely of long-term professional soldiers augmented by a secretly enlisted short-term "frontier guards."

Tracing its traditions back to the Germanic-dominated Austria-Hungarian Army of World War I, the Hungarian Army was heavily influenced by German tactics, procedures, and operational doctrine. Rearmament began in 1939, as Hungary followed Germany's example in rejecting the post–World War I treaties. Some tanks were purchased and an attempt was made at mechanization. Nevertheless, a shortage of money, combined with the treaty limitations, led to an army that entered the war with obsolete equipment. Most of the artillery dated from World War I and most of the armor proved too light for combat conditions on the eastern front, where the Hungarian Army did most of its fighting.

The Hungarian Army entered the war orga-

Hungarian Army Order of Battle 1941–1944

Divisions	1941	1944
Infantry	27	1
Armored	0	2
Cavalry	0	1
Light	0	1
Mixed	0	8
Reserve	0	8
Total	27	21

nized into three army districts, each with three corps. The corps were responsible for raising and training the troops and units within their areas. Each corps controlled three divisions and support troops. The divisions themselves had one regular army regiment at full strength in peacetime and one reserve regiment of professional cadre, which would be augmented by mobilized troops in war. Thus Hungary had nine divisions and support corps-level troops on 1 September 1939.

Regaining Transylvania from Romania with German support in 1940, Hungary added two more divisions to its order of battle. Still, equipment remained a problem throughout the war. The small mobile group that accompanied the German Army into Russia had to use requisitioned civilian vehicles to transport its infantry. Moreover, the Hungarian Army had to expand as German manpower needs increased throughout the war. An additional 200,000 troops were mobilized in 1942. Hungarian units later suffered heavily during the Stalingrad and Kursk (qq.v.) campaigns.

Although the Hungarian Army was a well-trained and proficient force, it lacked the modern equipment and mobile training needed to function efficiently on the battlefields of World War II. With its fate tied increasingly to that of Germany, Hungary's armed forces were forced to fight to the bitter end against a more numerous and better-equipped Soviet Army. The results were catastrophic; more than 75 percent of all Hungarian troops were killed or captured before the war's end.

Carl O. Schuster

Additional Reading

Abbott, Peter, et al., *Germany's Eastern Front Allies 1941–45* (1983).

Madej, Victor, *Southeastern Axis Armies Handbook* (1982).

Army, Indian

Until 1947, India was part of the British Empire. For almost 200 years, Britain relied heavily on Indian regiments for its overseas campaigns, and World War II was no exception. The Indian Army expanded from 200,000 regulars in 1939 to a total force of 2.5 million in 1945, the largest volunteer army in world history. The pre-independence use of "Indian" embraces people who are now called Pakistani or Bangladeshi. In the Indian divisions, there were also British units (especially artillery) and Gurkhas (q.v.) from the independent state of Nepal. The majority of the officers were British (until 1918, all had been). Between the wars, some Indians were trained at Sandhurst, and an Indian Military Academy was established at Dehra Dun. In 1939, there were 1,000 Indian officers, and by 1945, there were 16,000.

Originally, the main role of the Indian Army was the defense of India itself and internal security. During World War II, India's main contribution was in the Far East, but its divisions also played a prominent role in the Mediterranean theater. Indian divisions were organized and equipped in the same way as their British counterparts. Three Indian divisions served in North Africa, never less than two at any one time. The Indian 4th Division arrived in Egypt in 1939 and played a key part in General Archibald Wavell's (q.v.) defeat of the Italians in Libya in 1940–1941. It then moved to the Ethiopian front to take part, alongside the Indian 5th Division, in the conquest of Italian-held Ethiopia. The outstanding feature of this campaign was the capture, by two divisions, of the rugged Keren mountain feature, a position thought by the Italians to be impregnable. After Keren the 4th Division returned to North Africa. The 5th Division followed in May 1942 after the final surrender of Italian forces in North Africa.

In the middle of 1942, the 5th Division returned to the Far East and was replaced by the Indian 10th Division from Iraq. As the desert campaign ebbed and flowed, these units were present at every significant battle, including Operation CRUSADER, el Alamein battles, and the final breakthrough in Tunisia. Here, as at Keren, the mountain warfare expertise of the 4th Division, learned before the war on India's northwest frontier, proved invaluable.

In 1939, the British decided not to use Indian units on the European mainland. Manpower shortages, however, reversed that decision, and three Indian divisions—the 4th, 8th, and 10th—plus the 43rd Gurkha Brigade, took part in the Italian campaign. They saw some of the most severe fighting, including initial landings, the crossing of the Sangro, Sennio, and Garigliano Rivers, Monte Cassino (q.v.), the Liri Valley, and the Gothic Line (q.v.).

Indian troops passing through the ruins of Cassino, 16 March 1944. (IWM NA 12895)

Indian Army units also played a part in two minor operations. In 1941, Britain intervened in Persia, Iraq, and Syria (q.v.) to protect vital oil supplies and to keep a supply route into the southern Soviet Union open. The Indian 8th and 10th Divisions were involved in the defeat of pro-Nazi regimes in all three countries. In 1944, a civil war between Communist and pro-monarchy forces threatened to break out in Greece in the wake of the German withdrawal. British forces were sent from Italy to hold the ring, and the Indian 4th Division served there until the end of 1946.

With independence in 1947, World War II was the last time this magnificent army fought under the British flag. It was a fitting finale. According to Philip Mason, who served in the Indian civil service and defense department for twenty years: "With every reason to doubt the possibility of a British victory, in the teeth of Indian politicians who demanded that the British should quit India, the fighting units of the Indian Army were not only faithful to their colors, but again and again displayed heroic valor . . . their victory brought independence within two years. Their

defeat would have postponed indefinitely anything worth calling independence."

Philip Green

Additional Reading
Mason, Philip, *A Matter of Honour: An Account of the Indian Army, Its Officers, and Men* (1974).
Mollo, Boris, *The Indian Army* (1986).

Army, Italian
The Italian Army was less ready for modern warfare than all the other major armies in World War II. The main reasons for this unpreparedness stem from a misunderstanding of the lessons of World War I, combined with decisions made by key military leaders to comply with the wishes of the Fascist government in power.

At the end of World War I, the principal aim of all Italian political and military leaders was to demobilize the army (which had reached a maximum strength of three million) and reduce it to a peacetime footing. Demobilization was neither easy nor quick, because both the government and opposition worked to stall the process, while at the same time blaming the other in order to save face with a confused public. Furthermore, deciding on the exact structure of the new army was very difficult in the turbulent postwar years. Ten different ministers of war, each with vastly different ideas, served between November 1918 and October 1922.

The first reorganization, attempted in 1919, was driven primarily by economic considerations. It called for an army of 210,000 men organized into thirty infantry and two cavalry divisions (four regiments per division). Economic, social, and political forces all caused modifications in the plan. Over the course of the next five years at least four more completely different organizations were considered. This state of affairs had, of course, negative consequences for the army's efficiency. Every new change was followed by crises, and the continuous reorganizations, even if only partially implemented, adversely affected overall preparedness.

Compounding the problems of the Italian Army, Italy entered the period of Fascist political control. The Fascist seizure of power brought about the birth of another political-military organization, the *Milizia Volontaria per la Sicurezza Nazionale* (Voluntary Militia for the National Security). The initial purpose of these units was to give some form of organization and official recognition to the Fascist street fighting units. Over time, however, the *Milizia* evolved into something of a second army. Quite apart from the cost (no small amount) of this second army, the *Milizia* drew its troops from the normal yearly manpower pool and also was armed and equipped from army inventories. Thus, the *Milizia* became a serious drain on the Italian Army. As the "armed expression of the Fascist Party," the *Milizia* also acquired its political strength at the expense of the army.

Between 1926 and 1934, the army's structure finally started to stabilize around a force of thirty infantry, four mountain, and three cavalry divisions. The divisions were based on the more agile triangular structure, with three infantry regiments supported by one artillery regiment. With these types of units, the army participated in the Ethiopia campaign, the Spanish civil war, and the occupation of Albania (qq.v.). Each of the three operations was very different in nature and very expensive in terms of equipment and weapons. These losses were very difficult to replace with the Italian Army's minuscule operating budget. Nonetheless, they should have provided valuable experience that could have been translated into improved tactical and operational doctrine and equipment for the major war to come. Unfortunately, the experiences only tended to confirm, in the minds of the military and political leaders, the Fascist gibberish about their own invincibility. Thus no lessons were learned, and no improvements were made.

The Ethiopian campaign is a case in point. For a fairly small operation, it required a very large investment in resources. Almost 25 percent of the army was committed and several classes of reservists were mobilized. The operation also required the large-scale use of air, land, and sea logistical assets. Final victory over Ethiopia was obtained with relatively low casualties, giving the Fascist Party hacks more fuel to stoke the myth. This completely glossed over the fact that a modern European army had bulldozed its way over a handful of primitive tribesmen.

The Italian military also drew some dangerous conclusions about the nature of mobile warfare. The success of light mobile units against the poorly armed tribesmen led to the conclusion that the strengths of the divisions could be reduced to increase mobility, all without sacrificing combat power. The resulting structure was something called a "divisional hybrid." No other major army in the world had anything even vaguely comparable. In fact, it was a hollow division. Politically, however, it was a popular move. The reductions in heavy equipment and the divisional support structures freed up manpower to create more divisions, thereby creating more senior officer positions.

As World War II approached, the Italian Army was once again in the throes of another major reorganization. The big idea this time was something called "binary divisions," which really were little more than reinforced brigades. Again, this move increased the number of divisions on paper, all without increasing manpower and equipment requirements. Weapons and equipment were the army's principal weaknesses. Ammunition was comparatively plentiful, but it was obsolete.

The Italian armored forces were in a similar situation. At the start of the war, only the very light and fast tankette-type car was available in large numbers. What passed for a medium tank in the Italian Army weighed only eleven tons. By the time of the fighting in the Libyan desert, an improved thirteen- to fifteen-ton version began to appear in the armored units. When the fighting actually started, motor vehicles of any sort were very scarce. Plans were laid for the military to requisition civilian vehicles in time of need, but no consideration was given to the problems

A

Italian Army Order of Battle

Divisions	1940	1943
Infantry	57	67
Armored	3	5
Cavalry	3	3
Mountain	5	6
Motorized	2	5
Parachute	0	2
Airlanding	0	1
Colonial	14	0
Milizia	3	0
Coastal Defense	0	25
Total	87	114

of standardization of repair parts and supplies for these items.

Hobbled by all these staggering handicaps, the Italian Army entered the war with seventy divisions, of which three were armored, three cavalry, two motorized, five mountain, and fifty-seven infantry. Added to this force were the *Milizia* and colonial units. The cavalry divisions had three regiments, all the other divisions had two (plus supporting artillery). Each regiment had three battalions. The divisions generally had one mixed engineer battalion, one antitank company, one machine gun or mortar battalion, and the divisional services.

Altogether, the typical infantry division could muster a little more than 10,000 men, thirty-six guns, 420 vehicles of various types (including motorcycles), and 1,750 pack and draft animals. This structure proved so light that within a few months of the start of the war each division received a legion of *Milizia*. Consisting of only 1,200 troops, the *Milizia* legion was far too light to give the division the equivalent of the third regiment. On the other hand, it was often the only maneuver force available to Italian divisional commanders. Later, Italian divisions fighting in Greece received full "third regiments," while those in Yugoslavia were reinforced by many independent units of battalion size.

Only one-third of the division's thirty-six guns were of 100mm caliber, while the remainder were 75mm. Thus, the caliber of Italian artillery was smaller than other armies, where the standard size was 105mm. During the course of the war, the different types of divisional units were modified on the grounds of experience gained, especially antitank and mobility units. The rate of events, however, ran too fast for the army to keep pace, and more often, changes introduced were too little too late, or of poor quality.

By the end of the war, the army had fielded five armored, five motorized or semi-motorized, three cavalry, six mountain, two parachute, one airlanding, and sixty-seven infantry divisions. In addition, the army had twenty-five coastal divisions, static defense units composed of variable numbers of regiments and battalions manned by older troops and armed with whatever was available. All these units were organized into eleven field armies and thirty-one corps. They were deployed in France, Albania, northern and eastern Africa, Yugoslavia, Greece, and Russia, and of course, in Italy itself.

Badly armed and equipped, commanded by generals who often were not up to the task, the Italian Army did not play a decisive role during its thirty-nine months of war. This despite large-scale human sacrifice. In 1943, a new German-puppet Italian Army was created in northern Italy called the Army of the Italian Social Republic (q.v.).

Francesco Fatutta

Additional Reading

Badoglio, Pietro, *Italy and the Second World War* (1948).

Barclay, Glen, *The Rise and Fall of the New Roman Empire* (1973).

U.S. Army, Military Intelligence Division, *Handbook on the Italian Military Forces* (1943).

Army, Italian Social Republic (1943–1945)

On 12 September 1943, Benito Mussolini (q.v.) was freed by German paratroops from his confinement on Gran Sasso (q.v.) Mountain, and immediately transferred to Vienna, and later to Munich. After a couple of days, he reached German Chancellor Adolf Hitler (q.v.) in Rastenburg, and during the meeting between the two dictators, a new state was established. The actual foundation of the *Repubblica Sociale Italiana* (Italian Social Republic) dates from 18 September 1943, when Mussolini in a public speech promised that: "Italy would have again put herself on a war footing beside Germany, Japan and all the other [Axis] countries." The RSI became known as "Salò Republic," from the name of the small town on the shores of Lake Garda where the government established its seat. The RSI included nearly all of northern and central Italy, that part of the country still under German control. This situation meant the RSI was no more than a puppet state.

The RSI laboriously reconstituted an armed forces under the command of Marshal Rodolfo

Graziani (q.v.). From many smaller units and fragments, the RSI Army was able to form four divisions ("Monterosa," "San Marco," "Littorio," and "Italia"). Initially, they were trained in Germany and sent back to northern Italy. The primary mission of these units was counterinsurgency and antipartisan actions. This was especially true for the "Monterosa" and "San Marco" Divisions, the first to come back to Italy and the most politicized. Only a very few RSI units ever saw action against the Allied forces. Some fought at Anzio (q.v.) and at Garfagnana, where, near the end of the war, the "Italia" Division briefly faced the Brazilian 1st Division.

The RSI Navy, with almost nothing to put to sea, had its own land unit, the strong (respected by the Germans) "Decima Mas," commanded by Prince Junio Valerio Borghese (q.v.). This unit was fiercely loyal and fought well in northeastern Italy against the Yugoslav partisans.

The RSI Air Force had some strong fighting units, particularly those of torpedo bombers and fighters. The torpedo bombers units, flying the obsolete S.M. 79, fought in the Anzio zone, in the Ionian and Aegean Seas, and hit Allied shipping as far away as Gibraltar. In the end, they sacrificed themselves almost to the last man. The fighter units were used with some success against the rising onslaught of Allied bombers over northern Italy. Sometimes marked with a double insignia (Italian-Republican and German), they flew the modern Italian-made Macchi MC.205 and Fiat G.55, and the German-made Messerschmitt Bf-109G.

The RSI also formed a militia organization, the *Guardia Nazionale Repubblicana* (National Republican Guards), which included the former Black Shirts (q.v.). These units were used mainly on a territorial basis. Another RSI paramilitary organization was the *Brigate Nere* (Black Brigades), created by RSI Minister of the Interior Alessandro Pavolini. These well-paid units were especially brutal and employed heinous techniques in antipartisan actions. This was largely responsible for the outbreak of civil war in northern Italy.

When the Axis front collapsed in April 1945, the RSI went with it, even though Pavolini wanted to convert all of Valtellina into a gigantic fortress and resist to the last man. The RSI lived its last tragic day on 28 April 1945, when Mussolini and some of his Fascist leaders were executed by Italian partisans.

Francesco Fatutta

Additional Reading

Deakin, F.W., *The Brutal Friendship: Mussolini,*

Hitler, and the Fall of Italian Fascism (1962).

Pansa, G., *L'Esercito di Salò* (1970).

Army, New Zealand

The sense of nationhood in New Zealand grew at the turn of the century. Like Australia, it was strengthened in war, first in South Africa, where the New Zealanders excelled at guerrilla warfare, and then in World War I, where they paid a terrible price for their involvement.

New Zealand had a very small permanent force of regulars, some 500 men, which was complemented by a 12,000-member territorial force structured so that on the outbreak of war it could expand into one infantry division, one medium artillery brigade, and coastal defense troops.

New Zealand was organized into three districts: northern (Auckland), central (Wellington), and southern (Whangarei). Field troops consisted of four rifle regiments, three infantry battalions, sixteen assorted artillery batteries, three combat engineers companies, and three signal depots. Coastal defense troops consisted of three infantry battalions, two heavy coastal batteries, and antiaircraft units.

When war broke out in 1939, New Zealand lent its support to Great Britain, as it had previously, by forming New Zealand Forces Overseas. Troops were sent to train in Egypt and subsequently saw action in Greece, Crete, North Africa, and Italy. When Japan threatened after 1941, New Zealand forces became involved in the Pacific putting a severe strain on the country's manpower resources.

In 1941, in Greece (q.v.), the New Zealand troops resisted the German advance strongly. When, perhaps foolishly, they were ordered to Crete (q.v.), they made the Germans suffer. However, they were forced to withdraw and lost as many as half their force as POWs. The New Zealand 2nd Division, which fought bravely, was essentially the nation-in-arms. It was considered by most to be one of the best. It often supported British units when they assaulted enemy lines. Even so, many British leaders, particularly Sir Alan Cunningham (q.v.), tended to treat them (and the Australians) with disdain.

Before El Alamein (q.v.), the New Zealanders suffered at the hands of the *Afrika Korps* (q.v.) at Mersa Matrúh (q.v.), but showed their determination in a night attack on Ruweisat Ridge (q.v.) during that preliminary battle of Alamein. During the main battle of Alamein in 1942, they held the crucial sector of the Allied line. Under a rolling barrage, their 5th Brigade advanced and after bitter close-quarter fighting secured all its objectives. Afterward, they played a vital role in the victorious Operation SUPERCHARGE, leading the decisive assaults that followed a superb enveloping movement, clinching the battle of Mareth (q.v.). Led by General Bernard Freyberg (q.v.), the New Zealanders became a efficient, although diminishing, force.

Of special note was the 28th Maori Battalion. Its members would dance the *"Haka"* before going into battle and then sweep across their taken ground with great style. The Maoris were the only all-volunteer unit in the New Zealand forces. A remarkable 16,000 of them signed up. Most served in *Pakeha* units at home, but some 3,000 fought in the Maori Battalion, which suffered 612 killed.

From November 1943, the New Zealanders fought in Italy under the U.S. Fifth Army. They were prominent in the battle of Monte Cassino (q.v.) in February 1944, although they were withdrawn before the final assault. The long siege exacted a high toll.

A total of 146,000 New Zealanders served in their army during World War II, 98,000 of them overseas. To put the numbers in perspective, nearly 60 percent of the male population between the ages of eighteen and forty-five were mobilized. New Zealand casualties totaled 33,000, with some 6,000 killed. There was heroism as well as sacrifice, with the awards of eight Victoria Crosses and one Bar (second award), nearly 200 Distinguished Service Orders and twenty-four Bars, 262 Military Crosses and thirteen Bars, and some 3,000 Mentions in Dispatches (*see* Medals and Decorations).

Chris Westhorp

Additional Reading

Mollo, Andrew, *The Armed Forces of World War II* (1981).

Wood, Frederick L.W., *The New Zealand People at War: Political and External Affairs* (1958).

Army, Norwegian

Norway is a large, mountainous, and heavily forested country that is thinly populated, making for good defensive territory. Prior to World War II, however, the Norwegians neglected their own defense needs in favor of domestic political priorities. As a result, they had a badly trained and inadequately equipped force, possessing neither armored vehicles nor antitank weapons. They sought to maintain a neutral status (expecting that would provide security against attack), while believing at the same time that Britain would protect them in the event of any invasion. Thus, on the eve of World War II, the Norwegian Army was little more than a provincial infantry force. They were not, however, totally apathetic, and a volunteer battalion fought for Finland in the 1939–1940 Winter War (q.v.).

The army was organized on a militia basis with fixed cadres. There were nearly 13,000 men in the *Landstorm*, or territorial force, together with some 2,000 permanent soldiers in the *Landvärn*, or active army. They had a total of six divisions plus a number of supporting elements, including sixteen infantry regiments, three dragoon regiments, four artillery regiments, and engineer and air units.

The 1st, 2nd, and 5th Divisions, based at Holden, Oslo, and Trondheim, respectively, each had one cavalry, one artillery, and three infantry regiments. The 2nd Division also had the Royal Guard (four rifle companies) and the 5th Division had an engineer battalion. The 3rd and 4th Divisions, at Kristianland and Bergen respectively, each had two infantry regiments, a mountain artillery battalion, and a cyclist company. The 6th Division, based at Harstad near Narvik, had three infantry regiments, two independent infantry battalions, a mountain artillery battery, and an engineer battalion.

Armed with Krag-Jørgensen rifles, Madesn machine guns, mortars, and light artillery pieces, the Norwegians had the potential to offer significant resistance. Their politicians, however, hampered them by authorizing only a partial mobilization at the start of the war. By the time the full extent of the situation was apparent, a great many of the Norwegian military supply centers were captured.

After the Allies withdrew from Norway (*see* Norway 1940), King Haakon VII (q.v.), along with his government and many members of the *Storting* (Parliament), left for Britain to establish a government-in-exile. General Otto Ruge (q.v.), the Norwegian commander in chief, remained behind with his troops, but after sixty-two days of resistance he had little option but to surrender his command at Trondheim. The Norwegian Army effected well its holding operations and tactical withdrawal, given the means at its disposal. It tried to buy time with minimal losses, but it was doomed to fail in the end.

Many Norwegian soldiers managed to escape to Britain. Encouraged by their government, they continued the fight, retraining as SOE (q.v.) guerrillas and returning to Norway to establish an effective resistance network with which to fight the German occupiers. Norwegian ships, aircraft, and men formed into several combat units, including an infantry brigade and six air squadrons. Many also served with various British units. The Norwegian government-in-exile continued supportive broadcasts to the Norwegian people and assisted all Norwegians seeking safety in exile.

Chris Westhorp

Additional Reading

Andenas, Johs., O. Riste, and M. Skodvin, *Norway and the Second World War* (1966).

Derry, Thomas K., *The Campaign in Norway* (1952).

Mollo, Andrew, *The Armed Forces of World War II* (1981).

Army, Polish

When Poland was reborn in 1918, it immediately had to form an army to defend its independence. When the Polish-Soviet War (q.v.) came to an end in the fall of 1920, the Polish Army had 900,000 troops. Poland retained compulsory two-year military service. Immediately after the war, the 300,000-man Polish Army consisted of ten corps organized into thirty infantry divisions, ten cavalry brigades, ten heavy artillery regiments, and five tank battalions. During the 1920s, the planned mobilization potential of the Polish Army was sixty divisions, but that level was never achieved. Poland also had a 30,000-strong Frontier Defense Corps.

The worldwide depression of 1929–1935, which saw Poland's gross national product drop by 50 percent, hampered all efforts to develop a military industry and modernize Poland's armed forces. In 1936, a modernization plan was finally introduced in response to the rapid rise of German and Soviet military strength. The plan called for the expenditure of $900 million over a four- to six-year period. By the start of World War II, however, only a small portion of the plan had been realized. In general, the Polish war industry achieved the goals for hand-held weapons and machine guns. It fell somewhat short in the areas of mortars and ammunition. Under a licensing agreement with Bofors, the country also started producing antiaircraft and antitank guns, but the actual numbers were far from sufficient.

By the time the war started, the Polish Army had approximately 1.2 million rifles, 41,000 machine guns, 3,500 antitank rifles, 1,200 mortars, 1,200 antitank guns, 462 antiaircraft guns, and

Polish Army Order of Battle 1939–1945

	September 1939	May 1940	West 1945	East 1945
Divisions				
Infantry	39	2	2	14
Armored	0	0	1	0
Mountain	2	0	0	0
Totals	41	2	3	14
Brigades				
Cavalry	11	0	0	0
Mechanized	2	1	0	0
Armored	0	0	1	5
Parachute	0	0	1	0
Total	13	1	2	5

3,388 artillery pieces of various sizes. They also had 574 reconnaissance Whippet tanks, 211 light tanks, and 100 assorted armored vehicles. All in all, the Polish Army was very poorly motorized. Its total number of motor vehicles was somewhere between 5,000 to 6,000 plus 1,200 motorcycles. The railroad was the major source of Polish mobility. Despite these slim mobility resources, Polish doctrine continued to stress maneuver as derived from their experiences of the 1920 war. This disparity between doctrine and means was especially stark when confronted by an enemy with hundreds of thousands of motor vehicles at its disposal.

On 30 April 1938, the Polish military introduced Plan W, its new flexible mobilization plan. It spoke of drafting 1.3 million new conscripts and raising thirty-nine infantry divisions, eleven cavalry brigades, two armored brigades, and three independent tank battalions. The majority of these units were to be mobilized in the event of a national emergency, while the remaining eleven divisions were to be called up only after the announcement of a general mobilization.

The structure of the Polish high command changed several times between the world wars. Having returned to power in 1926, Marshal Józef Piłsudski (q.v.) retained the dual posts of minister of military affairs and inspector general of the armed forces (GISZ). In case of war, this latter post automatically became the commander in chief. After his death in 1935, the office of inspector general/commander in chief passed to Marshal Edward Śmigły-Rydz (q.v.). The following year, the Committee for the Defense of the Polish Commonwealth (KOR) was created. It was headed by the president of Poland, and included the GISZ, the minister of military affairs, the chief of the general staff, and several key cabinet ministers. The KOR had its own standing office, which was authorized to conduct a wide array of functions relating to the preparation of the armed forces for war.

As both Soviet and German military might grew, Polish contingency plans adapted accordingly and became more defensive in nature. Separate plans were developed to fight either adversary. The general framework for Plan "East" was ready at the beginning of 1939, while Plan "West" did not go beyond the initial stages of a Polish-German war.

In 1939, the Polish Army was organized into the following field armies and operational groups:

Narew	— two infantry divisions, two cavalry brigades;
Modlin	— two infantry divisions, two cavalry brigades;
Pomorże	— five infantry divisions, one cavalry brigade;
Poznań	— four infantry divisions, two cavalry brigades;
Łódź	— five infantry divisions, two cavalry brigades;
Kraków	— seven infantry divisions, one cavalry brigade, one motorized brigade, one mountain brigade.

The strategic and operational reserves were deployed as follows:

Wyszkow	— three infantry divisions in support of the north;
Kutno	— two infantry divisions in support of the Pomorże and Poznań armies;
Tarnów	— two infantry divisions in support of the south;
Prusy	— the main strategic reserve of eight infantry divisions, one cavalry brigade, and two tank battalions positioned in the vicinity of Radom and Kielce.

When the Poles learned of a buildup of German forces in Slovakia in July 1939, they hastily formed a weak army called Karpaty, consisting of two mountain brigades and various national defense units.

The Poles delayed general mobilization until 30 August 1939. As a result, many Polish units, particularly reserve formations, never reached their full strength. The Germans attacked on 1 September 1939. When the Soviets attacked on 17 September, the last hope for a successful defense vanished. The Polish Army in Poland ceased to exist on 5 October 1939. During the campaign, the Poles lost some 210,000 killed and wounded, 580,000 captured by the Germans, and more than 200,000 captured by the Soviets. Approximately 100,000 Polish soldiers and officers escaped into Romania, Hungary, and the Baltic states. A considerable number made their way to either France or the Middle East, where Polish forces-in-exile were being formed.

During command-level talks between Polish and French military officials held in Paris in May 1939, an agreement was reached to form units from Polish immigrants. At that time, about 500,000 Poles lived in France, and it was estimated that about 10 percent of them were suitable for military service. After Poland fell, a government-in-exile was formed in Paris headed by General Władysław Sikorski (q.v.). He also held the posts of minister of military affairs and commander in chief of the Polish armed forces. A new Polish Army was formed from the Polish immigrant community, along with Polish officers and soldiers filtering in from Hungary, Romania, the Baltics, and occupied Poland.

By June 1940, the reconstituted Polish armed forces numbered 84,500 troops, including 1,374 seamen in Britain and 9,556 airmen in Britain and France. The Podhale Rifle Brigade fought in Norway and Narvik (qq.v.), and the Independent Carpathian Rifle Brigade was formed in the Middle East. By the time the Germans invaded France, Polish ground forces consisted of two infantry divisions, a motorized brigade, several specialist units, and two more divisions in the process of organization.

After France capitulated, only about 30 percent of the Polish Army managed to escape to Great Britain. The 1st Grenadier Division was destroyed in the fighting in Lorraine. The 2nd Rifle Division crossed over into Switzerland only to be interned there. Those forces fleeing to Britain eventually formed the Polish I Corps, consisting of the 1st Armored Division, the 4th Infantry Division, and the 1st Independent Parachute Brigade. The 1st Armored Division took part in the Allied invasion of Normandy (q.v.), and the 1st Independent Parachute Brigade jumped during Operation MARKET-GARDEN.

Polish units were also raised from Polish officers and soldiers captured in the 1939 fighting, as well as Poles deported to labor camps in Siberia between 1939 and 1941. On the basis of an August 1941 agreement between Sikorski and Soviet premier Josef Stalin (q.v.), a Polish force of 96,000 was formed. The new army was supposed to operate against the Germans on the eastern front, but there were conflicts and tensions between Soviet authorities and Polish commanders right from the start. The British also brought pressure to have the Polish forces transferred to the Middle East. Thus, in August 1942, General Władysław Anders (q.v.) led 74,000 Polish soldiers and several thousand accompanying civilians to Palestine via Iran. They joined the Carpathian Rifle Brigade, already fighting in Libya, and formed the Polish II Corps.

Near the end of 1943, Polish II Corps transferred to the Italian front. In May 1944, the 48,000-man corps consisted of the 3rd Carpathian Rifle Division, the 5th Kresowa Infantry Division, the 2nd Armored Brigade, and an artillery group. The II Corps played a key role in the Allied drive on Rome, including its celebrated capture of the German stronghold at Monte Cassino (q.v.). In April 1945, II Corps took Bologna. During the Italian campaign, II Corps suffered 17,000 casualties; yet by the end of the war, its ranks had swelled to near army size by a steady stream of Poles previously impressed in the *Wehrmacht*.

After the war, the Polish armed forces in the west numbered close to 200,000, including 14,000 in the air force and 4,000 in the navy. During the fighting, this exile force sustained 43,500 casualties, including 7,600 dead. When the Polish armed forces demobilized in 1946, only a small number returned to Communist-dominated Poland. Many Poles remained in Britain and formed a tight-knit exile community.

After the evacuation of General Anders's force to the Middle East, hundreds of thousands of Poles still remained in the Soviet Union. For the most part, they were persons previously expelled from the Polish territory taken by the Soviets in 1939. In May 1943, the Germans discovered the mass graves of Polish officers murdered by the Soviet NKVD (q.v.) at Katyń (q.v.). When the Polish government in London requested an independent investigation from the International Red Cross, the Soviets used this as a pretext to sever diplomatic relations. The Soviets then started to form the basis of a Polish political power that would be dependent on Moscow. The Union of Polish Patriots was formed in May 1943 in Moscow, and from this organization arose the first formations of the Polish People's Army (PPA) that would fight alongside the Red Army.

The first PPA unit formed was the 1st Infantry Division, named ironically after Poland's national hero, Tadeusz Kościuszko, who had led a Polish revolt against the Russians. The division first saw action at Lenino in October 1943 and suffered severe losses. More units were added, first bringing the PPA up to corps size and then army size. In 1944, it was designated the First Polish People's Army, under the command of General Zygmunt Berling (q.v.). By the time the Soviets crossed the Bug River in July 1944, it consisted of five infantry divisions, a tank brigade, and artillery units amounting to about 107,000 troops. The First Polish People's Army was on the Vistula River opposite Warsaw during the 1944 Rising (q.v.) but was unable to reach the city and aid the rebelling Polish Home Army.

As the Red Army pushed west across Poland, the government formed by the Soviet-backed Polish Committee of National Liberation expanded the Polish People's Forces under the Soviet supreme command. It raised a second army and formed the nucleus for a third. The nominal commander of these forces was Marshal Michał Rola-Żymierski. By March 1945, the total size of the PPF amounted to fourteen infantry divisions, an armored corps, and sixteen artillery brigades. The total number of troops was around 400,000, half of which forming frontline units. As the Second Polish People's Army moved toward Dresden, the First Polish People's Armies took part in the April 1945 attack against Berlin (q.v.). Total Polish casualties for the Berlin operation came to 30,500.

By the end of World War II, there were more than 620,000 Poles in various Polish armies, east and west. They were the first of the Allies to fight the Axis. During the war, the Poles fought on five different European fronts: Norway, North Africa, Italy, Western Europe, and Eastern Europe.

Marian Zgórniak

Additional Reading

Anders, Władysław, *An Army in Exile: The Story of the Second Polish Corps* (1949).
Broń, Barwa I., *Wojsko Polskie* (1984).
Garliński, Józef, *Poland in the Second World War* (1985).
Imar, K., *With the Tanks of the 1st Polish Armoured Division* (1946).
Mollo, Andrew, *The Armed Forces of World War II* (1981).
Zaloga, Steven, and Victor Madej, *The Polish Campaign 1939* (1985).

Army, Romanian

The Romanian Army was the main ally of Nazi Germany on the eastern front. Romanian motives for the attack against the Soviet Union were the recuperation of Bessarabia and northern Bukovina, ceded to the Soviet Union in July 1940. There were ideological reasons as well. Like German chancellor Adolf Hitler (q.v.), Romanian dictator Marshal Ion Antonescu (q.v.) believed strongly in the necessity of defeating Bolshevism by military methods.

On 2 July 1941, when the German Eleventh Army launched its attack across the Prut River, six Romanian divisions started to move into Bessarabia. In this province and in northern Bukovina, tens of thousands of Jews were massacred by Romanian military units and the survivors were deported to Trans-Dniestria—a part of Ukraine between the Dniester and Bug Rivers under Romanian administration.

On 18 August 1941, Romanian Fourth Army launched a large-scale attack on Odessa. However, the city was not captured until mid-October and then only with the help of German reinforcements. Between 5 August and 15 October 1941, Eighteen Romanian divisions fought to capture Odessa, suffering heavy losses. From the start of the war to the capture of Odessa, the Romanians acknowledged 70,000 dead and 100,000 wounded. A large-scale massacre of local Jews followed the capture of Odessa. The perpetrators were Romanian military units.

At the beginning of 1942, General Ion Iacobici, chief of the Romanian Army staff, opposed Antonescu's decision to send more troops to the eastern front. Iacobici cited the dubious military efficiency of the Romanian units, heavy losses, lack of training, and severe problems related to logistics and the nondelivery of certain heavy armaments promised by the Germans. As a result, he was dismissed by Antonescu.

During the summer of 1942, twenty-seven Romanian divisions fought on the eastern front. On 7 June 1942, Romanian units were massively involved in the final offensive against Sevastopol (q.v.). In the Caucasus (q.v.) operations, Romanian troops were also an important help to the Germans.

The Romanian Third and Fourth Armies were heavily involved in the battle of Stalingrad (q.v.). General Petre Dumitrescu's (q.v.) Romanian Third Army was in the line west of Stalingrad and was separated from the Hungarian Second Army by the Italian Eighth Army. The Romanian Fourth Army under General Constantinescu was positioned south of Stalingrad. On 19 November 1942, a strong Soviet armored force broke through the Romanian Third Army despite the desperate counterattacks of generals Radu and Michail Lascar. Three days later, twenty German divisions and two Romanian divi-

Romanian Army Order of Battle 1940–1943

Divisions	1940	1943
Infantry	19	19
Armored	1	1
Cavalry	0	6
Mountain	0	4
Motorized	0	1
Total	20	31

sions were encircled. About 30,000 Romanians from the Third Army were captured by the Soviets. From these prisoners, Soviet authorities and Romanian Communist émigrés built the pro-Soviet and pro-Communist Tudor Vladimirescu Division.

After the disaster of Stalingrad, sharp official notes were exchanged between General Erich von Manstein (q.v.), and General Ilia Steflea (q.v.), chief of the Romanian Army staff. Responding to German accusations concerning the poor results shown by the Romanian units, General Steflea cited the following as causes of the disaster of the Third Romanian Army: a front of 156 kilometers, slow cooperation of German units, and the lack of antitank weapons and tanks. General Radu's 1st Armored Division belonging to the Romanian Third Army, for example, had about 100 Czech tanks that were unable to oppose the Soviet T-34s.

The Romanian armies again suffered heavy losses during the recapture of Odessa by the Soviets in April 1944. About half of the 195,000 men of the German Seventeenth Army holding Crimea were Romanians. Many of these troops, realizing that, like Stalingrad, they would be the last evacuated, surrendered to the Red Army in northern Crimea. After several months of calm, the front line that had stabilized between Iasi and Kishinev was broken, and the Soviet units captured fifteen German divisions and several Romanian divisions.

On 23 August 1944, a coup overthrew Marshal Antonescu and Romania capitulated, left the Axis, and on 26 August, declared war on Germany. These events were catastrophic for Germany, which lost not only Romanian oil, but also its whole defensive system in southeastern Europe. Put under Soviet military command, Romanian military units fought with losses up to 40 and 50 percent against the Germans. Twenty-seven Romanian divisions fought the Germans in northern Transylvania at Debrecin and Budapest (q.v.) in Hungary and in Czechoslovakia. Smaller Romanian military units, including an armored regiment and subunits belonging to a railway brigade, fought in Austria as well.

Radu Ioanid

Additional Reading

Erikson, John, *The Road to Berlin* (1984).
———, *The Road to Stalingrad* (1975).
Mollo, Andrew, *The Armed Forces of World War II* (1981)

Army, Soviet

After the Russian Revolution and the subsequent civil war, the Soviet military developed along lines and patterns similar to those of most nations. The great Soviet tactician, Marshal Mikhail Tukhachevsky (q.v.), established the training goals and guidelines for the Red Army. Principles of war and tactics were taught at the higher military academy named after the Soviet's foremost military strategist, Mikhail Frunze. As a result of interwar political struggles, neither of those leaders was alive at the start of World War II, but their methods and techniques did survive.

As the decade of the 1930s drew to a close, the Soviets had the opportunity to observe their equipment and tactics in action. The first such action was the Spanish civil war (q.v.), where the Soviets sent small units and military equipment to participate on the side of the Republicans. Although the military units did not fare particularly well, the equipment received invaluable live-fire testing. Despite serious doctrinal shortcomings, careful attention to after-action evaluations allowed the Soviet generals to identify weaknesses, and develop or refine their tactical doctrine accordingly.

The next action was the Winter War (q.v.) with Finland. It too proved less than successful, even embarrassing. The Finns, with significantly less manpower and equipment, were able to withstand Soviet military strength far longer than they should have. Again, the Soviet leaders were able to learn from their mistakes in this nearly abortive effort. They altered their command and control procedures, inasmuch as the political situation would allow.

In the summer of 1941, the Soviets had five fronts (army groups) facing the Germans from the Baltic to the Black Sea. The Soviet forces included 134 divisions, 6,000 tanks, and 8,000 aircraft massed along the borders of the nations already captured by the Germans. In addition to Soviet Premier Josef Stalin (q.v.), the principal military players included Semen Timoshenko (q.v.), the commisar of defense; Georgy Zhukov (q.v.), the chief of the general staff; and the five front commanders, Markian Popov, Nikolai Kuznetsov, Dimitry Pavlov (qq.v.), Mikhail Kirponos, and I.V. Tyulenov.

In the initial German attack in June 1941, forty Soviet divisions were destroyed or captured. Within three months, Popov and Kuznetsov were relieved, Kirponos was killed in action, and Stalin had Pavlov executed. (Pavlov was replaced by Timoshenko as Western Front commander.) Only Tyulenov survived the initial German onslaught. Ironically, he still commanded the Soviet Trans-Caucasus Front at the conclusion of the war.

The fronts facing Poland and Hungary and standing in the path of the German march toward Moscow each contained three or four armies, with

Table 1

Soviet Army Divisional and Corps Strengths

Unit Type	No. of Troops	Automatic Weapons	Artillery (over 75mm)	AT Weapons	Motor Vehicles	Horses	Tanks
Rifle Division c. 1943	9,619	1,082	44	262	180	3,840	0
Cavalry Division c. 1943	4,600	230	24	130	100	6,800	0
Artillery Division c. 1944	9,700	168	180	288	1,530	—	0
Tank Corps c. 1944	10,980	517	42	289	1,610	—	208
Mechanized Corps c. 1944	15,020	895	38	443	2,120	—	197

eight to ten divisions each. These fronts were heavily armored and straddled major avenues of approach across the Soviet Union. By contrast, Tyulenov's Southern Front had only two armies with eight divisions each. The terrain in the south, however, clearly favored the defense.

With many young and inexperienced commanders at division and army level, the Soviets were inept in the initial days of the war. A lesson not learned in the Spanish and Finnish wars was use of forces as combined arms. This was particularly evident in the use of such specialized troops as engineers and artillery. Soviet commanders tended to spread these units out equally among subordinate commands without regard to terrain. As a result, those forces—in short supply to begin with—that could most assist in the defense when used in mass formations at appropriate defensive positions, were fragmented to the extent that they became ineffective. The Soviets also lacked the supplies and equipment to maintain fully operational combat forces. Finally, the basic Soviet maneuver element, the rifle corps, was a huge organization that proved nearly impossible to manage.

To correct all of these problems, the Soviet high command, the *Stavka* (q.v.), reduced the division commander's span of control by removing specialized units from within divisions and assigning them to armies, or fronts. The rifle corps itself was eliminated, and the infantry division was reduced to about 11,000 troops. Tank elements from the mechanized corps were kept as separate brigades and attached to armies or fronts as needed. To further reduce the front commander's span of control, no more than six armies were assigned to a front. This allowed more flexibility and better control of the maneuver elements.

The Soviets were able to introduce two important new weapons in the months following the German attack. The first weapon, the *Katyusha,* was a multiple rocket launcher with devastating firepower. The second weapon, unveiled at the end of summer 1941, was the T-34 tank. Although weighing only twenty-six tons, the T-34 had a low profile, and its extra-wide tracks allowed it to traverse terrain that mired down the German *Panzers.* Initially used by inexperienced troops following commands and orders from inexperienced leaders, the T-34 merely held its own. As the war progressed, however, the crews and commanders became much more proficient. In the terrain of western Russia, ideally suited for swift, massive, and armor-heavy forces, the T-34 became one of the most formidable weapons of World War II.

By the spring of 1942, Soviet factories were producing high volumes of tanks. Colonel General Yakov Fedorenko, the chief of Armored Forces Administration, started forming the Soviet armored units into a new organization called a tank corps. A tank corps consisted of three tank brigades of fifty-three tanks each, plus a mechanized rifle brigade. Later in 1942, the Soviets started to form tank armies, usually consisting of two tank corps and one mechanized corps. The Soviet tank and mechanized corps were roughly the equivalent of the German *Panzer* and *Panzergrenadier* divisions.

Following the huge Soviet losses during Operation BARBAROSSA, the *Stavka* reorganized the divisions and corps, and created a sixth front on the battlefield. The Bryansk Front, commanded by General Andrei Yeremenko (q.v.), was placed into position between Timoshenko's Western and Kirponos's Southwestern fronts. In addition, a reserve front was established southwest of Moscow, under the command of Zhukov. This reserve was meant as a blocking force if Germany's Army Group Center pushed toward the Soviet capital.

During this period, the Soviets reinstituted the political commissar system among their combat units. A holdover from the days of the revolution, it quickly proved useless. The Soviet commissar was a strange mixture of political zealot and a military commander. Some had military experience (usually in the revolution), but this was not a requirement. The commissar's sole responsibility was to insure the Communist Party's goals were executed by military leaders, regardless of the soundness of any specific action. Nikolai Vashugin, political commissar of the Southwestern Front, was typical. Unhappy with the slowness of advance by a mechanized corps, he took personal command and led the corps to total defeat, including leading a tank unit into a swamp where it had to be abandoned. Typically, he committed suicide, but not before he decimated sorely needed units.

The commissar system fell into disrepute, for obvious reasons, and eventually was replaced by assistant commanders for political affairs. This change was more than in name, as the old commissars held "dual command" to the extent that no order could be issued or carried out without their signature. They could, however, issue orders (as Vashugin did) over the objections of the military commander. The political affairs officers, however, saw their responsibility limited to ensuring proper political indoctrination of all soldiers within a unit. In 1942, their title was changed to deputy commander for political affairs, but the concept of a single commander was firmly established, and the military leaders were able to execute their orders without the blessing of the commissars or political affairs officers.

Although the new reorganizations, the introduction of new weapons, and increasing the number of fronts in the battle did not stop the Germans, it did slow them down. When the harsh Russian winter arrived, the Soviets were able to place strong defensive rings around Moscow (q.v.) and prevent the capture of the city. The Germans estimated the Soviets had lost 2.5 million soldiers and half of their tanks and aircraft in the days following the June 1941 invasion. In the three defensive rings set up around Moscow, the Soviets still managed to mass eighty rifle divisions, two motorized infantry divisions, and thirteen tank brigades armed with the newly produced T-34s.

The Soviet chain of command, by this time fully developed and solidified, flowed downward from Stalin, through the *Stavka* and general staff, to the front commanders. These commanders, in turn, developed operational orders from national policy, and passed them down through army and division levels. The political officers had a shorter chain of command, as they each had a direct link to Lavrenty Beria, chief of the NKVD (qq.v.). After the commissars were replaced by the political affairs officers, the order process became more simplified. The political affairs officers, however, still had direct access to Beria through former commissar channels. They could not affect the missions of the field commanders, but they could report on any unacceptable political actions by the officers in the units. By this implicit control, the party continued to influence the political thinking, if not the military decisions, of its subordinates in the field.

As Soviet forces, in combination with the harsh winter, brought the Germans to a standstill, the Soviet high command formulated a counterattack and initiated it in early December 1941. Although not highly successful, it did drive the Germans back sufficiently so that Moscow was no longer threatened. The organization of the Soviet military, as developed and refined through the first six months after the invasion, remained basically the same for the remainder of the war.

When the Soviets started their counteroffensive in the spring of 1942, the military focused on one basic principle of war—mass. At Stalingrad (q.v.), Zhukov commanded three fronts that included 1,100 aircraft, 894 tanks, and more than 500,000 troops (with an additional 500,000 in reserve). He also had an average of 210 artillery pieces per kilometer on a sixty-five-kilometer battlefront. With this enormous concentration

TABLE 2

Soviet Army Order of Battle 1941–1945

Divisions	
Rifle	413
Guards Rifle	121
Motorized	24
Guards Motorized	2
Cavalry	69
Guards Cavalry	17
Mountain	22
Artillery	90
Corps	
Tank	31
Guards Tank	12
Mechanized	30
Guards Mechanized	9

Note: The Soviets never fielded this many divisions at the same time. Many Soviet divisions were destroyed and reformed, often more than once.

of forces, preceded by a thorough artillery preparation of the battlefield, the Soviets were able to start their own push toward the German homeland.

From 1942 through early 1944, the Soviets generally had three fronts on line pushing westward at any given time. On either flank they had additional forces, usually a front, whose mission was to protect the flanks of the main force and eliminate any enemy pockets that might be bypassed. In 1944, having gained the strategic initiative and having the Germans virtually in full retreat, the Soviets put four to six fronts on the battle line, with additional fronts continuing to protect the flanks.

Prior to 1942, the Soviets normally used a single front to conduct offensive operations. During the Moscow counteroffensive, they developed and perfected the use of groups of fronts, and the practice became entrenched in Soviet doctrine. The Soviets also organized second echelon forces at both the army and front level into "mobile groups." These units were organized to exploit a weakened enemy, driving deep into his rear areas to secure military objectives.

It is often noted that the Germans were defeated by the Soviet weather as much as by Soviet military power. That is an oversimplification. As a result of their massive territory, and the relative distance of their capital from their borders, the Soviets had the dubious luxury of allowing the invader to penetrate deep into their interior without it being fatal. They wisely moved their railroad rolling stock safely into the eastern provinces, preventing capture of these vital assets. Thus, the Soviets still had the transportation system readily available to move their troops to the western front lines when they went on the counteroffensive.

The structure and organization of the Soviet Army changed very little after World War II. Soviet strategy, based on experience in the "Great Patriotic War," continued to call for deep penetration into an enemy's reserves, followed by exploitation and encirclement of enemy pockets. Soviet doctrine continued to stress mass piled upon mass in the attack. The World War II–era mobile groups were reorganized into the feared (by NATO) operational maneuver groups, with essentially the same mission: concentrate mass and mobility at the right time and with the maximum amount of fire support in order to exploit a locally outnumbered enemy.

Prior to the military cutbacks announced in late 1989, the Soviet Union had more than 1.8 million troops. For the successor Russian Army, the tactics developed and fine-tuned in the cauldron of World War II can be expected to remain the basic principles of war for any future mobilization or large-scale conflict.

Thomas Cagley

Additional Reading
Bialer, Seweryn (ed.), *Stalin and His Generals* (1984).
Djakov, Yuri L., and Tatjana S. Bushuyeva, *The Red Army and the Wehrmacht: How the Soviets Militarized Germany, 1923–33, and Paved the Way for Fascism* (1995).
House, Jonathan M., *Toward Combined Arms Warfare: A Survey of 20th Century Tactics, Doctrine, and Organization* (1984).
Kerr, Walter B., *The Russian Army: Its Men, Its Leaders, and Its Battles* (1944).
Moynahan, Brian, *Claws of the Bear: The History of the Red Army from the Revolution to the Present* (1989).
Seaton, Albert and Joan Seaton, *The Soviet Army: 1918 to the Present* (1966).
Shukman, Harold (ed.), *Stalin's Generals* (1993).
Sokolovsky, Vasily, *Soviet Military Strategy* (1968).

Army, Spanish

The 1936 uprising against the Spanish government split the army as it did the populace. Prior to the revolt, Spain's military consisted of two forces: the Peninsular Army and the more potent Army of Africa. The latter, composed of *Regulares* (native Moroccan volunteers under the command of Spanish officers), and the battle-tested Spanish Foreign Legion, gave the Nationalists a loyal force of approximately 24,000 men. The Army of Africa went over to the Nationalist side following their commander, General Francisco Franco (q.v.). The Peninsular Army, from general down to private, divided itself according to political, religious, economic, and local beliefs. It was estimated that in Spain proper, more than half of the army remained loyal to the government, while more than half of the officer corps sided with the Nationalists.

Both the Republican and the Nationalist armies were composed of a nucleus of professional military to which volunteers were attached. On the Republican side, Communists, anarchists, and other leftist groups formed militias to defend the republic. The Soviet Union, France, and Mexico sent needed military and nonmilitary materiel to the Republicans, while leftist volunteers flocked to Spain and formed the international brigades to combat the spread of Fascism (q.v.). The Nationalists also counted on their own militia of more than 50,000 armed combatants who aligned themselves with two major organizations: the ultra-traditionalist Carlist *Requétes* from Navarre, and the pro-Fascist *Falange Española*. While the Republican government received aid from like-minded governments, the Nationalists received aid from the right-wing governments of Italy and Germany.

When German armed forces invaded the Soviet Union on 22 June 1941, the Spanish government perceived this as a splendid opportunity to continue the crusade against Bolshevism that began during the Spanish civil war (q.v.). Spain's foreign minister, Ramon Serrano Suner, stated that Spain had a "blood debt" requiring repayment.

The call went out for Spanish volunteers to form a division to fight in Russia. While the majority of volunteers were regular Spanish Army officers and soldiers, there were in the beginning a substantial number of Falangists and students who served as soldiers. Initially, the Blue Division (so-called because of the blue shirts worn by the Falangists) was composed of four infantry regiments. It was later reduced to three to conform to the organization of the German Army. By the middle of July 1941, 18,000 volunteers reached their training base in Bavaria, where they were christened the 250th Infantry Division. The man selected by Franco to command this group of volunteers was General Augustin Muñoz Grandes, a trusted comrade from the Moroccan wars who also led an army corps during the civil war. In December 1942, Grandes was replaced by General Emilio Esteban Infantes.

On 20 August 1941, after brief but intensive training, the Spanish *guripas* (GIs) began their long journey to the sector of Russia occupied by Germany's Army Group North. The Blue Division became part of the XXXVIII *Korps* of the German Eighteenth Army, and was deployed around the banks of the Volkhov River. While stationed on its shores, the Blue Division fought pitched battles against Soviet forces trying to break the iron ring that was slowly strangling Leningrad (q.v.). Suffering heavy casualties, due to the Spanish penchant for close quarters combat and from the bitter cold, the Spaniards demonstrated their mettle. By 15 January 1942, after three months on the line, Spanish battle casualties numbered 3,000 killed, wounded, and missing. The situation was about to change, however, after the German defeats at Stalingrad and Kursk (qq.v.).

With those defeats Franco realized that Germany was incapable of winning the war. That, along with pressure from the Allies, forced him to recall the volunteers from the Soviet Union in October 1943. So as not to totally alienate German chancellor Adolf Hitler (q.v.), Franco replaced the division with the so-called Blue Legion, which was made up of between 1,000 and 1,500 men. The Blue Legion fought a retreating war along with the German Army, as the Red Army pushed into the *Reich*. By April 1944, the Blue Legion itself was called back to Spain, and official Spanish involvement in World War II came to an end.

Unofficially, some veterans of the Blue Division and Legion joined the *Waffen-SS* (q.v.) and fought to the bitter end, taking part in the defense of the *Reich* Chancellery under the command of *SS-Obersturmbannführer* Miguel Ezquerra Sanchez. In the end, Spain's "blood debt" to Nazi Germany cost 13,000 casualties, with more than 4,000 killed in action.

José Alvarez

Additional Reading

Kleinfeld, Gerald R., and Lewis A. Tambs, *Hitler's Spanish Legion: The Blue Division in Russia* (1979).

Payne, Stanley G., *Politics and the Military in Modern Spain* (1967).

Army, Swiss

Despite their modern-day reputation as peaceful, due to their neutral status, the Swiss have a historical record as a very belligerent people. Once among Europe's leading military forces and available for hire as mercenaries, the Swiss in their confederated cantonal system have a neutral outlook on the world's great quarrels, but they have nearly always been well-armed, well-trained, and not reticent about using force to defend their stance. Prior to World War II, however, the Swiss Army was starved of money and thus was not in the best state for conflict.

Switzerland is a high-technology manufacturing nation and a great deal of this ability went into arms manufacture, be it guns, tanks, or vehicles. Their 20mm Oerlikon antiaircraft gun saw considerable action during World War II with the Swiss Army and other countries. It was rated as a highly effective piece. The Swiss Air Force was part of the army, and defended its airspace with distinction, given its somewhat limited resources.

The real credit for Switzerland's emergence from the war without serious confrontation should go to General Henri Guisan, who encouraged a strategy of national defense that made the best use of topography. The Alpine Redoubt, as it was called, used the high mountains to prepare for an indefinite stand against any aggressor. Stores and other installations were placed in protective rock fortresses, and giant railway tunnels were mined through the Alps. The manpower came from the citizens' militia, the historical legacy of the Swiss confederation. Every able-bodied Swiss male was on active call.

The state of alert of Swiss forces varied during the war, but there was never any doubt on the part of other countries that they would be in a very tricky proposition should any of them invade.

Chris Westhorp

Additional Reading

Hartmann, Frederick H., *The Swiss Press and Foreign Affairs in World War II* (1960).

Schwarz, Urs, *The Eye of the Hurricane: Switzerland in World War II* (1980).

Army, U.S.

Much of the U.S. Army did not become involved in ground operations during World War II until the end of 1942, and in the case of many units, even later. It spent the preceding period studying the nature of weapons, organizations, and tactics and putting the conclusions it drew into practice. The results were tested in a series of large-scale maneuvers in the United States and then in initial combat experiences overseas. Many of the early decisions proved unworkable in Europe, and the army had to make many changes during the war. The final tactical system was an excellent product that dominated American military thought well into the 1950s.

Early in 1940, there were only two active army divisions within the continental United States. One was a traditional horse cavalry unit, the 1st Cavalry Division, and the other was the 2nd Infantry Division. The U.S. Army of the 1930s was really more of a border constabulary than an army in the European sense. The force was built around cavalry and artillery horses and infantry pack mules. Under the direction of Army Chief of Staff George C. Marshall (q.v.), the army (including the Army Air Forces) grew to a size of almost eight million troops, reorganized the structure of its divisions, deployed overseas on two fronts, and successfully fought a war for which it was remarkably unprepared. The U.S. Army's ability to transform itself into such a powerful force in the midst of a world war surely ranks as one of the most impressive feats of military history.

Ever since the American Civil War, military doctrine was based on General Ulysses S. Grant's strategy of annihilation and attrition as the proven means of gaining victory. The 1939 version of the army's capstone doctrinal manual, *FM 100–5, Field Service Regulations: Operations* stated: "An objective may sometimes be gained by maneuver alone; ordinarily it must be gained through battle." The strategy was clear. Wars were won by meeting the enemy's main forces directly and overwhelming them with superior power.

This philosophy continued to dominate strategic thinking right up to the eve of World War II. On 27 March 1941, the ABC-1 (American-British Conversations) staff agreement clearly established the U.S. position that the best means of defeating Germany would be a cross-channel invasion, a frontal attack in strategic terms. At all subsequent conferences, American planners continued to press for the direct approach. The U.S. Army that emerged, however, was organized and equipped in such a way that it could not really generate and sustain the massive combat power required by such a strategy. Instead, the force was developed to fight the war of mobility and maneuver it found doctrinally undesirable.

The single most influential architect of this new army was General Lesley J. McNair (q.v.). Initially chief of staff of general headquarters, and then commander of Army Ground Forces, McNair worked energetically to make the army lean and mobile. His basic orientation was readily apparent in the weapons with which the army was outfitted and in the organization and structure of the divisions. His primary aim was mobility and he built an army that was light and agile, but it lacked the overwhelming firepower required by the accepted strategy of annihilation.

Post–World War I doctrine saw the tank as an adjunct of the infantry. Accordingly, the army required tanks that were agile enough to go wherever the infantry could. McNair believed that tanks were best used against vulnerable targets like infantrymen, rather than against other tanks. Thus, American tanks evolved into machine gun carriers with only enough armor to provide defense against enemy machine guns. It was not until July 1940 that the War Department approved a design for a tank with a 75mm main gun. Ordnance Department officers cautioned that U.S. tanks were falling behind their European counterparts in both gun size and thickness of armor, but their warnings met with renewed demands for lightness and maneuverability.

If tanks were not intended for use against enemy tanks, tank killers were. However, the same demand for mobility limited tank killers to a 37mm gun, which was completely ineffective against most mainline European tanks. By 1943, the size of the gun increased to a mere 57mm, which still lagged well behind the German 75mm and 88mm models.

For infantry use against enemy armor, the U.S. introduced a light, portable rocket launcher known as the "bazooka." Like other U.S. antitank weapons, the bazooka was too small to penetrate the heavy frontal armor of German tanks. Many U.S. soldiers preferred to capture and use the enemy's more powerful *Panzerschreck*. Thus, the entire family of U.S. armor and anti-armor weapons suffered from the same flaw. Firepower was sacrificed for mobility; yet the prevailing U.S. operational philosophy relied on this missing firepower.

In 1939, the army had just 190,000 soldiers. By Pearl Harbor, its ranks swelled to 1.6 million troops organized into thirty-six active divisions. In 1942, Marshall initiated an even more rapid expansion based on the hopes of mounting a cross-channel invasion no later than the spring of 1943. When British reluctance slowed down the timetable for the invasion, Marshall likewise slowed down the expansion. From the end of 1942 to July 1943, McNair's Army Ground Forces grew only slightly from 1.9 million enlisted men to just under 2.5 million. After that, the expansion virtually halted.

TABLE 1

U.S. Army Divisional Strength

Division Type	No. of Troops	Automatic Weapons	Artillery (over 75mm)	AT Weapons	Motor Vehicles	Half-Tracks	Tanks
Infantry c. 1941	15,504	667	56	60	1,834	0	0
Infantry c. 1943	13,253	656	66	567	1,640	0	0
Infantry c. 1945	14,037	853	66	615	2,114	0	0
Armored c. 1942	14,620	2,554	54	0	2,971	733	390
Armored c. 1945	10,670	3,627	54	609	1,538	466	272
Airborne c. 1944	8,500	346	36	182	408	0	0

The obvious question was whether this relatively small force could support the American strategy. The last new division, formed in August 1943, was the U.S. Army's nineteenth. In contrast, the Soviet Union fielded some 400 divisions, Germany 300, and Japan 100. Even considering variations in divisional size among the various nations, the U.S. Army's total strength was comparatively small.

After the Germans unleashed *Blitzkrieg* (q.v.) on the world, the U.S. Armored Force enjoyed an autonomy rivaled only by that of the Army Air Forces. General Adna R. Chaffee (q.v.), the first chief of the armored force, used this independence to begin forming armored divisions for the mobile application of concentrated power. As time passed, however, the shock of *Blitzkrieg* faded and McNair was able to bring armor more closely under his direction where he could emphasize mobility rather than concentrated power.

In McNair's opinion, an armored division was "of value only in pursuit or exploitation," which were traditional cavalry roles. Thus, in September 1943, he effected a reorganization of the armored divisions to give them more flexibility and increase their value in assisting the infantry in much the same manner as the old cavalry. As a result of this restructuring, the basic concept was that infantry divisions (with attached tanks) were responsible for overpowering the enemy, while armored divisions conducted the exploitation. This was all consistent with his belief that tanks should not fight tanks. Unfortunately, tank-to-tank battles were unavoidable in the strategy of a cross-channel invasion.

McNair placed special emphasis on infantry divisions. He did not think they could accomplish their mission structured in the prewar "square" organization of 22,000 troops in four regiments. Here, too, his concern was mobility. By Pearl Harbor, he had converted the active army divisions to a lighter "triangular" configuration of 15,514 troops. By July 1943, his further streamlining pared divisional troop strength to 14,253. His divisions contained only the essential support elements needed for routine operations. Additional support was provided on an "as needed" basis from the corps or the field army. Nothing unessential was allowed to hinder the division's ability to move.

The triangular division of July 1943 had three infantry regiments, the divisional artillery, a headquarters company, a reconnaissance troop, a combat engineer battalion, a quartermaster company, an ordnance company, a signal company, and a military police platoon. All elements of the division, except the infantry units, were motorized. With the attachment of just six quartermaster truck companies, the infantry could be motorized too. The army infantry division was one of the most mobile in the world.

The artillery, somehow, seemed to have been left out of the plans to increase mobility. This is particularly odd because McNair was an artillery officer. The basic 105mm howitzer was a towed model that had great difficulty keeping up with the infantry. What they needed was a self-propelled gun, but the Americans were very late in fielding such weapons. Despite this shortcoming, American artillery performed exceptionally well. Much of this effectiveness can be attributed to the fact that artillery's combat role is much the same as its peacetime training, fire downrange at unseen targets. Artillery was especially adept at time on tar-

TABLE 2

U.S. Army Order of Battle 1941–1945

Divisions	1941	Europe 1945	Total * 1945
Infantry	30	49	66
Armored	5	16	16
Cavalry	1	0	1
Airborne	0	4	5
Mountain	0	1	1
Totals	36	70	89

*Note: Total strength at the end of the war includes all divisions: in Europe, in the Pacific theater, and in the United States and its territories.

get (TOT) missions, which involved surprise concentrations of multiple firing batteries on a given target.

Eighty-two of the eighty-nine American divisions mobilized were infantry or armor. The other divisions—motorized, cavalry, airborne, and light—were experimental to varying degrees. McNair did not like specialized units because he thought they emphasized specialized skills at the expense of general military proficiency. He preferred to develop standard units and give them special training only when they completed their standard training and when an imminent mission required something additional.

The cavalry division, of course, existed before the war, but its usefulness rapidly became outdated in the age of machine warfare. No plans were made to deploy cavalry units with their mounts. The 2nd Cavalry Division deployed to North Africa in early 1944, only to be disbanded. The 1st Cavalry Division served in the Pacific as dismounted infantry.

The same tonnage restrictions that prevented shipping horses overseas helped contribute to the demise of motorized divisions. Additionally, McNair's philosophy of pooling transportation assets at corps level made motorized divisions unnecessary in his eyes. The experiment was short-lived.

In a departure from his usual stand against specialized units, McNair recognized the need for formally trained and organized airborne divisions. The 82nd and 101st Airborne Divisions were formed in August 1942 as miniature infantry divisions with only 8,500 troops, but with normal divisional components plus a small organic antiaircraft battery. Each airborne division had one parachute infantry regiment and two glider regiments. These divisions had no organic aircraft and depended on the army air force pool of transport planes.

As fighting progressed into the rugged terrain of the Southwest Pacific and Italy, War Department officials turned their attention to specialized jungle and mountain units. The result was the formation of three light divisions in June 1943: the 89th Light Division (Truck), the 10th Light Division (Pack, Alpine), and the 71st Light Division (Pack, Jungle). These divisions added no additional manpower to the army as they were simply reorganizations of units already in existence. Tests of the 71st and 89th Divisions conducted during force-on-force maneuvers from February through August 1944 showed very clearly that these light divisions were incapable of sustaining themselves. As a result, they were converted back to standard divisions. Tests for the 10th Light Division produced equally negative results, but the War Department decided to retain it as a special mountain division. It deployed to Italy in December 1944.

Divisions were actually the largest U.S. units to deploy overseas. Once the divisions arrived, they were organized into corps and field armies as needed. "Type" corps and "type" armies, those having specific organic elements, were abandoned beginning in 1943 in favor of a more flexible system. Corps and armies became so many "containers" for divisions, battalions, and companies. They were grouped and regrouped as the situation required.

The corps consisted basically of just a commander and a small staff, who gave unity of effort and common purpose to the collection of units in combat, regardless of how much the individual units might be expended, exchanged, or replaced. Because the division contained only what was essential for routine operations, the corps became the key headquarters for employing and distributing all combat elements in the proper combination. Unless operating independently, the corps was supposed to be a pure combat agency. The field army was responsible for overall administrative and support functions, as well as having a combat role of its own.

The failure of the Hawaiian Department to follow up on the warning order it received prior to Pearl Harbor convinced Marshall a complete reorganization of the command and control system was needed. In March 1942, his reorganization started with the intent of streamlining the force for combat action. The General Headquarters, the Air Force Combat Command, the offices of the chiefs of the air corps, infantry, field artillery, coast artillery, and cavalry were all eliminated. In their places the Army Air Forces, Army Ground Forces, and Services of Supply were created to take over administration, supply, organization, and training of the entire force.

Streamlining the army to just three major commands left the general staff free to concentrate on the strategic direction of the war and the broad control of operations. McNair commanded the Army Ground Forces; General Henry Arnold (q.v.) commanded the Army Air Forces; and General Brehon Somervell (q.v.) became head of Services of Supply (later renamed Army Services Force).

The reorganization also provided for a central command post staff inside the War Department. The War Plans Division (soon renamed the Operations Division) was given this role. Brigadier General Dwight D. Eisenhower (q.v.), who became the first assistant chief of staff, Operations Division, was responsible for the "formulation of plans and the strategic direction of military forces in the theater of war." This arrangement allowed Marshall to remain completely abreast of the situation overseas without leaving his critical post in Washington.

Starting from little better than scratch, the U.S. Army grew into a powerful fighting force. It benefited greatly from Marshall's leadership and vision and was profoundly influenced by McNair's personal belief in mobility. At times, the army's structure conflicted with its operational doctrine, but it continued to adjust and develop to meet the needs of the situation. The final product was a complete combat organization that accomplished its wartime mission.

Kevin Dougherty

Additional Reading

Cline, Ray, *The War Department; Washington Command Post; The Operations Division* (1951).

Greenfield, Kent R., Robert R. Palmer, and Bell I. Wiley, *The Army Ground Forces: The Organization of Ground Combat Troops* (1947).

Perret, Geoffrey, *There's a War to Be Won: The United States Army in World War II* (1991).

Stanton, Shelby, L., *Order of Battle: U.S. Army, World War II* (1984)

Weigley, Russel, *Eisenhower's Lieutenants: The Campaigns of France and Germany, 1944– 1945* (1981).

Army, Yugoslavian

Yugoslavia, with its multiethnic composition, was a fractious country. Security, therefore, was of prime importance. Externally it had its enemies,

and the signing of the 1934 Balkan Pact allied Yugoslavia, Greece, Turkey, and Romania against the threat posed by Hungarian and Bulgarian border revisionists. Also in 1934, the underlying tension broke in France (Yugoslavia's patron among the great powers) when King Alexander was assassinated by a Macedonian gunman with Croatian *Ustaša* (q.v.) links, and acting with the connivance of Hungary and Italy.

The Royal Yugoslav Army, predominantly Serbian, with its duties of internal cohesion to accomplish, was a relatively large one. In 1938, it had some 134,000 enlisted plus 20,000 officers and NCOs. Furthermore, with military service compulsory for eighteen months, it could call up one million or more men in the event of war. By 1941, in fact, there were 700,000 under arms, but about half were poorly trained conscripts with only one month of service. The army received most of its arms from Czechoslovakia, although there were two large arms factories in Yugoslavia itself, at Valjevo and Višegrad.

At the time of the Axis invasion, the Yugoslav Army was divided into seven field armies containing thirty divisions and deployed across four sectors in a cordon defense. The seven army headquarters, in numerical order of organization, were at Novi Sad, Osijek, Nikšic and Skopje, Zagreb, Nis, Belgrade, and Ljubljana-Korlovac. In addition, there were major fortresses at Boka Kotorska and Šibenik.

The prewar structure is a little difficult to determine. Of the higher army units most divisions were infantry. A few were cavalry. Each infantry division had from two to four infantry regiments plus one or two artillery regiments. Each cavalry division had two brigades of two regiments each plus one cyclist battalion, one horse artillery group, and service units. There were also a number of engineer regiments. The infantry also included a royal guard and two alpine regiments, while the cavalry had one artillery and two royal guard regiments. There were a total of 200 assorted batteries all together.

The event which brought Yugoslavia into the war was a *coup d'état* in Belgrade. The government of Prince Paul (the regent because Alexander's heir, Peter II, was a minor), led by Air Force General Dušan Simović (q.v.) and royal guard units, signed the Axis Pact (q.v.) in 1941 provoking Serbian radicals in the military. The Serbs installed seventeen–year-old King Peter II (q.v.), whose government reversed the policy. The Germans reacted with fury, and invaded on 6 April 1941. They were followed by the Italians, who entered Dalmatia on

11 April. When the Hungarians entered, the total invasion force amounted to fifty-two divisions.

The new regime had no time to organize and prepare for the invasion. Prewar plans had assumed Allied control of Greece, creating a rear safe haven where Yugoslav forces could withdraw if hard pressed by invading forces. The collapse of Greece and Italy's occupation of Albania threw this plan into disarray. With their four groups of armies deployed to repel invasions from all directions, it was impossible for them to focus their combat power.

Yugoslav thinking and organization were better suited to World War I than to the rapid armored thrusts and air strikes of the German *Blitzkrieg* (q.v.). Secondary lines of defense were prepared and a gradual withdrawal into the mountainous interior planned. There a protracted campaign could be mounted. The immediate problem was that aside from the alpine units, mountain warfare training was neglected in favor of World War I–style infantry warfare. Despite the obvious military advantages of their home terrain, it was only in 1940 that a Guerrilla Operations Command *(Četnicka Kommanda)* was formed. It was supposed to maintain seven battalions of specialist troops; it never did, but it provided the basis for the later Četniks (q.v.).

Armaments were generally inadequate and often quite old, providing low firepower. The army was also heavily dependent on animals, which inhibited its speed and maneuverability. It also meant that given the wartime infantry division strength of 27,000, the army would need 900,000 animals, requiring more maintenance than machinery.

This recipe for disaster was compounded by the lack of training and experience throughout the army in the face of a seasoned enemy. The chain of command collapsed after just one day of war and the army disintegrated rapidly in the face of the Axis onslaught. After one week, Belgrade (q.v.) fell and the army was encircled in Bosnia. An attempted offensive in northern Albania collapsed on 17 April and the Yugoslavs capitulated. Almost 340,000 were taken prisoner.

Many army personnel did not surrender and instead went into hiding with their weapons. Serbians and loyal Royalists in the main, these men and women adopted the name Četnik. Under the leadership of Colonel Draža Mihailović (q.v.), they reemerged as an organization of trained guerrilla bands vowing to continue the war against the German occupiers and the collaborators (*see* Yugoslavia National Liberation).

Chris Westhorp

Additional Reading

Jukic, Ilijn, *The Fall of Yugoslavia* (1974).
Mollo, Andrew, *The Armed Forces of World War II* (1981).

ATS

See Auxiliary Territorial Service

Auxiliary Territorial Service (ATS)

On 9 September 1938, the Auxiliary Territorial Service was formed under the authority of British Army Order 199. The role of the women who joined the ATS was nominally in the noncombatant duties. The volunteers were given basic military training, which was followed by trade training. Following the outbreak of war in 1939, members of the ATS replaced soldiers in many units, performing duties as cooks, drivers, switchboard operators, and clerks.

As the war progressed, the size of the ATS was increased and volunteers were integrated into many British corps units, such as the Royal Corps of Signals, where they took over the duties of teleprinter operators in signal centers, as well as being involved in the administration of those units in the role of drivers, clerks, storekeepers, etc. ATS volunteers also served on antiaircraft sites during the Battle of Britain (q.v.), with many women operating antiaircraft guns and range-finding equipment alongside gunners of the Royal Artillery.

By September 1943, the total strength of the ATS units inside Britain was 207,398, with an additional 5,077 women serving at overseas stations. The distribution of tradeswomen employed within the corps of the British Army has been recorded as follows:

Antiaircraft Command (Royal Artillery)	56,178
Royal Army Ordnance Corps	22,648
Royal Army Service Corps	17,013
Royal Army Pay Corps	11,013
Royal Corps of Signals	10,588
Royal Electrical and Mechanical Engineers	6,208
Royal Engineer Postal Service	1,500

During the latter part of the war, as their numbers increased, the designations of many of the regiments in which they served were changed to become "mixed" regiments, thus denoting that the unit was composed of members of the parent corps and of the ATS. In August 1941, Her Royal Highness, the Princess Royal, was appointed as

An ATS depot crew fits the turret onto a Churchill tank. (IWM H 24517)

comptroller commandant of the ATS. Other royal women also became involved with the ATS, including Her Majesty Queen Elizabeth II, who, as Princess Elizabeth, joined the ATS when she was old enough, and trained as a driver.

The ATS had its own rank structure that equated to ranks in the British Army:

ARMY	ATS
Major General	Chief Controller
Brigadier	Senior Controller
Colonel	Controller
Lieutenant Colonel	Chief Commander
Major	Senior Commander
Captain	Junior Commander
Lieutenant	Subaltern
Second Lieutenant	Second Subaltern.

In the integrated units many of the established positions were designed to be filled by either male or female officers. Members of the ATS gave valuable service in most theaters of World War II. On 1 February 1949, the remaining cadre of the ATS was formed into the Women's Royal Army Corps.

Alan Harfield

Additional Reading

Bidwell, Shelford, *The Women's Royal Army Corps* (1977).
Cavadina, Ada, *This Was the A.T.S.* (1946).
Langstaff, C.K., *The Story of the Royal Army Service Corps, 1939–1945* (1955).
Priestly, John B., *British Women Go to War* (1943).
Sherman, M., *No Tears for the ATS* (1944).

B

See British Broadcasting Corporation

BBC

See British Broadcasting Corporation

BCRA

See Bureau Central de Renseignement et d'Action

Black *Reichswehr*

General Hans von Seeckt (q.v.), chief of staff of the German *Reichswehr,* realized that his army could not adequately defend Germany's borders with the 100,000 men permitted under the provisions of the Versailles Treaty (q.v.). In 1922, he authorized the creation of civilian labor detachments to be assigned to the *Reichswehr,* a force that became known as the "Black *Reichswehr.*" These "civilians" were given army uniforms, garrisoned at military bases, and received supplies and other logistical support from the army. These units were funded from various secret accounts and by German industrialists who stood to gain from rearmament.

Major Ernst Buchrucker, a former member of von Seeckt's general staff, was appointed to command this clandestine armed force, though overall supervision of the Black *Reichswehr* remained in the hands of a select group of men, including Schleicher and Von Bock, chosen to advise von Seeckt on military matters. The Black *Reichswehr* sought to operate secretly, but a number of political murders revealed its activities and proved to be a major embarrassment for von Seeckt. He had to admit the existence of the unit and attempted to justify it as necessary for Germany's defense.

By 1923, the Black *Reichswehr* began asserting its independence from the regular army. Since many of its members were previously associated with the *Freikorps* (q.v.), or were active in anti-re-publican student groups at universities, it became more involved with the plans and activities of right-wing extremists in Bavaria and Prussia who were seeking the overthrow of the Weimar Republic (q.v.) and its democratic institutions. Von Seeckt and the *Reichswehr* did not support these activities. Buchrucker, however, recognized that no *coup d'état* would be successful without the army's support. Although that support existed to some degree in Bavaria, the Black *Reichswehr* met with open hostility in Prussia.

Buchrucker therefore planned a coup similar to the Kapp *Putsch* (q.v.) to take place during the evening of 29–30 September 1923. Buchrucker mobilized nearly 4,000 men on 27 September but was ordered to demobilize immediately. On 30 September, however, Buchrucker and more than 500 men departed their headquarters at the Küstrin fortress and seized a number of military installations near Berlin. They raised the old imperial flag and held off an army siege for two days before surrendering. Von Seeckt imprisoned Buchrucker and ordered the Black *Reichswehr* dissolved.

Steven B. Rogers

Additional Reading

Bracher, Karl D., *The German Dictatorship* (1970).

Mau, Hermann, and Helmut Krausnik, *German History, 1933–1945: An Assessment by German Historians* (1959).

Watt, Richard M., *The Kings Depart: The Tragedy of Germany: Versailles and the German Revolution* (1968).

Black Shirts

On 1 February 1923, the Italian government officially established the *Milizia Volontaria per la*

Sicurezza Nazionale (Volunteer Militia for National Security) with the twofold purpose of grouping and drilling the preexisting "action squads" and constituting an armed force able to guarantee the country's internal security and the interests of the ruling *Partito Nazionale Fascista* (Fascist National Party). All members of PNF were to take part. The new militia was organized into 150 legions grouped in fourteen zone headquarters, with one group of legions for Sardinia and one autonomous legion for Fiume. All the active list personnel of the legions came to be called the *Camicie Nere* (Black Shirts), from the color of their uniform shirts. Aside from the shirt, they wore the same type of uniform as the Italian Army. They also wore two-pointed cloth patches with small *fasces* (named "black flames") instead of the standard Italian military corps star badges.

Almost right from the start, the Black Shirts went far beyond the traditional militia function and started to encroach on other armed forces, particularly the army. The same year they were formed, the Black Shirts sent three legions into Libya for military colonial operations. The Black Shirts underwent several reorganizations, with the number of the legions being progressively decreased. Theoretically, each legion consisted of two battalions and one machine gun company, with a cadre of active duty officers and soldiers. The bulk of the Black Shirt units consisted of locally recruited conscripts. Various problems, such as a shortage of personnel and weapons, prevented a homogeneous structure in all the legions, some of which had only one battalion.

During the 1936 invasion of Ethiopia (q.v.), eighty-three Black Shirt battalions were mobilized. Black Shirt units also took part in the Spanish civil war (q.v.) and the occupation of Albania (q.v.). During World War II, Black Shirts mobilized forty-six legions, one attached to each Italian Army division, plus a large number of autonomous legions and battalions. With only light armament and little formal training, the *Camicie Nere* were far less effective than their counterparts in the regular army. There were some exceptions, especially among the units that fought in the Soviet Union and in the Balkans. Some of the best Black Shirt battalions that performed well in the field were designated "M" (for Mussolini) battalions, and their men were allowed to wear a stylized red "M" on their black collar patches. When the Fascist government fell, the *Camicie Nere* continued to take its orders from the army command, as it had throughout the war.

Within the Black Shirts there existed several special branches with police functions in particular fields, such as railways, forests, harbors, roads, postal services, and borders. Special Black Shirt units were also charged with antiaircraft and coastal defense missions. At the outbreak of the war, the *Milizia Artiglieria Contro-Aerea* (Antiaircraft Artillery Militia) had 77,000 men in twenty-two territorial legions, with 200 batteries and an observation and listening network. The *Milizia Artiglieria Marittima* (Maritime Artillery Militia) had 35,000 men in ten legions.

Francesco Fatutta

Additional Reading
Hibbert, C., *Mussolini* (1971).
MacGregor-Haste, Roy, *The Day of the Lion: The Life and Death of Fascist Italy, 1922–1945* (1963).
Shermer, David, *Black Shirts* (1969).

Black Units in the U.S. Military

The role of black servicemen and black units in World War II was greatly influenced by their role in World War I. The poor military record of the 92nd Infantry Division and the problems of racial tensions convinced the military leadership that blacks lacked the capability for combat duty. Conversely, bad treatment and limitation to support roles caused bitterness in the black community. Accordingly, there were only 3,640 black enlisted men and three black line officers serving in the regular army in 1939. The navy accepted blacks only as stewards. The marines and army air corps were closed to blacks until 1942.

During the course of the war, large segregated units were formed. In February 1943, the 2nd Cavalry Division (Colored) was organized at Fort Clark, Texas. The 92nd Infantry Division (Colored) of World War I was reactivated in October 1942 at Fort Hauchuca, Arizona. The 93rd Infantry Division (Colored) was activated in May 1942 at Camp Clipper, California. In October 1942, the all-black 99th Pursuit Squadron was activated at Tuskegee Army Air Field, Alabama, under the command of Lieutenant Colonel Benjamin O. Davis, Jr. (q.v.).

The role of blacks in World War II was largely limited to support functions. One out of every five black soldiers was assigned to general engineer units responsible for manual labor. In port units, 77 percent of the men were black, and in transportation units 69 percent. A third of chemical troops, 22 percent of signal units, and 11 percent of ordinance units were black.

Even the black servicemen in combat divi-

Black GIs from a field artillery battalion dig in their M-2 caliber .50 machine gun along a highway west of Bastogne during the Ardennes Offensive. (IWM EA 47950)

sions spent little time fighting and much time in reserve. The 93rd Infantry Division served as a support unit for the Eighth Army in the South Pacific. The 2nd Cavalry Division, though trained as a combat division, was broken up into service units (engineer, port, and transportation battalions). There were, however, a few black units that did see combat. The 92nd Infantry Division arrived in Italy in August 1944. The division fought as part of the Fifth Army in Italy. In battle it suffered 616 killed and 2,187 wounded, and received 12,098 military decorations. Throughout most of the war the 92nd was commanded by Major General Edward M. Almond (q.v.), who later became famous as the commander of the X Corps in Korea.

Davis's airmen were one of the great success stories for blacks in World War II. The 99th Pursuit Squadron arrived in North Africa in April 1943, and was assigned as part of the 33rd Fighter Group, based at Fordjouna, Tunisia. After a rocky start caused mostly by prejudicial policies, the success of the squadron led to the June 1944 formation of the 332nd Fighter Group, the only all-black combat air group ever organized by the U.S. Army Air Forces.

Under Davis's command, the four-squadron group flew P-51 Mustangs in the European the-ater. The 332nd Fighter Group flew 15,533 sorties and 1,579 missions, 200 of which involved bomber escort. Davis's pilots earned 865 military decorations and shot down 111 enemy aircraft, nearly all of which were fighters. They destroyed 150 airplanes on the ground and destroyed more than 600 railroad boxcars and other rolling stock. In all the bomber escort missions it flew, the 332nd Fighter Group never lost a friendly bomber to enemy fighters. The 99th Pursuit Squadron won two Presidential Unit Citations (PUCs) over Italy, and the 332nd Fighter Group won another over Berlin.

By the end of the war, three million blacks had registered for service, and 695,264 were inducted. Many of these black servicemen experienced discrimination during their service, including the denial of combat roles, exclusion from certain types of jobs, and limiting the number of leadership positions open to blacks.

For the military leadership, upholding the principle of segregation often took precedence over military effectiveness. Accordingly, the fate of many black units was characterized by frequent reorganizations, conversions, and disbandment. In 1943, several war zones suffered severe manpower shortages. Despite this, 425,000 of the 504,000 black servicemen were still stationed in the United

TABLE 1

Black U.S. Army Combat Units in World War II

Unit	Higher Headquarters	Service
24th Inf Regt	Separate Regiment	Western Pacific
25th Inf Regt	93rd Inf Div	New Guinea
364th Inf Regt	Separate Regiment	Liberia, Alaska
365th Inf Regt	92nd Inf Div	Italy
366th Inf Regt	92nd Inf Div	Italy
367th Inf Regt	Separate Regiment	Liberia, Corsica
368th Inf Regt	93rd Inf Div	New Guinea
369th Inf Regt	93rd Inf Div	New Guinea
370th Inf Regt	92nd Inf Div	Italy
371st Inf Regt	92nd Inf Div	Italy
372nd Inf Regt	Separate Regiment	U.S., Hawaii
428th Inf Regt	Separate Regiment	Inactive Reserve
447th Inf Regt	Separate Regiment	Inactive Reserve
449th Inf Regt	Separate Regiment	Inactive Reserve
9th Cav Regt	2nd Cav Div	North Africa
10th Cav Regt	2nd Cav Div	North Africa
27th Cav Regt	2nd Cav Div	North Africa
28th Cav Regt	2nd Cav Div	North Africa
5th Recon Squadron	2nd Cav Div	North Africa
35th Recon Cav Squadron	2nd Cav Div	North Africa
758th Tank Bn	Fifth Army	Italy
761st Tank Bn[*]	26th, 71st, 79th, 87th, and 103rd Inf Divs	France, Belgium, and Germany
784th Tank Bn	Non-divisional	France
614th Tank Dest Bn[*]	Non-divisional	France
649th Tank Dest Bn	Non-divisional	U.S.
659th Tank Dest Bn	Non-divisional	U.S.
669th Tank Dest Bn	Non-divisional	U.S.
679th Tank Dest Bn	Non-divisional	France, Italy
795th Tank Dest Bn	Non-divisional	U.S.
827th Tank Dest Bn	Non-divisional	France
828th Tank Dest Bn	Non-divisional	U.S.
829th Tank Dest Bn	Non-divisional	U.S.
846th Tank Dest Bn	Non-divisional	U.S.
77th Field Arty Bn	2nd Cav Div	North Africa
79th Field Arty Bn	2nd Cav Div	North Africa
159th Field Arty Bn	2nd Cav Div	U.S.
333rd Field Arty Bn	Non-divisional	France
349th Field Arty Bn	VIII Corps	Germany
350th Field Arty Bn	XXI Corps	Germany
351st Field Arty Bn	Third Army	Germany
353rd Field Arty Bn	Non-divisional	U.S.
578th Field Arty Bn	Third Army	France, Germany
593rd Field Arty Bn	93rd Inf Div	New Guinea
594th Field Arty Bn	93rd Inf Div	New Guinea
595th Field Arty Bn	93rd Inf Div	New Guinea
596th Field Arty Bn	93rd Inf Div	New Guinea
597th Field Arty Bn	92nd Inf Div	Italy
598th Field Arty Bn	92nd Inf Div	Italy

(continued next page)

TABLE 1 *(continued)*

Unit	Higher Headquarters	Service
599th Field Arty Bn	92nd Inf Div	Italy
600th Field Arty Bn	92nd Inf Div	Italy
686th Field Arty Bn	Non-divisional	Germany
732nd Field Arty Bn	Non-divisional	U.S.
777th Field Arty Bn	Non-divisional	France
795th Field Arty Bn	Non-divisional	U.S.
930th Field Arty Bn	Non-divisional	U.S.
931st Field Arty Bn	Non-divisional	U.S.
969th Field Arty Bn*	Non-divisional	France, Germany
971st Field Arty Bn	Non-divisional	U.S.
973rd Field Arty Bn	Non-divisional	U.S.
993rd Field Arty Bn	Non-divisional	U.S.
999th Field Arty Bn	Non-divisional	France, Germany
49th Coast Arty Bn	Non-divisional	New Guinea, Philippines
76th AA Arty Gun Bn	Non-divisional	Pacific
77th AA Arty Gun Bn	Non-divisional	Pacific
90th AA Arty Gun Bn	Non-divisional	North Africa, Italy
99th AA Gun Bn	Non-divisional	U.S.
100th AA Gun Bn	Non-divisional	New Guinea
234th AA Gun Bn	Non-divisional	Saipan
235th AA Gun Bn	Non-divisional	U.S.
349th AA Searchlight Bn	Non-divisional	North Africa
338th AA Searchlight Bn	Non-divisional	U.S.
361st AA Searchlight Bn	Non-divisional	U.S.
369th AA Gun Bn	Non-divisional	Okinawa
374th AA Searchlight Bn	Non-divisional	New Guinea
394th AA Auto Weapons Bn	Non-divisional	New Guinea
395th AA Auto Weapons Bn	Non-divisional	New Guinea
450th AA Auto Weapons Bn	Non-divisional	North Africa, Italy
452nd AA Auto Weapons Bn	Non-divisional	France
458th AA Auto Weapons Bn	Non-divisional	U.S.
466th AA Auto Weapons Bn	Non-divisional	New Guinea
477th AA Auto Weapons Bn	Non-divisional	New Guinea
484th AA Auto Weapons Bn	Non-divisional	Burma
492nd AA Auto Weapons Bn	Non-divisional	North Africa
493rd AA Auto Weapons Bn	Non-divisional	North Africa
538th AA Auto Weapons Bn	Non-divisional	U.S.
790th AA Auto Weapons Bn	Non-divisional	U.S.
819th AA Auto Weapons Bn	Non-divisional	U.S.
846th AA Auto Weapons Bn	Non-divisional	U.S.
870th AA Auto Weapons Bn	Non-divisional	Okinawa
871st AA Auto Weapons Bn	Non-divisional	New Guinea
933rd AA Auto Weapons Bn	Non-divisional	Pacific
938th AA Auto Weapons Bn	Non-divisional	New Guinea
183rd Engr Combat Bn	Non-divisional	France
184th Engr Combat Bn	Non-divisional	France
317th Engr Combat Bn	92nd Inf Div	Italy
318th Engr Combat Bn	93rd Inf Div	New Guinea
1553rd Engr Hvy Pontoon Bn	Non-divisional	North Africa, Italy, France
1554th Engr Hvy Pontoon Bn	Non-divisional	North Africa, Italy

(continued next page)

TABLE 1 *(continued)*

Unit	Higher Headquarters	Service
1692nd Engr Combat Bn	Non-divisional	Philippines
1693rd Engr Combat Bn	Non-divisional	U.S.
1694th Engr Combat Bn	Non-divisional	Philippines
1695th Engr Combat Bn	Non-divisional	France
1696th Engr Combat Bn	Non-divisional	France
1697th Engr Combat Bn	Non-divisional	France
1698th Engr Combat Bn	Non-divisional	France
1699th Engr Combat Bn	Non-divisional	France
1700th Engr Combat Bn	Non-divisional	France
6495th Engr Hvy Pontoon Bn	2nd Cav Div	North Africa
6496th Engr Hvy Pontoon Bn	Non-divisional	North Africa

*Note: Presidential Unit Citation

States, and of the 79,000 black troops overseas, the vast majority were in service units. Many overseas commanders refused to accept black troops because they were convinced that blacks lacked morale and efficiency. Moreover, several foreign governments feared unrest among either black or white local populations.

One of the main reasons for objections against blacks in the armed forces was their low educational achievement as a group. The army tested their personnel with the Army General Classification Test (AGCT), which was designed to test an individual's learning ability. In contrast to white soldiers, more than 80 percent of black soldiers scored within the two lowest categories. Therefore, the segregated black units received a much higher percentage of low-scoring men than white units, which helped to perpetuate the myth of black inferiority. Accordingly, the War Department was convinced that black units needed more officers than corresponding white units. Extra officers were assigned to counterbalance the lack of military background and educational training of these troops.

The War Department's criteria for officers serving with black troops included that the officer should be white, and should have "experience with blacks," i.e., he should be a Southerner. Some black officers could be used, but the number had to be kept to a minimum, and the policy was to assign them to service units—since it was generally believed that blacks lacked combat leadership abilities.

Warrant officers in black units were black, and blacks could command blacks only. By the end of 1942, this policy began to create serious problems. It barred promotions and was a constant reminder of discrimination. Only in all-black units could black officers rise above the rank of first lieutenant. Whenever a new white officer was assigned to a unit having black officers, shifts were made in order to ensure that no black outranked a white. Black officers were considered to be a class somewhere between enlisted men and white officers. This downgraded them in the eyes of their troops, and, of course, strengthened the army's assumption that blacks lacked leadership qualities.

For white officers serving with black troops, this policy created a different set of problems. Generally, an assignment to a black unit was considered a punishment. It included extra responsibilities like additional guard and patrolling duties, and, since most military facilities were located in the South, dealing with frictions between local whites and black soldiers. The War Department's policy, therefore, created a situation in which many officers were willing to go to great lengths in order to get out of their assignments to black units. This caused frequent changes in command, which in turn lowered the morale of the troops.

The first cracks in the segregation policy finally came about in 1944 and 1945 as the result of the strains of war. To alleviate a critical shortage of American infantrymen, all-black volunteer infantry replacement platoons were partially integrated into infantry regiments of ten divisions in the European theater. More than 4,000 black soldiers volunteered for the program, almost all of them taking reductions in rank to do so. In the 1st Infantry Division's 16th and 18th Infantry Regiments, high losses led to the integration of black platoons into white companies. These experiences led the 1945 Gillen Board to recommend the integration of the army.

Despite the wartime successes, the official policy toward black servicemen did not change until July 1948, when President Harry S Truman (q.v.) signed an executive order requiring the desegregation of the U.S. armed forces. The performance of black soldiers in America's subsequent wars, from Korea to Vietnam to the Persian Gulf, thoroughly demolished all of the World War II–era myths. Davis later became the first black officer in the U.S. Air Force. On 1 October 1989, some forty-one years after President Truman's executive order, General Colin S. Powell became the first black to serve as the chairman of the Joint Chiefs of Staff, America's senior-ranking military officer.

During World War II no black Americans received the Medal of Honor, although evidence exists that at least four were recommended for the award. In an attempt to determine if that situation was the result of racially based policies and prejudices of the time, the U.S. Army in 1992 began a study of the World War II–era award records of black GIs. The result was a 272-page report titled "The Medal of Honor and African Americans in the United States Army During World War II," compiled by a team of military historians from Shaw University in Raleigh, North Carolina. The Shaw study found no official documents to prove that racial bias determined American award policies. The team did conclude, however, that the social climate of the times and widespread attitudes within the military—a direct reflection of the American society as a whole—virtually guaranteed that no black American would ever receive the nation's highest award.

As part of their mandate, the Shaw team recommended ten black Americans to receive belated Medals of Honor. All but one had received the nation's second-highest award, the Distinguished Service Cross, for their battlefield heroism. The list was reviewed by the Army Senior Officer Awards Board, and then by the members of the Joint Chiefs of Staff. Seven of the soldiers remained on the list after both reviews. The final hurdle was cleared when Congress authorized a special waiver to the statute of limitations that had expired in 1952.

On 13 January 1997, the awards were made in a special ceremony at the White House—the final official act of America's half-century commemoration of World War II. Of the seven who received the Medal of Honor, only former 1st Lieutenant Vernon J. Baker was still alive.

Antje Richter

Additional Reading

Arnold, John, *Buffalo Soldiers: The 92nd Infantry Division and Reinforcements in World War II, 1942–1945* (1990).

Dalfiume, Richard, *Desegregation of the Armed Forces, Fighting on Two Fronts, 1939–1953* (1969).

TABLE 2

Black Medal of Honor Winners of World War II

Name	Rank	Unit	Location	Date
Vernon J. Baker	1st Lt	370th Infantry Regiment	Viareggio, Italy	4–5 April 1945
Edward A. Carter, Jr.	Staff Sgt	56th Armored Infantry Battalion	Speyer, Germany	23 March 1945
John R. Fox *	1st Lt	366th Infantry Regiment	Sommocolonia, Italy	26 December 1944
Wiley F. James, Jr. *	Pfc	413th Infantry Regiment	Lippoldsberg, Germany	7 April 1945
Ruben Rivers *	Staff Sgt	761st Tank Battalion	Guebling, France	14 November 1944
Charles L. Thomas	1st Lt	614th Tank Destroyer Battalion	Climbach, France	14 December 1944
George Watson *	Pvt	29th Quartermaster Regiment	Porloch Harbor, New Guinea	8 March 1943

*Note: Killed in action

Francis, Charles E., *The Tuskegee Airmen: The Story of the Negro in the U.S. Air Force* (1956).

Furr, Arthur, *Democracy's Negroes: A Book of Facts Concerning the Activities of Negroes in World War II* (1947).

Lee, Ulysses, *The Employment of Negro Troops* (1966).

Osur, Alan M., *Blacks in the Army Air Forces During World War II* (1977).

Stillman, Richard J., *Integration of the Negro in the U.S. Armed Forces* (1968).

Wilson, Ruth, *Jim Crow Joins Up: A Study of Negroes in the Armed Forces of the United States* (1944).

Bletchley Park

Bletchley was an ugly Victorian mansion housing the Government Codes and Cypher School during World War II. It was located in Bedfordshire, England, sixty-five kilometers north of London and about halfway between Oxford and Cambridge. The location was convenient for the recruitment of university personnel, for as Ronald Lewin wrote, "It was from the Cam, rather than from the Isis, the men were soon to be drafted, who like that earlier cryptanalyst, Daniel, in the end proved able to dissolve doubts, read the writing, and make known the interpretations."

The major operation at Bletchley during the war centered on the Enigma (q.v.) cipher machine, which produced a category of intelligence known as ULTRA (q.v.). The technique was made possible because Britain's MI-6 (q.v.) was able to obtain a copy of the German's most secret cypher machine and break the codes used on it. The achievements at Bletchley led to several Allied successes.

During the latter part of the war, more than 10,000 men and women worked at Bletchley. Many of the specialists slept in their offices, but housing had to be found in the community for many of the required security, administrative, and operational personnel who could not be housed in the rows of wooden barracks constructed in the park.

Local farmers and shopkeepers were surprised to suddenly find in their midst many "strange, unusually dressed and rather disheveled eccentrics" speaking in drawling Oxford accents and looking for a place to dine or a copy of the London *Times*.

After the United States entered the war, many Americans worked there. Because of the British Official Secrets Act, it was not until 1974 that anything was known outside of official circles about the ULTRA operation.

Many cover stories had to be devised to justify the sudden posting of 10,000 people to a small, rural place like Bletchley Park and the installation of so many radio antennas in the area. It was all-important that the truth of what was happening there not leak out. When Nazi sympathizer William Joyce (q.v.) (Lord Haw Haw) suggested that some sort of secret operations were being conducted at Bletchley Park, the British Broadcasting Corperation (q.v.) published a story that radio antennas in the area were being used for local BBC broadcasts.

Paul J. Rose

Additional Reading
Lewin, Ronald, *ULTRA Goes to War* (1978).
Wingerbotham, F.W., *The Ultra Secrets* (1974).

Brandenburg Division

Although the British commandos and American rangers (qq.v.) are better known, Germany's commando force, *Division Brandenburg,* was the first special operations unit to see action in World War II. Not to be confused with the *Panzergrenadier* division of the same name, the *Brandenburgers* were subordinate to the *Abwehr* (q.v.), Germany's military intelligence service. They were the first German troops to invade Poland (q.v.) in 1939. Preceding the invasion by several days, they seized bridges, tunnels, and other key choke points and facilities. They conducted similar operations during the invasions of Denmark, Belgium and Flanders, France, the Balkans, and the Soviet Union (qq.v.). It was the *Brandenburgers,* not "local Nazis" who constituted the so-called Fifth Column that wreaked havoc in the Allied rear during Germany's early offensives. Their successes declined and losses increased after 1941, however, as ULTRA (q.v.) increasingly forewarned the Allies of *Brandenburger* operations.

Originally formed as independent "sabotage teams," the *Brandenburgers'* success in Poland led to their official establishment on 25 October 1939. By 1943, they grew to four operational regiments, including one paratroop. Moreover, the German Navy's reluctance to organize special operations forces led to the *Brandenburgers* training Germany's first frogman unit, which later sank a British steamer and a minesweeper in Gibraltar. By the spring of 1943, this unit grew into a *Küstenjäger* (Coastal Ranger) battalion modeled after Italy's 10th Light Flotilla (q.v.).

Candidates entering the Brandenburg Division had to meet the highest mental and physical criteria. Officers were expected to be multilingual. The five- to seven-month training course included reconnaissance, swimming, hand-to-hand combat, demolition, marksmanship (with both German and Allied weapons), conventional infantry training, and other specialized instruction. The resulting elite troops performed phenomenal feats, operating up to 200 kilometers behind enemy lines for weeks at a time. Nonetheless, their operations became increasingly costly as the war progressed. Few survived the war.

Carl O. Schuster

Additional Reading

Lucas, James, *Kommando: Germany's Special Forces of World War II* (1985).
Spaeter, Helmuth, *Die Brandenburger* (1992).

British Broadcasting Corporation (BBC)

British historian Asa Briggs wrote that ". . . the Second World War—unlike the Vietnam War twenty years later—was a war not of images but of words," and the history of the BBC during the war reveals the power of words traveling on the air. Ironically, politicians were unable to appreciate the impact of radio before the war. Neville Chamberlain (q.v.) wanted to drop all broadcasting in the event of war, while others believed that people simply would pay no attention to the radio in wartime. Indeed, radio broadcasting did not get off to a very auspicious start, with much of the programing being called by one contemporary critic "an endless stream of trivialities and silliness, apparently labouring under the delusion that in any time of crisis the British public becomes just one colossal moron."

Gradually, BBC Home Service did respond to the public's insatiable appetite for news and entertainment. Concerned about public morale, BBC had some 1,196 broadcasts during the war on food, many being presented on the popular morning program, *The Kitchen Front*. The Home Service began at 7:00 A.M. weekdays with Big Ben and the first news bulletin; then came *Up in the Morning Early*, an exercise program for men and women; and then, to put you in the proper mood, there was *Tune for Today, Lift Up Your Heart*. Programing on the Home Service consisted of regular news readings, popular dance tunes, classical music, plays, travel, educational programing, "talks" on a variety of arcane subjects, the popular homilies of J.B. Priestley, and "highbrow" shows like *The Brain Trust*, which made a celebrity of Sir Kenneth Clark.

To keep these words on the air, BBC had to overcome severe obstacles. Studios were destroyed and control rooms and transmitters put out of action. On 5 October 1940, a 500-pound German bomb crashed into Broadcasting House, coming to rest on the fifth-floor music library. Bruce Belfrage (q.v.), reading the nine o'clock news, reportedly remarked: "Carry on. It's all right," and his only error the rest of the newscast was to say, "Tonight's postscript will be given by Lloyd Lord." BBC had the further difficulty of laboring under the suspicion of Winston S. Churchill (q.v.), who viewed it as "an enemy within the gates doing more harm than good." Despite such attitudes, the war years further proved that BBC was listening to its audience, thus confirming its place in the daily lives of the British people.

BBC also beamed its radio waves at enemy-occupied Europe through the European Service. In January 1941, BBC instituted the popular "V for Victory" campaign, which so alarmed Joseph Goebbels (q.v.) that he called it an "intellectual invasion of the continent by British radio."

European Service broadcasts were also used for clandestine operational purposes. BBC cooperated with the SOE (q.v.) in its support of various resistance movements in Europe through a special message system of codes and signals that would alert resistance groups to the arrival of agents or containers by parachute drop. In this capacity, BBC played a vital role in maintaining contact between resistance groups and Britain. Concern over the integrity and accuracy of its news reports made BBC balk at stating in such a report that, for instance, the RAF in an operation suffered fewer losses than in reality, to temporarily cover a weakness.

Georges Bidault, the foreign minister of France, in the fall of 1944, expressed his appreciation of the job done by the BBC European Service this way: "It is thanks to you, dear familiar voices, that our minds stayed free, while our limbs were bound."

Richard A. Voeltz

Additional Reading

Briggs, Asa, *The War of Words: The History of Broadcasting in the United Kingdom,* Vol. III (1970).
Mansell, Gerard, *Let the Truth be Told, Fifty Years of BBC External Broadcasting* (1982).

Bureau Central de Renseignement et d'Action (BCRA)

The *Bureau Central de Renseignement et d'Action*

(Militaire), or Central Bureau of Intelligence and Action (Military), was the intelligence service of General Charles de Gaulle's (q.v.) London-based Free French Movement. Major André Dewavrin (code name "Colonel Passy") headed the organization designed to maintain contacts with occupied France and the French resistance (q.v.).

Friction and suspicion between the British and BCRA were common and sometimes serious. For security reasons, Britain's SOE (q.v.) insisted on decentralization of operations in France and cared very little about political affiliations. Concerned with postwar conditions, the Gaullists sought tight control and the BCRA worked against the Communist underground's influence. Conflicts continued even after liberation.

Richard Wires

Additional Reading

Dewavrin, André, *Souvenirs* (1951).
Reynaud, Paul, *In the Thick of the Fight: 1930–1945* (1955).

B

C

Camp X

Camp X was a secret World War II intelligence camp located near the Toronto-Kingston highway in Canada. There, secret agents were trained, guerrilla devices tested, and Hollywood-style dummy buildings were constructed to simulate important Nazi hideouts. Camp X was part of an extensive British security complex established in North America under the direction of Sir William Stephenson (q.v.), to replace the regular British secret service lost when Britain withdrew from the continent of Europe in 1940. The assassination of SS-*Obergruppenführer* Reinhard Heydrich (q.v.) was planned there.

Paul J. Rose

Additional Reading

Deacon, Richard, *A History of the British Secret Service* (1980).

CAP

See Civil Air Patrol

CCS

See Combined Chiefs of Staff

Četniks

There were two resistance organizations in Axis-occupied Yugoslavia: Tito's Communist partisans (qq.v.), who ended the war in firm control of the country, and the Četniks, named after Serbian guerrillas who resisted previous Turkish and Bulgarian occupations and who remained loyal to the legitimate prewar government.

Discovering the truth about the Četniks is difficult. Abandoned by the British in 1943 and subsequently caught between the Nazis and the Communists, few survived to tell the tale. Even if their story had been told in 1945, in the euphoria of victory not many would have listened. Generally, they were seen as at best ineffectual, at worst Nazi collaborators. With the passage of time and the ending of the Cold War, there are reasons to question this judgment.

Their formal allegiance to their king and government exiled in London must be stressed. Their leader was Colonel Draža Mihailović (q.v.), a regular officer who fought with distinction in the Serbian Army in World War I. After the Nazi invasion in April 1941, he was appointed both defense minister and commander of the Yugoslav Home Army—the Četnik's official title—by the exiled government.

The Četniks' resistance, unlike that of the Communists, who waited until Germany invaded the Soviet Union, began immediately, though low key. It was based almost entirely in Serbia, with its headquarters on Mount Ravna Gora. For much of the war, large areas of Serbia, including from time to time large towns, were firmly under Četnik control. Estimates of their strength tend to vary with the political beliefs of the writer. In 1964, the Yugoslav military journal *Belgrade* put it at a total of 60,000 supporters, but a group of British and U.S. officers who visited Serbia in 1943 thought there were 10,000 fully armed with another 60,000 actively involved, and a potential of a further 250,000 if arms were supplied. Michailović's senior commanders came mainly from the army and air force, the most prominent being Jovo Stevanović, Milo Andrejević, Bora Manić, and Dragutin Kerserović.

From September 1941, British officers were sent by the SOE (q.v.) Cairo office to coordinate with the Četniks. Captain Bill Hudson was the first, and the mission was eventually commanded by Brigadier Charles Armstrong. Many attacks were carried out against Axis troops and installations, especially on the strategic Belgrade-Salonika railway, and some success against shipping on the Danube was also claimed. In the main, however, Četnik policy, as laid down by their government, was to avoid action likely to lead to reprisals against civilians. Bitter experience in World War I and of the German reaction to resistance activity in 1941 lay behind this. The main goal, then, was to build up a trained force ready to rise in the event of a British invasion of Greece or Yugoslavia. The small amount of supplies sent by the British (less than 1,000 tons compared to the 40,000 sent to Tito) further explains the Četniks' relative inactivity. Nonetheless, as late as August 1943, an intercepted signal indicated that the Germans still regarded Mihailović as their main enemy and that they intended to destroy his forces.

At the end of 1943, after British officers had tried in vain to get the two resistance movements to cooperate, British support for the Četniks ceased completely and the partisans were thereafter recognized as the only resistance movement. Low levels of activity and suspicion of collaboration with the enemy were the reasons given. There were, however, grounds for believing that the SOE in Cairo was infiltrated by Communists who doctored information being passed to British prime minister Winston S. Churchill (q.v.). It was alleged, for example, that Četnik sabotage successes were credited to the partisans, and that situation maps showed large Četnik areas as being under partisan control.

That the Četniks did collaborate to some extent is undeniable. It must be understood that the Yugoslav conflict was essentially three-sided, and that alongside the anti-Axis resistance, a civil war between revolutionary Communism and the prewar government was taking place. British officers who served with the Četniks were adamant that most fighting between the two movements was started by the Communists, and that the Četniks usually cooperated with the Nazis only in self-defense.

After the British withdrawal, the Četniks were slowly but surely destroyed by the Communists. At the end of the war, many sought refuge in Austria, only to be sent back with their families by the British Army to almost certain death at Tito's hands—an event still surrounded by controversy. Up to 30,000 perished in this episode. General Mihailović escaped capture until March 1946, but was executed that July. Churchill, wiser now as to the true nature of Tito's politics, asked his successor, Clement Attlee (q.v.) to intervene, but in vain. Tito would not permit British and American officers who served with Mihailović to return to give evidence on his behalf. In 1948, a U.S. inquiry exonerated Michailović of Tito's charges, and President Harry S Truman awarded him a posthumous Legion of Merit.

The Četniks are tragic figures, pawns caught between the great powers and rival ideologies. Though reviled in 1945, hindsight indicates that their motivation was at least as patriotic as the partisans. They were, after all, fighting for a Yugoslavia free of both Nazi and Communist domination. In neighboring Greece, Britain intervened decisively in 1944–1945 to prevent a Communist takeover. Failure to follow a similar line in Yugoslavia—possibly because Churchill was misled by Communist sympathizers, but more likely for reasons of short-term expediency—resulted in Yugoslavia ending World War II and entering the Cold War in the Communist instead of the Western camp.

Philip Green

Additional Reading

Lees, Michael, *The Rape of Serbia (The British Role in Tito's Grab for Power 1943–1944)* (1990).

Sirc, Ljubo, *Between Hitler and Tito* (1989).

Civil Air Patrol (CAP)

The Civil Air Patrol was the civilian auxiliary of the U.S. Army Air Forces (USAAF). CAP was created on 1 December 1941, under the Office of Civilian Defense. CAP's first commander was Major General John F. Curry, a USAAF officer. The basic purpose of CAP was to organize America's light-plane resources into a unified national system that could be used for the war effort. Those resources included some 25,000 light aircraft operating from 2,500 airfields. In 1942, a cadet program was added to give young people between the ages of fifteen and seventeen aviation and premilitary training. Significantly, the cadet program included both young men and women. By 1942, CAP had some 75,000 adult members in more than 1,000 units throughout the country.

Right from the start CAP was a quasi-military organization. Organized along military lines and partially staffed with active duty officers, CAP's members wore U.S. Army uniforms with their own distinctive insignia. Both adult and cadet members received training both in general aviation subjects and in many non-aviation military areas including first aid, map reading, leadership, and close order drill. On 29 April 1943, the War Department assumed control of the CAP and assigned the USAAF the responsibility for supervising and directing its operations. CAP members, however, could quit at any time, and never came under the jurisdiction of U.S. military law.

CAP performed a wide array of tasks for the USAAF within the borders of the United States. All of CAP's pilots were volunteers, many of them flying their own planes. For the most part the only compensation they received was expenses, and quite often not even that. During the war, the CAP moved roughly 3.5 million pounds of mail and critical aviation spare parts, flew approximately 30,000 hours of dawn to dusk patrols along the southern borders, and flew 20,593 target-towing missions for antiaircraft machine gunner training schools. This last task was particularly hazardous, resulting in twenty-three lost aircraft, seven CAP members killed, and five seriously injured.

Perhaps CAP's Coastal Patrol was its most significant contribution to the war effort. Between 5 March 1942 and 31 August 1943, CAP pilots and aircraft flew submarine spotting missions along the 1,200-mile sea frontier from Halifax to the Florida Keys. At that point in the war German U-boats were sinking merchantmen and tankers in U.S. coastal waters at the rate of two and three a day. With the U.S. Navy and the USAAF spread very thin so early in the war, the CAP patrols gave the military hundreds of extra sets of eyes. Using radios donated by the major oil companies, the CAP patrols would summon army and navy bombers to deal with any spotted U-boat.

It was only a short matter of time before the light CAP planes started carrying bombs with jury-rigged external racks. During its eighteen months of service, CAP's Coastal Patrol flew 86,685 missions, for a total of 24 million miles. The patrol sighted and reported 173 U-boats, dropped bombs on fifty-seven of them, and actually sank two. Coastal Patrol pilots also summoned help for ninety-one vessels in distress and for 363 survivors of U-boat attacks. The cost was ninety CAP aircraft lost and twenty-six pilots or observers killed. The results now may appear disproportionate for the cost, but the major significance of the Coastal Patrol was that for a critical period of time it hindered the otherwise almost free reign of the sea lanes the U-boats enjoyed.

As a result of their wartime services, CAP flight crew members were awarded a total of 825 Air Medals. When the U.S. Air Force became a separate service in 1947, CAP went with it. CAP today remains the official auxiliary of the U.S. Air Force, and its cadet program has expanded to equal status with the high school Junior ROTC programs.

David T. Zabecki

Additional Reading
Civil Air Patrol, *CAPM 50-1, Introduction to Civil Air Patrol* (1960).

Coast Guard, U.S.
The outbreak of war in Europe immediately involved the 11,000-strong U.S. Coast Guard (USCG), which was by law an armed force at all times, although located in the Treasury Department. President Franklin D. Roosevelt (q.v.) proclaimed a state of national emergency and established a neutral zone in U.S. territorial waters, and nine USCG cutters soon took up neutrality patrol duties under near-combat conditions.

In January 1940, cutters began serving as floating weather and rescue stations in the mid-Atlantic. After the United States incorporated Greenland into its hemispheric defense system on 9 April, the USCG established the Greenland patrol. In October 1941, the USCG icebreaker *Northland* took the Norwegian trawler *Boskoe* into "protective custody" and captured three German radiomen ashore. This was the first American naval capture of World War II. Roosevelt transferred the USCG to U.S. Navy (USN) operational control on 1 November.

After 7 December 1941, the strength of the USCG increased rapidly, as did the number of its cutters and planes, from 25,000 men to 171,000 men and women, with 80,476 at sea and 51,173 temporary reservists. Additionally, 802 cutters, more than 7,000 smaller craft, and about seventy aircraft were deployed by mid-1945. The USCG brought its more traditional activities and skills, such as search and rescue, marine safety, port security, high explosive handling, control of merchant ship movements and anchorages, and aids to navigation in the form of buoy tenders and long-range navigation, to the far-flung battles and campaigns of this global struggle. Finally, the USCG totally manned 351 USN ships and 288 U.S. Army Transportation Corps vessels.

During the Battle of the Atlantic (q.v.), the USCG destroyed twelve submarines and earned numerous assists. The USCG cutter *Campbell* became the first to escort a convoy on 10 November 1941. To her also fell the distinction of being the first U.S. warship to sink a German U-boat, on

22 January 1942. The honor of being the second fell to the USCG cutter *Icarus* on 9 May. USCG pilots also helped escort convoys and sank a U-boat on 1 August. By May 1944, the USCG established eleven long-range navigation stations that ringed the North Atlantic. It also manned thirteen of the twenty-two weather and rescue stations that dotted the Atlantic. In September 1944, two cutters captured the *Externsteine,* the only German surface naval vessel to be taken at sea by U.S. naval forces. The USCG continued to respond to calls for rescue, often under enemy fire, and saved 4,243 lives in the Atlantic theater.

USCG transports *Joseph T. Dickman, Leonard Wood,* and *Samuel Chase* participated in the invasion of Northwest Africa (q.v.). As in all later landings in the European theater, coast guardsmen also augmented the crews of other vessels. Although the *Wood* lost twenty-one of her thirty-two landing craft in the first wave on the reef near Casablanca, and the *Dickman* lost two, they landed the vast majority of the soldiers safely. One USCG ensign, his boat crew, and the soldiers of three disabled amphibious vehicles ended up ashore miles from any friendly forces. During his three-and-a-half days ashore, the ensign fought off French troops, walked twenty miles for help, returned with a rescue force, captured some of the enemy, and then was wounded and made a prisoner until the end of the fighting. At Algiers, the *Chase* managed to land her troops while successfully dodging torpedoes and fighting off German planes, three of which she downed.

Besides its transports, *Chase, Dickman,* and *Wood,* the USCG manned three 328-foot landing ships, tank (LSTs), Flotilla 4's twenty-two 158-foot landing craft, infantry (large) [LCI(L)], and two 175-foot subchasers in the invasion of Sicily (q.v.). The landings went smoothly in spite of casualties from enemy machine guns and mines on the beaches. For two days, the USCG crews on the beach unloaded supplies to the point of exhaustion under heavy German air attacks, before resistance melted away. At Salerno (q.v.), the USCG manned the *Chase,* the *Dickman,* the LCI(L)s of Flotilla 4, and two LSTs. At Anzio (q.v.), four LSTs and a subchaser, which attacked and sank a German torpedo boat, were manned by the USCG.

In the Normandy (q.v.) invasion, ninety-seven USCG-operated vessels crossed the English Channel. Most of the sixty fast, wooden-hulled, eighty-three-footers of USCG Rescue Flotilla 1 sailed close to the troop transports, where heavy casualties were anticipated. As a last-minute addition, they were rushed across the Atlantic and specially rigged in Britain to pick up survivors.

The rescue cutters, equally divided between the American and British beaches, were credited with saving 1,438 lives. They ran the gauntlet of deadly shore batteries, strafing by airplanes, thickly strewn minefields, naval gunfire, and sometimes even friendly fire to race to the aid of persons in distress, take them aboard until almost swamped, take the survivors to larger ships, and then return to search for more. Less than thirty minutes after H-Hour, one even towed two disabled amphibious vehicles loaded with much needed artillery pieces to the beach. After D-Day, they shepherded the ships carrying troops and supplies to exploit the beachhead.

At UTAH Beach, the *Dickman* landed the first wave without a single casualty, but lost seven landing craft, mainly to mines, before finishing unloading by noon and steaming out, carrying wounded, as did all the transports that day. As headquarters ship for the assault force commander, the USCG-manned *Bayfield* remained on the scene until 25 June. Hundreds of casualties were treated aboard her, and several shot-up landing craft were repaired alongside her. At OMAHA Beach, the *Chase* unloaded her soldiers without damage to herself and steamed out that afternoon. Six of her landing craft were put out of action, mainly by mines.

Of the ten USCG-manned LSTs (six at OMAHA and UTAH Beaches and four at the British beaches) none were lost as they ferried back and forth across the Channel, bringing troops and vehicles including freight cars, and carrying back the wounded. LST-261 alone made fifty-three crossings. One LCI(L) of Flotilla 4 received ten direct hits from German shore artillery, and four others fell victim to mines. Despite their damage, each succeeded in landing most of their soldiers. The remaining craft performed a variety of tasks for several weeks after the invasion, including the salvage of damaged ships and craft.

On 28 June 1944, four days before Cherbourg was liberated, Commander Quentin R. Walsh, USCG, took sixteen sailors to reconnoiter the strongly fortified arsenal and adjacent waterfront. After a machine gun opened fire on them, they silenced the machine gun, killed several snipers, took close to 500 prisoners, and then bluffed the surrender of the fanatical Nazi garrison of Fort du Hamet to free fifty captive U.S. paratroopers.

For the landing in southern France (q.v.), the USCG-operated vessels consisted of the *Bayfield, Chase, Dickman, Cepheus, USCG* cutter *Duane,*

C

four LCIs, and two patrol craft. No USCG vessel was damaged, and casualties were limited to several men wounded by machine gun fire. That operation brought to a conclusion the USCG's combat activities in Europe.

Truman R. Strobridge

Additional Reading

Mercey, Arch A., and Lee Grove (eds.), *Sea, Surf, and Hell: The U.S. Coast Guard in World War II* (1945).

Willoughby, Malcom F., *The U.S. Coast Guard in World War II* (1957).

Colditz

The seemingly impregnable castle fortress of Colditz near Leipzig in the eastern German province of Saxony was used to house Allied POW officers who proved themselves particularly troublesome. Its official name was *Oflag* IVc (Officers' Camp IVc). It was commandeered by the German high command as early as 1938 for the specific purpose of a high security *Sonderlager,* or special camp for enemy officers.

The castle was built in 1080 on a rock promontory overlooking the River Mulde. Its foreboding look led to its name of "Dark Forest" from the Slavic tongue of the original local inhabitants. During the war, it remained surrounded by moats and streams and with plenty of armed guards.

Its principal inmates were British, French, Polish, and Dutch. During its four and a half years as a POW camp some 300 escape attempts were made. A good number were successful, including twelve by Frenchmen, eleven by Britons, and six by Dutch officers.

Chris Westhorp

Additional Reading

Eggers, Reinhold, *Colditz: The German Story* (1961).

Reid, Patrick R., *Colditz: The Full Story* (1984).

———, *Escape from Colditz* (1973).

Combined Chiefs of Staff (CCS)

The Combined Chiefs of Staff Committee was created by British and American leaders during the first Washington conference, code-named ARCADIA, held late December 1941 to early January 1942. Located in Washington, D.C., the CCS was made up of representatives of the heads of the armed forces of Great Britain and the United States, the British chiefs of staff, and the American Joint Chiefs of Staff.

The committee was assigned the task of handling the day-to-day coordination of the war effort between the two nations, from the allocation of shipping to various theaters, to the issuing of daily orders to Allied commanders in the field. Major strategic decisions were made at Allied wartime conferences—Casablanca, Teheran, Yalta, and Potsdam (*see* Conferences, Allied). When the CCS met in plenary session, all heads of services of both countries were present, as well as their ultimate superiors, Prime Minister Winston S. Churchill and President Franklin D. Roosevelt (qq.v.). As a highly effective device for the coordination of the war machines of two Allied but sovereign countries, the CCS was unprecedented in history, and undoubtedly made a significant contribution to the defeat of the Axis.

However, essential differences in industrial power, culture, and historical experience between the two nations were not extinguished, and surfaced in disputes over strategy. The two nations were not equal partners. Indeed, American domination of the wartime coalition and the CCS was apparent from the beginning, although the actions of Roosevelt and the initial inexperience of U.S. Army leaders in alliance politics masked this temporarily.

While Churchill and Roosevelt corresponded from the very beginning of World War II, contacts between military leaders in Great Britain and the United States did not begin in any significant way until after the fall of France in June 1940. In the autumn and winter of 1940, Roosevelt, concerned that any American aid sent to Britain would be wasted if the British possessed neither the will nor the capacity to resist Germany, ordered a number of high-level army and navy observers to go to Britain to assess its strategic situation. The British, knowing what was at stake, opened many doors for these missions. Although not all American reports were optimistic about Britain's chances of survival, a spirit of cooperation and friendliness between the military in both countries was established.

Meetings between British and American military leaders increased both in number and importance in 1941. In spring 1941, for example, secret bilateral staff talks were held in Washington, D.C., and it was agreed that if war broke out between the United States and Japan and Germany, the Allies would seek the defeat of Germany first, Germany being the greater threat. This "Germany first" decision, although made while the United States was still a "neutral power," became a keystone in subsequent Allied strategy.

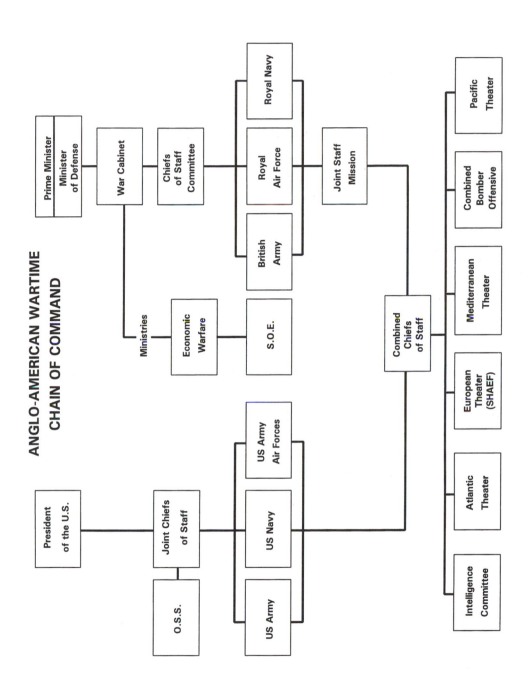

ANGLO-AMERICAN WARTIME
CHAIN OF COMMAND

Prime Minister / Minister of Defense

War Cabinet

Chiefs of Staff Committee

Royal Navy

Royal Air Force

British Army

Joint Staff Mission

Ministries

Economic Warfare

S.O.E.

Combined Chiefs of Staff

President of the U.S.

Joint Chiefs of Staff

O.S.S.

US Army Air Forces

US Navy

US Army

Intelligence Committee

Atlantic Theater

European Theater (SHAEF)

Mediterranean Theater

Combined Bomber Offensive

Pacific Theater

Thus, the establishment of the CCS at the Arcadia Conference was a natural progression. At Arcadia, Soviet representation to the CCS was considered but rejected, as the Russian front was regarded as separate, independent, and distant from the main focus of the Anglo-American war effort. Soviet political and cultural differences also played a part in the decision to exclude them. Nonetheless, the Soviets did have an important role in strategic decision making at subsequent Allied conferences. At Teheran, for example, Josef Stalin's (q.v.) strong support for Operation OVER-LORD, the planned Anglo-American invasion of France in 1944, was crucial in overcoming British reservations.

The most serious disagreements over strategy between the United States and Great Britain occurred during 1942, the first year of the CCS's existence. They were caused by the U.S. Army's BOLERO (q.v.) plan. Since BOLERO was eventually discarded and the Allies went ahead in November 1942 with the British plan to invade Northwest Africa (Operation TORCH [q.v.]), it is widely assumed that this meant Britain was dominant in the wartime coalition and was able to have its own preference for a peripheral strategy imposed over the U.S. Army's more direct approach, which called for an early invasion of France.

Roosevelt's insistence, for political reasons, on the involvement of American forces against Germany in 1942 ultimately determined that Operation TORCH was launched, as the BOLERO plan did not envision a major invasion of France before 1943. If he had supported the BOLERO plan, it is likely that it would have been carried out, for the enormous industrial and manpower resources of the United States were already apparent in 1942 and made it the preeminent member of the anti-Axis coalition.

The United States was eventually able to impose its ideas upon Allied strategy making through the CCS. Its direct strategy for the defeat of Germany was put into effect on D-Day, 6 June 1944, in Operation OVERLORD. This was in part because its representatives on the CCS became more skilled in persuading both the British military and politicians of both countries of the value of their strategic approach. In particular, they succeeded in winning Roosevelt over to their cause, and this proved decisive. By late 1943, he was determined to end the war in Europe as soon as possible and then to concentrate on the final destruction of Japan.

Differences between the United States and Great Britain should not be exaggerated. The CCS was a remarkable organization, which for the most part performed its demanding tasks with a high degree of skill and effectiveness. One only has to look at the noncooperation among the Axis powers to become aware of its importance in determining the ultimate victory of the Allies. If the Japanese had decided to participate in Hitler's invasion of the Soviet Union in June 1941, to take only one example of the possibilities open to a more unified Axis alliance, the consequences for the Soviets might well have been disastrous and could have resulted in a different outcome of World War II.

David Walker

Additional Reading

Churchill, Winston S., *The Grand Alliance* (*The Second World War*, Vol 3) (1950).

Matloff, Maurice, *Strategic Planning for Coalition Warfare, 1943–1944* (1959).

Matloff, Maurice, and Edward M. Snell, *Strategic Planning for Coalition Warfare, 1941–1942* (1953).

Combined Operations

Between the wars, the British armed forces paid little attention to amphibious matters. Money was short, more and more interest was being shown in the potential of airpower. Above all, recent memories of the World War I disaster at Gallipoli seemed to indicate that under modern conditions a large-scale amphibious assault on a defended shore was simply impossible. The Inter-Services Training and Development Centre at Portsmouth kept some interest alive. Its resources were small, but nonetheless some of its ideas proved worthy in World War II.

Necessity, however, is the mother of invention. By the end of summer 1940, German forces held the whole coastline of northwest Europe from the Arctic to the Bay of Biscay. It was obvious that the only way back onto the Continent for the British Army was by an amphibious landing. Historically, there was nothing new in this. Over the centuries this was Britain's normal method of intervening in European wars; for example, Wellington's campaign in Spain early in the nineteenth century. The four-year involvement in France in World War I represented a costly departure from this well-proven practice. If there was any doubt of the necessity for serious study of amphibious matters, then the fiasco of the Norway (q.v.) expedition in early 1940 served as a vivid reminder.

Thus a new directorate was set up, called at first Amphibious Operations, later Combined

Operations. The first chief was Admiral of the Fleet Sir Roger Keyes (q.v.), a veteran of amphibious operations at Gallipoli and Zeebrugge in the earlier war. After eighteen months, he was replaced by the charismatic Lord Louis Mountbatten (q.v.), and it was in this post that he first became a world figure. The directorate's mission was twofold: to raise, train, and employ the new commando (q.v.) forces, and to work out the tactics, training, and equipment needed for the eventual seaborne invasion of Europe. At that early stage, the British had no way of knowing that this would be carried out as a joint Anglo-American operation.

In practice, of course, there was little distinction between the two tasks. The lessons learned the hard way on a host of raids, some involving a handful of men, others the size of Saint Nazaire or Dieppe (qq.v.), were applied to the planning and execution of full-scale landings such as Sicily and Normandy. The contribution of Combined Operations can be seen in the part played by British forces in a whole series of successful Anglo-American amphibious assaults: Northwest Africa, Sicily, Italy, Anzio, Salerno, and Normandy (qq.v.).

Such assaults are among the most difficult operations of war. By the time they were executed, the Allies had complete command of both sea and air. They were lucky, too, in that the first major operation (the TORCH landings in Northwest Africa) was virtually unopposed, and thus offered an opportunity to learn valuable lessons at little or no cost. With that said, the complete success of this series of seaborne assaults on Axis Europe owes much to the work of the Combined Operations staff and its U.S. counterparts.

Special types of landing craft (q.v.) were designed and built, ranging in size from LSTs (landing ship, tank), oceangoing and 300 feet long, to the small LCIs and LCAs (landing craft, infantry, and landing craft, assault) carried by mother ships and used for the final runs to the shore. Some versions were modified to provide close fire support in the vital final stages of the assault. Whatever their size or role, all essentially were flat-bottomed and had blunt bow doors.

Once ashore, the assaulting infantry was alone until its own artillery arrived, and during this period had to rely on naval gunfire support. To control this, special artillery spotter teams, known as bombardment liaison officers, were trained to work both ashore and on board ship.

One of the difficulties of assaulting a fully defended coast is that there are no flanks to turn. A new element—airpower—was used to solve this. Wherever possible, airborne formations were parachuted some miles inland simultaneously with the beach assault to confuse the defenders and to give the attack more depth. Another lesson learned from earlier raids, particularly from the Dieppe disaster, was the need for prior reconnaissance to discover both the natural hazards, such as currents and hidden rocks or soft beaches, and cruel manmade obstacles such as mines. Small teams of specially selected and highly trained volunteers were used on these dangerous missions.

Once a bridgehead was secured it was important that it could be resupplied quickly and regularly, but until a port was captured, all supplies and follow-on units had to be funneled across the beach. The potential for a monumental logjam on the beach is obvious (to some extent this did happen in the Pacific at Guadalcanal in 1942). Again, the answer was to train specialized beach groups, joint army-navy units whose task was to police and organize the beach and ensure that anything that landed subsequent to the initial assault was dispatched in the right direction and to where it was needed.

All this effort had to be planned and coordinated from headquarters and operational centers hundreds of miles away. Command and control of this tri-service (and usually multinational) enterprise on the spot was needed, and during the early stages it had to be located afloat. This led to the development of special headquarters ships. After trial and error it was found that converted small passenger liners, with their luxurious saloons and dining rooms turned into plotting and operations centers, were ideal.

Some idea of the amount of coordination needed can be gauged from the figures for the Operation TORCH landings in Northwest Africa. Some 69,000 men were landed, with all their equipment, from sixty-seven ships using 408 landing craft and escorted by fifty-nine warships, including three battleships and seven carriers.

British naval historian A.C. Handy commented that without Adolf Hitler's (q.v.) 1940 victories none of this need have taken place. This is undoubtedly true. What is equally true is that the Allies' unbroken run of amphibious successes is one of the most remarkable features of World War II, and without them, Western Europe would either have remained under Nazi occupation, or exchanged Nazi for Communist masters. The considerable British contribution to this feat of arms was made possible by the efforts of Combined Operations.

Philip Green

Additional Reading

Fergusson, Bernard, *The Watery Maze: The Story of Combined Operations* (1961).

Saunders, Hillary St.G., *Combined Operations* (1952).

Commandos

By the middle of 1940, victorious Germany occupied the coast of northern Europe from the North Cape to the Pyrenees. In contrast, Great Britain, its army rescued from Dunkirk (q.v.) but without its heavy equipment, was barely strong enough to defend the United Kingdom, let alone contemplate an invasion of Europe. If it was to undertake any offensive operations it would have to be by unorthodox means. Thus was born the commando concept. On 6 June 1940, British prime minister Winston S. Churchill (q.v.) told the chiefs of staff: "Enterprises must be prepared with specially trained troops of the hunter class who can develop a reign of terror down the enemy coast." That the British, with their long maritime history, had to improvise in this way is somewhat surprising, but as recently as 1938, an amphibious exercise consisted of sailors rowing soldiers ashore in longboats. Clearly, little notice was being taken of modern ideas or technology.

Britain's desperate situation in 1940—the year of Dunkirk, the Battle of Britain (q.v.), and the Blitz—led to a swift response. The first unit, commanded by Lieutenant Colonel John Durnford-Slater of the Royal Artillery, paraded at Plymouth on 5 July, and six days later carried out its first raid, on Guernsey. Though small and achieving little, it was nonetheless a pointer to the future. By March 1941, there were eleven commando units, totaling 4,000 men. In February 1942, the Royal Marines (q.v.), with their great amphibious tradition, formed their own commando units as well. By the end of the war, commandos organized in brigade strength fought from the Arakan to the Arctic.

Initially, these units were called "Special Service," but understandably the initials "SS" were not popular. The term commando, once used by guerrilla columns harassing British forces in the Boer War, was adopted instead. This title was applied to both the individual soldier and complete units.

The men were all volunteers and came from many different regiments of the British Army. There were also volunteers from the Commonwealth and occupied Europe. They were not saints. Many were misfits in the army or civilian life before the war, but all had one essential quality: guts. Selection and training, carried out at Achnacarry in the Scottish Highlands, was rigorous. Those who failed to meet the required standards of physical and mental endurance, basic military skills, and, above all, ruthless determination to kill the enemy at close quarters were returned to their units.

Commando units were controlled by Headquarters, Combined Operations (q.v.), whose chief was initially Admiral Sir Roger Keyes (q.v.), and from October 1941, Admiral Lord Louis Mountbatten (q.v.). A commando unit comprised 450 men under a lieutenant colonel. It was divided into five troops of seventy-five, each in turn split into sections of fifteen men commanded by a sergeant. Though one troop was equipped with mortars and machine guns, the emphasis was on light automatic weapons. On occasion daggers and crossbows were used to kill sentries quietly.

Initially, operations were confined to small-scale raids across the English Channel, but they were soon to expand in size and extend geographically to all theaters of the war. Typical targets were radar sites, communication facilities, and economic installations, but above all, the aim was to kill Germans. Taking advantage of the Royal Navy's control of the sea, these raids were usually amphibious, but parachutes were also used.

In the dark days of 1940 and 1941, when Britain stood alone, virtually under siege, the offensive spirit after commandos and their successes in operations, like the Lofoten Islands and Saint Nazaire (q.v.), raised morale both in Britain and in occupied Europe. In the military sense, they reminded the large Allied conscript armies that even in the technological age of the tank, the four-engine bomber, and radar, the soldier on the ground still needed the age-old qualities of fitness, courage, and above all, the ambition and ability to kill the enemy in person. From their somewhat amateurish endeavors in the early years, lessons were learned, particularly about specialized equipment, the problems of interservice command in amphibious operations, and the need for airborne landings behind coastal defenses. These lessons were to pay dividends in later years.

By the end of 1942, the commandos and their American comrades, the rangers (q.v.), occupied a key place in the Allied order of battle. With their amphibious expertise, they played a prominent part in Allied landings in Sicily, Italy, and Normandy (qq.v.). Such elite forces attracted the best men and thus deprived routine line units of their most determined leaders, but in return they paid a considerable dividend. They sought action and carried the fight aggressively to the enemy in such a way that he could never relax in safety.

From their formation in 1940 until the end of the war, commandos were rarely out of action. Their memorial in Westminster Abbey contains a simple but appropriate quotation from the Second Book of Samuel: "They performed whatsoever the King commanded." Though British Army commandos were disbanded in 1946, the Royal Marines have performed this role with distinction ever since, most notably in Korea (where Number 41 Commando was awarded a U.S. Presidential Unit Citation), Aden, Borneo, and the Falklands.

Philip Green

Additional Reading
Durnford-Slater, J., *Commando: Memoirs of a Fighting Commando in World War Two* (1991).
Neillands, Robin, *By Sea & Land* (1987).
Saunders, Hillary St.G., *The Green Beret (The Story of the Commandos)* (1949).
Young, Peter, *Commando* (1969).

C

E

Eagle Squadrons

For more than a year before the United States entered World War II, some of its young men violated the U.S. Neutrality Acts (q.v.) and went through Canada to enlist in the Royal Air Force to fight Germany alongside the British. During the Battle of Britain (q.v.), the RAF accepted a few young American pilots but the effort was not well organized. Nonetheless, eight Americans fought in the RAF during the Battle of Britain, most of them serving with Number 609 Squadron. At first incorporated into all-British units, as more pilots volunteered for the RAF, the British decided to organize three squadrons of Americans, the so-called Eagle Squadrons.

The Eagle Squadron concept was first proposed by Charles Sweeny, a wealthy American in London, and was accepted by the secretary of state for air because of its public relations value. It conjured up images of a similar venture in World War I, the Lafayette Escadrille, and lent credibility to the role of Britain as a leader of an international coalition to defeat Nazism. In anticipation of the flow of recruits from the United States, the RAF established Number 71 Squadron, the first Eagle Squadron, at Church Fenton, 180 miles north of London, in September 1940. The first men to join the squadron arrived on 19 September 1940. Eugene Q. Tobin of Los Angeles, Andrew Mamedoff of Connecticut, and Vernon Keough of Brooklyn, were all expatriates who fought with the RAF in France and in Number 609 Squadron during the Battle of Britain. Number 71 Squadron's first commander was Squadron Leader Walter Myers Churchill, an English pilot and war hero.

During the fall of 1940, Number 71's personnel continued to grow. On 7 November 1940, the first aircraft arrived for the squadron, nine Hawker Hurricanes, as well as several additional American volunteers. Among the new pilots was a tall, rawboned Utah native, Chesley G. Peterson, who would become one of the youngest aces of the war and would command the Eagle Squadrons after their incorporation into the United States Army Air Forces in 1942. In January 1941, Squadron Leader Churchill was placed in charge of an RAF wing and was succeeded by American William E.G. Taylor, who had fought with the British since early in the war. The RAF declared the squadron operational early in February 1941, and moved it to Martlesham Heath, sixty-five miles northeast of London, for combat operations.

The RAF formed the second Eagle Squadron, Number 121, in mid-May 1941 at a Kirton-on-Lindsey base. RAF Fighter Command also appointed another Battle of Britain hero to lead Number 121 Squadron, Peter Powell, an ace with seven German planes to his credit. A third Eagle Squadron, Number 133, was activated on 1 August 1941 and stationed near RAF Station Duxford, five miles south of Cambridge. Its British commander, Squadron Leader George A. Brown, had been associated with Number 71 Squadron and proved to be an exceptional commander. Both new squadrons were equipped with Hawker Hurricanes. In August 1941, the RAF began swapping out the Hurricanes for the newer Spitfires in the Eagle Squadrons.

In all, 243 Americans fought in these three Eagle Squadrons while associated with the RAF. Almost one-third of these men were killed in action during World War II. The Eagle Squadrons acquitted themselves ably in combat. Number 71 Squadron, for example, accounted for three German Bf-109 fighters on its first combat engagement on 2 July 1941. Throughout the remainder of 1941 and most of 1942, the three Eagle Squadrons continued to serve in the RAF.

On the night of 7 December 1941, after they received news of the Pearl Harbor attack, representatives of the Eagle Squadrons visited the American ambassador in London to offer their service to the U.S. Army Air Forces. While they continued to operate with the RAF during the spring and summer of 1942, the U.S. Army Air Forces sent representatives to the Eagle Squadrons to gather information on tactics and organization and to lay the groundwork with the British for combined air operations against Germany. On 12 September 1942, the three Eagle Squadrons were incorporated into the U.S. Army Air Forces as the 334th, 335th, and 336th Fighter Squadrons. These units were combined into the newly activated 4th Fighter Group of the U.S. Eighth Air Force. Although they first operated with Spitfires, the group transitioned to P-47s in March 1943 and to P-51s in April 1944. The 4th Fighter Group served in combat in Europe from October 1942 through April 1945 and destroyed more enemy aircraft in the air and on the ground than any other fighter group of the Eighth Air Force.

Roger D. Launius

Additional Reading

Haugland, Vern, *The Eagle's War: The Saga of the Eagle Squadron Pilots, 1940–1945* (1982).

Maurer, Maurer, *Air Force Combat Units of World War II* (1983).

Einsatzgruppen

The term *Einsatzgruppen*, loosely translated from German, means Special Action Groups. These units followed into the Soviet Union closely on the heels of the invading German Army after Adolf Hitler (q.v.) launched Operation BARBAROSSA. *Einsatzgruppen* were responsible for the liquidation of Jews, Gypsies, Soviet political commissars, and anyone else deemed unfit by the *Reich*. The assembly of the *Einsatzgruppen* for the Russian campaign took place in the spring of 1941. The top officers consisted of the cream of the *Kripo* (Criminal Police), the *Gestapo* (q.v.), and the *Reich* Security Service. The enlisted men represented a motley collection of SS men, *Waffen-SS* (q.v.), regular police, locally recruited police, and auxiliaries recruited from local volunteer and native Fascist militia. Among them, Ukrainians, Lithuanians, Latvians, and Estonians were conspicuous in numbers and cruelty.

Einsatzgruppen were organized into four separate battalion-sized units of 500 to 900 men, and were identified by the letters A, B, C, and D. Each *Einsatzgruppe* was composed of a number of composite units called *Einsatzkommandos* and *Sonderkommandos*, the size of a company. These in turn were further broken down into platoon-sized units of *Teilkommandos* and special purpose squads.

Einsatzgruppe A was initially commanded by *SS-Brigadeführer* Dr. Walter Stahlecker and later by *SS-Brigadeführer* Heinz Jost. Its area of operations was the Baltic states. By far the largest number of executions was carried out by this group, which by the winter of 1941–1942 would boast of having executed 249,420 Jews, Gypsies, and political commissars.

Einsatzgruppe B, commanded by *SS-Brigadeführer* Arthur Nebe (q.v.), later head of the Criminal Police, and by *SS-Brigadeführer* Erich Naumann, was attached to Army Group Center with headquarters in Smolensk. Its theater of operations extended to the area pointing toward Moscow, including parts of Byelorussia. Its *Sonderkommandos* 7a, 7b, and 7c and *Einsatzkommando* 8 and 9 were active in Minsk, Mogilev, Sadrudubs, Krupa, and other places. Smolensk and the environs of Moscow were the special targets of these units. During the short five-month duration that Nebe held command, his unit was responsible for the execution of 45,000 people. It was Nebe who hosted *Reichsführer-SS* Heinrich Himmler (q.v.) during his visit to the front in 1941. Nebe ordered 100 people shot so that Himmler could see first-hand what a liquidation looked like. Himmler nearly fainted during the shootings.

Einsatzgruppe C, commanded by *SS-Brigadeführer* Dr. Otto Rasch and later by *SS-Brigadeführer* Max Thomas, was detailed to the area of operations behind Army Group South in the Ukraine. Its subordinate units were *Einsatzkommandos* 5 and 6. Its headquarters was located in Kiev and its operational range extended to the areas of Novo Ukrainka, Sokol, Tarnopol, Rovno, Stalino, and Kiev. By the winter of 1941–1942, Group C had executed 95,000 people. Dr. Rasch ensured that all the men in his command participated to the fullest in the executions, thus binding them to a certain comradeship of collective guilt.

Einsatzgruppe D, commanded by *SS-Brigadeführer* Otto Ohlendorf, operated in the area of the Crimea and Caucasus. In the one year he commanded Group D (June 1941–June 1942), Ohlendorf's men executed more than 90,000 people.

In the early days of the executions of the Eastern peoples, corpses were buried in mass graves in the woods. Burial had several disadvantages: the earth cover tended to collapse, and as a result, odors spread for miles around, and more earth had to be piled on top of the graves. Even more importantly, mass graves left telltale signs of the killing operation. The *Einsatzkommandos* normally lined up the victims in the front of a ditch and shot them in the back of the neck with submachine guns or other small arms. The mortally wounded toppled into their graves. Some commanders disliked this method, as it reminded them of the execution style used by the Soviet NKVD (q.v.).

As the tide of the war turned against Germany and its allies in late 1942 and the German retreat in Russia became imminent, an initiative was undertaken by the *Einsatzgruppen* to attempt to erase the evidence of their barbarous deeds. A special unit, known as *Kommando 1005,* commanded by *SS-Standartenführer* Paul Blobel, was activated for the purpose of reopening the mass graves of earlier victims and burning their remains. Exhuming and burning the bodies proved to be most effective in eradicating any trace of the mass graves.

For all the brutality displayed by the *Einsatzgruppen* during their operations in the Soviet Union, it is ironic to note that the commanders of these units were not illiterate Nazi thugs, but educated, cultured men. Most had advanced university degrees in law, economics, and, in one case, theology. *Einsatzgruppe* personnel underwent training in the town of Pretsch in Saxony. Marksmanship and political indoctrination filled most of their training hours. They were told that Slavs, Jews, and Gypsies of the East were considered *Untermenschen,* or subhumans, and had no place in Hitler's "New Order" for Europe. Thus, they were to be eliminated as they threatened life in the greater *Reich* and its newly acquired territories.

After the Allied victory in Europe in May 1945, the Allies commenced the trial of the major German war criminals at Nuremberg, beginning in November 1945 (*see* International Military Tribunal). The SS and *Gestapo* were branded as illegal criminal organizations and its members put on trial for war crimes. The trial of the *Einsatzgruppen* (Case 9, *USA* v. *Otto Ohlendorf, et al.*) brought the former commanders of the special action groups to justice.

The German Army also was not without guilt for the extermination of the Eastern peoples. The so-called Wagner-Heydrich Agreement of 1941 (named for General Eduard Wagner of the German Army and *SS-Obergruppenführer* Reinhard Heydrich [q.v.] on behalf of the SS) outlined the use of the special action groups in the rear areas of the army's operational zones. The military was to furnish petrol, food, quarters, and other logistical support to the *Einsatzgruppen.* This agreement tarnished the honor of the German Army, and closely linked it to the genocide that occurred on the eastern front.

John R. Dabrowski

Additional Reading

Dawidowicz, Lucy S., *The War Against the Jews 1933–45* (1975).

Höhne, Heinz, *The Order of the Death's Head* (1970).

Reitlinger, Gerald, *The SS: Alibi of a Nation, 1922–45* (1956).

F

FFI

See FORCES FRANÇAISES DE L'INTÉRIEUR

1st Special Service Force

The 1st Special Service Force was an American-Canadian special unit organized in 1942 for employment in particularly hazardous and difficult northern conditions. It originally was formed to undertake commando operations in snow-covered countries such as Norway and northern Italy (operations known collectively as Operation PLOUGH), and it was to have consisted of Canadians, Norwegians, and Americans. While this proved impractical, the force nevertheless was authorized in June 1942 and began training in the United States at Fort William Henry Harrison, Montana, in July.

Comprising a combat force of three regiments, each of two battalions of approximately 600 men and a "base echelon" or service battalion of about 600, the Special Service Force used American equipment and ranks. It was commanded by an American officer, Colonel Robert T. Frederick (q.v.). Canadians, administered under the auspices of the 1st Canadian Special Service Battalion, made up approximately one-third of the combat force. The senior Canadian officer acted as the commander's executive officer, while Canadians commanded a fluctuating number of the force's battalions. The Canadian contingent, however, was a one-time commitment, not to be reinforced.

The Canadians and Americans were not segregated in national units; all ranks were distributed throughout the regiment. Pay, honors, and military discipline were nevertheless administered by the troops' respective national governments, a point that caused some consternation given the higher pay scales of the American troops. Initial operational training included specialized parachute exercises, training in demolitions, infantry ground tactics, and winter warfare training under Norwegian instructors.

Operation PLOUGH was canceled in the fall of 1942, but the force remained in existence, undergoing further mountain and amphibious training to prepare it for action in the Mediterranean. In August 1943, it took part in the abortive invasion of Kiska, in the Aleutians, but was back training in the United States by 1 September. In mid-November, the force was assigned to General Mark W. Clark's (q.v.) Fifth Army for employment in the mountainous approaches to Cassino. In addition to its standard equipment of rifles, mortars, and machine guns, the force had parachutes, winter equipment, and flamethrowers. To augment its mobility and firepower, 1,190 trucks and 600 T-24 tracked amphibious carriers, as well as a battalion of airborne artillery, were attached.

The force saw its first action in the Fifth Army's attack to free the Camino hill mass on either side of the Mignano gap on 2 December 1943—a prelude to the attacks on Cassino. The 1st Special Service Force was in almost continuous action for the next six weeks as the approaches to Cassino were cleared. It seized the two highest features of the American sector on the right flank of the Mignano gap, Mount la Difensa and Mount la Remetanea, using scaling ropes to surprise and drive the Germans from their reinforced caves and pillboxes on the summits. By 8 December, the Camino hills were in Allied hands. The force's first action cost 400 casualties. Its final action in the assault to free the gap was a Christmas Day attack on Hill 720, a rocky feature of the 4,000-foot peak of Mount Sammucro. The Canadian official history observed with dry understatement, "Canadians and Americans ate their Christmas dinner of field rations on their snow-covered objective."

The force's special mountain training was called upon again early in the new year as, augmented by two infantry battalions and additional artillery, it assaulted several German-held peaks in preparation for the final assaults on the Gustav Line (q.v.). After determined fighting by both sides on 6–7 January 1944, the force took its objectives, the intensity of the battles measured by the heavy casualties. In February, it fought with distinction in the Anzio (q.v.) bridgehead and earned the honor of spearheading the advance into Rome in June 1944.

The force was employed in a commando role in the invasion of southern France (q.v.) in August 1944, and remained there covering the Allies' right flank along the mountainous Franco-Italian frontier. Disbanded in December 1944 due to the difficulty of securing reinforcements from the manpower-starved Allies, the force earned a reputation for its fighting record and "extraordinarily high morale," a record unmarred by national jealousies. With grudging respect, the Germans called the 1st Special Service Force the "Devil's Brigade." After World War II, the force's lineage was continued with the formation of the U.S. Special Forces.

Paul D. Dickson

Additional Reading

Adleman, Robert H., and George Walton, *The Devil's Brigade* (1966).

Blumenson, Martin, *Salerno to Cassino* (1969).

Burhans, Robert D., *The First Special Service Force* (1947).

Nicholson, G.W.L., *Official History of the Canadian Army in the Second World War,* Volume II: *The Canadians in Italy, 1943–1945* (1956).

Forces Françaises de l'Intérieur (FFI)

The French Forces of the Interior was a blanket name for a wide range of regular and irregular military forces operating in German occupied France during World War II. To some extent, the people who joined such units were motivated by their shame and shock over the French military defeat and the German seizure of the entire French economy.

Some initial, spontaneous uprisings started in June 1940 after the fall of France, but the organized resistance received its strongest impulse from a patriotic appeal originating from Brigadier General Charles de Gaulle (q.v.) in London. Speaking to the people of occupied France via a BBC (q.v.) broadcast, de Gaulle said, ". . . I invite all French-

men, wherever they may be, to join me in action, in sacrifice and hope. Our country is in mortal peril. Let us fight to save her. *Vive la France.*"

It took a while for the French public to realize who de Gaulle was and where their patriotic duty lay; with de Gaulle or with the Nazi-allied Vichy regime of Marshal Phillipe Pétain (qq.v.). De Gaulle's magnificent speech, however, was a clarion call to battle that many Frenchmen and women (women were prominent in all resistance movements) could not resist. People from all walks of life, particularly former servicemen, flocked to the Gaullist banner.

Many former officers, acting alone or with friends, set up intelligence networks in anticipation of the day they could resume combat against the Nazis. Others, by taking boats from poorly guarded ports or by crossing the Pyrenees, joined de Gaulle's organization in London in the name of "Free France." All of these officers, including de Gaulle, were sentenced to death in absentia by the Vichy regime.

At first, resistance efforts were disorganized, but by September 1941 the *Comité National Français* (National French Committee, or CNF) had formed and sent delegations to twenty countries in Africa, Asia, and the Americas seeking recognition and support. Recognition of the CNF by the Soviet Union brought considerable internal Communist support, while reassuring many others that it would not become a Nazi-dominated organization. This recognition brought to de Gaulle's cause such prominent French leftists as Pierre Brossolette, Christian Peneau, Leon Blum (q.v.), and Jean Moulin (q.v.).

The FFI, commanded from London by General Marie Pierre Koenig (q.v.), consisted of many resistance organizations operating from early 1944 under the loose control of the *Comité Français de Libération Nationale* (French Committee of National Liberation). Among these units were the *Armée Secrète* (Secret Army), the *Maquis* (q.v.), the *Francs-tireurs et Partisans* (Sharpshooters and Partisans), and the *Organization de Résistance de l'Armée* (Army Resistance Organization).

The FFI operated in occupied France, sabotaging German operations and providing intelligence to the Allies prior to the June 1944 landings in Normandy (q.v.). By the time of the landings, the FFI numbered some 200,000. After the invasion, soldiers of the FFI fought as effective auxiliaries of Allied units, particularly in the Rhône Valley, Brittany, and Normandy. Over 150,000 members of the various resistance units enlisted or were inducted into the French First Army, fighting across France, through Germany, and into Czechoslovakia by the war's end.

When de Gaulle returned to France after the Normandy invasion, his major imperative was to have his forces take immediate control of any liberated area of France in order to prevent a Communist take-over. He understood that pre-empting the Communists was just as important as prosecuting the war against Germany. In this respect, de Gaulle's strategic vision was clearer than that of U.S. President Franklin Roosevelt (q.v.), who often criticized de Gaulle for "playing politics" rather than fighting the Germans. Many historians today credit de Gaulle's actions with keeping the Communists from taking control of post-war France.

After the liberation and before the establishment of stable government, many members of the FFI participated in a terrible settling of accounts, as French collaborators and suspected collaborators were subjected to drum-head trials and often summary executions. Historian Robert Aron estimated that these executions in the name of post-liberation purification totaled approximately fifty thousand.

Paul J. Rose

Additional Reading

Aron, Robert, *The Vichy Regime, 1940–1944* (1958).

Erlich, Blake, *Resistance: France 1940–1944* (1965).

Paxton, Robert O., *Vichy France: New Order 1940–1944* (1972).

F

Foreign SS Volunteers

Idealists, criminals, or pressed men? Crusaders against Communism or collaborators? These epithets have been used many times since 1945 to describe the thousands of men and some women who saw service in the ranks of the *Waffen-SS* (q.v.) formations and yet were not German.

The range of nationalities is extensive, embracing all the European countries including the neutral states of Sweden, Switzerland, and Spain. Moreover, the numbers for these nationalities varied greatly, from the estimated 50,000 men and women of Dutch nationality who served in *Waffen-SS* or SS-controlled security formations, down to some groups of mixed quality from South Africa, Great Britain, and even the United States.

Within these units were people who volunteered or were conscripted and chose to serve within the *Waffen-SS* for a wide variety of reasons. Some were pro-German and National Socialist in politics, idealists fighting for the "New Order."

TABLE 1

The Germanic Legions, 1940–1943

Unit Designation	Date Formed	Ethnic Composition	Major Campaigns
SS Infantry *Regiment Westland*	May 1940	Dutch	None
SS Infantry *Regiment Nordland*	May 1940	Flemish Danish Norwegian	None
SS Volunteer *Regiment Nordwest*	April 1941	Flemish Danish	None
Volunteer Legion *Niederlande*	July 1941	Dutch	Leningrad
Volunteer Legion *Flandern*	April 1941	Flemish	Leningrad
Free Corps *Danemark*	June 1941	Danish	Demyansk
Volunteer Legion *Norwegen*	August 1941	Norwegian	Leningrad
Finnish Volunteer Battalion of the *Waffen-SS*	June 1941	Finnish	Caucasus

Note: With the exception of the Finnish Volunteer Battalion, the Germanic legions were disbanded in 1943. Those volunteers who still wished to fight were transferred to newly raised or existing *Waffen-SS* units (*see* Table 2).

TABLE 2

The Foreign *Waffen-SS* Divisions, 1940–1945

Unit Designation	Date Formed	Ethnic Composition	Major Campaigns
5th SS *Panzer* Division *Wiking*	1940	Dutch Danish Norwegian Estonian	Rostow Caucasus Warsaw Hungary
11th SS Volunteer *Panzergrenadier* Division *Nordland*	March 1943	Norwegian Danish French Swiss	Croatia Leningrad Kurland Berlin
13th *Waffen-SS* Mountain Division *Handschar*	March 1943	Croatian & Albanian Muslims	Yugoslavia Hungary Austria
14th *Waffen-SS* Grenadier Division *Galizische Nr. 1*	July 1943	Ukrainian	Brody Slovakia Yugoslavia
15th *Waffen-SS* Grenadier Division *Lattische Nr. 1*	February 1943	Latvian	Novorzhev West Prussia Berlin
19th *Waffen-SS* Grenadier Division	January 1944	Latvian	Latvia Kurland
20th *Waffen-SS* Grenadier Division *Estnische Nr. 1*	January 1944	Estonian	Estonia Silesia Czech border
21st *Waffen-SS* Mountain Division *Skanderberg*	April 1944	Albanian Muslims	Albania Kossovo
23rd Volunteer *Panzergrenadier* Division *Nederland*	1945	Dutch	Leningrad Lithuania Kurland Oder
24th *Waffen-SS* Mountain Division	July 1942	Italian Austrian	Italy Yugoslavia
25th *Waffen-SS* Grenadier Division *Hunyadi Nr. 1*	June 1944	Hungarian	Czechoslovakia South Germany Nuremberg
26th *Waffen-SS* Grenadier Division *Hunyadi Nr. 2*	February 1945	Hungarian	Czechoslovakia Hungary
27th SS Volunteer *Grenadier* Division *Langemarck*	1943	Flemish Belgians	Estonia Pomerania Oder
28th SS Volunteer *Grenadier* Division *Wallonie*	1943	Walloon Belgians	Estonia
29th *Waffen-SS* Grenadier Division	1944	Italian	Italy Northern Italy
30th *Waffen-SS* Grenadier Division	1945	Russian	Northern France

(continued next page)

TABLE 2 *(continued)*

Unit Designation	Date Formed	Ethnic Composition	Major Campaigns
34th *Waffen-SS* *Grenadier* Division *Charlemagne*	1945	French	Poland Pomerania Berlin
35th SS Volunteer *Grenadier* Division *Landstorn Nederland*	1945	Dutch	Holland Arnhem Rheinland

Note: Most of these SS divisions either started or finished the war as smaller units.

Some were just adventurers or even criminals evading justice. Later in the war collaborators joined seeking to avoid direct retribution as the Allies or Red Army liberated their countries. Finally, toward the end of the war, some served only to get decent rations, the so-called hunger-volunteers.

Non-German volunteers came into the *Waffen-SS* in a number of distinct time phases. Small numbers of pro-German/National Socialist idealists came forward between 1939 and July 1941. After the invasion of the Soviet Union in 1941, the numbers rose with many seeking to fight in the "Crusade against Communism." These included many who were not even pro-German or politically inclined toward National Socialism, but who saw service as a chance to destroy the Soviet threat once and for all. This was particularly true of those from the Baltic states (q.v.) of Latvia and Estonia. After the German surrender at Stalingrad (q.v.) in 1943, another phase was entered, as the German forces needed every man they could muster in the east. The theme of a "European Crusade Against Bolshevism" was widely used, together with hard-sell propaganda and recruiting drives in areas so far untouched by *Waffen-SS* recruiting agencies—the Ukraine, the Balkans, and the POW camps of all nationalities.

In the final phase were those such as members of the Vichy French security units, the *Milice Français* (q.v.), who, on the liberation of France, fled into Germany and were conscripted into, rather than volunteered for, the *Waffen-SS* units. This pattern was repeated in other newly liberated states where collaborators sought to avoid retribution from the resistance groups. The final phase also included those from the Baltic states and the Balkans, who experienced previous Soviet occupation, and who took up arms in German service as a means to hold off the impending Soviet threat to their homelands. The "hunger-volunteers" also fall into this final phase, a phenomenon particularly true in the near-starvation conditions in Holland

in the winter of 1944 and spring of 1945, when service in the *Waffen-SS* meant food, drink, warm clothing, and a roof over one's head.

Initially in the 1939–1940 period, non-Germans were recruited into *Waffen-SS* units as a means to circumvent the *Wehrmacht*'s restrictions on SS recruiting within Germany. The effort was aimed primarily at ethnic Germans in Hungary and the Balkans. The idea to tap into suitable "Nordic blood" soon followed as war in the east loomed. Later, all the earlier racial restrictions (except for Jews) were dropped, as the scramble for able men grew more intense.

The non-German units of the *Waffen-SS*, principally the larger formations, had a good, in some cases outstanding, war record. Some of the smaller units, too, served well and gained a reputation for courage and ferocity above and beyond mere Axis propaganda. Other formations fell far short of expectations, some not even worth the propaganda value used against the Allies. The Bosnian and Albanian Muslim units were plagued by desertions and criminal activity. The Indian Legion, which transferred to the SS from *Wehrmacht* control in 1944–1945, was useful only for anti-British propaganda. Other minority formations failed to reach combat strength.

There were, however, outstanding soldiers among these non-Germans. Léon Degrelle (q.v.), commander of the Walloon SS Storm Brigade (later nominally a division) was one of the highest decorated men in the entire *Waffen-SS*. SS-*Hauptsturmführer* Frederik von Schalburg, commander of the *Freikorps Danmark* until killed in action in June 1943, was described by Heinrich Himmler (q.v.) as the finest Aryan specimen he had ever seen; von Schalburg was a Danish nobleman.

Many non-German *Waffen-SS* soldiers gained Germany's highest military decorations. Among the last to receive the Knights Cross to the Iron Cross were French and Latvian SS men fighting in

Recruiting office for the Waffen-SS *in Calais, France. (Photo taken shortly after the liberation of the town.)*
(IWM B 10730)

defense of Berlin. It is ironic that in the final battle for the *Reich* in Berlin in 1945, the *Führer's* bunker was defended by non-Germans: SS men from the *Nordland* Division, Scandinavians, plus Latvians and French SS. Of the top ten *Waffen-SS* divisions, the *Wiking* Division had a terrific combat reputation. Largely non-German, mostly Scandinavian, this unit fought solely in the east and advanced farther into the southern Russian front than any other formation in the summer of 1942.

Without doubt, the non-German volunteers of the *Waffen-SS* played a major role in sustaining Germany's war effort, and especially in the east, they enabled Germany to hold out for longer than many thought possible. In particular, the Belgian Walloons, Flemish, Dutch, and Scandinavian units performed military feats far in excess of their numbers. The Baltic units fought like tigers and continued to do so long after Germany's surrender in 1945. It was a final irony of the Cold War in the 1950s that small groups of Ukrainian SS and Latvian and Estonian SS survivors were crossing into the West to surrender to U.S. forces.

Stephen L. Frost

Additional Reading

Frischauer, Willi, *Himmler: The Evil of the Third Reich* (1953).

Hoffmann, Joachim, *Die Ostlegionen 1941–1942* (1986).

Keegan, John, *Waffen SS: The Asphalt Soldiers* (1970).

Landwehr, Richard, *Lions of Flanders: Flemish Volunteers of the Waffen-SS, 1941–1945* (1996).

Manvell, Roger, *SS and Gestapo: Rule by Terror* (1969).

Mewland, Samuel J., *Cossacks in the German Army, 1941–1945* (1991).

Seth, Ronald, *Jackals of the Reich: The Story of the British Free Corps* (1972).

Freikorps

Already active in the final weeks of World War I and during the general demobilization of the *Reichwehr* that followed, the volunteer troops of the *Freikorps* (former soldiers either unable or unwilling to find employment, and young rabble-rousers looking for a fight), were reorganized under the leadership of General Walther von Lüttwitz and the German General Staff (q.v.).

These irregular troops swore allegiance to Chancellor Friedrich Ebert's (q.v.) provisional government, more specifically to Defense Minister Gustav Noske, and they dreamed of a new Germany, not necessarily one with a democratically elected government. With the demobilization of the *Reichwehr,* Ebert and Noske relied on *Freikorps* units to provide security for the new national assembly and to put down the Communist-inspired *Spartakist* and the various soldier and worker council rebellions throughout the country.

The *Freikorps* was actually an amalgamation of different armed factions united around a single officer cadre. The new government legalized these units in January 1919, and called on all able-bodied German men to defend their homeland and to provide for public order in these times of civil unrest. Legalization also provided the National Association of German Officers, formed in late 1918 to preserve the leadership cadres of the imperial army, a means to advance its reactionary and counterrevolutionary nationalism within the framework of the new Weimar Republic (q.v.). Legalization also placed the *Freikorps* on an equal footing with the newly constituted *Volkswehr,* or people's army, and dependence on the former officers corps proved inevitable.

Freikorps volunteers fought in Upper Silesia to prevent Poland from seizing territory. Units also operated in the Baltic states under the pretext of fighting Soviet forces, although Germany viewed the region as an area of future settlement. By the summer of 1919, the *Freikorps* had become the most important political and military force in Germany with a half-million members and recruitment on the rise.

In accordance with the provisions of the Versailles Treaty (q.v.), the Weimar Republic was forced to drastically reduce the size of its military. The Allied Control Commission ordered the disbanding of the *Freikorps* in March 1920, but von Lüttwitz refused to comply and consolidated two brigades deployed outside Berlin. When it became clear to them that the Weimar government would not stand up to Allied demands, and alleging a Jewish-Bolshevik and anti-German conspiracy at work, the monarchist elements within the *Freikorps* launched the Kapp *Putsch* (q.v.) in March 1920 and called for the restoration of the kaiser. Even after this attempted coup, the Weimar government continued to rely on *Freikorps* units to suppress left-wing uprisings.

Steven B. Rogers

Additional Reading

Mau, Hermann, and Helmut Krausnik, *German History, 1933–1945: An Assessment by German Historians* (1959).
Watt, Richard M., *The Kings Depart: The Tragedy of Germany: Versailles and the German Revolution* (1968).

French Foreign Legion

The World War II French Foreign Legion (*Légion Étrangère*) had a widely diverse ethnic composition. Originally founded in the post–French Revolution period, the Foreign Legion officially became a fighting force in 1831. Historically welcoming volunteers regardless of nationality, the French Foreign Legion was a polyglot when World War II began. Initially, the French government questioned whether it should deploy the Foreign Legion during the war because of possible ethnic problems.

The presence of Germans in the Foreign Legion—up to 80 percent of *sous-officiers* (NCOs) were German—was the most immediate problem. Nazis infiltrated the Foreign Legion in an attempt to gain control by coercing German legionnaires to desert. The French quickly became aware of this effort and screened German legionnaires, isolating potentially subversive soldiers to road-building assignments. Jews and socialists joined the Foreign Legion for political asylum and were hidden in Africa, where they served as border guards and in other remote assignments.

Foreigners and refugees representing forty-seven countries were assigned to three special regiments of the Legion: the 21st, 22nd, and 23rd *Régiments de Marche de Volontaires Étrangères* (Marching Regiments of Foreign Volunteers—RMVE). Organized in October 1939, they trained for mountain duty in the Pyrenees. Each RMVE consisted of three battalions. Most officers were French reservists. Two infantry regiments of reservists also were formed: the 11th and 12th *Régiment Étrangère d'Infanterie* (REI).

Lieutenant Colonel Magrin-Vernerey commanded the legion's 13th Demi-Brigade, which was sent to help Finland fight the Soviet Union. Before the unit arrived, the conflict ended. The

13th was then sent to neutral Norway in May 1940 to help the Norwegian Army resist a German attack. The unit distinguished itself at Narvik (q.v.). Ironically, the 13th Demi-Brigade was one of the French units destroyed at Dien Bien Phu in the First Indo-China War.

When the "Phony War" (q.v.) ended, Legion units joined the forces resisting the spring 1940 German offensive, suffering high casualties at Inor Wood and Soissons. After the capitulation, the German division of France into occupied and free zones caused dissension within the legion. General Charles de Gaulle (q.v.) urged the legionnaires to support the Free French. This caused them to question their own sworn loyalty to the Legion itself. Confused about their legal status as legionnaires, many joined the British Army, transferred to different regiments, had their regiment disbanded, or simply deserted. The fall of France immediately resulted in fewer recruits, and a shortage of men as well as supplies plagued the legion.

Germany asked the Vichy (q.v.) government to disband the French Foreign Legion. The legion countered by posting German legionnaires to distant stations in Africa where German inspectors would be unlikely to find them. The Germans also wanted the return of Austrian, Czechoslovak, and Polish legionnaires, and Italy demanded the release of its nationals. Arrangements for soldiers who wanted to request repatriation were made, and 1,000 Germans asked to be released from duty. A separate battalion of these men was formed but not allowed to return to Germany.

French Foreign Legion units supporting the Free French actively campaigned in North Africa until 1943. For operations in Europe itself, remnants of various legion units were organized into one unit, the *Régiment de Marche de la Légion Étrangère* (RMLE), created on 1 July 1943 and armed with American equipment. The RMLE was joined by the 13th Demi-Brigade in 1944. The legionnaires were equipped and trained for the campaign in Italy, where they joined the U.S. Fifth Army in the liberation of Rome. The legion then landed in France in August 1944 and liberated the port at Toulon.

The legion continued the campaign into Germany, helping secure bridges over the Rhine River. The 13th Demi-Brigade took Colmar (q.v.) on 2 February 1945 in its last engagement. The RMLE captured Stuttgart in February, fighting from street to street. In April, it battled in the Black Forest, enduring snipers and ambushes. It crossed the Danube River into Austria at the time of ceasefire. The RMLE and 13th joined Allied troops in the Parisian victory parade, celebrating the liberation of France and Europe.

The World War II French Foreign Legion was complicated by the divisiveness of legionnaires concerning whether to support Free France or Vichy France. It also suffered from lack of recruits, desertion, and antiquated tactics. These circumstances limited the effectiveness of this legendary fighting force on World War II battlefields.

Elizabeth D. Schafer

Additional Reading

Anderson, Roy C., *Devils, Not Men: The History of the French Foreign Legion* (1987).
Porch, Douglas, *The French Foreign Legion: A Complete History of the Legendary Fighting Force* (1991).

Führerhauptquartier (FHQu)

Created in September 1939, the FHQu was made up of a loosely defined group of dignitaries and functionaries who usually accompanied Adolf Hitler (q.v.) wherever he went. The most prominent members of this retinue included chief of staff and operations chief of the OKW, Field Marshal Wilhelm Keitel and Colonel General Alfred Jodl (qq.v.); head of the Nazi Party chancellery, Martin Bormann (q.v.); press chief of the *Reich,* Otto Dietrich; senior liaison officers representing the *Luftwaffe,* the navy, and the SS; a liaison official from the Foreign Ministry; and four *Wehrmacht* adjutants. The first military commandant of FHQu was Major General Erwin Rommel (q.v.), who was succeeded in February 1940 by Lieutenant Colonel Kurt Thomas. (Like Rommel, Thomas also wound up in North Africa later, commanding a division made up of penal battalions.)

After spending part of the 1939 Polish campaign (q.v.) on his special train, code named *AMERIKA,* the *Führer* returned to his *Reich* Chancellery in Berlin. On May 1940, on the eve of the western campaign, FHQu was transferred to a prepared site in the Eiffel region, code named *FELSENNEST* (MOUNTAIN NEST). On 6 June, Hitler and his retinue moved to *WOLFSSCHLUCHT* (WOLF'S GORGE), near Givet, Belgium, and later the same month to *TANNENBERG* (FIR MOUNTAIN) in the Black Forest. From early July 1940 until the invasion of the Soviet Union, Hitler stayed either in Berlin or at the *Berghof,* except during the Balkan campaign in April 1941, when his command train was parked south of Wiener Neustadt (near a tunnel) for two weeks.

Two days after Operation BARBAROSSA was launched, Hitler and his entourage settled down at a specially prepared site in East Prussia, the *WOLFSSCHANZE* (WOLF'S LAIR), about four miles east of Rastenburg. Although Hitler moved around frequently, staying at Berlin, Munich, the *Berghof,* and at a special field headquarters in the Ukraine, near Vinnitsa (code named *WERWOLF*), *WOLFSSCHANZE* remained his chief residence for the next three and a half years.

With the Red Army approaching East Prussia, the FHQu was moved back to Berlin in November 1944. The following month, in preparation for the Ardennes offensive (q.v.), Hitler established himself in the woods west of Bad Nauheim, at *ADLERHORST* (EAGLE'S NEST), and stayed there until mid-January 1945. Thereafter, he and his entourage ran the crumbling *Reich* from Berlin, and it was in a bunker beneath the chancellery that he ended his life on 30 April 1945.

Ulrich Trumpener

Additional Reading

Bullock, Alan, *Hitler: A Study in Tyranny,* rev., ed. (1962).

Hoffmann, Peter, *Hitler's Personal Security* (1979).

O'Donnell, James P., *The Berlin Bunker* (1979).

F

G

Geheime Staatspolizei (Gestapo)

The *Gestapo (Geheime Staatspolizei)* or Secret State Police originated in Prussia. In April 1933, Hermann Göring (q.v.) established it in his capacity as head of the Prussian Ministry of the Interior. The *Gestapo,* however, was not created from scratch. He used the political police of the Weimar period as the basis for his new, Nazi-oriented Prussian political police. According to Robert Gellately, there was no real purge of the Weimar political police after 1933. A certain degree of "cleansing" occurred in some, though not all, areas of the country. Holdover policemen from the Weimar period were no more humane in their treatment of prisoners than the Nazi recruits to the *Gestapo.* They "acted with the greatest brutality . . . against the ever-increasing numbers of people who were declared opponents and criminals."

Starting in Bavaria in early 1933, Heinrich Himmler, chief of the SS (qq.v.), gradually took over the political police in all of Germany. This aggrandizement culminated in April 1934 with his absorption of the *Gestapo,* the largest political police force of the seventeen German states. Upon gaining control of the *Gestapo,* Himmler and Reinhard Heydrich (q.v.) moved their base of operations from Munich to Berlin.

Over time the *Gestapo*'s functions were many, ranging from ferreting out the many putative enemies of the Third *Reich* to providing part of the manpower for the *Einsatzgruppen* (q.v.), which carried out the major segment of the "Final Solution" (q.v.). The *Gestapo*'s task, in broad terms, was to oppose anything "directed at the existence and security of the state." It enjoyed broad powers including "police surveillance of political affairs." Heydrich used the claim that Germany was inundated with hidden enemies (the "camouflaged enemy" argument) to justify increases in the *Ge-* *stapo* budget, even after the purge of Ernst Röhm (q.v.) and the consolidation of Nazi power in 1934.

Gellately shows that the *Gestapo* was able to enforce Nazi racial policy only because of the active cooperation, indeed the collaboration, of many German citizens. Although their motives varied, Germans denounced fellow citizens suspected of engaging in "criminal" behavior, particularly in the so-called cross-ethnic area. After the promulgation of the 1935 Nuremberg Laws (q.v.), the Third *Reich* tried to prohibit contact, sexual or other, between Germans and Jews, Poles, and other "non-Aryans."

Contrary to popular opinion, the *Gestapo* was small. Precisely because of its small size and the often private character of the race "crimes" it enforced, the *Gestapo* relied on tip-offs from the populace. It became especially dependent on stool pigeons in the 1940s when thousands of Poles were forced to labor in the Third *Reich*'s factories and farms. The Nazi goal of segregating Poles from Germans, unrealistic to begin with, would never have had a chance of success without the system of "auto-surveillance" that evolved.

The concentration and extermination camps were operated not by the *Gestapo* but by Theodor Eicke's (q.v.) "Deaths Head" units and later by Oswald Pohl's (q.v.) WVHA (*see* SS). However, the *Gestapo* was closely associated with the camps because it arrested people and ordered their incarceration there. In addition, they were represented in the camps by a political section responsible for the prisoners' admission, records, and treatment, and also their release, which had to be authorized by a *Gestapo* office.

Many *Gestapo* practices were of questionable legality. This led to persistent conflict between the *Gestapo* and the civil authorities, some of whom tried to maintain a semblance of the rule of law.

Prisoners line up outside their cells at the Gestapo *prison and interrogation center at Breedonck, Belgium. (IWM B 10071)*

Himmler had many run-ins with Wilhelm Frick (q.v.), *Reich* minister of the interior, over who should control the *Gestapo,* and over its more questionable activities. They even squabbled over seemingly insignificant questions of title; for instance, whether Himmler in 1936 should become inspector, commander, or chief of the German police. Although he remained formally subordinate to Frick until 1944, Himmler won most of these struggles thanks to favorable rulings by Adolf Hitler (q.v.), the Third *Reich's* "Great Arbitrator." The *Gestapo* was given the exclusive right to exercise "protective custody" *(Schutzhaft),* under which "anyone could be sent to a concentration camp for an indefinite period." The courts had no power to order a prisoner's release, making any control of *Gestapo* excesses virtually impossible.

In June 1936, Hitler named Himmler chief of the German police. From then on all police forces, the political police (the *Sipo,* composed of the *Gestapo* and the plain-clothes criminal police, *Kripo),* and the regular uniformed police *(Orpo),* were under the control of one man, Himmler, who was simultaneously head of the SS, a Nazi Party organization. Heydrich was appointed head of the newly created *Sipo,* in addition to head of the SD (q.v.), another party organization. Quite intentionally, the process of incorporating the police into the SD/SS, begun by Himmler in 1933, took a major step forward. It probably reached its zenith in 1939 when the *Gestapo* and the SD were combined with the criminal police to form the RSHA (q.v.).

Jon Moulton

Additional Reading

Browder, George C., *Foundations of the Nazi Police State: The Formation of SIPO and SD* (1990).

Crankshaw, Edward, *Gestapo* (1956).

Delarue Jacques, *The History of the Gestapo* (1964).

Gellately, Robert, *The Gestapo and German Society: Enforcing Racial Policy 1933–1945* (1990).

Manvell, Roger, *SS and the Gestapo: Rule by Terror* (1969).

German-American Bund

The German-American Bund was the largest and most public of the many pro-Nazi groups active in the United States before Pearl Harbor. The organization had its roots in the Teutonia Association founded in 1927 and the Friends of the New Germany established in 1933. The Friends lost its hold after a directive came from Berlin cutting all ties to the NSDAP and requiring German citizens to resign from membership.

The bund held its first annual convention in Buffalo, New York, in March 1936. Fritz Kuhn, a former *Freikorps* (q.v.) soldier from Munich who gained U.S. citizenship in 1934, was its *Bundesleiter*. Although he declared at another convention in April 1936: "As an organization of American citizens we shall educate the American people to become friends of the New Germany," the American public saw a serious threat to democracy in the bund's anti-Semitic and pro-Fascist ideology.

Kuhn also heightened American suspicion in 1936, when he went to Berlin and met with Adolf Hitler (q.v.). After 1938, Kuhn emphasized American patriotism under the slogan "Free America." One of his deputies explained: "The only purpose of the Bund is to make better Americans of those of German blood."

A mass meeting for Washington's birthday on 20 February 1939 in Madison Square Garden was the bund's final hurrah. The German government and party organizations realized the United States was unfertile for the growth of Fascist extremism and withdrew their support. Kuhn was arrested by federal authorities and sentenced to prison for larceny and forgery. The bund was indicted by the Dies Committee on Un-American Activities as a Nazi agency.

Susan Pentlin

Additional Reading

Divine, Robert A., *The Reluctant Belligerent American Entry into World War II* (1965).
Drummond, Donald F., *The Passing of American Neutrality Party, 1937–1941* (1955).
Eisinger, Chester E. (ed.), *The 1940s: Profile of a Nation in Crisis* (1969).

German General Staff

The historical image of the German General Staff has assumed nearly mythical proportions. Its name conjures up vague images of faceless, ruthlessly efficient officers poring over maps and timetables, plotting world conquest with Teutonic precision. The misconception persists that only Adolf Hitler's (q.v.) meddling kept these professionals from winning World War II. The truth is much more complex.

The general staff's origins go back to the seventeenth century, but only in the nineteenth century did it begin to take on real power. By 1870, the general staff became the highest military planning authority in the nation, and its chief exercised independent command of Germany's armies in wartime. Over the next four decades, its influence expanded still more. In World War I, the general staff, though constantly embroiled in disputes with other elements in the kaiser's army, shaped political, economic, and social policies. Germany became a virtual military dictatorship by the end of the war.

At the end of World War I, the victorious Allies dictated in the Versailles Treaty (q.v.) that the Germans abolish their general staff. The Germans foiled this effort, preserving the nucleus of the staff in the *Truppenamt* (Troop Office) of the Defense Ministry's Army Directorate. More importantly, general staff officers dominated the postwar army to an extent they had never achieved under the kaiser. These were the officers who would build and direct Hitler's army. While they lost some of their overt political power, they still wielded a great deal of influence behind the scenes in the early 1920s.

As the armed forces—the *Reischwehr* was renamed the *Wehrmacht*—expanded following Hitler's rise in 1933, the army general staff tried without success to place itself at the top of a central command system that would control all three services, as well as the civilian economy. When war broke out on 1 September 1939, however, the general staff was only one branch—albeit a dominant one—the army high command (*Oberkommando des Heeres* or OKH). The Navy and the *Luftwaffe* remained independent, though all three services operated under the nominal control of the armed forces high command (*Oberkommando der Wehrmacht* or OKW) (q.v.), Hitler's personal military planning staff.

Within this hierarchy, the general staff was responsible for planning and directing operations on land, working from strategic guidance provided by the commander in chief of the army. A number of different branches—Operations, Organization, and Supply, for example—fulfilled their own separate parts of this larger mission. Each branch had its own chief, all of whom worked under the direction of the chief of the general staff.

The Germans had long since worked out a set of principles and practices that made their staff system a model for armies throughout the world. They kept their staffs small and placed great emphasis on flexibility, initiative, efficiency, and responsibility. Lines of authority were short, spheres of activity clear and rationally defined. Officers underwent a rigorous selection and training process before joining the general staff corps, which provided key staff officers down to division level, as well as filling the army general staff. This ensured commensurate levels of ability at every echelon. Moreover, German General Staff officers held a great deal more power than their counterparts elsewhere.

In most armies, a staff officer had no command authority. He merely advised the commander, then coordinated and directed the execution of the commander's orders. In the German Army, a chief of staff shared total responsibility with his commander. He could issue orders on his own authority in the commander's absence. In addition, he was duty-bound to voice any disagreements he had with his superior's plans. If still not satisfied, a chief of staff could protest to the chief of staff of the next higher echelon, and so on up the chain to the chief of the general staff. This system helped to ensure that a commander would hear alternative views—whether he liked it or not!

These practices, and the professionalism of the individual officers, were the basis for the general staff's effectiveness in planning and directing operations. That effectiveness can be seen, for example, in the attack on Yugoslavia in 1941, which went from concept to execution in only ten days. For all its efficiency, though, the fact remains that the general staff could not win the war for Germany. Several factors contributed to this situation.

The most obvious of these was Hitler's meddling. Its importance has been overstated—especially by former German generals—but it was nonetheless real. Hitler made himself commander in chief of the *Wehrmacht* in 1938. In December 1941 he went further, appointing himself commander in chief of the army as well—but not of the navy and *Luftwaffe*. As the war went on, he interfered at progressively lower levels, until he was moving battalions on the battlefield. General Franz Halder (q.v.), the chief of the general staff from 1938 to 1942, confided to his diary: "This so-called leadership is characterized by a pathological reacting to the impressions of the moment and a total lack of any understanding of the command machinery and its possibilities."

The *Führer* also ordered the army to conform to his *Führerprinzip* (q.v.) or Leadership Principle, which held that every commander had absolute authority over his subordinates, who in turn owed him unquestioning obedience. Thus, the principle of the staff officer's co-responsibility all but went by the wayside.

Hitler's shortcomings do not fully explain the German problems, however. The general staff demonstrated time and time again that it lacked real strategic vision. The invasion of the Soviet Union is the most glaring example. Hitler's generals actively encouraged his ambitions in this direction. The war also highlighted severe problems in the logistics and intelligence functions within the staff. Finally, the *Wehrmacht*'s command structure exacerbated Germany's problems. By the end of 1942, the OKH and the OKW became parallel and competing agencies, rather than levels in a smooth-running hierarchy. Rational, centralized strategic direction was no longer possible, and all the operational effectiveness in the world could not make up for that fact.

Geoffrey P. Megargee

Additional Reading
Görlitz, Walter, *History of the German General Staff* (1953).
Halder, Franz, *The Halder Diaries: The Private War Journals of Colonel General Franz Halder* (1976).
Seaton, Albert, *The German Army 1933-1945* (1982).
Wilt, Alan F., *War from the Top: German and British Decision Making during World War II* (1990).

Gestapo

See Geheime Staatspolizei

Gurkhas

The Gurkhas were unique in the Indian Army in that they were recruited from Nepal, an independent kingdom never part of the British Empire. Gurkha is the name of the race of sturdy mountain farmers from the hinterland of Nepal. Britons and Gurkhas first met as enemies in 1814. They developed a strong mutual respect and have since been wise enough to fight on the same side. Immediately after the 1814 war, Lieutenant Frederick Young raised the first Gurkha regiment for the East India Company, and subsequently, these hardy fighters served Britain in the Indian Mutiny, two world wars, and a host of minor conflicts too numerous to mention.

"The Almighty," said Field Marshal Sir William J. Slim, who commanded in action every formation from an infantry platoon to a multinational army, "created in the Gurkha an ideal infantryman . . . brave, tough, patient, adaptable, and skilled in fieldcraft." A British officer of World War I, Professor Ralph Turner, paid them an even stronger compliment: "Uncomplaining you endure hunger and thirst and wounds; and at the last, your unwavering lines disappear into the smoke and wrath of battle. Bravest of the brave, most generous of the generous, never had a country more faithful friends than you."

In World War II that bravery, generosity, and friendship was yet again placed at Britain's disposal. In 1939, there were ten Gurkha regiments, each with two battalions. With the agreement of the Nepalese government, each regiment was expanded to at least four battalions. Eventually, the total contribution was a staggering fifty-five battalions; some 250,000 men out of Nepal's population of eight million served in these units as infantrymen.

To lead such men in battle was a demanding task. Before the war only the very best officers that Sandhurst could produce were posted to Gurkha regiments. Among those who shone in World War II were Slim, commander of the 14th Army in Burma, and Major General Francis Tuker, who led the Indian 4th Division in North Africa.

In the Middle East and the Mediterranean, Gurkha units saw action in Iraq, Persia, Tobruk, Alamein, Tunisia (where Subedar Lalbahadur Thapa won the Victoria Cross), and Italy, most noticeably at Cassino (q.v.). They also formed part of the British force sent to Greece (q.v.) in 1944 to prevent a civil war. Typical of these units was the 1st Battalion, 2nd Gurkha Rifles, which on returning to India in December 1945, spent four and a half years of continuous active service in ten countries.

Gurkhas were prominent in the Far East as well, serving in Malaya and Burma, and behind Japanese lines with Major General Orde Wingate's (q.v.) Chindits. After V-J Day, they were part of British expeditions sent to keep the peace in Indonesia and Indochina.

The tiny kingdom of Nepal paid a high price for supporting its British allies in World War II. In all theaters, a total of 7,544 Gurkha soldiers were killed in action or died of wounds or disease, while another 1,441 were listed as missing and presumed dead. An additional 23,655 Gurkhas were severely wounded, amounting to an overall casualty rate of a staggering thirteen percent. On the other hand, Gurkhas won some 2,734 decorations for gallantry, including ten Victoria Crosses

Gurkha troops attacking a German position during the battle for the Mareth Line, 20 March 1943. (IWM NA 1096)

(seven in Burma) out of the total of 182 awarded in World War II.

The independence of India was not the end of this heroic story. While six regiments stayed with the Indian Army, four transferred to the British Army. In January 1948, these four—the 2nd, 6th, 7th, and 10th Gurkha Rifles—sailed for a new home in Malaya. In subsequent years, the Gurkhas provided the backbone of Britain's successful campaigns in Malaya and Borneo, and a battalion fought in the 1982 Falklands campaign.

Philip J. Green

Additional Reading
Farwell, Byron, *The Gurkhas* (1984).
Smith, E.D., *Britain's Brigade of Gurkhas* (1973).

G

H

Hitler Youth

The first efforts of the Nazi Party to establish a youth group date from March 1922 when a "Youth League of the National Socialist Workers Party" was founded. Led by Kurt Grubers, it encountered little success before 1926 when the organization was renamed "Hitler Youth, League of German Working Youth." Prior to the Nazis coming to power in January 1933, the leadership of the Hitler Youth was preoccupied with gaining an in-

dependent position within the Nazi Party. Many considered it part of the SA, including Baldur von Schirach (qq.v.) who was appointed *Reich* youth leader in 1931.

During the late 1920s, organizational details were established. Membership began at age fourteen, and at eighteen, each person joined the Nazi Party. In 1930, a League of German Girls (BDM or *Bund Deutscher Mädel*) was added to the Hitler Youth, and a year later, a League of Young Ger-

Hitler Youth c. 1936. (IWM MH 13441)

mans (BDJ or *Bund Deutsches Jungvolk*) was organized for those under fourteen years of age.

In January 1933, the Hitler Youth gained new importance and opportunities. Membership soared from just over 100,000 at the end of 1932 to more than 3.5 million in 1934. Its leaders sought to recruit all of Germany's youth, a goal never fully realized. The dominance of the Hitler Youth came from the exclusion or elimination of other youth groups, its takeover of additional youth activities, and its designation on 1 December 1936, as the Nazi organization legally responsible for the development of the German youth outside of the home and school. On 25 March 1939, membership became obligatory, but a sizeable portion of German youth remained disassociated. To a large degree, the Hitler Youth was an effective vehicle for spreading Nazi ideology among Germany's youth, and it remained an important instrument of control.

Robert G. Waite

Additional Reading

Brandenburg, Hans-Christian, *Die Geschichte der HJ. Wege und Irrwege einer Generation* 1968).

Klönne, Arno, *Jugend im Dritten Reich* (1982).
Koch, H.W., *The Hitler Youth: Origins and Development 1922–45* (1976).
Rempsel, Gerhard, *Hitler's Children: The Hitler Youth and the SS* (1989).

Home Guard

The Home Guard (initially called the Local Defense Volunteers) was a locally based, British militia which eventually totaled some 1.7 million members. Founded on 14 May 1940 as a means of countering airborne landings and saboteurs, the force initially consisted of volunteers hastily armed with whatever weapons—including shotguns, muskets, and Molotov cocktails—they could round up.

With the omnipresent threat of German invasion after the fall of France, British Army defensive plans increasingly relied on Home Guard battalions, the force's largest unit, to defend fortified positions, harass and slow enemy columns, provide security for important installations, and form the first line of defense against any airborne assault. This army interest led to a standardization of

Two members of the Home Guard set up their Vickers machine gun on the village green at Dorking, 1 December 1940. (IWM H 5842)

Home Guard procedures, organization, training, and equipping, thanks in large part to shipments of American and Canadian rifles. By 1941, the Home Guard was fully integrated into the British Army as a part-time auxiliary militia. In early 1942, the government began to draft men into the Home Guard.

Although never called upon to fight, the Home Guard contributed to Britain's war effort by shouldering the burden for home defense and by taking over mundane, time-consuming tasks, like guarding against saboteurs, manning antiaircraft and coastal artillery batteries, rounding up downed German airmen, and serving as coast watchers. This allowed the regular army to concentrate on the overseas fighting fronts. The Home Guard continued to perform these duties until December 1944, when the government, given the greatly diminished threat, disbanded the force.

David K. Yelton

Additional Reading

Collier, Basil, *The Defense of the United Kingdom* (1957).
Longmate, Norman, *The Real Dad's Army: The Story of the Home Guard* (1974).

I

Interallied Control Commission

The European Advisory Commission, set up after the Teheran Conference to formulate plans for postwar Germany, proposed the establishment of an Interallied Control Commission to replace the ministries of the defeated German government. The commission, representing the three major Allies (France was added at the Yalta Conference), operated under the executive authority of the Allied Control Council and was composed of the Allied military commanders.

After the Potsdam Conference, the control commission was set up in Berlin. The military commanders for the four zones of occupation, who governed their own zones according to the directives of their respective governments, met periodically to determine, by their unanimous agreement, policy for Germany as a whole. The permanent four-power control committee was charged with codifying this policy. The commission, each level of which was staffed by representatives of all the Allies, supervised twelve directories, which were analogous to the German government ministries. Real authority, however, was vested in the military commanders of the individual zones. Though the commission issued many directives, it failed to take the fundamental steps authorized at Potsdam toward the establishment of all-German agencies.

In its effort to demilitarize Germany, the commission not only abolished all military and paramilitary organizations, but also did away with the political unit of Prussia, which was regarded as synonymous with German militarism. While each zone proceeded to implement its own approach to de-Nazification, the commission formulated a policy in October 1946. The commission divided former Nazis into five categories, with corresponding sanctions. This decree provided a theoretically unified approach, although there continued to be differences in zonal policies.

One of the committee's concerns was the establishment of an industrial policy that would not only prohibit the production of war materials, but would also deprive Germany of an industrial capacity that could be shifted to military production. Following a Potsdam directive in November 1945, the Committee ordered the break up of the industrial cartel I.G. Farben, but no general regulation on industrial size and complexity was ever formulated. In March 1946, the commission issued its Level of Industry Plan prohibiting certain industries and limiting productive capacities in others. Due to the growing split between the former Allies, most of these provisions were never implemented.

On 1 January 1947, the Americans and the British merged the administration of their zones into a unified *Bizonia,* and on 20 December 1947, the United States ceased the delivery of German reparations to the Soviets. When France decided to cooperate with the United States and Great Britain by merging its zone of occupation with *Bizonia* in 1948, the Soviet Union protested, stating that the West was violating the occupation agreements. On 20 March 1948, the Soviet delegates walked out of the control council meeting, and the four-power administration of Germany formally ended.

Bernard A. Cook

Additional Reading

Balfour, Michael, *Four-Power Control in Germany and Austria, 1945–1946* (1956).

Gimbel, John, *The American Occupation of Germany: Politics and the Military, 1945–1949* (1968).

Zink, Harold, *The United States in Germany, 1944–1955* (1957).

International Red Cross
See RED CROSS

J

Jedburghs

Jedburgh teams were Allied groups sent into France and the Low Countries to assist resistance movements in assuming a more active role during and after the invasion of Western Europe. They received their name from Jedburgh, Scotland, where they trained. The teams were international, usually consisting of one American, one French, and one British member. Some personnel came from the United States Office of Strategic Services (OSS) (q.v.) and more from the British Special Air Service (SAS) (q.v.). These men provided leadership in guerrilla fighting rather than conducting espionage.

The function of the Jedburgh teams was similar to that of U.S. Special Forces A Teams in the Vietnam era. The members of the *Maquis* (q.v.) and their Jedburgh advisers contributed materially to the Allied victory in France. They expedited Allied movements, partly by blocking, or at least delaying, German troops, even, at times, whole German divisions. After the end of the war, many American "Jeds" or "Jedburghs," such as William F. Colby, achieved prominence in the Central Intelligence Agency (CIA), and in other capacities.

Benjamin R. Beebe

Additional Reading
Bank, Aaron, *From OSS to Green Berets: The Birth of Special Forces* (1986).
Brown, Anthony Cave, *Bodyguard of Lies* (1975).

K

Kleinkampfverbände (KKV)

Admiral Erich Raeder (q.v.) considered naval special forces units as unsavory and unnecessary. His resignation on 31 January 1943 as chief of the German Navy cleared the way for the *Kriegsmarine* to form its first special operations force. Designated *Kleinkampfverbände* (Small Fighting Units or KKV), the force was modeled after Italy's 10th Light Flotilla (q.v.), which had enjoyed such great success in the Mediterranean. Unfortunately, the KKV enjoyed few successes because Allied intelligence, primarily ULTRA (q.v.), provided advanced warning of their presence and operations. They suffered excessive casualties (over 80 percent) for the small gains achieved. Still, the KKV served to divert extensive Allied air and naval forces from other missions. In that respect, perhaps, their operations may have been successful.

Admiral Karl Dönitz (q.v.) appointed Rear Admiral Helmuth von Heye to command the KKV in February 1943. Absorbing the lessons of the German Army's *Küstenjäger* (Coastal Rangers) and the Italian special operations forces, Heye organized the KKV into *Marine Einsatz Kommandos* (Naval Assault Units, or MEKs), and subordinate flotillas. Training and selection followed the practices of the *Brandenburg* Division (q.v.), and were conducted under the auspices of the army's *Küstenjäger* and frogman schools. The first thirty volunteers, taken from all the services, arrived for training in November 1943. They saw combat for the first time at Anzio (q.v.) on 17 April 1944, sinking only one small patrol craft. Despite this inauspicious start, the force numbered three MEKs commanding fourteen flotillas by August 1944.

Employing a mixture of manned torpedoes, midget submarines, and remote-controlled explosive boats, KKV units ran an intense gauntlet of Allied fighter and naval patrols to reach their targets. The only confirmed sinkings by these units included one Allied patrol craft, two minesweepers, a corvette, and two steamers. KKV frogman flotillas, however, proved remarkably adept at destroying bridges in the Allies' rear areas. The Soviets, in fact, employed special bridge protection battalions to counter KKV operations—generally to little avail. Few German frogmen survived their "bridge busting" operations, and their casualties exceeded 90 percent.

Carl O. Schuster

Additional Reading

Lucas, James, *Kommando: German Special Forces in World War II* (1985).
Showell, Max, *The Kriegsmarine in World War II* (1989).

Kondor Legion

The *Kondor Legion* was the German expeditionary *Luftwaffe* force in the Spanish civil war (q.v.) and an important factor in the Nationalist victory. Late in July 1936, Hitler loaned the Spanish Nationalists ten Lufthansa Junkers Ju-52 trimotor aircraft in order to transport their troops from North Africa to Spain. Six Heinkel He-51 biplane fighters provided protection. Later these aircraft were transferred to the Nationalists. Subsequently, Hitler approved full-scale military intervention by *Luftwaffe* units, and in early November, ten bomber-version Ju-52s were sent to Spain.

Ostensibly known as the *Luftwaffe* Volunteer Corps and identified as Number 88, this German unit in Spain was popularly known as the *Kondor Legion*. The men were not volunteers; all were assigned and were rotated periodically. The *Kondor Legion* consisted of a bomber group, a fighter group, a reconnaissance group, a seaplane squadron, an antiaircraft group, and ground support elements. Its authorized strength was 5,136 men and about 100 aircraft. Members wore Spanish rank insignia and, while with the legion, were appointed one rank higher than their normal status. The legion was first commanded by General Hugo Sperrle (q.v.), followed by General Helmuth Volkmann, and finally by General Wolfram von Richthofen (q.v.).

Kampfgruppe 88, the bomber portion of the legion, was made up of three squadrons of Ju-52 bombers. The best German bombers in Spain were two new twin-engine medium models, the Dornier Do-17 ("Flying Pencil") and the Heinkel He-111. In 1937, the He-111 replaced the Ju-52s, which were then turned over to the Nationalists. Virtually all planes in the *Luftwaffe* inventory, including the Junkers Ju-87 *Stuka* dive bomber, were used in Spain.

The fighter force of the *Kondor Legion, Jagdgruppe* 88, consisted of three squadrons of nine aircraft each. The main German fighter was at first the outdated He-51. In the spring of 1937, the first and second squadrons received the new single-seat monoplane Messerschmitt Bf-109, forerunner of all modern fighters and the best in the civil war. The third squadron retained the He-51 armed with fragmentation bombs and used it exclusively for close ground support.

The reconnaissance group in the legion had two squadrons of Heinkel He-99 and He-70 (*Blitz*) monoplanes. He-59 and He- 60 seaplanes and one Ju-52 on floats were used in the seaplane squadron.

After their arrival in Spain, the Germans were involved in all major Nationalist operations of the war. The *Kondor Legion* played a key role in the defeat of the great Republican Ebro River offensive in the summer of 1938.

The Germans learned many vital lessons in tactics, maintenance, and employment of aircraft from their experience in Spain. The decision to test the latest aircraft caused them to abandon the close wingtip-to-wingtip formation in favor of the "Finger Four." The *Luftwaffe* also developed techniques of close ground support that proved invaluable early in World War II. By accident, they also discovered the effectiveness of the 88mm antiaircraft gun as an antitank and field artillery piece. Chief among the negatives was that they learned nothing about strategic operations.

About 19,000 Germans served in Spain at one time or another; 886 were casualties (298 killed). The legion downed 386 Spanish Republican aircraft (fifty-six by antiaircraft fire), against German losses of seventy-two. Additionally, 160 *Kondor Legion* aircraft were lost through accidents.

Spencer Tucker

Additional Reading

Elstob, Peter, *Condor Legion* (1973).
Killen, John, *The Luftwaffe: A History* (1967).
Proctor, Raymond, *Hitler's Luftwaffe in the Spanish Civil War* (1983).

Kreisau Circle

With approximately twenty active members, the Kreisau Circle (*Kreisauer Kreis*) was a small group of Christian intellectuals, professionals, and military officers formed in 1933 to oppose the Nazi regime. The leader of the group was Helmuth James *Graf* von Moltke (q.v.), the bearer of one of the most distinguished names in German history. The group took its name from the location of von Moltke's family estate in Kreisau, Silesia (now Krzyżowa, Poland).

The members of the Kreisau Circle regarded Adolph Hitler (q.v.) and his political movement as disastrous for the German nation. The group was dedicated to the principles of Christianity and universal humanity. Rather than plotting the overt overthrow of the Nazis, the Kreisau Circle concentrated on planning the political, social, and philosophical framework for a post-Hitler Germany. On 9 August 1943, the group drafted its "Basic Principles for the New Order," which outlined its objectives.

Loosely organized at best, the Kreisau Circle collapsed after von Moltke's arrest in January 1944. Some of the circle's members later became involved with the July Plot against Hitler (*see* Opposition to Hitler). Most of those were arrested and executed after the failure of the July Plot.

David T. Zabecki

Additional Reading

Balfour, Michael, and Julian Frisby, *Helmuth von Moltke: A Leader Against Hitler* (1972).
Klemperer, K. von., *German Resistance Against Hitler* (1992).
Moltke, Helmuth J. von, *Letters to Freye, 1939–1945* (1990).

L

Long-Range Desert Group (LRDG)

The LRDG conducted reconnaissance and sabotage activities behind Axis lines in North Africa. It was the first of the various groups in the British Army known as the "private armies." The LRDG was founded by New Zealand Major Ralph A. Bagnold with the encouragement of British General Archibald Wavell (q.v.). In 1917, Wavell entered Jerusalem with General Edmund H.H. Allenby and Colonel T.E. Lawrence ("of Arabia"), and he thus recognized the value of small irregular motorized forces that could observe and interfere with supplies and communications behind enemy lines. A shortage of reconnaissance aircraft also led Wavell to explore this option for keeping track of enemy activity to his flanks and front. In Bagnold, Wavell knew that he had the man who could make such a force work.

Bagnold had explored, navigated, and survived in the North African desert for years prior to the war and shared that expertise with his new unit. Many of his prewar associates received British Army commissions to help fill out the officer strength when Bagnold activated the LRDG in 1940. Most of the other ranks initially came from the New Zealand 2nd Division. Equipment and

A driver and a sergeant on an LRDG patrol. (IWM E 12378)

supplies were not problems for this high-priority unit, which received U.S.-made Chevrolet trucks that were heavily modified to endure desert traveling and survival. Modifications included the addition of machine guns, radiator overflow tanks, steel channels for extracting vehicles from soft sand, and storage capacity for everything needed to stay out on extended patrols.

Members of the LRDG needed extensive training in order to accomplish their mission. Some of this training included desert driving, vehicle recovery, desert survival, demolition techniques, radio operations, and coding/ciphering. Maintenance and maintenance training of all equipment was especially critical to ensure missions could be accomplished in the unforgiving desert. Precision in accomplishing this variety of tasks required a special breed of soldier. The LRDG mission required tremendous patience as well as stamina. It was not a unit for soldiers who constantly wanted to face and fight the enemy. As a result, the LRDG drew a higher than usual number of scientists and academicians.

LRDG's primary purpose was long-range reconnaissance behind enemy lines, and they excelled at it. It was not unusual for an LRDG patrol to quietly "lay up" beside a desert road or trail for two to three weeks to observe traffic. LRDG patrols also updated available maps, guided Allied units through the desert and enemy lines, and were equipped for limited minelaying and raiding. In 1941, the LRDG established supply dumps behind the Axis lines that extended their capacity even more. Later missions occasionally involved providing transportation for the Special Air Service (q.v.) and commando (q.v.) units on their raids, as well as working with Popski's Private Army, another behind-the-lines group with origins in the LRDG (*see* Peniakoff, Vladimir).

All these various Allied threats and activities behind German general Erwin Rommel's (q.v.) lines forced him to take protective action by redeploying combat troops to secure his lines and rear areas. An apt tribute to the LRDG from Rommel was that they "caused more damage than any other unit of equal size." The ultimate success of the Allies in Africa eventually eliminated the need for the LRDG and it was deactivated in 1942.

Steven D. Cage

Additional Reading

Sanderson, James D., *Behind Enemy Lines* (1966).

Shaw, W.B. Kennedy, *Long Range Desert Group* (1980).

Swine, Arthur, *The Raiders: Desert Strike Forces* (1968).

Warner, Philip, *Secret Forces of World War II* (1991).

L

M

Maquis

The *Maquis,* as an organization of the French resistance, did not exist until 1943. Prior to that time fugitives hid in the mountains, but the small groups had neither organization, arms, money, direction, nor a name. As more young Frenchmen fled the forced labor programs, however, they asked the resistance for help. These requests came as the interior resistance groups in the southern zone were negotiating a merger. *Combat,* the largest and most effective non-Communist resistance group, combined with *Libération* and *Franc-Tireur* to form *Mouvements Unis de la Résistance* (MUR).

Henri Frenay, the leader and founder of *Combat,* was named head of military affairs for MUR. The *Maquis* then became a branch of MUR, and Frenay appointed Michel Brault chief of the *Service Maquis.* This was a fitting appointment, since Brault is said to have named the group. On New Year's Eve 1942, as Frenay, Brault, and four others met to discuss the formation of MUR, a messenger brought word that some young partisans had evaded the labor draft, obtained arms, and were hiding in the mountains, determined to resist deportation to German factories. "In other words," said Brault, "they've taken to the *maquis*" (a Corsican word meaning underbrush). Thus the *Maquis* acquired organization and a name.

Although theoretically Frenay's responsibility, many *Maquis* units acted independently and were attached to no resistance organization. Brault made contact with them through departmental and regional chiefs, and the *Maquis* units usually followed instructions willingly, in return for food, arms, and ammunition—all of which were in short supply. Interior resistance groups received money from French general Charles de Gaulle's BCRA (qq.v.) in London. Neither arms nor money came in large amounts, because both de Gaulle and the Allies feared that well-armed resisters might complicate invasion and liberation plans, militarily and politically. Despite this, Frenay armed and trained as many *Maquisards* as possible, and by March 1943, four *Maquis* training schools were in place.

Most *Maquis* members were workers, students, and farmers, those most vulnerable to the compulsory labor service, *Service Travail Obligatoire.* Frenay recommended that redoubts, supplied by parachute drops, be established in the Alps, the Juras, the Pyrenees, and the Massif Central. He envisioned highly mobile units of no more than thirty men, provisioned from the redoubts using hit-and-run tactics on designated targets. For the most part, his recommendations were followed, because mountainous terrain was ideal for guerrilla warfare.

Numerous Jedburgh (q.v.) teams, which included one French- and one English-speaking Allied officer plus a radio operator, parachuted into *Maquis* combat areas. The American OSS, British SOE (qq.v.), and French Special Services also dropped individuals in to instruct *Maquisards* in weapon use and in demolition. They brought explosives, arms, money, and orders for specific missions. Seldom did the *Maquis* engage in set-piece battles. There was one tragic exception.

The Vercors, a natural fortress in southeastern France, was a *Maquis* base in 1943. The *Maquisards* devised a plot whereby men and arms could be gathered on Vercors plateau and attack the Germans from the rear as they faced the Allied invasion in southern France (q.v.). Timing was essential to the success of this operation so that reserve forces did not mass prematurely. Equally important was Allied support in the form of ammunition and weapons. The interior commanders never intended to defend the plateau. The plan miscarried in all respects. The reserve *Maquis* forces heard a coded BBC (q.v.) message, which was, in fact, never sent. The Allies dropped only light weapons, and German SS troops converged on Vercors. As a result, almost 3,000 *Maquisards* were encircled and annihilated. Although some *Maquisards* escaped, brutal reprisals fell upon French civilians.

In 1944, all resistance groups within France, including the *Maquis,* merged to form the FFI, the French Forces of the Interior (q.v.). The Allied high command hoped for 40,000 French resisters to support the invasion but doubted that number would join. In fact, the problem for the FFI was that there were three men for every gun. General D. Dwight Eisenhower (q.v.) estimated that the effectiveness of FFI's support was equal to fifteen regular divisions. Perhaps he was more diplomatic than accurate, but there is no doubt that the *Maquis* were effective saboteurs. They gave the Allies crucial intelligence information and harassed the German retreat. When the moment came, they made a significant contribution to the liberation of France.

Mary Anne Pagliasotti

Additional Reading
Frenay, Henri, *The Night Will End* (1976).
Schoenburn, David, *Soldiers of the Night: The Story of the French Resistance* (1980).

Merchant Marine
The merchant marine was the logistical tail controlling battlefield action during World War II. None of the Allied or Axis military forces could function without the flow of supplies brought by the ships of the merchant marine. The outcome of the fight between the British Eighth Army and the German *Afrika Korps* (q.v.) was determined in large measure by the supplies brought to them by merchant ships. The Soviet Union was able to remain in the war thanks to the supplies carried to it by merchant ships sailing from British and American ports. Japan fell when its merchant marine could no longer bring supplies from Southeast Asia to the home islands. Britain survived because the Germans were unable to destroy its merchant marine. The United States functioned as the Arsenal of Democracy (q.v.) only because merchant ships were able to enter and leave its ports. Germany needed its merchant marine to supply troops in Norway and Finland, and to support land operations along the Baltic Sea and Black Sea coasts. Italy lost Ethiopia when its merchant fleet could no longer reach that colony.

The merchant marine, while a necessary part

Merchant Marines of World War II

Country	Gross Registered Tonnage	Year of Data
British Empire	15,100,000	1945
Belgium	200,000	1945
Brazil	488,000	1939
Chile	176,000	1939
Denmark	500,000	1945
Egypt	110,000	1939
France	1,000,000	1945
Germany	4,493,000	1939
Greece	500,000	1945
Italy	3,449,000	1939
Netherlands	1,400,000	1945
Norway	3,000,000	1945
Portugal	270,000	1939
Romania	112,000	1939
Soviet Union	1,316,000	1939
Spain	1,069,000	1945
Sweden	1,630,000	1945
Turkey	225,000	1939
United States	40,100,000	1945
Yugoslavia	411,000	1939

of the military and naval supply system, was not actually a part of the armed forces of most countries. This fact in the Western countries was due to the strong union sentiment of merchant seamen. They saw the threat of conscription into the armed forces as a ploy to break their union organization. Through a strong desire to protect the gains in working conditions won after World War I, the merchant marine union members insisted on working peacetime hours and demanded extra pay for hazardous duty. The insistence on retaining peacetime working hours and pay scales caused serious conflicts between the military and the merchant marine.

At the start of the war, the British Commonwealth had the world's largest merchant fleet, with some 9,000 ships of more than 100 tons each. That was twice as many ships as its nearest rival, the United States. Among the other Allied countries, France had 1,300 merchant ships, the Netherlands 1,400, and Norway 1,800. The combined merchant navies of the Axis powers had more than 5,000 ships (Germany 2,000, Italy 1,000, and Japan 2,300) totaling some 9.6 million tons.

All of the belligerent countries and even some of the neutrals found it necessary to sail their merchant ships in convoys to protect them from hostile airplanes, surface ships, and submarines. A large minesweeping force had to be employed to keep the ports and coastal sea lanes free of mines.

A large percentage of a nation's naval, air, and military strength was allocated to protection of its merchant fleet for the survival of that country.

The merchant marine transported not only its nation's military needs but also civilian needs. While certain civilian imports and exports could be cut, the larger portion of the country's normal export/import trade had to continue. Trade was needed to earn foreign currency and provide the civilian work force with necessities and some luxuries so they would continue to support the war effort. All countries established governmental agencies to apportion military and civilian requirements against the shipping tonnage available.

Major preoccupations of the warring countries included merchant ship construction, repair, and seamen training. New ships were in constant demand to replace tonnage lost and to meet the need for increased numbers of ships to handle wartime requirements. New seamen were needed to replace those lost, injured, or sick, and to man new ships. Like the warring nations, the neutrals were affected by these problems, because the belligerents competed fiercely to charter all available noncommitted shipping in the world.

The merchant marine was a main element in the economic warfare (q.v.) conducted by both Allied and Axis countries. Both sides tried to impose their wills on the neutral nations by granting or withholding privileges the neutrals needed to operate their ships. Among the means used by the Allies to control neutral shipping were the withholding of fuel, closing portions of the sea lanes, interrupting voyages and searching ships, condemning cargoes as contraband, and refusing to allow neutrals to sail in Allied convoys. The Axis powers, because of their geographic position, were unable to use most of these methods to any great extent against neutral shipping. In fact, Axis attacks on neutral merchant ships led many of those countries to join the Allies.

Since German chancellor Adolf Hitler (q.v.) did not really expect general war to start in September 1939, the German merchant marine was scattered around the world. Much German shipping was lost by internment, scuttled to avoid capture, or seized at sea or in port. Italy's merchant fleet likewise was scattered around the world when Premier Benito Mussolini (q.v.) unexpectedly entered the war in June 1940, and much of it, like Germany's, was lost. The Japanese, having carefully planned their date of starting hostilities, were able to position their merchant fleet in friendly waters before the fighting started. Of the countries overrun by the Axis, Norway, the Netherlands, Den-

mark, Belgium, Greece, Estonia, and Yugoslavia all ordered their merchant fleets at sea to join up with Britain and continue the fight. Only France did not follow suit.

During World War II, three major and four minor campaigns were fought with merchant ships as the key objectives. The major fights took place in the North Atlantic, the Mediterranean, and the Pacific. The minor operations took place in the Black Sea, Baltic Sea, Arctic Ocean, and North Sea. These struggles lasted for years, with the North Atlantic and North Sea campaigns being fought from 1939 to 1945. (*See* Convoy Battle in the North Channel, Convoy Battle off Portugal, Convoy PQ-17, Convoy PQ-18, Barents Sea, Convoys HX-229 and SC-122, North Cape, Malta Relief Convoys, and Malta Convoy PEDESTAL.)

In the end the German, Italian, and Japanese merchant marines were destroyed. The British Commonwealth lost 2,350 merchant ships and some 20,000 merchant sailors. A total of more than 4,700 Allied merchant ships totaling more than 21 million tons were lost in the war. Axis owned or controlled merchant ship losses were as follows: Germany 1,800 ships for three million tons; Italy 560 ships for two million tons; and Japan 2,500 ships for 8.6 million tons. The side that won the battle of the merchant ship convoys won the war.

Charles H. Bogart

Additional Reading

Armstrong, Warren, *Battle of the Oceans: The Story of the British Merchant Marine* (1944).
Behrens, C.B.A., *Merchant Shipping and the Demands of War* (1955).
Risenberg, Felix, *Sea War* (1956).
Van der Vat, Dan, *The Atlantic Campaign* (1988).

MI-5

MI-5, formerly Section 5 of Military Intelligence, is roughly the equivalent of the FBI in the United States. It is the agency in Great Britain entrusted with internal security. MI-5 is also known as the "Security Service." In a 1952 security directive, the British Home Secretary stated the mission of MI-5 as:

> The Security Service is part of the Defence Forces of the country. Its task is the defence of the Realm as a whole, from external and internal dangers arising from attempts of espionage and sabotage, or from actions of per-

sons and organizations whether directed from within or without the country, which may be judged to be subversive of the State.

This directive accurately describes MI-5's mission, which since its creation in 1909 has been the principal countersubversion, countersabotage, and counterespionage organization in all British territory. In wartime, MI-5 comes under the Ministry of Defence. Counterintelligence outside the country is entrusted to a sister service, MI-6 (q.v.).

During World War I, MI-5 was extremely successful in neutralizing German spies in Britain. In a roundup on 5 August 1914, more than a dozen spies were caught in as many British cities. Seven spies were tracked down during the first fifteen days of May 1915. So effective was MI-5 that from then until the end of World War I, Britain was never again seriously troubled with German espionage agents. During this same period, British intelligence was deeply involved in plots to maneuver the United States away from neutrality and toward joining the war on the side of the Allies.

By the end of World War I, the Security Service had scored such a remarkable triumph and its reputation was so high that in almost every capitol in Europe the hand of British intelligence was imagined in almost every political move being made. The spymasters and their top agents remained in the shadows, mostly unhonored, their identities carefully concealed from the public.

During the period between the two world wars, MI-5 concentrated principally on investigating domestic Communists and monitoring the activities of Sir Oswald Mosely's (q.v.) British Fascists. New recruits for most British security functions came mainly from the ranks of ex-military officers, and investigations into their backgrounds were perfunctorily performed with family status being the most important consideration. This was the manner in which Kim Philby and others were recruited into MI-6 with devastating results, since they went on to become dangerous Soviet double agents.

In World War II, MI-5 had more difficulty in neutralizing enemy agents than during World War I. A flood of German refugees and improved German espionage methods made the job more complex. Counterintelligence not only kept track of German agents, but also Soviet, Spanish, and Italian as well. In the prewar period, in addition to Philby, Donald Maclean, Guy Burgess, Anthony Blunt, and John Cairncross slipped through the screening process to spy for the Soviets. They were active Soviet agents during and after World War II.

During World War II, MI-5 was superbly successful in recruiting German agents operating in Britain and using them as double agents as part of the famed "Double Cross" system (*see* Counterintelligence Operations). They were used to mislead the German high command as to British and American strategic plans right until the end of the war. A few of the most notable of these double agents were "Garbo," "Tricycle" (Dusko Popov), and "Zig Zag" (Edie Chapman). The period represents the omega of MI-5 successes.

At the end of the war, MI-5 underwent a series of internal organizational changes, but its basic structure of six divisions remained unchanged. These divisions are: A, administrative department; B, counterespionage; C, vetting and other defensive work; D, military liaison; E, alien activity; and F, surveillance.

During the postwar period, MI-5 experienced many security scandals and acquired a very poor reputation among fellow security agencies, particularly in the United States. Author John Le Carre used MI-5 as the model for his Smiley novels, calling it "The Circus," from the location of its London headquarters at Oxford Circus.

Charges that the Soviet Union's KGB penetrated the upper echelons of MI-5 have persisted for years. These charges were so widely believed that KGB agents contemplating defection to the West would avoid even passing through Britain if at all possible because of the fear of exposure.

Paul J. Rose

Additional Reading

West, Nigel, *MI-5 1945–1972: A Matter of Trust* (1982).

Wright, Peter, *Spy Catcher* (1987).

MI-6

MI-6, formerly Section 6 of Military Intelligence, is the agency charged with Britain's overseas intelligence operations. Also known as the Secret Intelligence Service, or SIS, MI-6 functions roughly parallel those of America's Central Intelligence Agency (CIA).

Spying is old, sometimes called the second oldest profession, but intelligence agencies are new, a product of the twentieth century. In 1909, the first intelligence agency came into being in Britain. It was financed from government funds and its employees were mostly civilians. The British Secret Service Bureau of 1909 was divided into two sections: Home Services (which later became MI-5), and Foreign Services (later MI-6). The new organization was a product of "spy mania." William Le Queux, an amateur spy and fiction writer of the time, orchestrated a spy scare based on spy hysteria and little else; thus providing what justification there was for the creation of history's first permanent intelligence agency.

MI-6 quickly became the model for intelligence agencies in France, Germany, later the United States, and elsewhere. Ironically, at the end of World War II, MI-6 ace Kim Philby, while a Soviet double agent, advised and assisted in the creation of the U.S. Central Intelligence Agency.

Consistent with the earliest British experience is the all too frequent inability of intelligence agencies, of whatever hue, to distinguish between fiction and reality. A high degree of paranoia is the hallmark of all intelligence organizations. They thrive best in an international climate of tension and external threat. Periods of peace and tranquility are perceived as threatening to their very existence. This is the legacy of the way in which the British Intelligence Bureau was created in 1909.

A study of MI-6 reveals a fluctuation in both its strength and its weaknesses greater than any other national intelligence service. In some periods there were spectacular successes, and in others there were long runs of nothing but dismal failures. Adolf Hitler's (q.v.) swift conquest of Western Europe in 1940 utterly destroyed MI-6's rather weak network on the Continent. The loss of Holland, long an MI-6 chief base for operations against the Germans, was a devastating blow.

Earlier, on 8 November 1939, MI-6 suffered a humiliating experience when Captains H.R. Stevens and S. Payne Best, key officers from the MI-6 center in The Hague, were lured to Venlo on the German border and kidnapped by agents of the *Abwehr* (q.v.) posing as anti-Nazis who could supply the British with important military intelligence. In one swoop, the Germans captured two of MI-6's most experienced officers and effectively destroyed their Dutch network.

In 1940, to replace the intelligence network that had been wiped out on the Continent, British Security Coordination (BSC) headquarters was established in the Rockefeller Center, in New York City, under the direction of Sir William Stephenson (q.v.), "the man called 'Intrepid.'" With able assistance from Colonel Charles H. Ellis and Commander Ian Fleming (q.v.) (of James Bond fame), Stephenson established what Sir Noel Coward called the "greatest Anglo-American intelligence enterprise in history." Such personalities as Leslie Howard, Greta Garbo, and Coward were used by Intrepid as secret agents. Stephenson and his organization also provided critical assistance in establishing America's first secret intelligence service, the OSS (q.v.). Camp X (q.v.), situated in Canada, was one of BSC's major bases of operation.

The greatest success of British intelligence during World War II, and perhaps of all time, was ULTRA (q.v.). Using duplicates of the Enigma (q.v.) cipher machines used by the German military, British scientists at Bletchley Park (q.v.), with some advanced Polish assistance, cracked the German communications code in an operation that came to symbolize British intelligence services at their best.

Actually, MI-6 had relatively little to do with the success of ULTRA. Since the ULTRA program came under the Government Code and Cypher School, a subsection of MI-6, the organization was hard-pressed to claim credit for its success. The view persisted that MI-6 was in such disarray at the beginning of the war that only the success of ULTRA prevented it from being disbanded. Critics of MI-6 claim that it has largely lived off the ULTRA reputation since then.

British intelligence services in general, not only MI-6, have a long tradition of secrecy unmatched in any other democracy. The British Official Secrets Acts are draconian in their impact on British society. Editors dare not expose, and sometimes not even comment upon, official secrets the way the press does in the United States. Former intelligence service employees are restrained from discussing or writing about such matters, and the government is both unrelenting and unforgiving in its struggle to enforce the laws.

Careful observers of the British intelligence services might agree with author John Le Carre that it has "an image but not a face." It is, however, an image that has been very carefully nurtured and preserved since 1909. The CIA and the KGB are much larger and possess greater resources, and certain other intelligence agencies may be much more ruthless than MI-6. As Paul Greengrass wrote, the British intelligence services were the "first players in Kipling's Great Game; they are its master craftsmen." For him, the British intelligence services embody the most noble and noteworthy of British qualities: "subtlety of mind, pragmatism, and an ironic detachment from naivetés which disfigure other nations."

Considering the famed British tendency to come through in a crisis, the ability of MI-6 to rise to the occasion in the future should not be discounted.

Paul J. Rose

Additional Reading

Deacon, Richard, *A History of British Secret Services* (1980).

Knightly, Phillip, *The Second Oldest Profession* (1987).

Milice Français

The *Milice* (militia) was a Fascist, paramilitary police force of approximately 29,000 members created by the Vichy (q.v.) government during the German occupation. It was commanded by Joseph Darnand (q.v.), whose appointment was forced on the Vichy regime by German chancellor Adolf Hitler (q.v.). Based on German demands, the Vichy government gave Darnand the title of secretary general in charge of law and order. This gave him power over the *Milice*, as well as all law enforcement agencies under Vichy control. German SS leader Heinrich Himmler (q.v.) was so pleased with Darnand's services that he made him an honorary *Obersturmbannführer* of the SS. Darnand took the oath of loyalty to Adolf Hitler as an officer of the *Waffen-SS* (q.v.).

The *Milice*'s mission was to destroy, by whatever means, any opposition to the Vichy regime or to German occupation. Perceiving resistance members as a minority of "outlaws and communists" (the Germans called them terrorists), the Vichy regime drew ever closer to the German *Gestapo* (q.v.) in an effort to crush the resistance. The French people tended to fear the brutality of the *Milice* more than that of the murderous German secret police.

Marshal Henri Philippe Pétain (q.v.), president of Vichy France, saw little alternative to cooperation with the Nazi occupiers. The very logic of the Pétain regime required order, which the Germans also demanded. His major objective and strategy, as he saw it, was to rid his government of German control through cooperation and ultimately to reestablish French sovereignty, at least in police and military affairs. Such cooperation tended to draw him ever deeper into a web of treasonous complicity from which he never succeeded in extricating himself.

The *Milice* was established and received Pétain's official blessing at a ceremony at the Hotel Thermal in Vichy on 6 January 1943. Pétain made it clear that he was the *Milice*'s only chief and confirmed the *Milice*'s role as the "best instrument of national reformation." In fact, Pétain's control of the Vichy government was, at this time, pure fiction. On Hitler's insistence, political power had passed to Pétain's premier, Pierre Laval (q.v.). Sub-sequently, the *Milice* under Darnand would be attached to the French chief of government, Laval, as a national militia.

Only some 10,000 members of the *Milice* were active at any one time, the remainder constituting a reserve. The regular military arm of the *Milice* was the *Franc-Garde*, which never exceeded a strength of 2,000. The *Milice* initially confined their operations to unoccupied France, but after December 1943 they became active throughout the entire country. After the D-Day landings in Normandy (q.v.), 3,000 *Milice* members were mobilized.

Under Darnand's leadership, collaboration with the Germans against the resistance movements reached its culmination in a bloody campaign against *Maquis* (q.v.) units operating in the Glieres Plateau in the Haute-Savoie in March 1944. The *Milice* cooperated with a German division in wiping out the *Maquis* stronghold, producing some 400 resistance casualties.

Paul J. Rose

Additional Reading

Gaulle, Charles de, *Memoires de Guerre* (1954).

Lottman, Herbert R., *Pétain: Hero or Traitor* (1985).

Milorg (Norwegian Military Resistance Organization)

The Norwegian resistance (q.v.) movement had a clear advantage in the country's geography. To the east, Norway shared a long border with neutral Sweden. Along Norway's rugged west coast, thousands of fjords and smaller inlets made it virtually impossible to seal the country off from the sea. Immediately after the fall of Norway, fishing boats began making undetected runs between Norway and Great Britain. What became known as the "Shetland Bus" routinely brought Norwegians to Britain to enlist in the Norwegian forces-in-exile, and brought weapons, military supplies, and agents back into Norway.

As early as September 1940, Norwegians in Britain were training as SOE (q.v.) agents. By the end of 1940, the cadre of what would become Norwegian Independent Company No. 1 infiltrated back into the country under the command of Lieutenant Martin Linge. In the spring of 1941, the SOE established contact with fledgling resistance groups inside Norway and helped organize former army officers into the *Militär Organisasjonen*, known as Milorg.

In October 1941 the Norwegian government-in-exile recognized Milorg as the Home Forces, the fourth branch of the Norwegian armed forces. Milorg, however, remained aloof from the SOE and its operations. The SOE continued to push for increased sabotage and direct terror actions against the Germans. Milorg, on the other hand, preferred to concentrate on building itself up as a "force in being" against the day it could rise up to assist a direct Allied landing in Norway. The Norwegian government-in-exile was uncomfortable with Milorg's leadership at the start of the war. This changed in 1943, when Milorg underwent a reorganization. Jens Christian Hauge, a twenty-eight-year-old lawyer, became the commander of Milorg for the remainder of the war.

After the Normandy (q.v.) landings in June 1944, the headquarters of Supreme Allied Commander General Dwight D. Eisenhower (q.v.) sent a directive to the Norwegian Home Forces stating very clearly that no direct Allied landing in Norway would be forthcoming. The Norwegian Home Forces, therefore, were ordered to refrain from direct action, and continue to train and or-ganize to disarm the Germans and prevent a "scorched earth" action when the German collapse came.

Following Eisenhower's directive, Milorg between October 1944 and the spring of 1945 established three clandestine bases in the mountains where entire units were trained and equipped. By the end of the war, Milorg's strength numbered 40,000.

Between 7 and 9 May 1945, Milorg mobilized and assumed control of official buildings and other strategic points in the country. Although Milorg's direct actions were limited in nature, it nonetheless helped tie down over 360,000 German troops in Norway right to the end of the war.

David T. Zabecki

Additional Reading

Andenas, Johs., O. Riste, and M. Skodvin, *Norway and the Second World War* (1966).
Riste, Olav, and Berit Nökleby, *Norway 1940–45: The Resistance Movement* (1970).

N

NAAFI

See Navy, Army, and Air Force Institute

Narodnyy Kommissariat Vnutrenniakh Del (NKVD)

The People's Commissariat for Internal Affairs, or NKVD, existed from July 1934 to March 1946. It was the overarching secret police and intelligence agency with which Soviet premier Josef Stalin (q.v.) prosecuted the purges (q.v.) of the mid-1930s. Under the direction of Lavrenty Beria (q.v.) from 1938, the NKVD incorporated both the internal affairs machinery and the state security organs. The latter were removed from the NKVD briefly from February to July 1941, and formed into the separate People's Commissariat for State Security (NKGB), under a Beria henchman, Vsevold N. Merkulov.

Following the shock of the German invasion in June 1941, the two agencies were reunited under Beria and the NKVD. In April 1943, the NKGB reemerged as a distinct entity under the titular authority of Merkulov, but still controlled by Beria, who remained czar of the entire state security and police apparatus throughout the war. Despite the maze of administrative convolutions, the purpose of the NKVD as the merciless executor of Stalin's will over the Soviet state never wavered.

The onset of war brought about a rapid expansion of NKVD powers—a fact mirrored by the rise of Beria himself to a position of importance second only to Stalin. In January 1941, Beria was promoted to the rank of general commissar of state security (equivalent to the military rank of marshal of the Soviet Union), and in late June, he joined Stalin, Molotov, Marshal Kliment Voroshilov, and Georgy Malenkov (qq.v.) as members of the newly established supreme wartime authority, the State Defense Committee (GKO). Beria's portfolio—and that of the NKVD—dominated all aspects of domestic policy, including armaments, munitions, and a variety of economic functions such as hydroelectric projects and military construction.

In addition to the foreign espionage mission that it shared with Soviet military intelligence (GRU), the NKVD ran the penal empire of forced labor camps, the infamous *Gulag*. It supervised mass deportations and executions of "anti-Soviet" populations in newly occupied or reconquered lands and controlled the Soviet partisan (q.v.) war effort behind German lines. Additionally, the NKVD terrorized the Red Army itself in the name of military counterintelligence through its armed special departments (OO-NKVDs).

Combat operations also played a defining role in the NKVD charter. Beria's Border Troops, NKVD Internal Troops, and NKVD Troops of Special Purpose *(Osnaz)* together represented the praetorian guard of Stalin's regime, a military force directly responsive to the party/state apparatus and divorced from Red Army command channels. Postwar estimates of NKVD regular troop strength range from one to two million men.

While NKVD formations were employed against the *Wehrmacht* at the front, their major mission was behind Soviet lines in blocking unauthorized retreats, conducting counterinsurgency operations, and repressing indigenous populations. According to analyst John Dziak, the support of Stalin allowed Beria to operate "his NKVD armies and divisions with an independence similar to that of SS and *Waffen-SS* units relative to the regular German military."

In 1946, Stalin elevated Beria to full membership on the ruling Politburo, but the latter had to relinquish his NKVD chair to his former deputy, S.N. Kruglov. Concurrently, the NKVD and

NKGB were retitled as ministries, becoming the MVD and MGB, respectively.

In the aftermath of Stalin's death in March 1953, Beria merged the two organs once again under his direct control—albeit briefly—in the ill-conceived coup d'état that ended with his own arrest and execution. The NKVD was renamed the *Komitet Gosudarstvenoy Bezopasnosti* (KGB) in 1954.

Stephen Donahue

Additional Reading

Andrew, Christopher, and Oleg Gordievsky, *KGB: The Inside Story of Its Foreign Operations from Lenin to Gorbachev* (1990).

Barron, John, *KGB: The Secret Work of Soviet Secret Agents* (1974).

Dziak, John J., *Chekisty: A History of the KGB* (1988).

Tolstoy, Nikolai, *Stalin's Secret War* (1981).

Nationalsozialistische Deutsche Arbeiterpartei (NSDAP)

On 12 September 1919, Adolf Hitler (q.v.) attended a meeting of a small organization in Munich known as the *Deutsche Arbeiterpartei* (DAP)—German Workers' Party. Still in the military, he was sent to spy on this group that considered itself a vehicle for national unity during the political turmoil that had plagued Bavaria. A speech by Gottfried Feder and a pamphlet by Anton Drexler prompted Hitler to join the DAP. Hitler subsequently left the army. He soon emerged as the leading public speaker of the DAP and a well-known figure among other right-wing groups in Munich. His talents as a speaker enabled him to gain wide support and enough stature to restructure the DAP.

At a February 1920 mass rally, Hitler announced the renaming of the DAP as the National Socialist German Workers' Party (*Nationalsozialistische Deutsche Arbeiterpartei*—NSDAP or Nazi Party), and a new program, the "Twenty-five Points," which mirrored his views. The party grew quickly under his leadership, numbering about 3,000 members by January 1921. The old guard, the original members of the DAP, however, resented Hitler's dictatorial methods and challenged him in July 1921. Their efforts failed, and his control was further strengthened. He initiated immediate changes in leadership and structure and established its paramilitary arm, the *Sturmabteilung*—(SA) (q.v.).

With a solid base in Munich and the party firmly under his control, Hitler began focusing recruitment efforts on right-wing groups in other parts of Bavaria. He traveled from town to town, speaking and meeting with local sympathizers. The SA also grew rapidly, recruiting the unemployed, veterans, and the disgruntled. As political tensions mounted in the Weimar Republic (q.v.) during 1923, he believed the time had arrived for an armed insurrection led by him and the NSDAP but carried out with other right-wing groups. The Beer Hall *Putsch* (q.v.) launched in Munich on 8 November 1923, failed, but it taught Hitler important lessons.

The era of violence that spawned the Nazi Party was ending as economic recovery returned to Germany. Furthermore, Hitler found himself in a position where he and his movement had to act on behest of the other conspirators. He also concluded that a policy of legality for the NSDAP, working within the political system, was its only chance of coming to power. Placed on trial after the aborted *Putsch,* he turned a fiasco into a triumphant defense for his party and an indictment of the republic. He spelled out his program and found a responsive court that gave him the minimum sentence.

With Hitler in prison until December 1924, the NSDAP floundered, splitting into two factions. After his release, however, he began to regain his authority, first in Munich, then in the rest of Bavaria before moving to northern Germany, where the party was growing rapidly under Gregor Strasser. The northern faction was based primarily in cities and it focused on the plight of the urban proletariat. Hitler, however, had serious ideological reservations with this emphasis, but he feared splitting the NSDAP. At a conference in Bamberg in February 1926, he reestablished party unity. He secured the support of Strasser and some of his capable followers, including Joseph Goebbels (q.v.), whom Hitler then sent to organize Berlin.

As the party resumed its activities throughout Germany, it remained unclear which direction Hitler would lead the NSDAP, particularly during these years of prosperity and political stability. This calm also gave Hitler the time needed to strengthen the party organization and to centralize its administration. An important feature was the appointment of regional leaders, the *Gauleiter,* all of whom were intensely loyal to Hitler. Recruitment efforts focused increasingly on industrial workers and in urban areas, as the NSDAP attempted to win the proletariat over from Marxism and socialism.

The party appeared to have adopted the so-called urban plan, a political program that was anti-capitalist, anti-Communist, and anti-Semitic. Still, considerable efforts were made, particularly in south Germany in 1927, to gain the support of the middle class. The shift back to the right was sealed by the results of the May 1928 election when, hopeful of an electoral breakthrough, the NSDAP posted candidates in all thirty-five districts. The NSDAP gained only twelve seats in the *Reichstag*. It lost heavily in urban districts but made impressive gains in rural areas and small towns. The urban plan was formally abandoned at an August leadership meeting when the emphasis was shifted to the so-called rural-nationalist plan.

The NSDAP sent its speakers, who gave expression to the fears and anxieties of the lower middle class, to the rural areas and small towns. Rallies and speeches were held in almost every village. Its affiliate organizations, many only recently established, also emphasized this new message. The results were impressive; NSDAP candidates received 6.4 million votes in the September 1930 election and secured 107 seats in parliament. Membership soared to 130,000. The party was rapidly gaining momentum, but now the problem was to turn the new voters into followers, the source of real political power. Crucial to the electoral success was the SA, whose ranks swelled with the unemployed. It hung the campaign posters, guarded Nazi rallies, and disrupted opponents' meetings.

Membership continued to increase, as did the number of votes won at the ballot box. However, indications that the NSDAP would flounder on its own inner contradictions grew as it failed to gain power. Furthermore, the November 1932 local elections were a severe disappointment, as economic recovery and political stability became more prevalent. Although the NSDAP was viewed by other opponents of the republic as a coalition partner, Hitler turned down an offer to serve as vice chancellor. In mid-December 1932, Hitler and his party were rescued when Franz von Papen (q.v.) proposed a coalition government led by Hitler, whose mass party would provide the rightists the popular base essential to carry out the conservative program of eradicating the democratic government. Hitler accepted, and he become the *Reich* chancellor on 30 January 1933.

Once in power, the party's membership soared from about 850,000 to 1.5 million by late March 1933. Most new members were opportunists, and many came from the ranks of the civil service and professions. As head of the new coalition government, Hitler used his power to appoint the so-called old- fighters, members prior to 1933,

to a number of state positions. He thereby placed these alienated fanatics, who had little or no political experience, in positions of responsibility. Their lack of administrative skills actually served as an obstacle to the party's ambitions, but Hitler assuaged an important and loyal faction.

In addition to auxiliary and paramilitary organizations, the NSDAP began to establish institutions that paralleled existing elements of the government. For example, on 1 April 1933, Hitler created a party bureau to oversee foreign policy; a short time later special Nazi courts were organized. The new government also systematically eliminated independent centers of power, such as labor unions and political parties, and replaced them with Nazi-sponsored organizations. Within six months of coming to power, the Nazi Party controlled most areas of political and economic life. All party authority continued to be embodied in Hitler as the *Führer* of the Nazi Party, who shifted his movement from an instrument of revolution to a parallel bureaucracy. Party congresses and rituals remained important elements of German life, and the annual party rallies were often the occasion for issuing decrees of far-reaching significance, such as the infamous 1935 Nuremberg Laws (q.v.).

With the outbreak of war, the party assumed new responsibilities, as Hitler assigned it to maintain morale among the population. The party was also to guarantee that there would be no repeat of the November 1918 revolution. In addition, party dignitaries received administrative appointments in the newly occupied areas, thereby extending its power and stature. Party organizations spread rapidly to these areas. Within Germany proper, important changes were also taking place, such as the reform of the legal system that began in 1942 that made it a vehicle of Nazi ideology.

During the final years of the war, as the *Reich* faced new uncertainties, party officials increasingly lacked focus and direction. A few leaders, such as Goebbels, Albert Speer, Heinrich Himmler, and Martin Bormann (qq.v.), continued to compete for Hitler's favor and each gained enormous power. As the Allied forces advanced against the *Reich,* administrative chaos swept through the occupied areas with party officials fleeing. At home, party authority was further centralized in an effort to hold the country together. One of the party's final efforts was the *Volkssturm* (q.v.), the mobilization in October 1944 of those men who could still bear arms. With the defeat of Nazi Germany, the party collapsed and its members were arrested.

Robert G. Waite

Additional Reading

Kater, Michael H., *The Nazi Party: A Social Profile of Members and Leaders* (1983).

Nyomarky, Joseph, *Charisma and Factionalism in the Nazi Party* (1967).

Orlov, Dietrich, *The History of the Nazi Party, 1919–1933* (1971).

———, *The History of the Nazi Party, 1933–1945* (1973).

Navies, Bulgarian and Romanian

The naval balance in the Black Sea was decidedly in favor of the Soviet Union as World War II approached. None of the other Black Sea countries even approached the Soviet Union in naval power. Of the four Black Sea nations, Germany was allied with the two weakest, Romania and Bulgaria. Neither country had the resources to develop an independent navy and both were surrounded by hostile countries.

By necessity, both nations maintained relatively large armies to which their navies were subordinate. Moreover, Romania and Bulgaria were traditional enemies, and their units could not be safely expected to work in proximity, much less in cooperation. The Germans did not see this as a significant problem since Adolf Hitler (q.v.) believed the Soviet Union would fall in less than eight weeks, long before any naval actions could affect the outcome. That held true while the *Luftwaffe* maintained air supremacy, but Germany's Black Sea allies were unable to protect Germany's southern flank. That problem grew more serious as the *Luftwaffe*'s strength waned. By 1942, German and Italian units were sent as reinforcements, but they were not enough.

Romania's fleet was stronger than Bulgaria's, but it had only three modern units. Its 250 officers and 3,000 men were poorly trained, since the fleet had little money for training, operations, or maintenance. Romania lacked shipyard facilities and skilled workers to conduct any but the most routine repairs to its ships. Thus, all major equipment repairs required the import of foreign technicians, or were sent to Italy, using up precious foreign currency reserves. The situation was little changed by early 1941, despite much effort to improve its shipyards and build up a reserve of trained labor. By 1942, Romania developed the ability to produce small ships and even two small submarines. Nonetheless, its shipyards lacked all but the most rudimentary ability to build and repair modern naval equipment. On any given day, one or two of the new units, and the majority of the older units, had their speed or serviceability reduced by material deficiencies.

Romania's naval air arm was limited to two squadrons of slow obsolescent aircraft with limited range and firepower. As a result, Romania could not interdict the Soviet convoys supporting besieged Odessa and later, Sevastopol (q.v.), or prevent their evacuation. Its naval deficiencies became even more apparent as the war dragged on, and the Romanian Navy was reduced to protecting coastal convoys and patrolling the minefields of the western Black Sea. Although its surface units managed to sink two Soviet submarines, Romania's only modern submarine, the *Delflinui*, did not participate in any offensive operations because its employment was inhibited by material problems and a torpedo shortage.

Forced to surrender its navy after World War I, Bulgaria had an even smaller fleet, with four torpedo boats, two minesweepers, and six motor patrol boats, all of World War I vintage. The entire force was based in Varna and numbered less than 3,000 personnel. Even the Salonika Agreement of 1938, which removed all armaments restrictions on Bulgaria, had little effect on its navy, because there was very little cash, and the army and air force had higher precedence. The Bulgarian Navy needed and received much German help as the war progressed, but it never expanded beyond a basic coastal patrol force. More significantly, employment of Bulgaria's Navy was complicated by the fact that Bulgaria never declared war on the Soviet Union. Its primary mission was the patrolling and maintenance of the coastal minefields that constituted the foundation of the German antisubmarine warfare effort in the western Black Sea.

Despite extensive German assistance and reinforcement, neither the Bulgarian nor the Romanian Navies achieved anything near full operational capability. Germany placed less and less reliance on these small fleets as the war progressed and the momentum turned against the Axis. Their reliability declined as the Soviet armies draw nearer their borders. It was only the Soviet's loss of their own naval bases, Axis air supremacy, and the siphoning of Soviet naval crewmen into the ground war that prevented the Axis naval shortcomings from having a significant effect on the war.

Carl O. Schuster

Additional Reading

Madej, Victor, *Southeastern Europe Axis Armies Handbook* (1982).

Tarnstrom, Ronald L., *Handbooks of the Armed Forces: The Balkans,* Vols. 1 and 2 (1984).

Navy, Army, and Air Force Institute (NAAFI)

The organization known as NAAFI was formed in 1921 to provide a service to the three British armed services stationed on land-based establishments. The regimental canteens, which were gradually replaced by the NAAFI canteen, had provided recreational and social facilities, and the profits from these establishments were paid into the regimental funds. NAAFI, having replaced these local canteens, provided the same facilities, and in most camps much more. NAAFI paid a "rebate" to the regimental funds based on the total income at each station.

In 1939 an estimated 55 percent of the NAAFI staff were women; by 1943 that had risen to 85 percent. The "NAAFI girls" came from all walks of life, joining the organization from shops, restaurants, offices, and factories. The "girls" were all volunteers. During World War II they had to undergo basic training as members of the Auxiliary Territorial Service (ATS) (q.v.), and were subject to military regulations and discipline, the same as men who were employed by NAAFI.

The NAAFI buildings provided a meeting place for servicemen and women. The facilities usually consisted of a "dry canteen" (a restaurant), a "wet canteen" (a bar), and, where space permitted, a game room. In larger camps, the NAAFI facilities were divided into non-commissioned officers' and soldiers' rooms.

Many members of the NAAFI staff volunteered for service in combat and danger zones. Some became casualties, some became prisoners of war, and a number were decorated for gallantry. NAAFI continued in operation serving British forces after World War II. By the 1980 it had grown into a major world-wide trading company.

Alan Harfield

Additional Reading

Navy, Army, and Armed Forces Institute, *About NAAFI* (1981).

Williams, N. T., *Judy O'Grady and the Colonel's Lady* (1988).

Navy, Australian

In 1920, Australia possessed a navy of thirty-seven ships, including a battle cruiser. By 3 September 1939, this fleet had wasted away to seventeen ships. Its largest ship was a heavy cruiser and the personnel strength was 5,446 officers and men. During World War II, Australia fought two naval wars: from 1939 to 1942, it operated in the Indian and Atlantic Oceans and the Mediterranean Sea against Germany and Italy, and from 1942 to 1945, it operated in the Pacific Ocean against Japan.

Australia undertook two missions against Germany and Italy. Its navy provided convoy escort to and from Australia and New Zealand across the Indian Ocean, and it cooperated with the Royal Navy in holding the Mediterranean Sea against the Axis.

The notable occurrences for the Australian Navy were the sinking of the Italian cruiser *Bartolomeo Colleoni* by HMAS *Sydney* on 18 July 1940 north of Crete. The *Sydney*, in turn, was lost with all hands off west Australia on 19 November 1941, in action against the German raider *Kormoran*, which was also sunk. HMAS *Australia* sank the Vichy French destroyer *L'Audacieux* at Dakar (q.v.) on 23 September 1940. At least one of Australia's ten destroyers took part in all the naval engagements in the Mediterranean Sea from 1940 to mid-1942.

By the end of the war, the Australian Navy grew to 337 ships and 36,900 officers and men. However, all that strength was concentrated in the Pacific Ocean. Its losses to the Germans and Italians were one cruiser and two destroyers.

Charles H. Bogart

Additional Reading

Collins, John, *HMAS Sydney* (1971).

Gill, George Hermon, *Royal Australian Navy* (1968).

Navy, Brazilian

With the start of war in Europe in September 1939, Brazil established a neutrality patrol off its coast. To carry out this operation, it had a fleet consisting of a number of modernized pre-World War I ships, including two battleships, two cruisers, and six destroyers. The navy also had one old and four modern submarines, plus auxiliary craft. None of the ships had an antisubmarine capability. Six destroyers under construction for Brazil in Britain were taken over by the Royal Navy at the start of the war. Brazil also had nine destroyers under construction at home. Their completion was delayed by an inability to obtain needed parts from Europe.

In August 1942, the German U-boat *U-507* sank five Brazilian merchant ships off Brazil's coast, killing more than 400 seamen. As a result, Brazil declared war on Germany and Italy on 22 August. The Brazilian Navy was divided into two fleets, designated Northeastern, based at Bahia, and Southern, operating out of Rio de Janeiro. To support the Brazilian Navy in its war effort, the U.S. Navy transferred eight destroyer escorts, eight patrol craft, and eight subchasers in 1943 and 1944. The U.S. also provided Brazil the equipment to complete the warships it had under construction.

The principal duty of the Brazilian Navy during the war was to provide escort ships for merchantmen sailing to or from the Caribbean along the coast of South America. The Brazilian Navy escorted 3,164 merchant ships, losing only three. The navy itself lost the cruiser *Bahia,* the corvette *Camaqua,* the auxiliary *Vital de Oliviera,* and a total of 492 seamen in the war. No Axis ships or planes were destroyed by the Brazilian Navy. Even after Brazil declared war on Japan in May 1945, the Brazilian Navy continued to confine its operating area to the South Atlantic and the Caribbean. Because of U.S. pressure, the Brazilian Navy was unable to obtain any major combat ships during the war to prevent an upset in the naval balance in South America.

Charles H. Bogart

Additional Reading
Scheina, Robert L., *Latin America: A Naval History* (1987).

Navy, British

The Royal Navy (RN) of September 1939 was, by any conventional measure, more than a match for any combination of two of its likely European fleet opponents—Germany, the Soviet Union, and Italy. The Soviets, of course, eventually became an ally, while geographic considerations precluded the other two coordinating their naval operations effectively.

Nevertheless, the RN was ill-equipped for the type of war it was destined to fight. The RN's senior leadership had little appreciation for airpower's potential impact on naval operations and saw Germany's surface raiders and not its submarines (U-boats) as that country's primary threat to British commerce. The British admirals and then First Lord of the Admiralty Winston S. Churchill (q.v.), believed convoys and ASDIC (*see* Sonar) would deter the U-boat threat, leaving them free to blockade Germany into submission. It was a costly mistake from which it took the RN nearly three years to recover. Yet recover they did, and in doing so they saved their nation from defeat and paved the way for the eventual Allied victory.

The RN's mission in World War II was the same as it had always been: defend the empire, protect Britain's vital sea lanes, and project the empire's power against the enemy's shores wherever possible. In 1939, it was well equipped to carry out the first and third of these missions. It was not so well equipped to defend British trade. Although the need to convoy (*see* Convoys, Naval) was recognized and indeed implemented before the war started, the RN had only 150 short-range, sonar-equipped destroyers and no aircraft for escort duty. This was only a fraction of what was used to contain the U-boat threat in the previous war. Yet Britain was even more dependent on foreign imports, particularly oil, than it had been in 1914.

There were other problems as well. Antisubmarine warfare (ASW, q.v.) training was largely neglected in the interwar years. Few officers understood ASW, fewer still were familiar with sonar, and rare was the sonar operator who had more than minimal experience on the equipment. The little ASW training conducted before the war involved daylight tracking exercises against submarines whose initial positions were known. This gave the RN an exaggerated faith in its ability to find U-boats. That belief was exacerbated by the RN's traditional preference for seeking out the enemy for destruction. Many vitally needed convoy escorts were siphoned off to form "hunter-killer" groups that wastefully swept the Atlantic in fruitless searches for German U-boats. The only time they found one was when its torpedoes struck one of the hunting group's ships.

Despite prewar fleet exercises demonstrating that submarines could escape undetected on the surface at night, the RN neither expected nor trained against U-boats conducting night surface attacks. Evidence of German plans to conduct "wolf pack" attacks using groups of submarines also went unappreciated. As a result, convoys were poorly protected in the war's early years and their escorts were ill-prepared for U-boat tactics or the ferocity of the attacks.

The British also underappreciated antiaircraft defenses. RN ships entered the war with very light antiaircraft artillery (AAA) batteries. High angle defenses were particularly deficient. In contrast to American and Japanese practice, the secondary batteries on most British ships lacked the elevation and fire control equipment to engage high altitude or diving aircraft. Some progress was being made in installing close-in weapons systems as the war began, but on the whole, antiaircraft defenses remained insufficient throughout the war.

Radar (q.v.) was entering fleet service in 1939, but only on a handful of battleships and cruisers

TABLE 1

Royal Navy Order of Battle

		1 September 1939		8 May 1945
	Total	Under Construction	In European Waters	Total
Battleships	12*	5	10	14
Battle Cruisers	3**	0	2	1
Aircraft Carriers	6	6	5	11
Escort Carriers	0	0	0	35
Heavy Cruisers	15	0	6	9
Light Cruisers	32	19	26	24
Antiaircraft Cruisers	6	2	2	11
Destroyers	109	8	72	108
World War I Destroyers	58	0	58	0
Destroyer Escorts	15	20	10	83
Sloops/Corvettes	28	4	22	525
MTB/MGBs	18	0	12	320
Submarines	46	11	33	125
World War I Submarines	12	0	8	0
Minesweepers	19	5	16	1,028
World War I Minesweepers	23	0	23	0

Notes:
  *Two battleships were being modernized.
**One battle cruiser was being modernized.

before 1940. Convoy escort ships did not begin to receive radar until late 1941. After that, installations went quickly, which, combined with qualitative improvements in performance, ultimately helped turned the tide against the U-boats.

Airpower was one area where the RN entered the war at a severe disadvantage. Coastal Command, the RAF component on which the RN depended for its shore-based air support, was both small (less than two dozen aircraft) and improperly equipped for its mission. Its twin-engine Anson aircraft lacked the range, endurance, and weapons to be effective against anything heavier than small patrol craft.

The RN's sea-based airpower was little better. Although the RN pioneered fleet air operations in World War I, its perceptions of airpower in the early years of World War II were little different from that of other navies. It saw carrier-based airpower as an adjunct to the battle fleet. Carrier planes were supposed to scout out the enemy fleet, wear down its units with bombing and torpedo attacks, and guide the battle fleet to deliver the finishing blow. The RN's carrier force of six units was seen, therefore, as a special kind of cruiser or scouting force. Its air wings were not expected to deliver a decisive blow against the enemy, and they were nearly incapable of doing so.

The RN's air element, the Fleet Air Arm, was poorly equipped for modern naval air warfare. Having lost control of its carrier aircraft (*see* Carrier Borne Aircraft, British) to the RAF after World War I, the Admiralty only regained control in 1938. Moreover, Churchill saw no need for it to have modern aircraft such as the Spitfire. After all, the navy would be operating on the open ocean far away from first-rate enemy fighters. As a result, the RN's six aircraft carriers carried mixed air wings of obsolete biplanes and slow, underarmed, dual-purpose monoplanes. This, coupled with the small size of the British carrier air wings (less than forty planes each), limited their striking power. Thus their most effective attacks were against ships in port, as at Taranto (q.v.), or ships operating alone, as in the sinking of the *Bismarck* (q.v.). In the latter instance, torpedo planes from HMS *Ark Royal* crippled the battleship so it could be intercepted and destroyed. In effect, that operation seemed to reaffirm the RN's prewar doctrine for carrier employment.

The RN's battle fleet was either obsolete or obsolescent in 1939. Britain delayed modernizing its battle fleet during the 1930s in favor of operating it as a deterrent force. New construction was not ordered until 1937, and those ships would not be available for at least two more years. This placed the RN in an unenviable position in 1939. Only two of its battleships were updated and two were undergoing extensive modernization. As a result, the RN fought the war with a battle fleet that primarily dated back to World War I and had not been refitted since the late 1920s. This was to prove costly during the war. All but one of the battleships/battle cruisers the British lost in the war were these unmodernized capital ships that lacked adequate armor protection and AAA defenses. Only one of the new construction battleships that entered service after the war started was lost. No new battleship or battle cruiser construction was initiated after 1941. The construction of convoy escort ships enjoyed a higher priority.

British cruisers suffered from many of the same faults as battleships, but on the whole gave better service. Although not as large, fast, or heavily armed as their Italian and German counterparts, they were robust in service, and remained operational after absorbing exceptionally heavy punishment. More importantly, their radar sensors became increasingly superior after 1941. However, AAA batteries and on-board AAA ammunition remained a serious problem for the cruisers throughout the war.

The British destroyer and escort forces experienced the greatest improvements and growth during the war. They grew from 170 units in 1939, to nearly 1,000 vessels of all types by 1945. Half of the 1939 destroyer force served in World War I, and only a quarter of the force was less than ten years old. Their main batteries could not be used for air defense and they carried no radar before 1941. Still, they carried the best sonars, and eventually the best ASW weaponry, of any of the world's navies. It was this force that carried the brunt of the war and suffered the bulk of the RN's casualties. Their primary strength was in the boldness and competence of their commanders.

Minesweepers were another neglected arm in the RN. They were the first and last RN units to see action in the war, sweeping for mines from the war's first day until two years after it ended. Less than a dozen minesweepers were in service at the war's start, but plans were developed to requisition civilian craft for minesweeping upon mobilization. That brought approximately 100 vessels into service quickly, but they were only equipped with mechanical sweeping equipment and had no capability to sweep magnetic or other influence mines (*see* Mine Warfare, Naval).

German magnetic mines caught the British by surprise, requiring the rapid development of countermeasure equipment and the training of crews. Fighting mines became one of the most dangerous and widespread missions the RN undertook during the war. After late 1943, that mission even took precedence over ASW, when mines surpassed U-boats as a threat, particularly to Allied amphibious operations. In the RN, minesweepers also functioned as coastal convoy escorts, and occasionally as ocean escorts as well. The British had more than 1,000 minesweepers in service by 1 May 1944.

Despite its shortcomings, the RN still remained one of the world's most professional and proficient forces. Its preparations for war went smoothly. It instituted convoying quickly and efficiently and deployed surface hunting groups to locate and destroy German surface raiders. The RN also delivered the British Army to France, quickly and without loss. The British drew merchant ships from trade and quickly converted them into fleet supply ships or auxiliary cruisers. Both types gave good service during the war, often deterring German surface raiders at great cost to themselves.

Nonetheless, the magnitude of the U-boat threat came as a surprise. Merchant shipping losses skyrocketed, and one U-boat even penetrated the RN's main base at Scapa Flow (q.v.) and sank the battleship HMS *Royal Oak*. That devastated British morale so much that only the later victory against the German pocket battleship *Graf Spee* (*see* Platte River) could alleviate it.

Initially, the war went badly for the RN. As a result of devastating German air attacks in the Norway and Narvik campaigns (qq.v.), the RN lost in a matter of weeks the aircraft carrier HMS *Glorious,* four destroyers, and two submarines. Several cruisers and auxiliaries were damaged as well. Then France departed from the war, and Italy entered it on the German side. As a result, the RN's escort load in the Atlantic doubled just as a new threat arose in the Mediterranean. The RN came through, however, evacuating its army from France (*see* Dunkirk) and inflicting far more damage on the *Kriegsmarine* than it suffered in return.

Meanwhile, the number of U-boats in the Atlantic continued to rise. The first "wolf pack" attack took place in October 1940. To many British citizens, shipping losses seemed to be approaching the catastrophic levels of World War I. Undeterred, the Royal Navy pressed on.

The British seized Iceland in 1940 and from there, increased surface ship patrols in the Greenland, Iceland, and United Kingdom "air gap." They also had to maintain patrols in the English Channel and conduct attacks against German shipping concentrations. British submarines deployed to the Mediterranean and North Seas to prey on Axis sea lanes.

It was a time of grave danger for Great Britain. Italy threatened Malta and the Suez Canal. Germany was preparing to invade (*see* Operation SEA LION), while its U-boats ravaged Britain's sea lanes. Fearing the British fleet, however, Grand Admiral Erich Raeder (q.v.) and German Army leaders insisted that the invasion could not be attempted unless the *Luftwaffe* achieved total air supremacy over the Channel and southern England. RAF's Fighter Command prevented that from happening in the famous Battle of Britain (q.v.), but it was the RN's fearsome reputation that made that battle necessary.

The RN spent much of 1940 setting the stage for the programs that ultimately would provide victory. Merchant ship and escort production increased. Older destroyers were modified to give them more range so they could escort convoys all the way across the Atlantic. Research into better ASW weapons, improved radars, and dual-purpose guns also increased. An operational research group was established to examine the best systems and tactics to employ in the war. ASW and sonar training schools were being established. Better planes were sought for the Fleet Air Arm, and more capable aircraft were acquired for the expanding RAF Coastal Command. Still, it would take time for these initiatives to take effect—time Great Britain did not seem to have in 1940.

If 1940 was full of serious setbacks for the RN, 1941 was almost catastrophic. Churchill, now prime minister, committed the RN to supporting the Soviet Union, which meant more convoys across a greater expanse of ocean. Naval losses in the Mediterranean—particularly Crete (q.v.)—and the Atlantic and Pacific Oceans approached decisive levels. That year the RN lost four battleships and two battle cruisers (40 percent of the force), while cruiser and destroyer losses approached similar levels.

By year's end, the Japanese entered the Indian Ocean, U-boats were sinking 250,000 tons of shipping a month, and the Italians regained nominal superiority in the Mediterranean. Although no one realized it at the time, the German surface threat was in recession. The sinking of the *Bismarck* in May marked the last major German surface raiding operation of the war.

The RN started 1942 as a growing but nevertheless increasingly strained force. It now was fighting a war that stretched across the entire globe. Its forces were under attack everywhere. RN carriers were being sunk in the Indian and Atlantic Oceans, and damaged in the Mediterranean. Its escorts were decimated in the Atlantic and its convoys attacked in the Mediterranean. Still, the RN met every commitment, and indeed, became more aggressive.

Despite catastrophic losses in the Arctic convoys, RN carriers and submarines attacked German bases and ships in Norway, struck Axis positions in Italy and Libya, and perhaps most importantly, ravaged the supply lines of German general Erwin Rommel's *Afrika Korps* (qq.v.) in the Mediterranean. The RN also delivered tanks, supplies, and reinforcements to British forces in Africa. By the end of 1942, it supported the massive amphibious assault that brought American forces onto North Africa. Then, as the Allied forces advanced, the RN's Mediterranean Fleet tightened its choke hold on Rommel's supply lines. By May, Rommel was forced back to Germany and all Axis forces in North Africa surrendered. None of that would have been possible without the RN's victory at sea in the Mediterranean.

Meanwhile, in the Atlantic, the tide of the U-boat campaign against Britain's ocean commerce reached its peak. U-boats sank 1.8 million tons of shipping in the final three months of 1942, and that trend continued into the next year. Churchill recognized the sea war was entering its decisive phase. Three more months of such losses and Britain would have to leave the war.

There was some good news on the horizon. The escort construction program was reaching fruition. Every convoy now had as many as twenty escorts, and all escorts had radar. Escort carriers were being produced in large numbers, and RAF Coastal Command had enough long-range patrol

TABLE 2

British Dominion Navies Order of Battle 1 September 1939

	Total	In European/ Atlantic Waters
Heavy Cruisers	2	0
Light Cruisers	6	1
Destroyers	9	6
Destroyer Escorts	7	0
Sloops/Corvettes	7	0

Note: These figures are not included in the totals for the Royal Navy (RN), but dominion units essentially operated as part of the RN. They were deployed under RN direction and operated under RN tactical control, except when functioning as a dominion tactical unit—i.e., the formation was that of the Canadian, Australian, New Zealand, or Indian navies.

bombers to provide continuous air surveillance coverage far out into the Atlantic. The gap in air coverage now was limited to the central North Atlantic, and the escort carriers operating in support of the convoys virtually covered that area. New weapons, both ship and airborne, were entering service.

U-boat attacks continued, but U-boat casualties were climbing. The U-boats brought Great Britain to within six weeks of leaving the war, but by July 1943, U-boat losses themselves had reached unacceptable levels. Admiral Karl Dönitz (q.v.), commander of the German Navy, withdrew his submarines from the Atlantic. Although the U-boat threat never completely disappeared, the danger was past. The RN was now free to concentrate on its power projection role, delivering ground troops back to the Continent.

The RN played the principal role in the combined Allied naval command that carried the ground troops onto the European continent. It was RN victories in the Mediterranean and the Atlantic that paved the way for the amphibious operations in Sicily, Italy, and Normandy (qq.v.). Whatever its shortcomings in the war's early years, the RN adapted quickly to the changing nature and fortunes of modern naval warfare. More significantly, its commanders and personnel demonstrated an unwavering commitment to supporting the forces ashore, regardless of the costs to themselves and their organization. From Dunkirk to Crete and the Dodecanese Islands (qq.v.), RN units sacrificed themselves to bring the troops home in the face of seemingly overwhelming adversity. That spirit and dedication was as much responsible for their ultimate victory as anything else.

Carl O. Schuster

Additional Reading

Barnett, Correlli, *Engage the Enemy More Closely, The Royal Navy in the Second World War* (1991).

Hough, Richard, *The Longest Battle* (1986).

Piekalkiewicz, Janusz, *The Sea War; 1939–1945* (1987).

Roskill, Stephen W., *The War at Sea, 1939–1945,* 4 vols. (1954–1961).

Navy, Bulgarian

See Navies, Bulgarian and Romanian

Navy, Canadian

The Royal Canadian Navy (RCN) underwent vast expansion during World War II, and by 1945, it was the third-largest Allied navy in terms of number of warships. The most vital task of this growing fleet of corvettes, frigates, and destroyers was convoy escort, and it was in the Battle of the Atlantic (q.v.) that it played its most decisive role. By mid-1943, the RCN contributed 50 percent of the close escorts for North Atlantic trade convoys. RCN warships also operated in Pacific and Arctic Oceans, and Mediterranean and Caribbean Seas, and took a major part in the D-Day landings in 1944. Beginning in late 1942, the RCN acquired larger units such as Tribal-class destroyers, light cruisers, and escort carriers to form the nucleus of a balanced fleet.

During the 1920s and 1930s, the RCN was threatened with extinction by cost-cutting governments but narrowly survived. At the outbreak of war in September 1939, it consisted of six destroyers, five minesweepers, and two small training vessels, with a permanent force of 1,774 men and 2,083 reserves. From this tiny base, the RCN grew to a force of 100,000 men and women and more than 360 warships, made possible by a massive Canadian shipbuilding program.

Shipyards on the Great Lakes and St. Lawrence River, and the Pacific and Atlantic coasts, produced 70 frigates, 122 corvettes, 194 minesweepers, and a host of trawlers, motor launches, motor torpedo boats, and landing craft. In addition, they built more than 400 merchant ships for the Allied war effort. This was a remarkable achievement considering the moribund state of the Canadian shipbuilding industry in 1939; the only naval vessels produced in Canada since 1918 had been four small minesweepers.

Not surprisingly, this rapid expansion was accompanied by severe growing pains as Naval Service Headquarters struggled to equip, man, and train its burgeoning fleet. Facilities had to be improvised from scratch. In the early years, this did not pose an insuperable problem because the Allied need for escort vessels was so desperate that ships in almost any condition were useful. By 1942–1943, the nature of the U-boat war had intensified to such a degree that only highly trained escort groups fitted with the most advanced types of radar, sonar, and HF/DF could successfully battle the wolf packs.

The RCN failed to keep pace technically with the U.S. and Royal Navies, and for a few months in early 1943, RCN escort groups were removed from the North Atlantic run. They were upgraded in British ports and temporarily deployed on the Gibraltar run, where they immediately proved their increased effectiveness. In January 1944, the equipment crisis resulted in the replacement of Vice Admiral Percy Nelles, chief of the naval staff, with Rear Admiral G.C. Jones. The worst effects of the crisis had been addressed by mid-1943, although less serious technical shortcomings continued to plague RCN warships until the end of the war.

Nevertheless, the RCN enjoyed considerable success in the Battle of the Atlantic and made up with numbers what it sometimes lacked in quality. Canada's rapid production of corvettes, the workhorses of the escort fleet, made end-to-end convoy escort possible in the North Atlantic in 1941. When the U-boat menace spread to new theaters in 1942, the RCN's escort commitments expanded in turn. German submarines penetrated Canadian coastal waters and even entered the mouth of the St. Lawrence River. Local convoys were organized in the Gulf of St. Lawrence and between Boston, Halifax, and Newfoundland, using scratch groups of corvettes, minesweepers, armed yachts, and motor launches. Six corvettes protected vital oil tanker traffic from the Caribbean Sea during the spring and summer of 1942, and then moved over to the American eastern seaboard to reinforce the U.S. Navy. That autumn, the RCN scraped together another seventeen corvettes to support Operation TORCH in the Mediterranean Sea. The corvettes scored U-boat kills in both the Caribbean and the Mediterranean.

The brunt of the battle, however, was always in the North Atlantic. From summer 1942 until autumn 1943, hard-pressed RCN escorts fought the German wolf packs in a long-running series of convoy battles, including SC-94, ON-127, SC-107, ONS-154, ON-166, SC-121, and ON-202/ONS-18. As the Atlantic campaign reached its climax in April–May 1943, the ocean area off Canada and Newfoundland, hitherto under British and then U.S. strategic direction, became a distinct Canadian theater under Rear Admiral L.W. Murray, commander in chief, Canadian Northwest Atlantic. Henceforth, he controlled all Allied aircraft and warships engaged in the escort of trade convoys in this region.

This delegation of operational authority revealed American and British recognition of the crucial role played by RCN escorts in the Battle of the Atlantic. It also was a tribute to the excellence of the RCN's control-of-shipping organization, radio-intercept network, and Operational Intelligence Centre. By 1944–1945, the RCN provided most of the close escort for North Atlantic trade convoys and formed eight mid-ocean support groups. Its most successful support group, EG-9, destroyed five German U-boats between March 1944 and February 1945.

The Atlantic escort fleet was the RCN's most decisive contribution to the war at sea, but the service played a significant role in other theaters as well. In the aftermath of Dunkirk (q.v.) in 1940, Canadian destroyers participated in the evacuation of Allied soldiers from France and in the extension of convoy for shipping in British waters. Three passenger liners converted into auxiliary cruisers assisted British and U.S. forces in the defense against surface raiders in the North Atlantic, Caribbean, and North Pacific.

The commissioning of four heavily-armed Tribal-class destroyers in late 1942 and early 1943 gave the RCN an added capacity for traditional fleet work. The British-based RCN Tribals operated with the Royal Navy in a variety of tasks, including runs with the Arctic convoys to Murmansk during the winter of 1943–1944. They were transferred to the 10th Destroyer Flotilla at Plymouth in the spring of 1944 to clear the English Channel of German surface units in advance of the D-Day landings. As part of a select group of destroyers and cruisers, the *Tribals* were in the thick of the action and fought with distinction, sharing in the destruction of several German destroyers and smaller warships.

In total, the RCN contributed more than 100 ships to Operation NEPTUNE, the naval component of the D-Day landings. In addition to the four *Tribals,* this force included thirty landing craft, sixteen minesweepers, two fleet destroyers, nine escort destroyers, eleven frigates, nineteen corvettes, and sixteen motor torpedo boats (MTBs). These warships formed two flotillas of MTBs, four antisubmarine support groups, and one minesweeping flotilla. Those not in wholly Canadian groups operated with British formations. RCN forces engaged in tasks as diverse as shore bombardment, minesweeping, and close escort, among others. Although ranking well behind U.S. and British naval contributions to Operation NEPTUNE in size, the RCN contingent was larger than all the other Allied naval forces combined.

Toward the end of the war, growth and success bred ambition and confidence at Naval Service Headquarters and a firm desire to establish a solid naval base for the postwar period. Two escort carriers being built in American shipyards for the Royal Navy were taken over and manned by the RCN. The aviation side, however, remained wholly in British hands. The two carriers saw action overseas in 1944–1945 and acquired valuable experience in naval aviation for the postwar fleet. In addition, the RCN obtained two light cruisers from the Royal Navy, and one of these, HMCS *Uganda,* joined the British Pacific Fleet in 1945 in time for the intense operations off Okinawa. Although the second cruiser did not get into action, together they formed the core of the "big-ship navy" favored by the naval brass in Ottawa.

During World War II, the RCN established a proud fighting tradition, something the fledgling service failed to do in World War I. The RCN lost twenty-four ships to enemy action and suffered 1,990 fatal casualties. In return, it shared in the destruction of thirty-three axis submarines and sank or captured forty-two enemy surface ships. RCN warships escorted more than 25,000 merchant ships from North America to the United Kingdom, carrying more than 180 million tons of cargo to fuel the war.

Robert C. Fisher

Additional Reading

German, Tony, *The Sea Is at Our Gates: The History of the Canadian Navy* (1990).

Milner, Marc, *North Atlantic Run: The Royal Canadian Navy and the Battle for the Convoys* (1985).

Tucker, G.N., *The Naval Service of Canada: Its Official History* (1952).

Navy, Cuban

In December 1941, Cuba declared war on the Axis and offered its air force and navy to the Allies to patrol the waters around Cuba. As all the arms possessed by Cuba were obsolete or obsolescent, it also applied to the United States for modern equipment. In 1941, the Cuban Navy consisted of seven gunboats of pre–World War I vintage with no antisubmarine capability. To provide the Cuban Navy with some antisubmarine patrol craft, twelve 83–foot and five 110-foot U.S. Coast Guard cutters were transferred to Cuba between 1942 and 1943. With American instructors on board, these vessels patrolled and escorted ships off Cuba and convoyed sea train ships between Port Everglades and Havana.

On 15 May 1943, one of these boats, the *CS-13* commanded by Ensign Mario Ramirez Delgado, in coordination with U.S. aircraft, sank the German submarine *U-176* between Florida and Cuba. On 9 December 1943, *U-129* sank the Cuban naval auxiliary *Libertad* off of San Salvador Island. After January 1944, no German naval craft operated near Cuban waters and the Cuban Navy

saw no further action. The *CS-13* was the only Latin American naval ship to sink an Axis warship in World War II, and it was also the smallest naval craft to sink a U-boat.

Cuba ended the war as it started, with no significant naval ships. Its navy remained a coastal patrol force.

Charles H. Bogart

Additional Reading

Scheina, Robert L., *Latin America—a Naval History* (1987).

Navy, Dutch

The war's outbreak found the Royal Netherlands Navy a small but highly professional and expanding force. Rising tensions in Asia resulted in a substantial building program scheduled for completion by 1944. With a long-standing tradition of neutrality in European wars, the bulk of Holland's navy was stationed in Asian waters protecting its colonial empire when the Germans invaded on 10 May 1940. Thus, it was in Asia, not Europe, that the navy's reputation was made.

With only one cruiser and a handful of minor combatants available in European waters, the Dutch had little time or forces (particularly in the face of German air supremacy) to do more than scuttle inoperable units, provide fire support to ground units along the rivers and coasts, and evacuate key government figures. That it fulfilled all of these tasks under desperate circumstances is a testament to the navy's effectiveness. All the surviving serviceable units, including incomplete hulks, made it to Britain to establish the Dutch-navy-in-exile. It was a phenomenal performance.

The units and crews in Britain were incorporated into formations of the Royal Navy. Dutch minesweeping and motor torpedo boats were manned and operated under flag officer, Portsmouth, while submarines were deployed to the Mediterranean. Several minesweepers and the destroyer *Isaac Sweers* also deployed to the Mediterranean in 1942. Additionally, the Dutch crewed a former *Campbeltown*-class Lend-Lease (q.v.) destroyer and manned several merchant aircraft carriers in the North Atlantic convoys.

Wherever its units served in the European theater, from British home waters to D-Day and the Mediterranean, the Dutch Navy established an enviable record for courage and efficiency. This is particularly remarkable because those units served not as national entities reading and sending signals in their own language, but as subordinates in for-

Dutch Naval Unit Locations on 10 May 1940

Type Ship	Europe	Caribbean	Far East	Number Lost during May 1940
Light Cruisers	1	0	4	0
Destroyers	2	0	6	1
Torpedo Boats	0	0	6	0
Gunboats	5	0	1	3
Patrol Escorts	0	1	0	0
MTBs	0	0	5	0
Minelayers	7	0	5	1
Minesweepers	7	0	11	5
Submarines	10	0	14	4

mations communicating in English. British tactics also differed from those of the Dutch Navy. Still, its Royal Navy counterparts expressed great satisfaction with the Dutch performance.

Dutch ships of World War II, like those of all European navies of the period, entered the war with few sensors and inadequate air defenses. Holland's electronic industry was developing radar and sonar, but no operational systems entered service before the German invasion. Moreover, the navy's tactics were based on the traditional missions of protecting colonial possessions and the sea lines of communications. Thus its units were trained primarily in convoy and standard line of battle tactics, with little regard for air defense. It was a costly error but one suffered by all navies in the early war years. None of these shortcomings, however, proved as critical in the European theater as they did in the Far East, where Japan's flyers pressed their attacks in greater numbers, and with more determination and effectiveness.

Carl O. Schuster

Additional Reading

Divine, A.D., *Navies in Exile* (1944).
Lenton, H.T., *Royal Netherlands Navy* (1967).

Navy, Finnish

Finland's navy was a small and highly professional force of approximately sixty combat ships, a handful of coastal defense batteries, and approximately 4,500 personnel. Its primary mission was coastal defense and it dedicated little effort to any warfare area that did not support this mission. Little attention was paid to antisubmarine warfare (ASW, q.v.). The Finns believed ASW would require more resources than they had, and that their seaborne trade could be protected behind defensive minefields. The Finnish Navy's only offensive capability rested in its five small submarines, which

were based on the German designs of World War I and employed primarily for minelaying. Mine warfare, in fact, was an activity in which the Finnish Navy excelled. More Soviet submarines were lost at sea to mines, both Finnish and German, than to any other single cause.

Finland's surface forces were centered around two relatively modern coastal defense ships, the *Väinämöinen* and *Ilmarinen*. Displacing less than 4,000 tons fully loaded, these ships were only lightly armored but carried a fair gun armament and a relatively strong antiaircraft suite. Nonetheless, they would have been easy prey for Soviet battleships and heavy cruisers. The Finns recognized this problem and intended to employ these units as mobile gun batteries protected by defensive minefields. The coastal defense ships would then provide the firepower to support the motor torpedo boat squadrons, which would attack the enemy's minesweeping forces by crossing the minefields. It was a strategy that had worked very well for the Soviets and the Turks in World War I. The submarines would then lay mines in and around the enemy's operating bases and attack his shipping. It was a successful strategy that did not break down until faced with overwhelming odds in the fall of 1944.

Finland sank one Soviet submarine during the Winter War (q.v.) of November 1939–March 1940. Its own losses were limited to a single 775-ton steamer and one escort vessel. The only naval shortcomings noted were in ASW and an inadequate supply of mines. Both deficiencies required German assistance to overcome and they proved very helpful.

When war with the Soviet Union resumed on 25 June 1941, the Finns were able to lay extensive minefields both off their coasts and at the entrance to the Gulf of Bothnia. As the war progressed, they reinforced these minefields and joined with the Germans in extending several major minefields around the Soviet naval base at Kronstadt, in the central Gulf of Finland, and at the mouth of that gulf. Finland deployed its submarines and surface units between these minefields to intercept Soviet units trying to slip through. This layered system of minefields, ASW nets, and combined air/naval patrols proved very effective over the next three years as the Soviets mounted ever-larger efforts to break through into the Baltic. Only Finland's departure from the war in September 1944 enabled the Soviets (with Finnish assistance) to freely dispatch submarines against Germany's Baltic sea lanes.

Finland lost only one coastal defense ship and five minor combatants in the Continuation War (*see* Finland, 1941–1944) and sank more than forty Soviet units in return, mostly via mining. The Finnish Navy was able to keep the Soviets off all but one of Finland's coastal islands until August of 1944. The following month, however, the Soviet Army forced Finland out of the war. The peace treaty that followed required the Finns to scrap their sole surviving coastal defense ship and all of their submarines and motor torpedo boats. It was an ignoble end for a proud force that had not been defeated in battle.

Carl O. Schuster

Additional Reading

Achkasov, V.I., and N.B. Pavlovich, *Soviet Naval Operations in the Great Patriotic War, 1941–1945* (1981).

Rohwer, Jurgen, and G. Hummelchen, *Chronology of the War at Sea: 1939–1945* (1974).

Navy, French

World War II witnessed one of the most troubled periods in the history of the French Navy. Between the June 1940 armistice and liberation in 1944, there were, in effect, two French navies. The bulk of the navy (*Marine Nationale*), commanded initially by Admiral Jean François Darlan (q.v.), remained under Vichy (q.v.) control. A much smaller force rallied to Charles de Gaulle (q.v.) in London, forming the Free French *Forces Navales Françaises Libres* (FNFL) commanded by Admiral Emile Muselier. The French Navy of 1945 had little in common with that of 1939. On the outbreak of hostilities, the French Navy was at its peak, but by 1945, it was second rank. A major colonial power requires a large fleet, and before the war France had the world's fourth-largest navy with more than 107,000 men and 800,000 tons of shipping. This included six battleships totaling 170,000 tons. Yet

in France, the army always took priority over the navy in terms of military spending. In the ten years prior to the outbreak of World War II, the navy received an average 20 percent of military expenditure, by comparison with 55 percent allocated to the army and 25 percent to the air force. Despite the naval limitations talks at Washington in 1921 and London in 1930 and 1936, the interwar period was a time of considerable rebuilding under the direction of two naval ministers, Georges Leygues and François Petri.

In line with rebuilding, the commander in chief, Admiral Darlan, introduced an intensive training program in 1929, and naval regulations were modernized in 1935. For strategic reasons, oil refineries were constructed in metropolitan France to fuel the fleet (completed in 1939), and extensive work began at a new naval base at Mers el-Kébir (q.v.).

It has been argued that at the start of 1939 the French Navy was a modern navy and that only five of its ships were more than thirteen years old. Admittedly, the five ships concerned were all battleships, so that only two, the *Dunkerque* and the *Strasbourg*, commissioned in 1934 and 1938, respectively, could be considered of any real value in combating ships of the German *Scharnhorst* and *Deutschland* classes, and the Italian *Cavour* class. Two other battleships, the *Jean Bart* and the *Richelieu*, were commissioned later, in 1941 and 1940.

In 1939, the main drawbacks were a shortage of carriers and a concomitant lack of experience in carrier-borne operations. French naval thinking, always one war behind, followed World War I experience by giving priority to battleships over carriers. Although credits were voted in 1938 for the construction of two carriers, work had only just begun when war broke out. This setback meant that French naval strategy would be temporarily retarded at the end of the war. Cognate with this was the overall problem of poor antiaircraft defense in 1939 coupled with a shortage of naval aircraft. The latter problem was due to internal politicking between the wars and the creation of a separate Air Ministry in 1928, which requisitioned all naval aircraft. Although these units were recuperated in 1932, a strained relationship between the air force and the navy existed until the defeat of France in June 1940.

In 1939, the *Aéronavale* had about 350 operational planes, with orders for more machines from the United States. The main handicap confronting antiaircraft defense was the absence of radar and a severe shortage of light antiaircraft guns and heavy machine guns to combat low-flying attacks and dive bombings. Nevertheless, the navy possessed excellent mobile heavy antiaircraft pieces, as demonstrated during the defense of Dunkirk (q.v.) in May and June 1940. Another serious disadvantage was the lack of antisubmarine detection. French sonar (q.v.) was still developing in the laboratories when war broke out.

Between September 1939 and June 1940, considerable cooperation existed between the *Marine Nationale* and the British Royal Navy. With ships freed from major Mediterranean Sea duties due to Italian neutrality, emphasis was placed on defending maritime trade in the Atlantic and hunting down German raiders. The French Navy also carried out convoy protection in the western Mediterranean and off the west coast of Africa. This was particularly necessary for the transport of French colonial troops from Morocco, Algeria, Tunisia, and French West Africa to metropolitan France.

Duties in the English Channel involved convoy protection, the maintenance of an Allied barrage in the Pas de Calais, minelaying, and minesweeping. To fulfill this latter task, fishing boats were requisitioned and converted into minesweepers. At the time, mines played an important part in Allied thinking, since in the first three months of the war 40 percent of Allied maritime casualties were attributed to magnetic mines. This toll was halved in 1940. In April and May 1940, French naval squadrons worked with the British at Trondheim and Narvik (q.v.). Despite combined naval superiority over the *Kriegsmarine,* the French were notably vulnerable to *Luftwaffe* attacks because of their inadequate antiaircraft defenses.

During the France (q.v.) campaign in May and June 1940, the French Navy participated in the evacuation of Dunkirk. Its main contribution to the Allied evacuation was the use of four coastal batteries and two mobile batteries under the command of Admiral Gabriel Aubrial, in the bridgehead around Dunkirk. French naval vessels participated in the evacuation from 29 May. Premier Paul Reynaud (q.v.) later admitted in his memoirs that the 337,000 Allied servicemen, including 110,000 French soldiers, evacuated from the harbor and beaches owed their escape: ". . . almost exclusively to English ships and were protected above all by English aircraft." He added that 300 French naval and merchant vessels were used in the operation, with numerous sorties by the *Aéronavale.* French naval losses were one-fifth of the total number of vessels used in the operation, and included two large destroyers, five light destroyers, and a supply ship.

The same month witnessed French naval operations off Genoa and in the Aegean following Italy's entry into the war on 10 June 1940. On 3 July, as a result of the French armistice of 22 June and British fears that the French Navy would fall into German and Italian hands, a French fleet was attacked by the British at Mers el-Kébir. A total of 1,297 French officers and men lost their lives, leading to deep bitterness against the British in naval circles.

So began France's tragedy as a divided nation. Those who accepted peace with Germany supported Marshal Philippe Pétain (q.v.). Those who wanted to continue the fight rallied to Charles de Gaulle and the Free French in London. Two diverging national interests in a period of European war resulted in two French navies. After the armistice with Germany and the naval engagement at Mers el-Kébir, the *Marine Nationale* found itself not only technically at war with the British, but also with the Free French. The flash points of this *guerre franco-française* were the naval actions at Dakar (q.v.) and Gabon. More often than not clashes were avoided, and a blind eye was turned, as Vichy vessels sailed past those of the Free French without any shots being fired.

The navy's main role under Vichy was to maintain shipping lanes with the French empire (raw materials and food supplies) and to defend

French Navy Order of Battle 1 September 1939

	In Service	Under Construction
Battleships	5	4
Pre–WW I Battleships	1	0
Battle Cruisers	2	0
Aircraft Carriers	1	2
Heavy Cruisers	7	0
Light Cruisers	11	3
Large Destroyers	32	4
Destroyers	29*	9
Torpedo Boats **	12	0
Sloops/Corvettes	36	12
World War I–era Sloops	28***	0
Subchasers	12	3****
MTB/MGBs	4	2
Submarines	75	25
Minesweepers	11	0

Notes:

  * Five destroyers in reserve.

  ** Light destroyers armed primarily with torpedoes.

  *** Five World War I sloops in reserve.

  **** Five subchasers dating from World War I were taken out of service on 3 September 1939.

the empire against all aggressors. In September 1940, Vichy-controlled naval units defended Dakar against an Allied invasion. The squadron included the recently completed battleship *Richelieu* and the cruisers *Georges-Leygues* and *Montcalm*. On 17 January 1941, units of Admiral Jean Decaux's Far-Eastern Fleet defeated a Thai squadron off Koh-Chang.

In June 1940, the *Marine Nationale* remained intact and undefeated in war. Admiral Paul Auphan, secretary of state for the navy prior to November 1942, claimed that, despite occupying large areas of France, the Germans and the Italians: "... had the good taste never to set foot on an armed ship, so that the service continued to function exactly as before." Thus the French Navy retained its autonomy until further tragedy struck in November 1942. Threatened by German tanks at the major naval base at Toulon (q.v.), the fleet scuttled itself to avoid capture. Sixty-one ships (240,000 tons), a major part of the Vichy Navy, were lost, although several submarines managed to slip away and join the Allies.

From 28 June 1940, a Free French fleet began to rally to the Allied cause at Gibraltar and then in London. It was later joined by naval forces based at Dakar, the West Indies, and Alexandria. The FNFL was led by Admiral Emile Muselier, under the *croix de lorraine* ensign. Muselier commented that when he took command: "Complete disorder reigned everywhere at first. I was given three rooms, without any furniture. I even drafted my first orders on a packing case."

Operating in a foreign country, without any headquarters staff, administration, or arsenals, his seemingly impossible task was to forge a navy loyal to de Gaulle's Free French. This was made up of a combination of sailors, officers, and vessels rallying to London, and the reallocation of interned French vessels that had been seized by the Royal Navy during Operation CATAPULT.

Among the units interned in Britain were two battleships, the *Courbet* and *Paris;* two large destroyers; eight light destroyers; five submarines; twenty-three gun boats, seventy-one patrol boats and auxiliary minesweepers, plus an additional 140 merchant ships and fishing boats. Further support was provided from Force X, interned at Alexandria, which included the battleship *Lorraine,* four cruisers, and the submarine *Surcouf,* which at the time was the biggest submarine in the world. The action between the French and British at Mers el-Kebir very nearly killed off the Free French naval forces in their infancy, so that in its early days only twenty officers and 500 men rallied to the FNFL.

Muselier's first priority was to put a stop to the British Operation CATAPULT.

By the end of 1940, the FNFL had 100 officers, 3,100 sailors, and 500 *fusiliers marins* (marines), who took part in operations at Dakar and Saint Pierre et Miquelon in September and December. From January 1941, the principal role of the FNFL for the next three years involved patrols in the North Sea and the protection of French merchant shipping on the Atlantic convoys. Because of politico-military tension between de Gaulle and U.S. president Franklin D. Roosevelt (q.v.), Free French forces did not take part in the Anglo-American landings and liberation of French Northwest Africa (q.v.) in November 1942.

In 1943, the Free French Navy participated in the liberation of Corsica and the Italian campaign. Totally integrated within Anglo-U.S. naval strategy (due to a logistical dependence on the Anglo-American allies to the tune of 84,000 tons), France had temporarily lost all naval autonomy. This would have implications during the D-Day landings.

The Free French naval forces participated in the Allied landings in both Normandy and southern France (qq.v.). The only French naval forces used in the first assault on the Normandy beaches were the *fusiliers marins*. Because Free French naval forces could only offer a modest contribution to Operation NEPTUNE, the French naval staff was not represented on the joint Allied naval staffs. The first major French unit to participate in the Normandy landings, General Jacques Leclerc's (q.v.) *2e Division Blindee* (2nd Armored Division), did not land until 2 August (D+55). Free French naval activity for the time being was confined to channel minesweeping and the use of motor torpedo boats and motor gunboats on Channel escorts.

The Free French made a greater contribution to naval and amphibious operations in southern France in August 1944. They cooperated in the battle for Toulon with the Royal Navy and U.S. Navy, and they provided convoy protection for the Allied landings and shore gunfire support from the cruisers *Montcalm* and *Georges-Leygues*.

Between September 1944 and May 1945, the French Navy had two main tasks: to sweep the mine-infested Channel waters and to reestablish links with the French Empire. Particular emphasis was placed on operations off French Indochina, which, since March 1945, had fallen under complete Japanese control. In 1945, French surface ships took part in reducing the Atlantic coast pockets held by the Germans in conjunction with

French land forces. Yet a great number of the heavily damaged Breton ports remained unusable, since the Germans held out in St. Malo, Brest (qq.v.), Lorrient, and Saint Nazaire until the end of the war in Europe.

During the war, the French lost 200,000 tons of shipping in actions against either the Germans or the British. Another 240,000 tons were scuttled. French ports and the key naval bases of Brest, Cherbourg, and Toulon were destroyed, either through Allied bombing or German rear-guard action. The French Navy entered the Cold War period with 65,000 men, 400,000 tons of shipping and five years of technical delay; 100,000 tons were old and obsolete, especially the seventeen submarines and the battleship *Lorraine* (commissioned in 1914). There was a serious shortage of rapid escort vessels, submarines, amphibious craft, and naval aircraft.

The only ships that appeared to be of any real value were the one aircraft carrier, the *Dixmude* (an American loan), the battleship *Richelieu,* four large cruisers, and four lighter cruisers of the La Galissonnière class. One positive development in 1945 was the inheritance of impregnable German submarine bases on the Atlantic coast (particularly at Saint Nazaire), the acquisition of a German type XXI submarine fitted with *Schnorkel* (Snorkels), and eight German destroyers.

France began its colonial war in Indochina (1945–1954) with equipment largely drawn from United States surplus, especially the *Dinassault* teams, made up of LCTs and light river craft operating in the deltas.

After four years of occupation and the resulting problems of conscience, the French nation was deeply divided. This division was reflected in the personnel crisis that affected French naval command in the postwar period. Times were hard for those officers who served under Vichy. None of the admirals who served in Vichy France after November 1942 retained their commands after the liberation. A debate in the French national assembly on 3 April 1946 revealed that 97 percent of the senior officers were discharged, so that only five admirals continued to serve in the French Navy after 1944. This meant imprisonment or temporary exile for some. All later received amnesty, though not necessarily reinstatement in rank, by 1958. Arguably, the loss of this experienced senior officer corps, related to other technical setbacks, led to a temporary decline in technical and strategic initiative, resulting in France's reduced naval capabilities until the mid-1950s.

Robert C. Hudson

Additional Reading

Auphan, Paul, and Jacques Mordal, *French Navy in World War II* (1959).

Heckstail-Smith, Anthony, *The Fleet That Faced Both Ways* (1963).

Navy, German

Germany's defeat in World War I had many dramatic repercussions on its fleet. Under the terms of the armistice, the bulk of its modern battle fleet had already surrendered to the Allies. In June 1919, the commander of the interned fleet ordered his crews to scuttle their ships. In retribution, the Allies immediately demanded that Germany surrender the bulk of the modern vessels that were not interned. The terms the Treaty of Versailles (q.v.) clearly indicated that the Allies did not wish to see a resurgence of German naval power. For the immediate postwar period, the German fleet was reduced to a minuscule size. In addition, Germany was not allowed to possess submarines, aircraft carriers, and motor torpedo boats. The Allies also imposed severe restrictions on the replacements for obsolete vessels. Furthermore, an overall limit of 15,000 men and officers was imposed, and each of them had to volunteer for a twelve-year tour of duty.

In the dark days of 1919, however, Germany's admirals were more concerned about ensuring the continued existence of the fleet, not the types of warships it would possess. Their concern was caused by the intrusion of radical politics into the heart of the navy. In October 1918, the sailors on many of the kaiser's most powerful warships mutinied when the admirals decided to risk the fleet one last time before delivering it whole under the terms of the armistice. This mutiny sparked a revolution that toppled the ancient dynasties of Germany, including the German emperor.

As a consequence of the resulting power vacuum, the Social Democratic Party was thrust into a position of power with which it might otherwise never have been entrusted. This party had no reliable means of enforcing its will on the revolutionary mobs. The means of doing so were provided by the expedient of raising paramilitary formations from the rapidly disintegrating army and navy. The bulk of those formations proved themselves to be as anti-Republican as they were opposed to Communism.

Three such formations were raised from the German Navy. In contrast to the mutineers of the High Seas Fleet, the majority of them were drawn from the ranks of the fleet's smaller ships and junior officers' corps. While all of them had checkered careers, the 2nd Naval Brigade under Captain Hermann Ehrhardt was by far the most infamous of them all. The other important naval formation was the 3rd Naval Brigade, which was commanded by Captain Wilfried Löwenfeld. Once these irregular formations helped crush the revolutionary opposition within Germany, some of them decided to eliminate the Social Democratic Party's control of the German government.

In March 1920, Ehrhardt's men participated in the vain attempt to impose a dictatorial government on Germany. Once they occupied Berlin, the commander of the German Navy, Admiral Adolf von Trotha, recognized their benefactor, Wolfgang Kapp as the legitimate political leader of Germany. Kapp and his cohorts, however, were quickly ousted by a general strike that allowed the Social Democrats to regain power. Von Trotha's action, and the role played by the Ehrhardt Brigade, combined to give the German Navy a collective black eye. Von Trotha and two senior admirals were forced to resign, while one of his aides, Captain Erich Raeder (q.v.), was shunted to a less prominent post.

In addition to the fallout from the failed overthrow attempt, now known as the Kapp *Putsch* (q.v.), the navy was trying to determine the ultimate fate of the two remaining naval brigades. Despite the anti-Republican sentiment displayed by both units, the navy decided to retain some of their personnel. Whole subordinate units were accepted from the Löwenfeld Brigade, whereas Ehrhardt's unit was accepted on a more selective basis. Strangely, the navy decided to retain Löwenfeld despite his telegram of support to Ehrhardt during the Kapp *Putsch*.

Despite its deactivation, some members of the Ehrhardt Brigade continued to add to Germany's political woes. During the early 1920s, they participated in several groups that assassinated public figures. They also provided paramilitary training and weapons to the various nationalist right-wing groups that were opposed to the German government. It appears they obtained some weapons and funds through an ex-Löwenfeld Brigade member who was retained by the German Navy, Lieutenant Commander Wilhelm Canaris (q.v.). One of the many groups that benefited from this source of illegal arms and equipment was the private army that served the radical German racist party NSDAP led by Adolf Hitler (qq.v.).

While Germany was still plagued by political instability after 1921, it was finally able to plan for the future. In this period, the command of the German Navy changed hands several times. Von Trotha's immediate successor was Admiral Paul Behncke, who served until 1924. That year, he was replaced by Admiral Hans Zenker, who in turn was replaced by Admiral Raeder in 1928. Raeder served as naval commander in chief until January 1943, providing the fleet with a degree of stability it had not enjoyed since the days of the kaiser.

In terms of personnel, the navy, like the army, took full advantage of the Versailles requirements and proceeded to weed out all "undesirable" elements. That category included Social Democrats, Communists, and even liberals. Officially, the new German armed forces deceived themselves as being apolitical. To that end, officers and men were forbidden from joining any political party.

The navy, however, was more concerned with isolating its personnel from left-wing radicals than it was about right-wing extremists. The majority of both active and retired naval officers supported conservative and nationalist movements. One of Adolf Hitler's earliest supporters was retired Admiral Ludwig von Schroeder. Another of his early naval supporters was Admiral Magnus von Levetzow, who had been cashiered because of his open support of the Kapp *Putsch*. After Raeder assumed command of the navy, von Levetzow served as Raeder's unofficial contact with the Nazi Party.

At the end of 1921, the German Navy, now known as the *Reichsmarine,* started to replace its antiquated vessels. For the most part, the early constructions, with the exception of the new destroyers, did not greatly exceed the limits imposed by the Treaty of Versailles. Although the Allies were well-informed of minor treaty violations, they did not make any official protests. For the time being, the *Reichsmarine* decided to capitalize on the Allied restraint and adhere to limitations of both the Treaty of Versailles and the Washington Naval Conference as much as possible. One prominent design feature of all the German light cruisers and heavier ships that followed the introduction of the cruiser *Emden* in 1925 was the existence of a prominent gap in their superstructure. These gaps were later filled with equipment for the storage and launching of seaplanes.

In 1928, Germany astounded the world when it unveiled the planned replacements for its old pre-dreadnoughts. Their design featured a displacement of 10,000 tons, a main armament of six 11-inch guns, a speed of 26 knots, and a very wide radius of action. In effect, Germany presented the world with a ship that could overpower any Washington Treaty cruiser and outrun most capital ships. The British popular press quickly described the new German ships as "pocket battleships," but the *Reichsmarine* officially described them as "armored ships," in conformity with the official text of the Versailles Treaty. The Allied naval powers asked Germany not to build these ships, but Germany countered with a proposal to forgo their construction in exchange for becoming a signatory to the Washington Naval Treaty. Since the wartime Allies were not prepared to open a breach in the Versailles Treaty, they refused the German offer.

In addition to understating tonnage figures, the German Navy was also involved in much more ominous subterfuges. It subsidized a Dutch submarine firm throughout the 1920s. The *Reichsmarine* played an active role in the solicitation of business for the firm, and provided key personnel, such as designers, engineers, and test inspectors. It also purchased and operated a small group of motorboats under the cover of a private company. They were used in experiments designed to test motor torpedo boats. Another enterprise provided flight training and refresher courses to former members of the German Naval Flying Corps.

The navy also financed the construction of civilian tankers and specialized freighters. The former were to be used as oceangoing supply ships and tankers for warships conducting commerce raiding. The freighter's designs allowed for installation of a heavy concealed main armament. Unlike the German Army, the *Reichsmarine* eschewed collaboration with the Soviets. It appears that the World War I Allies were more than aware of both the real treaty violations made by the *Reichsmarine* and the treaty-breaking potential of the others. Nonetheless, they contented themselves with mild protests.

In 1928, the *Reichsmarine* was rocked by a scandal that pierced the veil of secrecy that was placed over many of its projects. The naval officers most directly involved in these operations were Captain Walter Lohmann, and to a somewhat lesser extent the ubiquitous Commander Canaris. One of Lohmann's financial deals, the support of a film company, became public knowledge after the firm went bankrupt. In a short period of time reporters, following the convoluted trail of this company's shady financing, discovered its source. The *Reichsmarine,* like the German Army, financed these ventures through a special non-budgetary fund. The Lohmann scandal resulted in the end of Lohmann's, commander in chief Admiral Zenker's, and the defense minister's careers.

The new commander of the Navy, Raeder, was determined to avoid making the same mistakes. Despite the ill-effects of the Lohmann scandal, he managed to obtain parliamentary support for the navy's armored ship program. He also posed as the ideal example of the nonpolitical military officer, but his private sympathies were clearly with the German Right. Through Levetzow, he maintained a tenuous contact with Hitler, which was particularly important once the latter began to garner popular political support.

The fiction of a "nonpolitical" officer corps was severely strained during the turbulent last years of the ill-fated Weimar Republic (q.v.). Hitler's ideology and program were bound to have a profound impact upon the men of the young fleet. Like Hitler, they favored the awakening of German nationalism, the rebirth of Germany's military might, and the revision of Europe's disputed boundaries in Germany's favor. In time, large numbers of naval personnel were attending the mass rallies of the Nazi Party in civilian attire. One of Hitler's key deputies, Joseph Goebbels (q.v.), boasted in his diaries that the men of the fleet wholeheartedly supported them. One of the distinct highlights of Hitler's rapport with the men of the *Reichsmarine* came in May 1932 when he visited the light cruiser *Köln,* and outlined his large-scale plans for the rebuilding of the fleet.

Hitler and Raeder did not see quite eye to eye on German naval construction. The former was more than willing to limit the German Navy in exchange for a political agreement with Britain. Nonetheless, this minor disagreement did little to weaken the mass enthusiasm of the lower ranks for National Socialism. In fact, Hitler's accession to power in 1933 was widely celebrated in the messes of the fleet.

Initially, Hitler's assumption of power had little or no impact upon the fleet's construction plans. The German naval staff was quickly faced with the need to revamp the designs for the last three armored ships because of developments elsewhere. After many design changes these ships reemerged as the battle cruisers *Scharnhorst* and *Gneisenau.* They were much larger, faster, and more powerful than their armored ship predecessors, but they still retained the 11-inch gun. In part, this was as much due to expediency as to Hitler's reluctance to annoy the naval powers by a dramatic increase in armament caliber. Nonetheless, the construction of these ships, and his decision to begin building submarines, were blatant breaches of the Versailles Treaty. In March 1935, he announced that Germany was unilaterally freeing itself from the military clauses of the treaty. At the same time, the *Reichsmarine* was ominously renamed *Kriegsmarine*.

In June 1935, Hitler's diplomacy achieved a major coup when his special envoy to Britain managed to obtain its agreement on new limits for German naval construction. The British entered into the Anglo-German Naval Treaty (q.v.) because it put a voluntary brake on German rearmament at sea. They were not anxious to engage in a new battleship-building race with Germany. On the other hand, Hitler believed that he might obtain British support for, or at least tacit disinterest in, his plans for central Europe. He did not lose much, because Germany did not have the necessary industrial capacity to build a substantial fleet.

The mid- to late 1930s saw a remarkable resurgence of German naval power. By late 1938, Germany was approaching the outer limits permitted by the Anglo-German Naval Treaty. As German-British relations were then at an all-time low, due to constant aggression in central Europe, Hitler authorized the navy to prepare a much more ambitious naval construction program. The subsequent Plan Z (q.v.) was surreptitiously approved and begun without any official fanfare in January 1939. In April, he repudiated both the Anglo-

German Naval Treaty and the German-Polish Nonaggression Pact. Hitler finally realized that Britain would not stand by idly while he set out to attain hegemony over continental Europe. On 1 September 1939, Hitler gambled and launched the invasion of Poland. Both Britain and France decided to respect their commitment to Poland and declared war on 3 September 1939.

During the whole lifetime of the Nazi regime, the leadership of the *Kriegsmarine* clung tenaciously to the myth of the nonpolitical armed forces. This was, however, increasingly more difficult as the internal and external excesses of the Hitler regime became more obvious.

In regard to the regime's anti-Semitic policy, for example, the navy restricted itself to protests against measures taken against certain individual officers and civilians. The *Kriegsmarine* intervened on behalf of officers of full or partial Jewish ancestry who had served in World War I. This cautious policy explains why an officer of partial Jewish ancestry attained the rank of admiral during World War II.

The only time the navy made a strong protest over the regime's racial policy was in the aftermath of the infamous *Kristallnacht* (q.v.) of November

German Navy Order of Battle

	1 September 1939		4 May 1945
	In Service	Under Construction	
Battleships	0	4	0
Battle Cruisers*	2	0	0
Pre-dreadnought Battleships†	2	0	0
Pocket Battleships‡	3	0	0
Aircraft Carriers	0	2	0
Heavy Cruisers	2	3	1
Light Cruisers	6	4	2
Scout Cruisers	0	4	0
Destroyers	22	10	15
Torpedo Boats§	11	9	11
Subchasers	12	7	6
MTB/MGBs	15	12	12
Minesweepers	22	10	8
World War I Minesweepers	36	0	16
Submarines	63	30	393

Notes:

* These were the Scharnhorst and Gneisenau, which were included as fast battleships in Plan Z, but were operationally classified as battle cruisers by the *Kriegsmarine* during the war.

† These obsolete pre-World War I units normally operated as training ships, but they were employed for shore bombardmant in the Baltic during the Polish campaign.

‡ These were classified as "armored ships" in German service.

§ These were essentially small destroyers that carried multiple torpedo banks.

1938. At that time a small delegation of officers, including Raeder, dared to voice their reaction to the outrage. They were uncritically satisfied with Hitler's explanation that a few overzealous followers had acted on their own initiative. Raeder chose to deal with the regime's continual persecution of the churches by attending religious services on a regular basis in uniform. He also made every effort to encourage other officers to do the same.

In regard to Hitler's foreign policy, the same trend of official aloofness was apparent. The navy had no qualms about participating in the nonintervention hoax of the Spanish civil war (q.v.); nor did it have any scruples about Hitler's decision to have the *Admiral Scheer* bombard a small Spanish town in retaliation for an aerial attack on the *Deutschland*. It welcomed the great escalation of its strength through the adoption of Plan Z, though it clearly violated the terms of all the naval agreements Germany had accepted after 1933.

Furthermore, the navy never questioned the ultimate goals of Hitler's foreign policy. The only exception to this trend occurred during the Sudetenland crisis of late 1938. At that time, two officers on the naval operations staff warned of the dangers inherent in Hitler's claims on Czechoslovakia. To date, we still do not know what Raeder did with either of these two memorandums. Given these trends, one should not be surprised to learn that the navy did not play a major role in the German opposition, or in diminishing the ill effects of Hitler's occupation policies.

Only three naval officers were executed because of complicity in 20 July 1944 plot. Of these, one was the disgraced commander of the German counterintelligence service, Admiral Canaris. Another was Berthold von Stauffenberg, brother of Hitler's would-be assassin; the third was a junior naval officer, Alfred Kranzfelder.

During World War II, the *Kriegsmarine* attempted to cut Britain's overseas lifelines with all the means at its disposal. Surface raiders, both regular warships and disguised merchant cruisers, participated in this campaign with varying success. The early loss of the *Admiral Graf Spee* (*see* Platte River) was a major setback for this campaign, but the loss of the *Bismarck* (q.v.) marked the end of the surface fleet's participation in the Atlantic. In addition, the fleet never fully recovered from the losses incurred as a consequence of the German invasion of Norway (q.v.).

For the most part, the brunt of the German naval campaign was borne by the U-boat arm. While U-boats inflicted serious damage on Allied shipping during the early years of the war, they eventually were conquered by the Allies' increasing military and technological strength. By 1943, they were finally forced by substantial losses to withdraw from the Atlantic. Both the surface and subsurface branches of the fleet suffered from the failure to fully develop a naval air arm, and the carrier *Graf Zeppelin* was the first casualty of that shortcoming.

Unfortunately, the surface fleet, which never even reached the level of the Anglo-German Naval Treaty, could not come to the aid of the U-boats. The Channel Dash (q.v.) of the *Scharnhorst, Gneisenau,* and *Prinz Eugen* served to underline this fact. The failure of an attack by the *Lützow* and *Admiral Hipper* in the company of six destroyers brought about Raeder's retirement in early 1943. Even his successor, Grand Admiral Karl Dönitz (q.v.), could not greatly influence the course of the war.

In December 1943, the *Scharnhorst* was sunk in a futile convoy attack in the Arctic Ocean. The *Tirpitz* was finally sunk by the RAF in November 1944. The remainder of the major German surface vessels remained inactive until the Soviets began to advance on Germany itself. Those ships then attempted to intervene on the German and Polish coastlines as floating artillery support groups. In time, Allied air forces managed to sink all but two of Germany's remaining big ships.

Dönitz hoped his new submarines, particularly the Type XXI, would allow the *Kriegsmarine* to resume the Battle of the Atlantic (q.v.). Unfortunately, his hopes were destined to be dashed by the constant aerial attacks on the submarine construction centers. In fact, the first Type XXI U-boat to go on a war cruise did so just days before the termination of hostilities.

On 30 April 1945, Hitler committed suicide in his bunker in Berlin as the Soviet Army mounted its final assault on Nazi Germany. Hitler's last will and testament named Dönitz as his successor. While the honor indicated that Hitler had changed his opinion of the merits of the German fleet, it was intended more as a slap in the face to army and *Luftwaffe* generals. It was a hollow achievement for the *Kriegsmarine*.

May 1945 saw the unconditional surrender of Germany to the Allies. Like its predecessor after World War I, the *Kriegsmarine* handed over its few surviving vessels to the Allies. Both Raeder and Dönitz were among the war criminals tried at Nuremburg. Raeder received a life sentence for his participation in crimes against peace, but was released on humanitarian grounds in 1955. Dönitz received a ten-year sentence for both war crimes and crimes against peace and was released at the end of 1956.

Peter K.H. Mispelkamp

Additional Reading
Humble, Richard, *Hitler's High Seas Fleet* (1971).
Porten, Edward von der, *The German Navy in World War II* (1969).
Rust, Eric, *Naval Officers Under Hitler: The Story of Crew 34* (1991).
Thomas, Charles S., *The German Navy in the Nazi Era* (1990).
Tarrant, V.E., *The Last Year of the Kriegsmarine; May 1944–May 1945* (1996).

Navy, Italian

The Italian Navy won no victory laurels in World War I. During the interwar years it sought to rebuild by assuming France as its potential enemy. While the navy received the smallest part of the Italian defense budget, it was able to rebuild its fleet into a formidable fighting machine.

On 10 June 1940, when Italy went to war, the fleet consisted of six battleships, seven heavy cruisers, twelve light cruisers, sixty-one destroyers, seventy-seven torpedo boats, 114 submarines, ninety-six motor torpedo boats, and numerous auxiliaries. Unfortunately, many of those ships were in the process of refitting, as the navy had been instructed to plan on war breaking out in 1942. During the war, a number of new ships were added to the total. Losses by the end of 1943 were three battleships, twenty-one cruisers, 175 destroyers and escorts, 151 submarines, and 125 motor torpedo boats. What ships were left were either lost while serving with the cobelligerent navy (which operated with the Allies 1944–1945), or were dispersed among the Allies as victory spoils at the end of the war.

The Italian fleet, while having numerical superiority over the Royal Navy and moral superiority over the dispirited French Navy at the start of the fighting, was never able to gain control of the Mediterranean Sea. This failure was due to various reasons. First, all aircraft belonged to the Italian Air Force, which was only charged with "cooperating" with the fleet. Since no aircraft were under naval control, they were never available to act in concert with the fleet to gain control of the seas. Second, the navy never overcame its feeling of inferiority to the Royal Navy. Third, the navy's prewar planning was directed against France and not Great Britain. Fourth, a shortage of fuel oils hampered

the navy from carrying out extensive offensive operations. Fifth, the navy's main operational capability was squandered in defensive operations to maintain Axis supply lines between Italy and North Africa. Sixth, the fleet's electronic gear was inferior to that of the Royal Navy.

At the start of the war, the Italian Navy was faced with four tasks: (1) prevent the French and British fleets from raiding the northwest coast of Italy; (2) maintain the supply lines to Albania and the Dodecanese Islands; (3) keep open the sea route to Libya; and (4) protect the colonies of Eritrea and Ethiopia from invasion. To these tasks were later added the missions of submarine warfare in the Atlantic and support of the Italian Expeditionary Force on the eastern front. Yet from the start of the war, the Italian Navy found itself responding to Royal Navy offensive operations and was never able to gain and hold the initiative.

Two major strategic mistakes made at the start of the war haunted the Italian Navy. The first was its inability to obtain ports and airfield concessions in Tunisia after the French armistice. The free use of these airfields and ports would have allowed the Italian Navy to dominate the narrow sea lane between Sicily and North Africa. The second was the failure to capture Malta (q.v.). At the start of the war, Malta's defenses were weak and the British government was not committed to its defense. The capture of Malta would have protected the supply routes from Italy to Libya from the Royal Navy and Royal Air Force. Malta's capture would also have denied its use by the British.

The Italian Navy started the war by laying an offensive minefield off Alexandria, Egypt, and conducting offensive sweeps near Malta. Its first sea combat took place on 12 June 1940, when Royal Navy surface craft sank the gunboat *Berta* off Tobruk, Libya, and the Italian submarine *Bagnolini* sank the cruiser HMS *Calypso*.

As a precursor of the way the war at sea would be fought, a successful bombardment by French surface craft was carried out on Genoa and Savona, Italy, on 13 June 1940. Then, on 27 June, Italian destroyers and cruisers were pressed into service as cargo vessels to deliver goods and men to Libya. The use of fighting ships as cargo and transport vessels had serious consequences, including a decline in naval combat efficiency in both equipment and personnel, and an expenditure of fuel oil out of proportion to the supplies delivered. A cargo ship delivers more tonnage for less fuel expenditure on the same hull displacement. Finally, British reconnaissance was able to carry out effective searches in Italian waters, while Italian aerial recon-

	1 September 1939		9 Sept 1943
	In Service	Under Construction	
Battleships	2 (+2)*	2	6***
Heavy Cruisers	7	0	5
Light Cruisers	12	3	4
Antiaircraft Cruisers	0	0	2
World War I–era Cruisers	3	0	0
Large Destroyers	15	0	1
Destroyers	41	2	28
World War I–era Destroyers	2	0	2
Destroyer Escorts	4	0	3
Torpedo Boats**	43	0	41
World War I–era Torpedo Boats	18	0	9
Sloops/Corvettes	1	1	28
Subchasers	1	0	0
MTB/MGBs	53	18	90
Submarines	112	2	50

Notes:

  * Two older battleships were being modernized.

  ** Light destroyers armed primarily with torpedoes.

  *** Includes the *Roma* which was sunk by the *Luftwaffe* on 9 Sept 1943.

naissance was disappointing or nonexistent. Italian Air Force considerations often overrode naval needs or the aircrews assigned to assist the navy flew inappropriate aircraft and were untrained for their missions.

The Italian submarine force, while sinking the HMS *Calypso* and successfully sailing the submarine *Finzi* into the Atlantic past Gibraltar on 13 June 1940, had a disastrous first month of warfare. During June, nine submarines were lost; eight more were lost and others heavily damaged over the next two months. Brave, dedicated, and experienced personnel were unable to overcome the boats' technical deficiencies, which made them slow divers, poor crew habitats, and indifferent weapon systems.

The first major surface action took place on 9 July 1940 off the foot of Italy. Italian and Royal Navy battleships, cruisers, and destroyers clashed in an exchange of gunfire that did little damage to either side. Although fought 200 miles off the Italian coast, no Italian aircraft entered the battle due to faulty communications. Ship type for ship type, most Italian vessels were faster than their Royal Navy counterparts, but they gained speed by having less armor.

The next surface engagement was a cruiser action on 17 July 1940 at the entrance to the Aegean Sea. The cruiser *Colleoni* was sunk and the *Bande Nere* damaged. Italian aircraft flying from

fields only an hour away took over five hours to respond to their request for support. These two actions shook the fleet's faith in itself and its air force.

The Italian fleet was further shaken on the night of 12 October 1940 when British cruisers sank one destroyer and two escorts, while suffering no damage in return. Technical superiority in radar gave the Royal Navy the victory. Disaster struck the Italian fleet on the night of 12–13 November 1940 when aircraft from the HMS *Illustrious* struck the port of Taranto (q.v.) and heavily damaged the battleships *Littorio*, *Duilio*, and *Cavour*.

Misfortune further dogged the Italian fleet when on 27 November 1940 it engaged a British force of battleships and cruisers with a like force off the southern coast of Sardinia. Due to incomplete information from air force reconnaissance aircraft, the Italian fleet did not know the British force was covering a convoy bound for Malta. Once the battle started, the Italian Navy overestimated the British strength and broke off action, allowing the convoy to reach Malta safely.

December 1940 to January 1941 saw the navy used to support the Italian Army in Cyrenaica. In order to save the situation there, the navy was pressed into transportation service from February to June 1941, to move the German *Afrika Korps* (q.v.) from Italy to North Africa.

During this period, the Italian fleet moved 450,000 tons of supplies to Libya. The only interruption came on 16 April when British destroyers struck one of the convoys off Kerkenah Banks, sinking three escorts, three merchantmen, and forcing two others aground.

When the war started, the Italian Navy had seven destroyers, six escorts, five motor torpedo boats, eight submarines, plus auxiliaries and merchantmen at Massawa, Eritrea, on the Red Sea. By January 1941, it lost four submarines and one destroyer. In March, the remaining four submarines reached Italy by sailing around Africa. At the same time, many of the merchant ships and large auxiliaries broke out for Japanese or Argentine ports. The remaining ships were lost in battle or scuttled on 1 April 1941 in the wake of an overwhelming British assault on Eritrea.

On 28 October 1940, Italy attacked Greece (q.v.) from positions in Albania. This greatly increased the navy's commitment in keeping open the supply lines from Italy to the Balkans and the Dodecanese Islands. The commitment grew even greater on 5 March 1941 when British troops landed in Greece to support that country. It was not until 30 April 1941 that the combined German and Italian force conquered Greece, with Crete (q.v.) finally falling on 31 May 1941. During this time, the navy delivered successfully to Greece and Crete all but a tiny fraction of the supplies entrusted to its care.

In order to support the German and Italian armies in Greece, the Italian Navy carried out a number of offensive sweeps to cut British supply lines. On 28 March 1941, an Italian battleship and cruiser force encountered four British cruisers south of Crete. In a running battle, the British were able to escape, thanks to the intervention of British torpedo planes, which disrupted the Italians by forcing them to maneuver to defend themselves. During the aerial attacks, the cruiser *Pola* was hit while 100 miles southwest of Cape Matapan (q.v.). That night, the Italian Navy sent the cruisers *Zara* and *Fiume* with four destroyers to assist the *Pola*. In a night action the British—with the help of radar—sank three cruisers and two destroyers, with no loss to themselves.

The Italian Navy started the war with a reserve of 1.8 million tons of fuel oil, but that reserve was used up by the summer of 1941. British blockade prevented any importation of fuel oil except by land. To conduct sustained offensive operations, the navy needed 200,000 tons of oil a month. The blockade meant only 50,000 tons per month were available, and that had to be husbanded for fleet

operations, which precluded sea training. The submarine force also had not achieved the success hoped for due to technical shortcomings and the need to employ the boats for reconnaissance purposes in place of aircraft. By the end of 1941, the submarine force lost nineteen boats in the Mediterranean.

One of the few bright spots was the navy's 10th Light Flotilla (q.v.). Using frogmen and explosive motor speed boats, it scored a number of successes, including penetration of Gibraltar harbor to sink and damage several ships, sinking of the HMS *York* at Suda Bay, and knocking out of action the battleships HMS *Valiant* and HMS *Queen Elizabeth* in Alexandria (q.v.) harbor. Another success was the Italians' antisubmarine ships, which sank twenty Allied submarines by January 1942.

The period July 1941 to April 1943 was a time of convoy battles. The Royal Navy operating from Malta attempted to disrupt the flow of supplies from Italy to North Africa, while the Italians attempted to cut off Malta from Gibraltar and Alexandria. During these battles, both sides scored successes but neither was able to deliver the knockout blow in 1941 or 1942. The Royal Navy brought through to Malta just enough supplies to keep it in action against the *Afrika Korps* supply lines. The Italian Navy, either by using its warships as transports or by escorting convoys to Libya and Cyrenaica, was able to keep the *Afrika Korps* alive. Due partly to inadequate ports, however, it was unable to deliver the extra tons of supplies that would allow the *Afrika Korps* to achieve victory.

In sustained fighting, both sides lost heavily in cruisers, destroyers, submarines, and merchant ships. In the end, the Royal Navy prevailed, thanks to adequate fuel supplies, technological superiority, and an industrial base able to maintain its ships. Before the *Afrika Korps* succumbed in May 1943, the Italian Navy had delivered 85 percent of the supplies and 92 percent of the personnel entrusted to it for transport to North Africa. Throughout that period, a number of major surface actions took place.

While the convoy battles were being fought, the Italian Navy was engaged in three other major operations: submarine warfare in the Atlantic, sea control in the Aegean and Adriatic, and support of the eastern front. Initial success in those areas turned to defeat in 1943.

By the summer of 1943, the defeat of the Italian Navy was complete. It was unable to challenge the Allied landings in Sicily (q.v.) on 9 June 1943, or on the Italian mainland on 3 September, 1943. While still possessing a formidable strength on paper, the fleet was short of fuel and in desperate need of maintenance. With its fleet bottled up and under pressure from all sides, the Italian government requested an armistice. It was granted on 9 September, provided the fleet surrendered to the Allies at Malta. In 1944, a cobelligerent Italian Navy was formed out of some of the surrendered escort vessels, but in the end the Italian Navy lost all of its ships as war prizes to the Allies.

Charles H. Bogart

Additional Reading

Borghese, J.V., *The Sea Devils* (1954).
Bragadin, Marc, *The Italian Navy in World War II* (1957).
Mollo, Andrew, *The Armed Forces of World War II* (1981).
Roskill, S.W., *The War at Sea* (1954).

Navy, Polish

The first of the Allied navies to see combat, the Polish fleet distinguished itself in an unequal struggle. A small force serving a poor country sharing an extensive border with two hostile powers, there was little it could do to alter the outcome of any war with its neighbors. Its commander, Vice Admiral Józef Unrug (q.v.), a former U-boat captain in the Imperial German Navy, accurately foresaw the future once the Ribbentrop-Molotov Pact (q.v.) was signed on 24 August 1939. Two days later, he dispatched the fleet's three newest destroyers to Britain. Unrug and his staff then withdrew to the naval base at Hel, where they held out to become the last Polish unit to surrender on 2 October 1939. Meanwhile, escaped units and trainees went on to serve their country in other theaters.

While Poland's three destroyers, *Grom, Blyksawica,* and *Burza,* made their way to safety, the remainder of the fleet prepared for war. Minefields were laid off the coast and supplies and ammunition loaded aboard the major combatants while the small units patrolled offshore. Nothing, however, could prepare them for the onslaught of the German *Luftwaffe*. The first air raid struck Gydnia at noon, sinking the torpedo boat *Mazur* almost immediately. The minelayer *Gryf,* the old destroyer *Wicher,* and eight minesweepers put to sea. Constantly attacked by German aircraft, the small task force was gradually whittled down over the next two days before the heavily damaged ships were caught in port and sunk by German destroyers. Only the minesweepers survived to lay mines in the Gulf of Danzig before escaping to Sweden.

Poland's five submarines deployed on 1 September in what proved a fruitless struggle. Facing a concentrated *Kriegsmarine* and overwhelming German air supremacy in the constricted waters of the southern Baltic, the submarines were quickly overwhelmed. Three were critically damaged in the first four days.

The fourth, *Orzel,* on patrol off Gydnia, suffered a catastrophic engineering casualty and had to withdraw to neutral Tallin, Estonia, for repairs. There she became involved in a diplomatic tug-of-war as Germany and the Soviet Union pressured Estonia, into surrendering the submarine to them. The *Orzel* then made its escape on 18 September, the day after the Soviet Union invaded Poland. Lacking a magnetic compass and navigational charts (all had been removed to prevent its escape), the submarine slipped out of the harbor and returned to the waters off Gydnia to attack German shipping. Finding few targets and hearing of Warsaw's fall, the *Orzel* departed the Baltic and made her way to Britain, arriving there on 14 October. The previously damaged submarine *Wilk* also made the treacherous journey in the final days of September. The remaining three submarines fled to Sweden where their crews were interned.

The units in Britain were later joined by the training ships *Iskra* and *Wilia,* which were in the Mediterranean when the war broke out. Using the trainees from those ships and volunteers from Polish nationals in Britain, the Polish navy-in-exile began to train new crews for ships to be obtained from the Royal Navy; the first of which was a *Greyhound*-class destroyer. Meanwhile, the Polish destroyers and submarines made themselves useful, patrolling off the British coast and Norway. The destroyer *Grom* and the submarine *Orzel* were lost during the German invasion of Norway (q.v.)

Polish Navy Order of Battle
September 1939

Ship Type	1 September 1939	Lost During Sept. 1939
Large Destroyers	2	0
Destroyers	2	1
Torpedo Boats	1	1
Minelayers	1	1
Submarines	5	3*
Minesweepers	8	8†
River Gunboats	12	12
Total	31	26

Notes:
*Three submarines were interned.
†Five minesweepers were sunk and three were interned.

while the *Burza* was heavily damaged during the evacuation of Dunkirk (q.v.).

This did not, however, end the Polish Navy's participation in World War II. Raising additional recruits from refugees and former soldiers, the navy went on to man an additional three *Hunt*-class destroyers, a squadron of motor gunboats (MGBs), three more submarines, and several minesweepers during the war. These units served in such diverse actions as the destruction of the *Bismarck* (q.v.), the escorting of convoys to Murmansk, and the amphibious assaults in Sicily and Normandy (qq.v.).

Like most European navies, Poland's fleet made little provision for air defense in its units and paid accordingly. Nonetheless, in Allied service, its personnel adapted quickly to the new tactics and equipment needed to survive modern naval combat. In every action, Polish seamen were noted for their courage, proficiency, and determination. Unfortunately, the majority of them did not receive a warm welcome when they returned home after the war. Facing persecution from the Soviet-dominated government controlling Poland after the war, many of them fled westward again or faced imprisonment in the country for whose cause they had fought so well.

Carl O. Schuster

Additional Reading
Dickens, Peter, *Narvik: Battles in the Fjords* (1974).
Divine, A.D., *Navies in Exile* (1944).
Piekalkiewicz, Janusz, *The Sea War* (1979).

Navy, Romanian

See NAVIES, BULGARIAN AND ROMANIAN

Navy, South African

The Republic of South Africa's Navy was formed on 15 November 1921 when three trawlers were presented to that country by Britain. Financial problems, however, led to the dissolution of the South African Navy in 1933.

When South Africa declared war against Germany on 6 September 1939, its navy consisted of two officers and three enlisted men. The government set out to build a coastal naval force. As a start, two whale catchers were commissioned in September to act as patrol ships. Over the next six years, the navy operated some seventy-five ships of 100 to 350 tons each. Only eleven were not commercial conversions. The main operational emphasis was on antisubmarine warfare and minesweeping.

The South African Navy was involved in four major operations during the war: (1) the assignment of five antisubmarine trawlers and eight minesweeping trawlers to operate in the eastern Mediterranean; (2) a patrol line set up off the Cape of Good Hope to intercept Vichy French ships carrying contraband between Indochina and France, or blockade runners making for German or Japanese ports; (3) antisubmarine escort to Allied convoys off the southeast and southwest coast of Africa (due to the scarcity and smallness of the escorts, 132 merchant ships were lost to U-boats and surface raiders in the waters of South Africa); and (4) minesweeping off South Africa's shores. Mines were laid off South Africa between 1940 and 1942 by German surface raiders. These mines damaged three ships and sank one. Total South African naval losses in the war were five ships.

Charles H. Bogart

Additional Reading
Goosen, J.C., *South Africa's Navy* (1973).
Turner, L.C.F., et al., *War in the Southern Ocean* (1961).

Navy, Soviet

The Soviet Navy entered World War II as a rapidly expanding force whose only experienced leaders were purged or executed in the months before the war. Like the other Soviet armed forces, the navy was ill-prepared for the German onslaught of 22 June 1941. Units were caught in port, bases overrun, and operations inhibited by German minefields and aerial supremacy.

The Soviet Navy fought hard, if not always competently, and suffered heavily in the process. It evacuated thousands of Soviet soldiers, sailors, and technicians against overwhelming odds. Moreover, the Soviet Navy was the first Allied navy to conduct a successful amphibious assault against the Axis. Its proficiency in all naval warfare areas improved as the war progressed, but the Soviet Navy never achieved operational equality with its opponents. Nonetheless, its record is an enviable one for a fleet whose logistical infrastructure was destroyed early in the fighting, and whose best people were siphoned off into the ground war.

Like German chancellor Adolf Hitler, Soviet premier Josef Stalin (qq.v.) had hoped to have a large oceangoing fleet to challenge the Royal Navy's maritime preeminence by 1945. Unlike Hitler, however, Stalin recognized his economic shortfalls and moved aggressively to correct them. The Soviets recruited foreign technicians and shipyard workers to design and build ships, submarines, and shipyards. New shipyards were built, including Severomorsk on the White Sea and Komsomolsk in the Pacific. Stalin also drafted thousands of Soviet workers into shipyard training programs and employed thousands of slave laborers to expand the inland river and canal system. It proved a fortuitous program. The new shipyards at Gorki and Severomorsk were outside German bomber range and could build their ships and submarines unhindered. More significantly, the river and canal system enabled the Soviets to transfer up to destroyer-size units among its three western fleets without exposure to Axis attack.

The Soviet naval air arm also grew during this period, as the Soviet hierarchy recognized the growing importance of airpower to fleet operations. Stalin swept away airpower doubters by the late 1920s and directed the development of a naval air strike force in addition to a naval air reconnaissance element. He wanted aircraft carriers and his agents approached American, British, and German designers to obtain plans and technical assistance to build such ships. Conservative like all navies, the Soviet Navy wanted a hybrid design with both large guns and an air wing.

The American designs came the closest. Displacing nearly 70,000 tons, the proposed units would have been equipped with sixteen 16-inch guns as well as an air wing of thirty to forty-five aircraft. Antiaircraft armament was to have been generous by European standards. It is highly doubtful, however, if this hybrid design was within the Soviet Union's capability to produce.

The German *Graf Zeppelin* design would have been more practical, but the Nazi regime hesitated to provide technical drawings, even after the signing of the Molotov-Ribbentrop Pact (q.v.) of 23 August 1939. Thus, Stalin had to content himself with a large shore-based naval air arm, and he gave the navy a high priority for land-based aircraft acquisition. His efforts resulted in a navy with the world's largest naval air arm by 1 September 1939.

The rapid expansion of the Soviet fleet stretched the country's economic and personnel resources to the breaking point, and Stalin's purges (q.v.) eliminated many of the country's few experienced leaders and managers. Thus, the Soviet Navy entered the war as a "hollow fleet" with a large number of new units and few experienced leaders to handle them. Moreover, the chaos engendered by the purges made it impossible to meet the increasingly unrealistic production goals. Also, most of its new construction suffered from severe material and technical shortcomings.

The damage control arrangements were poor, engineering systems unreliable, antiaircraft armament inadequate, and all units lacked the electronic sensors so important to modern naval warfare. More significantly, Stalin's purges eliminated most of those who were in a position to detect and solve those problems. This combination of poor material and inexperienced leadership was a recipe for disaster.

The navy's shortcomings did not surface during the short wars against Poland and Finland, but its performance was not auspicious either. Stalin ordered the navy to orchestrate an incident to justify his planned seizure of Estonia, and its performance in this episode typified its early operations in the war. A Soviet submarine, *SHCH-303,* was

Soviet Navy Order of Battle
1 September 1939/22 June 1941

Ship Type	Northern Fleet	Baltic Fleet	Black Sea Fleet	Pacific Fleet
Aircraft Carriers	0 / 0	0 / 0	0 / 0	0 / 0
Battleships	0 / 0	2 / 2	1 / 1	0 / 0
Heavy Cruisers	0 / 0	0 / 0	0 / 0	0 / 0
Medium Cruisers	0 / 0	1 / 2	0 / 2	0 / 0
Light Cruisers	0 / 0	0 / 0	0 / 0	0 / 0
World War I Cruisers	0 / 0	1 / 1	4 / 4	0 / 0
Flotilla Leaders	0 / 0	2 / 2	3 / 3	0 / 2
Modern Destroyers	4 / 4	6 / 12	5 / 8	0 / 6
World War I Destroyers	3 / 3	6 / 6	5 / 5	2 / 2
Torpedo Boats	3 / 3	8 / 8	4 / 4	5 / 5
Motor Torpedo Boats	0 / 2	48 / 48	84 / 84	134 / 135
Submarines	14 / 15	55 / 69	23 / 44	76 / 87
Total	24 / 27	129 / 150	129 / 155	217 / 237

positioned to sink the Soviet tanker *Metallist,* while a group of motor torpedo boats stood by to rescue the "survivors" and identify the "Polish" submarine *Orzel* (which was interned in the Estonian port of Tallin) as the perpetrator. In the event, the *SHCH- 303* emptied its torpedo magazine without hitting the tanker, and a motor torpedo boat had to sink the *Metallist.* The tanker crew, not aware of the plan, was rescued by Estonian fishing boats and exposed the episode as a fraud. It was not an impressive beginning.

The Soviet Navy accomplished nothing in the war against Poland and little more in the fighting against Finland. Stalin had ordered a close blockade of the Finnish coast, but the action was deterred by the treacherous reefs and intensive minefields that lay off that coast. The Soviets sank only one Finnish and two neutral merchant ships in the Winter War (q.v.), and they lost one submarine in the process. Some lessons were learned but there was little time or incentive to apply those lessons in a navy just recovering from the purges.

The German invasion caught the entire Soviet command structure off guard. The disastrous early days following the German invasion exposed the navy's deficiencies at a heavy cost. The bulk of the surface fleet was not serviceable and therefore could not get underway during the critical first few days of the invasion. Within a week, the Soviets lost twelve submarines and nearly fifty surface ships, most through scuttling. German airpower and mines took out the rest.

Still, the navy put up a credible performance in the Baltic and Black Seas. Minefields were laid around Saareema Island, off Tallin, and outside Sevastopol. Several Axis ships were lost on those minefields. The Soviet Black Sea Fleet actually conducted offensive sweeps off Romanian ports, sinking several merchant ships and shelling supply depots, but it lost one destroyer to Axis mines and several other ships to Axis air strikes. In the Baltic, Libau, Riga, and Tallin were all successfully evacuated, albeit at a heavy cost. The Soviet Northern Fleet conducted several small-scale amphibious landings along the Arctic coast to keep the German Arctic front off balance. Every Soviet naval action, however, brought out the *Luftwaffe* with predictable results—heavy Soviet losses. Still, the Soviets persevered.

The Black Sea Fleet was the most aggressive. It supported the Soviet Coastal Army in defending Odessa, running the German aerial gauntlet to deliver more than 100,000 tons of supplies and 35,000 fresh reinforcements and shelling German and Romanian coastal positions and convoys.

The Black Sea Fleet conducted the Allies' first major amphibious assault on 21 September 1941 when Captain Sergei Gorshkov (q.v.) landed the Soviet 3rd Naval Infantry Regiment at Grigorevka. His landing drove the Romanian 13th Infantry Division away from the coast and reopened the port of Odessa to sea traffic. Ultimately, however, the German drive on Sevastopol (q.v.) forced the Soviets to evacuate Odessa. Once again, the Black Sea Fleet came through and evacuated the 50,000 defenders and nearly 70,000 civilian workers and key technicians to Sevastopol.

The process of supporting a besieged army and evacuating wounded and key personnel was repeated there as well. In effect, the Germans had to fight the Soviet Coastal Army three different times as a result of the Black Sea Fleet's operations. Evacuations and amphibious operations became the Black Sea Fleet's *raison d'etre* for the war. It got better with each landing, and in doing so, made the reputation of the man who would lead the Soviet Navy through most of the Cold War, Fleet Admiral Sergei Gorshkov.

The basic pattern of operations for each fleet was set by October 1941. The Northern Fleet had the fewest units and the greatest operational freedom. Its ports were only subject to intermittent German air attacks, and the Arctic coastline was too long and deep to be protected continuously by minefields and coastal defense batteries.

The Baltic Fleet was effectively bottled in its own ports by extensive Axis minefields and by a layered combination of minefields and net booms supported by air and naval patrols starting in 1942. Most of its light units were transferred via the inland river/canal system to the Northern and Black Sea Fleets where they could be employed more efficiently.

The Black Sea Fleet's operations were hindered by the loss of its major support facilities and the shallow waters of its coastal areas, which were easily and effectively mined by both sides. Nonetheless, the Black Sea Fleet had the most success, conducting more than seventy amphibious assaults and the largest Soviet naval operations of the war.

The Soviet Navy's fortunes did not improve until the Axis lost air supremacy over the eastern front in 1944. Suddenly, it became possible to conduct combined naval/air operations over all three fleet areas with a corresponding increase in freedom of employment. Axis naval and shipping losses picked up, although the Soviets proved relatively inept at those operations. Finland and Romania left the war in September 1944 and with their departure went the last barriers to Soviet naval operations in the northern Baltic and Black Seas, respectively. The Northern Fleet was able to land special reconnaissance and amphibious assault units in support of the Arctic Army's advance across northern Finland and Norway.

Although the Soviet Navy neither conducted major fleet operations nor demonstrated any clear proficiency at anything other than tactical amphibious assaults, it fulfilled the mission requirements laid upon it by the Soviet high command. It also provided nearly 500,000 personnel, including some of its best officers and sailors, to the ground war. The Soviet Union's military strategy precluded a large and independent navy. Stalin's military strategy required a fleet that supported the army by protecting its coastal flank, attacking the enemy's rear, and providing logistical support. From that perspective, the Soviet Navy's operations were a success and provided the lessons and traditions that served the Soviet Navy through the Cold War era.

Carl O. Schuster

Additional Reading

Achkasov, V.I., and N.B. Pavlovich, *Soviet Naval Operations in the Great Patriotic War 1941–1945* (1979).

Herrick, Robert W., *Soviet Naval Theory and Policy* (1988).

Isakov, Ivan S., *The Red Fleet in the Second World War* (1947).

Ruge, Frederick, *The Soviets As Naval Opponents: 1941–1945* (1979).

Navy, U.S.

Although Pearl Harbor signaled official United States entry into World War II, preparations for global conflict, and, indeed, actual fighting by the navy predated the 7 December attack. Ending of an arms embargo, institution of a draft during peace, the Destroyers for Bases Deal (q.v.) with Great Britain, and passage of Lend-Lease (q.v.) all highlighted Washington's gradual but perceivable movement toward the Allied side in 1939–1941.

In terms of command structure, President Franklin D. Roosevelt appointed Frank Knox (qq.v.) as secretary of the navy in July 1940, a position he held until his death in April 1944. James V. Forrestal (q.v.) succeeded him in that post. Admiral Harold R. Stark replaced Admiral William D. Leahy (qq.v.) as chief of naval operations (CNO) in 1939. While the Navy Department maintained sizeable forces in the Pacific, it also strengthened the prewar Atlantic Squadron. Wash-

ington reorganized Atlantic naval units, called the Patrol Force, into the Atlantic Fleet under the leadership of Admiral Ernest J. King (q.v.) in February 1941. Admiral Husband E. Kimmel was commander in chief of both the United States Fleet and the Pacific Fleet.

These naval officers and their staffs did not wait for the war to come to their shores before preparing for American participation. Both U.S. and Royal Navy planners, meeting in Washington, concluded that defeating Adolf Hitler (q.v.) would have top priority. The March 1941 ABC-1 staff agreement also discussed cooperation, division of responsibility, and provided a framework for American involvement at sea. In practice, the establishment of neutrality patrol days after the start of the European war had presaged American convoy duties in the Atlantic. In April 1941, King formed task forces to operate near Panama, in the Gulf of Mexico, in the Caribbean Sea, and in the North Atlantic. Stark set up various sea frontier areas extending from a section of the North American coast outward for 200 miles. In addition to these moves, the August 1941 Placentia Bay Conference between Roosevelt, British prime minister Winston S. Churchill (q.v.), and their staffs not only produced the Atlantic Charter (q.v.), but also reviewed the U.S. Navy's role in convoy protection.

Not surprisingly then, the "war of nerves" in the North Atlantic soon escalated dramatically. On 4 September 1941, *U-652* fired several torpedoes at the USS *Greer* (q.v.), while the *Greer* was tracking the submarine with British assistance. While neither the German sub nor the destroyer's counterattack struck home, Roosevelt then issued his famous "shoot-on-sight" order to the navy regarding Axis warships. In mid-September, Convoy HX-150 became the initial cross-ocean expedition guarded by American naval vessels. These events soon culminated in open warfare with the torpedoing of the USS *Kearny* (q.v.) in October. While that destroyer limped into port, a U-boat sank the USS *Reuben James* (q.v.) in late October with heavy loss of life. Thus, even before December 1941, the navy engaged in hostilities in the Atlantic.

Within two weeks of the Hawaii attack, Roosevelt appointed Admiral King commander in chief, United States Fleet. (The navy changed the original abbreviation CINCUS to COMINCH.) Admiral Royal E. Ingersoll (q.v.) took King's place as Atlantic Fleet commander (CINCLANT) for most of the war. While unintended, the roles of COMINCH and CNO confused the chain of command in Washington. That led Roosevelt in March 1942 to dispatch Stark to London as commander Naval Forces Europe (COMNAVEU) and concentrate power in King's hands. King served as both CNO and COMINCH, as well as belonging to the Joint Chiefs of Staff (JCS) and the Anglo-American Combined Chiefs of Staff (CCS) (q.v.). Here, he had primary responsibility for U.S. naval operations during World War II.

As previously noted, the crucial Battle of the Atlantic (q.v.) did not begin with the December declarations of war against the Axis. While the German Navy at the start of the global conflict had fewer than fifty submarines ready for action, it succeeded in dealing severe blows to America's merchant fleets in early 1942. In the last half of January alone, Berlin's forces sank thirteen vessels. By May, the Eastern Sea Frontier managed to cut losses with the establishment of a coastal escort system assisted by air cover. The Germans then moved south. But even in that month, Hitler's submarines on patrols destroyed an average of 10,000 tons each, and forty American merchantmen went to the bottom on the Arctic and Atlantic routes. Moreover, the U.S. Navy sank only six U-boats through mid-1942 and seventeen for the whole year. Inexperience and the need for a clear, consistent approach to antisubmarine warfare (ASW, q.v.) characterized the disappointing effort.

In addition to the Atlantic patrols, the U.S. Navy also dispatched a task force, that initially included the carrier USS *Wasp,* to Britain in March 1942 to support British naval units. In the same year, American warships helped escort merchant ships on the difficult run to northern Russia. American naval historian Samuel Eliot Morison called the futile struggle to save Convoy PQ-17 (q.v.) in early July ". . . the grimmest convoy battle of the entire war."

Early 1943 saw the establishment of additional passage lanes for merchant vessels. The U.S. Navy assumed primary responsibility for several routes in the central Atlantic. Then, a "convoy conference" in March 1943, along with late analysis by King's staff, set the stage for the introduction of "hunter-killer groups" in the Atlantic consisting of an escort carrier and supporting warships. As the Allies grappled with vessel deployment, German technology as well as poor weather conditions hampered effective use of scientific advancements in radar and sonar (qq.v.).

The establishment of the U.S. Tenth Fleet in May 1943 highlighted American attempts to provide an umbrella organization for escort protection. While King exercised overall command, in practice, Rear Admiral Francis S. Low, the Fleet's chief of staff from its inception until January 1945,

effectively organized ASW. Although the Tenth Fleet directed Atlantic operations, Low and his officers studied the Pacific conflict as well and outlined overall procedures for dealing with submarines throughout the world.

Despite significant Allied losses, German wolf packs began to falter in the face of coordinated air-sea operations in the spring. The first U.S. hunter-killer squadron included the escort carrier USS *Bogue* and four destroyers. As the *Bogue* and her sister ships fanned out over the Atlantic, they destroyed sixteen German submarines by August. While the European Axis had lost fewer than 110 submarines in 1942, more than 260 went down the next year. Even the use of snorkels, advanced torpedoes, and planned new submarine models did not reverse the German decline.

Increased experience in ASW, cryptography, coordinated use of planes and ships, combined with expanded construction and technological progress in fields as varied as radar and weaponry (depth charges, for example), led to Allied domination of the Atlantic after 1943. The final figures were impressive indeed. The navy, with Allied assistance, convoyed thousands of vessels in this theater and delivered several million men and their logistic support to the Atlantic war. The Germans lost 781 U-boats out of more than 1,170 boats deployed. The U.S. Navy sank approximating 25 percent of those submarines.

Certainly the ASW aspect of the Atlantic war mandated both intraservice and internation cooperation. Yet strong Anglo-American differences colored wartime decisions, especially regarding the invasions of Northwest Africa, Italy, and France. In addition, the Pacific offered a different scenario: two separate, but specifically American-led, commands.

In December 1941, King selected Admiral Chester W. Nimitz to head the Pacific Fleet replacing Kimmel. Washington appointed Nimitz commander in chief, Pacific Ocean areas. There, he shared responsibility for the war against Japan with army General Douglas MacArthur, in charge of the southwest Pacific area.

The ongoing need to adjust construction and assignment priorities given the changing fortunes of this global war affected various engagements, including the projected assault on occupied France. Needless to say, this question, combined with an occasionally perplexing chain of command in the Pacific, posed problems for King.

The debate over fighting the Axis extended to specific regions. Britain, for instance, believed the Allies should emphasize Mediterranean operations, while the Americans felt the invasion of the Con-

U.S. Navy Order of Battle
1 September 1939

Ship Type	In Service	Under Construction	In Atlantic/ European Waters
Aircraft Carriers	7	0	1
Battleships	15	6	4
Heavy Cruisers	18	0	5
Light Cruisers	13	2	5
World War I Cruisers	10	0	0
Antiaircraft Cruisers	0	4	0
Modern Destroyers	89	3	11
WW I–era Destroyers	51	0	15
WW I–era Subchasers	11	0	4
Motor Torpedo Boats	2	0	0
Submarines	46	11	0
WW I–era Submarines	12	0	12
Minesweepers	0	10	0
WW I–era Minesweepers	26	0	7
Total	300	36	64

tinent through France would lead to victory. This sometimes uneasy relationship manifested itself in the command structure for the invasion of Northwest Africa (q.v.), scheduled for late 1942. Historically, Britain perceived the Mediterranean within its own "sphere of influence," but the United States was now furnishing both firepower and military strength for the campaign. Consequently, the Allies divided leadership positions accordingly. Lieutenant General Dwight D. Eisenhower (q.v.) directed overall operations as commander in chief, Allied Expeditionary Force. British officers filled his major subordinate posts.

Both the U.S. and Royal Navies had distinct objectives in Operation TORCH. Great Britain assumed primary responsibility for the attack on Mediterranean North Africa, while the Americans concentrated on the Atlantic beachheads. Although British Admiral Sir Andrew B. Cunningham (q.v.) served as Allied commander in chief Mediterranean, in practice he centered his attention on the British sector and allowed the U.S. Navy's Rear Admiral H. Kent Hewitt (q.v.) to direct the Western Naval Task Force himself.

As expected at first, the U.S. Navy lacked sufficient craft for a full-scale amphibious assault. At the beginning of June 1942, for instance, Hewitt had only a scattering of ships functioning under his control. On 8 November, however, his strengthened Task Force 34 landed Major General George S. Patton (q.v.) and 35,000 men in Morocco to take Casablanca. Combined Allied units composed the Central Task Force that struck at Oran, and the

Eastern Naval Task Force containing troops and craft from both countries attacked Algiers. British warships under Vice Admiral James F. Somerville supported the latter two landings. Hewitt's fleet including three battleships, seven cruisers, thirty-eight destroyers, as well as transports and other vessels, assisted by airpower from the carrier USS *Ranger* and several auxiliary carriers.

Bad weather, lack of experience, and initial French naval opposition hampered the three-pronged American invasion of the Northwest African beaches. Despite these hindrances, Hewitt's transports disembarked the army. Soon the airfield at Port Lyautey in French Morocco became a key installation for convoy protection in the Atlantic. Port Lyautey proved to be an exception, for after Operation TORCH, the Royal Navy generally dominated the Allied offensive in the Mediterranean. Hewitt temporarily went back to his post with the Atlantic Fleet.

Hewitt's (and the U.S. Navy's) absence from the Mediterranean was short-lived, for in January 1943, at the Casablanca Conference, the Allies decided to invade Sicily (q.v.). Beyond that action, however, British and American strategists could not as yet agree on other Mediterranean operations. Indeed, Sicily occupied immediate attention as the Allies delayed the often-debated frontal attack on Fortress Europe (q.v.). Thus, preparations commenced for Operation HUSKY. Vice Admiral Hewitt again commanded the American fleet during that landing. Eisenhower and Allied naval leaders ordered Hewitt's Western Naval Task Force to put Patton's Seventh Army ashore, while the British landed elsewhere on the island. Hewitt argued in vain for a daytime amphibious operation supported by extensive naval gunfire beforehand. The assault, on 10 July 1943, illustrated the value of offshore gunnery support for these landings.

In the summer of 1943, the Allies discussed the attack on Italy. Eisenhower remained in charge of the Mediterranean until preparations for Operation OVERLORD took him to Britain. British General Sir Henry Maitland Wilson (q.v.) replaced him in December 1943 as supreme Allied commander Mediterranean.

Once again, Hewitt led the U.S. amphibious squadrons for Operation AVALANCHE. He directed the Western Naval Task Force under Admiral of the Fleet Sir Andrew Cunningham. Hewitt commanded both the British Northern Attack Force, and the American Southern Attack Force as well as other units. He suggested lengthy prelanding bombardment, but to no avail. His orders were to land Lieutenant General Mark W. Clark's (q.v.) U.S. Fifth Army at Salerno (q.v.). Despite delayed and changed plans, Hewitt again successfully disembarked the Allied forces on 9 September 1943. There, as at Sicily, fire from ships off the coast played a significant role in the attack.

A third major amphibious attack revolved around Operation SHINGLE, directed at Anzio (q.v.) and Nettuno, near the Italian capital. There, Rear Admiral Frank J. Lowry and Major General John P. Lucas (q.v.), both Americans, led the Allied operation. While Lowry's fleet skillfully landed the Anglo-American ground forces on 22 January 1944, bloody fighting soon developed as six German divisions battled the invaders. Allied strategists had not committed enough troops to the campaign. The Allies finally moved into Rome on 4 June, after extended combat.

The final great assault in the Mediterranean centered on southern France (q.v.) in 1944. Considerable debate ensued regarding this operation, designated first ANVIL and then DRAGOON. Whatever the case, British objections made this invasion tentative until less than a week before its projected D-Day. Hewitt finally convinced planners to permit an extensive bombardment prior to the attack and a daylight landing on the beachheads. While the U.S. Navy generally did not assign ships bigger than cruisers to the Mediterranean, battleships augmented U.S. firepower for Operation DRAGOON.

Hewitt had three experienced subordinates, Lowry, and Rear Admirals Bertram J. Rodgers and Spencer S. Lewis leading main assault units carrying troops from three divisions. Other warships supported these groups. Army-navy-air coordination marked the successful 15 August 1944 landings. Within six weeks, almost 325,000 troops and more than 68,000 vehicles were ashore.

Positive Anglo-American relations furnished the framework for success in the Mediterranean. Yet sometimes traditional hegemony (British) clashed with significant military and naval commitments (U.S.). Furthermore, the question of clear organization and decision making regarding the use of airpower occasionally clouded army-navy execution, for example, the battle for Sicily. Hewitt, Cunningham, their staffs, and officers from both navies deserve credit since the Allies generally dealt successfully with these potentially damaging problems. While Anzio became a near-debacle after the troops were landed, both Operations HUSKY and AVALANCHE established an Allied foothold in the Mediterranean, and Operation DRAGOON drew upon the accumulated experience of those invasions. The final months of the European war in the Mediterranean theater centered primarily on ground operations.

As the Allies were embarking on the various amphibious assaults in the Mediterranean, they also were formulating plans for the postponed attack on France. In January 1944, Eisenhower became supreme Allied commander for Operation OVERLORD and Operation NEPTUNE, its naval component. Admiral Sir Bertram Ramsay (q.v.) served as his chief naval subordinate, with Rear Admiral Alan G. Kirk (q.v.) leading the American flotilla. Plans called for a combined paratrooper-amphibious offensive with landings centered on five areas. The U.S. had responsibility for the OMAHA and UTAH beachheads, while the British Commonwealth forces attacked points designated SWORD, JUNO, and GOLD.

Admiral Stark directed Naval Forces Europe and headed U.S. Twelfth Fleet, but his work centered on administrative matters rather than the Normandy operations. Kirk divided his mostly U.S. Western Task Force into two groups, led by Rear Admirals Don P. Moon and John L. Hall (q.v.). Rear Admirals Morton L. Deyo and Carleton F. Bryant commanded the ships furnishing cover fire for Kirk's fleet. The U.S. Navy assembled almost 2,500 vessels for the expedition.

Despite the threat of mines, Kirk's armada landed soldiers at UTAH Beach on 6 June 1944. By the close of that day more than 21,000 men were ashore. At OMAHA Beach, offshore gunfire, especially from destroyers, assisted progress despite heavy losses. Of approximately 34,000 men landed there by the end of D-Day, 2,000 were casualties. Both navies' warships served in each sector. Once the beaches were secured, troops and materiel followed. Within two weeks of D-Day, 315,000 troops were ashore in the American sector. The Army seized Cherbourg in late June aided by Rear Admiral Deyo's forces.

OVERLORD and DRAGOON concluded the great naval operations of the European war. Although naval craft trucked inland to the Rhine helped transport army units, the U.S. Navy turned its attention elsewhere. The navy in the Mediterranean became a task force of the European command's Twelfth Fleet in April 1945, and Washington appointed Vice Admiral William Glassford to head Naval Forces Northwest African Waters in the same month. V-E Day in May 1945 brought the expected reassignments to other theaters. By mid-June, Stark noted that all American warships had departed Britain. Hewitt replaced Stark as COMNAVEU later that year.

Edward J. Sheehy

Additional Reading

Morison, Samuel Elliot, *History of United States Naval Operations in World War II,* 15 vols. (1947–1957).

Potter, E.B. (ed.), *Sea Power: A Naval History* (1981).

Nazi Party

See Nationalsozialistische Deutsche Arbeiterpartei

Newspapers and Magazines, Soldiers'

During World War II in Europe, service newspapers and magazines were published for soldiers by soldiers, although often heavily laden with very unsubtle propaganda. Newspapers and magazines were important to the overall morale of troops, enabling them to maintain some link with the home front, family, and prewar habits, as well as providing war news from the various fronts. Allied troops were particularly interested in any news from the Russian front, which was seen as being crucial to the duration of the war. Newspapers, magazines, and cheap paperbacks provided something else: entertainment, escapism, and an alternative to gambling and drinking. For many soldiers, the greatest contentment came from lounging around with a book, newspaper, or magazine.

Among the U.S. forces, a whole series of publications were produced at camp, unit, or regimental level, including the *Field Artillery Journal, Army Motors, 45th Division News* (the first U.S. Army newspaper published on European soil in World War II), *Air Force Magazine,* and *Bureau of Naval Personnel Magazine.*

The two best-known American service publications were *Stars and Stripes* and *Yank.* The former, a newspaper for U.S. military personnel, was produced periodically since the American Civil War as either a weekly or a daily. It was published in 1918 as a weekly for U.S. soldiers in Europe but was discontinued in 1919. Revived in 1942, *Stars and Stripes* first appeared as a weekly, finally moving to a daily format. The European edition of *Stars and Stripes* had a circulation of more than 1,000,000 in 1945. In 1942, a Pacific edition of the newspaper was also established. *Stars and Stripes* contained war news, editorials, features, and cartoons that were of interest to American forces overseas.

Many excellent writers, editors, and photographers worked for the newspaper, including cartoonist Bill Mauldin (q.v.) who created the memorable characters of Willie and Joe (q.v.). A front page from 25 April 1942 featured pictures of General George C. Marshall (q.v.) inspecting troops in Northern Ireland, information about leaves and furloughs for U.S. forces in the British Isles, war news, home front news, e.g., "U.S. Rations Gasoline in 17 East States," and a special article entitled "Dear Mom: I've Met Two Heroes," written by a soldier about not bragging over American abundance in the face of scarcity in the British Isles. *Stars and Stripes* was intended to be the newspaper by enlisted men, for enlisted men.

The first British issue of *Yank,* the U.S. Army weekly magazine, appeared on 8 November 1942. *Yank* contained the usual cartoons, including the very popular Sad Sack (q.v.) drawn by George Baker (q.v.), pin-ups of movie stars, beauty contestants in swim suits, and other photos and features. It also published large numbers of its soldier readers' poems, stories, letters, and accounts of combat. Another popular section was "News from Home: What Goes on in Your Home State," which brought the troops news of county fairs, local elections, and even the purchase of a new fire truck. The motto of *Yank* was "By the men . . . for the men in the service."

The main editorial office was located in New York, with a separate editorial staff for a navy edition. Yank also maintained offices worldwide, from Washington, D.C., to the Marianas. The managing editors and the hundreds of editorial and production staff came from the enlisted ranks, but the magazine was still subject to sharp scrutiny by U.S. military censors. Yet despite such censorship, both *Yank* and *Stars and Stripes* still managed to reflect some of the realities of military service for the average enlisted man, as humorously revealed in this poem that appeared in *Yank,* written by Staff Sergeant Franklin M. Willment, entitled "Obituary":

> Under a friendly tavern spigot.
> Lay out my grave and write my ticket.
> My life was raw but always cricket.
> And Bacchus my partner and guide.
>
> This be the verse that you grave for me:
> "Here lies a GI where he longs to be
> With a flask on his hip and a blonde on his
>   knee
> And a quart of shellac in his hide."

The British and Commonwealth forces, of course, had their own newspapers and magazines. *Parade,* the Middle East theater weekly, came in a slick, pictorial format, and was first published in Cairo in August 1940. The *Union Jack,* which amalgamated with the *Eighth Army News,* first appeared in September 1943 three times a week. Soon *Union Jack* became the "Daily Newspaper for the British Fighting Services." First published in Tunis, the Italian invasion quickly produced an Italian edition. Features in the newspaper included sports, short stories, and a section by Lance Corporal Bernard Brett called "Now We're Talking." Also included were reprints of articles from home magazines as well as articles by political and military commentators. There was the required war news, and a daily Italian lesson.

The popularity of the American and British newspapers grew rapidly. In fact, one press in Italy in 1943, produced 380,000 daily copies of both *Eighth Army News* and *Union Jack,* 20,000 *Stars and Stripes* (Italian edition), and 100,000 *Crusaders,* the British Eighth Army weekly.

The Commonwealth troops also had their own newspapers and magazines. The Canadians had their *Maple Leaf,* the Australians in the Middle East had their *A.I.F. News,* while South African forces in that theater had a weekly called *Springbok,* with items in both English and Afrikaans. The New Zealanders in Italy had a weekly called *New Zealand Times.* Wherever soldiers went, newspapers were sure to follow them.

In the German Army, *Wehrmacht* propaganda staffs issued newspapers for the troops. German soldiers also came into contact with so-called occupation newspapers. They were German newspapers in style, format, and content, designed to facilitate communication between the German occupation authorities and the local population. German military commands would sometimes guarantee purchase of from 30,000 to 40,000 copies for the offices, staffs, and agencies of the occupation authority. The army also facilitated distribution through army canteens and clubs to the troops in the area. A particularly successful example of such a newspaper was the *Deutsche Zeitung in Norwegen.* The popular military journals, *Die Wehrmacht, Unser Heer,* and *Ostfront Illustrierte* fell under the control of the Nazi Party, despite vigorous objections from the armed forces that they needed a medium to communicate directly with the German public and soldier. *Signal,* a lavishly illustrated magazine, made its appearance in 1941. Not designed for soldiers, its mission was to impress Europeans with German military might. It was printed in fifteen languages, achieving a circulation of 1,600,000. The SS (q.v.) had its own newspaper, *Schwarzes Korps,* which became increasingly popular and influential as it came to be viewed as a significant forum for Nazi ideology. As the war drew to a close, and newsprint almost disappeared, so did most German newspapers of any kind. What did appear resembled posters or handbills more than traditional newspapers or magazines.

Books were also very popular among soldiers. First Pocket Books, then other American publishers, came out with cheap, easily mailed, and easily thrown away when moving out, "Armed Services Editions" of fiction and nonfiction. The Special Services Division of the U.S. Army sent four million books and ten million magazines overseas each month, many of them "pony" sized editions meant to save paper and reduce weight. In April 1945, *Stars and Stripes* conducted a survey that found among American soldiers in Europe the most popular book titles were: *The Pocket Book Dictionary; The Pocket Book of Cartoons; The Pocket Book of Boners;* the humorous *See Here Private Hargrove* (the best-selling paperback of the war); Erle Stanley Gardner's *The Case of the Curious Bride;* surprisingly, Emile Zola's *Nana;* and the *Pocket Book of Verse.* The British had no Pocket Books, but they did have Penguin Books. Like their American counterpart, the popularity of Penguins among British soldiers was due partly to their compact size. They could easily slip into a compartment in the gas mask haversack. Paul Fussell writes that "when the British army battle dress was devised, the troops found that the outer pocket above the left knee, intended for an entrenching tool in combat and used sometimes for carrying a field dressing, conformed exactly to the shape of a Penguin." Hence it was dubbed the "Penguin pocket."

Newspapers, magazines, and books were part of the routine of war for many soldiers in World War II, giving them a sense of belonging, identity, and pride, as well as preserving a tenuous bond with the civilian world.

Richard A. Voeltz

Additional Reading

Anglo, Michael, *Service Newspapers of the Second World War* (1977).

Ellis, John, *The Sharp End: The Fighting Man in World War II* (1980).

Fussell, Paul, *Wartime: Understanding and Behavior in the Second World War* (1989).

Hale, Oron J., *The Captive Press in the Third Reich* (1964).

Mauldin, Bill, *Up Front* (1945).

Nisei Units in the U.S. Army

Japanese began immigrating to Hawaii in the 1860s and to California in the early 1900s. They tended to remain on the West Coast where, from the beginning, they faced open public hostility. All Japanese children were excluded from public schools by the San Francisco Board of Education in 1909. In some western states, they were denied, by law, the right to own land.

Given this hostile attitude, it might not be surprising, after the Japanese attack on Pearl Harbor, that anti-Japanese hysteria provoked the internment of 110,000 Japanese Americans, both citizen and noncitizen, in ten high security relocation centers. Although less harshly run and not intended for extermination purposes, they were an American form of the infamous German concentration camps (q.v.).

People of Japanese ancestry could not become citizens unless born in the United States, because the first American immigration law passed in 1790 stated only "free whites" could be naturalized. Japanese Americans were thus classified as *Nisei,* born in the United States; *Issei,* an immigrant alien in the United States; or *Kibei,* an American citizen educated mostly in Japan.

After the Japanese attack on Pearl Harbor, suspicion was immediately directed at all people of Japanese ancestry as potential "fifth columnists." The *Issei* and the *Kibei* were looked upon with even greater suspicion than the *Nisei.* The distrust and prejudice against these groups was so great that a campaign was conducted to amend the U.S. Constitution so that children born in the United States of parents ineligible for citizenship would themselves be ineligible.

Morton Grodzin's book, *Americans Betrayed: Politics of the Japanese Evacuation,* explains how the malicious campaign for relocation got under way. West Coast newspapers, law enforcement officials, and Congressmen carried on a hysterical and untruthful campaign demanding the mass evacuation of all ethnic Japanese, both citizens and aliens, for alleged treasonable activities. Even a highly respected writer like Walter Lippmann used his syndicated column to call these Japanese-Americans "the Fifth Column on the Coast," and two Hearst newspapers, the *Los Angeles Times* and the *San Francisco Examiner,* called for their internment. One article in the Hearst press stated:

> Everywhere that the Japanese have attacked to date, the Japanese population has risen to aid the attackers, Pearl Harbor [sic], Manila. What is there to make the Government believe that the same wouldn't be true in California?

California Attorney General (and future U.S. Supreme Court Chief Justice) Earl Warren, while admitting that Japanese-Americans "have in the past and do now represent the highest standards of American citizenship," declared himself in favor of their internment. Secretary of the Navy Frank Knox (q.v.), told reporters, without citing any evidence, that "the most effective fifth column work of the entire war was being done in Hawaii" by Japanese Americans.

In a memorandum to the secretary of war, dated 14 February 1942, Lieutenant General John L. DeWitt, commander of the Western Defense Command and the Fourth Army, argued,

> Japanese race is an enemy race and while many second and third generation Japanese born in the United States soil, possessed of United States citizenship, have become 'Americanized,' the racial strains are undiluted.

He went on to add in a statement so ridiculous as to invite derision: "The very fact that no sabotage has taken place to date is disturbing and confirming indication that such action will take place."

Lippmann, using the same specious argument as DeWitt, wrote that inactivity to date is not a sign that there is nothing to be feared. "It is a sign," he wrote, "that the blow is well organized and that it is held back until it can be struck with maximum effect." Both statements implied that the fact they had been good, loyal citizens to date could be interpreted to mean that they were biding their time before striking. This was not only irrational but also unrealistic thinking.

It is a sad commentary on the mean-spirited and racist wartime atmosphere when such otherwise reasonable and moderate men as Lippmann and Warren were convinced that such illogical and unrealistic thinking was valid and that the Constitution had to be set aside so that American citizens could be deprived of their fundamental rights of due process of law and the writ of habeas corpus. It was also proof of the growing panic fed by unreasonable fears of a possible Japanese landing on the West Coast.

Such thinking and concerns prompted President Franklin D. Roosevelt (q.v.) to sign Executive Order No. 9066, dated 19 February 1942, authorizing and directing the secretary of war, or any military commander designated by the secretary, to establish "military areas" and exclude there from "any and all persons" deemed a threat to national security. The Supreme Court did not rule on the constitutionality of this order until 1944, when it was upheld by a six to three vote in the case of *Korematsu* v. *the U.S.* (323 U.S. 214), with Justices Roberts, Murphy, and Jackson dissenting.

As early as 17 June 1942, the U.S. War Department declared the *Nisei* unacceptable for military service "except as may be authorized in special cases." They earlier had been exempt from the draft by being placed in a 4-C (enemy aliens) classification. In July 1942, Dillon S. Meyers, director of the War Relocation Authority, requested John J. McCloy, assistant secretary of war, to revise army policy to allow *Nisei* "to volunteer and to serve and be drafted like other American boys." He felt it important for the future of Japanese citizens that the *Nisei* "have the opportunity to prove their patriotism in a dramatic manner, in view of the race-baiting pressure groups and their ceaseless clamor that a 'Jap is a Jap' regardless of citizenship or upbringing."

By a "dramatic manner," Meyers meant that they be allowed to fight in their own units rather than being integrated with other American troops. The case for the *Nisei* to serve was strengthened in early 1942 when the Japanese American Citizens League passed a resolution strongly urging the right of the *Nisei* to serve in the armed forces.

Some of the first *Nisei* recruits accepted for service were taken by army intelligence for training in Japanese, with a view toward using them as scouts, translators, and interpreters in the Pacific war. Oddly, the most qualified in this respect were the *Kibei*, who then were considered the most disaffected element among the Japanese Americans. Nevertheless, 167 Japanese Americans were recruited for language schools before the end of 1942. They rendered valuable service in the Pacific theater. Other recruits were sent to Oakland, California, for further processing.

All Japanese Americans were asked to answer two questions on a loyalty questionnaire: (1) Would the internee serve in combat with the United States Army?, and (2) Would he swear allegiance to America and denounce the Japanese emperor? Many, particularly the *Issei* and *Kibei*, felt the latter question unfair because they wanted to maintain their ethnic and cultural identity—the *Issei* were barred by law from becoming Americans and the *Kibei*, although American citizens, were under suspicion—and still had to prove their loyalty to the United States. All resented the incarceration of Japanese Americans. More than 20 percent of the *Nisei* answered both questions in the negative as a protest against the unconstitutional treatment of their families and friends. These men were considered disloyal and were kept in internment.

On 10 June 1942, the 100th Infantry Battalion, consisting of Japanese American troops, was activated as a separate battalion of six rifle companies. The original troops came from the Hawaiian Territorial Guard. The unit trained at Camp McCoy, Wisconsin, and landed in Oran, Northwest Africa, on 2 September 1943. Attached to the 34th Infantry Division, the 100th Infantry Battalion landed at Salerno (q.v.) and fought at Monte Cassino (q.v.).

A second Japanese American unit, the 442nd Regimental Combat Team (RCT), was formed on 1 February 1943 and trained at Camp Shelby, Mississippi. It went to Italy that June and joined the 100th Infantry Battalion attached to the 34th Infantry Division. From that point the history of the two units became intertwined. The first battalion of the 442nd RCT remained at Camp Shelby. Redesignated the 171st Infantry Battalion (Separate), it was the replacement source for the 442nd. In Italy, meanwhile, the 100th Infantry Battalion became the first battalion of the 442nd, but retained its own numerical designation. Including the 100th Infantry Battalion, the 442nd RCT consisted of three rifle battalions, an antitank company, a cannon company, a service company, plus the 522nd Field Artillery Battalion and the 232nd Engineer Company (Combat). The engineer unit was the only one initially formed with *Nisei* officers.

In September 1944, the 442nd RCT was transferred to France. It fought in the Vosges Mountains and was attached to the 36th Infantry Division for the Rhineland campaign (q.v.). In November 1944, the unit moved to the French-Italian border. In March 1945, it returned to Italy and was attached to the 92nd Infantry Division for the Po Valley campaign (q.v.). On 15 July 1946, the 442nd Regimental Combat Team was invited to Washington, D.C., and paraded down Constitution Avenue to the Ellipse, where it was presented the Presidential Unit Citation by President Harry S Truman.

The 100th/442nd was one of the most (perhaps *the* most) decorated units in the U.S. Army. Its individual soldiers won a Medal of Honor, fifty-two Distinguished Service Crosses, 343 Silver Stars, and approximately 3,600 Purple Hearts. The unit earned four Presidential Unit Citations and two Meritorious Unit Citations. In the postwar years, two of its members, Masayuhi Matsunaga and Daniel Inouye, became U.S. Senators. Appropriately, the motto of the 100th/442nd was "Go for Broke."

Approximately 33,000 *Nisei* fought for the United States. Following the war some 500 Japanese Americans renounced their American citizenship, left the United States, and moved to Japan because of strong resentment at their treatment.

Eventually, however, the laws that kept Japanese Americans from participating fully in American economic and political life were changed by presidential, congressional, and court action. In 1988, Congress passed a law apologizing on the part of the United States for the wartime treatment of Japanese Americans, and providing $20,000 restitution to each of approximately 60,000 surviving internees.

Paul J. Rose

Additional Reading

Duus, Masayo Umezawa, *Unlikely Liberators* (1983).

Grodzin, Morton, *Americans Betrayed: Politics and the Japanese Evacuation* (1949).

Meyer, Dillon S., *Uprooted Americans* (1971).

Tanaka, Chester, *Go for Broke* (1982).

N

NKVD

See NARODNYY KOMMISSARIAT VNUTRENNIKH DEL

NSDAP

See NATIONALSOZIALISTISCHE DEUTSCHE ARBEITERPARTEI

Oberkommando der Wehrmacht (OKW)

The High Command of the German armed forces or OKW, was an institution that, in most respects, never lived up to its name. Born out of power struggles within the German military, the OKW evolved into little more than a mouthpiece for Chancellor Adolf Hitler (q.v.), with no true authority over the high commands of the three armed services. This development destroyed the German chance to have a unified, coherent command structure.

The OKW's roots can be traced to World War I, when the army general staff controlled politics, industry, and society to an unprecedented degree. German military thinkers in the postwar period agreed that such a system would need to be reestablished, and even strengthened, should Germany ever be faced with another major war. The question was who would be in charge of a unified high command?

Several elements within the German defense establishment wanted to be at the top of the command structure. Their power struggles took on new intensity in 1933, after Hitler came to power and expressed his decision to expand the military. General Werner von Blomberg (q.v.), the minister of defense, naturally thought that his ministry should be the nucleus of any centralized command system. He appointed Colonel Walter von Reichenau (q.v.) to head the Ministerial Office. One of the first prominent army officers to express support for the Nazis, Reichenau worked to influence relations between the armed forces and the party. He also shared Blomberg's views on the Defense Ministry's place in a future high command.

Meanwhile, the commander in chief of the army, General *Freiherr* Werner von Fritsch, and the chief of the general staff, General Ludwig Beck (qq.v.), worked to reestablish the authority exercised by the army in World War I. Although they were rivals to some extent, each saw himself as the logical choice to head the new high command. They compromised in order to resist von Blomberg and von Reichenau. Their efforts continued throughout the mid-1930s, as the two sides traded memoranda, enacted conflicting regulations, and vied for influence with the *Führer.* Von Fritsch and Beck, since they controlled officer assignments, even tried to fill the Defense Ministry (renamed the War Ministry in 1935) with their own supporters. However, the men they chose—notably General Wilhelm Keitel and Colonel Alfred Jodl (qq.v.)—soon switched allegiances.

Ironically, these maneuverings did little to facilitate the creation of a rational, centralized command structure. Von Blomberg, Reichenau, Fritsch, Beck, and the others shared a common background of service in the German General Staff (qq.v.) corps. In a general sense, they had a common goal, but their internal struggles prevented them from forming a united front. While they fought, the leaders of the navy and the *Luftwaffe*—Admiral Erich Raeder and Hermann Göring (qq.v.)—staked out their own positions. They had no intention of subordinating themselves to the army or the War Ministry, and their relationship with Hitler ensured their services' continued independence.

In February 1938, Hitler took the opportunity to settle the conflict in a way that suited him. Distrusting Blomberg and Fritsch, he ousted them and declared himself commander in chief of the *Wehrmacht* (*see* Blomberg-Fritsch Crisis). The War Ministry became the *Oberkommando der Wehrmacht,* with General Keitel as its chief. The former Ministerial Office became the Armed Forces Operations Office *(Wehrmachtführungsamt).* This office handled the OKW's purely military tasks. General Jodl took charge there in August 1939.

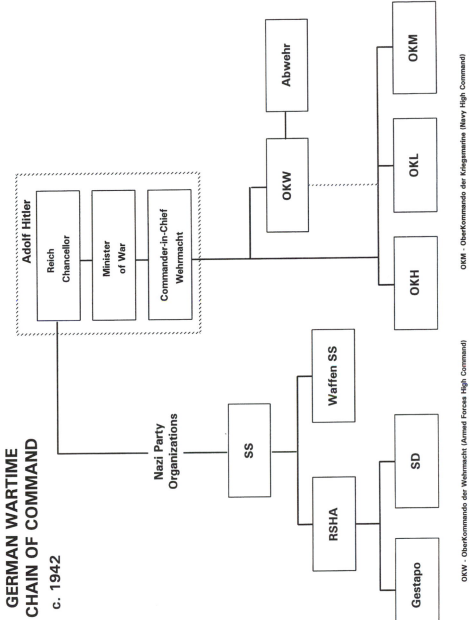

GERMAN WARTIME CHAIN OF COMMAND
c. 1942

Adolf Hitler
- Reich Chancellor
- Minister of War
- Commander-in-Chief Wehrmacht

Abwehr

OKW

OKH

OKL

OKM

Nazi Party Organizations

SS

Waffen SS

RSHA

Gestapo

SD

OKM - OberKommando der Kriegsmarine (Navy High Command)
OKL - OberKommando der Luftwaffe (Air Force High Command)

OKW - OberKommando der Wehrmacht (Armed Forces High Command)
OKH - OberKommando des Heeres (Army High Command)

What emerged was a poor compromise. The OKW was in place, but it was in no way the "armed forces general staff" that Blomberg and Reichenau had envisioned. The commanders in chief of the armed services still held considerable power. Hitler, as commander in chief of the *Wehrmacht,* soon began to take a more active role than any of the generals had envisioned, a development that Keitel and Jodl proved unable or unwilling to resist. Thus, the OKW found itself stuck between uncooperative subordinates and a megalomaniac.

The situation only worsened after the war broke out. In February 1940, Hitler gave the OKW responsibility for planning and executing the invasions of Denmark and Norway (qq.v.). Scandinavia was thus the first of what came to be called the "OKW theaters of war," which eventually included France, Italy, North Africa, the Balkans, and the occupied areas of Poland and Russia. After September 1942, the army high command (OKH), specifically, the general staff, remained responsible only for the combat zone on the eastern front.

This situation led to a number of problems. First of all, the OKW's workload, along with Hitler's intransigence, removed any possibility that the OKW could function as a strategic planning staff. Second, relations between the leaders of the OKW and the OKH became strained as each fought for resources to fight its segment of the war. Neither staff had overall authority, so Hitler had to settle every conflict. Third, the OKW still did not have complete authority over navy, *Waffen*-SS, or *Luftwaffe* units in its theaters; to some extent these services fought their own wars. Fourth, the OKW did not have the personnel or the organizational structure to carry out its expanded duties. It continued to rely on the OKH for support in a number of critical functions, resulting in greater confusion and further divisions of loyalty between the two staffs.

Only the professionalism of the many staff officers within the OKW and the OKH allowed this unwieldy system a measure of efficiency. At lower levels, officers within the two headquarters worked together to iron out differences with a minimum of delay. Informal networks developed by which the various offices kept themselves informed of events. The common traditions and practices of the general staff corps bound the structure together.

In the final analysis, one must bear in mind that the OKW's place in the command system was more a symptom of Germany's problems than a cause of its defeat. Infighting and strategic blunders by Hitler and his top generals lie at the root of the debacle. Germany's chaotic command arrangements simply serve to highlight the deeper malaise within the Third *Reich.*

Geoffrey P. Megargee

Additional Reading

Craig, Gordon, *The Politics of the Prussian Army* (1956).

Detwiler, Donald, Charles B. Burdick, and Jürgen Rohwer (eds.), *World War II German Military Studies: A Collection of 213 Special Reports on the Second World War Prepared by Former Officers of the Wehrmacht for the U.S. Army* (1979).

Taylor, Telford, *Sword & Swastika: Generals and Nazis in the Third Reich* (1952).

Warlimont, Walter, *Inside Hitler's Headquarters, 1939–45* (1964).

Wilt, Alan F., *War from the Top: German and British Decision Making During World War II* (1990).

ODESSA

Following the end of World War II, former SS (q.v.) members created a secret organization called ODESSA *(Organisation der Ehemaligen SS Angehörigen)* to aid their fellow associates in evading Allied authorities looking for war criminals. Posing as a social welfare group, ODESSA assisted SS, *Gestapo* (qq.v.), and other high-ranking Nazis in numerous ways by providing them with legal assistance if apprehended, helping them escape from prison, furnishing false identity papers, and smuggling them out of Germany or other European countries.

The underground escape network, also known as *Die Spinne* (The Spider), led through Austria or Italy, and then on to Spain. From there, those fleeing Europe would make their way to the Middle East or South American countries friendly toward the Nazis, especially to Chile, Paraguay, and Argentina. The organization funded its underground activities through enormous assets and monies the SS spirited out of Germany before the war's end.

Susanne Teepe Gaskins

Additional Reading

Infield, Glenn B., *Secrets of the SS* (1982).

Wechsberg, Joseph (ed.), *The Murderers among Us: The Simon Wiesenthal Memoirs* (1967).

Office Of Strategic Services (OSS)

In June 1942, the new intelligence unit formed by William J. Donovan (q.v.), the Office of the Co-ordinator of Information (COI), was reorganized as the OSS under the U.S. Joint Chiefs of Staff (JCS). Within the European Theater of Operations, OSS activities were directed from two primary field bases: London and Algiers. In both locations, the OSS built upon and expanded the COI frameworks already in place.

The COI had been operating in London since November 1941. In its first seven months of operation, it established modest branches for the conduct of espionage (secret intelligence, or SI), clandestine warfare (special operations, or SO), and intelligence research and analysis (R&A). By early 1944, the London base grew into an organization with fourteen branches and 2,000 personnel.

The two principal components of the London base were the SO branch, and the newer Counterespionage Service (X-2), established in June 1943. Modeled after British example, the OSS depended heavily on the training and experience of its British counterparts. As a result, SO and X-2, respectively, functioned as junior partners to the British Special Operations Executive (SOE) (q.v.) and section V of the Secret Intelligence Service (SIS, or MI-6). In return, SO and X-2 were incorporated fully into the SOE and MI-6 (q.v.) structures (including access to ULTRA [q.v.]). It would have taken the OSS years to build up such structures on its own.

Full access to British resources came at the cost of complete operational independence. Donovan, however, viewed the SI espionage function as a long-range (i.e., postwar) strategic interest that the U.S. could not allow to be co-opted by any foreign power. This attitude resulted in confrontations with the British government, which refused to authorize independent intelligence activities based from the United Kingdom. During this early period, the London SI branch concentrated on building up its fledgling structures in Madrid, Lisbon, Bern, and Stockholm. Donovan did not obtain authorization from the JCS to conduct independent intelligence collection operations until October 1943. Even then, it came over the vigorous objections of MI-6 and the U.S. theater command (which deferred to MI-6 in the matter).

OSS operations in Algiers had a far wider latitude from the start. The COI first penetrated Vichy-controlled Northwest Africa in January 1942. Headquartered in Tangier, the COI fielded ten case officers operating under State Department cover in Casablanca, Algiers, Oran, and Tunis. By mid-1942, the OSS was actively laying the intelligence and special operations groundwork for the Allied invasion of Northwest Africa, Operation TORCH. Northwest Africa was the first key test for the OSS, and the success of Operation TORCH was pivotal in garnering political support for the OSS both in Washington and among the theater military commanders.

Following Operation TORCH, the OSS selected Algiers as its headquarters for the Mediterranean Theater of Operations. There were several key differences between the Algiers and London bases. At its peak, personnel strength of OSS/Algiers was only about one-third the size of the London base. Furthermore, X-2 and R&A activities at Algiers were relatively limited, and SO/Algiers did not mount major operations until mid-1944. SI/Algiers, on the other hand, prospered. Operating in a U.S.-dominated theater, it also had the advantages of being distanced from overbearing MI-6 tutelage and control of assets, combined with the logistical support available from the U.S. military. Moreover, the French colonies of Northwest Africa provided a fertile agent recruiting ground for the penetration of France.

From Algiers, the OSS supported the Allied invasions of Sicily and Salerno (qq.v.) in July and September 1943. During the Italian campaign, both SI and SO branches were instrumental in developing a potent resistance force in northern Italy. OSS/Algiers received backing in this operation from Allen Dulles's (q.v.) Swiss-based OSS station.

In July 1944, the bulk of OSS/Algiers relocated to Caserta, north of Naples, to accompany the advancing U.S. Fifth Army. The SI branch remained in Algiers, attached to the U.S. Seventh Army to support the invasion of southern France (q.v.) in August 1944. Later, the successful landing was described in official accounts as the "best briefed invasion of the war"—a direct reference to voluminous, accurate intelligence reporting received from SI/Algiers-controlled agent networks in southern France.

Also in support of the southern France invasion a joint SO/SOE command, the Special Operations Center (SPOC), was established at Algiers in May 1944. The SPOC controlled twenty-five three-man Jedburgh (q.v.) teams, and commanded the operational groups (OG). The OGs were uniformed SO irregular combat platoons of about thirty soldiers each inserted behind German lines to bolster resistance efforts and to block, harass, and divert *Wehrmacht* forces.

Meanwhile, the OSS London base was gear-ing up to support the Normandy (q.v.) invasion. SO/London was operating as a de facto asset of the SOE since January 1943. From early on, small teams of SO/SOE undercover operatives were inserted throughout northern Europe to establish liaison and train local resistance movements. In May 1944, the two units were formally integrated as the Special Forces Headquarters (SFHQ), a joint command with the mission to organize the politically divided French resistance organizations in support of the coming invasions. In early to mid-1944, SFHQ operatives coordinated the resistance in widespread attacks on German troop and supply convoys, railways and bridges, fuel and munitions dumps, communications, and command and control facilities. Following D-Day on 6 June 1944, these operations were augmented by the Jedburgh teams.

The overriding mission of SFHQ was to prevent German armored and paratroop reserves from mounting a full-scale counterattack against the Allied beachhead in Normandy. SI and MI-6 mounted a joint operation, code named SUSSEX, in support of this critical endeavor. A series of two-man cells were inserted by parachute to provide a surveillance "*cordon sanitaire*" on the approaches to Normandy. Specific targets, including rail depots, roadways, airfields, and bridges over the Seine and Loire Rivers over which the *Wehrmacht* armored columns would have to pass, were divided between SI (OSSEX) and MI-6 (BRISSEX). Between 9 April and 31 August 1944, fifty-two teams parachuted into northern France (q.v.), spanning a rough arc from Avranches, southeast to Orleans, and north of Paris to Amiens. While plagued with disjointed ground contacts and radio procedures, the SUSSEX operation produced credible intelligence in support of the landings.

MI-6 had long viewed the espionage penetration of the German *Reich* itself as implausible. The obstacles, indeed, were myriad and severe. Indigenous resistance groups did not exist within the *Reich* (a fact that precluded special operations), very few dedicated anti-Nazis were known among the German population, and the *Gestapo* (q.v.) continued to hold ruthless sway over a cowed citizenry.

Nevertheless, the spiraling disorganization within Germany wrought by the Allied bombing offensive made it possible for SI/London to insert thirty-four teams into the *Reich* between September 1944 and April 1945. Technical problems with communications equipment caused serious problems, and less than one-third were able to report back. A handful of agent teams dispatched by SI/Italy, meanwhile, successfully infiltrated the forti-fied Nazi "redoubt" area. Their casualty rate, however, exceeded 50 percent. Despite the questionable intelligence benefits, SI/London did succeed in what MI-6 thought to be a futile task.

Once the Allies were firmly established on the Continent, the nature of the war shifted to the sort of conventional slugging match that left little room for clandestine operations and irregular warfare. As the Allied armies pushed the Germans back into Germany, the primary role of SI increasingly shifted to one of tactical support of frontline units.

The OSS represented a large-scale commitment to irregular warfare and intelligence that was unprecedented in U.S. military planning. As a fledgling enterprise, its operational education suffered many growing pains. Staffed largely by amateurs, the OSS struggled initially to define its wartime role to both itself and to the traditional military hierarchy. Both theater bases, however, did achieve notable successes in the SI and SO arenas.

The singular circumstances of the two theater bases shaped their contrasting operational styles. OSS/London focused its efforts on SO, while OSS/Algiers ". . . functioned principally as an SI operations center." In London, independent activities by SI were hampered by bureaucratic struggles. Conversely, SI/Algiers combined its advantages of greater political and geographic maneuvering room, with earlier opportunities to hone techniques in the recruitment, infiltration, and running of agent networks. The key result was that SI/Algiers outproduced the combined efforts of MI6 and French Intelligence in supporting the southern France invasion.

Ultimately, however, the OSS was not a cardinal instrument of Allied strategy in Europe. British historian John Keegan observed: "The often spectacular and controversial nature of clandestine operations . . . have given SOE and OSS a prominence out of all proportion to their overall contribution to the war effort."

How successful then was the OSS? An inordinate amount of fighting took place over turf with the navy and the army. Donovan had to fight for a charter, manpower authorizations, and other resources. Starting from scratch under wartime conditions, the OSS achieved moderate success. Would we have won the war without the OSS? The answer is yes, but over a longer period of time.

The OSS was not allowed by General Douglas McArthur to operate in the Pacific Theater. President Harry S Truman (q.v.) disbanded the OSS on 1 October 1945. The OSS, and the legacy of the SI and SO branches, however, provided distinct paternity to the Central Intelligence Agency (CIA) created in 1947.

Stephen Donahue

Additional Reading

Alsop, Stewart, and Thomas Braden, *Sub Rosa: The OSS and American Espionage* (New York: 1964).

Breuer, William B., *The Secret War with Germany: Deception, Espionage, and Dirty Tricks 1939–1945* (1988).

Persico, Joseph E., *Piercing the Reich: The Penetration of Nazi Germany by American Secret Agents During World War II* (1979).

Roosevelt, Kermit, *The Overseas Targets: War Reports of the OSS (Office Of Strategic Services)* Vol. II (1976).

Smith, Richard Harris, *OSS: The Secret History of America's First Central Intelligence Agency* (1972).

OKW

See OBERKOMMANDO DER WEHRMACHT

Organisation Todt

To further consolidate political power through unemployment relief, Adolf Hitler (q.v.) created the Office of the General Inspectorate of the German Highway System *(Reichsautobahn)* in 1933 to oversee the construction of a modern road network. Fritz Todt (q.v.), an engineer, National Socialist, and later minister for armaments and munitions, directed this major public works project. He was so successful with road building that Hitler designated Todt in May 1938 to take control of defensive fortification construction along the *Reich*'s western frontiers.

Die Organisation Todt (OT), though never officially assigned the name, was organized initially within the *Reichsautobahn* as the governmental liaison with the construction industry, and thus became the guardian of West Wall (q.v.) fabrication.

By late 1938, hundreds of private construction firms and hundreds of thousands of German workers were mobilized for the project. As World War II erupted, OT became an independent and increasingly regimented state enterprise controlling all facets of construction by 1945. Although its officers and supervisory personnel routinely carried firearms and its workers wore uniforms, OT remained distinct from party or *Wehrmacht* incorporation for the duration of its existence.

The increasingly paramilitary nature of OT became evident as its workers quickly followed the German attack into France and Belgium and Flanders (qq.v.) in May 1940, rebuilding bridges, railways, and roads destroyed during the advance in order to maintain lines of supply and communication with the *Reich*. Such tasks became standard fare for OT throughout occupied Europe. Other notable projects carried out by OT during the period of German expansion included the building of airfields for the *Luftwaffe* campaign against Britain, gun emplacements on the Channel Islands (q.v.), and hardened submarine pens along the west coast of France and Norway. The OT's huge challenge of building an impenetrable Fortress Europe (q.v.) ultimately failed, however, due to scarcity of time, manpower, and materiel.

By 1942, as *Blitzkrieg* gave way to attrition warfare, OT experienced serious manpower shortages as large numbers of skilled German workers were conscripted into the *Wehrmacht*—more than two million employees were inducted between 1939 and 1943. The loss of OT's charismatic leader in a February 1942 plane crash further eroded organizational efficiency and morale. Yet Todt's replacement, Albert Speer (q.v.), proved most capable and spearheaded an ongoing reorganization of OT administration. Henceforth, a newly created OT central headquarters in Berlin, under the direction of Xaver Dorsch, became the authority for issuing directives and allocating manpower to seventeen regional OT project groups.

Centralized authority was supplemented by the inclusion of foreign manpower as the only practical solution to meet OT's immense construction demands, especially once war with the Soviet Union stagnated. While many French and Belgian workers had voluntarily joined OT after June 1940, more were needed. Within two years, an astounding 90 percent of the OT work force were non-German; by March 1943, nearly 700,000 foreign workers labored under OT command.

Forced labor, especially from Soviet prisoners of war and Slavs from occupied territory, became a necessity as Hitler's obsession to forestall invasion of the greater *Reich* led to the construction of the Atlantic Wall (q.v.) and V-weapon sites in the west. Such *Ostarbeiter* (Eastern Worker) battalions suffered harshly under Nazi racial hatred, as did the Jews in OT-controlled labor camps. Late in the war, OT attempted to appease foreign laborers in an effort to increase efficiency, but the grueling hours, Nazi brutality, appalling living conditions, and Allied successes overrode any chance of reconciliation.

By mid-1944, OT shifted emphasis from Atlantic Wall construction to the repair of a transportation network disabled by the Allied preinvasion bombardment. Soon withdrawn into the fatherland, the OT's organization and performance suffered as German resistance collapsed during the final year of fighting. Yet, in the final analysis, *Organisation Todt* proved to be an integral element in the *Reich's* war effort and served as a unique attempt to manage private construction enterprise within a dictatorial governmental structure.

William E. Fischer, Jr.

Additional Reading
Kumpf, Walter, *"Organisation Todt im Krieg,"* in *Bilanz des Zweiten Weltkrieges: Erkenntnisse und Verpflichtungen für die Zukunft,* edited by Helmut Arntz (1953).

OSS

See OFFICE OF STRATEGIC SERVICES

P

Partisans, Soviet

The partisans were Soviet irregular forces operating behind German lines on the eastern front. One week after the German attack swept across the Soviet frontier, Moscow issued a 29 June 1941 directive outlining the shape of the overall war effort. Contained in this address was one paragraph that provided the mandate for the future Soviet partisan movement: "In areas occupied by the enemy, guerrilla units, mounted and on foot, must be formed; . . . to blow up bridges and roads, damage telephone and telegraph lines, set fire to forests, stores, transports. In the occupied regions conditions must be made unbearable for the enemy . . . They must be hounded and annihilated at every step . . ."

On 18 July, the Central Committee followed with a directive specifying that partisan units would be organized along existing Soviet territorial boundaries. While the Communist Party and NKVD (q.v.) provided the mechanism for political control of these irregulars, the partisan units were intended from the outset to support Red Army operations.

The immense scale of Soviet defeats in 1941 precluded partisan warfare from having any significant impact on operations that year. The vast German encirclement battles that shattered Soviet defenses left several million Soviet soldiers trapped behind enemy lines. The majority of those isolated troops were captured by the Germans and shipped to POW camps. The remainder, particularly Red Army officers, *Zampolits* (party political officers), and NKVD personnel, formed the trained (if temporarily disorganized) nucleus that set the stage for a revival of partisan operations in early 1942.

During the bitter winter of 1941–1942, partisan detachments ranged in size from twenty to 200 troops. By late summer 1942, the detachments were redesignated "brigades" for command purposes, in order to reflect their increased size of 350 to 2,000 troops per unit. Partisan commanders organized their units from Red Army stragglers, local civilians in occupied areas, and party/NKVD/army partisan-support teams parachuted behind German lines. On 30 May 1942, the partisans acquired formal, national-level organization in Moscow with the creation of the Central Staff of the Partisan Movement.

The net military effect of partisan operations is open to debate. Partisan contributions occasionally were significant, but never decisive. Partisan attacks succeeded in harassing and sometimes temporarily impeding German movement and communications in the rear areas, yet failed to inflict any fundamental disruption. The most successful type of partisan operation came on those occasions where full-scale offensives were launched behind German lines and closely coordinated in immediate support of Red Army attacks.

From July to August 1943, the central staff ordered the partisan "War on the Rail Tracks" immediately prior to and during the Soviet counteroffensives at the Orel and Bielgorod-Kharkov shoulders of the Kursk (q.v.) salient. The partisans conducted thousands of demolition attacks, well-timed with the Red Army offensive. The results, however, were disappointing. The attacks were widely dispersed, with many falling against secondary rail lines. The main trunk lines, while damaged, remained operational. One year later, the partisan railroad war was continued on a similar scale; this time in conjunction with Operation BAGRATION, the Red Army's Byelorussian offensive (q.v.) launched in June 1944.

The increased size and organization of partisan units beginning in 1942 proved a two-edged sword. The small local units, always short of ammunition and supplies, wore down under the weight of their own operations, or simply fell apart internally. The larger, more successful units, were easier for the Germans to hunt down and destroy; they made bigger targets.

If tangible military success proved elusive to the partisans, they nonetheless achieved a certain level of political control in the German rear areas. By virtue of the partisan presence, most of the German-occupied areas were never wholly absent of Soviet authority to some degree. In areas under partisan control, the Soviet system, to include a party administration and even collective farms, was preserved. Localized partisan ruling bodies, known as *Orgtroikas,* were established as tripartite groupings of party, government, and NKVD members. The *Orgtroikas* provided continuity of Soviet presence and authority in the occupied areas, and the infrastructure for the reimposition of Soviet political organization in the reconquered lands.

Stephen Donahue

Additional Reading

Armstrong, John A. (ed.), *Soviet Partisans in World War II* (1964).

Howell, Edgar M., *The Soviet Partisan Movement, 1941–1944* (1957).

Munoz, Antonio, J., *The Kaminski Brigade: A History* (1995).

Partisans, Yugoslavian

At the outset of the German invasion of Yugoslavia, Tito (qq.v.), the leader of the Communist partisan resistance group, immediately began to unite his forces for war. He trained men from all over the country, then sent them back to their local areas to lead the fight against the Germans. They were instructed not to engage superior forces and to save every injured man possible. This strategy seemed to work in the beginning and the partisans actually wrested control of large portions of Serbia from the Germans.

When negotiations stalled and broke off with the other Yugoslav resistance group, the Četniks (q.v.), Tito transformed his guerrilla band into a well-trained and disciplined army, with training schools and even a naval detachment. With the help of the British, he built twenty-three brigades of 3,000 to 4,000 troops each, and fought off five German offensives.

In light of this success, British prime minister Winston S. Churchill (q.v.) requested to meet with Tito to discuss future operations. Churchill wanted to conduct British operations from Yugo-slavia. Tito rejected that and even went so far as to say that he would resist the Allies by force if necessary. Tito's rebuff, coming only three months after the Allies had supported the partisans with 1,000 air support sorties, infuriated Churchill, who came to regret his support of the partisans.

Although the Soviet Union never offered aid to Tito's forces, the Soviets were invited to enter Yugoslavia. Soviet Marshal Fyodor Tolbukhin (q.v.) entered Belgrade with partisan assistance, and along with the partisans, fought to take back the country by breaking the back of the 350,000-strong German Army Group E under General Alexander Löhr (q.v.). By the end of August 1944, the Germans were in full retreat.

James Lussier

Additional Reading

Brown, Alec, *Mihailovich and Yugoslav Resistance* (1943).

Davidson, Basil, *Partisan Picture* (1945).

Lindsay, Franklin, *Beacons in the Night: With the OSS and Tito's Partisans in Wartime Yugoslavia* (1995).

Political Warfare Executive (PWE)

The PWE was formed in August 1941 from portions of the BBC (q.v.), Ministry of Information, and SO1 of the Special Operations Executive (SOE) (q.v.) to conduct psychological warfare against enemy military and civilian populations to destroy their morale and will to resist. The British considered such activities the "fourth arm" of warfare. The PWE carried out "white" (overt) and "black" (covert) operations against enemy and enemy occupied nations worldwide.

PWE helped produce BBC overt radio broadcasts and delivered its own clandestine programs from transmitters erected at its country base at Woburn Abbey south of London. The organization also produced "white" and "black" propaganda leaflets, forgeries, posters, pamphlets, and small gadgets. The Royal Air Force distributed the majority of PWE items to enemy civilian and military populations, but significant quantities were also distributed by SOE agents and resistance groups.

General Sir Robert Bruce Lockhart served as PWE director, assisted by Major General Dallas Brooks. Lockhart was a member of the Foreign Office and had direct access to the prime minister, foreign secretary, and chiefs of staff on all psychological warfare matters. The organization's 530 civilian and military personnel consisted of Britons and refugees from every European nation, and were divided into geographic departments according to their talents or expert knowledge of an enemy or enemy occupied country, its culture, or people. The varied mission of the organization was reflected in its diverse and rather odd membership that represented numerous cultures and peacetime professions. PWE members served in all Allied psychological warfare divisions that were combined Anglo-American commands in Europe, Asia, and the Pacific.

Clayton D. Laurie

Additional Reading
Cruickshank, Charles G., *The Fourth Arm: Psychological Warfare, 1938–1945* (1977).
Nicholas, Elizabeth, *Death Be Not Proud* (1973).

P

R

RAF

See AIR FORCE, BRITISH

Rangers

In the spring of 1942, U.S. Army Chief of Staff General George C. Marshall sent Colonel Lucian K. Truscott, Jr. (qq.v.) to London to coordinate the participation of American troops in British commando (q.v.) raids against German-occupied Europe. On 26 May, Truscott proposed to Marshall that because the American forces would be under British control, they should be organized along commando lines. This suggestion was approved and Major General Russell Hartle, commanding general of the United States Army Northern Ireland Forces, was instructed to organize the new unit as soon as possible.

The new unit would be battalion-size and would be filled by the best quality soldiers. Emphasis was placed on leadership, physical fitness, patrolling, marksmanship, demolitions, small boat handling, and mountaineering. Hartle selected William O. Darby (q.v.), a field artillery captain, to lead the unit.

Major General Dwight D. Eisenhower (q.v.), then chief of the Operations Division of the U.S. War Department general staff, told Truscott he felt the unit should be called something other than "commandos" because the name was so clearly identified with the British. Truscott chose the name "rangers," which was associated with special American units that fought before, during, and after the American Revolution, particularly the famous ranger force of Robert Rogers. Thus, on 19 June 1942, Darby activated the 1st Ranger Battalion at Carrickfergus, Northern Ireland.

Beginning 1 August, six officers and fifty-five enlisted rangers were attached to Numbers 3 and 4 Commandos and the Canadian 2nd Division for the raid on Dieppe (q.v.). The ill-fated landing took place on 19 August, with the U.S. Rangers suffering six killed and four captured. Because of the broadening scope of the war, Dieppe proved to be the only operation in which the U.S. Rangers fought under control of the British. Instead of being deactivated, however, the rangers were retained as an American version of the commandos.

Throughout World War II, six ranger battalions were activated with the 6th Battalion operating in the Pacific. The 1st Battalion participated in the initial Northwest Africa landings at Arzeu, Algeria, and in the Tunisian battles. The 1st, 3rd, and 4th Battalions combined as the ranger force to spearhead the landings at Gela and Licata, during the invasion of Sicily, and at Salerno and Anzio (qq.v.). The 2nd and 5th Battalions participated in the D-Day landings at OMAHA Beach, with Companies D, E, and F of the 2nd Battalion capturing the gun emplacements at Pointe du Hoc.

Throughout these diverse operations, the rangers suffered from not having their own separate headquarters. The missions of the individual battalions were dictated by the various headquarters to which they were assigned or attached. While some commanders used the rangers in accordance with their special skills, others did not. The most telling example occurred at Cisterna during the Anzio operation, where the 1st and 3rd Battalions were committed as conventional infantry and suffered 761 killed or captured out of 767 committed.

The efficiency of the rangers was also degraded through heavy casualties, who were replaced by soldiers who had not benefited from the extensive training of the original rangers. Thus, toward the end of the war, the battalions lacked the cohesion and training they had earlier enjoyed. With the rapid demobilization following the war, the rangers were inactivated. They were reactivated in the early 1950s, and have since formed part of the U.S. special operations forces.

Kevin Dougherty

Additional Reading

Darby, William O., and William H. Baumer, *Darby's Rangers: We Led the Way* (1980).

Fergusson, Bernard, *The Watery Maze: The Story of Combined Operations* (1961).

Ladd, James, *Commandos and Rangers of World War II* (1978).

Red Cross

The International Red Cross was active in alleviating the distress of World War II victims—both military and civilian—and in initiating postwar, international, humanitarian law reforms. Founded in 1863 by Henri Dunant, who was shocked at the nonexistent medical care for the wounded at the battle of Solferino, the International Red Cross's purpose in war is to relieve physical suffering of war victims.

In World War II, the Red Cross's membership consisted of independent states. Delegates agreed to provide aid for war casualties, acknowledging that the voluntary medical corps would be protected as neutrals and no political distinctions would be made between soldiers requiring medical care.

The devastating total war aspect of World War II stimulated the Red Cross's demand for the legalization of international humanitarian codes, especially concerning the civilian population. The World War II activities of the Red Cross were called the third front, or the humanitarian front. Previous diplomatic conventions concerning war victims were ineffectual, and several nations refused to allow Red Cross volunteers to minister the sick and wounded (especially in the Soviet Union and Asian countries).

The European and American public did not wholly endorse international relief organizations at the outbreak of World War II, making it difficult for these organizations to receive sufficient financial and political support. Sentiments changed as the war escalated, and by 1944, American membership reached 36 million. Women volunteers staffed Red Cross facilities on the home front, and patriotic Americans readily gave donations.

At field, base, and ship hospitals, thousands of volunteers tried to mitigate the catastrophic wartime circumstances. Red Cross volunteers, at home and abroad, prepared care packages with necessities and comforts such as food, blankets, books, pencils and paper, and tobacco for distribution to soldiers, prisoners, convalescents, and civilians. In the camps, volunteers offered doughnuts, refreshments, and entertainment, such as playing records on phonographs and dancing, for war-weary soldiers.

Red Cross personnel also policed maintenance of prisoners of war. The 1929 Geneva Convention stipulated that Red Cross inspectors could visit prison camps and inspect the prisoners. The Red Cross inspectors recorded prisoners' names and serial numbers for the Red Cross's Central Tracing Agency in Geneva, so that family members could contact the prisoners and learn of their location and condition.

The Red Cross staff ensured that prisoners received comforts and medical care. In countries that had not signed the Geneva Convention, such as the Soviet Union, Red Cross officials were not permitted to examine the camps or regulate guard treatment of prisoners. Conversely, nearly five-sixths of the Soviet prisoners held by Axis captors suffered because they were not provided Red Cross protection. In the spring of 1945, Red Cross workers were able, on occasion, to visit concentration camp victims, removing some of the sickest and most infirm to neutral countries. Red Cross packages and personal messages and letters from home were delivered to as many people as possible, including prisoners, soldiers, and internees.

During World War II, the Red Cross was the only liaison between the belligerent powers. Max Huber, president of the Red Cross during World War II, asserted that the Red Cross's mission was "to improve the rules of the law of nations safeguarding humanitarian interests in time of war." While Red Cross members repatriated wounded and sick prisoners of war, Huber initiated diplomatic talks among interested nations, discussing problems exemplified by the war.

After and as a reaction to World War II, the first drafts of the 1949 Geneva Convention, known as the "Law of the Red Cross," emphasized these crucial points. The most prominent article stated that an impartial humanitarian body, understood to be the Red Cross, would serve as neutral volunteers to care for wounded soldiers in future conflicts. The document specified hospital zones and hygienic conditions for prisoners of war, and conditions for repatriation of prisoners with diseases or bodily losses (arms, legs, digits).

The rights of civilians were put into print for the first time. More importantly, the convention guaranteed: the rights of family communication (when separated); adequate supply of food, clothing, and shelter; the right to maintain local culture

R

and public officials; the prohibition of torture and hostages; the opportunity of employment; and the maintenance of civilian hospitals.

Although it was a neutral intermediary, the Red Cross was influential in establishing guidelines for the conduct of war, humanizing it as much as possible. The Red Cross, however, could only negotiate with countries as a mediator for humanity; it could not enforce laws. As a result, many of its humanitarian efforts were failures. The Red Cross developed legal bases to apply during war and educated the public and governments about human rights. As a result of his work as an international humanitarian, Max Huber was awarded the Nobel Peace Prize in 1945.

Elizabeth O. Schafer

Additional Reading

Durand, Andre, *From Sarajevo to Hiroshima: History of the International Committee of the Red Cross* (1984).

Korson, George G., *At His Side: The Story of the American Red Cross Overseas in World War II* (1945).

A British Tommy and three GIs play a game of snooker in a Red Cross Club at a replacement center "somewhere in Britain." (IWM EA 9011)

Red Orchestra

Known in German as *Die Rote Kapelle,* the Soviet's Red Orchestra was one of the most successful intelligence networks in World War II. The chief of a spy network, in the jargon of the German secret service, was known as a *Kapellmeister* or orchestra leader. In this jargon, a soloist of major importance was the "pianist" or radio operator playing on his lonely radio transmitter, known as a music box. Many such operators constituted an orchestra.

Under the brilliant direction of Leopold Trepper (q.v.) a Polish Jew, the network controlled informers, agents, and operations throughout Nazi-occupied Europe. The network was set up during the 1930s and was ready to go into action as soon as the war started and the Soviet regular network of NKVD (q.v.) agents was ousted from the country.

Trepper penetrated the very heart of the German General Staff (q.v.) so successfully that German operational plans, in the words of Giles Perault, "were in the hands of the Russians even before they had reached the German commanders at the front." Even such a critical historian as David Dallin wrote: "Seen in historical perspective the apparat . . . gave a performance that was remarkable and unique . . . Never before had espionage played as prominent a role in wartime as it did for the Soviet Union in 1941–44." Heinrich Himmler (q.v.) stated that the Red Orchestra "cost Germany 200,000 soldiers." After interviewing Trepper, Himmler stated that everything the Germans knew about spying was obsolete.

The Red Orchestra had many operating cells throughout Europe, but one of the most interesting and effective was operated in Berlin by Lieutenant Harro Schultze-Boysen and Arvid Harnack. Some writers consider Schultze-Boysen the "greatest spy of all time." Their beautiful wives, Mildred (Fish) Harnack, an American from Milwaukee, and Libertas Schultze-Boysen were used to sexually attract young officers to serve as agents. Libertas was described by *Gestapo* (q.v.) officials as being "disturbingly beautiful." Investigators were forbidden from interrogating her alone for fear they would succumb to her charms.

The Schultze-Boysen/Harnack group was discovered and its members executed in the Berlin-Plotzensee prison on 19 February 1943, the women by guillotine, the men by hanging. The last words of the emaciated and prematurely grey Mildred Harnack before her decapitation were: "And I loved this country so much." Libertas Schultze-Boysen screamed: "Let me keep my young life."

Trepper tried mightily to alert Soviet premier Josef Stalin (q.v.) to the German buildup and the pending invasion of the Soviet Union in June 1941. At least two of Trepper's reports were shown to Stalin, who admitted Trepper previously had sent valuable information. Stalin, however, questioned how Trepper "failed to detect at once that this was a crude piece of British propaganda." Only after the initial debacle during the invasion was Stalin willing to believe intelligence information by his own agents.

Paul J. Rose

Additional Reading

Accoce, Pierre, and Pierre Quet, *The Lucy Ring* (1967).
Boysen, Elsa, *Harro Schultze-Boysen* (1967).
Höhne, Heinz, *CODE-WORD: DIRECTOR, The Story of the Red Orchestra* (1970).
Tarrant, V.E., *The Red Orchestra; The Soviet Spy Network Inside Nazi Europe* (1995).

Reichssicherheitshauptamt (RSHA)

The *Reichssicherheitshauptamt* (Main Security Office of the *Reich*) was one of the greatest terror organizations that ever existed. Established by Heinrich Himmler (q.v.) one month after the start of World War II, the RSHA under Reinhard Heydrich and later Ernst Kaltenbrunner (qq.v.) united the most powerful police forces in Nazi Germany: the *Sipo* or Security Police (which included the *Gestapo* (q.v.) or Secret Police, and the *Krips* or Criminal Police), and the SD (q.v.). The only major police units not included in the RSHA were the regular or uniformed patrolmen *(Orpo),* under Kurt Daluege (q.v.), which constituted yet another division of the SS (q.v.).

The formal organization of the RSHA comprised seven main departments, two of which were mixed *Sipo/* SD and responsible for administration. The next two were the former *Sipo* agencies, the *Gestapo* and Criminal Police, and the last three were the former SD offices (German spheres of life under Otto Ohlendorf, foreign intelligence under Walter Schellenberg [q.v.], and ideological intelligence under Franz Six). In other words, the only offices to be truly amalgamated were the first two; the remaining departments retained their previous identity.

Some historians have gone so far as to claim that the RSHA really was nothing new, as all its component parts were already under Heydrich before 1939. In any case, a good deal of tension existed between the operational departments of the

RSHA, especially between the three SD departments and the *Gestapo.*

The RSHA had a myriad of duties. The *Gestapo* and *Kripo* continued to be responsible for internal security, broadly interpreted, and the three SD departments of the RSHA also performed their previous duties while expanding some of them. Ohlendorf increased his investigations into all aspects of German life, at least until he was throttled by Joseph Goebbels (q.v.) and others in 1944.

The foreign intelligence department even took over the *Abwehr* (q.v.) in 1944, although it was a hollow victory. Following the *Wehrmacht* conquests of Poland, Norway, Denmark, France (qq.v.) and other countries, the *Gestapo* assumed responsibility for security and for activities related to the Holocaust (q.v.) in those countries. In addition, SD members of the *Gestapo* and Criminal Police were the backbone of the SD-led Special Action Groups (*Einsatzgruppen,* q.v.) in Poland and the Soviet Union, whose job it was to round up and murder the eastern "enemies" of the Third *Reich:* Jews, priests, Red Army commissars, Jehovah's Witnesses, Gypsies, and others.

The size of the RSHA remains controversial. Reliable estimates for the *Gestapo* and Criminal Police are available, but the same is not true for the SD. Estimates for the SD are "extremely difficult" to come by because the SD was composed of three categories of officer: full-time, salaried officials; part-time, unsalaried men; and clandestine members.

In addition, although the three branches of the RSHA (*Gestapo, Kripo,* and SD) kept their identities, several thousand members of the *Gestapo* and of the Criminal Police were also members of the SD. The following are estimates of the RSHA at its peak: *Gestapo,* 32,000–35,000; Criminal Police, 15,000–20,000; SD, more than 7,000; and other "attached personnel" including the *Einsatzgruppen,* 21,000. These totals exclude the "clandestine" members of the SD like the "V-men" (trusted informers).

Jon Moulton

Additional Reading

Browder, George C., *Foundations of the Nazi Police State: The Formation of Sipo and SD* (1990).
Delarue, Jacques, *The History of the Gestapo* (1964).
Höhne, Heinz, *The Order of the Death's Head* (1970).

ROA

See RUSSIAN LIBERATION ARMY

Royal Marines

Britain's Royal Marines (RM) entered World War II with little doctrinal preparedness beyond the traditional roles of sea soldiers. By the end of the conflict, the RM performed a variety of roles and created a solid basis for the role of commando troops in the postwar period.

The interwar years saw the RM performing their accustomed duties of ships' guards/gunnery parties/ad hoc intervention forces. There was some study of and experimentation with formations similar to the U.S. Marine Corps advanced base forces, ultimately resulting in the Mobile Naval Base Defence Organization (MNBDO). The MNBDO was heavy in coast defense and antiaircraft guns and was thus not geared to seize territory.

With the outbreak of war, the 12,400–man Royal Marines continued their traditional duties aboard British capital ships. Both the Norway campaign and the Battle of France (qq.v.) saw the participation of various RM units. The only campaign in which a MNBDO saw action was the ill-fated British defense of Crete (q.v.) in May 1940.

With Britain totally ejected from Europe, Prime Minister Winston S. Churchill (q.v.) pressed for the establishment of a combined operations headquarters that would coordinate the British armed forces' efforts to provide forcible entry along enemy-held coasts. Royal Marines, along with army formations, began to develop a variety of units for amphibious operations: commando troops, landing ship and amphibian operators, fire support, special boat missions, beach parties, coastal and antiaircraft artillery, etc.

From 1941 to 1943, there was an RM division, but it was eventually seen as redundant to the army's efforts and that a better contribution would be made in concentrating on smaller amphibious-related tasks. Thus, the division and MNBDO assets were assigned to fulfilling the corps' other missions.

RM units participated in most of the major landings in the European theater, in addition to a large number of commando raids and the Rhine crossings. Throughout the conflict, the RM continued its traditional duties aboard capital ships and in various gunnery roles. One of the more unusual assignments was the manning of antiaircraft guns on "HM Ship Forts" (similar to oil-rig platforms) in the Thames estuary. The male marines were supplemented by the "Marens" of the Women's Royal Navy Service (*see* WRNS). Casualties numbered approximately 2,500 killed and 3,000 wounded.

Michael E. Unsworth

Additional Reading

Gladd, James D., *The Royal Marines, 1919–1980* (1980).

Lockhart, Sir Robert H.B., *The Marines Were There: The Story of the Royal Marines in the Second World War* (1973).

RSHA

See R<small>EICHSSICHERHEITSHAUPTAMT</small>

Russian Liberation Army (*Russkaia Osvoboditel'naia Armiia* [ROA])

Throughout centuries of warfare, soldiers have fought for governments and countries not their own, but without parallel in modern times was military service by non-Germans in the German service in World War II. Large numbers served in the *Waffen-SS* (q.v.). On an incredibly larger scale, however, was military or paramilitary service by perhaps a million Soviets of various nationalities in the *Wehrmacht* as auxiliaries *(Hilfswillige),* later called "volunteers" and mixed into German units. Spontaneously, separate formations of Eastern European troops emerged, ranging in size from company to brigade strength. Many of them only nominally under German command. Eastern legions were units based on specific nationalities.

The first phases of the war in the Soviet Union brought into German custody millions of Soviet soldiers. German authorities selected individuals as early as July 1941. In December 1941, the first larger units were put together from Soviet prisoners of war. Because conditions in POW camps and the roads leading to them were genocidal at worst and brutal at best, recruitment was made easier by promises of rations and decent treatment.

Apart from sheer survival, other factors were important in this transfer of allegiance. There was the memory of how they or their families and friends were treated during the forced collectivization, industrialization, and terror campaigns unleashed by Soviet premier Josef Stalin (q.v.) in the 1930s. Furthermore, the Soviet government did not recognize POW status for its soldiers, and it had not signed the Geneva Convention. Imprisonment by the enemy was tantamount to desertion and treason. The average Soviet soldier was deemed expendable on the front as well as in prison camp.

Although the rights, rations, and treatment of the peoples of Eastern Europe improved gradually, service was difficult. German chancellor Adolf

Hitler (q.v.) and his henchmen were convinced that victory was theirs. Assistance offered by "inferior people" against other inferior people was not needed. Hitler planned for *Lebensraum* (q.v.) through a policy of domination, organization, and plunder of Eastern Europe. How could various Soviet peoples dare hope of establishing autonomous or independent political entities? Only on the fringes of the Nazi regime was there opposition to such schemes. Yet, despite these biases, eventually several million *Untermenschen* (subhumans, as the Nazis called them) worked for the Nazi regime, which was incapable of waging a genuine war of liberation.

Gradually, Russians as well as many Germans concluded that the Soviet Union could be defeated only by Russians. What was needed was a leader, a "Russian de Gaulle," who could be used by Germany. He was found in Lieutenant General Andrei Andreevich Vlasov (q.v.), who was captured in July 1942 on the Volkhov front. Vlasov, by now profoundly and genuinely hostile to Stalin's regime, wanted to use Germany to build an independent and federated Russian state after defeating Bolshevism. Both sides wanted to exploit each other; the Nazi regime was in a much better position to do so.

Only after the tide of war had turned dramatically and defeat was staring Germany in the eye, did Hitler, on the urging of Heinrich Himmler (q.v.), authorize an anti-Soviet movement, the Committee for the Liberation of the Peoples of Russia (KONR). The committee's armed forces were popularly known as Russian Liberation Army (ROA). Both the committee and its army were led by Vlasov. This movement was the most important so far. Although doomed to fail, the committee issued a remarkably independent and futuristic document, the Prague Manifesto.

Advanced planning allowed the ROA to develop quickly into a limited but credible force after January 1945. It contained not only Eastern European troops, but also recruits from POW and labor camps. The ROA had a complete staff, two divisions, a reserve brigade, and an antitank brigade. A third division was planned. A small air force was also authorized and partially equipped. Eventually, several Cossack units were attached to the ROA, doubling its size on paper to 100,000 men. Almost all officers were former Red Army officers, for whom there was a training school. Although dependent at first on Germany for rations and equipment, the ROA became independent in the final weeks of the war.

The first ROA division of about 20,000 men transferred to the Oder front, where it saw limited but inconclusive action against Red Army units. Because Vlasov believed that Germany had already lost the war, he and his commanders had no intention of being drawn into futile fighting. The decision was made against German threats to withdraw the entire ROA into Austria or Bohemia; survival was now what mattered. Many officers believed they might still have the opportunity to continue fighting Stalin's regime on the side of the Western Allies—a desperate misunderstanding they shared with many of their German colleagues. The West, as well as Stalin, saw KONR and its army as Nazi collaborators.

In Bohemia, the ROA was straddled precariously between the retreating German forces and the rapidly advancing Allied armies. With the bulk of the division stationed near Prague, the ROA supported the Prague uprising in a demonstration of its opposition to Nazi Germany—and to ingratiate itself with Czechs and the Western Allies. The Czech National Committee, wanting to liberate Prague from German control, was placed in a political bind because the Allies had already decided that the Red Army would enter Prague. Thus, the ROA was forced to move westward toward the U.S. Army with whom some senior officers were negotiating terms of surrender. In the meantime, the remaining ROA forces were moving from southern Germany into southern Bohemia.

On 12 May 1945, after several units managed to cross American lines, the Allies effectively dissolved the ROA. Vlasov and most of the men and officers were captured by or handed over to the Red Army. The higher-ranking officers were tried in Moscow for treason and collaboration with the enemy and executed in 1946. The Soviet regime could not admit that its opponents might have been driven by quite patriotic motives. The lesser ranks disappeared into the *Gulag,* from which most survivors emerged after the amnesty of 1955.

World War II was a traumatic test of survival for the Soviet state and the socioeconomic and political foundations upon which it rested. The attitudes and actions of millions of its citizens raised fundamental questions about the Communist regime and the depth of disaffection in Soviet society.

N.H. Gaworek

Additional Reading

Andreev, Catherine, *Vlasov and the Russian Liberation Movement: Soviet Reality and Émigré Theories* (1987).

Hoffmann, Joachim, *Die Geschichte der Wlassow-Armee* (1984).

Newland, Samuel J., *Cossacks in the German Army, 1941–1945* (1990).

S

SA

See STURMABTEILUNG

SAS

See SPECIAL AIR SERVICE

SBS

See SPECIAL BOAT SECTION

Schutzstaffel SS

Schutzstaffel means literally "guard staff" or "protective guard." It is sometimes translated "elite guard," but the SS is often referred to simply as the Black Shirts.

The SS was the most important and the most typical of all Nazi institutions. It showed the real face of the regime: tendencies only partially visible in other Nazi organizations were most fully developed in the SS. It institutionalized the essence of the Nazi regime, namely its totalitarian terror. It was responsible for the murder of more than five million Jews and approximately eight million non-Jews: Poles, Russians, Gypsies, Jehovah's Witnesses, asocials, and members of any other group classified by the Nazis as an enemy. In addition, it was responsible for killing some 70,000 Germans declared incurably ill or insane in the so-called euthanasia program.

The SS was founded in 1925 as an elite force within the SA (q.v.). Originally Adolf Hitler's (q.v.) personal bodyguard, it grew in stages. The General SS *(Allgemeine-SS)* was formed in the late 1920s. It combined several functions: it was the SS's personnel pool, and also that part of the SS where honorary members joined. These members could wear the honorary members' badge and more im-

portantly, were left alone by the SS. They had no duties and performed no services beyond contributing to the SS's coffers. For a time it was prestigious to belong. Heinrich Himmler (q.v.) solicited members from among the German elite, especially industrialists. This was his means of expanding SS influence into the most important sectors of German society.

Only in 1929 did Himmler become head of the SS with the rather grandiose title of *Reich* Leader SS. Called by some a school teacher because of his pedantic manner, he proved to be a gifted organizer. He established so many agencies that the SS is sometimes called the octopus. In 1931, he created the SD (q.v.) or Security Service. It was the Nazi party's intelligence-gathering arm, first within the SS and the party, later within the *Reich,* and eventually in territories under Nazi control. The first head of the SD and its guiding hand until 1942 was Reinhard Heydrich (q.v.). Assassinated by Czech partisans in Prague, he was replaced by Ernst Kaltenbrunner (q.v.), an Austrian ex-Catholic like Hitler.

In 1933, a full-time headquarters guard *(Leibstandarte Adolf Hitler)* was established. The first concentration camp guards were also recruited and trained. These were the early "Death's Head" units; their training has been called an education in sadism. Himmler's single most important activity in the months following the "seizure of power" was to absorb the political police in one German state after another. By the spring of 1934, he took over all of them except the Prussian. Then, on 20 April 1934, Himmler gained control of the Prussian political police, or *Gestapo* (q.v.), as well.

Hermann Göring (q.v.) created the *Gestapo* in April 1933 out of the Prussian political police of the Weimar period. Its function from 1919 to 1933 had been defensive: to combat acts against the state such as treason. To that end it had the right to detain and incarcerate political opponents. After 1933, the *Gestapo's* functions turned offensive: to promote the ideological goals of the Third *Reich*. To do that it expanded the powers formerly exercised by the Weimar political police, especially "protective custody" *Schutzhaft,* which eliminated the courts as a source of protection for the arrested. Göring added another twist in Prussia: following Himmler's lead in Bavaria, he set up the concentration camps.

The *Gestapo,* which had been part of the government of Prussia before 20 April 1934, became part of the SS. Göring relinquished control of the *Gestapo* somewhat reluctantly. One of his motives was to enlist Himmler's help in eliminating Ernst Röhm (q.v.) and other SA leaders in June. Then, on 26 July 1934, following the Röhm purge (*see* Night of the Long Knives), Hitler broke the SS out of the SA, making it an independent Nazi Party organ. This was Himmler's reward for services rendered. Himmler achieved real power with Röhm's purge.

In 1936, Hitler appointed Himmler chief of all German police forces. This was a critical decision, for it meant the merger of the regular uniformed police (the order police or *Orpo: Ordnungspolizei*), and the criminal police or detectives *(Kripo: Kriminalpolizei)* with the SS. Thereafter, Germany found itself in the unusual position for a European state of having its police forces under the control of a party organ and not part of a governmental agency like the Ministry of the Interior. The resulting confusion of party and state organs was undoubtedly a conscious move on Hitler's part. By June 1938, most high-ranking *Gestapo, Kripo,* and *Orpo* officers were given equivalent SS rank. The government picked up the tab for all the police forces and most parts of the SS. The SD was an exception as its budget was always covered by the party treasurer.

The *Waffen-* or Armed SS was another branch of the SS. It got its real start in the late 1930s. It expanded rapidly under Himmler's tutelage, reaching 50,000 men in 1939, 594,000 in June 1944, and 910,000 at its peak in the autumn of 1944. All *Waffen-SS* (q.v.) units that participated in World War II were integrated into the *Wehrmacht* chain of command. In many cases more fanatical than regular army divisions, they were among the most highly decorated military formations on the German side in the war. On the other hand, they were responsible for many violations of the law of land warfare. The *Wehrmacht* generally distrusted the *Waffen-SS.* There is some indication that the army high command (OKH) purposely sent SS units to do some of the nastiest fighting with the expectation they would be decimated, and many were.

In 1939, Hitler authorized the creation within the SS of the *Reich* Security Main Office or RSHA (q.v.), with Heydrich as its first head. This new office merged the political police *(Gestapo)* and the criminal police *(Kripo)* into a new formation, the Security Police *(Sicherheitspolizei or Sipo).* The Security Service (SD) was also a part of the RSHA. In time, RSHA absorbed all political intelligence-gathering functions. More importantly, it became one of the greatest terror machines in history.

The notorious *Einsatzgruppen* (q.v.) in Russia operated out of the RSHA. So, too, did Adolf Eichmann (q.v.). His "desk" in the *Gestapo* was responsible for the deportation of millions of Jews from all over Nazi-occupied Europe to the death camps in Poland (*see* Concentration Camps). These camps were run by yet another branch of the SS, the Main Economic and Administration Office or WVHA, whose head was Oswald Pohl (q.v.).

The concentration camps were of two general types, the regular concentration camps and the extermination camps. Prisoners were sent to regular camps like Ravensbrück and Dachau if the official intent was to keep them alive. Even so, many died there. Prisoners were sent to extermination camps like Auschwitz and Treblinka if they were members of a racial or other group slated for destruction. Later in the war, some of these unfortunates were spared in order to work for the SS as virtual slaves.

Due to this slave labor, the WVHA gained great economic power during the war, both in Germany and in the occupied countries. At one point, six million prisoners were being used for labor. From Bordeaux to the Ukraine, men and women were arrested and shipped off to Poland or Germany as slave laborers. German industry, desperate for workers, set up factories near the concentration camps and paid the SS sub-minimal wages for the use of camp prisoners.

After the war began, the WVHA often confiscated and then expanded businesses in conquered lands: armaments works, quarries, construction firms, shoe factories, soft drink and mineral water plants, building materials companies, etc., all were incorporated into the SS. Large sums of money were involved. Occasionally there was graft, but if detected, Himmler dealt with it severely. He promised the death penalty for any SS man found guilty of corruption by an SS court.

There is one famous case in this regard, that

A formation of SS trumpeters. (IWM HU 28425)

of Karl Koch, an SS colonel in charge of the Buchenwald concentration camp, near Weimar. One of Himmler's inspectors, Konrad Morgen, happened upon what looked like a case of graft there and decided to pursue it. Morgen obtained Himmler's approval for his investigations and for Koch's later trial. The result was that the commandant of Buchenwald was eventually convicted by an SS court and executed.

During the war, SS officials became rulers of

occupied territories in Czechoslovakia, Poland, and Russia. Himmler acquired the title RKFVD (*Reich* Commissioner for the Strengthening of Germanism), giving him broad and vague powers. "Higher SS and Police Leaders" (HSSPF), police commanders in charge of the security forces in occupied lands and nominally subordinate to the civil administrators like Hans Frank (q.v.) in the General Government of Poland (q.v.), became feudal barons. They reported to RSHA headquarters.

Hitler, typically, authorized the establishment of a number of conflicting governmental bodies in the eastern areas conquered by the *Wehrmacht,* like Alfred Rosenberg's (q.v.) *Reich* Ministry for Eastern Territories. The *Wehrmacht* also had responsibility for portions of these areas. The result was overlapping jurisdictions and struggles between the contending parties who usually worked at cross-purposes. The SS often won these struggles. It had control of information and could accuse Rosenberg and army officers of being squeamish. Being squeamish was anathema to Himmler and the SS, who fancied themselves as being tough. Hitler appreciated the hard line taken by the SS and often supported Himmler in interagency disputes.

What were some of the main characteristics of the SS? Its ideology was an extreme version of Nazism, which meant there was not much to it. Its main tenets were racism and a perverted form of social Darwinism. Many SS members were racial fanatics who talked constantly about "pure" and "corrupted" blood. Race was a constant preoccupation of Himmler. Himmler touted his SS as an elite of Aryan blood. The idea of a racial aristocracy attracted some members of the middle and upper classes.

Related ideals of "hardness" and "realism" appealed to many World War I veterans. All applicants for membership in the Black Shirts had to be of good "Aryan" stock. In the beginning, Himmler personally went over every applicant's photo with a magnifying glass trying to spot any features that might indicate racial impurity. In the early years, candidates had to supply proof of "Aryan" descent from 1750 on. Periodically during the war, however, this and other race requirements were relaxed. Tracing one's family records was usually possible due to excellent records kept by the German states, municipalities, and churches. "Family researchers" would help trace ancestors, for a fee. Several high SS officers had their racial purity questioned. This was especially true of Heydrich, but extended to Himmler and even to Hitler himself. SS men were allowed to marry only after receiving approval from the Race and Resettlement Main Office (RuSHA), a sizable organization.

SS treatment of prisoners depended on their race. Norwegians were at the top as members of the Nordic race; Jews, Poles, Russians, Ukrainians, and "Red" Spaniards were at the bottom. In the concentration camps, dehumanization was practiced systematically. Poles, for example, were forced to kill their fellow Poles, Jews to kill Jews. They were given a cigarette for the job. The key to understanding the psychology of the SS is its cynicism in dealing with opponents of the Nazi regime.

The SS ideology was also decidedly anti-Christian. Many Nazi leaders were anti-Christian but were ambivalent about it, as the churches were conservative. However, within the SS there was a reversion to paganism, that is, to pre-Christian Germany, and some went so far as to invoke Woton. Before joining the SS, most applicants had to leave their church. Another facet of the SS ideology was its egalitarianism. Himmler's goal was the complete elimination of social class barriers within the SS. In that sense, the ideology was radically democratic. Ranks, however, were not eliminated. Quite the contrary. The SS was also characterized by its extreme militarism. The clearest examples of this are the *Einsatzgruppen* in the east and the *Waffen-SS.*

The power of the SS grew immensely during World War II due to the slave labor in the concentration camps, the RuSHA's activities, and the *Waffen-SS.* By 1943, the SS enjoyed a near monopoly of power inside Germany. Outside the *Reich* it shared power with the *Wehrmacht* and some civilian administrators like the *Reich* commissioner of the Ukraine or the governor general of Poland. Himmler continued to add titles to his already bloated stack. In August 1943, he was appointed minister of the interior. From then on he was no longer under the nominal control even of the former minister, Wilhelm Frick (q.v.).

Following the 20 July 1944 attempt on Hitler's life, the *Führer* made Himmler head of Germany's "Replacement Army." *Wehrmacht* officers were prominent among those who attempted to kill Hitler and he no longer trusted the traditional officer corps. *Waffen-SS* officers became generals of entire armies. In 1944, Himmler absorbed the *Wehrmacht's* intelligence arm, the *Abwehr.* The SS also infiltrated the civil service, including the judiciary, through the practice of honorary appointments to the SS. In other words, the SS began to swallow up parts of business, the governmental bureaucracy, and even the armed forces. SS leaders became industrial captains. A merging of elites occurred. SS terror became less and less restrained.

By 1940, the SS had emancipated itself from the Nazi Party. It was an organization related to, but not controlled by, the party. The process began in 1934 with the blood purge of Ernst Röhm and the SA. Because the SA had lost power in 1934, it was more truly a party organ than the SS. Nazi Germany is usually considered a police state. It was that in two senses: (l) it was the opposite of a *Rechtsstaat,* a state governed by law, and (2) the police, fused with the SS, became the most powerful of the ruling elites.

The police exercised power over both their obvious enemies and the other Nazi elites, who feared the SS. Even the *Wehrmacht* officer corps was apprehensive of the SS. The *Wehrmacht* seemed resigned to the fact that it would eventually be subordinate to the SS. SS plans for the postwar period included the elimination of the older, traditional German elites and their replacement with a new group of leaders based on race. The *Waffen-SS* would replace the *Wehrmacht.* The SS also would rule huge areas of land in the east, especially the Ukraine. It would supply the leaders of the thousand-year *Reich.*

Jon Moulton

Additional Reading

Browder, George C., *Foundations of the Nazi Police State* (1990).

Höhne, Heinz, *The Order of the Death's Head* (1970).

Koehl, Robert L., *The Black Corps* (1983).

SD

See SICHERHEITSDIENST

Secret Intelligence Service

See MI-6

SHAEF

See SUPREME HEADQUARTERS, ALLIED EXPEDITIONARY FORCE

Sicherheitsdienst (SD)

The *Sicherheitsdienst* (SD), or Security Service, was established by Heinrich Himmler (q.v.) in 1931 as the intelligence gathering and counterespionage organ of the Nazi Party's SS, with Reinhard Heydrich (qq.v.) as its head. To assist him after 1933, Heydrich attracted young men with academic degrees to the SD, men like Werner Best,

Otto Ohlendorf, and Walter Schellenberg (q.v.). They are often termed the SD intellectuals. Initially, the SD was one of many Nazi information services, but by June 1934, deputy party chief Rudolf Hess (q.v.) declared it to be the party's sole espionage agency. It still had competition from non-party services, such as the *Abwehr* and the Foreign Ministry's *Informationsstelle.*

By all accounts, the SD was one of the most complex of all the many SS organizations. As Browder points out, "the SD" didn't exist. Instead, the name was used interchangeably to refer to the "total SD," the "functional SD," or after 1939, to one of the three SD departments of the RSHA (q.v.). Each had a different self-image, mission, and often membership. The "total SD" consisted of men completely dedicated to the ideological goals of the regime, true believers who saw themselves as the elite of the elite. The "functional SD" was composed of men who worked in one of the three SD offices that became Departments III, VI and VII of the RSHA. Their self-image was that of scientific researchers, idealists who would serve the highest principles of the Third *Reich* and would act as its guide and conscience, and even as its loyal opposition.

The several missions of the SD led to a "crisis of identity" by the mid-1930s that was never overcome. From Himmler's point of view, the "schizophrenia" of the several SD divisions had certain advantages. He could give illegal orders to those who were both police and SD members and expect them to be carried out. In addition, SD men who needed an excuse for engaging in "dirty work" had one: they could rationalize their unpleasant activities as the exception to their normal, respectable duties.

The SD's multiple mission and organization also enabled it to recruit completely "different and incompatible types." Indeed, membership in the SD was extremely heterogeneous. Recruits included anyone from university professors to amoral opportunists, retired soldiers, policemen to rootless misfits. Some of the men were truly idealistic as they understood it, others were "radical enforcers" of the Hitler doctrine, with little concern for legal or moral matters.

In addition to its persistent identity crisis, the SD had to contend with two other problems throughout its existence. The first arose as a result of the absorption by the SS of the German political police between March 1933 and April 1934. Like the SD, *Gestapo* (q.v.) detectives were engaged in intelligence gathering and they were more skilled at it than the SD. In addition, there were many more *Gestapo* than SD agents. What then was the SD's *raison d'être* after 1934? In fact, *Gestapo* exercise of the domestic espionage function seems to a large extent to have rendered the SD superfluous.

In July 1937, Heydrich tried to clarify the missions of the *Gestapo* and the SD through his "functional order" *(Funktions-befehl)*. He allotted all executive tasks, including the pursuit of individual opponents of the regime, to the *Gestapo.* The SD, on the other hand, was relegated to identifying the ideological enemy, drafting reports on general conditions inside Germany—Otto Ohlendorf's remarkable "Reports from the Reich"—and a role in foreign intelligence. Heydrich's attempt at rationalizing SD and *Gestapo* functions was only partially successful. After 1937, the SD was reduced to an auxiliary of the *Gestapo,* and the two agencies retained overlapping jurisdictions.

The second major problem encountered by the SD resulted from its investigative mission. Beginning in 1933, SD spying aroused the ire of several *Gauleiter* and other high Nazis. They demanded the SD be disbanded. Himmler came to the SD's defense and was forced to promise some modest restraints, not always observed, on SD snooping into party matters.

Despite recurring rumors that the SD would be dissolved or assimilated by the *Gestapo,* it continued to exist. Himmler had several reasons for retaining it. He wanted to perpetuate the SD's monopoly as the movement's surveillance organ. He also wanted the SD as a political check on police officers retained by the new regime after 1933, many of whom were not party members. Also, the SD made it easier for the SS to integrate those members of the *Gestapo* and other police agencies who were not yet members of the Nazi Party or the SS. This was accomplished by strongly encouraging suitable members of the regular police (*Orpo*) and especially of the security police (*Sipo*) to become members of the SD.

Unlike some other SS branches, the SD remained a party body throughout the Third *Reich.* This meant that it was financed by the party, but party financing meant that the SD was chronically and persistently short of funds. Like the other problems, this one was never solved before the SD disintegrated at the end of the war.

Jon Moulton

Additional Reading

Browder, George C., *Foundations of the Nazi Police State: The Formation of Sipo and SD* (1990).

Buchheim, Hans, "The SS—Instrument of Domination," in Helmut Krausnick, et al., *Anatomy of the SS State* (1968).

Smersh

Smersh was the Soviet military counterintelligence organization from 1943 to 1946. The word *Smersh* was the acronym derived from the slogan, *"Smert' Shpionam"* (Death to Spies), and the colloquial Soviet reference to what was formally titled the Main Administration of Counterintelligence (GUKR) of the People's Commissariat for Defense (NKO).

Smersh evolved from the network of armed special departments (*Osobye otdely,* or OO) operated by the Soviet state security apparatus (*Cheka*) since July 1918. From their inception, the OOs were charged with an unequivocal mandate: ensure the absolute political loyalty of the Soviet armed forces to the Communist Party. The OOs were empowered with, and frequently exercised, the most draconian methods in "combating counterrevolution" within the military and enforcing the party's will.

Beginning in July 1941, during the height of the German offensive, the state security OOs, now part of the People's Commissariat of Internal Affairs (NKVD), engaged in vigorous reprisals against Red Army troops retreating from shattered Soviet front lines. Charges of spying, desertion, self-mutilation, "panic-mongering," and "abandoning weapons and battle stations," kept OO-NKVD execution squads very busy during that period.

In April 1943, the OOs were detached from the NKVD with the creation of the GUKR-NKO (*Smersh*). While ostensibly subordinated to the Soviet defense organs, *Smersh* in fact answered directly to the supreme Soviet wartime authority, the State Committee of Defense (GKO) chaired by Josef Stalin (q.v.). In making *Smersh* his personal instrument, Stalin outflanked both the NKO and the infamous NKVD chief, Lavrenty Beria (q.v.), in tightening his unqualified control over the military. A Stalin protege, Viktor Semenovich Abakumov, ex-boss of OO-NKVD, was installed as the chief of *Smersh.* Similarly, *Smersh* personnel of all ranks were drawn from the most politically dependable officers of the former OO-NKVD.

Smersh was organized along functional lines into "administrations." The First Administration was responsible for the detection and neutralization of dissent and "anti-Soviet" opposition within the military. Composed of regular "Chekists" culled from the NKVD, it saturated the military with operatives at every level.

The Second Administration (operations) collected intelligence and inserted agents behind enemy lines. It also combined with regular NKVD forces for rear-area security, and for security in the reconquered Soviet territories. These operations included mass arrests, deportations, and executions.

The Third Administration (intelligence) was responsible for intelligence collection, management, and dissemination throughout *Smersh*. Here, it operated closely with the Main Intelligence Administration (GRU) of the armed forces general staff.

The Fourth (investigative) and Fifth (tribunals) Administrations worked in tandem to investigate and prosecute those arrested on suspicion of anti-Soviet activity. Sentences pronounced by these tribunals, each of which consisted of three *Smersh* officers, were without appeal and swiftly carried out.

In May 1945, *Smersh* conducted a search through Berlin for members of the Nazi hierarchy, and claimed to have recovered the remains of Adolf Hitler and Joseph Goebbels (q.v.) in the garden of the *Reich* Chancellery.

In the years following the war, *Smersh* established vetting and screening commissions (PFK) in eastern and central Europe to process the massive influx of displaced Soviet citizens within the Soviet zones of occupation. This task included handling those returned by the Western Allies. Tens of thousands of Soviet nationals were forcibly repatriated into the arms of *Smersh* and the NKVD. PFKs rated each refugee according to political reliability. Those deemed undesirable were either executed summarily, or in the majority of cases, put on prison trains to the *Gulag*, the system of forced labor camps operated by the NKVD. *Smersh* also played an active role in conducting counterintelligence operations against U.S., British, and French forces in the Allied occupation zones.

In May 1946, the wartime *Smersh* was retitled GUKR of the newly upgraded Ministry for State Security (MGB). It continued throughout the Cold War period as the Third Chief Directorate of the Committee for State Security (KGB), and remains today—in diminished form—within the Russian Federal Ministry for Security (MBRF).

Stephen Donahue

Additional Reading

Andrew, Christopher, and Oleg Gordievsky, *KGB: The Inside Story of Its Foreign Operations from Lenin to Gorbachev* (1990).

Dziak, John J., *Chekisty: A History of the KGB* (1988).
Romanov, A.I. *Nights Are Longest There: A Memoir of the Soviet Security Services* (1972).

SOE

See SPECIAL OPERATIONS EXECUTIVE

Special Air Service (SAS)

The Special Air Service (SAS) was the outgrowth of the Small Scale Raiding Force, developed under a concept authored by Lieutenant David Stirling (q.v.) in April 1941. Stirling, a former Scot's Guards officer who served in the commando "Layforce" prior to a parachuting accident, believed that small-scale, deep penetration raids against enemy targets in the rear areas would be more productive with less cost in men and equipment. His concept was approved by the British high command and he recruited his men, from former members of "Layforce" and other soldiers in the Middle East.

SAS training stressed expertise in soldier skills, including parachuting and explosives, but also stressed independent thought in covert operations. Working in small teams of four men, usually in conjunction with the Long-Range Desert Group (q.v.), SAS was credited with destroying almost 200 German aircraft and tons of munitions in western Africa. Originally designated Number 62 Commando, and later, the Small Scale Raiding Force, the SAS was officially designated the 1st SAS Regiment in February 1943. By January 1944, the SAS included two British, two French, and one Belgian regiment, all operational at the end of the war.

SAS Operations were conducted in Sicily (q.v.), and in Western Europe to the end of the war. Prior to D-Day and in the months afterward, SAS teams, working in conjunction with the French resistance, were credited with creating disorganization in depth of the German elements facing General George S. Patton's (q.v.) U.S. Third Army, enabling the success of the Third Army breakout and swift seizure of Paris (q.v.) that followed. The SAS was credited with the development of many new weapons and techniques used to destroy aircraft, including high-speed jeeps armed with three machine guns for quick travel behind enemy lines. Colonel R.B. "Paddy" Mayne, commander of the 1st SAS Regiment after Stirling was captured in North Africa, was one of the most decorated British soldiers of World War II.

Lieutenant Colonel (later Colonel) David Stirling, DSO, with an SAS Jeep Patrol, 18 January 1943. (IWM E 21338)

British military authorities judged the need for SAS to be marginal after the war and the regiments were disbanded in 1947. The SAS was later resurrected in the British defense establishment. With its trademark tan-colored berets, the SAS remains one of the premier special operations forces in the world today.

Richard P. Ugino

Additional Reading
Beraghty, Tony, *Inside the SAS* (1980).
Ladd, James, *Commandos and Rangers of World War II* (1978).

Special Boat Section (SBS)

Founded in July 1940 by Captain Roger J.A. Courtney, the Special Boat Section of Britain's Combined Operations Special Service Brigade played a key role in the Western Allies' successful amphibious operations of World War II. Although better known for conducting clandestine raids and sabotage operations, the reconnaissance of enemy harbors, beach approaches, and landing areas constituted the bulk of the Special Boat Section's missions. Direct action missions (e.g., demolition of enemy rail communications, bridges, and ammu-

nition dumps) generally followed reconnaissance operations in SBS priorities.

This emphasis on reconnaissance was the primary difference between the SBS and the Special Air Service's (SAS) (q.v.) Special Boat Squadron, formed in July 1942. The latter concentrated on direct action missions and suffered proportionally higher casualties in the process. There was no official connection between the two organizations. Their training and operations, however, were very similar, taking both units to the most dangerous areas of the war, onto enemy coastlines and into territory well behind enemy lines. Theirs was a war of small unit actions, stealth, shock, and surprise.

The SBS began as the Combined Operations Folboat Troops (later designated the 1st Special Boat Section), following Captain Courtney's demonstration of the concept for the commander of Combined Operations, Admiral Sir Roger Keyes (q.v.). The unit's designation came from their use of "folboats" (folding boats), which were portable canvas canoes that could easily be disassembled, folded up, and hidden or stored in small cramped spaces.

The SBS originally was intended to conduct limpet mine attacks against enemy ships at anchor or in harbor. The initial twelve-man section con-

ducted their training on the Scottish Island of Arran before moving on to Alexandria, Egypt, in February 1941. There, they were assigned as part of "Layforce" (Numbers 7, 8, and 11 Commandos). After some initial familiarization training, the 1st SBS was assigned to Alexandria's 1st Submarine Squadron. Once there, they became absorbed in the preparations for Operation CORDITE, Britain's planned invasion of Rhodes.

In support of that operation, the 1st SBS conducted several submarine-launched reconnaissance missions against the Italian-held beaches, harbors, and coastal defenses. Although CORDITE subsequently was called off as a result of German successes in Greece, Crete, and North Africa (qq.v.), these initial operations set the stage for what would become the SBS's primary mission in the war—supporting preparations for Allied amphibious operations. In that capacity, SBS teams generally were delivered to the target area by submarine or fast surface craft, paddling their final approach to the target in their folboats. Operating completely on their own, devoid of any outside support, the SBS units relied on their superb training, courage, and wit to conduct their mission and escape.

The 1st Special Boat Section spent most of 1941 and early 1942 conducting coastal raids against Axis airfields and radio stations, inserting agents, and even rescuing British soldiers from Crete. By mid-1942 the 1st SBS was absorbed into the SAS. Captain Courtney, meanwhile, was recalled to the United Kingdom to form the 2nd Special Boat Section. It was this unit that constituted the primary core of the SBS, and which provided Combined Operations with its coastal and maritime special operations element.

The 2nd SBS was first employed in the buildup for Operation TORCH, the Allied landings in Northwest Africa (q.v.). Initially used to land Allied agents and negotiating teams—including U.S. General Mark W. Clark (q.v.)—and to evacuate Free French General Henri Giraud (q.v.) from France, the 2nd SBS went on to carry out essential beach, coastal, and inland reconnaissance, navigation beacon emplacement, and channel marking operations in support of the Operation TORCH landings.

Following its successes in Operation TORCH, the 2nd SBS went on to participate in every Allied landing conducted in the European and Burma theaters. Not every mission was an unqualified success, but SBS losses were amazingly light during the war, affecting less than 15 percent of the total force. Throughout, SBS personnel demonstrated a flexibility, determination, and innovative approach that almost always guaranteed success. Drawing personnel from every service, the SBS became a magnet for unconventional thinkers and doers who more than reflected the unit's self-assured and flippant motto, *"Excreta Tauri Astutos Frustrantor"* (Bullshit Baffles Brains).

The SBS was a cost-effective unit whose strength never exceeded 300 men. Disbanded in 1945, the missions but not the personnel of the SBS were taken over by the Royal Marines Boom Patrol Detachment. That unit later became the Royal Marines Special Boat Squadron that, contributed so significantly to Britain's successful Falkland Islands campaign in 1982.

Carl O. Schuster

Additional Reading
Courtney, G.B., *SBS in World War II* (1986).
Ladd, James, *Commandoes and Rangers of World War II* (1971).
Lodwick, John, *The Filibusters* (1947).

Special Operations Executive (SOE)

The Special Operations Executive (SOE) was formed in July 1940 with elements from the British Foreign Office (Propaganda Branch), the War Office, and the Special Intelligence Service (Military Intelligence Research and Section D). In August 1941, the propaganda element broke off and became the Political Warfare Executive (PWE) (q.v.). The SOE came under the Ministry of Economic Warfare, with Hugh Dalton as director until February 1942, followed by Lord Selborne. The mission of the SOE was to create havoc and unrest, and incite revolution by the people of occupied Europe against their Nazi conquerors.

SOE operatives worked in occupied countries with regional offices in Bern, Stockholm, Madrid, Lisbon, and Tangier, and intermediate headquarters in Cairo, New York, Algiers, and Bari, Italy. The main headquarters was at 64 Baker Street, London.

SOE strength numbered around 13,000. Recruitment was based on "who-knew-who," or the "Old Boy Network," which enhanced the organization's security. As far as anyone knows, the Germans never penetrated any SOE headquarters. Soviet operatives, however, worked inside from time to time. These included Ormond Uren, Kim Philby, and James Klugmann. One disaster for the SOE involved Klugmann, a known Communist Party member, who transmitted distorted information against General Draža Mihailović and his Yugoslav Ćetniks (qq.v.), and in favor of Marshal

Tito and his partisans (qq.v.). Klugmann's disinformation, fed through the Cairo office to London, was influential in British abandonment of Mihailović.

SOE training schools were set up in southern England and Scotland. Recruits were trained in small arms, sabotage, climbing, parachuting, boating, and the art of clandestine operations—evasion, following suspects, changing identities, etc.

Agents infiltrated their target country either by small ship, submarine, or more commonly, air-drop. Often, SOE agents had to hitch a ride with other intelligence agents, which sometimes created strains and rivalries among the secret services. Because of the nature of the SOE mission (creating havoc, unrest, and revolution), other intelligence agents found it difficult to accomplish their own missions without being detected. To these other agencies, it was better to keep the local police and *Gestapo* (q.v.) unalarmed and unsuspecting. This basic difference in operational philosophies further intensified the rivalries and hostilities.

In August 1941, an intelligence liaison was established between Great Britain and the Soviet Union. The agencies tasked for this mission were the SOE and the NKVD (q.v.), forerunner of the KGB. This relationship did not work out well. While the SOE was willing to share information, the NKVD was paranoid about its security, and refused to share data with its British counterparts. The SOE's relations with its American counterparts in the Office of Strategic Services (q.v.), on the other hand, were outstanding. In one instance, Sir William Stephenson (q.v.) coordinated intelligence efforts resulting in the successful Allied naval victory at Cape Matapan (q.v.).

The SOE had considerable success in Norway, Denmark, and Belgium in sustaining resistance movements in occupied countries. The SOE also sent 1,800 agents and 10,000 tons of war materiel into France. It was in the Netherlands, however, that the SOE suffered a serious setback. Dubbed code name *ENGLANDSPIEL* by the Germans, the *Abwehr* (q.v.) located a Dutch SOE radio operator in March 1942 and forced him to continue sending messages to London. For more than two years, the operator omitted prearranged mistakes in the messages that were supposed to alert London that he had been compromised; but London never noticed anything wrong. As a result, forty air-inserted SOE agents were captured, as well as half of the SOE operatives in Holland and several in Belgium.

The SOE had little success in Germany and Austria. In Greece, the SOE had difficulty keeping the monarchists and Communists focused against the Germans.

For the most part, the SOE accomplished what it set out to do—harass the enemy and keep the resistance movements going. Many historians argue that the SOE was little more than a nuisance, a thorn in the German's side. It did, however, manage to divert troops that may otherwise have been used on the eastern and western fronts. The SOE was disbanded in January 1946.

William H. Van Husen

Additional Reading

Cookridge, E.H., *Inside the SOE* (1966).

Foot, Michael R.D., *SOE: An Outline History of the Special Operations Executive, 1940–46* (1984).

Fuller, Jean Overton, *The German Penetration of SOE France, 1941–44* (1975).

Pincher, Chapman, *Too Secret Too Long* (1984).

Spetsnaz

Although Soviet special designated forces, or *Spetsnaz*, enjoyed a brief flurry of publicity and speculation during the Cold War's final years, their activities in World War II have remained largely unknown and unappreciated in the West. Much of this is the result of the traditional Soviet secrecy about such operations, combined with a general lack of Western appreciation of the Soviet role in the war.

Special operations were an integral part of Soviet military doctrine even prior to World War II. Every offensive conducted by the Soviets from the Spanish civil war (q.v.) to the final drive on Berlin (q.v.) was preceded by special operations, including both direct actions and reconnaissance. The importance of such operations to Soviet military doctrine continued throughout the postwar period. From the invasions of Hungary in 1956 and Czechoslovakia in 1968, to the 1979–1989 Afghan War, Soviet *Spetsnaz* led the way.

The first Soviet special purpose forces were formed during the regime's early days in 1917. Originally organized under the *Cheka* (the Communist Party's secret police) to combat the party's enemies in the struggle for power, their mission expanded during the Russian civil war to conducting reconnaissance and disrupting the enemy's rear areas by sabotage, reconnaissance, and assassination.

By 1939, the Soviet Union had two special purpose forces (SPFs). That of the party was organized under the NKVD (q.v.), the new name for the secret police. The other SPF belonged to the GRU, the general staff's military intelligence. Other specially designated troops included special assault engineers and the airborne forces, but they were intended for overt military duties and had specific missions within conventional military operations. Only the NKVD's *Osoboga Nazhacheniya (Osnaz)* and the GRU's *Spetsialnoye Nazhacheniya (Spetsnaz)* were designated for covert operations in an enemy's rear.

In 1938, the *Osnaz* was the larger and better organized of the two groups, primarily because the GRU, like the rest of the Soviet military, was decimated by Premier Josef Stalin's purges (q.v.). *Osnaz* assassins and special action detachments operated almost at will throughout the United States and Europe during the 1930s, killing Stalin's exiled opponents and eliminating foreign Communist leaders who, in Stalin's view, had failed to accept Soviet leadership.

During the Spanish civil war, both the *Osnaz* and *Spetsnaz* were active in the Nationalist and Republican rear areas, conducting sabotage, assassination, and espionage operations. The GRU's best-known special operations were conducted by Major (later General) Mamsurov as part of the Republican XIV Special Corps, which controlled all guerrilla groups operating in the Nationalist rear after 1937. In 1939, Mamsurov's group spirited the Spanish gold reserves out of the country and smuggled them to the Soviet Union.

Both *Spetsnaz* and *Osnaz* were active during the invasion of Poland (q.v.), the Finnish Winter War (q.v.), and the seizure of the Baltic states. Operations in Poland were limited to the seizure by *Spetsnaz* units of key military facilities just ahead of the Soviet advance. Mamsurov commanded a *Spetsnaz* detachment that was assigned to conduct prisoner snatches and raids in the Finnish rear, and *Osnaz* troops were supposed to conduct assassinations and sabotage in the Finnish capital. Neither set of operations was successful, however.

Soviet SPF operations enjoyed almost total success in the Baltic countries. *Osnaz* units infiltrated the various capitals and seized political leaders and radio stations, while the *Spetsnaz* detachments sabotaged military communications facilities and captured key bridges along the invasion routes across those countries. Once the Baltics and eastern Poland were occupied, *Osnaz* detachments rounded up likely opponents to Soviet rule and either deported or executed them.

Both the NKVD and the Red Army were planning to conduct special operations in German-occupied Europe, but they were preempted when

the Germans launched Operation BARBAROSSA. Driven on the defensive, the Soviet SPFs were employed to establish and train "stay behind" networks to report on German rear area operations and force movements. They also trained, organized, and commanded partisan units in the Axis rear.

Although the operations of the two organizations overlapped in many ways, *Osnaz* units generally concentrated on operations directed at reestablishing the party's authority over the population or the partisans' leadership. *Spetsnaz* units generally concentrated on attacking German military facilities and leadership, although the *Osnaz* occasionally conducted similar operations. Both organizations serviced espionage networks in the Axis rear and conducted acts of assassination and sabotage.

The *Spetsnaz* units of the Soviet Navy conducted small raids against German coastal forces and bases in the Arctic and Black Seas. German soldiers manning isolated posts on Finland's and Norway's Arctic coasts had great respect and fear for these units. The Romanians also came to have reason to fear them.

The 22 September 1941 Soviet amphibious landing against Romanian forces besieging Odessa was preceded by a naval *Spetsnaz* attack against the headquarters of the Romanian 13th Division, which was responsible for defending the targeted landing area. The small thirty-man Soviet detachment disrupted the division by destroying its headquarters' communications center and killing many of its officers. The combination of the headquarters frantically reporting the attack, followed by total silence, led many of the division's subordinate units to believe the headquarters had been overrun. The subordinate units, therefore, abandoned their own positions and retreated, rather than risk being encircled. As a result, the Soviet main landing force easily penetrated nearly ten kilometers inshore within a few hours of landing. It took the Romanians several days to restore the front.

The most common direct action, or commando-type, missions conducted by Soviet SPFs were those undertaken by the "reconnaissance-miners" in support of army operations. First employed offensively in mid-1942, these units operated in teams of five to six men. Their missions were diversionary in nature, intended either to isolate the battlefield along the army's primary axis of advance, or to divert German attention and forces away from the main axis. More than 100 such teams supported the Soviet offensive at Stalingrad (q.v.) in late 1942. These units proved so effective that by October 1942 every Soviet front (army group) had a battalion of "guards engineers" assigned. Designated *Otdelny Gvardevskiy Batal'on Minerov,* or separate guards battalions, these OGBM troops are the direct forerunners of the *Spetsnaz* battalions of the post–World War II Soviet and Russian Armies.

OGBM troops generally crossed the front lines at night to attack targets within tactical depth (fifty kilometers). They usually parachuted into target areas at operational depth (100–250 kilometers). In June 1944, at least two OGBM brigades supported the Soviet Byelorussian offensive (q.v.) against German Army Group Center. Those units, in combination with partisan forces, successfully isolated the battlefield by destroying railroads, bridges, and communications facilities to a depth of more than 200 kilometers along the Soviet axis of advance. Another OGBM brigade supported the Soviet Fourteenth Army's drive into Norway, so crippling German communications that they never were able to establish a cohesive front, despite fighting on terrain favorable to the defender.

Both *Osnaz* and *Spetsnaz* units preceded the Soviet advances into Slovakia, Romania, Hungary, and Bulgaria. Delivered by air or sea, these detachments facilitated the ground advance by subverting government forces in those countries, fomenting rebellion, and assassinating key pro-German officials. The SPF units also tried to seize key bridges and facilities forward of the Red Army advances into Vienna and Berlin (qq.v.), but the lack of supporting sympathizer networks complicated the efforts, producing marginal results.

In general, Soviet special purpose forces enjoyed much success in World War II, while learning many valuable lessons in the process. Those lessons were applied with maximum effect during the advances into Europe and in Manchuria during the final months of the war. More significantly, perhaps, SPFs served the Soviet Union well in the rapid and efficient seizure of key capitals during the early stages of the Cold War. The success of these operations, however, was limited to areas where the Soviet's had local sympathizers to assist the covert deployments and support the SPF units. Such operations were not as successful in the areas where those sympathizers were not present, e.g., Finland, Germany, and Hungary. Nonetheless, the threat of Soviet special operations tied down considerable opposing forces and drew disproportionate command attention from both the Germans in World War II and the Western commanders during the period of the Cold War.

Carl O. Schuster

Additional Reading

Burgess, William H., III (ed.), *Inside Spetsnaz* (1990).
Leonov, Viktor, *Blood on the Shores* (1993).
Suvorov, Viktor, *Spetsnaz: The Story of the Soviet SAS* (1987).

SS

See SCHUTZSTAFFEL

Stavka

In Russian, *Stavka* means the "quarters of the commander in chief," an appropriate name for the Soviet military staff that commanded the armed forces during World War II. The *Stavka* was born on 23 June 1941, the day after the Germans attacked the Soviet Union and General Dimitry Pavlov's (q.v.) forces collapsed in total disarray. The original *Stavka* was chaired by Marshal Semen Timoshenko and had Soviet premier Josef Stalin, General Georgy Zhukov, Foreign Minister Vyacheslav Molotov, Marshal Kliment Voroshilov, Marshal Semyon Budenny, and Admiral Nikolai Kuznetsov (qq.v.) as members. Shortly after its creation, Voroshilov and Budenny lost any influence in decision making, although they remained members. Throughout most of the "Great Patriotic War" the influential members of the *Stavka* were Nikolai Voronov, Alexsandr Vasilevsky (qq.v.), and Andrei Khrulev.

Although Timoshenko was the nominal head, Stalin held and exercised power to establish policy and make final decisions regarding military operations. As a rule, the *Stavka's* directions and policies tended to be militarily sound, particularly after the Soviet's counteroffensive was initiated.

Prior to creation of the *Stavka* the Soviet military was controlled by a cumbersome Commissariat for Defense, subordinate to the Council of People's Commissars. Born out of the revolution and an intense desire to prevent class control, the commissariat met political needs but failed to meet military or security needs. As a result, there was no qualified senior military staff to evaluate either leaders or operational plans and orders. Further, although there existed national level plans for providing logistical support to military operations, the commissariat was unable to adequately plan for that support. Thus, military and tactical needs were considered primarily with the focus on political effects, and decisions were most frequently made by nonmilitary commissars.

The *Stavka* controlled the Soviet General

SOVIET WARTIME CHAIN OF COMMAND

```
                    ┌─────────────────────┐
                    │  State Committee    │
                    │   for Defense       │
                    │     (Goko)          │
                    └─────────────────────┘
         ┌──────────────────┴──────────────────┐
  ┌─────────────┐                      ┌─────────────────┐
  │ Praesidium  │                      │    Supreme      │
  │             │                      │    Command      │
  └─────────────┘                      │    (Stavka)     │
         │                             └─────────────────┘
  ┌─────────────────┐           ┌──────────────┴──────────────┐
  │  Soviet of      │    ┌───────────────┐            ┌──────────────┐
  │  People's       │    │  Red Army     │            │  Soviet Navy │
  │  Commissars     │    │ General Staff │            └──────────────┘
  └─────────────────┘    └───────────────┘
  Commissariats    ┌────────┬────────┼────────┬────────┐
  ┌────────────┐ ┌───────┐ ┌──────────┐ ┌──────────┐ ┌──────────┐
  │ Internal   │ │Fronts │ │Air Force │ │Artillery │ │  Rear    │
  │ Affairs    │ └───────┘ └──────────┘ └──────────┘ │ Services │
  └────────────┘                                     └──────────┘
  ┌────────────┐
  │   NKVD     │
  └────────────┘
  ┌────────────┐
  │  SMERSH    │
  └────────────┘
```

Staff, which in turn issued the orders and operational directives to fronts (army groups) and other field units. Stalin placed his own unique stamp on the *Stavka* directing that the senior officers make frequent visits to the forward battle areas. Vasilevsky spent a total of nearly two years at the various fronts during the thirty-six months he was the chief of the general staff.

In its initial phases, the *Stavka* did not function well. Stalin, as the supreme leader of the Soviet Union (no matter what title he assumed) tinkered with all of the organizations until he got them precisely the way he wanted them. He assumed more and more of the military leadership duties, and shuffled officers in and out of key positions on a regular basis. He replaced Zhukov as chief of the general staff, and it was Stalin's directions that kept the members of the general staff in forward positions throughout the war.

The *Stavka* kept Stalin fully informed of all military operations. This was accomplished by two daily briefings, as well as at least one daily telephone update. These briefings, in addition to members of the general staff and the *Stavka*, would include other important members of the Soviet Politburo.

All military actions ordered by Stalin and planned by the *Stavka* were passed directly to representatives of the army fronts in attendance, or directly to an officer on the general staff. By having this direct connection between the supreme headquarters and the primary operational organizations, the Soviets introduced a unique concept of military planning. Although not initially successful, it eventually proved effective.

The *Stavka* continued to function as the military staff presiding over all Soviet military forces right up to the end of the Soviet Union. The final version of the organization consisted of eleven members, with the chairman being the secretary general of the Soviet Union, in his role as commander in chief of the Soviet armed forces.

Thomas Cagley

Additional Reading
Bialer, Seweryn, *Stalin and His Generals* (1984).
Garder, Michael, *A History of the Soviet Army* (1966).
Seaton, Albert, and Joan Seaton, *The Soviet Army: 1918 to the Present* (1986).

Sturmabteilung (SA)

The SA, also known as Brownshirts or Stormtroopers, was the main Nazi paramilitary formation in the 1920s and early 1930s. In other words,

it was the Nazi Party's private army. This must be understood, however, in a special sense. To be sure, the SA was organized along military lines, trained in the use of firearms, and taught combat techniques. It was also "frequently deployed in violent situations" prior to 1933. But unlike most armies, members of the SA were volunteers "and free to leave the organization" at any time. Moreover, the SA's main function was not to conquer territory or defeat an enemy army. Rather, it was propaganda.

The idea for the SA was Adolf Hitler's (q.v.). It began in 1920 as the *Ordnerdienst* (Order Service) under Emil Maurice. In August 1921, it changed its name to the *Turn-und Sportabteilung* (Gymnastic and Sport Division) with a new leader, Hans Ulrich Klintzsch, who greatly expanded its membership. Finally, it became the *Sturmabteilung* (Storm Detachment) in November 1921. Hermann Göring (q.v.) became the SA head in 1923, with Ernst Röhm (q.v.) SA-Führer from 1924 to 1926, the real leader.

A former army officer, Röhm wanted the SA to cooperate with the *Reichswehr* (German armed forces) in order to undermine the Versailles Treaty (q.v.). By February 1923, he transformed the SA into a paramilitary formation. Now largely in the service of the *Reichswehr,* the SA participated in military exercises alongside other rightist defense leagues. "With this, the SA—and therewith the essential instrument of power for his control of the party—was wrested from Hitler's hands; in practical terms, he was now not much more than a very successful agitator in the service of the *Reichswehr.*" The consequences of this transformation for the SA's future development and for Hitler's relationship with the *Reichswehr* were great. Hitler swore "never again to enter into such arrangements with the *Reichswehr,*" whereas the *Reichswehr* mistakenly felt that it could enlist the Nazi Party's assistance at will.

The pre-1924 SA was partly responsible for Hitler becoming involved in the abortive 1923 Beer Hall *Putsch* (q.v.) following which the SA was banned nationally. Röhm simply renamed it and continued training. Hitler, however, was determined to prevent a repetition of November 1923. In February 1925, he issued his "Basic Guidelines" for the reorganized Nazi Party. He also invited Röhm to reconstitute the SA but on his terms. Before that could happen, however, he broke with Röhm over the question of the nature of the SA. For lack of a charismatic leader to replace Röhm, Hitler held off reconstituting the SA in 1925. SA units sprouted up in various Nazi districts, but they were not under the control of a central SA

A formation of SA troops in front of the Feldherrnhalle in Munich, commemorating the Beer Hall Putsch. (IWM MH 11613)

office. Instead, they were "completely dependent on the local party leader."

Not until 29 October 1926 was the SA reestablished with Franz von Salomon as its new leader. Von Salomon established a number of economic enterprises, including insurance and cigarette companies, in part to meet internal SA needs and in part to fund the SA. In 1930–1931, the SA experienced a number of revolts, all of which were easily suppressed by Hitler, who then reformed it. In September 1930, Hitler named himself "supreme SA leader," and in October, he recalled Röhm from Bolivia and made him again the day-to-day administrator with the title "SA chief of staff," effective 5 January 1931. Once again, Röhm set about transforming the SA into a paramilitary force, this time with the goal of creating a new "People's Army" once the Nazis came to power. Before accepting the position of SA chief of staff, he discussed with Hitler the role of the SA after the Nazis came to power, but Hitler fobbed him off with a number of ambiguous statements. This had serious repercussions after 1933.

By 1931, the Depression was in full swing. Unemployment surged and recruits inundated the SA. Time and again, Röhm had to reorganize his formation to accommodate this influx. In order to combat the effects of the Depression, Röhm continued von Salomon's SA-homes, SA-kitchens, SA-assistance office, and created his own special groups. The SA became a miniature welfare state with services in some ways superior to the German government's.

On 13 April 1932, the Weimar government's minister of the interior outlawed the SA. This was a heavy blow to the NSDAP, but thanks to the machinations of General Kurt von Schleicher (q.v.), the ban lasted only two months. SA growth continued. By the end of January 1933, the SA had approximately 700,000 men. This meant that the 100,000-man *Reichswehr* would probably have been incapable of controlling both the SA and the Communists had the Schleicher government, using Article 48 of the Weimar constitution, declared a state of emergency. On 30 January 1933, President Paul von Hindenburg (q.v.) appointed Hitler chancellor. That night, an exhilarated SA participated in the great torchlight march past the new chancellor's window.

In the first six months of 1933, the SA participated in the "revolution from below" and thus helped Hitler and the party "coordinate" the private and public sectors. On 22 February 1933, the Prussian minister of interior, Göring, commissioned SA men as "auxiliary police." They now enjoyed a privileged legal status and could legally use force against their enemies. The first SA concentration camps also appeared at this time.

After the "coordination" of early 1933 had run its course, the SA no longer had any visible role to play and the "repressed question" reappeared: What will be the SA's future tasks? Hitler's rise to power had made the SA superfluous. Despite this, it continued to grow rapidly. On 1 November 1933, it absorbed a substantial portion of the *Stahlhelm* veteran's organization. By mid-1934, the SA's program of intimidation, violence, and disruption threatened to discredit and even undermine Hitler's administration. Hitler had a choice: he could "redress the SA's grievances" or bring the SA "forcibly to heel." He chose the latter (*see* Night of the Long Knives).

What happened to the SA after 1934? It remained in existence but with a significantly reduced membership and largely ceremonial functions. It also participated in ideological indoctrination and premilitary training of German youth. After June 1934, very few of the SA's surviving former leaders carved out successful careers in the SA, SS, or the party.

Jon Moulton

Additional Reading

Fischer, Conan, *Stormtroopers: A Social, Economic, and Ideological Analysis, 1929–35* (1983).
Merkl, Peter, *The Making of a Stormtrooper* (1980).
Reiche, Eric G., *The Development of the SA in Nuremberg, 1922–1934* (1986).

Supreme Headquarters, Allied Expeditionary Force (SHAEF)

SHAEF was a military staff agency created by the Combined Chiefs of Staff (q.v.) to prepare for and execute an invasion of northern Europe, the goal of which was to destroy or secure the surrender of Germany's armed forces. SHAEF's mission was entrusted to General Dwight D. Eisenhower (q.v.), formerly the commander of Allied forces in the Mediterranean theater. As supreme Allied commander, Eisenhower commanded all land, sea, and air forces designated for use in the invasion, including the British 21st Army Group commanded by Field Marshal Sir Bernard L. Montgomery (q.v.), and the U.S. 6th and 12th Army Groups commanded by Generals Omar N. Bradley and Jacob L. Devers (qq.v.), respectively.

When Eisenhower took official command of SHAEF in February 1944, he found that much of its organization and mission had already been pre-pared by its predecessor unit, the Chief of Staff, Supreme Allied Command (COSSAC). COSSAC had planned a cross-channel attack on France, code named OVERLORD, and developed a military staff and organization to serve the then unnamed supreme commander. Eisenhower accepted most of COSSAC's scheme but made a few changes based on his experience in the Mediterranean theater. Among these changes were personnel additions, most notably the addition of General Walter Bedell Smith (q.v.) as chief of staff, and a number of organizational changes designed to integrate British and American staffs and promote a spirit of cooperation between their members.

SHAEF was organized to maximize efficiency by minimizing waste and duplicated effort. Five subordinate substaffs, known simply as G-1, G-2, G-3, G-4, and G-5 were created to oversee the specific tasks necessary for the success of the commander's mission.

The operations and planning section, G-3, was in many ways the heart of SHAEF. This staff coordinated the efforts of all Allied military forces, including some French resistance groups, to ensure both international and interservice cooperation. It issued orders and developed standing operating procedures to guide the activities of lower echelons. In addition, G-3 ran the war room, keeping it updated with situation summaries, weekly reports, weather forecasts, and other information necessary for operational decision making.

For the gathering of information and intelligence, SHAEF turned to its G-2 section. The duties included locating enemy forces, estimating their strengths, estimating likely enemy courses of action, and evaluating the importance and validity of strategic information. Among the many sources serving G-2 were the Office of Strategic Services (OSS) (q.v.), the Joint Intelligence Office in London, and the intelligence offices attached to the army groups in the field.

G-1 and G-4 were administrative sections, in charge of personnel and logistics, respectively. These two sections were charged with keeping the armies supplied with men and materiel. Consequently, these staff sections were more concerned with government resources, appropriations, and transport than they were directly with events on the battlefront. These staffs were vital links in the chain of command between the various Allied war departments in the home countries and the military commanders in the field.

Of all the general staff sections, perhaps the least understood and appreciated was G-5, SHAEF's civil affairs division. This staff was re-

ALLIED CHAIN OF COMMAND IN NORTHWEST EUROPE, 1944 - 1945

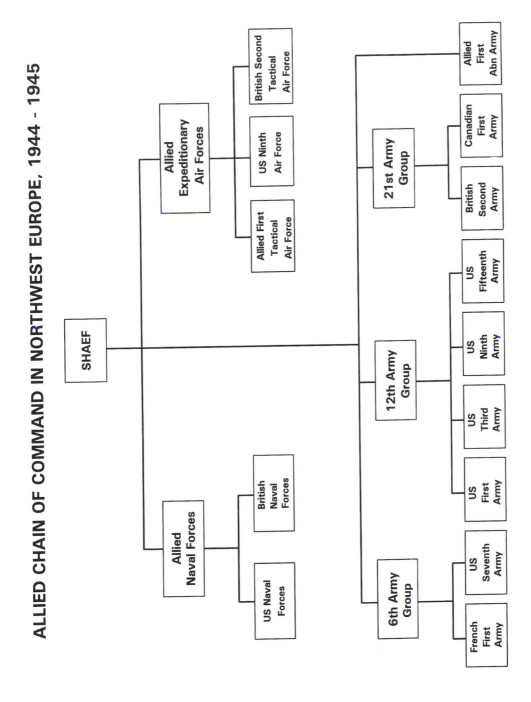

sponsible for the well-being of the populations of occupied and liberated areas. This concern was of paramount importance, since civil disturbances in the rear areas could easily disrupt the war effort at the front. Among its many tasks were the repair of water and sewage services, the supervision of food production and distribution, and the restoration of police, public safety, health, and local governmental institutions. Given the severity of the physical damage and the confusion and dislocation of war, G-5's task would prove one of the most arduous and important of SHAEF's duties.

SHAEF's organization was also aided by a number of special staff sections, including divisions for psychological warfare, public relations, medicine, communications, and air defense. Coordinating the activities of the special and general staff sections was an adjutant general's section that prepared and filed orders and directives.

SHAEF's headquarters was initially located at Bushy Park outside of London, but as D-Day approached, it moved to Portsmouth to be near the invasion embarkation points. Once Allied forces clearly established a foothold on the Continent, SHAEF again moved, this time to the town of Granville on the Normandy peninsula. Following the liberation of Paris, SHAEF claimed Versailles as its permanent home.

From a forward command post near Reims, SHAEF staff sections had access to every area of the front. It was in Reims, on 7 May 1945, that German General Alfred Jodl (q.v.) signed the instrument of surrender, thereby bringing SHAEF's mission to a successful conclusion. SHAEF officially disbanded on 14 July 1945, and its personnel were freed for other duties. In many ways, SHAEF was the organizational forerunner of the Supreme Headquarters, Allied Powers Europe (SHAPE), the military headquarters of the postwar North Atlantic Treaty Organization (NATO). SHAPE uses almost the same uniform shoulder sleeve insignia as SHAEF.

Richard Leiby

Additional Reading

Eisenhower, Dwight D., *Crusade in Europe* (1948).
Morgan, Frederick, *Overture to Overlord* (1950).
Pogue, Forrest C., *The Supreme Command* (1954).

T

10th Light Flotilla, Italian

Italy was the only nation in the European theater to develop naval special forces prior to the war. Although the unit was not fully functional when Italy entered the war on 10 June 1940, naval special forces soon demonstrated they could strike anywhere and any time—sinking ships in Gibraltar, Crete, Alexandria, and even the Black Sea. Their most successful operation was the sinking of British battleships HMS *Valiant* and *Queen Elizabeth* in Alexandria (q.v.), Egypt, in December 1941. They also planned subsequent operations in New York City and other critical Allied ports, but Italy was forced out of the war before the plans could reach fruition.

The Italian Navy first began working on the equipment and training of this unit in October of 1935. Basing their training and requirements on the lessons from their special operations in World War I, they concentrated on the use of midget submarines, manned torpedoes, limpet mines, explosive boats, and scuba diving gear. The first systems and personnel were identified by July 1939. The mission was assigned to the 1st Light Flotilla (changed to the 10th Light Flotilla in September 1940). The unit's first special missions were directed against Alexandria and Gibraltar in August and September 1940. Both met with failure and the unit commander, Vittorio Moccagatta, decided that tighter security as well as greater training was needed to prevent a repeat of those failures.

Subsequent operations and planning were decentralized to reduce the possibility of compromise. These measures paid off almost immediately. The next three attacks were successful, sinking a cruiser and 42,000 tons of shipping. Although the 10th Light Flotilla was never able to penetrate Malta's harbors, the British Royal Navy never felt that any of its harbors were safe from the commando attacks. In fact, British and Germans both paid the Italians the compliment of copying the 10th Light Flotilla's tactics and equipment for their own naval special forces. Many modern navies also have similar units patterned after this pioneering Italian formation.

Carl O. Schuster

Additional Reading
Borghese, J. Valero, *Sea Devils* (1956).

U

UDTs
See UNDERWATER DEMOLITION TEAMS

Underwater Demolition Teams (UDTs)

Originally designated "naval combat demolition units," the U.S. Navy's underwater demolition teams are the organizational ancestors of today's sea-air-land (SEAL) teams. In World War II, they were more commonly known as "frogmen." Contrary to popular belief, these units were initially formed to support amphibious operations in the European theater, but they saw far more use in the Pacific. Casualties were often heavy (more than 50 percent on D-Day at Normandy [q.v.]), but their operations were critical to the success of the Allied landings on both theaters.

Their roots can be traced to the Navy Bomb Disposal School established by Lieutenant Commander Draper Kauffman on the grounds of American University in Washington, D.C., during the fall of 1942. He expanded the training and mission of his units in early 1943 in response to reports that Germany was installing obstacles on French beaches. Kauffman convinced the navy that his teams were ideal for removing such obstacles and he received support to establish the first UDT school in Fort Pierce, Florida, in March 1943. A cadre of 500 former Seabees, British Commandos (q.v.), U.S. Army Rangers (q.v.), and a "handful" of navy scouts and rangers formed the first group of trainees and instructors.

Each trainee had to be able to swim two nautical miles and received eight weeks of training in hand-to-hand combat, scouting, ordnance disposal, and beach reconnaissance techniques. That was followed by "Hell Week," during which the trainees were kept awake as long as possible while being given a series of difficult mental and physical challenges. Overall attrition in training exceeded 60 percent, mostly during Hell Week. The first class graduated in July 1943 and its first operational employment in an amphibious landing was in the Pacific Kwajalein operation in February 1944.

The organization, tactics, and procedures of the UDTs differed greatly between the theaters. European teams went in at night with the first boat wave and primarily conducted obstacle clearance operations. By contrast, Pacific teams operated in daylight well in advance of the landing and generally had a naval gunfire unit assigned in direct support. Also, they did scouting, beach survey, and reconnaissance as well as obstacle clearance operations. The Pacific theater used the standard navy UDT organization, which consisted of sixteen officers and eighty enlisted men. It was divided into a headquarters platoon of four officers and twenty enlisted men, which controlled four subordinate platoons of three officers and fifteen enlisted men. This organization was never used in the European theater, which employed teams of one naval officer with ten enlisted personnel (five navy and five U.S. Army Engineers).

UDTs only saw action twice in the European theater. Some sixty-six mixed UDTs participated in Normandy and in the southern France (qq.v.) landings. Their beach clearance operations were critical to the success of those landings. The UDTs were better known for their more numerous and significant Pacific operations, where most of the U.S. Navy's eighteen UDTs were employed. The British used similar teams for the first time at the Normandy landings. The British teams were known as Landing Craft Obstacle Clearance Units (LOCUS).

Carl O. Schuster

Additional Reading

Casey, Robert J., *Torpedo Junction: With the Pacific Fleet from Pearl Harbor to Midway* (1942).

Morison, Samuel Eliot, *History of United States Naval Operations in World War II,* 15 vols. (1947–62).

United Services Organization (USO)

The United Service Organization, or USO, was formed in February 1941, by representatives from the YMCA, YWCA, the National Catholic Community Service, the National Jewish Welfare Board, the Salvation Army, and the Traveler's Aid—International Social Service of America. Not under U.S. government direction or financed by the government, it was staffed mainly by volunteers and financed by voluntary contributions.

The USO provided a place off the military base where service people could relax by dancing and enjoying refreshments. The organizers expected that, in the words of an official document, "wholesome social contact" would take place between service people and local civilians. A major part of the USO mission was to provide stage entertainment. Top Hollywood talent, and lesser figures too, flew by the thousands all over the world entertaining troops under USO auspices. The most famous entertainer to serve the USO was Bob Hope (q.v.), and he continued to do so for nearly five decades after the end of World War II. The USO, according to its figures at the end of the war, served more than a billion persons. It performed its mission very creditably.

Roland V. Layton

Additional Reading

Carson, J.M., *Home Away from Home: The Story of the USO* (1946).

Ustaša

On 10 April 1941, Ante Pavelić (q.v.), the leader of the pro-Fascist Croatian Party, and until that moment a refugee in Italy, proclaimed the establishment of the *Nezavisna Država Hrvatska* (Independent State of Croatia). The new state also annexed the whole of Bosnia and Herzegovina. Along with a regular army, the *Hrvatsko Domobranstvo* (Croatian Territorial Military Force), Pavelić also established a voluntary party paramilitary force, the *Ustaša,* which was organized along the lines of the Italian Black Shirts (q.v.).

Initially, the *Ustaša* comprised five active battalions with a strength of about 750 men each, two railway security battalions, and two special units: the *Crna Legija* (Black Legion), and the *Poglavnik Tjelesni Zdrug* (Ante Pavelić Bodyguard Battalion). Officially, the task of these units was to maintain security inside national borders. Very soon, however, their exaggerated nationalism turned into extreme anti-Serbian feelings combined with religious fanaticism, all of which were directed against the Serbians, the Orthodox, and the Moslem minorities living in Bosnia and the border regions.

The *Ustaša* committed countless crimes and slaughtered many defenseless civilians. This in turn created a huge divide (almost impossible to bridge) between the different communities and religions, with obvious advantages for the partisan forces under the leadership of Tito (q.v.). When the *Ustaša* started fighting Tito's partisans, their numbers grew. In 1942, the *Ustaša* had 25,000 under arms. The following year they had almost twice that many, organized into a dozen brigades. When the Italian Army surrendered on 8 September 1943, the operational field of the *Ustaša* broadened, and their numbers increased to almost 100,000 by 1944.

The fratricidal fighting between the *Ustaša* and the Communist partisan units had unbelievable costs in casualties for both sides. The Croatian Army proved incapable of handling the guerrilla-style fighting that emerged, and in 1944 it all but came under *Ustaša* control. Army brigades were paired with *Ustaša* brigades to form *Ustaša* divisions; seventeen mixed divisions were formed and fought doggedly until the end of the war—and also for several months after May 1945—with the hopelessness of people who had nothing else to lose.

The *Ustaša* wore black uniforms in either the Italian or German style. On their caps, officers wore a grenade badge with the Croatian white and red checkered national insignia and the letter "U." The same letter was worn on the red, white, and blue collar patches. The troops did not always wear these patches and sometimes only wore the letter "U" on their steel helmets.

Francesco Fatutta

Additional Reading

Roberts, Walter R., *Tito, Mihailović, and the Allies, 1941–1945* (1973).

Strugar, V., *Jugoslavija 1941–1945* (1970).

V

Volkssturm

The German *Volkssturm,* established on 25 September 1944 and publicly unveiled on 18 October, was a Nazi Party–controlled national militia with a twofold mission. First, the *Volkssturm* was a means to motivate German civilians to fight fanatically in the defense of their homes. Second, it was a local defense auxiliary designed to strengthen the *Wehrmacht.* According to *Volkssturm* founder and Party Chancellery Chief Martin Bormann (q.v.), meeting the second goal would depend on the success of the *Volkssturm* in attaining the first. Adolf Hitler (q.v.) always feared that a militia could damage home front morale, but Bormann convinced him that a fully indoctrinated, party-led militia could unleash the rage of the supposedly superior German race. Appropriately, the Nazi's christened their new force the *Volkssturm,* (literally, "the people's assault").

Bormann dominated *Volkssturm* decision making in crucial organizational, personnel, and administrative matters, while his local minions, the party's *Gauleiters* and *Kreisleiters,* administered the *Volkssturm* within their jurisdictional areas. Bormann's theoretical coequal, *Reichsführer-SS* Heinrich Himmler (q.v.), commander of the Replacement Army, controlled military aspects like training, conferring more responsibility than power. Once mobilized, however, *Volkssturm* battalions, the force's largest units, came under *Wehrmacht* command.

To minimize the economic consequences of mobilizations, *Volkssturm* personnel were divided into four separate levies. Levy IV contained those men who could serve as security guards, but were physically unfit for combat. All civilian boys aged sixteen to nineteen who were not antiaircraft auxiliaries served in Levy III. These youngsters underwent six weeks of indoctrination and basic military instruction in the Hitler Youth (q.v.) premilitary training camps, where they remained segregated from the older *Volkssturm* men. Before entering the *Wehrmacht* or *Waffen-SS,* Levy II units, activated only when their home district *(Kreis)* came under attack, contained all adult men who performed essential jobs (e.g., highly skilled factory workers, top managers). Because Levy I units could serve anywhere in their home region *(Gau)* they contained men in occupations like farming or construction work, deemed less essential.

Volkssturm units performed a wide variety of tasks. They provided labor for everything from constructing field fortifications to unloading trains and barges. *Volkssturm* men served as guards for bridges and factories, prisoners of war, and concentration camp inmates, and conducted patrols to keep watch on local foreign laborers. *Volkssturm* units, particularly in eastern Germany, assisted in the evacuation of economically useful goods, and occasionally provided refugee columns with security escorts. All of these contributions, though unspectacular, helped the *Wehrmacht* shift some of its dwindling manpower from rear echelon to combat formations.

The primary *Volkssturm* mission, however, was support of the *Wehrmacht* in combat, and in most instances, it failed dismally. Inferior combat performance usually stemmed from the fact that *Volkssturm* units were poorly armed and inadequately trained. The *Wehrmacht* itself lacked equipment, and German industry, crippled by bombing, could not hope to arm and clothe even a substantial fraction of the *Volkssturm's* six million members. Neither the Nazi Party's highly publicized collection drives nor industry's efforts to produce crude, cheap, simplified rifles could meet the immense needs. *Volkssturm* units generally received poor quality equipment, usually captured weapons for which ammunition was in very short supply. In fact, the only weapon that *Volkssturm* men had in adequate numbers was the *Panzerfaust* antitank rocket, for which they often lacked training. All this limited combat effectiveness and destroyed the troops' will to fight. As a result, low morale, defeatism, dereliction of duty, desertion, and mass surrender were common among *Volkssturm* battalions.

Although *Volkssturm* combat performance as a whole was dismal, some units fought quite well, particularly against the Soviets, whom most Germans had come to fear and hate. In Berlin (q.v.), Breslau, along the Oder and Neisse Rivers in East Prussia, *Volkssturm* battalions fought well alongside regular soldiers. On the western front, the *Volkssturm* generally performed quite poorly, but in some areas of the Siegfried Line (q.v.), on the upper Rhine, in Nuremberg, Leipzig, and else-where some *Volkssturm* men proved tough opponents. The crucial element in all *Volkssturm* successes was the assistance of regular army units, both before and during combat. Left alone, *Volkssturm* battalions were simply too weak to have anything but a temporary tactical impact. In the end, the *Volkssturm* did very little to prevent the military defeat of Nazi Germany, and more importantly, it proved unable to turn German civilians into fanatical warriors.

David K. Yelton

Additional Reading

Mammach, Klaus, *Der Volkssturm: Das letzte Aufgebot 1944/45* (1981).
Sevdewitz, Max, *Civil Life in Wartime Germany: The Story of the Home Front* (1945).

WAAC

See WOMEN'S AUXILIARY ARMY CORPS

Waffen-SS

The *Waffen-SS* was the armed army auxiliary and only one part of Heinrich Himmler's all-encompassing *Schutzstaffel* (qq.v.). The *Waffen-SS* has its origins in the personal bodyguard units formed by Adolf Hitler (q.v.) in the early 1920s. At Himmler's insistence, a broad expansion of armed SS units began in 1939. The term *Waffen-SS* was widely used after the 1940 campaign in the west.

The SS and Josef "Sepp" Dietrich (q.v.), as head of the *Stabswache* (Headquarters Security Guard), were instrumental in the "Night of the Long Knives," the blood purge of Ernst Röhm's SA (qq.v.) in 1934. First raised in Berlin in March 1933, the *Stabswache* expanded to become the *"Leibstandarte Adolf Hitler"* (Hitler's Life Guard) or LAH. The LAH became the first field regiment (later division) and most famous of all *Waffen-SS* units.

In 1936, the *SS-Verfügunstruppe* (Special Ready Troops) or SSVT were formed as fully armed, motorized, battalion- strength formations throughout Germany. Designed for both political and paramilitary security functions, the SSVT became the training apparatus and cadre for the later *Waffen-SS* formations. Himmler appointed retired army General Paul Hausser (q.v.) to supervise SSVT military training. Dietrich, however, continued to jealously guard the independence of his LAH, which earned the nickname "asphalt soldiers" for their many ceremonial duties. By 1939, there were three SSVT regiments. With much pomp, the SSVT participated in the occupations of Austria and Czechoslovakia.

Along with the rise of the SSVT, there was a parallel rise of the *Totenkopfverbände* (Death's Head Detachments), intended as concentration camp guards and internal security troops. By mid-1938, four such regiments were in existence. These later became the *Totenkopf* Division (later designated as the 3rd SS *Panzer* Division *Totenkopf*), which consisted mainly of men from the *Totenkopfverbände*.

Recruitment into the *Waffen-SS* required the highest standards in physical fitness, height, and even teeth. Above all, the candidate had to establish proof of a racially pure genealogy. Discipline was harsh. Absolute, unquestionable loyalty to Hitler was demanded. *"Meine Ehre heisst Treue"* (My Honor Is Loyalty) was its prominent motto. Recruits tended to come overwhelmingly from the working class—young men in search of superior identity. The majority of officer candidates also came from the same stock. Men from traditional military families tended to opt for the army, not the "upstart" *Waffen-SS*. Thus officers and units had considerable growing pains, as reflected in the *Waffen-SS*'s initial high casualty rates.

Eventually, the strict racial requirements for all *Waffen-SS* soldiers were relaxed, then thrown to the winds, as the war progressed and the German cause became more desperate. By early 1944, more than half of all *Waffen-SS* soldiers were not native Germans, representing at least fifteen other nationalities. Peak wartime strength was more than one million. At the end of the war the *Waffen-SS* had thirty-three divisions plus other formations, but most were not at full strength or quality. Forty-one separate divisions were raised over the course of the war, and in some cases the same division number was recycled.

The great effort to recruit foreigners "of Nordic blood" began in 1940. At least 125,000 West Europeans served in the *Waffen-SS*; some were impressed, but most volunteered. The Dutch alone contributed 50,000; Walloons and Flemings, 20,000 each; at least 15,000 French; 6,000 Danes; and 5,000 Norwegians. The *Nordland* Regiment was formed from Norwegian and Danish volunteers. The *Westland* Regiment (later the *"Wiking"* Division) comprised Belgian and Dutch volunteers. The French *Charlemagne* Division was decimated in its only battle—Berlin. Most of these West Europeans served on the eastern front against the "racially inferior" Slavs and Bolsheviks. From

the east, it obviously was more difficult to desert and go home.

Despite the cruelty with which Germany occupied the conquered Soviet states, a significant number of volunteers came from those indigenous populations and the Balkans; 100,000 Ukrainians served in the *Waffen-SS*. Two Russian divisions were formed. Inhabitants of the Crimea with Germanic heritage were outstanding soldiers. Croatian and Moslem forces were raised in Yugoslavia to

Waffen-SS Divisions

Unit and Title	Date Formed	Composition
1st SS-*Panzerdivision-Leibstandarte Adolf Hitler*	1933	German
2nd SS-*Panzerdivision-Das Reich*	1939	German
3rd SS-*Panzerdivision-Totenkopf*	1940	German
4th SS-*Panzergrenadierdivision-Polizei*	1940	German Police
5th SS-*Panzerdivision-Wiking*	1940	German/Scandinavian
6th SS-*Gebirgsdivision-Nord*	1940	German
7th SS-*Freiwilligen-Gebirgsdivision-Prinz Eugen*	1942	Ethnic German
8th SS-*Kavalleriedivision-Florian Geyer*	1942	German/Ethnic German
9th SS-*Panzerdivision-Hohenstaufen*	1943	German
10th SS-*Panzerdivision-Frundsberg*	1943	German
11th SS-*Freiwilligen-Panzergrenadierdivision-Nordland*	1942	German/Scandinavian
12th SS-*Panzerdivision-Hitlerjugend*	1943	German (Hitler Youth)
13th *Waffen-Gebirgsdivision der SS-Handschar*	1943	Yugoslav
14th *Waffen-Grenadierdivision der SS-Galizische Nr.1*	1943	Ukrainian
15th *Waffen-Grenadierdivision der SS-Lettische Nr.1*	1943	Latvian/German
16th SS-*Freiwilligen-Panzergrenadierdivision-Reichsführer-SS*	1943	German/Ethnic German
17th SS-*Panzergrenadierdivision-Götz von Berlichingen*	1943	German/Ethnic German
18th SS-*Freiwilligen-Panzergrenadierdivision-Horst Wessel*	1944	German/Ethnic German
19th *Waffen-Grenadierdivision der SS-Lettische Nr.2*	1944	Latvian
20th *Waffen-Grenadierdivision der SS-Estnische Nr. 1*	1944	Estonian
21st *Waffen-Gebirgsdivision der SS-Albanische Nr.1–Skanderberg*	1944	Albanian
22nd SS-*Freiwilligen-Kavalleriedivision-Maria Theresa*	1944	Ethnic German/German
23rd *Waffen-Gebirgsdivision der SS-Kama*	1944	Yugoslav
23rd SS-*Freiwilligen-Panzerdivision-Nederland*	1945	Dutch
24th *Waffen-Gebirgsdivision der SS-Karstjäger*	1944	Italian/Ethnic German
25th *Waffen-Grenadierdivision der SS-Hunyadi Nr.1*	1944	Hungarian
26th *Waffen-Grenadierdivision der SS-Hunyadi Nr.2*	1944	Hungarian
27th SS-*Freiwilligen-Grenadierdivision-Langemarck*	1945	Flemish/Belgian
28th SS-*Freiwilligen-Grenadierdivision-Wallonie*	1945	Walloon/Belgian
29th *Waffen-Grenadierdivision der SS-Russische Nr.1*	1944	Russian
29th *Waffen-Grenadierdivision der SS-Italische Nr.1*	1945	Italian
30th *Waffen-Grenadierdivision der SS-Russische Nr.2*	1944	Russian
31st SS-*Freiwilligen-Grenadierdivision*	1945	German
32nd SS-*Freiwilligen-Panzerdivision-Böhmen-Mahren*	1945	German
33rd *Waffen-Grenadierdivision der SS-Januar 30.*	1945	German
34th *Waffen-Grenadierdivision der SS-Charlemagne*	1945	French
35th SS-*Freiwilligen-Grenadierdivision-Landstorm Nederland*	1945	Dutch
36th SS-*Polizei-Grenadierdivision der SS*	1945	German Police
37th *Waffen-Grenadierdivision-Dirlewanger*	1945	German
38th SS-*Freiwilligen-Kavalleriedivision-Lüztow*	1945	Ethnic German
39th SS-*Panzergrenadierdivision-Nibelungen*	1945	SS Cadets

ineffectively battle Tito's (q.v.) partisans and anti-Nazi Serbians. There were some Albanian SS volunteers, but most deserted. By early 1943, 22,000 Latvians and Estonians volunteered. First formed in brigades, then in grenadier divisions, these quality troops fought to the end in the Kurland pocket and in Berlin (qq.v.).

A few ridiculous chapters enrich the *Waffen-SS* history. The "Legion of St. George" or *"Britisches Freikorps"* was formed as an attempt to lure British and Canadian POWs—a maximum of sixty volunteered by the war's end. The Germans made some attempt to recruit American POWs, but less than a dozen came forth. Three *Waffen-SS* battalions of the "Indian National Army" were raised from POWs captured in North Africa and Italy to fight their British masters.

The German Army always was critical of the *Waffen-SS*, especially in the formative years. Despite army criticism and rivalry (ruthlessness in general and the crimes committed by individuals) several *Waffen-SS* units were among Germany's finest, repeatedly proving their fighting ability. By the end of 1942, Hitler gave *Panzer* and *Panzergrenadier* units priority in men and equipment. The *SS Panzer* divisions were used as "fire brigades" for Hitler's hot spots from 1942 to 1945.

Waffen-SS generals were known for their Nazi fervor and aggressiveness, but few were brilliant soldiers. Among the finest *Waffen-SS* generals was Paul Hausser, prewar inspector of training, commander of the *"Das Reich"* motorized division, and commander of the *SS II Panzerkorps* in Normandy (q.v.). Felix Steiner was innovative and influential, particularly in the early days. As commander of the *SS II Panzerkorps* in September 1944, Willi Bittrich saved the German western front at Arnhem (q.v.). The ruthless Theodor Eicke (q.v.), former inspector of concentration camps, commanded the *Totenkopf* Division until he was killed. The "Butcher of Warsaw," Erich von dem Bach-Zelewski, was the most brutal, slaughtering partisans and civilians in the east. He later "sold out" his comrades at the postwar trials to save his own hide. In sharp contrast to Hausser stands Sepp Dietrich, who eventually commanded the entire Sixth *Panzer* Army. An old crony of Hitler's, he was not even competent at the divisional level.

Despite the unsavory character of the organization, the *Waffen-SS* produced its share of authentic combat heros. In June 1944, Michael Wittmann (q.v.), history's greatest tank commander, personally destroyed more than twenty-five British armored vehicles in five minutes, effectively halting the entire British 7th Armoured Division.

Kurt *"Panzer"* Meyer (q.v.) was a hero in Greece, and then commanded the *Hitlerjugend* Division in Normandy. Fritz Klingenberg, with a handful of men, captured the mayor and city of Belgrade. Otto Skorzeny (q.v.) was World War II's most extraordinary commando. Belgian SS *"Wallonien"* leader Léon Degrelle (q.v.) was the most highly decorated non-German. Despite his questionable competence as a commander, Sepp Dietrich was a brave combat soldier.

The *Waffen-SS* was responsible for a number of documented atrocities during the war, as well as the routine brutality with which they conducted all operations in the east. In 1940, the *Totenkopf* Regiment massacred some 100 British prisoners at Le Paradis. The 12th SS *Panzer* Division, *Hitlerjugend*, slaughtered forty Canadian POWs in Normandy in 1944. The 2nd SS *Panzer* Division *(Das Reich)*, killed every man, woman, and child in the French village of Oradour-sur-Glâne (q.v.) in 1944. *Kampfgruppe Peiper* of the 1st SS *Panzer* Division murdered more than 120 American soldiers and 200 Belgian civilians in what became known as the Malmedy Massacre (q.v.). The 16th SS *Panzergrenadier* Division *(Reichsführer-SS)*, murdered 2,700 Italian civilians at Arno in 1944. The *Waffen-SS* also supplied soldiers for the *Einsatzgruppen* (q.v.), which carried out mass murder in the east. Although the postwar veterans of the *Waffen-SS* claim to have been "soldiers like any other," such claims do not stand up under close scrutiny.

Samuel J. Doss

Additional Reading

Keegan, John, *Waffen-SS: The Asphalt Soldiers* (1970).
Quarrie, Bruce, *Hitler's Samurai: The Waffen-SS in Action* (1986).
Reitlinger, Gerald, *The SS: Alibi of a Nation* (1957).
Simpson, Kieth, *Waffen-SS* (1990).

WASPs

See WOMEN'S AIR FORCE SERVICE PILOTS

WAVES

See WOMEN ACCEPTED FOR VOLUNTEER EMERGENCY SERVICE

Werewolves

The Werewolves were intended to be a German

military operation patterned on resistance movements in Axis-occupied Europe. German men and women, mostly young members of Nazi Party organizations, trained for guerrilla duties in areas held by the Allies. A field manual adapted from literature prepared for Axis troops fighting Soviet partisans (q.v.) was used. The prospect of fighting German guerrillas during and after the war concerned Allied leaders, including General Dwight D. Eisenhower (q.v.).

Werewolf effectiveness was limited by swift Allied advances, bombing of training areas, and, most of all, by German war weariness. Grand Admiral Karl Dönitz's (q.v.) V-E Day order to cease Werewolf activity effectively ended the movement, even though isolated incidents occurred for several months. The major Werewolf success was the killing of the mayor of Aachen on 24 March 1945, for having cooperated with American authorities.

Benjamin R. Beebe

Additional Reading

Miksche, F.O., *Secret Forces: The Technique of Underground Movements* (1950).

Whiting, Charles, *Hitler's Werewolves: The Story of the Nazi Resistance Movement, 1944–1945* (1972).

White Rose

The White Rose was the name of a German student resistance group formed in Munich in the spring of 1942. Its members wrote anti-Nazi leaflets and distributed them clandestinely among selected audiences of students, professional people, and intellectuals. Coming from middle- and upper-middle-class families, the most important activists included Hans Scholl, twenty-five, and his sister Sophie, twenty-one (qq.v.), Alexander Schmorell, twenty-five, Christoph Probst, twenty-three, and Willi Graf, twenty-four.

All of the men were medical students, but as members of the *Wehrmacht* had to alternate study at the university with service as medics on different fronts. Hans Scholl, who spearheaded the group, became good friends with the others at Munich University, sharing philosophical and cultural interests as well as increasing moral indignation at the repression and excesses of the Nazi regime. Sophie Scholl joined the group when she enrolled as a student of biology and philosophy in May 1942.

At the time of Sophie's arrival in Munich, Hans and Alexander penned the first leaflet of the White Rose. It denounced National Socialism (q.v.) as the scourge of humanity and called for passive resistance against the regime. In June 1942, Professor Kurt Huber, a conservative nationalist and popular lecturer in philosophy at Munich University, attended a literary reading group, at which Hans and some others vented critical remarks about the cultural decay under Nazism. Huber echoed those comments and exclaimed: "Something must be done, and it must be done now." He came to collaborate with Hans in the drafting of several of the leaflets. Two further pamphlets, appearing in June and July, asserted that 300,000 Jews had been murdered in Poland, called the present state a dictatorship of evil, and advocated sabotage of war industries, educational institutions, and public organizations as a way of hastening the elimination of the regime.

With their term ending in the summer, the medical students were assigned front duty in southern Russia and Sophie a tedious job in a factory. When the students of the White Rose reassembled in Munich in November 1942 for the new term, their recent experiences had intensified their determination to engage in opposition to the Nazi cause. They now made efforts to establish cells of resistance in major German cities and to link up with the national opposition movement.

By January 1943, they had contact with circles in Hamburg, Vienna, Ulm, Stuttgart, Salzburg, Frankfurt, Freiburg, Saarbrücken, and Berlin. Also in January, a fifth leaflet, drafted by Hans and revised by Huber, appeared and issued a "Call to All Germans" to dissociate themselves from the gangsterism of the Nazis, projecting a German federal state and basic civil rights as the foundation of the "New Europe." In the first weeks of February, Hans, Alexander, and Willi repeatedly adorned public buildings with anti-Hitler slogans.

On 18 February, Hans and Sophie scattered the last leaflet, written entirely by Huber, on the stairs and window ledges of Munich University. A custodian observed them and had them arrested. The other members of the White Rose were rounded up by the *Gestapo* (q.v.) in the next few days or weeks. Roland Freisler (q.v.), the notorious president of the People's Court, presided over the trials that followed. On 22 February the Scholls and Probst were sentenced to die, and their execution followed within hours. Huber, Schmorell, and Graf were tried later and executed in July and October. Seven members of the Hamburg branch of the White Rose suffered a similar fate. A dozen or more members of the Munich group received prison sentences varying from six months to ten years.

The White Rose actually found few adherents among German students. The leaflets, however, found their way into concentration camps and were smuggled into Sweden and Switzerland. From there they were sent to London, reprinted, and dropped by Allied airplanes over German cities. Their message testified to the spirit of resistance and the existence of "another" Germany.

George P. Blum

Additional Reading

Dumbach, Annette E., and Jud Newborn, *Shattering the German Night: The Story of the White Rose.* (1986)

Scholl, Inge, *Students Against Tyranny: The Resistance of the White Rose, Munich 1942–1943* (1970).

Women Accepted for Volunteer Emergency Service (WAVES)

During World War II, the United States overcame severe manpower shortage by using women to fill many noncombat positions. In early 1942, the navy asked Dean Virginia Gildersleeve of Columbia University to head an advisory council concerning women reservists. On 30 June 1942, the navy established the women's reserve of the U.S. naval reserve, nicknamed WAVES (Women Accepted for Volunteer Emergency Service).

The WAVES, whose mission was to release men for duty at sea, were to serve until six months after the war. The law restricted the WAVES rank structure to one lieutenant commander and thirty-five lieutenants, and prohibited service outside the continental United States or on board naval vessels and combatant aircraft. Mildred McAfee (q.v.), president of Wellesley College, became the first director of the WAVES.

The WAVES began large-scale recruiting in the summer of 1942. Women had to be twenty years of age, of high moral character, in good health, and high school graduates, or have had two years of secondary schooling plus two years work experience. Officer candidates needed a college degree or two years of college plus two years of work experience. The navy used college campuses for training both officers and enlisted. Initially, boot training lasted six weeks but was later dropped to four. Women learned the fundamentals of navy life and underwent physical training. By mid-1945, more than 80,000 WAVES had completed boot training.

The WAVES stressed neatness and professionalism. Tough regulations on marriage and pregnancy hampered recruiting efforts. Initially, WAVES could marry no one in the armed forces, but later changes allowed marriage to navy personnel after completion of WAVE training. Pregnant WAVES were honorably discharged. There were relatively few disciplinary problems.

Because of the unexpected growth of the WAVES, the navy promoted McAfee to captain in late 1943. In late 1944, WAVES received permission to serve in Hawaii, Alaska, and American bases in the Caribbean.

Originally, WAVES performed traditional female tasks. They handled the huge paperwork generated by the wartime navy, serving as secretaries, stenographers, file clerks, receptionists, storekeepers, and public relations and personnel specialists. They took over the navy post offices and handled most of the mail. The navy hospital corps employed more than 13,000 female doctors, dentists, technicians, nurses, and physical therapists.

As the number of WAVES increased, they took on new duties. The navy bureau of personnel used WAVES to help distribute welfare and recreation funds for new ships and stations, and to handle problems related to ships lost at sea. In the office of the chief of naval operations, WAVES handled the communications network with a few WAVES trained to monitor Japanese broadcasts. Mathematicians and technicians worked in the Bureau of Ordnance as gunnery instructors and wrote abstracts of battle reports comparing naval ordnance.

The Bureau of Yards and Docks assigned women to purchase real estate, work on secret war plans, and devise camouflage techniques. Women engineers in the Bureau of Ships aided in ship construction and the development of sonar (q.v.) systems. At the Potomac River Naval Command, WAVES tested airplanes in the wind tunnel. Others worked in the port director's offices and routed ships into harbor, attended convoy conferences, assigned anchorages, and debriefed naval gun crews from merchant ships.

The Bureau of Aeronautics employed almost one-third of the WAVES, who served as control tower operators, taught instrument flying, and packed parachutes. Many aviation machinist's mates were women.

The 86,000 WAVES proved their worth during the war, and their ability opened thirty-eight of the sixty-two enlisted ratings to women reservists. Although most left the navy at the end of the war, a few remained, and in 1948, the Women's Armed Forces Integration Act permitted women to join the regular navy and the naval reserve.

Laura Matysek Wood

Additional Reading
Alsmeyer, Marie Bennet, *The Way of the WAVE* (1981).
Butler, Elizabeth Allen, *Navy WAVES* (1989).

Women's Air Force Service Pilots (WASPs)

Prior to Pearl Harbor, initial enthusiasm for American women fliers serving the U.S. military was spurred by famed aviatrix Jacqueline Cochran (q.v.). Cochran herself seized the opportunity on 17 June 1941 to ferry a Lockheed Hudson bomber across the Atlantic to Britain. Although her offer to form an American women's ferrying division was rejected, she was able to recruit a small detachment to assist the British Air Transport Auxiliary.

Confident of the inevitability of a U.S. women's program, Cochran returned to the United States in the fall of 1942, chagrined to learn that a plan without her consultation was already underway. Nancy Harkness Love, wife of Major Robert Love of the Air Transport Command's Ferrying Division, began to assemble especially qualified women pilots for ferry duty as part of the Women's Auxiliary Ferrying Service (WAFS) based at New Castle Army Air Base, Delaware.

Love's concept for her women pilots was different from Cochran's. Love was interested in female pilots with an average of more than 1,000 hours flying time, who could join the Ferrying Division with a minimum of military indoctrination and procedure. Cochran, conversely, wanted her women completely militarized and subject to the same training procedures as male cadets, and she wanted to be administratively in charge.

Through the intercession of General Henry H. "Hap" Arnold (q.v.), Cochran was given permission to recruit her own Women's Flying Training Detachment, based at barely equipped Howard Hughes Field in Houston, Texas. Women pilots of both the WAFS and the WFTD were ineligible for military flight pay due to lack of congressional approval. Thus, they initially became part of the federal civil service, pending future legislation.

Orientation training for the WAFS at New Castle was in many cases far below the skill levels of many of the women, some of whom had more flying hours than their instructors. For her WFTD, however, Cochran sought more modestly experienced fliers (initially 200 hours, then dropped to 35), but ones who possessed a more

typically military character. Indeed, she intended to prove the viability of an all-women's training course evenly matched to that of male cadets. As the women's dual programs progressed, the WAFS spread beyond Delaware to Dallas, Texas; Romulus, Michigan; and Long Beach, California. The WFTD officially located at Avenger Field, Sweetwater, Texas.

In July 1943, the U.S. War Department announced the consolidation of the women pilot groups in the Army Air Forces. Cochran became director of women pilots, and Love continued to direct specifically the activities of the women in the Ferrying Division of the Air Transport Command. Both WAFS and WFTD were merged and the entity became known as the Women's Air Force Service Pilots (WASPs).

During the war, the WASPs ferried Bell P-39 and Republic P-47 fighters, and on some special assignments, B-17 and B-29 bombers (even the experimental jet YP-59A). They delivered more than 12,000 aircraft of all types, logging more than 60 million miles. WASPs also performed the more strenuous duties of test-flying recently repaired planes, and towing air target sleeves for student aerial and antiaircraft gunners.

Of the 25,000 women who applied, 1,830 were accepted. In all, 1,074 WASPs graduated from the program, and thirty-eight died during training or operational duty. Regardless of their obvious success, the WASPs remained misunderstood in the perceptions of the general public and the military hierarchy. Besides the misdirected bias against women serving in previously traditional male roles, the WASPs were seen as a glamorous frivolity and the beginnings of encroachment upon the employment opportunities of returning male service members.

In 1944, Congress considered a bill to militarize the WASPs and standardize their pay, health, and hospitalization benefits. The bill, however, was defeated by special interests, and the entire WASPs program was deactivated on 20 December 1944. For her work as director of women pilots, Cochran was awarded the Distinguished Service Medal in 1945. Further efforts to gain veteran's status for the WASPs continued into the 1970s. It finally was achieved through the support of General Arnold's son, and the WASPs were finally given military veteran status in 1979.

William Camp

Additional Reading
Boles, Antoinette, *Women in Khaki* (1953).
Wood, Ethel M., *We Were WASPs* (1946).

Women's Auxiliary Army Corps (WAAC)

During World War II, 140,000 women joined the Women's Auxiliary Army Corps. In the spring of 1941, Republican Congresswoman Edith Nourse Rogers introduced legislation for an affiliated women's corps. The War Department worded the bill carefully so that women would not have full military status.

Laggardly congressional procedure delayed the bill's passage until General George C. Marshall (q.v.) pressured legislators. In March 1942, the Women's Auxiliary Army Corps (WAAC) finally was approved. Its director was Oveta Culp Hobby (q.v.), former president of the Texas League of Women Voters.

Volunteers had to be between twenty and thirty-five years old. The applicants' maturity and education were important factors, as well as prior work experience. Both single and married women applied, and many ethnic groups—Puerto Rican, Chinese, Japanese, and Native American—were represented. Although 94 percent of WAACs were white, approximately 4,000 black women served in segregated units.

Women enlisted for a variety of reasons. Frequently they had a relative or boyfriend in combat and thought their service would shorten the war. Others applied to escape a dull home life, to acquire a previously unavailable job, to advance professionally, for economic reasons, or for adventure. Volunteers applied at army recruiting stations where they underwent an interview, aptitude test, psychological and physical evaluation, and analysis of an essay addressing "Why I Desire Service." The first WAACs were selected on basis of the applicants' geographic region.

At the 1st WAAC Training Center at Fort Des Moines, Iowa, WAACs learned first aid, military customs, map reading, defense against chemical and air attack, company and supply administration, physical training and drill, and military protocol. By September 1942, the first class graduated and entered the field in a variety of positions: nursing, administrative, clerical, mechanics, motor transport, supply, and radio.

The European theater was the first foreign field to host WAACs. The U.S. Eighth Air Force requested a WAAC battalion in 1943. Applicants considered for service abroad were judged on stricter standards. Applicants' immaturity and emotional instability were key factors for being denied service because the European theater was considered extraordinarily demanding. In Europe, the women served in postal and telephone positions and often had access to military secrets and confidential files.

The WAACs suffered many slanderous attacks. Military opinion of the WAACs varied from tolerance to derision. Some male officers improperly disciplined or promoted women on factors other than merit. Many WAACs were not employed in positions equal to their qualifications and had to endure twelve-hour shifts, sexual harassment, lack of mentors, and low morale. They also complained of inadequate training and preparation.

WAACs faced more gender discrimination when Red Cross workers refused to provide them aid, stating their purpose was to serve men, not women. As a result of numerous factors—fear, apathy, ridicule, the inability to adjust to military lifestyle, family opposition—some women abruptly quit WAAC service. They did not risk punishment or court-martial because they were not in full military service.

Hostility toward WAACs was manifested in the 1943 slander campaign in which they were falsely charged with promiscuity. Although women were prohibited from combat duty, many men resented that women could enlist, and many spread slanderous rumors in order to alarm the women's families, who, it was hoped, would demand they discontinue service. In reality, few WAACs were dismissed for gross misconduct or immorality. The military initiated a public relations campaign to rehabilitate the WAACs' image.

In foreign service, WAACs endured overwork, clothing shortages, and improper attire for cold and hot climates. Some women requested discharges or deserted. Psychological maladies resulted in many desertions, and tests analyzing moral standards and social background were used to prevent parents or police from signing up criminals, prostitutes, or the mentally ill. Hobby gained control of the recruiting process and required all applicants to have a satisfactory aptitude test score and two years of high school.

In June 1943, the WAAC was disbanded to become the Women's Army Corps (WAC), according the women full military status. One-fourth of the WAAC did not transfer to the new service. In the conversion period, a transfer required stricter qualifications, a more rigorous medical examination, and recommendation by the woman's former commander. The women were converted at their equivalent WAAC rank.

The best WACs were sent in 1944 to assist in the Normandy (q.v.) invasion. Some earned Purple Hearts for wounds received during bombings in Britain. They also served in France and Germany, following the fighting forces and helping to restore normalcy as cities were retaken and occupied. After V-E Day, some WACs stayed in Germany to help with the postwar transitions. For the most part, though the WAC was demobilized when the hostilities ended.

World War II women veterans received benefits, and in 1948, women were ensured roles in regular military service. More than 2,000 women transferred from the wartime WAC to the peacetime equivalent. Although women were limited to the rank of colonel in World War II, they were promised more distinguished and significant opportunities in the military. Even so, the U.S. Army did not get its first female general officer until 1970. Some short-term aspects of the WAAC (and WAC) program seem to be failures, but the long-term results opened professional military careers for women.

Elizabeth D. Schafer

Additional Reading
Goldman, Nancy Loring (ed.), *Female Soldiers— Combatants or Noncombatants: Historical and Contemporary Perspectives* (1982).

WAACs plotting the position of bombers in the flight control room of a medium bomber station in Britain. (IWM AP 10138)

Holm, Jeanne, *Women in the Military* (1982).
Treadwell, Mattie E., *The Women's Army Corps* (1954).

Women's Royal Navy Service (WRNS)

During World War I, the Women's Royal Enlisted Navy (WREN), established in 1917 by Sir Eric Geddes, first lord of the Admiralty, operated as auxiliary volunteers for the Royal Navy (RN). Approximately 7,000 women performed clerical and domestic tasks, as well as serving as electricians and telegraphists, filling torpedoes, and repairing mine nets. The group was demobilized in 1919.

In World War II, the Women's Royal Navy Services (WRNS) served a similar duty. In 1939, the RN decided to renew the naval auxiliary with roles similar to the other military auxiliaries. The RN auxiliaries, known as WRNS, replaced male navy personnel in routine but necessary chores. Often, their jobs required technical ability as well as confidentiality. WRNS initially entered at the lowest enlisted rank, regardless of their age, experience, or status, before advancing to officer ranks. British naval officers trained WRNS at the Royal Naval College in Greenwich.

In many RN families, service as WRNS was expected for daughters and wives. The British public regarded WRNS as the most selective and glamorous (and smallest) of the military service groups for women. WRNS volunteers were recruited mostly from the upper middle and upper classes and were required to present three references attesting to their moral character and ability.

Despite this attempt at segregation of wartime workers by social class, some WRNS trained for positions such as mechanics and worked alongside working class women. Most of their own officers encouraged the WRNS to serve in more lofty positions, like officers' secretaries, or other duties considered appropriate for higher-class women, thus remaining segregated socially.

Applicants had to be between eighteen and forty-five years old. Women with prior naval experience or special qualifications were accepted up to the age of forty-nine. After an interview and reference check, volunteers signed up for a four-year enlistment. By 1941, 8,000 women had joined the WRNS.

WRNS were the only auxiliary service not regulated by military discipline, and their officers used patriotism to motivate them. Wearing a dark blue uniform, WRNS performed a myriad of duties. They drove automobiles and vehicles, delivered messages via motorcycle, worked at the post office and as telephone operators, performed clerical tasks, and cooked and hosted in the officers' messes. They also transported supplies from ship to ship or to docks, and serviced seaplanes.

Some of the WRNS' most important service came with the shore communication units. WRNS qualified as radio operators transmitted, received, intercepted, coded, and deciphered messages. Their training period for this special duty lasted from three to six months and was conducted by naval officers. WRNS also were responsible for tracking merchant ships and determining the location and range of targets. They even assisted in sinking the German battleship *Bismarck* (q.v.).

Despite their conscientious service to the RN, WRNS encountered slander and negative propaganda launched against them. Rumors circulated that WRNS were promiscuous and immoral. WRNS occasionally were confronted by officers and enlisted men making sexual advances, and were harassed verbally and sometimes physically. WRNS endured other discriminatory and morale lowering obstacles. Like other auxiliaries, WRNS were paid lower wages and given smaller rations than men. Often the WRNS' work—plotting ship and aircraft locations on giant maps from wireless messages—was boring and monotonous.

When the war ended, married WRNS were demobilized first. Women were dismissed based on their age and service. They received four weeks' pay and clothing coupons. Many WRNS married while in the service or soon afterward to satisfy their desire for emotional and economic security in what they considered a turbulent and chaotic society.

WRNS' wartime service was appreciated for the most part by naval officers. Perhaps this admiration and acceptance was because of the WRNS' close ties with naval relatives and traditions or their affiliation with Britain's upper classes. For the most part, WRNS were able to function well during and after the war, receiving more praise than criticism for their service in World War II.

Elizabeth D. Schafer

Additional Reading
Drummond, John D., *Blue for a Girl: The Story of the W.R.N.S.* (1960).
Schweitzer, P., L. Hilton, and J. Moss (eds.), *What Did You Do in the War, Mum?* (1985).
Scott, Peggy, *British Women in War* (1940).

A WRNS radio mechanic preparing to flight test a piece of equipment. (IWM A 9115)

X

XX Committee

One of the major Allied intelligence triumphs of World War II, the XX (or Twenty) Committee offered British authorities a ready means for passing disinformation to the German high command virtually until war's end. Early on, MI-5 (q.v.) realized the strategic possibilities of double agents. By the summer of 1940, all six *Abwehr* (q.v.) agents operating in Britain were actually under the control of the Security Service's B1(a) Branch.

Admiral John Godfrey (q.v.), director of naval intelligence, took the lead in urging the services to exploit the deception potential this afforded. Godfrey's prompting eventually led to the January 1941 creation of the W Board, an informal gathering of the directors of service intelligence, along with MI-5 and MI-6 (q.v.) representatives, that offered guidance on disinformation to be passed through double agents.

The actual disinformation and harmless true intelligence lay with an offshoot of the W Board, the Twenty Committee. The Twenty Committee (from the Roman numerals XX—a double cross) acted as a conduit between B1(a) and the rest of Britain's intelligence community in matters of deception material passed through the "special means" of double agents (*see* Counterintelligence Operations).

Soon integrated with John Bevan's (q.v.) London Controlling Section, the Twenty Committee became the linchpin of Allied deception measures leading up to D-Day. ULTRA (q.v.) decrypts provided a handy check on German reception of disinformation as well as a warning of the arrival of new agents, enabling the Twenty Committee to manipulate the *Abwehr*'s appreciation of Allied defenses. Apart from its role in the massive deception leading up to the Normandy invasion, the Twenty Committee (q.v.) also saved civilian lives by passing on false information about the effects and accuracy of German V-1 attacks and bombing raids. A model success in the art of strategic deception, the Twenty Committee ranks among Britain's greatest contributions to the Allied war effort.

Mark Rummage

Additional Reading

Howard, Michael, *British Intelligence in the Second World War*, Vol. 5, *Strategic Deception* (1990).
Masterson, John C., *The Double-Cross System in the War of 1939–1945* (1972).